The Great Conversation

The Great Conversation

A Historical Introduction to Philosophy

Norman Melchert

Lehigh University

Mayfield Publishing Company

Mountain View, California
London • Toronto

Library of Congress Cataloging-in-Publication Data

Melchert, Norman Paul.
The great conversation : a historical introduction to
philosophy / by Norman Melchert.
         p.   cm.
   Includes bibliographical references and index.
   ISBN 0–87484–952–7
   1. Philosophy—Introduction.   2. Philosophy—
History.   I. Title.
BD21.M43   1990
190—dc20   90-45038
                                              CIP

Manufactured in the United States of America
10 9 8 7 6 5 4 3

Mayfield Publishing Company
1240 Villa Street
Mountain View, California 94041

Sponsoring editor, James Bull; managing editor, Linda
Toy; production editor, Sondra Glider; manuscript editor,
Sally Peyrefitte; text and cover designer, Gary Head;
illustrator, Betsy Nute.
   The text was set in 10.5/12 Berkeley Old Style by
TypeLink and printed on 50# Finch Opaque by R. R.
Donnelley & Sons Co.

Cover: *The School of Athens* by Raphael, fresco, 1510–11,
Papal Apartments, the Vatican, Rome. Scala/Art Resource

Text credits appear on a continuation of the copyright
page, p. 587.

For Matthew, Andrew, and Stephen

Contents

A Word to Instructors

Like most philosophy teachers, I have taught introduction to philosophy many times and in many ways. We all have our favorites. What I came to prize is hard to do: a treatment fundamentally historical, having enough continuity that it doesn't seem like unconnected little bits, set in a fairly rich cultural and intellectual context, containing several complete works and many words by the philosophers themselves, presenting the development of thought about major issues, and concentrating on the arguments. *The Great Conversation* is my best try at satisfying these criteria. In addition to many shorter selections integrated with the text, the book offers three complete classics: Plato's *Euthyphro* and *Apology* and Descartes' *Meditations*.

It is not a history of philosophy; it is an introduction to that history for beginning students. In writing a book like this, one has hard choices to make. One of the basic ones is whether to try to say a bit about everything or to say more about fewer things. I have chosen the latter. So there is one representative of Medieval philosophy, Augustine, whom I chose over Aquinas as being more accessible and engaging. Of the classical rationalists you will find only Descartes, and of the empiricists Hume. The most controversial choices are bound to be those closest to us. In my judgment, Wittgen-

stein and Heidegger are the major players in the two main philosophical movements of our century. They are difficult. But with care, they can be made intelligible—and intensely interesting—to students.

As its title suggests, this book presents the development of philosophy as a conversation about some of humankind's deepest and most persistent concerns. The idea of a conversation across the centuries is obviously metaphorical, but is here made concrete by way of an unusual number of cross-references, both within the text and in footnotes. When constructing an argument or making a claim, one philosopher almost always has others in mind, correcting, disagreeing, supporting, or enlarging what the other has said. I try to present these ongoing debates without imposing my own evaluations as much as possible, though I realize no one can escape a point of view. I have found that the excitement of studying philosophy is greatly increased for students when they understand it to be dynamic in this way.

Instructors using this book should be able to help students become part of this conversation, so that they understand it sympathetically and, little by little, develop the ability to join in with reasoned views and arguments of their own.

A Word to Students

Before dinner one night I recounted to a small group of professors—scientists and engineers—the story of how Socrates had come to interrogate his fellow citizens so doggedly and irritatingly, behavior that undoubtedly contributed to their antagonism toward him and to his eventual death at their hands. When an oracle had declared that there was no man wiser than he, Socrates was doubtful, and so he set out to test the correctness of the oracle by questioning others. He wanted to discover whether others knew things he did not. The results of such questioning, he found, were persistently negative; people did not seem to know what justice really was, or courage, or piety, or beauty. Worst of all, they did not seem to know the things they thought they knew. And so Socrates concluded that the oracle was, after all, right. He was wiser, at least in this: that he did not claim to know what he actually did not know.

The response of the professors was to ask, "Is this true, or are you making it up?" I was astonished. This story, I thought, was a part of our history that every educated person must surely know. But on reflection I realized that I was being naive. Why should they have known this? And why should they be expected to have a sense of the significance of Socrates for our age? Where in their largely scientific education would it have turned up?

What is true for these highly intelligent and technically proficient professors is true as well for most of us, including most college students. Ours is a particularly unhistorical age. It is the spirit of the times to be interested in the latest products, not only of our advancing technologies, but also of our writers and thinkers and perhaps especially of our moviemakers and musical performers. Paying attention only to the present, however, is like hearing just snatches of a conversation. Its meaning is unclear, and one is likely to give it an interpretation that it will not bear. For we *are* engaged in a conversation, one that reaches back to earliest times and that, barring catastrophe, will be carried on beyond us.

The topics in that conversation include some of the deepest and most persistent concerns of our species. What sort of creatures are we? What sort of world do we inhabit? What, if anything, can we know to be true? How ought we to behave and live? There are lots of opinions about these matters. But there is a particular way of addressing them that we have come to call philosophy. Socrates is, we might say, the patron saint of those who ask and seek to answer these questions in that way. What way is this? We would not be wrong to call it "rational." But the only way really to appreciate what that means is to follow the participants in this great conversation as they struggle with these deep and difficult questions.

This book is designed to help its readers understand some of the major milestones in this conversation. Since it is partly through this history that we have become who we are—as individuals and as members of a culture—an acquaintance with this conversation helps us to understand ourselves—

our times and our human nature. And it should make current conversations bearing on these topics more meaningful.

I take the metaphor of a conversation quite seriously. So we will listen in, as it were, as Democritus tries to solve a problem posed for him by Parmenides. We will overhear Aristotle as he criticizes his teacher, Plato. We will take note while Descartes tries to put philosophy on firm foundations, something he thinks none of his predecessors had managed to do. And we will struggle to understand Heidegger's view that this whole conversation is, in a certain way, now *finished*. I will represent this ongoing debate sympathetically and *internally*, trying to refrain from imposing my own evaluations as much as possible. But I will take pains to point out the relevance of one thinker's arguments to those of another.

One of my convictions about philosophy is that it is *interactive*. When making a claim or constructing an argument, a philosopher nearly always has other philosophers in mind. That is what makes a conversation. One of the best ways to grasp the significance of an argument is to see what it is an argument *against*, as well as what it is an argument *for*. It helps a lot to understand who our thinker is arguing with or, perhaps, to see that the argument is actually elaborating and correcting an earlier view in the light of others' objections to it.

To help you get a feel for this conversational context, I include a large number of cross-references in the text. Taking the little time required to follow up these references will help you to understand what a philosopher thinks is at stake and why it matters that we get it right. A philosopher is someone who cares deeply about the right answer to some fundamental problem, who feels intensely the importance of some question. To understand philosophy, you need to identify these questions and feel their urgency. Pursuing these cross-references should help you do just that. I hope you will get the feeling of joining a conversation in progress and finding that a first-rate discussion is going on.

Pursuing the cross-references will also help you to avoid a mistaken impression that many newcomers to philosophy get: that this is hard-to-understand talk about something very abstract. Philosophy is never (well, hardly ever) that. Philosophers write about the most concrete things there are—about us and our lives and the world we live in. What they write *is* sometimes hard to understand. But because it is about real issues that make a difference in our lives, it is worth the effort required to understand it.

Since philosophy is interactive, you should also pose your own questions to these thinkers. I hope that you will be not just an observer of this conversation, but a participant. One of my own teachers, a little white-haired man with a thick German accent, used to say, "Whether you will philosophize or won't philosophize, you *must* philosophize." He meant by this that we all work out answers to these questions in the living of our lives. And if this is true, surely we are wise to listen to Socrates, who tells us that, for a human being, the unexamined life is not worth living. Philosophy offers you an opportunity to improve your own present views about important matters by comparing your views with some of the best that humans have thought through the ages.

There are two stages in this process. The first stage is *understanding*. This requires that you not react too quickly to what you read on the basis of your own present views. Before you say that some philosopher's opinions are "obviously" wrong or that his arguments are absurd, make an effort at sympathetic appreciation; try to feel what it would be like to "inhabit" a world in which such views make good sense. In short, first try to see things from the philosopher's point of view, however strange it may seem to you. The second stage is *evaluation*, in which you try to reach some reasoned judgment of your own about the matter at hand. One of the best ways to do this is to write something that expresses your views, to play—if only tentatively and provisionally—the game called philosophy for yourself.

When you pose your own questions to these thinkers, you will sometimes find an answer that satisfies you. Sometimes you won't. More often you will find there are too many answers, all with some plausibility. And then you must choose.

But this is all to the good. Reflecting on the ideas in this book should help you to choose *more wisely* than you otherwise would. Part of wisdom is being willing to take responsibility for one's life. You can fulfill that responsibility better if you make your choices with your eyes more fully open, being more alive to the options available.

I will not try to give a comprehensive treatment of each thinker but will focus attention on four major concerns shared by those we call philosophers, together with some characteristic questions that express each one:

Metaphysics: What is the nature of reality?

What kinds of things are there?

Is there a God?

What, if anything, is the soul?

Is free will a possibility?

Epistemology: What is knowledge?

What—if anything—can we know?

Are there different kinds of knowledge?

What is truth?

Ethics: What is good?

Are certain actions right or wrong? If so, which? And why?

How should we live?

Human nature: What kind of creature is a human being?

One motif, or theme, will appear again and again, most of our philosophers constructing some variation of their own on the theme. We can express the theme in various ways: knowledge versus skepticism, belief versus doubt, objectivism versus relativism. The issue is whether there is available to us a perspective, a point of view, or a method that will get us beyond the prejudices and assumptions peculiar to ourselves as individuals or as members of a culture. Is there a way to understand the world, ourselves, and human good that is universally acceptable, that is more than just the expression of how we happen to have been brought up or of the peculiarities of our own narrow experience?

This problem, which first came into prominence in classical Greece, has persisted to this day. For the most part, as we will see, the Western philosophical tradition has been one of resisting skepticism and relativism—though it is significant that philosophers have felt again and again that they *needed* to combat these views. Apparently they often felt like frontline soldiers fending off the barbarian hordes of chaos, darkness, and disorder. Whether relativism actually yields such chaos is, of course, itself an issue. Not everyone agrees.

Our own age has the distinction, perhaps, of being the first age ever in which the basic assumptions of most people, certainly of most educated people, are relativistic. So the theme we will be tracing has a peculiar poignancy for us. We will want to understand how we came to this point and what it means to be here. We will want to understand the arguments on both sides of the relativism issue.

Starting before Socrates, we will follow the thread of the conversation into our own century. Exciting things have been happening in all the major areas of philosophy. And the relativism debate is very much alive.

Acknowledgments

I want to thank Lehigh University for a year's leave of absence, during which the first half of the book was written, and the University of Kent in Canterbury for providing a wonderfully hospitable setting in which to write it. I owe a debt of thanks to my students over the years, especially those who from time to time encouraged me to write a book like this. My colleagues in the faculty seminar at Lehigh, whose great conversation I have prized and benefited from, have made this a much better book than it could possibly have been without them. I especially thank John Hare for both his encouragement and his criticisms. I profited from suggestions made by the publisher's readers: Linda Bomstad, California State University Sacramento; Jacquelyn Kegley, California State University Bakersfield; Don Porter, College of San Mateo; Merrill Ring, California State University Fullerton; Cynthia Rostankowski, San Jose State University; Anita Silvers, San Francisco State University; and especially from those by Raymond Herbenick, University of Dayton, whose careful reading and page-by-page criticisms have clearly made this a better book. Many of my sentences were made less awkward by Sally Peyrefitte, who also organized the citations in a clear and helpful way. And I thank Marianne Napravnik for assistance in more ways than I can briefly set down.

Books, like philosophies, are written by persons, not minds. We all have personal debts which are greater than mere words can express. Mine is greatest to my wife, Novi.

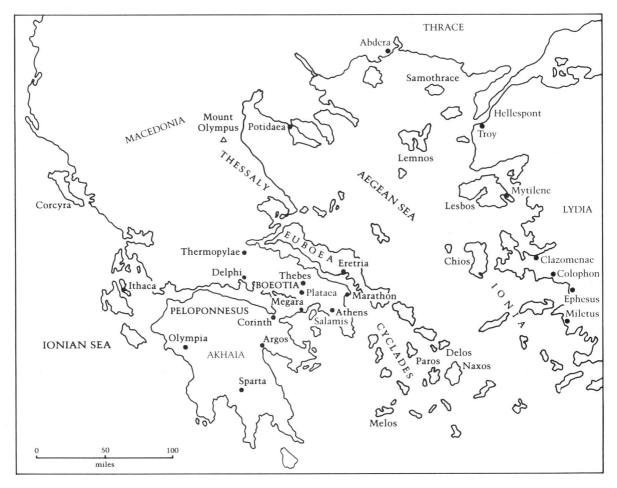

Map 1
The Greek Mainland

Map 2
Southern Italy and Sicily

I was aware that the reading of all good books
is indeed like a conversation with the noblest men
of past centuries who were the authors of them,
nay a carefully studied conversation,
in which they reveal to us
none but the best of their thoughts.

—RENÉ DESCARTES

What is education?
I should suppose that education was the curriculum
one had to run through
in order to catch up with oneself,
and he who will not pass through this curriculum
is helped very little by the fact that he was born in
the most enlightened age.

—SØREN KIERKEGAARD

1

Homer:
Heroes, Gods, and Excellence

Imagine that the year is 399 B.C.E.[1] The place is Athens (see map 1). You are one of 501 citizens gathered as jurors to conduct a trial according to the laws of the city. The defendant is elderly, seventy years of age. His name is Socrates. He is accused of impiety, that is, of not believing in the city's gods. He is also, in close connection with this charge, accused of corrupting the youth of Athens. You know something of Socrates. He is a stonemason, but he hasn't practiced his profession much for many years. He is neither wealthy nor a member of one of the old aristocratic families. What he mostly does is hang around in public places and talk to people. Or rather, he asks them questions. You have heard a few of these sessions, and you have to admit he is clever; he can often show people that they don't know what they are talking about. You can see why some might find his questions irritating. Whether any good comes of these talks is hard to say.

Still, that he should be brought to trial is rather puzzling. He seems harmless enough. So, you begin to wonder what lies behind this trial.

The trial of Socrates has come to be thought of as a touchstone; it takes us to the heart of what philosophy is. Was he guilty of the charges brought against him? What was it, anyway, that he stood for? Is that something valuable or not? A person trying to understand the argument about Socrates today also needs to understand something of Greek culture up to that time: Greek religion and society, the intellectual life of the preceding hundred years, and the mind-set of Socrates' contemporaries. We will fill in this background now and discuss Socrates in due course.

Let's begin by looking at the first lines of Homer's poem, *The Iliad*. (Here is a suggestion: Read quotations, especially poetry, aloud; you will find that they become more meaningful.)

Anger be now your song, immortal one,
Akhilleus' anger, doomed and ruinous,
that caused the Akhaians loss on bitter loss
and crowded brave souls into the undergloom,
leaving so many dead men—carrion
for dogs and birds; and the will of Zeus was done.

Begin it when the two men first contending
broke with one another—
   the Lord Marshall
Agamémnon, Atreus' son, and Prince Akhilleus.

Among the gods, who brought this quarrel on?
The son of Zeus by Lêto. Agamémnon
angered him, so he made a burning wind
of plague rise in the army: rank and file
sickened and died for the ill their chief had done
in despising a man of prayer.

(ILIAD 1, 11–12)[2]

1

The Iliad is a poem about a brief period during the Trojan war.* This war came about when Paris, son of Priam (the king of Troy), seduced and stole away Helen from her home in Akhaia, in southern Greece. Helen was the wife of Menelaos, king of Sparta and brother to Agamemnon. Agamemnon, king of Argos, was commander of the collected Greek forces that besieged Troy (see map 1) for more than nine years to recover Helen, to avenge the wrong, and—not just incidentally—to gain honor, glory, and plunder.

Why should we begin our account of the great conversation with Homer? Xenophanes, whom we meet later,† answers this very question by saying that "from the beginning all have learnt in accordance with Homer."[3] For centuries, Homer was the great teacher of the Greeks. To discover what was truly excellent in battle, governance, counsel, sport, the home, and human life in general, the Greeks looked to Homer's tales. These stories provided a picture of the world and man's place in it that was characteristically Greek. The poems of Homer molded the Greek mind and character; philosophy begins against the Homeric background.

There are other strains in Greek culture, older and more primitive than Homer: religions celebrating fertility and the earth, cults of ecstasy promising communion with gods, purification from sin or pollution, and immortality. Furthermore, these cults never entirely disappear. In fact, when the classical period ends in the fourth century B.C.E., they reawaken and grow enormously in influence. But in the beginning of our story, it is the religion, virtues, and world view of Homer's heroes that dominate Greece. It is the culture of conquerors who swept in several waves into that area from the north and east. So, we need to understand something of Homer.

The poet begins by announcing his theme: anger, specifically, the excessive anger of Akhilleus (Achilles), which brings death and destruction to many Greeks and almost costs them the war. So we might expect that the poem has a *moral* aspect. Moreover, in the sixth line of the passage we read, "And the will of Zeus was done." Notice that Homer simply takes for granted that Zeus, king of the gods, exists and is familiar to his readers. Further on we learn that Zeus is not alone among the gods; he has at least one son (also known as Apollo). We learn that the gods are interested in the affairs of men; Apollo has sent a plague on the Greek army because Agamemnon offended him. From the first stanzas of the poem, then, we can see that Homer's world is one of kings and princes, heroic but flawed, engaged in gargantuan projects against a background of gods who cannot safely be ignored.

The story Homer tells goes roughly like this. In a raid on a Trojan ally, the Greeks captured a girl, the daughter of a priest of Apollo. She was awarded to Agamemnon as part of his spoils. The priest comes to plead for her return, offering ransom, but is rudely rebuffed. He appeals to Apollo, who sends the plague. The Greeks, wanting to know what is causing the plague, ask their seer, Kalkhas, who explains the situation and advises that the girl be returned. Agamemnon is furious; to be without his prize while the other warriors keep theirs goes against the honor due him. He finally agrees, but he demands Akhilleus' prize, an exceptionally lovely woman, in exchange. The two heroes quarrel bitterly. Enraged, Akhilleus retreats to his tent and refuses to fight any more.

Since Akhilleus is the greatest of the great among the Greek warriors, his anger has serious consequences. The war goes badly for the Greeks. The Trojans fight their way to the beach and begin to burn the ships. Patroklos, Akhilleus' dearest friend, pleads with him to relent; if Akhilleus won't have pity on his comrades, Patroklos says, then at least let him take Akhilleus' armor and fight in his place. Akhilleus agrees. This tactic has some success, but Patroklos, driving the Trojans back from the ships, is killed by Hektor, another son of Priam and the greatest of the Trojan warriors.

---

*The date of the war is uncertain; scholarly estimates tend to put it near the end of the thirteenth century B.C.E. The poems we know as *The Iliad* and *The Odyssey* took form in song and were passed along in an oral tradition from generation to generation. They were written down some time in the eighth century B.C.E. Tradition ascribes them to a blind bard known as Homer, but the poems as we have them may be the work of more than one poet.

†See Chapter 2, "Xenophanes: The Gods as Fictions."

Akhilleus' rage now turns on Hektor and the Trojans, and he rejoins the war to wreak havoc among them. Finally, he kills Hektor and drags his body behind his chariot—a very bad thing to do. As the poem ends, Priam goes alone into the Greek camp to plead with Akhilleus for the body of his son. He and Akhilleus weep together, for Hektor and for Patroklos, and Akhilleus gives up the body.

This summary emphasizes the human side of the story. From that point of view, *The Iliad* can be thought of as the story of the tragedy that excess and pride lead to and of the humanization of Akhilleus. The main moral is the same as that expressed by a motto at the celebrated oracle at Delphi: "Nothing too much."* *Moderation* is what Akhilleus lacked, and his lack of it led to disaster. At the same time, the poem celebrates the "heroic virtues": strength, courage, physical prowess, and the kind of wisdom that consists in the ability to devise clever plans to achieve one's ends. These characteristics, together with moderation, make up for Homer and his audience the model of human excellence.

Throughout the story there is also the counterpoint of the gods, who look on, are appealed to, take sides, and interfere. For instance, when he is sulking about Agamemnon's having taken his woman, Akhilleus prays to his mother, the goddess Thetis (Akhilleus has a mortal father). He asks her to go to Zeus and beg Zeus to give victory to the Trojans. She does so, saying,

> Now Lord Marshal
> Agamémnon has been highhanded with him,
> has commandeered and holds his prize of war.
> But you can make him pay for this, profound
> mind of Olympos!
> Lend the Trojans power,
> until the Akhaians recompense my son
> and heap new honor upon him!
>
> (ILIAD 1, 28)

---

*This was one of several mottoes that had appeared mysteriously on the temple walls. No one could explain how they got there, and it was assumed that Apollo himself must have written them.

Zeus frets that his wife Hera will be upset, but he promises, saying,

> I shall arrange it.
> Here let me bow my head, then be content
> to see me bound by that most solemn act
> before the gods. My word is not revocable
> nor ineffectual, once I nod upon it.
>
> (ILIAD 1, 28)

We learn here that although there are numerous gods, one is supreme. Other gods may appeal to him, and if he promises by nodding his head, *it will be done*. (Recall the sixth line of the poem.) Homeric religion, while certainly not a monotheism, is not exactly a true polytheism. The powers that govern the world, though many, seem to be under the rule of one. That rule gives a kind of order to the universe; the world is not a chaos. There are even suggestions in Homer that Zeus himself, though the most powerful of the gods, is under the domination of Fate. Some things simply *will be*, and even Zeus cannot alter them.

Moreover, this order, though it may not be designed particularly with human beings in mind, is basically a just order. Zeus is the power who sees to it that certain customs are enforced: that oaths are kept, that suppliants are granted mercy, and that the rules governing guest and host are observed. These are the rules that Paris violated so grossly when he stole Helen away from Menelaos' house. Homer suggests that the Greeks eventually win the war because Zeus has an interest in punishing the violation of these customs. Again, Agamemnon does wrong in taking Akhilleus' woman, so Zeus promises that Akhilleus' honor will be avenged.

The Homeric idea of justice is not exactly the same as ours, however. We must see it in relation to the aim, the desire, the ambition of both men and gods in Homer's world. What men and gods alike covet is honor and glory. Agamemnon is angry not primarily because his woman was taken back to her father but because his honor is offended. Booty is valued not for its own sake so much as for the honor it conveys—the better the loot a warrior is awarded, the greater the honor bestowed. Achilles is overcome by rage because Agamemnon has humiliated him and thus deprived him of the honor due him. Therefore, Thetis begs Zeus to let the Trojans prevail until the Greeks recompense Akhilleus "and heap new honor upon him."

What is just in this social world is that each person receive the honor that is due him. So Nestor, wise counsellor of the Greeks, argues when he tries to make peace between Agamemnon and Akhilleus.

> Lord Agamémnon,
> do not deprive him of the girl, renounce her.
> The army had allotted her to him.
> Akhilleus, for your part, do not defy
> your King and Captain. No one vies in honor
> with him who holds authority from Zeus.
> You have more prowess, for a goddess bore you;
> his power over men surpasses yours.
>
> (ILIAD 1, 20–21)

Nestor tries to reconcile them by pointing out what is just, what each man's honor requires. Unfortunately, his good advice is heeded by neither.

The gods are also interested in honor. It has often been remarked that Homer's gods reflect the society that they allegedly govern; they are powerful, jealous of their prerogatives, quarrel among themselves, and are not above a certain deceitfulness, although some sorts of evil are simply beneath their dignity. The chief difference between human beings and gods is that human beings are bound for death and the gods are not. Greeks often refer to the gods simply as "the immortals." Immortality makes possible a kind of happiness or blessedness among the gods that is impossible for human beings.

As immortals, the gods are interested in the affairs of mortals, but only insofar as they are entertained or their honor touched. They are spectators of the human comedy—or tragedy; they watch human affairs the way we watch the soaps. There is a famous section in *The Iliad* where Zeus decides to sit out the battle about to rage on the plain below and simply observe. He says,

> Men on both sides may perish,
> still they are near my heart. And yet, by heaven,
> here I stay, at ease upon a ridge.
> I'll have an ample view here.
>
> (ILIAD 20, 474)

Such entertainment the gods may enjoy! At times they seem to forget all about humans, as the warriors of Homer's tale might well ignore their slaves and servants. For instance, after Zeus grants Thetis' prayer in Akhilleus' behalf, the gods sit down to a banquet. Some tension is felt, for Hera is not pleased that her husband has promised to aid the Trojans. But the spell is broken by bandy-legged Hephaistos, the master of the forge, who reminds them humorously that Zeus cannot be successfully resisted.

> To Mother my advice is—what she knows—
> better make up to Father, or he'll start
> his thundering and shake our feast to bits.
> You know how he can shock us if he cares to—
> out of our seats with lightning bolts!
>
> (ILIAD 1, 30)

He serves them "nectar of sweet delight." Then we read:

> And quenchless laughter
> broke out among the blissful gods
> to see Hêphaistos wheezing down the hall.
> So all day long until the sun went down
> they spent in feasting, and the measured feast
> matched well their hearts' desire.
>
> (ILIAD 1, 31)

The gods, too, deserve and demand the honor due them. We have already seen what can happen if it is not accorded. The plague was sent by Apollo because Agamemnon refused to accept the ransom offered by Apollo's priest for his daughter. When humans do not respect the prerogatives of the gods, do not give them due honor, they are guilty of arrogance, or **hubris**. In this state, a human being in effect thinks of himself as a god; he forgets his finitude, his limitations, his mortality. And *hubris* is punished by the gods, as hero after hero discovers to his dismay.

The gulf between Homeric gods and mortals—even those like Akhilleus who are accorded the dignity of half-divine parentage—is clear and impassable. In closing this brief survey, we need to emphasize two aspects of this gulf. First, no immortality worth prizing is believed in or aspired to by those whose thoughts were shaped by Homer. There is a kind of shadowy existence after death, but the typical attitude toward it is expressed by Akhilleus when he is visited in the underworld by Odysseus.

> Let me hear no smooth talk
> of death from you, Odysseus, light of councils.
> Better, I say, to break sod as a farm hand
> for some poor country man, on iron rations,
> than lord it over all the exhausted dead.[4]

(ODYSSEY 11, 201)

For these conquerors, who glory in the strength of their bodies, it seems impossible to suppose that there could be anything after death to compare. They know they are destined to die, believe that death is effectively the end of life, and take the attitude of Hektor when faced with Akhilleus.

> Death is near, and black, not at a distance,
> not to be evaded. Long ago
> this hour must have been to Zeus's liking
> and to the liking of his archer son.
> They have been well disposed before, but now
> the appointed time's upon me. Still, I would
> not die without delivering a stroke,
> or die ingloriously, but in some action
> memorable to men in days to come.

(ILIAD 22, 525)

Again, even at the end, the quest for honor is paramount.

The second conclusion is a corollary to the first. It is best expressed by Pindar, a poet of the sixth century B.C.E., but the thought is thoroughly Homeric.

> Seek not to become Zeus,
> For mortals a mortal lot is best.

> Mortal minds must seek what is fitting
> at the hands of the gods,
> knowing what lies at our feet
> and to what portion we are born.
> Strive not, my soul, for an immortal life,
> but use to the full the resources
> that are at thy command.[5]

Mortal thoughts for mortals. Human beings are not divine, not gods, not immortal. Let them strive for *excellence*, to "use to the full the resources" at their command (and no people, perhaps, has surpassed the Greeks in this). Let it be, however, an excellence appropriate to the "portion" allotted to humans. Not for the Greeks the deification of rulers in Persian or Roman fashion.* No blurring of the line by worshipping living men (although dead heroes, like saints, may occasionally receive sacrifice and prayer). Here too, in its estimate of the status human beings have in the world, the Homeric tradition praises moderation.

Notes

1. In this text, B.C.E. ("before the common era") and C.E. ("common era") are used instead of the traditional B.C. and A.D.
2. Homer, *The Iliad*, trans. Robert Fitzgerald (New York: Anchor Books, 1975). All quotations in the text are taken from this translation. References are to book and page numbers. Fitzgerald uses spelling that more closely approximates Greek spelling (thus Akhilleus rather than Achilles). This text follows his spellings.
3. Kathleen Freeman, *Ancilla to the Pre-Socratic Philosophers* (Cambridge, Mass.: Harvard University Press, 1948), 22.
4. Homer, *The Odyssey*, trans. Robert Fitzgerald (New York: Anchor Books, 1963). References are to book and page numbers.
5. Pindar, *Isthmia V and Pythia III*, trans. W. K. C. Guthrie, in *The Greeks and Their Gods* (Boston: Beacon Press, 1950), 113–14.

---

*There were exceptions. Heroes or rulers were occasionally given divine honors, and some, like Akhilleus, were considered only half mortal. But deification was not the norm.

2

Nature Philosophers

We can think of Homer as opening the conversation whose course we intend to trace. This idea is, of course, somewhat artificial, and in two senses. First, the Homeric tradition is just one of several traditions in Greece itself, as we learned earlier. For several centuries, however, it was the dominant one; Homer is allocated pride of place among the teachers of the Greeks. That is our justification for beginning with him.

Second, the Greek city-states are not the only sources of this conversation. Even if it is true that philosophic thought begins there, other sources also feed into our story. In particular, we will need to pay close attention to the Hebrew tradition, which was taking shape at the same time as Homeric bards were singing of Troy. But that tradition, together with its Christian successor—while enormously influential and making significant contributions to the conversation—did not by itself lead to philosophy. We will wait to consider it until such time as philosophers were forced to pay attention to what it had to say.

Let's turn now to the first recognizably philosophical voices: those of the nature philosophers, or proto-scientists, of Ionia (see map 1). It is seldom entirely clear why certain thinkers raised in a certain tradition become dissatisfied enough to try to establish a new one. The reason is even more obscure here. We have a scarcity of information regarding these thinkers. Although most of them

wrote books, these writings are almost entirely lost, some surviving in small fragments, others known only by references to them and quotations or paraphrases by later writers. As a group, these thinkers are usually known as the "pre-Socratics." This name testifies to the pivotal importance put on Socrates by his successors.

For whatever reason, a tradition grew up in which questions about the nature of the world took center stage, a tradition that was not content with stories about the gods. Thinkers were trying to *reason* their way to an answer; the Homeric tales must have seemed to them impossibly crude. We have noted that in Homer's poems Zeus and the other gods are simply taken for granted. Others had asked, "How did the gods come to be what they are?" Hesiod, for instance, in the eighth century B.C.E. tells of the origins of all things, of the birth of heaven and earth and of Homer's gods. "Birth" here is to be taken quite literally, for the stories are explicitly sexual. This should not be too surprising to us, for if we look about and ask, "Where do things come from?" the phenomena of sexual reproduction present an obvious and inescapable model. This model is rationally unsatisfactory, however, if we want to account for the origin of everything. If we are told that all things come from an original pair, we are immediately faced with the question, "And what does the original pair come from?"

Thales: Water and Gods

Some such dissatisfaction must have been felt by Thales of Miletus (a Greek seaport on the shore of Asia Minor—see map 1), whom Aristotle calls the founder of philosophy. We know very little about Thales, and part of that is arguably legendary. So, our consideration will be brief and somewhat speculative. He is said to have held that the cause and "element" of all things was water and that all things were filled with gods. What could these two rather obscure sayings mean?

Concerning the first, it is striking that Thales supposes there *is* some one thing which is both the origin and the underlying nature of all things. It is surely not obvious that wine and bread and stones and wind are really the same stuff despite all their differences. It is equally striking that Thales chooses one of the things that occur naturally in the world of our experience to play that role. Notice that it is neither Zeus nor Kronos (Zeus' father, according to Hesiod) nor Rhea (the earth-goddess mother who bore him) who plays this role. It is water. Here we are clearly in a different world of thought from that of Homer. The motto seems to be: Account for what you can see and touch in terms of things you can see and touch. This idea is a radical departure from anything prior to it.

Why do you think Thales chooses water to play the role of the primeval stuff? Aristotle speculates that Thales must have noticed that water is essential for the nourishment of all things and that without moisture seeds will not develop into plants. We might add that Thales must have noticed that water is the only naturally occurring substance that can be seen to vary from solid to liquid to gas. The fact that the wet blue sea, the white crystalline snow, and the damp and muggy air seem to be the very same thing despite their differences could well have suggested that water might take even more forms.

At first glance, the saying that all things are full of gods seems to go in a quite different direction. If we think a moment, however, we can see that it is quite consistent with the saying about water. What is the essential characteristic of the gods, according to the Greeks? Their immortality. To say that all things are full of gods, then, is to say in effect that *in* them—not, note well, outside them or in addition to them—is a principle that is immortal. But this suggests that the things of experience do not need explanations from outside themselves as to why they exist. Moreover, tradition appeals to the gods as a principle of action. Why did lightning strike just *there*? Because Zeus was angry with *that man*. But to say that all things are themselves full of gods may well mean that we do not have to appeal *beyond* them to explain why they happened. They have the principles of their behavior within themselves.

Both sayings, then, point thought in a direction quite different from the tradition of Homer and Hesiod. They suggest that if we want to understand this world, then it is to this world we should look, not to another. As we'll see, this view is quite congenial to Aristotle himself* (with certain qualifications); perhaps that is why he chooses the ideas of Thales to represent the beginnings of philosophical thought. Thales seems to have been the first to have tried to answer the question, Why do things happen as they do? in terms that are not immediately personal. It is almost impossible to overestimate the significance of this shift for the story of Western culture.

Anaximander: The Boundless

Let's grant that Thales has made a significant move. What next? Although he may have done so, we have no evidence that Thales addresses the question of *how* water accounts for everything else. If all is, in some sense, water, why does it seem as though many things are *not* water, that water is just one kind of thing among the many kinds that exist? Thales leaves us with a puzzle for which there is no clear solution.

---

*See p. 153–154.

There is something else unsatisfactory about his suggestion: even though water has those unusual properties of appearing in several different states, water itself is not unusual. It is, after all, just one of the many things that need to be explained. If we demand explanations of dirt and bone and gold, why should we not demand an explanation for water as well?

Although again we are speculating, it is reasonable to suppose that problems such as these led to the next stage in our story. We can imagine Anaximander, a younger fellow citizen from Miletus born about 612 B.C.E., asking himself—or perhaps asking Thales—these questions. *How* does water produce the many things of our experience? And *why* is water so special? The conversation develops.

Like Hesiod, Anaximander is interested in origins, but like Thales, he wants a "naturalistic" account of origins. At least, he wants one that does not appeal to the "supernatural" gods of Homer and Hesiod; as we'll see, the "divine" is not rejected, just reinterpreted. Assuming that there is nothing special about water, that it needs explanation just as much as any other kind of thing, we can reconstruct Anaximander's reasoning thus:

1. Given any state of things *X*, it had a beginning.
2. To explain its beginning, we must suppose a prior state of things *W*.
3. But *W* also must have had a beginning.
4. So, we must suppose a still prior state *V*.
5. Can this go on forever? No.
6. So there must be something which itself *has no beginning*.
7. We can call this *the infinite* or *the boundless*.

It is from this, then, that all things come.

We are ready now to appreciate a passage of Aristotle's, in which he looks back and reports the views of Anaximander.

Everything either is a beginning or has a beginning. But there is no beginning of the infinite; for if there were one, it would limit it. Moreover, since it is a beginning, it is unbegotten and indestructible. . . . Hence, as we say, there is no source of this, but this appears to be the source of all the rest, and "encompasses all things" and "steers all things," as those assert who do not recognize other causes besides the infinite. . . . And this, they say, is the divine; for it is "deathless" and "imperishable" as Anaximander puts it, and most of the physicists agree with him (*IEGP*, 24).[1]

Only the infinite or the boundless, then, can be a beginning for all other things. It *is* a beginning, as Aristotle puts it; it does not *have* a beginning. Because it is infinite, moreover, it has not only no beginning but also no end—otherwise it would have a limit and not be infinite.

It should be no surprise that the infinite is called "divine." Recall the constant characteristic ascribed by the Greeks to the gods: they are immortal; they cannot die. As Anaximander points out, this is precisely the key feature of the boundless.

Here we have the first appearance of a form of reasoning that we will meet again when later thinkers try to justify belief in a god (or God) conceived in a much richer way than Anaximander is committed to.* Yet even here some of the key features of later thought are already present. The boundless "encompasses all things" and "steers all things." Those familiar with the New Testament will be reminded of Paul's statement that in God "we live and move and have our being" (Acts 17:28).[2]

We should note that Aristotle remarks almost casually that those who use this language "do not recognize other causes besides the infinite." Here he hints at what he considers a defect in the view of Anaximander: it is too abstract to account in detail for the nature and behavior of the myriads of species and individuals we actually find in the world. What we need is not one big cause but many little causes.† But that is getting ahead of our story; we will return to this point.

---

*For an example, see Thomas Aquinas's third proof of the existence of God (Chapter 15).
†See pp. 154–156.

We have seen how Anaximander deals with one of the puzzles bequeathed to him by Thales. It is not water but the boundless that is the source and "element" of all things. What about the other problem? How does the boundless produce the many individual things of our experience?

The first point to note is that the ancient Greeks tend to adopt a fourfold classification scheme into which they fit all the many things there are. These four categories are "the hot," "the cold," "the dry," and "the moist." Most things are a mixture of these four; as you may know, they are the basis for much of Greek medicine. A feverish person, for instance, has too much of the hot, a person with the sniffles too much of the moist, and so on. At this early stage of thought, no clear distinction is made between heat as a *property* of a thing and the thing that is hot. There is just "the hot" and "the cold," what we might think of as hot-stuff and cold-stuff. In fact, these stuffs are virtually indistinguishable from what later came to be called earth (the cold), air (the dry), fire (the hot), and water (the moist). The universe was composed of various mixtures of these stuffs.

This classification scheme allows for a certain simplification of the problem at hand, which is how the many things of the world are produced by the infinite or boundless. If Anaximander could show how these four separate out, the basic problem would be solved; the rest would be details and could be solved along similar lines. To solve the problem, he uses an analogy. If you take a circular pan filled with water, put bits of limestone, granite, and lead in it (what you need is a variety of different weights), and then somehow get the water to swirl about, you find that the heavier bits move toward the middle and the lighter bits to the outside. Like goes to like; what starts as a jumble, a chaos, begins to possess some order. Anaximander is apparently familiar with this simple experiment and makes use of the principle involved to solve his problem.

If the infinite were swirling, like the water in the pan, in a *vortex motion*, then what was originally indistinguishable in it would become separated

out according to its nature. But what reason do we have for thinking that the boundless engages in such a swirling, vortex motion? Here Anaximander would ask you to look up. Every day we see the heavenly bodies in their swirl around the earth: the sun, the moon, and even—though much more slowly—the stars. Did you ever lie on your back out in a very dark, open spot (a golf course is a good place) for a long time and look at the stars? You can see them move, too, although it takes a long while to become conscious of their movement.*

Furthermore, it seems clear that the motions observable in the world exemplify the principle of the water in the pan. What is the lightest of the elements? Anyone who has stared at a camp fire for a few moments will have no doubt about the answer. The sticks stay put, but the fire leaps up, away from the cold earth toward the sky. And what bodies do we see in the sky whirling about the earth: the immensely hot, fiery sun and the other bright but less hot heavenly bodies.

According to the geography accepted at the time, moreover, the habitable earth was surrounded by an ocean of water, which was surrounded in turn by the air. Thus, we have an ordered, sorted world: earth (cold and heavy) in the middle, water (wet and not quite so heavy), then air, and in an outermost ring the fiery element—all in a continuous vortex motion that both produces and sustains the order. This explanation seems plausible and fits the observable data. What more could one ask?

We know more about Anaximander's views. He explains why we see not a ring of fire in the sky but rather spots (the ring is hidden for the most part by an opaque covering). He calculates (inaccurately) the orbits of the sun and moon. He offers an explanation of why the earth stays where it does (it rides on air—what we might call the frisbee principle). He gives us a non-Zeusian explanation of thunder and lightning (caused by the wind compressed in

---

*Copernicus, of course, turns this natural view inside out. The stars only *appear* to move; in actuality, Copernicus suggests, it is *we* who are moving. See pp. 280–281.

clouds). He suggests that humans originated inside other animals (fish, in particular). We needn't stop to discuss most of these points.[3] There is one more principle, however, that we need to give some attention.

Anaximander tells us that existing things "make reparation to one another for their injustice according to the ordinance of time" (*IEGP*, 34). Several questions arise here. What existing things? No doubt it is the opposites of hot and cold, wet and dry that Anaximander has in mind, but why does he speak of injustice? How can the hot and cold do each other injustice, and how can they "make reparation" to each other? There can be little doubt of the answer. He presupposes a principle of balance in nature that must ultimately be served, however much one or the other element seems to have gotten the upper hand. The hot summer is hot at the expense of the cold; it requires a cold winter to right the balance. A too dry winter, we still tend to think, will have to be paid for by a too wet spring. Thus, each season encroaches on the "rights" due to the others and does them an injustice, but reparation is made in turn when each gets its due—and more. This keeps the cycle going.

Notice two points in particular. First, this view is, in its own way, an extension of the Homeric view that requires a certain moderation in human behavior. Too much of anything—too much anger, too much pride—brings down the wrath of the gods. Here, Anaximander imagines a cosmic principle of moderation at work in the elements of the world. It is as if he were saying to Homer, "You are right, but your view is too limited; the principle applies not only within the human world but also in the universe at large."

The second point, however, is equally important. This principle is not imposed on reality from without; it is not applied by the gods. Anaximander conceives it as immanent in the world process itself. Thus, he says, does the world work. In this he is faithful to the spirit of Thales, and in this both of them depart from the tradition of Homer, the first and foremost "teacher of the Greeks." His explanations are framed impersonally. It is true

that there is "the boundless" that "steers all things." But the Homeric gods who intervene at will in the world have vanished. To explain particular facts in the world, no will, no purpose, no intention is needed. The gods turn out to be superfluous.

You can easily see that a cultural crisis is on the way. If the Homeric tradition is still alive and flourishing, if it still forms the conscious and unconscious background to the religious, artistic, political, and social life of Greek cities, what will happen when this new way of thinking begins to take hold? We mustn't, however, get too far ahead. There are other voices we need to hear before we can understand that crisis.

Xenophanes: The Gods as Fictions

From what we know about Anaximander, it seems that his criticism of the Homeric tradition was implicit rather than explicit. He was intent on solving his problems about the nature and origins of the world. Although his results were at odds with tradition, we have no record that he took explicit notice of this. Not so with Xenophanes.

A native of Colophon, about forty miles north of Miletus (see map 1), he was, like Thales and Anaximander, an Ionian Greek living on the eastern shores of the Aegean Sea. We are told that he fled in 546 B.C.E. when Colophon was taken by the Persians and that he lived at least part of his life thereafter in Sicily. (The Greek world at that time encompassed not only Greece proper but the lands from western Asia Minor to southern Italy, including the many smaller and greater islands between.) Xenophanes was a poet and apparently lived a long life of more than ninety-two years.

Xenophanes is important to our story because he seems to have been the first to state clearly the religious implications of the new nature philosophy. He explicitly criticizes the Homeric conception of the gods on two grounds. First, the way Homer pictures the gods for us is unworthy of our admiration or reverence:

Homer and Hesiod have attributed to the gods all those things which in men are a matter for reproach and censure: stealing, adultery, and mutual deception (*IEGP*, 55).

What he says is true, of course. It has often been remarked that Homer's gods are morally no better (and in some ways maybe worse) than the band of ruthless warrior barons on whom they are so clearly modelled. Magnificent in their own fashion they are, but flawed, like a large and brilliant diamond containing a vein of impurities. What is significant about Xenophanes' statement is that he not only notices this but clearly expresses his disapproval. He thinks it is *shameful* to portray the gods as though they are no better than human beings whom good men regard with disgust. That Homer, to whom all Greeks of the time look for guidance in life, should give us this view of the divine seems intolerable to Xenophanes. This moral criticism is further developed by Plato.* It is the negative side of a more exalted notion of divinity for both Xenophanes and Plato.

This kind of criticism makes sense only on the basis of a certain assumption: that Homer is not simply mirroring the truth for us but inventing stories. Several sayings of Xenophanes make this assumption clear.

> The Ethiopians make their gods snub-nosed and black; the Thracians make theirs gray-eyed and red-haired (*IEGP*, 52).
>
> And if oxen and horses and lions had hands, and could draw with their hands and do what man can do, horses would draw the gods in the shape of horses, and oxen in the shape of oxen, each giving the gods bodies similar to their own (*IEGP*, 52).

Here we have the first recorded version of the saying that god does not make men in his own image but that men make the gods in their own image. This, Xenophanes tells us, is what Homer and Hesiod have done. This point has often been made since Xenophanes' time by atheists and agnostics. Was Xenophanes, then, a disbeliever in the divine? No, not at all. No more than Anaximander, who says the infinite sees all and steers all. Xenophanes tells us there is

> one god, greatest among gods and men, in no way similar to mortals either in body or mind (*IEGP*, 53).

Several points in this brief statement stand out. There is only one god. Xenophanes takes pains to stress how radically different this god is from anything in the Homeric tradition. It is in "no way similar to mortals." This point is brought out in some positive characterizations he gives us of this dissimilar god.

> He sees all over, thinks all over, hears all over.
>
> He remains always in the same place, without moving; nor is it fitting that he should come and go, first to one place and then to another.
>
> But without toil, he sets all things in motion by the thought of his mind (*IEGP*, 53).

This god is very different from human beings indeed. We see with our eyes, think with our brain, and hear with our ears. We seldom remain in the same place for more than a short time; indeed, if we are strict enough about what constitutes the "same place," we might come to agree with Heraclitus, who argues that we and all things are constantly moving from one place to another.* Furthermore, if we want to set anything besides ourselves in motion, just thinking about it or wishing for it isn't enough. In all these ways we are different from the one god.

Yet there is a similarity after all, and Xenophanes' "no way similar" must be qualified. The one god sees and hears and thinks; so do we. He

---

*See *Euthyphro* 6a, for instance. This criticism is expanded in Plato's *Republic*, Book II, where Plato explicitly forbids the telling of Homeric and Hesiodic tales of the gods to children in his ideal state.

*See pp. 17–18.

does not do it in the *way* we do it; the way it is done is indeed "in no way similar." But god is intelligent, and so are we.

Here is a good place to comment on an assumption that seems to have been common among the Greeks. Where there is order, there is intelligence. Order, whether in our lives or in the world of nature, is not self-explanatory; only intelligence can supply the explanation. It's not clear whether this assumption is ever explicitly argued for or justified. It lies in the background as something almost too obvious to comment on. We can find common experiences to give it some support, and perhaps these are common enough to make it *seem* self-evident—but it is not. For example, consider the state of things on your desk or tools in your workshop. If you are like me, you find that these things, if left to their own devices, degenerate slowly into a state of chaos. Soon it is impossible to find what you want when you need it, and it becomes impossible to work. What you need to do then is *deliberately* and with some *intelligent plan in mind* impose order on the chaos. Order is the result of intelligent action, it seems. It doesn't just *happen*.

Whether this assumption is correct is an interesting question, one about which modern physics and evolutionary biology have had interesting things to say.* Modern mathematicians tell us that however chaotic the jumble of books and papers on your desk, there exists some mathematical function according to which they are in perfect order. However, we are getting ahead of our story. For the Greeks, the existence of order always presupposes an ordering intelligence. We find this assumption at work in the views of the divine given us by Anaximander and Xenophanes.

Let's consider a saying that shows us how closely Xenophanes' criticism of the traditional gods relates to the developing nature philosophy.

She whom men call "Iris," too, is in reality a cloud, purple, red, and green to the sight (*IEGP*, 52).

In *The Iliad*, Iris is a minor goddess, a messenger for the other gods. For instance, after Hektor has killed Patroklos, Iris is sent to Akhilleus to bid him arm in time to rescue Patroklos' body.[4] She seems to have been identified with the rainbow, which many cultures have taken as a sign or message from the gods. (Compare its significance to Noah, for example, after the flood in Genesis 9:12–17.)

Xenophanes tells us that rainbows are simply natural phenomena which occur in natural circumstances and have natural explanations. A rainbow, he thinks, is just a peculiar sort of cloud. This idea suggests a theory of how gods are invented. Natural phenomena, especially those that are unusual, particularly striking, or important to us, are personified and given lives that go beyond what is observable. Like the theory that the gods are invented, this theory has often been held. It may not be stretching things too far to regard Xenophanes as its originator.

It is clear that there is a kind of natural unity between nature philosophy and criticism of Homer's gods. They go together and mutually reinforce one another. Together they are more powerful than either could be alone. We will see that they come to pose a serious threat to the integrity of Greek cultural life.

There is one last theme in Xenophanes that we should address. Poets in classical times typically appealed to the Muses for inspiration and seemed often to think that what they spoke or wrote was not their own—that it was literally in-spired, or breathed into them, by these goddesses. Thus Hesiod, at the beginning of his *Theogony* (birth of the gods) writes:

The Muses once taught Hesiod to sing
Sweet songs, while he was shepherding his lambs
On holy Helicon; the goddesses
Olympian, daughters of Zeus who holds
The aegis, first addressed these words to me:
"You rustic shepherds, shame: bellies you are,
Not men! We know enough to make up lies

---

*See p. 289 for an example. Here Descartes claims that a chaos of randomly distributed elements, if subject to the laws of physics, would *by itself* produce an order like that we find in the world. For more recent views, see the fascinating book by James Gleick, *Chaos: Making a New Science* (New York: Penguin Books, 1987).

Which are convincing, but we also have
The skill, when we've a mind, to speak the truth."

So spoke the fresh-voiced daughters of great Zeus
And plucked and gave a staff to me, a shoot
Of blooming laurel, wonderful to see,
And breathed a sacred voice into my mouth
With which to celebrate the things to come
And things which were before.[5]

Hesiod clearly claims here that his words are not just his. They are breathed into his mouth by the daughters of Zeus himself. As such, they are not just the lying tales that shepherds are likely to tell. They are the very truth itself. No doubt this is more than a literary conceit; there are experiences of inspiration when one seems to be no more than a mouthpiece for powers greater and truer than oneself. Hesiod may well have had such experiences. Whether such experiences guarantee the *truth* of what one says in such ecstatic states is, of course, another question. Listen to Xenophanes.

The gods have not revealed all things from the beginning to mortals; but, by seeking, men find out, in time, what is better.

No man knows the truth, nor will there be a man who has knowledge about the gods and what I say about everything. For even if he were to hit by chance upon the whole truth, he himself would not be aware of having done so, but each forms his own opinion.

Let these things, then, be taken as like the truth . . . (*IEGP*, 56).

This is a very rich set of statements. Let us consider them in six points.

1. Xenophanes is deliberately, explicitly, denying Hesiod's claim of inspiration. He might well have had just this passage in mind (though there were lots of similar claims made). The gods have *not* revealed to us in this way "from the beginning" what is true. If we were to ask him why he is so sure about this, he would no doubt remind us of the unworthy picture of deity painted by the poets and of the natural explanations that can be given for phenomena they ascribe to the gods. Xenophanes' point is that the poet's claim of divine revelation is no guarantee of the poem's truth.

2. How, then, is it appropriate to form our beliefs? By "seeking," Xenophanes tells us. This idea is extremely vague. How, exactly, are we to seek? No doubt he is thinking of methods of the Ionian nature philosophers, but we don't have a very good idea of just what they were. So we don't get much help at this point.

Still, his remarks are not entirely without content. What he envisages is a process of moving toward the truth. If we want the truth, we should face not the past but the future. It is no good looking back to the tradition, to Homer and Hesiod, as though they had already said the last words. We must look to ourselves and to the results of our seeking. He is confident, perhaps because he values the results of the nature philosophers, that "in time"—not all at once—men will discover "what is better." They may not succeed in finding the truth, but their opinions will be "better," or more "like the truth."

3. It may be that we know some truth already. Perhaps there is someone who even knows "the whole truth." But even if he did, that person could not know for certain that it *is* the truth. To use a distinction Plato later makes much of, the person would not be able to distinguish his knowledge of the truth from mere opinion.* (Plato, as we'll see, does not agree.) There is, Xenophanes means to tell us, no such thing as *certainty* for limited human beings such as ourselves. Here is a theme that later skeptics take up.†

4. It does not follow from this somewhat skeptical conclusion that all beliefs are equally good. Xenophanes is very clear that although we may not ever be certain we have reached the truth, some beliefs are better or more "like the truth" than others. How we are to tell which are more truthlike he unfortunately does not tell us. Again we have a problem that many later thinkers take up.

5. Here we have a new direction for thought. Until now thought has basically been directed out-

---

*See pp. 106–108.
†See, for instance, the discussions by Sextus Empiricus (pp. 194–197) and Montaigne (pp. 277–279). Similar themes are found in Descartes' first *Meditation* and in the pragmatists (pp. 467, 478).

wards—to the gods, to the world of men, to nature. Xenophanes directs thought back upon itself. His questioning questions itself. How much can we know? How can we know it? Can we reach the truth? Can we reach certainty about the truth? These are the central questions that define the branch of philosophy called epistemology, or theory of knowledge. It seems correct to say that Xenophanes is its father.

6. If we ask, then, whether there is anyone who can know the truth *and* know that he knows it, what is the answer? Yes. The one god does, the one who "sees all over, thinks all over, hears all over." In this answer, Xenophanes carries forward that strain of Homeric tradition which emphasizes the gulf between humans and gods. The most important truth about humans is that they are not gods.* Xenophanes' remarks about human knowledge seem designed to drive that point home once and for all.

Notes

1. Quotations from John Manley Robinson's *An Introduction to Early Greek Philosophy* (Boston: Houghton Mifflin Co., 1968) are cited in the text using the abbreviation *IEGP*.
2. Biblical quotations in this text are taken from the Revised Standard Version.
3. If you would like to pursue these details (and others pertaining to the pre-Socratics), I heartily recommend the excellent treatment by John Manley Robinson. A more extensive treatment with original Greek texts is found in G. S. Kirk and J. E. Raven, *The Presocratic Philosophers* (Cambridge: The University Press, 1957).
4. Homer, *The Iliad*, trans. Robert Fitzgerald (New York: Anchor Books, 1975), bk. 18, p. 441.
5. Hesiod, *Theogony*, trans. Dorothea Wender, in *Hesiod and Theognis* (New York: Penguin Books, 1973), 23–24.

---

*Compare the poem of Pindar, part of which is quoted on p. 5.

3

Problems in Nature Philosophy

As we have seen, the Ionian philosophers are proposing interesting and novel views of nature and the gods. Subsequent thinkers are building on the work of their predecessors or reacting to puzzles implicit in their views. The great conversation is well under way.

If we reflect on the state of such opinion around the year 500 B.C.E., on the views of Thales, Anaximander, Xenophanes, and others not mentioned here, we should be able to see a puzzle at the heart of it that has not been resolved. The variegated world we live in, with all its multiplicity, has been explained as the product of one single cause: water or the boundless or the one god. But it has not been made clear on what principle the one source and the many products are related. In what sense is it, exactly, that reality—so obviously many different things—is "one"? This is the problem of "the one and the many." In some lectures given in 1906–1907, William James, an American psychologist and philosopher, was to call it "the most central of all philosophic problems."[1] It is first addressed as such by Heraclitus.

Heraclitus: The One and the Many

Heraclitus is said to have been at his peak (probably corresponding to middle age) shortly before 500 B.C.E. A native of Ephesus (see map 1), he was,

like the others we have considered, an Ionian Greek living on the shores of Asia Minor. We know that he wrote a book, of which about one hundred fragments remain. He had a reputation for writing in riddles and was often referred to in Roman times as "Heraclitus the obscure." His favored style seems to have been the epigram, the short, pithy saying that condenses a lot of thought into few words. Despite his reputation, most modern interpreters find that the fragments reveal a powerful and unified view of the world and man's place in it. Furthermore, Heraclitus is clearly an important influence on subsequent thinkers such as Plato and the Stoics.

The most characteristic feature of his thought is that reality is a flux.

All things come into being through opposition, and all are in flux, like a river (*IEGP*, 89).[2]

There are two parts to this saying, one about opposition and one about flux. Let's begin with the latter and discuss the part about opposition later. Plato ascribes to Heraclitus the view that "you cannot step twice into the same river." If you know anything at all about Heraclitus, it is probably in connection with this famous saying. What Heraclitus actually says, however, is slightly different.

Upon those who step into the same rivers flow other and yet other waters (*IEGP*, 91).

17

You can, he says, step several times into the same river. Yet it is not the same, for the waters into which you step the second time are different waters. The unity of things that are different—even sometimes opposite—is a theme Heraclitus plays in many variations.

> The path traced by the pen is straight and crooked.
>
> Sea water is very pure and very impure; drinkable and healthful for fishes, but undrinkable and destructive to men.
>
> The way up and the way down are the same (*IEGP*, 93–94).

The road from Canterbury to Dover is the road from Dover to Canterbury. They are "the same," just as it is the same water that is healthful and destructive, the same movement of the pen that is crooked (when you consider the individual letters) but also straight (when you consider the line written).

Consider the river. It is the same river, although the water of which it is composed is continuously changing. A river is not identical with the water that makes it up but is a kind of structure or pattern that makes a unity of ever-changing elements. It is a *one* that holds together the *many*. So it is, Heraclitus tells us, with "all things." All things are in flux, like the river, ever changing, and the river is for that reason a fit symbol for reality.

Another appropriate symbol for this flux is fire.

> This world-order, the same for all, no god made or any man, but it always was and is and will be an ever-living fire, kindling by measure and going out by measure (*IEGP*, 90).

Is Heraclitus here expressing disagreement with Thales? Is he telling us Thales is wrong in thinking that water rather than fire is the source of all things? In one sense Heraclitus is disagreeing, but in another sense he is not. Remember that at this early stage of thought the very language in which thoughts can be expressed is itself being formed. This means that thought itself is somewhat crude. As we observed earlier, the distinction between "hot-stuff" and "fire that is hot" has not yet been made. Heraclitus is reaching for abstractions that he hasn't quite got and cannot quite express. What he wants to talk about is the "world-order." This is, *we* would say, not itself a *thing* but an abstract *pattern* or *structure* in which the things of the world are displayed. Heraclitus, though, hasn't quite got that degree of abstraction, so he uses the most ethereal, least solid thing he is acquainted with to represent the world-order: fire.

We can be certain, moreover, that Heraclitus does not have ordinary cooking fires primarily in mind. Recall the view of Anaximander that the outermost sphere of the universe, in which the sun and stars are located, is a ring of fire. If you have ever been to Greece on a particularly clear day, especially on or near the sea, you can see even through our polluted atmosphere that not only the sun but the entire sky shines. The heavens are luminous, radiant. It is not too much to say the sky *blazes*. It is this luminous *aither*, as it was called, in which the gods are supposed to live. Olympus is said to be their home because its peak could be seen immersed in this fiery element. Notice the epithet Heraclitus gives to fire. He calls it "ever-living." And what, for the Greeks, deserves this accolade? Only, of course, the divine.

It is, then, the world-order itself that is immortal, divine. Heraclitus represents it as fire, the most ethereal and least "substantial" of the elements. No god made *that*, of course, for the world-order is itself eternal and divine.

This divine fire is both the *substance* of the world and its *pattern*. In its former aspect it is ever "kindling by measure and going out by measure." This thought is also expressed in the following fragments.

> The changes of fire: first sea, and of sea half is earth, half fiery thunderbolt . . .
>
> All things are an exchange for fire, and fire for all things; as goods are for gold, and gold for goods (*IEGP*, 91).

The sea, we learn, is a mixture, half earth and half fire. And all things are in continuous exchange.

Earth is washed into the sea and becomes moist; sea becomes air, which merges with the fiery heavens, from which rains fall and merge again with earth. If Heraclitus were able to use the distinction between things and patterns, he might say that *as a thing* fire has no priority over other things. It is just one of the four elements taking part with the others in the constant cycles of change. But *as pattern*, as world-order, it does have priority, for this pattern is eternal and divine. He does not, of course, say this; he can't. If he were able to, he might be less "obscure" to his successors.

We need now to go back to the first part of our original fragment, where Heraclitus says that "all things come into being through opposition." What can this mean? Compare the following statements.

War is the father and king of all. . . .

It is necessary to understand that war is universal and justice is strife, and that all things take place in accordance with strife and necessity (*IEGP*, 93).

Strife, opposition, war. Why are these elevated into universal principles? To see what Heraclitus is saying, think about some examples. A lyre will produce music, but only if there is a tension on the strings. The arms of the lyre pull in one direction, the strings in the opposite. Without this opposition, there is no music. Consider the river. What is it that makes a river a river? It is the force of the flowing water struggling with the opposing forces of the containing banks. Without the opposition between the banks and the water, there would be no river. Think of a sculpture. It is the result of the efforts of the artist and the chisel fighting the resistance of the stone. Now, if we think not about physical phenomena but about society, we see the same is true. What is justice, Heraclitus asks, but the result of the conflict between the desires of the wealthy and the desires of the poor? Were either to get the upper hand absolutely, there would be no justice. Tension, opposition, and conflict, he tells us, are *necessary*. Without them the universe could not persist. If we look carefully at each of these examples, we see that each consists of a unity of diverse elements. The lyre, the river, the statue,

and justice are each a *one* composed in some sense of *many*. In every "one," "many" strive.

In *The Iliad* Akhilleus laments the death of Patroklos, saying,

Ai! let strife and rancor perish from the lives of gods and men. . . .[3]

To this cry Heraclitus is supposed to have said,

He did not see that he was praying for the destruction of the whole; for if his prayers were heard, all things would pass away . . . (*IEGP*, 93).

Strife, then, is necessary. Yet it produces not chaos but the opposite; in fact, the divine world-order is the guarantee that a balance of forces is maintained. The result is this:

To god all things are beautiful and good and just; but men suppose some things to be just and others unjust (*IEGP*, 92).

Again we see the Homeric contrast between gods and mortals, and again the contrast is to the disadvantage of mortals. God, the divine fire, the world-order, sees things as they are; and they are good. Strife is not opposed to the good; strife is its necessary presupposition. Mortals, like Akhilleus, only "suppose," and what they suppose is false.

It is not characteristic of men to be intelligent; but it is characteristic of god (*IEGP*, 98).

We are now ready to consider the most explicit version of Heraclitus' solution to the problem of the one and the many. To do that, I must introduce a term that I will usually leave untranslated. It is a term that has numerous meanings in Greek and has had a long and important history, stretching from Heraclitus to the Sophists, to Plato and Aristotle, into the writings of the New Testament and the Christian church fathers, and beyond. The term is **logos**.

Logos is derived from a verb meaning "to speak" and refers first of all to the word or words that a speaker says. But as in English, a term is easily stretched beyond the simple, literal meaning. As we can ask for the latest "word" about the economy, the Greek can ask for the *logos* about the economy, meaning something like "message" or "discourse." This meaning easily progresses to the *thought* expressed in a discourse. Since such thought is typically backed up by reasons or has a rationale behind it, *logos* also comes to mean "rationale" or "argument." Arguments are composed of conclusions and the reasons offered for those conclusions. So, an argument has a typical pattern or structure to it, which is the job of *logic* to display. (Our term "logic" is derived from *logos*.) *Logos*, then, can also mean a structure or pattern, particularly if the pattern is a rational one.

You can see that *logos* is a very rich term, containing layers of related meanings: word, message, discourse, thought, rationale, argument, pattern, structure. When the word is used in Greek, it reverberates with all these associations. We have no precise equivalent in English, and for that reason I usually do not translate it.

As we have seen, Heraclitus claims that all things are part of a process of continuous change and that part of what makes them the things they are is a tension between opposite forces. This world of changes is not a chaos but is structured by a world-order that is divine in nature; in itself, therefore, it is good and beautiful. Unfortunately,

the many do not understand such things. . . .*

Though the logos is as I have said, men always fail to comprehend it, both before they hear it and when they hear it for the first time. For though all things come into being in accordance with this logos, they seem like men without experience (*IEGP*, 94).

There is a *logos*, Heraclitus now tells us, by which "all things come into being." What else is this but the structure or pattern of the world-order that we

had met before? But now the conception is deepened. The *logos* is not what it is just accidentally. It has a rationale that can be seen to be reasonable and right. It is not understood, however, by "the many." Heraclitus contrasts, as Socrates does later, the few who are wise, who listen to the *logos*, and the many who are foolish.

Why is it that the many do not understand the *logos*? Is it so strange and distant that only a few people ever have a chance to become acquainted with it? Not at all.

Though they are in daily contact with the *logos* they are at variance with it, and what they meet appears alien to them.

To those who are awake the world-order is one, common to all; but the sleeping turn aside each into a world of his own.

We ought to follow what is common to all; but though the *logos* is common to all, the many live as though their thought were private to themselves (*IEGP*, 94–95).

All people are "in daily contact" with this *logos*. It is all about us, present in everything that happens. You can't do or say anything without being immersed in it. Yet we ignore it. We are like sleepers who live in private dreams rather than in awareness of this rational pattern of things that "is common to all." We each manufacture a little world of our own, no doubt distorted by our own interests, fears, and anxieties, which we take for reality. In so doing, we miss the *logos* and become foolish rather than wise. What is it, after all, to be wise?

Wisdom is one thing: to understand the thought which steers all things through all things.

The one and only wisdom is willing and unwilling to be called Zeus (*IEGP*, 88).

To be wise is to understand the nature and structure of the world. To be wise is to see that all is and must be ever changing, that strife and opposition are necessary and not evil, and that if appreciated apart from our narrowly construed interests, they

---

*His term "the many" usually applies to all the individual things of which the world is composed; here, of course, it means "most people."

are good and beautiful. To be wise is to grasp the *logos*, the "thought which steers all things."* To be wise is to participate in the perspective of Zeus.

Why is this wisdom both "willing and unwilling" to be called by the name of Zeus? We can assume it is willing because Zeus is the common name for the highest of the gods, for the divine; to have such wisdom makes one a participant in the divine. Acting according to the *logos* is manifesting in one's life the very principles that govern the universe. However, such wisdom refuses the name of the Zeus of the Homeric tradition, who is immoral, unworthy, and no better than one of the many who do not understand the *logos*. Heraclitus, we see, agrees with the criticisms of traditional religion offered by Xenophanes.

Hesitant to reinforce these traditional pictures of deity, Heraclitus tells us:

Thunderbolt steers all things (*IEGP*, 89).

As we have just seen, there is a "thought" (a *logos*) that steers all things. Now we are told it is "thunderbolt." Thus we are brought back to the idea that a divine fire both *is* the world-order and manifests itself *in* that world-order. Reluctant to use the name of Zeus, Heraclitus chooses the most dramatic form of fire familiar to early man: lightning, the weapon Zeus supposedly uses to enforce his will. This "fire" is also the *logos*, the pattern or structure providing the unity of the world. This is what makes one world out of the many things.

Perhaps men are not to be too much blamed, however, for their lack of wisdom. For

Nature loves to hide.

and

The lord whose oracle is at Delphi neither speaks out nor conceals, but gives a sign (*IEGP*, 96).

---

*Compare Anaximander, p. 9. Heraclitus here identifies that which "steers all things" as a *thought*. This theme is later developed by the Stoics. See pp. 190–191.

Even though the *logos* is common to all, even though all our experience testifies to it, discerning this *logos* is difficult. It is rather like a riddle; the answer may be implicit, but it is still hard to make out. Solving the problem is like interpreting the ambiguous pronouncements of the famous oracle at Delphi, located north and west of Athens (see map 1). You could go there and ask the oracle a question, as Croesus, king of the Lydians (see map 1), once did. He wanted to know whether to go to war against the Persians. He was told that if he went to war a mighty empire would fall. Encouraged by this reply, he set forth, only to find the oracle's pronouncement validated by his own defeat.

How, then, is the riddle to be unraveled? How can we become wise, learning the secrets of the *logos*? This is a question, remember, that we have asked before. Xenophanes tells us that by "seeking" we can improve our opinions, but that is pretty uninformative.* Does Heraclitus advance our understanding any? To some degree he does. Two fragments that seem to be in some tension with each other address this issue:

Those things of which there is sight, hearing, understanding, I esteem most.

Eyes and ears are bad witnesses to men if they have souls that do not understand their language (*IEGP*, 96).

We can come to understand the world-order, then, not by listening to poets, seers, or self-proclaimed wise men but by using our eyes and ears. Yet we must be careful, for the senses can deceive us, can be "bad witnesses." They must be used critically, and not everyone "understands their language." These few remarks do not, of course, take us very far. We will see later philosophers filling in this picture and varying it in several ways.

Finally, Heraclitus draws from his view of the *logos* some significant conclusions for the way humans should live.

---

*See p. 14.

It is not good for men to get all they wish.

If happiness consisted in bodily pleasures we ought to call oxen happy who find vetch to eat.

It is hard to fight against impulse; for what it wants it buys at the expense of the soul.

Moderation is the greatest virtue, and wisdom is to speak the truth and to act according to nature, giving heed to it (*IEGP*, 97, 101).

Why is it not good for men to get all they wish?* If they did so, they would destroy the necessary tensions that make possible the very existence of both themselves and the things they want. They would overstep the bounds set by the *logos*, which allows the world to exist at all—a "many" unified by the "one." Desires must be limited not for prudish or puritanical reasons but because opposition is the very life of the world-order. Suppose someone has a taste for sweets and indulges that taste without limit. He soon finds himself ill or, if he persists, dead. Akhilleus indulges his impulse to anger with disastrous results. Of course, such impulses are "hard to fight against." Why? Because indulging them at all strengthens them, and we cannot help indulging them to some degree. Indulging an impulse seems to diminish the resources of the soul to impose limits on that impulse. Such indulgence is bought "at the expense of the soul."

That is why wisdom is difficult and why it is missed by the many. They, like cattle, seek to maximize their bodily pleasures. In doing so, they are "at variance" with the *logos*, which requires of every force that it be limited. That is why "moderation is the greatest virtue" and why it is so rare.

Note that Heraclitus ties his ethics intimately to his vision of the nature of things. The *logos* without is to be reflected in the *logos* within. Wisdom is "to speak the truth and to act according to nature." To speak the truth is to let one's words (one's *logos*) be responsive to the *logos* that is the world-order. To speak falsely is to be at variance with that *logos*. All one's actions should reflect that balance, that moderation nature displays to all who understand its ways. In the plea for moderation, Heraclitus reflects the main moral tradition of the Greeks since Homer, but he sets it in a larger context and justifies it in terms of the very nature of the universe itself and its divine *logos*.

In his exaltation of the few over the many, Heraclitus also reflects Homeric values.

One man is worth ten thousand to me, if only he be best.

For the best men choose one thing above all the rest: everlasting fame among mortal men. But the many have glutted themselves like cattle (*IEGP*, 104).

The Homeric heroes seek their "everlasting fame" on the field of battle. Heraclitus, we feel, would seek it on the field of virtue.

In Heraclitus, then, we have a solution to the problem of the one and the many. We do live in one world, a *uni*-verse, despite the multitude of apparently different and often conflicting things we find in it. It is made one by the *logos*, the rational, divine, firelike pattern according to which things behave. Conflict does not destroy the unity of the world; unless it goes to extremes, such tension is a *necessary condition of its very existence*. And if we see and hear and think rightly, we can line up our own lives according to this same *logos*, live in a self-disciplined and moderate way, and participate in the divine wisdom.

---

*It is time to acknowledge that when the Greeks talk in this way about "men" they probably do not mean to include women. Women were not citizens in ancient Athens, for example. It does not follow, of course, that what the Greeks say about "man" has no relevance for women of today. Here is a useful way to think about this. Aristotle formulated the Greek understanding of man in terms of *rational animal*, a concept that can apply to human beings generally. What the Greeks say about "man" may well apply to women too, although one should be on guard lest they sneak masculinity too much into the generic "man." Their mistake (and not theirs alone!) was to have underestimated the rationality and humanity of women. I will sometimes use the term "man" and the pronoun "he" in this generic sense but will often paraphrase it with "human being" or some other substitute.

Parmenides: Only the One

Parmenides introduces the strangest thought so far. His view is hard for us to grasp. Once we see what he is saying, moreover, we find it hard to take seriously. So we need to make a special effort to understand. It helps to keep in mind that Parmenides is not an isolated figure independent of any context; he is a participant in the great conversation and constantly has in mind the views of his predecessors and contemporaries, some of which are familiar to us.

What makes the argument of Parmenides so alien to us is its conclusion; most people simply cannot believe it. The conclusion is that there is no "many"; only "the one" exists. We find this hard to believe because our experience is so obviously manifold. There is the desk, and here is the chair. They are two; the chair is not the desk and the desk is not the chair. So, at least, it seems. If Parmenides is to convince us otherwise, he has his work cut out for him. He is well aware of this situation and addresses the problem explicitly.*

Parmenides was not an Ionian, as were Thales, Anaximander, Xenophanes, and Heraclitus. This fact is significant because, in a sense, geographical location is not intellectually neutral. Different places develop different traditions. Parmenides lived at the opposite edge of Greek civilization in what is now the southern part of Italy, where there were numerous Greek colonies. He came from a city called Elea (see map 2), which, according to tradition, was well governed in part through Parmenides' efforts. Plato tells us that Parmenides once visited Athens in his old age and conversed with the young Socrates. If this is so, Parmenides must have been born about 515 B.C.E. and lived until at least the year 450.

Parmenides wrote a book, in verse, of which substantial parts have come down to us. In the prologue, he claims to have been driven by horse and chariot into the heavens and escorted by maiden goddesses into the presence of a goddess who speaks to him:

> Welcome, youth, who come attended by immortal charioteers and mares which bear you on your journey to our dwelling. For it is no evil fate that has set you to travel on this road, far from the beaten paths of men, but right and justice. It is meet that you learn all things—both the unshakable heart of well-rounded truth and the opinions of mortals in which there is no true belief (*IEGP*, 108–9).

Such language might seem to be a throwback to the kinds of claims made by Hesiod.* Parmenides is telling us that the content of his poem has been revealed to him by divine powers. Is this philosophy? In fact, it is. The content of the revelation is an **argument** and the goddess admonishes him to

> judge by reasoning the much-contested argument that I have spoken (*IEGP*, 111).

The claim that this argument was revealed to him by a goddess may reflect the fact that the argument came to him in an ecstatic or inspired state. Or, it may just be a sign of how different from ordinary mortal thought the "well-rounded truth" really is. In either case, the claim that the poem is a revelation is inessential. We are invited to judge it, not just to accept it; we are to judge it "by reasoning." And this is the key feature of philosophy.†

Note that the goddess reveals to him two ways: the truth and the "opinions of mortals," which deal not with truth but with **appearance**. His poem is in fact set up in two parts, "The Way of Truth" and "The Way of Opinion." Because it is the former that has been influential, we'll concentrate on it.

---

*His pupil, Zeno, constructs paradoxes about plurality and motion that seem to hammer the final nails into the coffin of our common sense; they make common sense seem *self-contradictory*!

---

*Look again at Hesiod's description of his inspiration by the Muses, pp. 13–14.

†Compare Socrates on "examining" a statement that is put forward, pp. 61–63.

What, then, is this argument which yields such strange conclusions? It begins with something Parmenides thought impossible to deny.

> Thinking and the thought that it is are the same; for you will not find thought apart from what is, in relation to which it is uttered (*IEGP*, 110).

Consider any thought, Parmenides urges us. You will see that it is always a thought of something—of something which *is*. If you think, "This desk is brown," you are thinking what *is*, namely, the desk and its color. If you think "This desk is not brown," once more you are thinking of what *is*, namely the desk. Suppose you say, "But I am thinking that it is *not brown*; so I am thinking of what *is not*." Parmenides will reply that "not brown" is just an unclear way of expressing the real thought, which is that the desk *is*, let us say, gray. If you are thinking of the desk, you are thinking of *it* with whatever color it has. To think at all, he tells us, is to think that something *is*.

> For thought and being are the same (*IEGP*, 110).

They are "the same" in much the same way that for Heraclitus the way up and the way down are the same.* If you have the one, you also have the other. The concept of "being" is just the concept of "what is," as opposed to "what is not." Thinking and being, then, are inseparable.

This is Parmenides' starting point. It seems rather abstract and without much content. How can the substantial conclusions we hinted at be derived from such premises? The way to do it is to derive a corollary of this point.

> It is necessary to speak and to think what is; for being is, but nothing is not (*IEGP*, 111).

You cannot think of "nothing." Why not? Because nothing *is not*. And to think is (as we have seen) to think of what *is*. If you *could* think of nothing, it would (by the first premise) be *something*. But that is contradictory. Nothing cannot be something! Nothing "is not." And if anything is clear, it is that "something" *is*.

That still does not seem very exciting. Yet from this point remarkable conclusions follow (or seem to follow; whether the argument is a sound one we will examine later).* In particular, all our beliefs that involve manyness in one way or another are shown to be false. You believe, for example, that this book you are reading is one thing and the hand you are touching it with is another. So you believe there are *many* things. But if Parmenides' argument is correct, that belief is a false one. There is *in reality* no distinction between them. Parmenides describes ordinary mortals who do not grasp that fact in this way:

> For helplessness guides the wandering thought in their breasts; they are carried along deaf and blind alike, dazed, beasts without judgment, convinced that to be and not to be are the same and not the same, and that the road of all things is a backward-turning one (*IEGP*, 111).

This is harsh! The language he uses makes it clear that he has in mind not only common folks but also philosophers—Heraclitus in particular. It is Heraclitus who insists more rigorously than anyone else that "to be and not to be are the same" (to be straight, for instance, and not straight).† Whatever is, Heraclitus tells us, is only temporary; all is involved in the universal flux, coming into being and passing again out of being. In that sense, "the road of all things" is indeed "a backward-turning one." You may be reminded of the phrase common in funeral services: "Ashes to ashes, dust to dust."

Parmenides tells us, however, that to think in this way is to be blind, deaf, helpless, dazed—no better than a beast. Things cannot be so. For consider: to say that something "comes into being" is to imply that it formerly *was not*. But this is some-

---

*See p. 18.

*See the critique by Democritus on pp. 27–28.
†See the remark on p. 18 about the path traced by the pen.

thing that one can neither imply, nor say, nor even think sensibly, for it involves the notion of "not being." And we have seen that not being *cannot be thought.* It is inconceivable, for "thought and being are the same." So we are confused when we speak of something coming into being. We do not know what we are saying.

The same argument holds for passing away. The fundamental idea involved in passing away is that something leaves the realm of being (of what is) and moves into the realm of not being (of what is not). This, as we should by now easily see, is equally inconceivable. Passing away also involves the notion of what is not. But *what is not* cannot be thought. And if it cannot be thought, it cannot be. There is no "realm of not being." There couldn't be.

Parmenides summarizes the argument.

> How could what is perish? How could it have come to be? For if it came into being, it is not; nor is it if ever it is going to be. Thus coming into being is extinguished, and destruction unknown (*IEGP*, 113).

But if there can be no coming into being and passing away, then there can be no Heraclitean flux. Indeed, the common experience that things do have beginnings and endings must be an illusion.

> For never shall this prevail: that things that are not, are. But hold back your thought from this way of inquiry, nor let habit born of long experience force you to ply an aimless eye and droning ear along this road; but judge by reasoning the much-contested argument that I have spoken (*IEGP*, 111).

We have already examined the last part of this passage, but it is important to see what contrasts with the "reasoning" that Parmenides commends. We are urged not to let our thought be formed by "habit born of long experience." Parmenides acknowledges that experience is contrary to the conclusions he is urging upon us. *Of course* the senses tell us that things change, that they begin and end. But, he says, do not rely on sensory experience. You must rely on reasoning alone. You must go wherever the argument takes you, even if it contra-

dicts common sense and the persuasive evidence of the senses.*

In urging us to follow reason alone, Parmenides stands at the beginning of one of the major traditions in Western philosophy. Although too much importance should not be placed on such categorization, it is useful to give that tradition a name. It is usually called **rationalism**. Parmenides is rightly considered the first rationalist philosopher.

Notice the contrast to the Ionian nature philosophers. They all try to explain the nature of things observed; they start with the assumption that the world is composed of many different things changing in many different ways. It never occurs to them to question this assumption. Heraclitus, remember, explicitly says that he esteems most the things of which there are sight and hearing and understanding.† This reliance on the senses Parmenides rejects resolutely.

He is not finished, however, in deriving surprising conclusions from his principles. If we grant his premises, he tells us, we must also acknowledge that what is

> is now, all at once, one and continuous (*IEGP*, 113).

> Nor is it divisible, since it is all alike; nor is there any more or less of it in one place which might prevent it from holding together, but all is full of what is (*IEGP*, 114).

What is must exist "all at once" because time cannot affect it. Time itself must be unreal, an illusion, for the present can only be identified as the present by distinguishing it from the past (which is *no longer*) and from the future (which is *not yet*). But this shows that the notions of past and future both involve the unthinkable notion of "what is not." So, "what is" must exist all at once in a continuous

---

*We will see this theme repeated by Socrates; if it is true that as a young man Socrates conversed with Parmenides (as Plato tells us), it is likely that he learned this principle from him. For an example, see p. 99.

†In the seventeenth and eighteenth centuries, such reliance on sensory data will be called empiricism and will be starkly contrasted to rationalism. For an example, see pp. 340–341.

present. This thought will be exploited by St. Augustine in his notion of God.*

Moreover, *what is* must be indivisible; what is cleaves inseparably to what is. Why? Well, what could separate what is from what is? Only *what is not*. And what is not *cannot be*. All is "full of what is." It follows, of course, that there cannot be a vortex motion, as Anaximander thought, scattering stuff of different kinds to different places, because there cannot be things of different kinds. It is "all alike." There is not "any more or less of it in one place which might prevent it from holding together."† Why? Because if there were "less" in some place, this could only be because it is mixed with some nonbeing. And there is no nonbeing. So there cannot be a "many." The problem of the one and the many should never have come up!

It also follows that being must be uncreated and imperishable, without beginning or end. If *what is* had come into being, it must have arisen from not being. But this is impossible. To perish, it would have to pass away into nothingness. But nothingness is not. So being cannot perish. "For never shall this prevail: that things that are not, are."

We can characterize *what is* in the following terms. It is one, eternal, indivisible, and unchanging. If experience tells you otherwise, Parmenides says, so much the worse for experience.

If you think about it for just a moment, you can see that Parmenides has thrust to the fore one of the basic philosophical problems. It is called the problem of *appearance and reality*. Parmenides readily admits that the world *appears* to us to be many and to change continuously and that the things in it seem to move about. What he argues is that it is not so *in reality*. In reality, he holds, there is just the one. Any convictions we have to the contrary are just "the opinions of mortals in which there is no true belief."

We are all familiar with things not really being what they appear to be. Sticks in water appear to be bent when they are not. Roads sometimes appear to be wet when there is no water on them, and so on. The distinction is one we can readily understand. What is radical and disturbing about Parmenides' position is that *everything* with which you could possibly come in contact through your senses is allocated to the appearance side of the dichotomy. Nowhere do we sense what really is. Can this be right? This problem puzzles many a successor—or at least *appears* to do so!

Because these views are so strange, so alien to the usual ways of thinking, it is worth noting the response of Parmenides' contemporaries and successors. Do they dismiss him as "that crazy Eleatic" who denies multiplicity and change? Do they think of him as a fool and charlatan? Not for the most part. They take him very seriously. Plato, for example, always treats Parmenides with respect. Why? Because he, more successfully than anyone else up to his time, does what they are all trying to do: to follow reason wherever it leads. If his conclusions are uncongenial, that means only that his arguments must be examined carefully for any errors. Parmenides provides for the first time a coherent, connected argument—something you can really wrestle with. Succeeding philosophers have to come to terms with Parmenides in one way or another. Even though few accept his positive views, his influence is great, and his impact is still felt today.

Notes

---

*For Augustine, however, it is only God who enjoys this atemporal kind of eternity; time has a certain reality for Augustine—created and dependent, but not ultimate. See pp. 228–229.

†Anaximenes, a nature philosopher we are not considering, holds that air, when compressed, becomes cloud, then water, then earth and stone. When more rarefied, it becomes fire. Parmenides argues that such an explanation for the many kinds of things we seem to experience is impossible, because such compression and rarefaction implicitly involve nonbeing.

1. William James, "Pragmatism: A New Name for Some Old Ways of Thinking," in *Pragmatism and the Meaning of Truth* (Cambridge, Mass.: Harvard University Press, 1978), 64.
2. Quotations from John Manley Robinson's *An Introduction to Early Greek Philosophy* (Boston: Houghton Mifflin Co., 1968) are cited in the text using the abbreviation *IEGP*.
3. Homer, *The Iliad*, trans. Robert Fitzgerald (New York: Anchor Books, 1975), bk. 18, p. 439.

4

Atomist Nature Philosophy:
The One and the Many Reconciled

Anaximander and the other nature philosophers have proceeded on the assumption that the world is pretty much as it seems. We learn of it, as Heraclitus tells us, by sight, hearing, and understanding. We need only to set forth the elements of which it is made, its principles of organization, and the sources of its alteration. This might be difficult to do because the world is complex and human minds are limited. But there doesn't seem to be a shadow of suspicion that sight and hearing on the one hand (the senses) and understanding (reasoning) on the other hand might come into conflict. Yet that is precisely the outcome of Parmenidean logic. The world as revealed by our senses *cannot* be reality. And the force of that "cannot" is the force of reason itself. Parmenides has *proved* it. These arguments of Parmenides shake Ionian nature philosophy to its core.

Clearly, it is difficult simply to acquiesce in these results. It is not easy to say that our sensory convictions about the manyness of things, their changeableness, and their motion are all illusory. Several notable thinkers attempt to reconcile the arguments of Parmenides and his pupil Zeno with the testimony of the senses. Empedocles and Anaxagoras, in particular, struggle with these problems, but it is generally agreed that neither of them really resolve the issue.[1] It is not until we come to the atomists that we find, in principle, a satisfactory resolution.

Two figures are preeminent in the development of atomist thought: Leucippus and Democritus.

About the former we know very little; two ancient authorities doubt even that he existed. Others, however, attribute to Leucippus the key idea that allows the Parmenidean argument to be met. About Democritus we know much more. He lived in Abdera, a city of Thrace in northern Greece (see map 1), during the middle of the fifth century B.C.E. He wrote voluminously, perhaps as many as fifty-two books, of which well over two hundred fragments are preserved. He is also thoroughly discussed by later philosophers such as Aristotle, so we have a fairly complete notion of his teachings.

We need not try to sort out the separate contributions of Leucippus and Democritus. (We can't do so with certainty in any case.) They seem together to have developed the view known as **atomism**, to which we now turn.

The Key

In a work entitled *Of Generation and Corruption* (concerned with coming into being and passing away), Aristotle summarizes the Parmenidean arguments against these kinds of change and then says:

> Leucippus, however, thought he had arguments which, while consistent with sense perception, would not destroy coming into being or passing away or the multiplicity of existing things. These he conceded to be appearances, while to those who upheld the "one" he

conceded that there can be no motion without a void, that the void is not-being, and that not-being is no part of being; for what is, in the strict sense, is completely full (*IEGP*, 196).

Notice that Aristotle does not say simply that Leucippus disagrees with Parmenides. To disagree with an opinion is easy—too easy. What is needed is a *reason* to disagree. Aristotle says that Leucippus has, or thinks he has, *arguments*. These arguments concede some things to the "monists" (the believers in the "one"), but they show that these concessions are not as damaging to common sense as the monists had thought. The acceptable parts of the monistic argument could be reconciled with sense perception, with beginning and ending, and with multiplicity. What are these arguments?

Surprisingly, a follower of Parmenides, Melissus, gives us a hint toward an adequate solution:

. . . if there were a many, they would have to be such as the one is (*IEGP*, 148).

Melissus does not accept that there is a many. He just tells us that *if* there were a many, each of the many would have to have the same characteristics as Parmenides ascribes to the one. Each would have to be all-alike, indivisible, full, and eternal. What Leucippus does is to accept this principle and to say there are many such "ones." There are, in fact, an infinite number of them. Democritus was to call them "atoms."

From all we have seen so far, however, this is mere assertion; we need an argument. It goes like this. We must grant to Parmenides that being and not-being are opposites. And of course not-being *is not*. It doesn't follow from these concessions, though, that there is no such thing as empty space. Such space is empty in precisely this sense: It contains no *things* or *bodies*. Nonetheless, it may have *being*. Empty space, which Democritus calls "the void," is *not* the same as not-being. It only seems so if you do not distinguish *being* from *body*. But we can distinguish *what-is-not-at-all* from *what-does-not-contain-any-body*.

Once that distinction is recognized, we can see that Parmenides' argument confuses the two. He argues that there can be only a "one" because if

there were "many" they would have to be separated by *what is not*; and what is not *is not*. So there cannot be a many; what is must be all full and continuous. The atomists argue that there is an ambiguity here. What is *can* be separated from what is—by the void. So there *can* be a many. The void does not lack being altogether. It only lacks the kind of being characteristic of *things*. Democritus also calls the void "no-thing"—not, note carefully, "nothing" (nothing at all), which he acknowledges *is not*. No-thing (the void) is a *kind of being* in which no body exists. He puts the point this way:

No-thing exists just as much as thing (*IEGP*, 197).

A diagram may help to make this clear.

Parmenides

Being	Not-Being
is	is not

Democritus

Being		Not-Being
Thing No-Thing		is not
(Body) (Void)		
is		

We noted earlier the struggle to develop a language adequate to describe reality. Language begins, as the language of children does, tied to the concrete. Only with great difficulty does it develop enough abstraction—enough distance, as it were, from concrete things—to allow for the necessary distinctions. The language of Parmenides simply lacks the concepts necessary to make these crucial distinctions. Leucippus and Democritus are in effect forging new linguistic tools for doing the job of describing the world. This is a real breakthrough: it makes possible a theory that does not deny the evidence of the senses and yet is rational (i.e., does not lead to contradictions).

The World

We need to sketch this theory in some detail. Reality consists of atoms and the void. Atoms are so tiny that they are mostly, perhaps entirely, invisible to us. Each of them is indivisible (the word "atom" comes from roots that mean "not cuttable").* Because they are indivisible, they are also indestructible; they exist eternally. Atoms are in constant motion, banging into each other and bouncing off, or maybe just vibrating like motes of dust in a stream of sunlight. Such motion is made possible by the existence of the void; the void provides a place into which a body can move. Their motion, moreover, is not something that must be imparted to them from outside. It is their nature to move.

These atoms are not all alike, although internally each is homogeneous, as Melissus argues it must be. Atoms differ from each other in three ways: in shape (including size), in arrangement, and in position. Aristotle gives us examples to illustrate these ways. A differs from N in shape, AN differs from NA in arrangement, and Z differs from N in position. As the atoms move about, some of them hook into others, perhaps of the same kind, perhaps different. If enough get hitched together, they form bodies that are visible to us. In fact, such compounds or composites are what make up the world of our experience. Teacups and sparrow feathers differ from each other in the kinds of atoms that make them up and in the different arrangements of the atoms in a body. Light bodies differ from heavy bodies, for example, because the hooking together is looser and there is more void in them. Soft bodies differ from hard because the connections between the atoms are more flexible.

The atomists can explain coming into being and passing away as well. A thing comes into being when the atoms which make it up get hooked together in the appropriate ways. It passes away again when its parts disperse or fall apart.

These principles are obviously compatible with much of the older nature philosophy, and the atomists adopt or adapt a good bit of the tradition. The structure of the universe, for instance, is explained by a vortex motion or whirl that separates out the various kinds of compounds. Like tends to go to like, just as pebbles on a seashore tend to line up in rows according to their size. And we get a picture of the world that is, in its broad features, not very different from that of Anaximander. There is, however, one crucial and very important difference.

Anaximander has said that the boundless "encompasses all things" and "steers all things." Xenophanes claims that the one god "sets all things in motion by the thought of his mind." Heraclitus identifies the principle of unity holding together the many changing things of the world as a divine *logos*, or thought. But Democritus' principles leave no room for this kind of intelligent direction to things. Remember: what exist are atoms and the void. Democritus boldly draws the conclusions from this premise. If we ask why the atoms combine to form a world or why they form some particular thing in this world, the only answer is that they *just do*. The only reason that can be given is that these atoms happened to be the sort, and to be in the vicinity of other atoms of a sort, to produce the kind of thing they did produce. There is no further reason, no intention or purpose behind it.*

Nothing occurs at random, but everything occurs for a reason and by necessity (*IEGP*, 212).

This is, in one sense, the final destination of the pre-Socratic Greek speculation about nature. It begins by casting out the Homeric gods. It ends by casting out intelligence and purpose altogether from the governance of the world. Everything happens according to laws of motion that govern the wholly mechanical interactions of the atoms. In these happenings, mind has no place.

---

*What we call "atoms" nowadays are, as we well know, not indivisible. We also know, since Einstein, that matter and energy are convertible. Nonetheless, physicists are still searching for the "ultimate building blocks" of nature. Perhaps they are what scientists call "quarks." But whether that is so or not, the ancient atomists' assumption that there are such building blocks and that they are very tiny indeed is alive and well in the late twentieth century.

---

*Compare the nonpurposive character of evolutionary accounts of the origin of species with creationist accounts.

The Soul

If mind or intelligence cannot function as an explanation of the world-order, it is nonetheless obvious that it plays some role in human life. Democritus owes us an explanation of human intelligence that is compatible with his basic principles. His speculations are interesting and suggestive, though still quite crude. This problem is one we cannot claim to have solved completely even in our own day.

An atomist's account of soul and mind must, of course, be compatible with his general view of reality: that what exist are atoms and the void. According to Democritus, the soul is composed of exceedingly fine and spherical atoms; in this way, soul interpenetrates the whole of the body. Democritus holds that

> spherical atoms move because it is their nature never to be still, and that as they move they draw the whole body along with them, and set it in motion (*IEGP*, 222).

Soul-atoms are in this sense akin to fire-atoms, which are also small, spherical, and capable of penetrating solid bodies and (as Heraclitus has observed) are strikingly good examples of spontaneous motion. The soul or principle of life is, like everything else, *material*.

Living things, of course, have certain capacities that nonliving things do not. They experience sensations (tastes, smells, sights, sounds, pains). Some, at least, are capable of thought, and humans seem to have a capacity to know. Can Democritus explain these capacities using his principles regarding atoms and the void?

Think first about sensations. There doesn't seem to be too much difficulty in explaining tastes. Sweet and sour, salt and bitter are just the results of the variety of different shapes of atoms in contact with the tongue. What is sweet, Democritus says, consists of atoms that are "round and of a good size," the sour of "bulky, jagged, and many-angled" atoms, and so on (*IEGP*, 200). These are speculations that are not grounded in anything like modern experimental method, but the kind of ex-

planation is surely familiar to those who know something of modern chemistry.

Smells are explained along analogous lines. Sounds, too, are not difficult; Democritus explains them in terms of air being "broken up into bodies of like shape . . . rolled along with the fragments of the voice."[2] Vision is the sense most difficult to explain in terms of an atomistic view. Unlike touch, taste, and even hearing, it is a "distance receptor." With sight it is as though we were able to reach out to the surfaces of things at some distance from us without any material means of doing so. In this respect, the eye seems quite different from the hand or the tongue.

Democritus holds that sight is not really different, however. Like the other senses, it works by contact with its objects, only in this case the contact is more indirect than usual. The bodies that atoms combine to make up are constantly giving off "images" of themselves, he tells us. These images are themselves material, and so composed of atoms, but they are exceptionally fine. These "effluences" strike the eye and stamp their shape in the soft and moist matter of the eye, whereupon it is registered in the smooth and round atoms of soul present throughout the body.

This kind of explanation is regarded by most of his Greek successors as very strange. Aristotle even calls it a great absurdity. It may not strike us as absurd. Indeed, it seems somewhere near the truth.

It does have a paradoxical consequence, though, that Democritus recognizes and is willing to accept. It means that our senses *do not give us direct and certain knowledge of the world*. If you think a moment, you will see that this is indeed an implication of his view. Our experience of vision is a product, in the mathematical sense. It is the outcome of a complex set of interactions between the object seen, the intervening medium, and our sense apparatus. Exactly what our experience is when we look at a distant mountain is not a simple function of the characteristics of the mountain. That experience depends also on whether the air is clear or foggy, clean or polluted. It depends on whether it is dawn, dusk, or noon. Moreover, what we experience depends on what kinds and proportions of rods and cones we have in our eyes, on complex sending mechanisms in the optic nerve, and the condition of the visual center in the brain.

Democritus cannot express his point in these contemporary terms. Nonetheless, this is exactly his point. Similar explanations also apply to the other senses. It was recognized in ancient times that honey, for example, can taste sweet to a healthy person and bitter to a sick one. Clearly, the difference depends on the state of the receptor organs. What is the character of the honey itself? Is it both sweet and bitter? That seems impossible. Democritus draws the conclusion that it is neither. Sweetness and bitterness, hot and cold, red and blue exist only in us, not in nature.

> Sweet exists by convention, bitter by convention, color by convention; but in reality atoms and the void alone exist (*IEGP*, 202).

To say that something exists by **convention** is to say that its existence depends upon us.* In nature alone it is not to be found. But this means that we cannot rely on our sense experience to tell us what the world is really like. In a way, Parmenides was right after all!†

> It is necessary to realize that by this principle man is cut off from the real (*IEGP*, 203).

We are "cut off from the real" because whatever impact the real has on us is in part a product of our own condition. This is true not only of the sick person but also of the well one. The sweetness of the honey to the well person depends on the sensory receptors just as much as the bitterness to the sick one. Neither has a direct and unmediated avenue to what honey really is.‡

Later philosophers exploit these grounds in skeptical directions, doubting that we can have any reliable knowledge of the world at all. For Democritus, however, they do not lead to utter skepticism:

> There are two forms of knowledge: one legitimate, one bastard. To the bastard sort belong all of the following: sight, hearing, smell, taste, touch. The legitimate is quite distinct from this. When the bastard form cannot see more minutely, not hear nor smell nor taste nor perceive through the touch, then another, finer form must be employed (*IEGP*, 203–4).

He seems to be telling us that the senses can take us only so far, because they have a "bastard" parentage (i.e., they are the products of both the objects perceived and the perceiving organs). But there is "another, finer" and "legitimate" form of knowledge available to the soul. This knowledge is no doubt based on reasoning. Its product is the knowledge that what really exist are atoms and the void. At this point, we would like reasoning to be explained in terms of the atomistic view, as the senses have been explained. No such explanation is offered. This is not surprising; indeed, many think that a satisfactory account of reasoning on these materialistic principles is only now, after the invention of the computer, beginning to be constructed. But that, of course, is reaching far ahead of our story.

Notes

1. For a discussion of these thinkers, see John Manley Robinson, *An Introduction to Early Greek Philosophy* (Boston: Houghton Mifflin Co., 1968), 151–94. Quotations from this work are cited in the text using the abbreviation *IEGP*.
2. Quoted in G. S. Kirk and J. E. Raven, *The Presocratic Philosophers* (Cambridge: Cambridge University Press, 1960), 423.

---

*For a fuller discussion of the distinction between nature and convention, see Chapter 6, "*Physis* and *Nomos*."
†See p. 25.
‡Galileo and Descartes, creators of the new science in the seventeenth century, draw a distinction between *primary* and *secondary* qualities of things that is very like Democritus' distinction. See pp. 283–284.

5

The Rise of Athens

When we think of "the glory that was Greece," we think inevitably of Athens (see map 1). To this point, however, we have mentioned Athens scarcely at all. Greek culture, as we have seen, ranged from the southern parts of Italy and Sicily in the west, to the Ionian settlements on the shores of Asia Minor, to Thrace in the north. Important contributions to the great conversation about the nature of the world and the place of human beings in it were made from all those areas. But in the fifth and fourth centuries B.C.E., Greek culture came more and more to center in one city: Athens. The story of how this came about is a fascinating tale related for us by the Greek historian Herodotus and pieced together by modern writers from his history and many other sources. For our purposes, we need to understand several key elements of the rise of Athens. What kind of city was Athens in that time, what was it like to live in Athens, and how was it different from other cities?[1]

Although we have used the terms Greece and Greek culture, there was at the beginning of the fifth century (i.e., around 500 B.C.E.) nothing like a unified Greek state. People lived in and owed allegiance to a large number of city-states. A city-state (a *polis*) was an area—an island, perhaps, or an arable plain with natural boundaries of mountains and the sea—in which one city was dominant. The city was usually fortified and offered protection to the farmers, who sometimes lived within the walls and sometimes outside in smaller villages. The prominent city-states of that time were Thebes, Corinth, Argos, Sparta, and Athens, but there were

many more. Among these city-states there were often rivalries, quarrels, shifting alliances, and wars.

Two things happened around the beginning of the fifth century that contributed to the preeminence of Athens among the city-states: the beginnings of democracy in government and the Persian wars.

Democracy

For nearly a century, ever since the reforms of Solon, the common people had had some voice in the government of Athens. According to the constitution of Solon, the powers of government were divided among several bodies according to their functions. There was an executive body, composed of nine archons, elected year by year. A Council, made up of "the best men" (aristocrats or patricians), made the important decisions. It met on an outcropping of rock called Areopagus (or Hill of Ares, the god of war) and according to tradition, was founded by the goddess Athena.* All free men belonged to the Assembly, which had no initiative power but could veto measures that were excessively unpopular. A fourth body, the People's Council, acted as a steering committee for the Assembly. This structure was modified over the years, but it took on the character of an ideal; again and

---

*See, for instance, the third part of Aeschylus' trilogy, *Oresteia*.

again reforms of various kinds were justified as being a return to the constitution of Solon.

During a large part of the sixth century, Athens was ruled by "tyrants." This word did not originally have all the negative connotations it now has. It simply meant "boss" or "chief" and was applied to a ruler who was not a hereditary king but had seized power some other way. Some of the tyrants of Athens respected Solon's constitution, while arranging for their friends to be elected archons, but at least one tyrant was killed to restore the democracy.

In 508 B.C.E., there was a quarrel concerning citizenship for immigrants. A large influx of immigrants had led the aristocrats, fearful for their power, to attempt a purge of the citizenship rolls. Instead, a proposal to extend citizenship to many more of the immigrants was passed by the Assembly. The chief archon, backed by the force of a king of Sparta, attempted to exile seven hundred households and dissolve the People's Council. The Council refused to go, however, and the citizens of Athens came out in arms. After a three-day siege of the Acropolis, the Spartan king and his cohort left for home, and reforms that greatly increased the democratic nature of the government were instituted. Citizenship was extended (though not to include women or slaves), the People's Council was enlarged and its duties greatly expanded, and the Areopagite Council was relegated to the status of a supreme court. Land ownership was still required of anyone wanting to become an archon, but the citizens now had the principal control of major decisions. It was to be so for the next hundred years and, with some exceptions, for some time after that.

The Persian Wars

The Greek colonies on the shores of Asia Minor were always in a precarious state. Their language and heritage bound them to the Greek mainland, but their geographical situation made them of natural interest to whatever power was dominant to the east. These Greek cities paid taxes to the rising Persian power, but in 499 they rebelled. Athens sent twenty ships to aid these Greeks, and in the fighting they burnt Sardis, one of the principal Persian cities. The rebellion was put down by Persia, and anxiety began to increase among mainland Greeks. The Persians now had reason to take revenge and, having reasserted their control over the Asian Greek cities, were free to concentrate on the mainland.

In 490, the Persians came in force across the Aegean, conquered a coastal island, and landed at Marathon. In a famous battle on the plain twenty-six miles north and east of Athens, the Greeks under Miltiades, an Ionian general, defeated the Persians, killing 6,400 of them. The victory had an exhilarating effect on the democratic city of Athens, which had supplied most of the soldiers for the battle.

It was clear to the Athenians, however, that the Persians were not about to be stopped by the loss of one battle, no matter how decisive at the time. Herodotus represents the Persian monarch Xerxes, who had recently succeeded his father Darius, as saying:

> I will bridge the Hellespont [see map 1] and march an army through Europe into Greece, and punish the Athenians for the outrage they committed upon my father and upon us. As you saw, Darius himself was making his preparations for war against these men; but death prevented him from carrying out his purpose. I therefore on his behalf, and for the benefit of all my subjects, will not rest until I have taken Athens and burnt it to the ground, in revenge for the injury which the Athenians without provocation once did to me and my father [the burning of Sardis]. . . . If we crush the Athenians and their neighbours in the Peloponnese, we shall so extend the empire of Persia that its boundaries will be God's own sky, so that the sun will not look down upon any land beyond the boundaries of what is ours (*Histories* 7.8).[2]

There was much debate in Athens about how to meet the danger. One party favored land-based defenses, citing the former victory at Marathon. The other party, led by Themistocles, favored building up the navy and a defense by sea. After much infighting, the Athenians decided on a large increase in fighting ships of the latest style—and just in time. In the year 480, Xerxes, lashing ships together to make a bridge, led an army of perhaps 200,000 men across the Hellespont (which separates Asia from Europe), brought Thrace under submission, and began to advance south toward Athens. Advice was sought, in time-honored fashion, from the Oracle at Delphi (see map 1). The oracle was not favorable. A second plea brought this response:

> That the wooden wall only shall not fall, but help you and your children (*Histories* 7.141).

How should this opaque answer be interpreted? Some believed that wooden walls on the hill of the Acropolis would withstand the aggressor. Themistocles argued that the "wooden wall" referred to the ships that had been built and that they must abandon Athens and try to defeat the Persians at sea. Most of the Athenians followed Themistocles, though some did not.

First, however, it was necessary to stop the advance of the Persian army. Many saw it as a threat against Greece as a whole, not just against Athens. A force led by Spartan soldiers under the Spartan king Leonidas met the Persians at Thermopylae, eighty miles northwest of Athens (see map 1). Greatly outnumbered, the Greeks fought valiantly, inflicting many deaths, but were defeated. Leonidas was killed.

The Persians took Athens, overwhelmed the defenders on the Acropolis, and burned the temples. However, the main Athenian forces, in ships off the nearby island of Salamis, were still to be dealt with. On a day splendid in Greek history, Xerxes sat on a mountain above the bay of Salamis (see map 1) and saw the Greeks tear apart his navy. Themistocles' strategy had worked. The next spring (479), however, the Persians occupied Athens again. It took a great victory by the combined Athenian and Spartan armies at Plataea to expel the Persians for good.

These victories had several results. Athens, which had borne the brunt of the defense of Greece, became preeminent among the city-states. It had displayed its courage and prowess for all to see and took the lead in forming a league for the future defense of the Greek lands. In time, the league turned into an Athenian empire. Other states paid tribute to Athens, which saw to their protection, and Athens became a great sea power.

Athens also became very wealthy. It was not only the tribute from the allies, although that was significant. With their control of the sea, Athenians engaged in trading far and wide. A large and wealthy merchant class grew up, and Athens became the center of Greek cultural life. Pericles, the most influential leader of the democratic city in the middle of the fifth century, led the city to build the magnificent temples on the Acropolis. He was influential in encouraging Greek art and sculpture, supported the new learning, and was a close associate of certain philosophers. A speech of his, commemorating fallen soldiers in the first year of the tragic war with Sparta, gives a sense of what it meant to Athenians to be living in Athens at that time. Only part of it, as represented for us by the historian Thucydides, is quoted here. (Suggestion: Read it aloud.)

> Let me say that our system of government does not copy the institutions of our neighbours. It is more a case of our being a model to others, than of our imitating anyone else. Our constitution is called a democracy because power is in the hands not of a minority but of the whole people. When it is a question of settling private disputes, everyone is equal before the law; when it is a question of putting one person before another in positions of public responsibility, what counts is not membership of a particular class, but the actual ability which the man possesses. No one, so long as he has it in him to be of service to the state, is kept in political obscurity because of poverty. And, just as our political life is free and open, so is our day-to-day life in our relations with each other. We do not get into a state with our next-door neighbour if he enjoys himself in his own way, nor do we give him the kind of black looks which, though they do no real harm, still do hurt people's feelings. We are free and tolerant in our private lives; but in public affairs we keep to the law. This is because it commands our deep respect.

We give our obedience to those whom we put in positions of authority, and we obey the laws themselves, especially those which are for the protection of the oppressed, and those unwritten laws which it is an acknowledged shame to break.

And here is another point. When our work is over, we are in a position to enjoy all kinds of recreation for our spirits. There are various kinds of contests and sacrifices regularly throughout the year; in our own homes we find a beauty and a good taste which delight us every day and which drive away our cares. Then the greatness of our city brings it about that all the good things from all over the world flow in to us, so that to us it seems just as natural to enjoy foreign goods as our own local products.

Then there is a great difference between us and our opponents in our attitude towards military security. Here are some examples: Our city is open to the world, and we have no periodical deportations in order to prevent people observing or finding out secrets which might be of military advantage to the enemy. This is because we rely, not on secret weapons, but on our own real courage and loyalty. . . .

Our love of what is beautiful does not lead to extravagance; our love of the things of the mind does not make us soft. We regard wealth as something to be properly used, rather than as something to boast about. As for poverty, no one need be ashamed to admit it: the real shame is in not taking practical measures to escape from it. Here each individual is interested not only in his own affairs but in the affairs of the state as well. . . . We do not say that a man who takes no interest in politics is a man who minds his own business; we say that he has no business here at all. . . .

Again, in questions of general good feeling there is a great contrast between us and most other people. We make friends by doing good to others, not by receiving good from them. . . . We are unique in this. When we do kindnesses to others, we do not do them out of any calculations of profit or loss: we do them without afterthought, relying on our free liberality. Taking everything together then, I declare that our city is an education to Greece, and I declare that in my opinion each single one of our citizens, in all the manifold aspects of life, is able to show himself the rightful lord and owner of his own person, and do this, moreover, with exceptional grace and exceptional versatility. . . . Mighty indeed are the marks and monuments of our empire which we have left. Future ages will wonder at us, as the present age wonders at us now. We do not need the praises of a Homer, or of anyone else whose words may delight us for the moment, but whose estimation of facts will fall short of what is really true. For our adventurous spirit has forced an entry into every sea and into every land; and everywhere we have left behind us everlasting memorials of good done to our friends or suffering inflicted on our enemies.[3]

Such was the spirit of the Golden Age of classical Athens: proud, confident, serenely convinced that the city was "an education to Greece"—and not without reason. Twenty-five hundred years later, we still are moved by their tragedies, laugh at their comedies, admire their sculpture, are awed by their architecture, revere their democracy, and study their philosophers.

Notes

1. *The Pelican History of Greece* by A. R. Burn (New York: Penguin Books, 1984) is a lively treatment of these matters. A standard source is J. B. Bury, *A History of Greece* (London: Macmillan and Co., 1951). The Greek historians Herodotus, Thucydides, and Xenophon are also quite readable.
2. Quotations from Herodotus, *The Histories* (New York: Penguin Books, 1972), are cited in the text by title, book number, and section number.
3. Thucydides, *History of the Peloponnesian War*, trans. Rex Warner (New York: Penguin Books, 1954), 2.35–41.

6

The Sophists:
Rhetoric and Relativism

The social situation in fifth-century Athens called for innovations in education. The "best men" in the old sense no longer commanded a natural leadership. What counted was actual ability, as Pericles said, so men sought to develop their abilities. The aristocracy's education centering on Homer and the traditional virtues was no longer entirely adequate. Most citizens received an elementary education that made them literate and gave them basic skills. If a father wanted his son to succeed in democratic Athens, however, more was needed.

To supply this need, there arose a class of teachers offering what we might call higher education. Many of these teachers were itinerant, moving from city to city as the call for their services waxed and waned. They were professionals who charged for their instruction. The best of them became quite wealthy, since there was a substantial demand for their services. We can get a sense of what they claimed to provide for their students and for the eagerness with which they were sought out from the beginnings of Plato's dialogue, *Protagoras*. As we'll see, Protagoras was one of the greatest of these teachers. Socrates is the speaker.

Early this morning, when it was still pitch dark, Hippocrates, Apollodorus' boy, the brother of Phason, started hammering at my door with his staff; and when someone opened up, he came rushing straight in and said at the top of his voice: "Socrates, are you awake or asleep?" And recognizing his voice I said:

"Oh, it's Hippocrates. Nothing up, is there?" "Nothing but good," he said.

"That," I said, "really would be good news. But what is it, and why have you come round at this hour?"

"Protagoras has come," he said, standing beside me.

"Yes," I said, "the day before yesterday. Have you only just found that out?"

"Of course," he said; "well, yesterday evening, that is . . . but then it occurred to me that it was too late. But as soon as I slept off my fatigue, I got straight up and was on my way here, as you see."

Knowing how bold and volatile he is, I remarked: "But what has this got to do with you? You don't have some charge to bring against Protagoras, do you?"

"Indeed I do, Socrates," he laughed: "that he alone is wise [*sophos*], but is not making me wise."

"Oh yes he will, by Zeus," I said; "if you give him money and persuade him, he will make you wise too."

"Oh by Zeus and all the gods, if it were just a question of money," he said, "I should spare none of my own or my friends' possessions.* But that is just what I came to see you about—to get you to talk to him for me. For I am rather young. . . ." (*Protagoras* 310a–e).[1]

Note the eagerness expressed by Hippocrates— and for education, too! What could this education

---

*Protagoras was paid in the following way. Before the instruction he and his pupil would go to the temple; there the student would vow to pay, when the course was finished, whatever he then thought Protagoras' instruction was worth. It is said that when he died, Protagoras was wealthier than five Phidiases. (Phidias was the most famous sculptor in Athens.)

be that excited such desire in a young man? What did the **Sophists**, as these teachers were called, offer?

While they wait for day to dawn, Socrates tries in his questioning fashion to see whether Hippocrates really knows what he is getting into. Not surprisingly, it turns out that he doesn't. Undaunted, they set off and come to the home where Protagoras is staying. After some difficulty (the servant at the door is sick of Sophists and slams the door in their faces), they meet Protagoras, who is in the company of a number of other young men and fellow Sophists. Socrates makes his request.

It so happens that Hippocrates here desires to associate with you. So he wishes to learn what, if he does associate with you, the outcome of his studies will be (*Protagoras* 318a).

Protagoras answers:

If you associate with me, young man . . . then you will be able, at the end of your first day in my company, to go away a better man; and the same will happen on the next day, and each day after that you will continue to grow better and improve (*Protagoras* 318a).

Socrates, of course, is not satisfied with this answer. If Hippocrates were to associate with a famous painter, then each day his painting might improve. If he studied with a flutist, his flute playing would get better. But in what respect, exactly, will associating with Protagoras make Hippocrates "a better man"?

"You ask a good question, Socrates," said Protagoras, hearing me say this, "and I'm always pleased to reply to a good question. . . . The course of instruction is *good planning* [*euboulia*] both of his own affairs, to the end that he would best manage his personal estate, and of the *city's* [*polis*], to the end that he would be in the strongest position to conduct, in speech and action, the common business of the city" (*Protagoras* 318d–319a).

Here we have the key to the excitement of Hippocrates and to the demand for this instruction from the rising middle class of Athens. The Sophists claim to be able to teach the things that foster success, both personal and political, in this democratic city. Many of them also teach specialized subjects such as astronomy, geometry, arithmetic, and music. Nearly all are committed to the new learning developed by the nature philosophers. They are self-consciously "modern," believing they represent progress and enlightenment as opposed to ignorance and superstition.

However, it is their claim to teach "excellence" or "virtue" (the Greek word *arete* can be translated either way) both in mastering one's own affairs and in providing leadership in the city that makes them popular.* The excellences they claim to teach are the skills, abilities, and traits of character that make one competent, successful, admired, and perhaps even wealthy.

The term "sophist" has rather negative connotations for us. A "sophism," for instance, is a fallacy that looks good but isn't, and "sophistry" is verbally pulling the wool over someone's eyes. The term did not always have such connotations. "Sophist" comes from the Greek *sophos*, meaning wise. The term was applied in the fifth century to many earlier wise men, including Homer and Hesiod. Undoubtedly, the best of the Sophists, such as Protagoras, were neither charlatans nor fools. In connection with their teaching the young, they also made important contributions to the great conversation. They were philosophers who had to be taken seriously; for this reason, they are of interest to us.

Rhetoric

All of the Sophists taught **rhetoric**, the principles and practice of persuasive speaking. Some of the Sophists, Gorgias for example, claimed to teach nothing but that. Clearly, in a society such as dem-

---

*The Greek *arete* (ahr-e-tay) can apply to horses and knives, to flutists and cobblers, as well as to human beings as such. It has to do with the excellence of something when it does well what it is supposed to do. So, it goes beyond the sphere of morality but includes it. Though usually translated "virtue," this English word is really too narrow. I will often use the broader term "excellence," and especially "human excellence," when what is in question is not someone's excellence as a teacher or sailor but as a human being.

ocratic Athens this art would be very valuable. Suppose, for instance, that you are brought into court by a neighbor. If you hem and haw, utter only irrelevancies, and cannot present the evidence on your side in a coherent and persuasive way, you are likely to lose whether you are guilty or not. Or suppose you feel strongly about some issue that affects the welfare of the city; only if you can stand up in the Assembly of citizens and speak persuasively will you have any influence. You must be able to present your case, marshal your arguments, and appeal to the feelings of the audience. This is the art the Sophists developed and taught.

In one of his dialogues, Plato represents Gorgias as claiming to teach

> the power to convince by your words the judges in court, the senators in Council, the people in the Assembly, or in any other gathering of a citizen body (*Gorgias* 452e).[2]

> The rhetorician is competent to speak against anybody on any subject, and to prove himself more convincing before a crowd on practically every topic he wishes (*Gorgias* 457b).

We need to understand what rhetoric means to the Sophists because its philosophical consequences are deep. The central idea is that by using the principles of persuasive speaking, one can make a case for any position at all. It follows that if there are, as we often say these days, two sides to every issue, someone skilled in rhetoric should be able to present a persuasive argument for each side. In fact, this idea was embodied in one of the main teaching tools of the Sophists.

A student was encouraged to construct and present arguments on both sides of some controversial issue. He was not judged to be proficient until he could present a case as persuasive on one side as on the other. This method, presumably, was designed to equip a student for any eventuality; one never knew on what side of some future issue one's interests would lie.

A humorous story about Protagoras and one of his students illustrates this method. Protagoras agreed to teach a young man how to conduct cases in the courts. Since the young man was poor, it was

agreed that he would not have to pay his teacher until he won his first case. Some time elapsed after the course of instruction was over, and the student did not enter into any cases. Finally Protagoras himself brought the student to court, prosecuting him for payment. The student argued thus: If I win this case, I shall not have to pay Protagoras, according to the judgment of the court; if I lose this case, I will not yet have won my first case, and so I will not have to pay Protagoras according to the terms of our agreement; since I will either win or lose, I shall not have to pay the sum. Protagoras, not to be outdone by his student, argued as follows: If he loses this case, then by the judgment of the court he must pay me; if he wins it, he will have won his first case and therefore will have to pay me; so, in either case, he will have to pay me.

The story is probably apocryphal, and the arguments may be "sophistical" in the bad sense. But it is not easy to see what has gone wrong. The example is not far from the flavor of much of the Sophists' teaching.

The philosophical interest of this technique can be seen if we recall certain meanings of the term *logos*, which connotes speech, thought, argument, and discourse. What the Sophists were training their students to do was to present opposite *logoi*. There was the *logos* (what could be said) on one side, and there was the *logos* on the other. The presumption was that for every side of every issue a persuasive *logos* could be developed. Some Sophists seem to have written works consisting of just such opposed *logoi*, presumably as examples and practice pieces for their students.

In this connection, we must note a phrase that became notorious later on. It seems to have expressed a boast made by Protagoras and some of the other Sophists. They claimed to teach others *how to make the weaker argument into the stronger*. Suppose you are in court with what looks like a very weak case. The principles of rhetoric, if cleverly applied, could turn your argument into the stronger one—in the sense that it would be victorious.

Such a technique has profoundly skeptical implications. Think back to Heraclitus.* He believes,

*See especially p. 20.

or perhaps simply takes for granted, that there is one *logos* uniting the many changing things of the world into one world-order. This *logos* is "common to all." Although many men deviate from the *logos*, it is there and available to all. The wise are those who "listen to the *logos*" and order their own lives in accord with the pattern of the world-order. Think of Parmenides, who acknowledges that there is such a thing as the way of opinion but holds that it is quite distinct from the way of truth, in which "thought and being are the same."*

The practice of the Sophists shows that thought and being are *not* the same. Thought and being fall apart; there is no necessary correlation at all. No matter what the reality is, thought can represent it or misrepresent it with equal ease. If a *logos* that will carry conviction can be constructed on any side of any issue, how is one to tell when one is in accord with Heraclitus' *logos* and when one is not? How is one to discriminate the truth from mere opinion?

The Sophists' answer is that one cannot. All we have—and all we ever can have—are opinions. Parmenides writes of two ways, the way of truth and the way of opinion. The former represents the way things *are*. The latter sets forth the way things *appear*. What the Sophists have done is raise doubts about our ability to discern reality (the way things *are*) at all. They suggest that human beings are confined to appearances; truth is beyond us. For human beings, things *are* as they *seem* to us to be. No more can be said.

They agree with Democritus that we are "cut off from the real" by the conventional nature of our sense experience.† But unlike Democritus, they hold that there is no other avenue to the truth. Democritus thinks that intelligence or mind can penetrate where the senses fail us; he holds that reasoning can reveal what the eyes and ears cannot— that reality is composed of atoms and the void. However, if the Sophists are right in their conviction that an equally persuasive *logos* can be constructed on every side of every issue, then the appeal to reasoning cannot be sustained. For one can reason equally well for and against atoms and the void—or, indeed, anything else!

As you can see, the Sophists tend to be skeptical about their predecessors' claims to reveal the truth. They are skeptical of human ability to come to know the truth at all. You should be able to see how this **skepticism** is intimately related to the way they conceive and teach rhetoric. If rhetoric can make a convincing case for absolutely anything, then what can one know?

Such skepticism does not reduce them to silence, however. A person can still talk intelligibly about how things *seem*, even if not about how they really are. No doubt many of the theories of the nature philosophers are understood in just this way; they are plausible stories that represent the way the world seems to be. These stories represent probabilities at best, not the truth; but probabilities are the most that human beings can hope to attain. Without trying to penetrate to the core of reality, the Sophists are content with appearances. Without insisting on certainty, they are content with plausibility. Without knowledge, they are content with opinion.

The skeptical attitude is displayed in a statement by Protagoras concerning the gods. He is reported to have said:

> Concerning the gods I am not in a position to know either that they are or that they are not, or what they are like in appearance; for there are many things that are preventing knowledge, the obscurity of the matter and the brevity of human life (*IEGP*, 269).[3]

This statement seems to have been the basis for an accusation that Protagoras was an atheist. We know that he was at one time banished from Athens and that certain of his books were burned; it is likely that such statements were among those that aroused the anger of the citizens. (We will see a parallel in the case of Socrates.) Protagoras does not, however, deny the existence of the gods. He says that in light of the difficulty of the question and because of the brevity of human life, we are prevented from knowing about the gods. His view is not that of the

---

*See p. 24.

†See p. 31.

atheist, then, but that of the agnostic. The only reasonable thing to do, he says, is to suspend judgment on this issue. This is the view of the skeptic.

Relativism

The Sophists' point of view is best summed up in a famous saying by Protagoras. It is the first sentence of a book entitled *On Truth*. Unfortunately, it is the only part of the book that has come down to us.

Of all things the measure is man: of existing things, that they exist; of non-existing things, that they do not exist (IEGP, 245).

Protagoras' statement that man is the "measure" of all things means that there is no criterion, standard, or mark by which things can be judged, except the man himself. We cannot jump outside our skins to see how things look independently of how they appear to us. *As they appear to us, so are they.*

Clearly, he means, in the first instance at least, that things are as they appear to the individual man. A common example is the wind. Suppose to one person the winds feels cold and to another it feels warm. Can we ask whether the wind is cold or warm *in itself*—apart from how it *seems*? How could that be settled? Protagoras draws the conclusion that this question has no answer. If the wind seems cold to the first one, then to that person it *is* cold; and if it seems warm to the second, then it *is* warm—to him. About the warmth or coldness of the wind no more than this can be said. The first person cannot correct the second, and the second cannot correct the first. Each is the final judge of how the wind *seems*. Since it is not possible to get beyond such seemings, each individual is the final judge of how things are (to that individual, of course.)

This doctrine is the heart of a viewpoint known as **relativism**. It is the first appearance of one of the focal points of this book. From this point on, we see the major figures in our tradition struggling with the problems raised by relativism and the

skepticism about our knowledge of reality that attends it. Most of them oppose it. Some are willing to make certain concessions to it. But it has never been banished for long, and in one way or another it reappears throughout our history to pose its disturbing questions. In our own century, many have adopted some form of it. It is the merit of the Sophists that they set out the question in the clearest of terms and force us to come to grips with it.

We have now its essence. We need yet to understand what recommends it and what its implications are.

One implication that must have been obvious is that well-meaning citizens, not clearly prejudiced by self-interest, could disagree about the course the city should take. Another is that a well-wrought and persuasively delivered speech on any side of an issue could in fact convince a court or assembly of citizens. If you put these two observations together, it is not hard to draw the conclusion that the *best logos* about an issue is simply the one that does the best job of convincing. How can one judge which of two opposing *logoi* is the best, if not in terms of success? (An independent "logic," in terms of which one might judge that a certain persuasive device was "fallacious," had not yet been developed.) However, if there is no way to tell which *logos* is best except by observing which one *seems* best, then knowledge cannot be distinguished from opinion.* The best opinion is simply that which is most acceptable. But that means it may differ from culture to culture, from time to time, and even from individual to individual. There is no truth independent of what *seems* to be true. What seems true to one person or at one time may not seem true to another person or at another time. The best *logos* (what passes for truth) is relative to the individual, the culture, or the time. These observations and arguments were surely among those which motivated the sophists to adopt their relativism.

There was another factor. Greeks in general, and Athenians in particular, had expanded their hori-

*See how strenuously Plato struggles against this view (Chapter 10, "Knowledge and Opinion").

zons. They continued to distinguish, as Greeks always had done, between themselves and "barbarians," whom they took to be inferior to themselves. But the more they traveled and became acquainted with the customs and characters of other nations, the harder it became to dismiss them as stupid and uncivilized. This exposure to non-Greek ways of doing things exerted a pressure on thought. These ways came more and more to be seen not as inferior but as just different. There is a famous example given by the historian Herodotus, who was himself a great traveler and observer.

> Everyone without exception believes his own native customs, and the religion he was brought up in, to be the best. . . . There is abundant evidence that this is the universal feeling about the ancient customs of one's country. One might recall, in particular, an anecdote of Darius. When he was king of Persia, he summoned the Greeks who happened to be present at his court, and asked them what they would take to eat the dead bodies of their fathers. They replied that they would not do it for any money in the world. Later, in the presence of the Greeks, and through an interpreter, so they could understand what was said, he asked some Indians, of the tribe called Callatiae, who do in fact eat their parents' dead bodies, what they would take to burn them. They uttered a cry of horror and forbade him to mention such a dreadful thing. One can see by this what custom can do, and Pindar, in my opinion, was right when he called it "king of all."[4]

Physis and Nomos

The Sophists developed this notion that custom was "king of all" in terms of a distinction between *physis* and *nomos*. The word *physis* is the term for what the nature philosophers were studying. It is usually translated as "nature" and means the characteristics of the world, or things in general, independent of what human beings impose on it. As you can see, it is the word from which our "physics" is derived.

Nomos is the word for custom or convention, for those things that are as they are because human beings have decided they should be so. In America cars are driven on the right side of the road, in England on the left. Neither practice is "natural" or by *physis*. This is a clear example of convention. We drive on one side in America and on the other side in England simply because we have agreed to. In the case Herodotus refers to, it is not so clear that an explicit decision is responsible for how the Greeks and the Indians care for their dead. These are practices that probably go back into prehistory. Still, it is clear enough that neither practice is "by nature." Herodotus assigns the difference to custom, which is certainly *nomos*, for it is possible that, difficult as it might be, Greeks and Indians alike might take thought and change their practices. The mark of what is true by *physis* is that it is not up to us to decide, nor can we change the pattern if we want to. If by agreement we can change the order of certain things (e.g., which side of the road to drive on), then these things exist by *nomos*, not by *physis*.

There is an important corollary. Let us talk in terms of "the way things are." The way things are may be due to *physis* or to *nomos*. If they are due to *physis*, then we cannot go against them. For instance, it is part of the way things are that taking an ounce of strychnine will, unless immediate remedies are taken, cause one to die. It is not possible to swallow an ounce of strychnine, take no remedy, and continue to live. The connection between taking strychnine and death is a matter of *physis*. It does not depend on our decisions.

It is also part of the way things are that poisoning another human being is punished in some way. Yet it is possible (and it has happened) that someone might poison another and not receive punishment. Perhaps the killer is never discovered, or perhaps his lawyer is particularly skilled in rhetoric. If the way things are can be evaded, provided one is lucky or clever enough, then those connections are established by *nomos* and not by *physis*. It is for this reason that in cases of *nomos* we are likely to talk in terms of what a person "ought" to do: what is "right" or "appropriate," or "good" to do. It is neither right nor appropriate to follow the laws of nature. With respect to them, we have no choice. But conventions, customs, or laws that exist by *nomos* have a "normative" character to them. They state what we *should* do but may *fail* to do. It is possible to go against them. We should not, in England, drive on the right; but we can. Murderers should be punished, but they sometimes are not.

The distinction is an important one, and the credit for making it clearly must go to the Sophists. But how, you might ask, did they use it?

The question about the gods can be put clearly using this terminology. Do the gods exist by *physis* or by *nomos*? To answer that they exist by nature is to claim that their existence is quite independent of whatever humans believe about them. To say that the gods exist only by *nomos* amounts to saying that they are dependent on our belief; they have no reality independent of what we happen to believe about them. It is clear that the skeptical and relativistic nature of Sophist thought favors the latter alternative. Certain Sophists may have said that if it seems to you the gods exist, then they do exist— for you.* However, the agnosticism of Protagoras is probably more representative.

The distinction between *nomos* and *physis* is also applied to the virtues and, in particular, to justice. If a settled community like a city-state is to survive, then it is necessary that a certain degree of justice should prevail. Agreements must be kept, deceptions must be exceptions, and each individual must be able to count on others to keep up their end of things. So much is clear.† But is justice, which demands these things, something good by nature? Or is it merely a convention, foisted on individuals perhaps against their own best interest? Is justice a matter of *physis*, or is it entirely *nomos*? This question is important. It is extensively debated by the Sophists and, as we will see, by Plato and his successors.

It is clear what answers the Sophists must give to this question. They can look back to the institu-

tion of democracy, which is obviously a change made by human beings. They can see the process of laws being debated and set down. They observe decisions being made and sometimes reversed again. Clearly, forms of government, laws, and customs are matters of *nomos*. They are made by and can be altered by human decisions.

If one wants to know what is right or just, the obvious thing to do is to consult the laws. Is it just to keep agreements made? Then the laws will say so. How much tax is owed? The laws will tell you. For matters not covered explicitly by law, you can only look to the customs of the people. Where else can one look? Just as there is no sense in asking whether the wind in itself is either cold or warm (apart from the way it seems to those who feel it), so is there no sense in asking whether a given law is "really" just. If it seems just to the people of Athens, say, then it is just (for the Athenians).

For clarity's sake, let's call this sense of justice conventional justice. Conventional justice is defined as whatever the conventions (the *nomoi*) of a given society lay down as just.

We can contrast with this the idea of natural justice. Heraclitus, for instance, holds that

> all human laws are nourished by the one divine law. For it governs as far as it will, and is sufficient for all things, and outlasts them (*IEGP*, 103).

His idea is that human laws do not have their justification in themselves. They are "nourished," or get their sustenance, from a "divine law." This divine law, of course, is "common to all," the one *logos*, which is the same as the world-order. So human laws are not self-sufficient, in Heraclitus' view. Because people are commonly "at variance" with the *logos*, furthermore, we can infer that human law, too, may diverge from the *logos*. It makes sense for Heraclitus to contrast conventional justice with real or natural justice. He believes not only that there is a court of appeal from human law, which might fail to be really just, but also that human beings can know what that divine law requires.

An example of such an appeal is found in Sophocles' play *Antigone*. Following a civil war, Creon, king of Thebes, proclaims that the body of

---

*Does this sound cynical to you? Or might they have been sincere?

†Justice in this context is clearly something more than the justice of Homeric heroes giving each other the honor due to each (see p. 3–4). What is needed in settled city-states is more extensive than what is needed by warrior bands. Some notion of fair play or evenhandedness seems to be involved. The nature of justice is a perennial problem, and we will return to it.

Polyneices, leader of the opposition, should remain unburied. This was, in Greek tradition, a very bad thing; only if one's body was buried could the spirit depart for Hades. Polyneices' sister, Antigone, defies the decree and covers the body with dirt. Before the king she acknowledges that she knew of the proclamation and defends her action in these words.

> It was not Zeus who published this decree,
> Nor have the Powers who rule among the dead
> Imposed such laws as this upon mankind;
> Nor could I think that a decree of yours—
> A man—could override the laws of Heaven
> Unwritten and unchanging. Not of today
> Or yesterday is their authority;
> They are eternal; no man saw their birth.
> Was I to stand before the gods' tribunal
> For disobeying them, because I feared
> A man?[5]

Both Heraclitus and Antigone suggest that beyond conventional justice there is another justice. If the laws established by convention violate these higher laws, it may be permissible to violate the conventions. For the Sophists, however, no such appeal is possible. One might not like a law and therefore work to change it, but there is no appeal to another kind of law to justify its violation. Their skepticism about any reality beyond appearances and their consequent relativism rule out any such appeal.

A certain conservatism seems to be a consequence of this way of looking at justice. Protagoras, for instance, in promising to make Hippocrates a "better man," one able to succeed in Athenian society, would scarcely teach him that Athens is profoundly mistaken in her ideas of justice. He certainly would not turn him into a rebel and malcontent, or even into a reformer. That is no way to attain the admiration of one's fellow citizens; that is the way to earn their hostility and hatred. So it is likely that the Sophists taught their students to adapt to whatever society they found themselves in. If it seemed right to Athens, then it was right for Athens.

Some of the Sophists, though, drew different conclusions. The justice embodied in laws and customs is, they held, a matter of *nomos*. In the conventional sense, what is just is relative to the society you are in. There is also, however, a natural justice; moreover, we can know its content. But it is not, as Heraclitus thought, the "nourisher" of conventional justice; it is its opposite. A Sophist named Antiphon writes:

> . . . life and death are the concern of nature, and living creatures live by what is advantageous to them and die from what is not advantageous; and the advantages which accrue from law are chains upon nature, whereas those which accrue from nature are free (*IEGP*, 251).

Antiphon is telling us that if we only observe, we can see that a *natural* law governs the affairs of men and other living creatures: the law of self-preservation. Like all laws, it carries a punishment for those who violate it: death. Unlike conventional laws, this punishment necessarily follows the violation of the law. That is what makes it a natural law rather than a matter of convention. All creatures, he says, follow this law by seeking what is "advantageous" to themselves.

In contrast to this natural law, the restraints conventional justice places on human behavior are "chains upon nature." Antiphon goes as far as to claim that

> most of the things which are just by law [in the conventional sense] are hostile to nature (*IEGP*, 251).

It is natural, then, and therefore right or just (in the sense of *physis*) to pursue what is advantageous. Some of the time your advantage may coincide with the laws of the city. This is generally true because they represent the interests of many citizens of the city, who will haul you into court if you break the laws. But it is not always so; most of the things just by law, Antiphon says, are hostile to nature. Antiphon gives us this remarkable piece of advice:

> A man will be just, then, in a way most advantageous to himself if, in the presence of witnesses, he holds the laws of the city in high esteem, and in the absence

of witnesses, when he is alone, those of nature. For the laws of men are adventitious, but those of nature are necessary; and the laws of men are fixed by agreement, not by nature, whereas the laws of nature are natural and not fixed by agreement. He who breaks the rules, therefore, and escapes detection by those who have agreed to them, incurs no shame or penalty; if detected he does (*IEGP*, 250–51).

If you incur no "shame or penalty" by breaking the conventional laws (i.e., if you are not caught), then you have not brought any disadvantage upon yourself by doing so. Furthermore, the law of self-preservation bids you break the conventional laws. This law takes precedence over the conventional laws because it is "necessary" and "natural." Only *its* prescriptions cannot be evaded. Antiphon drives the point home:

If some benefit accrued to those who subscribed to the laws, while loss accrued to those who did not subscribe to them but opposed them, then obedience to the laws would not be without profit. But as things stand, it seems that legal justice is not strong enough to benefit those who subscribe to laws of this sort. For in the first place it permits the injured party to suffer injury and the man who inflicts it to inflict injury, and it does not prevent the injured party from suffering injury nor the man who does the injury from doing it. And if the case comes to trial, the injured party has no more of an advantage than the one who has done the injury; for he must convince his judges that he has been injured, and must be able, by his plea, to exact justice. And it is open to the one who has done the injury to deny it; for he can defend himself against the accusation, and he has the same opportunity to persuade his judges that his accuser has. For the victory goes to the best speaker (*IEGP*, 252–53).

"For the victory goes to the best speaker." We come around again to rhetoric. No matter which of the sophistic views of justice you take, rhetoric is of supreme importance. Whether you say that conventional justice is the only justice there is or hold that there is a natural justice of self-preservation, it is more important to *appear just* than to *be just*. According to the former view, appearances are all

anyone can know; according to the latter, the way you appear to others determines whether you obtain what is most advantageous to yourself.

The Sophists produced a theory of the nature of conventional justice as well. It is not clear how widespread it was; there was no unified sophistic doctrine. But it is of great interest and was picked up in the nineteenth century by Friedrich Nietzsche, who made it a key point in his attempt at a "revaluation of values." It is represented for us by Plato in the *Gorgias*, where it is presented by Callicles.

But in my opinion those who framed the laws are the weaker folk, the majority. And accordingly they form the laws for themselves and their own advantage, and so too with their approval and censure, and to prevent the stronger who are able to overreach them from gaining the advantage over them, they frighten them by saying that to overreach others is shameful and evil, and injustice consists in seeking the advantage over others. For they are satisfied, I suppose, if being inferior they enjoy equality of status. That is the reason why seeking an advantage over the many is by convention said to be wrong and shameful, and they call it injustice. But in my view nature herself makes it plain that it is right for the better to have the advantage over the worse, the more able over the less. And both among all animals and in entire states and races of mankind it is plain that this is the case—that right is recognized to be the sovereignty and advantage of the stronger over the weaker. For what justification had Xerxes in invading Greece or his father in invading Scythia? And there are countless other similar instances one might mention. But I imagine that these men act in accordance with the true nature of right, yes and by heaven, according to nature's own law, though not perhaps by the law we frame. We mold the best and strongest among ourselves, catching them young like lion cubs, and by spells and incantations we make slaves of them, saying that they must be content with equality and that this is what is right and fair. But if a man arises endowed with a nature sufficiently strong, he will, I believe, shake off all these controls, burst his fetters, and break loose. And trampling upon our scraps of paper, our spells and incantations, and all our unnatural conventions, he rises up and reveals himself our master who was once our slave, and there shines forth nature's true justice (*Gorgias* 483b–484a).

Callicles' basic idea is that we are by nature equipped with certain passions and desires. It is natural to try to satisfy these. Although the weak may try to fetter those who are strong by imposing a guilty conscience on them, the strong do nothing contrary to nature if they exert all their power and cleverness to satisfy whatever desires they have. Such behavior may be conventionally frowned upon, but it is not, in itself, unjust. In Plato's dialogue, Socrates tries to sum up what Callicles has said.

> . . . that the more powerful carries off by force the property of the weaker, the better rules over the worse, and the nobler takes more than the meaner? Have you any other conception of justice than this, or is my memory right? (*Gorgias* 488b).

To this Callicles replies,

> No, that is what I said then and still hold to (*Gorgias* 488b).

Note how dramatically this contrasts with the ethics of the Greek tradition. Compare it, for instance, to Heraclitus, who holds that it is not good for men to get all they wish, that "moderation is the greatest virtue."*

Callicles holds that enjoyment consists not in moderating one's desires but in satisfying them to the fullest extent. The really happy man is the one who is strong enough to do this without fear of retaliation. Here we have the very opposite of the "nothing too much" doctrine at Delphi—the negation of the tradition of self-restraint.

The views of the Sophists are bold and innovative, a response to the changing social and political situation, particularly in democratic Athens. But they are more than just reflections of a particular society at a given time. They constitute a serious critique of the beliefs of their predecessors and a challenge to those who come after them. These views force us to face the question: Why shouldn't we be Sophists too?

Notes

1. Quotations from Plato's *Protagoras*, trans. B. A. F. Hubbard and E. S. Karnofsky, in *Plato's Protagoras* (Chicago: Chicago University Press, 1982), are cited in the text by title and section numbers.
2. Quotations from Plato's *Gorgias*, in *The Collected Dialogues of Plato*, ed. E. Hamilton and H. Cairns (Princeton: Princeton University Press, 1961), are cited in the text by title and section number.
3. Quotations from John Manley Robinson's *An Introduction to Early Greek Philosophy* (Boston: Houghton Mifflin Co., 1968) are cited in the text using the abbreviation *IEGP*.
4. Herodotus, *The Histories*, (Penguin Books, 1972), bk. 3, sec. 38.
5. Sophocles, *Antigone*, trans. H. D. F. Kitto, in *Sophocles: Three Tragedies* (London: Oxford University Press, 1962), ll. 440–50.

*See p. 22.

7

The Decline of Athens

Athens and Sparta at War

In the context of the sophistic movement, we are philosophically prepared to understand Socrates and his disciple, Plato. But to understand why Socrates was brought to trial, we need to know something of the war. It was called the Peloponnesian War by Thucydides, who lived through it and wrote its history in a fascinating book by that title. The Peloponnesus is the large peninsula at the southern tip of mainland Greece connected by the narrow Isthmus of Corinth to Greece proper. It was named for a largely mythical ancestor, Pelops, supposedly the grandson of Zeus and the grandfather of Agamemnon and Menelaos of Trojan War fame. In the fifth century B.C.E., the dominant power on the peninsula was the city-state of Sparta (see map 1).

Sparta was quite unlike Athens. The Spartans had taken an important role in the defeat of the Persians, but thereafter, unlike Athens, they had followed a more cautious and defensive policy. Sparta was primarily a land power; Athens ruled the seas. While the Spartans had allies, mostly in the Peloponnesus, Athens had created an empire dominating most of the north of Greece and most of the islands in the Aegean. Sparta was not democratic. Rule in Sparta was in the hands of a relatively small portion of the population, which was in effect a warrior class. Their way of life was

austere and, as we say, spartan—devoted not to wealth and enjoyment but to rigorous training and self-discipline. They were supported by a large slave population called Helots and by other subject peoples in the area who paid tribute.

Perhaps it was inevitable that two such formidable powers in close proximity and so different would clash. They cooperated well enough in repelling the Persian invasion, but when that danger was past, their interests diverged. Thucydides tells us:

> It was by a common effort that the foreign invasion was repelled; but not long afterwards the Hellenes [the Greeks' name for themselves] . . . split into two divisions, one group following Athens and the other Sparta. These were clearly the two most powerful states, one being supreme on land, the other on the sea. For a short time the war-time alliance held together, but it was not long before quarrels took place and Athens and Sparta, each with her own allies, were at war with each other. . . . So from the end of the Persian War till the beginning of the Peloponnesian War, though there were some intervals of peace, on the whole these two Powers were either fighting with each other or putting down revolts among their allies. They were consequently in a high state of military preparedness and had gained their military experience in the hard school of danger. . . .

> What made war inevitable was the growth of Athenian power and the fear which this caused in Sparta[1] (HPW 1.18, 23).

War may indeed have been inevitable, but its coming was tragic. In the end, it led to the defeat of Athens and to the weakening of Greece in general. It meant the beginning of the end of the Golden Age of Greece.

The war itself was long and drawn out, lasting from 431 to 404 B.C.E. with an interval of seven years of relative peace in the middle. It was immensely costly to both sides, both in terms of men lost and wealth squandered. Athenian arrogance led to much foolishness: an ill-considered and disastrous expedition to conquer Sicily, for instance, and refusal of peace terms, which at one point would have been possible and reasonably honorable. We will not go into the details of the war; they can be found in Thucydides or any of a number of modern histories.* But war does things to a people, especially a long and inconclusive war fought with increasing desperation. And we need to have a sense for the temper of the times.

The war intensified the internal struggles within the city-states. Athens had been democratic for eighty years by the beginning of the war; nevertheless, tension between the descendants of the old aristocracy and the *demos*, or common people, still remained. These divisions were even more intense in other city-states, for Athens encouraged the development of democracy in her allies and appealed to the people (as opposed to the aristocrats) in cities she hoped to bring into her empire. These moves were resisted by the aristocratic or oligarchical parties in these states, who were often supported by Sparta. There was much infighting, which led to exile for defeated parties, to executions, and sometimes to civil wars. Those who lost these internal struggles sometimes offered their services to external foes of the winners—not infrequently even to Persia, who was still interested. Thucydides records the events in Corcyra (see map 1) after the victory of the democratic side over the oligarchs.

> . . . they seized upon all their enemies whom they could find and put them to death. They then dealt with those whom they had persuaded to go on board

the ships, killing them as they landed. Next they went to the temple of Hera and persuaded about fifty of the suppliants there to submit to a trial. They condemned every one of them to death. Seeing what was happening, most of the other suppliants, who had refused to be tried, killed each other there in the temple; some hanged themselves on the trees, and others found various other means of committing suicide. During the seven days that Eurymedon [an Athenian naval commander] stayed there with his sixty ships, the Corcyreans continued to massacre those of their own citizens whom they considered to be their enemies. Their victims were accused of conspiring to overthrow the democracy, but in fact men were often killed on grounds of personal hatred or else by their debtors because of the money they owed. There was death in every shape and form. And, as usually happens in such situations, people went to every extreme and beyond it. There were fathers who killed their sons; men were dragged from the temples or butchered on the very altars; some were actually walled up in the temple of Dionysus and died there. . . .

Later, of course, practically the whole of the Hellenic world was convulsed, with rival parties in every state—democratic leaders trying to bring in the Athenians, and oligarchs trying to bring in the Spartans (*HPW* 3.81–82).

We can see here the disintegration of the traditional Greek ideal of moderation; people "went to every extreme and beyond it." Moreover, the arguments of the more extreme Sophists found a parallel in concrete political undertakings. Naked self-interest came more and more to play the major role in decisions no longer even cloaked in terms of justice. Perhaps worst of all, Thucydides says, the very meaning of the words for right and virtue changed. When that happens, confusion reigns while moral thought and criticism become impossible.

The people of the island of Melos off the coast of the Peloponnesus (see map 1), who were originally colonists from Sparta, had remained neutral in the war. Athens sent an expedition to the island seeking their alliance. Thucydides reports a discussion between the ruling oligarchs of the island and the Athenian commanders. There are doubts about the authenticity of the dialogue, but it seems to represent the spirit of the times. The Melians have

---

*See suggestions, p. 36, fn. 1.

agreed that a dialogue should be the form of the discussion. We can think of each side as attempting to present the most persuasive *logos*.

> Athenians: Then we on our side will use no fine phrases saying, for example, that we have a right to our empire because we defeated the Persians, or that we have come against you now because of the injuries you have done us—a great mass of words that nobody would believe. And we ask you on your side not to imagine that you will influence us by saying that you, though a colony of Sparta have not joined Sparta in the war, or that you have never done us any harm. Instead we recommend that you should try to get what it is possible for you to get, taking into consideration what we both really do think; since you know as well as we do that, when these matters are discussed by practical people, the standard of justice depends on the equality of power to compel and that in fact the strong do what they have the power to do and the weak accept what they have to accept (*HPW*, 5.89).

The Melians argue that conquering them will not in fact be in the interest of Athens. In other words, they argue as "practical people." They do not have much success, however, and at last appeal to the gods, who will protect them because they "are standing for what is right against what is wrong" (*HPW*, 5.104). To this the Athenians reply:

> So far as the favor of the gods is concerned, we think we have as much right to that as you have. Our aims and our actions are perfectly consistent with the beliefs men hold about the gods and with the principles which govern their own conduct. Our opinion of the gods and our knowledge of men lead us to conclude that it is a general and necessary law of nature to rule whatever one can. This is not a law that we made ourselves, nor were we the first to act upon it when it was made. We found it already in existence, and we shall leave it to exist for ever among those who come after us. We are merely acting in accordance with it, and we know that you or anybody else with the same power as ours would be acting in precisely the same way (*HPW* 5.105).

The Athenian general who is represented as making this speech might have gone to school under Antiphon! He even frames the character of the law of self-interest in the same terms; it is "necessary" and not manmade. In effect, he claims this is a law of *physis*, not just a matter of *nomos*. For that reason, so the argument goes, the Athenians are perfectly justified in conquering Melos if they have the power to do so.

The Melians, not wise in these matters of power politics, refuse to surrender. After a siege, the Athenians

> put to death all the men of military age whom they took, and sold the women and children as slaves. Melos itself they took over for themselves, sending out later a colony of 500 men (*HPW* 5.116).

Such hardness was common on all sides.

After the death of Pericles in the early years of the war, Athens had no natural leader. Leadership tended to flow to those who could speak persuasively before the Assembly. These leaders were called "demagogues," those who could lead (*agoge*) the *demos*. Policy was inconstant and sometimes reversed, depending on who was the most persuasive speaker of the day. Dissatisfaction with democracy began to grow, especially in quarters traditionally allied with the "best people." When Athens was finally defeated in 404, treachery on the part of these enemies of democracy was suspected but could not be proved.

According to the terms of the peace treaty imposed on Athens, she had to receive returning exiles (most of whom were antidemocratic), agree to have the same friends and enemies as Sparta, and accept provisional government by a Council that came to be known as the Thirty. A new constitution was promised, but naturally the Thirty were in no hurry to form a new government. Supported by a cohort of Spartan men-at-arms, they carried out a purge of "wrongdoers," executing criminals and those who had opposed surrender. But their rule soon involved the persecution of any dissidents, as well as people they just didn't like, and the expropriation of their property to support the new system. They claimed, of course, to be enforcing virtue. In classic fashion, they tried to involve as many

Athenian citizens as possible in their adventures to prevent them from making accusations later. Socrates, as we learn, was one of five persons summoned to arrest a certain Leon of Salamis. (He refused.) The rule of the Thirty became, in short, a reign of terror. Ever after, Athenians could not hear the words "the Thirty" without a shudder.

This rule lasted less than a year. Exiles, joined by democratic forces within the city, attacked and defeated the forces backing the Thirty. Their leader Critias was killed in the fighting, the others were exiled, and democracy was restored. Though a bloodbath was resisted, bad feelings on all sides continued for many years.

Because of the war and its aftermath, Athenians lost confidence in their ability to control their own destiny. The satisfaction in their superiority expressed so well by Pericles disintegrated. Men seemed torn by forces beyond their ability to control in a world that was not well ordered, whether by the gods or by something like the Heraclitean *logos*. The world and human affairs seemed chaotic, beyond managing.

The Greeks had always believed, of course, that humans were not complete masters of their own fate. This belief was expressed in the ideas that the gods intervene in human affairs for their own ends and that no one can escape his fate. We find such ideas in the works of Homer and in the tragedies of Aeschylus and Sophocles. But in the time of the war, these notions were tinged with a new sense of bitterness and despair. The third of the great Greek tragedians, Euripides, expresses the new mood.

Hippolytus, in the play by that name, is devoted to Artemis (the Roman Diana), goddess of the woodlands, of the hunt, and of chastity. His father's wife (who is not his mother), Phaedra, falls passionately in love with him under the influence of Aphrodite (Venus). She is literally sick with love, sick, she says, to death. Her nurse first admonishes her in classic fashion.

> I have learned much
> from my long life. The mixing bowl of friendship,
> the love of one for the other, must be tempered.
> Love must not touch the marrow of the soul.

> Our affections must be breakable chains that we
> can cast them off or tighten them. . . .
> The ways of life that are most fanatical
> trip us up more, they say, than bring us joy.
> They're enemies to health. So I praise less
> the extreme than temperance in everything.
> The wise will bear me out

(HIPPOLYTUS 251–66).[2]

Temperance, moderation in all things, is her message. It is not wise to let one's passions get such a hold that they are beyond control. It is the old message that comes down through the philosophers from Homer. Her words suggest that Phaedra should give up her passion.

But upon learning the object of Phaedra's love and her inability or unwillingness to give it up, the nurse changes her mind.

> In this world second thoughts, it seems, are best.
> Your case is not so extraordinary,
> beyond thought or reason. The Goddess in her anger
> has smitten you, and you are in love. What wonder
> is this? . . .
>
> The tide of love,
> at its full surge, is not withstandable. . . .
>
> He who has read the writings of the ancients
> and has lived much in books, he knows
> that Zeus once loved the lovely Semele. . . .
> Yet all these dwell in heaven.
> They are content, I am sure, to be subdued
> by the stroke of love. . . .
>
> We should not in the conduct of our lives
> be too exacting

(HIPPOLYTUS 436–68).

Here we have the nurse as rhetorician, constructing a plausible *logos* to suit the one who hears her. She even appeals to the example of the gods; if they give in to their passions, she says, why should you think it wrong for you to do the same? Phaedra, hanging on to her virtue as best she can despite her acknowledged love, gives this reply:*

---

*Is it necessary to point out that we have here a critique of the practice of rhetoric? On what grounds is it criticized?

This is the deadly thing which devastates
well-ordered cities and the homes of men—
that's it, this art of oversubtle words.
It's not the words ringing in the ear
that one should speak, but those that have the power
to save their hearer's honorable name

(HIPPOLYTUS 486–89).

The nurse responds:

This is high moralizing! What you want
is not fine words, but the man!

(HIPPOLYTUS 490–91).

To Phaedra's protests that this is "wicked, wicked!"
and her refusal to listen to such "shameful" words,
the nurse admits,

O, they are shameful! But they are better than
your noble-sounding moral sentiments.
"The deed" is better if it saves your life:
than your "good name" in which you die exulting

(HIPPOLYTUS 500–503).

Here again we have the morality of certain Sophists. What is important is that you save your life. Considerations of honor and morality must be held strictly in second place. It is quite the opposite of the Homeric morality; Akhilleus, for instance, and Hektor too, are quite ready to die for honor and glory; death is, by comparison, unimportant.

As the play develops, the nurse tells Hippolytus of Phaedra's love for him. He rejects it and vows to tell his father, Theseus, who is out of the city at the time. When Phaedra learns of this, she kills herself and leaves a note (to save her good name) accusing Hippolytus of rape. Theseus returns, reads the note, and curses his son. The consequence is Hippolytus' death in an accident; only then does Theseus learn of his innocence.

The play is framed at beginning and end by speeches of the two goddesses, Aphrodite and Artemis, respectively. Aphrodite vows to take vengeance on Hippolytus because he despises her and worships only chastity. This she does, using Phaedra as her tool. Artemis at the end vows to avenge

Hippolytus by destroying some favorite of Aphrodite's. (Some vengeance!) The impression left by the play is that humans are mere pawns in the hands of greater powers—powers which are in opposition to each other, which make no sense, which have no rhyme or reason in some higher unity of purpose. Led this way or that by passions we cannot control, we are bound for destruction. The chorus laments near the end:

The care of God for us is a great thing,
if a man believe it at heart:
it plucks the burden of sorrow from him.
So I have a secret hope
of someone, a God, who is wise and plans;
but my hopes grow dim when I see
the deeds of men and their destinies.

For fortune is ever veering, and the currents of life are
shifting
shifting, wandering forever

(HIPPOLYTUS 1102–10).

We have the hope, the chorus says, that our lives are more than "sound and fury, signifying nothing." We would like to believe that there is a wise plan to our lives. But if we look about us at the world—and, the Sophists would say, what else can we do?—we find no such reason to hope. Men's fortunes are "ever veering, and the currents of life are shifting, shifting, wandering forever."

So things must have looked in the last decades of the fifth century in Athens.

Aristophanes and Reaction

Although the Sophists were obviously popular in some circles, they were hated and feared in others. They were a phenomenon that both depended on and fostered the kind of democracy Athens practiced: direct democracy where decisions were made by whichever citizens were present in the Assembly on a given day. Political power rested directly with the people in this system, but the masses, of course, tended to be at the mercy of those who possessed the rhetorical skills to sway them in the direction of their own interests: the "demagogues." The old families who could look back to the "good old days" when the "best people" made the decisions were never happy in this state of affairs. As we have seen, they tried, when they could, to reverse the situation—not always with better results!

Among those who were unhappy were certain intellectuals, including a writer of comedies named Aristophanes. One of his plays, *The Clouds*,* is a satire on the new education provided by the Sophists and on the sophistic movement in general. It is worth a look not only because it gives us another point of view on the Sophists but also because he makes Socrates a principal character in the play. In fact, Socrates is presented in *The Clouds* as the leading Sophist, who runs a school called "The Thinkery" to which students come to learn—provided they pay. When we first see Socrates, he is hanging in the air, suspended in a basket.

> You see,
> only by being suspended aloft, by dangling
> my mind in the heavens and mingling my rare thought
> with the ethereal air, could I ever achieve strict
> scientific accuracy in my survey of the vast empyrean.
> Had I pursued my inquiries from down there on the ground,
> my data would be worthless. The earth, you see, pulls down
> the delicate essence of thought to its own gross level
>
> (CLOUDS, p. 33).[3]

This is, of course, attractive nonsense. As we'll see, Socrates neither had a "Thinkery," charged for instruction, nor was interested in speculations about the heavens and earth. Most important, although he did share the Sophists' interest in human affairs, Socrates was one of their most severe critics. Aristophanes' picture of Socrates is satire painted with a broad brush.

Socrates' students are represented as engaging in scientific studies to determine, for example, how far a flea can jump and out of which end does a gnat tootle. But that is not the main interest of the play. Strepsiades, a man from the country who has married an extravagant city wife and has a son who loves horse racing, is worried about the debts they have piled up. In particular, several of his son's debts are coming due, and he hasn't the money to pay them. So he decides to send his son to the Thinkery to learn the new sophistic logic, which can make the weaker argument into the stronger. He thinks that by getting his son to learn these rhetorical tricks he may be able to avoid paying back the money.

Strepsiades is at first unable to persuade his son to go. So he becomes a student himself. He does not prove an apt pupil, however, and Socrates eventually kicks him out, but not before he has learned a thing or two. When he meets his son, Pheidippides, he again tries to force him to go to the school.

PHEIDIPPIDES: But Father,
what's the matter with you? Are you out of your head?
Almighty Zeus, you must be mad!

STREPSIADES: "Almighty Zeus!"
What musty rubbish! Imagine, a boy your age still believing in Zeus!

PHEIDIPPIDES: What's so damn funny?

STREPSIADES: It tickles me when the heads of toddlers like you
are still stuffed with such outdated notions. Now then,
listen to me and I'll tell you a secret or two
that might make an intelligent man of you yet.
But remember: you mustn't breathe a word of this.

PHEIDIPPIDES: A word of what?

STREPSIADES: Didn't you just swear by Zeus?

PHEIDIPPIDES: I did.

STREPSIADES: Now learn what Education can do for you:
Pheidippides, there is no Zeus.

PHEIDIPPIDES: There is no Zeus?

---

*First performed in Athens in 423 B.C.E., the eighth year of the war.

STREPSIADES: No Zeus. Convection-Principle's in power now.
Zeus has been banished
(*Clouds*, pp. 75–76).

The "convection principle" is our old friend the vortex motion or cosmic whirl, by means of which the nature philosophers explain the structure of the world. In the form given this principle by the atomists, as we have seen, there is no need for—indeed, no room for—any intelligent purpose at all. Everything is caused to happen necessarily, in a completely mechanical fashion. Zeus has indeed been "banished."

Aristophanes, far from conceding that this is progress, deplores the new thought. The old methods of education are farcically confronted with the new by means of two characters, dressed in the masks of fighting cocks, called the just *logos* and the unjust *logos*. (In this translation, they are called "Philosophy" and "Sophistry," respectively.) After some preliminary sparring and insult trading, the just *logos* speaks first.

PHILOSOPHY: Gentlemen,
I propose to speak of the Old Education, as it flourished once
beneath my tutelage, when Homespun Honesty, Plainspeaking, and Truth
were still honored and practiced, and throughout the schools of Athens
the regime of the three D's—DISCIPLINE, DECORUM, and DUTY—
enjoyed unchallenged supremacy.
Our curriculum was Music and Gymnastics, enforced by that rigorous discipline summed up in the old adage:
BOYS SHOULD BE SEEN BUT NOT HEARD. . . .

SOPHISTRY: Ugh, what musty, antiquated rubbish. . . .

PHILOSOPHY: Nonetheless, these were the precepts on which I bred a generation of heroes, the men who fought at Marathon. . . .
No, young man, by your courage I challenge you. Turn your back upon his blandishments of vice,

the rotten law courts and the cheap, corrupting softness of the baths.
Choose instead the Old, the Philosophical Education. Follow me
and from my lips acquire the virtues of a man:—
A sense of shame, that decency and innocence of mind that shrinks from doing wrong.
To feel the true man's blaze of anger when his honor is provoked.
Deference toward one's elders; respect for one's father and mother . . .
(*Clouds*, pp. 86–89).

This speech is applauded roundly by the chorus, who say that the unjust *logos* will have to produce "some crushing *tour de force*, some master stroke" to counter these persuasive comments. The unjust *logos* is not at a loss.

SOPHISTRY: Now then, I freely admit
that among men of learning I am—somewhat pejoratively—dubbed
the Sophistic, or Immoral Logic. And why? Because I first
devised a Method for the Subversion of Established Social Beliefs
and the Undermining of Morality. Moreover, this little invention of mine,
this knack of taking what might appear to be the worse argument
and nonetheless winning my case, has, I might add, proved to be
an *extremely* lucrative source of income. . . .
—Young man,
I advise you to ponder this life of Virtue with scrupulous care,
all that it implies, and all the pleasures of which its daily practice
must inevitably deprive you. Specifically, I might mention these:
Sex. Gambling. Gluttony. Guzzling. Carousing. Etcet.
And what on earth's the point of living, if you leach your life
of all its little joys?

Very well then, consider your natural needs.
Suppose, as a scholar of Virtue, you commit
some minor peccadillo,
a little adultery, say, or seduction, and suddenly
find yourself
caught in the act. What happens? You're ruined,
you can't defend yourself
(since, of course, you haven't been taught). But
follow me, my boy,
and obey your nature to the full; romp, play,
and laugh
without a scruple in the world. Then if caught in
flagrante,
you simply inform the poor cuckold that you're
utterly innocent
and refer him to Zeus as your moral sanction.
After all, didn't he,
a great and powerful god, succumb to the love
of women?
Then how in the world can you, a man, an ordinary mortal,
be expected to surpass the greatest of gods in
moral self-control?
Clearly, you can't be
(*Clouds*, pp. 91–94).

To his father's satisfaction, Pheidippides is persuaded to study with the Sophists. But the climax
comes when the son turns what he has learned, not
on the creditors, but on his father. After a quarrel,
he begins to beat his father with a stick. This is not
bad enough; he claims to be able to prove that he is
right to do so!

PHEIDIPPIDES: Now then, answer my question:
    did you lick me when I was a little boy?

STREPSIADES: Of course I licked you.
    For your own damn good. Because I loved you.

PHEIDIPPIDES: Then *ipso facto*,
    since you yourself admit that loving and lick-
    ings are
    synonymous, it's only fair that I—for your own
    damn good,
    you understand?—whip you in return.
        In any case by what right do you whip me

but claim exemption for yourself?
    What do you think I am? A slave?
Wasn't I born as free a man as you?
    Well?

STREPSIADES: But . . .

PHEIDIPPIDES: But what?
    Spare the Rod and Spoil the Child?
    Is that your argument?
        If so,
    then I can be sententious too. *Old Men Are Boys
    Writ Big*,
    as the saying goes.
        A fortiori then, old men logically deserve
    to be beaten more, since at their age they have
    clearly less
    excuse for the mischief that they do.

STREPSIADES: But it's unnatural! It's . . . *illegal!*
    Honor your father and mother.
        That's the law.
        Everywhere.

PHEIDIPPIDES The *law?*
    And who made the law?
        An ordinary man. A man like you or me.
    A man who lobbied for his bill until he per-
    suaded the people to make it law.
        By the same token, then, what prevents
    me now
    from proposing new legislation granting sons
    the power to
    inflict corporal punishment upon wayward
    fathers?. . .
        However, if you're still unconvinced,
    look to Nature for a sanction. Observe the
    roosters,
    for instance, and what do you see?
        A society
    whose pecking order envisages a permanent
    state of open
    warfare between fathers and sons. And how do
    roosters
    differ from men, except for the trifling fact that
    human
    society is based upon law and rooster society
    isn't?
(*Clouds*, pp. 122–24).

Strepsiades is forced by the "persuasive power" of this rhetoric to admit defeat: "The kids," he says, "have proved their point: naughty fathers should be flogged." But when Pheidippides adds that since "misery loves company" he has decided to flog his *mother*, too, and can prove "by Sokratic logic" the propriety of doing so, that's the last straw. Strepsiades cries out:

> By god, if you prove *that*,
> then for all I care, you heel,
> you can take your stinking Logics
> and your Thinkery as well
> with Sokrates inside it
> and damn well go to hell!
> (*Clouds*, p. 126).

Disillusioned by the promise of sophistry, Strepsiades admits he was wrong to try to cheat his creditors. Convinced that the new education is, as the just *logos* has put it, the "corrupter and destroyer" of the youth, he ends the play by burning down the Thinkery. The moral is drawn, as it typically is, by the chorus—in this case a chorus of Clouds representing the goddesses of the new thought.

> . . . this is what we are,
> the insubstantial Clouds men build their hopes upon,
> shining tempters formed of air, symbols of desire;
> and so we act, beckoning, alluring foolish men through their dishonest dreams of gain to overwhelming
> ruin. There, schooled by suffering, they learn at last
> to fear the gods
> (*Clouds*, p. 127).

The Clouds is surely not a fair and dispassionate appraisal of the sophistic movement. It is partisan in the extreme, a caricature by a traditionalist deeply antagonistic to the changes Athenian society was going through. And yet it poses some serious questions. Is there a way to distinguish between *logoi* independently of their persuasiveness? If not, is argument just a contest that the most persuasive must win? And if Strepsiades can think of no logical rejoinder to his son's sophisms, what is the outcome? Are arson and violence the only answer? But if that is so, in what sense is that answer superior to the rhetoric that it opposes? Isn't it just employing another tool of force, less subtle than the verbal manipulations of the rhetorician?

What is put in question by the Sophists and Aristophanes' response to them is this: Is there any technique by which people can discuss and come to agree on matters important to them that does not reduce to a power struggle in the end? It is the intellectual parallel to the question that lurked in the Melian debate. Is there something that can be identified as being reasonable, as opposed to being *persuasive*? Can human beings, by discussing matters together, come to know the truth? Or is it always just a question of who wins?

This is the question that interests Socrates.

Notes

1. Quotations from Thucydides, *History of the Peloponnesian War*, trans. Rex Warner (New York: Penguin Books, 1954), are cited in the text using the abbreviation *HPW*. References are to book and section numbers.
2. Quotations from Euripides' *Hippolytus*, trans. David Grene, in *Euripides I*, ed. David Grene and Richard Lattimore (Chicago: University of Chicago Press, 1965), are cited in the text by title and line numbers.
3. Quotations from Aristophanes' *Clouds*, trans. William Arrowsmith (New York: New American Library, 1962), are cited in the text by title and page numbers.

8

Socrates:
To Know Oneself

Some philosophers are important just for what they say or write. Others are important also for what they are—for their personality and character. No better example of the latter exists than Socrates.

Socrates wrote nothing, save some poetry written while he was waiting to be executed; he is said to have written a hymn to Apollo and to have put the fables of Aesop into verse. But those have not survived. His impact on those who knew him, however, was extraordinary, and his influence down to the present day has few parallels.

The fact that he wrote nothing poses a problem, of course. We have to look to other writers for our knowledge of him. Aristophanes is one source, but such farce must be taken with more than one grain of salt. Another source is Xenophon, who tells numerous stories involving Socrates but is philosophically rather unsophisticated.* Aristotle, too, discusses him. But our main source is Plato, a younger companion of Socrates and a devoted admirer.

Plato didn't, however, write a biography, nor did he write a scholarly analysis of his master's thought. He has left us a large number of dialogues, or conversations, in most of which Socrates is a participant, often the central figure. These might be very reliable, if Plato had carried with him a tape recorder and then transcribed the conversations. But of course he couldn't have. These

dialogues were all written after Socrates' death, many of them long after. And there can be no doubt that in the later dialogues Plato is putting ideas of his own into the mouth of Socrates. We should not think there is anything dishonest about this practice. The ancient world would have accepted it as perfectly in order; Plato surely believed that his own ideas were a natural development from those of Socrates and that in this way he was honoring his master. But it does pose a problem if we want to discuss the historical Socrates rather than Plato's Socrates.

No definitive solution to this problem may ever be found. One scholar recently acknowledged that "in the end we must all have to some extent our own Socrates."[1] Still, some things are reasonably certain.

The dialogues of Plato can pretty well be sorted into three periods: the early, the middle, and the late. The early dialogues, such as *Euthyphro, Crito,* and the *Apology* are thought to represent quite accurately Socrates' own views and ways of proceeding. They seem to have been written soon after his death. In these dialogues, Socrates questions various persons about the nature of piety, courage, justice, or virtue/excellence (*arete*).* The outcome of the conversation is usually negative in just this sense: no agreed upon solution is reached. The

---

*Note: This is not Xenophanes, the pre-Socratic philosopher discussed in Chapter 2.

---

*The meaning of this important word is discussed on p. 38.

57

participant, who at the dialogue's beginning claims to know something, is forced to admit ignorance. If realizing that you don't understand something you previously thought you did is progress, then there is also a positive side to these early dialogues. The participants do learn something—i.e., how little they know. And they clear the ground of untenable views.

In the middle dialogues, such as *Meno, Phaedo, Symposium*, and the monumental *Republic*, Socrates is still the main protagonist. But here we find positive doctrines aplenty, supported by many arguments. Here Plato works out his own solutions to the problems posed by the Sophists and by the negative outcome of Socratic questioning.

The last set of dialogues contain further developments and explore difficulties raised by the doctrines of the middle period. Here Socrates begins to play a lesser role; in the very late *Laws*, he disappears altogether.

We will discuss Socrates primarily as he appears in the early dialogues and read two short dialogues, plus a selection from another. But before reading those, we need to learn something about his character and person.

Character

Socrates was born in 470 or 469 B.C.E. His father was a stonemason and perhaps a minor sculptor. It is thought that Socrates pursued this same trade as a young man. His mother was a midwife. As we'll see, Socrates calls himself a "midwife" in the realm of thought. It is interesting to note that one of the duties of a Greek midwife in classical times was to determine whether the child was a bastard (presumably by way of resemblance to the "father"). In a similar way, Socrates claims not to be able to give people ideas but to help others deliver themselves of ideas and to determine their truth by examining their "resemblance" to other ideas expressed in the conversation. The question is always this: is the person talking to Socrates being *consistent*? We see

numerous examples of his "midwifery." He was married to Xanthippe, a woman with a reputation for shrewishness, and had three sons, apparently rather late in life.

No one ever claimed that Socrates was good looking, except in a joke. In a charming work designed to let us see "great and good men" in their "lighter moods," Xenophon reports on an impromptu "beauty contest" held at a banquet. The contestants are Critobulus, a good looking young man, and Socrates. Socrates is challenged to prove that he is the more handsome.

s: Do you think beauty exists in man alone, or in anything else?

c: I believe it is found in horse and ox and many inanimate things. For instance, I recognize a beautiful shield, sword or spear.

s: And how can all these things be beautiful when they bear no resemblance to each other?

c: Why, if they are well made for the purposes for which we acquire them, or well adapted by nature to our needs, then in each case I call them beautiful.

s: Well then, what do we need eyes for?

c: To see with of course.

s: In that case my eyes are at once proved to be more beautiful than yours, because yours look only straight ahead, whereas mine project so that they can see sideways as well.

c: Are you claiming that a crab has the most beautiful eyes of any animal?

s: Certainly, since from the point of view of strength also its eyes are best constructed by nature.

c: All right, but which of our noses is the more beautiful?

s: Mine, I should say, if the gods gave us noses to smell with, for your nostrils point to earth, but mine are spread out widely to receive odours from every quarter.

c: But how can a snub nose be more beautiful than a straight one?

s: Because it does not get in the way but allows the eyes to see what they will, whereas a high bridge walls them off as if to spite them.

c: As for the mouth, I give in, for if mouths are made for biting you could take a much larger bite than I.

s: And with my thick lips don't you think I could give a softer kiss?[2]

After this exchange, the banqueters take a secret ballot to determine who is the more handsome. Critobulus gets every vote, so Socrates exclaims that he must have bribed the judges! It must have been nearly impossible to resist caricaturing this odd-looking man who shuffled about Athens barefoot and peered sideways at you out of his bulging eyes when you spoke to him. Aristophanes was not the only writer of comedies to succumb to the temptation.

We see several things about Socrates in this little excerpt: (1) it was not for his physical attractiveness that Socrates was sought after as a companion; he was acknowledged on all sides to be extraordinarily ugly, though it seems to have been an interesting kind of ugliness; (2) we see something of Socrates' humor; here it is light and directed at himself, but it could also be sharp and biting; (3) we have our first glimpse of the typical "Socratic method," which proceeds by question and answer, not by long speeches; and (4) we see that Socrates here identifies the good or the beautiful in terms of usefulness or advantage; and this is typical of his views on these questions of value.

We learn that he served in the army several times with courage and distinction. In Plato's *Symposium*, an account of a party akin to Xenophon's banquet, Alcibiades, a brilliant young man we shall hear more of, gives the following testimony.

. . . we were both sent on active service to Potidaea [see map 1], where we messed together. Well, to begin with, he stood the hardships of the campaign far better than I did, or anyone else, for that matter. And if—and it's always liable to happen when there's fighting going on—we were cut off from our supplies, there was no one who put such a good face on

it as he. But on the other hand, when there was plenty to eat he was the one man who really seemed to enjoy it, and though he didn't drink for choice, if we ever pressed him he'd beat the lot of us. And what's the most extraordinary thing of all, there's not a man living that's ever seen Socrates drunk. . . .

Then again, the way he got through that winter was most impressive, and the winters over there are pretty shocking. There was one time when the frost was harder than ever, and all the rest of us stayed inside, or if we did go out we wrapped ourselves up the eyes and tied bits of felt and sheepskins over our shoes, but Socrates went out in the same old coat he's always worn, and made less fuss about walking on the ice in his bare feet than we did in our shoes. . . .

And now I must tell you about another thing "our valiant hero dared and did" in the course of the same campaign. He started wrestling with some problem or other about sunrise one morning, and stood there lost in thought, and when the answer wouldn't come he still stood there thinking and refused to give it up. Time went on, and by about midday the troops noticed what was happening, and naturally they were rather surprised and began telling each other how Socrates had been standing there thinking ever since daybreak. And at last, toward nightfall, some of the Ionians brought out their bedding after supper—this was in the summer, of course—partly because it was cooler in the open air, and partly to see whether he was going to stay there all night. Well, there he stood till morning, and then at sunrise he said his prayers to the sun and went away (*Symposium* 219–220d).[3]

Alcibiades goes on to tell how Socrates saved his life and in a retreat showed himself to be the coolest man around, so that

you could see from half a mile away that if you tackled him you'd get as good as you gave—with the result that he and Laches both got clean away (*Symposium* 221b).

He sums up his view by saying that

he is absolutely unique; there's no one like him, and I don't believe there ever was. . . .

Anyone listening to Socrates for the first time would find his arguments simply laughable. . . . He talks about pack asses and blacksmiths and shoe-makers and tanners, and he always seems to be say-ing the same old thing in just the same old way, so that anyone who wasn't used to his style and wasn't very quick on the uptake would naturally take it for the most utter nonsense. But if you open up his argu-ments and really get into the skin of them, you'll find that they're the only arguments in the world that have any sense at all, and that nobody else's are so godlike, so rich in images of virtue, or so peculiarly, so entirely pertinent to those inquiries that help the seeker on his way to the goal of true nobility (*Sympo-sium* 221c–222a).

It is somewhat ironic to hear Alcibiades talking of "true nobility" here. He was for a time a close asso-ciate of Socrates but in later life became notorious for lechery and lust for power. He was suspected of being responsible for the mutilation of statues of Hermes (often set by the gates or doors of Athenian houses) and was put on trial while he was away on a military mission. Eventually he deserted and of-fered his services as a general to the Spartans. The common opinion was that Alcibiades was hand-some and brilliant but also treacherous and despi-cable. Nonetheless, there is no reason to doubt the testimony to Socrates that Plato here puts into his mouth.

The party is invaded by a bunch of revelers; ev-eryone drinks a great deal, many leave, and some fall asleep. Near morning, only three persons are still awake: Agathon the host, Aristophanes (yes, the comic playwright), and Socrates. They are still drinking and arguing, now about whether one and the same person could write both tragedies and comedies.

But as he clinched the argument, which the other two were scarcely in a state to follow, they began to nod, and first Aristophanes fell off to sleep, and then Agathon, as day was breaking. Whereupon Socrates tucked them up comfortably and went away. . . . And after calling at the Lyceum for a bath, he spent the rest of the day as usual, and then, toward evening, made his way home to rest (*Symposium* 223d).

He "spent the rest of the day as usual." How was that? Socrates' days seem to have been devoted mainly to conversations in the public places of Athens. He was not independently wealthy, as you might suspect; Alcibiades' remark about "the same old coat he'd always worn" seems to have been ac-curate. Xenophon tells us that

he schooled his body and soul by following a system which . . . would make it easy to meet his expenses. For he was so frugal that it is hardly possible to imag-ine a man doing so little work as not to earn enough to satisfy the needs of Socrates (*Memorabilia* 1.3.5).[4]

He was temperate in his desires and possessed re-markable self-control with regard not only to food and drink but also to sex. He apparently refrained from the physical relationship that was a fairly common feature of friendships between older men and their young protégés in ancient Athens.* Al-though he used the language of "love" freely, he held that the proper aim of such friendships was to make the "beloved" more virtuous, self-controlled, and just. No doubt he believed that the young could not learn self-control from someone who did not display it. By common consent the judgment of Alcibiades was correct: Socrates was unique.

Is Socrates a Sophist?

In *The Clouds*, Aristophanes presents Socrates as a Sophist. There are undeniable similarities between them, but there are also important differences. We need to explore this a bit.

Socrates clearly moves in the same circles as the Sophists; he converses with them eagerly and of-ten, and his interests are similar. His subject matter is human affairs, in particular *arete*—excellence or virtue. As we have seen, the Sophists set them-selves up as teachers of such excellence. Socrates does not. He cannot do so, he might insist, because he does not rightly know what it is. And no one can claim to teach what he doesn't understand. None-

---

*See, for example, the complaint of Alcibiades in *Symposium* 217a–219d.

theless, he explores this very area, trying to clarify what human excellence consists in, whether it is one thing or many (e.g., courage, moderation, wisdom, justice), and whether it is the kind of thing that can be taught at all.

We have noted that many of the Sophists also teach specialized subjects, including geometry, astronomy, and nature philosophy in general. Socrates apparently was interested in nature philosophy as a youth but gave it up because it could not answer the questions that really intrigue him, such as Why are we here? and What is the best kind of life? Human life is what fascinates him. So he and the Sophists share a community of interest.

Young men associate themselves with Socrates, too, sometimes for considerable periods of time, and consider him their teacher. He does not, as we noted in connection with Aristophanes' "Thinkery," have a school. And *he* does not consider himself a teacher. In fact, we will hear his claim that he has never taught anyone anything. (This takes some explaining, which we will do later.) So he is unlike the Sophists in that regard, for they *do* consider that they have something to teach and are proud to teach it to others.

Socrates is unlike the Sophists in another regard. He takes no pay from those who associate themselves with him. This is, of course, perfectly consistent with his claim that he has nothing to teach. Xenophon adds that Socrates "marvelled that anyone should make money by the profession of virtue, and should not reflect that his highest reward would be the gain of a good friend" (*Memorabilia* 1.2.7).

Like the Sophists, Socrates is interested in the arts of communication and argument, in techniques of persuasion. But it is at just this point that we find the deepest difference between them, the difference that perhaps allows us to deny that Socrates is a Sophist at all. For the Sophists, these arts (rhetoric) are like strategies and tactics in battle. The whole point is to enable their practitioner to *win*. Argument and persuasion are thought of as a kind of strife or contest where, as Antiphon put it, "victory goes to the best speaker." No concern for *truth* underlies the instruction of the Sophists; the

aim is *victory*. This is wholly consistent with their denial that truth is available to human beings, with their skepticism and relativism. If all you can get are opinions anyway, then you might as well try to make things appear to others as they appear to you. That is what serves your self-interest. And rhetoric, as they conceive and teach it, is designed to do just that.*

For Socrates, on the other hand, the arts of communication, argument, and persuasion have a different goal. His practice of them is designed not to win a victory over his opponent but to advance toward the truth. He is convinced that there is a truth about human affairs and that we are capable of advancing toward it, of shaping our opinions so that they are more "like truth," to use that old phrase of Xenophanes.† Socrates could never agree that if a man *thinks* a certain action is just, then it *is* just—not even "for him." So he is neither a relativist nor a skeptic. Justice, Socrates believes, is something quite independent of our opinions about it. And what it is needs investigation.

Socrates' way of proceeding coheres well with this conviction about truth. He usually refrains from piling up fine phrases in lengthy speeches that might simply overwhelm his listeners; he does not want them to agree with his conclusions for reasons they do not themselves fully understand and agree to. So he asks questions. He is very insistent that his listeners answer in a sincere way, that they say what they truly believe. Each person is to speak for himself. In the *Meno*, for instance, Socrates professes not to know what virtue is. Meno expresses surprise, for surely, he says, Socrates listened to Gorgias when he was in town. Yes, Socrates admits, but he does not altogether remember what Gorgias said; perhaps Meno remembers and agrees with him. Meno admits that he does. Then Socrates says,

> Let us leave Gorgias out of it, since he is not here. But Meno, by the gods, what do you yourself say that virtue is? (*Meno* 71d).[5]

---

*See Antiphon quote on p. 45.
†Look again at the fragment from Xenophanes on p. 14.

So Meno is put on the spot and has to speak for himself. Again and again Socrates admonishes his hearers not to give their assent to a proposition unless they really agree.

The course of Socrates' conversations generally goes like this. Someone, often Socrates himself, asks a question: "What is piety?" or "Can human excellence be taught?" In response to the question, an answer is put forward, usually by someone other than Socrates. Socrates in turn proposes they "examine" whether they agree or disagree with this proposition. The examination proceeds by further questioning, which leads the person questioned to realize that the first answer is not adequate. A second answer that seems not to pose the difficulties of the first is put forward, and the pattern repeats itself. A good example is found in *Euthyphro*, to which we'll turn shortly. In the early, more authentically Socratic dialogues, we are usually left at the end with an inconsistent set of beliefs; it is clear that we cannot accept the whole set, but neither Socrates nor his partner knows which way to go. Thus the participant is brought to admit that he doesn't understand the topic at all—although he thought he did when the conversation began.

This technique of proposal-questions-difficulties-new proposal-questions is a technique that Plato calls **dialectic**. Socrates thinks of it as a way, the very best way, of improving our opinions and perhaps even coming to knowledge of the truth.* What is the connection between dialectic and truth? The connection is this: so long as people sincerely say what they believe and are open to revising this on the basis of good reasons, people can *together* identify inadequate answers to important questions. There really can be no doubt that certain answers won't do, that they are false. But if you can be sure that certain answers won't do and if you can pare away one after another of those, you

are surely circling around and in toward the truth about the matter.

Such a dialectical procedure works, however, only in certain conditions: each participant must say what that person really believes, and no one must be determined to hang on to a current belief "no matter what." In other words, the aim must be, not victory over the other speaker, but truth. Dialectic is the somewhat paradoxically cooperative enterprise in which each assists the others by raising objections to what the others say.

The cooperative nature of dialectic consists in the fact that communication is not one-way; Socrates does not deliver sermons. Anyone can ask the questions. In Plato's dialogues, it is usually Socrates who asks, but not always. Sometimes he gives his partner in the conversation the choice of either asking or answering questions. The procedure seems paradoxical because the aim is to find flaws in what the other person puts forward. No doubt this was not always well received; it was certainly one of the factors that led to hostility toward Socrates. You had to be a certain kind of person to benefit from a conversation with Socrates, as a passage from the *Gorgias* makes clear.

Here the topic is rhetoric, or the art of persuasion. At issue is whether persuasion can lead to knowledge of truth or whether it is restricted to opinion. Socrates says to Gorgias, who teaches rhetoric,

> Now, if you are the same kind of man as I am, I should be glad to question you; if not, I will let you alone. And what kind of man am I? One of those who would gladly be refuted if anything I say is not true, and would gladly refute another who says what is not true, but would be no less happy to be refuted myself than to refute, for I consider that a greater benefit, inasmuch as it is a greater boon to be delivered from the worst of evils oneself than to deliver another. And I believe there is no worse evil for man than a false opinion about the subject of our present discussion (*Gorgias* 458a).

This is a crucial passage for understanding Socrates' technique. He is in effect telling us that he will converse only with those who have a certain

---

*In the *Symposium*, Socrates attributes this method to a woman named Diotima. Although women are not prominent among the ancient philosophers whose works have been preserved, there are hints here and there that they played a larger role in the pursuit of wisdom than is superficially apparent. See Kathleen Wider, "Women Philosophers in the Ancient Greek World: Donning the Mantle," in *Hypatia*, Vol. 1, No. 1, Spring 1986.

character. Progress in coming to understand the truth is as much a matter of character as intelligence. If you care more for your reputation, for wealth, for winning, or for convincing others that *your* opinion is the right one, Socrates will leave you alone. Or, if you insist on talking with him, you are bound to leave feeling humiliated rather than enlightened; for *your* goals will not have been reached. In order to make progress, he says, you must be such a person as he himself claims to be. You must be just as happy to be shown wrong as to show someone else to be wrong. No—you must be even happier, for if you are weaned from a false opinion, you have escaped a great evil.

It is worth expanding on this point a bit. To profit from a conversation with Socrates, you must (1) be open and honest about what you really do believe; and (2) not be so wedded to any one of your beliefs that you consider an attack on it as an attack on yourself. In other words, you must have a certain objectivity with respect to your own opinions. You must be able to say, "Yes, that is indeed an opinion of mine, but I shall be glad to exchange it for another if there is good reason to do so." This outlook skirts two dangers: wishy-washiness and **dogmatism**. People with these virtues are not wishy-washy, because they really do have opinions. But neither are they dogmatic, because they are eager to improve their opinions. We might ask to what extent people must have this attitude if they are to be able to learn at all.

This attitude does, in any case, seem to characterize Socrates. At this point, the character and aims of Socrates stand as a polar opposite to those of the Sophists. There could never have been a day on which Socrates taught his students "how to make the weaker argument into the stronger." To take that as one's aim is to show that one cares not for the truth but only for victory. To teach the techniques that provide victory is to betray one's character, to show that one is looking for the same thing oneself: fame, wealth, and the satisfaction of one's desires. That is why the Sophists taught for pay and grew wealthy. That is why Socrates refused pay and remained poor. And that is why the portrait Aristophanes gives us in *The Clouds* is only a caricature—not the real Socrates.

What Socrates "Knows"

Socrates' most characteristic claim concerns his "ignorance." In his conversations, he claims not to know what human excellence, courage, or piety is. He begs to be instructed. Of course, it is usually the "instructors" who get instructed, who learn that they don't know after all. How shall we understand Socrates' claim not to know?

In part, surely, he is being ironic, especially in begging his partner in the conversation to instruct him. It is a *role* that Socrates is playing, the role of ignorant inquirer. But there is more to it than that. With respect to those large questions about the nature of human excellence, it is fairly clear that Socrates never does get an answer that fully satisfies him. He really *does not know*. Even where he might be fairly certain, moreover, he must allow that the next conversation might contain questions raising new difficulties and destroying his certainty. In this respect, too, his "ignorance" is not just a sham and show.

Nonetheless, there are things Socrates "knows." Some assertions have survived all the examination, scrutiny, and rude questions through the years. These are claims that neither Socrates nor any of his conversational partners have been able to undermine; these claims have *stood fast*. Before we examine some of the early dialogues, it will be useful to identify several of them. Let us discuss each one briefly.*

We Ought to Search for Truth

In his conversation with Meno, Socrates says,

> . . . I would contend at all costs both in word and deed as far as I could that we will be better men, braver and less idle, if we believe that one must search for things one does not know, rather than if

---

*Because in this section I make use of material from several of the middle dialogues, I cannot claim with certainty to be representing the "historical Socrates." In line with the earlier remark that each of us must to some degree construct our own Socrates, you might think of the picture painted here as "Melchert's Socrates."

we believe that it is not possible to find out what we do not know and that we must not look for it (*Meno* 86b–c).

This remark occurs in the context of an argument we will examine later* that the soul is directly acquainted with truth before it enters a human body. This argument has the practical consequence that we may hope to recover the knowledge we had before birth. Socrates says he is not certain about every detail of this argument, but of that consequence he *is* certain. Again, we can see the Sophists lurking in the background; for it is they who claim that knowledge of truth is not possible for human beings, each of us being the final "measure," or judge, of what seems so to us. Socrates is sure that this doctrine (relativism) will make us worse persons, less brave and lazier. And he is certain that to be brave and less idle is to be a better person. So one thing that "stands fast" for Socrates is that we ought to search for the truth and not despair of finding it. This is a corollary of another thing he "knows": courage and industry make for better persons than do cowardice and idleness.

Human Excellence Is Knowledge

Socrates seems to have held that human excellence consists in knowledge. No doubt this strikes us as slightly odd; it seems overintellectualized, somehow. Knowledge, we are apt to think, may be one facet of being an excellent human being, but how could it be the whole of it?

The oddness is dissipated somewhat when we note what sort of knowledge Socrates has in mind. He is constantly referring us to the craftsmen—to "blacksmiths and shoemakers and tanners," as Alcibiades said—and to such professions as horse training, doctoring, piloting a ship. In each case, what distinguishes the "expert" from a mere novice is the possession of knowledge. The physician is the one who *knows* what is good to eat and what not and what medicines cure which diseases. The pilot *knows* how to take you safely to Ionia or to Egypt. The tanner turns hides into useful leather

because he *knows* what must be done. Such knowledge is not just having abstract intellectual propositions in your head; it is knowledge of *what* to do and *how* to do it. The Greek word here is *techne*, from which our "technology" comes. This *techne* is a kind of applied knowledge. What distinguishes the competent doctor, horse trainer, blacksmith, then, is that they possess a *techne*. The amateur or novice does not.

Socrates claims that human excellence is a *techne* in exactly this same sense. What does the doctor know? He knows the human body and what makes for its health—its physical excellence. What does the horse trainer know? He knows horses—their nature and how they can be made to respond so that they will turn into excellent beasts. In a quite parallel fashion, the expert in human excellence (or virtue)—if there is one—would have to know human nature, how it functions, and wherein its excellence consists.*

Just as the shoemaker must understand both his materials (leather, nails, thread) and the *use* to which shoes are put—the point of having shoes at all—so those who wish to live well must understand themselves and what the point of living is. And just as one who has mastered the craft of shoemaking will turn out fine shoes, Socrates thinks, so one who has mastered the "craft" of living will live well. In the *Gorgias*, for instance, Socrates argues in this way:

SOCRATES: Now is not the man who has learned the art of carpentry a carpenter?

GORGIAS: Yes.

SOCRATES: And he who has learned the art of music a musician?

GORGIAS: Yes.

SOCRATES: And he who has learned medicine a physician? And so too on the same principle, the man who has learned anything becomes in each case such as his knowledge makes him?

GORGIAS: Certainly.

SOCRATES: Then according to this principle he who has learned justice is just (*Gorgias* 460b).

---

*See pp. 97–98.

*See Aristotle's development of just this point, pp. 173–175.

Notice that learning justice does not just produce an abstract understanding of what justice is; the one who learns justice becomes a just person, as the one who learns flute playing becomes a good flutist. *Without* the knowledge of justice it is not possible to be consistently just (though one might act justly by accident). *With* the knowledge of justice one will act justly. So, Socrates claims that knowledge is both necessary to this human excellence and sufficient to produce it. For that reason, he holds that human excellence *is* knowledge.

In the *Meno* we find another argument with the same conclusion. Socrates gets agreement that human excellence must be something beneficial. But if we consider the various things called "virtues," we can see that they may sometimes be beneficial and sometimes not. This is certainly true of wealth, health, and strength; whether they are an advantage depends on how they are used. Each can be used foolishly, to the possessor's detriment. But it is true even of attributes such as courage.

s: Consider whichever of these you believe not to be knowledge but different from it; do they not at times harm us, at other times benefit us? Courage, for example, when it is not wisdom but like a kind of recklessness: when a man is reckless without understanding, he is harmed, when with understanding, he is benefited. —Yes.

s: The same is true of moderation and mental quickness; when they are learned and disciplined with understanding they are beneficial, but without understanding they are harmful? —Very much so.

s: Therefore, in a word, all that the soul undertakes and endures, if directed by wisdom, ends in happiness, but if directed by ignorance, it ends in the opposite? —That is likely.

s: If then virtue is something in the soul and it must be beneficial, it must be knowledge (*Meno* 88b–c).

The conclusion that human excellence consists in knowledge faces one difficulty. If it is knowledge, then it should be teachable. Recall Socrates' conversation with Protagoras. He points out that if

a father wanted his son to be a painter, he would send him to someone who knew painting. If he wanted him to learn the flute, he would send him to someone who was an expert in flute playing. But where are the teachers of human excellence? Socrates could not allow that the Sophists were such. And he disclaims any knowledge of what such excellence consists in, so he can't teach it. But if there are no teachers, perhaps it isn't knowledge after all.

Socrates is able to resist this conclusion by a device that we'll examine soon.* For now, it is enough to note that this is one thing he does claim to "know": that human excellence is wisdom or knowledge.

All Wrongdoing Is Due to Ignorance

This thesis is a corollary to the claim that excellence is knowledge. All people, Socrates holds, always act in the belief that what they are doing is good or will produce good. No one ever intends to do what one *believes* is evil. If what we do is nonetheless evil or wicked, we do so because our beliefs are not properly informed. We believe to be good what is in fact evil. But that is to believe something false, and to believe false things is not to know the truth. And not to know the truth is to be ignorant. So whoever acts wrongly does so out of ignorance, not out of an evil will. If we knew better, we would do better.

For a comparison, let us look again to Euripides' *Hippolytus*, where Phaedra (who is, you remember, in love with her stepson) struggles with her passion.

We know the good, we apprehend it clearly.
But we can't bring it to achievement. Some
are betrayed by their own laziness, and others
value some other pleasure above virtue.[6]

Here Phaedra expresses an opinion opposed to that of Socrates: we do sometimes "know the good," she says, and yet fail to do it. One can imagine Euripides and Socrates debating this point in the marketplace. Perhaps Euripides even writes this play as he does and puts these words into

---

*See pp. 97–98.

Phaedra's mouth as part of an ongoing argument. Socrates does not agree; he believes it is not possible to apprehend the good clearly and not do it. Neither laziness nor pleasure can stand in the way. For human excellence *is* knowledge.

This view is connected intimately to Socrates' practice. He is not a preacher exhorting his fellow men to live up to what they know to be good. He is an inquirer trying to discover exactly what human excellence is. All people would, he assumes, automatically do the best they know how. If people can be brought to understand what human excellence consists in, the proper behavior will follow. For they will do the best they know.

This view has seemed mistaken to many people. Not only Euripides disagrees. Among others, so do Aristotle, St. Paul, and Augustine.*

The Most Important Thing of All Is to Care for Your Soul

There is a final cluster of things Socrates seems to "know." They all hang together and are represented in the dialogues we'll be reading. So I will just mention several of them briefly here.

Among the striking and unusual propositions that Socrates thinks have survived all the "examination" are these:

- It is worse to do harm than to suffer it;
- A good individual cannot be harmed in either life or death.

These have to do with the soul. The most important part of a human being, Socrates believes, is not the body but the soul; from the knowledge in the soul flow all those actions that reveal what a person really is. Indeed, Socrates even seems to *identify* himself with his soul. For that reason, the most

important task any person has is to care for the soul. And to that end nothing is more crucial than self-knowledge. Just as the shoemaker cannot make good shoes unless he understands his material, you cannot construct a good life unless you *know yourself*.

In the *Apology*, Socrates says that for a human being "the unexamined life is not worth living." In particular, we need to know what we *do* know and what we *do not* so that we can act wisely, and not foolishly. For foolishness is behavior based on false opinions. As you can see, this concern with the soul animates Socrates' practice; it is in pursuit of such self-knowledge that he questions his contemporaries—both for their sake and for his. One of the two mottoes at the Delphic Oracle might be the motto for Socrates' own life and practice as well: "Know Thyself."

Notes

1. W. K. C. Guthrie, *Socrates* (Cambridge: Cambridge University Press, 1971), 4.
2. Xenophon, *Symposium* V, trans. W. K. C. Guthrie, in *Socrates*, pp. 67–68.
3. Quotations from Plato's *Symposium* and *Gorgias*, in *The Collected Dialogues of Plato*, ed. E. Hamilton and H. Cairns (Princeton: Princeton University Press, 1961), are cited in the text by title and section number.
4. Xenophon, *Memorabilia*, in *Xenophon: Memorabilia and Oeconomicus*, ed. E. C. Marchant (London: William Heinemann Ltd., 1923), are cited in the text by title and book and section number.
5. Quotations from Plato's *Meno*, trans. G. M. A. Grube, in *Plato's Meno* (Indianapolis: Hackett Publishing Co., 1980), are cited in the text by title and section number.
6. Euripides, *Hippolytus*, trans. David Grene, in *Euripides* I, ed. David Grene and Richard Lattimore (Chicago: University of Chicago Press, 1965), ll. 380–84.

---

*See pp. 172, 209, and 230–235.

9

The Trial and Death
of Socrates

We are now ready to read several of the early dialogues of Plato, in which Socrates is the major figure. They must have been written reasonably soon after Socrates' death, and many people would have been witnesses of his trial and his conduct afterwards; so, scholars think they present as accurate a picture of "the historical Socrates" as we can find. We'll read *Euthyphro* and *Apology* in their entirety and selections from *Phaedo*.

The best way to proceed is to begin by giving each dialogue in turn a quick reading (they are all quite short). Don't try to understand everything the first time; just get a feel for it. Reading them aloud with a friend, each taking a part, would be ideal. After each dialogue has been read, go to the commentary and questions that follow. Reread the dialogue section by section, going back and forth between Plato's text and this one. Try to answer the questions asked as they occur; a good plan is to write out brief answers. You will be amazed at how rich these brief works are.

References to the Plato text are to page numbers from a standard Greek text, which are printed in the margins. These pages are divided into sections *a* through *e*.

Socrates Examines Euthyphro

Note: From sections 10a to 11a, there occurs a convoluted and confusing argument that most people find impossible to follow. I omit it in favor of a commentary following the dialogue, which I hope will be clearer. At this point, see pages 78–79.

Euthyphro

Euthyphro is surprised to meet Socrates near the king-archon's court, for Socrates is not the kind of man to have business with courts of justice. Socrates explains that he is under indictment by one Meletus for corrupting the young and for not believing in the gods in whom the city believes. After a brief discussion of this, Socrates inquires about Euthyphro's business at court and is told that he is prosecuting his own father for the murder of a laborer who is himself a murderer. His family and friends believe his course of action to be impious, but Euthyphro explains that in this they are mistaken and reveal their ignorance of the nature of piety. This naturally leads Socrates to ask, What is piety? and the rest of the dialogue is devoted to a search for a definition of piety, illustrating the Socratic search for universal definitions of ethical terms, to which a number of early Platonic dialogues are devoted. As usual, no definition is found that satisfies Socrates.

The Greek term hosion means, in the first instance, the knowledge of the proper ritual in prayer and sacrifice, and of course its performance (as Euthyphro himself defines it in 14b). But obviously Euthyphro uses it in the much wider sense of pious conduct generally (e.g., his own) and in that sense the word is practically equivalent to righteousness (the justice of the Republic), the transition being by way of conduct pleasing to the gods.

Besides being an excellent example of the early, so-called Socratic dialogues, Euthyphro contains several passages with important philosophical implications. These include those in which Socrates speaks of the one Form, presented by all the actions that we call pious (5d), as well as the one in which we are told that the gods love what is pious because it is pious, it is not pious because the gods love it (10d). Another passage clarifies the difference between genus and species (11e). The implications are discussed in the notes on those passages.

2   EUTHYPHRO:[1]   What's new, Socrates, to make you leave your usual haunts in the Lyceum and spend your time here by the king-archon's court? Surely you are not prosecuting anyone before the king-archon as I am?

SOCRATES: The Athenians do not call this a prosecution but an indictment, Euthyphro.

b   E: What is this you say? Someone must have indicted you, for you are not going to tell me that you have indicted someone else.

S: No indeed.

E: But someone else has indicted you?

S: Quite so.

E: Who is he?

S: I do not really know him myself, Euthyphro. He is apparently young and unknown. They call him Meletus, I believe. He belongs to the Pitthean deme, if you know anyone from that deme called Meletus, with long hair, not much of a beard, and a rather aquiline nose.

E: I don't know him, Socrates. What charge does he bring against you?

c   S: What charge? A not ignoble one I think, for it is no small thing for a young man to have knowledge of such an important subject. He says he knows how our young men are corrupted and who corrupts them. He is likely to be wise, and when he sees my ignorance corrupting his contemporaries, he proceeds to accuse me to the city as to their mother. I think he is the only one of
d   our public men to start out the right way, for it is right to care first that the young should be as good as possible, just as a good farmer is likely to take care of the young plants first, and of the

3   others later. So, too, Meletus first gets rid of us who corrupt the young shoots, as he says, and then afterwards he will obviously take care of the older ones and become a source of great blessings for the city, as seems likely to happen to one who started out this way.

E: I could wish this were true, Socrates, but I fear the opposite may happen. He seems to me to start out by harming the very heart of the city by attempting to wrong you. Tell me, what does he say you do to corrupt the young?

b   S: Strange things, to hear him tell, for he says that I am a maker of gods, and on the ground that I create new gods while not believing in the old gods, he has indicted me for their sake, as he puts it.

E: I understand, Socrates. This is because you say that the divine sign keeps coming to you.[2] So he has written this indictment against you as one who makes innovations in religious matters, and he comes to court to slander you, knowing that such things are easily misrepresented to the
c   crowd. The same is true in my case. Whenever I speak of divine matters in the assembly and foretell the future, they laugh me down as if I were crazy; and yet I have foretold nothing that did not happen. Nevertheless, they envy all of us who do this. One need not worry about them, but meet them head-on.

S: My dear Euthyphro, to be laughed at does not matter perhaps, for the Athenians do not mind anyone they think clever, as long as he does not teach his own wisdom, but if they think that he makes others to be like himself they get angry,
d   whether through envy, as you say, or for some other reason.

E: I have certainly no desire to test their feelings towards me in this matter.

S: Perhaps you seem to make yourself but rarely available, and not to be willing to teach your own wisdom, but I'm afraid that my liking for people makes them think that I pour out to anybody

---

1. We know nothing about Euthyphro except what we can gather from this dialogue. He is obviously a professional priest who considers himself an expert on ritual and on piety generally, and, it seems, is generally so considered. One Euthyphro is mentioned in Plato's *Cratylus* (396d) who is given to *enthousiasmos*, inspiration or possession, but we cannot be sure that it is the same person.

---

2. In Plato, Socrates always speaks of his divine sign or voice as intervening to prevent him from doing or saying something (e.g., *Apology* 31d), but never positively. The popular view was that it enabled him to foretell the future, and Euthyphro here represents that view. Note, however, that Socrates dissociates himself from "you prophets" (3e).

anything I have to say, not only without charging a fee but even glad to reward anyone who is willing to listen. If then they were intending to laugh at me, as you say they laugh at you, there would e be nothing unpleasant in their spending their time in court laughing and jesting, but if they are going to be serious, the outcome is not clear except to you prophets.

E: Perhaps it will come to nothing, Socrates, and you will fight your case as you think best, as I think I will mine.

S: What is your case, Euthyphro? Are you the defendant or the prosecutor?

E: The prosecutor.

S: Whom do you prosecute?

4 E: One whom I am thought crazy to prosecute.

S: Are you pursuing someone who will easily escape you?

E: Far from it, for he is quite old.

S: Who is it?

E: My father.

S: My dear sir! Your own father?

E: Certainly.

S: What is the charge? What is the case about?

E: Murder, Socrates.

S: Good heavens! Certainly, Euthyphro, most men b would not know how they could do this and be right. It is not the part of anyone to do this, but of one who is far advanced in wisdom.

E: Yes, by Zeus, Socrates, that is so.

S: Is then the man your father killed one of your relatives? Or is that obvious, for you would not prosecute your father for the murder of a stranger.

E: It is ridiculous, Socrates, for you to think that it makes any difference whether the victim is a stranger or a relative. One should only watch whether the killer acted justly or not; if he acted c justly, let him go, but if not, one should prosecute, even if the killer shares your hearth and table. The pollution is the same if you knowingly keep company with such a man and do not cleanse yourself and him by bringing him to justice. The victim was a dependent of mine, and when we were farming in Naxos he was a servant of ours. He killed one of our household slaves in drunken anger, so my father bound him hand and foot and threw him in a ditch, then sent a man here to enquire from the priest what should d be done. During that time he gave no thought or care to the bound man, as being a killer, and it was no matter if he died, which he did. Hunger and cold and his bonds caused his death before the messenger came back from the seer. Both my father and my other relatives are angry that I am prosecuting my father for murder on behalf of a murderer when he hadn't even killed him, they say, and even if he had, the dead man does not deserve a thought, since he was a killer. For, they e say, it is impious for a son to prosecute his father for murder. But their ideas of the divine attitude to piety and impiety are wrong, Socrates.

S: Whereas, by Zeus, Euthyphro, you think that your knowledge of the divine, and of piety and impiety, is so accurate that, when those things happened as you say, you have no fear of having acted impiously in bringing your father to trial?

E: I should be of no use, Socrates, and Euthyphro 5 would not be superior to the majority of men, if I did not have accurate knowledge of all such things.

S: It is indeed most important, my admirable Euthyphro, that I should become your pupil, and as regards this indictment challenge Meletus about these very things and say to him: that in the past too I considered knowledge about the divine to be most important, and that now that he says I am guilty of improvising and innovating about b the gods I have become your pupil. I would say to him: "If, Meletus, you agree that Euthyphro is wise in these matters, consider me, too, to have the right beliefs and do not bring me to trial. If you do not think so, then prosecute that teacher of mine, not me, for corrupting the older men, me and his own father, by teaching me and by exhorting and punishing him." If he is not convinced, and does not discharge me or indict you instead of me, I shall repeat the same challenge in court.

E: Yes, by Zeus, Socrates, and, if he should try to c indict me, I think I would find his weak spots and the talks in court would be about him rather than about me.

S: It is because I realize this that I am eager to become your pupil, my dear friend. I know that other people as well as this Meletus do not even seem to notice you, whereas he sees me so sharply and clearly that he indicts me for ungodliness. So tell me now, by Zeus, what you just now maintained you clearly knew: what kind of thing do you say that godliness and ungodliness are, both as regards murder and other things; or is the pious not the same and alike in every action, and the impious the opposite of all that is pious and like itself, and everything that is to be impious presents us with one form[3] or appearance in so far as it is impious?

E: Most certainly, Socrates.

S: Tell me then, what is the pious, and what the impious, do you say?

E: I say that the pious is to do what I am doing now, to prosecute the wrongdoer, be it about murder or temple robbery or anything else, whether the wrongdoer is your father or your mother or anyone else; not to prosecute is impious. And observe, Socrates, that I can quote the law as a great proof that this is so. I have already said to others that such actions are right, not to favour the ungodly, whoever they are. These people themselves believe that Zeus is the best and most just of the gods, yet they agree that he bound his father because he unjustly swallowed his sons, and that he in turn castrated his father for similar reasons. But they are angry with me because I am prosecuting my father for his wrongdoing. They contradict themselves in what they say about the gods and about me.

S: Indeed, Euthyphro, this is the reason why I am a defendant in the case, because I find it hard to accept things like that being said about the gods, and it is likely to be the reason why I shall be told I do wrong. Now, however, if you, who have full knowledge of such things, share their opinions, then we must agree with them too, it would seem. For what are we to say, we who agree that we ourselves have no knowledge of them? Tell me, by the god of friendship, do you really believe these things are true?

E: Yes, Socrates, and so are even more surprising things, of which the majority has no knowledge.

S: And do you believe that there really is war among the gods, and terrible enmities and battles, and other such things as are told by the poets, and other sacred stories such as are embroidered by good writers and by representations of which the robe of the goddess is adorned when it is carried up to the Acropolis? Are we to say these things are true, Euthyphro?

E: Not only these, Socrates, but, as I was saying just now, I will, if you wish, relate many other things about the gods which I know will amaze you.

S: I should not be surprised, but you will tell me these at leisure some other time. For now, try to tell me more clearly what I was asking just now, for, my friend, you did not teach me adequately when I asked you what the pious was, but you told me that what you are doing now, prosecuting your father for murder, is pious.

E: And I told the truth, Socrates.

S: Perhaps. You agree, however, that there are many other pious actions.

E: There are.

S: Bear in mind then that I did not bid you tell me one or two of the many pious actions but that form itself that makes all pious actions pious, for you agreed that all impious actions are impious and all pious actions pious through one form, or don't you remember?

E: I do.

S: Tell me then what this form itself is, so that I may look upon it, and using it as a model, say that any action of yours or another's that is of that kind is pious, and if it is not that it is not.

E: If that is how you want it, Socrates, that is how I will tell you.

S: That is what I want.

E: Well then, what is dear to the gods is pious, what is not is impious.

---

3. This is the kind of passage that makes it easier for us to follow the transition from Socrates' universal definitions to the Platonic theory of separately existent eternal universal Forms. The words *eidos* and *idea*, the technical terms for the Platonic Forms, commonly mean physical stature or bodily appearance. As we apply a common epithet, in this case pious, to different actions or things, these must have a common characteristic, present a common appearance or form, to justify the use of the same term, but in the early dialogues, as here, it seems to be thought of as immanent in the particulars and without separate existence. The same is true of 6d where the word "Form" is also used.

S: Splendid, Euthyphro! You have now answered in the way I wanted. Whether your answer is true I do not know yet, but you will obviously show me that what you say is true.

E: Certainly.

S: Come then, let us examine what we mean. An action or a man dear to the gods is pious, but an action or a man hated by the gods is impious. They are not the same, but quite opposite, the pious and the impious. Is that not so?

E: It is indeed.

S: And that seems to be a good statement?

b E: I think so, Socrates.

S: We have also stated that the gods are in a state of discord, that they are at odds with each other, Euthyphro, and that they are at enmity with each other. Has that, too, been said?

E: It has.

S: What are the subjects of difference that cause hatred and anger? Let us look at it this way. If you and I were to differ about numbers as to which is the greater, would this difference make us enemies and angry with each other, or would we proceed to count and soon resolve our difference

c about this?

E: We would certainly do so.

S: Again, if we differed about the larger and the smaller, we would turn to measurement and soon cease to differ.

E: That is so.

S: And about the heavier and the lighter, we would resort to weighing and be reconciled.

E: Of course.

S: What subject of difference would make us angry and hostile to each other if we were unable to come to a decision? Perhaps you do not have an

d answer ready, but examine as I tell you whether these subjects are the just and the unjust, the beautiful and the ugly, the good and the bad. Are these not the subjects of difference about which, when we are unable to come to a satisfactory decision, you and I and other men become hostile to each other whenever we do?

E: That is the difference, Socrates, about those subjects.

S: What about the gods, Euthyphro? If indeed they have differences, will it not be about these same subjects?

E: It certainly must be so.

e S: Then according to your argument, my good Euthyphro, different gods consider different things to be just, beautiful, ugly, good, and bad, for they would not be at odds with one another unless they differed about these subjects, would they?

E: You are right.

S: And they like what each of them considers beautiful, good, and just, and hate the opposites of these?

E: Certainly.

S: But you say that the same things are considered

8 just by some gods and unjust by others, and as they dispute about these things they are at odds and at war with each other. Is that not so?

E: It is.

S: The same things then are loved by the gods and hated by the gods, and would be both god-loved and god-hated.

E: It seems likely.

S: And the same things would be both pious and impious, according to this argument?

E: I'm afraid so.

S: So you did not answer my question, you surprising man. I did not ask you what same thing is both pious and impious, and it appears that what

b is loved by the gods is also hated by them. So it is in no way surprising if your present action, namely punishing your father, may be pleasing to Zeus but displeasing to Kronos and Ouranos, pleasing to Hephaestus but displeasing to Hera, and so with any other gods who differ from each other on this subject.

E: I think, Socrates, that on this subject no gods would differ from one another, that whoever has killed anyone unjustly should pay the penalty.

c S: Well now, Euthyphro, have you ever heard any man maintaining that one who has killed or done anything else unjustly should not pay the penalty?

E: They never cease to dispute on this subject, both elsewhere and in the courts, for when they have

committed many wrongs they do and say anything to avoid the penalty.

s: Do they agree they have done wrong, Euthyphro,
and in spite of so agreeing do they nevertheless
say they should not be punished?

E: No, they do not agree on that point.

s: So they do not say or do anything. For they do not
venture to say this, or dispute that they must not
pay the penalty if they have done wrong, but I
d   think they deny doing wrong. Is that not so?

E: That is true.

s: Then they do not dispute that the wrongdoer
must be punished, but they may disagree as to
who the wrongdoer is, what he did and when.

E: You are right.

s: Do not the gods have the same experience, if indeed they are at odds with each other about the
just and the unjust, as your argument maintains?
Some assert that they wrong one another, while
others deny it, but no one among gods or men
e   ventures to say that the wrongdoer must not be
punished.

E: Yes, that is true, Socrates, as to the main point.

s: And those who disagree, whether men or gods,
dispute about each action, if indeed the gods
disagree. Some say it is done justly, others unjustly. Is that not so?

E: Yes, indeed.

9   s: Come, now, my dear Euthyphro, tell me, too,
that I may become wiser, what proof you have
that all the gods consider that man to have been
killed unjustly who became a murderer while in
your service, was bound by the master of his
victim, and died in his bonds before the one
who bound him found out from the seers what
was to be done with him, and that it is right for a
son to denounce and to prosecute his father on
behalf of such a man. Come, try to show me a
b   clear sign that all the gods definitely believe this
action to be right. If you can give me adequate
proof of this, I shall never cease to extol your
wisdom.

E: This is perhaps no light task, Socrates, though I
could show you very clearly.

s: I understand that you think me more dull-wit-
ted than the jury, as you will obviously show

them that these actions were unjust and that all
the gods hate such actions.

E: I will show it to them clearly, Socrates, if only
they will listen to me.

c   s: They will listen if they think you show them
well. But this thought came to me as you were
speaking, and I am examining it, saying to myself: "If Euthyphro shows me conclusively that
all the gods consider such a death unjust, to
what greater extent have I learned from him the
nature of piety and impiety? This action would
then, it seems, be hated by the gods, but the
pious and the impious were not thereby now
defined, for what is hated by the gods has also
been shown to be loved by them." So I will not
insist on this point; let us assume, if you wish,
that all the gods consider this unjust and that
d   they all hate it. However, is this the correction
we are making in our discussion, that what all
the gods hate is impious, and what they all love
is pious, and that what some gods love and
others hate is neither or both? Is that how you
now wish us to define piety and impiety?

E: What prevents us from doing so, Socrates?

s: For my part nothing, Euthyphro, but you look
whether on your part this proposal will enable
you to teach me most easily what you promised.

e   E: I would certainly say that the pious is what all
the gods love, and the opposite, what all the
gods hate, is the impious.

s: Then let us again examine whether that is a
sound statement, or do we let it pass, and if one
of us, or someone else, merely says that something is so, do we accept that it is so? Or should
we examine what the speaker means?

E: We must examine it, but I certainly think that
this is now a fine statement.

10   s: We shall soon know better whether it is. Consider this: Is the pious loved by the gods because it is pious, or is it pious because it is loved
by the gods?

E: I don't know what you mean, Socrates.
. . . .

11   s: I'm afraid, Euthyphro, that when you were asked
what piety is, you did not wish to make its nature
clear to me, but you told me an affect or quality of
it, that the pious has the quality of being loved by

b all the gods, but you have not yet told me what the pious is. Now, if you will, do not hide things from me but tell me again from the beginning what piety is, whether loved by the gods or having some other quality—we shall not quarrel about that—but be keen to tell me what the pious and the impious are.

E: But Socrates, I have no way of telling you what I have in mind, for whatever proposition we put forward goes around and refuses to stay put where we establish it.

c S: Your statements, Euthyphro, seem to belong to my ancestor, Daedalus. If I were stating them and putting them forward, you would perhaps be making fun of me and say that because of my kinship with him my conclusions in discussion run away and will not stay where one puts them. As these propositions are yours, however, we need some other jest, for they will not stay put for you, as you say yourself.

E: I think the same jest will do for our discussion, Socrates, for I am not the one who makes them go round and not remain in the same place; it is d you who are the Daedalus; for as far as I am concerned they would remain as they were.

S: It looks as if I was cleverer than Daedalus in using my skill, my friend, in so far as he could only cause to move the things he made himself, but I can make other people's move as well as my own. And the smartest part of my skill is that I am clever without wanting to be, for I would rather have your statements to me remain unmoved e than possess the wealth of Tantalus as well as the cleverness of Daedalus. But enough of this. Since I think you are making unnecessary difficulties, I am as eager as you are to find a way to teach me about piety, and do not give up before you do. See whether you think all that is pious is of necessity just.

E: I think so.

S: And is then all that is just pious? Or is all that is 12 pious just, but not all that is just pious, but some of it is and some is not?

E: I do not follow what you are saying, Socrates.

S: Yet you are younger than I by as much as you are wiser. As I say, you are making difficulties because of your wealth of wisdom. Pull yourself together, my dear sir, what I am saying is not diffi-

cult to grasp. I am saying the opposite of what the poet said who wrote:

> You do not wish to name Zeus, who had done it, and who made all things grow, for where b there is fear there is also shame.

I disagree with the poet. Shall I tell you why?

E: Please do.

S: I do not think that "where there is fear there is also shame," for I think that many people who fear disease and poverty and many other such things feel fear, but are not ashamed of the things they fear. Do you not think so?

E: I do indeed.

S: But where there is shame there is also fear. For is there anyone who, in feeling shame and embarc rassment at anything, does not also at the same time fear and dread a reputation for wickedness?

E: He is certainly afraid.

S: It is then not right to say "where there is fear there is also shame," but that where there is shame there is also fear, for fear covers a larger area than shame. Shame is a part of fear just as odd is a part of number, with the result that it is not true that where there is number there is also oddness, but that where there is oddness there is also number. Do you follow me now?

E: Surely.

S: This is the kind of thing I was asking before, whether where there is piety there is also justice, d but where there is justice there is not always piety, for the pious is a part of justice. Shall we say that, or do you think otherwise?

E: No, but like that, for what you say appears to be right.

S: See what comes next: if the pious is a part of the just, we must, it seems, find out what part of the just it is. Now if you asked me something of what we mentioned just now, such as what part of number is the even, and what number that is, I would say it is the number that is divisible into two equal, not unequal, parts. Or do you not think so?

E: I do.

e S: Try in this way to tell me what part of the just the pious is, in order to tell Meletus not to wrong us any more and not to indict me for ungodliness, since I have learned from you sufficiently what is godly and pious and what is not.

E: I think, Socrates, that the godly and pious is the part of the just that is concerned with the care of the gods, while that concerned with the care of men is the remaining part of justice.

13 S: You seem to me to put that very well, but I still need a bit of information. I do not know yet what you mean by care, for you do not mean the care of the gods in the same sense as the care of other things, as, for example, we say, don't we, that not everyone knows how to care for horses, but the horse breeder does.

E: Yes, I do mean it that way.

S: So horse breeding is the care of horses.

E: Yes.

S: Nor does everyone know how to care for dogs, but the hunter does.

E: That is so.

S: So hunting is the care of dogs.

b E: Yes.

S: And cattle raising is the care of cattle.

E: Quite so.

S: While piety and godliness is the care of the gods, Euthyphro. Is that what you mean?

E: It is.

S: Now care in each case has the same effect; it aims at the good and the benefit of the object cared for, as you can see that horses cared for by horse breeders are benefited and become better. Or do you not think so?

E: I do.

S: So dogs are benefited by dog breeding, cattle by cattle raising, and so with all the others. Or do you think that care aims to harm the object of its care?

E: By Zeus, no.

S: It aims to benefit the object of its care?

E: Of course.

S: Is piety then, which is the care of the gods, also to benefit the gods and make them better? Would you agree that when you do something pious you make some one of the gods better?

E: By Zeus, no.

S: Nor do I think that this is what you mean—far from it—but that is why I asked you what you meant by the care of gods, because I did not believe you meant this kind of care.

E: Quite right, Socrates, that is not the kind of care I mean.

S: Very well, but what kind of care of the gods would piety be?

E: The kind of care, Socrates, that slaves take of their masters.

S: I understand. It is likely to be a kind of service of the gods.

E: Quite so.

S: Could you tell me to the achievement of what goal service to doctors tends? Is it not, do you think, to achieving health?

E: I think so.

e S: What about service to shipbuilders? To what achievement is it directed?

E: Clearly, Socrates, to the building of a ship.

S: And service to housebuilders to the building of a house?

E: Yes.

S: Tell me then, my good sir, to the achievement of what aim does service to the gods tend? You obviously know since you say that you, of all men, have the best knowledge of the divine.

E: And I am telling the truth, Socrates.

S: Tell me then, by Zeus, what is that excellent aim that the gods achieve, using us as their servants?

E: Many fine things, Socrates.

14 S: So do generals, my friend. Nevertheless you could easily tell me their main concern, which is to achieve victory in war, is it not?

E: Of course.

S: The farmers too, I think, achieve many fine things, but the main point of their efforts is to produce food from the earth.

E: Quite so.

S: Well then, how would you sum up the many fine things that the gods achieve?

b E: I told you a short while ago, Socrates, that it is a considerable task to acquire any precise knowledge of these things, but, to put it simply, I say that if a man knows how to say and do what is pleasing to the gods at prayer and sacrifice, those are pious actions such as preserve both private houses and public affairs of state. The opposite of these pleasing actions are impious and overturn and destroy everything.

c S: You could tell me in far fewer words, if you were willing, the sum of what I asked, Euthyphro, but you are not keen to teach me, that is clear. You were on the point of doing so, but you turned away. If you had given that answer, I should now have acquired from you sufficient knowledge of the nature of piety. As it is, the lover of inquiry must follow his beloved wherever it may lead him. Once more then, what do you say that piety and the pious are? Are they a knowledge of how to sacrifice and pray?

E: They are.

S: To sacrifice is to make a gift to the gods, whereas to pray is to beg from the gods?

E: Definitely, Socrates.

d S: It would follow from this statement that piety would be a knowledge of how to give to, and beg from, the gods.

E: You understood what I said very well, Socrates.

S: That is because I am so desirous of your wisdom, and I concentrate my mind on it, so that no word of yours may fall to the ground. But tell me, what is this service to the gods? You say it is to beg from them and to give to them?

E: I do.

S: And to beg correctly would be to ask from them things that we need?

E: What else?

e S: And to give correctly is to give them what they need from us, for it would not be skillful to bring gifts to anyone that are in no way needed.

E: True, Socrates.

S: Piety would then be a sort of trading skill between gods and men?

E: Trading yes, if you prefer to call it that.

S: I prefer nothing, unless it is true. But tell me, what benefit do the gods derive from the gifts they receive from us? What they give us is obvious to all. There is for us no good that we do not receive from them, but how are they benefited by what they receive from us? Or do we have such an advantage over them in the trade that we receive all our blessings from them and they receive nothing from us?

15

E: Do you suppose, Socrates, that the gods are benefited by what they receive from us?

S: What could those gifts from us to the gods be, Euthyphro?

E: What else, do you think, than honour, reverence, and what I mentioned just now, gratitude?

b S: The pious is then, Euthyphro, pleasing to the gods, but not beneficial or dear to them?

E: I think it is of all things most dear to them.

S: So the pious is once again what is dear to the gods.

E: Most certainly.

S: When you say this, will you be surprised if your arguments seem to move about instead of staying put? And will you accuse me of being Daedalus who makes them move, though you are yourself much more skillful than Daedalus and make them go round in a circle? Or do you not realize that our argument has moved around and come again to the same place? You surely remember that earlier the pious and the god-beloved were shown not to be the same but different from each other. Or do you not remember?

c

E: I do.

S: Do you then not realize now that you are saying that what is dear to the gods is the pious? Is this not the same as the god-beloved? Or is it not?

E: It certainly is.

S: Either we were wrong when we agreed before, or, if we were right then, we are wrong now.

E: That seems to be so.

S: So we must investigate again from the beginning what piety is, as I shall not willingly give up before I learn this. Do not think me unworthy, but concentrate your attention and tell the

d

truth. For you know it, if any man does, and I must not let you go, like Proteus, before you tell me. If you had no clear knowledge of piety and impiety you would never have ventured to prosecute your old father for murder on behalf of a servant. For fear of the gods you would have been afraid to take the risk lest you should not be acting rightly, and would have been ashamed before men, but now I know well that you believe you have clear knowledge of piety and im-

e   piety. So tell me, my good Euthyphro, and do not hide what you think it is.

E: Some other time, Socrates, for I am in a hurry now, and it is time for me to go.

S: What a thing to do, my friend! By going you have cast me down from a great hope I had, that I would learn from you the nature of the pious

16   and the impious and so escape Meletus' indictment by showing him that I had acquired wisdom in divine matters from Euthyphro, and my ignorance would no longer cause me to be careless and inventive about such things, and that I would be better for the rest of my life.

Now read the dialogue more slowly, section by section, using the following comments and questions as an aid.

Read 2a–5a   Note that Euthyphro is surprised to find Socrates at court. His surprise indicates that Socrates is neither the sort who brings suit against his fellow citizens nor the sort one would expect to be prosecuted.

Q1. Why does Socrates say that Meletus is likely to be wise? (2c)

Q2. What sort of character does Socrates ascribe to Meletus here? Is Socrates sincere in his praise of Meletus?

Q3. There seem to be two charges against Socrates. Can you identify them? (2c, 3b)

It is well known that Socrates claims to have a "divine sign" that comes to him from time to time. We hear of it again in the *Apology*. That the gods should speak to men in signs does not strike the ancient Greeks as a strange notion. Usually the gods speak through oracles, prophets, or seers. When Agamemnon wants to know why his troops are being wasted with plague, he calls on Kalkhas, who is described as

> wisest
> by far of all who scanned the flight of birds.
> He knew what was, what had been, what would be.[1]

When Oedipus seeks the cause for his city's distress, he calls the blind seer Tiresias. So the idea that the gods make their will known to men is a familiar one.

Euthyphro claims this ability for himself saying that he "foretells the future." He assumes (mistakenly) that Socrates too claims this ability for himself, and he concludes that it is out of envy for this talent that Meletus and the others are pressing charges. Moreover, Socrates' "sign" from the gods, Euthyphro thinks, would also explain the accusation that Socrates is introducing "new gods."

Does Socrates believe in the "old gods"? There can be little doubt that his view of the Olympians is much the same as that of Xenophanes or Heraclitus: the stories of Homer cannot be taken literally. (See *Euthyphro* 6a.) Yet he always speaks reverently of "god" or "the god" or "the gods" (these three terms being used pretty much interchangeably). And he feels free to use traditional language in speaking about the divine; so he writes that last hymn to Apollo and would probably have agreed with Heraclitus that the divine is "willing and unwilling to be called Zeus."*

Moreover, Xenophon tells us that Socrates behaves in accord with the advice given by the Priestess at Delphi when asked about sacrifice and ritual matters: "Follow the custom of the State: that is the way to act piously." Xenophon goes on to tell us:

> And again, when he prayed he asked simply for good gifts, "for the gods know best what things are good."

_____

*See p. 20.

Though his sacrifices were humble, according to his means, he thought himself not a whit inferior to those who made frequent and magnificent sacrifices out of great possessions. . . . No, the greater the piety of the giver, the greater (he thought) was the delight of the gods in the gift.[2]

There seems every reason to suppose that Socrates is pious in the conventional sense. Still, he would not have held back his beliefs if asked directly about the gods; as he says in 3d, his "liking for people" makes it seem as though he pours out to anybody anything he has to say. And traditionalists might well take exception to some of that.

What of the "sign"? Was that an introduction of new gods? There is no reason to believe that Socrates ever thought of it as such. It seems to be analogous to what we would call the voice of conscience, though clearly it was much more vivid to him than to most of us. It never, he tells us, advises him positively to do something; it only prevents him. And it is clearly not anything like Euthyphro's future-telling. (Note that in 3e he separates himself from "you prophets.") But he clearly thinks of the sign as the voice of the divine, however that is best conceived.

Q4. Why is Euthyphro in court?
Q5. What does Euthyphro claim to know?

Read 5a–6e We now know what the topic of this conversation is to be. Socrates says he is "eager" to be Euthyphro's pupil.

Q6. Why does Socrates say he wants Euthyphro to instruct him? Do you think he really expects to be helped?
Q7. Do you think this is going to be a serious inquiry? Or is Socrates just having some sport with Euthyphro?

Notice in 5d the three requirements that must be met to satisfy Socrates. He wants to know what the "pious" or the "holy" or the "godly" is (all these words may translate the Greek term).

1. A satisfactory answer will pick out some feature that is the same in every pious action.
2. This feature will not be shared by any impious action.
3. It will be that feature (or the lack of it) that *makes* an action pious (or impious).

What Socrates is searching for, we can say, is a *definition* of piety or holiness. He wants to know *what it is* so that it can be recognized when it appears. It is like wanting to know what a crow is: we want to know what features all crows have that are not shared by eagles and hedgehogs and the possession of which ensure that this thing we see before us is indeed a crow.*

Would a knowledge of what piety is be useful if one were on the brink of being brought to trial for impiety? A Sophist might not think so at all. At that point, the typical Sophist would construct a dazzling rhetorical display that would emotionally engage the jury on his side. But Socrates, as is typical, wants to know the truth. He wants to know the truth even more than he wants to be acquitted. We can think of this as one aspect of his persistent search to know himself. Who is he? *Has* he been guilty of impiety? Only an understanding of what piety truly is will tell.

Q8. What does Euthyphro say piety is?
Q9. What does Socrates focus on as the likely reason he is on trial?
Q10. What is Socrates' objection to the definition Euthyphro has proposed?

Note particularly the term "form" in 6d–e. It clearly does not mean "shape," except perhaps in a most abstract sense. The form of something is made up of whatever it is that makes it the kind of thing it is. The form may sometimes be shape, as the "form" of a square is to be an area bounded by equal straight lines and right angles, but it need not

---

*There are a number of different kinds of definition. For a critique of Socrates' kind, see Wittgenstein's notion of "family resemblances" in Chapter 26.

be. When we ask in this sense for the "form" of an elephant, we are asking for more than an outline drawing. What we want is what the biologist can give us; we are asking what an elephant *is*. Notice that the biologist can do this not only for elephants but also for mammals—and no one can draw the geometrical shape of a mammal. (True, you can draw a picture of *this* mammal or *that* mammal, but not a picture of a mammal *as such*. Yet it can be given a definition.) In the same way, it is perfectly in order to ask for the "form" of abstract qualities like justice, courage, or piety.

Read 7a–9b   Here we have Euthyphro's second attempt at answering Socrates' question.

Q11. What is Euthyphro's second answer?
Q12. Why does Socrates exclaim, "Splendid!"?
Q13. What is the difference between answering "in the way" he wanted and giving a "true" answer?

Note the characteristic Socratic admonition in 7a: "Let us examine what we mean." How does this examination proceed? He reminds Euthyphro of something he admitted earlier—that there is "war among the gods" (6b). And the question is whether that admission is *consistent* with the definition Euthyphro now proposes; do the two fit harmoniously together, or do they clash?

Q14. How does Socrates derive the conclusion (8a) that "the same things then are loved by the gods and hated by the gods"? Is this a correct derivation from the statements Euthyphro previously agreed to?
Q15. What further conclusion follows? Why is that disturbing?

In 8b, Socrates drives the disturbing consequence home by applying it to Euthyphro's own case. Socrates is never one to leave things up in the air, unconnected to practical life. If this is a good understanding of piety, then it ought to illumine the matter at hand. But of course, Euthyphro cannot admit that his own prosecution is loved by some of the gods and hated by others—that it is

both pious and impious. He protests that *none* of the gods would disagree that "whoever has killed anyone unjustly should pay the penalty."

Now, this is *sneaky*. Can you see why? It is a move that might slide past a lesser antagonist. But Socrates picks it up immediately.

Q16. What do people dispute about concerning wrongs and penalties? And what not?

So Socrates drives Euthyphro back to the issue: in light of the admission that the gods quarrel, what reason is there to think that prosecuting his father is an instance of what the gods love and thus an example of piety?

Q17. Do you agree that Socrates has put Euthyphro in an untenable position here?

Read 9c–11d   Socrates takes the lead here and proposes a modification to the earlier definition. Euthyphro embraces the suggestion with enthusiasm in 9e. Be sure you are clear about the new definition.

Again we get the characteristic invitation to "examine" this new attempt. In 9e, Socrates backs it up with this question: "Or do we let it pass, and if one of us, or someone else, merely says that something is so, do we accept that it is so?" He is asking whether there are any *reasons* why this should not be accepted. The mere fact that someone—anyone—says that it is so does not make it so. Do you agree with Socrates here?

In 10a, we get an important question, one that reverberates through later Christian theology and has a bearing on whether there can be an **ethics** independent of what God or the gods approve. Is a secular ethics possible? Suppose we agree that in normal circumstances it is wrong to lie (allowing that a lie may be justified in unusual situations). And suppose, for the sake of the argument, we also agree that God or the gods hate lying (in those normal circumstances). What is it, we still might ask, that *makes* lying wrong? Is it the fact that it is hated by the divine power(s)? Or is there something about lying itself that makes it wrong—and *that* is why the divine hates it? To ask these questions is a way of asking for the "form" of wrongness. (You should look again at the three requirements for a satisfactory definition in 5d and on page 77; it is the *third* requirement that is at issue.)

Socrates is asking an exactly parallel question here. Suppose we agree, he says, that what all the gods love is pious and what they all hate is impious; the question remains whether it is this love and hate that *explains* or *accounts for* the piety of the pious. Suppose it is. Then some behavior is pious or holy *simply because* that behavior pleases the gods. It follows that if the gods loved lying, stealing, or adultery, it would make it right to lie, steal, or sleep with your neighbor's wife. The alternative is that there is something about these actions which make them wrong—and that is why the gods hate them.

It is worthwhile to add a word about the consequences of this distinction for the possibility of a secular ethics. Suppose there is something about lying that makes it wrong, and that is why the gods hate it. If we could identify what that is, we would have a reason not to lie whether we believed in the gods or not. If, on the only hand, the *only* reason lying is wrong is that the gods hate it, then if one does not believe in the gods, one would have no reason to refrain from lying; ethics would be intrinsically tied to religion. An atheist might in the latter case, but not in the former, think that if God does not exist, then everything is permitted. So in the former case, but not in the latter it seems, a secular ethics is possible. The question Socrates raises is a basic and important one.

Assuming that the alternatives are clear, which one should we prefer? There is no doubt about Socrates' answer: the pious is *not* pious because the gods love it; rather, the gods love what is pious because of what it *is*. In the omitted section, Socrates piles up analogies to explain this. Let us take just one of them. There is a difference, surely, between your carrying a plate and the plate's being carried by you, even though they always occur together. The difference can be brought out in this way: the plate is carried by you *because* you are carrying the plate, and not vice versa. You don't

carry the plate *because* it is being carried. So there is a relation of dependence between them; the passive "being carried" depends on an active "carrying." Think of it this way. Suppose someone asks why anyone should think that this plate is being carried; a natural answer would be "Because I am carrying it." On the other hand, suppose someone asks why you are carrying this plate; it would be a *joke* to reply, "Because it is being carried by me."

There is a similar difference, Socrates says, between loving and being loved. These, too, are not the same. And a similar relation of dependence holds: *X*'s being loved depends on someone loving *X*, but not vice versa. If we ask *why* the gods love the pious, we cannot answer, "Because it is being loved by them." To give that answer would be just as farcical as to claim that I am carrying this plate because it is being carried by me. But if the gods don't love the pious because it is loved by them, there must be something about the pious *itself* that accounts for their love of it.

That is why Socrates complains in 11a that Euthyphro has not answered his question. He says that Euthyphro has told him only "an affect or quality" of the pious—i.e., that it is loved by the gods. But, he claims, Euthyphro has not yet made its "nature" clear. What he wants to know is what the pious *is*, what its "form" is. To be told only that the pious is what all the gods love is to learn only about *how it is regarded by them*. Euthyphro has spoken only of something quite external; he has not revealed a single thing about what it really is!

You might think of it this way. For all that Euthyphro's definition tells us, piety could be *this*, or *that*, or some altogether *different* thing. If we want to know what to do in order to be pious and what to avoid so as not to be impious, it doesn't help to be told simply to "do what all the gods love." We need to know what that *is*.

Q18. Is this a good argument? Suppose, in response to the question, "*Why* do the gods love the pious?" one were to reply: "They just *do*!" Is Socrates *assuming* that there must be a reason? Is he assuming what he needs to prove? Think about this.

Socrates probably calls Daedalus (in 11c) his "ancestor" because Daedalus was the mythical "patron saint" of stonemasons and sculptors. He was reputed to be such a cunning craftsman that his sculptures took life and ran away.

Q19. Why is Socrates reminded of Daedalus here?

Read 11e–end   Again Socrates makes a suggestion, this time that piety and *justice* are related somehow. It seems a promising line to investigate, but some clarifications are needed. Are they identical? Or is one a part of the other? And if the latter, which is part of which?

Q20. Which answer do they settle on? Why?
Q21. In what way are the fear/shame and odd/number distinctions analogous?
Q22. What are the two kinds of "care" that are distinguished? (13a–c and 13d–e)
Q23. Which one is the relevant one? Why?

In 14c we reach a crucial turning point in the dialogue. Note that Socrates here says they were on the verge of solving the problem, but Euthyphro "turned away." If only he had answered a certain question, Socrates says, he "should now have acquired . . . sufficient knowledge of the nature of piety." But Euthyphro didn't answer it.

Apparently Socrates feels that they were on the right track. Let us review. Piety is part of justice. It is that part which consists in care of the gods. The kind of care at issue is the kind that slaves offer their masters. Such service on the part of slaves is always directed to some fine end (health, ships, houses). The question arises: to what fine end is service to the gods devoted? To put it another way, what is the *point* of piety? What is it *for*? What is "that excellent aim that the gods achieve, using us as their servants?" Remember that for Socrates the good is always something *useful* or *advantageous*. He is here asking—on the tacit assumption that piety is something good—what the advantage is that piety produces. We can identify the good things produced by service to doctors. What good things are produced by service to the gods? If one

could answer this question, the nature of piety might finally be clarified. It would be service to the gods for the sake of X. All we need to know is what X is.

Unfortunately, all Euthyphro can say with regard to X is that it is "many fine things." When pressed harder, he in effect changes the subject, although he probably doesn't realize he is doing so. He says in 14b that "to put it simply," piety is knowing "how to say and do what is pleasing to the gods at prayer and sacrifice." This certainly does not answer the question of what aim the gods achieve through our service!

Let us, however, briefly consider Euthyphro's statement. First, it *does* go some way toward answering our earlier question of what we should do to be pious. Euthyphro's answer is in fact the traditional answer common to most religions: pray and offer sacrifice. That answer would have been the standard one in Athens, and it is a little surprising that it comes out so late in the dialogue. It corresponds to the advice of the Delphic Oracle to "follow the custom of the state."

Second, Euthyphro's statement mentions some advantages to being pious in this way: preserving "both private houses and public affairs of state." But this is puzzling. Why does Socrates not accept this as an answer to the question about the nature of X, for the sake of which we ought to be pious in just this way?

No answer is given in the dialogue; perhaps it must just remain puzzling. But here is a suggestion. Socrates, at the end of the Peloponnesian War, may simply be unable to believe this is true. No doubt Athens had offered many prayers and had made all the required sacrifices during the war. Athens had prayed for victory, just as Sparta must have prayed for victory. Yet Athens not only lost, she did irreparable damage to herself; such piety, it seemed, did *not* preserve private houses and public affairs. If the promised advantages do not materialize, then, Socrates would conclude, *this* kind of piety is not after all a good thing. Perhaps the exasperation evident in 14c expresses Socrates' view that it is by this time in history all too clear piety can't be *that*. It can't be a kind of "trading skill" between gods and men. And on the assumption that piety *is* a good thing, it must be something quite different from Euthyphro's version of it. So the nature of *X* remains unclarified.

Well, this is rather speculative but not, I think, implausible. As we'll see, Jesus and the Christians have an answer about the nature of *X*. We find it clearly, for instance, in St. Augustine.* It is an answer that Socrates is close to but does not quite grasp. It demands that we rethink the nature of God and the relations of man to God altogether. But that is a story for later.

Socrates, regretfully, feels it is necessary to follow his "teacher," and once more takes up his questioning in 14c. There is a fairly simple argument running through these exchanges, but it is not easy to pick it out. Let me try to identify the steps; check the text to see that I am getting it right.

1. Piety is prayer and sacrifice. (This is Euthyphro's latest definition, now up for examination.)
2. Prayer and sacrifice are begging from the gods and giving to the gods.
3. The giving must, to be "skillful," be giving what they need.
4. Giving what they need is benefiting them.
5. But we cannot benefit the gods.
6. If our giving does not benefit the gods, the only alternative is that this giving "pleases" them.
7. But that is just to say that they like it, it is dear to them—it is what they love.
8. And that returns us to the earlier definition: that piety is what all the gods love.

The crux of the argument is, no doubt, premise 5. It is expressed by Euthyphro in a surprised question in 15a and accepted by Socrates. Why can't we benefit the gods? No reasons are given here, but they are not hard to find. The gods, recall, were the immortals; as such they were also the happy ones. To think of them as having needs that mere mortals could supply would have seemed to many Greeks—especially to those who had the "high" view of "the

god" characteristic of Xenophanes, Heraclitus, and Socrates—as impious in the extreme. We receive all our benefits from them. To think that we could benefit them would be arrogance and *hubris* of the first rank.

Q24. Do you agree with this view? What do you think of this argument? Has the discussion really come full circle?

Q25. What characteristic of Socrates do you think Plato means to impress upon us in Socrates' next to last speech?

Q26. Has Euthyphro learned anything in the course of this discussion?

Q27. Have you? If so, what?

Socrates Defends Himself

As with the *Euthyphro*, you should first skim the text quickly, then come back to it a second time, using the commentary and questions as guides. Remember: Write out answers to the questions.

Apology

The Apology[1] professes to be a record of the actual speech that Socrates delivered in his own defence at the trial. This makes the question of its historicity more acute than in the dialogues in which the conversations themselves are mostly fictional and the question of historicity is concerned only with how far the theories that Socrates is represented as expressing were those of the historical Socrates. Here, however, we are dealing with a speech that Socrates made as a matter of history. How far is Plato's account accurate? We should always remember that the ancients did not expect historical accuracy in the way we do. On the other hand, Plato makes it clear that he was present at the trial (34a, 38b). Moreover, if, as is generally believed, the Apology was written not long after the event, many Athenians would remember the actual speech, and it would be a poor way to

---

*See pp. 237–238.

1. The word *apology* is a transliteration, not a translation, of the Greek *apologia* which means defence. There is certainly nothing apologetic about the speech.

vindicate the Master, which is the obvious intent, to put a completely different speech into his mouth. Some liberties could no doubt be allowed, but the main arguments and the general tone of the defence must surely be faithful to the original. The beauty of language and style is certainly Plato's, but the serene spiritual and moral beauty of character belongs to Socrates. It is a powerful combination.

Athenian juries were very large, in this case 501, and they combined the duties of jury and judge as we know them by both convicting and sentencing. Obviously, it would have been virtually impossible for so large a body to discuss various penalties and decide on one. The problem was resolved rather neatly, however, by having the prosecutor, after conviction, assess the penalty he thought appropriate, followed by a counter-assessment by the defendant. The jury would then decide between the two. This procedure generally made for moderation on both sides.

Thus the Apology is in three parts. The first and major part is the main speech (17a–35a), followed by the counter-assessment (35a–38c), and finally, last words to the jury (38c–42a), both to those who voted for the death sentence and those who voted for acquittal.

17   I do not know, men of Athens, how my accusers affected you; as for me, I was almost carried away in spite of myself, so persuasively did they speak. And yet, hardly anything of what they said is true. Of the many lies they told, one in particular surprised me, namely that you should be careful not to be deceived by an accomplished speaker like me.

b   That they were not ashamed to be immediately proved wrong by the facts, when I show myself not to be an accomplished speaker at all, that I thought was most shameless on their part—unless indeed they call an accomplished speaker the man who speaks the truth. If they mean that, I would agree that I am an orator, but not after their manner, for indeed, as I say, practically nothing they said was

c   true. From me you will hear the whole truth, though not, by Zeus, gentlemen, expressed in embroidered and stylized phrases like theirs, but things spoken at random and expressed in the first words that come to mind, for I put my trust in the justice of what I say, and let none of you expect anything else. It would not be fitting at my age, as it might be for a young man, to toy with words when I appear before you.

One thing I do ask and beg of you gentlemen: if you hear me making my defence in the same kind of language as I am accustomed to use in the market place by the bankers' tables,[2] where many of you have heard me, and elsewhere, do not be surprised or create a disturbance on that account. The

d   position is this: this is my first appearance in a law-court, at the age of seventy; I am therefore simply a stranger to the manner of speaking here. Just as if I were really a stranger, you would certainly excuse me if I spoke in that dialect and manner in which I

18   had been brought up, so too my present request seems a just one, for you to pay no attention to my manner of speech—be it better or worse—but to concentrate your attention on whether what I say is just or not, for the excellence of a judge lies in this, as that of a speaker lies in telling the truth.

It is right for me, gentlemen, to defend myself first against the first lying accusations made against me and my first accusers, and then against the later accusations and the later accusers. There have been

b   many who have accused me to you for many years now, and none of their accusations are true. These I fear much more than I fear Anytus and his friends, though they too are formidable. These earlier ones, however, are more so, gentlemen; they got hold of most of you from childhood, persuaded you and accused me quite falsely, saying that there is a man called Socrates, a wise man, a student of all things in the sky and below the earth, who makes the

c   worse argument the stronger. Those who spread that rumour, gentlemen, are my dangerous accusers, for their hearers believe that those who study these things do not even believe in the gods. Moreover, these accusers are numerous, and have been at it a long time; also, they spoke to you at an age when you would most readily believe them, some of you being children and adolescents, and they won their case by default, as there was no defence.

What is most absurd in all this is that one can-

d   not even know or mention their names unless one of them is a writer of comedies.[3] Those who maliciously and slanderously persuaded you—who

---

2. The bankers or money-changers had their counters in the market place. It seems that this was a favourite place for gossip.

3. This refers in particular to Aristophanes, whose comedy, *The Clouds*, produced in 423 B.C., ridiculed the (imaginary) school of Socrates.

also, when persuaded themselves then persuaded others—all those are most difficult to deal with: one cannot bring one of them into court or refute him; one must simply fight with shadows, as it were, in making one's defence, and cross-examine when no one answers. I want you to realize too that my accusers are of two kinds: those who have accused me recently, and the old ones I mention; and to think that I must first defend myself against the latter, for you have also heard their accusations

e first, and to a much greater extent than the more recent.

Very well then. I must surely defend myself and

19 attempt to uproot from your minds in so short a time the slander that has resided there so long. I wish this may happen, if it is in any way better for you and me, and that my defence may be successful, but I think this is very difficult and I am fully aware of how difficult it is. Even so, let the matter proceed as the god may wish, but I must obey the law and make my defence.

Let us then take up the case from its beginning.

b What is the accusation from which arose the slander in which Meletus trusted when he wrote out the charge against me? What did they say when they slandered me? I must, as if they were my actual prosecutors, read the affidavit they would have sworn. It goes something like this: Socrates is guilty of wrongdoing in that he busies himself studying things in the sky and below the earth; he makes the worse into the stronger argument, and he teaches these same things to others. You have

c seen this yourselves in the comedy of Aristophanes, a Socrates swinging about there, saying he was walking on air and talking a lot of other nonsense about things of which I know nothing at all. I do not speak in contempt of such knowledge, if someone is wise in these things—lest Meletus bring more cases against me—but, gentlemen, I have no part in it, and on this point I call upon the majority of you as witnesses. I think it right that all those of you who have heard me conversing, and

d many of you have, should tell each other if anyone of you have ever heard me discussing such subjects to any extent at all. From this you will learn that the other things said about me by the majority are of the same kind.

Not one of them is true. And if you have heard from anyone that I undertake to teach people and

e charge a fee for it, that is not true either. Yet I think it a fine thing to be able to teach people as Gorgias of Leontini does, and Prodicus of Ceos, and Hippias of Elis.[4] Each of these men can go to any city and persuade the young, who can keep company without anyone of their own fellow-citizens they

20 want without paying, to leave the company of these, to join with themselves, pay them a fee, and be grateful to them besides. Indeed, I learned that there is another wise man from Paros who is visiting us, for I met a man who has spent more money on Sophists than everybody else put together, Callias, the son of Hipponicus. So I asked him—he has two sons—"Callias," I said, "if your sons were colts or calves, we could find and engage a supervisor for them who would make them excel in their

b proper qualities, some horse breeder or farmer. Now since they are men, whom do you have in mind to supervise them? Who is an expert in this kind of excellence, the human and social kind? I think you must have given thought to this since you have sons. Is there such a person," I asked, "or is there not?" "Certainly there is," he said. "Who is he?" I asked, "What is his name, where is he from? and what is his fee?" "His name, Socrates, is Evenus, he comes from Paros, and his fee is five

c minas." I thought Evenus a happy man, if he really possesses this art, and teaches for so moderate a fee. Certainly I would pride and preen myself if I had this knowledge, but I do not have it, gentlemen.

One of you might perhaps interrupt me and say: "But Socrates, what is your occupation? From where have these slanders come? For surely if you did not busy yourself with something out of the common, all these rumours and talk would not have arisen unless you did something other than most people. Tell us what it is, that we may not

d speak inadvisedly about you." Anyone who says that seems to be right, and I will try to show you what has caused this reputation and slander. Listen then. Perhaps some of you will think I am jesting,

---

4. These were all well-known Sophists. Gorgias, after whom Plato named one of his dialogues, was a celebrated rhetorician and teacher of rhetoric. He came to Athens in 427 B.C., and his rhetorical tricks took the city by storm. Two dialogues, the authenticity of which has been doubted, are named after Hippias, whose knowledge was encyclopedic. Prodicus was known for his insistence on the precise meaning of words. Both he and Hippias are characters in the *Protagoras* (named after another famous Sophist).

but be sure that all that I shall say is true. What has caused my reputation is none other than a certain kind of wisdom. What kind of wisdom? Human wisdom, perhaps. It may be that I really possess this, while those whom I mentioned just now are

e wise with a wisdom more than human; else I cannot explain it, for I certainly do not possess it, and whoever says I do is lying and speaks to slander me. Do not create a disturbance, gentlemen, even if you think I am boasting, for the story I shall tell does not originate with me, but I will refer you to a trustworthy source. I shall call upon the god at Delphi as witness to the existence and nature of my

21 wisdom, if it be such. You know Chairephon. He was my friend from youth, and the friend of most of you, as he shared your exile and your return. You surely know the kind of man he was, how impulsive in any course of action. He went to Delphi at one time and ventured to ask the oracle—as I say, gentlemen, do not create a disturbance—he asked if any man was wiser than I, and the Pythian replied that no one was wiser. Chairephon is dead, but his brother will testify to you about this.

b Consider that I tell you this because I would inform you about the origin of the slander. When I heard of this reply I asked myself: "Whatever does the god mean? What is his riddle? I am very conscious that I am not wise at all; what then does he mean by saying that I am the wisest? For surely he does not lie; it is not legitimate for him to do so." For a long time I was at a loss as to his meaning; then I very reluctantly turned to some such investigation as this: I went to one of those reputed wise,

c thinking that there, if anywhere, I could refute the oracle and say to it: "This man is wiser than I, but you said I was." Then, when I examined this man—there is no need for me to tell you his name, he was one of our public men—my experience was something like this: I thought that he appeared wise to many people and especially to himself, but he was not. I then tried to show him that he thought himself wise, but that he was not. As a result he came to

d dislike me, and so did many of the bystanders. So I withdrew and thought to myself: "I am wiser than this man; it is likely that neither of us knows anything worthwhile, but he thinks he knows something when he does not, whereas when I do not know, neither do I think I know; so I am likely to be wiser than he to this small extent, that I do not think I know what I do not know." After this I ap-

e proached another man, one of those thought to be wiser than he, and I thought the same thing, and so I came to be disliked both by him and by many others.

After that I proceeded systematically. I realized, to my sorrow and alarm, that I was getting unpopular, but I thought that I must attach the greatest importance to the god's oracle, so I must go to all those who had any reputation for knowledge to examine its meaning. And by the dog,[5] gentlemen of

22 the jury—for I must tell you the truth—I experienced something like this: in my investigation in the service of the god I found that those who had the highest reputation were nearly the most deficient, while those who were thought to be inferior were more knowledgeable. I must give you an account of my journeyings as if they were labours I had undertaken to prove the oracle irrefutable. After the politicians, I went to the poets, the writers of

b tragedies and dithyrambs and the others, intending in their case to catch myself being more ignorant than they. So I took up those poems with which they seemed to have taken most trouble and asked them what they meant, in order that I might at the same time learn something from them. I am ashamed to tell you the truth, gentlemen, but I must. Almost all the bystanders might have explained the poems better than their authors could.

c I soon realized that poets do not compose their poems with knowledge, but by some inborn talent and by inspiration, like seers and prophets who also say many fine things without any understanding of what they say. The poets seemed to me to have had a similar experience. At the same time I saw that, because of their poetry, they thought themselves very wise men in other respects, which they were not. So there again I withdrew, thinking that I had the same advantage over them as I had over the politicians.

d Finally I went to the craftsmen, for I was conscious of knowing practically nothing, and I knew that I would find that they had knowledge of many fine things. In this I was not mistaken; they knew things I did not know, and to that extent they were wiser than I. But, gentlemen of the jury, the good craftsmen seemed to me to have the same fault as

---

5. A curious oath, occasionally used by Socrates, it appears in a longer form in the *Gorgias* (482b) as "by the dog, the god of the Egyptians."

the poets: each of them, because of his success at his craft, thought himself very wise in other most important pursuits, and this error of theirs over-

e shadowed the wisdom they had, so that I asked myself, on behalf of the oracle, whether I should prefer to be as I am, with neither their wisdom nor their ignorance, or to have both. The answer I gave myself and the oracle was that it was to my advantage to be as I am.

As a result of this investigation, gentlemen of

23 the jury, I acquired much unpopularity, of a kind that is hard to deal with and is a heavy burden; many slanders came from these people and a reputation for wisdom, for in each case the bystanders thought that I myself possessed the wisdom that I proved that my interlocutor did not have. What is probable, gentlemen, is that in fact the god is wise and that his oracular response meant that human wisdom is worth little or nothing, and that when

b he says this man, Socrates, he is using my name as an example, as if he said: "This man among you, mortals, is wisest who, like Socrates, understands that his wisdom is worthless." So even now I continue this investigation as the god bade me—and I go around seeking out anyone, citizen or stranger, whom I think wise. Then if I do not think he is, I come to the assistance of the god and show him that he is not wise. Because of this occupation, I do not have the leisure to engage in public affairs to any extent, nor indeed to look after my own, but I live in great poverty because of my service to the god.

c Furthermore, the young men who follow me around of their own free will, those who have most leisure, the sons of the very rich, take pleasure in hearing people questioned; they themselves often imitate me and try to question others. I think they find an abundance of men who believe they have some knowledge but know little or nothing. The result is that those whom they question are angry,

d not with themselves but with me. They say: "That man Socrates is a pestilential fellow who corrupts the young." If one asks them what he does and what he teaches to corrupt them, they are silent, as they do not know, but, so as not to appear at a loss, they mention those accusations that are available against all philosophers, about "things in the sky and things below the earth," about "not believing in the gods" and "making the worse the stronger argument;" they would not want to tell the truth, I'm sure, that they have been proved to lay claim to

knowledge when they know nothing. These people are ambitious, violent and numerous; they are con-

e tinually and convincingly talking about me; they have been filling your ears for a long time with vehement slanders against me. From them Meletus attacked me, and Anytus and Lycon, Meletus being vexed on behalf of the poets, Anytus on behalf of the craftsmen and the politicians, Lycon on behalf of the orators, so that, as I started out by saying, I

24 should be surprised if I could rid you of so much slander in so short a time. That, gentlemen of the jury, is the truth for you. I have hidden or disguised nothing. I know well enough that this very conduct makes me unpopular, and this is proof that what I say is true, that such is the slander against me, and

b that such are its causes. If you look into this either now or later, this is what you will find.

Let this suffice as a defence against the charges of my earlier accusers. After this I shall try to defend myself against Meletus, that good and patriotic man, as he says he is, and my later accusers. As these are a different lot of accusers, let us again take up their sworn deposition. It goes something like this: Socrates is guilty of corrupting the young and of not believing in the gods in whom the city believes, but in other new divinities. Such is their

c charge. Let us examine it point by point.

He says that I am guilty of corrupting the young, but I say that Meletus is guilty of dealing frivolously with serious matters, of irresponsibly bringing people into court, and of professing to be seriously concerned with things about none of which he has ever cared, and I shall try to prove that this is so. Come here and tell me, Meletus. Surely

d you consider it of the greatest importance that our young men be as good as possible?[6] —Indeed I do.

Come then, tell the jury who improves them. You obviously know, in view of your concern. You say you have discovered the one who corrupts them, namely me, and you bring me here and accuse me to the jury. Come, inform the jury and tell them who it is. You see, Meletus, that you are silent and know not what to say. Does this not seem

---

6. Socrates here drops into his usual method of discussion by question and answer. This, no doubt, is what Plato had in mind, at least in part, when he made him ask the indulgence of the jury if he spoke "in his usual manner."

shameful to you and a sufficient proof of what I say, that you have not been concerned with any of this? Tell me, my good sir, who improves our young

e   men?   —The laws.

That is not what I am asking, but what person who has knowledge of the laws to begin with? —These jurymen, Socrates.

How do you mean, Meletus? Are these able to educate the young and improve them?   —Certainly.

All of them, or some but not others?   —All of them.

Very good, by Hera. You mention a great abun-
25   dance of benefactors. But what about the audience? Do they improve the young or not?   —They do, too.

What about the members of Council?   —The Councillors, also.

But, Meletus, what about the assembly? Do members of the assembly corrupt the young, or do they all improve them?   —They improve them.

All the Athenians, it seems, make the young into fine good men, except me, and I alone corrupt them. Is that what you mean?   —That is most definitely what I mean.

b   You condemn me to a great misfortune. Tell me: does this also apply to horses do you think? That all men improve them and one individual corrupts them? Or is quite the contrary true, one individual is able to improve them, or very few, namely the horse breeders, whereas the majority, if they have horses and use them, corrupt them? Is that not the case, Meletus, both with horses and all other animals? Of course it is, whether you and Anytus say so or not. It would be a very happy state of affairs if only one person corrupted our youth, while the others improved them.

c   You have made it sufficiently obvious, Meletus, that you have never had any concern for our youth; you show your indifference clearly; that you have given no thought to the subjects about which you bring me to trial.

And by Zeus, Meletus, tell us also whether it is better for a man to live among good or wicked fellow-citizens. Answer, my good man, for I am not asking a difficult question. Do not the wicked do some harm to those who are ever closest to them, whereas good people benefit them?   —Certainly.

d   And does the man exist who would rather be harmed than benefited by his associates? Answer, my good sir, for the law orders you to answer. Is

there any man who wants to be harmed?   —Of course not.

Come now, do you accuse me here of corrupting the young and making them worse deliberately or unwillingly?   —Deliberately.

What follows, Meletus? Are you so much wiser at your age than I am at mine that you understand that wicked people always do some harm to their
e   closest neighbours while good people do them good, but I have reached such a pitch of ignorance that I do not realize this, namely that if I make one of my associates wicked I run the risk of being harmed by him so that I do such a great evil deliberately, as you say? I do not believe you, Meletus, and I do not think anyone else will. Either I do not
26   corrupt the young or, if I do, it is unwillingly, and you are lying in either case. Now if I corrupt them unwillingly, the law does not require you to bring people to court for such unwilling wrongdoings, but to get hold of them privately, to instruct them and exhort them; for clearly, if I learn better, I shall cease to do what I am doing unwillingly. You, however, have avoided my company and were unwilling to instruct me, but you bring me here, where the law requires one to bring those who are in need of punishment, not of instruction.

And so, gentlemen of the jury, what I said is clearly true: Meletus has never been at all con-
b   cerned with these matters. Nonetheless tell us, Meletus, how you say that I corrupt the young; or is it obvious from your deposition that it is by teaching them not to believe in the gods in whom the city believes but in other new divinities? Is this not what you say I teach and so corrupt them?   —That is most certainly what I do say.

Then by those very gods about whom we are talking, Meletus, make this clearer to me and to the
c   jury: I cannot be sure whether you mean that I teach the belief that there are some gods—and therefore I myself believe that there are gods and am not altogether an atheist, nor am I guilty of that—not, however, the gods in whom the city believes, but others, and that this is the charge against me, that they are others. Or whether you mean that I do not believe in gods at all, and that this is what I teach to others.   —This is what I mean, that you do not believe in gods at all.

d   You are a strange fellow, Meletus. Why do you say this? Do I not believe, as other men do, that the sun and the moon are gods?   —No, by Zeus, jurymen, for he says that the sun is stone, and the moon earth.

My dear Meletus, do you think you are prosecuting Anaxagoras? Are you so contemptuous of the jury and think them so ignorant of letters as not to know that the books of Anaxagoras[7] of Clazomenae are full of those theories, and further, that the young men learn from me what they can
e buy from time to time for a drachma, at most, in the bookshops, and ridicule Socrates if he pretends that these theories are his own, especially as they are so absurd? Is that, by Zeus, what you think of me, Meletus, that I do not believe that there are any gods?   —That is what I say, that you do not believe in the gods at all.

You cannot be believed, Meletus, even, I think, by yourself. The man appears to me, gentlemen of the jury, highly insolent and uncontrolled. He seems to have made this deposition out of inso-
27 lence, violence and youthful zeal. He is like one who composed a riddle and is trying it out: "Will the wise Socrates realize that I am jesting and contradicting myself, or shall I deceive him and others?" I think he contradicts himself in the affidavit, as if he said: "Socrates is guilty of not believing in gods but believing in gods," and surely that is the part of a jester!

Examine with me, gentlemen, how he appears
b to contradict himself, and you, Meletus, answer us. Remember, gentlemen, what I asked you when I began, not to create a disturbance if I proceed in my usual manner.

Does any man, Meletus, believe in human affairs who does not believe in human beings? Make him answer, and not again and again create a disturbance. Does any man who does not believe in horses believe in equine affairs? Or in flute music but not in flute-players? No, my good sir, no man could. If you are not willing to answer, I will tell
c you and the jury. Answer the next question, however. Does any man believe in divine activities who does not believe in divinities?   —No one.

Thank you for answering, if reluctantly, when the jury made you. Now you say that I believe in

divine activities and teach about them, whether new or old, but at any rate divine activities according to what you say, and to this you have sworn in your deposition. But if I believe in divine activities I must quite inevitably believe in divine beings. Is that not so? It is indeed. I shall assume that you
d agree, as you do not answer. Do we not believe divine beings to be either gods or the children of gods? Yes or no?   —Of course.

Then since I do believe in divine beings, as you admit, if divine beings are gods, this is what I mean when I say you speak in riddles and in jest, as you state that I do not believe in gods and then again that I do, since I believe in divine beings. If on the other hand the divine beings are children of the gods, bastard children of the gods by nymphs or some other mothers, as they are said to be, what man would believe children of the gods to exist, but not gods? That would be just as absurd as to
e believe the young of horses and asses, namely mules, to exist, but not to believe in the existence of horses and asses. You must have made this deposition, Meletus, either to test us or because you were at a loss to find any true wrongdoing of which to accuse me. There is no way in which you could persuade anyone of even small intelligence that it is not the part of one and the same man to believe in
28 the activities of divine beings and gods, and then again the part of one and the same man not to believe in the existence of divinities and gods and heroes.

I do not think, gentlemen of the jury, that it requires a prolonged defence to prove that I am not guilty of the charges in Meletus' deposition, but this is sufficient. On the other hand, you know that what I said earlier is true, that I am very unpopular with many people. This will be my undoing, if I am undone, not Meletus or Anytus but the slanders and envy of many people. This has destroyed many
b other good men and will, I think, continue to do so. There is no danger that it will stop at me.

Someone might say: "Are you not ashamed, Socrates, to have followed the kind of occupation that has led to your being now in danger of death?" However, I should be right to reply to him: "You are wrong, sir, if you think that a man who is any good at all should take into account the risk of life or death; he should look to this only in his actions, whether what he does is right or wrong, whether
c he is acting like a good or a bad man." According to

---

7. Anaxagoras of Clazomenae, born about the beginning of the fifth century B.C., came to Athens as a young man and spent his time in the pursuit of natural philosophy. He claimed that the universe was directed by Nous (Mind), and that matter was indestructible but always combining in various ways. He left Athens after being prosecuted for impiety.

your view, all the heroes who died at Troy were inferior people, especially the son of Thetis who was so contemptuous of danger compared with disgrace.[8] When he was eager to kill Hector, his goddess mother warned him, as I believe, in some such words as these: "My child, if you avenge the death of your comrade, Patroclus, and you kill Hector, you will die yourself, for your death is to follow immediately after Hector's." Hearing this, he despised death and danger and was much more afraid to live a coward who did not avenge his

d   friends. "Let me die at once," he said, "when once I have given the wrongdoer his deserts, rather than remain here, a laughingstock by the curved ships, a burden upon the earth." Do you think he gave thought to death and danger?

This is the truth of the matter, gentlemen of the jury: wherever a man has taken a position that he believes to be best, or has been placed by his commander, there he must I think remain and face danger, without a thought for death or anything else,

e   rather than disgrace. It would have been a dreadful way to behave, gentlemen of the jury, if, at Potidaea, Amphipolis and Delium, I had, at the risk of death, like anyone else, remained at my post where those you had elected to command had ordered me, and then, when the god ordered me, as I thought and believed, to live the life of a philosopher, to examine myself and others, I had aban-

29   doned my post for fear of death or anything else. That would have been a dreadful thing, and then I might truly have justly been brought here for not believing that there are gods, disobeying the oracle, fearing death, and thinking I was wise when I was not. To fear death, gentlemen, is no other than to think oneself wise when one is not, to think one knows what one does not know. No one knows whether death may not be the greatest of all blessings for a man, yet men fear it as if they knew that it is the greatest of evils. And surely it is the most

b   blameworthy ignorance to believe that one knows what one does not know. It is perhaps on this point and in this respect, gentlemen, that I differ from the majority of men, and if I were to claim that I am wiser than anyone in anything, it would be in this, that, as I have no adequate knowledge of things in the underworld, so I do not think I have. I do

know, however, that it is wicked and shameful to do wrong, to disobey one's superior, be he god or man. I shall never fear or avoid things of which I do not know, whether they may not be good rather

c   than things that I know to be bad. Even if you acquitted me now and did not believe Anytus, who said to you that either I should not have been brought here in the first place, or that now I am here, you cannot avoid executing me, for if I should be acquitted, your sons would practise the teachings of Socrates and all be thoroughly corrupted; if you said to me in this regard: "Socrates, we do not believe Anytus now; we acquit you, but only on condition that you spend no more time on this investigation and do not practise philosophy, and if you are caught doing so you will die;" if, as I say,

d   you were to acquit me on those terms, I would say to you: "Gentlemen of the jury, I am grateful and I am your friend, but I will obey the god rather than you, and as long as I draw breath and am able, I shall not cease to practise philosophy, to exhort you and in my usual way to point out to any one of you whom I happen to meet: Good Sir, you are an Athenian, a citizen of the greatest city with the greatest reputation for both wisdom and power;

e   are you not ashamed of your eagerness to possess as much wealth, reputation and honours as possible, while you do not care for nor give thought to wisdom or truth, or the best possible state of your soul?" Then, if one of you disputes this and says he does care, I shall not let him go at once or leave him, but I shall question him, examine him and test him, and if I do not think he has attained the goodness that he says he has, I shall reproach him because he attaches little importance to the most

30   important things and greater importance to inferior things. I shall treat in this way anyone I happen to meet, young and old, citizen and stranger, and more so the citizens because you are more kindred to me. Be sure that this is what the god orders me to do, and I think there is no greater blessing for the city than my service to the god. For I go around doing nothing but persuading both young and old among you not to care for your body or your

b   wealth in preference to or as strongly as for the best possible state of your soul as I say to you: "Wealth does not bring about excellence, but excellence brings about wealth and all other public and private blessings for men."

Now if by saying this I corrupt the young, this advice must be harmful, but if anyone says that I

---

8. The scene between Thetis and Achilles is from the *Iliad* (18, 94ff).

give different advice, he is talking nonsense. On this point I would say to you, gentlemen of the jury: "Whether you believe Anytus or not, whether you acquit me or not, do so on the understanding

c that this is my course of action, even if I am to face death many times." Do not create a disturbance, gentlemen, but abide by my request not to cry out at what I say but to listen, for I think it will be to your advantage to listen, and I am about to say other things at which you will perhaps cry out. By no means do this. Be sure that if you kill the sort of man I say I am, you will not harm me more than yourselves. Neither Meletus nor Anytus can harm me in any way; he could not harm me, for I do not

d think it is permitted that a better man be harmed by a worse; certainly he might kill me, or perhaps banish or disfranchise me, which he and maybe others think to be great harm, but I do not think so. I think he is doing himself much greater harm doing what he is doing now, attempting to have a man executed unjustly. Indeed, gentlemen of the jury, I am far from making a defence now on my own behalf, as might be thought, but on yours, to prevent you from wrongdoing by mistreating the god's

e gift to you by condemning me; for if you kill me you will not easily find another like me. I was attached to this city by the god—though it seems a ridiculous thing to say—as upon a great and noble horse which was somewhat sluggish because of its size and needed to be stirred up by a kind of gadfly. It is to fulfill some such function that I believe the god has placed me in the city. I never cease to rouse each and every one of you, to persuade and reproach you all day long and everywhere I find my-

31 self in your company.

Another such man will not easily come to be among you, gentlemen, and if you believe me you will spare me. You might easily be annoyed with me as people are when they are aroused from a doze, and strike out at me; if convinced by Anytus you could easily kill me, and then you could sleep on for the rest of your days, unless the god, in his care for you, sent you someone else. That I am the kind of person to be a gift of the god to the city you might realize from the fact that it does not seem

b like human nature for me to have neglected all my own affairs and to have tolerated this neglect now for so many years while I was always concerned with you, approaching each one of you like a father or an elder brother to persuade you to care for virtue. Now if I profited from this by charging a fee for

my advice, there would be some sense to it, but you can see for yourselves that, for all their shameless accusations, my accusers have not been able in

c their impudence to bring forward a witness to say that I have ever received a fee or ever asked for one. I, on the other hand, have a convincing witness that I speak for truth, my poverty.

It may seem strange that while I go around and give this advice privately and interfere in private affairs, I do not venture to go to the assembly and there advise the city. You have heard me give the reason for this in many places. I have a divine sign

d from the god which Meletus has ridiculed in his deposition. This began when I was a child. It is a voice, and whenever it speaks it turns me away from something I am about to do, but it never encourages me to do anything. This is what has prevented me from taking part in public affairs, and I think it was quite right to prevent me. Be sure, gentlemen of the jury, that if I had long ago attempted to take part in politics, I should have died long ago,

e and benefited neither you nor myself. Do not be angry with me for speaking the truth; no man will survive who genuinely opposes you or any other crowd and prevents the occurrence of many unjust

32 and illegal happenings in the city. A man who really fights for justice must lead a private, not a public, life if he is to survive for even a short time.

I shall give you great proofs of this, not words but what you esteem, deeds. Listen to what happened to me, that you may know that I will not yield to any man contrary to what is right, for fear of death, even if I should die at once for not yielding. The things I shall tell you are commonplace and smack of the lawcourts, but they are true. I

b have never held any other office in the city, but I served as a member of the Council, and our tribe Antiochis was presiding at the time when you wanted to try as a body the ten generals who had failed to pick up the survivors of the naval battle.[9] This was illegal, as you all recognized later. I was

---

9. This was the battle of Arginusae (south of Lesbos) in 406 B.C., the last Athenian victory of the war. A violent storm prevented the Athenian generals from rescuing their survivors. For this they were tried in Athens and sentenced to death by the assembly. They were tried in a body, and it is this to which Socrates objected in the Council's presiding committee which prepared the business of the assembly. He obstinately persisted in his opposition, in which he stood alone, and was overruled by the majority. Six generals who were in Athens were executed.

the only member of the presiding committee to oppose your doing something contrary to the laws, and I voted against it. The orators were ready to prosecute me and take me away, and your shouts were egging them on, but I thought I should run any risk on the side of law and justice rather than join you, for fear of prison or death, when you were engaged in an unjust course.

This happened when the city was still a democracy. When the oligarchy was established, the Thirty[10] summoned me to the Hall, along with four others, and ordered us to bring Leon from Salamis, that he might be executed. They gave many such orders to many people, in order to implicate as many as possible in their guilt. Then I showed again, not in words but in action, that, if it were not rather vulgar to say so, death is something I couldn't care less about, but that my whole concern is not to do anything unjust or impious. That government, powerful as it was, did not frighten me into any wrongdoing. When we left the Hall, the other four went to Salamis and brought in Leon, but I went home. I might have been put to death for this, had not the government fallen shortly afterwards. There are many who will witness to these events.

Do you think I would have survived all these years if I were engaged in public affairs and, acting as a good man must, came to the help of justice and considered this the most important thing? Far from it, gentlemen of the jury, nor would any other man. Throughout my life, in any public activity I may have engaged in, I am the same man as I am in private life. I have never come to an agreement with anyone to act unjustly, neither with anyone else nor with any one of those who they slanderously say are my pupils. I have never been anyone's teacher. If anyone, young or old, desires to listen to me when I am talking and dealing with my own concerns, I have never begrudged this to anyone, but I do not converse when I receive a fee and not when I do not. I am equally ready to question the rich and the poor if anyone is willing to answer my questions and listen to what I say. And I cannot justly be held responsible for the good or bad conduct of these people, as I never promised to teach them anything

and have not done so. If anyone says that he has learned anything from me, or that he heard anything privately that the others did not hear, be assured that he is not telling the truth.

Why then do some people enjoy spending considerable time in my company? You have heard why, gentlemen of the jury, I have told you the whole truth. They enjoy hearing those being questioned who think they are wise, but are not. And this is not unpleasant. To do this has, as I say, been enjoined upon me by the god, by means of oracles and dreams, and in every other way that a divine manifestation has ever ordered a man to do anything. This is true, gentlemen, and can easily be established.

If I corrupt some young men and have corrupted others, then surely some of them who have grown older and realized that I gave them bad advice when they were young should now themselves come up here to accuse me and avenge themselves. If they were unwilling to do so themselves, then some of their kindred, their fathers or brothers or other relations should recall it now if their family had been harmed by me. I see many of these present here, first Crito, my contemporary and fellow demesman, the father of Critoboulos here; next Lysanias of Sphettus, the father of Aeschines here; also Antiphon the Cephisian, the father of Epigenes; and others whose brothers spent their time in this way; Nicostratus, the son of Theozotides, brother of Theodotus, and Theodotus has died so he could not influence him; Paralios here, son of Demodocus, whose brother was Theages; there is Adeimantus, son of Ariston, brother of Plato here; Acantidorus, brother of Apollodorus here.

I could mention many others, some one of whom surely Meletus should have brought in as witness in his own speech. If he forgot to do so, then let him do it now; I will yield time if he has anything of the kind to say. You will find quite the contrary, gentlemen. These men are all ready to come to the help of the corruptor, the man who has harmed their kindred, as Meletus and Anytus say. Now those who were corrupted might well have reason to help me, but the uncorrupted, their kindred who are older men, have no reason to help me except the right and proper one, that they know that Meletus is lying and that I am telling the truth.

Very well, gentlemen of the jury. This, and maybe other similar things, is what I have to say in

---

10. This was the harsh oligarchy that was set up after the final defeat of Athens in 404 B.C. and that ruled Athens for some nine months in 404–3 before the democracy was restored.

c my defence. Perhaps one of you might be angry as he recalls that when he himself stood trial on a less dangerous charge, he begged and implored the jury with many tears, that he brought his children and many of his friends and family into court to arouse as much pity as he could, but that I do none of these things, even though I may seem to be running the ultimate risk. Thinking of this, he might

d feel resentful toward me and, angry about this, cast his vote in anger. If there is such a one among you—I do not deem there is, but if there is—I think it would be right to say in reply: My good sir, I too have a household and, in Homer's phrase, I am not born "from oak or rock" but from men, so that I have a family, indeed three sons, gentlemen of the jury, of whom one is an adolescent while two are children. Nevertheless, I will not beg you to acquit me by bringing them here. Why do I do none of these things? Not through arrogance, gen-

e tlemen, nor through lack of respect for you. Whether I am brave in the face of death is another matter, but with regard to my reputation and yours and that of the whole city, it does not seem right to me to do these things, especially at my age and with my reputation. For it is generally believed, whether it be true or false, that in certain respects Socrates is

35 superior to the majority of men. Now if those of you who are considered superior, be it in wisdom or courage or whatever other virtue makes them so, are seen behaving like that, it would be a disgrace. Yet I have often seen them do this sort of thing when standing trial, men who are thought to be somebody, doing amazing things as if they thought it a terrible thing to die, and as if they were to be immortal if you did not execute them. I think these men bring shame upon the city so that a stranger,

b too, would assume that those who are outstanding in virtue among the Athenians, whom they themselves select from themselves to fill offices of state and receive other honours, are in no way better than women. You should not act like that, gentlemen of the jury, those of you who have any reputation at all, and if we do, you should not allow it. You should make it very clear that you will more readily convict a man who performs these pitiful dramatics in court and so makes the city a laughingstock, than a man who keeps quiet.

c Quite apart from the question of reputation, gentlemen, I do not think it right to supplicate the jury and to be acquitted because of this, but to teach and persuade them. It is not the purpose of a juryman's office to give justice as a favour to whoever seems good to him, but to judge according to law, and this he has sworn to do. We should not accustom you to perjure yourselves, nor should you make a habit of it. This is irreverent conduct for either of us.

d Do not deem it right for me, gentlemen of the jury, that I should act towards you in a way that I do not consider to be good or just or pious, especially, by Zeus, as I am being prosecuted by Meletus here for impiety; clearly, if I convinced you by my supplication to do violence to your oath of office, I would be teaching you not to believe that there are gods, and my defence would convict me of not believing in them. This is far from being the case, gentlemen, for I do believe in them as none of my accusers do. I leave it to you and the god to judge me in the way that will be best for me and for you.

[The jury now gives its verdict of guilty, and Meletus asks for the penalty of death.]

e There are many other reasons for my not being angry with you for convicting me, gentlemen of the jury, and what happened was not unexpected. I am

36 much more surprised at the number of votes cast on each side, for I did not think the decision would be by so few votes but by a great many. As it is, a switch of only thirty votes would have acquitted me. I think myself that I have been cleared on

b Meletus' charges, and not only this, but it is clear to all that, if Anytus and Lycon had not joined him in accusing me, he would have been fined a thousand drachmas for not receiving a fifth of the votes.

He assesses the penalty at death. So be it. What counter-assessment should I propose to you, gentlemen of the jury? Clearly it should be a penalty I deserve, and what do I deserve to suffer or to pay because I have deliberately not led a quiet life but have neglected what occupies most people: wealth, household affairs, the position of general or public orator or the other offices, the political clubs and factions that exist in the city? I thought myself too honest to survive if I occupied myself with those

c things. I did not follow that path that would have made me of no use either to you or to myself, but I went to each of you privately and conferred upon him what I say is the greatest benefit, by trying to persuade him not to care for any of his belongings before caring that he himself should be as good and

as wise as possible, not to care for the city's possessions more than for the city itself, and to care for
d   other things in the same way. What do I deserve for
being such a man? Some good, gentlemen of the
jury, if I must truly make an assessment according
to my deserts, and something suitable. What is
suitable for a poor benefactor who needs leisure to
exhort you? Nothing is more suitable, gentlemen,
than for such a man to be fed in the Prytaneum,[11]
much more suitable for him than for any of you
who has won a victory at Olympia with a pair or a
team of horses. The Olympian victor makes you
e   think yourself happy; I make you be happy. Besides, he does not need food, but I do. So if I must
make a just assessment of what I deserve, I assess it
37   at this: free meals in the Prytaneum.

When I say this you may think, as when I spoke
of appeals to pity and entreaties, that I speak arrogantly, but that is not the case, gentlemen of the
jury; rather it is like this: I am convinced that I
never willingly wrong anyone, but I am not convincing you of this, for we have talked together but
a short time. If it were the law with us, as it is else-
b   where, that a trial for life should not last one but
many days, you would be convinced, but now it is
not easy to dispel great slanders in a short time.
Since I am convinced that I wrong no one, I am not
likely to wrong myself, to say that I deserve some
evil and to make some such assessment against myself. What should I fear? That I should suffer the
penalty Meletus has assessed against me, of which I
say I do not know whether it is good or bad? Am I
then to choose in preference to this something that
I know very well to be an evil and assess the pen-
c   alty at that? Imprisonment? Why should I live in
prison, always subjected to the ruling magistrates
the Eleven? A fine, and imprisonment until I pay it?
That would be the same thing for me, as I have no
money. Exile? for perhaps you might accept that
assessment.

I should have to be inordinately fond of life,
gentlemen of the jury, to be so unreasonable as to
suppose that other men will easily tolerate my
company and conversation when you, my fellow
d   citizens, have been unable to endure them, but

found them a burden and resented them so that
you are now seeking to get rid of them. Far from it,
gentlemen. It would be a fine life at my age to be
driven out of one city after another, for I know very
well that wherever I go the young men will listen to
e   my talk as they do here. If I drive them away, they
will themselves persuade their elders to drive me
out; if I do not drive them away, their fathers and
relations will drive me out on their behalf.

Perhaps someone might say: But Socrates, if you
leave us will you not be able to live quietly, without
talking? Now this is the most difficult point on
which to convince some of you. If I say that it is
38   impossible for me to keep quiet because that
means disobeying the god, you will not believe me
and will think I am being ironical. On the other
hand, if I say that it is the greatest good for a man to
discuss virtue every day and those other things
about which you hear me conversing and testing
myself and others, for the unexamined life is not
worth living for man, you will believe me even less.

What I say is true, gentlemen, but it is not easy
b   to convince you. At the same time, I am not accustomed to think that I deserve any penalty. If I had
money, I would assess the penalty at the amount I
could pay, for that would not hurt me, but I have
none, unless you are willing to set the penalty at
the amount I can pay, and perhaps I could pay you
one mina of silver.[12] So that is my assessment.

Plato here, gentlemen of the jury, and Crito and
Critoboulus and Apollodorus bid me put the penalty at thirty minae, and they will stand surety for
the money. Well then, that is my assessment, and
they will be sufficient guarantee of payment.

*[The jury now votes again and sentences Socrates to
death.]*

c   It is for the sake of a short time, gentlemen of
the jury, that you will acquire the reputation and
the guilt, in the eyes of those who want to denigrate
the city, of having killed Socrates, a wise man, for
they who want to revile you will say that I am wise
even if I am not. If you had waited but a little while,
this would have happened of its own accord. You
see my age, that I am already advanced in years and
close to death. I am saying this not to all of you but
d   to those who condemned me to death, and to these

---

11. The Prytaneum was the magistrates' hall or town hall of Athens
in which public entertainments were given, particularly to Olympian victors on their return home.

---

12. One mina was 100 drachmas, equivalent to, say, twenty-five
dollars, though in purchasing power probably five times greater. In
any case, a ridiculously small sum under the circumstances.

same jurors I say: Perhaps you think that I was convicted for lack of such words as might have convinced you, if I thought I should say or do all I could to avoid my sentence. Far from it. I was convicted because I lacked not words but boldness and shamelessness and the willingness to say to you what you would most gladly have heard from me, lamentations and tears and my saying and doing

e   many things that I say are unworthy of me but that you are accustomed to hear from others. I did not think then that the danger I ran should make me do anything mean, nor do I now regret the nature of my defence. I would much rather die after this kind of defence than live after making the other kind. Neither I nor any other man should, on trial

39 or in war, contrive to avoid death at any cost. Indeed it is often obvious in battle that one could escape death by throwing away one's weapons and turning to supplicate one's pursuers, and there are many ways to avoid death in every kind of danger if one will venture to do or say anything to avoid it. It is not difficult to avoid death, gentlemen of the jury,

b   it is much more difficult to avoid wickedness, for it runs faster than death. Slow and elderly as I am, I have been caught by the slower pursuer, whereas my accusers, being clever and sharp, have been caught by the quicker, wickedness. I leave you now, condemned to death by you, but they are condemned by truth to wickedness and injustice. So I maintain my assessment, and they maintain theirs. This perhaps had to happen, and I think it is as it should be.

c   Now I want to prophesy to those who convicted me, for I am at the point when men prophesy most, when they are about to die. I say gentlemen, to those who voted to kill me, that vengeance will come upon you immediately after my death, a vengeance much harder to bear than that which you took in killing me. You did this in the belief that you would avoid giving an account of your life, but I maintain that quite the opposite will happen to you. There will be more people to test you, whom I

d   now held back, but you did not notice it. They will be more difficult to deal with as they will be younger and you will resent them more. You are wrong if you believe that by killing people you will prevent anyone from reproaching you for not living in the right way. To escape such tests is neither possible nor good, but it is best and easiest not to discredit others but to prepare oneself to be as good as

possible. With this prophecy to you who convicted me, I part from you.

e   I should be glad to discuss what has happened with those who voted for my acquittal during the time that the officers of the court are busy and I do not yet have to depart to my death. So, gentlemen, stay with me awhile, for nothing prevents us from talking to each other while it is allowed. To you, as

40 being my friends, I want to show the meaning of what has occurred. A surprising thing has happened to me, judges—you I would rightly call judges. At all previous times my usual mantic sign frequently opposed me, even in small matters, when I was about to do something wrong, but now that, as you can see for yourselves, I was faced with what one might think, and what is generally thought to be, the worst of evils, my divine sign has not opposed me, either when I left home at dawn,

b   or when I came into court, or at any time that I was about to say something during my speech. Yet in other talks it often held me back in the middle of my speaking, but now it has opposed no word or deed of mine. What do I think is the reason for this? I will tell you. What has happened to me may well be a good thing, and those of us who believe death to be an evil are certainly mistaken. I have

c   convincing proof of this, for it is impossible that my customary sign did not oppose me if I was not about to do what was right.

Let us reflect in this way, too, that there is good hope that death is a blessing, for it is one of two things: either the dead are nothing and have no perception of anything, or it is, as we are told, a change and a relocating for the soul from here to another place. If it is complete lack of perception,

d   like a dreamless sleep, then death would be a great advantage. For I think that if one had to pick out that night during which a man slept soundly and did not dream, put beside it the other nights and days of his life, and then see how many days and nights had been better and more pleasant than that night, not only a private person but the great king would find them easy to count compared with the

e   other days and nights. If death is like this I say it is an advantage, for all eternity would then seem to be no more than a single night. If, on the other hand, death is a change from here to another place, and what we are told is true and all who have died are there, what greater blessing could there be, gentle-

41 men of the jury? If anyone arriving in Hades will

have escaped from those who call themselves judges here, and will find those true judges who are said to sit in judgement there, Minos and Radamanthus and Aeacus and Triptolemus and the other demi-gods who have been upright in their own life, would that be a poor kind of change? Again, what would one of you give to keep company with Orpheus and Musaeus, Hesiod and Homer? I am willing to die many times if that is true. It would be a wonderful way for me to spend
b my time whenever I met Palamedes and Ajax, the son of Telamon, and any other of the men of old who died through an unjust conviction, to compare my experience with theirs. I think it would be pleasant. Most important, I could spend my time testing and examining people there, as I do here, as to who among them is wise, and who thinks he is, but is not.

What would one not give, gentlemen of the jury, for the opportunity to examine the man who led the great expedition against Troy, or Odysseus,
c or Sisyphus, and innumerable other men and women one could mention. It would be an extraordinary happiness to talk with them, to keep company with them and examine them. In any case, they would certainly not put one to death for doing so. They are happier there than we are here in other respects, and for the rest of time they are deathless, if indeed what we are told is true.

You too must be of good hope as regards death, gentlemen of the jury, and keep this one truth in mind, that a good man cannot be harmed either in
d life or in death, and that his affairs are not neglected by the gods. What has happened to me now has not happened of itself, but it is clear to me that it was better for me to die now and to escape from trouble. That is why my divine sign did not oppose me at any point. So I am certainly not angry with those who convicted me, or with my accusers. Of course that was not their purpose when they accused and convicted me, but they thought they were hurting me, and for this they deserve blame.
e This much I ask from them: when my sons grow up, avenge yourselves by causing them the same kind of grief that I caused you, if you think they care for money or anything else more than they care for virtue, or if they think they are somebody when they are nobody. Reproach them as I reproach you, that they do not care for the right things and think they are worthy when they are not

42 worthy of anything. If you do this, I shall have been justly treated by you, and my sons also.

Now the hour to part has come. I go to die, you go to live. Which of us goes to the better lot is known to no one, except the god.

As we begin to delve into the character of Socrates as Plato portrays it in this dialogue, we should be struck by his single-mindedness. If it should turn out that death is a "change from here to another place," how would Socrates spend his time there? He would continue precisely the activities that had occupied him in this life; he would "examine" all the famous heroes to see which of them is wise. And why does he think of such examination as so important, as a "service to the god"? No doubt because it undermines *hubris*, that arrogance of thinking one possesses "a wisdom more than human."

Read 17a–18a   In this short introductory section, Socrates draws a contrast between himself and his accusers, characterizes the kind of man he is, and reminds the jury of its duty.

Q1. How is the contrast between persuasion and truth drawn? List the terms in which each is described.
Q2. What kind of a man does Socrates say that he is?
Q3. What is his challenge to the jury?

Read 18b–19a   Socrates makes a distinction between two sets of accusers.

Q4. Identify the earlier accusers and the later accusers. How do they differ?
Q5. Why is it going to be very difficult for Socrates to defend himself against the earlier accusers?

Read 19b–24b   Here we have Socrates' defense against the "earlier accusers." He tries to show how his "unpopularity" arises from his practice of questioning. He describes the origins of this occupation of his and discusses the sort of wisdom to which he lays claim.

Q6. What are the three points made against him in the older accusations?

Q7. What does Socrates say about each of these accusations?

Q8. How does Socrates distinguish himself from the Sophists here?

We have mentioned the Oracle at Delphi before. One could go there and, after appropriate sacrifices, pose a question. The "Pythian" (21a) was a priestess of Apollo who would, in the name of the god, reply to the questions posed. We have noted that it was characteristic of the Oracle to reply in a riddle. So it is not perverse for Socrates to wonder what the answer to Chairephon's question means. What sort of wisdom is this in which no one can surpass him? He devises his technique of questioning to clarify the meaning of the answer.

Note that several times during his speech Socrates asks the jury not to create a disturbance (20e, 27b, 30c). We can imagine that he is interrupted at those points by hoots, hissing, catcalls, or their ancient Greek equivalents.

Q9. Which three classes of people did Socrates question? What, in each case, was the result?

Q10. What conclusion does Socrates draw from his investigations?

Read 24b–28a At this point, Socrates begins to address the "later accusers." He does so in his usual question-and-answer fashion. Apparently, three persons submitted the charge to the court: Meletus, Anytus, and Lycon. Meletus seems to have been the primary sponsor of the charge, seconded by the other two. So Socrates calls Meletus forward and questions him. As in the *Euthyphro*, two charges are mentioned. Be sure you are clear about what they are.

In 24c Socrates tells the jury his purpose in cross-examining Meletus. He wants to demonstrate that Meletus is someone who ought not to be taken seriously, that he has not thought through the meaning of the charge, and that he doesn't even care about these matters. In short, Socrates is about to demonstrate before the jury—before their very eyes!—not only what sort of man Meletus is, and that he is not wise, but also what sort of man Socrates is. It is the truth, remember, that Socrates is after; if the jury is going to decide whether Socrates is impious and a corrupter of youth, they should have the very best evidence about what sort of man they are judging. Socrates is going to oblige them by giving them a personal demonstration.

He begins by taking up the charge of corrupting the youth. If Meletus claims that Socrates corrupts the youth, he must understand what corrupting is. To understand what it is to corrupt, one must also understand what it is to improve. And so Socrates asks him, "Who improves them?"

Q11. Does Meletus have a ready answer? What conclusion does Socrates draw from this? (24d)

When Meletus does answer, Socrates' questions provoke him to say that all the other citizens improve the youth and only Socrates corrupts them!

Q12. How does Socrates use the analogy of the horse breeders to cast doubt on Meletus' concern for these matters?

Starting in 25c, Socrates presents Meletus with a dilemma. The form of a dilemma is this: two alternatives are presented between which it seems necessary to choose, but each alternative has consequences that are unwelcome, usually for different reasons. The two alternatives are called the "horns" of a dilemma, and there are three ways to deal with them. One can "grasp" one of the horns (i.e., embrace that alternative with its consequences); one can "grasp" the other horn; or one can (sometimes, but not always) "go between the horns" by finding a third alternative that has not been considered.

Q13. What are the horns of the dilemma that Socrates presents to Meletus?

Q14. How does Meletus respond?

Q15. How does Socrates refute this response?

Q16. Supposing that this refutation is correct and that one cannot "pass through" the horns, what is the consequence of embracing the other horn? How does Socrates use the distinction between punishment and instruction?

Again Socrates drives home the conclusion that Meletus has "never been at all concerned with these matters." If he had been, he surely would have thought these things through. As it is, he cannot be taken seriously.

At 26b, the topic switches to the other charge. As the examination proceeds, we can see Meletus becoming angrier and angrier, less and less willing to cooperate in what he clearly sees is his own destruction. No doubt this is an example—right before the jury's eyes!—of Socrates' earlier description (21d–e) of the typical response to his questioning. We might think Socrates is not being prudent here in angering Meletus and his supporters in the jury. But again, it is for Socrates a matter of the truth; this is the kind of man he is. And the jury should see it if they are going to judge truly.

Q17. Socrates claims that Meletus contradicts himself. In what way?

Q18. What "divine activities" must the jury have understood him to be referring to? (27d–e)

Q19. What does Socrates claim will be his undoing, if he is undone?

Read 28b–35d   Socrates is now finished with Meletus, satisfied that he has shown him to be thoughtless and unreliable. He turns to more general matters relevant to his defense. He first imagines someone might say that the very fact that he is on trial for his life is shameful. How could he have behaved in such a manner as to bring himself to this?

Q20. On what principle does Socrates base his response? Do you agree with this principle? (Compare the speech of the nurse in *Hippolytus* on page 51.)

Q21. To whom does Socrates compare himself? Do you think the comparison is apt? How do you think this would have struck an Athenian jury?

Q22. Socrates refers to his military service; in what respects does he say his life as a philosopher is like that?

Q23. Why does he say that to fear death is to think oneself wise when one is not? Do you agree with this? If not, why not?

In 29c–d Socrates imagines that the jury might offer him a "deal," sparing his life if only he ceased practicing philosophy. Xenophon tells us that during the reign of the Thirty, Critias and another man, Charicles, in fact made such a demand of Socrates: they forbade him to hold conversations with the young. If this story is accurate, it may be that Socrates has this demand in mind. Or it may be that there had been talk of such a "deal" before the trial.

Q24. What does Socrates say his response would be? (Compare Acts 5:29 in the Bible.)

Q25. Why does he say that "there is no greater blessing for the city" than his service to the god? What are "the most important things"? Do you agree?

In the section that begins in 30b, Socrates makes some quite astonishing claims:

- If they kill him, they will harm themselves more than they harm him.
- A better man cannot be harmed by a worse man.
- He is defending himself not for his own sake but for theirs.

All these claims seem to turn the usual ways of thinking about such matters completely upside down. Indeed, to our natural common sense they seem incredible. Surely they must have seemed so to the jury as well.

Q26. Can you write a brief paragraph to make sense of these remarkable claims? (This will take some thought.)

Q27. What use does Socrates make of the image of the "gadfly"?

Socrates feels a need to explain why, if he is so wise, he has not entered politics. There are two reasons, one being the nature of his "wisdom." He focuses here on the other reason: his "sign" prevented it. If it had not, he says, there is little doubt that he would "have died long ago" and could not have been a "blessing to the city" for all these years.

He cites two incidents as evidence of this, one occurring when the city was democratic, one under the rule of the Thirty. He is trying to convince the jury that he is truly apolitical, since he was capable of resisting both sorts of government. In both cases, he resisted alone because the others were doing something contrary to law, and in both cases he was in some danger. Why should he feel the need to establish his political neutrality? Surely because there was a political aspect to the trial—not explicit, but in the background.

In 33a, he gets to what many people feel is the heart of the matter. Let us ask: Why was Socrates brought to trial at all? There was his reputation as a Sophist, of course—all those accusations of the "earlier accusers." There was the general hostility that his questioning generated. There was his "divine sign." But it is doubtful that these alone would have sufficed to bring him to court. What probably tipped the balance was the despicable political career of some who had at one time been closely associated with him, in particular Critias, leader of the Thirty, and Alcibiades, the brilliant and dashing young traitor. This kind of "guilt by association" is very common and very hard to defend against. If these men had spent so much time with Socrates, why hadn't they turned out better? Socrates must be responsible for their crimes! This could not be mentioned in the official charge because it would have violated the amnesty proclaimed by the democracy after the Thirty were overthrown. But it is hard not to believe that it is lurking in the background.

How does Socrates defend himself against this charge? He makes another remarkable claim. He has *never*, he says, "been anyone's teacher." For that reason, he cannot "be held responsible for the good or bad conduct of these people, as I never

promised to teach them anything and have not done so." This requires some explaining.

In the *Meno*, where the topic is whether virtue can be taught, Socrates invites Meno to join in a search for what virtue is. Meno asks,

> How will you look for it, Socrates, when you do not know at all what it is? How will you aim to search for something you do not know at all? If you should meet with it, how will you know that this is the thing that you did not know? (*Meno* 80d).[3]

In response to this puzzle, Socrates calls over a slave boy who has never studied geometry. He draws a square on the ground and divides it equally by bisecting the sides vertically and horizontally. (Draw such a square yourself.) He then asks the boy to construct another square with an area twice the original area. This is a nice problem. Clearly, if the original area is four, we want a square with an area of eight. But how can we get it? (Before you go on, think a minute and see if you can solve it.)

Socrates proceeds by asking the boy questions. The first, rather natural suggestion is to double the length of the sides. But on reflection, the boy can see (as you can, too) that this gives a square of sixteen. Wanting something between four and sixteen, the boy tries making the sides of the new square one and one-half times the original. But this gives a square of nine, not eight. Finally, at a suggestion from Socrates, the boy sees that taking the diagonal of the original square as one side of a new square solves the problem. (Do you agree that this solves the problem? How can you be sure?)

What is the relevance of this to Meno's puzzle? And to Socrates' claim never to have been anyone's teacher? The crucial point is that the boy can just "see" that the first two solutions are wrong. And when the correct solution is presented, he "recognizes" it as correct. But he has never been taught geometry! And his certainty about the correct solution does not now rest on the authority of Socrates, who might assure him that this is certainly true. Socrates does no such thing; and even if he would, the boy's knowledge would not be *based* on that. So Socrates doesn't *teach* him this truth!

This leaves us with another puzzle. How could the boy have recognized the true solution as the true one? Consider this analogy. You are walking down the street and see someone approaching. At first she is too far away to identify, but as she gets nearer you say, "Why, that's Joan!" Now, what must be the case for you to "recognize" Joan truly? There can be no doubt: you must already have been acquainted with Joan in some way. That alone is the condition under which recognition is possible.

Socrates thinks the slave boy's case must be similar. He must already have been acquainted with this truth; otherwise, it is not possible to explain how he recognizes it when it is present before him. But when? Clearly not in this life. Socrates draws what seems to be the only possible conclusion: that he was acquainted with this truth before birth and that it was always within him. (This is taken as evidence that the soul exists before the body, but that is not our present concern.) Coming to know something is just recognizing what, in some implicit sense, one has within oneself all along. What Socrates does is ask the right questions or present the appropriate stimuli. But he doesn't "implant" knowledge; he doesn't teach.

In the dialogue *Theatetus*, Plato represents Socrates as using a striking image.

> I am so far like the midwife that I cannot myself give birth to wisdom, and the common reproach is true, that, though I question others, I can myself bring nothing to light because there is no wisdom in me. . . . Those who frequent my company at first appear, some of them, quite unintelligent, but, as we go further with our discussions, all who are favored by heaven make progress at a rate that seems surprising to others as well as to themselves, although it is clear that they have never learned anything from me. The many admirable truths they bring to birth have been discovered by themselves from within. But the delivery is heaven's work and mine (*Theatetus* 150c–d).[4]

Here, then, is the background for the claim that Socrates has never taught anyone anything. His role is not that of teacher or imparter of knowledge and wisdom but that of "midwife" (recall that this was his mother's profession), assisting at the birth of ideas which are within the "learner" all along. This is why he says—though he could not have explained all this to the jury—that he cannot be held responsible for the behavior of men like Critias and Alcibiades.

Q28. What additional arguments does Socrates use in 33d–34b?

Q29. Why does he refuse to use the traditional "appeal to pity"? See particularly 35c.

Read 35e–38b   The verdict has been given, and now, according to custom, both the prosecution and the defense may propose appropriate penalties. Meletus, of course, asks for death.

Q30. What penalty does Socrates first suggest? Why?

Q31. Why does he resist proposing exile?

Q32. What does he say is "the greatest good" for a man? Why?

Q33. What does he finally offer?

Read 38c–end   After being sentenced to death, Socrates addresses first those who voted to condemn him and then his friends. To both he declares himself satisfied. He has presented himself for what he is; he has not betrayed himself by saying only what they wanted to hear in order to avoid death.

Q34. What does Socrates say is more difficult to avoid than death? And who has not avoided it?

Q35. What does he "prophesy"?

Q36. What "surprising thing" does he point out to his friends? What does he take it to mean?

Q37. What two possibilities does Socrates consider death may hold? Are there any he misses?

Q38. What is the "one truth" that Socrates wishes his friends to keep in mind? How does he try to comfort them?

Because of a religious observance involving a ship sent to the island of Delos (see map 1), it was not possible to execute Socrates immediately. Nearly a month passed, which Socrates spent in prison. His friends visited him regularly and spent long days in the usual conversations. They also made clandestine arrangements to allow him to escape and leave the state; apparently, the authorities would not have been unhappy if he had.

On the morning when the ceremonial ship was spotted off the coast south of Athens, an old friend, Crito, came to visit Socrates. His purpose was to try one last time to convince Socrates to escape. In a dialogue called *Crito*, Plato claims to record the conversation between the two friends.

Crito argues that Socrates should escape. As you might by now expect, Socrates replies that they must together "examine" whether to act that way or not. He adds an interesting characterization of himself. "I am the kind of man," he says, "who listens only to the argument that on reflection seems best to me" (*Crito* 46b).[5] By "reflection" he surely means that kind of dialectical examination in which the weaknesses of a position are deliberately sought out. The word for argument here is our old friend, *logos*. When Socrates is facing a choice, he chooses the alternative backed up by the best *logos*, unless perhaps his "sign" decides it for him by forbidding one of the alternatives.

This raises an interesting question. Would his sign ever oppose a choice favored by the best *logos*? Apparently not. Xenophon says that Socrates held it was not right to consult oracles in matters within the scope of human capacity, but that where humans could not know, it was appropriate to do so. His "divine sign" probably functioned in the same way, neither displacing nor contradicting rational deliberation but filling in when rational deliberation was not sufficient. This is rather speculative but seems to fit the evidence.

In any case, the question of escape seems to be one about which they can deliberate. And Socrates is committed to whatever course of action can be backed by the best argument. He asks Crito whether certain statements they had earlier agreed on "stay the same" in these new circumstances.

What Socrates wants to know is whether things look different now that he is facing death. Look again at *Euthyphro* 11d, where the complaint is that propositions, like the statues of Daedalus, will not "stay put." There Socrates says that he would rather have his arguments "remain unmoved than possess the wealth of Tantalus as well as the cleverness of Daedalus."

They agree that some statements "stay the same" even in these circumstances. Among them is the assumption that a part of ourselves is harmed by unjust actions. That is, *we* can harm *ourselves*—the "more valuable" part of ourselves, no less!—by acting unjustly. No other person can harm us in that way; we have to do it to ourselves. Other views also seem to stay put:

- It is not good to be governed by what the majority (the many) say.
- What is important is not life, but the good life.
- The good life, the beautiful life, and the just life are one and the same.

In light of these agreements, the question is then put: Should Socrates escape? An examination of this question produces an argument that we can summarize as follows:

1. One must never do wrong. The reason given is that to do wrong is "in every way harmful and shameful to the wrongdoer" (*Crito* 49b). It is neither wise nor prudent, for it harms that part of ourselves which is "more valuable."
2. One must not return wrong for wrong done. This is a corollary that follows directly from 1.
3. To injure people is to do wrong. Socrates recognizes that most people will not agree, but in light of the opinions that "stay the same," the disagreement of the many is no argument against it. So:
4. One must never injure anyone. This follows from 1 and 3.
5. To violate a just agreement is to injure people. There is not likely to be much disagreement about this principle.

6. To escape would be to violate a just agreement. In support of this principle, Socrates imagines that the laws of Athens come and interrogate him as he has questioned others. The laws point out that he has been satisfied with them all his life and that he had plenty of opportunity to leave Athens if he had been displeased with them but has not done so. In effect he has agreed to live under their rule, accepting their protection. To escape now that they have ruled against him would be to violate this agreement. And that would be tantamount to an attempt to destroy them and would be unjust. So:

7. To escape would be wrong. This follows from 3 and 5 and 6. Therefore:

8. Socrates must not escape. This follows from 1 and 7.

What are we to say about this argument? It convinces both Socrates and Crito; should it convince us? Socrates would surely approve if we did a little "examining" of this argument (*logos*) on our own.

There are always two ways to criticize an argument: (1) you can point out that it is not *logically* sound, that the conclusion doesn't *follow* from the reasons given; you are claiming in this case that you could accept all the reasons offered but that they do not compel you to accept the conclusion; (2) you can point out that some of the reasons are not true or acceptable; in that case—even if the argument is *logically* all right, so that *if* the premises were true you *would* have to accept the conclusion—you again don't have to accept the conclusion.

Socrates' argument seems to be logically sound. In fact, it seems to be *valid*, i.e., to exhibit the strongest sort of logical goodness. In a **valid** argument, it is *impossible* for the premises to be true while the conclusion is false. If you accept all the reasons Socrates gives, you should also accept the conclusion. But do you have to accept all the premises? Perhaps the ones most open to doubt are 3, 4, and 6. A good exercise is to "examine" these for yourself and see whether you should accept them. If you do not accept them, try to identify the reasons why you do not. You might imagine the ghost of Socrates standing before you, casting his sideways glance at you and pressing you to explain exactly why you don't think his reasons are good reasons. With regard to 6, you may want to look at the dialogue itself and pay close attention to what the laws say to Socrates.

At the end, ask yourself this question: Should Socrates have escaped?

Phaedo

The *Phaedo* is supposed to be a record of a conversation Socrates had with his friends on the day of his death. The topic is the soul, particularly whether the soul is immortal. An appropriate topic for philosophical discussion on the last day of one's life, you might think. Perhaps that was the topic, but there are good reasons for doubting that all the arguments for the soul's immortality are really Socratic. This dialogue seems to be slightly later than the others we have read; we are probably hearing Plato himself elaborating and expanding on his master's beliefs.

There is no reason, however, to doubt the authenticity of Plato's portrait of the serene manner in which Socrates died. That fits with everything else we know about him from any source. We'll read only the end of the dialogue.

Death Scene

In the Phaedo, *a number of Socrates' friends have come to visit him in prison on the last day of his life, as he will drink the hemlock at sundown. The main topic of their conversation is the nature of the soul and the arguments for its immortality. This takes up most of the dialogue. Then Socrates tells a rather elaborate myth on the shape of the earth in a hollow of which we live, and of which we know nothing of the splendours of its surface, the purer air and brighter heavens. The myth then deals with the dwelling places of various kinds of souls after death. The following passage immediately follows the conclusion of the myth.*

114d No sensible man would insist that these things are as I have described them, but I think it is fitting for a man to risk the belief—for the risk is a noble one—that this, or something like this, is true about our souls and their dwelling places, since the soul is evidently immortal, and a man should repeat this to himself as if it were an incantation, which is why I have been prolonging my tale. That is the reason why a man should be of good cheer about his own soul, if during life he has ignored the pleasures of the body and its
e ornamentation as of no concern to him and doing him more harm than good, but has seriously concerned himself with the pleasures of learning, and adorned his soul not with alien but with its own ornaments, namely moderation, right-
115 eousness, courage, freedom, and truth, and in that state awaits his journey to the underworld.

Now you, Simmias, Cebes, and the rest of you, Socrates continued, will each take that journey at some other time but my fated day calls me now, as a tragic character might say, and it is about time for me to have my bath, for I think it better to have it before I drink the poison and save the women the trouble of washing the corpse.

When Socrates had said this Crito spoke:
b Very well, Socrates, what are your instructions to me and the others about your children or anything else? What can we do that would please you most? —Nothing new, Crito, said Socrates, but what I am always saying, that you will please me and mine and yourselves, by taking good care of your own selves in whatever you do, even if you do not agree with me now, but if you neglect your own selves, and are unwilling
c to live following the tracks, as it were, of what we have said now and on previous occasions, you will achieve nothing even if you strongly agree with me at this moment.

We shall be eager to follow your advice, said Crito, but how shall we bury you?

In any way you like, said Socrates, if you can catch me and I do not escape you. And laughing quietly, looking at us, he said: I do not convince Crito that I am this Socrates talking to you here and ordering all I say, but he thinks that I am the
d thing which he will soon be looking at as a corpse, and so he asks how he shall bury me. I

have been saying for some time and at some length that after I have drunk the poison I shall no longer be with you but will leave you to go and enjoy some good fortunes of the blessed, but it seems that I have said all this to him in vain in an attempt to reassure you and myself too. Give a pledge to Crito on my behalf, he said, the opposite pledge to that he gave to the jury. He pledged that I would stay, you must pledge
e that I will not stay after I die, but that I shall go away, so that Crito will bear it more easily when he sees my body being burned or buried and will not be angry on my behalf, as if I were suffering terribly, and so that he should not say at the funeral that he is laying out, or carrying out, or burying Socrates. For know you well, my dear Crito, that to express oneself badly is not only faulty as far as the language goes, but does some harm to the soul. You must be of good cheer, and say you are burying my body, and bury it in any
116 way you like and think most customary.

After saying this he got up and went to another room to take his bath, and Crito followed him and he told us to wait for him. So we stayed, talking among ourselves, questioning what had been said, and then again talking of the great misfortune that had befallen us. We all felt as if we had lost a father and would be orphaned for
b the rest of our lives. When he had washed, his children were brought to him—two of his sons were small and one was older—and the women of his household came to him. He spoke to them before Crito and gave them what instructions he wanted. Then he sent the women and children away, and he himself joined us. It was now close to sunset, for he had stayed inside for some time. He came and sat down after his bath and conversed for a short while, when the officer of the
c Eleven came and stood by him and said: "I shall not reproach you as I do the others, Socrates. They are angry with me and curse me when, obeying the orders of my superiors, I tell them to drink the poison. During the time you have been here I have come to know you in other ways as the noblest, the gentlest, and the best man who has ever come here. So now too I know that you will not make trouble for me; you know who is responsible and you will direct your anger against them. You know what message I bring.

d   Fare you well, and try to endure what you must as easily as possible." The officer was weeping as he turned away and went out. Socrates looked up at him and said: "Fare you well also, we shall do as you bid us." And turning to us he said: How pleasant the man is! During the whole time I have been here he has come in and conversed with me from time to time, a most agreeable man. And how genuinely he now weeps for me. Come, Crito, let us obey him. Let someone bring the poison if it is ready; if not, let the man prepare it.

e   But Socrates, said Crito, I think the sun still shines upon the hills and has not yet set. I know that others drink the poison quite a long time after they have received the order, eating and drinking quite a bit, and some of them enjoy intimacy with their loved ones. Do not hurry; there is still some time.

117   It is natural, Crito, for them to do so, said Socrates, for they think they derive some benefit from doing this, but it is not fitting for me. I do not expect any benefit from drinking the poison a little later, except to become ridiculous in my own eyes for clinging to life, and be sparing of it when there is none left. So do as I ask and do not refuse me.

Hearing this, Crito nodded to the slave who was standing near him; the slave went out and after a time came back with the man who was to administer the poison, carrying it made ready in a cup. When Socrates saw him he said: Well, my good man, you are an expert in this, what must one do?   —"Just drink it and walk around un-

b   til your legs feel heavy, and then lie down and it will act of itself." And he offered the cup to Socrates who took it quite cheerfully, Echecrates, without a tremor or any change of feature or colour, but looking at the man from under his eyebrows as was his wont, asked: "What do you say about pouring a libation from this drink? Is it allowed?"   —"We only mix as much as we believe will suffice," said the man.

c   I understand, Socrates said, but one is allowed, indeed one must, utter a prayer to the gods that the journey from here to yonder may be fortunate. This is my prayer and may it be so.

And while he was saying this, he was holding the cup, and then drained it calmly and easily.

Most of us had been able to hold back our tears reasonably well up till then, but when we saw him drinking it and after he drank it, we could hold them back no longer; my own tears came in floods against my will. So I covered my face. I was weeping for myself—not for him, but for my misfortune in being deprived of such a com-

d   rade. Even before me, Crito was unable to restrain his tears and got up. Apollodorus had not ceased from weeping before, and at this moment his noisy tears and anger made everybody present break down, except Socrates. "What is this," he said, "you strange fellows. It is mainly for this reason that I sent the women away, to avoid such

e   unseemliness, for I am told one should die in good omened silence. So keep quiet and control yourselves."

His words made us ashamed, and we checked our tears. He walked around, and when he said his legs were heavy he lay on his back as he had been told to do, and the man who had given him the poison touched his body, and after a while tested his feet and legs, pressed hard

118   upon his foot and asked him if he felt this, and Socrates said no. Then he pressed his calves, and made his way up his body and showed us that it was cold and stiff. He felt it himself and said that when the cold reached his heart he would be gone. As his belly was getting cold Socrates uncovered his head—he had covered it—and said—these were his last words—"Crito, we owe a cock to Asclepius;[1] make this offering to him and do not forget."   —"It shall be done," said Crito, "tell us if there is anything else," but there was no answer. Shortly afterwards Socrates made a movement; the man uncovered him and his eyes were fixed. Seeing this Crito closed his mouth and his eyes.

Such was the end of our comrade, Echecrates, a man who, we would say, was of all those we have known the best, and also the wisest and the most upright.

---

1. A cock was sacrificed to Asclepius by the sick people who slept in his temples, hoping for a cure. Socrates obviously means that death is a cure for the ills of life.

Read 114d–115e   About fifteen people were present. Plato, it is said, was absent because he was ill. By this point in the conversation they have agreed that the soul is immortal and that the souls of the just and pious, especially if they have devoted themselves to wisdom, dwell after death in a beautiful place.

Q1. What are said to be the "ornaments" of the soul?

Q2. What harm, do you think, can it do the soul to "express oneself badly"?

Read 116–end   Socrates seems to have kept his calm and courage to the end—and his humor. There is a little joke about burial at 115c. Xenophon, too, records this:

A man named Apollodorus, who was there with him, a very ardent disciple of Socrates, but otherwise simple, exclaimed, "But Socrates, what I find it hardest to bear is that I see you being put to death unjustly!" The other, stroking Apollodorus' head, is said to have replied, "My beloved Apollodorus, was it your preference to see me put to death justly?" and smiled as he asked the question.[6]

The simple majesty of the final tribute is, perhaps, unmatched anywhere.

Notes

1. Homer, *The Iliad*, trans. Robert Fitzgerald (New York: Anchor Books, 1975), bk. 1, p. 13.
2. Xenophon, *Memorabilia*, trans. E. C. Marchant, in *Xenophon IV*, ed. E. C. Marchant and O. J. Todd (Cambridge: Harvard University Press, 1979), bk. 1, 3, 2–3.
3. Plato, *Meno*, trans. G. M. A. Grube, in *Plato's Meno* (Indianapolis: Hackett Publishing Co., 1980).
4. Plato, *Theatetus*, in *The Collected Dialogues of Plato*, ed. E. Hamilton and H. Cairns (Princeton: Princeton University Press, 1961).
5. Plato, *Crito*, trans. G. M. A. Grube, in *The Trial and Death of Socrates* (Indianapolis: Hackett Publishing Co., 1975).
6. Xenophon, *Apology 28*, trans. O. J. Todd, in *Xenophon IV*, ed. E. C. Marchant and O. J. Todd (Cambridge: Harvard University Press, 1979).

10

Plato:
Knowing the Real and the Good

When Socrates died in 399 B.C.E., his disciple and admirer Plato was just thirty years old. He lived fifty-two more years. That long life was devoted to the creation of a philosophy that would justify and vindicate his master, "the best, and also the wisest" man (*Phaedo* 118) he had ever known. It is a philosophy whose influence has been incalculable in the West. Together with that of his own pupil Aristotle, it forms one of the two foundation stones for nearly all that is to follow; even those who want to disagree first have to pay attention. In a rather loose sense, everyone who thinks about philosophy at all is either a "Platonist" or an "Aristotelian." Not without cause did Alfred North Whitehead write in 1929 that "the safest general characterization of the European philosophical tradition is that it consists of a series of footnotes to Plato."[1]

Plato apparently left Athens after Socrates' death and traveled quite widely. About 387 he settled again in his home town and established a school near a grove called "Academus," from which comes our word "academy." There he inquired, taught, and wrote the dialogues.

Let us briefly review the situation leading up to Socrates' death. These are extremely troubled times. A drawn out, ugly war with Sparta ends in humiliation, accompanied by internal strife between democrats and oligarchs, culminating in the tyranny of the Thirty, civil war, and their over-

throw. The Sophists, meanwhile, have been teaching doctrines that seem to undermine all the traditions and cast doubt on everything people hold sacred. And the intellectual situation in general, though it will look active and fruitful from a future vantage point, surely looks chaotic and unsettled from close up. It is a war of ideas no one has definitely won. You have Parmenides' One versus Heraclitus' flux, Democritus' atomism versus the skepticism of the Sophists, and the controversy over *physis* and *nomos*. Some urge conformity to the laws of the city; others hold that such human justice is inferior to the pursuit of self-interest, which can rightly override such "mere" conventions.

In this maelstrom appears Socrates—ugly to look at, fascinating in character, incredibly honest, doggedly persistent, passionately committed to a search for the truth, and convinced that *none* of his contemporaries know what they are talking about. Plato is not the only one entranced. But clearly Plato has genius of his own, and he takes the Socratic task on his own shoulders. Animating Socrates' practice, as we have seen, is the conviction that there is a truth about the matters he investigates; but Socrates seldom feels he has found it. Plato sets for himself the goal—nothing less!—of refuting skepticism and relativism. He intends to *demonstrate*, contrary to the Sophists, that there is a truth about reality and that it can be known. And he intends to show, contrary to Democritus, that this reality is not indifferent to moral and religious values.

His basic goal, and in this he is typically Greek, is to establish the pattern for a good state.* If you were to ask him, "Plato, exactly what do you mean by 'a good state'?" he would have a ready answer. He would say that a good state is one in which a good man can live a good life. And if you pressed him about what kind of man was a good man, he would acknowledge that here was a hard question, one needing "examination." But he would at least be ready with an example. And by now you know who the example would be. It follows that Athens as it existed in 399 was not, despite its virtues, a good state, for it had executed Socrates.

To reach this goal of setting forth the pattern of a good state, he has to show that there is such a thing as goodness—and not just by convention. It couldn't be that if Athens thought it was a good thing to execute Socrates then it *was* a good thing to execute Socrates. Plato *knew in his heart* that was wrong. But now he has to *show* it was wrong. Mere assertion was never enough for Socrates, and it won't do for Plato, either. He will construct a *logos*, a *true logos*, a *dialectic* to show us the goodness that exists in *physis*, not just in the opinions of people or the conventions of society. And he will show us how we can come to know what this goodness is and become truly wise. These, at least, are his ambitions.

Knowledge and Opinion

We sometimes make the following contrast: do you only *believe* that, or do you *know* it? This contrast between mere belief, or *opinion*, and knowledge is important for Plato. Indeed, he uses it to derive surprising conclusions—conclusions that make

up the heart and center of his philosophy. It is on this distinction that his critique of the sophistic relativism and skepticism turns.

The Sophists argue, you will recall, that if someone thinks the wind is cold, then it is cold—for that person.* And they generalize this claim. "Of *all* things, the measure is man," asserts Protagoras. In effect, all we can have are opinions or beliefs. If a certain belief is satisfactory to a certain person, then no more can be said. We are each the final authority of what seems right to us. We are restricted to appearance; knowledge of reality is beyond our powers. This is the heart of their skepticism and relativism.

Plato tries to meet this challenge in three steps. First, he has to clarify the distinction between opinion and knowledge. Second, he has to show that we do have knowledge. Third, he needs to explain the nature of the objects that we can be said to know.

Making the Distinction

What is the difference between knowing something and just believing? The key seems to be this: you can believe falsely, but you can't know falsely. Suppose that at a certain time, call it T1, you claim to know that John is Kate's husband. Later, at T2, you find out that John is really unmarried and has never been anyone's husband. What will you then say about yourself at T1? Will you say, "Well, I *used to know* (at T1) that John was married, but now I know he is not"? This would be saying, "I did know (falsely) that John was married, but now I know (truly) that he is not." Or will you say, "Well, I *thought I knew* (at T1) that John was married, but I *didn't know it at all*"? Surely you will say the latter. If we become convinced that one of the things we claim to know turns out to be false, we retract that claim. We do not claim to know things we believe are false. We can put this in the form of a principle: Knowledge involves truth.

---

*His *Republic* is an attempt to define an ideal state. The *Laws*, perhaps his last work, is a long and detailed discussion trying to frame a realistic constitution for a state that might actually exist.

*See p. 41.

Believing or having opinions is quite the opposite. If at T1 you *believe* that John is married to Kate and you later find out he isn't, you won't retract the claim that you did believe that at T1. You will simply say, "Yes, I did believe that; but now I believe (or know) it isn't so." It is quite possible to believe something false; it happens all the time. Believing does not necessarily involve truth.

We can, of course, believe truly. But even so, belief and knowledge are not the same thing. In the *Meno*, Plato has Socrates say:

> For true opinions, as long as they remain, are a fine thing and all they do is good, but they are not willing to remain long, and they escape from a man's mind, so that they are not worth much until one ties them down by (giving) an account of the reason why. . . . After they are tied down, in the first place they become knowledge, and then they remain in place. That is why knowledge is prized higher than correct opinion, and knowledge differs from correct opinion in being tied down (*Meno* 98a).[2]

To have true opinions is a fine thing, as far as it goes. There is a problem, though, if all you have is true beliefs; they don't "remain long." They "escape from a man's mind," Plato tells us, because they are not "tied down." What could tie them down? An "account of the reason why." In the *Republic*, Plato compares people who have true opinions without knowledge to blind people who yet follow the right road (*R* 506c).[3] Imagine a blind woman who wanders along, turning this way and that. It just happens that each of her turnings corresponds to a bend in the road, but her correct turnings are merely an accident. She might equally well go straight over the cliff at the next bend. By contrast, we who can *see* the road, have a "reason" why we turn as we do; we can see that the road bends here to avoid the precipice. We *know* that we must turn left here precisely because we can give an account of *why* we turn as we do. Our belief that we must turn left here is "tied down" by our "reason" that there is a cliff dead ahead.

We can connect this contrast between even *true* belief and knowledge with the practice of Socrates.

It is his habit, as we have seen, to "examine" others about their beliefs. And we can now say that surviving such examination is a necessary condition for any belief to count as knowledge. It is only a negative condition, however, because such survival doesn't *guarantee* truth; perhaps we simply have not yet come across the devastating counterexample. Plato wants more than such survival. In addition to a lack of reasons for giving up a belief, he wants to supply positive reasons for holding on to it. What he hopes to supply is a *logos* that gives "the reason why."

We have here a second and a third point of distinction between knowledge and belief (even true belief). Not only does knowledge invariably involve truth, it "remains in place." And it endures in this way because it involves "the reason why."

And this leads to a final difference. In the *Timaeus*, Plato tells us that

> the one is implanted in us by instruction, the other by persuasion; . . . the one cannot be overcome by persuasion, but the other can (*Timaeus* 51e).[4]

The instruction in question will be an explanation of the reason why. But what is persuasion? Can there be any doubt that Plato has in mind here all the tricks and techniques of rhetoric? If you truly know something, he is saying, you will understand *why* it is so. And that will protect you from clever fellows (advertisers, politicians, public relations experts) who use their art to "make the weaker argument appear the stronger." Opinion or mere belief, on the other hand, is at the mercy of every persuasive talker that comes along. If you believe something but don't clearly understand the reason why it is so, your belief will be easily "overcome" by persuasion. Compare yourself, for instance, to the blind woman at the bend of the road just before the cliff. She might easily be persuaded to go straight ahead; no one could persuade you to do so.

As you can see, Plato draws a sharp and clear line between opinion and knowledge. We can summarize the distinction in a table.

Opinion	Knowledge
is changeable	endures or stays put
may be true or false	is always true
is not backed up by reasons	is backed up by reasons
is the result of persuasion	is the result of instruction

So far even a Sophist need not quarrel; he could agree that such a distinction can be made. But he would claim that it cannot be *applied* because all we ever have are opinions. We can perhaps understand what it would be like to have knowledge, but it doesn't follow that we actually have any. So Plato has to move to his second task; he has to demonstrate that we can in fact know certain things.

We Do Know Certain Truths

The clearest examples are the truths of mathematics and geometry. Think back to the slave boy and the problem of doubling the area of a square. The correct solution is to take the diagonal of the original square as a side of the square to be constructed. That solution can be seen to be correct because an "account" or explanation can be given: the "reason why." Look again at the diagram.

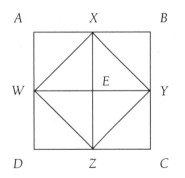

The reason why the square *WXYZ* is double the original square *WEZD* is that the larger square *ABCD* is four times the original, and *WXYZ* is made up of four triangles, each of which is half of a subsidiary square, each of which is itself the size of the original. Since four halves is two, we have a square

twice the size of *WEZD*. This *logos* or "account" gives the reason why this is the correct solution. Once you (or the slave boy) understand this rationale, it will not be easier to persuade you otherwise than to persuade you to go straight over the cliff edge. What we have here, then, is an opinion that is true, will endure, is backed up by reason, and is the result of instruction. In other words, we have not *just* opinion—we have knowledge.

This example (and innumerable others of the same kind can be constructed) is absolutely convincing to Plato. There can be no doubt, he thinks, that this solution is not just a matter of how it seems to one person or another. About these matters cultures do not differ. There is no sense in which man is the "measure" of this truth. It is not conventional or up to us to decide; we only recognize it. Relativism, at least as a general theory, is mistaken. Skepticism is wrong. We *do* have knowledge of the truth.*

But two important questions are still unsettled. First, what exactly do we have knowledge *about* when we know that this is the correct solution to the problem? Socrates probably drew the squares in the sand. Are we to suppose that he drew so accurately that the square made on the diagonal was really twice the area of the original? Not likely. The truth the slave boy came to know, then, is not a truth about that sand drawing. What is it about, then? Here is a puzzle. And Plato's solution to this puzzle is the key to understanding his whole philosophy.

The second question is whether this kind of knowledge can be extended to values and morality. Can we know that deception is unjust in the same

---

*The prominence of mathematical knowledge in Plato's philosophy is a reflection of earlier Pythagorean themes. Pythagoras and his followers had developed both geometry and arithmetic, had given a mathematical analysis of music, and had held in an obscure way that the universe was composed of numbers. They also believed that mathematical study was a means to purify the soul. The conviction these geometrical examples carry was not seriously shaken until the discovery (or invention) of non-Euclidean geometries in the late nineteenth century. With consistent alternatives available, it suddenly became plausible that geometrical truths were due to convention (*nomos*) after all.

sense and with the same certainty as that a square on the diagonal is twice the size of an original square? We address the first of these questions now and come back to the second later.

The Objects of Knowledge

Plato would say that Socrates' sand drawing is not the object of the slave boy's knowledge. Let's make sure we see Plato's point here. "I agree," you might say, "that Socrates' sand drawing is not exact. But we can do much better than sand drawings nowadays. Surely we can draw, or construct, a square exactly double the size of a given square!" Ah, but can we? Or, to put it more precisely, *could* we? Suppose the area of the original square is 4; then we want a square that is 8—not, note well, 7.999999999. And not 8.000000001 either.

There are two interesting points here. One is that we could not *draw* or *make* such a square, except perhaps by accident. Our instruments are not precise enough for that. The second is that even if we had such a square before us, we could not *know* that it was such a square, for all our measuring instruments are valid only within a certain range of error. The slave boy's knowledge (and yours), it seems, cannot be *derived* from the drawing you see before you; and neither is it *about* that drawing. Yet it is true, and it does constitute knowledge. Plato puts the point in this way:

> Then what about the actual acquiring of knowledge? Is the body an obstacle when one associates with it in the search for knowledge? I mean, for example, do men find any truth in sight or hearing, or are not even the poets forever telling us that we do not see or hear anything accurately, and surely if those two physical senses are not clear or precise, our other senses can hardly be accurate, as they are all inferior to these. Do you not think so?
>
> I certainly do, he said.
>
> When then, he asked, does the soul grasp the truth? For whenever it attempts to examine anything with the body, it is clearly deceived by it.
>
> True.
>
> Is it not in reasoning if anywhere that any reality becomes clear to the soul?

> Yes.
>
> And indeed the soul reasons best when none of these senses troubles it, neither hearing nor sight, nor pain nor pleasure, but when it is most by itself, taking leave of the body and as far as possible having no contact or association with it in its search for reality. (*Phaedo* 65a–c).[5]

Plato's views about the soul are hinted at in this passage; we'll ignore them now and discuss the soul explicitly later.* What is of immediate interest to us is the contrast between the senses as information gatherers and "reasoning." The senses (sight, hearing, and the rest) never get it right, Plato tells us; they are not "precise" or "accurate." We "grasp" the truth only through *reasoning*—through a *logos* or "account" that gives us the "reason why." But we *can* grasp it that way.

Here Plato agrees with Parmenides, who admonishes us not to trust our senses but to follow reasoning alone.† In this sense, Plato too is a "rationalist." You should be able to see, from the example we have considered, why he thinks this is the only way to proceed. (There is a role for the senses in the formulation of opinion about the world of experience, as we'll see, but they cannot give us *knowledge*.)

You should also be able to see that Plato agrees with Heraclitus about the world revealed to us through the senses.‡ Consider the drawing of the square again. Suppose we did get it just right; the area is exactly 8. But of course we drew it with a pencil, pen, or laser—with some physical material. What is to prevent it, once drawn correctly, from turning incorrect in the very next moment? Suppose a molecule of ink or a particle of light gets displaced? It might bounce in and out of correctness from nanosecond to nanosecond. It seems like a continual flux. And that is just what Heraclitus thinks it is. But our solution doesn't bounce in and out of truth that way. It "remains in place."

---

*See "The Soul," later in this chapter.
†You might like to review briefly what Parmenides says; see pp. 23 and 25.
‡See pp. 17–18.

Once again, the truth we know cannot be about the world disclosed to our senses. Nothing in that world "remains in place."

Plato holds that both Parmenides and Heraclitus are correct. They aren't in fact contradicting each other, even though one holds that reality is unchangeable and eternal and the other that reality is continually changing. Both are correct because each is talking about a *different reality*. The one is revealed to us through the senses, the other through reasoning. You are familiar with the reality of Heraclitus; it is just the everyday world we see, hear, smell, taste, and touch. The other world is not so ordinary. And we must say more about it.

We need to go back to the question, what is our truth about the square a truth *about*? Obviously, not about any square you could see, but what then? Plato's answer is that it is a truth about the Square Itself. And this is an object that can be apprehended only by the intellect, by thinking and reasoning. Still, it is an object, a reality; why should we suppose that the senses are our only avenue to the realities there are? It is, moreover, a public object, for you and I (and indeed anyone) can know the same truths about it. In fact, it is perhaps more public than sense objects. The square I see as red you may see as green, but we all agree that a square may be doubled by taking its diagonal as the base of another square.

Here is another feature of this reality, the Square Itself. It is not some particular square or other. It is not, for instance, one with an area of 4 rather than 6 or 10 or 19 5/8. This principle is true not only for squares with an area of 4 but for *any* square. It is a characteristic, we might say, common to all squares. So if our truth is a truth about the Square Itself, this must be a very unusual object! It is an object that is in some sense *shared* by all the particular squares that ever have or ever will exist.

Here we are reminded of what Socrates is looking for. Remember that when Socrates questions Euthyphro he isn't satisfied when presented with an *example* of piety. What he wants is something common to all pious actions, present in no impious actions, and which accounts for the fact that the pious actions are pious. He wants, he says, the

"form" of piety.* Plato takes up the term **Form** and uses it as the general term for the objects of knowledge. In our example, what we know is something about the Form of the Square. We may use the terms "Form of the Square" and "the Square Itself" interchangeably. What we can know, then, are Forms (the Square Itself, the Triangle Itself) and how they are related to each other.

About the world of the senses, Plato tells us, no knowledge in the strict sense is possible. Here there are only opinions. That world doesn't "stay put" long enough for us to know it; knowledge, remember, "endures" and therefore requires an object that also endures. The Square Itself does not fluctuate like visible and tangible squares. Therefore, it can qualify as an object of knowledge.

Up to this point we have traced Plato's reasoning about the Forms on the basis of the assumption that we do have some knowledge. Let us recapitulate the major steps.

a. Knowledge is enduring, true, rational belief based on instruction.
b. We do have knowledge.
c. This knowledge cannot be about the world revealed through the senses.
d. It must be about another world, one that endures.
e. This is the world of Forms.

Let us call this the Epistemological Argument for the Forms. Epistemology, you may recall, is the fancy term for the theory of knowledge—what knowledge is and what it is about.† And Plato has here concluded from a theory of what knowledge is that its objects must be realities quite different from those presented by the senses. These are realities that, like Parmenides' One, are eternal and unchanging, each one forever exactly what it is.

This very statement, however, reveals that Parmenides was not wholly right. For there is not just One Form—or the Form of the One—but many. There is the Square Itself, the Triangle Itself, the

---

*See *Euthyphro* 6d–e.
†See "A Word to Students," p. xvii.

Equal Itself, and indeed, as we shall see, the Just Itself, the Good Itself, and the Form of the Beautiful as well. The reality that is eternal is not a blank One but a most intricately related, immensely complex pattern of Forms. This pattern is reflected partly, though not entirely, in our mathematical knowledge. It is what mathematics is about.

This Epistemological Argument is one leg supporting the theory of Forms, but it is not the only one. Before we turn to a further consideration of the nature of Forms and their function in Plato's thought, let us look briefly at two more reasons why Plato believes in their reality.

In a late dialogue where Socrates is no longer the central figure, Plato puts the following question into the mouth of Parmenides:

> How do you feel about this? I imagine your ground for believing in a single form in each case is this. When it seems to you that a number of things are large, there seems, I suppose, to be a certain single character which is the same when you look at them all; hence you think that largeness is a single thing (*Parmenides* 132a).

Socrates, who is answering the questions, agrees. This argument, which we might call the Metaphysical Argument* for the Forms, goes like this. Consider two things that are alike. Perhaps they are both large or white or just. Think of two large elephants, Huey and Gertrude. They have a certain "character" in common. Each is large. Now, what they have in common (largeness) cannot be the same as either one; largeness is not the same as Huey and it is not the same as Gertrude. Nor is it identical with the two of them together, since their cousin Rumble is also large. What they share, then, must be distinct from them, taken either separately or together. Let us call it the Large Itself. Alternatively, we could call it the Form of the Large.

This argument starts not from the nature of knowledge and its difference from opinion, but from the nature of *things*. That is why we can call

this a "metaphysical" argument. The similarities among things require that there be something they have in common. What they have in common cannot be just another thing of the same sort as they are. Gertrude, for example, is not something that other pairs of things could share in the way they can share largeness; each of two other things can be large, but it is nonsense to suppose that each can be Gertrude. What Gertrude and Huey have in common must be something of another sort altogether. It is in fact, Plato holds, a Form.

Finally, let us look at a Semantic Argument for the Forms. **Semantics** is a discipline that deals with words, in particular with the meanings of words and how words are related to what they are about. In the *Republic* we read:

> We are accustomed to assuming one Form in each case for the many particulars to which we give the same name (*R* 596a).

The interesting phrase here is "to which we give the same name." What Plato has in mind here is the fact that we have names of several different kinds. "Gertrude" is a name, and it stands for a certain elephant—for Gertrude, in fact. But "elephant" also seems to be a name, yet it functions quite differently from "Gertrude." The latter names or picks out or stands for one particular thing in the world, namely Gertrude. But we give the name "elephant" to Gertrude and Huey and Rumble and all the other elephants there ever have been or ever will be. Why? Because, Plato suggests, we are assuming that one Form is common to them all. Just as the name "Gertrude" names some particular elephant, the name "elephant" names the Elephant Itself, or the Form Elephant. Whenever we give the same name to many particulars, Plato tells us, it is legitimate to assume that there is a Form that we are naming.

This line of reflection offers an answer to a somewhat puzzling question: how do *general* words get their meaning? What we call "proper names" seem to get their meaning by standing for or naming some object. "Socrates" is meaningful (not just a noise) because it stands for Socrates,

---

*For an explanation of the term "metaphysics," see "A Word to Students," p. xvii.

and "Gertrude" gets its meaning by naming Gertrude. This theory tells us that general terms like "man" or "elephant" get their meaning in the same basic way. They too stand for something; they too are names. But they are the names of Forms, not of particular things that our senses could allow us to meet.

What we have in Plato's philosophy is a single answer to three problems that any philosophy striving for completeness must address. Let us summarize.

Problem One. Assuming that we do have some knowledge, what is our knowledge about? What are the objects of knowledge? Plato's answer is that what we know are the Forms of things.

Problem Two. The particular things that we are acquainted with can be grouped into kinds on the basis of what they have in common. How are we to explain these common features? Plato tells us that what they have in common is a Form.

Problem Three. Some of our words apply not to particular things but to all things of a certain kind. How are we to understand the meaning of these general words? Plato's theory is that these general terms are themselves names, and that they function just as proper names do—except that what they name is not a particular thing but a Form.

The Reality of the Forms

We have, then, a number of lines of investigation—epistemological, metaphysical, and semantic—all of which seem to point in the same direction. In addition to the world of sense so familiar to us, there is another world, the world of Forms. The Forms are not anything we can smell, taste, touch, or see, but that is not to say they are unreal or imaginary. To suppose that they must be unreal if our senses do not make contact with them is just a prejudice; we could call it the Bias Toward the Senses. But Plato believes he has already exposed this as a *mere* bias. Consider again the problem of

doubling the size of a square. We *know* the (or at least one) correct solution for this problem, but what we know cannot be about squares we draw or see. Yet what we know is true. So there must really be something that this knowledge is about; otherwise, what we know would not be true. In the *Republic* we read:

> Does the man who has knowledge know something or nothing? . . .   —I will answer, he said, that he knows something.
> Something that is, or is not?   —Something that is, for how could that which is not be known? (*R* 476e).

You can't know what *isn't*, Plato tells us, for the simple reason that in *that* case there isn't anything there to know. You can only know what *is*.* In other words, if you do know something, there must really be something in reality for you to know. In the case of doubling the square, what you know concerns a set of Forms and their relations to each other. So there must *be* Forms; they cannot be merely unreal and imaginary.

There is a further and more radical conclusion. The Forms are not only *not unreal*, they are *more real* than anything you can see or hear or touch. What is Plato's argument for this surprising conclusion? We need to recall the distinction between knowledge and opinion.[†] If we reflect a little, however, we can see that we ought to have a threefold division rather than a twofold one; in addition to knowledge and opinion, there is Invincible Ignorance. Plato tells us that "what fully is, is fully knowable, and what in no way is, is altogether unknowable" (*R* 477a). It is not possible to know what *isn't*, what in no way exists or is real; there is nothing there to know. About "it" we are ignorant—not just ignorant for the time being or in such a way that we might learn, but *invincibly* ignorant. We then have three capacities to correlate with their objects.

---

*This is a narrower version of the Parmenidean principle that thought and being always go together (see p. 24). Plato accepts that *thought* might diverge from being, but the thought that meets the tests of *knowledge* will not. That is why we value it.
†Review the chart on p. 108.

Knowledge	Opinion	Invincible Ignorance
—of what is—	—?—	—of what is not—

What corresponds to opinion in the same way as reality and nothingness correspond to knowledge and ignorance? Opinion, Plato suggests, stands midway between knowledge and ignorance. It is more than ignorance but less than knowledge. Since it is a capacity of ours, there must be objects that answer to it; when we have an opinion, it is always an opinion *about something*. The natural solution is to find something midway between *what is* on the one hand and *what is not* on the other hand. Can we find something of which it is accurate to say that it *both is and is not*?

> It is now left for us, it seems, to find that which partakes of both being and nonbeing, and correctly cannot be called one or the other absolutely, in order that, if it appears, we can rightly call it the opinable, thus applying the extreme terms to the extremes, and the intermediate to the intermediate. Is that not so?   —It is.
>
> These things being established, I shall say, I want a word with, and an answer from, the good fellow who does not believe that there is a Beautiful itself or any Form of Beauty itself, which remains eternally the same in all respects, but who believes that many beautiful things exist. . . . We shall say to him: "My dear sir, of all those many beautiful things, is there one which will not also appear ugly? And is there one of those just actions which will not also appear unjust? and of pious actions, one that will not appear impious?"
>
> Not one, he said, for inevitably those beautiful things will appear ugly under certain circumstances, and so with the other things included in your question.
>
> What about the many things that are double? Are they any less half than double?   —Not one of them.
>
> So with things big and small, light and heavy, does any predicate we apply to them apply to them any more than its opposite?   —No, he said, each of these things partakes of both opposites.
>
> Is then each of the many things, more than it is not, that which anyone might call it? . . .
>
> Can you put them in a better place than between being and non-being? (*R* 478e–479c).

We can find something that both is and is not, Plato tells us here. And it corresponds to opinion. What is it? It is none other than that set of particular things Heraclitus identified as the flux: the world of our experience. For it is not true, Plato claims, that anything in this world just *is* beautiful; even the beauty of Helen of Troy faded with age. And even at her prime, someone could have come up with a set of lights under which she would have appeared ugly. It would be true to say of Helen that she both was and was not beautiful. Gertrude the elephant is large, but not in comparison to Mount Everest. In comparison to Mount Everest, Gertrude is small, even tiny. So Gertrude is both large and not large. And this kind of reflection applies to absolutely everything in the sensory world. How these things are regarded depends on the perspective taken, the aspect considered, the comparisons in mind. Moreover, all of them come into being and pass away again. None just *is*. Each of them can *appear* now this way, now that. We should now fill in the question mark in the chart above:

—about the world of experience—

Notice that we have reached the conclusion that Plato wants us to reach. The Forms are *more real* than anything you can experience by means of your senses. They are eternally, unchangingly, exactly what they are. Even if every square thing ceased to exist, the Square Itself would remain. In comparison to the Forms, Helen and Gertrude—and just and pious actions—are only partly real. They surely have some reality; they are not *nothing*. But they are less real than the Forms, for they do not endure. And of them we can have no knowledge; about them the best we can hope for is opinion. They don't "stay put" long enough to be known. As Plato charmingly puts it, these things are always "rolling around between nonbeing and pure being"; they are the "wandering intermediate grasped by an intermediate capacity" (*R* 479d).

Plato thinks that in a sense there are two worlds. There is the world of the Forms, which can be known, but only by reasoning, by the intellect. This is the most real world. And there is the world of the many particular, ever-changing things that make up the flux of our lives. These can be sensed; about them we may have opinions, but they cannot be known. This world is real, but less real than the world of the Forms.

It is clear that Plato needs to go on. No one could be satisfied to stop at this point. Even if we grant that he is right to this point (and let us grant it provisionally), we now must insist on an answer to a further question. How are the two worlds related? With this question we arrive at the most interesting part of Plato's answer to sophistic skepticism and relativism.

The World and the Forms

If Plato is right, reality is not at all what it seems to be. Rather, what seems to be is only partly real; reality itself is quite different. For convenience' sake, let us use the term "the world" to refer to this flux of things about us that appear to our senses: rivers, trees, desks, elephants, men and women, runnings, promisings, sleepings, customs, laws, and so on. This corresponds closely enough to the usual use of that term; however, the world must now be understood as less than the whole of reality, and none of it entirely real. We can then put Plato's point in this way: in addition to the world, there are also the Forms; and they are what is truly real. This much, he would add, we already *know*. For we have given an account (a *logos*) of the reason why we must believe in the reality of the Forms.

How Forms Are Related to the World

We must now examine the relationship between the two realities. Let us begin by thinking about shadows. We could equally well consider photographs, mirror images, and reflections in a pool of water. A shadow is in a certain sense less real than the thing that casts it. It is less real because it doesn't have any independent existence; its shape depends wholly on the thing that it is a shadow of (and of course the light source). Think about the shadow shapes you can make on a wall by positioning your hands in various ways in front of a strong lamp. Shaping your hands one way produces the shape of a rabbit; another way, an owl. What the shadow is depends on the shape of your hands. The shape of your hands does *not*, note well, depend on the shape of the shadow. If you put your hands in your pockets, your hands and their shape still exist, but the shadows vanish. This is the sense in which shadows are less real; your hands have an independent existence, but the shadows do not.

Both shadows and hands are parts of the world. So there are different degrees of reality *within* the world, too. Could we use the relationship between shadows and hands to illuminate the relationship between world and Forms? This is in fact what Plato does in a famous diagram called the Divided Line. Plato here calls the world "the visible" and the Forms "the intelligible," according to how we are acquainted with them.

> It is like a line divided into two unequal parts, and then divide each section in the same ratio, that is, the section of the visible and that of the intelligible. You will then have sections related to each other in proportion to their clarity and obscurity. The first section of the visible consists of images—and by images I mean shadows in the first instance, then the reflections in water and all those on close-packed, smooth, and bright materials, and all that sort of thing. . . .
>
> In the other section of the visible, place the models of the images, the living creatures around us, all plants, and the whole class of manufactured things (R 509e–510a).

Let us draw Plato's line, labeling as much of it as he has so far explained.

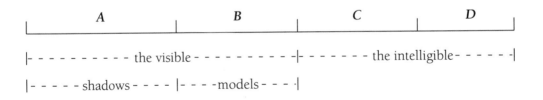

The lengths of the various line parts are significant, not in themselves but in relation to each other. The relation between segment A and segment B is the same as the relation between $A + B$ and $C + D$: as A is to B, so $A + B$ is to $C + D$. Plato intends the relationship between the line segments to mirror the fact that shadows and the models that cast them are related to each other in the same way the world (the visible) is related to the Forms (the intelligible).

Let's take a more realistic example than shadows of arbitrarily shaped hands. Imagine that we live at the bottom of a canyon. Our society has a very strong taboo against looking up, which has been handed down by our earliest ancestors from generation to generation. We do not look up to the rim of the canyon and the sky beyond. The sun shines down into the canyon during the middle part of each day, and we can see the shadows of the canyon walls move across the canyon floor from west to east. Eagles live high up in the canyon wall, but they never come down to the canyon floor, preferring to forage for their food in the richly supplied plains above. We have never seen an eagle, nor are we likely to.

We do see the shadows of eagles as they glide from one wall of the canyon to the other. Sometimes the eagles perch directly on the edge of the canyon wall and cast shadows of a very different shape, of many different shapes, in fact; sometimes they perch facing west, sometimes north, and so on. We do not know that these are eagle shadows, of course, for we are not acquainted with eagles. All we know are the shadows.

Could we come to know anything about eagles? We could. If we collected all the shadow shapes that we had seen, we could get a pretty good idea of what an eagle looks like and at least some idea of its behaviors. We might even get a kind of science of eagles on this basis; from certain shadows we might be able to make predictions about the shapes of others, and these predictions might often turn out to be true. The concept "eagle" would be merely a construct for us, of course; it would be equivalent to "that (whatever it is) which accounts for shadows of this sort." We would think of eagles as the things that explain such shadows, the things

making intelligible that there should be such a pattern of shadows as we experience. But we would never have any direct contact with eagles.

One day, an eagle is injured in a fight and comes fluttering helplessly down to the canyon floor. This has never happened before. We catch the injured bird and nurse it back to health. While we have it in our care, we examine it carefully. We come to realize that this is the creature responsible for the shadows we have been observing with interest all these generations. We already know a good bit about it, but now our concept of "eagle" is no longer just a construct. Now we have the thing itself in our sight. And we can *see* just what features of eagles account for the correctness of that shadow science we have constructed. We can say that this creature *explains* the shadows we were familiar with; it *makes it intelligible* that our experience of those shadows was what it was; now we *understand* why those shadows had just the shapes they did have and no others.

We can also say that this great bird is what *produces* these shadows; we now see that the shadows are *caused by* creatures like this; birds of this kind are *responsible for* the existence of those shadows.

So we are attributing two kinds of relations between eagles themselves and their shadows, which we'll call the relations of Making Intelligible and of Producing.

Remember now that our example has been framed entirely within the sphere of the world, what Plato calls "the visible." So we have been discussing what falls only within the A and B portions of the Divided Line. Now we need to apply the relations between A and B to the relations between $A + B$ and $C + D$. In other words, we need now to talk about the relationship between the world and the Forms, between "the visible" and "the intelligible."

Let us return to our example. While we have the eagle in our care, we examine it carefully, take measurements, X rays (imagine that although we know nothing of astronomy, since we never look up, our science is otherwise quite advanced), do behavioral testing, and come to understand the bird quite thoroughly. What do we learn? We learn a lot, of course, about this particular eagle (we have named him "Charlie"). But we are learning not only about Charlie but about the *kind* of creature that produces and makes intelligible the shadows we have long observed. So we are learning about eagles in general. It is true that if we generalize from this one case only, we may make some mistakes. Charlie may in some respects not be a typical eagle, but we can ignore this complication for the moment.

If we are learning about eagles, not just about Charlie, then we could put it this way: we are getting acquainted with what makes an eagle an eagle (as opposed to an owl or an egret). This is very much like, we might reflect, coming to understand what makes pious actions pious. Socrates says that he wants to know not just which actions are pious, you remember, but what it is that makes them pious rather than impious. He wants to understand the Form of the Pious. So we can say that we are coming to know the Form of the Eagle. This Form is what *explains* or *makes intelligible* the fact that this particular bird is an eagle. We might go as far as to say that it is what *makes* Charlie an eagle; his having this Form rather than some other *produces* Charlie-as-eagle. It is what is *responsible* for the fact that Charlie is an eagle.

It may be that Charlie is not a perfect eagle. And further acquaintance with eagles would doubtless improve our understanding of what makes an eagle an eagle, of those characteristics that constitute "eaglehood." If we were to improve our understanding of the Eagle Itself, we might well reach the same conclusion reached about the squares: that *no* visible eagle is a perfect example of the type or Form. Still, any particular eagle must have the defining characteristics of the species; it must "participate" in the Form Eagle, or it wouldn't be an eagle at all. What is this "participation" in a Form? We can now say that it is strictly analogous to the relationship between eagle shadows and actual eagles. Actual eagles "participate" in the Form Eagle in this sense: the Form makes the actual eagle intelligible and accounts for its existence as an eagle. So again there are two kinds of relationships, this time between the Form Eagle and particular eagles: the relationships of Making Intelligible and of Produc-

ing. The relationship on the Divided Line between $A + B$ and $C + D$ is indeed analogous to the relationship between A and B.

We should remind ourselves, too, that Forms have a kind of independence actual eagles lack. Should an ecological tragedy kill all the eagles in the world, the Form Eagle would not be affected. We might never again *see* an eagle, but we could perfectly well still *think about* eagles; we could, for instance, regret their passing and recall what magnificent birds they were.* The *intelligible* has this kind of superiority to the *visible*: it *endures*. And this, Plato would conclude, is a sign that the Form (the object of thought) is *more real* than those things (the objects of sight) that participate in it. And it is a sign that in Forms we have the proper objects of *knowledge*, which must itself endure.

Lower and Higher Forms

Let us return to the Divided Line. We need to note that the section of the Line representing the Forms is itself divided. There are, it seems, two kinds of Forms, just as there are two kinds of things in the visible world (images and the models which they image). We need to understand why Plato thinks so and why he thinks this distinction is important.

> Consider now how the section of the intelligible is to be divided. —How?
> In such a way that in one section the soul, using as images what before were models, is compelled to investigate from hypotheses, proceeding from these not to a first principle but to a conclusion. In the second section which leads to a first principle that is not hypothetical, the soul proceeds from a hypothesis without using the images of the first section, by means of the Forms themselves and proceeding through these. —I do not, he said, quite understand what you mean (R 510a–b).

---

*Those of you familiar with *Star Trek IV: The Voyage Home* may recall that Kirk and Spock in the twenty-third century could still *think about* humpback whales, long after they became extinct.

This is indeed rather difficult, and we cannot blame the listener for his puzzlement. Let us try to make it clear.

At the beginning we had only images (shadows) of eagles. Then we caught Charlie and had a model that accounted for the images. When we went on to develop our understanding of the Form Eagle, we were using Charlie in the same way we had earlier used the shadows. We were, as Plato says, "using as images what before were models." At that point we could see Charlie, but we could not see the Form Eagle. Just as our idea of an actual eagle was a mere *construct* for us before we caught Charlie (we could now call it a *hypothesis*), so the Form Eagle is for us at this point a construct or hypothesis. We posit the Form in order to explain Charlie. Once we have such Forms we can reason from them back to things in the world such as other eagles; we proceed "from these not to a first principle but to a conclusion." The conclusion is about the world. Such forms give us explanations of the things in the world.

While they do give us explanations, Plato adds, they do not give us *complete* explanations. Our hypotheses about eagles will make use of concepts of bone, muscle tissue, and blood. These concepts themselves need explanation. They might be explained in terms of cell structures, protein molecules, and amino acids; and these in terms of atomic structures, protons, neutrons, electrons, and perhaps finally quarks.

Plato doesn't know about any of these latter concepts, but the *structure* he points out is mirrored in these reflections. We do not need to—indeed, Plato would say that we cannot—rest content with hypotheses at the first level of the intelligible. They themselves need to be accounted for at a higher level, until we come at last (he believes) "to a first principle that is not hypothetical." What he has in mind is some principle that does not require explanation by a further principle; it is not "hypothetical"; it is not just *posited* as a supposition; it is something we can *see*. Just as our hypothesis about eagles ceased to be just a hypothesis when we saw Charlie, so a First Principle is one we can just *see* to be true—because of what it is.

The difference between *C* and *D* in the Divided Line is just this: the Forms in *D* make intelligible and produce the Forms in *C* (much as chemical elements make intelligible and produce bones and sinews and blood). If you should ask what it is that makes the highest of these principles—the First Principle—intelligible, you betray that you have not yet gotten the point. This Principle is intelligible *in itself*. It needs only to be seen to be understood.

Plato calls the discipline that constructs the hypothetical Forms at the lower level "science." Science uses the actual things of the world (Charlie, for instance) as its "images," constructing "models" that account for these "images." He calls the discipline that moves from the lower hypothetical Forms to the higher First Principles "dialectic."*

> Understand also that by the other section of the intelligible I mean that which reason itself grasps by the power of dialectic. It does not consider its hypotheses as first principles, but as hypotheses in the true sense of stepping stones and starting points, in order to reach that which is beyond hypothesis, the first principle of all that exists. Having reached this and keeping hold of what follows from it, it does come down to a conclusion without making use of anything visible at all, but proceeding by means of Forms and through Forms to its conclusions which are Forms (*R* 511b–c).

Dialectic, then, is a purely intellectual discipline, no longer relying on the world of sense at all. It is a search for the *ultimate presuppositions* of all our hypothetical explanations and proceeds through awareness of Forms alone. If by such dialectical reasoning we should come to such an ultimate presupposition, we will, Plato assures us, have discovered "the first principle of all that exists."

We obviously need to explore what Plato has to say about this First Principle. But first let us amplify our understanding of the Divided Line by adding some further characterizations.

---

*Note that the term "dialectic" is used in a narrower sense here than that discussed in connection with Socratic question-and-answer method. For a comparison, see p. 62.

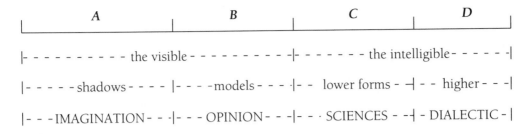

The sciences, even such sciences as geometry and astronomy, are only stages on the way to true and final understanding. They are not yet the place "where a man may find rest from travelling and the end and purpose of his journey" (*R* 532e). The sciences may "grasp reality to a certain extent"; they do that because they concern Forms. But because they do not themselves lead us to a First Principle, they are still

> dreaming about reality, unable to have a waking view of it so long as they make use of hypotheses and leave them undisturbed and cannot give a reasoned account of them (*R* 533b–c).

It is for dialectic to give this "reasoned account." In doing so it is

> doing away with hypotheses and proceeding to the first principle where it will find certainty. It gently draws the eye of the soul, which is really buried in a kind of barbaric mire, and leads it upwards, using the sciences we have described as assistants and helpers in the process of turning the soul around (*R* 533c–d).

We'll return shortly to this image of "turning the soul around." For now we need to note that dialectic, in leading to the First Principle, is supposed also to provide us with *certainty*. This is very important to Plato; indeed, the quest for certainty is a crucial theme in the rest of Western philosophy. Why should Plato suppose that acquaintance with the First Principle will be accompanied by certainty, by "rest from travelling"? Surely because it is no longer merely hypothetical. The truth of the First Principle need no longer be supported by principles beyond itself. It does not cry out for ex-

planation; it does not beckon us on beyond itself. Its truth is evident. To see it—with "the eye of the soul"—is to understand. Here we need no longer anxiously ask, "But is this really true?" Here we know we are not just "dreaming." Here the soul can "rest."

The Form of the Good

The examples we have considered recently—doubling the square, Charlie, and the Forms they participate in—are examples from mathematics and the world of natural science. But we should not forget that there are other Forms as well: Piety, Justice, Beauty, and the Good. We'll soon explore the dialectic involved in the Form of Justice and say at least something about Beauty. But if we want to illuminate Plato's First Principle, it is to the Form of the Good that we shall have to look.

Let us begin by asking why Plato should think of Goodness Itself as that Form to which dialectic will inevitably lead us in the search for the ultimate presupposition. As we consider this, we should remember that in moving higher and higher on the Divided Line we are always gaining clearer, less questionable explanations of *why something is the way it is*.

In the dialogue *Phaedo*, Plato supposedly relates a conversation that Socrates had with his friends on the day of his death. At one point in the conversation Socrates says,

> When I was a young man I was wonderfully keen on that wisdom which they call natural science, for I thought it splendid to know the causes of everything, why it comes to be, why it perishes and why it exists (*Phaedo* 96a).

He relates that he was unable to make much progress toward discovering those causes and became discouraged until hearing one day someone read from a book of Anaxagoras.* Socrates heard that Mind directs and is the cause of everything.

> I was delighted with this cause and it seemed to me good, in a way, that Mind should be the cause of all. I thought that if this were so, the directing Mind would direct everything and arrange each thing in the way that was best. If then one wished to know the cause of each thing, why it comes to be or perishes or exists, one had to find what was the best way for it to be, or to be acted upon, or to act. On these premises then it befitted a man to investigate only, about this and other things, what is best (*Phaedo* 97c–d).

Socrates procured the books of Anaxagoras and read them eagerly. But he was disappointed. For when it came down to cases, Anaxagoras cited as causes the standard elements of Greek nature philosophy—air and water and such.

> That seemed to me much like saying that Socrates' actions are all due to his mind, and then in trying to tell the causes of everything I do, to say that the reason that I am sitting here is because my body consists of bones and sinews, because the bones are hard and are separated by joints, that the sinews are such as to contract and relax, that they surround the bones along with flesh and skin which hold them together, then as the bones are hanging in their sockets, the relaxation and contraction of the sinews enable me to bend my limbs, and that is the cause of my sitting here with my limbs bent (*Phaedo* 98c–d).

Are these facts about his body the true explanation of why Socrates is sitting there in prison? It does not seem to Socrates to even be the right kind of explanation. These considerations do not even mention

> the true causes, that after the Athenians decided it was better to condemn me, for this reason it seemed best to me to sit here and more right to remain and to

endure whatever penalty they ordered. . . . To call these [other] things causes is too absurd. If someone said that without bones and sinews and all such things, I should not be able to do what I decided, he would be right, but surely to say that they are the cause of what I do, and not that I have chosen the best course, even though I act with my mind, is to speak very lazily and carelessly. Imagine not being able to distinguish the real cause from that without which the cause would not be able to act as a cause (*Phaedo* 98d–99b).

Why is Socrates sitting in prison? The true explanation is that the Athenians *decided* it was *better* to condemn him and that Socrates has *decided* that not escaping was for the *best*. The behaviors of the various bodily parts are not irrelevant, but they are not the "real cause." They are just conditions necessary for that real cause to have its effect. We do not get a satisfactory explanation until we reach one that mentions what is *good*; better and best are just the comparative and superlative of the good.

This suggests that explanations in which we can "rest" must be framed in terms of what is good. Since all explanations proceed by citing Forms, the ultimate explanation of everything must be in terms of the Form of the Good. The Form of the Good, then, must play the part of First Principle. In the final analysis, to understand why anything is as it is, we must see that it is so because it participates in this Form.

That is why Plato thinks the Form of the Good is the First Principle. But what is it? To call this First Principle the Form of the Good is not very illuminating. It doesn't tell us any more than Socrates knows about the pious at the beginning of his examination of Euthyphro. Socrates knows that he is looking for the Form of the pious, but he also knows that he doesn't know what that is. In just this sense, we might now ask Plato, "What is this Form which plays such a crucial role? Explain it to us."

At this point Plato disappoints us; he tells us plainly that he cannot give such an explanation.*

---

*A pre-Socratic nature philosopher. You may recall that Socrates mentions him in the speech at his trial: *Apology* 26d.

*Small wonder! There is much debate today on exactly this question, though it is usually not put in terms of Plato's Forms.

He says that "our knowledge of it is inadequate" (*R* 505a). When he is pressed to discuss it, he says, "I fear I shall not be able to do so," but he does agree to describe "what appears to be the offspring of the Good and most like it" (*R* 506d–e). He provides an analogy that illuminates the relationship between this highest of Forms and both the other Forms and the world. But it doesn't give us an "account" of the nature of the Form of the Good itself.

Consider sight, Plato suggests. What makes sight possible? Well, the eyes, for one thing. But eyes alone see nothing; there must also be the various colored objects to be seen. Even this is not enough, for eyes do not see colors in the dark. To eyes and objects we must add light. Where does light come from? From the sun.

> . . . it is the sun which I called the offspring of the Good, which the Good begot as analogous to itself. What the Good itself is in the world of thought in relation to the intelligence and things known, the sun is in the visible world, in relation to sight and things seen. . . .
>
> Say that what gives truth to the objects of knowledge, and to the knowing mind the power to know, is the Form of Good. As it is the cause of knowledge and truth, think of it also as being the object of knowledge. Both knowledge and truth are beautiful, but you will be right to think of the Good as other and more beautiful than they. As in the visible world light and sight are rightly considered sun-like, but it is wrong to think of them as the sun, so here it is right to think of knowledge and truth as Good-like, but wrong to think of either as the Good, for the Good must be honoured even more than they (*R* 508b–509a).

Knowledge, truth, and beauty are all good things. For Plato this means that they participate in the Form of the Good. This Form alone makes it intelligible that there should be such good things. You might ask in wonderment, why is there such a thing as knowledge at all? What accounts for that? If Plato is right here, you will not find a satisfactory answer to your question until you discover why it is for the best that knowledge should exist; and discovering that is equivalent to seeing its participation in the Form of Goodness Itself.

However, although knowledge is a good thing, Plato cautions us that it must not be thought of as identical with Goodness. It is no more identical with Goodness than Charlie is identical with the Form Eagle. That Form explains Charlie, but, as we saw, it has an existence quite independent of Charlie. The Form of the Good surpasses all the other Forms as well as the visible world in beauty and honor. If we think again about the Divided Line, we can now say that the Form of the Good is at the point farthest to the right of that Line, at the very end of section *D*. It makes intelligible everything to the left of it.

This ultimate Form not only makes everything else intelligible, it also is responsible for the very existence of everything else.

> You will say, I think, that the sun not only gives to the objects of sight the capacity to be seen, but also that it provides for their generation, increase, and nurture, though it is not itself the process of generation.   —How could it be?
>
> And say that as for the objects of knowledge, not only is their being known due to the Good, but also their being reality, though the Good is not being but superior to and beyond being in dignity and power (*R* 509b).

Just as the sun is responsible for the world of sight, is actually its cause, so the Form of the Good is the cause of the reality of everything else. Here we see that the two relations of Making Intelligible and of Producing are both applied to the relationship between the Form of the Good and everything else that is. To emphasize the uniqueness of this Form, Plato goes so far as to say that it is "beyond being." Since we usually understand what is beyond being to be *nothing at all*, this is a dark saying. And Plato does not do much to make it clear.*

Let us pause and see what Plato claims to have accomplished. He has proved, he believes, that we do have knowledge; so, wholesale skepticism is a

---

*It is as if the Form of the Good were not the point farthest to the right on the Divided Line but were pushed right off the end. Plato seems to be saying that this Form is strictly incomparable to everything else, both other Forms and the world. Yet it is responsible for them all. Later Christian thinkers took this as an "anticipation" of the Judeo-Christian concepts of God and creation. See, for instance, St. Augustine, pp. 223–225. For a different understanding of the idea of "beyond being," see Martin Heidegger, p. 575.

mistake. This knowledge is not dependent on what individuals or cultures happen to think; so, relativism is a mistake. Moreover, knowledge must have objects that endure; so, this knowledge must be of realities other than those in the world. So, there are Forms, whose being is eternal and unchanging. Knowledge of these Forms enables us to understand not only them and their relations to each other but also the things in the world, which owe their being and characteristics to participation in these Forms. And supreme among the Forms is that of Goodness. Therefore, atomism is a mistake.

But how does it follow that atomism is a mistake? Recall the central claim of the atomists: What exists is made up of atoms and the void. Nothing else. Plato, however, thinks he has proved that there are Forms, indeed, that these are the most real things of all. And Forms are radically different from atoms, since each atom is a tiny particular thing and a Form can be shared by many particulars.

Moreover, Democritus holds that events happen necessarily, mechanically, according to how the atoms happen to combine and fall apart again. No purpose, no goal, no direction toward the best can be discerned in the world.* But Plato thinks he has given us reason to believe that a complete explanation must be like the one given by Socrates in prison; it will have to explain why what happens is for the best and so will involve the Form of the Good. Science, pursued to its basic presuppositions, reveals a world with a moral and religious dimension.

It follows that reality is not, as Democritus thinks, indifferent to values; a kind of piety toward reality is quite in order. Democritus would overthrow the traditional religion altogether. Plato is no happier than his philosophical predecessors with the Homeric picture of the gods; *belief* in such gods was insupportable. Yet religious *attitudes* could be preserved. We shall soon see how Plato's metaphysical viewpoint—that values are realities, too—affects what he says about practical matters such as justice and the good state. But first we need to conclude this part of our consideration with his most famous story, the Myth of the Cave.

*See p. 29.

The Love of Wisdom

What Wisdom Is

There is a progress in the soul that corresponds to the degrees of reality in things. This idea is indicated in the various divisions of the Divided Line. Contemplating the images of worldly things is analogous to the use of *imagination*; indeed, mental images are quite like shadows and mirror images in their dependence on things. About the things and events of the world we can have *probable beliefs* or *opinions*. When we reason about them we are involved in the Forms, considered as hypothetical; here is the domain of *science*. Finally, we reach *understanding* through the process of dialectic, which takes us upward to the highest Forms on which all the others depend.

We can think of this progress as progress toward wisdom. A wise person would understand everything in the light of the Forms, particularly the Form of the Good. To produce such wise individuals is the aim of education. The progress toward wisdom is illustrated for us in a dramatic myth told in the seventh book of the *Republic*. As you read it, keep the Divided Line and the analogy of the sun in mind. You will also see that Plato is thinking of his master, Socrates.

> Next, I said, compare the effect of education and the lack of it upon our human nature to a situation like this: imagine men to be living in an underground cave-like dwelling place, which has a way up to the light along its whole width, but the entrance is a long way up. The men have been there from childhood, with their neck and legs in fetters, so that they remain in the same place and can only see ahead of them, as their bonds prevent them from turning their heads. Light is provided by a fire burning some way behind and above them. Between the fire and the prisoners, some way behind them and on a higher ground, there is a path across the cave and along this a low wall has been built, like the screen at a puppet show in front of the performers who show their puppets above it.   —I see it.
>
> See then also men carrying along that wall, so that they overtop it, all kinds of artifacts, statues of

men, reproductions of other animals in stone or wood fashioned in all sorts of ways, and, as is likely, some of the carriers are talking while others are silent. —This is a strange picture, and strange prisoners.

They are like us, I said. Do you think, in the first place, that such men could see anything of themselves and each other except the shadows which the fire casts upon the wall of the cave in front of them. —How could they, if they have to keep their heads still throughout life?

And is not the same true of the objects carried along the wall? —Quite.

If they could converse with one another, do you not think that they would consider these shadows to be the real things? —Necessarily.

What if their prison had an echo which reached them from in front of them? Whenever one of the carriers passing behind the wall spoke, would they not think it was the shadow passing in front of them which was talking? Do you agree? —By Zeus I do.

Altogether then, I said, such men would believe the truth to be nothing else than the shadows of the artifacts? —They must believe that.

Consider then what deliverance from their bonds and the curing of their ignorance would be if something like this naturally happened to them. Whenever one of them was freed, had to stand up suddenly, turn his head, walk, and look up toward the light, doing all that would give him pain, the flash of the fire would make it impossible for him to see the objects of which he had earlier seen the shadows. What do you think he would say if he was told that what he saw then was foolishness, that he was now somewhat closer to reality and turned to things that existed more fully, that he saw more correctly? If one then pointed to each of the objects passing by, asked him what each was, and forced him to answer, do you not think he would be at a loss and believe that the things which he saw earlier were truer than the things now pointed out to him? —Much truer.

If one then compelled him to look at the fire itself, his eyes would hurt, he would turn round and flee toward those things which he could see, and think that they were in fact clearer than those now shown to him. —Quite so.

And if one were to drag him thence by force up the rough and steep path, and did not let him go before he was dragged into the sunlight, would he not be in physical pain and angry as he was dragged along? When he came into the light, with the sunlight filling his eyes, he would not be able to see a single one of the things which are now said to be true. —Not at once, certainly.

I think he would need time to get adjusted before he could see things in the world above; at first he would see shadows most easily, then reflections of men and other things in water, then the things themselves. After this he would see objects in the sky and the sky itself more easily at night, the light of the stars and the moon more easily than the sun and the light of the sun during the day. —Of course.

Then at last, he would be able to see the sun, not images of it in water or in some alien place, but the sun itself in its own place, and be able to contemplate it. —That must be so.

After this he would reflect that it is the sun which provides the seasons and the years, which governs everything in the visible world, and is also in some way the cause of those other things which he used to see. —Clearly that would be the next stage.

What then? As he reminds himself of his first dwelling place, of the wisdom there and of his fellow prisoners, would he not reckon himself happy for the change, and pity them? —Surely.

And if the men below had praise and honours from each other, and prizes for the man who saw most clearly the shadows that passed before them, and who could best remember which usually came earlier and which later, and which came together and thus could most ably prophesy the future, do you think our man would desire those rewards and envy those who were honoured and held power among the prisoners, or would he feel, as Homer put it, that he certainly wished to be "serf to another man without possessions upon the earth" and go through any suffering rather than share their opinions and live as they do? —Quite so, he said, I think he would rather suffer anything.

Reflect on this too, I said. If this man went down into the cave again and sat down in the same seat, would his eyes not be filled with darkness, coming suddenly out of the sunlight? —They certainly would.

And if he had to contend again with those who had remained prisoners in recognizing those shadows while his sight was affected and his eyes had not settled down—and the time for this adjustment would not be short—would he not be ridiculed? Would it not be said that he had returned from his upward journey with his eyesight spoiled, and that it was not worthwhile even to attempt to travel upward? As for the man who tried to free them and lead them upward, if they could somehow lay their hands on him and kill him, they would do so.   —They certainly would (R 514a–517a).

To love wisdom is to be motivated to leave the Cave. At each stage, Plato emphasizes how difficult, even painful, the struggle for enlightenment is. It is much easier, much more comfortable, to remain a prisoner in relative darkness and occupy oneself with what are, in reality, only shadows.

The myth gives us an interesting picture of education. Plato draws the consequences explicitly.

We must then, I said, if these things are true, think something like this about them, namely that education is not what some declare it to be; they say that knowledge is not present in the soul and that they put it in, like putting sight into blind eyes.   —They surely say that.

Our present argument shows, I said, that the capacity to learn and the organ with which to do so are present in every person's soul. It is as if it were not possible to turn the eye from darkness to light without turning the whole body; so one must turn one's whole soul from the world of becoming until it can endure to contemplate reality, and the brightest of realities, which we say is the Good.   —Yes.

Education then is the art of doing this very thing, this turning around, the knowledge of how the soul can most easily and most effectively be turned around; it is not the art of putting the capacity of sight into the soul; the soul possesses that already but it is not turned the right way or looking where it should. This is what education has to deal with.   —That seems likely (R 518b–d).

We should be reminded here of Socrates and the slave boy. The capacity to understand is already there. All Socrates needs to do is point the boy in the right direction, and that he does with his questions. Education is not stuffing the mind with facts, Plato tells us, but turning the soul to face reality, trusting that the student will recognize the truth when confronted by it. Recall Socrates' claim that

he has never *taught* anyone anything.* Here is a whole philosophy of education in a nutshell.

This "turning of the soul" is not easy to do. The prisoners in the cave are quite convinced that the shadows they see are the most real of things and are not happy to be told that they suffer from an illusion. Wisdom can be resisted.

Have you never noticed in men who are said to be wicked but clever, how sharply their little soul looks into things to which it turns its attention? Its capacity for sight is not inferior, but it is compelled to serve evil ends, so that the more sharply it looks the more evil it works.   —Quite so.

Yet if a soul of this kind had been hammered at from childhood and those excrescences had been knocked off it which belong to the world of becoming and have been fastened upon it by feasting, gluttony, and similar pleasures, and which like leaden weights draw the soul to look downward—if, being rid of these, it turned to look at things that are true, then the same soul of the same man would see these just as sharply as it now sees the things towards which it is directed.   —That seems likely (R 519a–b).

If we can resist wisdom and be comfortable in the cave enjoying the pleasures of feasting, drinking, and so on, what motivation is there to engage in a struggle that Plato insists is both difficult and dangerous? Why should we not simply spend our lives pursuing the pleasures that are available to us in the world? What reason has an educator to think that he could be at all successful in turning the souls of others toward reality and truth? We need now to talk not just of what wisdom is, but of the *love* of wisdom.

Love and Wisdom

The theme of Plato's dialogue *Symposium*, from which Alcibiades' tribute to the character of Socrates was taken,† is love. After dinner each guest is

---

*See *Apology* 33b and Chapter 9, pp. 97–98.
†Review pp. 59–60.

obliged to make a speech in praise of love. When Socrates' turn comes, he protests that he cannot make such a flattering speech as the others have made, but he can, if they like, tell the truth about love.* They urge him to do so.

Socrates claims to have learned about love from a wise woman named Diotima, who instructed him by the same question-and-answer method he now uses on others.† I'll abbreviate the speech in which Socrates relates her instruction, keeping the question-and-answer mode. This very rich discussion of love is found in *Symposium* 198a–212b.

Q: Is love the love of something or not?

A: Of something.

Q: Does love long for what it loves?

A: Certainly.

Q: Is this something that love has, or something love lacks?

A: It must be what love lacks, for no one longs for what he or she has.

Q: What does love love?

A: Beauty.

Q: Then love must lack beauty?

A: Apparently so.

Q: Is love ugly, then?

A: Not necessarily. For just as opinion is a middle term between ignorance and knowledge, so love may be between beauty and ugliness.

Q: Is love a god?

A: No. For the gods lack nothing in the way of beauty or happiness. For that reason, the gods do not love beauty or happiness either. Nor do the gods love wisdom, for they are wise and do not lack it.

Q: What is love, then?

A: Midway between mortals and the gods, love is a spirit that connects the earthly and the heavenly. [Think of the world and the Forms.]

Q: What is the origin of love?

A: Love is the child of Need and Resource (the son of Craft). It is a combination of longing for what one does not have and resourcefulness in seeking it.

Q: But what, more exactly, is it that love seeks?

A: Love seeks the beautiful. And the good.

Q: To what end?

A: To make them its own.

Q: And what will the lover gain by making the beautiful and the good his own?

A: Happiness.

Q: Does everyone seek happiness?

A: Of course.

Q: Then is everyone always in love?

A: Yes and no. We tend to give the name of love to only one sort of love. Actually, love "includes every kind of longing for happiness and the good." So those who long for the good in every field—business, athletics, philosophy—are also lovers.

Q: For how long does a lover want to possess that good that he or she longs for?

A: Certainly not for a limited time only. To think so would be equivalent to wanting to be happy for only a short time. So the lover must want the good to be his or hers forever.

Q: How could a mortal attain this?

A: By becoming immortal.

Q: So a mortal creature does all it can "to put on immortality"?

A: Evidently.

Q: Could this be why lovers are interested not just in beauty but in procreation by the means of such beauty?

A: Yes. It is by breeding another individual as like itself as possible that mortal creatures like animals and humans attain as much of immortality as is possible for them. Such a creature "cannot,

---

*This should remind you of the contrast Socrates draws between rhetoric and his own plain speaking at the very beginning of the *Apology*. About love, it must be noted that the Greeks had distinct words for several different kinds of love; in this their language was more discriminating than ours. The kind of love Socrates is here discussing is *eros*, from which our term "erotic" is drawn.
†See again the footnote on p. 62.

like the divine, be still the same throughout eternity; it can only leave behind new life to fill the vacancy that is left in its species by obsolescence."

Q: Is there any other way to approach immortality?

A: Yes, by attaining the "endless fame" that heroes and great benefactors of humankind attain. Think, for example, of Akhilleus and Homer and Solon.

Q: So some lovers beget children and raise a family, and others "bear things of the spirit . . . wisdom and all her sister virtues," especially those relevant to "the ordering of society, . . . justice and moderation"?

A: Yes. And the latter will especially be concerned to share these goods with friends and, with them, to educate each other in wisdom.

Q: Is there a natural progression of love?

A: Yes.

At this point, we need to hear Plato's words themselves. Diotima is speaking as if someone were to be initiated into a cult devoted to love.

Well then, she began, the candidate for this initiation cannot, if his efforts are to be rewarded, begin too early to devote himself to the beauties of the body. First of all, if his preceptor instructs him as he should, he will fall in love with the beauty of one individual body, so that his passion may give life to noble discourse. Next he must consider how nearly related the beauty of any one body is to the beauty of any other, when he will see that if he is to devote himself to loveliness of form it will be absurd to deny that the beauty of each and every body is the same. Having reached this point, he must set himself to be the lover of every lovely body, and bring his passion for the one into due proportion by deeming it of little or of no importance.

Next he must grasp that the beauties of the body are as nothing to the beauties of the soul, so that wherever he meets with spiritual loveliness, even in the husk of an unlovely body, he will find it beautiful enough to fall in love with and to cherish—and beautiful enough to quicken in his heart a longing for such discourse as tends toward the building of a noble nature. And from this he will be led to contemplate the beauty of laws and institutions. And when

he discovers how nearly every kind of beauty is akin to every other he will conclude that the beauty of the body is not, after all, of so great moment.

And next, his attention should be diverted from institutions to the sciences, so that he may know the beauty of every kind of knowledge. . . . And, turning his eyes toward the open sea of beauty, he will find in such contemplation the seed of the most fruitful discourse and the loftiest thought, and reap a golden harvest of philosophy, until, confirmed and strengthened, he will come upon one single form of knowledge, the knowledge of the beauty I am about to speak of.

And here, she said, you must follow me as closely as you can.

Whoever has been initiated so far in the mysteries of Love and has viewed all these aspects of the beautiful in due succession, is at last drawing near the final revelation. And now, Socrates, there bursts upon him that wondrous vision which is the very soul of the beauty he has toiled so long for. It is an everlasting loveliness which neither comes nor goes, which neither flowers nor fades, for such beauty is the same on every hand, the same then as now, here as there, this way as that way, the same to every worshiper as it is to every other.

Nor will his vision of the beautiful take the form of a face, or of hands, or of anything that is of the flesh. It will be neither words nor knowledge, nor a something that exists in something else, such as a living creature, or the earth, or the heavens, or anything that is—but subsisting of itself and by itself in an eternal oneness, while every lovely thing partakes of it in such sort that however much the parts may wax and wane, it will be neither more nor less, but still the same inviolable whole (*Symposium* 210a–211b).

These are the steps, Plato tells us, that love involves. It is important to recognize that he sees these as making up a natural progression; there is nothing arbitrary about this series. In discussing these stages, let us call someone who is in love a "lover," remembering all the while that one can love in ways other than sexual. A lover, then, is someone who lacks that which will make him or her happy. What will make the lover happy is to possess the beautiful and the good—forever. For that the lover longs, yearns. And the lover is resourceful in seeking what he or she lacks. It is this resourcefulness, propelled by longing, that moves the lover up the ladder of love. At each stage the lover is only partially satisfied and is therefore powerfully motivated to discover whether there might be something still more satisfying.

Being in the world, the lover naturally begins in the world. His or her first object is some beautiful body. But if the lover is resourceful, he or she will soon discover that the beauty in this body is not unique to that individual. It is shared by every beautiful body. What shall the lover do then? Although Plato does not say so explicitly, we might conjecture that at this point it is easy for the lover to go wrong by trying to possess each of these bodies in the same way as he or she longed to possess the first one—like Don Juan. We might think of it like this. Don Juan (with 1003 conquests in Spain alone) has moved beyond the first stage of devotion to just one lovely body. He now tries to devote to *each* the same love that he devoted to the one. This is bound to be unsatisfying; if a single one does not satisfy, there is no reason to think that many ones will satisfy.

How does Plato describe the correct step at this point? The lover of "every lovely body" must "bring his passion for the one into due proportion by deeming it of little or of no importance." Rather than trying to multiply the same passion many times, the discovery of beauty in many bodies must occasion what we might call a "sublimation" of the original passion. It must be transferred to a more appropriate *kind* of object. Indeed, it is at this point that the lover first becomes dimly aware of the Form of Beauty.* The resourcefulness of love makes it clear that only this sort of object is going to satisfy; only this sort of object *endures*.

The lover, moreover, discovers that a beautiful soul is even more lovely than a beautiful body, finding it so much more satisfying that he or she will "fall in love with" and "cherish" a beautiful soul even though it is found "in the husk of an unlovely body." (Could Plato here be thinking of the physical ugliness of Socrates?) The lover will, in fact, come to love *all* beautiful souls.

The next step is to "contemplate the beauty of laws and institutions." Presumably the transition from lovely individual souls to a pleasing social order is a small one. The harmony, moderation, and justice that make for individual beauty of soul are the same virtues that make for a beautiful society. But it is one more step away from the original passion for possession of an individual beautiful body; when this stage is reached, the lover "concludes that beauty of the body is not, after all, of so great moment."

Once in the sphere of "spiritual loveliness," the lover comes to long for knowledge. Plato speaks movingly here of "the beauty of every kind of knowledge," and supposes that the lover—not yet satisfied—will explore all the sciences. Here the lover will find an "open sea of beauty," in contemplation of which he or she will be able to bring forth "the most fruitful discourse and the loftiest thought, and reap a golden harvest of philosophy."

But even this is not the last stage. And we must note that Diotima cautions Socrates at this point to "follow . . . as closely as you can." The final stage, then, must be difficult to grasp and appreciate. Indeed, those who have not attained it might well be unable to appreciate it fully. It is, in fact, a kind of mystical vision of the Form of Beauty Itself.* Note the rapturously emotional language Plato uses here. There can be little doubt that he is describing an experience that he himself had, one to which he ascribes a supreme value.

It is called a "wondrous vision," an "everlasting loveliness which neither comes nor goes, which neither flowers nor fades." Like all the Forms, the Form of Beauty is eternal. The object of this vision is not any individual thing; it is not a face, not hands, not "anything that is of the flesh." Nor is it "words" or "knowledge." It is nothing human or

---

*Recall the doctrine of learning by recollection (pp. 97–98). The beautiful individual is the "occasion" for recollecting what the soul previously knew, Beauty Itself. Only by a prior acquaintance with this Form can the lover recognize the beloved as beautiful.

*The language Plato uses to describe this experience is remarkably similar to the language of Christian mystics describing the "beatific vision" of God.

worldly. But it subsists "of itself and by itself in an eternal oneness, while every lovely thing partakes of it." The religious character of the vision is indicated by the term "worshiper," which Plato applies to the lover who attains this "final revelation."

We began this discussion of love in order to find an answer to a question. Why, we wondered, would anyone be motivated to leave the Cave and make the difficult ascent to the sunlight, leaving behind the easy pleasures of worldly life? We now have Plato's answer. It is because we are all lovers.* We all want to be happy, to possess the beautiful and the good, forever. This is what we lack and long for. And to the extent of our resourcefulness and cleverness, we will come to see that this passion cannot be satisfied by the possession of one beautiful body or even of many. We will be drawn out of the Cave toward the sun, toward the beautiful and the good in themselves, by the very nature of love. Plato is convinced that there is within each of us already a motivation that, if followed, will lead us beyond shadows to the Forms. The educator does not need to implant that in us; it is already there. All the educator needs to do is point us in the right direction.

Wisdom, which for Plato is equivalent to seeing everything in the light of the Forms, particularly in the light of the highest Forms of Beauty and Goodness, is something we all need, lack, and want. Wisdom alone will satisfy. Only wisdom, where the soul actually participates in the eternality of the Forms, will in the end bring us as close to immortality as mortals can possibly get.

But this conclusion is not yet quite accurate. As stated, it assumes the Homeric picture of human beings as mortal through and through.† This was not Plato's considered view. And we need now to enquire into his theory of the soul.

The Soul

The Immortality of the Soul

Plato thought about his central problems throughout a long life. And it is apparent, particularly in his doctrine of the soul, that his thought was not full-blown at its first appearance but developed complexities unimagined at the beginning. Scholars dispute whether this development involves some inconsistency, whether his later thought is in conflict with the earlier. Some say yes, some say no. There is no doubt that there is at least a tension between the earlier and the later views of the soul. In this introductory treatment I will ignore these problems, presenting a picture of the soul that will be oversimplified and less than complete but true in essentials to Plato's views on the subject.[6]

At the end of his defense to the jury, Socrates, because his divine sign does not oppose him, concludes that "there is good hope that death is a blessing." He thinks one of two things must be true: either death is a dreamless sleep, or we survive the death of the body and can converse with those who died before. But he does not try to decide between them.*

In various dialogues, Plato offers a number of arguments to demonstrate that the latter is the true possibility—that the soul is immortal. We find such an argument in the story of Socrates and the slave boy.† According to Socrates, the boy is able to recognize the truth when it is before him because he is remembering or recollecting what he was earlier acquainted with. But if that is so, then he—or rather his soul—must have existed before he was born, and in such a state that he was familiar with the Forms. Similarly, in judging two things to be *equal* we are using a concept that we could not have gained from experience, for no two worldly things are ever exactly equal. Plato concludes that

*Actually, this is not quite Plato's view. He thinks there are distinctly different sorts of people, and only some of them are lovers of wisdom. But I take here the more democratic view and give you all the benefit of the doubt!
†You might like to look back to the discussion of this Homeric view on p. 5.

*See *Apology* 40a–41c.
†In *Meno* 82b–86b, discussed on pp. 97–98.

before we began to see or hear or otherwise perceive, we must have possessed knowledge of the Equal itself if we were about to refer our sense perception of equal objects to it, and realized that all of them were eager to be like it, but were inferior (*Phaedo* 75b).

If we had knowledge of the Equal "before we began to see or hear or otherwise perceive," then we must have been acquainted with this Form before our birth.

We may have doubts about the adequacy of this argument for the preexistence of the soul; if we could give another explanation of how we come to know the truth or of how we develop ideal concepts like "equal," it might be seriously undermined. But even if it were a sound argument, it would not yet prove that the soul is immortal. For even if our souls do antedate the beginnings of our bodies, it is still possible that they dissipate when our bodies do (or some time after). In that case, the soul would still be mortal.

Plato considers this possibility, but he has other arguments. Recall Socrates in his prison cell. Why is he there? As we have seen, it is not because his body has made certain movements rather than others. At least, this is a very superficial explanation. Socrates is still in prison because he has thought the matter through (with Crito) and as a result has decided not to escape.

Now Plato contrasts two kinds of things: those that move only when something else moves them and those that move themselves. To which class does the body belong? It must, Plato argues, belong to the first class; for a corpse is a body, but it doesn't move itself. When does *your* body move? It can move (in the same manner a corpse moves) when someone carries you somewhere. But it can also move if *you* move it. The difference between living and nonliving bodies is that the former possess a principle of activity and motion within themselves. Such a principle of energy, capable of *self-motion* is exactly what we call a soul.

Any body that has an external source of motion is soulless, but a body deriving its motion from a source within itself is animate or besouled (*Phaedrus* 245e).

So a soul is essentially a self-mover, a source of activity and motion. It is because Socrates is "besouled," capable of moving himself, that he remains in prison. No explanation that does not involve Socrates' soul can be adequate. Therefore, his remaining in prison cannot be explained by talking only about his body, for the body is moved only by something other than itself.

It is precisely because the body is not a self-mover that it can die. The body must be moved either by a soul or by some other body. But if the soul is a self-mover, if it is inherently a source of energy and life, if it does not depend on something outside itself to galvanize it into action—then the soul cannot die.

All soul is immortal, for that which is ever in motion is immortal. But that which while imparting motion is itself moved by something else can cease to be in motion, and therefore can cease to live; it is only that which moves itself that never intermits its motion, inasmuch as it cannot abandon its own nature; moreover this self-mover is the source and first principle of motion for all other things that are moved (*Phaedrus* 245c).

We might say that life is the very essence of the soul. And it is immortal because "it cannot abandon its own nature." It cannot die.

There are other arguments for this conclusion, but let us be content with these.

If the soul is an entity or a source of energy distinct from the body, if it survives the body's decay, and if the soul is somehow the *essential self*, then Socrates was right in not being dismayed at death. But Plato goes further. It must be the task of those who love wisdom to *maximize* this separation of soul from body even in this life. It is not through the capacities of the body, as we have seen, that we can come to know the reality of the Forms. The body confuses and distracts us. Only the intellect, through reason, can lead us through the sciences, via dialectic, to our goal: the Beautiful and the Good. And these are the capacities of the soul.

It follows that it should be the aim of those who seek to be wise to separate the soul as far as possible from the body and accustom it to gather itself and collect itself out of every part of the body and to dwell by itself as far as it can both now and in the future, freed, as it were, from the bonds of the body (*Phaedo* 67c–d).

Moreover, the pursuit of philosophy, which is the practice of the love of wisdom, leads to the desire to "free the soul," to release it from its bondage to the body. But if the separation of the soul from the body in actual fact is death, it follows that

those who practise philosophy in the right way are in training for dying and they fear death least of all men (*Phaedo* 67e).

If we understand by "the world" what we indicated above, then it is accurate to say that Plato's philosophy contains a drive toward otherworldliness. Our true home is not in this world but in another. The love of wisdom, as he understands it, propels us out and away from the visible, the changeable, the bodily—out and away from the world. The most extreme expression of this drive is the assertion that philosophy, the love of wisdom, is a "training for dying." It is true that one who has climbed out of the Cave into the sunlight of the Forms may return to the darkness below, but only for the purpose of encouraging others to make that turn which will allow them to see the eternal realities.

Yet this is not a philosophy of pure escape from the world. The otherworldly tendency is balanced by an emphasis on the practical, this-worldly usefulness of acquaintance with the Forms. But in order to see this practical side of Plato at work, we must talk about the internal structure of the soul.

The Structure of the Soul

When a subject is both difficult and important, Plato often constructs a myth. The Myth of the Sun presented the Form of the Good. The struggle toward wisdom is the subject of the Myth of the Cave. And to help us comprehend the soul, Plato tells The Myth of the Charioteer.*

As to soul's immortality then we have said enough, but as to its nature there is this that must be said. What manner of thing it is would be a long tale to tell, and most assuredly a god alone could tell it, but what it resembles, that a man might tell in briefer compass. Let this therefore be our manner of discourse. Let it be likened to the union of powers in a team of winged steeds and their winged charioteer. Now all the gods' steeds and all their charioteers are good, and of good stock, but with other beings it is not wholly so. With us men, in the first place, it is a pair of steeds that the charioteer controls; moreover, one of them is noble and good, and of good stock, while the other has the opposite character, and his stock is opposite. Hence the task of our charioteer is difficult and troublesome (*Phaedrus* 246a–b).

Now of the steeds, so we declare, one is good and the other is not, but we have not described the excellence of the one nor the badness of the other, and that is what must now be done. He that is on the more honorable side is upright and clean-limbed, carrying his neck high, with something of a hooked nose; in color he is white, with black eyes; a lover of glory, but with temperance and modesty; one that consorts with genuine renown, and needs no whip, being driven by the word of command alone. The other is crooked of frame, a massive jumble of a creature, with thick short neck, snub nose, black skin, and gray eyes; hot-blooded, consorting with wantonness and vainglory; shaggy of ear, deaf, and hard to control with whip and goad (*Phaedrus* 253d–e).

We are presented with a picture of a soul in three parts, two of which contribute to the motion or activity of the whole and one whose function is to guide the ensemble. The soul is not only internally complex, however; it is beset by internal conflict. The two horses are of very different sorts and struggle against each other to determine the direction the soul is to go. For this reason, "the task of the charioteer is difficult and troublesome."

---

*The image Plato uses here may well have been suggested by chariot racing in the Olympic games.

In the *Republic*, Plato tells a story to illustrate one type of possible conflict in the soul.

> I have, I said, heard a story which I believe, that Leontius, the son of Aglaion, as he came up from the Piraeus on the outside of the northern wall, saw the executioner with some corpses lying near him. Leontius felt a strong desire to look at them, but at the same time he was disgusted and turned away. For a time he struggled with himself and covered his face, but then, overcome by his desire, pushing his eyes wide open and rushing toward the corpses: "Look for yourselves," he said, "you evil things, get your fill of the beautiful sight!" —I've heard that story myself.
>
> It certainly proves, I said, that anger sometimes wars against the appetites as one thing against another. —It does (*R* 439e–440a).

This story also gives us a clue to further identification of the two horses in the Myth of the Charioteer. The black, unruly and hot-blooded steed is desire, or appetite. Leontius *wants* to look at the corpses. Though he struggles against it, he is finally "overcome by his desire."

This desire is opposed by what Plato calls the "spirited" part of the soul, which corresponds to the white horse. When we call someone "animated" (in the sense this has in ordinary speech), we are calling attention to the predominance of "spirit" in that person. Children "are full of spirit from birth," Plato tells us. Spirit is what makes people become angry at wrongs and fight injustice; it is what drives the athlete to victory and the soldier to battle. It is, Plato tells us, "by nature the helper of reason, if it has not been corrupted by a bad upbringing" (*R* 440e–441a).

The two horses, then, represent desire and spirit. What of the charioteer? Remember that the function of the charioteer is to guide the soul. What else could perform this guiding function, from Plato's point of view, than the rational part of the soul? Think of a desperately thirsty man in the desert. He sees a pool of water and approaches it with all the eagerness that deprivation is able to create. But when he reaches the pool, he sees a sign: "Danger: Do not drink. Polluted." He experiences conflict within. His *desire* urges him to drink. But *reason* tells him that such signs usually indicate the truth, that polluted water will make him very ill and may kill him, and that if he drinks he will probably be worse off than if he doesn't. He decides not to drink. In this case, it is the rational part of him that opposes his desire. His reason guides him away from the water and tries to enlist the help of spirit to make that decision effective.

Desire, spirit, and reason, then, make up the soul. Desire *motivates*, spirit *animates*, and reason *guides*. In the gods, these parts are in perfect harmony. The charioteer in a god's soul has no difficulty in guiding the chariot. In humans, though, there is often conflict, and the job of the rational charioteer is hard.*

Plato supposes that any one of these parts may be dominant in a given person. This allows for a rough division of people into three sorts, according to what people take pleasure in.

> One part, we say, is that by which a man learns; the second is that with which he gets angry; as for the third part, . . . we . . . have called it the appetitive part because of the violence of the appetites for food, drink, sex, and other things which follow from these. We have also called it the money-loving part because such appetites are most easily satisfied by means of money. . . .
>
> Of these three, one rules in the soul of one man, I said, another in another's, whichever it happens to be. —That is so.
>
> That is why we say that there are three primary kinds of men, the philosophic, the lover of victory, and the lover of profit. —There certainly are (*R* 580c–581c).

Plato uses the idea of three kinds of men in his plan for an ideal state, as we'll see.† But first we need to examine his views on how the various parts of the soul *should* be related. This will allow us to see the practical use to which Plato thought the Forms could be put.

---

*There is a saying by Democritus, the atomist: "It is hard to fight with desire; but to overcome it is the mark of a rational man."
†See "The State," later in this chapter.

Justice

Plato believes that he has met the challenge of skepticism. We do have knowledge; knowing how to double the square is only one example of innumerable other things we either know or can come to know. Relativism is also a mistake, he thinks; for the objects of such knowledge are public and available to the intellect of all. It is by introducing the Forms that he has solved these problems. They are the public, enduring objects about which we can learn through reasoning and instruction. They are the realities that account for and make intelligible all else and give even the fluctuating things of the world such stability as they do have.

We might not be satisfied yet, however. We might say, "That's all very well in the sphere of geometry and the like, but what about ethics and politics? Is there knowledge here, too?" And we might remind Plato of that passage where Socrates reminds Euthyphro that even the gods dispute with each other—not about numbers, lengths, and weights, but about "the just and the unjust, the beautiful and the ugly, the good and the bad" (*Euthyphro* 7d). If we are to meet the challenge of skepticism and relativism, we must do it in this sphere, too. Can we *know*, for instance, that justice is good rather than bad? Are there public objects in this sphere, too, about which rational persons can come to agreement? Or, in this aspect of human life, is custom "king of all"?* Is it true here, as the Sophists argue, that *nomos* rules entirely, that justice, for example, is merely conventional? Unless this challenge can be met, Plato has not succeeded. Skepticism and relativism, ruled out of the theoretical sphere, will reappear with renewed vigor in our practical life. And Plato will neither be able to *prove* that Athens was wrong to have executed Socrates nor be convincing about the structure of a good state.

Justice seems to be a fundamental virtue for a community. And Plato makes the problem of justice one of the main themes in the *Republic*. He is asking the Socratic question: What is justice? For Plato, this is equivalent to asking about the Form of Justice. The particular question is this: Is the Form of Justice related to the Form of the Good? And if so, how? Or, to put it in more familiar terms, is justice something good or not?

As we have seen, Antiphon argues that conventional justice, which forbids deception, stealing, and breaking contracts, may not be in the interest of the individual. And when it is not to his advantage, there is nothing wrong with violating the conventional rules, following the law of self-preservation, and being (in the conventional sense) unjust. If you can deceive someone and get away with it when it is to your advantage, that is what you should do.

In the *Republic*, Plato presents another Sophist, Thrasymachus, arguing the same case. Since, he claims, the rules of justice are purely conventional and are made by those with the power to make them, it will seldom be to the advantage of an individual to be just.* In fact, for most of us

> the just is really another's good, the advantage of the stronger and the ruler, but for the inferior who obeys it is a personal injury. . . .
>
> The just is everywhere at a disadvantage compared with the unjust. First, in their contracts with one another: whenever two such men are associated you will never find, when the partnership ends, the just man to have more than the unjust, but less. Then in their relation to the city: when taxes are to be paid, from the same income the just man pays more, the other less; but when benefits are to be received, the one gets nothing while the other profits much; whenever each of them holds a public office, the just man, even if he is not penalized in other ways, finds that his private affairs deteriorate through neglect while he gets nothing from the public purse because he is

---

*Quoted by Herodotus from Pindar, after he tells the story of the Greeks and Indians before Darius (p. 42). Review the *nomos/physis* controversy that follows.

*This principle is sometimes humorously called "The Golden Rule: He who has the gold, makes the rule." Another version of it is the principle that might makes right.

just; moreover, he is disliked by his household and his acquaintances whenever he refuses them an unjust favour. The opposite is true of the unjust man in every respect. I repeat what I said before: the man of great power gets the better deal (R 343c–344a).

From Thrasymachus' point of view, being just is "high-minded foolishness," whereas being unjust is "good judgment" (R 348c–d). If the question is which gives a person "the most profitable life" (R 344e), there can be, in the opinion of Thrasymachus, no doubt about the answer.

We should note that Plato accepts this as the right question. Which life is the *most profitable*, or the *most advantageous*, or provides the *greatest happiness*? To accept this as the right question is to adopt what we can call the Self-Interest Theory of Rationality.* According to this theory, a course of action can be rational only if it is in your long-term self-interest. What Plato tries to show is that being just *is* in your long-term self-interest because it is the only way to be happy. He also tries to show that justice is valuable for itself.

As we saw earlier, Plato takes for granted that everyone desires to be happy. And no one doubts that what makes you truly happy (enduringly happy) is good. Happiness, moreover, is one thing that everyone admits is good *by nature*. The search for happiness is not merely conventional. These ideas suggest a strategy. If Plato can show that, contrary to the assertions of Thrasymachus, it is the just man who is the happy man, then he has also shown that justice is good—good not only according to *nomos* but good by *physis*.

But is the just man the happy man? That question is posed in the most radical way possible by another participant in the dialogue of the *Republic*, Glaucon, who tells the following story. It is about Gyges,

a shepherd in the service of the ruler of Lydia. There was a violent rainstorm and an earthquake which broke open the ground and created a chasm at the place where he was tending sheep. Seeing this and marvelling, he went down into it. He saw, besides many other wonders of which we are told, a hollow bronze horse. There were window-like openings in it; he climbed through them and caught sight of a corpse which seemed of more than human stature, wearing nothing but a ring of gold on its finger. This ring the shepherd put on and came out. He arrived at the usual monthly meeting which reported to the king on the state of the flocks, wearing the ring. As he was sitting among the others, he happened to twist the hoop of the ring towards himself, to the inside of his hand, and as he did this he became invisible to those sitting near him and they went on talking as if he had gone. He marvelled at this and, fingering the ring, he turned the hoop outward again and became visible. Perceiving this he tested whether the ring had this power and so it happened. If he turned the hoop inwards he became invisible, but was visible when he turned it outwards. When he realized this, he at once arranged to become one of the messengers to the king. He went, committed adultery with the king's wife, attacked the king with her help, killed him, and took over the kingdom (R 359d–360b).

The story of the Ring of Gyges poses this question: Is justice something good only for its consequences? Or is it something good in itself, regardless of its consequences? We are invited to imagine a situation in which we could evade all bad consequences for behaving unjustly. We could behave as unjustly as we like while invisible, and no one could pin it on us. If we took a fancy to anything, we could just take it. Would *anyone* possessing such a ring fail to take advantage of it? Remembering that we all want to be happy, would it be at all sensible (i.e., *rational*) to refuse to use the ring to gratify our desires—knowing that we would never be caught or punished?

If justice is the true good, then it follows that it would be *better* to refrain from these actions; it would be more advantageous not to steal, kill, or commit adultery, even though we could get away with it. We would be *happier* being just, even

---

*This theory has been enormously influential in Western thought; it is pretty well taken as self-evident in economics, for example. It has been seriously challenged recently by Derek Parfit in his fascinating book, *Reasons and Persons* (Oxford: Clarendon Press, 1984).

though we would have to do without many things that would satisfy our desires. Glaucon imagines two extreme cases.

The extreme of injustice is to have a reputation for justice, and our perfectly unjust man must be granted perfection in injustice. We must not take this from him, but we must allow that, while committing the greatest crimes, he has provided himself with the greatest reputation for justice; if he makes a slip he must be able to put it right; he must be a sufficiently persuasive speaker if some wrongdoing of his is made public; he must be able to use force, where force is needed, with the help of his courage, his strength, and the friends and wealth with which he has provided himself.

Having described such a man, let us now in our argument put beside him the just man, simple as he is and noble, who . . . does not wish to appear just but to be so. We must take away his reputation, for a reputation for justice would bring him honour and rewards, and it would then not be clear whether he is what he is for justice's sake or for the sake of rewards and honour. We must strip him of everything except justice and make him the complete opposite of the other. Though he does no wrong, he must have the greatest reputation for wrongdoing so that he may be tested for justice by not weakening under ill repute and its consequences. Let him go his incorruptible way until death with a reputation for injustice throughout his life, just though he is, so that our two men may reach the extremes, one of justice, the other of injustice, and let them be judged as to which of the two is the happier (*R* 361a–d).

Perhaps the just man languishes in prison, dirty, cold, and half-starved; all he has is justice. The unjust man, meanwhile, revels in luxuries and the admiration of all. Plato is being challenged to show that the just man is, despite all, the happier of the two—that *he* is the one who has the good life. If he can demonstrate this, he will have shown that the Form of Justice is involved in the Form of the Good, that no one who participates in the former can be excluded from participation in the latter. It is this bit of dialectic we now want to understand.

We should note at this point, however, that we have so far been discussing whether justice has the advantage over injustice without being very clear about the nature of justice. We have assumed we know what it is we are talking about; as Socrates makes clear, however, this is often an unwarranted assumption. And we now have to address this Socratic question directly: What is justice? Only if we are clear about that can we hope to answer the question whether it is something good, even apart from its consequences.

To answer the question, Plato draws on his description of the soul. As we have seen, there are three parts to the soul: reason, spirit, and appetite. Each has a characteristic function. In accord with its function, each has a peculiar excellence. Just as the function of a knife is to cut, the best knife is the one that cuts smoothly and easily; so the excellence of anything is the best performance of its function. What are the functions of the various parts of the soul?

The function of appetite or desire is to motivate a person. It is, if you like, the engine that supplies the energy driving the whole mechanism. If you never wanted anything, it is doubtful that you would ever *do* anything. Your heart might beat and your lungs take in air, but there would be no *actions* on your part. So appetite is performing its function and doing it well when it motivates you strongly to achievement.

Spirit's function is to animate life, so that it is more than the dull drudgery of satisfying wants. Without spirit, life would perhaps go on, but it wouldn't be enjoyable; it might not even be worth living. Spirit is "doing its thing" if it puts sparkle into your life, determination into your actions, and courage into your heart. It supplies the pride and satisfaction that accompanies the judgment that you have done something well. And it is the source of indignation and anger when you judge that something has been done badly.

It is the task of the rational part of the soul to pursue wisdom and to make such judgments. And it performs this task with excellence when it judges wisely, in accord with knowledge. Such knowledge, we have seen, involves acquaintance with the Forms, including at its apex a vision of the Form of the Good. The rational part of the soul, then, works out by reasoning the best course of action. Its function is to guide or rule the other two parts. Desire, one could say, is blind; reason gives it sight. Spirit may be capricious; reason gives it sense.

Just as the body is in excellent shape when each of its parts is performing its function properly—heart, lungs, digestive system, muscles, nerves, and so on—so the whole soul is excellent when desire, spirit, and reason are each functioning well. The excellent human being is one who is strongly motivated, emotionally vivacious, and rational. Such a person, Plato believes, will also be *happy*.

For what is the source of unhappiness? Isn't it precisely a lack of harmony among the various parts of the soul? Desire wants what reason says it may not have. Spirit rejoices at what reason advises is an inappropriate object. These are cases in which the parts of the soul are not content to perform their proper function. Each wants to usurp the function of another. When, for example, you want what reason says is not good for you, it may be that your motivation is so great that it overrides the advice given. In that case, desire takes over the guiding function, which properly belongs to reason. But, in that case, you will do something unwise; and if it is unwise, you will suffer for it. And that is no way to be happy.

On the assumptions that we all want to be happy and that being happy is what is good, the good life for human beings is the one in which each part of the soul performs its functions excellently—where reason makes the decisions, supported by spirit, and desire is channeled in appropriate directions. The good and happy person is the one who is internally harmonious. Though we do not all realize it, this internal harmony is what we all most want; for that is the only way to be happy.

But what does this have to do with justice? Plato's answer is that we have in the harmonious soul a kind of image of the very nature of justice itself. Consider an analogy: If we look at a community and ask what would make it just, we can see that it is a harmony among the members of the community—each member contributing what he or she is best suited for, none envious of the others or striving to have what the others have. Justice is, to put it in a short phrase, "each doing his own." It is evidenced by a lack of conflict among the persons involved, a harmonious cooperation among those who rule, those who defend, and those who produce. (As we shall see, Plato's ideal state is made up of three classes, which mirror the three functions of the soul.)

Since this harmonious division of functions is justice on the large scale of the state and since it is mirrored in the internal structure of the soul, we may call the harmonious soul itself "just." Let us call a person whose soul is "just" in this sense "internally just." So we have an idea of the Just State and a perfectly parallel idea of the Internally Just Man. What we still lack, however, is a relation between the two. For all we have said, there may be no *connection* between them at all; a just state could be composed of internally unjust persons, and an internally unjust person might participate in a just state. The parallelism between internal justice and social justice may be sheer accident.

What Plato needs to show is that *social justice* is something *good for the individual*. Social justice involves keeping promises, refraining from deception, stealing, and so forth. To meet the challenge set forth by Thrasymachus and Glaucon, Plato needs to show that such behavior is good in itself, not only for its consequences. He thinks he has shown us that happiness (the good) consists in a harmonious soul. So *internal justice* is good in itself. It would be absurd to think that happiness is prized for its consequences! But will the internally just person also be externally just? Will he or she treat others justly? That is what remains to be shown.

Near the end of the *Republic*, Plato constructs another memorable image.

> Let us in our argument fashion an image of the soul. . . .   —What kind of image?
> One of the kind that are told in ancient legends about creatures like the Chimera, Scylla, Cerberus,

and many others in whose nature many different kinds had grown into one.   —We are told of such creatures.

Fashion me then one kind of multiform beast with many heads, a ring of heads of both tame and wild animals, who is able to change these and grow them all out of himself.

A work for a clever modeler, he said. However, as words are more malleable than wax and such things, take it as fashioned.

Then one other form, that of a lion, and another of a man, but the first form is much the largest, and the second second.   —That is easy and it is done.

Gather the three into one, so that they somehow grow together.   —All right.

Model around them on the outside the appearance of being one, a man, so that anyone who cannot see what is inside but only the outside cover will think it is one creature, a man.   —Done.

Let us now tell the one who maintains that injustice benefits this man, and that justice brings him no advantage, that his words simply mean that it benefits the man to feed the multiform beast well and make it strong, as well as the lion and all that pertains to him, but to starve and weaken the man within so that he is dragged along whithersoever one of the other two leads. He does not accustom one part to the other or make them friendly, but he leaves them alone to bite and fight and kill each other.   —This is most certainly what one who praises injustice means.

On the other hand, one who maintains that justice is to our advantage would say that all our words and deeds would tend to make the man within the man the strongest. He would look after the many-headed beast as a farmer looks after his animals, fostering and domesticating the gentle heads and preventing the wild ones from growing. With the lion's nature as his ally, he will care for all of them and rear them by making them all friendly with each other and with himself.   —This is most definitely the meaning of him who praises justice (R 588b–589b).

Plato uses this image to make the connection between the harmonious, internally just man on the one hand and the socially just man on the other. To be unjust to one's fellow man is to allow the beast within to rule—against the better judgment and wisdom of the man within (who represents reason). But that means that each of the internal parts of the soul is no longer "doing its own." Harmony and happiness are destroyed, and the good is lost.*

The internally just person, on the other hand, fostering the excellent functioning of each part of the soul in inner harmony, allows "the man within" to master the beast and tame the lion. The various parts are "friendly with each other." The external result of this inner harmony is social justice, for the beast will not wildly demand what reason says it is not proper to want.

> Can it benefit anyone, I said, to acquire gold unjustly if when he takes the gold he enslaves the best part of himself to the most vicious part? . . .
>
> If he then enslaves the most divine part of himself to the most ungodly and disgusting part and feels no pity for it, is he not wretched and is he not accepting a bribe of gold for a more terrible death than Eriphyle when she accepted the necklace for her husband's life? . . .
>
> How then and by what argument can we maintain, Glaucon, that injustice, licentiousness, and shameful actions are profitable, since they make a man more wicked, though he may acquire more riches or some other form of power?   —We cannot.
>
> Or that to do wrong without being discovered and not to pay the penalty is more profitable? Does not one who remains undiscovered become even more vicious, whereas within the man who is discovered and punished the beast is calmed down and tamed?   —Most certainly (R 589d–591b).

Here, then, is Plato's answer to Glaucon, Adeimantus, and Thrasymachus. In the last analysis, it is more profitable to be just than to be unjust because injustice inevitably involves disharmony in the soul. And that is unhappiness. And unhappiness is not the good.

Social justice, then, is correlated with internal justice (justice in the *polis* with justice in the *psyche*). Where each part of the soul is "doing its thing"—reason making the decisions, supported

---

*Compare this to Heraclitus' aphorism on p. 22, where he says that what impulse wants it buys "at the expense of the soul." Giving in to impulse is—in terms of Plato's image—feeding the beast. The beast grows strong at the expense of the lion and the man.

by the lion of the spirit and a domesticated appetitive beast—there is happiness. And happiness is the good. So the Form of Justice involves the Form of the Good. It is good for us to be just, even though we suffer for it.

Plato claims that by such dialectical reasoning we can have knowledge in the sphere of practice as well as in the theoretical sphere. By such dialectic, he believes that he has defeated the skepticism and relativism of the Sophists and vindicated the practice of his master, who went around "doing nothing but persuading both young and old among you not to care for your body or your wealth in preference to or as strongly as for the best possible state of your soul" (*Apology* 30b).

The State

We will not discuss Plato's views of the ideal state in any detail, but we must note several political implications of doctrines we have already canvassed. Like his views on the soul, his views on an ideal community developed throughout his lifetime, and his later thought manifests some deep changes in attitude and outlook. We will, however, focus on the more famous doctrines of the middle-period *Republic*.

We have observed that Plato sees a parallelism between the internal structure of a soul and the structure of a community. Just as the parts of the soul have different functions, the parts of a community (individual men and women) differ in their capacities and abilities. They can be grouped into three classes: (1) Some will be best fitted to be laborers, carpenters, plumbers, stonemasons, merchants, or farmers; these can be thought of as the *productive* part of the community; they correspond to the part of the soul called "appetite;" (2) Others, who are adventurous, strong, brave, and in love with danger, will be suited to serve in the army and navy; these form the *protective* part of the state, and they correspond to spirit in the soul; (3) Some, a very few, who are intelligent, rational, self-controlled, and in love with the search for wisdom, will be

suited to make decisions for the community; these are the *governing* part; and obviously their parallel in the soul is the rational part.

Up to this point, we have more or less been taking for granted that the search for wisdom is something open to everyone. But this is not in fact Plato's view. Here he is following Socrates, who always contrasts the *few* who know with the *many* who do not. Plato goes further; a foundational principle for Plato's ideal state is that there are, and always will be, only a few who are fit to rule. Obviously, Plato is consciously and explicitly rejecting the foundations of Athenian democracy as it existed in his day, where judges were selected by lot rather than by ability and where laws could be passed by any majority of the citizens who happened to show up in the Assembly on a given day. It is *not* the case, Plato urges, that everyone is equally fit to govern. Where democracy is the rule, rhetoric and persuasion carry the day, not reason and wisdom.

He is not, of course, in favor of tyranny or despotism, either; we can think of these as forms of government where the strong rule—i.e., whoever has the power to seize the reins. Nor does he favor oligarchy, or rule by the wealthy. Who, then, are these "few" who are fit to be rulers? Consider again the harmonious, internally just soul. In such a soul, reason rules. So in the state:

> Cities will have no respite from evil, my dear Glaucon, nor will the human race, I think, unless philosophers rule as kings in the cities, or those whom we now call kings and rulers generally and adequately study philosophy, until, that is, political power and philosophy coalesce, and the various natures of those who now pursue the one to exclusion of the other are forcibly debarred from doing so (*R* 473c–d).

Who are these philosophers?

> . . . we shall rightly call a philosopher the man who is easily willing to learn every kind of knowledge, gladly turns to learning things, and is insatiable in this respect (*R* 475c).

The philosopher kings will be those who love wisdom and are possessed of the ability to pursue it, those who have the ability to *know*. Since, as we have seen, knowledge is always knowledge of the Forms, philosopher kings will be those who have attained such knowledge, especially knowledge of the Form of Justice and the Form of the Good. For how can one rule wisely unless one knows what is good for the community and what is just?

This is supported by an analogy, some form of which Plato uses again and again.

> Imagine something like this happening on board one or many ships: the owner surpasses all on board in size and strength, but he is hard of hearing, somewhat short-sighted and his knowledge of seafaring is of the same quality. The sailors are quarreling about the steering, each of them thinking that he should be the pilot, though he has never learned the art of navigation; he cannot point to anyone who taught him or to a time when he learned it; moreover, they maintain that navigation cannot be taught and are ready to cut to pieces anyone who says it can. They are always crowding round the owner begging him and doing everything they can to get him to entrust the rudder to them. Sometimes, if they do not succeed while others do, they execute these others or throw them overboard, and they overpower their noble owner with drugs, or wine, or in some other way. Then they rule over the ship and enjoy its stores; drinking and feasting they sail as such men are likely to do. Further, the man who is clever at devising how they may rule by persuading or forcing the owner they call a navigator and a pilot who knows ships; anyone else they blame as useless. They do not even understand that a true navigator must pay attention to the seasons of the year, the sky, the stars, the winds, and all that pertains to his craft if he really is to be the master of a ship. Nor do they think it possible to acquire the art and practice of navigation whether people want one to steer or not and therewith the art of navigation. When this happens on ships, do you not think that the true pilot will be called a stargazer, a prattler, a good-for-nothing by those who sail on ships managed in that way?   —I certainly do, said Adeimantus.
>
> I do not think you require us to examine this parable in detail to see that it resembles the attitude of cities towards the true philosophers, but you understand my meaning.   —I certainly do (R 488a–489a).

It is indeed a fairly transparent analogy, the details of which do not need much comment. But we need to make explicit something that Plato takes for granted here. The analogy assumes that there *is* a body of knowledge available to the statesman similar to that utilized by the navigator. It assumes that this can be taught and learned and that it involves some theory which can be applied by the skilled practitioner. Clearly, the knowledge of statecraft, which Plato here compares to knowledge of the art of navigation, involves acquaintance with the Forms.

In a similar way, Plato compares the statesman to a doctor (*Gorgias* 463a–465e). We would never entrust the health of our bodies to just *anybody*. We rely on those who have been trained in that craft by skilled teachers. Furthermore, just as not everyone is by nature qualified to be a doctor, not everyone is fit to rule. Because the education necessary to reach the higher level of the Forms is rigorous and demanding, only a few will be able to do it. And for that reason, government in the best state will be by the few: the few who are wise.

A large part of the *Republic* is devoted to a description of the social and educational arrangements that will make it possible to produce philosophers who are kings and kings who are philosophers. Though these discussions are interesting, we will omit them here. We still need, however, to ask about the many. If only the few will ever make it to wisdom, what are the many to do? If they cannot *know* the good, how can they be depended on to *do* the good? And if they do not do the good, won't the state fall apart in anarchy and chaos?

The state can be saved from this fate by the principle that, for purposes of action, right opinion will be as effective as knowledge. If you merely guess that the cliff is directly ahead and as a result turn left, you will avoid falling over just as surely as if you knew that it was. The problem then, is to assure that the large majority has correct beliefs. They may not be able to follow the complicated dialectical reasoning demonstrating the goodness of justice, but they should be firmly persuaded that it pays to be just.

Such right opinion is inculcated by the education of the young, which is directed by the guardians or rulers, who know what is best. There are detailed discussions in the *Republic* about what sort of stories the young should be told and what sort of music should be allowed. Consider music. It is clear that the young cannot be allowed to listen to whatever kind of music they desire; for there is music that feeds the many-headed beast within and encourages passions that will destroy the harmony of a good state. (You might ask yourself what Plato would say about the popular music of today.) Music and stories should both encourage the belief—which Plato thinks can be demonstrated dialectically to the few—that the best and happiest life is a life of moderation and rational self-control, a life of justice.

There is in Plato's state, then, a distinct difference between the few and the many. The latter are brought up on a carefully censored educational regime; it would not be unfair to call the diet offered to the many propaganda, for it is persuasive rather than rational. The few, of course, are those who know what is best, for they have attained knowledge of the Forms. They arrange the education of the others so that they will attain as much goodness as they are capable of.

With respect to knowledge, Plato is both an optimist and a pessimist: an optimist about the few, a pessimist about the many. It is worth noting that Plato is in effect jettisoning one of the basic principles of his master, Socrates: that "the unexamined life is not worth living for a man" (*Apology* 38a). Plato seems to have concluded that for most people this sets the standard too high. They will do best not under Socratic "examination," but conditioned by censorship, propaganda, indoctrination, and persuasion under the guidance of those for whom such dialectical examination leads to a knowledge of the Forms.

Those who find these elitist, antidemocratic consequences disturbing have reason to go back to their presuppositions. We will find subsequent philosophers raising serious questions both about the Forms and about Plato's view that some—but not all—of us are capable of knowing them.

Problems with the Forms

Plato offers a complete vision of reality, including an account of how knowledge is possible, an ethics that guides our practical lives, and a picture of an ideal community. As we have seen, all these aspects of reality involve the Forms. The Forms are the most real of all the things there are. They serve as the stable and enduring objects of our knowledge. The Forms of Goodness, Justice, and Beauty function as guides to our goals, our behaviors, and our creative drives. And knowledge of them is the foundation for a good state.

But are there such realities? It is not only the political consequences that lead people to raise this question. It is raised in Plato's own school, and serious objections are explored—and not satisfactorily answered—by Plato himself in a late dialogue, the *Parmenides*. Here the leading character is made out to be Parmenides himself, the champion of the One, from whom Plato undoubtedly derives his inspiration in devising the doctrine of the eternal and unchanging Forms.

Parmenides examines the young Socrates:

> I imagine your ground for believing in a single form in each case is this. When it seems to you that a number of things are large, there seems, I suppose, to be a certain single character which is the same when you look at them all; hence you think that largeness is a single thing.
>
> True, he replied.
>
> But now take largeness itself and the other things which are large. Suppose you look at all these in the same way in your mind's eye, will not yet another unity make its appearance—a largeness by virtue of which they all appear large?
>
> So it would seem.
>
> If so, a second form of largeness will present itself, over and above largeness itself and the things that share in it, and again, covering all these, yet another, which will make all of them large. So each of your forms will no longer be one, but an indefinite many (*Parmenides* 131e–132b).

The argument begins with a statement we used before in justification of the introduction of the

Forms.* But then what happens is that an unacceptable conclusion is derived. Let us see if we can follow the argument.

Think again about Gertrude and Huey, the two elephants. Both are large. Let the small letters *g* and *h* represent Gertrude and Huey. Let the capital letter *L* represent the property they share of being large.† Then we have

Lg   *Lh*

According to the arguments for the Forms, this common feature means that Gertrude and Huey "participate" in a Form—The Large. Let's represent this by *F*. So we add the following to our diagram:

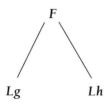

It is the Form *F* that *makes* the two elephants large and *makes it intelligible* that they are just what they are, i.e., large.

Now Plato also regularly thinks of the Forms as *possessing* the very character that they engender in the particulars. Or, to put it the other way around, he says that individual things "copy" or "imitate" the Form. When writing about the Form of Beauty, for example, Plato says that it is in itself beautiful, that it exemplifies "the very soul of the beauty he has toiled for so long," that it possesses "an everlasting loveliness."‡ Particular individuals are beautiful just to the extent that they actually have that Beauty which belongs in preeminent fashion to the Form.

_____

*See p. 111.

†We here use a convention of modern logicians, for whom small letters symbolize individuals and large letters represent properties or features. The property symbols are written to the left of the individual symbols.

‡See p. 125.

If that is right, then Largeness must itself be large. So we have to add this feature to our representation:

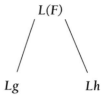

But now a problem stares us in the face: now the Form and the two elephants *all* have something in common—Largeness. And according to *the very principle Plato uses* to generate the *F* in the first place, there will now have to be a *second F* to explain what the first *F* shares with the individuals! And that, of course, will also be Large. So we will have to put down:

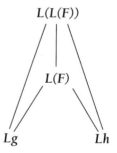

And now you can probably see how this is going to go. There will have to be a third *F*, a fourth, a fifth, and so on and on and on. We will no longer have just one Largeness, but two, three, four. . . . As Plato acknowledges through the character of Parmenides, each Form "will no longer be one, but an indefinite many." We are on the escalator of an *infinite regress*.

Moreover, at any stage of the regress what is real is supposed to depend on there already being a level above it, which explains the features at that stage. So this is what philosophers call a *vicious infinite regress*. For any stage to exist, there must actually be an infinite number of stages in reality, on which its existence depends. We thought we were explaining something about Gertrude and Huey. But this explanation now dissipates itself in the requirement for a never-ending series of explanations—and all of exactly the same sort. This is bad news for Plato's theory of Forms.

Still further, this argument can be applied to any characteristic whatever. It is traditionally formulated in terms of the Form of Man. Heraclitus and Socrates are both men; so there must be a Form of Man to explain this similarity. If that Form is itself a man, you have a third man. In this guise the argument has a name. It is called the **Third Man Argument**. It could as well be called the Third, Fourth, Fifth, Sixth . . . Man Argument.

The Forms are posited to explain the fact of knowledge, the meaning of general terms, and the common features of individuals.* But the Third Man Argument shows that—on principles accepted by Plato himself, at least in his middle period—the Forms *do not explain what they are supposed to explain.*

Like all such paradoxes derived from a set of premises, this indicates that something is wrong. But it does not itself tell us *what* is wrong. Some solution to the problem is needed. As we will see, Aristotle offers a solution.

Notes

1. A. N. Whitehead, *Process and Reality* (1929; reprint, New York: Harper Torchbooks, 1960), part II, p. 63.
2. Plato, *Meno*, trans. G. M. A. Grube, in *Plato's Meno* (Indianapolis: Hackett Publishing Co., 1980).
3. Quotations from Plato's *Republic*, trans. G. M. A. Grube, in *Plato's Republic* (Indianapolis: Hackett Publishing Co., 1974), are cited in the text using the abbreviation R. References are to section numbers.
4. Quotations from Plato's *Timaeus, Parmenides, Symposium, Phaedrus,* and *Gorgias,* in *The Collected Dialogues of Plato,* ed. E. Hamilton and H. Cairns, (Princeton: Princeton University Press, 1961), are cited in the text by title and section numbers.
5. Quotations from Plato's *Phaedo*, trans. G. M. A. Grube, in *Plato's Phaedo* (Indianapolis: Hackett Publishing Co., 1977), are cited in the text by title and section numbers.
6. A discussion of these problems may be found in W. K. C. Guthrie, "Plato's Views on the Nature of the Soul," in *Plato II: A Collection of Critical Essays,* ed. Gregory Vlastos (Notre Dame, Indiana: University of Notre Dame Press, 1978), 230–243.

*Review p. 112.

11

Aristotle:
The Reality of the World

The year was 384 B.C.E. Socrates had been dead for fifteen years; Plato had begun his Academy three years earlier. In northern Thrace, not far from the border of what Athenians called civilization, a child was born to a physician in the royal court of Macedonia. This child, named Aristotle, was destined to be the second father of Western philosophy.

At the age of eighteen he went to Athens, where bright young men from all over desired to study, and enrolled in the Academy. He stayed there for twenty years, as student, researcher, and teacher, until the death of Plato in 347. He then spent some time traveling around the Greek islands, pursuing research in what we would call marine biology. For a short time he went back to Macedonia, where he had a position at court as a tutor to the young Alexander, later known as "The Great," who was shortly to complete his father's ambition of conquering and unifying the known world.

By 335, Aristotle was back in Athens, where he founded a school of his own, the Lyceum. He remained there until 323, when he was apparently forced to flee—lest, he said, the Athenians "should sin twice against philosophy."[1] He died the following year at the age of 63.

Aristotle and Plato

Let us begin by drawing some comparisons between Aristotle and his teacher, Plato.[2] First, Plato was born into an aristocratic family with a long history of participation in the political life of the city. Aristotle's father was a doctor. These backgrounds not only influence but also can serve as symbols of their different interests and outlook. The influence of Plato on Aristotle's thought is marked; still, Aristotle is a quite different person with distinct concerns, and his philosophy in some respects takes quite a different turn. Here are some contrasts.

Otherworldliness

As we saw, there is a strong drive toward otherworldliness in Plato.* One feels in Plato a profound dissatisfaction with the familiar world of sense, which is to him no more than a pale shadow of reality. The real is quite different—unchanging,

———————
*See p. 129.

eternal, and unperceivable. The aim of philosophy, the love of wisdom, is to grasp by intellect this otherworldly reality, the Forms, and ultimately to escape the Heraclitean flux altogether and so to be caught up in contemplation of the True, the Good, and the Beautiful. Philosophy is a dying away from sense and desire.

Aristotle, by contrast, does not seem to suffer the same discontents. While he develops a profound view of the divine and its relation to the world, he does not seem driven to denigrate life in this world as something to be fled from. Life in this world, if not perfect, is as good as one could reasonably expect. The snails and octopuses he studies so avidly, dissects, classifies, and writes about, are nothing if not real things. And philosophy is not an escape from them, but a way of comprehending them.

The Objects of Knowledge

Plato is a combination of rationalist and mystic. He is committed to the idea that reality is ultimately rational. The Forms are perfectly definite realities, hanging together in perfectly rational ways, just as geometrical forms make up a perfectly systematic whole. Mathematics, in fact, seems to embody the ideal of knowledge, and reasoning is the way to discover truth. Yet, it seems that even reason is not ultimately sufficient. Eventually, when you get far enough up the hierarchy of the Forms, you just have to "see" the truth (with "the mind's eye"). Thus Diotima in the *Symposium* is supposed to have spoken about the "vision" of Beauty when the lover comes to "see the heavenly beauty face to face."*

It is perhaps for this reason that Plato—unable to describe what must be seen—offers us in crucial places the memorable Myths of the Sun and the Cave. These fit with the idea that teaching is "turning the soul toward reality." The myths point us in a direction where we might be able to see for ourselves what language is inadequate to describe.

Aristotle, much more down to earth, is convinced that language is quite capable of expressing the truth of things. This truth concerns the sensible world, and our knowledge of it begins with actually seeing, touching, and hearing the things of the world. The senses, while not sufficient in themselves to lead us to knowledge, are the only reliable avenues along which to pursue knowledge. We must be careful, of course, and mistakes are easy to make. But we can come to know and adequately express real knowledge of the changing world about us.

Human Nature

Plato is sure that the real person is the soul, not the body. Souls inhabit bodies for a time but are neither bound to nor dependent on them for their existence. The body is nothing more than a temporary and ultimately unreal prison. Our souls possess knowledge of the Forms before we are born, and with determination, intelligence, and virtue, we can enjoy a blessed communion with the Forms after death.

Aristotle's view of human beings is more complicated. There is some question whether the things he says about this topic can all be harmonized into one account. But the main theme is simple. Man is a "rational animal." The person is not identical with a soul-thing distinct from the body; a person is an animal of a certain special sort. As such, a person has a soul of a certain, very special sort. But the soul is not a thing; it is simply the "form" of the particular sort of body that a man has. Human beings are not "tandem" creatures composed of a "stoker" and a "captain." A person is one unified creature. What we get in Aristotle is a (basically) this-worldly account of the soul.*

Relativism and Skepticism

Plato is preoccupied, one might even say obsessed, with the problem of refuting Protagorean relativ-

---

Symposium 211e; see the discussion on pp. 124–126.

*There is a complication here which should be noted. See the discussion of *nous*, later in this chapter.

ism and skepticism. This is terribly important to him; it matters enormously. We can sense in his writing the passionate concern to prove these doctrines wrong. Its urgency is the motivational source behind his introduction of the Forms to serve as the unchanging, public objects of knowledge.

Plato is convinced that it was sophistic relativism and skepticism that had really killed Socrates, not the particular members of that jury. It is the views they had come to hold—that every opinion is as true as every other, that what seems good to someone *is* good (for that person), that if it seems right for Athens to condemn Socrates, then it is right. Plato knows in his heart that this is not right. So there must be standards that are more than just conventional, standards that are not just *nomos* but have a reality in *physis*. Hence the Forms, the dialectic about Justice, the subordination of everything else to the Form of the Good, and his outline of an ideal state. In a sense, this is Plato's *one* problem; it almost seems as if everything else in Plato gets its sense from that one center.

To that problem Aristotle seems almost oblivious, as though it were not on his horizon at all. The explanation may be partly that he believes Plato has succeeded in refuting the skeptics, so it doesn't have to be done again. But there is probably more to it. As a biologist, he knows that not every opinion about crayfish, for example, is equally good, so he isn't overwhelmed by the arguments of the skeptics. So he pursues his research and writes up his results, which, he believes, do constitute knowledge of the sensory world. The only problem, philosophically speaking, is to analyze the processes by which we attain such knowledge and to set out the basic features of the realities disclosed.

Ethics

Plato wants and thinks we can get the same kind of certainty in rules of behavior that we have in mathematics. Dialectic, reasoning about the Forms, can lead us to moral truths. And the ultimate vision of the Form of the Good will provide a single standard for deciding practical questions. Apprehen-

sion of the latter seems to promise, in a flash of insight, the solution for all questions of value—but only for the few specially qualified individuals able to make the tortuous journey out of the Cave.

Characteristically, Aristotle is much less inclined to make such grandiose claims. We ought not, he advises, to ask for more certainty in a given subject matter than the subject matter allows. In matters of practical decision, we are not likely to get the same certainty we can get in mathematics. He proceeds, therefore, in a more cautious and specific way, discussing particular virtues and the conditions under which it is and isn't reasonable to hold people responsible for the exercise of these virtues. There is no suggestion that ethical knowledge is something restricted to a small coterie of specially trained experts. The ordinary citizen, he holds, is quite able to make good decisions and to live a good life.* And appeal to the Form of the Good is in any case quite useless in these matters.

The Greek poet Archilochus had written in the seventh century,

> The fox knoweth many things, the hedgehog one great thing.[3]

Two quite different intellectual styles are exemplified by Plato and Aristotle. Plato is a man with one big problem, one passion, one concern; everything he touches is transformed by that concern. Aristotle has many smaller problems. These are not unrelated to each other, and there is a pattern in his treatment of them all. But he is interested in each for its own sake, not just in terms of how they relate to some grand scheme. Plato is a hedgehog. Aristotle is a fox.

It is quite possible to overdraw this contrast, however. There is a very important respect in which Aristotle is a "Platonist" from beginning to end. He agrees with his teacher without qualification that knowledge—to be knowledge—must be certain and enduring. And for that to be so, knowledge must be of objects that are themselves free

---

*Here it must be remembered that in Athens there were many slaves and that women were not citizens.

from the ravages of time and change. For both Plato and Aristotle, knowledge is knowledge of forms.* But they understand the forms differently—and thereby hangs the tale to come.

Logic and Knowledge

The Sophists' claim to teach their pupils "to make the weaker argument appear the stronger" has been satirized by Aristophanes, scorned by Socrates, and repudiated by Plato. But until Aristotle does his work in logic, no one gives a good answer to the question, just what makes an argument weaker or stronger anyway? An answer to this question is absolutely essential for appraising either the success of the Sophists or those who criticize them. Unless you have clear criteria for discriminating weak from strong arguments, bad arguments from good, the whole dispute remains in the air. Are there standards by which we can divide arguments into good ones and bad ones? Aristotle answers this question.

He does not, of course, answer it once and for all—though for two thousand years many people will think he very nearly has. Since the revolution in logic of the last hundred years, we can now say that Aristotle's contribution is not the last word. But it is the first word, and his achievement remains a part of the much expanded science of logic today.

It is undoubtedly due in part to Aristotle's ability to produce criteria distinguishing sound arguments from unsound ones that he can take the sophistic challenge as lightly as he does. To Aristotle, the Sophists can be dismissed as the perpetrators of "sophisms," of bad arguments dressed up to look good. They are not such a threat as they seem, because their arguments can now be *shown* to be bad ones.

But it is not mainly as an unmasker of fraudulent reasoning that Aristotle values logic.* Logic, the science of *logos*, would prove a valuable instrument in gaining knowledge of all kinds. Aristotle thinks of logic not so much as a science, but as a *tool* to be used in every intellectual endeavor, allowing the construction of valid "accounts" and the criticism of invalid ones. As his universal intellectual tool, logic is of such importance that we need to understand at least the rudiments of Aristotle's treatment of the subject.

It will be useful, however, to work toward the logic from more general considerations. Why should we care about logic? What can it do for us? We need to think again about *wisdom*.

Aristotle begins the work we know as *Metaphysics* with these memorable words:

> All men by nature desire to have knowledge. An indication of this is the delight that we take in the senses; quite apart from the use that we make of them, we take delight in them for their own sake, and more than of any other this is true of the sense of sight. . . . The reason for this is that, more than any other sense, it enables us to get to know things, and it reveals a number of differences between things (M 1.1).[4]

This delight is characteristic even of the lower animals, Aristotle tells us, though their capacities for knowledge are more limited than ours. They are curious and take delight in the senses and in such knowledge as they are capable of. Some of the lower animals, though not all, seem to have *memory*, so that the deliverances of their senses are not immediately lost. Memory produces *experience*, in the sense that one can learn from experience. (We have learned that taking aspirin relieves a headache; we do not totally understand why.) Some of the animals are quite good at learning from experience. Humans, however, are best of all at this; in

---

*Note that "form" is here uncapitalized. I will use the capitalized version, Form, only when referring to Plato's independent, eternal reality. For Aristotle's forms, an uncapitalized version of the word will do.

*Aristotle does not himself use the term "logic," which is of a later origin. What we now call "logic" is termed by his successors the "organon," or "instrument" for attaining knowledge. In the seventeenth and eighteenth centuries, this use of logic is contrasted with experience and attacked as sterile.

humans, *universal judgments* can be framed in *language* on the basis of this experience. We not only see numerous black crows and remember them but also form the judgment that all crows are black and use this statement together with others to build up a knowledge of that species of bird.

We regard those among us as wisest, Aristotle says, who know not only that crows are black but also why they are so. Those who are wise, then, have knowledge of the *causes* of things, which allows them to use various arts for practical purposes (as the doctor is able to cure the sick because he knows the causes of their diseases). And knowing the causes allows the wise person to teach others how and why things are the way they are.

Wisdom, then, either is or at least involves knowledge. And knowledge involves both *statements* (*that* something is so) and *reasons* (statements *why* something is so). Furthermore, for the possession of such statements to qualify as wisdom, they must be true. As Plato has pointed out, falsehoods cannot make up knowledge.

It is Aristotle's intention to clarify all this, to sort it out, put it in order, and show how it works. So he has to do several things. He has to (1) explain the nature of *statements*—how, for instance, they are put together out of simpler units called *terms*; (2) explain how statements can be *related* to each other so that some can give "the reason why" for others; and (3) give an account of what makes statements *true* and *false*. These tasks make up the logic.

Terms and Statements

When Aristotle discusses terms, the basic elements that combine to form statements, he is also discussing the world. In his view, the terms we use can be divided according to the *kinds* of things they pick out. He insists that things in the world can *be* in a number of different ways.* Correlated with the different *kinds of things there are*—or different ways things can be—are different *kinds of terms*. These kinds, called **categories**, are set out this way:

*One of the mistakes made by Parmenides and others, he claims, is failing to recognize that being comes in kinds.

Every uncombined term indicates substance or quantity or quality or relationship to something or place or time or posture or state or the doing of something or the undergoing of something (*C* 4).

Aristotle gives some examples:

Substance—man or horse
Quantity—two feet long, three feet long
Quality—white or literate
Relationship—double, half, or greater
Place—in the Lyceum, in the market place
Time—yesterday or last year
Posture—reclining at table, sitting down
State—having shoes on, being in armor
Doing something—cutting, burning
Undergoing something—being cut, being burnt

He does not insist that this is a complete and correct list. But you can see that categories are very general concepts, expressing the various *ways* in which being is manifested. Such distinctions exist and must be observed.

None of these terms is used on its own in any statement, but it is through their combination with one another that a statement comes into being. For every statement is held to be either true or false, whereas no uncombined term—such as "man," "white," "runs," or "conquers"—is either of these (*C* 4).

Neither "black" nor "crow" is true or false. But "That crow is black" must be one or the other. Terms combine to make statements. For example, we might combine terms from the list above to make statements like these:

A man is in the Lyceum.
A white horse was in the market place yesterday.
That man reclining at table was burning rubbish last year.

Terms can be combined in a wide variety of ways, but there are, Aristotle believes, certain standard and basic forms of combination to which all other combinations can be reduced. This means there is a limited number of basic forms that statements can take.

The clue to discovering these basic forms is noting that every statement is either true or false. Not every sentence we utter, of course, is either true or false. "Close the door, please," is neither. It may be appropriate or inappropriate, wise or foolish, but it isn't the right kind of thing to be true or false. It is not, Aristotle would say, a *statement*. Aristotle's own example is a prayer; it is, he says, "a sentence, but it is neither true nor false (I 4).

Statements (the kinds of things that can be true and false) say something. And they say something *about* something. We can then analyze statements into two parts: there is the part indicating what we are talking about, and there is the part indicating what we are saying about it. Call the first part the *subject* and the second part the *predicate*. Every statement, Aristotle believes, displays (or can be reformulated to display) a pattern in which some term plays the role of subject and another term the role of predicate. It will be convenient to abbreviate these parts as *S* and *P*, respectively.

Not every term, however, can play both roles. And this is of very great importance for Aristotle, for it allows him to draw the most fundamental distinction on which his whole view of reality is based.

> What is most properly, primarily, and most strictly spoken of as a substance is what is neither asserted of nor present in a subject—a particular man, for instance, or a particular horse (C 5).

Look back to the list of terms on page 145. There is one kind of term that stands out from the rest: **substance**. Although there are several kinds of substance (as we shall see), the kind that is "properly, primarily, and most strictly" called substance is distinguishable by the kind of role the term for it can play in statements—or rather, the kind of role

it *cannot* play. Terms that indicate such substances can play the role only of subject, never of predicate. They can take only the *S* role in statements, not the *P* role.

Consider the term "Socrates." This term indicates one particular man, namely Socrates himself. And it cannot take the *P* place in a statement; we can say things about Socrates—that he is wise, or snub-nosed—but we cannot use the term "Socrates" to say something about a subject. We cannot, for example, say "Snub-nosed is Socrates," except as a fancy and poetic expression for "Socrates is snub-nosed." In both of these expressions, "Socrates" is in the *S* place and "is snub-nosed" in the *P* position. In both, "is snub-nosed" is used to say something about Socrates. It is not *spatial* position in the sentence that counts, then, but what we could call *logical* position. In a similar way, it is clear that Socrates cannot be "present in" a subject, in the way the color blue can be present in the water of the Aegean Sea or knowledge of Spanish can be present in those who know the language.

Things *are*, Aristotle holds, in all these different ways. Some things have being as qualities, some as relations, some as places, and so on. But among all these, there is one *basic* way in which a thing can be: *being an individual substance*, a thing, like Socrates. All the other ways of being are parasitic on this. They are all *characteristics* of these basic substances; our terms for them express things we can say *about* these primary substances. For example, we can say that Socrates is five feet tall (Quantity), that he is ugly (Quality), that he is twice as heavy as Crito (Relationship), that he is in prison (Place), and so on. But that *about which* we say all these things, of which they all are (or may be) true, is some particular individual. And that Aristotle calls *primary substance*.

> . . . the reason why primary substances are said to be more fully substances than anything else is that they are subjects to everything else and that all other things are either asserted of them or are present in them (C 5).

Primary substances are "sub-jects" lying under their qualities, states, relationships, and so forth. That is why they cannot be predicated of other things.

It is clear that Aristotle will reject the Platonic Forms. We shall explore what he says about the Forms more fully later, but here he says that those things which are "more fully substances than anything else" are particular, individual entities such as this man, this horse, this tree, this snail. These are not shadows of more real things, as Plato held; they are the most real things there are. Everything else is real only in relation to them.

For now, however, we want to concentrate not on this metaphysical line of reasoning, but on the logical. Let us review. The wise person is the one who knows—both what is and why it is. Such knowledge is expressed in statements. Statements are composed of terms put together in certain definite ways. All of them either are already or can be reformulated to be subject–predicate statements, in which something is said about something. And the ultimate subjects of statements are primary substances.

Before we leave this topic, we need to note a complication. We can say, "Socrates is a *man.*" This conforms to our *S-P* pattern. But we can also say, "*Man* is an animal." This seems puzzling. How could "man" play the role of both *P* (in the first statement) and *S* (in the second)? If primary substances (individual things) are the ultimate subjects of predication, shouldn't we rule out "Man is an animal" as improper? Yet it is a very common kind of thing to say; indeed, biology is chock full of such statements!

Aristotle solves this problem by distinguishing two senses of "substance."

> But people speak, too, of secondary substances, to which, as species, belong what are spoken of as the primary substances, and to which, as genera, the species themselves belong. For instance, a particular man belongs to the species "man," and the genus to which the species belongs is "animal." So it is these things, like "man" and "animal," that are spoken of as secondary substances (*C* 5).

Individual humans, he notes, belong to a *species*: the species man. And a human is a kind of animal. So "animal" is a *genus*, under which there are many species: men, lions, whales, and so on. We can think of species and genera as substances, too, in a secondary sense. They are substances—and so can play the role of *S* in statements—by virtue of being forms embedded in primary substances (the individual people, lions, whales). A genus or species has no reality apart from all those real particular things that make it up, but we can think of it as a derivative kind of substance, about which we can say lots of interesting things.

The admission of species and genera as secondary substances, however, must not be understood to undermine his insistence that what is fully real is always the individual thing.

Truth

So far Aristotle has been dealing with issues of *meaning*. We turn now to what he has to say about *truth*. In one of the most elegant formulations in all philosophy, using only words any four-year-old can understand, Aristotle defines truth.

> To say that what is is not, or that what is not is, is false and to say that what is is, or that what is not is not, is true (*M* 4.7).

Grass, let us assume, is green. Then to say of it that it is green is to say something true about it. To say that it is not green—red or blue, perhaps—is to say something false. Contrariwise, the snail in my garden is not a mathematician. If I say that it is not a mathematician, I speak truthfully, whereas if I say that it is a mathematician, I speak falsely. Truth represents things as they are. Falsehood says of them that they are other than they are. This view of truth is not the only possible one.* We should,

---

*For other views of truth, see Hegel's claim that the truth is not to be found in isolated statements, but is only the *whole* of a completed system of knowledge (Chapter 21, "Reason and Reality: The Theory of Idealism"), and the pragmatist view that truth consists of all that a community of investigators would agree upon if they inquired sufficiently long (Chapter 24, pp. 468–469).

therefore, have a name for it. Let us call it the **Correspondence Theory of Truth**, because it holds that a statement is true just when it "corresponds" to the reality it is about. We can also call it the Classical View of Truth.

Reasons Why: The Syllogism

We can now say that the wise man is one who is able to make true statements, or say true things about whatever subject he discusses. But he is able to do more than that; he is able to "give an account" of *why* what he says is true. In Aristotle's terminology, he is able to give the causes why things are as he says they are.

With this we come to logic proper. The study of statements and their component parts, and of truth, is preliminary to the study of *reason-giving*. In giving the cause why a certain statement is true, the wise man offers other statements. Will these constitute good reasons for what he claims to know or not? If he is truly wise, they presumably will; but to discover whether someone is wise, we may have to decide whether what he says is true and whether the reasons he offers for what he says are sound. Giving a reason is giving an **argument**: offering premises for a conclusion. Perhaps it will be only a weak argument, perhaps a strong one. How can we tell? Aristotle is committed to the view that we cannot determine the strength of an argument on the basis of how far it convinces us, or even most people. To Aristotle, the Sophist's reliance on persuasiveness as the key to goodness in argument must seem like Euthyphro's third answer to Socrates' questions about piety—that it gives at best a property of good arguments, not the essence of the matter. Aristotle is trying to find what it is about an argument that explains why people should—or should not—be convinced.

Remember that for Aristotle all statements have an *S-P* form; they all say something about something. Such statements may either affirm that something is the case ("Grass is green") or deny it ("My snail is not a mathematician"). Call the former affirmative statements and the latter negative statements.

Moreover, *S-P* statements may either be about *all* of the subject ("All whales are mammals") or only about *some* of the subject ("Some dogs are vicious"). The former statements can be called universal, since they predicate something of each and every item talked about; each and every whale, for instance, is said to be a mammal. The latter statements can be called particular; our example does not say something about each and every dog, only about this or that dog or some collection of dogs. These distinctions give us a fourfold classification of statements. It will be useful to draw a chart, with some examples of each.

	Universal	Particular
Affirmative	All men are mortal. (All *S* is *P*.)	Some men are mortal. (Some *S* is *P*.)
Negative	No men are mortal. (No *S* is *P*.)	Some men are not mortal. (Some *S* is not *P*.)

Such are the different forms that statements may take. There are some interesting logical relationships between these forms. For example, a universal affirmative statement is the *contradictory* of a particular negative statement. To say that these are contradictories is to say that if either of them is true, the other must be false; and if either is false, the other must be true. (Look at the chart and check whether this is so.) Universal negatives and particular affirmatives are likewise contradictories.

Let us now ask how reasons may be given to support the truth of such statements. Again, an example is useful. Suppose that someone claiming to be wise asserts that "All men are mortal." Understanding that wisdom includes not only knowing truths but also knowing their causes or reasons, we ask her why this is so. In response, she says, "Because animals are mortal, and all men are animals." She has given us an argument:

All animals are mortal.

All men are animals.

Therefore: All men are mortal.

Aristotle calls this kind of argument a *syllogism*. Every syllogism is made up of three statements. In the three statements are three terms (here the terms are "man," "animal," and "mortal"), two terms in each statement. Two of the statements function as reasons for the third. These are the premises, and what is to be proved is the conclusion.

Consider the terms that occur in the conclusion; each of these occurs also in just one of the premises. And the third term, which Aristotle calls the *middle* term, occurs once in each of the premises. It is the middle term that links the two terms in the conclusion. The fact that the middle term is related to each of the others in a certain specific way is supposed to be the *cause* or the *reason why* the conclusion is true.

One of Aristotle's greatest achievements is the realization that what makes a syllogism good or bad not only has nothing to do with its persuasiveness, but it also has nothing to do with its subject matter. Its goodness or badness as a piece of reason-giving is completely independent of what it is about. It is not because it is about men and animals rather than gods and spirits or snails and mollusks that it either is or is not successful. Its success is wholly a matter of its *form*.* So we can abstract from the subject matter altogether in discussing its success. We might as well use letters of the alphabet instead of meaningful terms in the statements. In fact, this is exactly what Aristotle does. How good an argument is, then, depends only on how terms are related to each other in the various kinds of statements.

We can represent the relevant structure or form of this example in the following way, using *S* for the subject of the statement we want to prove, *P* for its predicate, and *M* for the middle term that is supposed to link these together:

All *M* is *P*.

All *S* is *M*.

Therefore: All *S* is *P*.

Remember, all that matters is how the terms are related to each other. What the terms *mean* doesn't matter. This suggests that if our original argument was a good one, so will any other argument that has this same form be a good one. What counts is form, not content.

But what is it for *any* argument to be good? Let us remind ourselves of the point and purpose of giving arguments in the first place. The point is to answer *why*. An argument is a good one, then, if it answers this question. A good argument should give a *reason why* of the following sort: if that reason is true, then the conclusion must also be true. A poor argument, correspondingly, is one where the premises might well be true, but even if they are, they do not "force" the truth of the

---

*Form is here contrasted with content, or subject matter; it is not the Platonic contrast between the ultimate reality and the world of the senses.

conclusion—which may then be false. Poor arguments give poor reasons, not in the sense that the reasons are necessarily unbelievable or untrue, but in the sense that they are not *reasons why* we should believe the conclusion is true.

Now we can ask, is the syllogism above a good argument? It should be obvious that it is. (Not all syllogisms are so obviously either bad or good; Aristotle uses obviously good ones like this as axioms to prove the goodness of less obvious ones.) If it is not obvious, it can easily be made so. Remembering that correctness is a matter of form, not content, let us take the terms as names for shapes. Then we can represent the argument in the following way:

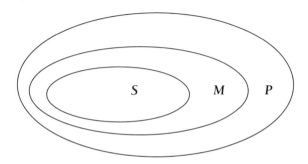

Simply by looking at these shapes, we can now see that if all of S is included in M, and all of M is included in P, then all of S must be included in P. It couldn't be any other way. But that is exactly what a good argument is supposed to do: to show you that, given the truth of the premises, the conclusion must also be true. It gives you a reason why the conclusion is true. So this argument form is a good one. And our original argument, which is an instance of this form, is also a good one. When an argument is good in this sense (*if* the premises are true, then the conclusion *must* be true) the argument is called **valid**.

Let us consider another syllogism.

No sparrows are mammals.
No mammals are plants.
Therefore: No sparrows are plants.

Each of these statements is true. But is this a valid argument? Do the reasons offered guarantee, or force, or make true the conclusion? It has this form:

No *S* is *M*.
No *M* is *P*.
Therefore: No *S* is *P*.

If that is a correct argument form, then any other argument having that form must be correct. This suggests a method of testing for goodness in arguments. Try to find another argument which has the same form as this one but which has true premises and a false conclusion. If you can, you have shown that these reasons, with terms arranged like that in those kinds of statements, do *not* guarantee the truth of the conclusion. The middle term is not doing its job of linking the subject and the predicate of the conclusion. So the argument is not a good one. Can we find such an argument? Easy.

No Toyotas are Mercedes.
No Mercedes are inexpensive.
Therefore: No Toyotas are inexpensive.

You can see (check to be sure you do) that this argument has the same form as the argument about sparrows. But here, although the premises are both true, the conclusion is false. In a good argument, however, the conclusion *must* be true if the premises are true. So this argument is no good. The reasons offered do not give us the *reason why* the conclusion is true (since it *isn't* true). Since it is form that accounts for goodness in arguments, then if this argument is no good, neither is the one about sparrows—even though the conclusion in that example happens to be true. That is the problem; it just *happens* to be true; it is not true *because* the premises are true. So the argument doesn't do the job that arguments are supposed to do. It doesn't give the *reason why*. It is an *invalid* argument.

On the basis of fairly simple examples such as these, Aristotle develops a complex system of logic. He tries to set out all the correct and all the incorrect forms of reasoning.* The result is a powerful tool both for testing arguments and for constructing arguments that tell us the cause or reason why things are as they are. In its latter use, logic is called *demonstration*. What can be demonstrated, we can know.†

Knowing First Principles

Can everything knowable be demonstrated? Can we give reasons for everything? Aristotle's answer is no:

> For it is altogether impossible for there to be proofs of everything; if there were, one would go on to infinity, so that even so one would end up without a proof (*M* 4.4).

Giving a proof for a statement, as we have seen, means constructing a syllogism; that means finding premises from which the statement logically follows. But we can ask whether there is also a proof for these premises. (Why should we believe *them*?) If so, other syllogisms can be constructed with these premises as their conclusions. But then, what about the premises of these syllogisms? This kind of questioning, like the child's *why?* can go on

indefinitely. And so we will continue to be unsatisfied about the truth of the statement we were originally seeking reasons to believe. But this means, as Aristotle says, that "it is impossible for there to be proofs for everything."

The chain of demonstrations must come to an end if we are to have knowledge. But where can it end? Socrates has an answer to this question.* If, as he thinks, our souls existed before we were born and had lived in the presence of the truth, then we might be able to "recollect" the truth when we were reminded of it. This recollection would not be demonstrative, needing argument and premises and such; it would be an immediate recognition of the truth. But Aristotle cannot use this Socratic solution. As we'll discover, he can see no reason to believe that our souls existed before we were born, nor does he think there are independently existing Forms we could have been acquainted with.

So Aristotle is faced with this problem: since not everything can be known by demonstration, how do we come to know that which cannot be demonstrated? If we are to avoid an infinite regression, there must be starting points for our proofs.

> The starting point of demonstration is an immediate premise, which means that there is no other premise prior to it (*PA* 1.2).

We can call these immediate premises *first principles*. If we are to have knowledge by demonstration, our knowledge of these starting points must not be inferior to what we prove from them. In fact, Aristotle says, they must be even better known. About them we must have the most certainty of all.

> . . . since we know and believe through the first, or ultimate, principles, we know them better and believe in them more, since it is only through them that we know what is posterior to them. . . . This is because true, absolute knowledge cannot be shaken (*PA* 1.2).

---

*Aristotle is mistaken in thinking that syllogisms of this sort exhaust the forms of correct reasoning; we now know that there are many more correct forms. He also neglects, or gives an inadequate picture of, so-called inductive reasoning. But his achievement is impressive nonetheless.

†Here you should ask yourself: does Aristotle resolve the puzzle posed by the Sophists' teaching of rhetoric? For them, remember, an argument is a good one just in case it is convincing. The criterion for goodness is success. Do Aristotle's logical rules provide a criterion independent of success? How would Aristotle explain the fact that it is often possible to construct a convincing *logos* on both sides of a question?

---

*Discussed on pp. 97–98.

This means that we must be more certain about what makes something an animal than about what makes something a monkey; in geometry, we must know the definition of line with greater clarity than that of isosceles triangle.

But how are such principles to be known? We can't just start from nothing and—by a leap across a chasm of nothingness—get to knowledge. In this respect Socrates was right.

> All instruction and all learning through discussion proceed from what is known already (PA 1.1).

This seems paradoxical. It is as though we were required to know *something* prior to our coming to know *anything*. But this is impossible.

The key to resolving the paradox, Aristotle holds, is not the preexistence of the soul but the recognition that things may be "known" in several senses. What Aristotle does is to show how knowledge of these first principles *develops*. This is a characteristically Aristotelian tactic. Instead of saying that we either know or we don't know, Aristotle shows us how knowledge develops from implicit to more and more explicit forms. What is presupposed is not full-blown, explicit, and certain knowledge (such as Socrates supposed the soul had in its preexistence), but a series of stages, beginning in a *capacity* of a certain sort. Though it is incredible to think that we are born knowing how to double a square (and just can't remember it), it makes good sense to think we are born with capacities of various kinds. One relevant capacity, moreover, is one that human knowers share with other animals. Knowing begins in perceiving.

Aristotle agrees with Plato that perceiving something is not the same as knowing it. The object of perception is always an individual thing, but knowledge is of the universal; perception can be mistaken, but knowledge cannot. But these facts don't lead Aristotle, as they lead Plato, to disparage the senses, to cut them off from reality, and to install knowledge in another realm altogether. Per-

ception is not knowledge, but it is where knowledge begins. (It is surely of crucial importance to note here that when Plato thinks of knowledge, his first thought is of mathematics; when Aristotle thinks of knowledge, his first thought is of biology.)

We noted earlier that some animals have memory in addition to their faculties of sense perception. Thus they can retain traces of what they perceive in numerous particular encounters with their environment. These traces build up into what Aristotle calls "experience." And experience is the source of a *universal*, a sense of the unity of the many things encountered. Aristotle compares it to a rout ending in battle: individual men are fleeing, each in his own way (many perceptions are pouring into the soul); one turns and stands (memory), then another (solidifying the memory), and another (experience), until finally a battle line is formed (One is made out of Many).

> As soon as one individual percept "has come to a halt" in the soul, this is the first beginning of the presence there of a universal. . . . Then other "halts" occur among these (proximate) universals, until the indivisible genera or (ultimate) universals are established. E.g., a particular species of animal leads to the genus "animal," and so on. Clearly it must be by induction that we acquire knowledge of the primary premises, because this is also the way in which sense-perception provides us with universals.[5]

How do we come to know the first principles, from which demonstrations may then proceed? By **induction**, Aristotle tells us. Imagine the biologist observing creatures in a tidal pool. At first, he can distinguish only a few kinds, those very different from each other. As he keeps watching very closely, new differences (as well as new similarities) offer themselves to his observation. He begins to group these creatures according to their similarities, bringing the Many under a variety of Ones. Then all these Ones are united under further universal principles, until finally all are classified under the One heading of "animals." "Is this like the one I saw a moment ago? Yes. So there is that kind; and that is different from this kind. Still, they are alike in a certain respect, so they may be species of the same genus. . . ." Eventually, the biologist comes to group the creatures according to characteristics they do and do not share with each other. His perception provides him with "universals" under which he groups or organizes the various kinds of things that he has been observing.

These universals provide something like definitions of the natural kinds of things that exist. The wider one's experience of a certain field, the more firmly these inductive definitions are grounded. The first principles of any field are arrived at in this way. Thus we can come to know what a plant is, what an animal is, what a living creature is. And these definitions can serve as the starting points, the ultimate principles of any science.

Not everything, as we have seen, can be known by demonstration. What cannot be demonstrated must be grasped some other way. That way is induction from sense perceptions. But what is there in us that is capable of such a grasp? It is clearly not the senses, nor memory, nor even experience. On the other hand, it is not our reasoning ability, for the capacity in question has nothing to do with proof. Aristotle uses a term for this capacity of ours that has no very adequate English counterpart: **nous**. It is sometimes translated as "mind" and sometimes as "intuition"; the English term "mind" seems too broad and "intuition" too vague. *Nous* is the name for that ability we have to grasp first principles by abstracting what is essential from many particular instances present to our senses.*

---

*Do we really have such a faculty? Can we get certain points from which the rest of our knowledge can be logically derived? Modern philosophy from the seventeenth century on will be preoccupied with these questions. What if we don't? Are we thrown back again into that sophistic skepticism and relativism from which both Plato and Aristotle thought they had delivered us? See, for example, Montaigne, who thinks we are (Chapter 16, "Skeptical Thoughts Revived") and Descartes, who is certain we are not (*Meditations*).

The World

Aristotle discusses his predecessors often and in detail.* He believes that something can be learned from all of them and that by showing where they go wrong we can avoid their mistakes and take a better path. Such a dialectical examination of the older philosophers does not amount to knowledge, for it is neither demonstration of a truth nor insight into first principles. But it clears the ground for both and is therefore of considerable importance.

His fundamental conviction about the work of his predecessors is that they go wrong by not *observing* closely enough. With the possible exception of Socrates and certain of the Sophists who were interested in other things, they had all been searching for explanations that would make the world intelligible. But these explanations either are excessively general (Thales' water, Anaximander's boundless, and the rather different *logos* of Heraclitus), or seem to conclude that there is no intelligibility in the world at all (Parmenides condemns the world to the status of mere appearance, and Plato believes only the Forms are completely intelligible). Even Democritus, who was from a theoretical point of view superior to all but Plato, misses the intelligibility in the observable world and tries to find it in the unobservable atoms.

Aristotle, drawing on his own careful observations, is convinced that the things which make up the world have principles of intelligibility *within* them.† In order to explain their nature, their existence, and the changes they regularly undergo, it is necessary only to pay close attention to *them*. The world as it offers itself to our perception is not an unintelligible, chaotic flux from which we must

---

*In, for example, *Physics* I and *Metaphysics* I. The book you are now reading is itself an example of the Aristotelian conviction expressed in the next sentence.

†In this regard, Aristotle is carrying on the tradition begun by Thales but improving on it by making explanations more specific and detailed. See the discussion of Thales' remark, "All things are full of gods," p. 8.

flee to find knowledge. It is made up of things—the primary substances—that are ordered; the principles of their order are internal to them, and these principles, through perception, can be known.

Nature

What Aristotle calls "nature" is narrower than what we have been calling "the world." Within the world there are two classes of things: artifacts, which are things made for various purposes by people (and by some animals), and "nature-facts." There are beds, and there are boulders. These two classes differ in important respects. The basic science concerned with the world (what Aristotle calls "physics") deals with boulders, but only in a derivative sense with beds. Aristotle draws the distinction in the following way.

> Of the things that exist, some exist by nature, others through other causes. Those that exist by nature include animals and their parts, plants, and simple bodies like earth, fire, air, and water—for of these and suchlike things we do say that they exist by nature. All these obviously differ from things that have not come together by nature; for each of them has in itself a source of movement and rest. This movement is in some cases movement from place to place, in others it takes the forms of growth and decay, in still others of qualitative change. But a bed or a garment or any other such kind of thing has no natural impulse for change—at least, not insofar as it belongs to its own peculiar category and is the product of art (*PH* 2.1).

Of course, beds and garments change, too. But they change not because they are beds and garments but because they are made of natural things like wood and wool. It is by virtue of being wood that the bedstead changes, develops cracks and splinters, not by virtue of being a bedstead. The sword rusts not because it is a sword but because it is made of iron.

Nature, then, is distinguished from art and the products of art because it "has in itself a source of movement and rest." We should note that Aristotle

understands "movement" here in a broad sense: there is (1) movement from place to place, also called local motion, (2) growth and decay, and (3) change in qualities. (We usually call only the first of these "movement.") Natural things, then, change in these ways because of what they are, not because something else acts upon them. A bed, for example, may move from place to place, but only if someone moves it; it does not grow or decay; and any change in its qualities is due either to the action of some other entity on it (I paint my bed red) or to a property of the natural substance it is made of (the wood in the bedstead fades from dark to light brown). By contrast, a beaver moves about from place to place on its own, is born, matures, becomes wiser with age, and dies because this is the *nature* of beavers.

Nature, then, is the locus of change. Aristotle is convinced that if we only observe closely enough, we can understand the principles governing these changes. Nature is composed of primary substances that are the *subjects* of change. They change in two ways: (1) they come into being and pass away again; (2) while in existence, they vary in quality, quantity, relation, place, and so on. About natural substances we can have knowledge. And since Aristotle agrees with his teacher Plato that knowledge is always knowledge of the real, it follows that nature is as real as anything could be!

The Four "Becauses"

The wise person, as we have seen, knows not only what things are but also why. Aristotle sees that all his predecessors are asking why things are the way they are and giving these answers: because of water, because of the boundless, because of opposition and the *logos*, because of atoms and the void, because of the Forms. What none of them sees is that this is not *one* question but *four* distinct questions.

> Some people regard the nature and substance of things that exist by nature as being in each case the proximate element inherent in the thing, this being

itself unshaped; thus, the nature of a bed, for instance, would be wood, and that of a statue bronze. Antiphon produces as evidence of this the fact that if you were to bury a bed, and the moisture that got into it as it rotted gained enough force to throw up a shoot, it would be wood and not a bed that came into being. For his view is that its arrangement according to the rules of an art, is an accidental attribute, whereas its substance is what remains permanently, and undergoes all these changes (*PH* 2.1).

People who think this way identify the substance of a thing—its nature—with the element or elements it is made of. Thales, for instance, thinks that the nature of all things is water; everything else is nonessential, just accidental ways in which the underlying substance happens, for a time, to be arranged. The underlying substratum, however, is eternal; that is the real stuff!

Those who think this way are taking the why-question in one very specific sense. They answer, "Because it is made of such and such stuff." Aristotle does not want to deny that this is one very proper answer to the why-question. Why is this statue what it is? Because it is made of bronze. The answer points to the *matter* from which it is made. Let us call this kind of answer to the why-question an indication of one type of **causation**: the Material Cause.

While this may be a correct answer, it is not, Aristotle insists, a complete answer to the why-question. That should be obvious enough; lots of bronze is not formed into statues. Consider some wood that has not been made into a bed. We could call such wood a "potential bed," but it is not yet a *bed*. It is the same, he says,

with things that come together by nature; what is potentially flesh or bone does not yet have its own nature until it acquires the form that accords with the formula, by means of which we define flesh and bone; nor can it be said at this stage to exist by nature. So in another way, nature is the shape and form of things that have a principle of movement in themselves—the form being only theoretically separable from the object in question (*PH* 2.1).

Bone is what accords with "the formula" for bone—the definition that sets out the essential characteristics of bone. The elements of which bone is composed are not yet themselves bone; they are at best potential bone and may be formed into bone. In the case of bronze, there is no statue until it takes the shape of a statue. So here is another reason why a thing is the thing it is: it satisfies the requirements for being that sort of thing.

Aristotle here uses the term *form* for both the shape of something simple like a statue and for the definition of more complex things like bone. This is in accord with the usage for the term that comes down from Socrates and Plato. However, Aristotle adds this qualification: "the form being only theoretically separable from the object in question." He means that we can consider just the form of some substance independently of the material stuff that makes it up; but we must not suppose on that account that the form is really separable from the thing. Aristotle's forms are not Plato's Forms. The form of a thing is not an independent object, but just its-having-the-characteristics-that-make-it-the-thing-that-it-is.

So we can answer the why-question in a second way by citing the form. Why is this bit of stuff bone? Because it has the characteristics mentioned in the definition of bone. Aristotle calls this the Formal Cause.

But there must be something else, particularly in cases where a substance comes into being, such as a mouse or a man. There is the material stuff out of which mice and men are made, and each has its proper form. But what explains the fact of their *coming to be*?

Thus, the answer to the question "why?" is to be given by referring to the matter, to the essence, and to the proximate mover. In cases of coming-to-be it is mostly in this last way that people examine the causes; they ask what comes to be after what, what was the immediate thing that acted or was acted upon, and so on in order (*PH* 2.7).

Here is a third answer to the why-question. This answer names whatever triggered the beginning of the thing in question, what Aristotle calls the "proximate mover." This sense of cause comes closest to our modern understanding of causes. For Aristotle, though, such causes are always themselves substances ("man generates man"), whereas for us causes tend to be conditions, events, or happenings. This cause is often called the Efficient Cause.

There is one more sense in which the why-question can be asked. We might be interested in the "what for" of something, particularly in the case of artifacts. Suppose we ask, "Why are there houses?" One answer is that cement and bricks and lumber and wallboard exist. Without them (or something analogous to them) there wouldn't be any houses. This answer cites the Material Cause. Another answer is that there are things which satisfy the definition for a house, an answer naming the Formal Cause. A third answer cites the fact that there are house builders—the Efficient Cause. But even if we had all these answers, we would not be satisfied. What we want to know is why there are houses in the sense of what purpose they serve, what ends they satisfy.

Why are there houses? To provide shelter from the elements for human beings. If it were not for this purpose they serve, there would be no such things; the materials for houses might exist, but they would not have come together in the sort of form that makes a house a house. When we answer the why-question in this way, Aristotle says we are giving the Final Cause.*

> It is clear, then, that there are causes, and that they are as many in number as we say; for they correspond to the different ways in which we can answer the question "why?" The ultimate answer to that question can be reduced to saying what the thing is . . . or to saying what the first mover was . . . or to naming the purpose . . . or, in the case of things that come into being, to naming the matter. . . . Since there are these four causes, it is the business of the natural scientist to know about them all, and he will give his answer to the question "why?" in the manner of a natural scientist if he refers what he is being asked about to them all—to the matter, the form, the mover, and the purpose (*PH* 2.7).

Is There Purpose in Nature?

The most controversial of the four "becauses" is the last. We say there is a purpose for artifacts (houses, for example), but only because *human beings* have purposes. We need, want, desire shelter; so we form an intention that shelters should exist. We think, plan, and draw up a blueprint, then gather the materials together and assemble a house. But the crucial thing here is the intention—without that, no houses. To say that there are Final Causes in nature seems like imputing intentions to nature. We might be able to answer the question, what is a sheep dog for? since sheep dogs serve our purposes. But does it even make sense to ask what *dogs* are for?[6] In a humorous sketch Bill Cosby asks, "Why is there air?" He answers that the purpose of air is to have something to blow up basketballs with. But that is obviously a joke.

Yet Aristotle holds seriously that the question about Final Causes applies to natural facts just as much as to artifacts. There may be some things that are accidental by-products (two-headed calves and such), and they may not have a purpose. Such accidents, he says, occur merely from "necessity." But accidents apart, he thinks natural facts are inherently purposive.

Aristotle does not, however, think that there are *intentions* resident in all things; intentions are formed after deliberation, and only rational animals can deliberate. But that does not mean that nature in general is devoid of *purposes*, for the concept of purpose is broader than that of intention.

> Of things that come to be, some serve a purpose, others do not; of those that do, some come to be in accordance with an intention, others do not, although in both cases they serve a purpose. Plainly, then, even apart from things that happen according to necessity, or to what is usual, there are some things that can have a purpose. Things that serve a purpose

---

*Compare Socrates' answer to the question about why he is in prison, pp. 118–119.

include everything that might have been done intentionally, and everything that proceeds from nature. When such things come to be accidentally, we say that they are as they are by chance (*PH* 2.5).

But why couldn't everything in nature happen by chance, without purpose, according to sheer necessity? This is what Democritus thinks the world is like—the accidental product of the necessary hooking up of atoms.* Why is that a mistake?

Aristotle has two arguments. (1) He draws on his close observations of nature to conclude that

all natural objects either always or usually come into being in a given way, and that is not the case with anything that comes to be by chance (*PH* 2.8).

Chance or accident makes sense only against a background of regularity, of what happens "either always or usually." Roses come from roses and not from seeds of wheat; therefore, a rose coming from a rose is no accident. But since everything must occur either by chance or for a purpose, it must happen for some purpose. (2) Art (meaning something like the art of the physician or house builder) either completes nature or "imitates nature." But there is purpose in art, so there must be purpose in nature as well.†

Teleology

The idea that natural substances are *for* something is called **teleology**, from the Greek word *telos*, meaning end or goal. We can get a better feel for this by thinking about a concrete example. Consider a frog. Let it be a common leopard frog such as children like to catch by the lake in the summer time. We can consider the frog from two points of view: (1) at a given time we can examine a kind of cross-section of its history, and (2) we can follow its development through time.

At the moment when he is caught by little Johnny, the frog has certain characteristics. Johnny might list them as spottedness, four-leggedness, and hoppiness. A biologist would give us a better list amounting to a definition of what a frog is. This "what-it-is" the frog shares with all other frogs; it is what makes it a frog rather than a toad or a salamander. This is what Aristotle calls its form.

But of course it is one particular frog, the one Johnny caught this morning. It is not "frog in general," or "all frog," or "all the frog there is." What makes it the particular individual that it is? Surely it is the matter composing it; this frog is different from the one Sally caught, because even though they share the same form, each is made up of different bits of matter.

So in a cross-section it is possible to distinguish form from matter. But now let us look at the history of the frog. Each and every frog develops from a fertilized egg into a tadpole and then into an adult frog. At each of these temporal stages, moreover, one can distinguish form and matter. The egg is matter that satisfies the definition for eggs; the tadpole has the form for tadpoles; the frog satisfies the formula for frogs. These stages are related in a regular, orderly way. As Aristotle puts it, this development is something that happens "always or usually." There is a determinate pattern in this history. And it is always the same.

In the egg, Aristotle will say, there is a potentiality to become a frog. It won't become a toad. This means that it has a direction programmed into it, so to speak. There is a goal or end *in* the egg, which is what determines the direction of development. The term for this indwelling of the goal is **entelechy**. The goal, or *telos*, is present *in* the egg. The goal (being a frog) is not present, of course, in actuality—otherwise, the egg would not be an egg but already a frog. The egg has *actually* the form for an egg, but the form frog is there *potentially*. If it were not, Aristotle would say, the egg might turn into anything! (Note that the Final Cause toward which the egg and tadpole develop is itself a form; the goal is to actualize the form of a frog.)

This indwelling of the end, entelechy, is what Aristotle means by the purpose that is in natural

---

*See p. 29.

†Are these sound arguments? The key move in the development of modern science is their rejection. See p. 283.

things. Such things have purpose in the sense that there is a standard direction of development for them; they move toward an end. Natural things, particularly living things, look in two directions. They look back to earlier forms (which contained the later forms potentially) and forward to still later forms (which they contain potentially). Earlier forms are potentially what they will later become actually. The tadpole is the potentiality of there being an actual frog. The frog is the actuality the tadpole tends toward.

Science, Aristotle says, can grasp not only the nature of static and eternal things, such as Plato's Forms, but also the nature that changes and develops. Knowledge is of forms; in this Plato was right. But the forms are not outside the natural world; they are within it, guiding and making intelligible the changes that natural substances undergo either always or usually. The concepts of the four causes, plus actuality and potentiality, are the tools by which science can succeed in this task.

First Philosophy

> It is from a feeling of wonder that men start now, and did start in the earliest times, to practice philosophy (M 1.2).

Practicing philosophy, Aristotle makes clear, is not the basic activity of human beings. They must first see to the necessities of life, and only when these are reasonably secure will they have the leisure to pursue wisdom. For the wise person, as we have seen, wishes to know, wishes to know everything, and wishes to know the causes in every case. So far does human wonder go.

There need not be any practical payoff to such knowledge. Indeed, Aristotle is quite convinced that there will not be. There are, of course, practical sciences such as medicine, which do have practical consequences. But the most uniquely human pursuit of knowledge is characterized by a delight in knowing "for its own sake." In a certain sense, Aristotle says, this pursuit is "more than human, since human nature is in many respects enslaved"

(M 1.2). So much of our activity is devoted to the necessities of just staying alive that we are enslaved to the needs of our own nature. The knowledge that does nothing more than satisfy wonder, in contrast, is more than human because it would be free from this bondage. It is akin to the knowledge god would have. For it would be what the wise person seeks—knowledge of everything and the causes of everything, for its own sake. In its concern for causes, such "divine" knowledge would have as its principal objects those things which are "first" or "primary" or independent of everything else. If there were such knowledge, we could call it "first philosophy."

Aristotle is convinced that we can and do have knowledge of the world of nature. Nature is the sphere of individual substances subject to change. And we can understand these substances in terms of (1) the matter that makes them up, (2) their form (or definition, or essence), (3) the trigger that sets them going, and (4) the end toward which they strive. Understanding change or development in such substances involves also the notions of potentiality and actuality.

Familiar as we are with the world of nature, we wonder now whether that is all there is.

> If there is no other substance apart from those that have come together by nature, natural science will be the first science. But if there is a substance that is immovable, the science that studies it is prior to natural science and is the first philosophy. . . . It is the business of this science to study being qua being, and to find out what it is and what are its attributes qua being (M 6.1).

Biology, we might say, studies *being qua living being*; or to put it another way, the biologist is interested in *what there is* just insofar as it is *alive*. There are in fact a variety of sciences, theoretical and practical, each of which cuts out a certain area of what there is—of being—for study. Each such science brings its subject matter together under some unifying first principles. And this question must inevitably arise: Is there some still higher unity to what there is? Is being *one*? Is it unified by some principles that are true of it throughout?

If so, this too must be an area of knowledge, and the wise person's wonder will not be satisfied until it is canvassed and understood. This science would be concerned with the characteristics or attributes of being in an unqualified sense: of *being qua being*. If there is such a science, it is "first" in the sense that it would examine the principles taken for granted by all the special sciences. It would ask about the ultimate causes of all things. If, says Aristotle, natural substances are the only ones there are, then natural science will be this first science or philosophy. But if there are other substances— ones not subject to change—then the science that studies those will be first philosophy.* So first philosophy, also called **metaphysics**, looks for the ultimate principles and causes of all things. What are they?

Not Plato's Forms

As we have seen, Plato gives an answer to this very question. The ultimate realities are the Forms, he says, and ultimately the Form of the Good. But Aristotle criticizes this answer severely. Not only are the Forms subject to the Third Man Problem, they present many other difficulties.† Let us briefly explore some of them.

The things of this world are supposed to derive their reality from their "participation" in the Forms. But nowhere does Plato explain just what this "participation" amounts to. Without such an account, however, all we have are "empty phrases" and "poetic metaphors" (M 1.9).

The Forms are themselves supposed to be substantial realities—indeed, the most real of all the things there are. Aristotle's comment is this:

In seeking to find the causes of the things that are around us, they have introduced another lot of objects equal in number to them. It is as if someone who wanted to count thought that he would not be able to do so while the objects in question were relatively few, and then proceeded to do so when he had made them more numerous (M 1.9).

To say that the Form Human is the cause of humans is simply to multiply the entities needing explanation. If it is difficult to explain the existence and nature of human beings, it is certainly no easier to explain the existence and nature of humans-plus-the-Form-Human.

Third, the Forms are supposed to be what many individuals of the same kind have in common. Yet they are supposed to be individual realities on their own. But, says Aristotle, these requirements conflict. If the Forms are indeed individual substances, it makes no sense to think of them being shared out among other individual substances.* If, on the other hand, they are universal in character (nonindividual), there is no sense in thinking of them as things that exist separately from particulars. Being-a-man, Aristotle holds, is realized not in a substantial Form independently of all men, but precisely and only in *each individual man*. Because the "friends of the Forms" are unable to explain how such substances are both individual and universal,

they make them the same in form as perishable things (since we know them), talking of "the man himself" and "the horse itself," just adding the word "self" to the names of sensible objects (M 7.16).

But this is completely useless as an explanation.

Finally, there is no way to understand how the Forms, eternally unchanging, account for changes. They are supposed to be the first principles and causes of whatever happens in the world. But

one is most of all bewildered to know what contribution the forms make either to the sensible things that are eternal or to those that come into being and perish; for they are not the cause of their movement or of any change in them (M 1.9).

---

*Aristotle seems to be assuming here that the cause which accounts for the entire world of changing substances cannot itself just be a changing substance; if it were, it would itself need accounting for. So it must be—if it exists—something unchanging. If nature is defined as the sphere of those things that change because of a source of movement or change within them, an ultimate, unchanging cause of natural things would be beyond nature.

†Review the Third Man Argument on pp. 138–140.

---

*Review the discussion of substance on p. 146.

By "the sensible things that are eternal," Aristotle means the things in the natural world whose movement is (as he thought) regular and everlasting: the sun, moon, and the fixed stars. How can fixed and eternally stable Forms explain the changes either in these things or in the more unstable items on earth?

The outcome of Aristotle's critical appraisal of his master's metaphysics is a thoroughgoing rejection of the Forms. The fundamental things that exist, have to be things that are *individual* and can exist *independently* of other things. Plato's Forms do not satisfy either requirement. The Forms are supposed to be the common features of things that are individual, but such features, Aristotle believes, have no independent being; they depend for such being as they have on individual substances (of which they are the qualities, relations, and so on). The sensible things of nature, humans and beavers, surely exist; but being mortal and having a broad, flat tail are qualities existing only as modifications of these. Whether anything beyond these individual entities exists is still an open question. But if it does, it too will be substantial, individual, and capable of independent existence. It will not be a "common feature" of individual things.*

What of Mathematics?

The most convincing arguments for the Forms seem to be mathematical in nature. Socrates is not talking about his sand figure, so Plato concludes that Socrates is talking about the Square Itself, the Triangle Itself, and the Equal. Aristotle wishes to avoid drawing this conclusion. So how does he deal with mathematics?

The natural scientist, in studying changeable things, deals with subjects like the shape of the moon and the sphericity of the earth.

> Such attributes as these are studied by mathematicians as well as by natural scientists, but not by virtue of their being limits of natural bodies. The mathematician is not interested in them as attributes of whatever they are attributes of, and so he separates them. For these attributes can be conceptually separated from movement, without this separation making any difference or involving any false statement (*PH* 2.2).

The crucial point is that we can "conceptually" separate attributes of things and consider them on their own, without supposing that they must be independent things. To use one of Aristotle's favorite examples, consider a snub nose. As a natural thing, a nose is a compound made up of form and matter; as such, it is of interest to the natural scientist but not to the mathematician. What makes it "snub," though, is its being curved in a certain way. And we can consider the curve alone, abstracting away from the matter in the nose. When we do this, we are taking up the mathematician's point of view. But the fact that we can adopt this viewpoint does not mean the Curvedness exists in some sense independently of noses. There need be no Form of the Curve to make mathematics intelligible.

There is no argument, Aristotle holds, from mathematics to the reality of Platonic Forms independent of the world of nature. Mathematics is a science that, like natural science, has the world of nature as its only object. But it does not study it *as nature*; it studies only certain abstractions from natural things, without supposing that such abstractions are themselves things.

Substance and Form

When we considered Aristotle's categories, it was already apparent that certain terms were more basic than others.* These terms could play only the role of subjects in statements; they picked out substances. Now Aristotle reinforces this conclusion, looking more directly at things themselves.

> There are many ways in which the term "being" is used, corresponding to the distinctions we drew earlier, when we showed in how many ways terms are used. On the one hand, it indicates what a thing is and that it is this particular thing; on the other, it

---

*We can think of these reflections as a critique of Plato's metaphysical argument for the Forms (see p. 111). In the following section, Aristotle examines the epistemological argument.

*See pp. 145–147.

indicates a thing's quality or size, or whatever else is asserted of it in this way. Although "being" is used in all these ways, clearly the primary kind of being is what a thing is; for it is this alone that indicates substance. When we say what kind of thing something is, we say that it is good or bad, but not that it is three feet long or that it is a man; but when we say what a thing is, we do not say that it is white, hot, or three feet long, but that it is a man or a god. All other things are said to be only insofar as they are quantities, qualities, affections, or something else of this kind belonging to what is in this primary sense. . . . Neither what is good nor what is sitting down can be referred to independently of a substratum. Clearly, then, it is because of the substance that each of these terms "is"; so what is primarily—not in the sense of being something, but of just quite simply being—is substance (M 7.1).

We can ask many different questions about any given thing: how old is it? how large is it? what color is it? what shape is it? is it alive? does it think? Answers to each of these questions tell us something about the thing in question, describing a way the thing *is*, saying something about its *being*. But one question, Aristotle argues, is basic, namely, *what is it?* We may learn that it is thirty years old, six feet tall, white, fat, and thinking of Philadelphia, but until we learn that it is a *man* all these answers hang in the air. Aristotle puts it this way: that answer gives us the "substance." And substance is *what is* in the basic, fundamental, primary sense.

This is the first answer to the metaphysical question about *being qua being*. For something to be, in the primary sense, is for it to be a substance. But more must be said. What is it that makes a given object a substance?

If we think back to the discussion of nature, we recall that natural things are composed of matter and form (the latter being expressed in a formula or definition). Could it be the matter that makes an object a substance? No. Matter, considered apart from form, is merely potentially something. If you strip off all form, you are tempted to say that what is left is sheer, undifferentiated, characterless something. But even that would be wrong, because every "something" has some character or form that differentiates it from something else. This "prime matter" can't be anything at all, on its own. It cannot have an independent existence; it exists only *as formed*. So matter cannot be what accounts for, or what makes or causes, something to be a substance. For what accounts for something being a substance must be at least as substantial as the substances it produces.

What of the other alternative? Could it be form that makes a portion of being into a substance? In a series of complex arguments, Aristotle argues that this is in fact the case. But not just any form makes the substance *what it is*. The form responsible for the substantiality of substances he calls the **essence** of the thing. *Essences* are expressed by definitions telling us *what things are*.

Johnny's frog may weigh five ounces, but weighing five ounces is not part of the essence of that frog. The proof is that if the frog eats well and gains weight, it does not cease to be a frog. What it is that makes it a frog remains the same whether it weighs five, six, or seven ounces. The definition of frog allows a variation in many of the qualities and quantities Johnny's frog might have. But not in all. It could not cease to be amphibious and still be a frog. Amphibiousness is part of the essence of what it is to be a frog. All natural things (and artifacts, too), Aristotle holds, have an essence: a set of characteristics without which they would not be the things they are.

> Why, for instance, are these materials a house? Because of the presence of the essence of house. One might also ask, "Why is this, or the body containing this, a man?" So what one is really looking for is the cause—that is, the form—of the matter being whatever it is; and this in fact is the substance (M 7.17).

We are, remember, looking for first principles and causes. We want to know what it is that makes a bit of matter what it is. We know that natural things are substances; they can exist independently and individually. But what makes this bunch of bricks a house, this mass of protoplasm a human? The answer is that each satisfies the definition of the essence of that thing. The presence of the essence house in the one case and the essence human in the other is the cause of each one being what it is.

So here we come to a second answer. Even more basic than substances composed of form and matter is the form itself. This form—essence—is the very substance of substance itself.

This should be no surprise. Thinking back to the account Aristotle gives of natural substances, we can see how prominent form is. There are four causes, four explanations of why something is the particular substance it is. The material cause cannot be fundamental, as we have seen. But think about the other three: the form or essence of the thing; the final cause or goal, which is itself a form; and the efficient cause. Even this latter must involve a form, for it must be something actual, and actualities always embody form; as Aristotle likes to say, "man begets man." The trigger explaining the coming into being of a substance with the form of human is another already existing substance, actually embodying that very form. From all three points of view, then, form is the principal cause of the substantiality of things.

Aristotle gives us a simple example. Consider a syllable, *ba*. What makes this a syllable? There is the "matter" that makes it up: the elements *b* and *a*. But it is not the matter that makes these into the syllable *ba*, for these elements might also compose *ab*. So it must be the form. Moreover, the form cannot itself be an element, or we would need to explain how it is related to the *b* and the *a* (i.e., we would have the Third Man problem). So the form must be something else.

> But this "something else," although it seems to be something, seems not to be an element; it seems in fact to be the cause of . . . that [the *b* and the *a*] being a syllable . . . ; in each case it is the thing's substance, since that is the ultimate cause of a thing's being (M 7.17).

So form is the substance of things. But substance is what can exist independently and as an individual entity. This raises a very interesting possibility. Might there be substances that are not compounds of matter and form? Might there be substances that are *pure forms*?

All of nature is made up of material substances in which matter is made into something definite by the presence of form within it. But might there be something more fundamental than nature itself, in just the way that form is more basic than the compounds it forms? If there were any such substances, knowledge of them might be what the wise person seeks. Wisdom is knowing the being and causes of things. If there were substances of pure form, they would be less dependent and more basic than the things of nature, since even natural things depend on form for their substantiality. Knowledge of such "pure" substances would therefore be the knowledge most worth having, the most divine knowledge; it would satisfy our wonder in the highest degree. We need now to explore this possibility.

Pure Actualities

One thing is clear. If there are such purely formal substances, without any matter, they would be pure *actualities* as well. They couldn't involve any "might be's," for the principle of potentiality is matter and they would have no matter. Nor could such substances admit of any change, for every change is a movement from something potential to something actual (e.g., from tadpole into frog). The realm of nature is the realm of change: any natural thing might now be this, might later be that, and might eventually not be at all; it has a potential to be other than it is at any given time. But that is possible because a natural thing is formed matter, which is potentially this, potentially that. A substantial form, not being material, would not be potential, either. It *could not change*. But then it would be eternal as well.

A second thing is also clear. These would be the *best* things. Why? Think again about natural things, for example, the frog that Johnny caught. When is that frog at its very best? Surely when it is most froggy—hopping around, catching flies, doing all the things frogs most typically do. It is not at its best when it has a broken leg, nor when it is feeling listless, nor when it is a mere tadpole. In Aristotle's terms, the frog is best when the form that makes it a frog (the essence) is most fully actualized in the matter—when it most fully is *what it is*. If it is hindered from being at its best, then it must have some potentiality to be less than its best; and all potentiality is due to matter (the principle of potentiality).

If there are substances lacking matter and potency altogether, substances that are fully actual, then they must be the best substances. For they cannot fail to display all the perfection of their form. But are there any such substances—perfect, immaterial, and eternal—pure actualities without the possibility of change? If so, what are they like?

God

In the world of nature, the best things would be those that come closest to these ideals. Aristotle believes these are the heavenly bodies that move eternally in great circles. They change their positions constantly, but in a perfectly regular way, without beginning or ending.* But even such eternal motion is not self-explanatory.

> There is something that is always being moved in an incessant movement, and this movement is circular. . . : and so the first heaven will be eternal. There must, then, be something that moves it. But since that which is moved, as well as moving things, is intermediate, there must be something that moves things without being moved; this will be something eternal, it will be a substance, and it will be an actuality (M 12.7).

Think about baseball. A bat may impart movement to a ball, but only if put into movement by a batter. The bat is what Aristotle calls an "intermediate" mover; it moves the ball and is moved by the batter. The batter himself is moved to swing the bat by his desire to make a hit. Aristotle would put it this way: making a hit is the final cause (the goal) that moves him to swing as he does. So the batter

himself is only an "intermediate" mover. He moves as he does for the sake of making a hit. The goal of making a hit in turn exists for the sake of winning the game, which has as *its* goal the league championship. In the world of baseball, the ultimate final cause putting the whole season in motion is the goal of winning the World Series. Each batter is striving to embody the form of Member of a Team That Wins the World Series.

Let's return to the world of nature, containing the eternal movements of the heavenly bodies. Is there any final or ultimate mover here? There must be, Aristotle argues; otherwise we could not account for the movement of anything at all. Not all movers can be "intermediate" movers. If they were, that series would go on to infinity, but there cannot be any actually existing collection of infinitely many things. There must, then, be "something that moves things without being moved."

Moreover, we can know certain facts about it. It must itself be eternal, since it must account for the eternal movement of the heavenly bodies and so cannot be less extensive than they. It must be a substance, for what other substances depend on cannot be less basic than they. And, of course, it must be fully actual; otherwise, its being what it is would cry out for further explanation—for a mover for it.

What kind of cause could this *unmoved mover* be? Let's review the four causes. It clearly couldn't be a material cause, since that is purely potential. It couldn't be an efficient cause, for the eternal movement of the heavens does not need a temporal trigger. It is not the formal cause of a compound of form and matter, since it contains no matter. It could only be a *final cause*. This conclusion is driven home by an analogy.

> Now, the object of desire and the object of thought move things in this way: they move things without being moved (M 12.7).

Our baseball example already indicated this. What sets the whole baseball world in motion is a goal, namely, winning the World Series. Within the world of baseball, there is no further purpose. That goal is not there for the sake of anything else. It

---

*His reasons for thinking so are complex, involving a theory of the nature of time; we will not discuss that theory here. It can be found in *Physics* IV, 10–14. His theory was combined with the astronomy of the second century Alexandrian, Ptolemy, and was to dominate scientific thinking until the beginnings of modern science in the sixteenth century. For a fuller discussion of this Aristotelian/Ptolemaic theory of the universe, see "The World God Made for Man," in Chapter 16.

moves the players, managers, umpires, and owners, but without being moved itself.* It is "the object of desire and thought," and functions as such as a final cause. It is what they all "love."

> The final cause then moves things because it is loved, whereas all other things move because they are themselves moved. . . . But since there is something that moves things, while being itself immovable and existing in actuality, it is not possible in any way for that thing to be in any state other than that in which it is. . . . The first mover, then, must exist; and insofar as he exists of necessity, his existence must be good; and thus he must be a first principle. . . .
>
> It is upon a principle of this kind, then, that the heavens and nature depend (*M* 12.7).

The ultimate cause of all things is a final cause; it is what all other things love. Their love for it puts them in motion, just as the sheer existence of a bicycle stimulates a boy or girl into activity; delivering papers, mowing lawns, and saving to buy it. As the object of desire and love, this first mover must be something good. Can we say anything more about the nature of this unmoved mover?

> Its life is like the best that we can enjoy—and we can enjoy it for only a short time. It is always in this state (which we cannot be), since its actuality is also pleasure. (And that is why waking, sensation, and thought are the most pleasant of things, whereas hopes and memories are pleasant because of them.) . . . If, then, God is always in the good state which we are sometimes in, that is something to wonder at; and if he is in a better state than we are ever in, that is to be wondered at even more. This is in fact the case, however. Life belongs to him, too; for life is the actuality of mind, and God is that actuality; and his independent actuality is the best life and eternal life. We assert, then, that God is an eternal and most excellent living being, so that continuous and eternal life and duration belong to him. For that is what God is (*M* 12.7).

There must be such an actuality, Aristotle argues, to explain the existence and nature of changing things. As the final cause and the object of the "desire" in all things, it must be the best. What is the best we know? The life of the mind.* So God must enjoy this life in the highest degree.

God, then, is an eternally existing, living being who lives a life of perfect thought. But this raises a further problem. What does God think about? Aristotle's answer to this question is reasonable, but puzzling, too.

> Plainly, it thinks of what is most divine and most valuable, and plainly it does not change; for change would be for the worse. . . . The mind, then, must think of itself if it is the best of things, and its thought will be thought about thought (*M* 12.9).

It would not be appropriate for the best thought to be about ordinary things, Aristotle argues. It must have only the best and most valuable object. But that is itself! So God will think only of himself. He will not, in Aristotle's view, have any concern or thought for the world. He will engage eternally in a contemplation of his own life—which is a life of contemplation. His relation to the world is not that of *creator* (the world being itself everlasting needs no efficient cause), but of *ideal*, inspiring the world to produce its very best in imitation of the divine perfection. God is not the origin of the world, but its goal. Yet he is and must be an actually existing, individual substance, devoid of matter, and the best in every way.

God, then, is to *the* world as winning the World Series is to the "world" of baseball. He functions as the unifying principle of reality, that cause to which all other final causes must ultimately be referred. There is no multitude of ultimate principles. The world is one world. As Aristotle puts it,

> The world does not wish to be governed badly. As Homer says: "To have many kings is not good; let there be one" (*M* 12.10).

---

*You may object that there are further goals: fame, money, and so on. And you are right. But that just shows that the "world" of baseball is not a self-contained world; it is not *the* world, but has a place in a wider setting.

---

*This is discussed in more detail later in this chapter. See "The Highest Good."

The Soul

Plato holds that the essence of a person is found in the soul and that the soul is an entity distinct from the body. Souls exist before their "imprisonment" in a body and survive the death of the body. The wise man tries to dissociate himself as much as possible from the obscure and harmful influences of the body. The practice of philosophy, the love of wisdom, is a kind of purification making a soul fit for blessedness after death.

Aristotle argues against the otherworldliness implicit in such views. One of the causes of such otherworldliness, Aristotle holds, is a too narrow focus.

> Till now, those who have discussed and inquired about the soul seem to have considered only the human soul; but we must take care not to forget the question of whether one single definition can be given of soul in the way that it can of animal, or whether there is a different one in each case—for horse, dog, man, and god, for instance (*PS* 1.1).

The term "soul" is the English translation of the Greek *psyche*. And that is the general word applied to life. So, things with *psyche*—ensouled things—are living things. But not only humans are alive. Aristotle is raising the question whether soul or life or *psyche* is something shared in common among all living things. If you think only about the life characteristic of humans, you might well think of soul as something quite other than nature; but if you pay attention to the broader context, you may find that you have to give a very different account of soul. Again we see Aristotle the biologist at work, trying to organize and classify all living things, humans being just one species among many.

Levels of Soul

There is "one definition of soul in the same way that there is one definition of shape" (*PS* 2.3). Just as there are plane figures and solid figures, and among the latter there are spheres and cubes, so souls come in a variety of kinds. Aristotle adds,

In the case both of shapes and of things that have souls the one thing is potentially present in what follows it; the triangle is potentially present in the quadrilateral, for instance, and the nutritive soul in the sensitive. We must, then, inquire, species by species, what is the soul of each living thing—what is the soul of a plant, for instance, or what is that of a man or a beast (*PS* 2.3).

The general definition of soul involves life: "that which distinguishes what has a soul from what has not is life" (*PS* 2.2). But the point here is that souls may differ from each other as triangles differ from rectangles; the latter are constructed on the basis of triangles, which are more fundamental (every rectangle is composed of two triangles). Similarly, there are more primitive souls (or forms of life) and more complex forms built upon them. Aristotle distinguishes three general levels of soul: that of plants, that of beasts, and that of humans.

The most fundamental of these forms is that of the plants,

> for clearly they have within themselves a faculty and principle such that through it they can grow or decay in opposite directions. For they do not just grow upwards without growing downwards; they grow in both directions alike, and indeed in every direction—provided they are always nourished and, so continuously living—for as long as they can receive nourishment. This nutritive faculty can be separated from the other faculties, but the other faculties cannot exist apart from it in mortal creatures. This is clear in the case of plants, since they have none of the other faculties of the soul. It is because of this primary principle that life belongs to living beings (*PS* 2.2).

Nutritive soul, the capacity to take in nourishment and convert it to life, is basic to living things and is found in plants and animals alike. Plants, however, do not share the higher levels of soul. They live and reproduce and so have a kind of soul, but without the capacities of movement, sensation, and thought.

We should pause a moment to consider reproduction. Why do plants (as well as animals) reproduce? This is a question concerning causes; we know now the fourfold answer Aristotle will give. Because it is so different from the standard answers to such a question, we need to note particularly that for Aristotle the answer is incomplete if it makes no mention of the final cause. What is the final cause for reproduction? For what end does the plant make use of its capacities for nutrition?

> . . . the most natural function of any living being that is complete, is not deformed, and is not born spontaneously is to produce another being like itself . . . so that it may share, as far as it can, in eternity and divinity; that is what they all desire, and it is the purpose of all their natural activities. . . . They cannot, however, share in eternity and divinity continuously, since it is not possible for any perishable thing to remain forever numerically one and the same thing; so they participate in it in the only way in which they can, some to a greater, some to a lesser degree; and what persists is not the thing itself but something like it, what is not numerically, but only in species, one with it (*PS* 2.4).

This is an application of the principle uncovered in first philosophy. There is an unmoved mover, existing eternally in perfect independence and actuality. This is the final cause of whatever else exists. So the fact that plants and animals reproduce can be explained by their "desire" to share, as far as possible, the eternity and divinity that caps off the universe. Each thing imitates God in the way possible for it. God's eternal existence is responsible for the fact that the mature pine tree drops its cones and new plants of that very same species grow up. For the continuation of the same kind of being is as close as mortal beings can come to a kind of eternity.*

More complex forms of soul are built upon the nutritive soul and are never found in nature without it. The next level can be called the level of sensitive soul; it belongs to the animals.

> Plants possess only the nutritive faculty, but other beings possess both it and the sensitive faculty; and if they possess the sensitive faculty, they must also pos-

sess the appetitive; for appetite consists of desire, anger, and will. All animals possess at least one sense, that of touch; anything that has a sense is acquainted with pleasure and pain, with what is pleasant and what is painful; and anything that is acquainted with these has desire, since desire is an appetite for the pleasant (*PS* 2.3).

Animals, then, have sensations and desires in addition to the faculties of nutrition and reproduction. This is a distinctive level of soul. Some animals, though not all, also have the capacity for locomotion.

Finally, there is soul that has the capacity to think, which we can call the rational faculty. Among naturally existing species, it seems to be characteristic only of human beings. Whether there is something unique and special about this kind of soul we'll consider in due course.

In general, then, there are three kinds or levels of soul: nutritive, sensitive, and rational. They correspond to three great classes of living things: plants, animals, and human beings. They are related in such a way that higher kinds of soul incorporate the lower, but the lower can exist without the higher.

Soul and Body

We need now to ask how souls are related to bodies. Can we give the same sort of answer for each of the kinds of soul? Plato, concentrating on human beings, holds that souls are completely distinct entities, capable of existence on their own. That is not so plausible in the case of plant and animal souls. What does Aristotle answer?

Actually, Aristotle gives two answers, and that fact has been the cause of much subsequent debate. There is a general answer and an answer that pertains specifically to the rational form of soul. Let's look first at the general answer. The scene is set by a remark about the proper way to talk about soul.

> It is probably better to say not that the soul feels pity or learns or thinks, but that man does these things with his soul; for we should not suppose that the

---

*Compare Plato's discussion of love, pp. 124–125.

movement is actually in the soul, but that in some cases it penetrates as far as the soul, in others it starts from it; sensation, for instance, starts from the particular objects, whereas recollection starts from the soul and proceeds to the movements or their residues in the sense organs (PS 1.4).

This view of soul is one that firmly embeds soul in the body and makes man a quite unitary being. Man is not thought of as a dual being in such a way that certain of his operations can be assigned to the body and certain others to the soul. It is not the soul that feels or learns or thinks while the body eats and walks; it is the *person* that does all these things. It would be no more sensible, Aristotle holds, to say that the soul is angry than that the soul weaves or builds. Souls do none of these things; human beings do them all. Sensation is not something the soul accomplishes; it cannot occur at all without a body, sense organs, and objects to which those sense organs are sensitive. Recollection has its effects in bodily movements (for example, remembering an appointment makes you run to catch the bus). A person is *one being* with *one essence*.

But what exactly is a soul, and how is it related to a body? We must remind ourselves of the results of Aristotle's investigations of being qua being. The basic things that exist are substances, and in natural substances there is a material substratum that is made into the substance it is by a form.

> Bodies more than anything else seem to be substances, and particularly natural bodies, since they are the first principles of everything else. Some natural bodies have life, some do not; by life we mean self-nutrition, growth, and decay. Every natural body, then, that possesses life will be a substance, and a composite substance, too. Since body is of this kind—that is, possessing life—the soul will not be a body, for the body is not one of the things asserted of a substratum; it is rather substratum or matter itself. The soul, then, must be a substance inasmuch as it is the form of a natural body that potentially possesses life; and such substance is in fact realization, so that the soul is the realization of a body of this kind (PS 2.1).

Suppose you have before you a living being (whether plant, animal, or human makes no difference just now). Subtract from it—in thought—its life. What you have left is a body that *could* be alive, but isn't—a body that is potentially alive. In one sense it is just a body, like a stone or a stove. But in another sense it isn't, for stones and stoves are not even potentially alive; they are not organized in the right way to be alive. Walt Disney can make stoves talk, perhaps, but only in cartoons. There are no talking stoves in reality, precisely because a stove is not the sort of body that is potentially alive.* The body from which we have in thought abstracted life, however, is such a body. It cannot now engage in nutrition or sensation or thought, but it could. It is a kind of "substratum" that could support life—*matter* that could have the *form* of a living thing.

Remember that "form" does not stand for shape (except in very simple cases) but for the essence, the definition, the satisfaction of which makes a thing the substance it is. Remember also that form is the principle of actualization or realization; it is what makes a bit of matter into an actual thing. And remember that form is itself substance: the very substance of substances.

Now you can understand Aristotle's view of soul as "the form of a natural body that potentially possesses life" and as the "realization of a body of this kind." Restore—in thought—life to that body from which you earlier abstracted it. Now it is capable of performing all the activities that are appropriate to that kind of being; it feeds itself and perhaps sees, desires, and thinks. And its being capable of those activities is the *same* as its having certain essential characteristics. Having those characteristics is having a form of a certain kind; having that form is having a soul.

> We have, then, said in general what the soul is: it is a formal substance. That means that it is the essence of a body of a particular kind (PS 2.1).

---

*From Aristotle's point of view, the reincarnationist idea that a human soul might enter into the body of a lower animal is absurd. Cows and dogs do not have the right sorts of bodies (including brains) to support human souls.

Aristotle offers us several examples. Suppose that an axe were a natural body. Then its "formal substance" would be "being an axe." And that would be its soul. But axes are not alive, any more than stones or stoves. They don't actually have souls, since the soul is the principle of life in living things. The analogy should show you, though, what *kind* of thing a soul is. Similarly, Aristotle says, "If the eye were an animal, its soul would be sight; for sight is the formal substance of the eye" (*PS* 2.1). From these examples it should be clear that the soul, so conceived, is not a separable entity; for neither "being an axe" nor sight have any existence independent of actual axes and eyes.

It should be no surprise, then, to hear Aristotle say rather offhandedly,

> We do not, therefore, have to inquire whether the soul and body are one, just as we do not have to inquire whether the wax and its shape, or in general the matter of any given thing and that of which it is the matter, are one (*PS* 2.1).

This problem, which so occupies Plato and for which he constructs so many proofs, is simply one that we do not have to inquire into! The answer is *obvious*, as obvious as the answer to the question whether the shape of a wax seal can exist independently of the wax.

Aristotle gives a brief indication of how this view works in practice. Consider anger. Some people define anger as a disposition to strike out or retaliate in response to some perceived wrong. Its definition therefore involves beliefs, desires, and emotions—all mental states of one sort or another. Others say that anger is just a bodily state involving heightened blood pressure, tensing of muscles, the flow of adrenaline, and so on. Nothing mental needs to be brought into its explanation. What would Aristotle say? He contrasts the viewpoint of the natural scientist with that of the "logician," by which he means one who seeks the definition of such states.

> The natural scientist and the logician would define all these affections in different ways; if they were asked what anger is, the one would say that it was a

desire to hurt someone in return, or something like that, the other that it was a boiling of the blood and the heat around the heart. Of these, one is describing the matter, the other the form and the definition; for the latter is indeed the definition of the thing, but it must be in matter of a particular kind if the thing is going to exist (*PS* 1.1).

If Aristotle is right, psychology and physiology in fact study the same thing. The former studies the form, and the latter the matter. From one point of view anger is a mental state, from the other a physical state. There need be no quarrel between the psychologist and the physiologist. Certain kinds of physical bodies have capacities for certain kinds of activities, and the exercise of those activities is their actuality and form; it is their life—their soul.*

Think of the body of Frankenstein's monster before it was jolted into life. What the tragic doctor provided for the body was a soul. But what is that? He didn't plug a new *thing* into that body; he just *actualized* certain *potentialities* the body already had. The doctor made it able to walk and eat, to see and talk, to think. Having a soul is just being able to do those kinds of things.

This, then, is Aristotle's general account of the relation of soul and body. Souls are the forms (the essential characteristics) of certain kinds of bodies, and as such they do not exist independently of bodies. This means, of course, that a soul does not survive the death of the body to which it gives form. Neither does sight survive the destruction of the eyes.

This general account, however, stands in tension with his account of the rational soul, or perhaps just a part of the rational soul, to which we now turn.

Nous

For the most part, Aristotle's account of the soul is thoroughly "naturalistic." Soul is just how naturally existing, living bodies of a certain kind function; it

---

*This paragraph has a very contemporary ring to it. It expresses a view called functionalism, the dominant theory of mind in recent cognitive science.

is not an additional part separable from such bodies. In this regard, things with souls are thoroughly embedded in the world of nature. Aristotle extensively discusses the capacities of such living beings. These are discussions of the activities of soul.

Sensation, for example, is an organism's ability to receive the *form* of a substance in its environment without taking in its matter. So the eye picks up the color of a thing, the ear its sound, the tongue its taste, and so on. The senses are adapted to the final cause of preserving the life of the organism. They provide information on which animals can act in pursuit of their goals. And they provide data that humans develop through imagination and thinking into true judgments about the world. In other words, sensation provides the data for science, the statements of which can correspond in a truthful way to reality.*

We need not go into further details of Aristotle's psychology. Much of it, while suggestive in its general outlines, is outdated in detail. But we need to address what he says about whether *all* of the soul can be considered as just the form of a living body. Might there be some part of some souls (the human and rational ones) that is separable and can have a kind of independent existence?

Sensation is passive, simply registering the characteristics of the environment. But thinking or knowing is not a passive registration of such features (otherwise, mirrors and calm pools would know what is reflected in them). Thinking is, in fact, active in the highest degree, as his discussion of the contemplative actuality of God has made clear. As we have seen, Aristotle calls our capacity to grasp first principles inductively from many instances, our ability to theorize about the world, *nous*. Can *nous* (translated below as "mind") be simply one aspect of the form of living human bodies?

Although his discussion is somewhat obscure, it seems he is convinced that *nous* (or at least the active part of it) must be something capable of independent existence. What are his reasons?

(1) He draws an analogy to sight. What is required to see, visually to know, that this Ferrari is

red? There seem to be three factors: (a) the red car; (b) an appropriate sense organ; and (c) light. Note that the first two are not sufficient. The capacity to register the qualities of an object, though essential, is by itself too passive to count as knowledge. Something more active is required. (Think of cream cheese kept near garlic; it absorbs the garlic smell, but does it *smell* the garlic?)

> There is the mind that is such as we have just described by virtue of the fact that it becomes everything; then, there is another mind, which is what it is by virtue of the fact that it makes everything; it is a sort of condition like light. For in a way light makes what are potentially colors become colors in actuality. This second mind is separable, incapable of being acted upon, mixed with nothing, and in essence an actuality (*PS* 3.5).

The passive power of *nous* can potentially "become everything," can register the color of the car, the smell of the garlic, the taste of honey. It can take in the forms of things without absorbing their matter. But without some active power in the mind that "makes everything" the way light makes colors visible, you couldn't distinguish between a knowing human being and the cream cheese.* Active *nous* is required to turn these passive registrations—which are only potentially knowledge—into actual knowledge.

Moreover, this power must itself be an actuality; as we have seen, only an actuality can turn something that is potentially *X* into something actually *X*. Since knowledge is actual, an actual power must exist in the mind to produce it. Aristotle takes these considerations to establish the distinctness of the active and passive powers of *nous*. In fact, he speaks not just of two powers but of two minds. The second mind, he says, is "mixed with nothing" and "separable" from the first. To say it is mixed with nothing must mean that it is a pure form unmixed with matter. If you think a moment, you should be able to see that it must be a pure form if

---

*Compare the discussion of induction on pp. 152–153.

*Compare Plato on the function of the Form of the Good (p. 120). What Plato attributes to the highest Form, Aristotle makes a capacity of the rational soul itself.

it can actualize *everything*; if it were mixed with matter, it would be some definite thing and would lack the required plasticity. If it is not some definite thing, however, it cannot be some part of the body. And that is the first reason why Aristotle concludes that it is separable from the body.

(2) Aristotle seems, moreover, to have been unable to find any "organ" or bodily location for this activity. Sight is located in the eyes, hearing in the ears, and so on. But where could the faculty of knowing be? Reflecting on his general view of the soul, Aristotle writes:

> Clearly, then, the soul is not separable from the body; or, if it is divisible into parts, some of the parts are not separable, for in some cases the realization is just the realization of the parts. However, there is nothing to prevent some parts being separated, insofar as they are not realizations of any body (*PS* 2.1).

Sight is the "realization" of the eye. But what part of the body could have as its function something as infinitely complex as thinking and knowing? The seat of sensation and emotions, Aristotle thinks, is the heart. The brain he considers an organ for cooling the body. Without a knowledge of the microstructure of the brain, it must have seemed to him that there is nothing available in the body to serve as the organ of thought, so the active part of *nous* must be separable from the body.

It is not only separable, Aristotle holds; it is eternal and immortal.

> . . . it alone is immortal and eternal; we do not remember this because, although this mind is incapable of being acted upon, the other kind of mind, which is capable of being acted upon, is perishable. But without this kind of mind nothing thinks (*PS* 3.5).

Why should active *nous* be eternal? Because it is not material; it is not the form of a material substance (i.e., of part of the body). It is rather one of those substantial forms which can exist separately. Lacking matter, it also lacks potentiality for change and is fully and everlastingly what it is. If *nous* is eternal and immortal, it must, like the soul of Socrates and Plato, have preexisted our birth. But,

Aristotle insists, we do *not remember* anything we know before birth—because there is nothing there to remember. We did not *know* anything before birth. Active *nous*, remember, is like the light. It lights up what the senses receive; it makes actual what is so far only a potentiality for knowledge. But it is not itself knowledge; it only works material delivered to it by the senses into knowledge.* Without this matter from the senses, there is no actuality—no knowledge. And before birth there were no senses or sense organs to produce this material.

Aristotle cannot and does not accept the Socratic and Platonic doctrine of recollection as an explanation of knowing. For similar reasons, it does not seem that *nous* can be anything like personal immortality, in which an individual human being survives death and remembers his life. Active *nous*, in fact, seems quite impersonal.

A number of questions arise, but Aristotle does not give us answers. Is *nous* numerically the same thing in all individuals, or is there a distinct *nous* for each person? What is the relation between *nous* and God, to which it bears some striking resemblances? How, if *nous* is independent and separable, does it come to be associated with human souls at all?

These questions give rise to a long debate, partly about what Aristotle means, partly about what truth there is to all this. In the Middle Ages, for instance, Jewish, Muslim, and Christian thinkers, trying to incorporate Aristotle into a broader theological context, wrestle determinedly with these problems. But for our purposes it is enough to register his conviction that there is something about human beings, and particularly about them as knowers, that cannot be accounted for in purely naturalistic terms. There is a part of the soul that is, after all, otherworldly.

---

*Immanuel Kant's view of the relation between concepts and percepts is very similar to this account of *nous*. Like *nous*, concepts alone cannot give us any knowledge; they structure, or interpret, or "light up" the deliverances of the senses; knowledge is a product of the interplay of "spontaneous" conceptualization and "receptive" sensation. (See p. 379.) It is also interesting to compare this discussion of *nous* with Heidegger's view of the "clearing" in which things become present. See Chapter 27, "Modes of Disclosure."

The Good Life

Because Aristotle's views of knowledge, reality, and human nature are so different from Plato's, we might expect his views of the good for man to differ as well. So they do. They do not disagree much over specific goods; both, for instance, defend the traditional virtues of moderation, justice, and courage. Moreover, Aristotle is as insistent as Plato that adherence to such virtues can be rationally justified. And the general form of justification is the same; both strive to show that the virtuous person is the happy person. So there is a large measure of agreement. But the whole approach to ethics is quite different, for in repudiating the Forms, Aristotle denies the claim of Socrates and Plato that knowledge—in the strict, scientific sense—is possible in this sphere. He makes this quite explicit in the following paragraphs.

> Our treatment will be adequate if we make it as precise as the subject matter allows. The same degree of accuracy should not be demanded in all inquiries any more than in all the products of craftsmen. Virtue and justice—the subject matter of politics—admit of plenty of differences and uncertainty. . . .
>
> Then, since our discussion is about, and proceeds from, matters of this sort, we must be content with indicating the truth in broad, general outline. Since our statements are about things that are generally such and such, and that is also the character of our starting point, we must be content with conclusions of the same sort. This is how we should also estimate every statement made here. The educated man looks for as much precision in each subject as the nature of the subject allows (*NE* 1.3).

When he talks about knowledge of the natural world, Aristotle always insists that it is knowledge of its universal and unchanging aspects. Aristotle never repudiates Plato's principle that knowledge in the strict sense (science) must be certain; and to be certain, its objects must be eternal and unchanging. We can know the essences of natural things (of a certain species of fish, for example) because this essence never changes. Individual fish

of that species may vary within certain limits, and each individual is born, changes, and dies. But the species remains unchanging.*

Theoretical knowledge like this, when disciplined by demonstration and insight into first principles, is quite different from what we can expect in the realm of ethics. The subject matter in ethics is practical—choice, character, and action. Ethics is a practical art; it is better not to call it a science. It is more like navigation than astronomy. It aims at wisdom about what to do and how to live. We always act in some particular situation or other, so ethics must pay attention to *particulars* as well as universals. Because particulars are often just "generally such and such," they cannot be known with the kind of scientific certainty available for universals, and we ought not to expect too much exactness here (*NE* 7.7). Rather, we "must be content with indicating the truth in broad, general outline." But then, as Aristotle says, "the educated man looks [only] for as much precision . . . as the nature of the subject allows."

There are two consequences of looking at ethics this way. First, we should not be surprised if those who are not particularly knowledgeable sometimes make better decisions than those who are. For what counts here is experience of particulars, not just knowledge of what is universally true. Second, we ought not to expect young people to be very good at these matters, for "they are inexperienced in the practical side of living" and tend to be "ruled by their emotions" (*NE* 1.3). There may be child prodigies in music and mathematics, but there are no child prodigies in ethics.

This focus on the practical and particular is the basis of Aristotle's rejection of Plato's Form of the Good as the apex of the wise person's wisdom. If Plato were right here, not only should there be a science of the good, it should be one unified science. But, Aristotle says, there is no one such science of the good. What we find instead is a multitude of goods; there is a good of medicine, a good of generalship, a good pertaining to politics, and so

---

*Aristotle has no theory of the evolution of species. There were hints of such a view in at least one of the pre-Socratic philosophers (Empedocles), but Aristotle explicitly repudiates it.

on. Each has its own end (health, victory, and well-being, for example) and must be judged in terms of the good it aims at.

Worse yet, even if there were a single unique Form of the Good, knowledge of it would be useless. Aristotle tells us that in all the arts and sciences

> people aim at some good and try to find where they fall short; yet they leave aside knowing this Idea [Form]! It would be unreasonable for all craftsmen to be unaware of it, if it is so useful, and not even try to find it. It is hard to see how a weaver or builder will benefit in his art, by knowing this Idea [Form] of the good* (*NE* 1.6).

It is not, then, by a theoretical knowledge of the highest realities that we should try to address our practical problems of choice and action. Yet we must try to be as rational as possible. We can think of Aristotle as making the attempt to apply reason to the somewhat recalcitrant facts of human nature, in order to shape it into the best that it can be. The aim of ethics is not, after all, purely "theoretical." It should have a practical payoff.

> . . . we are not studying in order to know what virtue is, but to become good, for otherwise there would be no profit in it (*NE* 2.2).

What is it, then, to "become good," and how can we do so?

Happiness

Aristotle begins his main treatise on ethics, the *Nicomachean Ethics*, with these words:

> Every skill and every inquiry, and similarly, every action and choice of action, is thought to have some good as its object. This is why the good has rightly been defined as the object of all endeavor (*NE* 1.1).

Whenever we do something, we have some end in view. If we exercise, our end is health; if we study,

our end is knowledge or a profession; if we earn money, our end is security. And we consider that end to be good; no one strives for what he or she considers bad.*

> Now, if there is some object of activities that we want for its own sake (and others only because of that), and if it is not true that everything is chosen for something else—in which case there will be an infinite regress, that will nullify all our striving—it is plain that this must be the good, the highest good. Would not knowing it have a great influence on our way of living? Would we not be better at doing what we should, like archers with a target to aim at? (*NE* 1.2).

We often do one thing for the sake of another. But this cannot go on forever, or there will be no point to anything we do. What we want to find is some end that we want, but not for the sake of anything else: something we prize "for its own sake." That would be something good, not just good, but the highest good, since there is nothing we want that *for*. If we can identify something like that and keep it clearly before our eyes, as an archer looks at the target while shooting, we will be more likely to attain what is truly good.

Is there anything like that?

> What is the highest good in all matters of action? As to the name, there is almost complete agreement; for uneducated and educated alike call it happiness, and make happiness identical with the good life and successful living. They disagree, however, about the meaning of happiness (*NE* 1.4).

Everyone wants to be happy. And the question, "Why do you want to be happy—for what?" seems to be senseless. This is the end, the final goal. Money we want for security, but happiness for its own sake. Yet, for us as well as for Aristotle, there is something unsatisfying about this answer, some-

---

*The term *Eidos*, which we have been translating as "Form," is sometimes also rendered "Idea." We must only remember that such Platonic "Ideas" are not subjectively located in our minds.

*This is true in general. Both Socrates and Plato, however, hold it is universally true. For that reason, they hold that if we know what is good, we will do what is good. But Aristotle believes there are exceptions when a person can, in some sense, act contrary to what he himself considers to be his best judgment. See the view expressed in Euripides' *Hippolytus*, quoted on p. 65. As we shall see, St. Paul and Augustine both agree with Aristotle that such inner conflict is possible. See pp. 209, 220–231, and 235.

thing hollow. For we immediately want to ask: "What is happiness, anyway?"

Many people, Aristotle notes, think that happiness is pleasure; in fact, they live as though that were so. But that cannot be correct. For the good of every creature must be appropriate to that creature's nature; it couldn't be right that the good life for human beings was the same as "the kind of life lived by cattle" (*NE* 1.4). It is true that "amusements" are pleasant, and that they are chosen for their own sake. Within limits, there is nothing wrong with that. But

> it would be absurd if the end were amusement and if trouble and hardship throughout life would be all for the sake of amusing oneself. . . . It would be stupid and childish to work hard and sweat just for childish amusement (*NE* 10.6).

Other people think that happiness is a matter of fame and honor. Again, there is something to be said for that; it is more characteristically human than mere pleasure. Aristotle does not want to deny that honor is something we can seek for its own sake; still

> it seems to be more superficial than what we are looking for, since it rests in the man who gives the honor rather than in him who receives it, whereas our thought is that the good is something proper to the person, and cannot be taken away from him (*NE* 1.5).

Here Aristotle is surely drawing on the tradition of Socrates, who believes that "the many" could neither bestow the greatest blessings nor inflict the greatest harms and that it is not possible for a bad man to harm a good man.* The highest good, happiness, must be something "proper to the person" that "cannot be taken away." The problem with honor and fame is that you are not in control of them; whether they are bestowed or withdrawn depends on others. If you take honor as your end, you give your happiness as a hostage into the hands of others. This seems unsatisfactory to Aristotle.

How, then, shall we discover what happiness is?

---

*See *Apology* 30d, 44d.

We might achieve this by ascertaining the specific function of man. In the case of flute players, sculptors, and all craftsmen—indeed all who have some function and activity—"good" and "excellent" reside in their function. Now, the same will be true of man, if he has a peculiar function to himself. Do builders and cobblers have functions and activities, but man not, being by nature idle? Or, just as the eye, hand, foot, and every part of the body has a function, similarly, is one to attribute a function to man over and above these? In that case, what will it be? (*NE* 1.7).

A woman is a flutist by virtue of having a certain function to perform: playing the flute. In a similar way, an eye is defined by its function: it is a thing for seeing with. These reflections help us identify what makes a flute player *good*, namely, excellence in flute playing, which is indeed the end each flutist strives to attain. An eye is good if it performs its function well, i.e., gives clear and accurate images. If we could discover a function characteristic of human beings as such—not as flutists or cobblers, but just *in virtue of being human*—we might be able to identify the good appropriate to them. Aristotle thinks we can discover such a function.

> The function of man is activity of soul in accordance with reason, or at least not without reason (*NE* 1.7).

Let's examine this statement. Aristotle is claiming that there is something in human beings analogous to the function of a flutist or cobbler: "activity of soul in accordance with reason."* What does that mean? And why does he pick on that, exactly?

If we are interested in the function of a human being, we must pay attention not only to *accidental* capacities, abilities, and activities. We must focus on what makes a human being human: the soul. As we have seen, soul is the realization of a certain kind of body; it is its life and the source of its actuality as an individual substance. It is the *essence* of a living thing. A dog is being a dog when it is

---

*In one important respect, Aristotle is Plato's faithful pupil. Look again at the functions of the soul for Plato (p. 130). Which one is dominant?

doing essentially doglike things. And human beings are being human when they are acting in essentially human ways. Now what is peculiarly characteristic of humans? We already know Aristotle's answer to that: humans are different from plants and the other animals because they have the *rational* level of soul. So the function of a human being (not qua mother, carpenter, or president, but qua human) is living according to reason, or at least, Aristotle adds, "not without reason." This addition is not insignificant. It means that although an excellent human life is a rational one, it is not limited to purely intellectual pursuits. There are excellences (virtues) that pertain to the physical and social aspects of our lives as well. The latter he calls the *moral* virtues.

Furthermore, although the function of the cobbler is simply to make shoes, the best cobbler is the one who performs this function with excellence, i.e., makes excellent shoes. As Aristotle says, "function comes first, and superiority in excellence is superadded." If that is so, then

> the good for man proves to be activity of soul in conformity with excellence; and if there is more than one excellence, it will be the best and most complete of these (*NE 1.7*).

Doing what is characteristic of humans to do, living in accord with reason, and in the most excellent kind of way, is the good for humans. And if it is the human being's good, it is also what constitutes happiness.

> It seems as though everything that people look for in connection with happiness resides in our definition. Some think it to be excellence or virtue; others wisdom; others special skill; whereas still others think it all these, or some of these together with pleasure, or at least not without pleasure. Others incorporate external goods as well (*NE 1.8*).

Happiness is not possible without excellence or virtue (*arete*), any more than a flutist is happy over a poor performance. It surely includes wisdom, for excellent use of one's rational powers is part of being an excellent human being. Special skills are almost certainly included, for there are many necessary and useful things to be done in a human life, from house building to poetry writing. And it will include pleasure, not because pleasure is itself the good—we have seen it cannot be that—but because the life of those who live rationally with excellence is in itself pleasant.

> The feeling of pleasure belongs to the soul, and pleasure for each individual consists of what he is said to be a lover of—horses for horse lovers and plays for theater lovers. In the same way, justice is pleasant for the man who loves justice; and in general, things that conform to virtue are pleasant for him who loves virtue. The things thought pleasant by the vast majority of people are always in conflict with one another, because it is not by nature that they are pleasant; but those who love goodness take pleasure in what is by nature pleasant. This is the characteristic of actions in conformity with virtue, so that they are in themselves pleasant to those who love goodness. Their life has no extra need of pleasure as a kind of wrapper; it contains pleasure in itself (*NE 1.8*).

Does a happy life "incorporate external goods as well," as some say? Aristotle's answer is, yes—at least in a moderate degree.

> It is impossible (or at least not easy) to do fine acts without a supply of "goods." Many acts are done through friends, or by means of wealth and political power, which are all, as it were, instruments. When people are without some of these, that ruins their blessed condition—for example, noble birth, fine children, or beauty. The man who is quite hideous to look at or ignoble or a hermit or childless cannot be entirely happy. Perhaps this is even more so if a man has really vicious children or friends or if they are good but have died. So, as we have said, happiness does seem to require this external bounty (*NE 1.8*).

A certain amount of good fortune is a necessary condition for happiness. One would not expect the Elephant Man, for example, to be entirely happy, nor a person whose children have become thoroughly wicked. This means, of course, that your happiness is not entirely in your own control. Self-sufficiency in happiness may be a kind of ideal, but in this world it is not likely to be entirely realized.

One point needs special emphasis. The happy life, which is one and the same with the good life, is a life of *activity*. Happiness is not something that happens to you. Even though it may require a foundation in moderate good fortune, many goods will not guarantee happiness. Happiness is not something the world owes you or can give you. It is not passive. It is not rest. Think about the following analogy.

> At the Olympic games, it is not the handsomest and strongest who are crowned, but actual competitors, some of whom are the winners. Similarly, it is those who act rightly who get the rewards and the good things in life (*NE* 1.8).

Happiness is an *activity* of soul in accord with excellence.

And finally, Aristotle adds, "in a complete life." Just as one swallow does not make a summer, so "a short time does not make a man blessed or happy" (*NE* 1.7). There is a certain unavoidable fragility to human happiness.

> There are many changes and all kinds of chances throughout a lifetime, and it is possible for a man who is really flourishing to meet with great disaster in old age, like Priam of Troy. No one gives the name happy to a man who meets with misfortune like that and dies miserably (*NE* 2.9).

Virtue or Excellence (*Arete*)

The good for human beings, then, is happiness, and happiness is the full development and exercise of our human capacities "in conformity with excellence." But what kind of thing is this excellence? How is it attained? Is there just one excellence which is appropriate to human beings, or are there many? We often speak of the "virtues" in the plural—courage, moderation, justice, temperance, and so on; are these independent of one another, or

can you be an excellent human being only if you have them all? These are the questions we now address. (I shall speak in terms of "virtues" for the time being and postpone the question about their unity.)

In considering what kind of thing a virtue is, Aristotle notes that it is for our virtues and vices that we are praised and blamed. A virtue, then, cannot be a simple emotion or feeling, for two reasons: (1) we are in general blamed not for being angry as such, but for giving in to our anger, for nursing our anger, or for being unreasonably angry; and (2) we feel fear and anger without choosing to, but the virtues "are a sort of choice, or at least not possible without choice" (*NE* 2.5). Nor can the virtues be capacities we have by nature; again, we are called good or bad not because we are *capable* of feeling angry or *capable* of reasoning. We do not become good "naturally."

But if the virtues are not emotions or capacities, what can they be? Aristotle's answer is that they are *dispositions* or *habits*. To be courageous is to be disposed to do brave things. To be temperate is to have a tendency toward moderation in one's pleasures. These dispositions have intimate connections with choice and action. People who never do the brave thing when they have the opportunity are not brave, no matter how brave they happen to feel or what capacities they have. And the person who just happens to do a brave thing, in a quite accidental way, is not brave either. The brave person acts bravely whenever the occasion calls for it; and the more the person is truly possessed of that virtue, the more easily and naturally courageous actions come. There is no need to engage in fierce internal struggles to screw up the courage to act rightly.

So this is the answer to the first question. To have a virtue of a certain kind is to have a disposition to choose and to behave in ways appropriate to that virtue.

How are the virtues attained? This is our second question. They are not innate in us, though we have a natural capacity for them. They are, Aristotle tells us, learned. And they are learned as all habits are learned, by practice.

Where doing or making is dependent on knowing how, we acquire the know-how by actually doing. For example, people become builders by actually building, and the same applies to lyre players. In the same way, we become just by doing just acts; and similarly with "temperate" and "brave" (NE 2.1).

This leads, moreover, to a kind of "virtuous circle."

We become moderate through abstaining from pleasure, and when we are moderate we are best able to abstain. The same is true of bravery. Through being trained to despise and accept danger, we become brave; we shall be best able to accept danger once we are brave (NE 2.2).

So we learn these excellences by practicing behavior that eventually becomes habitual in us. And if they can be learned, they can be taught. Socrates seems forever unsure whether human excellence is something that can be taught.* Aristotle is certain that it can be and tells us how.

The point is that moral virtue is concerned with pleasures and pains. We do bad actions because of the pleasure going with them, and abstain from good actions because they are hard and painful. Therefore, there should be some direction from a very early age, as Plato says, with a view to taking pleasure in, and being pained by, the right things (NE 2.3).

A child can be taught virtue—moderation, courage, generosity, and justice—by associating pleasures and pains with them, by rewarding and punishing. A child needs to be taught to find pleasure in virtuous behavior and shame or pain in vice. If we can teach a person to build well or to play the lyre well in this way, we can also teach the more specifically human excellences. Why should we teach these virtues to our children? Aristotle has a clear answer: if they find pleasure in the most excellent exercise of their human nature, they will be happier people. Such happy people are also the virtuous and good, for the good person is the one who takes pleasure in the right things.

*See Meno and Chapter 9, pp. 97–98.

Our third question is whether virtue is one or many. Can a person be partly good and partly bad, or is goodness all or nothing? Plato and Socrates are both convinced that goodness is one. For Plato, knowledge of the Form of the Good is the only secure foundation for virtue; and that Form is one. Whoever grasped it fully would be good through and through. We might expect Aristotle to be more pluralistic. In fact, he says that Socrates and Plato are in one sense right and in one sense wrong. There are indeed many virtues, and they can perhaps even exist in some independence of each other. Often, a brave man is not particularly moderate in choosing his pleasures; James Bond would be an example. But in their perfection, Aristotle holds, you can't have one virtue without having them all. What will the brave man without moderation do, for example, when he is pulled in one direction by his bravery and in another by some tempting pleasure? Won't his lack of moderation hamper the exercise of his courage?

The unity of human excellence in its perfection is a function of the exercise of reason. If you follow reason, you will not be able to develop only one of these virtues to the exclusion of others. This use of reason Aristotle calls practical sense or practical wisdom. "Once the single virtue, practical sense, is present, all the virtues will be present" (NE 6.13).

To this "single virtue," which provides the foundation and unity of all the rest, we now turn.

The Role of Reason

Happiness is living the life of an excellent human being; you can't be an excellent human being unless you use your rational powers. But how, exactly, does Aristotle think that rationality helps in living an excellent life?

Let us consider this first: it is in the nature of things for the virtues to be destroyed by excess and deficiency, as we see in the case of health and strength—a good example, for we must use clear cases when discussing abstruse matters. Excessive or insufficient training destroys strength, just as too much or too little food and drink ruins health. The right amount, however, brings health and preserves it. So this applies to moderation, bravery, and the other virtues. The man who runs away from everything in fear, and faces up to nothing, becomes a coward; the man who is absolutely fearless, and will walk into anything, becomes rash. It is the same with the man who gets enjoyment from all the pleasures, abstaining from none: he is immoderate; whereas he who avoids all pleasures, like a boor, is a man of no sensitivity. Moderation and bravery are destroyed by excess and deficiency, but are kept flourishing by the mean (*NE* 2.2).

We can think of an emotion or an action as laid out on a line, the extremes of which are labeled "too much" and "too little." Somewhere between these extremes is a point that is "just right." This point Aristotle calls "the mean." It is at this "just right" point that human excellence or virtue flourishes.

But where on such a line does the mean lie? Aristotle is very clear that it does not necessarily lie in the geometrical middle. The amount of training right for a beginner is not the right amount for a world-class runner. Aristotle distinguishes between *the mean relative to the thing* and *the mean relative to us* and gives an example. Think about a trainer considering how much food to give his athletes. He may know that ten pounds is too much and two pounds too little. Does it follow that he should give them six (the mathematical mean)? Of course not. He has to consider each of the athletes and give *each one* an amount that is not too much and not too little *for him*.

So it is with the virtues.

In feeling fear, confidence, desire, anger, pity, and in general pleasure and pain, one can feel too much or too little; and both extremes are wrong. The mean and good is feeling at the right time, about the right things, in relation to the right people, and for the right reason; and the mean and the good are the task of virtue (*NE* 2.6).

Think about being angry. It is a matter of degree; you can be very angry or only a little angry. Aristotle's recommendation of *the mean relative to us* does not mean that you should always get only moder-

ately angry.* About certain things, in relation to a given person, and for some specific reason, it might sometimes be the right thing to be very angry indeed. But in relation to other times, occasions, persons, and reasons, that degree of anger might be altogether inappropriate. We should always seek the mean, but what that is depends on the situation in which we find ourselves.

Finding the mean in the situation is the practical role of *reason* in ethics. The virtuous or excellent person is the one who is good at rationally discovering the mean relative to us with regard to our emotions, our dispositions or habits, and our actions. How much, for instance, shall we give to charity? About these things we deliberate and choose. Because these are matters of degree and because the right degree depends on our appreciation of subtle differences in situations, being truly virtuous is difficult. As Aristotle says,

going wrong happens in many ways . . . , whereas doing right happens in one way only. That is why one is easy, the other difficult: missing the target is easy, but hitting it is hard (*NE* 2.6.)

This is why it is a hard job to be good. It is hard to get to the mean in each thing. It is the expert, not just anybody, who finds the center of the circle. In the same way, having a fit of temper is easy for anyone; so is giving money and spending it. But this is not so when it comes to questions of "for whom?" "how much?" "when?" "why?" and "how?" This is why goodness is rare, and is praiseworthy and fine (*NE* 2.9).

The capacity of reason to make such estimations of the mean, to answer the above questions, is what Aristotle calls *practical sense* or *practical wisdom*. (The Greek word is *phronesis*.) The person of practical wisdom is the one who uses reason to determine the mean whenever choices have to be made. Since virtue or excellence lies in the mean, and the mean is determined by reasoning, we can now also

---

*Nor is this a doctrine of relativism in the Sophist's sense. It is *not* the case that if Jones thinks it is right to get angry to a certain degree in a certain circumstance, then it *is* (therefore) right—not even *for Jones*. Jones can be *mistaken* in his judgment of the mean.

say that virtue is "disposition *accompanied* by right reason. Right reason, in connection with such matters is practical sense" (*NE* 6.13).

Aristotle does not give us a formula or an algorithm to use in making choices. He apparently thinks that no such formula is possible in practical matters pertaining to particular situations of choice. If a formula were possible, ethics could be a science rather than an art.* Nonetheless, there is a kind of standard for judging whether the right thing is being done. That standard is the virtuous and good person. The right thing to do in any situation is what the good person would do. In judging which are the best pleasures, for example, Aristotle's view is that

> the thing is as it appears to the good man. If this is true, as it seems to be and excellence and the good man, as good man, are the measure of each thing, then pleasures, too, will be the pleasures of the good man, and pleasant will apply to the things that please him (*NE* 10.5).

Protagoras holds that "man is the measure of all things." We have seen how this leads to a kind of relativism; if Jones thinks something is good, then it is good—to Jones. Aristotle disagrees and argues in this way: we do not take the sick man's word about whether the pudding is sweet, nor the word of someone who is color blind about the color of certain clothes; in the same way, not everyone is adept at judging the goodness of things. Protagorean relativism is a mistake, because it is not everyone, but only the good person, who is the "measure of each thing." In every situation, virtuous and good actions are defined by the mean. The mean is discovered by "right reason" or practical wisdom. So the "measure" of virtue and goodness will be the person who judges according to practical wisdom.

You might still want to ask, but how do we recognize these practically wise persons? To this question Aristotle has no very clear answer. Again, there is no formula for recognizing such persons. But that need not mean we cannot in general tell who they are. They tend to be those persons, we might suggest, to whom you would turn for advice.

Responsibility

The virtues, as we have seen, are dispositions to choose and behave in certain ways, according to right reason or practical wisdom. If we have these dispositions, we are called good; if we lack them, we are called bad. It is for our virtues and vices that we are praised and blamed. But there are situations in which someone does a bad thing yet is not blamed. The presence of certain conditions can make praise and blame inappropriate. Let's call these "excusing conditions."

Aristotle is the first to canvass excusing conditions systematically, and so to try to define when persons should not be held responsible for their actions. This is an important topic in its own right, useful "for those who are laying down laws about rewards and punishments" (*NE* 3.1). It has, moreover, been discussed in a variety of ways by subsequent philosophers. So we must look briefly at the way Aristotle begins this conversation.

> Praise and blame are accorded to voluntary acts; but involuntary acts are accorded pardon, and at times pity (*NE* 3.1).

It is only for actions that are voluntary that we are held responsible. But what are the conditions that make an action involuntary? He identifies two excusing conditions: compulsion and ignorance. Let us discuss each one briefly.

When someone acts under compulsion we mean, says Aristotle, that

> the principle of action is external, and that the doer . . . contributes nothing of his own—as when the wind carries one off somewhere, or other human beings who have power over one do this (*NE* 3.1).

---

*We will see that some later writers on ethics, the utilitarians, for example, try to supply such a formula (p. 452). Kant also tries to find a single principle from which the right thing to do can be derived. See pp. 391 and 394.

Now having your ship driven somewhere by a storm or being tied up and carried somewhere are particularly clear cases. If something bad should happen as a result of either of these, no one would blame you for it, for "the principle of action is external."

There are more debatable cases; for example, a captain in a storm throws his cargo overboard. Here the action is one that normally would be bad; it is not something the captain would ordinarily do. We might say that the storm forced him to do it to save the lives of his crew and passengers. Yet we can't say that he contributed "nothing of his own." He did make the decision; in that respect, the action was voluntary. Still, because this is what "all people of sense" would do in those circumstances, the captain is pardoned. Aristotle concludes that though such actions are voluntary if considered as particular acts, they are involuntary in a general way, or essentially—for no one would ordinarily choose them. And that is the ground on which we excuse the captain from blame.

Again Aristotle insists that we not try to find a precise formula for deciding such cases. He stresses how difficult such decisions may be.

> There are times when it is hard to decide what should be chosen at what price, and what endured in return for what reward. Perhaps it is still harder to stick to the decision.
> It is not easy to say if one course should be chosen rather than another, since there is great variation in particular circumstances (*NE* 3.1).

This does not mean, of course, that anything goes. The application of practical wisdom to such situations helps us discriminate whether something was done by compulsion.

Let us consider the second condition. What sort of ignorance excuses us from responsibility? It is not, Aristotle says, ignorance of what is right. Those who do not know what is right are not ignorant, but wicked! We do not excuse people for being wicked. (Here is the source of the adage that ignorance of the law is no excuse.)

If ignorance of the right does not excuse, neither does ignorance of what everybody ought to know. But

> ignorance in particular circumstances does—that is, ignorance of the sphere and scope of the action. . . . A man may be ignorant of *what* he is doing: e.g., when people say that it "slipped out in the course of a conversation": or that they did not know these things were secret (like Aeschylus on the mysteries); or like the man with the catapult, who wanted "only to demonstrate it," but fired it instead. Someone, as Merope does, might think his son an enemy; or mistake a sharp spear for one with a button. . . . One might give a man something to drink, with a view to saving his life, and kill him instead (*NE* 3.1).

It is ignorance about particular circumstances that makes an action involuntary and leads us to excuse the agent from responsibility. In such cases, a person can say: if I had only known, I would have done differently. The mark of whether that is true or not, Aristotle suggests, is regret. If someone does something bad through ignorance and later regrets doing it, that is a sign that he is not wicked. It shows that he would indeed have done it otherwise if he had known. And in that case he can truly be said to have acted involuntarily and deserve pardon.

Again, there are difficult cases. What about the person who acts in ignorance because he is drunk and is not in a condition to recognize the facts of the case? Here Aristotle suggests that it is not appropriate to excuse him, because he was responsible for getting himself into that state. The same is true for someone ignorant through carelessness; that person should have taken care. Here is, perhaps, a harder case.

> But perhaps the man's character is such that he cannot take care. Well, people themselves are responsible for getting like that, through living disorderly lives: they are responsible for being unjust or profligate, the former through evildoing, the latter through spending their time drinking, and so on. Activity in a certain thing gives a man that character; this is clear

from those who are practicing for any contest or action, since that is what they spend their time doing. Not knowing that dispositions are attained through actually doing things is the sign of a complete ignoramus (*NE* 3.5).

No one, Aristotle suggests, can be that ignorant.

There is further discussion of such cases, but this provides the main outlines of his views on responsibility. We can see that Aristotle assumes people must normally be held responsible for what they do, that compulsion and ignorance may be excusing conditions, and that he is rather severe in his estimation of when these conditions may hold. Although Aristotle does not explicitly say so, it is a fair inference that he considers the *acceptance* of responsibility and the sparing use of excuses as a part of the good life. By our choices and actions we create the habits that become our character. And so we are ourselves very largely responsible for our own happiness or lack thereof.

The Highest Good

When Aristotle defines the good for man as "activity of soul in conformity with excellence," he adds that "if there is more than one excellence, it will be the best and most complete of these." We need now to examine what the "best and most complete" excellence is.

The best activity of soul must be the one that activates whatever is best in us. And what is that? Think back to Aristotle's discussion of the human soul. It incorporates the levels of nutrition and reproduction, sensation, and reason. At the very peak is *nous*, or mind: the nonpassive, purely active source of knowledge and wisdom. Can there be any doubt that this, which contains no potentiality at all, is the best, the most divine part of us?

But if that is so, the activity that is best is the activity of *nous*. And such activity should be not only the highest good but also the greatest happiness for a human being. This is just what Aristotle claims.

This is the best activity (mind is the best in us; and "intelligible" things which are apprehended by the mind are the best objects in the world), and also the most continuous. We are better able to contemplate continuously than to *do* anything (*NE* 10.7).

The activity of *nous*—discovering and keeping in mind the first principles of things—Aristotle calls "contemplation." The life of contemplation is said to be the very best life partly because it is the exercise of the "best" part of us and partly because we can engage in it "continuously." But this claim has two other foundations. This life is both the most pleasant life and the most self-sufficient. For these reasons it is the happiest life.

We think it essential that pleasure should be mixed in with happiness, and the most pleasant of activities in accordance with virtue is admittedly activity in accordance with wisdom. Philosophy has pleasures that are marvelous for their purity and permanence. Besides, it is likely that those who have knowledge have a more pleasant life than those who are seeking it. Sufficiency, as people call it, will be associated above all with contemplation. The wise man, the just, and all the rest of them need the necessities of life; further, once there is an adequate supply of these, the just man needs people with and towards whom he may perform just acts; and the same applies to the temperate man, the brave man, and so on. But the wise man is able to contemplate, even when he is on his own; and the more so, the wiser he is. It is better, perhaps, when he has people working with him; but still he is the most self-sufficient of all (*NE* 10.7).

Aristotle dismisses honor as a candidate for the good, you will recall, on the grounds that it is too dependent on others. What is truly good, it seems, must be more "proper to the person, and cannot be taken away." The same point is here used to recommend the life of contemplation as the very best life, for it is more "self-sufficient" than any other, less dependent upon other people. The other virtues need the presence of other people for their exercise, while the wise man can engage in contemplation "even when he is on his own." And to Aristotle this seems to recommend such a life as the very best.*

Note that an assumption betrays its presence here, as it does elsewhere in Greek philosophy. Justice is inferior to wisdom, we are told, because the just man needs other people and material goods for the exercise of his virtue. It is almost as if justice itself would be better if it could be exercised independently of other people.

Suppose we ask why the just individual acts justly. From what Aristotle says, we suspect that it is not because other people need the individual's just acts or are benefited by them; it is just that he or she has come to see that this is the best way to live. This is the ground for Aristotle's recommendation of contemplation as well; it is the best way for an individual to live. "Best" always means "most self-sufficient" for Aristotle. So the life of contemplation is praised because it is a life independent of fortune—to the extent that is possible for a human being. We see clearly that Aristotle's ethics (and classical Greek ethics in general) is an ethics of self-perfection, or self-realization. There is not much in it that recommends caring for others for *their* sakes.†

This attitude underlies the rational justification for being virtuous in both Plato and Aristotle. They try to show that we should be just and moderate because, to put it crudely, it *pays*. True, neither argues that the consequences of virtue will necessarily be pleasing. Glaucon's picture of the perfectly just and perfectly unjust men had ruled out that sort of appeal.‡ Happiness is not related to virtue as a paycheck is related to a week's work. The relation for both Plato and Aristotle is internal; the just and virtuous life is recommended because it is *in itself* the happiest life (though they also believe that *in general* its consequences will be good). Although Aristotle always thinks of the good of a person as essentially involving the good of some community, and especially as involving friends, it remains true nonetheless that individuals are primarily interested in their own happiness. This may, we might grant, be a stimulus to achievement, but there is not much compassion in it.

Aristotle sums up his discussion of the contemplative life (the happiest of all) by *disagreeing* with Pindar's aphorism, "For mortals, a mortal lot is best."* The contemplation of the wise man, he tells us, will

> be more than human. A man will not live like that by virtue of his humanness, but by virtue of some divine thing within him. His activity is as superior to the activity of the other virtues as this divine thing is to his composite character. Now if mind is divine in comparison with man, the life of the mind is divine in comparison with mere human life. We should not follow popular advice and, being human, have only human ambitions, or, being mortal, have only mortal thoughts. As far as possible, we should become immortal and do everything toward living by the best that is in us (*NE* 10.7).

The activity of a wise human being, then, resembles the activity of God, the unmoved mover. Indeed, this is another case of God acting as a final cause, an ideal that draws all things, in this case the philosopher, to imitate his own self-sufficient activity to the extent possible. Because the best and most pleasant activity for any living creature is what most fully realizes its nature, contemplation—the life of reason—is the most happy life possible for human beings.

Notes

1. Quoted from Ps. Ammonius, *Aristotelis Vita*, in W. D. Ross, *Aristotle* (New York: Meridian Books, 1959), 14.
2. I am indebted here to Marjorie Grene's excellent little book, *A Portrait of Aristotle* (Chicago: University of Chicago Press, 1963), 38–65.
3. Quoted in J. M. Edmonds, *Elegy and Iambus with the Anacreontea II* (New York: G. P. Putnam's Sons, 1931), 175.

---

*Contemplation, for Aristotle, is not what is often called "meditation" these days. It is not an attempt to empty the mind, but an active life of study to uncover the wonder and the whys of things.
†Such compassion, or caring, under the names of "love" and "charity" (*agape*, not *eros*) comes into our story with the Christians. See pp. 206–207.
‡See p. 133.

---

*See p. 5.

4. All quotations from Aristotle's works are from *The Philosophy of Aristotle*, ed. Renford Bambrough (New York: New American Library, 1963), unless noted otherwise. Within this text, references to specific works will be as follows (numerical references are to book and section numbers).

C: Categories
I: On Interpretation
M: Metaphysics
PA: Posterior Analytics
PH: Physics
PS: Psychology
NE: Nicomachean Ethics

5. As quoted in Grene, *Portrait of Aristotle*, 105.

6. I owe this example to J. L. Ackrill, *Aristotle the Philosopher* (Oxford: Oxford University Press, 1981), 42.

12

Epicureans, Stoics, and Skeptics: Happiness for the Many

It is customary to discuss the development of philosophy in the Hellenistic and Roman periods after Aristotle in terms of three schools, or movements of thought. We will follow this practice, but without any claim to do full justice to these developments. We will look at only a few central tenets of these schools and show how they try to solve problems facing people of those times, problems not adequately addressed by the great systematic achievements of Plato and Aristotle.

To understand the appeal of these philosophies, however, we need to look at more than just their intellectual predecessors. A brief discussion of the altered social and religious climate will be useful. The era of the city-state was fading. After the war between Athens and Sparta, the regions of Greece engaged in a long series of struggles to achieve dominance, and some, Thebes and Macedonia for instance, managed it for a time (see map 1). But the struggles with shifting alliances and continual warfare wore down the belief that a city could be an arena for living a good life. People lost confidence in it, retreating into smaller units and leaving the politics of cities to be settled by rather crude military types. (The Epicureans, as we'll see, are prominent among those who seek their happiness not as citizens but as members of a smaller voluntary community.) Under Philip of Macedon and his son Alexander, vast territories were conquered and unified politically. And finally Rome established her dominance over the entire Mediterranean ba-

sin, bringing a kind of stability and enforced peace to the region. The Romans were good administrators and warriors and contributed much in the sphere of law but not much original philosophy.

With the loss of confidence in the cities went a loss of faith in the gods of the cities. In the era of empires, Athena seemed too restricted even for Athens. The Olympians had apparently failed, and their authority waned. It is true that the Romans took over the Greek pantheon and gave the old gods new names (Jove, Juno, Venus), but the vigor of the religion was gone. This didn't mean, however, that religion was dead or dying—far from it. The old religions of the earth (religions of fertility, ancestor worship, and ecstasy), suppressed for a time by the Homeric gods of the sky, had never disappeared. Now they flourished with new vigor. To this was added a flood of religious cults and ideas from the East, all seeming to promise what the new age demanded. There was a proliferation of initiations into sacred and secret mysteries, of mediators and saviors, of claims to esoteric knowledge comprising fantastic systems that populated the world with spirits, demons, gods, and powers, and of rites that promised a merging of the worshiper's very being with the being of some divinity.

Politicians, of course, made use of religion for their own ends, accepting (and encouraging) the accolades of divinity people laid upon them. Alexander was proclaimed a god; his successors liked the status it gave them and continued the practice.

The world seemed hostile and society brutal. People had lost control and grasped desperately at almost any promise to reestablish it. Fortune and Chance themselves came to seem divine and were worshiped and feared. Astrology, never a force in the Golden Age of Greece, "fell upon the Hellenistic mind," Gilbert Murray says, "as a new disease falls upon some remote island people."[1] The stars were thought to be gods, the planets living beings (or controlled by living beings).* Their positions in the heavens were consulted as signs of things happening and to happen on earth. The heavens were thought to be populated by myriads of spirits, powers, principalities, demons, and gods. And one never knew when they would cause some fresh disaster to overtake one.

The tradition established by Thales and his successors, never widespread in its influence in any case, was impotent to stop all this. Rational criticism had not completely disappeared, but it must have seemed to many thinkers that they were in a new dark age. People were anxious and afraid, their confidence broken.

What could those who wished to carry on the enterprise of the nature philosophers, of Socrates, Plato, and Aristotle, do to stem the tide? Let us look first at Epicurus.

The Epicureans

It is not possible for one to rid himself of his fears about the most important things if he does not understand the nature of the universe but dreads some of the things he has learned in the myths. Therefore, it is not possible to gain unmixed happiness without natural science (*PD* 12.143).[2]

---

*The philosophers were, perhaps, not altogether blameless in this. It was common to ascribe greater perfection to the heavenly bodies in their eternal course than to the changeable world we live in. And more than one philosopher spoke of them as divine. In Plato's later political thought, the supreme object of worship for the masses was to be the sun.

This passage strikes the key notes in the philosophy of Epicurus (341–270 B.C.E.). The aim of life is happiness. Happiness depends above all on ridding oneself of fears. And the basis for the removal of fear is science. We want to examine what fears Epicurus thinks stand in the way of happiness, what he thinks happiness is, why an understanding of the universe will help, and what kind of science will give us this understanding.

According to Epicurus,

pleasure is the beginning and end of the blessed life. We recognize pleasure as the first and natural good; starting from pleasure we accept or reject; and we return to this as we judge every good thing, trusting this feeling of pleasure as our guide (*LM* 129a).

The Greek word translated as pleasure is *hedone*, and the viewpoint expressed in the passage above is therefore called **hedonism**. As we have seen, Aristotle considers the view that pleasure is the good and rejects it.* It does not seem to him that something we share with the lower animals could be the distinctively human good. But Epicurus is unmoved by this argument. Just look about you, he seems to be saying. Every living thing, humans included, takes pleasure as a natural good; it is clearly one thing that is good not by convention but by *physis*. It is the ground of our acceptances and rejections, of what we pursue and what we avoid. And if we want to judge the goodness of some course of action, we ask whether there is more pleasure than pain involved in pursuing it.

His claim is not that this is the way it should be but that this is how it *is*. The things we judge to be good or evil are in fact measured by this standard of pleasure and pain. It is no use, Epicurus might say, to complain that this is unworthy of human beings; this is the way we are made—all of us. This fact levels things out and defeats the elitism of the philosophers. Perhaps only a few are capable of the tortuous dialectic that leads to the vision of the Form of the Good. Not many can live the life of

---

*See pp. 173 and 178.

divine contemplation that Aristotle recommends as the highest good. But a pleasant life is available to all without difficulty.

It is in terms of pleasure and pain, then, that we must understand happiness.* The happy life is the pleasant life. And philosophy, Epicurus holds, is the study of what makes for happiness—nothing more, nothing less.

> Let no young man delay the study of philosophy, and let no old man become weary of it; for it is never too early nor too late to care for the well-being of the soul. The man who says that the season for this study has not yet come or is already past is like the man who says it is too early or too late for happiness (LM 122).

But what, exactly, can philosophy do for us to make us happy? Note that contrary to Aristotle's view, the pursuit of philosophy is not in itself the recipe for the happy life. Philosophy is basically a means for Epicurus. Though philosophical discussion with a group of friends is itself one of the great pleasures in life, Epicurus is not interested in philosophical speculation for its own sake. So only those parts of philosophy which serve the end of happiness are recommended. As he says,

> do not think that knowledge about the things above the earth, whether treated as part of a philosophical system or by itself, has any other purpose than peace of mind and confidence. This is also true of the other studies (LP 85b).

There is a single-minded practicality about Epicurus' thought that brushes to one side all that does not serve the goal. So we should not expect much from him in the way of new developments in science, logic, or epistemology; indeed, his contributions in these areas are mostly secondhand, as we will see. But in ethics he has some originality and has had some influence.

The study of philosophy can do two things for us. It can free us from certain fears and anxieties that spoil our happiness, and it can provide directions for maximizing the pleasant life. Let us look at each of these in turn.

There are pains and displeasures that are natural and cannot always be avoided, such as illness and separation from loved ones because of death. About these, however, Epicurus says that the intense pains typically do not last very long, while those that last a long time are usually not very intense; one way or another, these pains may be endured (PD 4; VS 4). But there are pains that are due to certain *beliefs* we hold, and for these there is a sure remedy: changing these beliefs. In fact, that is not only the expedient thing to do, he tells us, but also the right thing to do because the beliefs that cause us distress are *false*. So we can rid ourselves of these pains by a true apprehension of *the way things are*.*

What are these false beliefs that distress us? There are two sets of such beliefs in particular: those concerning the gods and those concerning death. About the gods, people are misled by the "myths," as Epicurus calls them, which permeate the cults of popular religion and official state piety as well. The heart of such myths is that the gods are always poking around in the universe to make things happen according to their whims and wishes, that they are interested in human affairs, and that they need to be propitiated if things are not to go badly with us. Such beliefs fill us with dread, Epicurus believes, because we never know when some god or demon or star power is going to crush us—perhaps for no reason we can discern at all. So we need to be always anxiously inquiring of the diviners, prophets, augurs, soothsayers, astrologers, and priests about what went wrong or whether this is a good time to do so and so and, if not, whether we can do something to make it a good time. (Usually, of course, we can, to the benefit of the "sage" in question.) Fear of the gods, then, is one of the most potent spoilers of contentment.

---

*This theme is taken up in the nineteenth century by the utilitarians. See Chapter 23.

*In the first century B.C.E. the Roman poet Lucretius wrote a long poem popularizing the views of Epicurus. Its title in Latin is *De Rerum Natura* ("on nature"). I borrow the phrase "the way things are" from Rolfe Humphries' version of that title in his very readable translation (Indiana University Press, 1969).

The other fear concerns death. It is the same anxiety that pulls Hamlet up short and prevents him from taking his own life:

> To die, to sleep;
> To sleep: perchance to dream: ay, there's the rub;
> For in that sleep of death what dreams may come
> When we have shuffled off this mortal coil,
> Must give us pause.[3]

Tradition was full of dreadful stories of the fates of the dead. Lucretius lists some of them: Tantalus, frozen in terror, fears the massive rock balanced above him; Tityos is food for the vultures; Sisyphus must forever roll his rock up the hill, only to see it crash down again; and so on (WTA, pp. 114–115).[4]

The good news Epicurus proclaims is that none of this is true. As Lucretius put it:

> Our terrors and our darknesses of mind
> Must be dispelled, not by the sunshine's rays,
> Not by those shining arrows of the light,
> But by insight into nature, and a scheme
> Of systematic contemplation.

(WTA, p. 24)

Now, of course, you want desperately to know what this "insight into nature" is that will dispel such terrors. It is nothing new; we are already familiar with it, but not exactly in this guise. What the Epicureans have in mind is the atomism of Leucippus and Democritus.* Why do they choose atomism as the philosophy that tells us "the way things are"? They never make that very clear. One suspects that Epicurus and Lucretius saw atomism as particularly serviceable in the role of terror dispeller.

Let us remind ourselves of a few of the main points of atomism.

1. Atoms and the void alone exist.
2. The common things of the world, including living things, are temporary hookings together of atoms.

---

*You may find it helpful to review that philosophy, looking especially at pp. 29–30.

3. The soul is material, made of very fine atoms, and is therefore mortal.
4. Whatever happens is mechanistically determined to happen according to the laws by which atoms combine and fall apart again.

Epicurus accepts atomism as an account of the way things are, except for a slight but crucial modification to the fourth point. The universal determinism envisaged by Democritus is modified so that room for our free will to act can be salvaged. If we were not free, how could we follow the prescriptions for happiness Epicurus sets out? Although the atoms *mostly* follow strictly determined mechanistic paths, *sometimes*, he holds, they "swerve" unaccountably. Lucretius presents the argument:

> If cause forever follows after cause
> In infinite, undeviating sequence
> And a new motion always has to come
> Out of an old one, by fixed law; if atoms
> Do not, by swerving, cause new moves which break
> The laws of fate; if cause forever follows,
> In infinite sequence, cause—where would we get
> This free will that we have, wrested from fate,
> By which we go ahead, each one of us,
> Wherever our pleasures urge? Don't we also swerve
> At no fixed time or place, but as our purpose
> Directs us?

(WTA, p. 59)

With this alteration, the rest of atomist metaphysics is acceptable to Epicurus. This is the "insight into nature" that will dispel the terrors of religious myths. But exactly how will it do this?

The gods, Epicurus maintains, surely exist. But like everything else, they too are composed of atoms and the void. Nonetheless, they seem to be immortal, being composed of exceedingly fine atoms and dwelling between the worlds, unaffected by the grosser impingements of worldly things. (Epicurus thinks there must be many worlds because space is infinite, and our world is clearly limited.) Moreover, we must acknowledge that they dwell in unchangeable blessedness. It follows that they have no concern with the world, nor with human affairs:

That which is blessed and immortal is not troubled itself, nor does it cause trouble to another. As a result, it is not affected by anger or favor, for these belong to weakness (*PD* 1).

To be concerned about human affairs, Epicurus thinks, would be an imperfection in the gods. How could they be blessed if they had to worry about what Jones is going to do tomorrow? To poke around in the world, changing this and adjusting that, would mean the gods' immortality would be in jeopardy, for they could not help but be affected by their interventions; and such bumps and bruises are what shake the atoms loose and lead to disintegration.

There is no reason, then, to fear the gods. They have no interest in us and do not intervene directly. The heavenly bodies, moreover, are not demons or divinities that rule our destinies. Sun and moon, planets and stars are composed of atoms and the void just like everything else. Their behavior can be explained in exactly the same kinds of ways we explain familiar phenomena on earth. So it is inappropriate—ignorant—to look to the heavens for signs and portents, to go to astrologers for predictions, and try to read the riddle of the future in the stars. After summarizing some of the traditional stories of the gods, Lucretius says:

All this, all this is wonderfully told,
A marvel of tradition, and yet far
From the real truth. Reject it—for the gods
Must, by their nature, take delight in peace,
Forever calm, serene, forever far
From our affairs, beyond all pain, beyond
All danger, in their own resources strong,
Having no need of us at all, above
Wrath or propitiation.

(*WTA*, p. 70)

So much, then, for fear of the gods. What of death? Remember that if atomism is correct, soul and body dissipate together in the event we call death. So there is no future life to look forward to. In what is probably Epicurus' best known saying, he draws the moral.

Accustom yourself to the belief that death is of no concern to us, since all good and evil lie in sensation and sensation ends with death. . . . Death, the most dreaded of evils, is therefore of no concern to us; for while we exist death is not present, and when death is present we no longer exist. It is therefore nothing either to the living or to the dead since it is not present to the living, and the dead no longer are (*LM* 124b–125).

Good and evil, of course, are pleasure and pain. These are the sources of happiness and unhappiness. Fear of death is predicated on the assumption that we will experience these sensations after death and perhaps be wretchedly unhappy. But that makes no sense at all, for "when death is present we no longer exist." What, then, is there to fear? Death "is of no concern to us."

Thus "insight into nature" can remove at least certain virulent strains of unhappiness from our lives. This is the negative benefit philosophy can confer, but it is not yet enough for happiness. We need also to know how to *live well*. And here too Epicurus gives guidance. The key point is clearly put in the following passage:

For the very reason that pleasure is the chief and the natural good, we do not choose every pleasure, but there are times when we pass by pleasures if they are outweighed by the hardships that follow; and many pains we think better than pleasures when a greater pleasure will come to us once we have undergone the long-continued pains. . . . By measuring and by looking at advantages and disadvantages, it is proper to decide all these things; for under certain circumstances we treat the good as evil, and again, the evil as good (*LM* 129b–130a).

The terms "Epicurean" or "hedonist" nowadays suggest someone who is a glutton for pleasures of every kind and indulges to excess in the satisfaction of every desire. This is a complete distortion of the philosophy of Epicurus; in his view, there is no better way to secure for oneself a life of misery than such sensual indulgence. If what you want is pleasure—the most pleasure—then you must be prudent in your pursuit of it.

When we say that pleasure is the end, we do not mean the pleasure of the profligate or that which depends on physical enjoyment—as some think who do not understand our teachings, disagree with them, or give them an evil interpretation—but by pleasure we mean the state wherein the body is free from pain and the mind from anxiety. Neither continual drinking and dancing, nor sexual love, nor the enjoyment of fish and whatever else the luxurious table offers brings about the pleasant life; rather it is produced by the reason which is sober, which examines the motive for every choice and rejection, and which drives away all those opinions through which the greatest tumult lays hold of the mind (*LM* 131b–132a).

To implement these general principles, we must make a distinction between different sorts of desire.

You must consider that of the desires some are natural, some are vain, and of those that are natural, some are necessary, others only natural. Of the necessary desires, some are necessary for happiness, some for the ease of the body, some for life itself (*LM* 127b).

The classification of desires, then, looks like this:

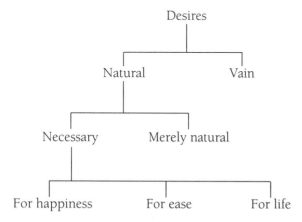

Let us fill in each of these categories with some plausible examples:

- vain desires: luxuries of all kinds, following fashion, keeping up with the Joneses
- merely natural desires: sexual desire (natural but not necessary)
- necessary for life: food, drink, shelter
- necessary for ease: a bed
- necessary for happiness: friendship

What philosophy can do for us is to make clear that not all desires are on a par and that satisfying some of them will cost more than it is worth. That is surely the case, Epicurus believes, with vain desires. It is likely to be the case with the merely natural desires; at least it is clear that following every sexual passion is a sure prescription for unhappiness. The point is that if we want to be happy, the crucial step is to control and limit our desires—to those which are necessary, if possible. Epicurus recommends the simple life, as the following sayings make clear:

Natural wealth is limited and easily obtained; the wealth defined by vain fancies is always beyond reach (*PD* 15.144)

Nothing satisfies him to whom what is enough is little (*VS* 68).

To be accustomed to simple and plain living is conducive to health and makes a man ready for the necessary tasks of life. It also makes us more ready for the enjoyment of luxury if at intervals we chance to meet with it, and it renders us fearless against fortune (*LM* 131a).

So this hedonist, who finds pleasure to be the only natural good, values the old Greek virtue of moderation after all. Now, however, it is recommended on the grounds that it will give us the pleasantest life possible. What of the other virtues, of justice, for instance? Justice is not something good in itself, Epicurus argues, thus taking the view that Glaucon and Adeimantus urge against Socrates (*PD* 31–38).* Justice arises when men

---

*See *Republic* Book II and pp. 132–133.

make a "compact" together not to injure one another, and it is reasonable to be just as long as that compact pays off—in increased pleasure, of course. Justice and the other virtues are praised, but only as *means* to a happy life for the individual (the "honesty is the best policy" syndrome).

We must say a word about friendship. The virtue of friendship is held in the highest esteem among the Epicureans. They are famous for it. Epicurus established in Athens a "Garden" in which his followers lived, sharing work, study, and conversation. In this Garden and in similar communities across the ancient world, men—including at least some women and slaves—cultivated this virtue. Friendship, they believed, is the key to the highest blessings this life holds. As Epicurus says,

> Of the things that wisdom prepares for insuring lifelong happiness, by far the greatest is the possession of friends (*PD* 27.148).

> Friendship dances through the world bidding us all to waken to the recognition of happiness (*VS* 52).

This blessing, Epicurus assumes, is open to all people—or at least to all who pursue their pleasures with prudence and moderation. So, he assures us, happiness is not restricted to the few. The many, too, may participate.

The Stoics

Our treatment of the Stoic philosophers will be even more incomplete than that of the Epicureans, because the Stoics work harder at developing all the major fields of philosophy. They make original contributions to logic, set forth a detailed theory of knowledge, and spend considerable effort on theories of the nature of the universe, elaborated over a period of five centuries by a succession of good minds. Although in many respects the Stoics are consciously opposed to the main principles of the Epicureans, the two schools share one belief: that

philosophy is to serve the aim of promoting the best and happiest life a human being could live. We'll concentrate on the Stoics' views in this area, discussing their other philosophical contributions only to clarify their views about ethics.

The founder of **Stoicism** was Zeno from Citium, a city in Cyprus.* Like several other important figures in this tradition, he was not a native Greek, though he came to Athens as a young man (in about 320 B.C.E.), studied there, and taught there until his death, about 260. The fact that Stoic teachers came from parts of the Mediterranean basin that Plato and Aristotle would have regarded as barbarian is a sign that times had changed for philosophy. Stoic doctrines from the first had a universality about them that reached beyond the parochial concerns of any city or nation; in this way, they were both a reflection of the enlarged political situation and an influence on it. Socrates had thought of himself as a citizen of Athens. The Stoics considered themselves citizens of the world.

The universality of Stoicism is shown in another way. It appealed to members of all social classes. Among its leading figures was a freed slave, Epictetus (c. 51–135 C.E.), and the Roman Emperor Marcus Aurelius (121–180 C.E.).

Let us begin with some reflections on happiness. Stoic ideas of happiness owe much to Socrates, Plato, and Aristotle, all of whom argue that what makes for a truly good life cannot depend on anything outside ourselves.† This ideal of independence or self-sufficiency is carried to the extreme by the Stoics, who claim that absolutely *nothing that happens* to the wise man can disturb his calm happiness. This may seem a startling suggestion.‡

---

*Note that this is not the Zeno of the paradoxes, the associate of Parmenides.
†Socrates holds that a good man cannot be harmed (*Apology* 41c–d) and Plato argues that happiness is a condition of the harmonious soul. Aristotle claims that "the good is something proper to the person and cannot be taken away from him" (see p. 173).
‡Compare Aristotle, p. 175. As you study Stoicism, ask yourself: is this an improvement on Aristotle?

How can this be? Epictetus puts his finger on the crux of the matter:

> Men are disturbed not by things, but by the views they take of things. Thus death is nothing terrible, else it would have appeared so to Socrates (E 5).[5]

This implies that what bothers us, what dismays us, what makes us unhappy is *up to us*. Happiness and unhappiness are not functions of events. They are in our control!

But how can that be? To understand this we need to appreciate a crucial distinction.

> There are things which are within our power, and there are things which are beyond our power. Within our power are opinion, aim, desire, aversion, and, in one word, whatever affairs are our own. Beyond our power are body, property, reputation, office, and, in one word, whatever are not properly our own affairs (E 1). [6]

This distinction between what is and what is not within our power makes possible the remarkable claims of the Stoic. When are we happy? When we get what we desire. Suppose now that we set our hearts on the things that are beyond our power—a beautiful body, a fine estate, fame, being chairman of the board. Reflection will surely convince you that these things are at best only partly in our power; circumstances must cooperate if they are to be ours. If these are what we really want, disappointment is sure to follow. If we don't get them, we will be unhappy. Even if we do get them, we will be continually anxious lest we lose them. And neither disappointment nor anxiety is part of a happy life.

What, then, is within our control? It is, Epictetus answers, "the use of the phenomena of existence" (E 6). The phenomena—what appears, what happens, the stuff of the world—are not in our control, but the *use* to which we put them is. How we view them, our opinions about them, whether we desire or fear them—all this is within our power. This is our proper business, the area of our concern. Of all that lies beyond this sphere, we

are advised to "be prepared to say that it is nothing to you" (E 1).

Suppose now that we have, by dint of determination and long practice (for this is what it would take), gotten to the point where we always make the distinction. We never set our hearts on the things that are not in our power to control. It seems we have gotten ourselves into a serious difficulty. Having enough food to eat (to take just one example) is not something entirely within our control. People who live in lands stricken by famine are evidence enough for that. Are we not to desire food? And if not, how are we to live? At this point, it seems as though the Stoics are condemned by their principles to starve virtuously, but perhaps contentedly, to death. Is there a way they can solve this problem?

The key to the solution is found in the positive advice the Stoic gives: to keep our wills in harmony with nature (E 4, 6, 13, 30; and M 2.9). But to understand this, we have to explore what the Stoics mean by "nature." We need not go into the details of their nature philosophy, but the central idea is crucial.

Whatever exists, according to the Stoics, is material or corporeal. Our only certainties come from sense experience, and sense experience always reveals the material. But like Heraclitus, they hold that the material world is ordered by a rational principle, a *logos*.* That is what makes the world a world rather than a chaos. This principle, which (like Heraclitus) they sometimes call the fiery element, is not just a passive pattern in things; it is the ordering of the world by and for a reason.† As the ordering principle of the world, it is appropriately called divine.

Thus God, for the Stoics, is not like the gods of the Epicureans, apart from the world and unconcerned with it. Nor is the Stoic God like the unmoved mover of Aristotle, independent and self-sufficient, related to the world only as an ideal that the world tries to emulate. Neither of these divinities could be known through the senses. The

---

*See pp. 19–21.
†See p. 18.

Stoics conceive of God (whom, again like Heraclitus, they are willing to call Zeus) as *immanent* in the world.* Whatever material being you come across has its divine element within it. So the Stoics are committed to a version of pantheism (God is all and all is God), though the term "God" emphasizes the *ordering* and the term "nature" the *ordered* aspects of things. Marcus Aurelius expresses these views:

> Universal Nature's impulse was to create an orderly world. It follows, then, that everything now happening must follow a logical sequence; if it were not so, the prime purpose towards which the impulses of the World-Reason are directed would be an irrational one. Remembrance of this will help you to face many things more calmly (M 7.75).

Everything "must follow a logical sequence." It is apparent that the Stoics are believers in Destiny or Fate. Whatever happens happens of necessity. But this is not a cause for despair, since Destiny is indistinguishable from Divine Providence. Whatever happens is determined by the divine reason, and so it must happen for the best.† As Epictetus says,

> As a mark is not set up for the sake of missing the aim, so neither does the nature of evil exist in the world (E 27).

Although "whatever will be, will be," it does not follow that we can simply drift. Your attitude toward what happens makes an enormous difference. For on that attitude your happiness or unhappiness depends.

> Demand not that events should happen as you wish; but wish them to happen as they do happen, and you will go on well (E 8).

Epictetus quotes from a hymn written by Cleanthes, one of the disciples of Zeno.

> Conduct me, Zeus, and thou, O Destiny,
> Wherever your decrees have fixed my lot.
> I follow cheerfully; and, did I not,
> Wicked and wretched, I must follow still.
>
> (E 51)

If we are to be happy, then, we must seek to keep our wills in harmony with nature. And we now can see that this is identical with keeping our wills in harmony with both reason and God, for nature is the sphere of events governed by the benevolent purpose of a rational deity. The Stoics sometimes speak of the soul as a microcosm (a little world) and compare it to the macrocosm of the universe. Our task, they hold, is to use our reason to order the microcosm in a way that mirrors the ordering of the macrocosm. This is possible for us because the reason within us is in fact a manifestation or aspect of the divine reason that orders the world as a whole. God not only is immanent in the macrocosm but also is present within each of us.

Now we can see how the Stoics address the problem raised earlier. Everything in nature has its own ordering principle within it, all bound in harmony with the great order of the whole. In living things there is a natural tendency toward certain ends—self-preservation in particular, together with all that serves that end. This is part of the Divine Providence and is not to be despised. This is why animals seek food and shelter; and this is why they naturally seek to preserve their species. To deny these natural tendencies would certainly not be to keep one's will in harmony with nature!

So the Stoics eat when hungry, drink when thirsty, and do what is necessary to preserve themselves from the weather. It is in accordance with nature so to do. But, and this point is crucial, they pursue these natural goals with equanimity, not being disturbed if their quest for them is frustrated. In regard to what is natural to a living being, the Stoics distinguish what is *preferred*, what is *shunned*, and what is *indifferent*. For human beings not only food and shelter are "preferred," but also skills, knowledge, health, reputation, and wealth. Their opposites are in the class of things "shunned,"

---

*See p. 20.
†Compare Heraclitus again, p. 19.

and many things are "indifferent"; about them one simply shouldn't care. The natural tendencies in human beings determine what falls in one class or another.

So there is nothing wrong with pursuing what is preferred. Where people go wrong, however, is in attributing some absolute value to all these things. And the mark of this wrong turn is their reaction when they do not get what they want: distress, despair, resentment, and general unhappiness. The wise person, by contrast, "uses such things without requiring them."[7] This attitude makes possible the equanimity of the Stoics, in which nothing that happens in the world can destroy their calm. There is only one thing to which the Stoic attaches absolute value: that his will should be in harmony with nature. In comparison with that, even the things "preferred" seem only indifferent.

This means that the *only* true good is virtue: a life in harmony with nature, reason, and God. Stoics and Epicureans carry on a running battle, over just this point. The Epicureans, of course, hold that the only good is pleasure, and everything else (including virtue) is good only in relation to that. Stoics typically respond in a most extreme fashion, denying not only that pleasure is the one true good, but also that it is even in the realm of the "preferred." Pleasure, according to the Stoics, is *never* to be pursued; it is not an appropriate end *at all*.

The Epicureans argue, as we have seen, that pleasure is the only natural good, the root of all our choosing. The Stoics reply that this is far from so. Our natural tendencies are for the acquisition of certain *things*, such as food, which is necessary for self-preservation. They do not deny that eating when hungry is pleasurable, but the pleasure is an *accompaniment* to the eating, not the end sought. Pleasure on its own won't keep one alive. People go wrong exactly here, in seeking the by-product instead of the end—A sure recipe, the Stoics think, for disaster. The virtuous will in fact lead a pleasant life. But if they make the pleasant life their object, they will miss virtue *and* the pleasure that accompanies it.

There are two corollaries to the view that only virtue is the good. First, the only thing that counts in estimating the goodness of an action is the intention of the agent. You can see why this must be so. An action is an attempt to change the world in some way; whether the action succeeds depends upon the cooperation of the world; the world is not entirely in the control of the agent; and so the goodness or badness of the *person* or the *action* cannot depend on the action's outcome. The outcome depends in part on the world's cooperation. But this means that a judgment on the agent must be a judgment on his intention. Cleanthes gives the example of two slaves sent out to find someone. The one slave searches diligently but fails to find him. The other loafs about and runs into him by accident. Which is the better man? (*SES*, 264). The Stoic has no doubt about the answer and takes it to show that results are to be considered indifferent. What counts is the state of your will; that is in your control, and that is what is absolutely good or bad. So the entire concentration of life must be put into the effort to set your will in harmony with nature. The outcome must be nothing to you.

This leads us to the second corollary. The important thing is to do one's *duty*. The notion of "duty" has not played a large role to this point. We hardly find it in Socrates or Plato, nor in Aristotle, nor Epicurus. These philosophers are asking this question: what is the best life for a human being to live? They never imagine that it might be a duty or an obligation to lead such a life. It is just a question of what the prudent or wise person would do. Why, we might wonder, does the notion of duty suddenly come to prominence in Stoic thought?

It has a natural home here because of the connection between the divine, rational principle that providentially guides the course of the world and the notion of *law*. It is law that shows us our duties. The principles governing the world are not only descriptions of how the world inevitably *does* go; they express how things, according to their natures, *should* go. So they take on for us the aspect of law reflected in civil law: they prescribe to us our duties and obligations.* The Stoics devote considerable attention to duties, distinguishing several classes of duties and examining particular cases. We need not explore the details, but we should note the one duty that is clear and always overriding: the duty to harmonize our intentions with the law of nature. This is the duty to be virtuous or to perfect ourselves. The microcosm of our soul *ought* to be in harmony with the order without. It is our first and most important task to see that it is. And this means that we must concern ourselves above all with the things in our power. Everything else must be, as Epictetus says, nothing to us in comparison. We began the discussion of Stoic thought by considering happiness. But now we can see that if we devote ourselves to virtue, to doing our duty, to the good, our happiness will take care of itself.†

As you can see, Stoic philosophy contains the resources to support the claim that whatever city or nation we belong to, we are first of all citizens of the world. All men are brothers, for all are "children" of the same God. The consideration we owe to our neighbors is not different from that we owe to strangers. All of us, Greeks, Romans, and barbarians, are part of the world and partake of the divine reason. Marcus Aurelius says:

> If the power of thought is universal among mankind, so likewise is the possession of reason, making us rational creatures. It follows, therefore, that this reason speaks no less universally to us all with its "thou shalt" or "thou shalt not." So then there is a world-law; which in turn means that we are all fellow-citizens and share a common citizenship, and that the world is a single city (*M* 4.4).

Finally, let us note one more point of contrast with the Epicureans. Stoics are much more tolerant of popular beliefs than the Epicureans (*SES*, 343–80). Stoics tend to tolerate the polytheism that permeates the times, think there is some truth in astrology, and even accept the legitimacy of divination (foretelling the future by interpreting signs). Though there is just one God, everything partakes of his nature. It is therefore easy to view the gods of popular religion as symbols of the sacredness of one aspect of nature or another. Since the entire cosmos is a harmony, why shouldn't the stars reflect what is happening and is to happen on earth? And since everything is necessarily connected with everything else, it seems not unreasonable that a diviner could "read" the signs and predict what is to come.

This tolerance is bolstered by the development of a system of allegorical interpretation, by which tales of the gods (in Homer and Hesiod, for example) are accepted as symbolic representations of truths that can be supported in a more scientific way. No doubt this tolerance on the part of the Stoics helps the spread of their doctrine, but it also makes Stoicism susceptible to corruption by what the tough-minded Epicurean atomists would call sheer superstition.

Let Gilbert Murray have the last word.

> The glory of the Stoics is to have built up a religion of extraordinary nobleness; the glory of the Epicureans is to have upheld an ideal of sanity and humanity stark upright amid a reeling world, and, like the old Spartans, never to have yielded one inch of ground to the common foe.[8]

---

*Is there a contradiction, or at least an unresolved tension, here in Stoic thought? If the law of nature (a notion we owe to the Stoics) describes what happens, and everything happens according to necessity, what room is there for deviation by human beings? But if it is not possible for us to deviate from the law, how could it prescribe duties to us? Doesn't the notion of duty presuppose that we might not do what it is our duty to do?

†Compare this thought with what Jesus says in the Sermon on the Mount: "Seek first the Kingdom of God and his righteousness, and all these things will be added to you as well" (Matthew 6:33).

The Skeptics

What has skepticism to do with happiness? We are apt to suppose that someone who doesn't know, or at least thinks he doesn't know, must on that account be *unhappy*. Aristotle, who holds that all men by nature desire to know, would surely think so. Moreover, we are almost all brought up as believers in something or other. Belief is as natural to us as breathing. What sense could it make to suspend all our beliefs, to get rid of that habit? And how could that make us happy? These are the perplexing questions we must now address. The ancient skeptics give some surprising answers to these questions.

Again we shall simplify, this time by focusing on only one of the several varieties of skeptical positions. Skepticism in the ancient world comes, we might say, in degrees; some are more skeptical than others. Let us consider the most radical group of skeptics, who call themselves by the name of a shadowy fourth-century figure Pyrrho, about whom little is known. From what we do know, it seems that Pyrrho is not interested in speculative or scientific philosophy, but only in the practical question of how best to live. But it is not sheer disinterest; it is what we might call principled disinterest. His pupil Timon is reported to have said that the nature of things is "indeterminable," meaning that we cannot determine that things are more like this than they are like that.[9] But why not? Let us review a little of the story we have been telling.

From the time of Parmenides it is maintained that a distinction must be drawn between things as they appear to us and things as they are in themselves. The core insight is that things may not appear as they really are. The realm of appearance is generally agreed to be the world of the senses, which sometimes deceive us about reality: the straight oar in water looks bent; square towers in the distance look round; honey tastes bitter to a sick person; and so on. So the question forces itself upon thinkers: is there some way to tell what things are really like? The usual answer is given in terms of intelligence or reason, and we have seen some of the results. Parmenides, following what he takes to be the best argument, asserts that reality is the One. Democritus holds that it is atoms and the void. For Plato, the independent world of eternally unchanging Forms constitutes the really real. And for Aristotle, reality is made up of individual substances that are composites of matter and form.

It is partly this diversity of answers that motivates the Pyrrhonists, who like to gather these and even more examples of disagreement among the philosophers. But sheer disagreement does not prove that nothing can be known about reality; some one of these views may well be correct and the others mistaken; or perhaps none of them are correct, but some future development of them might be. To support the claim that the nature of things is "indeterminable" more must be said.

The later Pyrrhonists systematize the arguments in favor of skeptical conclusions in a number of types or *modes* of reasoning. Our best source for these is a Greek physician, Sextus Empiricus, who lived in the second century C.E. Let us survey several of these modes.

The first mode stresses that the sense organs of animals differ from species to species. His arguments are rather primitive, since not much was known about the details of animal sense organs until recent times. But we can think of the registration of the world in the many-faceted eye of a fly, in the echolocation of a bat, and in what the frog's eye tells the frog's brain.[10] Cats and owls see much better in the dark than we do, and the olfactory world of the dog must be immensely rich compared to ours. In terms like these, we can understand these words of Sextus:

> But if the same things appear different owing to the variety in animals, we shall, indeed, be able to state our own impressions of the real object, but as to its essential nature we shall suspend judgment. For we cannot ourselves judge between our own impressions and those of the other animals, since we ourselves are involved in the dispute and are, therefore, rather in need of a judge than competent to pass judgment ourselves. . . . If, then, owing to the variety in animals their sense-impressions differ, and it is impossible to judge between them, we must necessarily suspend judgment regarding the external underlying objects (*OP* 1.59–61).[11]

Here we have some of the key notions of skepticism. Because the nature of the "external underlying objects" appears differently to creatures with different sense organs, we cannot confidently judge that these objects are as they appear to us. If they appear one way to us and another way to the bat or fly or frog, it would be arbitrary to pick one of those ways rather than another and say: that is how it really is. The result is that we must "suspend judgment."

The second mode concerns differences among human beings. These are particularly notable, Sextus tells us, with respect to objects of choice. He quotes poets and dramatists who exclaim about the variations in human preferences, and adds,

> Seeing, then, that choice and avoidance depend on pleasure and displeasure, while pleasure and displeasure depend on sensation and sense-impression, whenever some men choose the very things which are avoided by others, it is logical for us to conclude that they are also differently affected by the same things, since otherwise they would all alike have chosen or avoided the same things. But if the same objects affect men differently owing to the differences in the men, then, on this ground also, we shall reasonably be led to suspension of judgment. For while we are, no doubt, able to state what each of the underlying objects appears to be, relatively to each difference, we are incapable of explaining what it is in reality. For we shall have to believe either all men or some. But if we believe all, we shall be attempting the impossible and accepting contradictories; and if some, let us be told whose opinions we are to endorse (*OP* 1.87–88).

The message is the same; we must suspend judgment. What does that mean? It means that we do not say either yes or no; we do not affirm or deny any proposition about the real nature of the underlying objects. We do not say, as do the Stoics, that they are part of the divine nature, nor do we deny that. We do not say, as do the atomists, that reality is composed of atoms and the void, but neither do we deny it. We do not say, as do the Platonists, that the things of sense are shadows of the eternal Forms, but neither do we deny it.

Note carefully that we *can* state what the object *appears* to be. But we refrain from making any fur-

ther judgments. In terms of the appearance/reality distinction, the skeptic restricts himself to appearance. He is forced to this by the considerations in the "modes," of which we have examined only two. Some of the others concern the differences among our own organs of sense, the dependence of appearances on differing circumstances, and the differences in customs and laws.

There are also modes of a more formal character. These are standard ways in which the arguments of the dogmatic philosophers are criticized. A skeptic considers someone who affirms what is not *evident* dogmatic; and any claim about how things *really* are, independently of their appearance to our senses, is a claim about the nonevident. To be dogmatic, in this sense, is to claim to know something for which you have no evidence. So all the other schools of philosophy, with their theories about the reality beyond the appearances, are classified as dogmatic by the skeptics.

One of these more formal modes is based on an "infinite regress" argument and another on the charge of "circular reasoning." An infinite regress is generated when a claim *A* is supported by another claim *B* and *B* itself needs to be supported. If it is supported by *C*, the skeptic will ask how *C* is to be supported, and so on. Circular reasoning occurs when somewhere in the chain of supporting arguments appeal is made to what is in question, to what is supposed to be proved by those arguments. The argument goes in a circle.

Here is an example of Sextus making use of these modes. Suppose one of the "dogmatic" philosophers (a Platonist, perhaps, or a Stoic) has made some claim about the real nature of an object.

> The matter proposed is either a sense-object or a thought-object, but whichever it is, it is an object of controversy; for some say that only sensibles are true, others only intelligibles, others that some sensibles and some intelligible objects are true. Will they then assert that the controversy can or cannot be decided? If they say it cannot, we have it granted that we must suspend judgement; for concerning matters of dispute which admit of no decision it is impossible to make an assertion. But if they say that it can be decided, we

ask by what is it to be decided? For example, in the case of the sense-object . . . is it to be decided by a sense-object or a thought-object? For if they say by a sense-object, since we are inquiring about sensibles that object itself also will require another to confirm it; and if that too is to be a sense-object, it likewise will require another for its confirmation, and so on ad infinitum. And if the sense-object shall have to be decided by a thought-object, then, since thought-objects also are controverted, this being an object of thought will need examination and confirmation. Whence then will it gain confirmation? If from an intelligible object, it will suffer a similar regress ad infinitum; and if from a sensible object, since an intelligible was adduced to establish the sensible and a sensible to establish the intelligible, the Mode of circular reasoning is brought in (*OP* 1.170–72).

The key question here is, "By what is it to be decided?" These modes attempt to show that the question cannot be satisfactorily answered, for either the answer will itself be subject to that very same question or will assume what is to be proved. The moral is the same: we must suspend judgment.

All of the various modes circle around a central point, which we must now explore more explicitly. It can be called the problem of the **criterion**. Claims to knowledge and truth are a dime a dozen; the Hellenistic world, as we have seen, is filled with them (just as ours is)—religious, popular, and philosophical. The problem we face is how to decide among them. By what mark or standard or criterion are we to decide where truth and knowledge really lie? This problem faces thoughtful people in an insistent way, and numerous attempts are made to solve it. The skeptics argue, however, that this is an insoluble problem: *no* satisfactory criterion is to be found. In a chapter called "Does a Criterion of Truth Really Exist?" Sextus Empiricus writes:

Of those, then, who have treated of the criterion some have declared that a criterion exists—the Stoics, for example, and certain others—while by some its existence is denied, as by . . . Xenophanes of Colophon, who says—"Over all things opinion bears

sway";* while we have adopted suspension of judgement as to whether it does or does not exist. This dispute, then, they will declare to be either capable or incapable of decision; and if they shall say it is incapable of decision they will be granting on the spot the propriety of suspension of judgement, while if they say it admits of decision, let them tell us whereby it is to be decided, since we have no accepted criterion, and do not even know, but are still inquiring, whether any criterion exists. Besides, in order to decide the dispute which has arisen about the criterion, we must possess an accepted criterion by which we shall be able to judge the dispute; and in order to possess an accepted criterion, the dispute about the criterion must first be decided. And when the argument thus reduces itself to a form of circular reasoning, the discovery of the criterion becomes impracticable, since we do not allow them to adopt a criterion by assumption, while if they offer to judge the criterion by a criterion we force them to a regress ad infinitum. And furthermore, since demonstration requires a demonstrated criterion, while the criterion requires an approved demonstration, they are forced into circular reasoning (*OP* 2.18–20).

Let us note several points in this passage. First, any claim that some principle is a criterion for truth needs itself to be supported. We shall need a criterion to decide whether that support is successful or not. And any attempt to provide such a criterion will either be forced into the infinite regress of criteria by which to decide criteria by which to decide, or it will be circular, begging the question in favor of some assumed criterion. We can represent the infinite regress argument by a flow chart. (See figure on opposite page.)

The result once more is that we must suspend judgment. And if we suspend judgment about a criterion, it follows that judgment is suspended about each and every claim to knowledge; for each such claim depends on there being a criterion by which it is singled out from among all the claimants as true knowledge. So if we cannot solve the problem of the criterion, we must suspend judgment generally.

---

*See p. 14.

Second, note that Sextus does *not* claim there is no criterion of truth; about the question of whether there is or is not a criterion, the Pyrrhonian skeptic suspends judgment. There is a kind of skeptic who claims that nothing can be known. This kind is obviously subject to a devastating counter: he can be asked how he knows *that*. But Sextus is careful not to make any such claim. He does not know whether anything can be known or not. If he is pushed back a step and asked whether he knows that he does not know, he will presumably confess that he doesn't. His attitude throughout is one of *noncommitment* to any knowledge claims that concern how things really are.

The argument about the criterion seems like a very powerful argument indeed. It sweeps the board clean.

But this surely leads to a pressing question: how then can we live? If we make no judgments about the world we are in, are we not going to be paralyzed? To eat bread rather than a stone seems to depend on a judgment that bread will nourish you and a stone will not. Can we suspend judgments like that?

Here we must remember that the skeptic does not deny appearances. It is his claim that it is possible to live, and to live well, by restricting oneself to how things seem. Though there may not be a criterion for truth or knowledge about reality, there is a criterion for life and action. Sextus tells us that this practical criterion

> denotes the standard of action by conforming to which in the conduct of life we perform some actions and abstain from others. . . . The criterion, then, of the Skeptic School is, we say, the appearance, giving this name to what is virtually the sense-presentation. For since this lies in feeling and involuntary affection, it is not open to question. . . .
>
> Adhering, then, to appearances we live in accordance with the normal rules of life, undogmatically, seeing that we cannot remain wholly inactive (*OP* 1.21–23).

Sextus was a physician, a member of a school of medicine that followed similar principles. These doctors were unwilling to speculate about the

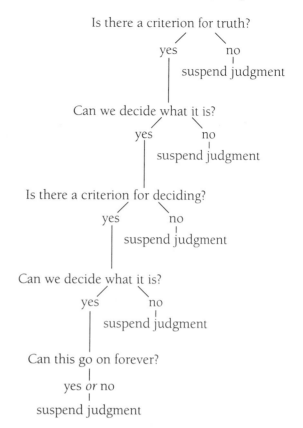

"real" nature of diseases, about underlying causes and unobservable entities—either physical or demonic—posited to explain illness. They wished to restrict themselves to what they observed, to appearances. If they observed that certain symptoms responded to certain medicines, they noted and remembered this. If they observed that diet positively affected the outcome of a certain disease, they had a rule to prescribe that diet for that disease. It was, we might say, empirical medicine rather than speculative. If medicine can be done in this way, then why can't life be lived according to the same principles?*

---

*One might question, of course, how successfully medicine can be done on such a restricted empirical base. Modern medicine does not restrict itself to what is observable but makes use of the theoretical constructions of modern science. Does the same hold for principles of living?

So if we are skeptics, we eat what experience has shown to be connected with health and behave in ways correlated with positive outcomes. We do not pronounce things to be truly good or truly bad, for about such claims we suspend judgment. But it is beyond question that bread *appears* to nourish us and scarcely less so that obedience to the law *appears* to be profitable. We do not worry about absolutes, either of truth or of goodness, for they are unattainable. But we follow appearances. In the matter of behavior, we conform to the customs of the land in which we live, for these customs express what appears to our fellow citizens to be good. We live "in accordance with the normal rules of life," but "undogmatically," not claiming that this is somehow the absolutely best or right thing to do.

As you can see, the relativism against which Plato struggles and which Aristotle thinks he has overcome is reborn. It is not reborn as a doctrine claiming to be the truth about matters, for no such claims are made. But since what appears in one way to a person or culture may appear differently to another person or culture, a *practical relativism* is the result. We might also note that skepticism tends to be a profoundly conservative view, for it will nearly always be the case that adaptation to customs and laws—whatever they may be—will appear to be the best way to live. Plato struggles to delineate the outlines of an ideal state, because he is convinced that there is an absolute goodness in reality that states might (and typically did) miss. And the Stoics think they have a criterion for correcting customs and laws in the appeal to the law of nature. But a skeptic has no such fulcrum on which to work the lever of reform. Skeptics are not great revolutionaries, religiously, politically, or morally.

On what grounds, then, could the skeptic recommend his views? There are two. One, which we have looked at in some detail, amounts to the argument that there really is no alternative. Every nonskeptical view founders in one way or another on the problem of the criterion. But the second ground is a more positive one and brings us to the connection between skepticism and happiness. As long as we seek certainty about the true nature of

things, we will be in doubt; if we are in doubt, we will be perturbed; as long as we are perturbed, we won't be happy. So the key to quietude and happiness is to give up the search for certainty. We must cease to be dogmatists and become skeptics.

For the man who opines that anything is by nature good or bad is for ever being disquieted; when he is without the things which he deems good he believes himself to be tormented by things naturally bad and he pursues after the things which are, as he thinks, good; which when he has obtained he keeps falling into still more perturbations because of his irrational and immoderate elation, and in his dread of a change of fortune he uses every endeavor to avoid losing the things which he deems good. On the other hand, the man who determines nothing as to what is naturally good or bad neither shuns nor pursues anything eagerly; and in consequence, he is unperturbed.

The Sceptic, in fact, had the same experience which is said to have befallen the painter Apelles. Once, they say, when he was painting a horse and wished to represent in the painting the horse's foam, he was so unsuccessful that he gave up the attempt and flung at the picture the sponge on which he used to wipe the paints off his brush, and the mark of the sponge produced the effect of a horse's foam. So, too, the Sceptics were in hopes of gaining quietude by means of a decision regarding the disparity of the objects of sense and of thought, and being unable to effect this they suspended judgment; and they found that quietude, as if by chance, followed upon their suspense, even as a shadow follows its substance (*OP* 1.27–29).

This quietude, or tranquillity of soul, is what the skeptic means by happiness. Or, if happiness is more than this, it is at least a necessary condition for happiness; without it no one can be happy. Though no one can escape trouble entirely, most people are doubly troubled, once by the pain or suffering and once by two further beliefs: that this is something bad or evil they are undergoing, and that either they do not (in some absolute sense) deserve it, or—worse yet—that they do. The skeptic at least does not suffer these further agonies. So the skeptics recommend their attitude, the suspension of judgment about all claims to truth, on the grounds that doing so provides a basis on which a happy life can be built.

These may seem rather minimal claims and their kind of happiness rather a pale one. It seems to be a retreat of some magnitude from the "high" view of happiness expressed, for instance, by Aristotle: activity of soul in accord with excellence. But perhaps the times did not realistically allow for more—for most people. Furthermore, the problem of the criterion still remains; unless this can be solved, maybe no more can reasonably be expected. This is a very real problem with which numerous future philosophers struggle.*

Notes

1. Gilbert Murray, *Five Stages of Greek Religion* (New York: Doubleday, Anchor Books, 1955), 139. I am indebted to this source for numerous points in this section.
2. All quotations from Epicurus' works are from *Letters, Principal Doctrines, and Vatican Sayings*, trans. Russel M. Geer (Indianapolis: Library of Liberal Arts, 1964). Within this text, references to specific works will be as follows: *PD*, *Principal Doctrines*; *LM*, *Letter to Menoeceus*; *LP*, *Letter to Pythocles*; and *VS*, *Vatican Sayings*.
3. William Shakespeare, *Hamlet*, act 3, sc. 1, lines 64–68.
4. Quotations from Lucretius, *The Way Things Are*, trans. Rolfe Humphries (Bloomington: Indiana University Press, 1969), are cited in the text using the abbreviation *WTA*. References are to page numbers of this edition.
5. Quotations from Epictetus, *The Enchiridion*, trans. Thomas W. Higginson (Indianapolis: Library of Liberal Arts, 1948), are cited in the text using the abbreviation *E*.
6. See also Marcus Aurelius, *Meditations*, trans. Maxwell Staniforth (New York: Penguin Books, 1964), 6.41. Quotations from this work are hereafter cited in the text using the abbreviation *M*.
7. Attributed to Chrysippus by Eduard Zeller in *Stoics, Epicureans, and Sceptics* (New York: Russell and Russell, 1962), 284–285. Subsequent quotations from this work are cited in the text using the abbreviation *SES*.
8. Murray, *Five Stages of Greek Religion*, 125.
9. Charlotte L. Stough, *Greek Scepticism* (Berkeley: University of California Press, 1969), 17.
10. There is a well-known study of interest in this connection: "What the Frog's Eye Tells the Frog's Brain," by J. Y. Lettvin, H. R. Maturana, W. S. McCulloch, and W. H. Pitts, *Proceedings of the Institute of Radio Engineers* 47 (1959): 1940–51.
11. Quotations from Sextus Empiricus, *Outlines of Pyrrhonism* (Cambridge, Mass.: Harvard University Press, 1955), are cited in the text using the abbreviation *OP*.

*See for example Augustine (p. 218) and particularly René Descartes (*Meditation III*) and Hegel (pp. 403–404).

13

The Christians:
Sin, Salvation, and Love

Although Augustine in the late fourth and early fifth centuries would come to consider Christianity the one true philosophy,* its whole mode of thought is different from that of the Greek tradition we have been examining. Question and answer, proposal and critique, dialectical argument, and the reliance on human experience and rationality mark the Greek philosophers from Thales to Sextus Empiricus. They do not all agree about the success of this way of searching for the truth. Aristotle is confident, the skeptics pessimistic. But they do all agree that there is no alternative to using our wits to unravel the mystery.

Suppose we provisionally take this to be the peculiar conviction of the philosopher.† Then we could well say that what we find in early Christianity and the Hebrew tradition out of which it grew is not philosophy, but prophecy. The mode of procedure is not discussion, but proclamation. The typical form is not "let us examine" but "Thus says the Lord!" The appropriate response is not questioning but acceptance, especially, perhaps, repentance. From the very beginning, this tradition emphasizes righteousness, human deviation from it, and what it means to live before God.

Nonetheless, it is important for the story of Western philosophy to understand the essentials of this tradition. For in becoming the major religious tradition of the West, Christianity has had an enormous influence on the way men have philosophized ever since. For more than a thousand years, Christianity provided a framework in which nearly all serious intellectual work was done; even since, its influence has never been lacking. In ethics particularly, the Christian ideal has been absorbed by many secular thinkers, while others have felt the need to attack it—thus indirectly manifesting its importance.* Let us try to capture something of the spirit, as well as the beliefs, of this tradition.

Background

Jesus, whom the Christians call "Christ" or "Messiah" (meaning "the anointed one"), was a Jew, as were all of his first followers; Christianity is a modification of the Jewish heritage. So if we want to understand the outlook and faith of the Christians,

---

*See pp. 214–215.

†Provisional because Augustine and other Christian philosophers will modify this conviction in an important way. See pp. 221 and 243–244.

---

*The two major ethical theories of modern times, utilitarianism and the duty-theory of Immanuel Kant, both develop Christian themes in a more or less secular way. See "Reason and Morality," in Chapter 20. See also Chapter 23. Nietzsche attacks the Christian ideal as self-deceptively grounded in weakness and resentment.

it is necessary to sketch something of the history in terms of which the Jewish or Hebrew people understood themselves. Perhaps more than any other people, the Jews have interpreted their own being and role in terms of the story of their origins and history. And this feature the Christians preserved. Their history was the history of the Hebrew people. Let us outline, then, certain central convictions which grew out of that history and which the Christians could take for granted.

Of the very first importance is the conviction that there is *one God*. We may be able to trace some development of this concept—from a kind of tribal deity, to a God superior to the gods of their neighbors, to one having the exclusive claim to worship—but by the time of the great prophets from the eighth to the sixth centuries B.C.E., it was already clear to the Hebrews that all other "gods" were mere pretenders, "idols" which it was sinful to reverence.

> Thus says the Lord, the King of Israel
> and his Redeemer, the Lord of hosts:
> "I am the first and I am the last;
> besides me there is no god. . . .
>
> "To whom will you liken me and make me equal,
> and compare me, that we may be alike?
> Those who lavish gold from the purse,
> and weigh out silver in the scales,
> hire a goldsmith, and he makes it into a god;
> then they fall down and worship!
> They lift it upon their shoulders, they carry it,
> they set it in its place, and it stands there;
> it cannot move from its place.
> If one cries to it, it does not answer
> or save him from his trouble."
>
>   (Isa. 44:6, 46:5–7)[1]

The one true god differs from idols in all these respects. He is not made by men; he cannot be seen or touched or carried; he is not restricted to any one place; and when you cry to him, he does help to save you from trouble. He is, moreover, "the first and the last," meaning that he has no beginning and no ending. He is eternal. He alone is worthy of worship and reverence.

He is the creator of the entire visible universe. The world is not eternal, as Aristotle thinks; nor is it God or an aspect of God, as the Stoics believed. God precedes and transcends the world, which is, however, wholly dependent on his power. The first words in the Hebrew scriptures are

> In the beginning God created the heavens and the earth (Gen. 1:1).

Moreover, God is entirely good, righteous, just, and holy. And this goodness is transmitted to the creation; on each of the "days" of creation, after God made light, the heavens, dry land, vegetation, animals, and human beings, we read that "God saw that it was good." Finding the world to be good, the Hebrews have a positive attitude toward it; the world is not something to flee or escape from; it is not just a shadowy image of true reality; and the body is not—as it is for Plato—a prison in which we are alienated from our true home. It is in this world that we have a home; it is here that God has put us; it is here that our tasks and purposes are to be accomplished and our happiness achieved. The shadowy existence in the underworld after death is not anything to desire.*

But this task and happiness are complicated by the fact of sin. In the well-known story of the first man and woman, we read that human beings have succumbed to the temptation to "be like God, knowing good and evil." (Gen. 3:5) Not content with their status, unhappy in obedience, unwilling not to play God themselves, humans have made themselves corrupt and find themselves outside the Garden. Of the first pair of brothers, one murders the other. And so it has been ever since.

The story that occupies the rest of the Hebrew scriptures concerns a series of attempts to remedy this situation. It is the story of how God, sometimes directly and sometimes through representatives, acts to reestablish his rule in a community of

---

*See for instance Psalms 39:3 and 88:3–5, 10–12. Compare also Homer's Akhilleus on p. 5. Belief in a "resurrection of the body" grew among Jews in the several centuries before Jesus, however. In Jesus' time, one party, the Sadducees, held out against the belief. See Mark 12:18–27.

righteousness and justice. It is often understood in terms of the concept of the "Kingdom of God." This story has intimate relationships to the self-understanding of the Jewish people (and the Christians). We sketch it briefly.

One tactic to clean up the unrighteousness of men would be to destroy them and start again. Something close to this is found in the story of Noah.

> The Lord saw that the wickedness of man was great in the earth, and that every imagination of the thoughts of his heart was only evil continually. And the Lord was sorry that he had made man on the earth, and it grieved him to his heart. So the Lord said, "I will blot out man whom I have created from the face of the ground, man and beast and creeping things and birds of the air, for I am sorry that I have made them." But Noah found favor in the eyes of the Lord (Gen. 6:5–8).

The outcome is a great flood, from which only Noah and his family are saved, together with a pair of each kind of animal. But not many generations pass before wickedness again becomes widespread, and people become arrogant enough to think they can build a tower that reaches to heaven. This presumption is punished by the confusing of their languages, so that they cannot understand each other and cooperate in finishing that venture.

A crux comes when God calls a certain man, Abram (later called Abraham), to leave his home, his culture, his nation, and to venture out to a new land.

> Now the Lord said to Abram, "Go from your country and your kindred and your father's house to the land that I will show you. And I will make of you a great nation, and I will bless you, and make your name great, so that you will be a blessing" (Gen. 12:1–2).

It is in terms of this promise and burden that the Hebrew people identify themselves. They trace their heritage back to Abraham and believe that they have a special place to play in the history of the world: it is their privilege—and responsibility—to be agents for the reestablishment of God's kingdom on earth. They consider that they have entered upon a covenant with God, the terms of which are to honor and reverence him, obeying him only, establishing justice among themselves, and so be a blessing to the rest of corrupt mankind—who can learn from them the blessings of righteousness. The long line of prophets find plenty to do in condemning the inconstancy of the Hebrews and recalling them to the terms of this covenant.

A second crux is the Exodus. After some generations, the children of Abraham, faced with famine in Palestine, move to Egypt. Eventually they are enslaved there and spend "four hundred years" suffering the considerable oppression of slaves. Against all odds, they leave Egypt under the guidance of Moses and establish themselves again in the land promised to Abraham. This remarkable occurrence, which leaves an indelible mark on the national character, is the sign and seal of their mission.

Corresponding to this deliverance from bondage and the establishment of the Hebrews as a nation is the giving of the Law ("Torah"). It is the Law that marks the Hebrews as distinct and unique. It defines them as a people. What has distinguished the Jews to this day is the continuous possession of that Law, which begins with these words,

> "I am the Lord your God, who brought you out of the land of Egypt, out of the house of bondage.
> "You shall have no other gods before me" (Exo. 20:2–3).

The Law goes on to forbid misusing God's name, killing, adultery, theft, false witness, and covetousness and to require keeping a Sabbath day holy and honoring one's parents. These statutes are well known as the Ten Commandments. But the Law also states in great detail how life is to be lived by the people of God, specifying dietary and health rules, principles of reparation for wrongs done, and regulations for religious observances.

The life of the Hebrew people in that continually troubled area of the Middle East is precarious.

They achieve some years of security and prosperity in the time of David and Solomon.* But thereafter it is a struggle to keep the community together. Surrounded by hostile nations, dominated for a time by the powerful Assyrians, exiled to Babylon, conquered by Alexander's armies, and finally made a province of the Roman Empire, they fight tenaciously for their heritage. They are constantly falling away from the Abrahamic covenant and the Law, if we are to judge by the succession of prophets who unsparingly condemn their waywardness and call them back again to God. Still, despite the people's "hardness of heart," as the prophets called it, there is truth in the boast of Josephus, the first century C.E. Jewish historian:

> Throughout our history we have kept the same laws, to which we are eternally faithful. [2]

During the period of foreign domination there grows up an expectation that God will soon send someone who will act decisively to establish God's kingdom of righteousness among men. This agent of God is sometimes conceived in terms of a political liberator who will expel the oppressors and restore the ancient kingdom of David; sometimes he is conceived in more cosmic and apocalyptic terms, as one who will institute a general judgment and destruction of all the wicked, together with the rescue of the faithful few. This hoped-for figure is given a variety of titles: Son of David, Son of Man, Messiah.

Together with the insistent hope that God will not fail in his promise to create a holy people, a righteous kingdom, these expectations provide a rich context for understanding the life of Jesus. Jesus is called by all of these titles and often calls himself "Son of Man." Christians will look back particularly to Isaiah's prophecy about a "Suffering Servant" who will create the kingdom not by might, but by bearing the burdens of the people.

> Behold, my servant shall prosper,
> he shall be exalted and lifted up,
> and shall be very high. . . .

Who has believed what we have heard?
And to whom has the arm of the Lord been revealed?
For he grew up before him like a young plant,
and like a root out of dry ground;
he had no form or comeliness that we should look
    at him,
and no beauty that we should desire him.
He was despised and rejected by men;
a man of sorrows and acquainted with grief;
and as one from whom men hide their faces
he was despised, and we esteemed him not.
Surely he has borne our griefs
and carried our sorrows;
yet we esteemed him stricken,
smitten by God, and afflicted.
But he was wounded for our transgressions,
he was bruised for our iniquities;
upon him was the chastisement that made us whole;
and with his stripes we are healed.
All we like sheep have gone astray;
we have turned every one to his own way;
and the Lord has laid on him the iniquity of us all.

(Isa. 52:13, 53:1–6)

These words, familiar to all who are acquainted with Handel's *Messiah*, are applied to the life, and particularly to the death, of Jesus. We must now turn to Jesus himself in order to see what about him leads so many to think of him in these terms.

Jesus

In the earliest Gospel* Mark introduces Jesus, after his baptism by John, with these words:

> Now after John was arrested, Jesus came into Galilee, preaching the gospel of God, and saying, "The time is

---

*This apex of the nation's power corresponds roughly to the time of the Trojan War.

*The word "gospel" means "good news." The four accounts we have of the life of Jesus (Matthew, Mark, Luke, and John) are called gospels because they present the good news that God has fulfilled his promises to Abraham in the life and death of Jesus. It should be noted that each of these accounts is written from a Christian perspective by one who believes that Jesus is Lord, Savior, and the expected Messiah. We have no hostile or even neutral accounts of his life.

fulfilled, and the kingdom of God is at hand; repent and believe in the gospel" (Mark 1:14–15).

That which the prophets have foretold and apocalyptic seers envisioned is now "at hand." The "kingdom of God" is about to be established, and Jesus sees himself as the one to whom that task falls.

That the kingdom is indeed at hand is manifest in the healing miracles of Jesus. According to the gospel writers, Jesus cures leprosy, gives sight to the blind and hearing to the deaf, casts out demons, and even brings the dead back to life. These miracles are signs of God's presence and power and stimuli to repentance and faith.

The attitude and behavior of Jesus bears out his sense of a new beginning. He is absolutely without any class consciousness, associating with poor and rich, learned and ignorant, righteous and sinner alike. A common complaint among those who carefully observe the Law is that he associates with outcasts and undesirables. He does not do so, of course, to sanction their sin, but to lead them to righteousness, as the following parable illustrates.

Now the tax collectors and sinners were all drawing near to hear him. And the Pharisees and the scribes murmured, saying, "This man receives sinners and eats with them."

So he told them this parable: "What man of you, having a hundred sheep, if he lost one of them, does not leave the ninety-nine in the wilderness, and go after the one which is lost, until he finds it? And when he has found it, he lays it on his shoulders, rejoicing. And when he comes home, he calls together his friends and his neighbors, saying to them, "Rejoice with me, for I have found my sheep which was lost." Just so, I tell you, there will be more joy in heaven over one sinner who repents than over ninety-nine righteous persons who need no repentance" (Luke 15:1–7).

Absolute indifference to wealth and worldly goods is characteristic of both his life and his teaching. Of himself he says,

"Foxes have holes, and birds of the air have nests; but the Son of man has nowhere to lay his head" (Luke 9:58).

And he emphasizes again and again that attachment to riches will keep one out of the kingdom. A wealthy man asks him what he must do to inherit eternal life. Jesus replies that he must keep the commandments. The man says he has done so all his life. Then,

Jesus looking upon him loved him, and said to him, "You lack one thing; go, sell what you have, and give to the poor, and you will have treasure in heaven; and come, follow me." At that saying his countenance fell, and he went away sorrowful; for he had great possessions.

And Jesus looked around and said to his disciples, "How hard it will be for those who have riches to enter the kingdom of God!" (Mark 10:21–23).

There are many sayings to the same effect. To be part of the Kingdom of God requires absolute singleness of mind; care for possessions distracts one from that intensity.

And he said to him, "Take heed, and beware of all covetousness; for a man's life does not consist in the abundance of his possessions" (Luke 12:15).

"No one can serve two masters; for either he will hate the one and love the other, or he will be devoted to the one and despise the other. You cannot serve God and mammon [riches].

"Therefore I tell you, do not be anxious about your life, what you shall eat or what you shall drink, nor about your body, what you shall put on. Is not life more than food, and the body more than clothing? Look at the birds of the air: they neither sow nor reap nor gather into barns, and yet your heavenly Father feeds them. Are you not of more value than they? And which of you by being anxious can add one cubit to his span of life? And why are you anxious about clothing? Consider the lilies of the field, how they grow; they neither toil nor spin; yet I tell you, even Solomon in all his glory was not arrayed like one of these. But if God so clothes the grass of the field, which today is alive and tomorrow is thrown into the oven, will he not much more clothe you, O men of little faith? Therefore do not be anxious, saying, 'What shall we eat?' or 'What shall we drink?' or 'What shall we wear?' For the Gentiles seek all these things; and your heavenly Father knows that you need them all. But seek first his kingdom and his righteousness, and all these things shall be yours as well" (Matt. 6:24–33).

What is this righteousness that is to take such an absolutely preeminent place in our aims? When a lawyer asks him what to do to inherit eternal life, Jesus answers,

> "What is written in the law? How do you read?" And he answered, "You shall love the Lord your God with all your heart, and with all your soul, and with all your strength, and with all your mind; and your neighbor as yourself." And he said to him, "You have answered right; do this, and you will live" (Luke 10:26–28).

The key to the righteousness of the kingdom is *love*. But "love," as we have noted, is a word with many meanings.* What does it mean here? With reference to God, it clearly means a kind of undivided and absolute devotion; it is the appropriate response to the creator who provides not only for us but also for the birds of the air and the lilies of the fields. This devotion will express itself in our observance of God's law concerning our fellow men. And that requires loving our "neighbors" as ourselves. No better explanation of this requirement can be given than the one Jesus gives to the lawyer who asks the question.

> "A man was going down from Jerusalem to Jericho, and he fell among robbers, who stripped him and beat him, and departed, leaving him half dead. Now by chance a priest was going down that road; and when he saw him he passed by on the other side. So likewise a Levite, when he came to the place and saw him, passed by on the other side. But a Samaritan, as he journeyed, came to where he was; and when he saw him, he had compassion, and went to him and bound up his wounds, pouring on oil and wine; then he set him on his own beast and brought him to an

inn, and took care of him. And the next day he took out two denarii and gave them to the innkeeper, saying, 'Take care of him; and whatever more you spend, I will repay you when I come back.' Which of these three, do you think, proved neighbor to the man who fell among the robbers?" He said, "The one who showed mercy on him." And Jesus said to him, "Go and do likewise" (Luke 10:30–37).*

Several things in this famous parable of the good Samaritan are worth comment. First, note that Jesus does not exactly answer the question he is asked, "Who is my neighbor?" Rather, he answers the question, "What is it to *act as a neighbor*?" And the closing line directs the lawyer's attention not outward, but to himself: Do likewise—see that *you* act as a neighbor. This redirecting of attention from externals to the condition of one's own heart is quite characteristic of Jesus.

Second, note that the key word here is "compassion." Jesus is explaining how he understands the second part of the Law. To love your neighbor as yourself is to have compassion, to "feel with" your fellow man, and to act in accord with that feeling. Just as we feel our own desires, anxieties, cares, pains, and joys, so are we to "feel with" the desires, anxieties, cares, pains and joys of others. And as we act to fulfill the intentions that grow out of these self-directed passions, so, like the Samaritan, must we act to satisfy the needs of others.

> "And as you wish that men would do to you, do so to them" (Luke 6:31).

Love, understood in this way, strikes a new note in our story. It is a conception quite foreign to the Greek philosophers. For them the basic human problem focuses on the control of the passions; by and large, they ascribe the locus of control to reason. Plato sees it as a struggle to subjugate the beast within, Aristotle as a matter of channeling the pas-

---

*See the discussion of love in Plato's *Symposium* (pp. 124–127). The word the New Testament writers use for love is *agape*. It is interesting to compare the *eros* that Socrates extols with the *agape* that Jesus holds is the key to the kingdom of God.

*Note the three types and their response to the injured man. The priest represents the religious leadership; Levites were lay assistants to the priests; and Samaritans were foreigners who were despised by the Jews.

sions by means of virtuous habits; the Stoics come close to recommending the elimination of feelings altogether.* For all of them, the goal is finding the best possible way to live. And though it is true that the Platonic wise man will return to the cave to try to enlighten those still in bondage, none of them would say that the best way to live necessarily involves an equal concern for others—feeling for them just as we feel for ourselves. What Jesus recommends is not the control or extinction of passion, but its *extension*; it is in universal compassion that we will find the kingdom of God. Nor do the Greek philosophers recommend the *universality* of concern we find in Jesus, though the Stoics perhaps come closest in thinking of all men as brothers. But not even a Stoic would say this:

> "Love your enemies, do good to those who hate you, bless those who curse you, pray for those who abuse you" (Luke 6:27).

> "If you love those who love you, what credit is that to you? For even sinners love those who love them" (Luke 6:32).

We do seem to have something genuinely new here.

A corollary to this love is a new virtue: humility. Humility is conspicuously lacking from the Greek lists of virtues, but it is nearly the very essence of perfection according to Jesus. For humility is the opposite of pride, and pride is the very root of sin. It is pride—wanting to be like God—that leads to the sin of Adam. And it is pride that sets human beings against each other; the proud man, glorying in his superiority, cannot consider his neighbor equal in importance to himself and so cannot love as Jesus requires.

Pride, particularly pride in one's righteousness or goodness, is the attitude most at variance with the kingdom of God.

He also told this parable to some who trusted in themselves that they were righteous and despised others: "Two men went up into the temple to pray, one a Pharisee and the other a tax collector. The Pharisee stood and prayed thus with himself, 'God, I thank thee that I am not like other men, extortioners, unjust, adulterers, or even like this tax collector. I fast twice a week, I give tithes of all that I get.' But the tax collector, standing far off, would not even lift up his eyes to heaven, but beat his breast, saying, 'God, be merciful to me a sinner!' I tell you, this man went down to his house justified rather than the other; for every one who exalts himself will be humbled, but he who humbles himself will be exalted" (Luke 18:9–14).*

Jesus issues numerous scorching denunciations of those—usually the wealthy and powerful—who consider themselves righteous but do not act as neighbors should act. Like Socrates, he thereby incurs hostility among those in a position to do him harm. Unlike Socrates, of course, he does not do so by asking questions. Like the prophets of old, Jesus thunders out condemnation; and it is not a claim to know that he tries to undermine, but pretensions to righteousness.† Here are two samples.

> "Woe to you, scribes and Pharisees, hypocrites! for you tithe mint and dill and cummin, and have neglected the weightier matters of the law, justice and mercy and faith; these you ought to have done, without neglecting the others. You blind guides, straining out a gnat and swallowing a camel!" (Matt. 23:23–24).

> "Woe to you, scribes and Pharisees, hypocrites! for you are like whitewashed tombs, which outwardly appear beautiful, but within they are full of dead men's bones and all uncleanness. So you also

---

*The Stoics, for example, oppose pity. In considering what behavior is appropriate when someone is weeping, Epictetus advises us not to be overcome; we should remember that his weeping has its source not in what has happened but in the view he takes of it. We may, perhaps, go as far as to groan with him, but, Epictetus says, "Take heed, however, not to groan inwardly, too" (*Enchiridion* XVI).

*The Pharisees claimed that they observed all the details of the Law. Tax collectors, working for the Roman occupiers, were generally despised; and it is true that many of them were corrupt. A "tithe" is one-tenth of one's income, which is what the Law required to be given for religious and charitable purposes.
†This difference, while significant, may be diminished by the observation that for Socrates virtue is knowledge. So one who claims to know what piety is, for example, would also—in Socrates' eyes—be claiming to be pious.

outwardly appear righteous to men, but within you are full of hypocrisy and iniquity" (Matt. 23:27–28).

His antagonism to mere outward observance leads him to deepen and internalize the Law. About the Law he speaks with authority, contrasting the *words* of the Law, which can be kept simply *by behaving* in certain ways, with the *spirit* of the Law, which requires an *attitude* of love. For example,

"You have heard that it was said to the men of old, 'You shall not kill; and whoever kills shall be liable to judgment.' But I say to you that every one who is angry with his brother shall be liable to judgment" (Matt. 5:21–22).

"You have heard that it was said, 'You shall not commit adultery.' But I say to you that every one who looks at a woman lustfully has already committed adultery with her in his heart" (Matt. 5:27–28).

"You have heard that it was said, 'An eye for an eye and a tooth for a tooth.' But I say to you, Do not resist one who is evil. But if any one strikes you on the right cheek, turn to him the other also" (Matt. 5:38–39).

This attitude to the Law, which the Jews hold so dear, brings him into severe conflict with the authorities. He seems to them to take the Law lightly; on several occasions, for example, they clash with him on the details of Sabbath observance. He is, moreover, popular among the common people and must seem to be undermining the authority of the Jewish leaders. They determine to put him to death.

Because of Roman law, they cannot execute Jesus themselves. So after a trial in the religious court in which he is convicted for blasphemy (putting himself in the place of God), the Jewish leaders bring him before the Roman governor, Pilate. Here he is accused of treason, of setting himself up as King of the Jews (a charge of blasphemy would not have impressed this cosmopolitan Roman). Pilate reluctantly accedes to their demands, and Jesus is crucified.

Each of the four Gospels ends with an account of the discovery, on the third day after Jesus' death, of an empty tomb and of numerous appearances of Jesus to his disciples. His followers come to believe that he has risen from the dead. And this is taken by them as a sign that he is indeed God's anointed, the suffering servant who takes upon himself in his death the sins of the world, thereby bringing in the Kingdom of God in an unexpectedly spiritual way. Their response is to set about making disciples of all nations.

The Meaning of Jesus

We have noted that all the Gospels are written by believers; they are shot through and through with the significance his followers attribute to Jesus after their experience of his resurrection. But it will be useful to discuss more explicitly some of the categories in terms of which his life and death are interpreted. For this purpose, we will look particularly at the Gospel of John and at some letters written by the greatest of the early missionaries, Paul.

John begins his Gospel with a majestic prologue.

In the beginning was the Word, and the Word was with God, and the Word was God. He was in the beginning with God; all things were made through him, and without him was not anything made that was made. In him was life, and the life was the light of men. The light shines in the darkness, and the darkness has not overcome it. . . .

The true light that enlightens every man was coming into the world. He was in the world, and the world was made through him, yet the world knew him not. He came to his own home, and his own people received him not. But to all who received him, who believed in his name, he gave power to become children of God; who were born not of blood nor of the will of the flesh nor of the will of man, but of God.

And the Word became flesh and dwelt among us, full of grace and truth; we have beheld his glory, glory as of the only Son from the Father. . . . And from his fulness have we all received, grace upon grace. For the law was given through Moses; grace and truth came through Jesus Christ. No one has ever seen God; the only Son, who is in the bosom of the Father, he has made him known (John 1:1–18).

It is Jesus, of course, who is being described as the Christ. But notice the exalted conception of him we have here. He is identified with the Word—the *logos*—who is eternal, "in the beginning" (a phrase meant to recall the first line of Genesis). The term *logos* has very rich philosophical connotations, as we have seen, which can hardly have been unknown to the author. Jesus is identified with this *logos*, the wisdom through which all things are made. He comes into the world, though he exists beyond the world, for the purpose of revealing God, whom no one has seen. Jesus, the Christ, is the visible image of God, enlightening men about God and their relation to him.

These remarkable claims are elaborated in a number of discourses that John attributes to Jesus. Jesus says, "He who has seen me has seen the Father" (John 14:9). He says, "I and the Father are one" (John 10:30). He calls himself "the light of the world" (John 8:12), "the bread of life" (John 6:48), and "the good shepherd" who "lays down his life for the sheep" (John 10:11).

If Jesus is the visible image of God, what are we to think of God?

> For God so loved the world that he gave his only Son, that whoever believes in him should not perish but have eternal life. For God sent the Son into the world, not to condemn the world, but that the world might be saved through him (John 3:16–17).

The God whom Jesus reveals is not Aristotle's unmoved mover, thinking true thoughts about himself. Nor is he akin to the gods of the Epicureans who live in blessedness, unconcerned with human beings. The message is that God is Love, that he cares for us, and will save us from our sinfulness through his Son Jesus, who took our sin upon himself in his death. The life and death of the Christ manifest the extremity of that Love and serve, in turn, as a model for life in the kingdom of God.

What is required is a "new birth," not of flesh and the will of man, but "of God."* And this new life—this is the gospel—is now available by trust in Jesus, the Christ.

Paul was a Jew, very strict about the observance of the Law, who was at first vigorously opposed to the new "sect" of Christians. While engaged in persecuting them, he saw a vision of Jesus and was converted, after which he devoted his life to spreading the gospel. He traveled extensively, establishing churches all over Asia Minor and Greece. He visited Athens and argued there with both the Jews and the philosophers, appalled by the "idolatry" he found there and preaching the one creator God and Jesus who rose from the dead.*

Paul comes to believe it is hopeless to try to attain the righteousness of the kingdom of God by observing the Law; no doubt this reflects in part his own zealous efforts before his conversion. All men, Paul holds, are inextricably caught in the web of sinfulness and cannot by their own (sinful) efforts "justify" themselves before the righteous judge. What we cannot do for ourselves has, however, been graciously done by God for us through Jesus.

> For no human being will be justified in his sight by works of the law, since through the law comes knowledge of sin.
>
> But now the righteousness of God has been manifested apart from the law, although the law and the prophets bear witness to it, the righteousness of God through faith in Jesus Christ for all who believe (Rom. 3:20–22).
>
> There is therefore now no condemnation for those who are in Christ Jesus. For the law of the Spirit of life in Christ Jesus has set me free from the law of sin and death (Rom. 8:1–2).

Having been freed from the burden of the Law and no longer needing to prove ourselves righteous, says Paul, allows us to participate in the Spirit of Christ and to love our neighbors and serve their needs. It really is Jesus, then, who has brought in the kingdom of God. Moreover, just as God raised Jesus from the dead, so will all who believe in him be raised to a blessed life with him.

---

*See Jesus' conversation with the Jewish leader Nicodemus in John 3:1–15.

*See Acts 17:16–34.

Our consideration of Christian teaching can be brought to a close with these words from another author.

We know that we have passed out of death into life, because we love the brethren. He who does not love remains in death. Any one who hates his brother is a murderer, and you know that no murderer has eternal life abiding in him. By this we know love, that he laid down his life for us; and we ought to lay down our lives for the brethren. But if anyone has the world's goods and sees his brother in need, yet closes his heart against him, how does God's love abide in him? Little children, let us not love in word or speech but in deed and in truth (1 John 3:14–18).

Notes

1. Biblical quotations in this text are taken from the Revised Standard Version.
2. Josephus, *Against Apion* 200:20; quoted in C. K. Barrett, ed., *The New Testament Background: Selected Documents* (London: S.P.C.K., 1956), 202.

14

Augustine:
God and the Soul

Augustine is not only a fascinating figure personally but also something of a turning point historically. He lived (354–430 C.E.) in the days of what we call "late antiquity," just as it began to merge into the medieval period. He draws on and brings together the results of nearly four centuries of debate and consolidation concerning Christian doctrine. And he melds that with what he takes to be the best in the heritage of the Greek philosophers—the tradition stemming from Plato. Both of these traditions are given a unique stamp by Augustine's penchant for introspection, his passionate search for happiness, and the impress of his undeniably powerful mind. He would himself say that if he had contributed anything of value, it was due entirely to the grace of God. This would not be merely an expression of modesty, such as it tends to be today; Augustine believes it to be the literal truth. Whether we agree with that or not, we can fairly say that no one else did as much to shape the intellectual course of the next thousand years.

The views of some philosophers can be discussed quite independently of their lives. Not so Augustine. We need to understand, then, at least the outlines of a tumultuous life much involved with the issues of his time.[1] There is no better introduction to his early years than his own *Confessions*, in which he reflects—before God but also before us all—on his youthful waywardness. By the time he wrote this reflective look at his life (in 397), he was forty-three years old, had been a

Christian for eleven years, a priest for eight years, and a bishop for two. We cannot hope here to imitate the richness of these meditations but will try just to get a feel for how he saw his life from the point of view he had reached.

Augustine was born in northern Africa, which had been Roman for many generations but was always precariously perched between the sea and the barbarian interior. Christianity had taken root there but, despite its legitimization by the emperor Constantine in 325, was still in competition with the old pagan beliefs and ways. Augustine was the child of a Christian mother, Monica, and a pagan father, who converted to Christianity before he died. Monica was the stronger influence, convinced all her life that her son would be "saved." But it was Patricius, his father, who resolutely determined that Augustine should be educated; he studied literature and rhetoric and, for a while, the law. His education was intense but narrow, concentrating on the masters of Latin style and consisting of enormous amounts of memorization of, for example, Virgil's *Aeneid*. He read very little philosophy.

Meanwhile, he lived the life of pleasure. The bishop he became, looking back on those days, puts it this way:

> I cared for nothing but to love and be loved. But my love went beyond the affection of one mind for another, beyond the arc of the bright beam of friend-

ship. Bodily desire, like a morass, and adolescent sex welling up within me exuded mists which clouded over and obscured my heart, so that I could not distinguish the clear light of true love from the murk of lust. Love and lust together seethed within me. In my tender youth they swept me away over the precipice of my body's appetites and plunged me in the whirlpool of sin (C 2.2).[2]

It is not just sex, however, on which the bishop focuses in "the whirlpool of sin." He is almost more perplexed over a single act that comes to represent for him the puzzling nature of human wickedness. He, together with some companions, had shaken down an enormous quantity of pears from a neighbor's tree and had stolen them away. And why did they steal the pears? Did they need them? No. Did they eat them? No. They threw them to the pigs.

Why, then, did they steal the pears? This is what puzzles Augustine. In a judicial inquiry, he notes, no one is satisfied until the motive has been produced: a desire of gaining some good or of avoiding some evil. But what was the good gained here? What evil was avoided? He concludes: "our real pleasure consisted in doing something that was forbidden" (C 2.4). But why was that a pleasure? Augustine's reflective answer is that the act was, in a perverse sort of way, an imitation of God who is the source of all good; it was an attempt to exercise a liberty that belongs to God alone: that of being unconstrained by anything outside himself (C 1.6). We come, then, even in this simple prank by a sixteen-year-old, to Augustine's analysis of the root of man's predicament: pride.

He also notes that he surely would not have stolen the pears on his own.

It was not the takings that attracted me but the raid itself, and yet to do it by myself would have been no fun and I should not have done it. This was friendship of a most unfriendly sort, bewitching my mind in an inexplicable way. For the sake of a laugh, a little sport, I was glad to do harm and anxious to damage another; and that without a thought of profit for myself or retaliation for injuries received! And all because we are ashamed to hold back when others say "Come on! Let's do it!" (C 2.9).

This power of the group to incite to evil deeds is expressed also in the following passage, in which Augustine sets out a very common experience of the young.

I was so blind to the truth that among my companions I was ashamed to be less dissolute than they were. For I heard them bragging of their depravity, and the greater the sin the more they gloried in it, so that I took pleasure in the same vices not only for the enjoyment of what I did, but also for the applause I won.

Nothing deserves to be despised more than vice; yet I gave in more and more to vice simply in order not to be despised. If I had not sinned enough to rival other sinners, I used to pretend that I had done things I had not done at all, because I was afraid that innocence would be taken for cowardice and chastity for weakness (C 2.3).

It is clear that the Christian bishop at age forty-three does not take lightly the peccadilloes of his youth. It is not prudishness or puritanical negativism that accounts for this, however; it is a considered judgment that pursuing such desires is a sure way to miss true happiness. But the young Augustine had a long way to go before he would see things this way.

He took a mistress, to whom he was apparently faithful for many years. They had a son. Augustine completed his education and became a teacher of rhetoric and literature, first in the provincial north African town of Thagaste, then in Carthage, the great city of Roman Africa. He was an able teacher and earned a reputation, for which he was most eager.

But he was eager for something else as well. At nineteen, he read a (now lost) work by Cicero, the great orator, which contains an exhortation to study philosophy. Augustine was carried away.

. . . the only thing that pleased me in Cicero's book was his advice not simply to admire one or another of the schools of philosophy, but to love wisdom itself, whatever it might be, and to search for it, pursue it, hold it, and embrace it firmly (C 4.4).

The young Augustine embraced this love of wisdom with a "blaze of enthusiasm." But where to look? He knew very little of classical philosophy, which is what Cicero surely had in mind. But in Augustine's circle in late fourth-century Africa, it was Christ who was portrayed as "the wisdom of God"; so Augustine turned to the Bible. But he was greatly disappointed. Not only did it seem to lack the polish of the best Roman poets, its conceptions seemed crude and naive to him. In Genesis, after Adam and Eve had disobeyed God, we read that they "heard the sound of the Lord God walking in the cool of the day." What a way to think of God!

Moreover, Christianity seemed unable to solve a great puzzle, which was to perplex Augustine sincerely for many years. The Christian God was proclaimed to be both almighty and perfectly good. But if this is so, where does evil come from? If the answer is the devil, the question can be repeated: where does the devil come from? If from God, then God is the source of evil. And if God is almighty, where else could the devil come from? But God is good; so how could he be the source of evil? Augustine could not see that the Christians had any satisfactory answer to this problem.

So, in his search for wisdom, he turned instead to the Manichees, among whom he was a "hearer" for nine years. Manicheanism was a syncretistic sect founded by the Babylonian Mani in the third century. Mani was martyred (some say crucified) by the religious establishment in 277 C.E., and that fact helped spread the sect widely. Mani's views were a combination of themes from the Persian religion of Zoroastrianism—particularly its theme of the opposition of light (goodness) and dark (evil)—and Christianity. Manicheanism is often thought of as one of the many Christian "heresies" prevalent during the first centuries of the Christian era, as the Church tried to sort out an orthodox view of revealed truth.

The doctrines of the sect are enormously complex, involving facets of astrology and half-digested bits of natural science, as well as borrowings from traditional religions. But the key beliefs are simple and provide a solution of sorts to the problem of evil. The reason there is evil in the world, say the Manichees, is that there *is* no omnipotent good power. Rather, there are two equal and opposed powers, one good and one evil. It has always been this way, they say, and will always be so.

But this opposition is not just "out there" in the world. It is resident within each of us, since we are ourselves a battleground between good and evil. That may not sound very profound; but the Manichees explain this dichotomy in a particular way. The good part of ourselves is the soul (composed of the light), and the bad part is the body (composed of the dark earth). A human being is literally part divine and part demonic.

I have known my soul and the body that lies upon it,
That they have been enemies since the creation of the worlds (*MP*, 49).[3]

In fact, the entire earth is the province of the evil power, since evil resides in matter as such. We are, however, *essentially souls*; and as souls we experience ourselves to be under the domination of a foreign power—matter, the body, the world.

These equivalences between good, God, and the soul on the one hand and evil and matter on the other also affect their interpretation of the Christian scriptures. God could not be the *creator* of the physical world, for obvious reasons. Nor could the Word literally become *flesh*, as the Gospel of John states. Nor could Christ die or suffer any other sort of evil. The Old Testament, with its God of wrath and vengeance, is very largely dismissed as a product of the evil power, and they suggest that the parts of the New Testament that speak of judgment and punishment by God are inauthentic additions by "Judaizing" editors. In their eyes, God remains unsullied by any contact with matter, and Christ only *appeared* to be born, to suffer and die.

The "gospel" of the Manichees is their proclamation of the essentially noncorruptible nature of the soul, which they identify with the true person. We can be saved from the domination of the evil power—matter—if we come to *know who we are.*

A man called down into the world saying: Blessed is he that shall know his soul (*MP*, 47).

The man was Mani, and this was the heart of his message.

Manicheanism, then, solves the *theoretical* problem of evil by the postulation of the two powers, and it solves the *practical* problem of evil by the doctrine that the soul is essentially good, untouched by the evil of the body. If one can only come to identify oneself with the soul, one will experience "salvation" from the evil. No doubt Augustine was not only troubled by the theoretical problem but also needed to be able to think of himself as "essentially good." This, then, was the first "wisdom" that he embraced in his enthusiasm for the truth.

He noticed, however, that some of the doctrines were obscure and that others seemed to conflict with the best astronomical knowledge of the day. When one of the Manichean "Elect," a certain Faustus, came to Carthage, Augustine determined to inquire about these things. He was disappointed for the second time. It became obvious that Faustus was not wise.*

Moreover, he found Manichean views unhelpful in a practical sense. Their key to salvation lay in knowledge, in a recognition of the true nature of the self as good. But this didn't seem to be of any help in actually changing one's life. It was too *passive*. (It may have been his experience as a Manichee that led to his later view that the root of sin lies not in the intellect but in the *will*.) The bishop he became reflects on his experience:

> I still thought that it is not we who sin but some other nature that sins within us. It flattered my pride to think that I incurred no guilt and, when I did wrong, not to confess it so that you might bring healing to a soul that had sinned against you (Psalm 41:4). I preferred to excuse myself and blame this unknown thing which was in me but was not part of me. The truth, of course, was that it was all my own self, and my own impiety had divided me against myself. My sin was all the more incurable because I did not think myself a sinner (C 5.10).

These notions of pride, guilt, and a divided self we need to examine in more detail. But because of these intellectual and spiritual dissatisfactions, Augustine began to drift away from the Manichees.

He began to read the philosophers and found himself attracted to skepticism. He left Africa and went to Rome, where again he taught rhetoric and literature. He attracted the attention of an influential Roman and was recommended to the more attractive post of Professor of Rhetoric in Milan. Here he was joined by his widowed mother and with her attended Christian services conducted by the Bishop of Milan, Ambrose. Ambrose was an immensely learned man, far more learned in the traditions of the Greek church fathers and Greek philosophy than Augustine (whose Greek skills were always imperfect). He was also an accomplished orator. At first, Augustine went simply to hear him speak, but he soon found himself listening to the content as well as the style. And he began to discover the possibility of a Christianity that was not naive and crude but that could bear comparison with the best thought of the day.

What made the Christianity of Ambrose a revelation to Augustine, who had, in a sense, been familiar with Christianity since his childhood? There seem to have been three things. (1) There was the idea of God and the soul as *immaterial* realities. Augustine had found great difficulty in thinking of either as other than some sort of *body*, even if very ethereal bodies. (Recall that the Manichees thought of God and the soul as light.) But if God is a body, God must, like other bodies, be excluded from some places; and this idea fits with the Manichean dualism of two equal realities. (2) The category of immaterial reality was drawn from philosophy, particularly from that of Plato and his successors. (Remember the Forms, especially the Form of the Good.)* Ambrose was not afraid to plunder the Greek philosophical tradition for help in making Christianity intelligible. (3) Finally, there was the possibility of giving allegorical interpretations to Scripture, particularly to the Old Testament. Taken allegorically rather than literally, many passages ceased to offend and took on the aspect of conveying deep spiritual truths.†

---

*Compare Socrates asking questions in Athens: *Apology* 21b–22c.

*See pp. 118–121.

†The Stoics had adopted a similar strategy with respect to the works of the pagan poets, as you may recall. See p. 193.

Augustine began to study the Bible seriously for the first time and to read philosophy. The Bible spoke of the Wisdom of God, and philosophers loved wisdom. Could Christianity contain the truth the philosophers were seeking? He began to suspect so. He grew more sure of it, then became virtually certain.

Yet he hesitated. What would happen if he became a Christian? In Augustine's view, this was a serious matter. His life would have to change drastically, for he was still preoccupied with worldly things: his career, his reputation, and sex. He had dismissed his mistress, who returned to Africa, and a marriage with an heiress was being arranged. Would he have to give all this up? Augustine was never one for half-measures, and it seemed to him that he would. But could he? He procrastinated. The bishop he had become expresses the agony he had felt at that time in the following way:

> . . . I was held fast, not in fetters clamped upon me by another, but by my own will, which had the strength of iron chains. The enemy held my will in his power and from it he had made a chain and shackled me. For my will was perverse and lust had grown from it, and when I gave in to lust habit was born, and when I did not resist the habit it became a necessity. These were the links which together formed what I have called my chain, and it held me fast in the duress of servitude. But the new will which had come to life in me and made me wish to serve you freely and enjoy you, my God, who are our only certain joy, was not yet strong enough to overcome the old, hardened as it was by the passage of time. So these two wills within me, one old, one new, one the servant of the flesh, the other of the spirit, were in conflict and between them they tore my soul apart (*C* 8.5).

The perversity of the will which leads to lust which leads to habit which becomes a virtual necessity forms a chain that will play a crucial role in Augustine's analysis of what is wrong with human beings and how it can be cured.

In a dramatic experience, which Augustine relates in the *Confessions*, the chain of necessity was broken. After hearing from a traveler the stories of several others who had renounced the world and devoted themselves to God, Augustine rushed into a garden in a tumult. "My inner self," he says, "was a house divided against itself." "I was my own contestant. . . ."

> . . . I felt that I was still the captive of my sins, and in my misery I kept crying, "How long shall I go on saying 'tomorrow, tomorrow'? Why not now? Why not make an end of my ugly sins at this moment?
>
> I was asking myself these questions, weeping all the while with the most bitter sorrow in my heart, when all at once I heard the sing-song voice of a child in a nearby house. Whether it was the voice of a boy or a girl I cannot say, but again and again it repeated the refrain "Take it and read, take it and read." At this I looked up, thinking hard whether there was any kind of game in which children used to chant words like these, but I could not remember ever hearing them before. I stemmed my flood of tears and stood up, telling myself that this could only be a divine command to open my book of Scripture and read the first passage on which my eyes should fall. . . .
>
> So I hurried back to the place where Alypius was sitting, for when I stood up to move away I had put down the book containing Paul's Epistles. I seized it and opened it, and in silence I read the first passage on which my eyes fell: Not in reveling and drunkenness, not in lust and wantonness, not in quarrels and rivalries. Rather, arm yourselves with the Lord Jesus Christ; spend no more thought on nature and nature's appetites. (Romans 13:13, 14) I had no wish to read more and no need to do so. For in an instant, as I came to the end of the sentence, it was as though the light of confidence flooded into my heart and all the darkness of doubt was dispelled (*C* 8.12).

Augustine had found the wisdom he had been searching for.

He gave up his career and his prospects for marriage. He retired for some months with some friends and his mother to a retreat where he studied and wrote. On Easter Day in 387, he was baptized by Ambrose, thus making the break with "the world" public. Not long thereafter, his mother having died, he returned to Africa, was made a priest (somewhat against his will), and in 391 was ordained bishop of Hippo, a city on the Mediterranean coast.

Thereafter he was engaged in practical affairs of the church: in serving as a judge (one of the tasks of a bishop in those days), in controversies to define and defend the faith, and in an enormous amount of writing. There are, of course, the sermons. But there are also letters and pamphlets and book after book in which Augustine explores the meaning of the faith he had adopted. In these the theme is—again and again—to try to *understand* what he has *believed*. For Augustine, faith must come first; understanding may follow (though on some difficult topics, such as the Trinity, even understanding will be only partial). This order of things may seem strange to some of us. We may think that unless we understand first, we will not know what it is that we are believing. But it is a reflection of Augustine's conviction that will is more fundamental than intellect and that only if the will is first directed by faith to the right end will the intellect be able to do its job rightly.*

With this point we are ready to leave the life of Augustine and focus on his philosophy. It is characteristic of Augustine's thought that we cannot do so without at the same time discussing his theology, or doctrine of God. For wisdom, Augustine is convinced, is *one*. And that means that philosophy and theology, understanding and faith, science and religion are inextricably bound together. What the lover of wisdom wants is the truth. And the truth is God. And God is most fully known by faith in Christ. We will not do full justice to this unity, but in selecting out certain themes that are of particular philosophical interest, we will try to keep in mind the whole context in which they play their part for Augustine. Part of Augustine's legacy is just this unity of thought. It sets the intellectual tone for a thousand years. Eventually, as we see, thinkers begin to try to take it apart again; the consequence is our largely secular modern world.

---

*Think about Socrates. We said that in order to benefit from a conversation with Socrates, you had to be a person of a certain *character*. The arrogant, the proud, the self-satisfied would only be humiliated. (See pp. 61–63.) Augustine agrees that character is more fundamental than intellect. But whereas Socrates thinks of virtue or character as a matter of knowledge, for Augustine it is a matter of faith, or commitment.

Wisdom, Happiness, and God

Augustine simply takes for granted that the pursuit of wisdom, philosophy, has just one aim: happiness. This was the common assumption in late antiquity, shared by the Epicureans, the Stoics, and the Skeptics. Augustine was never greatly interested in nature philosophy and eventually turned away from it as resolutely as Socrates had done.* The pursuit of understanding with respect to the natural world is not perhaps a positively bad thing; but as usually pursued it is unessential, distracting, merely the satisfaction of curiosity ("the lust of the eyes"). It could not make one happy.

What does interest Augustine intensely is the soul—his own soul first of all, then what that could teach him about the souls of all. For happiness and unhappiness are clearly conditions of the soul. That soul is happy which possesses what it most desires, provided that it most desires what wisdom approves. As we'll see, Augustine becomes convinced that the only proper object of desire is God. Shortly after his conversion he wrote some "soliloquies" in the form of dialogues between his soul and his reason:

A: Behold, I have prayed to God.

R: What, then, do you desire to know?

A: Those things for which I have prayed.

R: Sum them up, briefly.

A: I desire to know God and the soul.

R: And nothing more?

A: Nothing whatever (*SO* 2.7).

---

*See *Apology* 19c–d and p. 119. There are many in the modern world, of course, who see a close connection between science and happiness. The application of modern science cures diseases, lengthens life, eases labor, and increases enjoyment. Ancient science tended to be divorced from application and technology, except perhaps in medicine. The scientist and the "mechanic" belonged to different social classes. Whether Augustine would have been more friendly to modern science in its applications is uncertain, but his criticism of the Epicureans (below) makes it doubtful.

Note that he has already prayed to God, yet what he wants to know is God. If this sounds paradoxical, remember that Augustine thinks that belief must precede understanding, not follow it. To believe is to give one's assent to the testimony of others, to some authority. It is an act of the will. To understand is to grasp the matter in such a way that one sees the truth for oneself. Augustine quotes the Greek version of the prophet Isaiah again and again: "Unless you believe, you shall not understand." The will must be open to the truth, or the intellect cannot do its proper work. He believes in God, yearns for him, hopes in him, but he does not yet understand what he believes. And so he addresses God in faith, but with a prayer that he may understand and know both *that* God is and *what* God is. God and the soul make a pair for Augustine, because it is only God that can supply the happiness his soul longs for. And nothing else matters.

But we are getting ahead of our story. Philosophically speaking, we do not yet understand what justifies bringing God into it at all. To be sure, Augustine has gone through a dramatic conversion experience and believes that in turning his will away from worldly things to God, he has found the solution to the problem of happiness.* But what makes Augustine a philosopher is the fact that he is not satisfied simply to bask in the blessings of faith. He needs to *understand* what he has done, why it has produced the happiness that it has, and what justifies the turn to God. He never doubts that this can be understood. So we must go back to a stage of thought that is logically prior—though experientially subsequent—and ask whether the soul in pursuit of wisdom needs to take account of God at all.

The soul wants happiness. And for that reason it wants wisdom. For wisdom is nothing more than the knowledge of what makes for happiness.

Just as it is agreed that we all wish to be happy, so it is agreed that we all wish to be wise, since no one with-

out wisdom is happy. No man is happy except through the highest good, which is to be found and included in that truth which we call wisdom (*FCW* 2.9.102–3).

All humans desire to be happy. So all want to know what that highest good is which will provide such blessedness. Desiring that knowledge, all want to be wise. But they do not agree about what this highest good is. The Epicureans think it is pleasure, the Stoics think it is virtue, and the Skeptics think the best we can do is suspend judgment.

Can we make any progress in deciding the question about the highest good? Augustine thinks we can. Two things are evident: you cannot be happy unless you have what you desire; yet having what you desire does not guarantee happiness, for you must desire the right things. Certain things, if they are desired and attained, will produce misery rather than happiness. Augustine knows this from bitter experience.

Moreover, the appropriate objects of desire must be things that we cannot lose without desiring to (i.e., they must be things that cannot be taken away from us against our will), and they must be enduring.* If they could be taken away from us, we could not be secure in the enjoyment of them; and if they could fade or disappear on their own, we would fear their prospective loss even if we had them. What makes for happiness must *last*. These are among the truths that wisdom teaches.

But again we need to backtrack a bit. For, as we have seen, some philosophers—the skeptics—doubt whether any such truths can be known. They suggest that what Augustine here sets out as the requirements of wisdom are nothing more than opinions, just one more set of views among the interminable squabble of the schools. Augustine himself had been attracted to skepticism for a time. He feels the strength of this objection. And he sees that unless it is met, nothing else can stand firm. So we must take another logical step backwards.

*Compare Plato on the "turning" of the soul in the Myth of the Cave, pp. 121–123.

*This is by now a familiar point. See, for instance, p. 173.

Can the skeptical objections be met? Augustine believes they can be met, and decisively so. He admits that we can be deceived by the senses and that we can make purely intellectual mistakes. But there are three things we know with absolute certainty:

> . . . the certainty that I exist, that I know it, and that I am glad of it, is independent of any imaginary and deceptive fantasies.
>
> In respect of these truths I have no fear of the arguments of the Academics.* They say, "Suppose you are mistaken?" I reply, "If I am mistaken, I exist." A non-existent being cannot be mistaken; therefore I must exist, if I am mistaken. Then since my being mistaken proves that I exist, how can I be mistaken in thinking that I exist, seeing that my mistake establishes my existence? Since therefore I must exist in order to be mistaken, then even if I am mistaken, there can be no doubt that I am not mistaken in my knowledge that I exist. It follows that I am not mistaken in knowing that I know. For just as I know that I exist, I also know that I know. And when I am glad of those two facts, I can add the fact of that gladness to the things I know, as a fact of equal worth. For I am not mistaken about the fact of my gladness, since I am not mistaken about the things which I love. Even if they were illusory, it would still be a fact that I love the illusions (CG 11.27).

Skepticism, then, which denies or doubts whether we can have knowledge at all, is an error. Knowledge and certainty are possible. Truth is available to us, at least to this small extent.

Notice now what this truth is about: his own existence, his thought, and his feelings. (In some works we find a different trinity: existence, life, and knowledge; or existence, knowledge, and will.) In short, what we can know for certain concerns ourselves and, in particular, the soul.† One of the striking things about Augustine's thought is the degree to which it is "psychological." It is the interior life that interests him, and he is a master of subtle descriptions of this life. This interest is consonant with his epistemological views about what is best known to us.

The next question, obviously, is whether we can know *more* than this. In the spirit of the Platonic philosophers, Augustine turns to mathematics. He offers a number of examples, but the nicest one concerns a circle, from the center of which two radii are drawn to the circumference. Let the points at which the radii meet the circle be as close together as you like; it will still be the case that these two lines meet only at that point which is the center. You cannot draw it to look this way, but it is true nonetheless.* Furthermore, we know that between any two such lines, no matter how close together they are, innumerable other lines can be drawn. Moreover, we know that between any two such lines, no matter how close together and no matter how small the original circle, another circle can be inscribed! This is true, and we know it to be true (SO 20.35). And this truth is not something private to any one of us. It is knowledge common to all.

> Whatever I may experience with my bodily senses, such as this air and earth and whatever corporeal matter they contain, I cannot know how long it will endure. But seven and three are ten, not only now, but forever. There has never been a time when seven and three were not ten, nor will there ever be a time when they are not ten. Therefore, I have said that the truth of number is incorruptible and common to all who think (FCW 2.7.82–83).

Augustine concludes that mathematical truth exists and we can know it.

Perhaps, however, we grant that there is mathematical truth but doubt that there is such a thing as practical truth—truth about what we should desire to be happy, about the highest good. But, Augustine asks,

---

*The Academics were members of the Academy after Plato who turned to skepticism.
†At the beginning of modern philosophy in the seventeenth century, this theme will be picked up by René Descartes. See *Meditation II*.

*Compare discussion of Socrates' sand drawings on p. 108.

Will you deny that the incorrupt is better than the corrupt, the eternal better than the temporal, the inviolable better than the violable? (*FCW* 2.10.114).

Here is a truth that seems as secure to Augustine as the truths of mathematics. How could, for example, the beauty of a flower that lasts for a day be as good as an equivalent beauty that lasts for two days? And how could that be as good as the same beauty lasting forever? But this, notice, is a truth about what is "better," and so it has direct practical implications. Whatever is the highest good, whatever will actually fulfill the desire for happiness must be the best of all possible things. It must be incorruptible, eternal, inviolable. Otherwise, even if we possessed it, it could be taken away from us without our consent. To settle for less than such a good is to resign ourselves to unhappiness.

But if this is *true*, then this truth is itself eternal—as unchanging a truth as seven plus three makes ten. And it is a truth common to all. If two of us look at a tree, the tree is neither in me nor in you. It has an existence independent of either of us. In a similar way, these truths are not private possessions. I can know them, and you can know them; but their existence does not depend on either me or you.

These truths are clearly superior to us and to the powers of our minds. This is shown in two ways. We do not make judgments *about* them, as we judge about sensible things or even ourselves; we make judgments *according to* them. For example, we say of an apple not only that it is ripe, but that it is *too* ripe, or that it *ought to be* riper. And we often say that a person has not done what he ought to have done. In doing so, we judge *about* these things, but *according* to certain rules. And these rules we do not in turn judge about. Moreover, truth (unlike ourselves) is unchanging.

When a man says that the eternal is more powerful than the temporal, and that seven plus three are ten, he does not say that it ought to be so; he knows it is this way, and does not correct it as an examiner would, but he rejoices as if he has made a discovery.

If truth were equal to our minds, it would be subject to change. Our minds sometimes see more and sometimes less, and because of this we acknowledge that they are mutable. Truth, remaining in itself, does not gain anything when we see it, or lose anything when we do not see it. It is whole and uncorrupted. With its light, truth gives joy to the men who turn to it, and punishes with blindness those who turn away from it (*FCW* 2.12.134–35).

Let us review. We want to be happy, and in order to find happiness we desire to be wise. Wisdom will tell us what the highest good is. Possession of this good will make us happy. Such a good must be eternal, available to all, and superior to ourselves. But we have now found something with precisely those characteristics: truth itself.*

We possess in the truth, therefore, what we all may enjoy, equally and in common; in it are no defects or limitations. For truth receives all its lovers without arousing their envy. It is open to all, yet it is always chaste. No one says to the other, "Get Back! Let me approach too! Hands off! Let me also embrace it!" All men cling to the truth and touch it. The food of truth can never be stolen (*FCW* 2.14.145).

Truth is something we cannot lose against our will. And since it is superior to our minds, it is a candidate for being the highest good and the source of our happiness.

Now we have reached the point where we can *understand* (not just believe) why God must be brought into the picture. Think back to what Augustine claims to know: he exists, he lives, and he knows and feels. These facts are ordered in a kind of hierarchy. The latter facts presuppose the former; you cannot live unless you exist, and you cannot know and feel unless you are alive. Moreover, this is a hierarchy of value, for it is better to be alive than just to exist, and it is better to know and feel than just to live. These are the reasons we judge plants superior to rocks, animals to plants, and

---

*The common, public nature of truth is stressed also by Plato. See p. 110.

ourselves to all. At the top of this hierarchy is our own rational nature, by which we judge the rest and guide our own behavior. This is best of all among the things of experience. But what if there were something superior even to this? Would it not be right to acknowledge that as *God*, particularly if it were shown to be eternal and immutable?

But this is just what Augustine claims already to have shown! Truth itself exists. It is immutable and eternal. And it is superior to our reason. By definition, God is "that to whom no one is superior" (*FCW* 2.6.54).* So we can now say that, on the assumption that there is nothing superior to the truth, the truth itself is God. If there should exist something superior to the truth, then that is God. On either hypothesis, God exists! As Augustine puts it in a dialogue with a friend,

> You granted . . . that if I showed you something higher than our minds, you would admit, assuming that nothing existed which was still higher, that God exists. I accepted your condition and said that it was enough to show this. For if there is something more excellent than truth, this is God. If there is not, then truth itself is God. Whether or not truth is God, you cannot deny that God exists, and this was the question with which we agreed to deal. . . . This indubitable fact we maintain, I think, not only by faith, but also by a sure though somewhat tenuous form of reasoning, which is sufficient for the immediate question (*FCW* 2.15.153–54).

To this demonstration his friend, Evodius, exclaims:

> I can scarcely find words for the unbelievable joy that fills me. I accept these arguments, crying out that they are most certain. And my inner voice shouts, for truth itself to hear, that I cling to this: not only does good exist, but indeed the highest good—and this is the source of happiness (*FCW* 2.15.156).

Since his experience in the garden Augustine has believed this. But now he also understands it in a way that satisfies his reason. Others may follow this proof and come to understand it, too. But one's reason is not unaffected by one's will and desires; without a will to truth, even the best rational demonstration may fail to convince. As we'll see, in a certain sense Augustine holds that *will* is basic.

The Interior Teacher

Augustine struggles with the same epistemological problem that puzzles Socrates: what accounts for the fact that we can recognize the truth when we stumble upon it? Socrates solves the problem, you will recall, by positing the preexistence of the soul in a life where it dwelt in intimate contact with the truth. Though Augustine toys with this idea, it is fundamentally inconsistent with Christian doctrine, and in his mature thought he rejects it. But then he needs another solution.

He draws this solution from both Platonic and biblical sources, between which he sees a remarkable congruence. As a prelude to understanding his solution, we need to look at the background from which this solution is drawn. In his letter to the Church in Rome, St. Paul had written, concerning all people,

> For what can be known about God is plain to them, because God has shown it to them. Ever since the creation of the world his invisible nature, namely, his eternal power and deity, has been clearly perceived in the things that have been made (Rom. 1:19–20).

For Augustine, it is Plato and his followers, particularly Plotinus, who exemplify the truth of these scriptural remarks.* In the Platonists he recognizes a view of God as eternal, immutable, and immaterial. Consider Plato's doctrine of the Forms and, in particular, of the Form of the Good—source of

---

*This idea is the root from which a much more sophisticated and complex proof will be drawn by Anselm of Canterbury. See Chapter 15.

*Plotinus (204–270 C.E.) is a mystic who draws on Plato's doctrines to express his mystical experiences and to structure a vision of reality. We will discuss one important part of this vision (see pp. 223–224).

both the being and the intelligibility of all else. Plato explicitly compares the Good to the visible sun as the source of intelligible light, making truth visible. And he insists that only those who participate in the Form of the Good will be wise and that only those who have this knowledge will be truly virtuous and good. These pagan philosophers also have much to say about the *logos*, the principle of rationality or wisdom that informs the world.

Augustine remarks that some Christians are amazed when they learn of these congruences; he notes the speculation of some that Plato may have read these things in the works of the Hebrew prophets. His own view is that this is possible, but not likely. Nor is it a necessary explanation, if the words of Paul and John are taken seriously—if *all* are "enlightened" by the Word. Augustine himself is most of all impressed with the following fact:

> . . . that when the angel gave Moses the message from God, and Moses asked the name of him who gave the command to go and free the Hebrew people from Egypt, he received this reply, "I am HE WHO IS, and you will say to the sons of Israel, 'HE WHO IS has sent me to you.'" This implies that in comparison with him who really is, because he is unchangeable, the things created changeable have no real existence. This truth Plato vigorously maintained and diligently taught (*CG* 8.11).

The most profound truth about God, Augustine holds, is expressed in this phrase: "He Who Is." If we want to say most fundamentally *what* God is, we must say that he is *being*.* Moreover, what truly *is* must be both eternal and immutable. Of nothing but God is this true. Only God *is* in an eternal perfection that admits no change. This is a doctrine that he finds both in the Platonists and in the Scriptures.

All this is strikingly similar to the beginning of John's Gospel.† Here the Word (the *logos*) is said to be eternal, indeed to be God, and to be "the light that enlightens every man." In Augustine's view, philosophers had themselves been "enlightened" by that very light. And this view informs his attitude to the entire range of non-Christian literature and philosophy. Like Ambrose, he gives an allegorical interpretation to the command that the fleeing Hebrews should take with them the gold and silver of the Egyptians, whose slaves they had so long been. There is "gold" in the writings of the pagan thinkers, and Christians may plunder their insights with a good conscience without feeling a sense of betrayal to God. For God is the author of truth wherever it is to be found (*OCD* 2.40).

There are, from Augustine's point of view, definite limits to the truths found in pagan writings. We do not find there the assertions of John that "the Word became flesh and dwelt among us," and that "grace and truth came through Jesus Christ." Though they may have truth, they do not have the whole truth. In particular, they do not have the truth concerning the way of salvation; for though wisdom may have led them to see that "salvation" or blessedness lies in participating in the Goodness of God, they are without either a clear notion of sin (which separates us from God) or of the grace of Christ (which makes possible the return to God). They may *know*, but they are unable to *do*. Their knowledge is both a result of pride and a stimulus to pride. But pride, as we shall see, is what most fundamentally cuts us off from God. So although the best of the pagan writers know part of the truth and share in wisdom to some degree, although they have an idea of blessedness, they are impotent to reach it.

In deciding what may be taken from the writings of the pagans, Augustine's rule always is this: is it congruent with the Scriptures? And in the light of this rule, we can see that there is much in those writings that must be criticized and rejected—in particular, the continuing toleration for the worship of many gods and the vices that typically accompany such worship.

Let us now go back to the problem concerning recognition of the truth. For simplicity's sake, we shall set aside the whole area of truths about the

---

*To use Aristotle's terminology, this is to understand the "essence" of God. For *essence*, see p. 161.
†You should at this point review that important passage. Look back to p. 208.

changeable world and concentrate on intelligible truths, particularly those which make up the wisdom that leads to happiness. How do we come to recognize such truths *as true*? Consider the proposition that the immutable is better than the mutable. Augustine thinks we can know this with as much certainty as the truths of mathematics. How do we learn that this is so?

Note that we do not learn it by being *told* it is so. First, we can be told false things as well as true; and second, we cannot, in any case, learn anything at all by means of mere *signs*. The second reason is the deeper one and needs to be explored. Words are signs, Augustine tells us. Since they are signs, they stand for, or represent, some reality. Some words signify other signs, like the word "noun," but other words represent realities that are not themselves signs—"horse," for instance.

Knowledge may be expressed in terms of signs, though it needn't be. In any case, knowledge is not knowledge of the signs that express it. Knowledge is knowledge of the realities expressed by those signs. Suppose we read, "And their sarabelle were not altered" (an example Augustine takes from Daniel 3:27). Do we understand that? Probably not, because although we hear the word "sarabelle," we do not know what it stands for. Suppose we are told that sarabelle are head coverings. Then we do understand—provided we know what heads and coverings are. But we must be *acquainted* with the realities in question if we are to know whether something is true. In this case, an image of heads and coverings must be stored in the memory. We consult this memory to understand the words.

We do not, then, learn from words. Words at best are reminders of realities we already in some sense know. How, then, do we learn? In particular, how do we learn the truths of wisdom, e.g., that the immutable is better than the mutable? We do not remember them from a previous existence, nor do we learn them on hearing them expressed. Augustine's answer draws on the common heritage of Platonism and the Bible we have just sketched.

Regarding, however, all those things which we understand, it is not a speaker who utters sounds exteriorly whom we consult, but it is truth that presides within, over the mind itself; though it may have been words that prompted us to make such consultation. And He who is consulted, He who is said to dwell in the inner man, he it is who teaches—Christ—that is, the unchangeable Power of God and everlasting Wisdom. This Wisdom every rational soul does, in fact, consult. But to each one only so much is manifested as he is capable of receiving because of his own good or bad will (T 11.38).

Like Plato, Augustine compares the inner light, which he takes to be Christ, to the light of the sun.

Thus, as of the sensible sun, we may predicate three things: namely, that it is, that it shines, that it makes objects visible; even so may we predicate three things of that most mysterious God whom you long to know: viz., that He is, that He is apprehended, that He causes other things to be apprehended (SO 8.15).

We may exist, and sensible objects may exist, but we can see them only in the light of the sun. In the same way, the truth may exist without being grasped unless it is illuminated for us by "the true light that enlightens every man." (John 1:9). As we have seen, Augustine argues that these truths exist and exist independently of us. These truths either are God himself or are, as Augustine often holds, resident in the mind of God. (For Augustine, Plato's Forms have the status of Ideas in God's mind.) But our minds are finite and limited. What can make eternal truths available to us? Only an "illumination" of them by that light which is God's Wisdom itself. Note carefully, Augustine's view is that these truths of wisdom are lighted up for everyone. But not everyone comes to understand and accept them. Only as much is available to us as our will allows: the truth will escape one whose will is bad.*

Augustine's view of learning the truth is different from that of Socrates. But in one respect there is a striking similarity: both hold that no one ever teaches another person anything. Socrates claims

---

*Note how once again everything hangs on the will. We shall explore this in more detail below. Is this a dangerous principle? How might it be put to a bad use?

to be just a midwife, helping the hearers of his questions bring forth truths they already know and can recall. For Augustine, we learn by confronting realities directly, illuminated by the Interior Teacher, the Word of God, the Eternal Wisdom: Christ himself.

> Teachers do not claim, do they, that their own thoughts are perceived and grasped by the pupils, but rather the branches of learning that they think they transmit by speaking? For who would be so absurdly curious as to send his child to school to learn what the teacher thinks? But when they have explained, by means of words, all those subjects which they profess to teach, and even the science of virtue and of wisdom, then those who are called pupils consider within themselves whether what has been said is true. This they do by gazing attentively at that interior truth, so far as they are able. Then it is that they learn; and when within themselves they find that what has been said is true, they give praise, not realizing that they are praising not so much teachers as persons taught—provided that the teachers also know what they are saying (T 14.45).

God and the World

Augustine has come to believe in the God of the Christians. Here, he is convinced, is wisdom and the path to happiness. But he needs also to understand what he has come to believe. He has discovered a rational proof that God is. Both the Scriptures and the philosophers portray the nature of God as being itself. Could reason, employed in support of faith and enlightened by the divine light, also understand how this world is related to God? Augustine sees no reason why this could not, at least to some considerable degree, be understood.

Here too Augustine draws from the wisdom of the philosophers, especially from the Platonists. For as Augustine reads them, they express in a perfectly rational way, without relying on the authority of revelation, ideas that mesh remarkably well with the Scriptures. His borrowings are not uncritical, but they are extensive. For this reason, it will be useful to take a detour to the views of

Plotinus. Plotinus is the main source for a tradition called Neoplatonism, a tradition lasting well into the eighteenth century within which Augustine himself must be counted a distinguished figure.

The views of Plotinus are a blend of mystical insight with rational elaboration, the latter largely dependent on Plato. Mystical experience, which Plotinus is clearly familiar with, has certain characteristics that reappear in all ages and cultures. It is an experience of a particularly powerful and persuasive sort, in which the focus is an absolute unity. The multiplicity of things disappears; one is no longer able even to distinguish oneself from other objects. Mystics talk of this experience in terms of identity of the self with "the All," with "the One," or with "God." It is accompanied by an absolutely untroubled bliss.

Plotinus knows such experience firsthand, so he is certain that there is another, better reality than the one we ordinarily experience. When he tries to express this reality, he speaks in terms of **the One**. About this One, Plotinus holds, we can literally say nothing; for to predicate any properties of it would be to imply some multiplicity in it, some division. It is "ineffable." We cannot even say that it *is*. It resides in a majesty *beyond being*.* Plotinus allows that it can be given names, but none of these are to be understood literally; they are at best hints that point in a certain direction. Some of these names are "Unity," "the Transcendent," "the Absolute," "the Good," and "the Source."

Like Plato's Form of the Good, the One is the source of whatever else exists. But at this point, we must ask: why should anything else exist? The One is absolutely self-sufficient; it needs nothing.

But this is precisely the key. To make it clear, Plotinus uses a pair of analogies.

> What, then, is the One?
> It is what makes all things possible. Without it nothing would exist, neither Being, nor The Intelligence, nor the highest life, nor anything else. What is above life is the cause of life. The activity of life, being all things, is not the first principle. It flows from it as from a spring. Picture a spring that has no

---

*Compare Plato on the Form of the Good, p. 120.

further origin, that pours itself into all rivers without becoming exhausted of what it yields, and remains what it is, undisturbed. The streams that issue from it, before flowing away each in its own direction, mingle together for a time, but each knows already where it will take its flood. Or think of the life that circulates in a great tree. The originating principle of this life remains at rest and does not spread through the tree because it has, as it were, its seat in the root. The principle gives to the plant all its life in its multiplicity but remains itself at rest. Not a plurality, it is the source of plurality (*EP*, 173).[4]

The One is like the spring that, being itself full and lacking nothing, gives of itself without ever diminishing itself; or like the originating principle of the life in a great tree that remains at rest in the root, though the whole tree pulses with life. Plotinus thinks of all reality as an *emanation* from the One. To use another analogy, it is like the light that streams from the candle, while the light of the flame remains undiminished.

Note that this is the old problem of the one and the many: whence this plurality of beings, this multiplicity all about us? The answer is, they originate in the One.* If we ask why there are *so many*, the answer is that there must be as many as possible, for the One is ungrudging in its giving.

Every nature must produce its next, for each thing must unfold, seedlike, from indivisible principle into a visible effect. Principle continues unaltered in its proper place; what unfolds from it is the product of the inexpressible power that resides in it. It must not stay this power and, as though jealous, limit its effects. It must proceed continuously until all things, to the very last, have within the limits of possibility come forth. All is the result of this immense power giving its gifts to the universe, unable to let any part remain without its share (*EP*, 68).

---

*See the earlier discussion of this same problem by Heraclitus (pp. 19–21), Parmenides (p. 26), and Plato (p. 111ff). At the very beginning of the process of emanation, Plotinus holds, the One produces an image of itself in which it knows itself. This is "The Intelligence" of the passage quoted above. And the next "procession" is "The Soul," or the principle of life. Augustine reads this as a pagan version of the Christian Trinity: the One = the Father, the Creator; the Intelligence = the Word, Wisdom, the Christ; and the Soul = the Holy Spirit.

Just as there are all possible degrees of brightness in the emanation of light from a candle, until it vanishes at last in the darkness, so there will be found all degrees of being, intelligibility, and life in the world. Reality is partitioned in graded steps, which are, however, infinitely close to each other. No degree can be lacking; every possible level of being is represented, from the complete self-sufficiency of the One to vanishingly small realities near absolute nothingness. In the world as we see it, being and nothingness are mixed in all degrees.

We get the picture of a **great chain of being**, an image that is to be enormously influential for centuries.* It certainly has an impact on the thought of Augustine. How does he make use of these ideas in trying to understand what he has come to believe about God and the world?

As a Christian, Augustine is bound to believe that the world was *created*. But reason, he thinks, comes to that same conclusion. If something is not created, it is eternal; the eternal is unchanging; and the world is the domain of change (*C* 11.4). So it must be that the universe is not a self-sufficient reality but depends for both its being and its character on a reality beyond itself.

But how are we to understand the creation of the world? It could not be like the creation of buildings by stonemasons or of sculptures by artists. For in these cases people merely give new shape and form to realities that are already in existence. The creation of the world must account for those very realities. That is exactly what we discover in Genesis 1:3, where we read, "God said, 'Let there be light,' and there was light."

You did not work as a human craftsman does, making one thing out of something else as his mind directs. . . . Nor did you have in your hand any matter from which you could make heaven and earth, for where could you have obtained matter which you had not yet created, in order to use it as material for making something else? Does anything exist by any other cause than that you exist?

---

*For a fascinating study of the history of this idea, see Arthur Lovejoy, *The Great Chain of Being: A Study of the History of an Idea* (Cambridge, Mass.: Harvard University Press, 1936).

It must therefore be that you spoke and they were made. [Ps. 33:9] In your Word alone you created them (C 11.5).

Other than God himself, there is nothing but what he has made—again a rejection of Manicheanism. God "spoke" and the heavens and the earth *were*. Remember that in this context "your Word" represents not a spoken word but the *logos*, the Wisdom of God, the second person of the Trinity, who is "with God" and "is God," as John's Gospel tells us. It is through this rational, intelligent, and ultimately loving Word that God makes all things. And he makes them *ex nihilo*, or *out of nothing*.* The world, then, is entirely, without any exception, dependent upon God.

Because the world is created through Wisdom (compare Plotinus's Intelligence, Plato's Forms), the world is a rational and well-ordered whole. Here again the philosophers confirm the biblical tradition. At the end of each of the "days" of creation in the Genesis story, we read, "And God saw that it was good." How could it be otherwise, since God himself is good. For Augustine, as for Plotinus and Plato, there is a direct correlation between being and goodness. The more being something has (which means, of course, the more self-sufficient and eternal it is), the better it is. God, being completely self-sufficient and eternal, is completely good. The created world is less good than God. But still it is *good*. From the premise that the world is less good than God, one cannot conclude that it is therefore *bad*.

Here again Augustine parts company from the Manicheans. The source of evil is not to be found in body or matter, for these are creations of God and so are good. Not everything created is equally good, of course. As we have already seen, life is better than mere existence and intellect better than mere life. In fact, Augustine follows Plotinus here and urges that there is a continuous gradation of goodness in things. But even the lowest degree of existence has its correlative degree of goodness. Nothing God made is to be despised.

As you should be able to see, this brings Augustine right back to the problem of evil. It was to solve this problem that he embraced the dualism of the Manichees in the first place. But now, if God is good and the material world is good, he is faced again with the question: whence evil? The answer comes in two parts, the second of which we'll postpone until we talk about human nature. But the first part of the solution we can now state. Literally speaking, evil does not exist!

This is not to deny that we experience some things as evil, and truly so. It is to deny that evil has any reality of its own. If you were to make a list of all the things there *are*, evil would not be on the list. Nor would anything on the list be evil—insofar as it *is*. Being, remember, *is* goodness. Insofar as something *is*, then, it is *good*. What we call evil is just a *lack* of the being that something should have. Evil is the *privation of good*.

> For as, in the bodies of animate beings, to be affected by diseases and wounds is the same thing as to be deprived of health, . . . so also of minds, whatever defects there are are privations of natural good qualities, and the healing of these defects is not their transference elsewhere, but that the defects which did exist in the mind will have no place to exist, inasmuch as there will be no room for them in that healthiness (AE 2.10–25).

There is a kind of primitive magic that "cures" by moving the disease or wound out of the body and into, for example, a tree. From Augustine's point of view, this is to misconceive the nature of the problem altogether. For a disease or wound is not a "thing," having some reality of its own, nor is healing "removing" that thing. Disease is just the privation of healthiness, and healing is restoring the body to that condition of health (of being and goodness) in which there will be nothing lacking, leaving "no room" for the defect.

---

*It is of some importance here to note that Augustine's concept of creation is not identical with the emanation of Plotinus. For one thing, creation is the creation of a separate reality; creation is in no sense an extension of or a part of God's reality, as the light cast by the candle is the very same light as that of the flame. For Augustine, the world is in no sense divine. For another thing, creation is in some sense a free act. God did not have to create the world. But emanation is a necessary process.

Augustine is again making use of Plotinus here. For if we equate goodness and being, we must also equate evil and nothingness. And, as Parmenides already taught us, nothing *is not*. So ignorance is not a reality, but just the lack of knowledge; it is knowledge that is the reality and, therefore, good. Nor is weakness a reality, but simply the absence of strength; strength—that good thing—is the reality.

Since all created things are arranged in degrees of reality, they all participate to some degree in nothingness. Does this mean that they are all evil to some degree? They do not have the full degree of being and goodness that belongs only to God, but we ought not to call them "evil" on that score. It is irrational to complain that created things are not as good as God; to do so is tantamount to wishing that only God should exist and that there should be no created world at all! For what makes the world distinct from God is precisely its admixture of nonbeing. The very *being* of created things, remember, is good to some degree; and isn't it better that the created world exist rather than not? It adds to the sum total of being and goodness in reality.

If, by contrast, you complain not that some created thing could have been perfectly good, but that it could have been better than it is, your complaint is equally irrational. For there is already in existence something better than that; and to wish the thing you complain about to be better is to wish it not to be what it is, but to be that other thing (see *FCW* 2.5).

The conclusion is that evil only can exist where there is good. To put it another way, evil is parasitic on good. Whatever is, insofar as it is, is good; and if there is evil in it, the reason is only that it—like all things less than God—has some part in nothingness as well as being. But no aspect of its nature can be evil per se.

It is not only the goodness of the world that Augustine is concerned to understand. He is also puzzled by its temporality. Creation is the realm of change and impermanence. Yet God is eternal. How comes the one from the other? There is an additional sting in the problem of time for Augustine because the Manichees target time as an irrational element in the orthodox notion of creation. Remember that for them the two powers of light and darkness are both eternal, so that material things have no beginning. They ask the Christians what they take to be an unanswerable question: what was God doing before he made the world? The supposition is that God must have chosen to create the world at some particular time. But why at that time rather than some other? There seems to be no answer to this question, no reason why God should suddenly, after ages of noncreation, decide to make the world; but without an answer, there seems to be something irrational about believing in creation (as opposed to belief in the *eternal* conflict of light and darkness).

Apparently there was a snappy answer in circulation. Augustine says that he refuses to give it—though one can hardly help feeling that by repeating it he betrays some relish of it!

> My answer to those who ask "What was God doing before he made heaven and earth?" is not "He was preparing Hell for people who pry into mysteries." This frivolous retort has been made before now, so we are told, in order to evade the point of the question. But it is one thing to make fun of the questioner and another to find the answer. So I shall refrain from giving this reply (C 11.12).

Augustine's answer is, rather, a long and famous meditation on the nature of time and eternity. In it he establishes his view of God and God's relation to the created world. Let us see if we can follow his reasoning.

The first point is that God's eternity is not to be understood as everlastingness. God is not eternal in that he outlasts all other things; he is eternal in that he is not located in time at all. Those who imagine that God was idle through countless ages before engaging in the work of creation should think again.

> How could those countless ages have elapsed when you, the Creator, in whom all ages have their origin, had not yet created them? What time could there have been that was not created by you? How could time elapse if it never was?

You are the Maker of all time. If, then, there was any time before you made heaven and earth, how can anyone say that you were idle? You must have made that time, for time could not elapse before you made it.

But if there was no time before heaven and earth were created, how can anyone ask what you were doing "then"? If there was no time, there was no "then."

Furthermore, although you are before time, it is not in time that you precede it. If this were so, you would not be before all time. It is in eternity, which is supreme over time because it is a never-ending present, that you are at once before all past time and after all future time. . . . You made all time; you are before all time; and the "time," if such we may call it, when there was no time was not time at all (*C* 11.13).

So time was created along with the world. That is the way to answer the Manichees: deny that God exists in time, and the question they asked simply cannot arise. God did not create the world at a given time, since before the creation time itself did not exist.

Here we again see Augustine drawing on the resources of his philosophical tradition to understand a biblical concept. There may be a problem here. In the seventeenth century, Blaise Pascal would draw a sharp contrast between the God of revelation and the God of the philosophers.* It is for Pascal the difference between a God you can and a God you cannot worship. And many scholars subsequently have held that there is little biblical reason to understand God's eternity in this atemporal way. We must, I think, admit that this radically atemporal eternity is the eternity of mathematical truth, Plato's Forms, and the One of Plotinus. But Augustine sees no conflict at all between the Bible and the philosophers on this score. Again and again, he points out, the Scriptures proclaim the unchanging nature of God, and for Augustine God's eternity is just that "never-ending

present," that being "at once," he here describes. God, then, is outside of time, and time itself is a creation.

What, then, is time? It is something we are all intimately familiar with. But in a much-quoted sentence, Augustine says,

> I know well enough what it is, provided that nobody asks me; but if I am asked what it is and try to explain, I am baffled (*C* 11.14).

It is clear enough that there are three divisions to time: the past, the present, and the future. And yet these are profoundly puzzling. Think, for instance, of the past. The obvious thing about the past is that *it is no more*. There is a correlative fact about the future: *it is not yet*. Neither past nor future exists. The only aspect of time that has any existence, then, must be the present.

Consider, though, what we call a "long time." It seems evident that only what exists can be long. What does not exist cannot be either long or short, any more than it can be white or sweet or smell of roses. When, then, is time "long"? Not in the past, for the past does not exist; nor in the future, for a similar reason. But this leaves only one alternative. A long time must exist in the present.

Let us, Augustine says, "see if our human wits can tell us whether present time can be long" (*C* 11.15). What would you call a long time? A century? Can that exist in the present? Suppose we are in the first year of the century; then ninety-nine years are still in the future—and these *are not yet*. Perhaps only a year, then, can be in the present. But suppose it is April. Three months have passed, and eight are yet to come; so most of the year either *is no more* or *is not yet*. Most of the year does not exist, and what does not exist cannot be long. Shall we count only the present month, then, as the present? But suppose today is the twenty-third day; most of the month is in the past and exists no more, while some of it is yet to come.

This thought experiment can be repeated, as you can readily see, for hours, minutes, seconds, until this conclusion is forced upon us:

---

*When he died there was discovered sewn into the lining of his jacket a piece of paper recording an experience he had on the night of November 23, 1654. Part of it read: "FIRE—God of Abraham, God of Isaac, God of Jacob, not of the philosophers and scholars."

. . . the only time that can be called present is an instant, if we can conceive of such, that cannot be divided even into the most minute fractions, and a point of time as small as this passes so rapidly from the future to the past that its duration is without length. For if its duration were prolonged, it could be divided into past and future. When it is present it has no duration (*C* 11.15).

The present is just that knife edge where *what is not yet* becomes *what is no longer*, where the future turns into the past. The present itself "has no duration." So the present could not possibly be long. Where, then, does the time we call "long" exist? It cannot exist in the past or in the future, as we have seen. But now we see that it cannot exist in the present either. You can see why Augustine is baffled.

Nonetheless, with prayers to God for help, Augustine presses on. It is evident that we are aware of different periods of time; and we can compare them in length to each other. How do we do this? We can see only what exists; that much is certain. So we cannot see the past or the future. We may predict the future on the basis of what we are aware of in the present, and we can make inferences about past facts. But since only the present exists, it is only the present we can be aware of. How, then, are we aware of times that do not exist? Augustine again looks into his soul.

When we describe the past correctly, it is not past facts which are drawn out of our memories but only words based on our memory-pictures of those facts, because when they happened they left an impression on our minds, by means of sense-perception. My own childhood, which no longer exists, is in past time, which also no longer exists. But when I remember those days and describe them, it is in the present that I picture them to myself, because their picture is still present in my memory (*C* 11.18).

Augustine concludes that though there are three times, they are not—strictly speaking—past, present, and future. If we speak accurately, we should speak of a *present of things past* (the memory), a *present of things present* (direct awareness), and a *present of things future* (which he calls expectation). Where do these times exist? The answer is clear: in the mind; nowhere else.

It is in my own mind, then, that I measure time. I must not allow my mind to insist that time is something objective. . . . I say that I measure time in my mind. For everything which happens leaves an impression on it, and this impression remains after the thing itself has ceased to be. It is the impression that I measure, since it is still present, not the thing itself, which makes the impression as it passes and then moves into the past. When I measure time it is this impression that I measure. . . .

It can only be that the mind, which regulates this process, performs three functions, those of expectation, attention, and memory. The future, which it expects, passes through the present, to which it attends, into the past, which it remembers (*C* 11.27–28).

This clinches the argument. Time has no meaning apart from the mind, so it *must* have come into being along with creation. Our minds—vacillating and changeable—are not eternal. Minds are a part of creation. In possessing these powers of expectation, attention, and memory, our minds are the locale where time realizes itself. Our minds are in this respect a faint image of the mind of God, which also sees past, present, and future. But God does not see them fragmentarily, as we do. If our attention is focused on the past in memory, we cannot at the same moment be paying attention to the future. We cannot see it all; we must be selective. But to God, who lives in that "never-ending present," all time is known "at once."

If there were a mind endowed with such great power of knowing and foreknowing that all the past and all the future were known to it as clearly as I know a familiar psalm, that mind would be wonderful beyond belief. We should hold back from it in awe at the thought that nothing in all the history of the past and nothing in all the ages yet to come was hidden from it. It would know all this as surely as, when I sing the psalm, I know what I have already sung and what I have still to sing, how far I am from the beginning and how far from the end. But it is unthinkable that you, Creator of the universe, Creator of souls and bodies, should know all the past and all the future merely in this way. Your knowledge is far more wonderful, far more mysterious than this. It is not like the knowledge of a man who sings words well known to him or listens to another singing a familiar psalm. While he does this his feelings vary and his senses are divided, because he is partly anticipating words still to come and partly remembering words already sung. It is far otherwise with you, for you are eternally without change, the truly eternal Creator of minds. In the Beginning you knew heaven and earth, and there was no change in your knowledge. In just the same way, in the Beginning you created heaven and earth, and there was no change in your action. Some understand this and some do not: let all alike praise you (C 11.31; see also CG 11.21).

The nature of time is one of the most puzzling phenomena of nature. Augustine expresses the perplexities as well as anyone ever has. But his reflections on creation and time are not just an attempt to solve a theoretically interesting problem. The problem is urgent for Augustine because it concerns the relation between God and the Soul, the two foci of wisdom that bear on human happiness. Augustine's meditations on time reaffirm the sharp line of distinction between creation—even including its highest part, the mind—and God who created it. We are not divine or parts of the divine.* We, together with the whole temporal order, are absolutely dependent upon God for our very being. Still, our relation to time is part of the image of God within us. Unlike God, we are in time, subject to time; yet, like God to some degree, we are above it. God sees all time in a single moment. We cannot do that, but we do measure time and are aware of past, present, and future. We are not simply caught in the momentary present, as we might imagine a stone or perhaps even an insect to be. We project ourselves into the future and recollect our past. This relation to time, and particularly to our future, is the foundation for our free will, our responsibility, and our hope of happiness.

Moreover, time is significant not only for individuals but also for the human race. As a Christian, Augustine looks back to a sacred history (beginning with Adam, moving through Noah, Abraham, Moses, and the prophets to Christ) and looks forward to the culmination of God's kingdom in the future return of Christ as judge. To varying degrees, pagan thought diminishes the significance of time, often swallowing up the uniqueness of events in doctrines of circular eternal recurrence. The Socratic doctrine of reminiscence also fits the pattern: if learning is just recollecting what we have eternally known, then the moment of learning is not really very significant. It brings nothing new into being.* But for the Christians the course of events in history is tremendously significant; it occurs just once, and human decisions made in those never-recurring moments have a tremendous—an infinite—weight. For it is in time that our eternal destiny is settled. It is not surprising to find Augustine ending these meditations on time with expressions of awe and praise.

Human Nature and Its Corruption

What is man? He is certainly a creature of God, but that does not yet distinguish him from any other creature. The Platonistic tradition on which Augustine draws so heavily is unequivocal: a person is an immaterial soul, who may for a time inhabit a body. But the body is inessential to his being. If we look to the biblical story of creation, however, we get a view that seems to contradict this tradition. For we are told that God "formed man of dust from the ground, and breathed into his nostrils the breath of life" (Gen. 2:7). It seems obvious that man is here conceived to be a material being—a living body. Perhaps it is possible to understand the "breath of life" as the creation of an immaterial soul, but this seems somewhat strained.

*Here Augustine is at one with Homer (see p. 5) and in disagreement not only with the Manichees but also with more respectable philosophies such as Stoicism (see p. 191).

*This point of contrast between paganism and Christianity is the one focused on most insistently by Søren Kierkegaard in the nineteenth century. See pp. 438–440.

Augustine's thought about human nature is thus pulled in two directions, and we can see an uneasy tension in his efforts to reconcile these traditions. In trying to remain true to the biblical tradition, he emphasizes that man is a unitary being: one thing. God did not create a soul when he took up the dust of the earth; he created *man*. But Augustine also believes in the soul and accepts Platonic arguments about its immateriality and its distinctness from the body. But if man is one thing, how can he be composed of two things? We see that Aristotle solves this problem by considering the soul to be the form of a certain kind of living body; in the thirteenth century Thomas Aquinas will adapt this solution in his Christian Aristotelianism. But Augustine, drawing on the Platonic tradition, cannot take this line. And the result is an uneasy compromise. Man is one being, created by God, but he is composed of both body and soul, each a distinct created being.

How, then, are soul and body related to each other? Augustine tries to answer this question in the very definition of a soul.

> But if you want a definition of the soul, and so ask me—what is the soul? I have a ready answer. It seems to me to be a special substance, endowed with reason, adapted to rule the body (*GS* 13).

So a soul is, by its very nature, suited to "rule the body" by virtue of possessing reason. One thing is clear, then. The soul and its powers are superior to the body. This fact is crucial to Augustine's view of man's predicament, of what stands in the way of his happiness and how he may after all attain it.

Man was created by God and so is by nature something good. Yet on all sides we find him involved in evil. He was created in the image of God's justice, but he acts unjustly. He was created for happiness, but we see him miserable. Why? The biblical answer is that man has sinned. This seems precisely the right answer to Augustine. But, again, he wants to understand what that means. Augustine's analysis of sin and the way to blessedness draws heavily on his own experience. But to understand that experience he needs to come to terms with freedom and responsibility, with God's grace and foreknowledge, and above all with the nature of the will. These are perhaps the most original and penetrating parts of Augustine's philosophy. They are also among the most controversial.

Augustine takes the biblical story of the first human pair's sin quite literally. This interpretation introduces into his thought a certain complication that many later thinkers believe is inessential. Adam and Eve—created good, happy, and dwelling in the Garden with all of their needs satisfied—are tempted by the serpent to disobey the commandment of God. And they do. As punishment, they are made subject to death, driven out of the Garden, and forced into a struggle for survival. Their children inherit this status. They cannot "begin again" and take the position that Adam and Eve enjoyed before their sin. This status, into which they are simply born, is original sin. It is also shared by all of their descendants, including us. Original sin both is a penalty for the original sinful disobedience and is itself sinful. Its characteristics are ignorance (i.e., lack of wisdom) and what Augustine calls concupiscence, or wrong desire. If Augustine is right, we are in trouble from the very start of our lives. Look, he says, at infants.

> It can hardly be right for a child, even at that age, to cry for everything, including things which would harm him; to work himself into a tantrum against people older than himself and not required to obey him; and to try his best to strike and hurt others who know better than he does, including his own parents, when they do not give in to him and refuse to pander to whims which would only do him harm. This shows that, if babies are innocent, it is not for lack of will to do harm, but for lack of strength.
>
> I have myself seen jealousy in a baby and know what it means. He was not old enough to talk, but whenever he saw his foster-brother at the breast, he would grow pale with envy. . . . it surely cannot be called innocence, when the milk flows in such abundance from its source, to object to a rival desperately in need and depending for his life on this one form of nourishment (*C* 1.7).

Innocence and guilt, it should be noticed, are to be found not in outward actions but in desires, in such things as jealousy and the "will to do harm."

And this condition of the heart, directed away from God and to the world, is the very essence of sinfulness. We may call babies "innocent," but this is a very shallow judgment. They are innocent only in their lack of ability to do what they very much want to do. As Augustine allows, babies tend to grow out of crying and throwing tantrums. But this does not mean that their desires change; it may only mean that their concupiscence takes on more sophisticated and socially acceptable forms.

We need to understand the elements of sin more clearly. And we have to face the problem of how it could have originated in a world that was created good. What, then, is sin? It clearly has something to do with the motivation for action. So we need to understand motivation better. Whatever we do, Augustine says, is done from a desire for something. These desires Augustine calls "loves." We seek to delight in the possession of the object of our love. This delight appears to us as happiness. If we think that wealth will make us happy, we love riches. We are sure that if only we can possess riches, we will delight in them. So we are moved by this desire to act. We do what is necessary to become wealthy in order to attain that object of delight which we imagine will make us happy.

Remember that reality is ordered in a great chain of being, reaching from God to the merest speck of existence. This order is at the same time an order of value, for a thing's degree of being is an index to its degree of goodness. Clearly, the things of higher value should be loved more and the things of less value loved less. If our loves were rightly ordered, they would match the order of value in things themselves. In other words, there is an appropriate ordering of loves that matches perfectly the ordering of goodness in things. And this means that God, who is perfect being and goodness, should be loved most of all, and all the rest of creation in appropriate degrees corresponding to their goodness. In fact, the injunction of Jesus to love God absolutely, "with all your heart, and with all your soul, and with all your strength, and with all your mind," corresponds to the absolute value to be found in God. (Between God and creation there is an absolute gulf of both being and value.) The rule to love our neighbors as ourselves also fits

this ordering rule; for each of us has the same degree of value. Those who are perfectly virtuous—i.e., righteous—have their loves rightly ordered. They love all things appropriately, in accord with their worthiness to be loved.

Sin, we can now say, is disordered love. It is loving things inappropriately, loving more what is of lower value and loving less what is of higher or highest value. Since we are motivated to act by our loves, these sinful desires produce wicked acts: murder, theft, adultery, deception, and so on. For example, Jones loves money and is willing to kill his aged aunt to get it. What this means is that he loves money (which is less valuable) more than he loves the person who has it (who is more valuable). His desires are not ordered correctly, and the result is wickedness.

We have not yet plumbed the depths of sin, however. Two errors must be avoided. First, we may think that sin is just a *mistake*. We might think that vice and wickedness is simply not being aware of the true ordering of value in the world. This is akin to the view of Socrates, who holds that virtue is knowledge and vice ignorance. The person who acts wrongly, according to this view, simply doesn't *know* what is right. Augustine agrees that there is a kind of ignorance involved in sin. But it is not *simple* ignorance, for he holds that the light of Wisdom has "enlightened every man," and the rules of righteousness are written in the human heart. So if we are ignorant, we are *willingly* ignorant. We don't *want* to see the truth. We obscure it and then complain that it is too obscure to make out. Sin, then, is not just ignorance. Socrates and Plato are on that score too optimistic; if the problem with human beings is not simple ignorance, there is no reason to hope that simple education will solve the problem. What is needed is not education alone, but *conversion*. And that concerns the *will*.

The second error is to suppose that sin might be something that just *happens* to us. Our environment and developmental history might just have produced certain loves in us rather than others. Our wickedness may be just bad luck—the bad luck of a bad upbringing. And for luck no one is to blame. A key aspect of the notion of sin, however, is that we are to blame for it. For our sins we are punished, and justly so. Therefore something must be missing in this analysis.

We need to bring in the aspect of *will*. Augustine does this by offering an analysis of four basic emotions: desire, joy, fear, and grief.

> The important factor in those emotions is the character of a man's will. If the will is wrongly directed, the emotions will be wrong; if the will is right, the emotions will be not only blameless, but praiseworthy. The will is engaged in all of them; in fact they are all essentially acts of will (*CG* 14.6).

To desire something is not just to have a tendency to acquire it. To desire is to *consent* to that tendency, to acquiesce in it, to give in to it, to say yes to it—in short, to *will* it. In a similar way, to fear something is not just to be disposed to avoid something, perhaps with a feeling of panic added. To be afraid is to "disagree" that something should happen, and that disagreement is an act of will. What are joy and grief? They, too, are acts of will, joy being consent in the attainment of something desired and grief disagreement in the possession of something feared. In general, Augustine says that

> as a man's will is attracted or repelled in accordance with the varied character of different objects which are pursued or shunned, so it changes and turns into feelings of various kinds (*CG* 14.6).

We noticed at various points the prominence that Augustine gives to the concept of will. Here we see why. It is the character of the human will that accounts for emotions and actions alike. We may be motivated by our loves, but in the last analysis, these loves come down to will. And for what we will we are responsible. The will is *free*.

Sin, then, for which we are properly held responsible, is a matter of the will having gone wrong. As Augustine puts it,

> When an evil choice happens in any being, then what happens is dependent on the will of that being; the failure is voluntary, not necessary, and the punishment that follows is just (*CG* 12.8).

Note an important feature of this account of sin. Its root is not located in the body or anywhere in the material world. Its root is in the soul—precisely in that superior part of man which mirrors most clearly the image of God. The soul, which by means of reason is "fit to rule the body," consents instead to be the body's slave, preferring what is less good to what is better.

Again, of course, Augustine is rejecting the Manichean view of evil. If we really do manage to observe the injunction to know ourselves, what we will find is not the pure, unsullied soul that is part of God. What we will find is a rebel who has gone radically wrong by consenting to a disordered love life. The miser loves gold, but there is nothing wrong with gold. What is wrong is that the miser consents to putting his love for gold (which is worth less) above his love for justice (which is worth more). The lustful person loves beautiful bodies, but there is nothing wrong with beautiful bodies. What is wrong is that the love of sensual pleasures is preferred to the love of self-control "by which we are made fit for spiritual realities far more beautiful, with a loveliness which cannot fade" (*CG* 12.8).

But now we must face the question: how can this happen in a world created by a good God? Here we discover the second part of Augustine's solution to the problem of evil. The first part, you will remember, consisted in arguing that evil is not a reality but simply the privation of goodness. Whatever exists is good, simply in virtue of its *being*. The question now is whether this principle can be used in the sphere of moral evil, where it looks as though the bad will is itself a positive reality. Augustine is confident that it can.

The first thing to be established is that the will is itself a good thing. This is easily done, not only from the principle that all created things are good, but also from the reflection that without free will no one can live rightly. To live rightly is to choose to live rightly; no one can choose rightly without a free will; and since living rightly is acknowledged to be a good, the necessary condition for that good must itself be good (*FCW* 18.188–90).

There are, Augustine tells us, three classes of goods. There are great goods, such as justice, the mere possession of which guarantees a righteous life. There are lesser goods, such as wealth and physical beauty, which, though good, are not essential to the highest goods of happiness and a virtuous life. And then there are intermediate goods. Of these intermediate goods we can say that their possession does not guarantee either virtue or happiness, yet without them no one can be virtuous or happy. Such an intermediate good is free will. Whether it leads to happiness depends on what we will; and that is up to us.

Augustine thinks it obvious that the human race has made bad use of its free will; we have turned from the true and lasting good to lesser goods and have sought our happiness where it is not to be found. How are we to understand that?

> The will . . . commits sin when it turns away from immutable and common goods, towards its private good, either something external to itself or lower than itself. It turns to its own private good when it desires to be its own master; it turns to external goods when it busies itself with the private affairs of others or with whatever is none of its concern; it turns to goods lower than itself when it loves the pleasures of the body. Thus a man becomes proud, meddlesome, and lustful; he is caught up in another life which, when compared to the higher one, is death (*FCW* 19.199–200).

The result of such "turning away" from the highest goods, which, like truth, can be held in common by all and for which there need be no competition,* and the concomitant "turning towards" lower goods is pride, meddlesomeness, and lust. Note that when all pursue the goods that are common to all, a community can exist in peace and harmony. When each one loves goods that must be enjoyed privately, if at all, the result is discord and strife. Proud, meddlesome, and greedy individuals will never be at peace with one another. But pride is more than the result of sin. It is the very root of sin itself.

Why did the first couple disobey God's command? Augustine emphasizes that it was not because the command was difficult to obey; in fact,

nothing was easier. They simply had to refrain from eating the fruit of one of the many bountiful trees in the Garden. Why, then, did they disobey? The words of the serpent that tempted them suggest the answer. He said, "God knows that when you eat of it your eyes will be opened, and you will be like God, knowing good and evil" (Gen. 3:5). This is the key. They wanted to be "like God." It is only because their wills had already "turned away" from a determination to be obedient to the truth that the temptation had any power over them.

> It was in secret that the first human beings began to be evil; and the result was that they slipped into open disobedience. For they would not have arrived at the evil act if an evil will had not preceded it. Now, could anything but pride have been the start of the evil will? For "pride is the start of every kind of sin" (Ecclesiasticus 10:13). And what is pride except a longing for a perverse kind of exaltation? For it is a perverse kind of exaltation to abandon the basis on which the mind should be firmly fixed, and to become, as it were, based on oneself, and so remain. This happens when a man is too pleased with himself: and a man is self-complacent when he deserts that changeless Good in which, rather than in himself, he ought to have found his satisfaction. . . .
>
> We can see then that the Devil would not have entrapped man by the obvious and open sin of doing what God had forbidden, had not man already started to please himself. That is why he was delighted also with the statement, "You will be like gods." In fact they would have been better able to be like gods if they had in obedience adhered to the supreme and real ground of their being, if they had not in pride made themselves their own ground. . . . By aiming at more, a man is diminished, when he elects to be self-sufficient and defects from the one who is really sufficient for him.
>
> This then is the original evil: man regards himself as his own light, and turns away from that light which would make man himself a light if he would set his heart on it (*CG* 14.13).

Pride, then, is the cause of man's fall. Trying to lift himself above the place proper to him in the chain of being, he seeks to become "like God," to be "self-sufficient," based only on himself, the "ground" of his own being. In trying to rise above

---

*See pp. 218–219.

his place, he falls. For in this attempt at self-sufficiency, he is catapulted at once into anxiety and concern for his well-being, which he himself now has to guarantee. Not content with the true goods which are available to all, he finds himself engaged in ruthless competition with his fellow man for the lower goods. His loves settle upon the things in the world, and greed, lust, and covetousness reign among his desires. No longer is his will ordered according to the worthiness of goods to be desired, the order implicit in the created world. But, as though he were God, he creates his own order. The result is chaos and disorder, both within his own soul and between man and man.

The pride of sin shows itself also in the fact that the first couple, when confronted with their disobedience, made excuses.

> . . . the woman said, "The serpent led me astray, and I ate," and the man said, "The woman whom you gave me as a companion, she gave me fruit from the tree, and I ate." There is not a whisper anywhere here of a plea for pardon, nor of any entreaty for healing (CG 14.14).

One of the manifestations of sin is a refusal to admit that it is sin. Neither of the first humans would admit to sin; each tried to pin it on someone else.

The root of sin, then, is pride, and pride is setting ourselves up as the highest good when the highest good is something we properly should acknowledge as above us. Pride is the will turning away from God and to itself. And the result is a set of disordered loves.*

Suppose we ask, what causes that? Why does that happen? God, after all, created us good. We have free will, to be sure, but why do we use our freedom in that way?

> If you try to find the efficient cause of this evil choice, there is none to be found. For nothing causes an evil will, since it is the evil will itself which causes the evil act; and that means that the evil choice is the efficient cause of an evil act, whereas there is no efficient

cause of an evil choice. . . . It is not a matter of efficiency, but of deficiency; the evil will itself is not effective but defective. For to defect from him who is the Supreme Existence, to something of less reality, this is to begin to have an evil will. To try to discover the causes of such defection deficient, not efficient causes—is like trying to see darkness or to hear silence. . . .

> No one therefore must try to get to know from me what I know that I do not know (CG 12.6–7).

We can understand Augustine's argument in this way. Suppose that there were an answer to the question, Why do we sin? Suppose that we could find something that is the cause of the will's turning away from the highest good. Then that something would—since it has being—be something good. But something good cannot cause something evil. So there cannot be such a cause in being.

Yet we must remember that created wills, living in time and subject to change, are a mixture of being and nonbeing. If the will, like God's will, were unmixed with nothingness, then it could not fall. So there is a "cause" for sin in the sense that the incomplete being of the will is a *necessary condition* for sin. This is what Aristotle calls a "deficient" cause and compares to darkness or silence. Darkness is not a reality on its own; it is just the absence of light. Similarly, silence is the nonexistence of sound. A deficient cause is the absence of the fullness of being that would make sin impossible. The presence of such a deficient cause does not guarantee that the will turns away from God; it just makes that turning possible. So if we ask, then, what does cause the turning away of the evil will, the answer, literally, is *nothing*. The act is voluntary. For Augustine, this means that it cannot have an efficient cause. If it had an efficient cause it would occur necessarily and not be subject to just punishment.* Clearly Augustine is again relying on the Neo-

---

*Compare the *hubris* of the Greeks; see p. 4.

---

*Here we meet for the first time a theme that will puzzle philosophers down to the present day: does responsibility require exemption from the causal order of the world? Augustine thought the answer was an obvious yes. For other views see David Hume ("Rescuing Human Freedom," in Chapter 19) and Immanuel Kant (pp. 384–386).

platonic idea of the chain of being to solve this problem.

He has not yet solved it completely, however. Recall his doctrine of God. God exists "all at once" in a timeless eternity and "sees all things in a single moment." But that means that God knew—or foreknew—even before man was created that man would sin. So it was true that Adam was going to sin even before he chose to sin. And if that is so, did he really have any choice? Could he have refrained from sinning, even if he had wanted to? Doesn't God's foreknowledge take away man's free will?

Clearly Augustine needs to affirm both; free will is necessary for responsibility, and God's foreknowledge is a necessary consequence of his perfection. Can he have it both ways? "It does not follow," Augustine says,

> that there is nothing in our will because God foreknew what was going to be in our will; for if he foreknew this, it was not nothing that he foreknew. Further, if, in foreknowing what would be in our will, he foreknew something, and not nonentity, it follows immediately that there is something in our will, even if God foreknows it. Hence we are in no way compelled either to preserve God's prescience by abolishing our free will, or to safeguard our free will by denying (blasphemously) the divine foreknowledge. We embrace both truths, and acknowledge them in faith and sincerity, the one for a right belief, the other for a right life. . . . The fact that God foreknew that a man would sin does not make a man sin; on the contrary, it cannot be doubted that it is the man himself who sins just because he whose prescience cannot be mistaken has foreseen that the man himself would sin. A man does not sin unless he wills to sin; and if he had not willed to sin, then God would have foreseen that refusal (CG 5.10).

If God foresees that I am going to *freely will* something, then I will undoubtedly *will that thing freely*. But it would be a crazy mistake, Augustine thinks, to conclude that this somehow robs me of my free will. How could it not be my will if what God infallibly foresees is that I am going to exercise my will? So Augustine does not see that there is any conflict between God's omniscience and individual freedom.

Augustine's analysis of the human predicament, then, reveals us to be in a pretty sorry state. We are proud, determined to be masters of our own destiny, turned away from the highest goods and anxiously devoted to the lower; our desires are not ordered by the order of value in things. Furthermore, we are continually engaged in turning away from the source of our being. And we cannot escape responsibility for this descent into evil, with all its consequences, both personal and social.

Is there any way out of this desperate plight?

Human Nature and Its Restoration

The result of sin is a diminution in the very being of human beings; they become smaller—more ignorant, weaker, and less in control of themselves.* Their very will is divided. With one part of the mind they continue to acknowledge the truth of God and the righteousness of his law (since they cannot entirely put out the light that enlightens everyone); but with another part they love what is of lesser value. This was Augustine's own experience of his condition before his conversion. He often quotes a passage from St. Paul to the same effect.

> I do not understand my own actions. For I do not do what I want, but I do the very thing I hate. . . . I can will what is right, but I cannot do it. For I do not do the good I want, but the evil I do not want is what I do. Now if I do what I do not want, it is no longer I that do it, but sin which dwells within me (Rom. 7:15, 18–20).

Augustine is convinced that this condition is so desperate that the individual cannot rescue himself from it.†

---

*Recall the correlation of knowledge and strength with being, p. 226.
†See again Augustine's theory of the "chain" which sin forms, by which the soul becomes enslaved and loses its ability to do even what it truly wants to do (p. 215).

For by the evil use of free choice man has destroyed both himself and it. For as one who kills himself, certainly by being alive kills himself, but by killing himself ceases to live, and can have no power to restore himself to life after the killing; so when sin was committed by free choice, sin became victor and free choice was lost (*AE* 9.30).

Here, however, is the point where the distinctive "gospel" of Christianity comes into its own. What we cannot do for ourselves, God has done for us through his Son Jesus, the Mediator, who took upon himself the sins of the world. All that is required is to trust, by faith, that God has forgiven and received us, despite our turning away, and we will be healed.

This may seem simple enough. But once again there are problems in trying to understand it. We cannot save ourselves from our disordered loves, precisely because our loves are disordered. It would be as impossible as trying to lift ourselves off the ground by wrapping our arms around our own chests and lifting. The restoration of human nature—its re-creation—is no more possible for us than its original creation. So God has to do it. And he has in fact done it in Christ. All we need is to accept it by faith.

But is faith something we can do? This itself seems like an act of will. If our wills are divided against themselves, how can we wholeheartedly will to have faith? If we do not love God absolutely, what love that is actually present in us could lead us to do so?

This problem faces Augustine starkly because of the influence of a British monk, Pelagius. As Pelagius is usually understood, he emphasizes (a) the responsibility of individuals for their lives and (b) the justice of God. Each of us is responsible for keeping the law of God; and if we *ought* to keep the law, it must follow that we *can* keep it.* Otherwise, it would be unjust of God to punish us for not doing so. Therefore, he argues, perfection must be *possible* for us, since it is *demanded* of us. The impli-

cation is that each individual comes into the world as fresh and innocent as Adam, and each has the same opportunity to earn, or merit, the reward of eternal life. Whether a person is saved or not, then, is entirely up to the will of the individual.

You can see that this starting point is at direct odds with that of Augustine. It contradicts both his inability before his conversion to make the decision he knew he ought to make and the flaws in his continuing desire-structure that a scrupulous examination finds even after his conversion. It seems to be a moralism that makes the work of Christ inessential. And it is in conflict with many passages in the Scriptures. But it does dramatically pose the problem of what individuals can and cannot do to restore themselves to the sort of creature they were made to be.

Augustine spent the last decade of his life struggling against Pelagian views. He wrote treatise after treatise trying to clarify the situation and work out a satisfactory answer. Two things were never in doubt for him: our wills are free, and our salvation is a gift of God's grace. That there is a tension between these ideas is undeniable. But he thinks they can be reconciled. Let us see how.

First it is important to realize that we can never free ourselves from dependence upon God. Remembrance of this will be the surest way to guard against pride, which is, as we have seen, the root of sin. "What have you that you did not receive? If then you received it, why do you boast as if it were not a gift?" (1 Cor. 4:7) Augustine applies this principle of Paul's to the free will: that in itself is a gift, one of God's creations. Whenever we will anything, we are but exercising a power we owe to God.

But that is not enough, for the question concerns merit. If I use my will to turn to God in faith, is that something I do on my own, for which God owes me a reward? The very idea is repugnant to Augustine, for it would let pride back in at the very place where it should be most firmly excluded. It is precisely that turning back to God for which we owe God himself the greatest thanks. For what gift can compare with that? But, then, is it something we have done? Or did God do it in us?

Augustine wrestles with this puzzle again and again. Perhaps his most developed thought on the

---

*This principle, that "ought" implies "can," will be used in the eighteenth century by Immanuel Kant as one of the cornerstones of his moral philosophy. See pp. 396 and 398.

matter is that faith (the turning of our loves back to God) is something in our power. But whether it will be exercised or not depends on whether there are certain "inducements or invitations" present in us or our environment. We do not, after all, choose to take a candy bar unless there is a candy bar presented for us to choose. These inducements are not in our power but are a gift of God. Apparently God makes an offer that some cannot refuse, which is too good to turn down; though when they accept it, they are making use of their own free will. But such an offer of grace is so great that it overwhelms any effort to take pride in its acceptance. We do not boast about possessing a candy bar when it has been offered to us. The appropriate response is gratitude (*SL* 52–60).

There is a section in the *Confessions* where Augustine is searching his soul for evidence of continuing sins and temptations. He sets forth his struggles to get his loves in order with respect to sex, food, pleasures of eye and ear, curiosity, the opinions of others, speech, and self-complacency. And in this section there is a phrase that is repeated again and again:

Give me the grace to do as you command, and command me to do what you will! (*C* 10.29, 31, 37).

This phrase perfectly expresses that paradoxical combination of reliance on God's grace and determination to will the right which Augustine discovers when he tries to *understand* what he has come to *believe* in becoming a Christian. Our salvation—happiness, blessedness—is up to us. Yet it is wholly a product of God's grace; we have nothing that we have not received.

Let us say a bit more about the life in which Augustine claims to have found both wisdom and happiness. What is it like to live as a Christian? As we have seen, Augustine's theory of motivation holds that we are moved by our various "loves." Our loves are expressions of the will as we desire a variety of presumed goods. Since it is the interior life that really counts, the quality of our lives will be determined by the nature of our loves.

As we have seen, things in the world are ordered in value according to the degree of being they pos-

sess (the great chain of being principle). And the degree of value a thing possesses determines its worthiness to be loved. Happiness and virtue (which coincide as surely for Augustine as they do for Plato or the Stoics) consist in "ordered love," where our loves are apportioned according to the worth of their objects.

He lives in justice and sanctity who is an unprejudiced assessor of the intrinsic value of things. He is a man who has an ordinate love: he neither loves what should not be loved nor fails to love what should be loved; he neither loves more what should be loved less, loves equally what should be loved less or more, nor loves less or more what should be loved equally (*OCD* 1.27).

But we can now add two further distinctions.

Here is the first one. Some things are to be *used*, whereas others are to be *enjoyed*. And some may be both used and enjoyed.

To enjoy something is to cling to it with love for its own sake. To use something, however, is to employ it in obtaining that which you love, provided that it is worthy of love. For an illicit use should be called rather a waste or an abuse (*OCD* 1.4).

What is appropriately loved *for its own sake*? For Augustine there can be just one answer: only God alone. In loving the eternal truth, wisdom, and goodness of God we find blessedness. Here alone we can *rest*, content at last; for there exists no higher good to be enjoyed than the creator and restorer of our human nature. As Augustine says in a famous phrase,

. . . you made us for yourself and our hearts find no peace until they rest in you (*C* 1.1).

The enjoyment we seek is a never-ending delight in the object of our love, which nothing but the highest and eternal good will provide. All other things are to be used in the service of that end so that we may find the blessedness of that enjoyment. Even other humans, though we are to love them as we love ourselves, are not to be loved *for their own sake*. To do so would be a kind of idolatry, an attempt to find our end, our "rest" in them rather than in the source of all good. Delight in friends and neighbors or in our own talents and excellences must be a delight that always turns to gratitude by being referred to the One who provides it all. We must use a friend as a ladder on which to climb to those heights on which true enjoyment is to be found. And, since we are to love the friend as we love ourselves, we must use ourselves to bring the friend with us.

We can see now that Augustinian Christianity is totally different from that "trading skill" piety Socrates rejected in the *Euthyphro* (see 13a–15b and page 80). Euthyphro (and much religious practice in our own day) seeks to "use" the gods to attain some advantage and thinks that prayer and sacrifice (what the gods love) will induce them to give us what we need. Augustine absolutely rejects this notion of the "use" of what is highest. His emphasis on grace means that whatever good we have is already provided by God, so we have *nothing to trade with*. God is to be sought not for the sake of some worldly advantage we might gain from him, but for his own sake alone. In God we "rest"; he is not a means to some further end. God is to be *enjoyed*. And that good *X* (see page 81) produced by service to God is nothing external, but the transformation of our desire-structure so that our ordered loves enjoy and use each thing appropriately.

The second distinction corresponds to that between enjoyment and use. Augustine divides love into two kinds: charity and cupidity.

> I call "charity" the motion of the soul toward the enjoyment of God for his own sake, and the enjoyment of one's self and of one's neighbor for the sake of God; but "cupidity" is a motion of the soul toward the enjoyment of one's self, one's neighbor, or any corporeal thing for the sake of something other than God (*OCD* 3.10).

From cupidity comes both vice (by which Augustine means whatever corrupts one's own soul) and crime (which harms someone else). We try to enjoy what should only be used and destroy both ourselves and others. Greed, avarice, lust, and gluttony are all forms of cupidity. Cupidity is disordered love.

Charity, on the other hand, is ordered love, directed toward enjoying God and all other things only in God. If charity is the motivation for one's life, all will be well. "Love, and do what you will," Augustine tells us.[5] You can do whatever you want, provided that your motivation is charity. Charity will motivate us to behave appropriately to all things (i.e., in accord with their actual value). From charity will flow all the virtues: temperance, prudence, fortitude, and justice.*

We must never assume, however, that what motivates us is pure charity. Augustine's own self-examination revealed the cupidity that remained in his life even as a Christian bishop. The Christian may be "on the way" toward the blessedness of truly ordered loves but cannot expect to find it entire until the resurrection of the dead.

Augustine on Relativism

As we have seen, Augustine argues against skepticism. And everything we have seen so far should lead us to conclude that he is completely opposed to relativism as well. No believer in God could accept Protagoras' saying that *man* is the measure of all things. There is indeed a "measure," a standard by which to judge. But it could not be any created thing, much less a human being whose valuations are determined by a set of disordered loves.† More-

---

*Compare Aristotle on the unity of the virtues, p. 176. There is much similarity between his view and that of Augustine. But there is one great difference: for Augustine, charity (the source of the virtues) is a result of God's grace, not something we have in our control.

†Again, a comparison with Aristotle is instructive. Aristotle also disagrees with Protagoras; for him the "measure" is the good man (see p. 178), not just *any* man. Augustine might not disagree with this in principle, but he would ask: where is this good man to be found? Among men, he would say, there is but one without sin—the Christ, the incarnation of the Wisdom of God, the *logos*. *He* can be the "measure." Aristotle's "good man" might have many virtues, but from Augustine's point of view, he is puffed up with pride—which undermines them all.

over, if the doctrine of relativism is that (1) Jones can judge some particular action to be right, (2) Smith can judge *that very same action* to be wrong, and (3) both Jones and Smith are correct, then Augustine is certainly not a relativist.

Nonetheless, there is a sense in which Augustine can admit a good deal of what the relativist wishes to urge. Part of what makes relativism plausible are the differences in customs among the nations.* Another part of its plausibility is the conviction (which most people share) that it is usually wrong to lie, or steal, but *not always*. Augustine does justice to both these intuitions by recognizing that particular actions are always done out of particular *motivations* and in particular *circumstances*, which must both be taken into account when judging the goodness or badness, the rightness or wrongness of someone's act. Remember Augustine's rule: Love and do what you will. One crucial fact in the evaluation of all actions concerns the way they are motivated: is the motivation charity or cupidity, a sound will or an evil will? A second crucial fact is an appraisal of what the circumstances require.

Augustine's view on these issues comes up in a rather curious context. He is considering what to make of the fact that certain of the "patriarchs" whose stories are recorded in the Old Testament had more than one wife or had children by concubines. Did they act sinfully in behaving that way? Or, on the other hand, does this mean that the same behavior is acceptable today? His answer to both questions is no. The principle is this: one and the same *kind* of action may be quite differently motivated. And it is the motivation that counts. His comment on the patriarchs is in accord with this principle.

> The just men of antiquity imagined and foretold the Heavenly Kingdom in terms of an earthly kingdom. The necessity for a sufficient number of children was responsible for the blameless custom by which one man had several wives at the same time. And thus it was not virtuous for one wife to have several husbands, for one woman is not more fruitful

by this means, and it is rather a whorish evil to seek either wealth or children by common intercourse. With reference to customs of this kind, whatever the holy men of those days did without libidinousness, even though they did things that may not now be done in that way, is not blamed by the Scriptures (*OCD* 3.12).

> For if because of the times a man could then use many wives chastely, a man may nevertheless use one wife libidinously. I commend more a man who uses the fecundity of many wives for a disinterested purpose than a man enjoying the flesh of one wife for itself. In the first instance a utility congruous with the circumstances of the time is sought; in the second a cupidity implicated in temporal delights is satiated (*OCD* 3.27).

In ancient times it was allowable for men to have many wives, but now it is not allowable. Why? Because the circumstances then required numerous children to be produced swiftly; but that "utility" is not present now. What counts is not whether a man has one wife or many, but the state of his "loves": whether the motivation is *cupidity*, the desire to "enjoy the flesh" for its "temporal delights," or *charity*.* So neither is polygamy to be condemned absolutely, nor is monogamy to be universally praised. It all depends on what constitutes "a utility congruous with the circumstances of the time" and on the motivation.

It is clear that this principle gives Augustine great flexibility in one respect (with regard to outward behavior), while it constrains his judgment in a very rigorous way in another. An Augustinian will be very tolerant about any matter that is clearly nothing but *nomos* or convention, such as fashion. Whether more significant actions are judged good or bad depends partly on the motivation and partly on what is useful in the circumstances. Not everything is merely *nomos*, nor can a thief's idea of what is useful be our guide to action. But without a full knowledge of both motivation and circumstances, we should be very cautious about pronouncing judgment. As we shall see in the next section, there is even one sense in which such judgment is reserved to God.

---

*Recall the example of the Greeks before Darius cited by Herodotus (see p. 42) and the judgment that custom is king over all.

*Look again at the discussion of use and enjoyment, p. 237.

Augustine's discussion of these matters is certainly incomplete. But in pointing to these two factors, he makes a significant contribution to the debate about relativism. While allowing considerable relativity to moral judgments, Augustine is saved from a complete relativism by (1) the Neoplatonic conviction that reality itself is ordered in value, corresponding to the degrees of being, and (2) the thesis about motivation. It is not merely by a conventional agreement that (for example) eternal things are of more value than temporal things.* Nor is it just *nomos* by which charity is praised and lust, greed, and avarice are condemned. Here we reach values that cannot be relativized. The command of Jesus, for example, to love God without reserve and our neighbors as ourselves is *absolute*. Augustine goes as far as to say, "Scripture teaches nothing but charity, nor condemns anything except cupidity, and in this way shapes the minds of men" (*OCD* 3.10).

Similar considerations apply to justice. Some men, he says,

> misled by the variety of innumerable customs, thought that there was no such thing as absolute justice but that every people regarded its own way of life as just. . . . They have not understood, to cite only one instance, that "what you do not wish to have done to yourself, do not do to another"† cannot be varied on account of any diversity of peoples. When this idea is applied to the love of God, all vices perish; when it is applied to the love of one's neighbor, all crimes disappear. For no one wishes his own dwelling corrupted, so that he should not therefore wish to see God's dwelling, which he is himself, corrupted. And since no one wishes to be harmed by another, he should not harm others (*OCD* 3.14).

These remarks are found in a book entitled *On Christian Doctrine*. We are hearing the Christian bishop speak, appealing to his authoritative source, the Scriptures. Here is an interesting question: can this kind of absolutism about motivation (together with the relativism about action) be *un-derstood* as well as *believed*? Can an Augustinian provide a reasoned case for regarding the value of charity as nonrelative, analogous to the case Augustine provides for belief in God? Augustine does not explicitly try to do that, but certain hints toward a way to do it might be found in the last quotation.

In effect, then, Augustine makes two moves: (1) he breaks up the question about whether values are relative by saying that some are and some are not; and (2) he locates those that are not in the realm of motivation. Augustine is certainly not a relativist, but neither is he a simple absolutist. The subtlety of his analyses of the interior life serve him in good stead in advancing the conversation at this point.

The Two Cities

There is an old joke that there are just two kinds of people in the world: those who think that there are just two kinds of people and those who don't. Augustine is emphatically a member of the first group and in this displays his primary allegiance to the Christian heritage. The two kinds are the saved and the damned, those destined for eternal blessedness in heaven and those to be punished for their sins in hell.

But, as you might expect, Augustine's view is more sophisticated and subtle than that bare statement suggests. It is set forth in a book of more than a thousand pages that presents us with an entire philosophy of history. Augustine's intense interest in time and temporal progression is never merely speculative or introspective. In *The City of God* he brings together all he has learned in the forty and more years since first dedicating himself to the search for wisdom. Here he provides a unified interpretation of human history from creation to the end of the world.

The occasion for writing this magnum opus was the sack of Rome by a Gothic army under the leadership of Alaric in August of 410 C.E. The late Roman empire had been harried by barbarians from

---

*See p. 219.
†Luke 6:31 and Matt. 7:12. See p. 206.

the north and east for some time, but for a barbarian army to take Rome, the "eternal city," was a profound shock to every Roman citizen, Christian and pagan alike. People asked: "How could this happen?" Jerome, who had translated the Bible into Latin, wrote, "If Rome can perish, what can be safe?"[6]

Augustine's answer distinguishes "two cities," an earthly city and a heavenly city. The goal of each city is the same: peace. Members of the earthly city seek peace (harmony and order) in this life: such a peace is a necessary condition for happiness, the ultimate end of all men. For this reason states and empires are established, the noblest of them all (in Augustine's view) being the Roman empire. It is noblest in this respect: it succeeded in guaranteeing the earthly peace of its citizens better and for a longer time than any other state ever had.

Yet see to what a pass it had come! Why? To answer this question Augustine reaches back into his theory of motivation and applies its insights to Roman history. (Note again how everything is traced back to the soul and its relations with the highest good; God and the soul really do determine everything of interest in Augustine's world.) What motivated the founders of Rome and all its greatest statesmen? Like Homer's heroes, they wanted *glory*.*

> They were passionately devoted to glory; it was for this that they desired to live, for this they did not hesitate to die. This unbounded passion for glory, above all else, checked their other appetites. They felt it shameful for their country to be enslaved, but glorious for her to have dominion and empire; and so they set their hearts first on making her free, and then on making her sovereign (CG 5.12).

The best among the Romans directed this quest for glory into the "right path"; it "checked their other appetites," and they were exemplars of virtue, "good men in their way," as Augustine puts it (CG 5.12). Those virtues (personal moderation and devotion to the good of their country) led to Rome's

empire and greatness. The passion for glory can yield magnificent results, and Augustine is ready to acknowledge them in full.

> By such immaculate conduct they laboured towards honours, power and glory, by what they took to be the true way. And they were honoured in almost all nations; they imposed their laws on many peoples; and today they enjoy renown in the history and literature of nearly all races (CG 5.15).

And, Augustine adds (quoting from Matt. 6:2), "they have received their reward."

The passion for glory, however, is a peculiarly unstable motivation; it can lead as easily to vice and crime as to virtue. For the glory sought is the praise and honor of others. What happens if the others honor wealth and domination more than moderation and justice? The result is obvious. In fact, the earthly city is always a mix of virtue and vice—precisely because it is an *earthly* city. The aim of its citizens is to *enjoy* what they should only *use*: earthly peace, possessions, and bodily well-being. Since these are exclusive goods (if I possess an estate, you *necessarily* do not possess it), any earthly city is bound to generate envy and conflict and to tend toward its own destruction.*

In fact, this is the essence of the difference between the two cities. The one seeks its ultimate good here in this world, where nothing is stable and goods are competitively achieved. The other realizes that the only eternal good is found in God, which all can have in common. In fact, the difference is precisely that difference between disordered and ordered love we explored earlier.

> We see then that the two cities were created by two kinds of love: the earthly city was created by self-love reaching the point of contempt for God, the Heavenly City by the love of God carried as far as contempt of self. In fact, the earthly city glories in itself, the Heavenly City glories in the Lord. The former

---

*See pp. 3–5.

*It is the hope of Karl Marx and the communists that such envy and conflict can be overcome in *this* world; the key, they believe, is overcoming private property, so that the ground of envy is undercut. See Chapter 22.

looks for glory from men, the latter finds its highest glory in God, the witness of a good conscience. The earthly lifts up its head in its own glory, the Heavenly City says to its God: "My glory; you lift up my head." In the former, the lust for domination lords it over its princes as over the nations it subjugates; in the other both those put in authority and those subject to them serve one another in love, the rulers by their counsel, the subjects by obedience. The one city loves its own strength shown in its powerful leaders; the other says to its God, "I will love you, my Lord, my strength" (*CG* 14.28).

Pursuing earthly goods for their own sake is self-destructive, for it leads to competition, conflict, and disaster. And that is Augustine's explanation for Rome's fall. Rome was not, as some Christians held, particularly wicked; in fact, its empire was a magnificent achievement, characterized by the real, though flawed, provision of peace and order for its citizens. But it reaped the inevitable consequence of earthly cities, which set their loves on earthly glory.

For the same reason, the charge of some pagans that Rome fell because she had deserted the old gods for Christianity is rebutted. At the very best, service to lesser gods (as lesser goods) will provide only temporary, though not negligible, benefits. Only service to the one eternal good yields lasting peace and happiness.

Members of the heavenly city realize that here in this world they have no continuing home; they look for the fulfillment of their hopes in the life to come. Here they have a taste of blessedness, and through God's grace a beginning of true virtue can begin to grow on the ground of charity. But the culmination of these hopes lies beyond.

Nonetheless, citizens of the heavenly city duly appreciate the relative peace provided by the earthly city and contribute to it as they can. While on earth they consider themselves as resident aliens and follow the laws and customs of the society they are dwelling in, to the extent that doing so is consistent with their true citizenship. They *use* the arrangements of their society, but they do not settle down to *enjoy* them. In this world there are no lasting goods, and only what lasts can be enjoyed forever.

However, it would be incorrect to say that the goods which [the earthly] city desires are not goods, since even that city is better, in its own human way, by their possession. . . . These things are goods and undoubtedly they are gifts of God (*CG* 15.4).

So, with respect to laws that establish "a kind of compromise between human wills about the things relevant to mortal life," there is "a harmony" between members of the two cities. It is only when the earthly city tries to impose laws at variance with the laws of God that citizens of the heavenly city must dissent (*CG* 19.17).

There are, then, two kinds of people. They are distinguished by their loves. But this very fact—that it is motivation that makes the difference—removes the possibility that anyone can with certainty *sort* people into one class or the other. We might think Augustine would be tempted to equate membership in the Church with citizenship in the heavenly city, but he does not. The Church is, collectively, the custodian of the truth about God; individuals are another matter. We can tell who is on the church rolls, but we cannot tell for certain who is a member of the City of God. Only God can judge that.

Among the professed enemies of the City of God, Augustine tells us,

are hidden future citizens; and when confronted with them she must not think it a fruitless task to bear with their hostility until she finds them confessing the faith. In the same way, while the City of God is on pilgrimage in this world, she has in her midst some who are united with her in participation in the sacraments, but who will not join with her in the eternal destiny of the saints. . . .

In truth, these two cities are interwoven and intermixed in this era, and await separation at the last judgment (*CG* 1.35).

This epistemological obscurity concerning the saints (for us, though not for God) is a direct consequence of the fact that it is motivation, desire, and the order of a person's loves that make the difference. Behavior is always ambiguous; as we have seen, even the lust for earthly glory can sometimes produce human excellence of a high order. Once more it is the will that tells.

We shall not pursue the details of Augustine's interpretation of history in these terms. It is enough to say that *The City of God* understands human history as *meaningful*. It is not, as a distinguished historian once said, "just one damn thing after another." It has a narrative unity; there is plan and purpose in it; and the story found in the Christian Scriptures provides the key.*

Augustine's conviction is that we can get a perspective on history only if we see it from the viewpoint of eternity—through God's eyes, so to speak. But just that viewpoint has been communicated by God himself through his prophets, who prepared the way for the Christ, through the life, teachings, death, and resurrection of Jesus, and finally through the Church, which preserves and extends this "gospel." The story is about God's calling citizens of a heavenly city out of the sinful world. These will eventually enjoy blessedness in perfect peace with one another and rest in enjoyment of the one eternal good. For Augustine, all of history must be seen in relation to that end.

Christians and Philosophers

Augustine melds two traditions, the classical and the Christian. Certainly, tensions show up at various points in Augustine's work. But the degree of success he achieves makes him a peculiarly important figure. He is a culmination of the conversation that precedes him and one of the most influential contributors to the conversation still to come.

He is convinced that truth is one and that important contributions to our understanding of it have been made by both philosophers and prophets. But there is never any doubt which tradition has priority when there is a conflict: Augustine is first, last, and always a Christian, convinced that the one and only wisdom is most fully revealed in the Christ. Ready to acknowledge that pagan

thinkers have much to contribute, he uses only what he judges to be consistent with his Christian faith. The rest is subject to severe, sometimes savage criticism.

Augustine has put us in a good position to draw some broad contrasts between classical philosophy and Christianity. These are suggestive rather than exact but point out certain patterns that tend to recur.

Reason and Authority

Augustine is no despiser of reason. Not for him the *credo quia absurdum est* of some Church Fathers.* He wants to understand what he believes. He thinks that to a very large extent this can be done and so must use his reason.

Nevertheless, belief has the priority. It must have, for rational understanding could never by itself discover the truth about the Word becoming flesh or about the Trinity. These things must be believed on the authority of the prophets and apostles who bear testimony to them. This authority is founded on eyewitnesses and is handed on in the Church. The key that unlocks the mystery of life is *revealed*, not *discovered*. Thus at the heart of wisdom Augustine finds a place for authority. This authoritative witness must be *believed*, and belief is a matter of giving one's assent by an act of *will*. As Augustine never tires of saying: unless you believe, you will not understand.

Greek philosophy, on the other hand, takes the opposite point of view: unless I understand, the philosopher says, I will not believe. The extreme case is, of course, the skeptic, who, applying this exact principle, suspends judgment about virtually everything. But Xenophanes already set the pattern:†

> The gods have not revealed all things from the beginning to mortals; but, by seeking, men find out, in time, what is better.

---

*Review the major "chapters" in this story by looking again at Chapter 13.

*"I believe because it is absurd." This formula is attributed to Tertullian, a Christian writer of the second century.
†Review the discussion of the whole passage from which these words are taken, pp. 14–15.

These words express the essence of the spirit of Greek philosophy.

Here we have one of the great watersheds in the quest for wisdom: is wisdom something we can *achieve*, or is it something we must *receive*? Augustine is convinced that we must receive it because of the absolute distinction between God and humans (we are too limited to discover truth on our own), sin (we are too corrupted to do it), grace (God provides it for us), and gratitude and humility (the appropriate responses to the situation).

Greek philosophy, on the whole, is convinced that there is no alternative to trying to achieve wisdom on our own (though individual philosophers differ about how successful this quest can be). And part of this pattern is the value put on human excellence (especially intellectual excellence), self-sufficiency, and pride in one's attainments.

In a sermon, Augustine explores the divergence between one who says, "Let me understand that I may believe," and another who says, "Believe rather that you may understand." He acknowledges the deep divide between these two by his suggestion: "Let us go before a judge with this dispute, for neither of us is able to settle the issue on his own" (*SS* 43). Who does he suggest as a judge? There is no surprise here: it must be someone with authority to settle such disputes, and it must obviously be someone with more than merely human authority (or he would be a party to the dispute). So Augustine appeals to the *prophet*. And the prophet (Isaiah) says: "If you do not believe, you shall not understand."*

This problem of the choice between reliance on authority or reliance on our native wits comes up again when we discuss Aquinas, Descartes, Hume, and Kant.

---

*It is unfortunate for Augustine's appeal that the text of Isaiah 7:9 is unclear. Some translations render the last part as "you shall not continue" and others as "you shall not be established." However that may be, we should ask whether such an appeal is likely to win over the philosopher. You might try to answer this question by looking again at what the skeptic calls "the problem of the criterion." (See pp. 195–197.) Here again we may have a contrast between those William James calls the tough- and tender-minded.

Intellect and Will

Greek philosophers tend to see human problems and their solution in terms of ignorance and knowledge. This is particularly clear in Socrates, for whom virtue or excellence *is* knowledge. But the pattern is very broad, reflected in the importance of education for Plato's guardians, of practical wisdom and contemplation for Aristotle, and of knowledge of reality (in their different theories) by Epicureans and Stoics. Roughly, the pattern takes this form: inform the intellect and the rest of life will take care of itself.*

Augustine, expressing both the Christian tradition and his own experience, disagrees. Intellect may well be impotent—or worse—unless the will is straightened out. The basic features of human life are desire and love, which are matters of the will. What is needed is not (at first) education, but *conversion*; not inquiry, but *faith*.

Again we have a watershed, which correlates fairly well with the first one. From the point of view of the Christian, we cannot rely upon our reason alone; its use depends on the condition of the will, and the will is corrupted. Our predicament is, on the Christian view, a *deep* one; we are not in a position to help ourselves out of it, but—this is also crucial—help is available. From the point of view of the Greek philosophers, the human predicament may be serious, but well-intentioned intellectual work will lead us out of it. (Even the skeptics think happiness is attainable.) Reason can master desire.

There is a sense, then, in which Christian thinkers are more pessimistic about humanity than the Greek philosophers.

Augustine on Epicureans and Stoics

We can cap this contrast by noting Augustine's criticisms of several pagan philosophies that seemed serious rivals to Christianity's claim to wisdom.

---

*The contrast, put this baldly, is overdrawn. We have to remember that for Plato's view of education, the *love* of the good is a crucial factor, and this isn't just a matter of intellect. Still, there is something essentially right about it. Compare Descartes, p. 317.

Platonism is, of course, the one that seems to him nearest the truth. But the Platonists go wrong in allowing worship of powers greater than human beings but inferior to God. Augustine concedes that there are such powers (whether called angels, demons, or gods) but insists that devotion, prayer, and worship belong only to God. To think otherwise is the ultimate betrayal.

Augustine's interest in Epicurean and Stoic philosophies is sharpened because St. Paul is alleged to have debated with them in Athens (see Acts 17:18). Moreover, between them they seem to cover neatly the this-worldly possibilities for happiness, the Epicureans seeking it in the pleasures of a material world and the Stoics in the virtues of the soul.

Recall that Epicurus and Lucretius hold that there is no sense in which we survive our physical death; the soul is as physical as the body, and disperses when the body disintegrates. Augustine puts these two doctrines together and concludes that they recommend nothing but the pursuit of bodily pleasures.* He ascribes to them the slogan, "Let us eat and drink, for tomorrow we shall die," which expresses a hedonist's determination to experience as much of bodily pleasure as possible before death extinguishes all sensation.

This doctrine, Augustine says, is "more fitting for swine than for men." Moreover, it is a doctrine that will inevitably lead to injustice and the oppression of the poor (*SS* 150).† And the reason is by now a familiar one: they are trying to enjoy what should only be used and as a result are dominated by cupidity rather than charity. But the key error is their neglect of life after death. Epicureanism in this life makes sense only if they are right about consciousness ending in the grave, and of course Augustine is convinced that cannot be right.

The Stoics, who locate happiness in the virtues of the soul, are considered more worthy opponents. Augustine cannot help admiring their courage and steadfastness. But the crucial question is whether the Stoics have indeed found the key to blessedness. Augustine is convinced that they have not. Recall the advice of Epictetus: "Demand not that events should happen as you wish; but wish them to happen as they do happen, and you will do well." The Stoics' aim is to live in harmony with nature.* Augustine caustically asks:

> Now is this man happy, just because he is patient in his misery? Of course not! (*CG* 14.25).

It is real happiness that we are interested in, not just contentment with what the world happens to dish out; the Stoic version of happiness is just a makeshift second best. True happiness is delight in the possession of the highest good, to which only the Christian has the key.

But, Augustine suggests, what else could you expect? The Stoic, like the Epicurean, "puts his hope in himself" (*SS* 150). This is simply another display of pride, which is the root of human trouble in the first place. From Augustine's point of view, even the virtues of the pagans are but "splendid vices."

Summary

Augustine, great admirer of pagan learning, is also one of its most severe critics. He brings to the fore a number of "choice points" in which the Christian tradition differs from non-Christian rational philosophy. These traditions differ in their conceptions of God and of God's relation to the world; they differ about appeal to authority, about the priority of will or intellect in human nature, about whether pride is a virtue or a vice; and they differ in their conceptions of love. The general pattern on these issues that Augustine sets will dominate Western philosophy for a thousand years (although many variants are explored). But the fundamental questions that Augustine thinks he has settled will all come up for inquiry again at the beginning of the modern period.

---

*Is this justified? Or is he trading on an ambiguity in the term "body"? Does "body" mean the same for Epicurus as it does for Augustine, who believes in an immaterial soul?
†How fair to the Epicureans do you think this is? Review pp. 187–188. Could it be that Augustine is (in part) responsible for the "bad press" that Epicureans have gotten?

---

*This concept is discussed on pp. 190–191.

Notes

1. An excellent and readable biography is *Augustine of Hippo* by Peter Brown (London: Faber and Faber, 1967). A classic discussion of his philosophy is Etienne Gilson, *The Christian Philosophy of St. Augustine* (London: Victor Gollanz Ltd., 1961).

2. References to the works of Augustine will be as follows:

   C: Confessions, trans. R. S. Pine-Coffin (Harmondsworth, Middlesex, England: Penguin Books, 1961).

   FCW: On Free Choice of the Will, trans. Benjamin G. Hackstaff (New York: Macmillan Co., 1964).

   CG: The City of God, trans. Henry Bettenson (Harmondsworth, Middlesex, England: Penguin Books, 1972).

   OCD: On Christian Doctrine, trans. D. W. Robertson, Jr. (New York: Macmillan Co., 1958).

   SO: The Soliloquies of St. Augustine, trans. Rose Elizabeth Cleveland (London: Williams & Norgate, 1910).

   T: The Teacher and *GS, The Greatness of the Soul*, in *Ancient Christian Writers*, ed. Johannes Quasten and Joseph C. Plumpe (Westminster, Md.: Newman Press, 1964).

   AE: Saint Augustine's Enchiridion, trans. Ernest Evans (London: S.P.C.K., 1953).

   SL: The Spirit and the Letter, trans. John Burnaby, vol. 8 of *The Library of Christian Classics* (London: SCM Press, 1955).

   SS: Selected Sermons of St. Augustine, ed. Quincy Howe, Jr. (London: Victor Gollanz Ltd., 1967).

3. Quotations from a *Manichean Psalmbook* in Brown, *Augustine of Hippo* are cited in the text using the abbreviation *MP*. References are to page numbers.

4. Quotations from *The Essential Plotinus*, ed. Elmer O'Brien (Indianapolis: Hackett Publishing Co., 1980), are cited in the text using the abbreviation *EP*. References are to page numbers.

5. Quoted in Gilson, *Christian Philosophy of St. Augustine*, 140.

6. Quoted in Brown, *Augustine of Hippo*, 289.

15

Bits of Later
Medieval Philosophy

Augustine's influence in Western philosophy and theology was so great that when, in about 1150 C.E. Peter Lombard collected notable sayings of the church fathers in a *Book of Sentences*, ninety percent of the quotations were from Augustine's writings.[1] Augustine's work was clearly preeminent.

After the fall of Rome, intellectual work in the West was carried on largely within the Church. There were no independent centers of learning. It was churchmen who preserved libraries, copied manuscripts, and wrote books. Over most of this work presided the Augustinian spirit, with its convictions that Wisdom is one, that Scripture and Reason are essentially in harmony, and that the interesting and important topics are God and the soul.

Later Medieval philosophy, from the eleventh to the fifteenth centuries, is exceedingly rich and inventive—despite being carried on within bounds that later thinkers will find too confining. But, for the purposes of our story, we will sample just two small "bits" from it. We will examine an ingenious but perplexing "proof" for the existence of God formulated by Anselm of Canterbury. And we will sample very briefly a rival to Augustinian Platonism: the Christian Aristotelianism of Thomas Aquinas. Anselm and Thomas, both made saints of the Church after their deaths, exemplify some of the best, though by no means the only, philosophy

of this period. An understanding of at least some aspects of their thought will be helpful as we follow the great conversation into modern times.

Anselm: On That, Than Which No Greater Can Be Conceived

In about three pages, Anselm (1033–1109 C.E.) sets forth an argument, the conclusion of which is not only that God exists, but that he exists "so truly" that we cannot even *conceive* that he doesn't. This famous argument is known to history as the **Ontological Argument.***

Before formulating the argument, we should note something of the context Anselm is working

---

*The term "ontological" comes from the Greek word for *being*. The argument in question was given this name in the eighteenth century by one of its critics, Immanuel Kant, because (unlike the arguments of Aquinas) it does not begin from facts about the world, but goes straight from the *idea* of God to a conclusion about his *being*. Many thinkers find it important to distinguish two, or even more, distinct arguments because at least one form of the argument is pretty obviously invalid. Anselm himself does not do so; and we will interpret it as *one* argument. I will try to formulate this argument in its strongest form, while remaining fairly colloquial in manner. (Discussions of the soundness of this argument often bristle with technical-logical apparatus.)

in. Anselm was a priest and a bishop—the Arch-bishop of Canterbury, in fact. And from all ac-counts, his character and spirit were such as to merit his later sainthood. He is, moreover, steeped in the Augustinian tradition. The work in which the argument is found was first called *Faith Seeking Understanding** (a concept that should by now be familiar). It is, in Augustinian fashion, a meditative work, the first chapter of which is a prayer. Here Anselm resolves to "enter the inner chamber of [his] mind" and "shut out all thoughts save that of God" (*Proslogium* 1).[2] As you can see, questions about God and the soul again predominate—the former to be known most clearly by a withdrawal into the recesses of the latter. God is not sought by exploring the *world*. Anselm appeals to the Interior Teacher in these words:

> Teach me to seek thee, and reveal thyself to me, when I seek thee, for I cannot seek thee, except thou teach me, nor find thee, except thou reveal thyself (*Proslogium* 1).

He acknowledges that he cannot fully comprehend God; but he says,

> I long to understand in some degree thy truth, which my heart believes and loves. For I do not seek to un-derstand that I may believe, but I believe in order to understand (*Proslogium* 1).

In the preface, Anselm notes that he had written an earlier work (*Monologium*, or *Soliloquy*), in which he had tried to see how far—setting Scrip-ture aside—argument and reason could substanti-ate the central doctrines of Christianity. The an-swer was, pretty far—but not, of course, all the way. His aim there was to explore the truth, while making as few assumptions as possible. Because the arguments of this work were pretty involved, he began to wonder

whether there might be found a single argument which would require no other for its proof than itself alone; and alone would suffice to demonstrate that God truly exists (*Proslogium* preface, p. 1).

This argument he believes he has found—or has been taught by the Interior Teacher.

The argument begins with a rather abstractly stated expression of the *idea* of God, a definition, if you like, of what we have in mind when we use the word "God." God, says Anselm, is *that, than which no greater can be conceived.** Let us think about this a moment. Suppose you imagine or conceive a cer-tain being. Have you done it? Now ask yourself the question: can I conceive of something that is in some way "greater" than this? If you can, then it is not yet God that you have conceived.

Why does Anselm use this strangely convoluted phrase, *that, than which no greater can be conceived*? Why not just say, more simply, that God is the greatest being we can conceive? There are two rea-sons, I think: (1) Anselm doesn't want the idea of God to be limited by what *we* may be able to con-ceive, and (2) he doesn't want to suggest that a positive conception of God may be entirely com-prehensible to us. The strange phrase has this fea-ture: it pushes us out beyond everything familiar by forcing us to ask again and again: can some-thing greater than this be conceived?

Suppose, for instance, that you think of an oak tree. Now an oak tree has certain powers and abili-ties but also some very definite limitations. It is not very hard to think of something "greater" than that—something, perhaps, that can move, that can seek nourishment and flee danger, rather than hav-ing to suffer whatever occurs at the spot where it is rooted. It follows that God is not an oak tree.

Suppose we think of a creature that does not have these limitations, a wolf, perhaps. Again, it is not hard to think of something "greater" than a wolf—a creature, for instance, that can plan ahead, build a shelter, heat and cool it, preserve

---

*It was later titled *Proslogium*, or *A Discourse*. This is the title under which it is now known.

*Compare Augustine's formulation, p. 220.

food for the hard winter months. Since we can conceive something greater than a wolf, God is not a wolf.

What if we think of a human being? Is a human being something than which no greater can be conceived? Hardly. For surely a being would be greater if it were not subject to death. Of two human lives, each of which is well worth living and equally happy, we judge the longer one to be preferable. And humans have many other limitations besides mortality; we can surely conceive a being that knows more than any human knows, is more powerful than any human, is not so dependent on other things, and is not subject to the moral failures of human beings. So when we think of God, we are not thinking of a human being, but of something much greater.

Another line of thought that helps make this conception intelligible is to consider what sort of being would be worthy of worship. To worship something is to "bow the knee" before it, to be willing to abase oneself before it, to defer to it absolutely; to worship is to acknowledge the object worshiped as holy, and as wholly other. Suppose you think of something, and then you think of a second thing that is greater. Isn't your immediate reaction that the first thing is not something you could *worship*?

Until we reach the conception of *that, than which no greater can be conceived*, we have not yet thought of God. That is what we mean when we use the word "God." Although this conception is peculiarly abstract, it does seem to capture the crucial idea of God as the only being worthy of worship. Devotion to anything less would be idolatry.

Let us note one more thing about this conception of God before we move on to the argument that Anselm finds embedded in it. It is framed in terms of the great chain of being.* This Augustinian notion is so much a part of Anselm's outlook that it is simply taken for granted. That the world is ordered by the degrees of being and value (greatness) in its various parts must seem to Anselm so

obvious that it is beyond question. If you run up and down the chain, you find it easy to conceive of beings both lesser and greater; and your mind is inevitably carried to the idea of something that is not only *actually* greater than other existing things, but something than which you cannot even *conceive* a greater. And that, Anselm says, is what we mean by God.

But now the question arises: Is there a being answering to that conception? There really are oak trees and wolves and human beings. Is there a being than which nothing greater can be conceived?*

According to Psalm 14:1, "The fool says in his heart, 'There is no God.'" Let us consider this "fool." There are two ways he might think "There is no God." (1) He might just have these words in mind, without really understanding what they mean; in this case he is a fool only in a weak sense—he is ignorant of what he means by the words he is using. In this case we could easily explain to him what the words mean, and he would cease to be this kind of fool. (2) He might, however, understand what it is he is denying. This fool has the *idea* of God in mind, and presumably he understands the words, "that, than which no greater can be conceived." It is this second way of saying or thinking these words that is of interest. Anselm's "discovery" is that such a fool necessarily convicts himself of error every time he thinks, "There is no God."

For suppose the fool were right. Then *that, than which no greater can be conceived* would exist only in his understanding and not in reality. It would exist in the same way, Anselm says, as a painting exists in the mind of a painter who changes his mind before putting brush to canvas. The painter has the painting "in his understanding," as Anselm puts it; but it does not exist also in reality.

---

*Review the discussion of this Neoplatonic notion on p. 224.

*Anselm, of course, does not doubt that there is. But he wishes to *understand* what it is that he so firmly believes. Though Anselm is writing at the request of (and primarily for the enlightenment of) his Christian brothers, there can be little doubt that he thinks the proof he has discovered is valid quite independently of any Christian assumptions. It should convince *anyone* who thinks about God at all.

It is easy to see how this might be the case with the painting. But can it be the case that *that, than which no greater can be conceived* exists only in the understanding? Anselm invites us to consider that it does exist only in our understanding. But then, he says, it is not after all *that, than which no greater can be conceived*. For you can certainly conceive of something greater than *that*. You can think that it exists both in the understanding and in reality.

Such a being will be "greater" in the sense that it has more powers and is less dependent on other things; it occupies a higher place on the great chain of being. So it couldn't be true that *that, than which no greater can be conceived* exists only in our minds. God must exist in reality.

In fact, Anselm adds, this being exists so truly "that it cannot be conceived not to exist" (*Proslogium* 3). Most beings—trees, wolves, and humans, for example—you can imagine as never having existed. If an extra large comet had collided with the earth several billion years ago, none of them would have existed. Could *that, than which no greater can be conceived* be like these beings? Could it be the sort of thing that we can conceive as not existing? Again let us suppose that it were; then it would depend on the cooperation or good will of other things for its existence—or maybe on sheer good luck!

But then it wouldn't be *that, than which no greater can be conceived*, for we can surely conceive a greater being than that. We can conceive of a being that is not so dependent on other things. In fact, we can conceive of a being that we cannot even *conceive* as not existing.

> Hence, if that, than which nothing greater can be conceived, can be conceived not to exist, it is not that, than which nothing greater can be conceived. But this is an irreconcilable contradiction (*Proslogium* 3).

You cannot even conceive that God does not exist. You can, of course, say the words, "There is no God"; but, Anselm says, you cannot clearly think what they mean without falling into contradiction. What is contradictory cannot possibly be true. So what the fool says is necessarily false. It follows not only that God does exist but also that it is impossible that he does not.

Here is an analogy. You can *say* that one plus one equals three, but you cannot conceive that it is true. If you understand what one is and what three is, and if you understand the concepts of addition and equality, then you cannot possibly believe or even understand that one plus one equals three. To try to do so would be like trying to believe that three both *is* three and also *is not* three (but two). But that is impossible, a contradiction. It is necessarily false that three both is and is not three. Just so, it is necessarily false that *that, than which no greater can be conceived* does not exist. To try to believe it is true is like trying to believe that *that, than which no greater can be conceived* both does exist (since it *is* that, than which no greater can be conceived) and does not exist. But you can't believe both. So, you must believe that it does exist. You cannot even conceive that God does not exist. That God should not exist is as impossible as that one plus one should equal three.

Why, then, does the fool (in the second sense) say in his heart, "There is no God"? Because he is a dim-witted fool who believes contradictions! The nonexistence of God is something that cannot be rationally thought.

It is little wonder that Anselm exclaims,

> I thank thee, gracious Lord, I thank thee; because what I formerly believed by thy bounty, I now so understand by thine illumination, that if I were unwilling to believe that thou dost exist, I should not be able not to understand this to be true (*Proslogium* 4).

Even if Anselm *wanted* to disbelieve in God, he couldn't manage it. It would now be clear to him that the very sentence in which he expressed his disbelief is necessarily false.

Is Anselm's argument a sound one? Should we be convinced by it? Or is it a tissue of confusions and ambiguities? Discussion since the eleventh century has been intense, beginning with Gaunilo of Marmoutier, a monk who was Anselm's contemporary. The argument has had both defenders and critics down to the present day. It is not only the interest of its conclusion that attracts attention—though if the argument were sound, the conclusion might be of the greatest importance. But it is interesting also because it involves the very difficult notions of existence, conceivability, possibility, and necessity. And these are notions that run very deep in our conception of reality—whatever it might be like.

We will meet the argument again.*

Thomas Aquinas: What All Men Speak of as God

Thomas Aquinas was born in Italy in 1225 C.E. and died at the relatively young age of forty-nine in 1274. It was an exciting time for a brilliant young man to be growing up. A new institution was being established: the university. And new ideas were in the air. For centuries the intellectual atmosphere had been Neoplatonic and Augustinian. Of Aristotle, only the logical treatises and some commentaries on them had been available. But now more or less the whole of Aristotle's works were becoming available, though at first only in poor Latin translations: the ethics, the physics, the treatises on the soul, the metaphysics. With the new interest in Aristotle coincided (not just by accident) a revival of interest in the world. The world became a focus of attention in its own right, and people began again to investigate certain natural phenomena. One of the first sciences to be pursued was optics—still reflecting the Platonic and Augustinian preoccupation with light and illumination. But alchemists were investigating the properties of matter in conjunction with their magical quest for ways to transform base metals into gold. And other interests followed. It was no longer just God and the soul that mattered.

Thomas became a Dominican friar. He studied in Naples, and then in Cologne under Albert the Great, an early scientist, philosopher, theologian, and enthusiast for Aristotle. Thomas went to the new university in Paris, where he lectured and took part in "disputations," organized discussions in which a topic was set, a proposition on that topic put forward, and arguments given for and against it by students and teachers, with a "Professor" giving judgment at the end. These disputations set the pattern for medieval philosophy and for the writings of Thomas himself.

He wrote an incredible amount. No topic in philosophy or theology is untouched. Most of his work is in the severely ordered form that came to be known (later, with scorn) as "scholastic." A question is stated, and an answer is given. Then several objections to this answer are raised. Thomas gives his view and his reasons for accepting it. And there follows a reply to each of the objections. This pattern makes for comprehensiveness and attention to detail. It depends absolutely on the ability of writers and readers to distinguish good arguments from bad. And it requires enormous patience. In the hands of lesser intellectuals, it often degenerates into pedantry.

Thomas is without doubt one of the great philosophers. If we judge by his merits, he deserves as much attention as Plato, Aristotle, or Augustine. But in a selective introduction such as this book, hard choices have to be made. With some regret, we will restrict ourselves to a famous "bit" of his philosophy that concerns some much-discussed arguments for the existence of God. Because these can be understood only within the broad Aristotelian context that Thomas accepts, we must remind ourselves of certain Aristotelian themes.

Thomas accepts Aristotle's criticisms of the Platonic Forms.* The primary objects of our knowledge are the created things of the world about us; we know them because they leave traces of themselves in our sense organs—in the eyes, ears, and so on. Such traces are not themselves knowledge,

---

*See Descartes (*Meditation V*) and Kant (the ontological argument, Chapter 20). Here is an excellent exercise: try to evaluate the argument's goodness; if you think there is something wrong with it, try to say exactly what it is.

---

*Look again at pp. 159–160. It will also be useful to review the comparison of Aristotle to Plato on pp. 141–144.

of course. Animals have similar sensory experiences, but they are without knowledge (or at least without the linguistically expressible kind of knowledge humans have). Human beings convert sensory experience into *concepts* by a process of abstraction: a capacity of rational minds. And human knowledge is framed in terms of these concepts. We do not, then, have a direct intuition of intelligible realities, as both Plato and Augustine hold; all our knowledge comes *via the senses*.

Thomas works out these basic principles in detailed ways that we need not discuss. But it should be clear already how different is this view of our knowledge capacities from that of Augustine. Using our senses to understand the world about us is not a distraction from the important topics of God and the soul, but a means to their comprehension. We can begin nowhere else than with the world our senses disclose.

Thomas is of course familiar with Anselm's argument for God's existence. But Thomas is among those who do not think it a good argument. It is not that he thinks, as some Christians do, that *no* argument could prove this conclusion. As we'll see, he does think it can be proved. But this is the wrong sort of argument. It is not an argument appropriate to creatures such as we are—if Aristotle is basically right about human nature and its cognitive capacities. For Anselm's argument begins with the assumption that we have a grasp of *what God is*—of the "essence" of God, as Thomas would put it. But that is not something we can assume. *What* God is must be filled in by argument (or by revelation) just as much as *that* God is. For we do not have an intuition of intelligible realities; we cannot just grasp concepts out of the air. Since we are rational *animals*, all our knowledge must start from—though it may lead us beyond—the senses. And the senses do not inform us directly about the nature of God.

Anselm's argument in effect says that the existence of God is *self-evident*. Now something is *self-evident* if all you need to do in order to see that it is true is to understand it. And that is exactly what Anselm claims. If you understand what God is— *that, than which no greater can be conceived*—you

will see it is true that God exists. Aquinas says that God's existence *may* be self-evident *in itself*, or to God; but it is not self-evident *to us*. And the reason is that we get our concepts and our knowledge by abstraction from our experience, which does not contain any direct intuition of the essence of God.

So we must go by another path.

In answer to the question, "Whether God Can Be Known in This Life by Natural Reason?" Thomas says,

> Our natural knowledge begins from sense. Hence our natural knowledge can go as far as it can be led by sensible things. But our intellect cannot be led by sense so far as to see the essence of God; because sensible creatures are effects of God which do not equal the power of God, their cause. Hence from the knowledge of sensible things the whole power of God cannot be known; nor therefore can His essence be seen. But because they are His effects and depend on their cause, we can be led from them so far as to know of God *whether He exists*, and to know of Him what must necessarily belong to Him, as the first cause of all things, exceeding all things caused by Him.[3]

We must, then, begin from what we know best— the world that our senses tell us about—and proceed by reasoning until we find the *cause*. This is the key feature of the proofs Thomas offers: we ask in them for the cause of certain fairly obvious facts about the world. And we can (rationally) know about God exactly as much as we can know about this "cause of all things."

Thomas says that "the existence of God can be proved in five ways."[4] Like the proof of Anselm, these "five ways" have been subjected to exhaustive logical scrutiny, often in a forbidding forest of technical symbols.* I will present Thomas's arguments

---

*The evaluation of such arguments probably cannot be thoroughly done except by means of such a technical analysis, using the best logical apparatus available. If this is so, it means that for most of us a decision on whether the arguments are successful or not must be somewhat tentative. But a tentative view of them is at least a start. And it is better to hear them framed by a first-rate philosopher such as Thomas than in the sloppy forms in which they appear in popular culture.

in his own words and then add some interpretive remarks. In these remarks I will try to present the argument in as strong and sympathetic a way as I can. You may be inclined to try to criticize these arguments; and that's fine. But it is important that you first *understand* them.

The Argument from Motion

It is certain, and evident to our senses, that in the world some things are in motion. Now whatever is moved is moved by another, for nothing can be moved except it is in potentiality to that toward which it is moved; whereas a thing moves inasmuch as it is in act. For motion is nothing else than the reduction of something from potentiality to actuality. But nothing can be reduced from potentiality to actuality, except by something in a state of actuality. Thus that which is actually hot, as fire, makes wood, which is potentially hot, to be actually hot, and thereby moves and changes it. Now it is not possible that the same thing should be at once in actuality and potentiality in the same respect, but only in different respects. For what is actually hot cannot simultaneously be potentially hot; but it is simultaneously potentially cold. It is therefore impossible that in the same respect and in the same way a thing should be both mover and moved, i.e., that it should move itself. Therefore, whatever is moved must be moved by another. If that by which it is moved be itself moved, then this also must needs be moved by another, and that by another again. But this cannot go on to infinity, because then there would be no first mover, and consequently, no other mover, seeing that subsequent movers move only inasmuch as they are moved by the first mover; as the staff moves only because it is moved by the hand. Therefore it is necessary to arrive at a first mover, moved by no other; and this everyone understands to be God.

The first thing to note is the very broad and Aristotelian interpretation Thomas gives to "motion." He does not mean just change of place, though that is included. "Motion" includes change of all kinds, as the example of fire heating wood shows. And change is understood to be an alteration in something, by which it becomes *actually*

what it was until then only *potentially.** If the sun heats the sidewalk, so that you can't stand on it with bare feet, this is a change from actually being cool (but potentially hot) to actually being hot. The world is full of such changes or motions.

The next point is that each of these changes is brought about by something that is, in the appropriate way, *actual*. The curtains have the potentiality to fade; but they are not actually faded. Nor do they have an actual power to fade themselves. It takes the fading action of the sun to fade them. We might say that the sun has an actual fading power. In the same way, the wood (potentially hot) does not actualize that potentiality on its own; it takes something that is actually hot—the fire—to make the wood actually hot, too. And since the wood cannot be simultaneously actually hot and only potentially hot (actually cold), it cannot make itself hot. Similarly, it is only because the hand is actually in motion that the stick's potentiality to move is actualized.

In fact, Aquinas tells us, *nothing* can move itself. And we now can see why. For a thing T to move, or change, is for it to move from being potentially X to being actually X. It takes something that is actually X to accomplish this. But T isn't already actually X; X is what it is going to become. So it must be changed by something else, S, which is already X.

Therefore, everything that is moved must be moved by another thing. T must be changed by S. But here you can see a question: what accounts for the fact that S is actually X? Well, there are two possibilities. Either S is actualized by some third thing, R, or it is not. If it is not, then it is what Aquinas calls a "first" mover; it moves T without itself being moved by another. If, however, it is made X by R then the question repeats itself about R.

And now the question arises: could this sequence of movers go on to infinity? Might it be that there is no "first" mover at all, nothing that is the source of change without itself being changed by some other thing? Could it be that *everything* is moved by something else, which in turn is moved

---

*It may help to review what Aristotle says about the notions of actuality and potentiality. See pp. 157 and 162.

by something else? This is a tricky question. But on this question the soundness of the proof probably rests.

Thomas answers no. His reason is that if this were true, there would obviously be no "first" mover. But if there were no "first" mover, then there would not be any other movers either, since they move only insofar as they are moved by the "first" one. And, of course, if there were no other movers, then there would be no change at all. But this is obviously false. So the series cannot "go on to infinity." There must be a point at which change *originates*. This must be something that is not merely potential, but is fully and entirely actual. Otherwise, it would need something outside itself to actualize its potentialities.

It is important to guard against a misinterpretation here. Thomas is not thinking of a first thing in a temporal series. His argument is not that one change precedes another, a second precedes that, and so on, to the beginning of the world in time. In fact, Thomas does not think that reason can prove that the world had a beginning in time; if it were not revealed to us by God that the world did have a beginning, we could rationally conclude that the world is eternal, without beginning or end—as Aristotle in fact does. But for the purposes of proving the existence of God, this does not matter. An eternal world would need a "first" mover, a source of change, an actuality that was not merely potential, just as much as a temporally limited world.

We must think, not of a temporal series, but of nested sets of necessary conditions. A necessary condition for the wood's becoming hot is the presence of something actually hot. A necessary condition of that is something else in appropriate ways actual, and so on. That set of conditions cannot be infinite. There must be some condition that is itself *sufficient* to account for the rest, without requiring another condition beyond itself. This would be a "first" mover. And that, Aquinas says, is what "everyone understands to be God."

The Argument from Efficient Causality

In the world of sensible things we find there is an order of efficient causes. There is no cause known (neither is it, indeed, possible) in which a thing is found to be the efficient cause of itself; for so it would be prior to itself, which is impossible. Now in efficient causes it is not possible to go on to infinity, because in all efficient causes following in order, the first is the cause of the intermediate cause, and the intermediate is the cause of the ultimate cause, whether the intermediate cause be several, or one only. Now to take away the cause is to take away the effect. Therefore, if there be no first cause among efficient causes, there will be no ultimate, nor any intermediate, cause. But if in efficient causes it is possible to go on to infinity, there will be no first efficient cause, neither will there be an ultimate effect, nor any intermediate efficient causes; all of which is plainly false. Therefore it is necessary to admit a first efficient cause, to which everyone gives the name of God.

An efficient cause, you will recall, is the "trigger" that sets a process going.* Examples are the spark that produces the explosion, the moisture that sprouts the seed, and the stroke of the golf club that sends the ball flying. What we find in the world is a certain "order" of such causes. One obvious fact is that nothing can be the efficient cause of itself. The spark may be the cause of the explosion, but it cannot be the cause of the spark. To be its own cause, it would have to preexist itself. But that is absurd. This is what Thomas means when he says it is impossible for a cause to "be prior to itself." It cannot exist before it exists. The spark itself requires another efficient cause, perhaps a hammer striking a rock.

Another obvious fact is that if you take away the cause, you take away the effect as well. No hammer, no spark (or at least not this particular spark); no spark, no explosion (this particular explosion).

What we find in the world, then, is an "order" of such causes, one cause depending on another for its existence. Again, this order need not be a temporal one, though it may be. Thomas is not trying to prove that there was a temporally first event in the world's history. Even if the world is eternal, as Aristotle thinks it must be, every thing in it needs an efficient cause for its very existence; nothing causes itself to exist. We can think of this as a hierarchically

---

*See Aristotle, pp. 155–156.

ordered set of dependencies, rather than a temporally extended series of successive things.*

Again the question arises: could this series of dependencies be infinite? Could *every* cause exist (as the cause it is) only because it is brought into being (as a cause) by another? Thomas again says no. For if the series were infinite, there would be no cause that is "first." (A "first" cause would be that on which the existence of the whole causal order depends, while it depends on nothing beyond itself.) Take away this first cause, and there would be no intermediate causes, nor any ultimate effects. But, as we see, there are causes and effects. So there must be a first cause. And that is what everyone gives the name of God.

One commentator gives a helpful analogy[5] Suppose you are in your car, stopped at a light, and are hit from behind. You want to know the cause of this unfortunate effect. So you get out and see that the car that hit you had been stopped but was itself hit from behind. So you can't pin the effect on the driver of that car. As you look at the car behind that one, you find that it too was hit from behind, and so on. Who caused your accident? Clearly, the driver of some car that hit a second car, but was not hit in turn. He caused each of the other cars to cause an accident, ending in yours. He produced the whole series of causes. He is the "first" cause.

Suppose, however, that it were an infinitely long pileup. Then *no one* would have started the chain. But if no one started it, it would not have happened. Since it did happen, we can conclude there is someone who did start it. He is the first cause.

The Argument from Possibility and Necessity

We find in nature things that are possible to be and not to be, since they are found to be generated, and to be corrupted, and consequently, it is possible for them to be and not to be. But it is impossible for these always to exist, for that which can not-be at some time is not. Therefore, if everything can not-be,

then at one time there was nothing in existence. Now if this were true, even now there would be nothing in existence, because that which does not exist begins to exist only through something already existing. Therefore, if at one time nothing was in existence, it would have been impossible for anything to have begun to exist; and thus even now nothing would be in existence—which is absurd. Therefore, not all beings are merely possible, but there must exist something the existence of which is necessary. But every necessary thing either has its necessity caused by another, or not. Now it is impossible to go on to infinity in necessary things which have their necessity caused by another, as has already been proved in regard to efficient causes. Therefore we cannot but admit the existence of some being having of itself its own necessity, and not receiving it from another, but rather causing in others their necessity. This all men speak of as God.

To understand this argument, we must be clear about what Thomas means by "possibility" and "necessity." Both terms are applied by Thomas to *beings* of various sorts. And it seems that he thinks we have examples of both merely possible beings and necessary beings in our experience.

A merely possible being is a being that is "found to be generated, and to be corrupted." Such beings are the plants and animals, who begin to exist and cease again. Mountains and rivers, too, are merely possible beings: there was a time when the Rockies did not exist, and eventually erosion will wear them away; even the mighty Mississippi will eventually disappear, perhaps in the next ice age.

These are among the things of Aristotelian physics that have the principles of change within them. But there are two kinds of "natural" beings, corresponding to two ways in which they can change. *Merely* possible beings are beings that can change *essentially*—that is, they can change *from what they are* into *something else*. They can appear and disappear again. Fido is born, lives for a time, and dies. What Fido is made out of (his matter) is not born with him, nor does it disappear when he dies. But it appears *as Fido* when Fido is born and disappears *as Fido* when Fido dies.

This is what a "merely possible" being is. A necessary being, by contrast, is one that is neither gen-

---

*If you want an example of a causal relation of the efficient sort that is not temporally ordered, think of the depression of the sofa cushion, which is simultaneous with your sitting upon it. Your sitting is the efficient cause of the depression in the cushion, but they happen precisely together.

erated nor corrupted. So it is—at least in the realm of nature—without beginning or ending. As an Aristotelian in this regard, Thomas thinks there are such beings in our experience. The sun and moon and stars are such beings.* They are subject to change in place, of course, as the heavenly spheres revolve. But this change is "accidental" to their being. They do not change *essentially*, because *what they are* doesn't come into being and pass away again, as Fido does. Moreover, these necessary beings are constantly generating and regenerating the merely possible things below the heavenly spheres.

Now, *we* know that the sun, moon, and stars are not necessary beings in this sense. They, too, experience generation and corruption. So Aristotle and Thomas are mistaken in this claim. But we might ask whether *our* physics is committed to any necessary beings, in the sense Thomas gives to this term. One commentator suggests that the elementary particles, or energy quanta, are the modern version of Thomas's necessary beings.[6] Nowadays Thomas might cite the principle of the conservation of matter (or energy) as a principle that points to a kind of "necessary" being.

The important point is that "merely possible" beings depend upon "necessary" beings. There cannot *just* be merely possible beings. Thomas argues that since merely possible beings have an inherent tendency to disappear, if these were the only beings, they would eventually *all* disappear. And then there would be nothing in existence. In fact, this would already have happened! But if this had ever happened, then nothing would exist now—because *from nothing comes nothing.*

But as we can clearly see, a great many things now exist. So it follows, Thomas says, that "not all beings are merely possible." At least *something* must be a necessary being. Something must be such that it does not naturally tend to vanish.

Now consider the necessary beings that exist (whether the heavenly bodies or the elementary particles of modern physics). Where does the necessity of these beings come from? What explains or accounts for the fact that they are necessary? Some necessary beings may have their necessity given to them by other necessary beings. But (for reasons similar to those given in the last proof) this process of necessity-giving cannot go on to infinity. There must be some being which has its necessity "of itself," and which does not owe that to any other being. This being does not depend on anything beyond itself for its properties of being ungenerable and incorruptible. This being is in itself eternal and necessary in the most proper sense of the word. And this being, as Thomas says, "all men speak of as God."

The Argument from Grades of Value in Things

> Among beings there are some more and some less good, true, noble, and the like. But *more* and *less* are predicated of different things according as they resemble in their different ways something which is the maximum, as a thing is said to be hotter according as it more nearly resembles that which is hottest; so that there is something which is truest, something best, something noblest, and, consequently, something which is most being, for those things that are greatest in truth are greatest in being, as it is written in *Metaph.* ii. Now the maximum in any genus is the cause of all in that genus, as fire, which is the maximum of heat, is the cause of all hot things, as is said in the same book. Therefore there must also be something which is to all beings the cause of their being, goodness, and every other perfection; and this we call God.

This proof begins with the observation that the things we experience do not all have the same value. Some are better than others, some truer, some more noble. All of these comparative judgments, however, make sense only if we assume that in each case there is something which exemplifies those characteristics to a superlative degree.

Thomas uses the example, which he borrows from Aristotle, of hot things, which are judged more or less hot as they more or less resemble the

---

*This is an expression of that Aristotelian distinction between the perfection of the *celestial* spheres in contrast to the corruptibility of the *terrestrial* sphere. It is this distinction that modern astronomy, initiated by Copernicus, overthrows. See p. 282.

hotness of fire. (Again, *we* know there are many things hotter than ordinary fire, but that just means we have a longer scale by which to make such comparative judgments; perhaps we would judge heat in comparison with the temperature of atomic fusion in the sun, and cold in comparison with absolute zero.) Something is better than another thing, then, to the extent that it more closely resembles the best. Something is truer if it is more like the truth, and so on.

But that is not the only point on which this argument rests. It is not just that the comparative degrees in such things are measured by the superlative; their very being depends on a superlative. As Thomas says, fire is the cause of all hot things; and this must be actually existing fire. Again this is a *causal* proof. Thomas is claiming that if there were not in existence a superlative degree of goodness, truth, and being, the existence of any lesser degree would be inexplicable. So there must be a "maximum" best, noblest, truest, and so on.

But since the lower degrees actually exist, the maximum must also really exist. This maximum is what explains the fact that we observe all these degrees of goodness in things: it is their cause. This maximum "best" of all things, Thomas says, "we call God."

The Argument from the Governance of the World

We see that things which lack knowledge, such as natural bodies, act for an end, and this is evident from their acting always, or nearly always, in the same way, so as to obtain the best result. Hence it is plain that they achieve their end, not fortuitously, but designedly. Now whatever lacks knowledge cannot move towards an end, unless it be directed by some being endowed with knowledge and intelligence; as the arrow is directed by the archer. Therefore some intelligent being exists by whom all natural things are directed to their end; and this being we call God.

This proof is often called "the argument from design." It is probably the one that turns up most often in popular "proofs" of the existence of God, and it has a famous history.* The key idea is that intelligent beings act purposefully, arranging means suitable to achieve ends they have in mind. We plant and harvest and store, for example, so that we will have food in the winter when we know there will be none to gather. We can look ahead to a situation that does not now exist and can take steps to meet it satisfactorily.

This capacity is none too surprising in intelligent beings; perhaps it is even the main thing that constitutes intelligence. But when we look at the nonrational part of the world, we see the same thing. And this *is* surprising. We can hardly suppose that my Newfoundland dog, Shadow, grows a thick coat in the fall and sheds it in the spring because he foresees that otherwise he will be uncomfortable and perhaps even in danger of not surviving! Yet it is just as if he planned that rationally.

We see the same apparently rational planning wherever we look. Rabbits are quick so that they can escape foxes. Foxes are cunning so that they can catch rabbits. Moths are camouflaged to escape predators. And so on. Everything happens as though it were planned to happen that way. But we cannot believe that dogs, rabbits, moths, and foxes are doing that planning. Someone else must be doing it for them.

Here is an analogy. People sometimes wonder whether computers are intelligent. They can certainly do some remarkable things: solve problems, rotate images in three dimensions on a screen, guide spacecraft. A standard reply is that though they may *look* intelligent, the intelligence they display is not their own, but that of their designers and programmers. They have a "borrowed" intelligence.

Thomas is claiming something similar for naturally existing beings. They do remarkable things, things that seem inexplicable in the absence of intelligence. They act "always, or nearly always, in the same way, so as to obtain the best result." We cannot believe that they are themselves intelligent.

*See particularly the discussion by David Hume ("Is It Reasonable to Believe in God?" in Chapter 19). Darwinian modes of explanation also tend to undermine the argument.

So there must be "some intelligent being . . . by whom all natural things are directed to their end.*This being, Thomas says once more, "we call God."

What These Arguments Are Supposed to Prove

In thinking about these arguments, we must be careful not to read too much into the term "God." In particular, we must not fill out that term with all the richness of meaning it has in a Christian, Jewish, or other religious tradition; we shouldn't suppose Thomas thinks he has proved that God has all the qualities ascribed to him by these traditions. He is quite clear that he has not done that.

What he claims to have proved by these arguments is the existence of a being that is a first mover, a first efficient cause, has its necessity in itself, is the best of all existing beings, and is the intelligent designer of all the rest. Actually, these proofs do not quite show even that: they do not show that there is *one* being that has all these properties. But Thomas thinks that such uniqueness too can be proved and offers an argument for that later.

These characteristics make up a part, though only a part, of our traditional conception of God. And, given the history of the term, it is not unreasonable for Thomas to comment at the end of each of the proofs that the being whose existence is demonstrated is what we all understand by "God."

For Thomas, the significance of the proofs is that they provide a foundation on which he thinks all rational people should be able to agree. If we think about the matter clearly, he contends, we should all agree that *atheism is irrational*. This does not mean that the rational man will necessarily be a Christian. For some of the truths about God cannot be rationally demonstrated. The full significance of God is apparent only from revelation; and acceptance of such truths depends not on natural reason but on grace. But the message of the Bible and the doctrines of the church build upon the foundation that reason has laid.

---

*Note the persistence of the Greek assumption that where there is order, there is intelligence. See p. 13.

Skeptical Doubts—Again

Since Augustine rebutted skepticism in the late fourth century, there had been a broad consensus that human minds were capable of knowing the truth.* There were often sharp disagreements about what constituted the truth, but they were almost always conducted on this epistemological common ground. God had created the world, and he created human beings in his own image. It would not have been "suitable" for God to mismatch reality and the mind. In any case, it was through Wisdom, the *logos*, the second person of the Trinity, that everything was created. So it was natural to suppose that the pattern in reality was one that could be reproduced in the mind. As St. Thomas puts it, the rational mind is "adequate" to attain knowledge.

It is true that our minds are finite and limited. We cannot discover the whole truth on our own. But God has graciously come to our aid; he has revealed to us such truths as are consistent with our finite status and necessary for our salvation. These revealed truths, which we accept on the authority of the Scriptures and the Church, are not in conflict with the truths we can discover on our own. How could they be, since both come ultimately from the same God? Revealed truth supplements our rational knowledge, completes it, and provides an overall framework within which all correct believing and knowing are carried on.

We must add two further notes to this happy picture. (1) Knowledge is always understood in that very strong classical sense delineated by Plato when he distinguishes it from opinion.† In medieval philosophy, the requirement that knowledge "stays put" or "endures" is understood to mean that it involves *absolute certainty*. If you *know* something, you are certain of it; you are not about to be shaken by any stray wind that might blow some doubts your way. And, as with Plato, this feature is correlated with the fact that knowledge is some-

---

*Review his arguments on p. 218.
†See pp. 106–108.

thing for which reasons can be given. The reasons are sometimes based on logic, sometimes on experience, and sometimes on the Scriptures—often on a combination of them. But there is always "an account" that can be given.

(2) Knowledge, and the certainty that goes with it, is crucially important. It is absolutely essential to get it right, because your eternal salvation depends on getting it right. That is why heresy—erroneous belief—is so terrifying. The difference between correct, or orthodox, belief and heresy is the difference between *heaven* and *hell*. So it is not just an attempt to satisfy Aristotelian "wonder" that motivates the medieval theologians and philosophers.* Getting it right has an intensely personal and practical aspect.

All this is common ground in the thirteenth century. On these foundations Thomas builds a remarkably comprehensive system of thought. We can call it a system because it is cleanly ordered, its parts are interdependent, and it aspires to completeness. Like the thought of Augustine, it integrates classical philosophy with Christian faith. But there are two differences. It builds on Aristotle instead of Plato and Plotinus. And it expresses in a serenely rational way a confidence that the rational ordering of thought can mirror in a systematic way the rational ordering of reality.

Augustine is always caught up in one struggle or another—against the Manicheans or the Pelagians or those who would revive classical paganism. Compared with Thomas, Augustine—though an intense personality and a great thinker—writes *tracts*. Thomas writes as though he were already among the angels (who were, in fact, a favorite topic of his). The kind of confidence in the intellect that Thomas expresses has perhaps not been seen since Aristotle himself.

It is surprising to learn that this systematic synthesis, so marvelous in its way, is being undermined already in the fourteenth century. Doubts raise their ugly heads once again: doubts not about some detail, but about the very foundation that has been taken for granted in the centuries since Au-

gustine. It is even more surprising to learn that these doubts have their source not, as you might suspect, among some atheist or agnostic folks who can't accept the claims about revealed truth, but among theologians whose orthodoxy (at least on central issues) is beyond question.[7]

Two condemnations of heretical opinions, issued in 1270 and 1277 by the bishop of Paris, Etienne Tempier, have a dramatic effect on the thought of Christian philosophers. Certain Arab (Muslim) philosophers had written impressive commentaries on Aristotle, which are greatly admired among Christian thinkers. They bring out, however, certain Aristotelian opinions that are in conflict with Christian doctrine. Among the Aristotelian/Arab views that are condemned are these:

1. The opinion that the world is eternal (which conflicts with Christian views of creation)
2. The view that, with the possible exception of certain human actions, everything happens for sufficient causes (which conflicts with the possibility of miracles)
3. The opinion that substances are necessarily connected with their properties or "accidents" (which conflicts with Catholic interpretations of the eucharist, wherein the bread and the wine are said to *become* the body and blood of Christ while retaining the "accidents" of bread and wine)
4. The view that the soul is the form of a living body (which seems to conflict with individual immortality)

St. Thomas, of course, struggles with all these inconsistencies. He either interprets Aristotle in ways consistent with Christian doctrine or rejects certain Aristotelian views. But the condemnation has the following general effect: thinkers come to suspect that there might be a conflict between the best-reasoned view of some matter and the teachings of the Church. The authority of Aristotle in logic, natural philosophy, metaphysics, and ethics is substantial by this time. Thomas, for example, often refers to him simply as "the Philosopher." But if what Aristotle teaches can conflict with what the

---

*See Aristotle on wonder, p. 158.

Church clearly teaches, thinkers will have to be much more cautious about relying on classical thought to interpret Christian doctrine.

It is important also to note that these views are not *argued against*. They are not shown to be mistaken by a close rational critique; they are *condemned as heretical*.* It is obvious that one has to be mighty careful about relying on natural reason. Even the most careful and conscientious use of it might very well lead one astray. A gulf begins to yawn between revealed truth (which these thinkers do not question) and what the human mind could show to be likely. It is not that there are two truths; it is that what seems evidently true to unaided reason might in fact not—according to the "measure" of revelation—be true. And what seems untrue, revelation might pronounce to be true.

In conjunction with these condemnations, there is increased attention paid to one basic doctrine: the *omnipotence* of God. "I believe in God, the Father Almighty," begins the Creed. What does this mean? During the medieval period God's omnipotence is understood to mean that he can do anything that is not self-contradictory. He cannot make a cube with only five sides, since by definition a cube has six sides. Nor can he make something that did happen not happen; for in this case it would be true of some event x that x both happened and did not happen—and that is contradictory. But since contradictory expressions do not describe real possibilities, this is no real limitation on God's power. God can do anything that is possible. For any state of affairs that can be given a consistent description, then, God can realize that state of affairs. This doctrine is important partly because it protects the possibility of miracles.

Among those who derive some surprising consequences of this doctrine is William of Ockham (born in the 1280s and died about 1349). Ockham was English, taught at Oxford, and was embroiled in some nasty confrontations between his Franciscan order and the pope. Like all the major philosophers of the period, he thinks of himself first and foremost as a theologian. He is also a very acute

logician who makes some important contributions concerning the status of logical principles and the structure of knowledge. Any adequate treatment of Ockham's thought would have to include his logic. But we will concentrate on his emphasis on the omnipotence of God, specifically, the impact of this doctrine on views of the world and our knowledge of it.

Consider the following kind of case. You are sitting at a table, in good light, looking directly at a tangerine about three feet in front of your eyes. You are wide awake, not under the influence of any drugs, and are paying attention to what is before you. This seems to be the most favorable sort of case we can imagine for knowing something. We would ordinarily say that you know that there is a tangerine on the table.

But what does your knowledge consist in? It is clearly some state of yourself—what Ockham calls an "intuitive cognition." In standard cases, we think, this state is caused in part by the tangerine and in part by your sense organs and intellect. The first part of the cause is a matter of how the world is—that there happens to be a tangerine on the table. The second part is a matter of how you are—where you are, whether your eyes are open, whether you have learned what a tangerine is, and so on. In the standard case, your "intuitive cognition" of the tangerine depends both on the actual existence of a tangerine on the table and on a suitable state within you. Ockham does not deny this.

But now consider the impact that the doctrine of God's omnipotence has on this case. God, remember, can do anything that is not self-contradictory. This means that he can cause to happen anything whose description is not inconsistent. God has created a world that operates as we have described in the standard case above. But could God *directly* cause you to have that "intuitive cognition" of the tangerine? In the standard case, your experience is caused by the presence of the tangerine; but could God cause this experience without the mediation of the actual piece of fruit?

To answer this question, we must ask whether that would be self-contradictory. And it is easy to see that it is not. The presence of that piece of fruit on the table neither entails nor is entailed by your

---

*Compare the contrast drawn earlier between the philosopher and the prophet, p. 201.

"intuitive cognition" of it. Either, so far as logic goes, could exist without the other. So, God could cause you to have such an experience even in the absence of the tangerine.

What is the consequence of this line of reasoning? Evidently, our conviction that we *know* that the tangerine exists—even in this most favorable case—is mistaken. For knowledge, remember, involves absolute certainty that could not possibly be mistaken. But if God can produce in us the internal state that is usually caused by the tangerine even in the *absence* of the tangerine, there is a possibility that our "intuitive cognition" is mistaken.

At best, our belief that there is a tangerine in front of us is merely *probable* belief. It amounts to no more than what Plato calls "opinion." But since all our knowledge of the world rests ultimately on such favorable cases of "intuitive cognition," the claim to know is seriously undermined.

Ockham does not draw the completely skeptical conclusion that knowledge is impossible for us. But these reflections deal a serious blow to confidence in our ability to find such absolute knowledge. And, as you can see, the blow comes from a consideration of what God's omnipotence implies.

A similar conclusion follows about the causality we claim to find in the world independent of ourselves. A piece of cloth is brought near a flame and starts to burn. How are we to explain the burning? It might be possible for God to cause it directly, so that our usual account in terms of the causal efficacy of the fire would be mistaken.* Again, the best we can do is to give probable explanations of why things happen in the world. It seems that our explanations might always be mistaken. And if that isn't skepticism itself, it surely seems to move us toward skeptical doubts, especially if one insists at the same time that knowledge must involve absolute certainty.

This produces a very interesting situation. For more than a thousand years the assumption that reason and revelation are compatible has reigned. They are more than just compatible; for reason can supply foundations—with certainty—for revelation to build upon. Philosophy, the pursuit of wisdom by our human wits, has been treated as the "handmaiden" of theology, which in turn is the "queen" of the sciences. And suddenly the suspicion arises that perhaps natural reason and experience are not well suited for this task!

Let us ask what effect this has on, for instance, trying to prove the existence of God. Such proofs are a main part of the service that philosophy is supposed to provide to theology. Ockham himself is convinced that a certain form of proof is still possible. But we may get an idea of the effects of these more critical views of knowledge by looking at some propositions put forward in the late fourteenth century by Pierre d'Ailly, a cardinal of the Church. He is discussing Aristotle's argument for a first mover (which was adapted by St. Thomas in his "first way").* And he considers what a "captious debater" could say.

1) It is not unqualifiedly evident that something is moved; movement may be only apparent. . . .

2) Even if we grant that an object is in motion, we do not have to grant that it comes from some other object.

3) Granted that all motion is caused from another thing and granting that there is no infinite series of movers, we cannot infer a first unmoved mover. For the captious opponent could say that the first mover is unmoved for the present but not absolutely unmovable.

4) We cannot exclude the possibility that there is a circularity of causes and effects, i.e., A causes B, B causes C, and C causes A.

5) We cannot be sure that there is no infinity of essentially ordered causes. For God by His absolute power could create such an infinite series.

6) Moreover, the newness of things cannot be inferred from appearances. . . .

---

*We have here an anticipation of one of the most influential of all treatments of causality, that by David Hume in the eighteenth century. Hume does not depend on the doctrine of God's omnipotence; and the skeptical consequences are more determinedly drawn. See "Causation: The Very Idea," in Chapter 19.

---

*See again p. 253.

7)   The argument that if something exists anew it was produced is not evident.

8)   It is very difficult to explain what it means for one thing to be from another thing or to be effected or produced by another thing.[8]

This piling up of alternative possibilities that have not been definitively excluded seriously undermines our confidence in the "proof." At the very least, it shows us that a defender of the argument will have to do a lot more work if the argument is to succeed. It appears much less than certain that there must be a first mover, which all men call God.

It is important to note that d'Ailly does not intend to call the existence of God into question. Far from it. That God exists we know on the authority of the Scriptures and the Church. Rather, such reflections serve to undermine confidence in our natural ability to substantiate such truths apart from authority—at least with the certainty necessary for faith. (The cardinal allows that a *probable* argument for God's existence can be constructed.) Skepticism such as this, then, casts us more firmly than ever into the arms of the Church, which has such truths in its care. The moral is this: Aristotle and those who, like him, rely on our natural reason, should be approached with caution.

It seems then that the late Middle Ages is busily undoing what the earlier Middle Ages has done. It is engaging in a critique of the basic assumptions that have made the grand synthesis of classical and Christian thought possible. When several more ingredients are added to this furiously boiling pot—namely, the scientific revolution, the humanism of the Renaissance, and the impact of the Reformation on the Church—the modern era in philosophy will begin.

Notes

1. Jasper Hopkins, *A Companion to the Study of St. Anselm* (Minneapolis: University of Minnesota Press, 1972), 17.

2. Quotations from Anselm's *Proslogium*, in *St. Anselm: Basic Writings*, trans. S. N. Deane (La Salle, Ill.: Open Court Publishing Company, 1962), are cited in the text by chapter number.

3. Thomas Aquinas, *The Summa Theologica* I, question 12, article 12, in *Basic Writings of Saint Thomas Aquinas*, vol. 1, ed. Anton C. Pegis (New York: Random House, 1945), 109.

4. The quotations from the "five ways" all come from *The Summa Theologica* I, question 2, article 3, in Pegis, *Basic Writings of Saint Thomas Aquinas*, 21–23.

5. Patterson Brown, "Infinite Causal Regression," in *Aquinas: A Collection of Critical Essays*, ed. Anthony Kenny (London: Macmillan Co., 1969), 234–35.

6. Patterson Brown, "St. Thomas' Doctrine of Necessary Being," in Kenny, *Aquinas*, 172.

7. I am especially indebted in this section to Julius R. Weinberg's *Short History of Medieval Philosophy* (Princeton: Princeton University Press, 1964).

8. Cited in Weinberg, *Short History of Medieval Philosophy*, 287–88.

16

Moving from
Medieval to Modern

It is not clear just when the modern era begins. But it cannot be denied that something of immense significance happens in the sixteenth and seventeenth centuries that changes life and thought startlingly. In philosophy the beginnings of modernity are usually attributed to René Descartes (1596–1650). Though there are other plausible candidates for the title of "father of modern philosophy," it is the work of Descartes that sets the agenda for most of what we call "modern" in philosophy. Despite the fact that he shares many medieval concerns and convictions, Descartes sees clearly that a new beginning is required. He dramatically poses fundamental questions. And, although his own answers to these questions will satisfy few of his successors, they all see that an answer is required. Generations of philosophers will worry about solving the problems Descartes uncovers.

We can classify these problems under three heads. (1) Descartes, himself a distinguished mathematician and contributor to physics, sees with blinding clarity the need to assimilate the methods and results of the *new sciences* into our picture of the world. Copernicus, Kepler, and Galileo had recently reoriented thinking about both earth and the heavens. These new conceptions clash badly with the old. So some tearing down and rebuilding is called for.

(2) Paradoxically, and to some extent accidentally, *skepticism* has arisen once more from its ashes—this phoenix that first Plato and then Au-

gustine seek to slay.* Fueled by Reformation quarrels among the churches and lack of agreement among philosophers and scientists, the doubts of Sextus Empiricus spread rapidly among Renaissance intellectuals.† Descartes sees that skepticism cuts at the root of the claims made by science, philosophy, and religion alike. If we are going to rely on any one of them to tell us how things are, skepticism will have to be taken on again—and this time killed for good.

(3) Both of the first two problems mean that much closer attention will have to be paid to *knowledge*. Epistemological questions begin to take center stage. Can we know anything at all? And if so, by what means? Do the sciences give us knowledge of reality? If they do, how can we be sure of that? This preoccupation with epistemological questions is the principal heritage of Descartes. In ancient and medieval philosophy, questions about knowledge are just one sort of question among many others. But after Descartes they seem absolutely preeminent. *Unless you can solve these problems, no other problems can be solved.*

These are Descartes' problems: the problems of modern philosophy. But to feel the force of them *as problems* we need to back up a bit and sketch the

---

*For Plato's attempt at refutation, see p. 108; for Augustine's, p. 218.
†For a discussion of ancient skepticism, featuring the views of Sextus, see "The Skeptics," in Chapter 12.

context. His age is intellectually, and in other ways as well, one of the most tumultuous we have ever lived through. Though we are interested primarily in the intellectual ferment, we cannot help but note some of the social, political, and economic factors that make this an age of change. It will be useful to start with a review of the medieval picture of the world.

The World God Made for Man

Though there was by no means unanimity in the late Middle Ages about details, there was broad agreement about a certain picture of the world.[1] The universe, people thought, is a harmonious and coherent whole, created by an infinite and good God as an appropriate home for human beings, for whose sake it was made. It is difficult for us now to put ourselves into the place of medieval men and women and see the world as they saw it. We have been shaped by our education, which has very different presuppositions. But let us try.

It will help if we try to set aside all we have learned in school about the structure of the universe and attempt to recapture a more direct and naive interpretation of our experience. Consider the sky as you see it on a clear day or night. If you look *at* it, rather than *through* it, as those with our picture of the world tend to do, you will almost certainly conclude that it has a certain shape. It is *something* (as our term "the sky" tends to suggest). And the shape it has is roughly that of an upside down bowl. It is the roof of the earth, the "firmament" of Genesis 1 that God created to separate the primeval waters and make a place for dry land and living creatures. This view of the heavens is very common among primitive people and among children, too. We have to *learn* that the sky is not a thing.

This primitive view of the sky undergoes a great deal of rather sophisticated development by the later Middle Ages. But two things remain constant. It is still considered a thing. And its nature is defined in terms of its relation to the earth. The development is largely due to the efforts of ancient phi-

losophers (particularly Plato and Aristotle) and astronomers, especially an Egyptian astronomer of the second century C.E. named Ptolemy. How do they modify this primitive view?

For one thing, the earth is recognized to be roughly a sphere. So the heavens can't be completely analogous to the roof of a house or a tent. They, in fact, are spherical, too. The basic picture is of two spheres, the smaller one solid and stationary directly in the center of a much larger sphere, which is hollow and moving. The sphere in the center is, of course, the earth. And the outer sphere, composed of aether, a crystalline, weightless solid, is that of the stars, which revolve around the inner sphere once each day.

Astronomical observations complicate this picture considerably. Neither the sun nor the moon fit neatly into such a scheme, and they are given spheres of their own. Even more recalcitrant to neatness are those "wanderers" in the heavens, the planets. They seem to move in more complicated patterns, both speed and direction varying at irregular times. Much astronomical ingenuity had been devoted to the mathematical description of their paths; postulations of circles revolving around centers that are themselves revolving on circles are used to solve these problems. But the basic pattern is the same: each planet is assigned an aetherial sphere. Saturn occupies the sphere just below that of the fixed stars, and the moon occupies that nearest to the earth, with the sun and the other planets arranged between.

This universe is said to be finite. Aristotle holds that outside the outer sphere there is literally nothing—no matter, no space, not even a void.* For medieval Christians, however, there is something

---

*Aristotle did not accept the atomists' conception of a void, i.e., a space in which nothing exists. His reasoning depends on the notion of potentiality. Wherever there is space, there is potentially some substance. But potentiality is just the possibility of having some form; and what is formed into a substance is matter. So wherever there is space there is matter; matter never exists unformed; and the idea of empty space is a contradiction in terms. There could not be other worlds out in space beyond this world; this world is not just the only world there *is*, but the only world there *could be*.

beyond the sphere of the stars. It is often called simply Heaven, but sometimes also the Empyrean, the place of perfect fire or light; it is the dwelling place of God and the destination of saved souls. (Note that heaven, on this view, has a physical location.)

In this universe everything has its natural place. The earth is the center toward which heavy objects naturally fall. The heavy elements, earth and water, find their natural place as near this center as they can. Between the earth and the sphere of the moon is the natural home for the lighter elements, air and fire. But these four elements are continually being mixed up with one another and suffer constant change.*

This change is explained by the motions of the heavens. Aristotle supplies a mechanism to explain such change. The outermost celestial sphere rotates at great speed, as it must to return to the same position in only twenty-four hours. (Compare the speed at the inside of a merry-go-round with that at its edge.) This motion drags the sphere of Saturn (just inside it) along by friction; and this process is repeated all the way to the spheres of the sun and moon. These then produce changes in the air and on the earth below them: the tides, the winds, and the seasons, for example, and the generation of plants and animals. Why, we may wonder, does the sphere of the stars move, though? Dante, whose *Divine Comedy* is a perfect expression of this view of the world, offers an Aristotelian explanation.

> However, beyond all these [crystalline spheres], the Catholics place the Empyrean Heaven . . . ; and they hold it to be immovable, because it has within itself, in every part, that which its matter demands. And this is the reason that the *Primum Mobile* [or ninth sphere] moves with immense velocity; because the fervent longing of all its parts to be united with those of this most quiet heaven, makes it revolve with so much desire that its velocity is almost incomprehensible.[2]

The celestial spheres are quite different from anything on earth. Here on earth all is subject to change, generation, and decay. But the spheres in which the heavenly bodies are located revolve in immutable splendor. Only one conclusion can be drawn: terrestrial and celestial substances are made of different material and governed by different laws. Spiritual beings—angels, for instance, whom St. Thomas holds to be pure forms without matter—have their natural home in these more perfect regions.

The obvious fact that the heavens, particularly the sun, influence what happens here on earth means that what we today distinguish as astronomy and astrology are considered one science. Signs in the heavens—comets and eclipses, for instance—are considered omens that need interpretation. And the question of what they mean is scarcely distinguishable from the question of what the spiritual beings that dwell in those regions mean to convey by means of them. Virtually every astronomer is also an astrologer; as late as the seventeenth century, Kepler, recognized to possess unusually accurate astronomical data, is consulted for horoscopes. Reference to astrological phenomena is common in the work of Dante and Chaucer. Everything in the heavens is significant, since it all exists for the sake of man.

Here we come to the heart of the medieval world view. The earth is not only physically at the center of the universe; it is also the religious center. For on this stationary globe lives the human race, made in the image of God himself, the summit of his creative work. Around human beings everything revolves, both literally and symbolically. The earth is the stage whereon is enacted the great drama of salvation and damnation. It is on the earth that men fall from grace. It is to the earth that God's Son comes to redeem fallen men and women, graciously to save them from their sins and lead them to that heavenly realm in which they can forever enjoy blessedness in the presence of light eternal.

Nothing expresses this drama in its intimate connection with the medieval picture of the world better than Dante's great poem. The journey on which he is led, first by Virgil and later by Beatrice, traverses the known universe. As we follow that journey we learn both physical and religious

---

*See the pre-Socratic speculations about the vortex, p. 10.

truths, inextricably linked. Let us trace the outline of that journey.

Dante begins his great poem by telling us that he had lost his way and could not find it again.

> Midway life's journey I was made aware
>   That I had strayed into a dark forest,
>   And the right path appeared not anywhere.
> Ah, tongue cannot describe how it oppressed,
> This wood, so harsh, dismal and wild, that fear
> At thought of it strikes now into my breast.
>
> (INFERNO 1.1–6)[3]

The pagan poet Virgil appears and offers to lead him down through hell and up through purgatory as far as the gates of heaven. There he will be supplanted by another guide, as Virgil is not allowed into paradise. A vision of these moral and religious realities, embedded as they are in the very nature of things, should resolve Dante's crisis and show him the way again. It may also serve as a guide to the blessed life for all of us who read the poem.

The poem is a long and complex allegory, and it is possible to read it with an eye only to the values it expresses. But there is little doubt that Dante means its cosmology to be taken with equal seriousness, at least in its basic outlines. The point we need to see is that the cosmos, as envisaged by late medieval thinkers, is not an indifferent and value-less place; every detail speaks of its creator, and the "right path" is inscribed in the very structure of things.*

We can do no more than briefly indicate that structure. There are three books in the poem, *Inferno, Purgatorio,* and *Paradiso.* In each a portion of the physical and moral/religious universe is explored. The first thing to note is that to get to hell (the inferno), one goes *down*—deep into the earth. Hell is a complex place of many layers; as one descends, the sins of its occupants become more serious, the punishments more awful, and the conditions more revolting. After an antechamber in which the indifferent reside (offensive both to God

and to Satan), Dante and Virgil cross the river Acheron and find hell set up as a series of circles, descending ever deeper into the earth. The first circle is Limbo, in which are found the virtuous pagans, including Homer and Aristotle; this is Virgil's own home. Here there is no overt punishment; only the lack of hope for blessedness.

After this there are the circles containing, in an order of increasing evil:

These last are frozen up to their necks in ice at the very center of the earth, guarded over by Satan—the arch traitor—in whose three mouths are the mangled bodies of Judas, Brutus, and Cassius.

Virgil and Dante climb down past Satan and climb up again through a passage in the earth until they come out on the opposite side from which they began. There they find themselves on a shore, facing a mountain that rises to the sky. This is the mountain of Purgatory, where those who will ultimately be saved are purified of their remaining faults. Here there are seven levels (corresponding to the "seven deadly sins"), each populated by persons whose loves are not yet rightly ordered.*

---

*Dante's *Divine Comedy* was written in the first decades of the fourteenth century.

*For the concept of a proper ordering of one's loves, see Augustine, p. 231.

These have repented and will be saved, but they still love earthly things too much, or not enough, or in the wrong way. From the lower levels to the higher, the unpurged sins are ranked from more to less serious, those highest on the mountain being furthest from hell and closest to heaven. Let us list them in that "geographical" order, so that we can imagine Virgil and Dante mounting from the bottom of the list to the top:

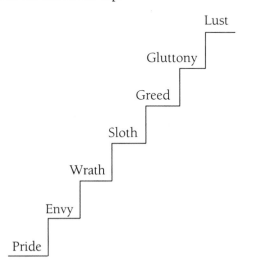

Those who dwell at each level are purging their predominant passion by suffering penances of an appropriate kind. The proud, for example, are bowed down by carrying heavy stones, so that they can neither look arrogantly about nor look down on their fellows. It is worth noting that the "spiritual" sins of pride, envy, and anger are judged to be more serious (farther from heaven) than the "fleshly" sins of gluttony and lust; this ranking roughly corresponds to the evaluations of church fathers such as Augustine, for whom pride is the root of all sin.*

At the top of the purgatorial mountain Virgil disappears, and Beatrice, who represents Christian love, takes his place. She transports Dante through the sphere of fire above the earth to the lowest celestial sphere, that of the moon. She answers Dante's question about why the moon seems to

---

*For Augustine on pride, see pp. 233–234.

have shadows on it and in the process gives a fine description of the celestial realm, which looks roughly like this:

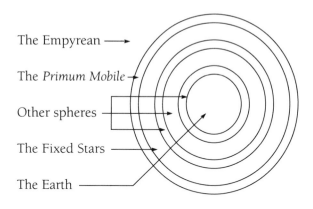

You can see that it conforms nicely to the Aristotelian/Ptolemic astronomical view we sketched earlier. Motion (energy) is imparted from outside toward the center, each of the spheres displaying in its own magnificent way the glory of God. This vision of the heavens as the visible image of the creator is summed up in the first canto of *Paradiso*.

> The glory of Him who moveth all that is
>   Pervades the universe, and glows more bright
>   In the one region, and in another less. . . .
>
> "All things, whatever their abode, [*Beatrice says*]
>   Have order among themselves; this Form it is
>   That makes the universe like unto God.
> Here the high beings see the imprint of His
>   Eternal power, which is the goal divine
>   Whereto the rule, aforesaid testifies.
> In the order I speak of, all natures incline
>   Either more near or less near to their source
>   According as their diverse lots assign.
> To diverse harbors thus they move perforce
>   O'er the great ocean of being, and each one
>   With instinct given it to maintain its course."
>
> (PARADISO 1.1–3, 103–14)

The spheres of paradise which Beatrice leads Dante through correspond to the various virtues, though Dante is careful to say that the appearance of the souls of the virtuous in each sphere is not to be taken literally. One and all, blessed souls inhabit the Empyrean realm with God himself.

The key notions in Dante's vision of the universe are order, harmony, justice, and, finally, love. The poem ends with Dante trying to describe, inadequately he admits, the vision of God. This vision is both intelligible and emotional. Its object both explains the universe and draws Dante's soul towards itself. In the end imagination fails to communicate the glory.

> But like to a wheel whose circling nothing jars
> Already on my desire and will prevailed
> The Love that moves the sun and the other stars.

(PARADISO 33.143–45)

Such is the world for late medieval man: harmonious, ordered, finite, displaying the glories of its creator. Physics, astronomy, and theology are one in a marvelous integration of life and knowledge. Everything in the universe embodies a goal and purpose set within it by the divine love, which governs all. To understand it is to understand this purpose, to gain guidance for life, and to see that absolutely everything depends on and leads to God.

The Humanists

One of the influences on that magnificent flowering of arts and letters we call the Renaissance is the rediscovery of classical poetry, histories, essays, and other writings, which followed by a century or two the recovery of Aristotelian philosophy. These Greek and Roman works breathe a spirit quite different from the extreme otherworldliness expressed in the self-denial of monk's vows, on the one hand, and from the arid disputations of scholastic theologians on the other. They present a model of style, both in language and life, that seems worthy of emulation. And a rather diffuse movement called "humanism" spreads gradually northward from Italy.

Some of the humanists are churchmen, but many are not. They belong to that aristocratic stratum of society which has leisure to cultivate the arts, paint, compose, or write. They are not, on the whole, antagonistic to the Church; nor do most of them pit the old pagan classical works against Christianity. On the contrary, they tend to see a profound harmony between Christianity and the classics. In this they are, of course, following in the steps of Augustine and Aquinas.* But there is a difference. These earlier theologians hold that pagan philosophy can be a servant to Christian understanding—but never its equal. Many humanists, however, tend to equate faith with virtue and move toward a kind of universalism: the virtuous sage is blessed, whether he knows of (or accepts) Christ as savior or not.

In a dialogue called "The Godly Feast," printed in 1522, Erasmus (the "prince of humanists") has one of the characters say,

> . . . whatever is devout and contributes to good morals should not be called profane. Sacred Scripture is of course the basic authority in everything; yet I sometimes run across ancient sayings or pagan writings—even the poets—so purely and reverently and admirably expressed that I can't help believing their authors' hearts were moved by some divine power. And perhaps the spirit of Christ is more widespread than we understand, and the company of saints includes many not in our calendar.[4]

One of his partners in the conversation, on being reminded of Socrates' attitude at his death, exclaims,†

> An admirable spirit, surely, in one who had not known Christ and the Sacred Scriptures. And so, when I read such things of such men, I can hardly help exclaiming, "Saint Socrates, pray for us!"[5]

In another dialogue, "The Epicurean," Erasmus argues that those who spend their lives pursuing fine food, sex, wealth, fame, and power in a quest

---

*To see how Augustine used Platonic philosophy in the service of the faith, see pp. 220–221. Aquinas did much the same for Aristotle.

†Contrast this with Dante's vision 200 years earlier, in which virtuous pagans are consigned—at best—to Limbo. See *Inferno*, Canto IV. For the last moments of Socrates' life, see *Phaedo*.

for pleasure actually miss the greatest pleasures: those of righteousness, moderation, an active mind, and a calm conscience. It is Epicurus, of course, who holds that pleasure is the one true good.* It follows that the *successful* Epicurean—the one who gets the most pleasure out of life—will live righteously and moderately, preferring the approval of God to the satisfaction of his bodily appetites. But these are precisely the virtues cultivated by the Christian!

> . . . if people who live agreeably are Epicureans, none are more truly Epicurean than the righteous and godly. And if it's names that bother us, no one better deserves the name of Epicurean than the revered founder and head of the Christian philosophy [Christ], for in Greek *epikouros* means "helper." He alone, when the law of Nature was all but blotted out by sins, when the law of Moses incited to lusts rather than cured them, when Satan ruled in the world unchallenged, brought timely aid to perishing humanity. Completely mistaken, therefore, are those who talk in their foolish fashion about Christ's having been sad and gloomy in character and calling upon us to follow a dismal mode of life. On the contrary, he alone shows the most enjoyable life of all and the one most full of true pleasure.[6]

This gives us an insight into why these thinkers are called humanists.[†] Their concern is the development of a full and rich human life—the best life for a human being to live. Their quest is stimulated by the works of classical antiquity, which they read, edit, translate, and imitate with eagerness. They live, of course, in a culture dominated by Christianity and express that quest in basically Christian terms. But their interests focus on the human. To that end they recommend and propagandize for what they call "humane studies": an education centering on the Greek and Latin clas-sics, on languages, grammar, and rhetoric. They are convinced that "the classics represent the highest level of human development."[7]

The ideal is a person who can embody all the excellences a human being is capable of: music, art, poetry, science, soldiery, courtesy, virtue, and piety. This renewed passion for human excellence is expressed in the art of Bellini, Titian, Tintoretto, Raphael, Holbein, Dürer, and Michelangelo. In these Renaissance painters and sculptors one finds the ideal human form, often in an idealized natural setting–whether the subject is the Christian Madonna and child or Greek gods and heroes. And sometimes classical and Biblical themes are found in the same painting.* The man who embodies this Renaissance ideal most completely is perhaps Leonardo da Vinci. His many accomplishments show what humans are capable of. He represents what humanists admired and worked for: a celebration of man as the central fact in all the created world.

In the 1480s, a twenty-four-year-old Italian wrote a preface to nine hundred theses that he submitted for public debate. As it turned out, the debate was never held, but the *Oration on the Dignity of Man* by Giovanni Pico della Mirandola has seldom been equalled as a rhetorical tribute to the glory of being human. We could say it is the apotheosis of humanism. Pico finds the unique dignity of man in the fact that human beings alone have no "archetype" they are predetermined to exemplify. Everything else has a determinate nature; it is man's privilege to be able to *choose* his own nature. He imagines God creating the world. All is complete, from the Intelligences above the heavens to the lowest reaches of earth.

> But, when the work was finished, the Craftsman kept wishing that there were someone to ponder the plan of so great a work, to love its beauty, and to wonder at its vastness. Therefore, when everything was done . . . , He finally took thought concerning the creation of man. But there was not among His

---

*See p. 187.

†Note that Erasmus here follows the lead of much Greek thought, from Homer to Epicurus. Pursuit of virtue is recommended on ground of *self-interest*. Why be moral? Because you will be happier that way. See the following pages: for Plato, pp. 131–132; for Aristotle, pp. 180–181; for Epicurus, pp. 184–189.

*We already find this unification in Dante; but there the classical is still severely subordinated to the Christian.

archetypes that from which He could fashion a new offspring, nor was there in His treasurehouses anything which He might bestow on His new son as an inheritance, nor was there in the seats of all the world a place where the latter might sit to contemplate the universe. All was now complete. . . .

At last the best of artisans ordained that that creature to whom He had been able to give nothing proper to himself should have joint possession of whatever had been peculiar to each of the different kinds of being. He therefore took man as a creature of indeterminate nature and, assigning him a place in the middle of the world, addressed him thus: "Neither a fixed abode nor a form that is thine alone nor any function peculiar to thyself have we given thee, Adam, to the end that according to thy longing and according to thy judgment thou mayest have and possess what abode, what form and what functions thou thyself shalt desire. The nature of all other beings is limited and constrained within the bounds of laws prescribed by Us. Thou, constrained by no limits, in accordance with thine own free will, in whose hand We have placed thee, shalt ordain for thyself the limits of thy nature. We have set thee at the world's center that thou mayest from thence more easily observe whatever is in the world. We have made thee neither of heaven nor of earth, neither mortal nor immortal, so that with freedom of choice and with honor, as though the maker and molder of thyself, thou mayest fashion thyself in whatever shape thou shalt prefer. Thou shalt have the power to degenerate into the lower forms of life, which are brutish. Thou shalt have the power, out of thy soul's judgment, to be reborn into the higher forms, which are divine."

O supreme generosity of God the Father, O highest and most marvelous felicity of man! To him it is granted to have whatever he chooses, to be whatever he wills.[8]

Man as "maker and molder" of himself, able "to have whatever he chooses, to be whatever he wills." What a concept! Pico exclaims, "Who would not admire this our chameleon?"[9] With such possibilities open to him, it is no wonder that human beings should develop in so many different ways. Along with the theme of an essential unity that runs through mankind, the diversity of individuals comes to be valued more and more. Individualism, the idea that there is value to sheer uniqueness, begins to counter the uniformity of Christian schemes of salvation. Portrait painters strive to capture the unique character of each one of their subjects. And variety and invention in music and literature are praised.

Finally, the humanists recapture some of the confidence that had characterized Athenians of the Golden Age. Man's failings are more apt to be caricatured as foolishness (as Erasmus satirically did in *Praise of Folly*) than to be condemned as sins. And this reveals a quite different attitude and spirit. Though they do not deny sin and God's grace, they tend to focus on the capability of man to achieve great things. As often happens in such cases, they thereby help to make great things happen.

Reforming the Church

The world view Dante expresses in his great poem was institutionalized in the Church. The Church was the keeper and protector of Christian truths and the harbor of salvation for those at sea in sin. But the institutional Church had strayed far from the precepts of humility and love enjoined by Jesus. It had become a means of securing worldly prestige, power, and wealth for those who were clever and ruthless enough to bend it to their will.

The Church in the West was dominated by the papacy in Rome, whose occupants had, through the centuries, succeeded in bringing under their control a great variety of incomes, privileges, and powers. Popes were engaged continually in political intrigues to establish and extend their power. More than one pope during this period exceeded in influence, wealth, and power any secular prince, king, or emperor. His court was more splendid, his staff more extensive, and his will more feared than theirs. For a king could, if need be, torture and kill the body; but the pope had the power to cast the soul into Hell. If displeased with a monarch, the pope could put an entire land under the "interdict," which meant that no masses and no sacraments could be celebrated there—a dire threat indeed for those who depended on them for their eternal salvation.

No one doubts—and few doubted even then—that the Church had grown corrupt. Already in the fourteenth century Dante had set several popes, bishops, friars, and priests in the Inferno. There had been numerous attempts at reform. The establishment of new monastic orders by St. Francis and St. Dominic had been motivated by a desire to recapture the purity of Christian life by renouncing wealth and power. Unfortunately, their very success ensured the acquisition of wealth and power, with all the inevitable outcomes. Heretical groups, such as the Albigenses in southern France, mixed moral rigor with unacceptable theologies. (The Albigenses were exterminated after a twenty-year "crusade" called for by Pope Innocent III.)

The notorious Inquisition was established in 1231 under Pope Gregory IX, and heresy hunting gained official sanction. Heresy was considered "the greatest of all sins because it was an affront to the greatest of all persons, God; worse than treason against a king because it was directed against the heavenly sovereign; worse than counterfeiting money because it counterfeited the truth of salvation; worse than patricide and matricide, which destroy only the body." If a heretic recanted under torture, he "might be granted the mercy of being strangled before being burned at the stake."[10]

From a philosophical point of view, we should note that the institution known as the Inquisition rests on several presuppositions: (1) that truth about God and man not only can be known, but is clearly identifiable and available to all; (2) that it is the Church who is the custodian of this truth; and (3) that whether one affirms these truths or not *matters terribly*. Perhaps even these assumptions do not suffice to justify such extreme measures; but it is clear both that these were actually in the background and that nothing less than these will do. These assumptions are the heritage of that blend of Judeo-Christian prophetism and classical Greek philosophy worked out first by Augustine using the Platonic tradition and later by Thomas Aquinas

using the Aristotelian. A further (but not irrelevant) question is to what extent the Inquisition was simply a technique used by those in power for consolidating their power and suppressing dissent.

Unless they could be assimilated into the structure of the Church, as the monastic orders were, reformers were harshly dealt with. The followers of John Wycliffe in England (the Lollards) were sent to the stake in 1401. Jan (John) Hus of Bohemia was burned in 1415. Savanarola of Florence was hanged and then burned in 1498. Meanwhile the Church, clutching its pomp and privileges, went from corruption to corruption. Here are a few examples. Pope Alexander VI had four illegitimate children (including Cesare and Lucrezia Borgia), though clerical celibacy was the rule. Pope Julius II led his own troops in armor to regain certain papal territories. And Leo X, made a Cardinal through family influence at the age of 13, is said to have exclaimed after his election as pope, "The papacy is ours. Let us enjoy it."[11]

Albert of Brandenburg, already bishop of two districts, aspired to be also Archbishop of Mainz, which would make him the top churchman in Germany. The price demanded by the Pope was high—ten thousand ducats. Since his parishes could not supply that fee, he paid it himself, borrowing the money at twenty percent interest from the banking house of Fugger. It was agreed that "indulgences" (we'll hear more about these later) would be sold in his territories; half of the income he could use to repay the loan and half would go to Rome to help build St. Peter's Cathedral.

Such examples, which could be multiplied indefinitely, called forth a steady stream of critical responses. In the eyes of many, they discredited the claim of the Church to be the repository of truth about God and man. But it was not until the protests of Martin Luther (1483–1546) that the situation was ripe for such moral objections to make a real difference. Luther's appeal for reform coincided with a new assertion of the rights of nations against domination by the church. Princes heard not only the cry for religious reform but also an opportunity to stop wealth and power from flowing interminably to Rome.

It was religious reform that Luther was interested in. But he could address the German nobility in terms that encouraged them to think of papal taxes, fees, and benefits as exploitation of the German people. For example:

> . . . it is painful and shocking to see that the head of Christendom, proclaiming himself the Vicar of Christ and the successor of St. Peter, lives in such a worldly and ostentatious style that no king or emperor can reach and rival him. He claims the titles of "Most Holy" and "Most Spiritual," but there is more worldliness in him than in the world itself. He wears a triple crown, whereas the mightiest kings wear only one. If that is like the lowly Christ or St. Peter, it is to me a new sort of likeness.

> What Christian purpose is served by the ecclesiastics called cardinals? I will tell you. In Italy and Germany there are many wealthy monasteries, institutions, benefices, and parishes. No better way has been devised of bringing them into Rome's possession than by creating cardinals and giving them bishoprics, monasteries, and prelacies as their property. . . . The consequence is that Italy is now almost devastated; monasteries are in disorder, bishoprics despoiled, the revenues of prelacies and all the churches drawn to Rome, cities devastated, land and people ruined, because no longer are services held or sermons preached. Why so? Because the cardinals must have their revenues. . . . Now that Italy is drained dry, they are coming into the German countries . . .

> If ninety-nine per cent of the papal court were abolished and only one per cent were left, it would still be large enough to deal with questions of Christian faith. At present there is a crawling mass of reptiles, all claiming to pay allegiance to the pope, but Babylon never saw the like of these miscreants. The pope has more than 3,000 secretaries alone, and no one can count the others he employs, as the posts are so numerous. It is hardly possible to number all those that lie in wait for the institutions and benefices of Germany, like wolves for the sheep. . . . It is not at all astonishing if princes, aristocracy, towns, institutions, country, and people grow poor. We ought to marvel that we still have anything left to eat.[12]

This is strong stuff, and it had its effect. But it is a *consequence* of Luther's views and not the heart of them. We need to understand the religious center from which such protests arose.

Luther was a monk troubled about his sins and in mortal terror of God's justice. His sins did not in fact seem so terrible in the eyes of the world, for he was a monk of a most sincere and strict kind. But he had early seen the point that God looks not to externals, but to motivations; and he could not be sure that his motives were pure.* No matter how much he confessed, he was never confident that he had searched out every tinge of selfishness, greed, lust, and pride. And these sins the righteous God would judge. Luther did penances of a rigorous sort, going as far as to scourge himself. But he could never be sure: had he done enough to make himself worthy of salvation? He suffered agonies of doubt and self-accusation.

> Though I lived as a monk without reproach, I felt that I was a sinner before God with an extremely disturbed conscience. I could not believe that he was placated by my satisfaction. I did not love, yes, I hated the righteous God who punishes sinners, and secretly, if not blasphemously, certainly murmuring greatly, I was angry with God.[13]

He was assigned by his superior to study the Bible and become a professor of theology. As he wrestled with the text of the Psalms and the letters of St. Paul, it gradually dawned on him that his anxieties about sin were misplaced. He was, to be sure, a sinner. But the righteous God, whom Luther had so much feared, had sent Jesus, his Son, the Christ, precisely to win forgiveness for such sinners. This was an undeserved gift of grace and needed only to be believed to be effective. Even though one was not just in oneself, God "justified" the unjust by means of the cross and resurrection of Christ, who had taken upon himself the sins of the world. Salvation did not have to be *earned*! It was a *gift*!

> . . . I began to understand that the righteousness of God is that by which the righteous lives by a gift of

---

*See the discussion of Jesus on pp. 206–208, and the similar point made by Augustine on pp. 231–232 and 238. It is perhaps significant that Luther was a monk of the Augustinian order.

God, namely by faith. And this is the meaning: the righteousness of God is revealed by the gospel, namely, the passive righteousness with which merciful God justifies us by faith, as it is written, "He who through faith is righteous shall live." Here I felt that I was altogether born again and had entered paradise itself through open gates. . . .

Thus that place in Paul was for me truly the gate to paradise. Later I read Augustine's *The Spirit and the Letter*, where contrary to hope I found that he, too, interpreted God's righteousness in a similar way, as the righteousness with which God clothes us when he justifies us.[14]

With this insight, the Reformation was born. The power of this idea was first demonstrated in relation to the indulgences being sold under the authority of the pope and Archbishop Albert of Mainz. An indulgence was a piece of paper assuring the purchaser of the remission of certain penalties—perhaps in this life, perhaps in purgatory, and perhaps escape from hell itself. The practice of promising such spiritual benefits in return for worldly goods can be traced back to the Crusades. Popes offered heavenly blessings in return for military service in the Holy Land against the Turks. But for those who could not serve or were reluctant to go, a payment in cash to support the effort was accepted instead. This practice had proved so lucrative that, as we have seen, it was extended for other purposes—including the repayment of loans for the purchase of an archbishopric.

The set of indulgences sponsored by Albert were peddled in 1517 by a Dominican monk named Tetzel, who advertised his wares with a jingle:

As soon as the coin in the coffer rings,
The soul from purgatory springs.[15]

Although prohibited in Wittenberg, where Luther was both parish priest and teacher of theology, indulgences were sold near enough that his parishioners traveled to buy them. They came back boasting that they could now do what they liked, for they were guaranteed heaven. Luther was troubled. Was this Christianity—to buy salvation for a few gold coins? Didn't this make a mockery of re-

pentance and the attempt to reform one's life? Indeed, didn't it make a mockery of God's grace, which was sold for worldly gain like any other commodity? On the eve of All Saints' Day, 1517, Luther posted ninety-five theses to the door of the Castle Church. He had drafted them quickly and meant them only to form the substance of a scholarly debate among theologians. But they caused a sensation, escaped his control, and were published and disseminated widely. Among the theses were these:

27. There is no divine authority for preaching that the soul flies out of purgatory immediately the money clinks in the bottom of the chest.

36. Any Christian whatsoever, who is truly repentant enjoys plenary remission from penalty and guilt, and this is given him without letters of indulgence.

43. Christians should be taught that one who gives to the poor, or lends to the needy, does a better action than if he purchases indulgences.

44. Because, by works of love, love grows and a man becomes a better man; whereas, by indulgences, he does not become a better man, but only escapes certain penalties.[16]

Let us think about Thesis 27 for a moment. Here Luther says there is no "divine authority" for Tetzel's rhyme. What does he mean by this? There clearly was ecclesiastical authority for it, at least in the sense that the selling of the indulgences was sponsored by an archbishop and the pope. But for Luther, who had spent five years trying to understand the Bible and who knew well the works of the early church fathers, particularly Augustine, this does not settle the matter at all. It didn't take a great deal of historical knowledge to discover that popes and councils of the Church had disagreed with one another and were often flatly in disagreement with the words of Scripture. So the fact that the practice was backed by the highest Church authority is just that for Luther—a fact. It does not make the practice *right*. Only a *divine* authority can determine that.*

---

*Compare the speech in which Antigone defends her action defying the king's command, p. 44.

What, then, does Luther mean by "divine authority"? Above all, he means the words and deeds of Christ. But secondarily, he means the testimony of the apostles who had known Jesus or of those (like Paul) to whom Christ had specially revealed himself. So Luther appeals to the Bible, that collection of the earliest records we have of the life and impact of Jesus. This was Luther's authority, against which the words of archbishops and popes alike had to be measured.

It is precisely here that his conflict with the established Church is sharpest. In a certain sense, the Church does not deny that Scripture is the ultimate authority; however, Scripture needs to be interpreted. And the proper interpretation of Scripture, according to the Church, is that given by the Church itself in the *tradition* that reaches back in a long, unbroken historical sequence to the apostles. Ultimately the authority to interpret Scripture resides in the pope, the successor of the apostle Peter, of whom Jesus had said, "You are Peter, and on this rock I will build my church" (Matt. 16:18).

In an interview with Cardinal Cajetan (during the tumult over indulgences) the cardinal reminded Luther of these points. Luther was unmoved. "'His Holiness abuses Scripture,' retorted Luther. 'I deny that he is above Scripture.' The cardinal flared up and bellowed that Luther should leave and never come back unless he was ready to say, 'Revoco'—'I recant.'"[17]

In a great debate at Leipzig in 1519, Luther went as far as to say,

A simple layman armed with Scripture is to be believed above a pope or a council without it.

His opponent in the debate replied,

When Brother Luther says that this is the true meaning of the text, the pope and councils say, "No, the brother has not understood it correctly." Then I will take the council and let the brother go. Otherwise all the heresies will be renewed. They have all appealed to Scripture and have believed their interpretation to be correct, and have claimed that the popes and the councils were mistaken, as Luther now does.[18]

This exchange gives the tenor of the arguments that continued for about four years while the Church was trying to decide what to do about the rebel. Luther appeals to the Scriptures against the Pope and the ecclesiastical establishment. They in turn point out the damaging consequences—heresy and the destruction of the unity of Christendom—if Luther is allowed to be right.

Meanwhile Luther was seeing more and more clearly the implications of his fundamental discovery that we are saved by God's grace alone, through faith in Christ's passion, death, and resurrection—implications that are thoroughly subversive of the institutional claims of the Church. Let us briefly list a few of the claims Luther was led to make.

1. Those in religious orders are not thereby superior to ordinary people.
2. Farmers and housewives can be as pleasing to God in their work as is a priest.
3. Each individual can approach God directly and does not need a priest or bishop as an intermediary.
4. The priesthood is simply an office established for the sake of good order.
5. There is no Scriptural justification for seven sacraments; these are inventions designed to bring Christian believers into bondage to the ecclesiastical hierarchy.
6. There is no Scriptural justification for enforcing celibacy on the clergy.
7. Since he is saved by the grace of God in Christ, a Christian has no need to do good works, to purchase indulgences, or to go on pilgrimages to earn his salvation.
8. A Christian will, however, do good works—the works of love and charity—out of gratitude to God who has saved him when he did not deserve it.

At last Luther was granted a hearing at a meeting of the leaders of the German nation in Worms. In response to a final demand that he recant his works, he declared,

Unless I am convicted by Scripture and plain reason—I do not accept the authority of popes and councils, for they have contradicted each other—my conscience is captive to the Word of God. I cannot and I will not recant anything, for to go against conscience is neither right nor safe. God help me. Amen.[19]

We should note that there are two separate claims that Luther makes here, though he does not separate them. One is that "Scripture and plain reason" are the grounds for belief. It is not right for authorities simply to *demand* conformity. That conformity must be justified; it must be shown to be legitimate by appeal to these grounds.

The second claim is that it is "neither right nor safe" to go against conscience. Luther does not clearly distinguish these because *his* conscience is in fact "captive to the Word of God," and he cannot imagine that any conscience could be legitimate unless it were bound to that source. But it is a separable claim. The attractiveness of this appeal to conscience explains in part the tremendous influence of the Reformation. It seems to many a clarion call to individualism and resistance to authority of all sorts—to follow one's own conscience, whatever it says. The reformers are in this way (like the humanists, with whom they lived in an uneasy love-hate relationship) a great influence in the emancipation of individual opinions from domination by great institutions—whether religious or secular.

In 1521 Luther was formally excommunicated from the Church, and the split between "Protestants" and "Roman Catholics" became official. There is much more to this story, but we have enough before us to draw some lessons relevant to our philosophical conversation.

For more than a thousand years there had been a basic agreement in the West about how to settle questions of truth. Some questions could be settled by reason and experience; the great authority on these matters for the past few centuries had been Aristotle, whom Aquinas had called simply "the Philosopher." But above these questions were others—the key questions about God and the soul and the meaning of life—which were answered by *authority*, not reason. And the authority had been that of the Church, as embedded in the decision-making powers of its clergy, focused ultimately in the papacy.

When Luther challenges this authority, he attacks the very root of a whole culture. It is no wonder that there is so much opposition. His appeal to the authority of Scripture sets up a standard for settling those higher questions that is different from the accepted one. And we can now see that the crisis Luther precipitates is a form of the old skeptical *problem of the criterion*, one of the deepest and most radical problems in our intellectual life.* By what criterion or standard are we going to tell when we know the truth? If a criterion is proposed, how do we know that it is the right one? Is there a criterion for choosing the criterion?

In the religious disputes of the following century, each side busies itself in demolishing the claims of the other side. Protestants show that if we accept the Catholic criterion, we can be sure of nothing, because—as Luther points out—popes and councils disagree with one another. If there are contradictions in the criterion itself, how can we choose which of the contradictory propositions to accept? Moreover, popes had certainly sanctioned abuses contrary to the spirit of the Scriptures; so the claim that the interpretations of the Church constitute the criterion seems more and more hollow.

Catholics, on the other hand, argue that reliance on one's individual conscience after reading Scripture could not produce certainty, for the conscience of one person may not agree with the conscience of another. Indeed, it is not long before the Protestants are as divided among themselves as they are united in opposing the Catholics. Luther's assumption that Scripture speaks unambiguously enough to serve *of itself* as a criterion begins to look rather naive, and the Roman insistence on the need for an authoritative interpreter of Scripture seems to be supported by the chaotic course of events.

---

*For a discussion of the problem about the criterion, see pp. 195–197.

The consequence is that each side appeals to a criterion that is not accepted by the other side; but neither can find a criterion to decide which of these criteria is the correct one!

This quarrel, moreover, is not just an intellectual and religious debate. A long series of savage and bloody quasi-religious wars ensues, in which princes try not only to secure territories, but also to determine the religion of the people residing in them.* Indeed, one outcome of these wars is that southern Germany is to this day overwhelmingly Catholic, whereas northern Germany is largely Protestant.

What the Reformation does, philosophically speaking, is to unsettle the foundations. Though the reformers only intend to call an erring Church back to its true and historical foundations, the consequences are lasting divisiveness, with those on each side certain of their own correctness and of the blindness (or wickedness) of their opponents. This unsettling of the foundations by the reformers is one of the factors that lies behind Descartes' attempt to sink the piles so deep that beliefs built on them could never again be shaken.

But these disputes of the Reformation are not the only source of Descartes' concern. We must consider next the revival of skeptical thought in the sixteenth century.

Skeptical Thoughts Revived

As we have noted, the recovery of ancient scientific and philosophical texts (in particular, the works of Aristotle) was followed by the recovery of Greek and Roman poetry, histories, and essays. Somewhat later still another rediscovery exerted an influence.[20] In 1562 the first Latin edition of a work by Sextus Empiricus was published, and within

seven years all his writings were available.* Sextus calls his views "Pyrrhonism," after one of the earliest Greek skeptics, Pyrrho. In this period of divisiveness and strife between Catholics and Protestants, Pyrrhonism strikes a responsive chord in more than one thinker who considers that an impasse has been reached. But we will focus on just one man, Michel de Montaigne.

Montaigne (1533–1592) was a Frenchman of noble birth who, after spending some years in public service as a magistrate, retired at the age of thirty-eight to think and write. His essays are one of the glories of French literature. We are interested not in his style, however, but in his ideas—ideas that a great many people begin to find attractive in the late sixteenth and early seventeenth centuries.

His point of view comes out most clearly in a remarkable essay called *Apology for Raymond Sebond*. Sebond had been a theologian of the fifteenth century who had exceeded the claims of Augustine, Anselm, and Aquinas by claiming not only that the existence and nature of God could be proved by reason, but also that rational proofs could be given for *all* the distinctive doctrines of Christianity. This is an astonishing claim; if true, it would mean that clear thinking alone would suffice to convince us all (Jews, Muslims, and pagans alike) that we should be Christians. No one had ever gone so far before. And, as you can imagine, Sebond attracted critics like clover attracts bees.

In his youth, Montaigne had translated Sebond's book into French at his father's request. Much later, he set out to defend Sebond's thesis. ("Apology" here means "defense," as it does in the title of Plato's account of Socrates' trial.) It is an unusual defense, however; and Sebond, had be been alive, might well have exclaimed that he needed no enemies with friends like this!

Montaigne's strategy is to assert first that Christianity depends entirely on faith and then to demonstrate extensively that Sebond's "proofs" of Christian beliefs are not in the slightest inferior to reasons offered for any other conclusion whatsoever. He claims that Sebond's arguments will

---

*Here you may be reminded of Socrates' point in *Euthyphro* 7b–d that the gods do not quarrel about length and weight and such matters, but about good and justice. Where there are accepted criteria (rules of measurement, for instance) for settling disputes, wars are unlikely. But where there are apparently irresolvable disagreements, involving appeal to differing standards, might may seem like the only thing that *can* make right.

*For a discussion of the skeptical philosophy of Sextus, see Chapter 12.

be found as solid and as firm as any others of the same type that may be opposed to them. . . .

Some say that his arguments are weak and unfit to prove what he proposes, and undertake to shatter them with ease. These must be shaken up a little more roughly. . . .

Let us see then if man has within his power other reasons more powerful than those of Sebond, or indeed if it is in him to arrive at any certainty by argument and reason (*ARS*, 327–28).[21]

Montaigne, then, is going to "defend" Sebond's claim to prove the doctrines of the faith by showing that his arguments are as good as those of his critics—because *none* of them are any good at all!

The essay is a long and rambling one, but with a method in its madness. It examines every reason that has been given for trusting our conclusions and undermines each with satire and skeptical arguments. Are we capable of knowing the truth because of our superiority to the animals? In example after example, Montaigne causes us to wonder whether we are superior at all. Have our wise men given us insight into the truth? He collects a long list of the different conceptions of God held by the philosophers, and then exclaims:

Now trust to your philosophy . . . when you consider the clatter of so many philosophical brains! (*ARS*, 383).

He adds,

Man is certainly crazy. He could not make a mite, and he makes gods by the dozen (*ARS*, 395).

Can we not at least rely on Aristotle, the "master of those who know"? But why pick out Aristotle as our authority? There are numerous alternatives.

The god of scholastic knowledge is Aristotle. . . . His doctrine serves us as magisterial law, when it is peradventure as false as another (*ARS*, 403).

Still, surely we can depend on our senses to reveal the truth about the world.

That things do not lodge in us in their own form and essence, or make their entry into us by their own power and authority, we see clearly enough. Because, if that were so, we should receive them in the same way: wine would be the same in the mouth of a sick man as in the mouth of a healthy man; he who has chapped or numb fingers would find the same hardness in the wood or iron he handles as does another. . . .

We should remember, whatever we receive into our understanding, that we often receive false things there, and by these same tools that are often contradictory and deceived (*ARS*, 422–24).

But can't we at least depend on science? Haven't scientists discovered the truth about things? Montaigne reminds us that in old times most people thought that the sun moved around the earth, though some thought the earth moved.

And in our day, Copernicus has grounded this doctrine so well that he uses it very systematically for all astronomical deductions. What are we to get out of that, unless we should not bother which of the two is so? And who knows whether a third opinion, a thousand years from now, will not overthrow the preceding two? (*ARS*, 429).

Well, maybe it is difficult or impossible to know the truth about the universe. But surely reason can demonstrate truth about right and wrong?

Truth must have one face, the same and universal. If man knew any rectitude and justice that had body and real existence, he would not tie it down to the condition of this country or that. It would not be from the fancy of the Persians or the Indians that virtue would take its form. . . .

But they are funny when, to give some certainty to the laws, they say that there are some which are firm, perpetual and immutable, which they call natural, which are imprinted on the human race by the condition of their very being. And of those one man says the number is three, one man four, one more, one less: a sign that the mark of them is as doubtful as the rest. . . .

It is credible that there are natural laws, as may be seen in other creatures; but in us they are lost; that fine human reason butts in everywhere, domineering and commanding, muddling and confusing the face of things in accordance with its vanity and inconsistency. . . .*

See how reason provides plausibility to different actions. It is a two-handled pot, that can be grasped by the left or the right (*ARS*, 436–38).

Finally Montaigne gives us a summary of the chief points of skeptical philosophy. Whenever we try to justify some claim of ours, we are involved either in a *circle*, or in an *infinite regress* of reason-giving. In neither case can we reach a satisfactory conclusion.

To judge the appearances we receive of objects, we would need a judicatory instrument; to verify this instrument, we need a demonstration; to verify the demonstration, an instrument: there we are in a circle!

Since the senses cannot decide our dispute, being themselves full of uncertainty, it must be reason that does so. No reason can be established without another reason; there we go retreating back to infinity.

Our conception is not itself applied to foreign objects, but is conceived through the mediation of the senses; and the senses do not comprehend the foreign object, but only their own impressions. And thus the conception and semblance we form is not of the object, but only of the impression and effect made on the sense; which impression and the object are different things. Wherefore whoever judges by appearances, judges by something other than the object.

And as for saying that the impressions of the senses convey to the soul the quality of the foreign objects by resemblance, how can the soul and understanding make sure of this resemblance, having of itself no communication with foreign objects? Just as a man who does not know Socrates, seeing his portrait, cannot say that it resembles him.

Now if anyone should want to judge by appearances anyway, to judge by all appearances is impossible, for they clash with one another by their contradictions and discrepancies, as we see by experience.

Shall some selected appearances rule the others? We shall have to verify this selection by another selection, the second by a third, and thus it will never be finished.*

Finally, there is no existence that is constant, either of our being or of that of objects. And we, and our judgment, and all mortal things go on flowing and rolling unceasingly. Thus nothing certain can be established about one thing by another, both the judging and the judged being in continual change and motion (*ARS* 454–55).

Let us pause to note one point in this juggernaut of an argument. Montaigne remarks that if the senses do not simply record external realities (as Aristotle assumes, using the image of a seal impressing its form on the wax), then our ideas may not correspond at all to those realities.† Even worse, we are never in a position to find out whether they do or not. We may be in the position of having only pictures, without ever being able to compare these pictures to what they are pictures of. Here is that depressing and familiar image of the mind as a prisoner within its own walls, constantly receiving messages but forever unable to determine which of them to trust, and utterly incapable of understanding what is really going on. This image plagues many modern thinkers, not least of all Descartes.

Like all radical skeptics, Montaigne is faced with the question of how to manage the business of living. To live, one must choose, and to choose is to prefer one course as better than another. But this seems to require precisely those beliefs (in both facts and values) that skeptical reflections undermine. Montaigne accepts the solution of Protagoras and Sextus Empiricus before him of simply adapting himself to the prevailing opinions. We see, he says, how reason goes astray—especially when it meddles with divine things. We see how

when it strays however little from the beaten path and deviates or wanders from the way traced and

---

*Note that Montaigne is making essentially the same point as Pico (p. 270). There are no determinate laws for human nature. But whereas Pico takes this to be the *glory* of man, Montaigne draws from it a *despairing* conclusion: the truth is unavailable to us.

---

*Here we have a statement of that problem of the criterion that was identified by Sextus. For a more extensive discussion of it, see pp. 195–197.
†For a discussion of Aristotle's view of sense experience, see p. 152.

trodden by the Church, immediately it is lost, it grows embarrassed and entangled, whirling round and floating in that vast, troubled, and undulating sea of human opinions, unbridled and aimless. As soon as it loses that great common highroad it breaks up and disperses onto a thousand different roads (*ARS*, 387).

> . . . since I am not capable of choosing, I accept other people's choice and stay in the position where God put me. Otherwise I could not keep myself from rolling about incessantly. Thus I have, by the grace of God, kept myself intact, without agitation or disturbance of conscience, in the ancient beliefs of our religion, in the midst of so many sects and divisions that our century has produced (*ARS*, 428).

You can see that skepticism is here being used as a defense of the status quo. Montaigne was born and brought up a Catholic. No one can bring forward reasons for deserting Catholic Christianity that are any better than Raymond Sebond's reasons for supporting Catholic Christianity. Reason supports the Roman view just as strongly as it supports the Protestant view or, indeed, any other view— which is, of course, *not at all*! So to keep from "rolling about incessantly," the sensible course is to stick with the customs in which one has been brought up.* In one of his sharpest aphorisms, Montaigne exclaims:

> The plague of man is the opinion of knowledge. That is why ignorance is so recommended by our religion as a quality suitable to belief and obedience (*ARS*, 360).

It is not knowledge, note well, that Montaigne decries as a plague, but the opinion that one possesses it. If you are reminded of Socrates, it is no coincidence.† He was known to his admirers as "the French Socrates."

---

*Note how different this religiosity is from both that of the Catholic Dante (for whom the "indifferent" are rejected by both God and Satan) and the reformer Luther (for whom commitment and certainty are essential to Christianity). Can it count as being religious at all? What do you think?

†For the claim that Socrates is the wisest of men because he knows that he doesn't know, see Plato's *Apology*, 20e–23b. Socrates, however, is not a Pyrrhonian sceptic; he does not doubt that knowledge is possible; he just confesses that (with some possible few exceptions), he does not possess it.

Such is Montaigne's "defense" of the rational theology of Raymond Sebond. In an age when everyone's conscience seems to demand that those who disagree are either blind or wicked, the view has a certain attractiveness. While despairing and pessimistic in one way, it seems at least to promote tolerance. Someone who is a Catholic in Montaigne's sense is unlikely to have any incentive to burn someone who differs. This is no doubt one, but only one, of the reasons for the spread of Pyrrhonism among intellectuals and even among some of the clergy.

Copernicus to Kepler to Galileo: The Great Triple Play

Renaissance humanism, the Reformation, and the undermining of accepted certainties by the new Pyrrhonists all contribute to a general sense of chaos and lost unity. But there is also a spirit of expectation. Something new is in the air; the tumults and controversies of the time are a testimony to it. The invention of the printing press together with a growing literacy spreads the new ideas. Imagination is enlarged by the discovery of the New World, and a sense of excitement is generated by the voyages around the globe. New wealth flowing into Europe from America and from the new routes to the East stimulates growth and a powerful merchant class. The isolation of Europe is coming to an end, and the reverberations are felt on every side—not least in the sphere of the intellect. The ancient authorities had been wrong about geography. Perhaps they were wrong about other things as well, and better understanding might lie in the future rather than in the past.

But nothing else can compare, in its long-term impact, with the development of the new science. More than all these other factors combined, this changes people's view of themselves, of the world, and of their place in it. Before we examine the philosophy of Descartes, who was himself a contributor to these new views, we need to look briefly at one tremendously significant shift in perspective—one that decisively overturns the entire Medieval world view and undermines forever the authority of its philosophical bulwark, Aristotle. It is traditionally called the Copernican Revolution. Though there were anticipations of it before Copernicus, and the revolution was carried to completion only in the time of Newton, it is the name of Copernicus we honor. For his work is the turning point. The key feature of that work is the displacement of the earth from the center of the universe.

We saw earlier how the centrality of the earth had been embedded in the accepted astronomical and physical theories. A stationary earth, moreover, had intimate links with the entire medieval Christian view of the significance of man, of his origins and destiny, and of God's relation to his creation. If the earth is displaced and becomes just one more planet whirling about in infinite space, we can expect consequences to be profound. And so they are, though the more radical consequences are not immediately perceived.

The earth-centered, multisphere universe had dominated astronomy and cosmology for eighteen hundred years. As developed by Ptolemy, with a complex system of epicycles to account for the "wanderings" of the planets, it was an impressive mathematical achievement, and its accuracy in prediction was not bad. But it never quite worked. And Copernicus (1473–1543) tells us that this fact led him to examine the works of previous astronomers to see whether some other system might improve accuracy. He discovered that certain ancient thinkers had held that the earth moved.

> Taking advantage of this I too began to think of the mobility of the Earth; and though the opinion seemed absurd, yet knowing now that others before me had been granted freedom to imagine such circles as they chose to explain the phenomena of the stars, I considered that I also might easily be allowed to try whether, by assuming some motion of the Earth, sounder explanations than theirs for the revolution of the celestial spheres might so be discovered.[22]

It is important to recognize that the heart of Copernicus' achievement is in the mathematics of his sys-

tem—in the geometry and the calculations that filled most of his 1543 book, *De Revolutionibus*. As he himself puts it, "Mathematics are for mathematicians."[23] He expects fellow astronomers to be the ones to appreciate his results; from non-mathematicians he expects trouble.

We cannot go into the mathematical details. But we should know in general what Copernicus does—and does not do. He does not entirely abolish the Ptolemaic reliance on epicycles centered on circles to account for apparent motion. His computations are scarcely simpler than those of Ptolemy. He retains the notion that all celestial bodies move in circles; indeed, the notion of celestial spheres is no less important for Copernicus than for the tradition. And he accepts the idea that the universe is finite—though considerably larger than had been thought. Even the sun is not set clearly in the center, as most popular accounts of his system state.[24]

But his treatment of the apparently irregular motions of the planets is a breakthrough. The planets appear to move, against the sphere of the fixed stars, slowly eastward. But at times they reverse course and move back westward. This "retrograde" motion remains a real puzzle as long as it is ascribed to the planets themselves. But Copernicus treats it as merely an *apparent* motion, the appearance being caused by the *actual* motion of the observers on an earth that is not itself stationary. And this works; at least, it works as well as the traditional assumptions in accounting for the observed phenomena. Moreover, it is aesthetically pleasing, unlike the inexplicable reversals of earlier theory. Copernicus' view, though not less complex and scarcely more accurate in prediction, allows for a kind of unity and harmony throughout the universe that the renegade planets had previously spoiled. Until the availability of better naked-eye data and the invention of the telescope (about fifty years later) these "harmonies" are what chiefly recommend the Copernican system to his astronomical successors.

At first some of them simply use his mathematics without committing themselves to the truth of this new picture of the universe. Indeed, in a preface to Copernicus' major work, a Lutheran theologian, Osiander, urges this path. Copernicus' calculations are useful, but to give up the traditional picture of the universe would mean an overhaul of basic beliefs and attitudes that most are not ready for. So if one could treat the system merely as a calculating device, without any claims to truth, one could reconcile the best of the new science with the best of ancient traditions.*

Johannes Kepler (1571–1630), however, is not content with this restricted view of the theory. A lifelong Copernican, he supplies the next major advance in the system by taking the sun more and more seriously as the true center. Oddly enough, his predilection for the sun as the center has its roots not so much in observation, or even in mathematics, as in a kind of mystical Neoplatonism, which takes the sun to be "the most excellent" body in the universe.† Its essence, Kepler says

> is nothing else than the purest light, than which there is no greater star; which singly and alone is the producer, conserver, and warmer of all things; it is a fountain of light, rich in fruitful heat, most fair, limpid, and pure to the sight, the source of vision, portrayer of all colours, though himself empty of colour, called king of the planets for his motion, heart of the world for his power, its eye for his beauty, and which alone we should judge worthy of the Most High God, should he be pleased with a material domicile and choose a place in which to dwell with the blessed angels.25

It may be somewhat disconcerting to hear this sort of rhetoric from one we honor as a founder of the modern scientific tradition; but it is neither the first nor the last time that religious or philosophical views function as a source of insights later confirmed by more exact and pedestrian methods.

Part of Kepler's quasi-religious conviction is that the universe is fundamentally mathematical in nature. God is a great mathematician, and his cre-

ation is governed by mathematically simple laws. This view can be traced back through Plato to the Pythagoreans, who hold (rather obscurely) that all things are numbers. In the work of Kepler and his successors, this conviction is to gain an unprecedented confirmation. Mathematics must be devised to fit the phenomena, and the phenomena are given a mathematical description.

Drawing on more accurate data compiled by the great observer of the heavens, Tycho Brahe, Kepler made trial after trial of circular hypotheses, always within the Copernican framework; but none of them exactly fit the data. He tried various other kinds of ovals without success. For the greater part of ten years he worked on the orbit of Mars. At last, he noticed certain regularities suggesting that the path of a planet might be that of an ellipse, with the sun at one of the two foci that define it. And that worked; the data and the mathematical theory fit precisely.

This became the first of Kepler's famous three laws. The second offers an explanation of the varying speeds that must be postulated in the planets' movement around these ellipses: The areas swept out by a line from the sun to the planet are always equal in equal intervals of time. The third law is more complicated, and we need not bother about its details; it concerns the relation of the speeds of planets in different orbits. In fact, Kepler formulated a great many laws; posterity has selected these three as particularly fruitful.

The significance of Kepler's work is that for the first time we are presented with a simple and elegant mathematical account of the heavens that matches the data; and it is sun-centered. For the first time we have a really powerful alternative to the medieval picture of the world. Its ramifications are many, however, and will take time to draw out. Part of this development is the task of Galileo.

Galileo Galilei (1564–1642) was, in 1609, the first to view the heavens through a telescope. The result was a multitude of indirect but persuasive evidences for the Copernican view of the universe. New stars in prodigious numbers were observed. The moon's topography was charted; it resembled the earth remarkably, a fact that cut against the distinction between terrestrial imperfection and celes-

---

*Here is foreshadowed one of the intense debates in current philosophy of science: should we understand terms in explanatory theories in a "realistic" way, or take such terms as mere "instruments" for calculation and prediction?

†In *Republic* 506d–509b, Plato uses the sun as a visible image of the Form of the Good (see pp. 241 ff). And in his later work, *Laws*, he recommends a kind of sun worship as the heart of a state-sponsored religion.

tial perfection. Sun spots were observed; it was not perfect either! And it rotated—it was not immutable! The moons of Jupiter provided an observable model of the solar system itself. The phases of Venus indicated that it moved in a sun-centered orbit.

Encouraged by the successful application of mathematics to celestial bodies, Galileo sets himself to use these same powerful tools for the description and explanation of terrestrial motion. Previous thinkers, influenced by Aristotle, had asked primarily *why* bodies move. Why do objects fall to earth when unsupported? Why does a projectile traverse the course it does? Aristotelian answers were at hand. A body falls because it is seeking its natural place. The significance of this answer can be seen by a thought experiment. Imagine that the earth is where the moon now is and that you let go of a rock some distance above the surface of the earth. What would happen? If Aristotle's answer were correct, the rock would not fall to the earth (where it *now* is) but would travel to the place where the center of the earth *used* to be; it would fly away from the earth.[26]

Place, not space, is primary in an Aristotelian world; place is a qualitative term, each place having its own essential character. The place at the center of the celestial spheres is the place of heavy elements. The concept of space, by contrast, which plays such a crucial role in the new science, is the concept of an infinitely extended neutral container with a purely mathematical description.

Note also that this Aristotelian explanation in terms of *final causes* gives no answer at all as to *how* an object falls; no specification of laws that describe its speed and trajectory is given.* But this is just what Galileo supplies in terms of a mathematical theory of motion. It is a theory that applies to *all* motion, terrestrial and celestial alike. For him, as for his two predecessors, the great book of nature is written in mathematical language. And we, by using that language, can understand it.

Let us set down some of the consequences of the new science. First, our sense of the size of the universe changes. Eventually it will be thought to be infinitely extended in space. This means it has *no center*, since in an infinite universe every point has an equal right to be considered the center. As a result, it becomes more difficult to think of human beings as the main attraction in this extravaganza, where quite likely there are planets similar to the earth circling other suns in other galaxies. The universe no longer seems a cozy home in which everything exists for our sake. Blaise Pascal, himself a great mathematician and contributor to the new science, would exclaim a hundred years after Copernicus, "The eternal silence of those infinite spaces strikes me with terror."[27]

Second, our beliefs about the nature of the things in the universe change. Celestial bodies are thought to be made of the same lowly stuff as we find on the earth, so that the heavens are no longer special—eternal, immutable, and akin to the divine. Furthermore, matter seems to be peculiarly *quantitative*. For Aristotle and medieval science alike, mathematics had been just one of the ways in which substances could be described. Quantity was only one of the ten categories, which together supplied the basic concepts for describing and explaining reality. Substances were fundamentally qualitative in nature, and science had the job of tracing their qualitative development in terms of changes from potentiality to actuality.*

But now mathematics seems to be a privileged set of concepts in terms of which to describe and explain things. Only by the application of geometry and mathematical calculation has the puzzle of the heavens been solved; and it is mathematics that can describe and predict the fall of rocks and the trajectory of a cannonball. Mathematics, it seems, can tell us what *really* is. The result is a strong push toward thinking of the universe in purely quantitative terms, as a set of objects with purely quantitative characteristics (size, shape, motion) that interact with each other according to fixed laws. It is no surprise that the implications of the new science move its inventors in the direction of atomism or, as they call it, "corpuscular-

---

*For a discussion of final causes, see pp. 156–158.

*See Aristotle's development of these ideas on pp. 154–157. For Aristotle's categories, see pp. 145–147.

ism.''* We will see this at work in Descartes' philosophy.

In the third place, the new science does away with teleological explanations, or final causes. The question about what *end* or *goal* a planet or a rock realizes in behaving as it does is simply irrelevant. Explanations of its behavior are framed in terms of mathematical laws that account for *how* it behaves. Why does it behave in a certain way? Because it is a thing of just this precise quantity in exactly these conditions, and things of that quantity in those conditions necessarily behave in accordance with a given law. It is no longer good enough to explain change in terms of a desire to imitate the perfection of God.†

As you can see, this way of viewing the universe puts *values* in a highly questionable position. If we assume that the valuable is somehow a goal, something desirable, what we all want—and this is the common assumption of virtually all philosophers and theologians up to this time—where is there room for such goals in a universe like this? A goal seems precisely to be a final cause, something that operates by drawing us onward and upward towards itself. But if everything simply happens as it must in the giant machine that is the universe, how can there be values, aspirations, goals?

It looks like knowledge and value, science and religion are being pulled apart again after two thousand years of harmony. Plato, and Aristotle after him, opposes the atomism of Democritus to construct a vision of reality in which the ultimate facts are not indifferent to goodness and beauty. Christian thinkers take over these schemes and link them intimately to God, the creator. But all this, expressed so movingly in Dante's *Divine Comedy*, seems to be in the process of coming unstuck again.

One more consequence of the new science will prove to be perhaps the most perplexing of all. It is a consequence drawn quite explicitly by Galileo, who sees that the quantitative, corpuscular universe makes the *qualities of experience* highly questionable. If *reality* is captured by mathematics and geometry, then the real properties of things are just their size, shape, velocity, acceleration, direction, weight: those characteristics treatable by numbers, points, and lines. But what becomes of those fuzzy, intimate, and lovable characteristics, such as warm, yellow-orange, pungent, sweet, and harmonious to the ear? It is in terms of such properties that we make contact with the world beyond us; it is they that delight or terrify us, attract or repel us. But what is their relation to those purely quantitative things revealed by Galilean science as the real stuff of the universe?

Our instinctive habit is to consider the apple to be red, the oatmeal hot, cookies sweet, and roses fragrant. But is this correct? Do apples and other such things really have these properties? Here is Galileo's answer:

> . . . that external bodies, to excite in us these tastes, these odours, and these sounds, demand other than size, figure, number, and slow or rapid motion, I do not believe; and I judge that, if the ears, the tongue, and the nostrils were taken away, the figure, the numbers, and the motions would indeed remain, but not the odours nor the tastes nor the sounds, which, without the living animal, I do not believe are anything else than names, just as tickling is precisely nothing but a name if the armpit and the nasal membrane be removed; . . . having now seen that many affections which are reputed to be qualities residing in the external object, have truly no other existence than in us, and without us are nothing else than names; I say that I am inclined sufficiently to believe that heat is of this kind, and that the thing that produces heat in us and makes us perceive it, which we call by the general name fire, is a multitude of minute corpuscles thus and thus figured, moved with such and such a velocity; . . . But that besides their figure, number, motion, penetration, and touch, there is in fire another quality, that is heat—that I do not believe otherwise than I have indicated, and I judge that it is so much due to us that if the animate and sensitive body were removed, heat would remain nothing more than a simple word.[28]

---

*The key notions of ancient atomism are discussed on pp. 29–31.
†Compare the teleological explanations of Aristotle (pp. 156–158) and Dante (pp. 266–268).

Galileo is here sketching a distinction between two different kinds of qualities: those which can be attributed to things themselves and those which cannot. The former are often called **primary qualities** and the latter **secondary qualities**. Primary qualities are those that Galilean mathematical science can handle: size, figure, number, and motion. These qualities are now thought to characterize the world—or what we might better call the *objective* world—exhaustively. All other qualities exist only *subjectively*—in us. They are caused to exist in us by the primary (quantitative) qualities of things.

Heat, for example, experienced in the presence of a fire, no more exists in the fire than a tickle exists in the feather brushing my nose. If we try to use the term "heat" for something out there in the world, it turns into "nothing but a name"—i.e., it does not describe any reality, since the reality is just the motion of "a multitude of minute corpuscles." The tickle exists only in us; and if the term "heat" (or for that matter "red" or "sweet" or "pungent") is to be descriptive, then what it describes is also only in us. Take way the eye, the tongue, the nostrils, and all that remains is figure and motion.

Democritus, the ancient atomist, draws the same conclusion. He remarks in a poignant phrase, "By this man is cut off from the real."* The problem that Galileo's distinction between primary and secondary qualities bequeaths to subsequent philosophers is this: if, in order to understand the world, we must strip it of its experienced qualities, where do those experienced qualities exist? If they exist only *in us*, what then are *we*? If they are mental, or subjective, what is the *mind*? And how is it related to the corpuscular world of the new science? Suppose we agree, for the sake of the mastery of the universe given us by these new conceptions, to kick experienced qualities "inside." Then how is this "inside" related to the "outside"? Who are these men that, in Democritus' phrase, are cut off from reality?

In this way, the new astronomy and physics, creating a picture of the universe as an immense *machine*, create also a whole nest of problems concerning man, mind, and experience—to say nothing of freedom and responsibility. Galileo, concerned as he is with the objective world, can simply relegate secondary qualities to some otherwise unspecified subjective realm. But the question will not go away: *what is the place of mind in this machine?*

Descartes, among others, sees the radical character of this problem and sets himself to solve it.

It is a new world, indeed. The impact of all these changes on a sensitive observer is registered in a poem by John Donne in 1611.

> And new philosophy calls all in doubt,
> The element of fire is quite put out;
> The sun is lost, and th' earth, and no man's wit
> Can well direct him where to look for it.
> And freely men confess that this world's spent,
> When in the planets, and the firmament
> They seek so many new; they see that this
> Is crumbled out again to his atomies.
> 'Tis all in pieces, all coherence gone;
> All just supply, and all relation:
> Prince, subject, father, son, are things forgot,
> For every man alone thinks he hath got
> To be a phoenix, and that then can be
> None of that kind, of which he is, but he.
> This is the world's condition now.[29]

Here is a lament founded on the new developments. Point after point recalls the detail we have just surveyed: Pyrrhonism, secondary qualities (why is the sun, source of light, heat, and color "lost"?), the moving earth, the expanding universe, corpuscularism, and in the last few lines, the new individualism, which seems to undermine all traditional authority. The medieval world has vanished; "'tis all in pieces, all coherence gone."

It did not go quietly, of course. The Roman Catholic Counter-Reformation tried to preserve as much as it could. The argument about Copernicanism, which seemed to be the key, was long and fierce; we all know the story of the Church's condemnation of Galileo's opinions and his recantation and house arrest. In 1633, the Church prohibited teaching or believing that the earth moved around the sun. And many Protestants were no

*See p. 31.

more friendly, citing biblical passages that seemed to support the claim that the earth was stationary.* These conservative forces were not interested in the new science per se, but in the fact that it seemed subversive of the "coherence" Christian society had enjoyed for so long. It questioned everything and seemed to turn it all upside down. When one part of a coherent world view is undermined, all the rest seems suddenly unstable.

But the new science proves irresistible, and in one way or another religion, morality, world view, and the structure of society would have to make peace with it. The question of what to make of this science is perhaps the major preoccupation of philosophers in the modern era.

Notes

1. I am indebted for much in this chapter to the excellent book by Thomas Kuhn, *The Copernican Revolution* (Cambridge: Harvard University Press, 1957).
2. Quoted in Kuhn, *Copernican Revolution*, 112.
3. Quotations from Dante, *The Divine Comedy*, in *The Portable Dante*, ed. Paolo Milano (New York: Penguin Books, 1947), are cited in the text by canto and line numbers.
4. Erasmus, "The Godly Feast," in *The Colloquies of Erasmus*, trans. Craig R. Thompson (Chicago and London: University of Chicago Press, 1965), 65.
5. Erasmus, "Godly Feast," 68.
6. Erasmus, "The Epicurean," in *Colloquies*, 549.
7. Ernst Cassirer, Paul Oskar Kristeller, and John Herman Randall, Jr., *The Renaissance Philosophy of Man* (Chicago and London: University of Chicago Press, 1948), 4.
8. Giovanni Pico della Mirandola, *Oration on the Dignity of Man*, in Cassirer, Kristeller, and Randall, *Renaissance Philosophy of Man*, 224–25.
9. Pico, *Oration*, 225.

10. Roland H. Bainton, *Christendom: A Short History of Christianity and Its Impact on Western Civilization* (New York: Harper and Row, 1964), 218.
11. Bainton, *Christendom*, 249.
12. Martin Luther, "An Appeal to the Ruling Class of German Nationality as to the Amelioration of the State of Christendom," in *Martin Luther: Selections from His Writings*, ed. John Dillenberger (New York: Anchor Books, 1981), 418–21.
13. Quoted in Dillenberger, "Preface to the Complete Edition of Luther's Latin Writings," in *Martin Luther*, 11.
14. Quoted in Dillenberger, *Martin Luther*, 11–12.
15. Quoted in Roland H. Bainton, *Here I Stand: A Life of Martin Luther* (London: Hodder and Staughton, 1951), 78.
16. Luther, "The Ninety-Five Theses," in Dillenberger, *Martin Luther*, 493–94.
17. Bainton, *Here I Stand*, 96.
18. Quoted in Bainton, *Here I Stand*, 117.
19. Quoted in Bainton, *Here I Stand*, 185.
20. I rely here on Richard H. Popkin's *History of Scepticism from Erasmus to Descartes* (Assen, Netherlands: Van Gorcum & Comp., N.V., 1960).
21. Quotations from Michel de Montaigne, *Apology for Raymond Sebond*, in *The Complete Works of Montaigne*, trans. Donald M. Frame (Palo Alto, Calif.: Stanford University Press, 1958), are cited in the text using the abbreviation *ARS*.
22. Quoted from Copernicus, *De Revolutionibus*, in Kuhn, *Copernican Revolution*, 141.
23. Quoted in Kuhn, *Copernican Revolution*, 142.
24. Kuhn, *Copernican Revolution*, 164–70.
25. Quoted in Edwin Arthur Burtt, *The Metaphysical Foundations of Modern Physical Science* (London: Routledge and Kegan Paul Ltd., 1924), 48.
26. Kuhn, *Copernican Revolution*, 86.
27. Blaise Pascal, *The Pensées*, trans. J. M. Cohen (New York: Penguin Books, 1961), sec. 91, p. 57.
28. Quoted in Burtt, *Metaphysical Foundations*, 78.
29. John Donne, "An Anatomy of the World," in *John Donne: The Complete English Poems* (New York: Penguin Books, 1971), 276.

---

*For example, Joshua 10:13, Ecclesiastes 1:4, 5, and Psalm 93:1.

17

René Descartes:
Doubting Our Way to Certainty

When he is just twenty-three years old, René Descartes (1596–1650) experiences a vision in a dream. He writes down:

> 10, November, 1619; I discovered the foundations of a marvellous science.[1]

This discovery decisively shapes the intellectual life of the young man. Before we focus on the philosophy of his *Meditations*, we need to understand something about that discovery and its importance for his method of approaching problems.

Descartes had received a good education, as he himself acknowledges. But he is dissatisfied. He had expected to obtain "a clear and certain knowledge . . . of all that is useful in life." Instead, he tells us,

> . . . I found myself beset by so many doubts and errors that I came to think I had gained nothing from my attempts to become educated but increasing recognition of my ignorance (*DM* 1.4, p. 113).[2]

Mathematics delights him "because of the certainty of its demonstrations and the evidence of its reasoning," though he is surprised that more has not been done with it. As for philosophy, he says,

> Seeing that it has been cultivated for many centuries by the most excellent minds, and yet there is still no point in it which is not disputed and hence doubtful,

I was not so presumptuous as to hope to achieve any more in it than others had done (*DM* 1.8, pp. 114–15).

What is a serious young man, who has always had "an earnest desire to learn to distinguish the true from the false," to do? (*DM* 1.10, p. 115).

> . . . I entirely abandoned the study of letters. Resolving to seek no knowledge other than that which could be found in myself or else in the great book of the world, I spent the rest of my youth travelling, visiting courts and armies, mixing with people of diverse temperaments and ranks, gathering various experiences, testing myself in the situations which fortune offered me, and at all times reflecting upon whatever came my way so as to derive some profit from it (*DM* 1.9, p. 115).

A striking move! He does not give up learning, but he does give up "letters"—learning what other men had written. In this, Descartes is both a reflection of the age and an immense influence furthering the individualism we earlier remarked on. Where would he seek truth? Not in the writings of the ancients, but in *himself* and in *the great book of the world*. Since he concludes—echoing Socrates—that hardly anyone knows anything worth learning, he would have to *discover* the truth.* If he is

---

*Do you find it surprising that two thousand years after Socrates someone should still echo the same complaint? Could we say the same today? If not, why not?

going to "learn to distinguish the true from the false," he would have to look to himself.

He joins an army (a traditional way to "see the world") and in his travels meets a Dutchman interested in mathematics and the new physics. Descartes' interest is sparked, and he begins to think about using mathematics to solve problems in physics. While working on these problems, he has his dream.

What is this "marvellous science" that formed the content of his "vision"? Apparently it is analytic geometry, which Descartes invented.* Descartes sees in a flash of insight that there is an isomorphism between algebraic symbols and geometry. He sees, moreover, that this opens the door to a mathematical treatment of everything that can be geometrically represented. But *nature* seems to be something that can be geometrically represented, natural things having size, figure, volume, and geometrical relations to each other. Suppose that the things in the world were just objects having such geometrical properties; suppose that whatever other properties they have can in one way or another be reduced to purely geometrical properties; then the stunning prospect opens up of a science of nature—a physics—that is *wholly mathematical.* Mathematics, the only discipline that impressed him in his college days as clear and certain, would be the key to unlock the secrets of nature. Surely this is a vision fit to motivate a research program! And that is exactly what it does.

For the rest of his life Descartes works on this program, in constant communication with the best minds at work on similar problems. In 1633 he is about to publish a *Treatise on the World,* when he learns of the Catholic Church's condemnation of Galileo and the burning of his books. He holds the treatise back, for in it he has endorsed the Copernican view of the moving earth. Four years later, however, he ventures to publish several works on light, on meteors, and on geometry. These are accompanied by a *Discourse on Method,* which we will examine in more detail. But we may first note something of the scope and character of his science.

He writes on a wide variety of topics: on the sun, moon, and the stars; on comets; on metals; on fire; on glass; on the magnet; on the human body, particularly on the heart and the nervous system (for which he gathers observations from animal bodies at a local slaughter house). He formulates several "laws of nature." Here are two influential ones:

> . . . that each thing as far as in it lies, continues always in the same state; and that which is once moved always continues to move.

> . . . that all motion is of itself in a straight line; and thus things which move in a circle always tend to recede from the centre of the circle that they describe (*PP* 2.37–39, p. 267).[3]

Newton will later adopt both of them, and so they pass into the foundations of classical physics; but they were revolutionary in Descartes' day. Both laws contradict Aristotelian assumptions built into the world view of medieval science. It had been thought that rest (at or near the center of the universe) is the natural state of terrestrial things, while the heavenly spheres revolve naturally in the most perfect of geometrical forms, perfect circles. To say that rest is not more "natural" than motion, and that motion is "naturally" in a straight line is radical indeed. It could make sense only in a world of infinite space, where there is no such thing as a natural center. And it fits only with a moving earth.

Descartes applies these principles to a world that he takes to be geometrical in essence. He tries to do without concepts of weight and gravity, for these seem to be "occult" qualities like those in the nonmathematical science of Aristotle. To say that a body falls because it has weight or because it is naturally attracted to another body seems to him no explanation at all; it is just attaching a name to a phenomenon and supposing that we thereby learn something. (These concepts trouble many of the early scientists, including Newton, who does use the concept of gravity but is never happy with it.)

For Descartes, bodies are sheer extended volumes. They interact according to mechanical principles that can be mathematically formulated. Given that a single body in motion would continue in that motion unless interfered with, and given

---

*So-called Cartesian coordinates are, of course, named for Descartes.

the laws of interaction, the paths and positions of interacting bodies can be plotted and predicted. Since extension is the very essence of body, there can be no vacuum or void. (You can see that if bodies are just extended volumes, the idea of such a volume containing *no body* is self-contradictory.) So the universe is full, and motion takes place by a continual recirculation of bodies, each displacing another as it is itself displaced. The fall of bodies near the earth is due to the action on them of other bodies in the air, which in turn are being pressed down by others out to the edges of the solar system. This system forms a huge vortex tightly bound in by the vortices of other systems, which force the moving bodies in it to deviate from otherwise straight paths into the roughly circular paths traced by the planets.*

The key idea, as you can see, is that everything in the material world can be treated in a purely geometrical and mathematical fashion. Descartes is one of the most vigorous promoters of that "corpuscularism" noted earlier.† Although he criticizes Democritus and the ancient atomists (for thinking that atoms are indivisible, for positing a void, for believing in gravity, and for not specifying the laws of interaction precisely), it is clear that the general outlines of Descartes' universe bear a striking resemblance to that earlier theory.‡ In particular, the *mechanistic* quality of the picture is identical. He states explicitly that "the laws of mechanics . . . are identical with the laws of Nature" (*DM* 5.54, p. 139).

The radical nature of this conception can be appreciated by noting a thought experiment Descartes recommends. Imagine, he says, that God creates a space with matter to fill it and shakes it up until there is thorough chaos. All that God then adds is a decree that this matter should behave according to the laws of Nature. What would be the result?

. . . I showed how, in consequence of these laws, the greater part of the matter of this chaos had to become disposed and arranged in a certain way, which made it resemble our heavens; and how, at the same time, some of its parts had to form an earth, some planets and comets, and others a sun and fixed stars. Here I dwelt upon the subject of light, explaining at some length the nature of the light that had to be present in the sun and the stars. . . . From that I went on to speak of the earth in particular: how, although I had expressly supposed that God had put no gravity into the matter of which it was formed, still all its parts tended exactly towards its centre; . . . how mountains, seas, springs and rivers could be formed naturally there, and how metals could appear in mines, plants grow in fields, and generally how all the bodies we call 'mixed' or 'composite' could come into being there (*DM* 5.43–44, p. 132).

Of course, Descartes does not actually succeed in demonstrating all that. No one yet has solved all these problems, and they are in fact insoluble with the limited resources that Descartes allows himself. But it is the conception and the daring it expresses that counts. This vision of a universe evolving itself in purely mechanistic ways has been enormously influential; and we haven't yet finished exploring its ramifications.

Descartes is quick to add that he does not infer from this thought experiment that the world was actually formed in that way, only that it could have been. Careful still about charges of heresy, he says it is "much more probable" that God made it just as it now is. But in either case, it is pretty clear that God is excluded from the day to day operations of the universe, which in Descartes' view proceeds as it must according to purely mathematical and mechanistic laws.

The Method

While working on these physical problems, and feeling certain that progress is being made virtually every day, Descartes asks himself why more progress hadn't been made in the past. It is surely not, he thinks, that he is more clever or intelligent than

---

*The notion of a cosmic vortex, a huge, swirling mass of matter, is already found in the speculations of Anaximander; see pp. 10–11. Compare also Parmenides' arguments against the existence of a void, pp. 24–26.

†See p. 282.

‡For the views of the atomists, see Chapter 4. Descartes' criticisms may be found in Part IV, CCII, of *The Principles of Philosophy*.

earlier thinkers. No, the problem is that they lacked something. And it gradually becomes clear to him that what they lacked is a *method*. They did not proceed in as careful and principled a way as they might have. Acceptance of obscurity, the drawing of hasty conclusions, avoidable disagreements, and general intellectual chaos were the results.

Descartes sets himself to draw up some rules for the direction of the intellect. It is of some importance to recognize that these rules of method formulate what Descartes takes himself to be doing in his scientific work. In particular, they are indebted to his experience as a mathematician. They are not picked arbitrarily, then, but are an expression of procedures that actually seem to be producing results. If only other thinkers could be persuaded to follow these four rules, he thinks, what progress might be made!

> The first was never to accept anything as true if I did not have evident knowledge of its truth: that is, carefully to avoid precipitate conclusions and preconceptions, and to include nothing more in my judgements than what presented itself to my mind so clearly and distinctly that I had no occasion to doubt it.
>
> The second, to divide each of the difficulties I examined into as many parts as possible and as may be required in order to resolve them better.
>
> The third, to direct my thoughts in an orderly manner, by beginning with the simplest and most easily known objects in order to ascend little by little, step by step, to knowledge of the most complex, and by supposing some order even among objects that have no natural order of precedence.
>
> And the last, throughout to make enumerations so complete, and reviews so comprehensive, that I could be sure of leaving nothing out (DM 2.18–19, p. 120).

He says of these four rules that he thought they would be "sufficient, provided that I made a strong and unswerving resolution never to fail to observe them" (DM 2.18, p. 120). They are difficult to follow, as any attempt to do so will convince you immediately. But let us explore their content more carefully.

The first one has to do with a condition for accepting something as true. It is pretty stringent. You want to avoid two things: "precipitate conclusions" (hastiness) and "preconceptions" (categorizing something before you have good warrant to do so). How do you do this? By accepting only those things which are *so clear and distinct that you have no occasion to doubt them.* Descartes clearly has in mind as models such propositions as "3 + 5 = 8" and "the interior angles of a triangle are equal to two right angles." Once you understand these, you really cannot bring yourself to doubt that they are true. Can you?

What do the key words "clear" and "distinct" mean? In *The Principles of Philosophy* (PP 1.45, p. 237) he explains them as follows. Something is "clear" when it is "present and apparent to an attentive mind, in the same way as we assert that we see objects clearly when, being present to the regarding eye, they operate upon it with sufficient strength." Seeing an apple in your hand in good light would be an example. We are not to accept any belief unless it is as clear as that. Nothing obscure, fuzzy, dim, indefinite, indistinct, vague, ambiguous—only what is *clear!*

By "distinct" he means "so precise and different from all other objects that it contains within itself nothing but what is clear." An idea not only must be clear in itself but also impossible to confuse with any other idea. Ideas must be as distinct as the idea of a triangle is from the idea of a square.

Ask yourself how many of *your* beliefs are clear and distinct in this way. Descartes is under no illusions about the high standard he sets. "There are even a number of people who throughout all their lives perceive nothing so correctly as to be capable of judging it properly." But the first rule of the method is to *accept nothing as true* that does not meet that high standard. In the first of the *Meditations* we shall see how much that excludes.

The second rule recommends analysis. Problems are typically complex, and an essential step in their solution is to break them into smaller problems. Anyone who has tried to write a computer program to solve a certain problem will have an excellent feel for this rule. Often more than half the battle is to discover smaller problems we already have the resources to solve, so that by combining the solutions to these more elementary problems we can solve the big problem. We move, by analysis, not only from the complex to the simple, but also from the obscure to the clear and distinct; and so we also follow the first rule.

The third rule recognizes that items for consideration may be more or less simple. It recommends beginning with the simpler ones and proceeding to the more complex. Here is a mathematical example. If we compare a straight line to a curve, we can see that there is a clear sense in which the straight line is simple and the curve is not; no straight line is more or less straight than another, but curves come in all degrees. If we know a line is straight, we know something perfectly definite about it; if we know it is curved, we do not. And it is in fact possible to analyze a curve into a series of straight lines at various angles to each other, thus "constructing" the more complex curve from the simple straights.

For Descartes, this serves as a model of all good intellectual work. There are two basic procedures: a kind of *insight* or *intuition* of simple natures (which must be clear and distinct), and then *deduction* of complex phenomena from perceived relations between the simples. A deduction, too, is in fact just an insight: insight into the connections holding between simples. Geometry, again, provides many examples. Theorems are proved by deduction from the axioms and postulates. The latter are simply "seen" to be true; for example, through two points in a plane one and only one straight line can be drawn. The same kind of "seeing" is required to recognize that each step in a proof is correct.

Deductions, of course, can be very long and complex, even though each of the steps is clear and distinct. That is the reason for the fourth rule: to set out all the steps completely (we all know how easily mistakes creep in when we take something for granted) and to make comprehensive reviews.

Descartes is extremely optimistic about the results we can obtain if we follow this method.

These long chains composed of very simple and easy reasonings, which geometers customarily use to arrive at their most difficult demonstrations, had given me occasion to suppose that all the things that can fall under human knowledge are interconnected in the same way. And I thought that, provided that we refrain from accepting anything as true which is not, and always keep to the order required for deducing one thing from another, there can be nothing too remote to be reached in the end or too well hidden to be discovered (*DM* 2.19, p. 120).

We will see this optimism at work when Descartes tackles knotty problems like the existence of God and the relation between soul and body. But first we need to ask: why does Descartes feel a need to address these *philosophical* problems at all? Why doesn't he just stick to mathematical physics?

For one thing, he is confident that his method will allow him to succeed where so many have failed. But a deeper reason is that he needs to show that his physics correctly describes the world, that it is more than just a likely story. In short, he needs to demonstrate that his physics is *true*. He is quite aware of the skeptical doubts of the Pyrrhonists, of the way they undermine the testimony of the senses and cast doubt on our reasoning. In particular, he is aware of the problem of the criterion.* Unless this can be solved, no certainty is possible.

Descartes thinks he has found a way to solve this problem of problems. He will outdo the Pyrrhonists at their own game; when it comes to doubting, he will be the champion doubter of all time. The first rule of his method already gives him the means to wipe the slate clean—unless, perhaps, there remains something that is *so clear and distinct that it cannot possibly be doubted*. If there were something like that, the rest of the method could gain a foothold, deductions could lead us to further truths, and perhaps, from the depths of doubting despair, we could be raised to the bliss of certainty.

---

*For a discussion of this problem by the ancient skeptics, see pp. 195–197. For the impact of skepticism nearer to Descartes' time, see pp. 277–279.

This is Descartes' strategy. And it is his attempt to *justify* his physics that makes Descartes not just a great scientist, but a great philosopher as well. We are now ready to turn to this philosophy as expressed in the *Meditations*.

The *Meditations*

The *Meditations on First Philosophy* is Descartes' most famous work. We will focus our attention on the text itself, as we did earlier with certain dialogues of Plato. It is a remarkably rich work; and if you come to understand it, you will have mastered many of the concepts and distinctions that philosophers use to this day. So it will repay careful study. I cannot emphasize too much that in this section it is the *text*, the words of Descartes himself you must wrestle with. It is he who is your partner in this conversation, and you must make him speak to you and—as far as possible—answer your questions. What I will do is offer some commentary on particularly difficult aspects, fill in some background, and ask some questions.

Though it is usually known just as the *Meditations*, the full title of the work is *Meditations on First Philosophy in Which the Existence of God and the Distinction of the Soul from the Body Are Demonstrated.* The title gives you some idea what to expect. But as you will see, his experience as a mathematician and physicist is everywhere present. It was first published in 1641.[†]

Although not represented in our text, the *Meditations* are prefaced by a letter to "the Wisest and Most Distinguished Men, the Dean and Doctors of the Faculty of Theology in Paris." The motivation behind this letter is fairly transparent. It had been just eight years since the condemnation of Galileo's opinions; and, as we have seen, Descartes had allied himself with the basic outlook of Galileo. The Faculty of Theology in Paris had indeed been an illustrious one for some centuries. If he could secure their approval, he could almost certainly escape Galileo's fate. The *Meditations*, as it turns out, was examined carefully by one of the theologians, who expressed his approval; but twenty-two years later it was nonetheless placed by the Roman Catholic Church on the *Index Librorum Prohibitorum* of books dangerous to read.*

Descartes had also asked one of his close friends, the priest and scientist Mersenne, to circulate the text to some distinguished philosophers, who were then invited to write criticisms of it. These criticisms, including some from his English contemporary, Thomas Hobbes, were printed along with Descartes' replies at the end of the volume.

In the letter to the theologians, Descartes refers to "believers like ourselves." He professes to be absolutely convinced that it is sufficient in these matters to rely on Scripture. But there is a problem. God's existence, he says, is to be believed because it is taught in Scripture. Scripture, on the other hand, is to be believed because God is its source. Now it doesn't take a lot of thought to realize that there is a circle here, a pretty tight circle. It comes down to believing that God exists because one believes that God exists. (Recall skeptics like Sextus and Montaigne, who maintain that all our claims to know are involved in such circular thinking.)

To break into the circle Descartes thinks it necessary to *prove rationally* that God exists and that the soul is distinct from the body. His claim that reason should be able to do this is no innovation; Augustine, Anselm, Aquinas and others had said as much before. Descartes, however, claims to have proofs superior to any offered by these thinkers.

He refers to some thinkers who hold that it is rational to believe the soul perishes with the body. Aristotle seems in the main to think so (though he waffles).[‡] Christian Aristotelians like Thomas Aquinas labor mightily, but inconclusively, to reconcile this view with the tradition of an immortal

---

*The *Index* was created in 1571 by Pope Pius V, after approval by the Council of Trent; the latter was a general council of the Roman Catholic church, called to deal with problems created by the Protestant Reformation. It set in motion the Catholic Counter-Reformation, and the *Index* was one of its tools.

[†]Numbers in the margins of the *Meditations* text refer to page numbers in the standard Latin text, edited by Adam and Tannery. References will be to these page numbers.

[‡]For Aristotle's view of the soul as "the form of a living human body" see pp. 165–168.

soul. Descartes thinks he has a proof of the soul that is direct, simple, and conclusive.* He claims, in fact, that his proofs will "surpass in certitude and obviousness the demonstrations of geometry." A strong claim indeed! You will have to decide whether you agree.

These are meditations on *first philosophy*. This is a term derived from Aristotle, who means by it a search for the *first principles of things*. First philosophy is also called **metaphysics**. In a letter to the man who translated his *Principles of Philosophy* from Latin into French, Descartes uses a memorable image.

> Thus the whole of philosophy is like a tree; the roots are metaphysics, the trunk is physics, and the branches that issue from the trunk are all the other sciences.[4]

Note that all the sciences, in 1641, are still counted as parts of philosophy, the love of wisdom.

So Descartes is inquiring into *what kinds of things there ultimately are*, about which physics and the other sciences give us more detailed information. What he wants to find is a set of concepts that will give us an inventory of the *basic kinds of being*. Aristotle calls such fundamental concepts "categories."[†]

Descartes' inventory of what there is actually looks fairly simple. We can diagram it this way:

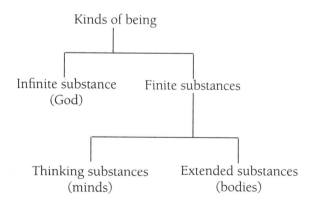

But by itself this chart isn't very informative. It is time to turn to the *Meditations* themselves, to see how Descartes fills in this schema and why it turns out just that way.

The text of *Meditations on First Philosophy* is printed at the end of this chapter, beginning on p. 305. You should read through one of the meditations quickly to get a general feel for the argument. After reading it, come back to the commentary and questions below, using them as a guide to go through the text again, this time paying close attention to Descartes' exact words. He is a careful and clear writer and says exactly what he means. If you proceed in this way, you will not only learn some philosophy but also gain skill in reading a text of some difficulty—a valuable ability. Writing out brief answers to the questions will increase your understanding. Repeat this procedure for each of the six meditations.

Read Meditation I: On What Can Be Called Into Doubt   Note the personal, meditative character of the writing. Descartes is inviting us to join him in thinking certain things through, asking us to mull them over and see whether we agree. He is not making authoritative pronouncements. Just as he reserves the right to be the judge of what *he* should believe, so he puts you on the spot. You will have to be continually asking yourself: Do I agree with this or not? if not, why not? This familiar first-person style is quite different from most of medieval philosophy; it harks back to Augustine's *Confessions* in the late fourth century.

Note that there are three stages in the "tearing down" of opinions, and one principle running throughout. The principle is that we ought to withhold assent from anything uncertain, just as much as from what we see clearly to be false. This is simply a restatement of the first rule of his method, but is of the greatest importance.* The three stages

---

*Descartes tends to use the terms "soul," "mind," and "spirit" interchangeably. They are all terms for "the thing that thinks." Some philosophers and theologians make distinctions among them.
†See p. 145.

---

*A brief look back at the four rules of the method will be of use at this point. See p. 290. It is the principle expressed in this first rule which the pragmatists in our century reject. (See Peirce's critique on p. 465.) Once, when a friend of mine stumbled on an unusually high first step of a staircase, I formulated what came jokingly to be known as Norman's First Law: Watch that first step; it's a big one. Good advice for appraising philosophical systems.

concern (a) the senses, (b) dreams, and (c) the evil demon hypothesis.

Q1. Aren't you *strongly* inclined to think, just like Descartes by the fire, that you *can't deny* that you are now reading this book which is "right there" in your hands?

Q2. What do you think of Descartes' rule that we shouldn't completely trust those who have cheated us even once? Does this rule apply to the senses?

Q3. *Could* you be dreaming right now? Explain.

Q4. What is the argument that even in dreams *some* things are not illusory? And what are they?

Q5. How does the thought of God, at *this* stage, seem to reinforce skeptical conclusions— *even* about arithmetic?*

Here Descartes avails himself of the techniques of the Pyrrhonists, who set argument against plausible argument until they find themselves no more inclined to judge one way than another. But he acknowledges that this equilibrium or suspension of judgment is difficult to achieve. "Habit" strongly inclines him to believe some of these things as "probable." Like Descartes, you almost certainly take it as *very* probable that you are now looking at a piece of paper, which is located a certain determinate distance before your eyes, that you indeed have eyes, and that 2 + 3 really does equal 5. And you almost certainly find it very hard *not* to believe these things. You very likely find yourself so committed to them that you almost *can't* doubt them. (Ask yourself whether this is the case.) How can we overcome these habits of believing? We now know, if Descartes is right so far, that we *should* doubt them. As a remedy against these habitual believings, Descartes determines *deliberately* (as an act of will) to suppose that all his prior beliefs are false.

Q6. Is this possible? Can *you* do it? How does the hypothesis of the evil demon help?

---

*Review the consequences William of Ockham draws from the doctrine of God's omnipotence (pp. 260–261).

Descartes now thinks that he has canvassed every possible reason for doubting. We cannot rely on our senses; we cannot even rely on our rational faculties for the simplest truths of mathematics, geometry, or logic. All our beliefs, it seems, are dissolved in the acid of skeptical doubt.

Q7. Before going on to *Meditation II*, ask yourself the question: Is there anything at all that I am *so certain* of that I could not *possibly* doubt it? (Meditate on this question a while.)

Read Meditation II: On the Nature of the Human Mind, Which Is Better Known Than the Body Descartes seems to have gotten nowhere by doubting. What to do? He resolves to press on, suspecting that the terrors of skepticism can be overcome only by enduring them to the end. The monster in the child's closet will only disappear if the child can muster the courage to look at it directly. If we avert our eyes in fear, we will not conquer.

The particular horror, of course, is that all our beliefs might be false—that nowhere would they connect at all with reality. If Descartes has carried us with him to this point, we know that we have lots of ideas and beliefs, but whether any one of them represents something that really *exists* must seem quite uncertain. Perhaps they are just webs of illusion, like those spun by a master magician—or the evil demon.

Descartes here represents a pattern of thought which deserves a name. Let us call it the representational theory of knowledge and perception, or the **representational theory** for short. The basic ideas of this theory are very widely shared in modern philosophy. We can distinguish five points.

1. We have no immediate or direct access to things in the world, only to the world of our ideas.
2. "Ideas" must be understood broadly to include all the contents of the mind, including perceptions, images, memories, concepts, beliefs, intentions, and decisions.
3. These ideas serve as *representations* of things other than themselves.

4. Much of what these ideas represent, they represent as "out there," or "external" to the mind containing them.
5. It is in principle possible for ideas to represent these things correctly; but they may also be false and misleading.

In *Meditation I*, Descartes draws a certain consequence of the representational theory. It seems that mind and world could be disconnected in a perplexing way, that even the most solid ideas might represent things all wrong—or maybe even not represent anything at all! This possibility, foreshadowed by the ancient skeptics and by William of Ockham in his reflections on God's omnipotence, provokes thinkers to try to find a remedy. What we need is a bridge across the chasm between mind and world; and it is clear that it will have to be built by inference and argument. We want *good reasons* to believe our ideas represent the "external" world truly. But the good reasons must be of a peculiar sort. It is as if we have to start this construction project while isolated on one side, restricted in our choice of materials to those available there. It is from the vantage point of the mind that we try to stretch the girders of our argument across the gulf to the world.

We will examine Descartes' effort to build such a rational bridge. Other thinkers after him will struggle with the problem. Hume will despair of a bridge, Kant will redefine the problem so as to make the gulf partially disappear, Hegel will deny that there is a gulf at all, and Kierkegaard will open it up again. In our century, there have been several attempts to show that the notion of a chasm needing to be bridged is itself an illusion.* In those first few pages of the *Meditations*, formulated in an incomparable way, is a dramatic rehearsal of the old skeptical worries about knowledge. They are now seen to hover around the theses of the representational theory of knowledge and perception.

To change the metaphor, we might remember Archimedes, who says, "Give me a lever long enough, and a place on which to rest it, and I can move the earth." Descartes thinks that if he can find just one certainty, he might, like Archimedes, do marvels. He might just build that bridge.

Q8. To what certainty does Descartes' methodical doubt lead? Is he right about that?*

The principle "I think, therefore I am" is often referred to as the *cogito*, from the Latin "I think" and we will use that shorthand expression from time to time.

Note that Descartes rejects the standard, long-accepted way of answering the question, What am I? (25–26). According to a tradition that goes back to Socrates (and is codified by Aristotle), the way to answer such a question is to give a *definition*. The traditional way to define something will tell you (a) what *genus* it belongs to, and (b) the *difference* between it and other things in that genus. Not surprisingly, this is called *definition by genus and difference*. A human being is said to belong to the genus *animal*; and the difference between a human and other animals is that a human is *rational*. Human beings, Aristotle says, are *rational animals*.

Descartes objects to such a definition because it simply calls for more definitions; you need next a definition of *animal* and a definition for *rational*. Then, presumably, you will require definitions for the terms used to define *them*. And so on.

This whole process has to come to ground somewhere. There must be some terms, Descartes thinks, that do not need definition of this sort, but whose meaning can just be "seen." These will be the *simple* terms. From these more complex terms can be built up. We see in Descartes' rejection of the traditional definition-procedure an application of the second and third rules of his method. He is

---

*Other thinkers, not represented in our volume, who struggle with this problem are John Locke (1632–1704) and George Berkeley (1685–1753). It is the latter who shows that Galileo's distinction between primary and secondary qualities (see p. 284) cannot resolve the problem; size and shape, as we experience them, are just as much ideas in the mind as are colors and smells. Berkeley's *Three Dialogues between Hylas and Philonus* is an accessible source for this argument.

---

*Descartes' central idea here is anticipated by Augustine in his refutation of the skeptics. See p. 218.

searching for something so simple, clear, and distinct that it just presents itself without any need for definition. He is looking for something *self-evident*. If that can be found, he can use it as a foundation on which to build more complex truths.

Q9. What, then, does Descartes conclude that he is?

Note that Descartes briefly considers the view that he may after all *be* a body, or some such thing, even though he does not *know* he is (p. 308).* But he does not try to refute it here; that proof comes in *Meditation VI*. Here he is interested in what he knows that he *is*—not in what he can infer that he *is not*.

Q10. Why does Descartes rule out the use of the imagination in answering the question, What am I?

Q11. What all is included in "thinking," as Descartes understands the term? (See 28.) Note how broad the term is for him.

Q12. Suppose I feel certain that I see a cat on the mat. Is it certain that there is a cat on the mat? What, in this situation, *can* I be certain of?

How difficult it is to stay within the bounds of what I know for certain! As Descartes says, his "mind enjoys wandering." And so it is with us. I, too, keep slipping back into the error of thinking that I know *sensible* things best—this desk, this computer keyboard, this hand. (Do you find that too?)

It is to cure this inclination to rely on the senses that Descartes considers the bit of wax. Read that passage once more (30–33). All the sensible qualities by means of which we recognize the wax can change. But we still judge that it is the same wax.

Q13. What qualities, then, belong to the wax essentially? (Here Descartes' physics shows itself.)†

Q14. Why is our imagination incapable of grasping these qualities of the wax? By what faculty *can* we understand it?

---

*This is the view that Thomas Hobbes urges against Descartes. See "Minds and Motives" in Chapter 18.
†Look again at pp. 288–289.

Q15. How does the wax example help to cure our habitual inclination to trust the senses?

Q16. How does "common usage" help to mislead us?

The distinction between *ordinary perception* and *judgment* is crucial for Descartes. It is illustrated by the hats and coats we see through the window. We say that we *see* men passing; but this is inaccurate, for they may be just robots dressed like men. What is actually happening in ordinary perception is that our intellect is drawing an *inference* on the basis of certain *data* (supplied by the senses) and issuing a *judgment*. Judging is an activity of the mind—indeed, as we'll see in *Meditation IV*, of the will.

Perceiving, then, is not a purely passive registration by the senses. Implicit in all perception is judgment, or *giving assent*. In ordinary perception, these judgments are apt to be obscure, confused, and just plain wrong. But fortunately they can be corrected by the application of ideas that are clear and distinct, e.g., the mathematical simples. (These points will be crucial in *Meditation IV*, where Descartes explains how it is possible for us to err.)

With respect to the bit of wax, the moral is that it is "grasped, not by the senses or the power of having mental images, but by the understanding alone." When based wholly on sense, our perception is "imperfect and confused." When directed, however, to "the things of which the wax consists" (the mathematically determinable simples of extension, figure, and motion), knowledge of the wax can be *clear and distinct*.

Now we can understand why Descartes introduces the wax example. If even here knowledge cannot be found in sensation, but only in a "purely mental inspection," then we should have less difficulty remembering that knowledge of *what we are* must also be approached in this way. Our tendency to think of ourselves as what we can *sense* of ourselves—these hands, this head, these eyes—is considerably undermined. Indeed, I must know myself "much more truly and certainly" even than the wax.

And there follows a remarkable conclusion: "I can't grasp anything more easily or plainly than my mind." (What would Freud have said to that?)

Read Meditation III: On God's Existence   In the first paragraphs Descartes resolves to explore more carefully his own mind. You might wonder whether he has any alternative, now that he has resolved to consider everything else "as empty illusions."

A momentous step is taken: he *solves* (or at least he thinks he solves) the problem of the criterion! Here are the steps.

a. He is certain that he exists as a thinking thing.
b. He asks himself: What is it about this proposition that accounts for my certainty that it is true?
c. He answers: The fact that I grasp it so clearly and distinctly that I perceive it could not possibly be false.
d. He concludes: Let this then be a general principle (a *criterion*): Whatever I grasp with *like* clarity and distinctness must also be true.

He then reviews (once more) the other things he had at one time thought were certainly true.

Q17. Why does he feel a need to inquire about the existence and nature of God?

Descartes now tries to make clear a crucial distinction between *ideas* on the one hand and *volitions, emotions,* and *judgments* on the other (37–38). This distinction is embedded in an inventory of the varied contents of the mind (which is all that we can so far be certain of). Here is a schematic representation of that inventory.

Q18. What is the key difference between ideas and judgments?
Q19. What is the key difference between judgments, on the one hand, and volitions and emotions on the other?
Q20. What question arises with respect to the ideas that seem to be acquired from outside myself?
Q21. What (provisional) examples does Descartes give of each class of ideas?

We need to comment on the notion of **innate ideas**. In calling them "innate," Descartes does not mean to imply that they are to be found in babies and mentally defective adults, as some of his critics suppose. He merely means there are some ideas that we would have even if nothing existed but ourselves. These ideas do not require external causes for their existence in us; every developed rational mind will possess them from its own resources. Thus, the idea of a *thing* can originate with the *cogito*, which gives me the certainty that I exist as a thing that thinks—even if nothing else exists. Perhaps my idea of an antelope is caused in me by seeing antelopes in a zoo (though this remains to be proved). But we would have the ideas of thing, thought, and truth in any case.

Q22. Why do you think Descartes believes the ideas of truth and thought are innate?
Q23. Why does Descartes think that some ideas do originate from objects outside himself? He gives two reasons (38).

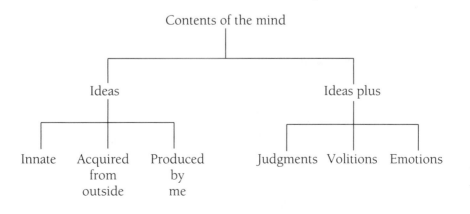

Q24. Are these two reasons conclusive?

Q25. What is the difference between being taught "by nature" and being taught "by the light of nature"? (See 38–39.) What is the **light of nature**?*

We come now to a point of terminology. Descartes distinguishes between *subjective* reality on the one hand and *formal* and *eminent* reality on the other. If we are going to understand Descartes' argument, we must be clear about how he uses these terms and keep his use firmly in mind.

It is easier to begin with formal reality. Something has formal reality if it is, in our terms, actual or existing. If there really are giraffes and angels, then giraffes and angels have formal reality. You also, because you exist, have formal reality. And when you form an image of a giraffe in your mind, that image also has formal reality—i.e., it actually exists *as an image* in your mind. So any idea actually present in a mind is formally real. This means that (if there are giraffes) both the idea of a giraffe (when being thought) and the giraffe you are thinking of are formally real. They are distinct realities, but related: the one *represents* the other.

What you are thinking about when you entertain an idea has *subjective* reality. Giraffes and angels have subjective reality whenever you think of them. But there are ideas whose objects have *only* subjective reality: the tooth fairy, for instance, or unicorns. These, of course, are examples of ideas "produced by us." But if we look carefully, we can see that they have not been invented out of nothing. The idea of a unicorn comes from the ideas of a horse and a single horn. And (though Descartes has not proved it yet) it may be that horses and horns are *formally* real. Already he remarks (41–42) that although one idea may be derived from others, this cannot go on to infinity: there must eventually be a *cause* for these ideas; and the reality

of that cause must be more than "merely subjective." If this were not so, we would have gotten something "from nothing." And the light of nature assures us that this is impossible. There is an old Latin saying: *ex nihilo nihil fit*, or "from nothing, nothing comes."

Descartes does not, of course, make these distinctions for their own sake. There is a problem he is trying to solve: given that I can be certain that *I* exist (together with all my ideas), can I be certain of the *formal* existence of anything else? Although thoroughgoing skepticism may have been refuted (we do know something in the *cogito*), we have not got beyond solipsism. **Solipsism** is the view that each of you (if there is anyone out there!) must state for yourself in this way: "I am the only thing that actually exists."

Another step in solving that problem is to note that there are *degrees of reality*: some things are more real than others. Descartes gives two examples, framed in terms of subjective reality (40), though the same is true for formal reality as well.

Q26. Why does the idea of *substance* contain more subjective reality than that of *modification or accident*? (Think of a fender and the dent in it.)*

Q27. Why does the idea of infinite substance have more subjective reality than that of finite substance?

On the basis of these distinctions, Descartes formulates a *causal principle*: that there must be at least as much reality in the cause as there is in the effect. A cause is said to be formally real when it has the same degree of reality as the effect it produces; it is said to be eminently real when it has even more reality than its effect.

Q28. After examining Descartes' examples (heat, stone), do you think this principle is revealed by "the light of nature"?

---

*It is interesting to compare this with what Augustine says about the Interior Teacher and the light within. (See Chapter 14.) Descartes' view is less explicitly theological and is a step on the road to secularization. It should also be compared to what Heidegger says about "the clearing" (p. 549).

---

*I owe this nice example to Ronald Rubin, the translator of these *Meditations*.

Q29. What about the *application* of this principle: that there must be at least as much *formal* reality in the *cause of an idea* as there is *subjective* reality in the *idea itself*?

Once more Descartes canvasses the various kinds of ideas he finds in himself as a thinking thing. He is looking for some idea of which he himself could not possibly be the cause. Such an idea must have a cause (since nothing comes from nothing). If (a) he is not the cause, and (b) there is a cause, then (c) he knows that he is not alone in the universe. Something else exists!

Descartes thinks his meditations to this point give him the materials with which to prove that God exists. In its bare bones, his argument looks like this:

> I have an idea of an infinitely perfect substance. Therefore, such a substance exists.

Now you no doubt think that, stated in this stark way, this is a terrible argument. And it is. But when properly filled in with other premises, Descartes thinks it is a proof that is as good as the best mathematical proofs.

Q30. Fill in the premises that complete Descartes' argument that God exists.
Q31. Why could not Descartes himself be the cause of his idea of God?

Meditation III contains two separate arguments for God's existence. The first one, which we have now examined, begins with the fact that each of us has an *idea* of God. The second one begins (48–51) with the fact that it is certainly true that I exist. The argument then addresses whether I could exist if God does not. It is an argument by exclusion; it considers the other plausible candidates for the cause of my existence and shows in each case that it won't do. Note that both of these arguments are *causal* arguments. The first inquires about the cause of my *idea* of God, the second about the cause of my own *existence*. Both make use of the causal principle Descartes has formulated.

Q32. Set down briefly, in numbered sentences, the essential steps of this second argument.
Q33. What does Descartes conclude is the origin of his idea of God? And why?

At the end of the third *Meditation*, Descartes feels he has achieved his aim. He now knows that he is not alone. In addition to himself there is at least one other being—a substance infinite in intelligence and power, and perfect in every way. This latter fact will prove to be of very great significance, for Descartes will use it to defeat the hypothesis of the evil demon; a perfect being could not be a deceiver. Thus he thinks he can overcome the deepest ground for skepticism about knowledge of the external world. But that is a line of argument pursued in the remaining meditations.

Read Meditation IV: On Truth and Falsity Note the transitional character of the first paragraph. Descartes sums up the argument so far, expresses his confidence that God's existence is more certain than anything else (except the *cogito*), and looks forward to further progress.

Q34. Is Descartes' assertion (53) that deception is an evidence of weakness rather than power plausible? Explain your answer.

Before God's existence was proved, it was unclear whether any of our beliefs were true. Now there is a new puzzle: how any of them can be false? (Do you see why this puzzle arises?) So Descartes has to provide an explanation of the obvious fact that we can and do make mistakes.

For the basic framework he depends upon the idea of the great chain of being.* He finds that he is an "intermediate" between God and nothingness, having less reality than God, whose perfection excludes error, but more reality than sheer nonbeing.

---

*For a more detailed discussion of this idea, see p. 224.

Error, in any case, is not a positive reality; it is only a defect, as weakness is only the absence of strength and cold the absence of heat. So it should not be too surprising that Descartes, and we, too, should be liable to error.

Two points he makes in passing are worth noting. (1) Why did God create me so that I could make mistakes? I don't know, he says, but if I could see the world as God sees it, it is quite possible that I would judge it to be for the best.*

Q35. How might recognizing that I am only a part of a larger whole help?

(2) Among the many things we do not know are God's purposes. It follows that Aristotelian final causes—the what for—are not appropriate in the explanations given by physics. Thus Descartes buttresses the mechanistic character of his (and the modern world's) scientific work. We can come to know *how* things happen, but not *why*.

A more detailed analysis of error can be given. It depends on another distinction: that between entertaining a belief, or having it in mind (which is the function of the *understanding*), and assenting to that belief, or accepting it (which is the function of the *will*).

Q36. How does this distinction between understanding and will explain the possibility of error?
Q37. In what way is the will more perfect than the understanding?
Q38. Can God be blamed for our errors?
Q39. How can we avoid error?

---

*Here is one expression of that attitude expressed in Leibniz and other later writers to the effect that "this is the best of all possible worlds." It is this optimism which Voltaire caricatures so savagely in *Candide*. These reflections of Descartes form part of a project known as theodicy—the justification of the ways of God to man. For another attempt at theodicy, see Hegel (pp. 423–426). And you might review the Stoic notion that evil does not exist in the world, but only in our perception of it (p. 191).

Read Meditation V: On the Essence of Material Objects and More on God's Existence   This brief meditation is a transition to the more important sixth meditation. Though Descartes says at the beginning that he wants to investigate whether anything can be known about material things (so far, only God and the soul are known), he doesn't solve that problem here. But he does take a significant step towards its solution. And, along the way, he discovers a third proof that God exists.

Again we find the typical Cartesian strategy at work. He wants to know whether material things exist independently of himself. How can he proceed? He can't just look to see, since he has put the testimony of the senses in doubt. So he must consider more carefully the *idea* of material things, which is all that is available to him. And again he finds that some of these ideas are confused and obscure, while others are clear and distinct. The latter are those of extension, duration, and movement—the qualities that can be treated geometrically or mathematically.*

Note that these mathematical ideas are not just imaginary inventions. I cannot put them together any way I like, as I can construct fantastic creatures by combining heads, bodies, and hides at will. I may not yet know whether there are any triangular things outside myself, but the idea of a triangle "can't be said to be nothing" (64–65). It has a *nature* that is "immutable and eternal." This nature does not depend upon me.

The point can be put in this way. Suppose you imagine a creature with wings covered with scales, a long furry tail, six legs, and an elephantlike nose covered with spikes. Then I ask you, does this creature have a liver? You will have to *invent* the answer. You cannot discover it. But if you imagine a triangle and I ask you whether the interior angles equal two right angles, you do not have to invent an answer. Even if you had never thought about that question before, you could investigate and discover that the answer is yes. With respect to these geometrical

---

*Review the discussion of the bit of wax in *Meditation II* and on p. 296.

properties, there are *truths*.* And these, remember, are the very properties that determine the essence of material things.

Since the idea of a material thing is the idea of something extended, and since extended things can be treated geometrically, it follows that the *idea* of a material thing is one which is clear and distinct. Material substances have an essence or nature that would make a *science* of them a possibility—if only we could be assured that they exist. And we know that such a science is a possibility merely from an examination of their ideas. So, provided we can discover a proof that some *formal* reality corresponds to the *subjective* reality of our ideas of material things, we can have a science of material things—a physics. Descartes offers such a proof in *Meditation VI*. In this way, then, he hopes to give a metaphysical foundation to his mechanistic physics.

The discovery that certain ideas have a nature or essence of their own, quite independent of our inventions, also supplies Descartes with material for a third proof of God's existence.† If we simply pay close attention to what is necessarily involved in our idea of *what* God is (his essence or nature), we can discover, Descartes argues, *that* God is (that he exists). God's existence is included in his essence. Notice that, unlike the first two arguments, this is not a *causal* proof.

Q40. Set out briefly, in numbered sentences, the essential points of this argument.

Q41. Is the argument, in your opinion, a sound one? Explain.

This last proof of God's existence allows Descartes to lay to rest a final worry that has been tormenting him. You really cannot help believing, he suggests, that your clear and distinct thoughts are true—while you are thinking them. But later you may not be so sure! You may then think you were dreaming what earlier seemed so certain. But now this worry can be dealt with. And *Meditation V* closes on a note of reassurance.

Q42. How are the dream and demon worries finally disposed of?

Q43. Can an atheist do science? (See the last paragraph.)

Read Meditation VI: On the Existence of Material Objects and the Real Distinction of Mind from Body We now know what the essence of material things is: to be such a thing is to be extended in space in three dimensions, to have shape and size, to endure, and to be movable and changeable in these dimensions. This is what a material thing would be—if there were any. At last we face the haunting question: Are there any?

The first thing to note is that they *can* exist.

Q44. What is Descartes' reason for thinking this?

If, moreover, we examine our *images* of material things, it seems that the imagination produces these images by turning "to the body" and looking "at something there" (p. 321). It is as though a representation of a triangle were physically stored in the body (or brain); and imagination is looking, not at a real triangular thing, but at that stored representation. Since we can undoubtedly form mental images, it certainly seems as though some material things exist, namely, our bodies.

But to make this clearer, Descartes draws a sharp distinction between *imagining* something and *conceiving* it.

Q45. How does the example comparing the triangle with the chiliagon help to clarify this distinction? (See 72–73.)

---

*Socrates thinks that we can never be taught anything other than what we in some sense already know; what we call learning is in fact just remembering. (See pp. 97–98.) Descartes alludes to this doctrine here; in discovering the properties of a triangle I am "noticing for the first time something that had long been in me without my having turned my mind's eye towards it." Descartes is not, however, committed to the Socratic doctrine of the preexistence of the soul as an explanation of this phenomenon, since he thinks God's creation of a soul possessing certain innate ideas will suffice.

†This proof is a version of the ontological argument first worked out by Anselm of Canterbury in the eleventh century. See Chapter 15.

We still have no proof, of course, that there are any bodies. But again, progress has been made; for we now have an account of how one of the faculties of the mind works—on the assumption that there really are bodies. If we can find a proof of this assumption, it will "fit" with what we know about our mental capacities.

Descartes now turns from imagining to sensing. In 74–76 he reviews first his reasons for confidence in the senses and then his reasons for doubt.* At the end of this review he concludes again that what he is taught "by nature" does not deserve much credence.

However, the situation is now very different from that of the first *Meditation*. For now he knows that God exists and is not a deceiver. And in short order Descartes offers proofs that the soul is distinct from the body and that material things exist. Both of these depend on clear ideas of the essence of material things, which he arrived at in the fifth *Meditation*.

Q46. Set out briefly, in numbered sentences, the essential steps in the argument that the soul can exist without the body.

Q47. Is there a tension between this conclusion and the assertion (81) that I am not in my body the way a sailor is in his ship?

Q48. Set out briefly, in numbered sentences, the essential steps in the proof that material things exist (78–80).

At this point Descartes has, he thinks, achieved his main objectives. Skepticism and solipsism have been defeated. The basic structure of reality has been

---

*In the course of this review he paraphrases one of the basic principles of Thomas Aquinas, who derives it from Aristotle: that there is no idea in the intellect which was not previously in the senses. This is, for instance, the foundation for Thomas's rejection of the ontological argument (see p. 352). Descartes allows that this principle is superficially plausible; but in the light of his skeptical doubts he considers it naive. Not only do we know that we have ideas before we know we have senses, we know that some of these ideas must be innate—i.e., they could not plausibly be derived from sensible experience. Such are the ideas of thing, thought, truth, and God.

delineated: God, souls, and material things. Reality, then, is composed of infinite substance and two kinds of finite substances—thinking and extended. The bridge has been built. Knowledge has been shown to be possible. Physics has been supplied with a foundation. And all this with a certainty that rivals that of geometry!

The rest of *Meditation VI* attends to a few details that are still left.

Q49. Compare what Descartes says in 81–82 to Galileo's view of "secondary qualities" (pp. 283–284).

Q50. If the senses present external things in such an inadequate way, what use are they?

Q51. How are we to account for certain errors the senses seem to lead us to (such as the pain in an amputated limb or the desire of a person with dropsy to drink)?

Q52. What is the final disposition of the problem arising from dreams?

What Has Descartes Done?

It is possible to argue whether Descartes is the last of the Medievals or the first of the Moderns. Like most such arguments about transitional figures, there is truth on both sides. But that both philosophy and our general view of the world have been different ever since is indisputable. Descartes develops a philosophy that reflects the newly developing sciences and, in turn, gives them a legitimacy they otherwise lack. A measure of his lasting influence is the fact that a significant part of philosophy since World War I has been devoted to showing that he was crucially wrong about some basic things (which would not be worth doing unless his influence was still powerfully felt).* Descartes is *our* ancestor.

Let us sum up several key features of his thought and then indicate where certain problems crop up.

---

*Among the critics are Martin Heidegger and Ludwig Wittgenstein. See the chapters on their philosophies.

A New Ideal for Knowledge

One commentator says of the Cartesian revolution that it "stands for the substitution of free inquiry for submission to authority, for the rejection of Faith without reason for faith *in* reason, and the replacement of Faith by Demonstration."[5] Though Descartes is far from trying to reject religious belief (indeed, he thinks he can rationally justify its two most important parts, God and the soul), in the last analysis everything comes down to what the rational mind finds clear and distinct enough to be indubitable. Nothing else will be accepted, regardless of its antiquity or traditional claims to authority. We each contain within ourselves the criterion for truth and knowledge. This radical individualism is qualified only by the conviction that rationality is the same for every individual (just as mathematics is the same for all). No longer can we put the responsibility for deciding what to believe on someone else, whether priest, pope, or king. It lies squarely on each of us.

Moreover, the ideal for such belief is the clarity and certainty of mathematics. Probability or plausibility is not enough. Being vaguely right is not enough. The habits of thought developed in us by nature are not enough. By analysis we can resolve problems into their simple elements; by intuition we can see their truth; and by demonstration we can move to necessary consequences. Knowledge has the structure of an axiomatic system. All this is possible. Anything less is unacceptable. To be faithful to this ideal is to free oneself from error and to attain truth.

In all this Descartes deserves his reputation as Prince of the Rationalists.* The ultimate court of appeal is Reason—the Light of Nature. We ought to rely on intellect rather than sense, on intuition and deduction rather than imagination; "for true

---

*Though (almost) all philosophers try to reach their conclusions rationally, a rationalist is one who emphasizes the *exclusive* role of reason in the formation of knowledge. For one of Descartes' most distinguished predecessors in this tradition, see the discussion of the pre-Socratic thinker, Parmenides, in Chapter 3.

knowledge of external things seems to belong to the mind alone, not the composite of mind and body" (82–83).

A New Vision of Reality

Descartes' metaphysics makes explicit and complete the world view that was emerging already in the work of Copernicus, Kepler, and Galileo. Our world is a giant mechanism, not unlike a clock (see Descartes' analogy in 84). It was, to be sure, created by God. But now it runs on the principles of mechanics, and our science is mechanistic in principle. If we abstract from the fact of creation, the entire material universe, including the human body, is just a complex machine. The world has become a *secular* world. What happens can be explained and predicted without reference to any purposes or intentions of the creator. We are, we might say, worlds away from the intrinsically purposive, inherently value-laden, God-directed world of the Medievals. Dante now begins to look like a fairy tale or, at best, a moral allegory with no literal truth value at all. It is, perhaps, no great surprise that the *Meditations* ends up on the *Index* of forbidden books.

There are, to be sure, human minds or souls, and they are not caught up in the mechanism of the material world. They are, in fact, radically free. Even God does not have more freedom than a soul (see *Meditation IV*). But as we'll see, this disparity between soul and body is not as much the solution to a problem as it is a problem in itself.

Problems

Great as Descartes' achievement is, he bequeaths to his successors a legacy of unsolved problems. There are those who refuse to accept his radical beginning point and remain true to a more traditional approach, usually Aristotelian. But his methodological doubt has been powerfully persuasive to many, and the continued progress of physics seems to be evidence that his basic view of the world is correct. For the next hundred and fifty years, Cartesianism, together with its variants, will be the dominating philosophy on the continent. As we'll see, different assumptions are at work in Britain, but even here the Cartesian spirit of independence is pervasive. Still, there are nagging worries. Let us note three of them.

The Place of Humans in the World of Nature Descartes is intent on legitimizing the new science. And this he does. But what place is there for us in the universe of the new physics? Is it plausible to think that we, too, are just cogs in this universal machine? We assume that we have purposes and act to realize certain values. But where is there room for purposes and values in this mechanistic world? Is our assumption just an illusion? We assume that we can make a difference in the outcome of physical processes. But if the world is a closed mechanism, how can this be? We experience ourselves as conscious beings, aware of ourselves and the world around us. But can a machine be conscious? These are very contemporary questions, the sort cognitive science aims to sort out and solve.

All these questions force themselves on us once we take Descartes' vision of the universe seriously. Descartes is not unaware of them. His basic strategy for dealing with them consists in the radical split that he makes between mind and body. Bodies, he holds, are parts of the mechanical universe; minds are not. Physics can deal with the body, but not with the mind. We know that we are not merely automata because (1) we can use language, and (2) we are flexible and adaptable in a way no machine could be; reason, Descartes says, "is a universal instrument which can be used in all kinds of situations." It is quite possible, he says, that we could construct a machine that utters words—even one that utters words corresponding to movements of its body. But it is not possible, he thinks, for a machine to "give an appropriately meaningful answer to whatever is said in its presence, as the dullest of men can do" (DM 6.56–57, p. 120).*

---

*This, of course, is precisely the aim of research on artificial intelligence. Will it be successful? Descartes bets not.

But merely dividing mind from body does not completely solve the problem. The question arises: how are they related?

The Mind and the Body Descartes concludes that the mind is one thing and the body another; each is so independent of the other that either could exist without the other. They are, moreover, of a radically different character. The essence of a mind is thinking; minds are in no sense extended objects. The essence of a material thing is extension; but extended things such as bodies cannot think. Still, he says, mind and body are so intimately related as to form "a single unified thing" (86).

But how can I be two things and yet one single thing? No explanation is given. Clearly he must insist that what happens to the body affects the mind, as when I get hungry, or am hurt, or open my eyes to a blue wall in daylight. And what the mind decides, the body may do, as when I choose to walk or eat an ice cream cone. There seems to be a two-way causal relation between mind and body. This view is called *interactionism*

. Yet it is completely puzzling how this can be. How can something that is not extended reach into the closed system of the mechanical world and work a change there, where all changes are governed by mechanical principles? And how can an alteration in the shape or position of certain material particles cause us to feel sad or think of Cleveland? No explanation is forthcoming. It seems entirely mysterious. To save the integrity of his physics, Descartes pushes the mental out of the physical world entirely. But then it is inexplicable how physics itself can be done at all, since it seems to depend on interactions between nonphysical minds and physical bodies. Here is the problem that Schopenhauer would later call "the world knot." It is safe to say that a philosophy that does not solve the mind-body problem cannot be considered entirely acceptable.

God and the Problem of Skepticism As we have seen, Descartes takes the skeptical problem very seriously. He pushes skeptical arguments about as far as they can be pushed. And he thinks that in the *cogito* he has found the key to overcoming skepticism. But even if we grant that each of us knows, by virtue of the *cogito*, that we exist, knowledge of the *world* depends on the fact that God is not a deceiver. And that depends on the proofs for the existence of God.

What if those proofs are faulty? Then we are back again in solipsism, without a guarantee that anything exists beyond ourselves. Are the proofs— or at least one of them—satisfactory? Descartes is quite clear that everything depends on that question; "the certainty and truth of all my knowledge derives from one thing: my thought of the true God" (71). He is sure that the proofs are as secure as the theorems of geometry. But is he right about that?

The Preeminence of Epistemology

In earlier philosophies there are many problems— the one and the many, the nature of reality, explaining change, the soul, the existence of God— and the problem of knowledge is just one among the rest. Descartes' radical skepticism changes that. After Descartes and until very recent times most philosophers think that epistemological problems are absolutely foundational. Among these problems of knowledge, the problem about knowing the external world is the sharpest and most dangerous. Can we know anything at all beyond the contents of our minds? Unless this skeptical question can be satisfactorily answered, nothing else can be done. Epistemology is, for better or worse, the heart of philosophy for the next several hundred years.

These are problems that Descartes' successors wrestle with, as we'll see. Next, however, we want to look at a figure who is often neglected in the history of modern philosophy, Thomas Hobbes. Hobbes is more interesting to us than to previous generations, perhaps, because he presents an alternative response to the new science. Some recent thought about the mind—that associated with artificial intelligence—can be thought of as a struggle to replace the paradigm of Descartes with that of Hobbes.

Meditation I:
On What Can Be Called Into Doubt

For several years now, I've been aware that I accepted many falsehoods as true in my youth, that what I built on the foundation of those falsehoods was dubious, and accordingly that once in my life I would need to tear down everything and begin anew from the foundations if I wanted to establish any stable and lasting knowledge. But the task seemed enormous, and I waited until I was so old that no better time for undertaking it would be likely to follow. I have thus delayed so long that it would be wrong for me to waste in indecision the time left for action. Today, then, having rid myself of worries and 18 having arranged for some peace and quiet, I withdraw alone, free at last earnestly and wholeheartedly to overthrow all my beliefs.

To do this, I don't need to show each of them to be false; I may never be able to do that. But, since reason now convinces me that I ought to withhold my assent just as carefully from what isn't obviously certain and indubitable as from what's obviously false, I can justify the rejection of all my beliefs if in each I can find some ground for doubt. And, to do this, I need not run through my beliefs one by one, which would be an endless task. Since a building collapses when its foundation is cut out from under it, I will go straight to the principles on which all my former beliefs rested.

Of course, whatever I have so far accepted as supremely true I have learned either from the senses or through the senses. But I have occasionally caught the senses deceiving me, and it's prudent never completely to trust those who have cheated us even once.

But, while my senses may deceive me about what is small or far away, there may still be other things that I take in by the senses but that I cannot possibly doubt— like that I am here, sitting before the fire, wearing a dressing gown, touching this paper. And on what grounds might I deny that my hands and the other parts of my body exist?—unless perhaps I liken myself to 19 madmen whose brains are so rattled by the persistent vapors of melancholy that they are sure that they're kings when in fact they are paupers, or that they wear purple robes when in fact they're naked, or that their heads are clay, or that they are gourds, or made of glass. But these people are insane, and I would seem just as crazy if I were to apply what I say about them to myself.

This would be perfectly obvious—if I weren't a man accustomed to sleeping at night whose experiences while asleep are at least as far-fetched as those that madmen have while awake. How often, at night, I've been convinced that I was here, sitting before the fire, wearing my dressing gown, when in fact I was undressed and between the covers of my bed! But now I am looking at this piece of paper with my eyes wide open; the head that I am shaking has not been lulled to sleep; I put my hand out consciously and deliberately and feel. None of this would be as distinct if I were asleep. As if I can't remember having been tricked by similar thoughts while asleep! When I think very carefully about this, I see so plainly that there are no reliable signs by which I can distinguish sleeping from waking that I am stupe-fied—and my stupor itself suggests that I am asleep!

Suppose, then, that I am dreaming. Suppose, in particular, that my eyes are not open, that my head is not moving, and that I have not put out my hand. Suppose that I do not have hands, or even a body. I must still admit that the things I see in sleep are like painted images which must have been patterned after real things and, hence, that things like eyes, heads, hands, and bodies are real rather than imaginary. For, even when
20 painters try to give bizarre shapes to sirens and satyrs, they are unable to give them completely new natures; they only jumble together the parts of various animals. And, even if they were to come up with something so novel that no one had ever seen anything like it before, something entirely fictitious and unreal, at least there must be real colors from which they composed it. Similarly, while things like eyes, heads, and hands may be imaginary, it must be granted that some simpler and more universal things are real—the "real colors" from which the true and false images in our thoughts are formed.

Things of this sort seem to include general bodily nature and its extension, the shape of extended things, their quantity (that is, their size and number), the place in which they exist, the time through which they endure, and so on.

Perhaps we can correctly infer that, while physics, astronomy, medicine, and other disciplines that require the study of composites are dubious, disciplines like arithmetic and geometry, which deal only with completely simple and universal things without regard to whether they exist in the world, are somehow certain and indubitable. For, whether we are awake or asleep, two plus three is always five, and the square never has more than four sides. It seems impossible even to suspect such obvious truths of falsity.

21   Nevertheless, the traditional view is fixed in my mind that there is a God who can do anything and by whom I

have been made to be as I am. How do I know that He hasn't brought it about that, while there is in fact no earth, no sky, no extended thing, no shape, no magnitude, and no place, all of these things seem to me to exist, just as they do now? I think that other people sometimes err in what they believe themselves to know perfectly well. Mightn't I be deceived when I add two and three, or count the sides of a square, or do even simpler things, if we can even suppose that there is anything simpler? Maybe it will be denied that God deceives me, since He is said to be supremely good. But, if God's being good is incompatible with His having created me so that I am deceived always, it seems just as out of line with His being good that He permits me to be deceived sometimes—as he undeniably does.

Maybe some would rather deny that there is an omnipotent God than believe that everything else is uncertain. Rather than arguing with them, I will grant everything I have said about God to be fiction. But, however these people think I came to be as I now am—whether they say it is by fate, or by accident, or by a continuous series of events, or in some other way—it seems that he who errs and is deceived is somehow imperfect. Hence, the less power that is attributed to my original creator, the more likely it is that I am always deceived. To these arguments, I have no reply. I'm forced to admit that nothing that I used to believe is beyond legitimate doubt—not because I have been careless or playful, but because I have valid and well-considered grounds for doubt. Hence, I must withhold my assent from my for-
22 mer beliefs as carefully as from obvious falsehoods if I want to arrive at something certain.

But it's not enough to have noticed this: I must also take care to bear it in mind. For my habitual views constantly return to my mind and take control of what I believe as if our long-standing, intimate relationship has given them the right to do so, even against my will. I'll never break the habit of trusting and giving in to these views while I see them for what they are—things somewhat dubious (as I have just shown) but nonetheless probable, things that I have much more reason to believe than to deny. That's why I think it will be good deliberately to turn my will around, to allow myself to be deceived, and to suppose that all my previous beliefs are false and illusory. Eventually, when I have counterbalanced the weight of my prejudices, my bad habits will no longer distort my grasp of things. I know that there is no danger of error here and that I won't overindulge in skepticism, since I'm now concerned, not with action, but only with gaining knowledge.

I will suppose, then, not that there is a supremely good God who is the source of all truth, but that there is an evil demon, supremely powerful and cunning, who works as hard as he can to deceive me. I will say that sky, air, earth, color, shape, sound, and other external things are just dreamed illusions that the demon uses to en-

23 snare my judgment. I will regard myself as not having hands, eyes, flesh, blood, and senses—but as having the false belief that I have all these things. I will obstinately concentrate on this meditation and will thus ensure by mental resolution that, if I do not really have the ability to know the truth, I will at least withhold assent from what is false and from what a deceiver may try to put over on me, however powerful and cunning he may be. But this plan requires effort, and laziness brings me back to my ordinary life. I am like a prisoner who happens to enjoy the illusion of freedom in his dreams, begins to suspect that he is asleep, fears being awakened, and deliberately lets the enticing illusions slip by unchallenged. Thus, I slide back into my old views, afraid to awaken and to find that after my peaceful rest I must toil, not in the light, but in the confusing darkness of the problems just raised.

Meditation II:
On the Nature of the Human Mind, Which Is Better Known Than the Body

Yesterday's meditation has hurled me into doubts so great that I can neither ignore them or think my way out

24 of them. I am in turmoil, as if I have accidentally fallen into a whirlpool and can neither touch bottom nor swim to the safety of the surface. I will struggle, however, and try to follow the path that I started on yesterday. I will reject whatever is open to the slightest doubt just as though I have found it to be entirely false, and I will continue until I find something certain—or at least until I know for certain that nothing is certain. Archimedes required only one fixed and immovable point to move the whole earth from its place, and I too can hope for great things if I can find even one small thing that is certain and unshakeable.

I will suppose, then, that everything I see is unreal. I will believe that my memory is unreliable and that none of what it presents to me ever happened. I have no senses. Body, shape, extension, motion, and place are fantasies. What then is true? Perhaps just that nothing is certain.

But how do I know that there isn't something different from the things just listed that I do not have the slightest reason to doubt? Isn't there a God, or something like one, who puts my thoughts into me? But why should I say so when I may be the author of those thoughts? Well, isn't it at least the case that I am something? But I now am denying that I have senses and a

25 body. But I stop here. For what follows from these denials? Am I so bound to my body and to my senses that I cannot exist without them? I have convinced myself that there is nothing in the world—no sky, no earth, no minds, no bodies. Doesn't it follow that I don't exist? No, surely I must exist if it's me who is convinced of something. But there is a deceiver, supremely powerful and cunning whose aim is to see that I am always deceived. But surely I exist, if I am deceived. Let him deceive me all he can, he will never make it the case that I am nothing while I think that I am something. Thus having fully weighed every consideration, I must finally conclude that the statement "I am, I exist" must be true whenever I state it or mentally consider it.

But I do not yet fully understand what this "I" is that must exist. I must guard against inadvertently taking myself to be something other than I am, thereby going wrong even in the knowledge that I put forward as supremely certain and evident. Hence, I will think once again about what I believed myself to be before beginning these meditations. From this conception, I will subtract everything challenged by the reasons for doubt that I produced earlier, until nothing remains except what is certain and indubitable.

What, then, did I formerly take myself to be? A man, of course. But what is a man? Should I say a rational animal? No, because then I would need to ask what an animal is and what it is to be rational. Thus, starting from a single question, I would sink into many that are more difficult, and I do not have the time to waste on

26 such subtleties. Instead, I will look here at the thoughts that occurred to me spontaneously and naturally when I reflected on what I was. The first thought to occur to me was that I have a face, hands, arms, and all the other equipment (also found in corpses) which I call a body. The next thought to occur to me was that I take nourishment, move myself around, sense, and think—that I do things which I trace back to my soul. Either I didn't stop to think about what this soul was, or I imagined it to be a rarified air, or fire, or ether permeating the denser parts of my body. But, about physical objects, I didn't have any doubts whatever: I thought that I distinctly knew their nature. If I had tried to describe my conception of

this nature, I might have said this: "When I call something a physical object, I mean that it is capable of being bounded by a shape and limited to a place; that it can fill a space so as to exclude other objects from it; that it can be perceived by touch, sight, hearing, taste, and smell; that it can be moved in various ways, not by itself, but by something else in contact with it." I judged that the powers of self-movement, of sensing, and of thinking did not belong to the nature of physical objects, and, in fact, I marveled that there were some physical objects in which these powers could be found.

But what should I think now, while supposing that a supremely powerful and "evil" deceiver completely devotes himself to deceiving me? Can I say that I have any of the things that I have attributed to the nature of physical objects? I concentrate, think, reconsider—but nothing comes to me; I grow tired of the pointless repetition.

27 But what about the things that I have assigned to soul? Nutrition and self-movement? Since I have no body, these are merely illusions. Sensing? But I cannot sense without a body, and in sleep I've seemed to sense many things that I later realized I had not really sensed. Thinking? It comes down to this: Thought and thought alone cannot be taken away from me. I am, I exist. That much is certain. But for how long? As long as I think—for it may be that, if I completely stopped thinking, I would completely cease to exist. I am not now admitting anything unless it must be true, and I am therefore not admitting that I am anything at all other than a thinking thing—that is, a mind, soul, understanding, or reason (terms whose meaning I did not previously know). I know that I am a real, existing thing, but what kind of thing? As I have said, a thing that thinks.

What else? I will draw up mental images. I'm not the collection of organs called a human body. Nor am I some rarified gas permeating these organs, or air, or fire, or vapor, or breath—for I have supposed that none of these things exist. Still, I am something. But couldn't it be that these things, which I do not yet know about and which I am therefore supposing to be nonexistent, really aren't distinct from the "I" that I know to exist? I don't know, and I'm not going to argue about it now. I can only form judgments on what I do know. I know that I exist, and I ask what the "I" is that I know to exist. It's obvious that this conception of myself doesn't depend

28 on anything that I do not yet know to exist and, therefore, that it does not depend on anything of which I can draw up a mental image. And the words "draw up" point to my mistake. I would truly be creative if I were to have a mental image of what I am, since to have a mental

image is just to contemplate the shape or image of a physical object. I now know with certainty that I exist and at the same time that all images—and, more generally, all things associated with the nature of physical objects—may just be dreams. When I keep this in mind, it seems just as absurd to say "I use mental images to help me understand what I am" as it would to say "Now, while awake, I see something true—but, since I don't yet see it clearly enough, I'll go to sleep and let my dreams present it to me more clearly and truly." Thus I know that none of the things that I can comprehend with the aid of mental images bear on my knowledge of myself. And I must carefully draw my mind away from such things if it is to see its own nature distinctly.

But what then am I? A thinking thing. And what is that? Something that doubts, understands, affirms, denies, wills, refuses, and also senses and has mental images.

That's quite a lot, if I really do all of these things. But don't I? Isn't it me who now doubts nearly everything, understands one thing, affirms this thing, refuses to affirm other things, wants to know much more, refuses to be deceived, has mental images (sometimes involuntarily), and is aware of many things "through his senses"? Even if I am always dreaming, and even if my creator does what he can to deceive me, isn't it just as true that I do all these things as that I exist? Are any of

29 these things distinct from my thought? Can any be said to be separate from me? That it's me who doubts, understands, and wills is so obvious that I don't see how it could be more evident. And it's also me who has mental images. While it may be, as I am supposing, that absolutely nothing of which I have a mental image really exists, the ability to have mental images really does exist and is a part of my thought. Finally, it's me who senses—or who seems to gain awareness of physical objects through the senses. For example, I am now seeing light, hearing a noise, and feeling heat. These things are unreal, since I am dreaming. But it is still certain that I seem to see, to hear, and to feel. This seeming cannot be unreal, and it is what is properly called sensing. Strictly speaking, sensing is just thinking.

From this, I begin to learn a little about what I am. But I still can't stop thinking that I apprehend physical objects, which I picture in mental images and examine with my senses, much more distinctly than I know this unfamiliar "I," of which I cannot form a mental image. I think this, even though it would be astounding if I comprehended things which I've found to be doubtful, unknown, and alien to me more distinctly than the one

which I know to be real: my self. But I see what's happening. My mind enjoys wandering, and it won't confine
30 itself to the truth. I will therefore loosen the reigns on my mind for now so that later, when the time is right, I will be able to control it more easily.

Let's consider the things commonly taken to be the most distinctly comprehended: physical objects that we see and touch. Let's not consider physical objects in general, since general conceptions are very often confused. Rather, let's consider one, particular object. Take, for example, this piece of wax. It has just been taken from the honeycomb; it hasn't yet completely lost the taste of honey; it still smells of the flowers from which it was gathered; its color, shape, and size are obvious; it is hard, cold, and easy to touch; it makes a sound when rapped. In short, everything seems to be present in the wax that is required for me to know it as distinctly as possible. But, as I speak, I move the wax toward the fire; it loses what was left of its taste; it gives up its smell; it changes color; it loses its shape; it gets bigger; it melts; it heats up; it becomes difficult to touch; it no longer makes a sound when struck. Is it still the same piece of wax? We must say that it is: no one denies it or thinks otherwise. Then what was there in the wax that I comprehended so distinctly? Certainly nothing that I reached with my senses—for, while everything having to do with taste, smell, sight, touch, and hearing has changed, the same piece of wax remains.

Perhaps what I distinctly knew was neither the sweetness of honey, nor the fragrance of flowers, nor a sound, but a physical object that once appeared to me one way and now appears differently. But what exactly is it of which I now have a mental image? Let's pay careful at-
31 tention, remove everything that doesn't belong to the wax, and see what's left. Nothing is left except an extended, flexible, and changeable thing. But what is it for this thing to be flexible and changeable? Is it just that the wax can go from round to square and then to triangular, as I have mentally pictured? Of course not. Since I understand that the wax's shape can change in innumerable ways, and since I can't run through all the changes in my imagination, my comprehension of the wax's flexibility and changeability cannot have been produced by my ability to have mental images. And what about the thing that is extended? Are we also ignorant of its extension? Since the extension of the wax increases when the wax melts, increases again when the wax boils, and increases still more when the wax gets hotter, I will be mistaken about what the wax is unless I believe that it can undergo more changes in extension than I can ever

encompass with mental images. I must therefore admit that I do not have an image of what the wax is—that I grasp what it is with only my mind. (While I am saying this about a particular piece of wax, it is even more clearly true about wax in general.) What then is this piece of wax that I grasp only with my mind? It is something that I see, feel, and mentally picture—exactly what I believed it to be at the outset. But it must be noted that, despite the appearances, my grasp of the wax is not visual, tactile, or pictorial. Rather, my grasp of the wax is the result of a purely mental inspection, which can be imperfect and confused, as it was once, or clear and distinct, as it is now, depending on how much attention I pay to the things of which the wax consists.

I'm surprised by how prone my mind is to error. Even when I think to myself non-verbally, language
32 stands in my way, and common usage comes close to deceiving me. For, when the wax is present, we say that we see the wax itself, not that we infer its presence from its color and shape. I'm inclined to leap from this fact about language to the conclusion that I learn about the wax by eyesight rather than by purely mental inspection. But, if I happen to look out my window and see men walking in the street, I naturally say that I see the men just as I say that I see the wax. What do I really see, however, but hats and coats that could be covering robots? I *judge* that there are men. Thus I comprehend with my judgment, which is in my mind, objects that I once believed myself to see with my eyes.

One who aspires to wisdom above that of the common man disgraces himself by deriving doubt from common ways of speaking. Let's go on, then, to ask when I most clearly and perfectly grasped what the wax is. Was it when I first looked at the wax and believed my knowledge of it to come from the external senses—or at any rate from the so-called "common sense," the power of having mental images? Or is it now, after I have carefully studied what the wax is and how I come to know it? Doubt would be silly here. For what was distinct in my original conception of the wax? How did that conception differ from that had by animals? When I distinguish the wax from its external forms—when I "undress" it and view it "naked"—there may still be errors in my judgments about it, but I couldn't possibly grasp the wax in this way without a human mind.

33 What should I say about this mind—or, in other words, about myself? (I am not now admitting that there is anything to me but a mind.) What is this "I" that seems to grasp the wax so distinctly? Don't I know myself much more truly and certainly, and also much more

distinctly and plainly, than I know the wax? For, if I base my judgment that the wax exists on the fact that I see it, my seeing it much more obviously implies that I exist. It's possible that what I see is not really wax, and it's even possible that I don't have eyes with which to see—but it clearly is not possible that, when I see (or, what now amounts to the same thing, when I think I see), the "I" that thinks is not a real thing. Similarly, if I base my judgment that the wax exists on the fact that I feel it, the same fact makes it obvious that I exist. If I base my judgment that the wax exists on the fact that I have a mental image of it or on some other fact of this sort, the same thing can obviously be said. And what I've said about the wax applies to everything else that is outside me. Moreover, if I seem to grasp the wax more distinctly when I detect it with several senses than when I detect it with just sight or touch, I must know myself even more distinctly—for every consideration that contributes to my grasp of the piece of wax or to my grasp of any other physical object serves better to reveal the nature of my mind. Besides, the mind has so much in it by which it can make its conception of itself distinct that what comes to it from physical objects hardly seems to matter.

34 And now I have brought myself back to where I wanted to be. I now know that physical objects are grasped, not by the senses or the power of having mental images, but by understanding alone. And, since I grasp physical objects in virtue of their being understandable rather than in virtue of their being tangible or visible, I know that I can't grasp anything more easily or plainly than my mind. But, since it takes time to break old habits of thought, I should pause here to allow the length of my contemplation to impress the new thoughts more deeply into my memory.

Meditation III:
On God's Existence

I will now close my eyes, plug my ears, and withdraw all my senses. I will rid my thoughts of the images of physical objects—or, since that's beyond me, I'll write those images off as empty illusions. Talking with myself and looking more deeply into myself, I'll try gradually to come to know myself better. I am a thinking thing—a thing that doubts, affirms, denies, understands a few things, is ignorant of many things, wills, and refuses. I also sense and have mental images. For, as I've noted, even though the things of which I have sensations or mental images may not exist outside me, I'm certain that

the modifications of thought called sensations and mental images exist in me insofar as they are just modifica-
35 tions of thought.

That's a summary of all that I really know—or, at any rate, of all that I've so far noticed that I know. I now will examine more carefully whether there are other things in me that I have not yet discovered. I'm certain that I am a thinking thing. Then don't I know what's needed for me to be certain of other things? In this first knowledge, there is nothing but a clear and distinct grasp of what I affirm, and this grasp surely would not suffice to make me certain if it could ever happen that something I grasped so clearly and distinctly was false. Accordingly, I seem to be able to establish the general rule that whatever I clearly and distinctly grasp is true.

But, in the past, I've accepted as completely obvious and certain many thoughts that I later found to be dubious. What were these thoughts about? The earth, the sky, the stars, and other objects of sense. But what did I clearly grasp about these objects? Only that ideas or thoughts of them appeared in my mind. Even now, I don't deny that these ideas occur in me. But there was something else that I used to affirm—something that I used to believe myself to grasp clearly but did not really grasp at all: I affirmed that there were things besides me, that the ideas in me came from these things, and that the ideas perfectly resembled these things. Either I erred here, or I reached a true judgment that wasn't justified by the strength of my understanding.

36 But what follows? When I considered very simple and easy points of arithmetic or geometry—such as that two and three together make five—didn't I see them clearly enough to affirm their truth? My only reason for judging that I ought to doubt these things was the thought that my God-given nature might deceive me even about what seems most obvious. Whenever I conceive of an all-powerful God, I'm compelled to admit that, if He wants, He can make it the case that I err even about what I take my mind's eye to see most clearly. But, when I turn to the things that I believe myself to grasp very clearly, I'm so convinced by them that I spontaneously burst forth saying, "Whoever may deceive me, he will never bring it about that I am nothing while I think that I am something, or that I have never been when it is now true that I am, or that two plus three is either more or less than five, or that something else in which I recognize an obvious inconsistency is true." And, since I have no reason for thinking that God is a deceiver—indeed, since I don't yet know whether God exists—the grounds for doubt that rest on the supposi-

tion that God deceives are very weak and "metaphysical." Still, to rid myself of these grounds, I ought to ask as soon as possible whether there is a God and, if so, whether He can be a deceiver. For it seems that, until I know these two things, I can never be completely certain of anything else.

37 The structure of my project seems to require, however, that I first categorize my thoughts and ask in which of them truth and falsity really reside. Some of my thoughts are like images of things, and only these can properly be called ideas. I have an idea, for example, when I think of a man, of a chimera, of heaven, of an angel, or of God. But other thoughts have other properties: while I always apprehend something as the object of my thought when I will, fear, affirm, or deny, these thoughts also include a component in addition to the likeness of that thing. Some of these components are called volitions or emotions; others, judgments.

Now, viewed in themselves and without regard to other things, ideas cannot really be false. If I imagine a chimera and a goat, it is just as true that I imagine the chimera as that I imagine the goat. And I needn't worry about falsehood in volitions or emotions. If I have a perverse desire for something, or if I want something that doesn't exist, it's still true that I want that thing. All that remains, then, are my judgments; it's here that I must be careful not to err. And the first and foremost of the errors that I find in my judgments is that of assuming that the ideas in me have a similarity or conformity to things outside me. For, if I were to regard ideas merely as modifications of thought, they could not really provide me with any opportunity for error.

38 Of my ideas, some seem to me to be innate, others acquired, and others produced by me. The ideas by which I understand reality, truth, and thought seem to have come from my own nature. Those ideas by which I hear a noise, see the sun, or feel the fire I formerly judged to come from things outside me. And the ideas of sirens, hippogriffs, and so on I have formed in myself. Or maybe I can take all of my ideas to be acquired, all innate, or all created by me: I do not yet clearly see where my ideas come from.

For the moment, the central question is about the ideas that I view as derived from objects existing outside me. What reason is there for thinking that these ideas resemble the objects? I seem to have been taught this by nature. Besides, I find that these ideas are independent of my will and hence of me—for they often appear when I do not want them to do so. For example, I now feel heat whether I want to or not, and I therefore take the idea or

sensation of heat to come from something distinct from me: the heat of the fire by which I am now sitting. And the obvious thing to think is that a thing sends me its own likeness, not something else.

I will now see whether these reasons are good enough. When I say that nature teaches me something, I mean just that I have a spontaneous impulse to believe it, not that the light of nature reveals the thing's truth to me. There is an important difference. When the light of nature reveals something to me (such as that my thinking implies my existing) that thing is completely beyond doubt, since there is no faculty as reliable as the light of nature by means of which I could learn that the thing is 39 not true. But, as for my natural impulses, I have often judged them to have led me astray in choices about what's good, and I don't see why I should regard them as any more reliable on matters concerning truth and falsehood.

Next, while my sensory ideas may not depend on my will, it doesn't follow that they come from outside me. While the natural impulses of which I just spoke are in me, they seem to conflict with my will. Similarly, I may have in me an as yet undiscovered ability to produce the ideas that seem to come from outside me—in the way that I used to think that ideas came to me in dreams.

Finally, even if some of my ideas do come from things distinct from me, it doesn't follow that they are likenesses of these things. Indeed, it often seems to me that an idea differs greatly from its cause. For example, I find in myself two different ideas of the sun. One, which I "take in" through the senses and which I ought therefore to view as a typical acquired idea, makes the sun look very small to me. The other, which I derive from astronomical reasoning (that is, which I make, perhaps by composing it from innate ideas), pictures the sun as many times larger than the earth. It clearly cannot be that both of these ideas are accurate likenesses of a sun that exists outside me, and reason convinces me that the one least like the sun is the one that seems to arise most directly from it.

All that I've said shows that, until now, my belief that 40 there are things outside me that send their ideas or images to me (perhaps through my senses) has rested on blind impulse rather than certain judgment.

Still, it seems to me that there may be a way of telling whether my ideas come from things that exist outside me. Insofar as the ideas of things are just modifications of thought, I find no inequality among them; all seem to arise from me in the same way. But, insofar as different ideas present different things to me, there obviously are great differences among them. The ideas of substances are unquestionably greater—or have more "subjective reality"—than those of modifications or accidents. Similarly, the idea by which I understand the supreme God—eternal, infinite, omniscient, omnipotent, and creator of all things other than Himself—has more subjective reality in it than the ideas of finite substances.

Now, the light of nature reveals that there is at least as much in a complete efficient cause as in its effect. For where could an effect get its reality if not from its cause? And how could a cause give something unless it had it? It follows both that something cannot come from nothing and that what is more perfect—that is, has more

41 reality in it—cannot come from what is less perfect or has less reality. This obviously holds, not just for those effects whose reality is actual or formal, but also for ideas, whose reality we regard as merely subjective. For example, it's impossible for a non-existent stone to come into existence unless it's produced by something containing, either formally or eminently, everything in the stone. Similarly, heat can only be induced in something that's not already hot by something having at least the same degree of perfection as heat. Also, it's impossible for the *idea* of heat or of stone to be in me unless it's been put there by a cause having at least as much reality as I conceive of in the heat or the stone. For, although the cause doesn't transmit any of its actual or formal reality to the idea, we shouldn't infer that it can be less real than the idea; all that we can infer is that by its nature the idea doesn't require any formal reality except what it derives from my thought, of which it is a modification. Yet, as the idea contains one particular subjective reality rather than another, it must get this reality from a cause having at least as much formal reality as the idea has subjective reality. For, if we suppose that an idea has something in it that wasn't in its cause, we must suppose that it got this thing from nothing. However imperfect the existence of something that exists subjectively in the understanding through an idea, it obviously is something, and it therefore cannot come from nothing.

And, although the reality that I'm considering in my

42 ideas is just subjective, I ought not to suspect that it can fail to be in an idea's cause formally—that it's enough for it to be there subjectively. For, just as the subjective existence of my ideas belongs to the ideas in virtue of their nature, the formal existence of the ideas' causes belongs to those causes—or, at least, to the first and foremost of them—in virtue of the causes' nature. Although one idea may arise from another, this can't go back to infinity; we must eventually arrive at a primary idea whose

cause is an "archetype" containing formally all the reality that the idea contains subjectively. Hence, the light of nature makes it clear to me that the ideas in me are like images that may well fall short of the things from which they derive, but cannot contain anything greater or more perfect.

The more time and care I take in studying this, the more clearly and distinctly I know it to be true. But what follows from it? If I can be sure that the subjective reality of one of my ideas is so great that it isn't in me either formally or eminently and hence that I cannot be the cause of that idea, I can infer that I am not alone in the world—that there exists something else that is the cause of the idea. But, if I can find no such idea in me, I will have no argument at all for the existence of anything other than me—for, having diligently searched for such an argument, I have yet to find one.

Of my ideas—besides my idea of myself, about

43 which there can be no problem here—one presents God, others inanimate physical objects, others angels, others animals, and still others men like me.

As to my idea of other men, of animals, and of angels, it's easy to see that—even if the world contained no men but me, no animals, and no angels—I could have composed these ideas from those that I have of myself, of physical objects, and of God.

And, as to my ideas of physical objects, it seems that nothing in them is so great that it couldn't have come from me. For, if I analyze my ideas of physical objects carefully, taking them one by one as I did yesterday when examining my idea of the piece of wax, I notice that there is very little in them that I grasp clearly and distinctly. What I do grasp clearly and distinctly in these ideas is size (which is extension in length, breadth, and depth), shape (which arises from extension's limits), position (which the differently shaped things have relative to one another), and motion (which is just change of position). To these I can add substance, duration, and number. But my thoughts of other things in physical objects (such as light and color, sound, odor, taste, heat and cold, and tactile qualities) are so confused and obscure that I can't say whether they are true or false—whether my ideas of these things are of something or of nothing. Although, as I noted earlier, that which is properly called falsehood—namely, *formal* falsehood—can only be found in judgments, we can still find falsehood of another sort—namely, *material* falsehood—in an idea when it presents what is not a thing as though it were a thing. For example, the ideas that I have of cold-

44 ness and heat are so unclear and indistinct that I can't

tell from them whether coldness is just the absence of heat, or heat just the absence of coldness, or both are real qualities, or neither is. And, since every idea is "of something," the idea that presents coldness to me as something real and positive could justifiably be called false if coldness were just the absence of heat. And the same holds true for other ideas of this sort.

For such ideas, I need not posit a creator distinct from me. I know by the light of nature that, if one of these ideas is false—that is, if it doesn't present a real thing—it comes from nothing—that is, the only cause of its being in me is a deficiency of my nature, which clearly is imperfect. If one of these ideas is true, however, I still see no reason why I couldn't have produced it myself—for these ideas present so little reality to me that I can't even distinguish it from nothing.

Of the things that are clear and distinct in my ideas of physical objects, it seems that I may have borrowed some—such as substance, duration, and number—from my idea of myself. I think of the stone as a substance—that is, as something that can exist on its own—just as I think of myself as a substance. Although I conceive of myself as a thinking and unextended thing and of the stone as an extended and unthinking thing so that the two conceptions are quite different, they are the same in that they both seem to be of substances. And, when I grasp that I exist now while remembering that I
45 existed in the past, or when I count my various thoughts, I get the idea of duration or number, which I can then apply to other things. The other components of my ideas of physical objects—extension, shape, place, and motion—can't be in me formally, since I'm just a thinking thing. But, as these things are just modes of substance, and as I am a substance, it seems that they may be in me eminently.

All that's left is my idea of God. Is there something in this idea of God that couldn't have come from me? By "God" I mean a substance that's infinite, independent, supremely intelligent, and supremely powerful—the thing from which I and everything else that may exist derive our existence. The more I consider these attributes, the less it seems that they could have come from me alone. So I must conclude that God necessarily exists.

While I may have the idea of substance in me by virtue of my being a substance, I who am finite would not have the idea of infinite substance in me unless it came from a substance that really was infinite.

And I shouldn't think that, rather than having a true idea of infinity, I grasp it merely as the absence of

limits—in the way that I grasp rest as the absence of motion and darkness as the absence of light. On the contrary, it's clear to me that there is more reality in an infinite than in a finite substance and hence that my grasp of the infinite must somehow be prior to my grasp of the finite—my understanding of God prior to my understanding of myself. For how could I understand that
46 I doubt and desire, that I am deficient and imperfect, if I didn't have the idea of something more perfect to use as a standard of comparison?

And, unlike the ideas of hot and cold which I just discussed, the idea of God cannot be said to be materially false and hence to come from nothing. On the contrary, since the idea of God is completely clear and distinct and contains more subjective reality than any other idea, no idea is truer *per se* and none less open to the suspicion of falsity. The idea of a supremely perfect and infinite entity is, I maintain, completely true. For, while I may be able to suppose that there is no such entity, I can't even suppose (as I did about the idea of coldness) that my idea of God fails to show me something real. This idea is maximally clear and distinct, for it contains everything that I grasp clearly and distinctly, everything real and true, everything with any perfection. It doesn't matter that I can't fully comprehend the infinite—that there are innumerable things in God which I can't comprehend fully or even reach with thought. Because of the nature of the infinite, I who am finite cannot comprehend it. It's enough that I think about the infinite and judge that, if I grasp something clearly and distinctly and know it to have some perfection, it's present either formally or eminently—perhaps along with innumerable other things of which I am ignorant—in God. If I do this, then of all my ideas the idea of God will be most true and most clear and distinct.

But maybe I am greater than I have assumed; maybe all the perfections that I attributed to God are in me
47 potentially, still unreal and unactualized. I have already seen my knowledge gradually increase, and I don't see anything to prevent its becoming greater and greater to infinity. Nor do I see why, by means of such increased knowledge, I couldn't get all the rest of God's perfections. Finally, if the potential for these perfections is in me, I don't see why that potential couldn't account for the production of the ideas of these perfections in me.

None of this is possible. First, while it's true that my knowledge gradually increases and that I have many as yet unactualized potentialities, none of this fits with my idea of God, in whom absolutely nothing is potential; indeed, the gradual increase in my knowledge shows that I am *imperfect*. Besides, I see that, even if my knowledge were continually to become greater and greater, it would never become actually infinite, since it would never become so great as to be unable to increase. But I judge God to be actually infinite so that nothing can be added to his perfection. Finally, I see that an idea's subjective being must be produced, not by mere potentiality (which, strictly speaking, is nothing), but by what is actual or formal.

When I pay attention to these things, the light of nature makes all of them obvious. But, when I attend less carefully and the images of sensible things blind my 48 mind's eye, it's not easy for me to remember why the idea of an entity more perfect than I am must come from an entity that really is more perfect. That's why I'll go on to ask whether I, who have the idea of a perfect entity, could exist if no such entity existed.

From what might I derive my existence if not from God? Either from myself, or from my parents, or from something else less perfect than God—for nothing more perfect than God, or even as perfect as Him, can be thought of or imagined.

But, if I derived my existence from myself, I wouldn't doubt, or want, or lack anything. I would have given myself every perfection of which I have an idea, and thus I myself would be God. And I shouldn't think that it might be harder to give myself what I lack than what I already have. On the contrary, it would obviously be much harder for me, a thinking thing or substance, to emerge from nothing than for me to give myself knowledge of the many things of which I am ignorant, which is just an attribute of substance. But surely, if I had given myself that which is harder to get, I wouldn't have denied myself complete knowledge, which would have been easier to get. Indeed, I wouldn't have denied myself *any* of the perfections that I grasp in the idea of God. None of these perfections seems harder to get than existence. But, if I had given myself everything that I now have, these perfections would have seemed harder to get than existence if they were harder to get—for in creating myself I would have discovered the limits of my power.

I can't avoid the force of this argument by supposing that, since I've always existed as I do now, there's no 49 point in looking for my creator. Since my lifetime can be divided into innumerable parts each of which is independent of the others, the fact that I existed a little while ago does not entail that I exist now, unless a cause "recreates" me—or, in other words, preserves me—at this moment. For, when we attend to the nature of time,

it's obvious that exactly the same power and action are required to preserve a thing at each moment through which it endures as would be required to create it anew if it had never existed. Hence, one of the things revealed by the light of nature is that preservation and creation differ only in the way we think of them.

I ought to ask myself, then, whether I have the power to ensure that I, who now am, will exist in a little while. Since I am nothing but a thinking thing—or, at any rate, since I am now focusing on the part of me that thinks—I would surely be aware of this power if it were in me. But I find no such power. And from this I clearly see that there is an entity distinct from me on whom I depend.

But maybe this entity isn't God. Maybe I am the product of my parents or of some other cause less perfect than God. No. As I've said, there must be at least as much in a cause as in its effect. Hence, since I am a thinking thing with the idea of God in me, my cause, whatever it may be, must be a thinking thing having in it the idea of every perfection that I attribute to God. And we can go on to ask whether this thing gets its existence from itself or from something else. If it gets its 50 existence from itself, it's obvious from what I've said that it must be God—for it would have the power to exist on its own and hence the power actually to give itself every perfection of which it has an idea, including every perfection that I conceive of in God. But, if my cause gets its existence from some other thing, we can go on to ask whether this other thing gets its existence from itself or from something else. Eventually, we will come to the ultimate cause, which will be God.

It's clear enough that there can't be an infinite regress here—especially since I am concerned, not so much with the cause that originally produced me, as with the one that preserves me at the present moment.

And I can't suppose that several partial causes combined to make me or that I get the ideas of the various perfections that I attribute to God from different causes so that, while each of these perfections can be found somewhere in the universe, there is no God in whom they all come together. On the contrary, one of the chief perfections that I understand God to have is unity, simplicity, inseparability from everything in Him. Surely the idea of the unity of all God's perfections can only have been put in me by a cause that gives me the ideas of all the other perfections—for nothing could make me aware of the unbreakable connection of God's perfections unless it made me aware of what those perfections are.

Finally, even if everything that I used to believe about my parents is true, it's clear that they don't preserve me. Insofar as I am a thinking thing, they did not even take part in creating me. They simply formed the matter in which I used to think that I (that is, my mind, which is 51 all I am now taking myself to be) resided. There can therefore be no problem about my parents. And I am driven to this conclusion: The fact that I exist and have an idea in me of a perfect entity—that is, God—conclusively entails that God does in fact exist.

All that's left is to explain how I have gotten my idea of God from Him. I have not taken it in through my senses; it has never come to me unexpectedly as the ideas of sensible things do when those things affect (or seem to affect) my external organs of sense. Nor have I made the idea myself; I can't subtract from it or add to it. The only other possibility is that the idea is innate in me, like my idea of myself.

It's not at all surprising that in creating me God put this idea into me, impressing it on His work like a craftsman's mark (which needn't be distinct from the work itself). The very fact that it was God who created me confirms that I have somehow been made in His image or likeness and that I grasp this likeness, which contains the idea of God, in the same way that I grasp myself. Thus, when I turn my mind's eye on myself, I understand, not just that I am an incomplete and dependent thing which constantly strives for bigger and better things, but also that He on whom I depend has all these things in Himself as infinite reality rather than just as vague potentiality and hence that He must be God. The whole argument comes down to this: I know that I 52 could not exist with my present nature—that is, that I could not exist with the idea of God in me—unless there really were a God. This must be the very God whose idea is in me, the thing having all of the perfections that I can't fully comprehend but can somehow reach with thought, who clearly cannot have any defects. From this, it's obvious that He can't deceive—for, as the natural light reveals, fraud and deception arise from defect.

But before examining this more carefully and investigating its consequences, I want to dwell for a moment in the contemplation of God, to ponder His attributes, to see and admire and adore the beauty of His boundless light, insofar as my clouded insight allows. As I have faith that the supreme happiness of the next life consists wholly of the contemplation of divine greatness, I now find that contemplation of the same sort, though less perfect, affords the greatest joy available in this life.

Meditation IV:
On Truth and Falsity

In the last few days, I've gotten used to drawing my mind away from my senses. I've carefully noted that I 53 really grasp very little about physical objects, that I know much more about the human mind, and that I know even more about God. Thus, I no longer find it hard to turn my thoughts away from things of which I can have mental images and toward things completely separate from matter, which I can only understand. Indeed, I have a much more distinct idea of the human mind, insofar as it is just a thinking thing that isn't extended in length, breadth, or depth and doesn't share anything else with physical objects, than I have of physical objects. And, when I note that I doubt or that I am incomplete and dependent, I have a clear and distinct idea of a complete and independent entity: God. From the fact that this idea is in me and that I who have the idea exist, I can clearly infer both that God exists and that I am completely dependent on Him for my existence from moment to moment. This is so obvious that I'm sure that people can't know anything more evidently or certainly. And it now seems to me that, from the contemplation of the true God in whom are hidden all treasures of knowledge and wisdom, there is a way to derive knowledge of other things.

In the first place, I know that it's impossible for Him ever to deceive me. Wherever there is fraud and deception, there is imperfection, and, while the ability to deceive may seem a sign of cunning or power, the desire to deceive reveals malice or weakness and hence is inconsistent with God's nature.

Next, I find in myself an ability to judge which, like 54 everything else in me, I've gotten from God. Since He doesn't want to deceive me, He certainly hasn't given me an ability which will lead me wrong when properly used.

There can be no doubt about this—except that it may seem to imply that I don't err at all. For, if I've gotten everything in me from God and He hasn't given me the ability to err, it doesn't seem possible for me ever to err. Thus, as long as I think only of God and devote all my attention to Him, I can't find any cause for error and falsity. When I turn my attention back to myself, however, I find that I can make innumerable errors. In looking for the cause of these errors, I find before me, not just the real and positive idea of God, but also the negative idea of "nothingness"—the idea of that which is completely devoid of perfection. I find that I am "intermediate" between God and nothingness, between the supreme entity and nonentity. Insofar as I am the creation of the supreme entity, there's nothing in me to account for my being deceived or led into error, but, insofar as I somehow participate in nothingness or the nonentity—that is, insofar as I am distinct from the supreme entity itself and lack many things—it's not surprising that I go wrong. I thus understand that, in itself, error is a lack, rather than a real thing dependent on God. Hence, I understand that I can err without God's having given me a special ability to do so. Rather, I fall into error because my God-given ability to judge the truth is not infinite.

55   But there's still something to be explained. Error is not just an absence, but a deprivation—the lack of knowledge that somehow ought to be in me. But, when I attend to God's nature, it seems impossible that He's given me an ability that is an imperfect thing of its kind—an ability lacking a perfection that it ought to have. The greater the craftsman's skill, the more perfect his product. Then how can the supreme creator of all things have made something that isn't absolutely perfect? There's no doubt that God could have made me so that I never err and that He always wants what's best. Then is it better for me to err than not to err?

When I pay more careful attention, I realize that I shouldn't be surprised at God's doing things that I can't explain. I shouldn't doubt His existence just because I find that I sometimes can't understand why or how He has made something. I know that my nature is weak and limited and that God's is limitless, incomprehensible, and infinite, and, from this, I can infer that He can do innumerable things whose reasons are unknown to me. On this ground alone, I regard the common practice of explaining things in terms of their purposes to be useless in physics: it would be foolhardy of me to think that I can discover God's purposes.

It also seems to me that, when asking whether God's works are perfect, I ought to look at all of them together, not at one in isolation. For something that seems imper-
56 fect when viewed alone might seem completely perfect when regarded as having a place in the world. Of course, since calling everything into doubt, I haven't established that anything exists besides me and God. But, when I consider God's immense power, I can't deny that He has made—or, in any case, that He could have made—many other things, and I must therefore view myself as having a place in a universe.

Next, turning to myself and investigating the nature of my errors (which are all that show me to be imperfect), I notice that these errors depend on two concur-
rent causes: my ability to know and my ability to choose freely—that is, my understanding and my will. But, with my understanding, I just grasp the ideas about which I form judgments, and error therefore cannot properly be said to arise from the understanding itself. While there may be innumerable things of which I have no idea, I can't say that I am deprived of these ideas, but only that I happen to lack them—for I don't have any reason to think that God ought to have given me a greater ability to know than He has. And, while I understand God to be a supremely skilled craftsman, I don't go on to think that He ought to endow each of his works with all the perfections that He can put in the others.

Nor can I complain about the scope or perfection of my God-given freedom of will—for I find that my will doesn't seem to me to be restricted in any way. Indeed, it
57 seems well worth noting that nothing in me other than my will is so great and perfect that it couldn't conceivably be bigger or better. If I think about my ability to understand, for example, I realize that it is very small and restricted and I immediately form the idea of something much greater—indeed, of something supremely perfect and infinite. And, from the fact that I can form the idea of this thing, I infer that it is present in God's nature. Similarly, if I consider my other abilities, like the abilities to remember and to imagine, I clearly see that they all are weak and limited in me, but boundless in God. My will or freedom of choice is the only thing I find to be so great in me that I can't conceive of anything greater. In fact, it's largely for this reason that I regard myself as an image or likeness of God. God's will is incomparably greater than mine, of course, in virtue of the associated knowledge and power that make it stronger and more effective, and also in virtue of its greater range of objects. Yet, viewed in itself as a will, God's will seems no greater than mine. For having a will just amounts to being able either to do or not to do (affirm or deny, seek or avoid)—or, better, to being inclined to affirm or deny, seek or shun what the understanding offers, without any sense of being driven by external forces. To be free, I don't need to be inclined towards both alternatives. On the contrary, the more I lean towards one alternative—either because I understand the truth or goodness in it,
58 or because God has so arranged my deepest thoughts—the more freely I choose it. Neither divine grace nor knowledge of nature ever diminishes my freedom; they increase and strengthen it. But the indifference that I experience when no consideration impels me towards one alternative over another is freedom of the lowest sort, whose presence reveals a defect or an absence of

knowledge rather than a perfection. For, if I always knew what was good or true, I wouldn't ever deliberate about what to do or choose, and thus, though completely free, I would never be indifferent.

From this I see that my God-given ability to will is not itself the cause of my errors—for my will is great, a perfect thing of its kind. Neither is my power of understanding the cause of my errors; whenever I understand something, I understand it correctly and without the possibility of error, since my understanding comes from God. What then is the source of my errors? It is just that, while my will has a broader scope than my understanding, I don't keep it within the same bounds, but extend it to that which I don't understand. Being indifferent to these things, my will is easily led away from truth and goodness, and thus I am led into error and sin.

For example, I've asked for the last few days whether anything exists in the world, and I've noted that, from the fact that I ask this, it follows that I exist. I couldn't fail to judge that which I so clearly understood to be 59 true. This wasn't because a force outside me compelled me to believe, but because an intense light in my understanding produced a strong inclination of my will. And, to the extent that I wasn't indifferent, I believed spontaneously and freely. However, while I now know that I exist insofar as I am a thinking thing, I notice in myself an idea of what it is to be a physical object and I come to wonder whether the thinking nature that's in me—or, rather, that *is* me—differs from this bodily nature or is identical to it. Nothing occurs to my reason (I am supposing) to convince me of one alternative rather than the other. Accordingly, I am completely indifferent to affirming either view, to denying either view, and even to suspending judgment.

And indifference of this sort is not limited to things of which the understanding is completely ignorant. It extends to everything about which the will deliberates in the absence of a sufficiently clear understanding. For, however strong the force with which plausible conjectures draw me towards one alternative, the knowledge that they are conjectures rather than assertions backed by certain and indubitable arguments is enough to push my assent the other way. The past few days have provided me with ample experience of this—for I am now supposing each of my former beliefs to be false just because I've found a way to call them into doubt.

If I suspend judgment when I don't clearly and distinctly grasp what's true, I obviously do right and am not deceived. But, if I either affirm or deny in a case of this 60 sort, I misuse my freedom of choice. If I affirm what is false, I clearly err, and, if I stumble onto the truth, I'm still blameworthy since the light of nature reveals that a perception of the understanding should always precede a decision of the will. In these misuses of freedom of choice lies the deprivation that accounts for error. And this deprivation, I maintain, lies in the working of the will insofar as it comes from me—not in my God-given ability to will, or even in the will's operation insofar as it derives from Him.

I have no reason to complain that God hasn't given me a more perfect understanding or a greater natural light than He has. It's in the nature of a finite understanding that there are many things it can't understand, and it's in the nature of created understanding that it's finite. Indeed, I ought to be grateful to Him who owes me absolutely nothing for what He has bestowed, rather than taking myself to be deprived or robbed of what God hasn't given me.

And I have no reason to complain about God's having given me a will whose scope is greater than my understanding's. The will is like a unity made of inseparable parts; its nature apparently will not allow anything to be taken away from it. And, really, the wider the scope of my will, the more grateful I ought to be to Him who gave it to me.

Finally, I ought not to complain that God concurs in bringing about the acts of will and judgment in which I err. Insofar as these acts derive from God, they are completely true and good, and I am more perfect with the ability to perform these acts than I would be without it. And, the deprivation that is the real ground of falsity and 61 error doesn't need God's concurrence, since it's not a thing. When we regard God as its cause, we should say that it is an absence rather than a deprivation. For it clearly is no imperfection in God that He has given me the freedom to assent or not to assent to things of which He hasn't given me a clear and distinct grasp. Rather, it is undoubtedly an imperfection in me that I misuse this freedom by passing judgment on things that I don't properly understand. I see, of course, that God could easily have brought it about that, while I remain free and limited in knowledge, I never err: He could have implanted in me a clear and distinct understanding of everything about which I was ever going to make a choice, or He could have indelibly impressed on my memory that I must never pass judgment on something that I don't clearly and distinctly understand. And I also understand that, regarded in isolation from everything else, I would have been more perfect if God had made me so that I never err. But I can't deny that, because some things are immune to error while others are not, the universe is more perfect than it would have been if all its parts were alike. And I have no right to complain about God's wanting me to hold a place in the world other than the greatest and most perfect.

Besides, if I can't avoid error by having a clear grasp of every matter on which I make a choice, I can avoid it 62 in the other way, which only requires remembering that I must not pass judgment on matters whose truth isn't apparent. For, although I find myself too weak to fix my attention permanently on this single thought, I can—by careful and frequent meditation—ensure that I call it to mind whenever it's needed and thus that I acquire the habit of avoiding error.

Since the first and foremost perfection of man lies in avoiding error, I've profited from today's meditation, in which I've investigated the cause of error and falsity. Clearly, the only possible cause of error is the one I have described. When I limit my will's range of judgment to the things presented clearly and distinctly to my understanding, I obviously cannot err—for everything that I clearly and distinctly grasp is something and hence must come, not from nothing, but from God—God, I say, who is supremely perfect and who cannot possibly deceive. Therefore, what I clearly and distinctly grasp is unquestionably true. Today, then, I have learned what to avoid in order not to err and also what to do to reach the truth. I surely will reach the truth if I just attend to the things that I understand perfectly and distinguish them from those that I grasp more obscurely and confusedly. And that's what I'll take care to do from now on.

63 *Meditation V:*
On the Essence of Material Objects and More on God's Existence

Many questions remain about God's attributes and about the nature of my self or mind. I may return to these questions later. But now, having found what to do and what to avoid in order to attain truth, I regard nothing as more pressing than to work my way out of the doubts that I raised the other day and to see whether I can find anything certain about material objects.

But, before asking whether any such objects exist outside me, I ought to consider the ideas of these objects as they exist in my thoughts and see which are clear and which confused.

I have a distinct mental image of the quantity that philosophers commonly call continuous. That is, I have a distinct mental image of the extension of this quantity—or rather of the quantified thing—in length, breadth, and depth. I can distinguish various parts of this thing. I can ascribe various sizes, shapes, places, and motions to these parts and various durations to the motions.

In addition to having a thorough knowledge of extension in general, I grasp innumerable particulars about things like shape, number, and motion, when I pay careful attention. The truth of these particulars is so 64 obvious and so consonant with my nature that, when I first think of one of these things, I seem not so much to be learning something novel as to be remembering something that I already knew—or noticing for the first time something that had long been in me without my having turned my mind's eye toward it.

What's important here, I think, is that I find in myself innumerable ideas of things which, though they may not exist outside me, can't be said to be nothing. While I have some control over my thoughts of these things, I do not make the things up: they have their own real and immutable natures. Suppose, for example, that I have a mental image of a triangle. While it may be that no figure of this sort does exist or ever has existed outside my thought, the figure has a fixed nature (essence or form), immutable and eternal, which hasn't been produced by me and isn't dependent on my mind. The proof is that I can demonstrate various propositions about the triangle, such as that its angles equal two right angles and that its greatest side subtends its greatest angle. Even though I didn't think of these propositions at all when I first imagined the triangle, I now clearly see their truth whether I want to or not, and it follows that I didn't make them up.

It isn't relevant that, having seen triangular physical objects, I may have gotten the idea of the triangle from external objects through my organs of sense. For I can think of innumerable other figures whose ideas I could 65 not conceivably have gotten through my senses, and I can demonstrate facts about these other figures just as I can about the triangle. Since I know these facts clearly, they must be true, and they therefore must be something rather than nothing. For it's obvious that everything true is something, and, as I have shown, everything that I know clearly and distinctly is true. But, even if I hadn't shown this, the nature of my mind would have made it impossible for me to withhold my assent from these things, at least when I clearly and distinctly grasped them. As I recall, even when I clung most tightly to objects of sense, I regarded truths about shape and number—truths of arithmetic, geometry, and pure mathematics—as more certain than any others.

But, if anything whose idea I can draw from my thought must in fact have everything that I clearly and distinctly grasp it to have, can't I derive from this a proof of God's existence? Surely, I find the idea of God, a supremely perfect being, in me no less clearly than I find the ideas of figures and numbers. And I understand as clearly and distinctly that eternal existence belongs to His nature as that the things which I demonstrate of a figure or number belong to the nature of the figure or number. Accordingly, even if what I have thought up in the past few days hasn't been entirely true, I ought to be **66** at least as certain of God's existence as I used to be of the truths of pure mathematics.

At first, this reasoning may seem unclear and fallacious. Since I'm accustomed to distinguishing existence from essence in other cases, I find it easy to convince myself that I can separate God's existence from His essence and hence that I can think of God as nonexistent. But, when I pay more careful attention, it's clear that I can no more separate God's existence from His essence than a triangle's angles equaling two right angles from the essence of the triangle, or the idea of a valley from the idea of a mountain. It's no less impossible to think that God (the supremely perfect being) lacks existence (a perfection) than to think that a mountain lacks a valley.

Well, suppose that I can't think of God without existence, just as I can't think of a mountain without a valley. From the fact that I can think of a mountain with a valley, it doesn't follow that a mountain exists in the world. Similarly, from the fact that I can think of God as existing, it doesn't seem to follow that He exists. For my thought doesn't impose any necessity on things. It may be that, just as I can imagine a winged horse when no such horse exists, I can ascribe existence to God when no God exists.

No, there is a fallacy here. From the fact that I can't **67** think of a mountain without a valley it follows, not that the mountain and valley exist, but only that whether they exist or not they can't be separated from one another. But, from the fact that I can't think of God without existence, it follows that existence is inseparable from Him and hence that He really exists. It's not that my thoughts make it so or impose a necessity on things. On the contrary, it's the fact that God does exist that necessitates my thinking of Him as I do. For I am not free to think of God without existence—of the supremely perfect being without supreme perfection—as I am free to think of a horse with or without wings.

Now someone might say this: "If I take God to have all perfections, and if I take existence to be a perfection, I must take God to exist, but I needn't accept the premise that God has all perfections. Similarly, if I accept the premise that every quadrilateral can be inscribed in a circle, I'm forced to the patently false view that every rhombus can be inscribed in a circle, but I need not accept the premise." But this should not be said. For, while it's not necessary that the idea of God occurs to me, it is necessary that, whenever I think of the primary and supreme entity and bring the idea of Him out of my mind's "treasury," I attribute all perfections to Him, even if I don't enumerate them or consider them individually. And this necessity ensures that, when I do notice that existence is a perfection, I can rightly conclude that the primary and supreme being exists. Similarly, while it's not necessary that I ever imagine a triangle, it is necessary that, when I do choose to consider a rectilinear figure having exactly three angles, I attribute to it proper- **68** ties from which I can rightly infer that its angles are no more than two right angles, perhaps without noticing that I am doing so. But, when I consider which shapes can be inscribed in the circle, there's absolutely no necessity for my thinking that all quadrilaterals are among them. Indeed, I can't even think that all quadrilaterals are among them, since I've resolved to accept only what I clearly and distinctly understand. Thus my false suppositions differ greatly from the true ideas implanted in me, the first and foremost of which is my idea of God. In many ways, I see that this idea is not a figment of my thought, but the image of a real and immutable nature. For one thing, God is the only thing that I can think of whose existence belongs to its essence. For another thing, I can't conceive of there being two or more such Gods, and, having supposed that one God now exists, I see that He has necessarily existed from all eternity and will continue to exist into eternity. And I also perceive many other things in God that I can't diminish or alter.

But, whatever proof I offer, it always comes back to the fact that I am only convinced of what I grasp clearly and distinctly. Of the things that I grasp in this way, some are obvious to everyone. Some are discovered only by those who examine things more closely and search more carefully, but, once these things have been discovered, they are regarded as no less certain than the others. **69** That the square on the hypotenuse of a right triangle equals the sum of the squares on the other sides is not as readily apparent as that the hypotenuse subtends the greatest angle, but, once it has been seen, it is believed just as firmly. And, when I'm not overwhelmed by prejudices and my thoughts aren't besieged by images of sensible things, there surely is nothing that I know earlier or more easily than facts about God. For what is more self-evident than there is a supreme entity—that God, the only thing whose existence belongs to His essence, exists?

While I need to pay careful attention in order to grasp this, I'm now as certain of it as of anything that seems most certain. In addition, I now see that the certainty of everything else so depends on it that, if I weren't certain of it, I couldn't know anything perfectly.

Of course, my nature is such that, when I grasp something clearly and distinctly, I can't fail to believe it. But my nature is also such that I can't permanently fix my attention on a single thing so as always to grasp it clearly, and memories of previous judgments often come to me when I am no longer attending to the grounds on which I originally made them. Accordingly, if I were ignorant of God, arguments could be produced that would easily overthrow my opinions, and I therefore would have unstable and changing opinions rather than true and certain knowledge. For example, when I consider the nature of the triangle, it seems plain to me—steeped as I am in the principles of geometry—
70 that its three angles equal two right angles: I can't fail to believe this as long as I pay attention to its demonstration. But, if I were ignorant of God, I might come to doubt its truth as soon as my mind's eye turned away from its demonstration, even if I recalled having once grasped it clearly. For I could convince myself that I've been so constructed by nature that I sometimes err about what I believe myself to grasp most plainly—especially if I remember that, having taken many things to be true and certain, I had later found grounds on which to judge them false.

But now I grasp that God exists, and I understand both that everything else depends on Him and that He's not a deceiver. From this, I infer that everything I clearly and distinctly grasp must be true. Even if I no longer pay attention to the grounds on which I judged God to exist, my recollection that I once clearly and distinctly knew Him to exist ensures that no contrary ground can be produced to push me towards doubt. About God's existence, I have true and certain knowledge. And I have such knowledge, not just about this one thing, but about everything else that I remember having proven, like the theorems of geometry. For what can now be said against my believing these things? That I am so constructed that I always err? But I now know that I can't err about what I

clearly understand. That much of what I took to be true and certain I later found to be false? But I didn't grasp any of these things clearly and distinctly; ignorant of the true standard of truth, I based my belief on grounds that I later found to be unsound. Then what can be said? What about the objection (which I recently used against myself) that I may be dreaming and that the things I'm now experiencing may be as unreal as those that occur to me in sleep? No, even this is irrelevant. For, even if I am dreaming, everything that is evident to my under-
71 standing must be true.

Thus I plainly see that the certainty and truth of all my knowledge derives from one thing: my thought of the true God. Before I knew Him, I couldn't know anything else perfectly. But now I can plainly and certainly know innumerable things, not only about God and other mental beings, but also about the nature of physical objects, insofar as it is the subject-matter of pure mathematics.

Meditation VI:
On the Existence of Material Objects and the Real Distinction of Mind from Body

It remains for me to examine whether material objects exist. Insofar as they are the subject of pure mathematics, I now know at least that they can exist, because I grasp them clearly and distinctly. For God can undoubtedly make whatever I can grasp in this way, and I never judge that something is impossible for Him to make unless there would be a contradiction in my grasping the thing distinctly. Also, the fact that I find myself having mental images when I turn my attention to physical objects seems to imply that these objects really do exist. For, when I pay careful attention to what it is to have a
72 mental image, it seems to me that it's just the application of my power of thought to a certain body which is immediately present to it and which must therefore exist.

To clarify this, I'll examine the difference between having a mental image and having a pure understanding. When I have a mental image of a triangle, for example, I don't just understand that it is a figure bounded by three lines; I also "look at" the lines as though they were present to my mind's eye. And this is what I call having a mental image. When I want to think of a chiliagon, I understand that it is a figure with a thousand sides as well as I understand that a triangle is a figure with three, but I can't imagine its sides or "look" at them as though they were present. Being accustomed to using images when I think about physical objects, I may confusedly picture some figure to myself, but this figure obviously is not a chiliagon—for it in no way differs from what I present to myself when thinking about a myriagon or any other many sided figure, and it doesn't help me to discern the properties that distinguish chiliagons from other polygons. If it's a pentagon that is in question, I can understand its shape, as I can that of the chiliagon, without the aid of mental images. But I can also get a mental image of the pentagon by directing my mind's eye to its five lines and to the area that they bound. And it's obvious to me that getting this mental image requires 73 a special mental effort different from that needed for understanding—a special effort which clearly reveals the difference between having a mental image and having a pure understanding.

It also seems to me that my power of having mental images, being distinct from my power of understanding, is not essential to my self or, in other words, to my mind—for, if I were to loose this ability, I would surely remain the same thing that I now am. And it seems to follow that this ability depends on something distinct from me. If we suppose that there is a body so associated with my mind that the mind can "look into" it at will, it's easy to understand how my mind might get mental images of physical objects by means of my body. If there were such a body, the mode of thinking that we call imagination would differ from pure understanding in only one way: when the mind understood something, it would turn "inward" and view an idea that it found in itself, but, when it had mental images, it would turn to the body and look at something there which resembled an idea that it had understood by itself or had grasped by sense. As I've said, then, it's easy to see how I get mental images, if we supposed that my body exists. And, since I don't have in mind any other equally plausible explanation of my ability to have mental images, I conjecture that physical objects probably do exist. But this conjecture is only probable. Despite my careful and thorough investigation, the distinct idea of bodily nature that I get from mental images does not seem to have anything in it from which the conclusion that physical objects exist validly follows.

Besides having a mental image of the bodily nature 74 that is the subject-matter of pure mathematics, I have mental images of things which are not so distinct—things like colors, sounds, flavors, and pains. But I seem to grasp these things better by sense, from which they seem to come (with the aid of memory) to the understanding. Thus, to deal with these things more fully, I

must examine the senses and see whether there is anything in the mode of awareness that I call sensation from which I can draw a conclusive argument for the existence of physical objects.

First, I'll remind myself of the things that I believed really to be as I perceived them and of the grounds for my belief. Next, I'll set out the grounds on which I later called this belief into doubt. And, finally, I'll consider what I ought to think now.

To begin with, I sensed that I had a head, hands, feet, and the other members that make up a human body. I viewed this body as part, or maybe even as all, of me. I sensed that it was influenced by other physical objects whose effects could be either beneficial or harmful. I judged these effects to be beneficial to the extent that I felt pleasant sensations and harmful to the extent that I felt pain. And, in addition to sensations of pain and pleasure, I sensed hunger, thirst, and other such desires—and also bodily inclinations towards cheerfulness, sadness, and other emotions. Outside me, I sensed, not just extension, shape, and motion, but also hardness, hot- 75 ness, and other qualities detected by touch. I also sensed light, color, odor, taste, and sound—qualities by whose variation I distinguished such things as the sky, earth, and sea from one another.

In view of these ideas of qualities (which presented themselves to my thought and were all that I really sensed directly), I had some reason for believing that I sensed objects distinct from my thought—physical objects from which the ideas came. For I found that these ideas came to me independently of my desires so that, however much I tried, I couldn't sense an object when it wasn't present to an organ of sense or fail to sense one when it was present. And, since the ideas that I grasped by sense were much livelier, more explicit, and (in their own way) more distinct than those I deliberately created or found impressed in my memory, it seemed that these ideas could not have come from me and thus that they came from something else. Having no conception of these things other than that suggested by my sensory ideas, I could only think that the things resembled the ideas. Indeed, since I remembered using my senses before my reason, since I found the ideas that I created in myself to be less explicit than those grasped by sense, and since I found the ideas that I created to be composed largely of those that I had grasped by sense, I easily convinced myself that I didn't understand anything at all unless I had first sensed it.

I also had some reason for supposing that a certain 76 physical object, which I viewed as belonging to me in a special way, was related to me more closely than any other. I couldn't be separated from it as I could from other physical objects; I felt all of my emotions and desires in it and because of it; and I was aware of pains and pleasant feelings in it but in nothing else. I didn't know why sadness goes with the sensation of pain or why joy goes with sensory stimulation. I didn't know why the stomach twitchings that I call hunger warn me that I need to eat or why dryness in my throat warns me that I need to drink. Seeing no connection between stomach twitchings and the desire to eat or between the sensation of a pain-producing thing and the consequent awareness of sadness, I could only say that I had been taught the connection by nature. And nature seems also to have taught me everything else that I knew about the objects of sensation—for I convinced myself that the sensations came to me in a certain way before having found grounds on which to prove that they did.

But, since then, many experiences have shaken my faith in the senses. Towers that seemed round from a distance sometimes looked square from close up; and huge statues on pediments sometimes didn't look big when seen from the ground. In innumerable such cases, 77 I found the judgments of the external senses to be wrong. And the same holds for the internal senses. What is felt more inwardly than pain? Yet I had heard that people with amputated arms and legs sometimes seem to feel pain in the missing limb, and it therefore didn't seem perfectly certain to me that the limb in which I feel a pain is always the one that hurts. And, to these grounds for doubt, I've recently added two that are very general: First, since I didn't believe myself to sense anything while awake that I couldn't also take myself to sense in a dream, and since I didn't believe that what I sense in sleep comes from objects outside me, I didn't see why I should believe what I sense while awake comes from such objects. Second, since I didn't yet know my creator (or, rather, since I supposed that I didn't know Him), I saw nothing to rule out my having been so designed by nature that I'm deceived even in what seems most obviously true to me.

And I could easily refute the reasoning by which I convinced myself of the reality of sensible things. Since my nature seemed to impel me toward many things that my reason rejected, I didn't believe that I ought to have much faith in nature's teachings. And, while my will didn't control my sense perceptions, I didn't believe it to follow that these perceptions came from outside me, since I thought that the ability to produce these ideas might be in me without my being aware of it.

Now that I've begun to know myself and my creator better, I still believe that I oughtn't blindly to accept ev-78 erything that I seem to get from the senses. Yet I no longer believe that I ought to call it all into doubt.

In the first place, I know that everything that I clearly and distinctly understand can be made by God to be exactly as I understand it. The fact that I can clearly and distinctly understand one thing apart from another is therefore enough to make me certain that it is distinct from the other, since the things could be separated by God if not by something else. (I judge the things to be distinct regardless of the power needed to make them exist separately.) Accordingly, from the fact that I have gained knowledge of my existence without noticing anything about my nature or essence except that I am a thinking thing, I can rightly conclude that my essence consists solely in the fact that I am a thinking thing. It's possible (or, as I will say later, it's certain) that I have a body which is very tightly bound to me. But, on the one hand, I have a clear and distinct idea of myself insofar as I am just a thinking and unextended thing, and, on the other hand, I have a distinct idea of my body insofar as it is just an extended and unthinking thing. It's certain, then, that I am really distinct from my body and can exist without it.

In addition, I find in myself abilities for special modes of awareness, like the abilities to have mental images and to sense. I can clearly and distinctly conceive of my whole self as something that lacks these abilities, but I can't conceive of the abilities' existing without me, or 79 without an understanding substance in which to reside. Since the conception of these abilities includes the conception of something that understands, I see that these abilities are distinct from me in the way that a thing's properties are distinct from the thing itself.

I recognize other abilities in me, like the ability to move around and to assume various postures. These abilities can't be understood to exist apart from a substance in which they reside any more than the abilities to imagine and sense, and they therefore cannot exist without such a substance. But it's obvious that, if these abilities do exist, the substance in which they reside must be a body or extended substance rather than an understanding one—for the clear and distinct conceptions of these abilities contain extension but not understanding.

There is also in me, however, a passive ability to sense—to receive and recognize ideas of sensible things. But, I wouldn't be able to put this ability to use if there weren't, either in me or in something else, an active power to produce or make sensory ideas. Since this active power doesn't presuppose understanding, and since it often produces ideas in me without my cooperation and even against my will, it cannot exist in me. Therefore, this power must exist in a substance distinct from me. And, for reasons that I've noted, this substance must contain, either formally or eminently, all the reality that is contained subjectively in the ideas that the power produces. Either this substance is a physical object (a thing of bodily nature that contains formally the reality that the idea contains subjectively), or it is God or one of His creations that is higher than a physical object (something that contains this reality eminently). But, since God isn't a deceiver, it's completely obvious that He doesn't send these ideas to me directly or by means of a creation that contains their reality eminently rather than formally. For, since He has not given

80 me any ability to recognize that these ideas are sent by Him or by creations other than physical objects, and since He has given me a strong inclination to believe that the ideas come from physical objects, I see no way to avoid the conclusion that He deceives me if the ideas are sent to me by anything other than physical objects. It follows that physical objects exist. These objects may not exist exactly as I comprehend them by sense; in many ways, sensory comprehension is obscure and confused. But these objects must at least have in them everything that I clearly and distinctly understand them to have—every general property within the scope of pure mathematics.

But what about particular properties, such as the size and shape of the sun? And what about things that I understand less clearly than mathematical properties, like light, sound, and pain? These are open to doubt. But, since God isn't a deceiver, and since I therefore have the God-given ability to correct any falsity that may be in my beliefs, I have high hopes of finding the truth about even these things. There is undoubtedly some truth in everything I have been taught by nature—for, when I use the term "nature" in its general sense, I refer to God Himself or to the order that He has established in the created world, and, when I apply the term specifically to *my* nature, I refer to the collection of everything that God has given *me*.

Nature teaches me nothing more explicitly, however, than that I have a body which is hurt when I feel pain, which needs food or drink when I experience hunger or thirst, and so on. Accordingly, I ought not to doubt that there is some truth to this.

81 Through sensations like pain, hunger, and thirst, nature also teaches me that I am not present in my body in the way that a sailor is present in his ship. Rather, I am very tightly bound to my body and so "mixed up" with it that we form a single thing. If this weren't so, I—who am just a thinking thing—wouldn't feel pain when my body was injured; I would perceive the injury by pure understanding in the way that a sailor sees the leaks in his ship with his eyes. And, when my body needed food or drink, I would explicitly understand that the need existed without having the confused sensations of hunger and thirst. For the sensations of thirst, hunger, and pain are just confused modifications of thought arising from the union and "mixture" of mind and body.

Also, nature teaches me that there are other physical objects around my body—some that I ought to seek and others that I ought to avoid. From the fact that I sense things like colors, sounds, odors, flavors, temperatures, and hardnesses, I correctly infer that sense perceptions come from physical objects that vary as widely (though perhaps not in the same way) as the perceptions do. And, from the fact that some of these perceptions are pleasant while others are unpleasant, I infer with certainty that my body—or, rather, my whole self which consists of a body and a mind—can be benefited and harmed by the physical objects around it.

82 There are many other things that I seem to have been taught by nature but that I have really accepted out of a habit of thoughtless judgment. These things may well be false. Among them are the judgments that a space is empty if nothing in it happens to affect my senses; that a hot physical object has something in it resembling my idea of heat; that a white or green thing has in it the same whiteness or greenness that I sense; that a bitter or sweet thing has in it the same flavor that I taste; that stars, towers, and other physical objects have the same size and shape that they present to my senses; and so on.

If I am to avoid accepting what is indistinct in these cases, I must more carefully explain my use of the phrase "taught by nature." In particular, I should say that I am now using the term "nature" in a narrower sense than when I took it to refer to the whole complex of what God has given me. This complex includes much having to do with my mind alone (such as my grasp of the fact that what is done cannot be undone and of the rest of what I know by the light of nature) which does not bear on what I am now saying. And the complex also includes much having to do with my body alone (such as its tendency to go downward) with which I am not dealing now. I'm now using the term "nature" to refer only to what God has given me insofar as I am a composite of mind and body. It is this nature that teaches me to avoid that which occasions painful sensations, to seek that which occasions pleasant sensations, and so on. But this nature seems not to teach me to draw conclusions about external objects from sense perceptions without first having examined the matter with my understanding—

for true knowledge of external things seems to belong to the mind alone, not to the composite of mind and body.

83   Thus, while a star has no more effect on my eye than a flame, this does not really produce a positive inclination to believe that the star is as small as the flame; for my youthful judgment about the size of the flame, I had no real grounds. And, while I feel heat when I approach a fire and pain when I draw nearer, I have absolutely no reason for believing that something in the fire resembles the heat, just as I have no reason for believing that something in the fire resembles the pain; I only have reason for believing that there is something or other in the fire that produces the feelings of heat and pain. And, although there may be nothing in a given region of space that affects my senses, it doesn't follow that there aren't any physical objects in that space. Rather I now see that, on these matters and others, I used to pervert the natural order of things. For, while nature has given sense perceptions to my mind for the sole purpose of indicating what is beneficial and what harmful to the composite of which my mind is a part, and while the perceptions are sufficiently clear and distinct for that purpose, I used these perceptions as standards for identifying the essence of physical objects—an essence which they only reveal obscurely and confusedly.

I've already explained how it can be that, despite God's goodness, my judgments can be false. But a new difficulty arises here—one having to do with the things that nature presents to me as desirable or undesirable and also with the errors that I seem to have found in my internal sensations. One of these errors seems to be 84 committed, for example, when a man is fooled by some food's pleasant taste into eating poison hidden in that food. But surely, in this case, what the man's nature impels him to eat is the good tasting food, not the poison of which he knows nothing. We can draw no conclusion except that his nature isn't omniscient, and this conclusion isn't surprising. Since a man is a limited thing, he can only have limited perfections.

Still, we often err in cases in which nature does impel us. This happens, for example, when sick people want food or drink that would quickly harm them. To say that these people err as a result of the corruption of their nature does not solve the problem—for a sick man is no less a creation of God than a well one, and it seems as absurd to suppose that God has given him a deceptive nature. A clock made of wheels and weights follows the natural laws just as precisely when it is poorly made and inaccurate as when it does everything that its maker wants. Thus, if I regard a human body as a machine made up of bones, nerves, muscles, veins, blood, and skin such that even without a mind it would do just what it does now (except for things that require a mind because they are controlled by the will), it's easy to see that what happens to a sick man is no less "natural" than what happens to a well one. For instance, if a body suffers from dropsy, it has a dry throat of the sort that regularly brings the sensation of thirst to the mind, the dryness disposes the nerves and other organs to drink, and the drinking makes the illness worse. But this is just as natural as when a similar dryness of throat moves a per- 85 son who is perfectly healthy to take a drink that is beneficial. Bearing in mind my conception of a clock's use, I might say that an inaccurate clock departs from its nature, and, similarly, viewing the machine of the human body as designed for its usual motions, I can say that it drifts away from its nature if it has a dry throat when drinking will not help to maintain it. I should note, however, that the sense in which I am now using the term "nature" differs from that in which I used it before. For, as I have just used the term "nature," the nature of a man (or clock) is something that depends on my thinking of the difference between a sick and a well man (or of the difference between a poorly made and a well-made clock)—something regarded as extrinsic to the things. But, when I used "nature" before, I referred to something which is *in* things and which therefore has some reality.

It may be that we just offer an extrinsic description of a body suffering from dropsy when, noting that it has a dry throat but doesn't need to drink, we say that its nature is corrupted. Still, the description is not purely extrinsic when we say that a composite or union of mind and body has a corrupted nature. There is a real fault in the composite's nature, for it is thirsty when drinking would be harmful. It therefore remains to be asked why God's goodness doesn't prevent *this* nature's being deceptive.

To begin the answer, I'll note that mind differs importantly from body in that body is by its nature divisible while mind is indivisible. When I think about my 86 mind—or, in other words, about myself insofar as I am just a thinking thing—I can't distinguish any parts in me; I understand myself to be a single, unified thing. Although my whole mind seems united to my whole body, I know that cutting off a foot, arm, or other limb would not take anything away from my mind. The abilities to will, sense, understand, and so on can't be called parts, since it's one and the same mind that wills, senses, and understands. On the other hand, whenever I think of a physical or extended thing, I can mentally divide it, and I therefore understand that the object is divisible.

This single fact would be enough to teach me that my mind and body are distinct, if I hadn't already learned that in another way.

Next, I notice that the mind isn't directly affected by all parts of the body, but only by the brain—or maybe just by the small part of the brain containing the so-called "common sense." Whenever this part of the brain is in a given state, it presents the same thing to the mind, regardless of what is happening in the rest of the body (as is shown by innumerable experiments that I need not review here).

In addition, I notice that the nature of body is such that, if a first part can be moved by a second that is far away, the first part can be moved in exactly the same way by something between the first and second without the second part's being affected. For example, if A, B, C, and **87** D are points on a cord, and if the first point (A) can be moved in a certain way by a pull on the last point (D), then A can be moved in the same way by a pull on one of the middle points (B or C) without D's being moved. Similarly, science teaches me that, when my foot hurts, the sensation of pain is produced by nerves distributed throughout the foot which extend like cords from there to the brain. When pulled in the foot, these nerves pull the central parts of the brain to which they are attached, moving those parts in ways designated by nature to present the mind with the sensation of a pain "in the foot." But, since these nerves pass through the shins, thighs, hips, back, and neck on their way from foot to brain, it can happen that their being touched in the middle, rather than at the end in the foot, produces the same motion in the brain as when the foot is hurt and, hence, that the mind feels the same pain "in the foot." And the point holds for other sensations as well.

Finally, I notice that, since only one sensation can be produced by a given motion of the part of the brain that directly affects the mind, the best conceivable sensation for it to produce is the one that is most often useful for the maintenance of the healthy man. Experience teaches that all the sensations put in us by nature are of this sort and therefore that everything in our sensations testifies to God's power and goodness. For example, when the **88** nerves in the foot are moved with unusual violence, the motion is communicated through the middle of the spine to the center of the brain, where it signals the mind to sense a pain "in the foot." This urges the mind to view the pain's cause as harmful to the foot and to do what it can to remove that cause. Of course, God could have so designed man's nature that the same motion of the brain presented something else to the mind, like the motion in the brain, or the motion in the foot, or a mo-

tion somewhere between the brain and foot. But no alternative to the way things are would be as conducive to the maintenance of the body. Similarly, when we need drink, the throat becomes dry, the dryness moves the nerves of the throat thereby moving the center of the brain, and the brain's movements cause the sensation of thirst in the mind. It's the sensation of thirst that is produced, because no information about our condition is more useful to us than that we need to get something to drink in order to remain healthy. And the same is true in other cases.

This makes it completely obvious that, despite God's immense goodness, the nature of man (whom we now view as a composite of mind and body) cannot fail to be deceptive. For, if something produces the movement usually associated with an injured foot in the nerve running from foot to brain or in the brain itself rather than in the foot, a pain is felt as if "in the foot." Here the senses are deceived by their nature. Since this motion in the **89** brain must always bring the same sensation to mind, and since the motion's cause is something hurting the foot more often than something elsewhere, it's in accordance with reason that the motion always presents the mind a pain in the foot rather than elsewhere. And, if dryness of the throat arises, not (as usual) from drink's being conducive to the body's health, but (as happens in dropsy) from some other cause, it's much better that we are deceived on this occasion than that we are generally deceived when our bodies are sound. And the same holds for other cases.

In addition to helping me to be aware of the errors to which my nature is subject, these reflections help me readily to correct or avoid these errors. I know that sensory indications of what is good for my body are more often true than false; I can almost always examine a given thing with several senses; and I can also use my memory (which connects the present to the past) and my understanding (which has now examined all the causes of error). Hence, I need no longer fear that what the senses daily show me is unreal. I should reject the exaggerated doubts of the past few days as ridiculous. This is especially true of the chief ground for these doubts—namely, my inability to distinguish dreaming from being awake. For I now notice that dreaming and being awake are importantly different: the events in dreams are not linked by memory to the rest of my life like those that happen while I am awake. If, while I'm awake, someone were suddenly to appear and then im-**90** mediately to disappear without my seeing where he came from or went to (as happens in dreams), I would justifiably judge that he was not a real man but a ghost—or, better, an apparition created in my brain. But, if I distinctly observe something's source, its place, and the time at which I learn about it, and if I grasp an unbroken connection between it and the rest of my life, I'm quite sure that it is something in my waking life rather than in a dream. And I ought not to have the slightest doubt about the reality of such things if I have examined them with all my senses, my memory, and my understanding without finding any conflicting evidence. For, from the fact that God is not a deceiver, it follows that I am not deceived in any case of this sort. Since the need to act does not always allow time for such a careful examination, however, we must admit the likelihood of men's erring about particular things and acknowledge the weakness of our nature.

Notes

1. Quoted in S. V. Keeling, *Descartes* (London, Oxford, New York: Oxford University Press, 1968).

2. Quotations from René Descartes' *Discourse on the Method of Rightly Conducting One's Reason and Seeking the Truth in the Sciences*, in *The Philosophical Writings of Descartes*, ed. John Cottingham, Robert Stoothoff, and Dugald Murdoch (Cambridge: Cambridge University Press, 1985), are cited in the text using the abbreviation *DM*. References are to part numbers and page numbers in the classic French edition, followed by page numbers in this edition.

3. Quotations from René Descartes, *The Principles of Philosophy*, in *The Philosophical Works of Descartes*, vol. 1, ed. Elisabeth S. Haldane and G. R. T. Ross (n.p.: Dover Publications, 1955), are cited in the text using the abbreviation *PP*. References are to the classic French edition, followed by the page numbers in this edition.

4. Quoted by Martin Heidegger in *The Way Back into the Ground of Metaphysics*, reprinted in *Existentialism from Dostoevsky to Sartre*, ed. Walter Kaufmann (New York: Meridian Books, 1957).

5. Keeling, *Descartes*, 252.

18

Thomas Hobbes:
Catching Persons in the
Net of the New Science

Descartes is one of the heroes of the new science. But for various reasons he stops short of supposing that geometrical mechanics can account for everything. The most obvious exceptions are mental activities: thinking, imagining, doubting, feeling, and willing. And since Descartes believes it is beyond question that each of us is first and foremost a thinking thing—and as free in our decisions as God himself—there can be no Cartesian physics of human beings. We, as thinkers, escape the net of mechanical causality.*

But do we really? Are Descartes' reasons for thinking we do conclusive? And what would be the result if human beings, too, were wholly and completely included in the physical world of Galilean/Cartesian science? Thomas Hobbes (1588–1679) makes the experiment and draws radical conclusions. It is a new world indeed, with shattering implications for human life.

We will make no comprehensive survey of Hobbes' philosophy. But it will prove useful to bring into our sense of the great conversation what Hobbes has to say about human beings, about our place in the world, and about what this means for our life together. In particular, we will ask what

status and justification any moral rules can have in a world such as the one Hobbes describes.

Hobbes accepts without reservation the Galilean/Cartesian physics of the nonhuman world. And he accepts and radicalizes the modern rejection of the medieval/Aristotelian picture of the world. It will be useful to contrast once more the salient features of this new science with the view of the world it was replacing.

1. Whereas for Aristotle and his medieval disciples, motion is development toward some fulfilling goal (a change from potentiality to actuality), for the new science, motion is simply a body's change of place in a neutral geometrical space.
2. Galileo substitutes the distinction between accelerated motion and constant motion for the Aristotelian distinction between motion and rest. For Galileo, rest is simply a limiting case of motion. In no sense is rest the culmination or fulfillment or goal of a motion.
3. Motion is the normal state of things; it does not require explanation, as in the medieval view. Only changes in motion (in direction or rate) need to be explained. And they are explained in terms of other motions.
4. Therefore, there is no natural center to the universe where things "rest." Since something in motion continues in a straight line to infinity unless interfered with, the universe is con-

---

*For Descartes' reasons see his argument for the distinctness of mind and body in *Meditation VI*. There is also his conviction that a rational being is *infinitely adaptable*; this, he thinks, distinguishes human beings from any conceivable automaton, no matter how cleverly designed. See p. 304.

ceived to be infinite rather than finite. And there are no privileged places in it.

5. Scientific explanation can no longer mention the final causes of things—those essences toward which development has been thought to strive. Final causes are derided as explanatorily barren, obscure, and even occult. In the geometrical world of Galileo and Descartes, all explanation is in terms of *contact*, of some prior impetus or push. It is as if the rich Aristotelian world with its four causes is stripped down to only the "efficient cause." Purposiveness is eliminated from the physical world.*

Now Hobbes comes along and insists that there is no reason why human beings should be considered exceptions in this world. In his comments on the *Meditations*, Hobbes claims to be unconvinced by Descartes' arguments concerning the independence of the mind from the body. For all Descartes has said, Hobbes thinks, the thing that thinks may just as well be a physical body! Indeed, Hobbes is convinced that "the subject of all activities can be conceived only after a corporeal fashion."[1] If so, then the mind cannot be thought of as a thing independent of the body. It becomes just one of the ways that bodies of a certain sort function.[†] Can this claim be plausible?

Method

Hobbes is as convinced as Descartes that method is the key to progress. He calls his method—which

he claims to have learned from Galileo and his friend William Harvey (who discovered the circulation of the blood)—the method of *resolution and composition*. The first stage, resolution, consists in the analysis of complex wholes into simple elements. It resembles Descartes' second rule.* In the second stage, the elements are reassembled, or composed again into a whole. This is analogous to Descartes' third rule. When we have both resolved and composed the complex whole we began with, we understand it better than we did before we applied the method. Both Galileo and Harvey offer impressive examples of successes attained by this method.

Galileo explains the path taken by a cannonball by imagining a projectile moving on a frictionless horizontal plane that suddenly comes to an end. At that point, the cannonball will tend both to move in the same direction (since things in motion tend to remain in motion) and to drop (since unsupported objects fall at a specific rate). The path is then *resolved* into these two tendencies, each of which can be mathematically expressed. And when synthesized or *composed* by the laws of motion, it can be seen that the path is that of a semiparabola. This principle can then be used to make predictions about the actual paths cannonballs take. These predictions (for instance, that the greatest distance is reached when the gun is at 45 degrees) are found to agree with the observations made by gunners in the field.

A somewhat different example is that of Harvey's work on the circulatory system. Here *resolution* is actually taking apart a complex object—dissecting the body of a human or other mammal. The elements figuring in the explanation of the behavior of the blood are the heart together with its chambers and valves, the arteries and veins, and the blood itself. When all these are understood in their complex relations to each other, i.e., when they are *composed* again into a whole, we understand what was previously puzzling to us.

We will see Hobbes trying to use these methods in understanding both mind and society. He aspires to be the Galileo or the Harvey of the human world.

---

*Compare Hobbes in this respect to the Greek atomists ("The World," in Chapter 4). You might also like to remind yourself of Plato's critique of this kind of nonpurposive explanation, pp. 119–121.
†Hobbes, like nearly all the moderns, is a great opponent of Aristotle. And yet this conclusion is basically Aristotelian. (See p. 167.) Likewise, his account of how we gain knowledge about the world is Aristotelian in spirit, if not in detail. In more than one way, Hobbes must be counted a "critical Aristotelian." Descartes, by contrast, clearly writes in the Plato-Augustine tradition. The principal difference between Hobbes and Aristotle is the former's repudiation of final causes, of potentiality, and of the essences that make them work. But this difference transforms everything it touches.

---

*See pp. 290–291.

Minds and Motives

Life, says Hobbes,

> is but a motion of limbs, the beginning whereof is in some principle part within; why may we not say, that all *automata* (engines that move themselves by springs and wheels as doth a watch) have an artificial life? For what is the heart, but a spring; and the nerves, but so many strings, and the joints, but so many wheels, giving motion to the whole body, such as was intended by the artificer? (*L*, 129).[2]

The distinction, in other words, between living and nonliving things is not to be found in a soul, or a life-principle, or in anything nonmaterial. Living things are just those things which *move* because they have a source of motion *within* them. They are not in principle different from automata or robots that we ourselves might make. In fact, we say that robots are alive, too; it is just that their life is *artificially created*. That doesn't make it any the less life. The internal motions causing the movements of automata are, in principle, no different from the heart, nerves, and joints of the human body. Living things, whether natural or artificial, are just matter in motion.

In a way, Descartes does not yet disagree. For he thinks that animals are just "machines"; and animals are undoubtedly alive. But what about the life of the mind? What of thought and feeling? What of desire, imagination, and memory? Can these too be plausibly considered just matter in motion? We have seen Descartes' negative answer. Can Hobbes make a positive answer plausible?

Let us begin with thinking. What are thoughts?

> . . . they are everyone a *representation* or *appearance*, of some quality or other accident of a body without us, which is commonly called an *object* (*L*, 131).

Note that Hobbes expresses no doubt that there are indeed bodies—objects—independent of ourselves. He seems simply not to take the Cartesian reasons for doubting seriously.* Descartes, notoriously, thinks there is a serious problem here—that all our experience might be just as it is while *nothing at all* corresponds to it in the world beyond our minds. That there are bodies, Descartes holds, is something that needs to be *proved*. Hobbes offers no proofs. It is as though he thinks it beyond question. *Of course* our thoughts represent bodies. *Of course* bodies really exist. To be sure, we are sometimes mistaken about them, but these mistakes give us no reason to withhold belief in external things altogether. In fact, if it were not for those objects, we would not have any thoughts at all!

> The original of them all is that which we call *sense*, for there is no conception in a man's mind which hath not first, totally or by parts, been begotten upon the organs of sense. The rest are derived from that original (*L*, 131).

The source of all our thoughts is to be found in sensation.† And sensation is an effect in us of the action of those external bodies upon our eyes, ears, nose, skin, and tongue. Motions are communicated to our sense organs from these bodies; these motions set up other motions in the sense organs; and these motions are in turn propagated by the nerves "inwards to the brain and heart." There the pressure of these motions meets a "counterpressure, or endeavor of the heart to deliver itself" (*L*, 131). Because this counterpressure is directed outward, we take the disturbance set up to be a representation or appearance of the object from which the motions originated. Here, then, are the origins of our experiences of colors, sounds, tastes, smells, hardness and softness, and so on. These experiences we call sensations, or, to use Hobbes' seventeenth-century term, "fancy."

---

*Here again Hobbes stands to Descartes as Aristotle to Plato. See pp. 142–143.

†For all Hobbes' tirades against Aristotle, this is a very Aristotelian view. It is the dead opposite of Descartes' belief in innate ideas (see p. 297). It means that he can have no tolerance for Descartes' first proof for the existence of God. In this respect, compare Thomas Aquinas' rejection of the ontological argument of St. Anselm on essentially similar Aristotelian grounds (see p. 252).

But what of these experiences themselves? Can a sensation of red or a smell of rose really be "resolved" into motions? Here is what Hobbes says. In the objects that cause them, these qualities are

> but so many several motions of the matter, by which it presseth our organs diversely. Neither in us that are pressed, are they anything else but divers motions; for motion produceth nothing but motion. But their appearance to us is fancy (L, 131).

It will pay us to consider this passage carefully, for it contains a crucial ambiguity. On the one hand Hobbes says that sensations are themselves nothing but motion; "for motion produceth nothing but motion." If we take that seriously, then Hobbes is what we call a **materialist**. The entire life of the mind is nothing more than matter in motion. For sensations are motions, and all the rest is built up out of sensations. There are no distinctive *mental qualities* at all. Mind is just matter, being moved in certain distinctive ways.

On the other hand, Hobbes says of these motions that "their appearance to us is fancy." Now if it is not the motions themselves that constitute the sensations, but their *appearance* to us, then the sensations must be distinct from the motions. Under this interpretation Hobbes is not a materialist at all; he is what we call an *epiphenomenalist*. An epiphenomenalist thinks there are unique mental qualities, that they are causally dependent upon physical states, but that they do not in turn affect the physical world. They more or less ride piggyback on the physical, but they have no physical effects.

Is Hobbes a materialist or an epiphenomenalist about the mind? It is probably impossible to decide. He talks both ways, probably because he is simply unaware of the distinction. His intentions, however, are fairly clear. He wants to be a materialist, to resolve everything—including all aspects of mental life—into matter in motion. Let us take his intentions to be more significant than his linguistic lapses from them. We will consider him, therefore, to be a materialist about the mind. In this way, he stands in dramatic opposition to Descartes, for whom mind is a radically different kind of substance from body. Descartes, then, is a metaphysical *dualist*, Hobbes a *monist*. For Hobbes there is only one kind of finite substance.

Sensations, the "original" of thought, are motions. But this poses a problem. Paraphrasing Galileo's laws of inertia, Hobbes admits that "when a body is once in motion, it moveth, unless something else hinder it, eternally" (L, 133). Why is it, then, that sensations do not remain with us? The answer is that in a way they do—but in a diminished way only. For new sensations are ever pouring in on us; and by these succeeding motions the previous ones are weakened. This "*decaying sense*," as Hobbes calls it (L, 133), is *imagination* and *memory*.

In this way Hobbes can give an account of dreams. The old motions that constitute imagination and memory are reactivated in us during sleep by some condition of the body. He allows, what Descartes makes so much of, that it is a hard matter sometimes to distinguish dreams from waking life. But he finds in this fact quite a different implication. It does not, for Hobbes, constitute a reason to doubt everything. What it does provide is an explanation for belief in satyrs, nymphs, fairies, ghosts, goblins, and witches. Because of the similarity to wakeful experience, the presence of such entities in dreams leads to belief in their reality. Superstitions, false prophecies, and religious certainties which are purely private, have the same source and constitute a threat, Hobbes thinks, to civil peace and well-being.

But let us return to thinking. When an image (the decayed motion left by a sensation) is combined with a sign, he says, we have *understanding*. And this is common to both humans and the higher animals. For instance, a dog who comes when his master whistles gives evidence that he understands what is wanted of him. The whistle is a sign connected in this case to images and tendencies to act. Hobbes, unlike Descartes, is quite content to speak of a dog as thinking this or that. The difference between the dog and ourselves is not absolute (that we have a soul, which the dog completely lacks) but is a matter of degree.

Because sense is the origin of all thinking, it is not possible for us to think of something we have not experienced. We can, of course, combine sense elements in novel ways to produce purely imaginative thoughts, of unicorns or centaurs, for instance. But things that are neither sensed nor invented on the basis of sensations are *inconceivable*. This has an important consequence: we can have, Hobbes says, no positive thought of God. "Whatsoever we imagine," he says, "is *finite*. Therefore there is no idea or conception of anything we call *infinite*" (*L*, 140). The terms we use of God do not really function to describe him; rather, they are signs of our intention to honor him.

Our thoughts, then, are derived from sense; they too are just motions in the matter of our brains. If we examine them, we find that they can roughly be grouped into two classes: *unregulated* and *regulated* thoughts. The first kind may seem to follow each other in a wholly random way. But it is not so. Upon careful observation, Hobbes tells us, we can see that their order mirrors previous successions of sense experiences. The appearance of randomness comes from the variety of our experiences. If at one time we *see* Mary with John, and then again with Peter, the *thought* of Mary may be accompanied by either that of John or that of Peter. But it will be associated in some way dependent on earlier experiences. In trying to find a pattern to unregulated thoughts, Hobbes is making a suggestion that will be developed into the doctrine of the *association of ideas*.*

More interesting, however, are regulated thoughts. These do not even have an appearance of randomness but exhibit a quite definite order. One thing Hobbes has in mind is the kind of thinking that looks for *means* to attain a certain end; a young woman wants to attract a certain man, and she thinks about how that might be done. Another kind of regulated thought consists in inquiry about the *consequences* of taking a certain action; a student considers what her life will be like if she changes her curriculum from history to engineer-

ing. In regulated thought about the world, we are always searching for either *causes* or *effects*.

Such a hunt for causes is usually carried out in *words*, which are useful both as aids to memory and as signs representing our thoughts to others. Hobbes is acutely conscious of the benefits we derive from having such objective signs of our inner thoughts. But he also warns us about the errors into which they can easily trap us.

> Seeing then that truth consisteth in the right ordering of names in our affirmations, a man that seeketh precise truth had need to remember what every name he uses stands for, and to place it accordingly, or else he will find himself entangled in words, as a bird in lime twigs, the more he struggles the more belimed (*L*, 142).

The cure for these evils of confusion is to be found in *definition*, to which Hobbes attributes the success of geometry, "the only science that it hath pleased God hitherto to bestow on mankind." (*L*, 142). Words need to be carefully defined, lest we find ourselves "entangled" in them like the bird in the lime twigs. In an often quoted phrase, Hobbes tells us that

> words are wise men's counters, they do but reckon by them; but they are the money of fools, that value them by the authority of an Aristotle, a Cicero, or a Thomas (*L*, 143).

Only a "fool" thinks that we can buy truth with the *words* of some authority.* A "wise man" realizes that they are only *signs* that, if properly used to "reckon" or calculate with, may possibly yield us a science.

We use words to *reason*, to think rationally about some matter. What is reasoning? Hobbes has a view of reasoning that some artificial intelligence researchers these days look back to as prophetic. Reasoning, he tells us, is "nothing but *reckoning*, that is adding and subtracting, of the consequences

---

*See the use to which David Hume puts this notion, Chapter 19.

*Augustine makes a similar point in a quite different context. See pp. 222–223.

of general names agreed upon for the marking and signifying of our thoughts" (L, 133–34). Reasoning, as the cognitive scientist nowadays says, is computation.

Whether we reason about the theoretical consequences of some geometrical axiom, about means to attain a certain end, or about the practical consequences of some course of action, these regulated thoughts are governed by *desire*. We wouldn't bother if we didn't *want* to find out the answer. So the motivation behind all our rational thinking is passion. Hobbes must now ask: can these desires and wants, these likes and dislikes, themselves be accounted for in terms of the metaphysics of motion?*

We have seen that living things are distinguished from nonliving things by having the origins of some of their motions within them. Hobbes must now give a more careful account of this. He distinguishes two sorts of motions peculiar to animals: *vital* and *voluntary* motions. Vital motions are such things as the circulation of the blood, the pumping of the heart, breathing, and digestion. Voluntary motions, by contrast, are those whose cause is to be found in some *imagination*. Jane imagines how pleasant it would be if John were to invite her to the movies; she walks out of her way in the hope that their paths will cross. It is clear that if imagination itself is nothing but the diminished motions of sense, voluntary motions such as walking in a certain direction have their origin in internal motions.

These small, perhaps infinitesimally small, beginnings of motion Hobbes calls *endeavor*. Endeavor can either be toward something (in which case it is called *desire*) or away from something (which is called *aversion*). In desire and aversion we find the sources of all human action.

Desire and aversion allow Hobbes to introduce certain value notions. What we desire, he says, we call *good*; what we wish to avoid we call *evil*. And these value distinctions are invariably founded on *pleasure* and *pain*, respectively: what gives us pleasure we call good; what causes pain we call evil.* It is important to realize that good and evil are not thought to attach absolutely to things. They are not properties that things have independently of our relation to them. The words "good" and "evil," Hobbes tells us,

> are ever used with relation to the person that useth them; there being nothing simply and absolutely so; nor any common rule of good and evil to be taken from the nature of the objects themselves; but from the person of the man, where there is no commonwealth; or, in a commonwealth, from the person that representeth it; or from an arbitrator or judge, whom men disagreeing shall by consent set up, and make his sentence the rule thereof (L, 150).

The idea that in a "commonwealth," or state, good and evil are not relative to *individuals* is one we will explore shortly. But in what Hobbes calls a "state of nature," where there are no monarchs and judges, good and evil strictly depend on "the person of the man." The *only* judgment possible is that of the individual; if she desires X, she judges X to be good; if he dislikes Y, he considers Y evil. And from those judgments there is (in the state of nature) no appeal.†

This analysis is an important step in Hobbes' materialistic program. Goodness is not a Platonic Form or an unanalyzable property that some things have. Everything is just body and motion. But some (living) bodies are related in certain ways to other bodies in such a way that the former bodies utter the words "That is good" about those latter bodies. They do so when the latter produce motions in the former that are pleasurable.

And what is pleasure? Pleasure, Hobbes tells us, is just "a corroboration of vital motion, and a help thereunto," while pains are a "hindering and trou-

---

*What is at stake here is whether *purpose* and *intention* can be given a mechanistic explanation. We have seen that Plato and, following him, Aristotle, think not. For this reason, Aristotle believes we need to ask about *final* causes in addition to the other three kinds. This question is still hotly debated.

---

*It is clear that Hobbes is a *hedonist*. See Epicurus, pp. 184–185.
†Compare the doctrine of Protagoras, the Sophist, who said, "Of all things, man is the measure" (p. 41).

bling the motion vital" (*L*, 150). Feeling good, in other words, is just having all our normal bodily processes working smoothly; the more active and untroubled they are, the better we feel. And what we all want is to feel good.

It seems, then, that regulated thoughts are regulated by desire, that desire is always for the good, and that "good" is our name for whatever produces pleasure. The end point of a train of regulated thoughts is some action on our part—an action we think will gain us some good. These actions, when caused by thoughtful desires in this way, are called "voluntary."

At this point Hobbes meets a natural objection. It is not, someone might claim, *desire* that is the cause of voluntary action; it is *will*. And willpower can override our desires. I desperately *want* another slice of that dark, rich chocolate cake; but I exercise my will and say, "Thank you, but no." Can Hobbes deal with this common experience?

He does so by asking what we mean by "*will*." It cannot be anything else, he thinks, than "*the last appetite in deliberating*" (*L*, 154). Will, then, *is* a desire. I do desire that slice of cake. But I also have desires that run counter to that desire: I want not to look piggish; I want not to gain too much weight. On this occasion, these latter desires outweigh the former; they are the ones that dictate my action. And so these are what we *call* my will. Will is nothing but *effective desire*. It is the desire that *wins*. Since we have already seen that Hobbes believes desire and aversion can be given an analysis in terms of matter in motion, there is no need to bring in nonmaterial mental factors to explain the origin of voluntary actions.*

Our voluntary actions, then, are governed in the last analysis by passion—by our desires and aversions, our loves and hates. And since the good we seek and the evil we try to avoid are rooted in our own pleasures and pains, action is always egoistic. It is my own good that I seek, if Hobbes is right—not yours. As Hobbes puts it, "of the voluntary acts of every man, the object is some *good to himself* (*L*, 165).

Moreover, we seek such good *continually*. It is not enough to act once for our own pleasure; the next moment demands other acts that have the same end. Happiness—or felicity, as Hobbes calls it—is just a life filled with the satisfaction of our desires.

> *Continual success* in obtaining those things which a man from time to time desireth, that is to say, continual prospering, is that men call *felicity*; I mean the felicity of this life. For there is no such thing as perpetual tranquility of mind, while we live here; because life itself is but motion, and can never be without desire, nor without fear, no more than without sense (*L*, 155).

In this life there can be no resting, no "tranquility." No sooner has one desire been fulfilled than another takes its place. And the reason Hobbes gives for this is that life itself is nothing but motion. (We have here a kind of principle of inertia for living things; just as things in motion tend to remain in motion, so the life of desiring tends to perpetuate itself.) So there is a perpetual striving for the satisfaction of desires; when this is successful over some period of time, we say that during that period a person is happy.*

All of us desire this felicity, Hobbes says. But it is easy to see that if we are not to be mere pawns of fortune, we must also control access to it. That is,

---

*It is clear that Hobbes is a *determinist*—i.e., one who thinks that for every event, including all human actions, there is a set of sufficient conditions guaranteeing its occurrence. All actions are caused; and the causes of these causes themselves have causes. This poses a problem, of course: the problem of freedom of the will. We saw that Descartes, who is not a materialist, can hold that our decisions escape this universal determinism that holds for the material world; even God, Descartes says, is not more free than we are. Hobbes cannot think so. He has a solution to this problem, but since the same solution is more elegantly set out by Hume, we will consider it in the next chapter. If you want a preview, see "Rescuing Human Freedom," in Chapter 19.

*Compare this notion of happiness to that of Epicurus ("The Epicureans," in Chapter 12). Note that there is a fundamental agreement: pleasure is the good. But note also that Hobbes makes no distinction between those desires it is and is not *wise* to try to fulfill. It is hard to see how he could—at least for the state of nature. Desires are just facts—any and all of them; they all, equally, demand satisfaction. And the strongest wins. That, Hobbes might say, is just how it is.

we must be guaranteed the *power* to satisfy whatever desires we may happen to have.

> . . . I put for a general inclination of all mankind, a perpetual and restless desire of power after power, that ceaseth only in death. And the cause of this, is not always that a man hopes for a more intensive delight, than he has already attained to; or that he cannot be content with a moderate power: but because he cannot assure the power and means to live well, which he hath present, without the acquisition of more (*L*, 158–59).

This kind of power is, of course, a relative matter. In a world of limited resources, if I gain more power to guarantee the satisfaction of *my* desires, I naturally diminish *your* power to satisfy your desires. In seeking to assure my own felicity, I threaten yours. So we are naturally competitors. I seek my good. You seek yours. And we each seek to increase our own power to assure that we at least do not lose those goods we now have.*

Although there are natural differences in our power, we are equal enough in natural gifts that each of us has reason to fear the other. As Hobbes says, even "the weakest has strength enough to kill the strongest" (*L*, 159). Because of this equality, the egoistic desire for happiness—plus the need to be assured of it by a continual increase of power—leads human beings to be enemies. So our *natural* condition (i.e., before any artificial arrangements or agreements among us) is one of *war*. Indeed, it is "such a war as is of every man against every man." In such a condition, Hobbes argues,

> there is no place for industry, because the fruit thereof is uncertain; and consequently no culture of the earth; no navigation, nor use of the commodities that may be imported by sea; no commodious building; no instruments of moving and removing, such things as require much force; no knowledge of the face of the earth; no account of time; no arts; no letters; no society; and which is worst of all, continual fear, and danger of violent death; and the life of man, solitary, poor, nasty, brutish, and short (*L*, 161).

Solitary, poor, nasty, brutish—and short! Such is our life in a state of nature.

Let us remind ourselves of what Hobbes claims to be doing here. He is trying to use the same method on human nature and society that Galileo and Harvey use on the nonhuman world. He resolves human beings into their component elements—the motions characteristic of living things—and finds this competitive and restless striving to be the result.

This analysis is supported, he believes, by observation. Hobbes lived during extremely troubled times in England. There was a long struggle between king and parliament over the right to make certain laws and collect taxes. This struggle reflected a broader quarrel between the old nobility and the established Church of England on the one hand and the rising middle classes and religious dissenters of a more radical Protestant sort on the other. Those on each side, in Hobbes' view, were trying to preserve against the other side the means of their own happiness.

The outcome was a protracted and bloody civil war, the execution of King Charles I, a period of government without a king under the Protectorate of Oliver Cromwell, and finally the Restoration of the monarchy under Charles II (to whom Hobbes had been a tutor in mathematics). The "state of nature" into which Hobbes resolves human society was very nearly the actual state of affairs during a good part of the seventeenth century in England. The war of all against all was not just a theoretical construct; it was an observed actuality.

Still, Hobbes does not intend his description of the state of nature to be a description of society at all times and places. Nor is it supposed to be a historical description of the state of society at some time in the distant past. It is intended to picture the results of an analytical decomposition of human society into its elements. Left to their own devices, the theory says, individuals will always act ego-

---

*If this seems unrealistic to you as a model of relations among individuals, consider political and economic rivalries among nations. As we will see, Hobbes has an explanation of how we have gotten beyond this competitive situation on the individual level. It is instructive to compare this picture of restless competitiveness to Augustine's two cities, pp. 240–243.

istically for their own good. And the inevitable consequence is a state of war—each of us fearing our neighbor and striving to extend our sphere of control at our neighbor's expense. This is the result of the *resolution* phase of Hobbes' method.

We now need to look at the *composition* phase, where the elements are put back together again. And here we are interested primarily in Hobbes' view of the ethical consequences.

The Natural Foundation of Moral Rules

Hobbes has "resolved" human society into its elements. Let us see how he thinks it can be "composed" back again into a whole. If Hobbes succeeds in this stage, we will have an explanation of the human world, including its ethical and political aspect, in purely mechanistic terms.

In the state of nature, human beings are governed by their egoistic passions, their endeavor to ensure their own happiness. And we have seen how this leads to the "war of everyone against everyone," a deadly competition for the power to guarantee for each person what he considers good. If this is our natural state, how can it be overcome? Partly, Hobbes says, by passion itself, and partly by reason.

One of the strongest passions is the *fear of death*. It is this fear, together with the desire for happiness, that motivates us to find a way to end the state of nature. We must remember that in the state of nature there are no rights and wrongs, no goods and bads, except where an individual thinks there are. We each take as much as we have power to take and keep. An individual's liberty extends as far as his power. But if a person in this state of nature realizes how unsatisfactory this condition is, he will see that

> it is a precept, or general rule of reason, *that every man ought to endeavor peace, as far as he has hope of obtaining it; and when he cannot obtain it, that he may seek and use all helps and advantages of war.* The first branch of which rule containeth the first and funda-

mental law of nature; which is, to *seek peace and follow it.* The second, the sum of the right of nature; which is, *by all means we can, to defend ourselves* (L, 163).

Hobbes speaks here of a *right* of nature and of a *law* of nature. What can he mean? In a universe composed merely of matter in motion, how can there be rights and laws *in nature*? Hasn't Hobbes already denied that there is any right or wrong independent of some monarch or judge to declare what is right and wrong?

There has been much debate about how Hobbes means these notions to be understood. If we interpret him sympathetically, however, it seems that a law of nature must simply be an expression of the way things go. Jones, who by nature seeks his own happiness and fears death, is worried about his future. This is just how it is. In reasoning about his situation, Jones sees that if peace were to replace war, then his fear of death would be relieved; and if he didn't have to be so afraid of his neighbors, he could more satisfactorily fill his own life with "felicity." The rule to "seek peace" is a rule that an egoistic but rational creature such as Jones will inevitably—naturally—come upon. He will reason that if he is going to have any chance of a good life, he has to get beyond this state of war. A *law of nature* for Hobbes is simply a rule of prudence that results from the shrewd calculation of a scared human being.

A *right* of nature must have a similar foundation. In the state of nature there are no "rights" in the usual sense. If, in a state of nature, someone injures me, I cannot complain that my "rights" have been infringed. All I can say is that I don't like it, and I will do whatever I can to see that it doesn't happen again! But precisely because there are no rules, I am *at liberty* to use whatever means I can muster to preserve my life and happiness. Hobbes uses the term "right" to refer to this liberty everyone has in the state of nature. So Jones having the "right" to defend himself is simply the fact that there are no rules that curtail his tendency to preserve his life and happiness. If, however, Jones (and everyone else) exercises this liberty without limit, the results will be, as we have seen, uniformly bad: the war of all against all.

This suggests to the rational person that some of the liberty we have in the state of nature must be given up. To give it up entirely, however, would make no sense at all; if Jones gave up the liberty of defending himself altogether, he would become the prey of everyone—and an egoistic agent could not rationally allow that. So this "right" of self-defense remains something that Jones will always retain.

We have, then, one right and one law, which are used by Hobbes as the foundation for a series of deductions. Once we have these, others "follow" in almost geometrical fashion. For instance, the second law, Hobbes tells us, is

> that a man be willing, when others are so too, as far forth as peace and defense of himself he shall think it necessary, to lay down this right to all things; and be contented with so much liberty against other men, as he would allow other men against himself (L, 163–64).

Each of us, according to this second law, should be content with as much liberty with respect to others as we are willing to allow with respect to ourselves. There should be—in order to end the state of war—a mutual limiting of rights, as far as this is of mutual benefit to each. (Note that Hobbes does not suppose that anyone would do this *altruistically*, or out of sheer good will. The motivation throughout is hedonistic and egoistic.)

This agreement to limit one's claims has the flavor of a *contract*. And, indeed, Hobbes' view is one version of a **social contract** theory.* But you can see that there is a difficulty at this point. Suppose Jones and Smith, in a state of nature, each agree to

_____

*The idea of a contract or agreement as the basis for society is taken up by a number of other political thinkers: Spinoza, Rousseau, and—most importantly for the founding of the American Republic—John Locke. They differ about whether the contract is with a sovereign (Hobbes) or among individuals (Locke) and about whether once entered into it could or could not be revoked. But social contract theories generally stress the rights of individuals and consent as the basis of legitimate government. As such they are both a reflection of and an influence on the individualism of the times.

limit their own liberty to the extent that the other does as well. Why should they believe each other? What reason do they have to trust each other to keep the promise? Is there anything to keep Smith from violating the contract if he thinks it is in his interest to do so and calculates that he can get away with it? It seems not. Hence, in a state of nature contracts and promises are useless. They are just words! This is a serious problem. It looks like you cannot get *here* from *there*—i.e., to a moral community from a state of nature. Can Hobbes solve this problem?

What is necessary to make the contract operative, Hobbes says, is "a common power set over them both, with right and force sufficient to compel performance" (L, 167). Only then, when punishment threatens, can Jones trust Smith to keep his promise. For only then will it clearly be in his self-interest not to break it. There is, then, a necessity for

> some coercive power, to compel men equally to the performance of their covenants . . . and such power there is none before the erection of a commonwealth (L, 168).

This is the rationale for that "great *Leviathan*," that "artificial man," that "mortal god," the state. It is the state, together with the power of enforcement that we agree to give it, that gets us beyond the state of nature. Only in such a community can moral and legal rules exist and structure our lives.

The details of Hobbes' political philosophy are of great interest. But we will pass them by. Our interest lies in the possibility of a world picture built on the foundations of the new science that *includes* human beings, together with their mental and moral life. And we now have an outline of what one such attempt looks like. Let us summarize a few of the main points.

1. Sensation, thought, motivation, and voluntary action are all analyzed in terms of matter in motion.
2. All events, including human actions, are subject to the same laws of motion that Galileo has discovered.

3. Only egoistic desires are recognized as motivators; so all actions are performed for the welfare of the agent.

4. If you peel off the veneer of civilization, what you are left with is individuals in conflict.

5. This conflict can be resolved on the basis of the very passions that produce it, provided people reason well about their individual long-term interest.

6. Morality and law are simply the best means available, the *only* means, to stave off imminent death and the possible loss of felicity. Being moral and law-abiding is no more than a smart strategy for self-preservation.

7. Unless these rules are enforced by a powerful ruler, everything will collapse again into the state of nature.

It is a stark vision that Hobbes gives us. He thinks that acceptance of modern science forces that view upon us. Is that correct? Or are there less forbidding alternatives?

Notes

1. Quoted in *Objections III with Replies* in *The Philosophical Works of Descartes*, vol. 2, ed. Elisabeth S. Haldane and G. R. T. Ross (n.p.: Dover Publications, 1955), 62.

2. Quotations from Thomas Hobbes, *Leviathan, or The Matter, Form, and Power of a Commonwealth, Ecclesiastical and Civil*, in *The English Philosophers from Bacon to Mill*, ed. Edwin A. Burtt (New York: Modern Library, 1939), are cited in the text using the abbreviation *L*. References are to page numbers.

19

David Hume:
Unmasking the Pretensions of Reason

The eighteenth century is often called the Age of Enlightenment. Those who lived through this period felt that progress was being made almost daily toward overthrowing superstition and arbitrary authority, replacing ignorance with knowledge and blind obedience with freedom. It is an age of optimism. One of the clearest expressions of this attitude is found in a brief essay by Immanuel Kant (the subject of our next chapter). Here, in 1784, he defines what his age understands by "enlightenment."

> *Enlightenment is man's emergence from his self-imposed immaturity. Immaturity is the inability to use one's understanding without guidance from another. This immaturity is self-imposed when its cause lies not in lack of understanding, but in lack of resolve and courage to use it without guidance from another. Sapere Aude!* "Have courage to use your own understanding!"—that is the motto of enlightenment.[1]

This call to think for oneself, to have the courage to rely on one's own abilities, is quite characteristic of the age. For Kant, the lack of courage is "self-imposed." To overcome it we need only the resolve not to be bound any more by those who set themselves up as our guardians.

It is so easy to be immature. If I have a book to serve as my understanding, a pastor to serve as my conscience, a physician to determine my diet for me, and

so on, I need not exert myself at all. I need not think, if only I can pay. . . . The guardians who have so benevolently taken over the supervision of men have carefully seen to it that the far greatest part of them (including the entire fair sex) regard taking the step to maturity as very dangerous, not to mention difficult. Having first made their domestic livestock dumb, and having carefully made sure that these docile creatures will not take a single step without the go-cart to which they are harnessed, these guardians then show them the danger that threatens them, should they attempt to walk alone. Now this danger is actually not so great, for after falling a few times they would in the end certainly learn to walk; but an example of this kind makes men timid and usually frightens them out of all further attempts.

Thus, it is difficult for any individual man to work himself out of the immaturity that has all but become his nature. He has even become fond of this state and for the time being actually incapable of using his own understanding.[2]

Working oneself out of this immaturity is "difficult," but not impossible—as had been clearly shown in the triumphs of the scientific revolution from Copernicus to that most admired of thinkers, Isaac Newton. It was Newton's triumphant integration of his predecessors' work into one unified explanatory scheme for understanding both terrestrial and celestial movements that symbolized what human efforts could achieve—if only they could be freed from the dead hand of the past. And thinkers throughout the eighteenth century busy themselves applying Newton's methods to other subjects: to the mind, to ethics, to religion, and to the state of society.

And yet none of them would think that they have arrived at the goal. Here again is Kant:

> If it is now asked, "Do we presently live in an *enlightened* age?" the answer is, "No, but we do live in an age of *enlightenment*."[3]

The key word is "progress." Newton showed that progress is really possible. And the conviction spreads that this progress can be extended indefinitely if only we can muster the courage to do, in one sphere after another, what Newton had done in physics and astronomy. We were not yet mature; but we were becoming mature.

How Newton Did It

It is almost impossible to exaggerate Newton's impact on the imagination of the eighteenth century. As a towering symbol of scientific achievement, he can be compared only to Einstein in the twentieth century. The astonished admiration his work evoked is expressed in a couplet by Alexander Pope.

> Nature and Nature's laws lay hid in night;
> God said, Let Newton be, and all was light.

Everyone has some idea of Newton's accomplishment, of how his theory of universal gravitation provides a mathematically accurate and powerful tool for understanding not only the motions of heavenly bodies but also such puzzling phenomena as the tides. We won't go into the details of this theory. But every science is developed on the basis of certain methods and presuppositions that may properly be called philosophical. It is these philosophical underpinnings that we must take note of, for they are crucially important to the development of the whole trend of thought in the eighteenth century—not least to the philosophy of David Hume.

How had Newton been able to pull it off? His methods are in fact not greatly different from those of Galileo and Hobbes. There are two stages (like Hobbes' resolution and composition), which he calls *analysis* and *synthesis*. But there is a particular insistence in some of his pronouncements that strike a note somewhat different from those we have heard before. He does not, he says, *frame hypotheses*. What does this mean? By a *hypothesis* he means a principle of explanation not derived from a close examination of the facts. The key to doing science, he believes, is to stay close to the phenomena; the big mistake is to jump prematurely to an explanation. Newton's own long and persistent series of experiments with the prism exemplifies this maxim. The fact that white light is not a simple phenomenon (as it seems to naive sight) is disclosed only by an immensely detailed series of investigations, which reveal its composition out of the many simpler hues of the rainbow. Only an analysis of *facts that disclose themselves to our senses* yields true principles of explanation.

> I frame no hypotheses; for whatever is not deduced from the phenomena is to be called an hypothesis; and hypotheses, whether metaphysical or physical, whether of occult qualities or mechanical, have no place in experimental philosophy.[4]

Principles of explanation are to be "deduced from the phenomena." This emphasis on paying close attention to the facts of experience has a long history in English philosophy even before Newton; it can be traced back through John Locke to Francis Bacon—and, indeed, it is Aristotelian in character. But in Newton its fruitfulness pays off in a way that had never been seen before. In Newton's work we find a suspicion of any principles that have not been derived from a close experimental examination of the sensible facts. We cannot *begin* with what *seems* right to us. Hypotheses, no matter how natural and right they may seem, must be subjected to the test of experience. Hypotheses not arrived at by way of careful analysis of the sensible facts are arbitrary—no matter how intuitively convincing they may seem. And Newton's success is, to the eighteenth-century thinker, proof that his methods are sound.

Note how different this emphasis is from the rationalism of Descartes. Always the mathematician, Descartes seeks to find starting points for science and philosophy that are intuitively certain, axioms that are "so clear and distinct" that they can not possibly be doubted. He is confident that reason, the "light of nature," will certify some such principles as knowable and known. So the whole structure of wisdom, in Descartes, is the structure of an axiomatic, geometrical system. Intuitive insight and deduction from first principles are the hallmarks of his way of proceeding.

But for eighteenth-century thinkers inspired by the example of Newton, this smells too much of arbitrariness. One man's intuitive certainty, they suspect, is another man's absurdity.* The only cure is to stick closely to the facts. The **rationalism** of Descartes is supplanted by the **empiricism** of thinkers like David Hume.

To Be the Newton of Human Nature

David Hume aspires to do for human nature what Isaac Newton did for nonhuman nature: to provide principles of explanation both simple and comprehensive.[5] There seem to be two motivations. First, Hume shares with many other Enlightenment intellectuals the project of debunking what they call "popular superstition." By this they usually mean the deliverances of religious enthusiasm together with the conviction of certainty that typically accompanies them.† (The era of religious wars based on such certainties is still fresh in the memory.) But these thinkers also mean whatever in philosophy cannot be demonstrated on a basis of reason and experience common to all men. Hume's prose betrays his passion on this score. Remarking on the obscurity, uncertainty, and error in most philosophies, he pinpoints the cause:

. . . they are not properly a science; but arise either from the fruitless efforts of human vanity, which would penetrate into subjects utterly inaccessible to the understanding, or from the craft of popular superstitions, which, being unable to defend themselves on fair ground, raise these entangling brambles to cover and protect their weakness. Chased from the open country, these robbers fly into the forest, and lie in wait to break in upon every unguarded avenue of the mind, and overwhelm it with religious fears and prejudices. The stoutest antagonist, if he remit his watch a moment, is oppressed. And many, through cowardice and folly, open the gates to the enemies, and willingly receive them with reverence and submission, as their legal sovereigns.

But is this a sufficient reason, why philosophers should desist from such researches, and leave superstition still in possession of her retreat? Is it not proper to draw an opposite conclusion, and perceive the necessity of carrying the war into the most secret recesses of the enemy? (*E*, 5–6).[6]

The basic strategy in this war is to show what the human understanding is (and is not) capable of. And this is what a science of human nature should give us. If we can show that "superstition" consists in claims to know what no one can possibly know, then we undermine its defenses in the most radical way.

Hume's second motivation is his conviction that a science of human nature is, in a certain way, fundamental. All the other sciences

have a relation, greater or less, to human nature. . . . Even *Mathematics, Natural Philosophy, and Natural Religion*, are in some measure dependent on the science of Man; since they lie under the cognizance of men, and are judged of by their powers and faculties. 'Tis impossible to tell what changes and improvements we might make in these sciences were we thoroughly acquainted with the extent and force of human understanding, and could explain the nature of the ideas we employ, and of the operations we perform in our reasonings (*T*, xix).

---

*They feel confirmed in this suspicion by the example of rationalist philosophy after Descartes. First-rate intellects like Malebranche, Spinoza, and Leibniz developed remarkably different philosophical systems on the basis of supposedly "self-evident" truths.

†"Enthusiasm" is the word eighteenth-century thinkers use to describe ecstatic forms of religion involving the claim that one is receiving revelations, visions, or "words" directly from God. This form of religion is far from dead.

Since all our intellectual endeavors are *products* of human understanding, an examination of that understanding itself should illumine them all. Such an inquiry will reveal how the mind works, what materials it has to operate on, and how knowledge in any area at all can be constructed.

Hume is aware that others before him have formulated theories of the mind (or human understanding). But they have not satisfactorily settled matters.

> There is nothing which is not the subject of debate, and in which men of learning are not of contrary opinions. . . . Disputes are multiplied, as if every thing was uncertain; and these disputes are managed with the greatest warmth, as if every thing was certain (*T*, xviii).

Consider the wide disagreement between Descartes and Hobbes, for instance. Descartes, as we have seen, believes that the freedom and rationality of our minds exempts them from the kind of causal explanation provided for material bodies. A mind, he concludes, is a thing completely distinct from a body. Hobbes, on the other hand, includes the mind and all its ideas and activities within the scope of a materialistic and deterministic science. "Mind," for Hobbes, is just a name for certain ways a human body operates. Who is right here?

From Hume's point of view, neither one prevails. Hobbes simply *assumes* that our thoughts are representations of objects that exist independently of our minds and that whatever principles explain those objects will also explain the mind. But surely Descartes has shown us that this is something that should not be assumed! Whatever our experience might be, whatever it "tells" us about reality, things could actually be different. That is the lesson of Descartes' doubt. Hobbes' assumption that sensations and thoughts generally represent realities accurately is nothing but a "hypothesis." And, Hume says (following Newton), we are to avoid framing hypotheses.

Descartes' positive doctrine of a separate mind-substance, however, is just as "hypothetical" as that of Hobbes. It is derived from principles that may *seem* intuitively obvious, but have not been "deduced from the phenomena." The problem is that neither pays close attention to the data available. Both of them fail because they did not have the example of Newton from which to learn. We do not have, Hume thinks, any insight or intuition into the "essence" of material bodies. Nor do we have such an intuition into the "essence" of minds. We have made progress in the physical realm only by sticking close to the experimental facts; we can hope to progress in constructing a science of human nature only if we do the same in that realm.

> For to me it seems evident, that the essence of the mind being equally unknown to us with that of external bodies, it must be equally impossible to form any notion of its powers and qualities otherwise than from careful and exact experiments, and the observation of those particular effects, which result from its different circumstances and situations. And tho' we must endeavour to render all our principles as universal as possible, by tracing up our experiments to the utmost, and explaining all effects from the simplest and fewest causes, 'tis still certain we cannot go beyond experience; and any hypothesis, that pretends to discover the ultimate original qualities of human nature, ought at first to be rejected as presumptuous and chimerical (*T*, xxi).

The Newtonian tone is unmistakable. What, then, are the *data* which a scientist of human nature must "observe" and from which he may draw principles "as universal as possible"? Hume calls them "perceptions," by which he means all the contents of our minds when we are awake and alert.* Among perceptions are all our ideas, including not only those of the sciences, but also ideas both arbitrary and superstitious. One of Hume's aims is to draw a line between legitimate ideas and ideas that are confused, unfounded, and nonsensical. To do this, he thinks it necessary to inquire about the *origin* of our ideas.

---

*Here Hume shows that he, like Descartes (and Locke and Berkeley, too), is committed to the representational theory (p. 294). Unlike Descartes, as we will see, Hume believes there are no legitimate inferences from ideas to things.

The Theory of Ideas

A science of human nature must concentrate on what is peculiarly human. A woman's height, weight, and hair color are characteristics of a human being; but these are properties she shares with nonhuman objects, which Newtonian science explains so well. It is human ideas, feelings, and actions that are distinctive and require special treatment. And it is on these that Hume focuses. Ideas are particularly important, since they are involved in nearly all the other activities that are characteristically human. What are ideas? And how do we come to have them?

Hume thinks that the contents of the mind he calls "perceptions" can be divided into two major classes: *impressions* and *ideas*.

> The difference betwixt these consists in the degrees of force and liveliness with which they strike upon the mind, and make their way into our thought or consciousness. Those perceptions, which enter with most force and violence, we may name *impressions*; and under this name I comprehend all our sensations, passions and emotions, as they make their first appearance in the soul. By *ideas* I mean the faint images of these in thinking and reasoning (*T*, 1).

You can get a vivid illustration of the difference between the two classes if you bring your hand down suddenly on the table (the sound you hear is an impression), and then, a few seconds later, recall that sound (the image of it in your memory is an idea).

Hume thinks that this difference is one we are all familiar with. There may be borderline cases such as a terrifying dream, in which the ideas are very nearly as lively as the actual impressions would be. But on the whole, the distinction is not only familiar, but clear. One other important distinction must be observed: that between *simple* and *complex*. The impression you have when you slap the table is simple; the impression you have when you hear a melody is complex. Complex impressions and ideas are built up from simples.

Hume is trying to pay close attention to the data. The next thing he notices is "the great resemblance betwixt our impressions and ideas" (*T*, 2). It seems as though "all the perceptions of the mind are double, and appear both as impressions and ideas" (*T*, 3). No, he adds, this is not quite correct. For you have the idea of a unicorn, but you have never experienced a unicorn impression. (Ah, you say; but I have seen a *picture* of a unicorn! True enough, but your experience on that occasion did not constitute an impression of a unicorn, but of a unicorn picture. Your idea of a unicorn is not the idea of a picture.) So you do have an idea that does not correspond to any impression; so not all our perceptions are "double."

But a closer look, Hume thinks, will convince us that although this principle does not hold for *complex* ideas, it does hold for all *simple* ideas. The idea of a unicorn, after all, is a very complex idea. We need not analyze it very far to notice that it is made up of two simpler ideas: that of a horse and that of a single horn. Impressions do correspond to these simpler ideas, for horses and horns we have all seen. So the revised principle is that to every *simple idea* corresponds a *simple impression* that resembles it.

If impressions and simple ideas come in pairs like this, so that there is a "constant conjunction" between them, the next question is: which comes first? Hume again notes that *in his experience* it is always the impression that appears first; the idea comes later.

> To give a child an idea of scarlet or orange, of sweet or bitter, I present the objects, or in other words, convey to him these impressions; but proceed not so absurdly, as to endeavour to produce the impressions by exciting the ideas. . . . We cannot form to ourselves a just idea of the taste of a pine-apple, without having actually tasted it (*T*, 5).

This suggests that there is a relation of *dependence* between them; Hume concludes that every simple idea has some simple impression as a causal antecedent. Every simple idea, in fact, is a *copy* of a preceding impression.* What is the origin of all our ideas? The impressions of experience—no impression, no idea.

This is an apparently simple principle. But Hume warns us that taking it seriously will have far-reaching consequences. It contains, in fact, a rule of procedure that Hume makes devastating use of.

> All ideas, especially abstract ones, are naturally faint and obscure: The mind has but a slender hold of them: They are apt to be confounded with other resembling ideas; and when we have often employed any term, though without a distinct meaning, we are apt to imagine it has a determinate idea, annexed to it. On the contrary, all impressions, that is, all sensations, either outward or inward, are strong and vivid: The limits between them are more exactly determined: Nor is it easy to fall into any error or mistake with regard to them. When we entertain, therefore, any suspicion, that a philosophical term is employed without any meaning or idea (as is but too frequent), we need but enquire, *from what impression is that supposed idea derived*? And if it be impossible to assign any, this will serve to confirm our suspicion (*E*, 13).

Every meaningful term, Hume tells us, is associated with an idea. Some terms, however, have no clear idea connected with them. We get used to them and think they mean something, but we are deceived. How can we discover whether a term really means something? Try to trace the associated idea back to an impression. If you can, it is a meaningful term that expresses a real idea. If you try and fail, then it is just noise or marks on paper.

Hume has here a powerful critical tool. It seems innocent enough, but Hume makes radical use of it. The rule is a corollary to Hume's Newtonian analysis of the phenomena. It is a result of the theory of ideas.

---

*Compare Hobbes, p. 329. Hume's theory of the origin of ideas is similar, but without the mechanistic neurological explanation, and also without the assumption that external objects are the cause of our impressions. In trying to stick to the phenomena, Hume considers both these claims to be merely "hypotheses." The perceptions of the mind are our *data*; beyond them we may not safely go.

The Association of Ideas

The results so far constitute the stage of analysis. What we find, on paying close attention to the contents of the human mind, are impressions and ideas, the latter in complete dependence upon the former. Hume now needs to proceed to the stage of synthesis; what are the principles that bind these elements together to produce the rich mental life characteristic of humans? Like Newton, he finds that the great variety of phenomena can be explained by a few principles, surprisingly simple in nature. These are principles of *association*, and correspond in the science of human nature to universal gravitation in the purely physical realm.

> It is evident that there is a principle of connexion between the different thoughts or ideas of the mind, and that, in their appearance to the memory or imagination, they introduce each other with a certain degree of method and regularity. . . . Were the loosest and freest conversation to be transcribed, there would immediately be observed something, which connected it in all its transitions. Or where this is wanting, the person, who broke the thread of discourse, might still inform you, that there had secretly revolved in his mind a succession of thought, which had gradually led him from the subject of conversation (*E*, 14).

Whether this observation is correct or not you should be able to test by observing your own trains of thought, or noting how one topic follows another in a conversation you are party to.

If Hume is right here, then the obvious next question is, What are these principles of association?

> To me, there appear to be only three principles of connexion among ideas, namely *Resemblance, Contiguity* in time or place, and *Cause* or *Effect*.
>
> That these principles serve to connect ideas will not, I believe, be much doubted. A picture naturally leads our thoughts to the original [Resemblance]: The mention of one apartment in a building naturally introduces an enquiry or discourse concerning the

others [Contiguity]: And if we think of a wound, we can scarcely forbear reflecting on the pain which follows it [Cause and Effect] (*E*, 14).

There is some question about whether this list of three principles of association is complete; Hume thinks it probably is and invites you to try to find more if you think otherwise. The world of ideas, then, is governed by the "gentle force" of association. He likens it to "a kind of Attraction, which in the mental world will be found to have as extraordinary effects as in the natural, and to shew itself in as many and as various forms" (*T*, 10, 12–13).

It is important to note that this "gentle force" operates entirely without our consent, will, or even consciousness of it. It is not something in our control, any more than we can control the force of gravity. If Hume is right, it just happens that this is how the mind works. He does not think it possible to go on to explain *why* the mind works the way it does; explanation has to stop somewhere, and, like Newton, he does not "frame hypotheses." But these principles can be "deduced from the phenomena."

Causation: The Very Idea

We now have the fundamental principles of the science of human nature Hume is trying to construct: an analysis into the elements of the mind (impressions and ideas), the relation between them (dependence), and the principles that explain how ideas interact (association). We are now ready for the exciting part: What happens when this science is applied?

One more distinction will set the stage.

All the objects of human reason or enquiry may naturally be divided into two kinds, to wit, *Relations of Ideas*, and *Matters of Fact*. Of the first kind are the sciences of Geometry, Algebra, and Arithmetic; and in short, every affirmation, which is either intuitively or demonstratively certain. *That the square of the hypothenuse is equal to the square of the two sides*, is a

proposition, which expresses a relation between these figures. *That three times five is equal to the half of thirty*, expresses a relation between these numbers. Propositions of this kind are discoverable by the mere operation of thought, without dependence on what is anywhere existent in the universe. Though there never were a circle or triangle in nature, the truths, demonstrated by Euclid, would forever retain their certainty and evidence.

Matters of fact, which are the second objects of human reason, are not ascertained in the same manner; nor is our evidence of their truth, however great, of a like nature with the foregoing. The contrary of every matter of fact is still possible; because it can never imply a contradiction, and is conceived by the mind with the same facility and distinctness, as if ever so conformable to reality. *That the sun will not rise to-morrow* is no less intelligible a proposition, and implies no more contradiction, than the affirmation, *that it will rise*. We should in vain, therefore, attempt to demonstrate its falsehood. Were it demonstratively false, it would imply a contradiction, and could never be distinctly conceived by the mind (*E*, 15–16).

The contrast drawn in these paragraphs is an important one. Let's be sure we understand it. Suppose we contrast these two statements:

A: Two plus three is not five.
B: The sun will not rise tomorrow.

Assume that the sun does rise tomorrow. Then both statements are false. But what Hume draws our attention to is that they are *false in different ways. A* is false simply because of the way in which the ideas "two," "plus," "three," "five," and "equals" are related to each other. To put them together as *A* does is not just to make a false statement; it is to utter a *contradiction*, to say something that cannot even be clearly conceived. As Hume puts it, we can know it is false "by the mere operation of thought." We do not have to make any experiments or look to our experience. The opposite of *A* can in turn be known to be true, no matter what is "anywhere existent in the universe."

However, we can clearly conceive *B* even though it is false. It is not false because the ideas in it are related the way they are; given the way they are related, it might possibly be true. We can clearly conceive what that would be like: we wake up to total and continuing darkness. Whether *B* is true or false depends on the *facts*, on what actually happens in nature. And to determine its truth or falsity we need to do more than just think about it. We need to consult our experience. The falsity of *B*, Hume says, cannot be *demonstrated*. Reason alone will not suffice to convince us of matters of fact; here only experience will do.

And he suggests one further difference between them: about *A* we can be certain; but with respect to propositions stating matters of fact, our evidence is never great enough to amount to certainty.*

At this point we need to remind ourselves once again that Hume is committed to sticking to the phenomena: the perceptions of the mind, its impressions and ideas. This is the data that needs explaining in a science of human nature. But now it is obvious that a question forces itself on us. Is that all we can know about?

We don't usually think so. We talk confidently of things beyond the reach of our senses and memory—of what's going on in the next room or on the moon, of what happened long before we were born, of a whole world of objects that exist (we think) quite independently of our minds; and many of us think it quite sensible to talk of God and the soul. All this is common sense. And yet it all goes far beyond the narrow bounds of Hume's

data. What can we make of this? Or rather, what can Hume make of it? He considers some examples:

- A man believes that his friend is in France. Why? Because he has received a letter from his friend.
- You find a watch on a desert island and conclude that some human being had been there before you.
- You hear a voice in the dark and conclude there is another person in the room.

In each of these cases, where someone claims to know something not present in his perceptions, you will find that a connection is being made by the relation of *cause and effect*. In each case a present impression (reading the letter, seeing the watch, hearing the voice) is *associated* with an idea (of the friend's being in France, of a person's dropping the watch, of someone speaking). And in each case, the idea is an idea of something not present. The way we get beliefs about matters of fact beyond the present testimony of our senses and memory is by relying on our sense of causal relations. The letter is an *effect* of our friend's having written and sent it; the watch was *caused* to be there on the beach by another person; and voices are *produced* by human beings. Or so we believe. It is causation that allows us to reach out beyond the limits of present sensation and memories.

> All reasonings concerning matter of fact seem to be founded on the relation of *Cause and Effect*. By means of that relation alone we can can go beyond the evidence of our memory and senses (*E*, 16).

This seems like progress, though it is hardly very new. Descartes, you will recall, escapes the solipsism of having his knowledge limited to his own existence by a causal argument for the existence of God.* But Hume now presses these investigations in a novel direction. How, he asks, do we arrive at the knowledge of cause and effect?

---

*Hume is here suggesting a revolutionary understanding of the kind of knowledge we have in mathematics. A contrast with Plato will be instructive. For Plato (see pp. 108–110), mathematics is the clearest case of knowledge we have. Not only is it certain and enduring; it is also the best avenue into acquaintance with absolute reality, for its *objects* are independent of the world of sensory experience—eternal and unchanging Forms. What Hume is suggesting is that mathematics is certain not because it introduces us to such a world of realities, but simply because of how it relates *ideas* to one another. Mathematics *has no objects*. This suggestion undermines in a radical way the entire Platonic picture of reality. It is further developed in this century by Ludwig Wittgenstein and the logical positivists. See pp. 499 and 508.

---

*You might review the argument in *Meditation III*, noting especially the role played by the causal principle that nothing comes from nothing.

The first part of his answer to this question is a purely negative point. We do not, and cannot, arrive at such knowledge independently of experience, or **a priori** (a term which simply means "independent of experience"). To put this in a now familiar way, our knowledge of causality is not a matter of the *relations of ideas*. Consider two events that are related as cause and effect. To use a typical eighteenth-century example, think about two balls on a billiard table, the cue ball striking the eight ball, causing the eight ball to move. Suppose we know all about the cue ball—its weight, its direction, its momentum—but have never had any experience whatsoever of one thing striking another. Could we predict what would happen when the two balls meet? Not at all. For all we would know, the cue ball might simply stop, reverse its direction, pop straight up in the air, go straight through, or turn into a chicken. Our belief that the effect will be a movement of the second ball is *completely* dependent on our having observed that sort of thing on prior similar occasions. Without that experience, we would be at a total loss.

> No object ever discovers, by the qualities which appear to the senses, either the causes which produced it, or the effects which will arise from it; nor can our reason, unassisted by experience, ever draw any inference concerning real existence and matter of fact. . . . *causes and effects are discoverable, not by reason, but by experience* (E, 17).

My expectation that the second billiard ball will move when struck is based entirely on *past experience* with balls and similar things. I have seen that sort of thing happen before. This seems entirely reasonable: I make a prediction on the basis of past experience. But if that prediction is reasonable, we ought to be able to set out the reason for it. Reasons can be given in arguments. Let us try to make the argument explicit.

1. I have seen one ball strike another many times.
2. Each time the ball which was struck has moved. Therefore:
3. The struck ball will move this time.

If we look at the matter this way, however, it is easy to see that (3) does not *follow* from (1) and (2). It seems quite possible that this time something else could happen. To be sure, none of us believes that anything else will happen; but it is precisely this belief, the belief that the first one *causes* the second to move, which needs explanation. Hume is searching for what, if anything, makes this a *rational* thing to believe. This time could be very different from all those past times. The ball *could* fail to move. So the argument is invalid and does not give us a good *reason* to believe that the second ball will move. Can we patch the argument up?

Suppose we add a premise to the argument.

1a. The future will (in the relevant respect) be like the past.

Now the argument looks valid. (1a), (1), and (2) do indeed entail (3). If we know that (1a) is true, then, in the light of our experience summed up in (1) and (2), it is rational to believe that the second billiard ball will move when struck by the first one. (We could call (1a) the principle of *the uniformity of nature*.)

But how do you know that (1a) is true? Think about that a minute. How *do* you know that the future will be like the past? It is surely not *contradictory* to suppose that the way events hang together might suddenly change; putting the kettle on the fire after today *could* produce ice. So (1a) is not true because of the relation of the ideas in it.* Whether (1a) is true or false must surely be a *matter of fact*. So if we know it, we must know it on the basis of experience. What experience? If we look back, we can see that the futures we were (at various points) looking forward to always resembled the pasts we were (at those points) recalling. This suggests another argument.

4. I have experienced many pairs of events which have been constantly conjoined in the past.

---

*You should review the discussion of the distinction between relations of ideas and matters of fact, p. 345.

5. Each time I found that similar pairs of events were constantly conjoined in the future. Therefore:

1a. The future will (in these respects) be like the past.

But it is clear that this argument is no better than the first one; we are trying to justify our general principle (1a) in *exactly* the same way as we tried to justify the expectation that the struck billiard ball would move (3). If it didn't work the first time, it surely won't work now. The fact that past futures resembled past pasts is simply no good reason to think that future futures will resemble their relevant pasts.

Yet we all think that is so. Don't we? Our practical behavior surely testifies to that belief; we simply have no hesitation in walking about on the third floor of a building, believing that it will support us now just as it always has in the past. We all believe in the uniformity of nature. But why? For what *reason*? Here is Hume's response to that question.

> These two propositions are far from being the same,
> *I have found that such an object has always been attended with such an effect, and*
> *I foresee, that other objects, which are, in appearance, similar, will be attended with similar effects.*
> I shall allow, if you please, that the one proposition may justly be inferred from the other: I know in fact, that it always is inferred. But if you insist, that the inference is made by a chain of reasoning, I desire you to produce that reasoning. The connexion between these propositions is not intuitive. There is required a medium, which may enable the mind to draw such an inference, if indeed it be drawn by reasoning and argument. What that medium is, I must confess, passes my comprehension; and it is incumbent on those to produce it, who assert, that it really exists, and is the origin of all our conclusions concerning matter of fact (*E*, 22).

Let us review. Hume is inquiring into the foundation of ideas about things that go far beyond the contents of our present consciousness. These ideas all depend on relations of cause and effect: they are effects caused in us by impressions of some kind.

But what is the foundation of these causal inferences? It can only be experience. But now we see that *experience cannot supply a good reason* for believing that my friend is in France—not even my impression that I hold in my hand a letter which which seems to have a Paris postmark. There is a gap between the premise and the conclusion; it seems always possible that the premise might be true while the conclusion is false; I might have such a letter even though she is not in France but is taking a holiday in Istanbul. The gap is certainly there; and it seems there is no possible *reason* that can fill that gap. Reason does not seem to be the right "medium" to fill the gap.

And so we have the first part of Hume's answer to the question about what justifies us in believing in so many things independent of our present experience: *not any reason!*

We must be careful here. Hume is not advising us, on that ground, to give up such beliefs; he thinks we could not, even if we wanted to. "Nature will always maintain her rights," he says, "and prevail in the end over any abstract reasoning whatsoever" (*E*, 27). The fact that these beliefs do not rest on any rational foundation is an important result in his science of human nature. And, as we'll see, its philosophical consequences are dramatic. But he acknowledges that these are beliefs living creatures such as ourselves really cannot do without. Our survival depends on them.

If we allow that these beliefs about the world are not rationally based, the next obvious question is this: What *is* their foundation? Hume suggests a thought experiment.

> Suppose a person, though endowed with the strongest faculties of reason and reflection, to be brought on a sudden into this world; he would, indeed, immediately observe a continual succession of objects, and one event following another; but he would not be able to discover any thing farther. He would not, at first, by any reasoning, be able to reach the idea of cause and effect; since the particular powers, by which all natural operations are performed, never appear to the senses; nor is it reasonable to conclude, merely because one event, in one instance precedes another, that therefore the one is the cause, the other the effect. Their conjunction may be arbitrary and

casual. There may be no reason to infer the existence of one from the appearance of the other. And in a word, such a person, without more experience, could never employ his conjecture or reasoning concerning any matter of fact, or be assured of any thing beyond what was immediately present to his memory and senses.

Suppose again, that he has acquired more experience, and has lived so long in the world as to have observed similar objects or events to be constantly conjoined together; what is the consequence of this experience? He immediately infers the existence of one object from the appearance of the other (E, 27–28).

This seems plausible. But what is the difference between the first and the second supposition? The only difference is that in the first case the man lacks sufficient experience to notice which events are "constantly conjoined" with each other. But what difference does this difference make? What allows him in the second case to make inferences and have expectations, when he cannot do that in the first case? If it is not a matter of reasoning, then there must be

some other principle, which determines him to form such a conclusion. This principle is CUSTOM or HABIT (E, 28).

Note carefully what Hume is saying. Our belief that events are related by cause and effect is a completely *nonrational* belief. We have no good reason to think this. So we also have no good reason to think what we do in fact think: that all those things we believe are going on beyond the range of our present impressions and memories really exist. We do believe these things. We cannot help it. But it is simply by virtue of a kind of natural instinct. That is just how human nature works: when we experience the *constant conjunction* of events, we form a habit of expecting the second when we observe the first. (We can think of Hume's thesis here as an ancestor of the contemporary psychological notion of conditioning.)

Custom, then, is the great guide of human life. It is that principle alone, which renders our experience useful to us, and makes us expect, for the future, a similar train of events with those which have appeared in the past. Without the influence of custom, we should be entirely ignorant of every matter of fact, beyond what is immediately present to the memory and senses (E, 29).

Hume is here turning upside down the major theme of nearly all philosophy before him. Almost everyone in the philosophical tradition has agreed that a person has a right to believe something only if a good reason can be given for it. This goes back at least to Plato.* The major arguments among the philosophers concern what can (and what cannot) be adequately supported by reason. This commitment to the rationality of belief is most prominent, of course, in a rationalist such as Descartes, who determines to doubt everything that cannot be certified by the "light of reason." The skeptics, on precisely these same grounds, argue that virtually nothing can be known, since virtually nothing can be shown to be reasonable. Hume seems to agree that virtually nothing can be shown to be reasonable; is he, then, a skeptic? We will return to this question.

For now, let us note his conclusion that almost none of our most important beliefs (all of which depend on the relation between cause and effect) can be shown to be rational. We hold them simply out of habit. Our tendency to form beliefs about the external world is just a *fact* about us; this is the way human nature works. Experiencing the constant conjunction of pairs of events leads us to expect the one when we experience the other. Hume does not try to explain *why* human nature functions this way—it just does. We should not try to frame hypotheses!

There is a corollary, which Hume is quick to draw. Sometimes a certain event is *always* conjoined with another event. But in other cases two events are more loosely connected in our experience, so that it is only *often*, or *mostly*, the case that when the one occurs the other also occurs. Water always boils when put on a hot fire, but it only sometimes rains when it is cloudy. These facts are

_____

*Review Plato's distinction of knowledge from opinion in terms of the former being "backed up by reasons" (pp. 106–108).

the foundation of *probabilistic* expectations. Our degree of belief corresponds to the degree of connection that our experience reveals between the two events. Again, note that for Hume this is not the result of a rational calculation. We do not *decide* to believe with a particular degree of assurance. It just happens. We *find ourselves* believing those things most confidently which are most regular in our experience. That is how we are made.*

One more fact about our causal beliefs needs to be accounted for. We have seen that they are founded on a habit, or custom, of expecting one event whenever we have observed it to be constantly conjoined with another event. But this does not seem to exhaust the notion of causality. When we say that X causes Y, we don't just mean that whenever X occurs Y also occurs. We mean that if X occurs, Y *must* occur, that X *produces* Y, that X has a certain *power* to bring Y into being. In short, we think that in some sense the connection between X and Y is a *necessary connection*. This is part of what we mean by the idea of a *cause*. Hume owes us an account of this aspect of the idea.

How can he proceed? The idea of cause is one of those metaphysical ideas we are all familiar with, but whose exact meaning is obscure. Hume has already given us a rule to deal with these cases: try to trace the idea back to an impression. What happens if we try to do that?

Think again about the billiard balls on the table. Try to describe with great care your exact experience when seeing the one strike the other. Isn't it your impression that the cue ball moves across the table, it touches the eight ball, and the eight ball moves? Is there anything else you observe? In particular, do you observe the *force* that *makes* the sec-

ond ball move? Do you observe the *necessary connection* between them? Hume is convinced that you do not.

> . . . we are never able, in a single instance, to discover any power or necessary connexion; any quality which binds the effect to the cause, and renders the one an infallible consequence of the other. We only find, that the one does actually, in fact, follow the other. . . . Consequently, there is not, in any single, particular instance of cause and effect, any thing which can suggest the idea of power or necessary connexion (*E*, 41).

Mental phenomena are no different. If I will to move my hand, my hand moves. If I try to recall the first line of "The Star Spangled Banner," I can (usually) do it. But no matter how closely I inspect these operations, all I can observe is one thing being followed by another. I never get an impression of the *connection* between them. All relations of cause and effect must be learned from experience; and experience can show us only "the frequent CONJUNCTION of objects, without being ever able to comprehend any thing like CONNEXION between them" (*E*, 46).

Where then do we get this idea of cause? Is it one of those ideas that is simply meaningless? Should we discard it? Try to do without it? That seems hardly possible. Yet a close inspection of all the data seems to confirm Hume's conclusion:

> . . . upon the whole, there appears not, throughout all nature, any one instance of connexion, which is conceivable by us. All events seem entirely loose and separate. One event follows another; but we can never observe any tie between them. They seem *conjoined*, but never *connected*. And as we can have no idea of any thing, which never appeared to our outward sense or inward sentiment, the necessary conclusion *seems* to be, that we have no idea of connexion or power at all, and that these words are absolutely without any meaning, when employed either in philosophical reasonings, or common life (*E*, 49).

"All events seem entirely loose and separate." And the conclusion *seems* to be that we have no idea of

---

*A qualification needs to be made here. While our degree of confidence in our beliefs is usually governed by this principle, there are exceptions. We can be misled by confusions in our terms, thinking that certain ideas have meaning when they do not. Or we can generalize too soon, on the basis of limited information. These mistakes lead to what Hume calls "superstition." A superstition is usually an erroneous belief, held with too high a degree of confidence, about causes and effects. Think about the bad luck supposedly associated with breaking a mirror or walking under a ladder.

cause at all—because there is no corresponding impression. But then it is really puzzling why this idea should be so natural, so pervasive, and so useful. It is an idea we all have, and one we can hardly do without.

This puzzle, Hume thinks, can be solved. He can explain why we have this idea. To understand this explanation, we have to go back to the fact that exposure to constant conjunctions of events builds up an associationistic *habit* of expecting one event on the appearance of the other. This habit is the key to understanding the concept of a cause.

> . . . after a repetition of similar instances, the mind is carried by habit, upon the appearance of one event, to expect its usual attendant, and to believe that it will exist. This connexion, therefore, which we *feel* in the mind, this customary transition of the imagination from one object to its usual attendant, is the sentiment or impression, from which we form the idea of power or necessary connexion. . . . When we say, therefore, that one object is connected with another, we mean only, that they have acquired a connexion in our thought, and give rise to this inference, by which they become proofs of each other's existence (E, 50–51).

Hume is able, in this way, to give a certain legitimacy to the concept of cause. In fact he ventures to give a *definition* of a cause. A cause, he says, is

> an object, followed by another, and where all the objects, similar to the first, are followed by objects similar to the second. Or in other words, *where, if the first object had not been, the second never had existed* (E, 51).

And there is a second definition equivalent to that which mentions our experience of the constant conjunction involved:

> an object followed by another, and whose appearance always conveys the thought to that other (E, 51).

In this way Hume explains why causation is a natural, universally shared concept among humans by giving us an account of how it arises: we all *feel* this tendency to expect a second event when we experi-

ence a first one, provided they have been uniformly connected in our past experience. And this feeling *in the mind* is the impression that gives rise to the idea of a necessary causal connection.

Although the concept is explained and we can understand how humans naturally come to have it, the concept itself is a *fiction*. We cannot help applying it to observed events, but nothing in our observation of those events *ever* gives us a warrant for so applying it.

Remember that the relation of cause and effect is the foundation of all our beliefs about matters beyond immediate consciousness. It follows that the entire world of common sense (and science, too) is a *construction*—one *without any reason behind it*. If knowledge is belief based on reason, there is precious little we can claim to know! The confidence of Descartes and Hobbes (in their different ways) that we have good reason to think modern science tells us the truth about reality seems very naive. And the major philosophical tradition since Plato and Aristotle, one dedicated to finding what is reasonable to believe, is shown to be built on sand. What do we have *reason* to believe about the nature of reality? Virtually nothing.

Again we should ask, Is this just skepticism all over again—this time on the foundation of an attempt to construct a science of human nature? But again, let us put off the question.

The Disappearing Self

Philosophers since Plato have struggled with the question about the nature of human beings. This metaphysical problem is puzzling and difficult because the phenomena of mind—consciousness, thinking, feeling, willing, deciding to act—seem to be so different from nonmental phenomena—size, motion, weight, inertia. Plato argues that a person is really an entity distinct from the body, a *soul*; residence in a body is a temporary state, and the soul survives the body's death. The tradition in the West generally follows him, though there are dissenters. The atomists and Epicureans think of the soul as material and mortal; Aristotle holds (with qualifications) that the soul is a functional aspect of a living body; the skeptics, of course, suspend judgment on the whole question.

In modern times, Descartes follows the lead of Plato, holding not only that the soul or mind is a distinct substance and immortal, but also that it is better known than any body could be. Hobbes, by contrast, interprets human beings in a thoroughly materialistic way. The issue is certainly not settled before the age of Enlightenment.*

Hume can hardly avoid dealing with the problem, since he claims to be constructing a science of human nature. The first thing we need to do, to the extent possible, is to clarify the meaning of the central term. What Plato called "soul" and Descartes the "mind," Hume names the "self." A self is supposedly a substance or thing, simple (not composed of parts), and invariably the same through time. It is the "home" for all our mental states and activities, the "place" where these characteristics are "located." (The terms in quote marks are, of course, used metaphorically.) My self is what is supposed to account for the fact that I am one and the same person today as I was at the age of four, even though nearly all my characteristics have changed over the years. I am larger, stronger, and smarter; I have different hopes and fears, different thoughts and memories; my interests and activities are remarkably different. Yet I am the *same self*. The thing that I most deeply am has not changed. This selfsame, identical thing—this is I. Or so the story goes.

It is clear what Hume will ask here. Remember his rule: If there is a term which is in any way obscure, or about which there is much controversy, try to trace it back to an impression.

> . . . from what impression cou'd this idea be derived? This question 'tis impossible to answer without a manifest contradiction and absurdity; and yet 'tis a question, which must necessarily be answer'd, if we

wou'd have the idea of self pass for clear and intelligible. It must be some one impression, that gives rise to every real idea. But self or person is not any one impression, but that to which our several impressions and ideas are suppos'd to have a reference. If any impression gives rise to the idea of self, that impression must continue invariably the same, thro' the whole course of our lives; since self is suppos'd to exist after that manner. But there is no impression constant and invariable (*T*, 251).

Let us be clear about the argument here. The term "self" is supposed to represent an idea of something that continues unchanged throughout a person's life. Since the idea is supposed to be a simple one, there must be a simple impression that is its "double." But there is no such impression, Hume claims, "constant and invariable" through life. It follows, according to Hume's rule, that *we have no such idea!* The term is one of those meaningless noises that we suppose (through inattention or confusion) means something, when it really doesn't.

This is a most radical way of undermining belief in the soul or self. Some philosophers claim to have such an idea and to be able to prove the self really exists. Others claim to be able to prove that it doesn't exist. But Hume undercuts both sides; they are just arguing about words, he holds, because neither side really knows what it is talking about. Literally! There simply is no such idea as the (supposed) idea of the self. So it doesn't make sense either to affirm it *or* to deny it.

This claim, of course, rests on the theory of ideas. It is only as strong as that theory is good. Is that a good theory? This is an important question; we will meet other philosophers who investigate this question.* But for now, let us explore in a bit more depth why Hume thinks there is no impression that corresponds to the (supposed) idea of the self. In a much-quoted passage, Hume says,

---

*Discussions of these various doctrines can be found as follows: Plato, pp. 127–129; Aristotle, pp. 165–168; atomism, pp. 30–31; Descartes in *Meditation VI*; and Hobbes on pp. 329–330.

*Kant, for instance, denies a key premise of the theory of ideas: that all our ideas (Kant calls them "concepts") arise from impressions. Some of our concepts, Kant claims, do not *arise out of* experience, though they may *apply to* experience. See pp. 369 and 375–376.

For my part, when I enter most intimately into what I call *myself*, I always stumble on some particular perception or other, of heat or cold, light or shade, love or hatred, pain or pleasure. I never can catch *myself* at any time without a perception, and never can observe any thing but the perception. When my perceptions are remov'd for any time, as by a sound sleep; so long am I insensible of *myself*, and may truly be said not to exist. And were all my perceptions remov'd by death, and cou'd I neither think, nor feel, nor see, nor love, nor hate after the dissolution of my body, I shou'd be entirely annihilated, nor do I conceive what is farther requisite to make me a perfect non-entity. If any one upon serious and unprejudic'd reflexion, thinks he has a different notion of *himself*, I must confess I can reason no longer with him. All I can allow him is, that he may be in the right as well as I, and that we are essentially different in this particular. He may, perhaps, perceive something simple and continu'd, which he calls *himself*; tho' I am certain there is no such principle in me (*T*, 252).

Again, Hume tries to pay close attention to the phenomena and tries not to frame hypotheses that go beyond them. If we look inside ourselves, do we find an impression of something simple, unchanging and continuing? He confesses that *he* can find no such impression; his suggestion that maybe *you* can, that maybe *you* are "essentially different" in this regard is surely ironic. His claim is that none of us ever finds more in ourselves than fleeting perceptions—ideas, sensations, feelings, and emotions.

So we have no reason to suppose that we are selves, or minds, or souls, if we understand those terms to refer to some simple substance that underlies all our particular perceptions. But what, then, are we? If we set aside any of us that are, perhaps, "essentially different," here is Hume's answer:

> . . . I may venture to affirm of the rest of mankind, that they are nothing but a bundle or collection of different perceptions, which succeed each other with an inconceivable rapidity, and are in a perpetual flux and movement. . . . The mind is a kind of theatre, where several perceptions successively make their appearance; pass, re-pass, glide away, and mingle in an infinite variety of postures and situations. There is properly no *simplicity* in it at any one time, nor iden-

tity in different; whatever natural propensity we may have to imagine that simplicity and identity. The comparison of the theatre must not mislead us. They are the successive perceptions only, that constitute the mind; nor have we the most distant notion of the place, where these scenes are represented, or of the materials, of which it is compos'd (*T*, 252–53).

The idea of self, like the idea of cause, is natural and inevitable. But, like the idea of cause, it too is a fiction. As selves or minds, we are nothing but a "bundle" of perceptions. Anything further is sheer, unsupported hypothesis. We have not only no reason to believe in a world of "external" things independent of our minds, but also no reason to believe in mind as a thing.*

In thinking of ourselves, Hume suggests, the analogy of a theater is appropriate. In this theater, an amazingly intricate and complex play is being performed. The players are just all those varied perceptions that succeed each other, as Hume says, with "inconceivable rapidity." But if we are to understand the analogy correctly, we must think away the walls of the theater, think away the stage, think away the seats and even the audience. What is left is just the performance of the play. Such a performance each of us *is*.

But what distinguishes one performance from another—the bundle of perceptions that I am from the bundle that you are? We might think that my bundle is distinguished from others by the fact that it is associated with my body. But this can't be the right answer, in Hume's terms. My awareness of my body is through an impression or idea. So the question arises for that impression or idea too: What makes *that* perception one of mine? Hume's answer is that personal identity must be a matter of the *relations between* the perceptions I call mine. But since Hume himself is never satisfied with his answer, we won't discuss it in detail. (This does not mean that a theory of this kind could not be defended.)

---

*This "bundle theory" of the self is remarkably like the Buddha's view of the self.

However, we do need to see how the bundle theory of the self bears on Descartes' *cogito*: "I think, therefore I am." Descartes takes this as something each of us knows with certainty. And in answer to the question, "What, then, am I?" he says, "I am a thing (a substance) that thinks." Hume is in effect saying that Descartes is going beyond what the phenomena reveal. A twentieth-century Humean, Bertrand Russell, puts it this way: The most that Descartes is entitled to claim is that there is thinking going on. To claim that there is a mind or self—a thing—doing the thinking is to frame a hypothesis, to go beyond the evidence available.[7] If this criticism is correct, it clearly undermines Descartes' dualistic metaphysics; we cannot know that the mind is a substance distinct from the body because we cannot know it is a substance at all! All we have is acquaintance with that bundle of perceptions.

Rescuing Human Freedom

Another topic a science of human nature must address is whether human actions are in some sense *free*. This question takes on a new urgency with the adoption of the mechanistic physical theories of Galileo and Newton. As long as the entire world is conceived in Aristotelian terms, where a key mode of explanation is teleological,* the question of freedom is not pressing. If *everything* acted for the sake of some end, pursuing its good in whatever way its nature allowed, human actions would seem to fit the general pattern of explanation neatly. Humans simply have more alternatives available than do petunias and snails and have to use their reason to make choices between the available goods. But the pattern of explanation is common to all things.

In the mid eighteenth century, however, the situation is quite different. Explanation in terms of ends or goals has been banished; explanation by

---

*An explanation is teleological if it makes essential reference to the realization of a goal or end state. Aristotle's discussion of "final causes" provides a good case study (see pp. 156–157).

prior causes is "in." The model of the universe is mechanical; the world is compared to a gigantic clock. Stones do not fall *in order to* reach a goal (their natural place); and oak trees do not grow because of a *striving* to realize the potentiality in them. Everything happens as it *must happen*, according to laws that make no reference to any end, goal, or good. Every movement takes place with the same inexorability as we find in the hands of a clock.

What about human actions in a world like this? Are they as strictly determined by law and circumstance as the fall of the stone? In the context of the new science, this question gains a new poignancy. How are we to think of our lives, now that we think of everything else in this mechanical way? The view that human actions constitute no exception to the universal rule of causal law is known as **determinism**. The successes of modern science give it plausibility. But it seems to clash with a deeply held conviction that sometimes we are *free* to choose, will, and act.

Descartes shows us one way to deal with this problem: Make an exception for human beings! Mechanical principles might govern material bodies, but they can get no leverage on a nonmaterial mind. The will, Descartes says, is completely free; even the will of God could not conceivably be more free than the human will. And by "free" he means "not governed by causal laws."

But Hume cannot take this way. For he is convinced we have no idea of a substantial self; and so we can have no reason to think such a nonmaterial mind or soul exists. Hume's solution to this puzzle is quite different from Descartes', and it is justly famous. Its basic pattern is defended by numerous philosophers (but not all) even today.

He begins by asserting that "all mankind" is and always has been of the same opinion about this matter. Any controversy is simply due to "ambiguous expressions" used to frame the problem. In other words, if we can get our terms straight, we should be able to settle the matter to everyone's satisfaction. What we need is a set of *definitions* for what Hume calls "necessity" on the one hand and "liberty" on the other.

I hope, therefore, to make it appear, that all men have ever agreed in the doctrine both of necessity and of liberty, according to any reasonable sense, which can be put on these terms; and that the whole controversy has hitherto turned merely upon words (*E*, 54).

We already know what Hume says about *necessity*. The idea of necessity is part of our idea of a cause but is a kind of fiction. It arises, not from impressions, but from that habit our minds develop when confronted with regular conjunctions between events. All we ever observe, when we believe that one event causes another, is the constant conjunction of events of the first kind with events of the second.

Are human actions caused? If we understand this as Hume thinks we must, we are simply asking whether there are *regularities* detectable in human behavior. And he thinks we all must admit that there are. He gives some examples (*E*, 55–61):

- Motives are regularly conjoined to actions: greed regularly leads to stealing, ambition to the quest for power.
- My actions are carried out in a context where I count on being able to predict yours; I depend on the regularity of your behavior.
- If a foreigner acts in unexpected ways, there is always a cause—some condition (education, perhaps) that regularly produces this behavior.
- Where we are surprised by someone's action, a careful examination always turns up some unknown condition that allows it to be fit again into a regular pattern.

If all that we can possibly mean by "caused" is that events are regularly connected, we should all agree that human behavior is caused. Why do some of us resist this conclusion? Because, Hume says,

men still entertain a strong propensity to believe, that they penetrate farther into the powers of nature, and perceive something like a necessary connexion between the cause and the effect. When again they turn their reflections towards the operations of their own minds, and *feel* no such connexion of the motive and the action; they are thence apt to suppose, that there is a difference between the effects, which result from material force, and those which arise from thought and intelligence (*E*, 61).

But this is just a confusion! In neither case, material or intelligent, is there any *constraint* observed. And Hume's account of causality has made that clear. Causality on the side of the objects observed is just regularity; on the side of the observer, it is the setting up of a habit or custom on the basis of those regularities. Causality and its accompanying fiction, necessity, apply as much to the mind (when considered as an object of reflection) as to the physical world.

What then of freedom or liberty?

. . . it will not require many words to prove, that all mankind have ever agreed in the doctrine of liberty as well as in that of necessity, and that the whole dispute, in this respect also, has been hitherto merely verbal. For what is meant by liberty, when applied to voluntary actions? We cannot surely mean, that actions have so little connexion with motives, inclinations, and circumstances, that one does not follow with a certain degree of uniformity from the other, and that one affords no inference by which we can conclude the existence of the other. For these are plain and acknowledged matters of fact. By liberty, then, we can only mean a *power of acting or not acting, according to the determinations of the will*; that is, if we choose to remain at rest, we may; if we choose to move, we also may. Now this hypothetical liberty is universally allowed to belong to everyone, who is not a prisoner and in chains (*E*, 63).

This requires some comment. Perhaps the most accessible way to understand Hume's point is to think of cases where a person is said to be *unfree*. Hume's example is that of a man in chains. What is it that makes this a case of unfreedom? Isn't it just this: that he cannot do what he *wants* to do? Even if he *yearns* to walk away, *wills* to walk away, *tries* to walk away, he will *be unable* to walk away. He is unfree because his actions are *constrained*—against his will, as we say.

Suppose we remove his chains. Then he is free, at liberty to do what he wants. And isn't this the very essence of freedom: to be able to do whatever it is that you want or choose to do? We could put this more formally in the following way:

A person *P* is *free* when the following condition is satisfied: *If P chooses to do action A, then P does A.*

If this condition were *not* satisfied (if *P* should choose to do *A*, but be *unable* to do it) then *P* would *not be at liberty* with respect to *A*.

Now we can see what Hume is up to. He wants to show us that it is possible to *reconcile* our belief in causality (or necessity) with our belief in human freedom. We do not have to choose between them. We can have both modern science and human freedom. Newtonian science and freedom to act would clash only if freedom entailed exemption from causality. But causes are simply regularities; and freedom is not an absence of regularity, but the "hypothetical" power to do something *if* we choose to do it. It is, in fact, a certain kind of regularity. It is the regularity of having the actions we choose to do follow regularly upon our choosing to do them.

There is no reason, then, in human liberty, to deny that a science of human nature—a causal science of a Newtonian kind—is possible. And Newtonian, mechanistic science is no reason to deny or doubt human freedom. In particular, human freedom gives us no reason to postulate a Cartesian mind, quite independent in its substance and operations of the basic laws of the universe. Hume's **compatibilism**, as it is sometimes called, is an important part of a kind of **naturalism**, a view that takes man to be a natural fact, without remainder.

Is It Reasonable to Believe in God?

After doubting everything doubtable, Descartes finds himself locked into solipsism—unless he can demonstrate that he is not the only thing that exists. The way he does this, you recall, is to try to demonstrate the existence of God. He looks, in other words, for a good reason to believe that something other than his own mind exists. If he can prove that God exists, he knows he is not alone; and, God being what God is, he will have good reason to trust at least what is clear and distinct about other things as well. Thus everything hangs, for Descartes, on whether it is reasonable to believe that there is a God.*

What does Hume say about this quest to show that belief in God is more reasonable than disbelief? We will review briefly two of the arguments Descartes presents, together with a Humean response to each, and then look at a rather different argument that was proving very popular in the atmosphere after Newton.

Descartes' first argument, you will recall, begins from the fact that we have an idea of God—an idea of an infinite and perfect being. Descartes argues roughly in the following way:

1. Such an idea requires a cause.
2. The cause must be equal in "formal" reality to the "subjective" reality of the idea.
3. I myself could not possibly be the cause.
4. The only plausible alternative cause is God himself. Therefore:
5. God exists.

Where could Hume attack this argument? Consider premise (3). This premise concerns the *origin* of a certain idea. As we have seen, Hume has a theory about the origin of ideas: Each and every one stems from some impression. Can Hume show that there is an impression which could be the origin of the idea of God?

Even those ideas, which, at first view, seem the most wide of this origin, are found, upon a nearer scrutiny, to be derived from it. The idea of God, as meaning an

---

*Earlier thinkers, too, from Aristotle on, think they can give good reasons for concluding that some ultimate perfection exists and is in one way or another responsible for all other things. Review the proofs given by Augustine (pp. 219–220), Anselm (pp. 248–251), and Aquinas (pp. 253–257). The arguments of Descartes are in *Meditations III* and *V*.

infinitely intelligent, wise, and good Being, arises from reflecting on the operations of our own mind, and augmenting, without limit, those qualities of goodness and wisdom (*E*, 11).

The idea of God, Hume says, also has its origin in impressions. We reflect on ourselves and find impressions of intelligence and a certain degree of goodness. Not perfect intelligence or complete goodness, of course. But we also have, from our impressions, the ideas of more and less. If we combine the idea of more with the ideas of intelligence and goodness, we get the idea of a being more intelligent and good than we are. We can reiterate this operation, over and over again, until we get the idea of a being that is perfectly intelligent and completely good. And this is the idea of God.*

If Hume is correct, you can see that he has undercut one of the premises Descartes uses in his first argument. He *can* be the origin of his idea of God, contrary to premise (3). Since the argument absolutely depends on the correctness of that premise, it no longer can give us a good reason to believe in God.

Think about Descartes' third argument, which goes something like this:

1. You cannot think of God without thinking that God exists, any more than you can think of a mountain without a valley or a triangle without three sides.
2. You do have the thought of God.
3. You must, therefore, think (believe) that God exists. Therefore:
4. God exists.

The first premise states a set of relations between ideas we have. The idea of a mountain necessarily involves the idea of a valley (or at least of a plain). In the same way, Descartes says, you cannot have the idea of God without also having the idea that he exists. You should remember, however, that Hume has drawn a sharp contrast between *relations of ideas* on the one hand and *matters of fact* on

the other. Propositions concerning the relations of ideas, he holds, are independent in their truth value of "what is anywhere existent in the universe." It may be that thinking of God entails thinking that he exists; but that concerns only how those *ideas* are related to each other. It has nothing whatever to do with whether God *in fact* exists. Yet it is the latter that Descartes is vitally concerned with; unless God exists *in fact*, he is stuck in solipsism. Likewise, it is this question that we, believers and nonbelievers alike, are interested in. Does God *in fact* exist? Simply pointing out that one thought involves another does not answer that question—even if one of the thoughts is the thought of God's existence.

If we analyze the argument this way, it may be quite correct through step (3). But the transition from (3) to (4) is illegitimate; for a relation among ideas—even a necessary relation—gets no grip on how things actually are in the world. If it did, then the truth of matters of fact could be discovered "by the mere operation of thought." And that cannot be done, Hume is convinced, because "the contrary of every matter of fact is still possible" (*E*, 15–16). In the realm of fact, it is just as possible that God does not exist as that God does exist—no matter how the ideas are logically related in our scheme of ideas. If it is God's existence as a matter of *fact* that we are interested in (and surely it is), then logical proof moving only within the realm of our ideas will not get us there. Belief in God's existence cannot be made reasonable, then, simply by considering the idea of God. About matters of fact we must consult *experience*.

The most popular argument for God during the Enlightenment, among common folk and intellectuals alike, does begin from experience. It can be called the *argument from design*. If there had ever been suspicions that the universe was not a perfectly ordered, magnificently integrated piece of work, Newton's work sets such suspicions at rest. The image of a great machine, or clockwork, dominates eighteenth-century thought about the nature of the world. And it suggests a powerful analogy. Just as machines (and clocks in particular) are the effects of intelligent design and workmanship, so the universe is the work of a master craftsman,

---

*Descartes foresees this line of argument and tries to block it. See his discussion in *Meditation III*, p. 313.

supremely intelligent and wonderfully skilled. Machines don't just happen. And neither does the world.

In a set of dialogues that Hume did not venture to publish during his lifetime, one of the participants sets out the argument:

> Look round the world: Contemplate the whole and every part of it: You will find it to be nothing but one great machine, subdivided into an infinite number of lesser machines, which again admit of subdivisions to a degree beyond what human senses and faculties can trace and explain. All these various machines, and even their most minute parts, are adjusted to each other with an accuracy which ravishes into admiration all men who have ever contemplated them. The curious adapting of means to ends, throughout all nature, resembles exactly, though it much exceeds, the productions of human contrivance; of human design, thought, wisdom, and intelligence. Since therefore the effects resemble each other, we are led to infer, by all the rules of analogy, that the causes also resemble, and that the Author of Nature is somewhat similar to the mind of man, though possessed of much larger faculties, proportioned to the grandeur of the work which he has executed. By this argument *a posteriori*, and by this argument alone, do we prove at once the existence of a Deity and his similarity to human mind and intelligence (D, 15).

Before considering Hume's appraisal of this argument, let us note several points. It is an argument, Hume says, *a posteriori*; i.e., it is an argument that depends in an essential way upon experience. Our experience of the world as an ordered and harmonious whole provides one crucial premise; our experience of how machines come into being provides another. Note also that it is an argument *by analogy*. Its structure looks like this (M = a machine; I = intelligence; W = the world):

1. M is the effect of I.
2. W is like M. Therefore:
3. W is the effect of something like I.

Finally, you should recognize that this, like Descartes' first two arguments, is a *causal* argument.

Both the first premise and the conclusion deal with causal relations.

Hume says many interesting things about this argument, partly through his spokesmen in the dialogue. Here we'll be brief, simply listing a number of the points he makes.

(1) No argument from experience ever can establish a certainty. The most that experience can yield is a certain probability (since experience is always limited and cannot testify to what is beyond its limits). So even if the argument is a good one (of its kind), it does not give us more than a probability that the "Author of Nature" is analogous to the mind of man.

(2) There is a sound principle to be observed in all causal arguments: that "the cause must be proportioned to the effect."

> A body of ten ounces raised in any scale may serve as a proof, that the counterbalancing weight exceeds ten ounces; but can never afford a reason that it exceeds a hundred. . . . If the cause be known only by the effect, we never ought to ascribe to it any qualities, beyond what are precisely requisite to produce the effect (E, 94).

If we look around at the world, can we say that it is perfectly good? That is hard to believe. If we think of this proof as an attempt to demonstrate the existence of God as he is traditionally conceived—infinite in wisdom and goodness—it surely falls short. For the proportion of goodness we are *justified* in ascribing to the cause (God) cannot far exceed the proportion of goodness (in the world) that needs to be explained.

(3) The analogy is supposed to exist between the productions of intelligent human beings and the world as an effect of a supremely intelligent designer. But a number of consequences follow if we take the analogy seriously.

a. Many people cooperate to make a machine; by analogy, the world may have been created through the cooperation of many gods.
b. Wicked and mischievous people may create technological marvels; by analogy, the cre-

ator(s) of the world may be wicked and mischievous.

c. Machines are made by mortals; by analogy, may not the gods be mortal?

d. The best clocks are a result of a long history of slow improvements; by analogy,

> Many worlds might have been botched and bungled, throughout an eternity, ere this system was struck out; much labor lost; many fruitless trials made; and a slow but continued improvement carried on during infinite ages in the art of world-making (D, 36).

The point here is not that any of these possibilities is likely but that analogies always have resemblances in certain respects and differences in others. How do we know which are the similarities in this case and which are the differences? Unless we have some principle to make this distinction, any one of these conclusions is as justified as the one theists wish to draw.

(4) Finally, we have to ask what we can learn from a single case. Here Hume applies his analysis of the idea of causality to the case of the cause of the world.

> It is only when two *species* of objects are found to be constantly conjoined, that we can infer the one from the other; and were an effect presented, which was entirely singular, and could not be comprehended under any known *species*, I do not see, that we could form any conjecture or inference at all concerning its cause. If experience and observation and analogy be, indeed, the only guides which we can reasonably follow in inferences of this nature; both the effect and cause must bear a similarity and resemblance to other effects and causes, which we know, and which we have found, in many instances, to be conjoined with each other (E, 101–2).

There is one respect in which this universe is entirely *unlike* the clocks and automobiles and stereos of our experience: it is, in our experience, "entirely singular." We can infer that the cause of a new stereo is some intelligent human because we have had past experience of the constant conjunction of stereos and intelligent designers. In this case, we

have had experience of instances of *both* the effects *and* the causes. To apply this kind of analogical reasoning to the universe, we would need past experience of the making of worlds; and in our experience of each making, there would have to have been a conjoined experience of an intelligent being. On the basis of such a constant conjunction, we could infer justly that this world, too, is the effect of intelligence. But since the universe is, in our experience, "entirely singular," we can make no such inference. These, and more, are the difficulties Hume finds in the design argument.

You can see that according to Hume's principles *any* causal argument for God is subject to this last criticism. But, even worse, any causal argument for the existence of *anything at all* beyond our own perceptions is undermined. We cannot, by causal reasoning, get beyond our own perceptions; causal judgments are always founded on experience—on the constant conjunction *within our experience* of pairs of events. To judge that some extra-mental object is the cause of some experience, we would need to be able to observe a constant conjunction of that perception with its extra-mental cause. To do that we would need to jump out of our own skins, to observe the perceptions in our minds from outside, and compare them with the external things correlated with them. And that is something we surely cannot do.

Descartes thinks we need to prove the existence of God in order to ground our belief that the material world (described by his physics) is more than merely a set of ideas. His argument involves the claim that God is the (extra-mental) cause of an idea he has. But if Hume is right about the origin of the concept of causality *within* experience, we could never have the evidence required to validate this claim. All we can do is relate perceptions to perceptions. And if Descartes is right that without *good reason* to believe in God we are caught within the web of our own ideas, then solipsism seems (rationally) inescapable.* A dismal and melancholy conclusion.

---

*Solipsism is explained on p. 298.

After reviewing these attempts to make belief in God reasonable, it seems that this must be our conclusion: We have so far not found good reason to believe in God. Now we must add that neither have we found good reason to believe in the existence of a material world independent of our perceptions. We can think of this as a radical consequence of the representational theory (p. 294). Hume shows us that if we begin from ideas in the mind, there is no way to build that bridge to the world beyond.

This is not, however, Hume's last word on the subject of religion. In a passage that has puzzled many commentators, one of Hume's characters goes on to say:

> A person, seasoned with a just sense of the imperfections of natural reason, will fly to revealed truth with the greatest avidity: While the haughty dogmatist, persuaded that he can erect a complete system of theology by the mere help of philosophy, disdains any further aid and rejects this adventitious instructor. To be a philosophical sceptic is, in a man of letters, the first and most essential step towards being a sound, believing *Christian* (D, 89).

What can we make of this? Is Hume serious here? Or, more importantly, is this a serious possibility, this combination of religious faith and philosophical skepticism? What would this be like?*

Understanding Morality

You and I find ourselves making judgments like this: "That was a bad thing Jones did," "Smith is a good person," "Telling the truth is the right thing to do," and "Justice is a virtue." You see twenty dollars on a desk in a room down the hall; no one is around, and you could pick it up; you say to yourself, "That would be wrong," and walk away. Such "moral" judgments are very important to us, both as evaluations of the actions of others and as guides to our own behavior. They are no less important to

society. A science of human nature ought to have something to say about this feature of human life, so Hume tries to understand our propensity to make judgments of this kind. His question is put in this way: Are these judgments founded in some way on reason? Or do they have some other origin?

Reason Is Not a Motivator

> Nothing is more usual in philosophy, and even in common life, than to talk of the combat of passion and reason, to give the preference to reason, and to assert that men are only so far virtuous as they conform themselves to its dictates. Every rational creature, 'tis said, is oblig'd to regulate his actions by reason; and if any other motive or principle challenge the direction of his conduct, he ought to oppose it, 'till it be entirely subdu'd, or at least brought to a conformity with that superior principle. . . . In order to shew the fallacy of all this philosophy, I shall endeavour to prove *first*, that reason alone can never be a motive to any action of the will; and *secondly*, that it can never oppose passion in the direction of the will (T, 413).

Hume's claim that "reason alone" can never motivate any action has clear moral implications. For moral considerations can be motivators. We sometimes refrain from taking something that belongs to another person, not because we are afraid of the consequences, but simply because we judge that it would be *wrong* to do so. Morality is a practical matter. It has implications for what we *do*. If reason alone cannot motivate an action, it seems to follow that morality cannot be a matter of reason alone.

But what does this mean, that reason alone can neither motivate an action nor oppose passion (e.g., desire or inclination)? Recall Hume's claim that "all the objects of human reason or enquiry may naturally be divided into two kinds, to wit, *Relations of Ideas* and *Matters of Fact*" (E, 15). If reason is going to motivate action, it must do so in one of these two ways. Let us examine each possibility.

Consider adding up a sum, which Hume takes to be a matter of the relations of ideas. Suppose I am totaling up what I owe to my dentist, Dr. Payne. Will this reasoning lead to any action? Not by it-

---

*Fideism, as this view is sometimes called, is explored in the work of Søren Kierkegaard. See "The Religious," in Chapter 22.

self, says Hume. If I *want* to pay Payne what I owe her, this reasoning will contribute to what I do: I will pay her the total and not some other amount. But in the absence of that (or another) want, the reasoning alone will not produce an action. The motivator is the want; and a want is what Hume calls a *passion*.

Consider next these examples of reasoning about matters of fact:

> Ask a man *why he uses exercise*; he will answer *because he desires to keep his health*. If you then enquire *why he desires health*, he will readily reply *because sickness is painful*. If you push your enquiries further and desire a reason *why he hates pain*, it is impossible he can ever give any. This is an ultimate end, and is never referred to any object.
>
> Perhaps to your second question, *why he desires health*, he may also reply that *it is necessary for the exercise of his calling*. If you ask *why he is anxious on that head*, he will answer *because he desires to get money*. If you demand why? *It is the instrument of pleasure*, says he. And beyond this it is an absurdity to ask for a reason. It is impossible there can be a progress *in infinitum*; and that one thing can always be a reason why another is desired. Something must be desirable on its own account, and because of its immediate accord or agreement with human sentiment and affection (*PM*, 268–69).

Here we have reasoning about matters of fact; it is a matter of fact that exercise is conducive to health, that health is required to pursue a profession successfully, and so on. But mere knowledge of these matters of fact will not motivate action unless one cares about the end to which they lead. And this caring is not itself a matter of reason. It is a matter of *sentiment* or *passion*. Hume draws the conclusion:

> It appears evident that the ultimate ends of human actions can never, in any case, be accounted for by *reason*, but recommend themselves entirely to the sentiments and affections of mankind, without any dependence on the intellectual faculties (*PM*, 268).

So reason alone can never motivate us to action. But Hume goes even further; he claims that reason can never oppose passion. One passion can oppose another. For example, as I contemplate the roller coaster ride, fear fights with the desire for thrills. Likewise, one rational proposition can be opposed to another when they are contradictories. But for reason to oppose passion, it would have to be a motivator in itself; and Hume argues that it is not. Reason, we might say, is *inert*.

> We speak not strictly and philosophically when we talk of the combat of passion and of reason. Reason is, and ought only to be the slave of the passions, and can never pretend to any other office than to serve and obey them (*T*, 415).

Reason can instruct us how to satisfy our desires, but it cannot tell us what desires to have.* Reason can only be the "slave" of the passions. In a few dramatic sentences, Hume drives this point home.

> Where a passion is neither founded on false suppositions, nor chuses means insufficient for the end, the understanding can neither justify nor condemn it. 'Tis not contrary to reason to prefer the destruction of the whole world to the scratching of my finger (*T*, 416).

What would Plato have said about this?[†] Plato's idea that reason can grasp the Good, and therefore should *rule* the passions, simply misses the point if Hume is right here. Reason is motivationally impotent; it cannot rule. Its role is that of a slave! The master says, "I want that," and it is the job of the slave to figure out how it can be got. The slave deals with *means*. Reason has an important place in action, since if we calculate wrong or make a mistake about the facts, we will be likely to miss our ends. But those ends are dictated by the nonrational part of our nature, the wants and desires, the passions and sentiments, that are simply given with that nature. If I truly prefer the destruction of the world to the scratching of my finger, reason cannot oppose me. There is nothing *irrational* about that.

---

*You might think there is an obvious exception: Can't reason tell me that it would be better for me if I didn't have this desire to smoke cigarettes? And isn't this a case of reason opposing a desire I have? What would Hume say?

†See Plato's discussion of the role of reason in the life of the just and happy person, pp. 134–136.

The Origins of Moral Judgment

What, then, of morality, which is supposed to govern human actions? It is clear that if moral judgments are to have any effect on actions, they cannot be purely rational judgments. They must be the expression of passions of some sort. This is just what Hume claims.

Let us again consider the two possible classes of things subject to reason. Could morality be simply a matter of the relations between ideas? It is plausible to think that there is a conceptual relation between the ideas of murder and wrong. All murder is wrong—because what "murder" means is "wrongful killing." So the connection in this case *is* a matter of relations of ideas. But this can hardly be all that is involved in morality, because morality is supposed to be applied to the facts. Just pointing out that murder involves the idea of wrongful killing is no help at all when we are asking of a certain action: is this murder—i.e., is this a wrongful killing? So morality, if it is going to have any practical effects, cannot be merely a matter of the relations between ideas.

Can morality be a matter of fact (the second province of reason)?

Take any action allow'd to be vicious: Wilful murder, for instance. Examine it in all lights, and see if you can find that matter of fact, or real existence, which you call *vice*. In whichever way you take it, you find only certain passions, motives, volitions and thoughts. There is no other matter of fact in the case. The vice entirely escapes you, as long as you consider the object. You can never find it, till you turn your reflexion into your own breast, and find a sentiment of disapprobation, which arises in you, towards this action. Here is a matter of fact; but 'tis the object of feeling, not of reason. It lies in yourself, not in the object. So that when you pronounce any action or character to be vicious, you mean nothing, but that from the constitution of your nature you have a feeling or sentiment of blame from the contemplation of it. Vice and virtue, therefore, may be compar'd to sounds, colours, heat and cold, which, according to modern philosophy, are not qualities in objects, but perceptions in the mind (*T*, 468–69).

This analysis should be compared to Hume's discussion of causation. When we observe carefully any instance of a causal relation, we never observe the causing itself. We claim that one event causes another on the basis of building up a habit (in ourselves) of expecting the one on the appearance of the other; the concept of "necessary connection" we attribute to the relation between the events is founded on a "feeling" in our minds. Moral judgments, Hume is saying, are perfectly parallel to judgments of causality. Here, too, we project onto the facts an idea whose origin is simply a feeling in the mind. In this case, the feelings are those of approval and disapproval, which are expressed in terms of the concepts "right/good" and "wrong/bad." No matter how closely you examine the facts of any action, you will never discover in them its goodness or badness. The moral quality of the facts is not read off them; it is a matter of how the author of the moral judgment "feels" about them.

In a famous passage that widely influences subsequent moral philosophy, Hume marks out clearly the distinction between *the facts* on the one hand (expressible in purely descriptive language) and *the value qualities of the facts* on the other (expressible in evaluations).

In every system of morality, which I have hitherto met with, I have always remark'd, that the author proceeds for some time in the ordinary way of reasoning, and establishes the being of a God, or makes observations about human affairs; when of a sudden I am surpriz'd to find, that instead of the usual copulations of propositions, *is*, and *is not*, I meet with no proposition that is not connected with an *ought*, or *ought not*. This change is imperceptible; but is, however, of the last consequence. For as this *ought* or *ought not*, expresses some new relation or affirmation, 'tis necessary that it shou'd be observ'd and explain'd; and at the same time that a reason should be given, for what seems altogether inconceivable, how this new relation can be a deduction from others, which are entirely different from it. But as authors do not commonly use this precaution, I shall presume to recommend it to the readers; and am persuaded, that this small attention wou'd subvert all the vulgar [i.e., common] systems of morality, and let us see, that the distinction of vice and virtue is not founded merely on the relations of objects, nor is perceiv'd by reason (*T*, 469–70).

Hume is here pointing to what is often called the fact/value gap, or the is/ought problem.* Reason can tell us what the facts are, but it cannot tell us how to value them.

We do make value judgments; it is hard to imagine human life without them. And Hume is not advising us to refrain from doing so, any more than he advises against making causal judgments. But a science of human nature tries to understand both kinds of judgment; what it discovers, Hume thinks, is that neither of them is founded on reason. Both have their origins in sentiment or feeling; both are projections onto a world in which they cannot be discovered.

The foundation, or "origin," of morality, then, is to be found in sentiment—in feelings of approval and disapproval—not in reason. A scientific examination of morality ought to do more than discover these foundations, however. It ought also to reveal what *kinds of things* we approve and disapprove, and why. Hume has many interesting things to say about this matter; we'll be brief.

Hume claims that we tend to approve of those things which are either *agreeable* or *useful*, either to *ourselves* or to *others*. Some things naturally elicit our immediate approval (e.g., white sand on a warm beach); those are the agreeable things. Others do not but are valued as means, useful in promoting the occurrence of agreeable things (e.g., a visit to Dr. Payne). Hume believes that we often feel a kind of approval for things agreeable to others, as well as to ourselves; e.g., we can take pleasure in another person's enjoyment of a good meal. If Hume is right, an egoistic account of human motivation (such as that of Hobbes) is inadequate.*

There is a passion in human beings that makes possible the apparent "disinterestedness" of moral judgments. Hume calls it *sympathy* or *humanity* or *fellow feeling*. Sympathy plays a large role in our moral judgments, since it is characteristic of moral judgments not to be purely self-interested. As evidence, Hume notes that we make moral judgments about figures in past history, where there is no possible impact on our present or future interests. So we tend to approve of benevolent or generous acts, even when they are not directed toward ourselves.

We will not follow the development of Hume's ideas about the particular virtues. But we should note one aspect. His insistence that morality is not founded on reason would seem to catapult him directly into moral relativism, since feelings seem so personal. What I approve, we may think, might be quite different from what you approve. But the insistence on sympathy as an original passion in human nature—within every individual—works toward a commonality in the moral sense of us all. It does not make moral disagreements between cultures or individuals impossible, but it is a pressure built into us all that explains the large agreement in moral judgment we in fact find.

Is Hume a Skeptic?

On topic after topic Hume sets himself against the majority tradition in the West. No doubt he feels this is only to be expected. Galilean and Newtonian science had overthrown traditional views about the nonhuman world; it should be no surprise that an attempt to apply the same methods to human nature should have the same result. Aristotle had defined man as a rational animal; ever since the emphasis had been on the "rational" aspect. In deciding what to believe, what to do, how to live, and how to judge, philosophers had looked to reason. The prerogatives of reason had lately been

---

*Reflection should tell you that this problem, too, is a consequence of the change produced by the development and acceptance of modern science. Dante's world contained no such gap; he could find the "right way" by discovering the facts about the universe. In general, where *final causes* are an intrinsic part of the *way things are* no such gap exists. For the ends of things are part of their very being. When final causes are cast out, however, values lose their rootedness in the way things are.

*Compare Hobbesian egoism, pp. 332–336.

exalted in an extreme way by Descartes, who held that we shouldn't accept *anything* unless it was attested by rational insight or rational deduction. What Hume thinks he has shown is that *if this is the right rule*, then there is *virtually nothing* we should accept.

Let us review.

a. The principles governing the way ideas succeed each other are nonrational principles: those of sheer mechanical association, analogous in their function to the principle of gravitation.
b. All knowledge of anything beyond our perceptions depends on the relation of cause and effect; but the origin of our idea of causality is a nonrational custom or habit that builds up in our minds whenever impressions succeed each other in a constant conjunction.
c. We have no reason to believe in a substantial self; any such belief is a fiction foisted on us by detectable mistakes.
d. We have no reason to believe in God.
e. Our actions are governed by nonrational passions.
f. Our liberty in action is not a matter of reason freeing us from the causal order, but simply a matter of nothing standing in the way of following those passions.
g. Moral judgments, too, whether used as guides to our own action or as evaluations of the actions of others, are founded on nonrational sentiments that are simply a given part of human nature.

In every area Hume discovers the passivity, the limits, the impotence of reason. There is no good reason to believe in an objective causal order, in the existence of a material world independent of our perceptions, in God, in a soul or self, or in objective moral values. These certainly seem to be skeptical themes. Is Hume, then, a skeptic?

He makes distinctions between several kinds of skepticism. Let us examine two. There is Descartes' type, which Hume calls "antecedent" skepticism, since it is supposed to come before any beliefs are deemed acceptable. About this sort he says:

It recommends an universal doubt, not only of all our former opinions and principles, but also of our very faculties; of whose veracity, say they, we must assure ourselves, by a chain of reasoning, deduced from some original principle, which cannot possibly be fallacious or deceitful. But neither is there any such original principle, which has a prerogative above others, that are self-evident and convincing: Or if there were, could we advance a step beyond it, but by the use of those very faculties, of which we are supposed to be already diffident. The CARTESIAN doubt, therefore, were it ever possible to be attained by any human creature (as plainly it is not) would be entirely incurable; and no reasoning could ever bring us to a state of assurance and conviction upon any subject (E, 103).

His criticism of Descartes' project is twofold. First, you cannot *really* bring yourself to doubt everything; belief is not that much under your control. You find yourself believing in, for example, the reality of the world independent of your senses whether you want to or not. Second, if you could doubt everything, there would be no way back to rational belief; to get back you would have to use your reasoning faculties, the competence of which is one of the things you are doubting.*

There is another kind of skepticism, however, which Hume thinks is quite useful. This is not an attempt to doubt everything in the futile hope of gaining something impossible to doubt, but an attempt to keep in mind "the strange infirmities of human understanding."

The greater part of mankind are naturally apt to be affirmative and dogmatical in their opinions. . . . But could such dogmatical reasoners become sensible of the strange infirmities of human understanding, even in its most perfect state, and when most accurate and cautious in its determinations; such a reflection would naturally inspire them with more modesty and reserve, and diminish their fond opinion of themselves, and their prejudice against antagon-

---

*Hume seems to be saying that we must be content with the things we are, in Cartesian terms, "taught by nature." See *Meditation III*. Is this criticism of Descartes correct? Compare also the critique of Descartes by Charles Peirce, pp. 465–466.

ists. . . . In general there is a degree of doubt, and caution, and modesty, which, in all kinds of scrutiny and decision, ought for ever to accompany a just reasoner (*E*, 111).

This "mitigated" skepticism, Hume says, makes for modesty and caution; it will "abate [the] pride" (*E*, 111) of those who are haughty and obstinate. It will teach us the limitations of our human capacities and encourage us to devote our understanding, not to abstruse problems of metaphysics and theology, but to the problems of common life.

In sponsoring such modesty about our intellectual attainments, Hume reflects Enlightenment worries about the consequences of dogmatic attachments to creeds that have only private backing. And if reason is really as broken-backed as Hume says, then dogmatic attachment to what appears rational is just as worrisome. One of the virtues of his examination of human nature, he feels, is that it makes such dogmatism impossible.

There might be an opposite worry, however. Could the consistently skeptical conclusions of Hume's philosophy undermine our lives to the point of paralysis? Hume himself reports, in an introspective moment, that after pursuing his researches for a while he finds himself

> ready to reject all belief and reasoning, and [to] look upon no opinion even as more probable or likely than another. Where am I, or what? From what causes do I derive my existence, and to what condition shall I return? Whose favor shall I court, and whose anger must I dread? What beings surround me? and on whom have I any influence, or who have any influence on me? I am confounded with all these questions, and begin to fancy myself in the most deplorable condition imaginable, inviron'd with the deepest darkness, and utterly depriv'd of the use of every member and faculty (*T*, 268–69).

Reason has no answer to these questions. Depressing indeed!

What is the solution?

> Most fortunately it happens, that since reason is incapable of dispelling these clouds, nature herself suf-

fices to that purpose, and cures me of this philosophical melancholy and delirium, either by relaxing this bent of mind, or by some avocation, and lively impression of my senses, which obliterate all these chimeras. I dine, I play a game of back-gammon, I converse, and am merry with my friends; and when after three or four hours' amusement, I wou'd return to these speculations, they appear so cold, and strain'd, and ridiculous, that I cannot find in my heart to enter into them any farther (*T*, 269).

We need not worry, he assures us, that the results of philosophical study will paralyze us by taking away all our convictions. "Nature," he says, "is always too strong for principle" (*E*, 110). Custom and habit, those nonrational instincts that are placed in our natures, will ensure that we don't sit shivering in terror at our lack of certainty.

But Hume does not mean that we should cease to pursue philosophy. Indeed, his conviction that nothing is more useful than the science of human nature remains untouched. Only such an enquiry into the nature and limits of human understanding can free us from the natural tendency toward dogmatism and superstition that plagues human society. All our knowledge falls into one of two camps: relations of ideas or matters of fact. The former concern logical and mathematical matters; these, Hume thinks, are irrelevant to real existence. The latter are based wholly on experience, can get us probability at best, and are founded in any case on mere instinct, which we cannot prove is reliable. Here are Hume's last words in *An Enquiry Concerning Human Understanding*.

> When we run over libraries, persuaded of these principles, what havoc must we make? If we take in hand any volume of school metaphysics, for instance; let us ask, *Does it contain any abstract reasoning concerning quantity or number?* No. *Does it contain any experimental reasoning concerning matter of fact and existence?* No. Commit it then to the flames: For it can contain nothing but sophistry and illusion (*E*, 114).

Hume represents a kind of crisis point in modern philosophy. Can anyone build anything on the rubble he leaves behind?

Notes

1. Immanuel Kant, "An Answer to the Question: What Is Enlightenment?" in *Perpetual Peace and Other Essays*, trans. Ted Humphrey (Indianapolis: Hackett Publishing Co., 1983), 41.
2. Kant, "What Is Enlightenment?" 41.
3. Ibid., 44.
4. From Newton's *Principia Mathematica*, General Scholium to Book III, reproduced in John Herman Randall, *The Career of Philosophy*, vol. 1 (New York: Columbia University Press, 1962), 579.
5. I have benefited from the excellent study of Hume by Barry Stroud: *Hume* (London: Routledge and Kegan Paul, 1977).
6. References to Hume's works are as follows:
   E: Enquiry Concerning Human Understanding, ed. Eric Steinberg (Indianapolis: Hackett Publishing Co., 1977).
   D: Dialogues Concerning Natural Religion, ed. Richard H. Popkin (Indianapolis: Hackett Publishing Co., 1980).
   T: A Treatise of Human Nature, ed. L. A. Selby-Bigge (Oxford: Oxford University Press, 1888).
   PM: An Enquiry Concerning the Principles of Morals, abridged in *Hume's Moral and Political Philosophy*, ed. Henry D. Aiken (New York: Hafner Publishing Co., 1948).
7. Bertrand Russell, *A History of Western Philosophy* (New York: Simon and Schuster, 1945), 567.

20

Immanuel Kant:
Rehabilitating Reason
(Within Strict Limits)

David Hume had published *A Treatise of Human Nature* at the early age of twenty-three. Immanuel Kant (1724–1804) published in 1781 the first of his major works, *The Critique of Pure Reason*, when he was fifty-seven. He enters the great conversation rather late in life because it has taken him some time to understand the devastating critique of Hume, "that acute man."

> I openly confess that my remembering David Hume was the very thing which many years ago first interrupted my dogmatic slumber and gave my investigations in the field of speculative philosophy a quite new direction (*P*, 5).[1]

> . . . since the origin of metaphysics so far as we know its history, nothing has ever happened which could have been more decisive to its fate than the attack made upon it by David Hume (*P*, 3).

Kant sets himself to solve what he calls "Hume's problem": whether the concept of cause is indeed objectively vacuous, a fiction whose origin can be traced to a merely subjective and instinctive habit of human nature. We have seen the skeptical consequences Hume draws from his analysis; these, we can imagine, are what wakes Kant from his "dogmatic slumber."

Human thought seems naturally to recognize no limits. It moves easily and without apparent strain from bodies to souls, from life in this world

to life after death, from material things to God. One aspect of Enlightenment thought is the acute consciousness of how *varied* thoughts become when they move out beyond the ground of experience—and yet how *certain* people feel about their own views. This is the dogmatism (or superstition) that Hume tries to debunk. Stimulated by Hume, Kant too feels this is a problem. It is true that in mathematics we have a clear example of knowledge independent of experience. But it does not follow (as thinkers like Plato suppose) that we can extend this knowledge indefinitely in a realm beyond experience. Kant uses a lovely image to make this point.*

> The light dove, cleaving the air in her free flight, and feeling its resistance, might imagine that its flight would be still easier in empty space. It was thus that Plato left the world of the senses, as setting too narrow limits to the understanding, and ventured out beyond it on the wings of the ideas, in the empty space of the pure understanding. He did not observe that with all his efforts he made no advance—meeting no resistance that might, as it were, serve as a support upon which he could take a stand, to which he could apply his powers, and so set his understanding in motion (*CPR*, 47).

---

*Plato believes that the non-sensible, purely intelligible world of Forms is not only knowable but also *more* intelligible than the world of experience, and *more* real, too. See pp. 109–114.

Could the dove fly even better in empty space? No, it could not fly there at all; it absolutely depends on some "resistance" to fly. In the same way, Kant suggests, human thought needs a medium that supplies "resistance," some discipline, to work properly. In a resistance-free environment, everything is equally possible (as long as formal contradiction is avoided), and the conflicts of dogmatic believers (philosophical, religious, or political) are inevitable.

Kant is convinced that Hume is right to pinpoint *experience* as the medium that disciplines reason, as the limit within which alone reason can legitimately do its work. But Kant doubts that Hume has correctly understood experience. Why? Because Hume's analysis has an unacceptable consequence. We did not explicitly draw this consequence when discussing Hume (because he does not draw it). But if Hume is right, Newtonian science itself is basically an irrational and unjustified fiction.* Recall that for Hume *all* our knowledge of matters of fact beyond present perception and memory are founded on the relation of cause and effect. And causes are nothing more than projections onto a supposed objective world from a feeling in the mind.

Kant is convinced that in Newtonian science we do have rationally justified knowledge. And if Hume's examination of reason forces us to deny that we have this knowledge, something must be wrong with Hume's analysis. What we need, Kant says, is a more thorough and accurate *critique of reason*—a critique that will lay out its *structure*, its *relationship to its objects*, and inscribe precisely the line that sets the *limits* within which it can legitimately work. Hume thinks that what we need is a science of human nature. Kant agrees; but he thinks it must be done better than Hume manages to do it. This is the project Kant sets for himself,

now that he has awakened from his dogmatic slumber and is no longer, like the dove, trying to fly in empty space.

He makes an absolutely revolutionary suggestion.

> Hitherto it has been assumed that all our knowledge must conform to objects. But all attempts to extend our knowledge of objects by establishing something in regard to them *a priori*, by means of concepts, have, on this assumption, ended in failure. We must therefore make trial whether we may not have more success in the tasks of metaphysics, if we suppose that objects must conform to our knowledge. . . . We should then be proceeding precisely on the lines of Copernicus' primary hypothesis. Failing of satisfactory progress in explaining the movements of the heavenly bodies on the supposition that they all revolved round the spectator, he tried whether he might not have better success if he made the spectator to revolve and the stars to remain at rest. A similar experiment can be tried in metaphysics, as regards the *intuition* of objects (*CPR*, 22).

This requires some explanation. Nearly all previous philosophy (and science and common sense, too) has made a very natural assumption—as natural as the assumption that the heavenly bodies revolve around us. But perhaps it is just as wrong.

What is that assumption? It is that we acquire knowledge and truth when our thoughts "conform to objects." According to this assumption, objects are *there*, quite determinately *being* whatever they are, completely *independent of our apprehension* of them. And when we know them, we have to "get it right" in the sense that our beliefs must be brought to *correspond* to these independently existing things. Aristotle's classical definition of truth expresses this assumption perfectly: to say of what *is* that it is, and of what *is not* that it is not, is true.* Truth (and knowledge, too) is a matter of getting what we *say* (or believe) lined up to correspond to what there *is*. The assumption is integral to the representational theory (p. 294).

---

*You can see that Hume ends up exactly where Descartes fears to be; in order to escape this fate for his own physics, Descartes thinks you need to prove the existence of a nondeceptive God. By undermining any such proofs, Hume finds himself unable to escape from solipsism—except by joining a game of backgammon and ignoring the problem.

---

*See Aristotle's discussion of this on pp. 147–148.

But Hume has shown us the impossibility of thinking about representation in this way. To know whether an idea corresponds to some independent object, we would have to be able to compare that idea with the idea-less object.* But the object can *only* be known via an idea. We may have ideas (like the idea of a cause) which are supposed to cross this gulf. Descartes thought he could use this idea to get from his idea of God to the reality of God. But the gulf is impassable. On the basis of mere concepts alone, we can know nothing at all about objects existing outside our minds. Ideas that have their origin in experience (e.g., green, warm, solid) can go no further than experience. And ideas that don't (e.g., cause) are mere illusions. By using such concepts we can know nothing at all about objects. All this follows if (a) we are acquainted only with the ideas in our experience, (b) objects are thought to exist independently of our experience, and (c) knowledge requires that we ascertain a correspondence between ideas and objects.

But what if this assumption is wrong? What if, to be an object at all, a thing has to conform to certain concepts? What if objects couldn't exist—simply couldn't *be* in any sense at all—unless they were related to a rational mind, set in a context of rational concepts and principles? Think about the motion of the stars from horizon to horizon. On the assumption that this motion is real, accurate understanding proves to be impossible. Copernicus denies this assumption. He suggests that this motion is only *apparent*. It is *contributed by us*, the observers. On this new assumption, we are able to understand and predict the behavior of these objects.

Perhaps, Kant is suggesting, the same is true in the world of the intellect. Perhaps the objects of experience are (at least in part) the result of a construction by the rational mind. If so, they have no reality independent of that construction. Like the motion of the stars, objects are merely apparent, not independently real. If this is so, it may well be that concepts like causation, which cannot be *abstracted* from experience (the lesson of Hume), still *apply* to experience, simply because objects of experience that are not structured by that concept are inconceivable. The suggestion is that the rational mind has a certain structure, and whatever is knowable by such a mind must necessarily be known in terms of that structure. This structure is not derived from the objects known. It is *imposed* on them—but not arbitrarily, since the very idea of an object not so structured makes no sense.

This is Kant's "Copernican Revolution" in philosophy. To the details of this novel way of thinking we will now turn.

Critique

If we are going to take seriously this possibility that objects are partially constituted—as objects—by the rational mind, we must examine how that constitution takes place. We need to peer reflectively behind the scenes and catch a glimpse of the productive machinery at work. So we are interested in the *processes* involved in knowing anything at all. A prior question, of course, is *whether* we can know anything at all. But Kant thinks that Newton's science has definitely settled that question. Assuming, then, that a rational mind can have some knowledge, we want to ask, How does it manage that? We need to engage in what Kant calls "critique." A "critical" philosophy is not one that criticizes, in the carping, censorious way where "nothing is ever right." Critique is the attempt to get behind knowledge claims and ask, What makes them possible?

The objects of human knowledge seem to fall into four main classes. We can see what Kant is up to if we frame a question with respect to each of these classes.

---

*Montaigne compares the problem to that of a man who does not know Socrates and is presented with a portrait of him. How can he tell whether it resembles Socrates or not? See p. 278. This perplexity is obviously a consequence of the representational theory, once one has become skeptical of inferences from our ideas to external things existing independently of these ideas.

1. How is *mathematics* possible?
2. How is *natural science* possible?
3. How is *metaphysics* possible?
4. How is *morality* possible?

These are, in Kant's sense, "critical" questions. We are not now going to develop mathematics, physics, metaphysics, or morality. But in each case we are going to look at the rational foundations on which these disciplines rest. What is it, for instance, about human reason that makes it possible to develop mathematics? What *structure, capacities,* and *concepts* must reason have for it to be *able* to do mathematics?

These are *reflective* questions, which together constitute a *critique of reason,* a critical examination of the way a rational mind works. Kant also calls this kind of investigation **transcendental**.* A transcendental inquiry reaches back into the activities of the mind and asks how it produces its results. If this kind of investigation succeeds, we'll know what the powers of reason are—and what they are not. We can, Kant thinks, determine the *limits* of rational knowledge. And this is most important. For if we can determine both the capacities and the limitations of human reason, we may be able to escape both of those evils between which philosophy has so often swung: *dogmatism* on the one hand, and *skepticism* on the other. From Kant's point of view, these extremes are well illustrated by Descartes and Hume, respectively.

Judgments

Since all our claims to know are expressed in the form of judgments, the first task is to clarify the different kinds of judgments there are. Hume had divided our knowledge into relations of ideas and

matters of fact.* Kant agrees that this is roughly right, but not precise enough. Hume's distinction runs together two quite different kinds of consideration. (1) There is an *epistemological* question involved: Does a bit of knowledge rest on experience, or not? (2) There is also a *semantic* question: How do the meanings of the words we use to express that knowledge relate to each other? Kant sorts these matters out, and the result is a classification of judgments (which might be known to be true) into *four* groups rather than into Hume's two.

1. Epistemological
   1a. A judgment is *a priori* when it can be known to be true without any reference to experience. "7 + 5 = 12" is an example.
   1b. A judgment is *a posteriori* when we must appeal to experience to determine its truth or falsity. For instance, "John F. Kennedy was assassinated," cannot be known independently of experience.
2. Semantic
   2a. A judgment is **analytic** when its denial yields a contradiction. Here is an example Kant gives: "All bodies are extended." This is analytic because the predicate "extended" is already included as part of the subject, "bodies." To say that there is some body that is *not* extended is, in effect, to claim there can be some extended thing that is not extended. And that is contradictory. If an analytic judgment is true, it is *necessarily true*. The opposite of an analytic judgment is *not possible*. Since it is analytic that every father has a child, it is not possible that there should be a father without a child. And every father necessarily has a child.
   2b. A judgment is **synthetic** when it does more than simply explicate or analyze a concept. Here are some examples: "Every event has a cause," "Air has weight," and "John F. Kennedy was assassinated." Consider the first

---

*The term "transcendental" must be carefully distinguished from the similar term "transcendent." See p. 381.

*Hume's discussion of these is found on pp. 345–346.

example. The concept *having a cause* is not part of the concept *being an event*. This is something Hume teaches us.* We can imagine that an event might simply occur without any cause. Even if we don't believe that ever happens, there is no contradiction in supposing it might. The opposite of synthetic judgments is always *possible*.

These two pairs can be put together to give us four possibilities. In Kant's view, every judgment that is a candidate for being knowledge will belong to one or another of these four classes. Let us give some examples.

- analytic *a priori*: "All bodies are extended." This is analytic, as we have seen, because "extended" is part of the definition of "body." It is *a priori* because we don't have to examine our experience of bodies to know it is true; all we need is to understand the meanings of the terms "body" and "extended."
- analytic *a posteriori*: This class seems empty; if the test for analyticity is examining a judgment's denial for contradiction, it seems clear that we do not *also* have to examine experience. Every analytic judgment must be *a priori*.
- synthetic *a posteriori*: Here belong most of our judgments about experience, judgments of science and common sense alike, from particular judgments (e.g., "The water in the tea kettle is boiling") to general laws (e.g., "Water always boils at 100°C at sea level").
- synthetic *a priori*: This is a puzzling and controversial class of judgments. If we were to know such a judgment as true, we would have to be able to know it quite independently of experience. This means that if such a judgment is true, it is true no matter what our experience shows us. Even if the events of experience were

organized in a completely different way, a true judgment of this kind would remain true. And yet it is *not* true because it is analytic; its denial is not logically contradictory.

We can represent these possibilities in a matrix:

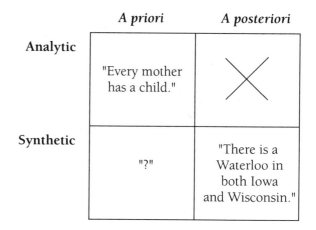

	A priori	*A posteriori*
Analytic	"Every mother has a child."	✕
Synthetic	"?"	"There is a Waterloo in both Iowa and Wisconsin."

There is something very odd about synthetic *a priori* judgments. Consider a judgment that is about experience. Suppose that it is synthetic, but that we can know it *a priori*. Because it is synthetic, its opposite is (from a logical point of view) a real possibility. And yet we can know—without appealing to experience—that this possibility is never realized! How can this be?

Kant believes that the solution to the dilemmas of past philosophy lies precisely in the recognition that we are in possession of synthetic *a priori* judgments. It is his Copernican revolution in philosophy that makes this recognition possible. Think: On the assumption that objects are realities independent of our knowing them, it would be crazy to suppose that we could know them without observing or experiencing them in some way; our thoughts about them would be one thing, the objects something quite different; and they could vary independently. What could possibly guarantee that things would match our thoughts *a priori*? On the traditional correspondence assumption, then, *a priori* knowledge that is synthetic would be impossible.

---

*Recall Hume's claim that "all events seem entirely loose and separate." Neither experience nor reason, he claims, ever discloses that necessary "connexion" which might link them inseparably together. See p. 350.

But suppose that objects *are* objects only because they are structured in certain ways by the mind in the very act of knowing them. Then it is not at all implausible to think that there might be *principles* of that structuring and that some of these principles might be synthetic. Moreover, a reflective, critical study of rationality might uncover them. And those principles would be known *a priori*—independently of the character of the objects they are structuring. So if Kant's Copernican revolution makes sense, there will be such *a priori* synthetic principles for every domain of objects.

It is time to give some examples of judgments Kant considers to be both *a priori* and synthetic. You may be surprised by some of them.

- All the judgments of mathematics and geometry
- In natural science, such judgments as "Every event has a cause"
- In metaphysics, "There is a God," and "The soul is a simple substance, distinct from the body"
- In morality, the imperative to treat others as ends, not merely as means to some end of your own

I do not mean to suggest that we *know* all these judgments, or that they are all true. That remains to be seen. But if you examine them, you should be able to see that they are all examples of judgments which would have to be known *a priori* (i.e., not from experience), if at all. And examination should also confirm, Kant thinks, that they are all synthetic. None of them is true simply in virtue of how the terms are related to each other.

Kant wants to understand how mathematics, natural science, metaphysics, and morality are possible. In the light of his Copernican revolution, we can see that he is asking how the rational mind structures its objects into the objects of mathematics, natural science, metaphysics, and morality. It must be that implicit in the foundations of all these disciplines are some judgments which are synthetic and *a priori*, judgments which do not arise out of experience but *prescribe* how the objects of experience *must* be. All four of these areas are con-

stituted by synthetic *a priori* judgments. The objects we encounter are—in part—*constructions*.

Kant sometimes calls *a priori* judgments "pure." By this, he means that they are not "contaminated" by experience. We can now restate his questions:

1. How is *pure* mathematics possible?
2. How is *pure* natural science possible?
3. How is *pure* metaphysics possible?
4. How is *pure* morality possible?

Let's examine his answers.

Geometry, Mathematics, Space, and Time

It would be useful to have a criterion by which we could distinguish *a priori* knowledge from *a posteriori* knowledge. Kant suggests that there are two tests we can use: *necessity* and *universality*.

> Experience teaches us that a thing is so and so, but not that it cannot be otherwise. First, then, if we have a proposition which in being thought is thought as *necessary*, it is an *a priori* judgment. . . . Secondly, experience never confers on its judgments true or strict, but only assumed and comparative *universality*, through induction. . . . Necessity and strict universality are thus sure criteria of *a priori* knowledge, and are inseparable from one another (*CPR*, 43–44).

As Hume has taught us, necessity cannot be discovered by means of experience; as far as experience tells us, all events are "entirely loose and separate." Further, we all know that experience is limited in extent; so experience cannot demonstrate that a proposition is universally true (i.e., true everywhere and at all times). It follows that if we nonetheless find a judgment that is either necessarily true or universally true, we can be sure that it does not have its justification in experience. Such a judgment must be *a priori*.

Mathematical truths are both necessary and universal. They are, therefore, clear examples of *a priori* judgments. But they also, Kant tells us,

> are all synthetic. This fact seems hitherto to have altogether escaped the observation of those who have analyzed human reason; it even seems directly opposed to all their conjectures, though it is incontestably certain and most important in its consequences. . . .
>
> It might at first be thought that the proposition 7 + 5 = 12 is a mere analytic judgment, following from the concept of the sum of seven and five, according to the principle of contradiction. But on closer examination it appears that the concept of the sum of 7 + 5 contains merely their union in a single number, without its being at all thought what the particular number is that unites them. The concept of twelve is by no means thought by merely thinking of the combination of seven and five; and analyze this possible sum as we may, we shall not discover twelve in the concept. We must go beyond these concepts by calling to our aid some intuition corresponding to one of them, i.e., either our five fingers or five points . . . ; and we must add successively the units of the five given in the intuition to the concept of seven. . . .
>
> All principles of geometry are no less analytic. That a straight line is the shortest path between two points is a synthetic proposition. For my concept of straight contains nothing of quantity, but only a quality. The concept of the shortest is therefore altogether additional and cannot be obtained by any analysis of the concept of the straight line. Here, too, intuition must come to aid us (P, 13–14).

What is Kant trying to show through these examples? Hume suggests that the truths of mathematics are simply matters of how ideas are related to each other—that they are analytic and can be known by appeal solely to the principle of contradiction. Kant argues that this is not so. For "7 + 5 = 12" to be analytic, the concept "12" would have to be implicitly included in the concept "7 + 5." But all that concept tells us, if Kant is right, is that two numbers are being added. It does not, of itself, tell us what the sum is.

What can tell us what the sum is? Only some *intuition*, Kant says.* An intuition is not anything mysterious or occult. By "intuition" Kant simply means the presentation of some sensible object to the mind. That is why we need the five fingers (or something similar). We must "add successively" the units presented in the intuition: we count, one finger at a time. Knowing that 7 + 5 = 12 is a *process*. We *construct* mathematics by inscribing it on a background composed of sensible objects or sets of objects.

But we need to understand these objects more clearly. Since geometry and mathematics are *a priori* disciplines, their objects cannot be the ordinary objects of sensible experience (e.g., apples and oranges), for those objects we can only know *a posteriori*, through experience. If mathematics were only about the objects of experience, then it could neither be necessary nor universal. We might know that *these* five oranges and *those* seven oranges happen to make twelve oranges. But we wouldn't know that *all* such groups of oranges (examined or not) make twelve and *must* make twelve. If we know this with necessity and universality (as we surely do), the objects that justify mathematical truths must themselves be known in a purely *a priori* manner. There must be *pure* intuitions, forms of *pure sensibility*. But what could they be?

> Now the intuitions which pure mathematics lays at the foundation of all its cognitions and judgments . . . are space and time. . . . Geometry is based upon the pure intuition of space. Arithmetic attains its concepts of numbers by the successive addition of units in time (P, 27).

Think about space a moment. According to our ordinary experience, space is filled with things. But suppose you "think away" all these things—all the household goods, the clothes, the houses, the earth itself, sun, moon, and stars. Have you thought

---

*Kant is the ancestor of a school in the philosophy of mathematics that still has distinguished adherents. The viewpoint is called "intuitionism" but might more accurately be termed "constructivism."

away space? Kant thinks not. (Newton would have agreed.) But you have "subtracted" (in this thought experiment) everything *empirical*—that is, everything that gives particular content to our experience. All that is left is a kind of container, a form or structure, in which empirical things can be put. But, since you have gotten rid of everything empirical, what is left is *pure*. And it can be known *a priori*. Geometry is the science of this pure intuition of space.*

But what is the status of the intuition itself? Could space simply be one more (rather abstract and esoteric) object independent of our perception of it? Kant doesn't think so. And the reason is this: The truths of geometry, like those of mathematics, are not probabilistic, but *necessary*. If you ask, "How *likely* is it that any given straight line is the shortest distance between its end points?" you demonstrate that you haven't *understood* geometry! Moreover, that a straight line in a plane is the shortest distance between two points is something we know to be *universally* true, not only for spaces that we have examined. If space were an object independent of our minds, this would be impossible. We would have to say that this is true *for all the spaces we have examined*, but beyond that, who knows? Geometers do not proceed in this manner. They neither make experiments concerning space nor suppose that unexamined space could have a different structure. Yet geometry is the science of space. How can this be?

The explanation must be this: Space is not something "out there" to be discovered; space is a form of the mind itself. It is a pure intuition providing a "structure" into which all our more determinate perceptions *must fit*. When you handle an apple, your experience is constituted on the one hand by sensations (color, texture, weight, and so on) and on the other hand by a form or structure into which these sensations fit (the pure intuition of space). About this intuited form, we can know necessary truths: truths that are synthetic but *a priori*. The apple as we experience it is not an object en-

tirely independent of our perception of it. Part of that very experience is constituted by the intuition of space, which we do not *abstract from* the experience, but *bring to* it.

This has an important consequence. We cannot experience the apple as it is *in itself*, independent of our perception of it. Why not? Because part of what it is to *be* an apple is to be in space; and space is an aspect of our experience that comes from the side of the subject. So the apple, as we can know it, is the apple *as it appears to us*, not the apple *as it is in itself*. What goes for the apple goes for the entire world. We can only know how things *appear*.

> . . . things as objects of our senses existing outside us are given, but we know nothing of what they may be in themselves, knowing only their appearances, i.e., the representations which they cause in us by affecting our senses. Consequently, I grant by all means that there are bodies without us, that is, things which, though quite unknown to us as to what they are in themselves, we yet know by the representations which their influence on our sensibility procures us, and which we call bodies. This word merely means the appearance of the thing, which is unknown to us but is not therefore less real (P, 33).

Just as space is the pure intuition that makes geometry possible, time is the pure intuition that makes mathematics possible. Geometrical figures are constructed on the pure (spatial) form in which external objects are experienced. Numbers and their relations are constructed on the pure (temporal) form in which any objects whatsoever (including all mental events) are experienced.

Kant has now answered his first question. Pure geometry and mathematics are possible because their objects are not independent of the knowing rational mind; space and time are pure forms of sensible intuition. He has shown, moreover, that geometry and mathematics essentially involve judgments that are synthetic (because they are constructive) and *a priori* (because they are necessary and universal).

Because experience is always experience in time (if it is experience of external objects, it is experience in space as well), it is made up of the *appear-*

---

*Kant is referring to Euclidean geometry, of course. Various non-Euclidean geometries were discovered in the nineteenth century.

ances of things; it is a *product* of contributions from two sides: the objective and the subjective. Nowhere can we know things as they are in themselves, independent of our contribution to their natures. It is not that we know things in themselves in a confused and inadequate way that can be continually improved. We do not know them at all! And we can know *a priori* just the part of their natures that we ourselves, as rational minds, necessarily supply in experiencing them.

Common Sense, Science, and the *A Priori* Categories

Pure mathematics does not exhaust our knowledge. We know many things in the course of our ordinary life and through Newtonian science. What is the application of Kant's Copernican revolution in these spheres? One thing we know already. Whatever common sense and science may reveal, they will not be able to penetrate behind the veil of our pure sensible intuitions, which structure all possible objects in space and time. In these fields, too, we will be unable to reach to things in themselves; all our knowledge will concern how these things *appear* to us.

To deal with his second question, how pure natural science is possible, Kant needs to clarify a distinction between two aspects or powers of the mind. He calls them *sensibility* and *understanding*. The former is a passive power, the ability to receive impressions. The latter is an active power, the power to think objects by constructing a representation of them using concepts.

> Our knowledge springs from two fundamental sources of the mind; the first is the capacity of receiving representations (receptivity for impressions), the second is the power of knowing an object through these representations (spontaneity [in the production] of concepts). Through the first an object is *given* to us, through the second the object is *thought*. . . . Intuition and concepts constitute, therefore, the elements of all our knowledge, so that neither concepts

without an intuition in some way corresponding to them, nor intuition without concepts, can yield knowledge. Both may be either pure or empirical. When they contain sensation (which presupposes the actual presence of the object), they are empirical. When there is no mingling of sensation with the representation, they are pure (*CPR*, 92).

Kant's general term for the contents of the mind is "representation." He is here telling us that our representations can be of several different kinds: pure or empirical, intuitive or conceptual. In fact, this gives us a matrix of four possibilities; let us set them out with some examples.

Representations

	Pure	Empirical
Intuitions (from sensibility)	Space and time	Sensations of red, warm, hard, etc.
Concepts (from understanding)	Straight, cause, substance, God, the soul	Cherry pie, otter, water, the sun, unicorn, etc.

We have not determined at this point whether all these representations actually *represent* something. But we do know that any concept which succeeds in representing something will have to do it in tandem with some intuition. For "neither concepts without an intuition in some way corresponding to them, nor intuition without concepts, can yield knowledge." The dove cannot fly in empty space.

Kant has contrasted sensibility with understanding, intuitions with concepts. But he is also convinced that they must work together.

> To neither of these powers may a preference be given over the other. Without sensibility no object would be given to us, without understanding no object

would be thought. Thoughts without content are empty, intuitions without concepts are blind. It is, therefore, just as necessary to make our concepts sensible, that is, to add the object to them in intuition, as to make our intuitions intelligible, that is, to bring them under concepts. . . . The understanding can intuit nothing, the senses can think nothing. Only through their union can knowledge arise (*CPR*, 93).

We have seen that there are *pure intuitions* that can be known *a priori* (space and time). There are also *nonpure* or *empirical* intuitions; these are Humean impressions or sensations. Kant thinks of sensations as the *matter* of sensible objects. We can illustrate by imagining a square cut out of wood. The spatial properties of the square can be known *a priori*, quite independent of whether the square is red or brown, warm or cold, smooth or rough. But it can only be *some particular square* if it is either red or some other color, either warm or not, either smooth or less than smooth. Our sensations determine which it is. They provide the "filling" or content for the purely formal intuition of a square.

Are *concepts* like this too? Can there be *pure concepts* as well as empirical concepts? Kant is convinced that we make use of pure, *a priori* concepts all the time. If there were concepts that we *necessarily* use in thinking *any* object whatsoever, these concepts would be *a priori* concepts. They would satisfy the two criteria of necessity and universality. Pure concepts would do for understanding what space and time do for sensibility: provide a structure within which alone objects could be known. Kant's idea here is that our thinking with concepts also has two sides: the empirical, derived from sensation, and the *a priori* (or formal), supplied by the structure of the *understanding*.* Like sensibility, the understanding brings something of its own to experience. In neither case is the mind just a blank tablet on which experience writes, as some philosophers have thought.

The question then forces itself upon us: What concepts do we have that apply to objects but are not derived from them? We are searching for a set of concepts we use necessarily in thinking of an object. And these will be *a priori* concepts. Kant calls them *categories*, since they will supply the most general characteristics of things: the characteristics it takes to qualify as a thing or object at all.*

But how can we discover these concepts? Critical philosophy, you will remember, is reflective or transcendental in nature. So we need to reflect on our thinking, to see whether there are some features of our thinking about objects that must be present no matter what the object is.

Let's begin by asking, What is it to think of an *object*, anyway? Consider the contrast between these two judgments:

A: "It seems as if there is a heavy book before me."
B: "The book before me is heavy."

What is the difference? In a certain sense, they both have the same *content*: book, heavy, before me. Yet there is a crucial difference. What is it? Isn't it just that B is a judgment about an *object*, whereas A *pulls back* from making a judgment about that object? A is a judgment, not about the book, but about *my perception*; it has only what Kant calls "subjective validity." B, however, is a judgment about *the book*. It is an "objective" judgment; whether true or false, it makes a claim that an object has a certain characteristic.

But in what does this difference consist? It can't consist in the empirical concepts involved: "book" and "heavy" and "before me" are the same in A and B. Nor can the difference be anything derived

---

*Check the examples again in the chart on p. 375.

*You can see that Kant embarked on a project similar to that of Aristotle: to discover the characteristics of being *qua* being. Aristotle also produces a set of categories, displaying the most general ways in which something (anything) can *be*. (See p. 145.) Kant goes about the project in a roughly similar way: he looks at the language in which we talk about objects. But between Kant and Aristotle there stands the Kantian Copernican revolution. And that makes a tremendous difference. Kant's "categories," the universal and necessary features of objects, originate in the structure of *thinking* about those objects. They apply not to being *as such*, but to being *as it is knowable* by rational minds like ours—i.e., to appearance.

from my experience of the book in the two cases, since my experience may be exactly the same in each. So the difference must be an *a priori* one. It seems to be a difference in the *manner* in which the judgments are made, or in the *form* of the judgments. If we can isolate the feature that distinguishes A from B, we will have put our finger on something necessary for objective judgments—i.e., for thinking about a world of objects. We will have isolated the contribution the *understanding* makes to our experience of an objective world.

In this case, Kant tells us, the distinguishing feature is that in B we are thinking in terms of a *substance* together with its *properties*. These concepts are not derived from what is *given* in my sensations (since the sensations are exactly the same in A). These concepts are *brought to* the experience of the book by the understanding in the very form of thinking of the book as an object. The book is a substance that has the property of being heavy. But this means that the concepts "substance" and "property" are *a priori* concepts. And that is just what we are looking for.

The point is this. In thinking of an objective world, thinking necessarily takes certain forms of organization. One of these forms consists of a kind of logical function or rule: *Structure experience in terms of substances having properties.* Unless thoughts take this logical form, Kant says, a world of objects simply cannot be thought at all. Without the application of these *a priori* concepts, there can be no objective world for common sense or science to know. So a world of objects is, like the world of sensible intuitions, a composite. There is an empirical aspect to it (expressed in empirical concepts like "book" and "heavy"). But there is also an *a priori* aspect to it (expressed in nonempirical concepts such as "substance" and "property"). Experience of an objective world requires both.

Kant works out an entire system of such *a priori* concepts or categories. He thinks he can do this by canvassing all the possible forms objective judgments can take. And he thinks he can do that because he assumes that logic (the science of the forms of judgment) is a closed and finished science; no essential changes, he observes, have oc-

curred in it since Aristotle.* For each possible form of judgment (he thinks there are twelve such forms) he finds an *a priori* concept that we bring to bear on sensations. In each case, the application of this concept produces an *a priori* characteristic of the objective world of our experience. So Kant identifies twelve categories—twelve general ways we know that any objective world *must* be. The fact that the world of our experience must be structured in terms of substances-having-properties is just one of these ways. We will examine only one other, passing over much of the detail of Kant's treatment.

The *a priori* concept of substance gets an opportunity, so to speak, to apply to experience because sensations come grouped together in various ways in *space*. Considered just as sensations, my experience of what I call the book hangs together in a certain way; the color, texture, shape, and so on seem to be closely associated—hanging together, for instance, as they move across my field of vision. If this were not so, I could scarcely unify these sensations under one concept and experience one object, the book. In a similar way, sensations also appear *successively in time*. This provides a foothold for another of the categories: *causation*.

We have examined Hume's powerful argument that our idea of cause is not an empirical idea—that it is not abstracted from our experience.† Hume concludes that the idea is a fiction, a kind of illusion produced in us by custom. So we cannot really know that objects are related to each other by cause and effect.

But what if the concept of causation (like the concept of substance) represents a necessary aspect of any world of objects? What if there simply couldn't *be* objects at all unless they were set in causal relations with each other? This is the possibility that Kant's Copernican revolution explores. Objects are what we know, both in common sense and in science. If knowing them requires that this

---

*We now know that Kant's list of the possible forms of judgments is not, as he thinks, complete. Logic has gone through a revolution since Kant's time.
†Review this argument on pp. 345–351.

knowledge be expressed in judgments making use of an *a priori* concept of causality, we could know (*a priori*) that objects are necessarily and universally causal and avoid Hume's skeptical conclusions.

Again Kant shows us that there is a difference between judgments that refer only to our perceptions and judgments that are about objects. It may *seem* to us that one thing follows necessarily upon another. But once we affirm the idea of a world of objects, we are committed to there being a rule that it *must* be so. Suppose that something unusual happens. What will we do? We will ask why. We will search for its cause. Will we allow the possibility that this event had no cause? Certainly not. But what if we search and search and do not discover its cause (e.g., the cause for a certain kind of cancer)? Will we finally conclude that it has no cause? Of course not. No degree of failure in finding its cause would ever convince us that it has no cause. *Every* event has a cause.

How do we know that? We have seen that it is not analytic. How do we know that this conviction is not a mere prejudice on our part? Our confidence cannot be based on an induction from past successes in finding causes, for that would never justify our certainty that even unexamined events must have causes. We've learned that from Hume. If we know that every event has a cause, we know it because part of the very idea of a world of objects is that events in it are structured by rules of succession. There *could not be* an objective world that was not organized by cause and effect.

Think of it this way: if there were no necessary order in the succession of events, this succession could not be distinguished from sheer fancy, dream, or imagination. Its being subject to a rule determining that when *X* happens, *Y* must necessarily happen is just what makes it objective. Again note the difference between judgments which refer only to perception and judgments which refer to something objective. In the latter, we understand the temporal succession of events in terms of a rule that *makes* the succession objective, a rule of causation. Structuring the world in that way is part of what makes it an objective world that can be experienced. Objective worlds (as opposed to subjec-

tive fancies) are just those that do have such a causal structure in time.

The concept of causality *does* apply to the world we experience—not because we discover it there, but because we bring it with us to the experience.

> This complete . . . solution of Hume's problem rescues for the pure concepts of the understanding their *a priori* origin and for the universal laws of nature their validity as laws of the understanding, yet in such a way as to limit their use to experience, because their possibility depends solely on the reference of the understanding to experience, but with a completely reversed mode of connection which never occurred to Hume: they are not derived from experience, but experience is derived from them.
>
> This is, therefore, the result of all our foregoing inquiries: "All synthetic principles *a priori* are nothing more than principles of possible experience" and can never be referred to things in themselves, but to appearances as objects of experience (P, 55–56).

Let us sum up. The principle that every event has a cause is, as we have seen, *synthetic* (the concept of causation is not included in the concept of an event, but is added to it). Hume is right that the causal principle cannot be known *a posteriori*, from experience. But we do know that the principle is true: it is a presupposition of Newtonian science. So we know it *a priori*. It is, then, one of the synthetic *a priori* judgments.

Now we can see that Kant has answered how science (including pure science) of nature is possible. Pure knowledge of nature is possible because nature itself (the objective world that is there to be known) is partially constituted by the concepts and principles that a rational mind must use in understanding it. We know *a priori* that nature is made up of substances-having-properties, though we can know only through experience which substances have what properties. We know *a priori* that the world is a causally ordered whole, though we can know only through experience which particular events cause what other events. Science, together with its pure or *a priori* part, is possible only because it is the knowledge of an objective world that is not entirely independent of either our sensibility or our understanding. It is possible only on the basis of Kant's Copernican revolution.

Let us just remind ourselves once more of the consequence: We have, and can have, no knowledge whatever about things as they are "in themselves." Our knowledge is solely about the way they appear to us. But, we must add, it does not follow that our knowledge is in any way illusory. It is not like a dream or a fancy of our imagination. The distinction, in fact, between illusion and reality is one drawn by us *within* this objective world of appearance—not *between* it and something else. Dreams and illusions are just sequences that cannot be ordered by the regularity of causal law; that is why they lack *objectivity* and are taken to be purely subjective phenomena. We are not capable of knowing anything *more real* than the spatiotemporal world of our experience, structured as it is by the categories of the pure understanding. This world may be "transcendentally ideal" (i.e., its basic features are not independent of the knowing mind), but it is *empirically real*.

This, perhaps, needs a bit more explanation.

Phenomena and Noumena

"Thoughts without content are empty," Kant says, and "intuitions without concepts are blind" (*CPR*, 93). Thoughts are made up of concepts united in various ways. But unless those concepts are given a content through some intuition, either pure (as in geometry) or empirical (as in physics), they are "empty"—sheer forms that for all we know may apply to nothing. They provide us with no knowledge. However, merely having an intuition of space, or of blue-and-solid, provides no knowledge either. Intuitions without concepts are "blind." To know, or to "see" the truth, we must have concepts that are applied to some matter.

We demand in every concept, first, the logical form of a concept (of thought) in general, and secondly, the possibility of giving it an object to which it may be applied. In the absence of such object, it has no meaning and is completely lacking in content, though it may still contain the logical function which is required for making a concept out of any data that may be presented. Now the object cannot be given to a concept otherwise than in intuition. . . . Therefore all concepts, and with them all principles, even such as are possible *a priori*, relate to empirical intuitions, that is, to the data for a possible experience. Apart from this relation they have no objective validity, and in respect of their representations are a mere play of imagination or of understanding (*CPR*, 259).

Kant insists on this point again and again, for we are

subject to an illusion from which it is difficult to escape. The categories are not, as regards their origin, grounded in sensibility, like the *forms of intuition*, space and time; and they seem, therefore, to allow of an application extending beyond all objects of the senses (*CPR*, 266).

We have ideas of, for example, "substance" and "cause." And it seems there is no barrier to applying them even beyond the boundaries of **possible experience**.* In fact, *nearly all previous philosophers* think we can do that! Plato, for example, is convinced that reality is composed of *substances* (the Forms) that cannot be sensed but are purely intelligible. Descartes asks about the *cause* of his idea of God. One of the presuppositions of traditional metaphysics is that these concepts can take us beyond the sphere of experience.† But, if Kant is right, these concepts

---

*See the principle restricting such concepts to possible experience, p. 378.

†Notice how Kant has turned completely upside down Plato's claim that knowledge is restricted to the purely intelligible world of Forms. For Kant, this realm beyond any possible sensory experience cannot be known at all; what we can know is the changing world of the senses, about which Plato thinks we can have only opinions. Here we have yet another example of the radical consequences of modern science for traditional epistemology and metaphysics; for Kant's confidence in knowledge of the sensory world rests ultimately on the achievement of Newton.

are nothing but *forms of thought*, which contain the merely logical faculty of uniting *a priori* in one consciousness the manifold given in intuition; and apart, therefore, from the only intuition that is possible for us, they have even less meaning than the pure sensible forms [space and time] (*CPR*, 266).

The categories, Kant claims, cannot be used apart from sensible intuitions to give us knowledge of objects. Why not? Because they are merely "forms of thought." Compare them to mathematical functions, like x^2. Until some number is given as x, we have no object. If a content for x is supplied, say 2 or 3, then an object is specified, in these cases the numbers 4 or 9. The categories of substance, cause, and the rest are similar. They are merely operators whose function is to unite "in one consciousness the manifold given in intuition." If a certain manifold of sensations is given, our possession of the concept "substance" allows us to produce the thought of a book; a different manifold of sensations produces (under the concept "substance") the thought of a printing press; and the category of "causation" allows us to think a causal relation between the two. Objects are the result of the application of the categories as operators to some sensible material.

It may be helpful to contrast Kant's *concepts* with Hume's *ideas*.* Their analyses of this central feature of our intellectual life are as different as can be. For Hume, you will recall, an idea is a kind of *copy* of an impression; so an idea must be analogous to an *image*. Every idea, for Hume, has a *content* that is determined by its ancestry in our experience. It is produced in us passively: no impression, no idea. For Kant, by contrast, a concept is understood as a kind of *formal rule* for uniting intuitions (among which Hume's impressions may be found). Concepts may be suggested by impressions, but they are far from mere copies. Nor are we passive with regard to concepts. The pure concepts (categories) are necessarily *brought to* experience by a rational mind; they do not just reflect experience, they *organize* it. Empirical concepts have the same organizing role, but not so universally. Since a concept

is just a formal rule for structuring some material, we can have concepts that reach beyond our experience. Kant holds that these concepts cannot give us *knowledge*, for without the sensible intuitions, there are no objects.

But it *seems* as though there are. This is the illusion.

> The categories . . . extend further than sensible intuition, since they think objects in general, without regard to the special mode (the sensibility) in which they may be given. But they do not thereby determine a greater sphere of objects (*CPR*, 271).

The category of substance, for instance, is not inherently limited to the objects of sensory experience, or even, for that matter, to space and time. It seems we can have the idea of a nonmaterial, nonspatial, nontemporal substance. Nothing easier! But this is profoundly illusory, if Kant is right. Why? Because the concept "substance" is not a complete concept in its own right. It is only a kind of *rule* for organizing some content or other. And the content must be given by intuition.

It is perhaps not impossible for there to be other forms of intuition than those available to us. We human beings, however, are limited to space, time, and sensation. To treat the categories as concepts that can give us knowledge beyond these limitations is to suppose that we have types of intuition that we do not have. And that is to fall into the illusion.

One common form of the illusion is the claim that we can know things as they are *in themselves*, apart from the way they appear to us through our powers of intuition. This is the illusion of speculative metaphysics. The illusion is reinforced because we do have the concept of **things-in-themselves**. Kant even gives it a name: something as it is in itself, independently of the way it reveals itself to us, is called a **noumenon**. This contrasts with a **phenomenon**, its appearance to us.

But it is crucial to observe that this concept of a noumenon is not a concept with any positive meaning. Its role in our intellectual life is purely negative; it reminds us that there are things we cannot know—namely what the things affecting

*See pp. 343–344.

our sensibility are *really* like (if by "really" we mean what they are like independently of our intuitions of them). The phenomenal world of appearance is all we can ever know.

Kant once more drives home the moral:

> *Understanding* and *sensibility*, with us, can determine objects *only when they are employed in conjunction*. When we separate them, we have intuitions without concepts, or concepts without intuitions—in both cases, representations which we are not in a position to apply to any determinate object (*CPR*, 274).

Reasoning and the Ideas of Metaphysics: God, World, and Soul

Kant's third question concerns metaphysics. The term "metaphysics" has a precise meaning for Kant. Metaphysics contrasts sharply with both common sense and science. We have seen that the entire range of possible experience is governed by the *pure intuitions* of space and time, as well as by the *pure categories* of the understanding. These, together with *sensations*, constitute the way things appear to us, the realm of *phenomena*. Beyond this realm our understanding is without footing. We know there are things that appear to us; but we are completely at sea about what they may be in themselves. "Out there" the dove cannot fly.

It may be useful to set out the basic pattern of Kant's epistemology as a series of steps that together constitute the world of all possible experience.

a. Noumena, or things in themselves,
b. Constitute the phenomenal world of appearance (objects), by
c. Producing in the knower a manifold of sensations (Humean impressions), which are
d. Apprehended through the intuitions of space and time (*a priori* forms of the knower's sensibility), and
e. Structured as substances in causal connections by the *a priori* categories of the understanding.

Experience of the empirical world lies at level (b). This is the domain in which common sense and science can do their work. Critical or transcendental philosophy reveals the levels (c) through (e) by what Kant calls a "critique of pure reason." Mathematics is done in (d).

Metaphysics looks in two directions. Understood in the traditional way, it is the discipline that tries to gain knowledge about level (a)—about things apart from their appearance to us. It is the attempt to go beyond experience in a *transcendent* direction, toward the *noumenal world*, which *transcends* all possible experience. But metaphysics can also look in the opposite direction: to the structures on the side of the subject that condition the being of objects. In this case Kant calls it *transcendental*. It is just that critique of pure reason we have been examining; it tries only to discern the *a priori* conditions of experience. Such a *transcendental* investigation, looking back into the knowing subject, Kant also calls *immanent*.

Not surprisingly, Kant thinks the transcendent kind of metaphysics is impossible. But his discussion of the reasons for the impossibility are full of interesting insights. First, Kant claims to be able to explain why the quest for metaphysical knowledge recurs with such inevitability (despite the critiques of the skeptics) and why it is so difficult to give up. Second, he finds a positive use for the fundamental metaphysical ideas—God, the world, and the soul—even though he denies that these ideas can give us knowledge. Finally, Kant's examination of these ideas propels us into the fourth of his major concerns, the practical use of reason, or morality.

The notion that we can get knowledge of things in themselves is, Kant says, "a *natural* and inevitable *illusion*" (*CPR*, 300). Something in the very structure of rationality gives us that notion; it has to do with *reasoning*. The aim of reasoning is to supply "the reason why" something is true. As we have seen numerous times already, the why-question can always be repeated; we can ask for the reason for the reason. Kant talks of this process as one that seeks the *conditions* which account for a given truth. Grass is green. Why? In answering this question, we refer to some condition in the world that explains that fact. Why is that condition the way it is? Again, we can supply a condition that explains that condition. And we could go on.

As you can see, the quest for reasons will not be satisfied until it finds some condition that doesn't need to be explained by a further condition. Reason is always searching for the *unconditioned*. We can think of this as Kant's version of the search for first principles. This has always been the task of first philosophy, or metaphysics. The search is for something intelligible in itself, which explains or makes intelligible all the rest.

> Without solving this question, reason will never be satisfied. The empirical use to which reason limits the pure understanding does not fully satisfy reason's own proper destination. Every single experience is only a part of the whole sphere of its domain, but the absolute totality of all possible experience is itself not experience. . . . the concepts of reason aim at the completeness, i.e., the collective unity, of all possible experience, and thereby go beyond every given experience. Thus they become *transcendent* (P, 70).

> . . . when reason, which cannot be fully satisfied with any empirical use of the rules of the understanding, as being always conditioned, requires a completion of this chain of conditions, then the understanding is forced out of its sphere. And then reason partly represents objects of experience in a series so extended that no experience can grasp it, partly even (with a view to complete the series) it seeks entirely beyond experience *noumena*, to which it can attach that chain; and so, having at last escaped from the conditions of experience, reason makes it hold complete (P, 74).

We can understand only what lies within the bounds of possible experience. But reason cannot be content with that. If those bounds are reached, reason still wants to ask why. Why is experience as a whole the way it is? Why is there experience at all? But this question can be answered only by transcending those boundaries. To ask for the condition that explains the "absolute totality of all possible experience" is no longer asking for the explanation of one phenomenon in terms of another—about which we might then ask the same question. It is asking for something absolute, for the uncon-

ditioned, which will necessarily involve knowledge of things in themselves.

And so arise, naturally and inevitably, those concepts of God, the world in itself, and the knowing subject or soul. These concepts are very different from all others. They are not empirical concepts abstracted from sensations. Nor are they *a priori* concepts structuring each and every one of our experiences. Kant gives them a special name: *Ideas of Pure Reason.**

> As the understanding stands in need of categories for experience, reason contains in itself the ground of ideas, by which I mean necessary concepts whose object *cannot* be given in any experience (P, 70).

Reason can try to trace out the ultimate conditions in three different directions: back into the *subject* (trying to construct an absolute psychological Idea), out into the *world* (trying to discover the cosmological Ideas), and toward the *absolute condition of anything at all* (searching for the theological Idea). And so we have reason inevitably constructing the ideas of soul, world, and God.

The Soul

The outcome of Descartes' strategy of methodical doubt is that he cannot doubt his own existence. And when he asks himself what he is, the answer seems obvious: a thing that thinks. He "knows" that he is a substance whose essential characteristic is to think. Descartes, as we have seen, further claims that this substance is simple (indivisible), that it doesn't change over time, and that it is immortal.

It is clear that Descartes is not doing empirical psychology here; there are no experiments, and he

---

*Kant has Plato explicitly in mind here. The term in Greek for what we usually call "Form" is translated as "idea." In Plato these are purely intelligible entities that can be understood, but not sensed. For Kant, of course, the Ideas are concepts, not realities; and they can give us no knowledge. But they are concepts whose aim seems to be the presentation of realities beyond any possible sensory experience. For Plato on the Forms, see pp. 109–114.

gathers no data. Kant calls this kind of thing **rational psychology**. Rational psychology is an attempt to understand the fundamental nature of the self by rational reflection on what the self *must* be if experience is to be possible. It is a quest for the *unconditioned condition* on the side of the subject. Kant is convinced that rational psychology is illusory, that there can be no such knowledge. But he also thinks that the illusion is a powerful one and difficult to resist. It arises from what Kant calls "the sole text of rational psychology," the judgment "I think" (*CPR*, 330). Reflection on this judgment alone seems to be enough to yield all the conclusions desired by the rational psychologist.

Is the soul a substance? It seems as though I can conclude that I am a substance. Here is the argument. Every thought I have can be preceded (at least implicitly) by the phrase, "I think." I think roses are lovely; I think eggs come from chickens; I think Kant is a great philosopher. All these thoughts belong to me; they are qualities or properties of myself. But what about the "I"? Could this *I* be simply a property or characteristic? Of what? The idea that *I* might be just a property of some other substance doesn't seem to make sense. *I* am the absolute subject of all these determinations. But this is just what we mean by substance; a substance is, by definition, that which cannot be predicated of anything else, but is the subject of properties.* So I, as a thinking thing, must be a substance.

This seems a persuasive argument; but, if Kant is right, it is a mere sophism. Remember that "substance" is one of the *a priori* categories. This means it is a concept that is purely formal in itself, without any content. Its whole function is to serve as a kind of rule for organizing sensible intuitions into experience. But where is the intuition that corresponds to the "I"? Kant agrees with Hume, who claims not to be able to find any perception of the self when he introspects.† When you say "I think,"

you are not peering at or describing your self. The whole content of what you think is expressed in what comes *after* that phrase.

> The 'I' is indeed in all thoughts, but there is not in this representation the least trace of intuition, distinguishing the 'I' from other objects of intuition.
> We do not have, and cannot have, any knowledge whatsoever of any such subject (*CPR*, 334).

Reason is always searching for the conditions that make experience possible. In looking back and back into myself, I seem to come upon the idea that there is a substance to which all these activities connected with thinking belong. But this is a kind of grammatical or logical illusion. Just because I need to express my thinking by using subject/predicate forms in which the "I" occurs, I cannot infer that *noumenal reality* is structured that way. I cannot transform a necessity of my mode of representing myself into a metaphysical necessity concerning my nature.

Kant says that the "I" in "I think" is just a kind of formal marker. Concepts like this (others are "now" and "here" and "this") are sometimes called *indexicals*; what is peculiar about them is that they have no determinate content but merely indicate something relative to the circumstances of utterance. About the term "I," Kant says, "we cannot even say that this is a concept, but only that it is a bare consciousness which accompanies all concepts" (*CPR*, 331). All knowledge, however, is through concepts. So the "I" is nothing more than an empty representation of an unknown X, "this I or he or it (the thing) which thinks" (*CPR*, 331). What I am in myself is completely unknown to me. For all that rational reflection can tell me, this X that I am may be anything at all. I do not know that I am a substance. The self or soul, then, is that unknown X to whom the world appears and by which it is structured into objects.

Similar reflections undermine the claims about the soul's simplicity, its unchanging nature, and its immortality. In each case a *merely subjective condition* of thinking is transformed into a concept of a *noumenal object*. The "I," however, is not an object

---

*This idea of substance can be traced back to Aristotle's discussion of the categories of being. Substance is basic in the sense that all other modes of being (qualities, relations, etc.) are parasitic on substance. See pp. 146–147 for a brief discussion of this point.
†For Hume on the self, see "The Disappearing Self," in Chapter 19.

and cannot be known as an object. Objects, remember, can be known in experience only through the application of concepts to intuitions. The "I" is a *subject* and *resists objectification*. As far as rational knowledge goes, the subject of thinking remains merely an *X*, which must express itself *as if* it were a simple substance, continuously the same through time, and so on. But what it is in itself remains a complete mystery.* The concept of "soul" is an empty idea.

Kant's denial of rational psychology is not equivalent to a denial of the possibility of an *empirical* psychology. Such a psychology, based on experience, is just as legitimate as Newtonian science of nature. Only let psychologists be aware that they are examining appearance, the world of phenomena, in this case, the world of inner phenomena in time. Let them not think that they can discern the ultimate nature of the subject of consciousness!

The World

When we reason about the world, our reasoning seeks completeness, closure. Whatever we experience in the realm of phenomena is conditioned by other things; reason seeks the final condition, a foundation on which it can rest. It is seeking a point where its why-questions can stop. But Kant believes our reason can find no satisfaction in its search for the totality of the world; in fact, it develops internal conflicts. For example, he tries to demonstrate that we cannot decide whether the world had a beginning in time—whether it is temporally finite or infinite. In fact, he has arguments that seem to show that each alternative is false! When reason runs into such a contradiction—he calls it an "antinomy"—this is a sign that reason is

overreaching its own powers. Trying to complete the search for the unconditioned, reason frustrates itself. The moral of the story is that the world *in itself* is unknowable.

A second question, one more pertinent to our concerns here, addresses whether we can know that the world in itself is ordered causally. Phenomena are subject to causal ordering, as we have seen, but only because phenomenal objects are constituted *as objects* by the category of causality. Does this category extend to noumena? No. But then an interesting possibility arises: that our wills might—in themselves—be *free*.

As we have seen, this problem arises with particular insistence in the modern era. The scientific revolution, which leads to thinking of the world in mechanistic ways (the big clock), raises the question about human actions: Are they, too, just a part of the mechanism?

Descartes takes one possible tack here: mind and all its manifestations are excluded from the universal determinism governing material bodies. For Descartes, will is as free in man as it is in God: *absolutely free*. It escapes the causal network; when I will to raise my arm, there is no worldly cause in existence sufficient to produce that action. It is *my* doing—mine alone!

Hobbes and Hume take another tack. Universal determination of events is not denied. Actions, too, have causes: the laws of nature determine what we do just as surely as they determine the fall of a stone. These philosophers try to rescue human freedom, however, by offering a hypothetical analysis of what it is to act freely: *If you can do what you want to do, then you are free.* This is a *conditional* account of freedom. In a free action, they say, there are no conditions to *constrain* us, to keep us from doing what we want. They believe that this view of freedom is quite compatible with the view that (a) our wants themselves have causes and (b) our wants cause our actions. So they hope to *reconcile* freedom of action with the new physics.*

---

*Some thinkers have taken this lack of direct insight into the nature of the self to open the door to the Hobbesian possibility that the subject might be a material body after all—perhaps just a human body with a certain type of brain. This is an interesting possibility. There is no evidence that Kant takes this view, though he does point out that the *supposed* simplicity of the soul is the only ground on which it can be distinguished from matter.

---

*Review the discussion by Descartes in *Meditation IV*, p. 316. For Hume's view, see "Rescuing Human Freedom," in Chapter 19.

We should not be surprised if Kant's Copernican revolution in philosophy were to transform the shape of this problem. For, from Kant's point of view, Descartes and Hobbes/Hume share an important presupposition: both sides assume that they are describing things (in this case the will, or human action) as they are independent of our knowing them. What happens if we recognize that things in themselves are unknown to us and that all we can know is their appearance?

Critical philosophy, Kant thinks, will resolve this puzzle in the nicest possible way.

a. We can agree with Descartes that freedom is exemption from causality. Kant calls it "the power of beginning a state *spontaneously*" (*CPR*, 464).
b. But we do not have to carve out a part of the world in which causal law does not apply. We can agree with Hobbes and Hume that Newtonian science applies without limits to everything we can possibly experience.

This surely seems like the best of both views! Kant thinks he can give us all this without the questionable moves of Descartes and Hume. Descartes' exemption of the will from causal determination is dubious; it seems like special pleading, a stratagem designed simply to preserve something we are loath to give up. And the definition of "free" that Hobbes and Hume offer is equally questionable; can our actions really be free if they have causes that reach back and back and back in an unbroken chain to some period before we were even born? If Kant can avoid both shortcomings, effectively preserve human freedom, and still allow science unlimited scope, what more could we ask?

What makes this possible, of course, is the distinction between phenomena and noumena, between things as they appear to us and things in themselves.

> Is it a truly disjunctive proposition to say that every effect in the world must arise *either* from nature *or* from freedom; or must we not rather say that in one and the same event, in different relations, both can be

found? That all events in the sensible world stand in thoroughgoing connection in accordance with unchangeable laws of nature is an established principle . . . and allows of no exception. The question, therefore, can only be whether freedom is completely excluded by this inviolable rule, or whether an effect, notwithstanding its being thus determined in accordance with nature, may not at the same time be grounded in freedom. The common but fallacious presupposition of the *absolute reality* of appearances here manifests its injurious influence. . . . For if appearances are things in themselves, freedom cannot be upheld. Nature will then be the complete and sufficient determining cause of every event. The condition of the event will be such as can be found only in the series of appearances; both it and its effect will be necessary in accordance with the law of nature. If, on the other hand, appearances are not taken for more than they actually are; if they are viewed not as things in themselves, but merely as representations, connected according to empirical laws, they must themselves have grounds which are not appearances (*CPR*, 466–67).

Every action, even every act of will, has two aspects: (1) it is something that appears in the world of our experience and (2) it is something in itself. As an appearance, part of the world of nature, it is governed by all the principles that constitute that realm. It appears in time and is related by the category of causality to other events that precede and follow it. In this aspect, every action is causally determined. But as a thing in itself, we cannot even say that it occurs in time! And the category of causality does not extend to what occurs beyond the bounds of experience. So it may well be that in itself an act of will is free in that *absolute* sense of Descartes', i.e., there are no causal conditions sufficient for producing it.

Both Descartes and Hume think you have to choose between a strong noncausal view of freedom and a weaker compatibilist view. If you choose the former, you are committed to events that are exceptions to scientific laws. If you choose the latter, you believe the will is not free (in this absolute sense). Descartes chooses the former, Hume the latter (but adds that acts can be free in another, hypothetical sense). Kant argues that if we keep in mind the distinction between phenomena and things in themselves, we don't have to choose! An act can be both free and determined: free in itself (since the category of causality does not reach so far) and yet causal as it appears to us. The notion that an act couldn't possibly be both is simply due to considering the things we experience as things in themselves. And that is a mistake that critical philosophy can keep us from making.

> Freedom is therefore no hindrance to natural law in appearances; neither does this law abrogate the freedom of the practical use of reason, which is connected with things in themselves, as determining grounds.
> Thus practical freedom, viz., the freedom in which reason possesses causality according to objectively determining grounds, is rescued; and yet natural necessity is not in the least curtailed with regard to the very same effects, as appearances (P, 86–87).

Most of this should now be intelligible to you. "Practical freedom" is freedom in action, freedom to decide what events should occur in the world. This freedom, Kant is convinced, is closely tied to reason and acting for reasons. We can act freely when we act for a reason and not just in response to nonrational causes. We'll address what Kant means by "objectively determining grounds" for action when we discuss his views on morality; for now it will be enough to understand that Kant is thinking that reason itself, in the form of a rational will, might be a certain kind of (spontaneous) causality. So that when you (an agent) act for good reasons, you bring into being events that *appear* in the causal order of the world, but *in themselves* may have a completely noncausal origin.

We need to be very careful, however. Kant does not claim he has proved that there are free actions, or that he has evidence that such free actions exist. Remember, the will in its aspect as free is the will considered noumenally. And about the noumenal world we can know nothing at all. Kant does not even claim to have proved that such freedom is possible. The most he will say is that "causality through freedom is at least *not incompatible with nature*" (CPR, 479). There is *no contradiction* in thinking of an act as free in itself, but determined as appearance.

This means that, from the viewpoint of critical theory, freedom remains merely an Idea of Reason. It is one of those Ideas to which reason is driven when it asks (this time) about the conditions under which it can itself make a difference in the world. But no empirical filling of that concept is available to give us knowledge. More will be said about freedom, however, when we come to the topic of morality.

God

We have seen how our reason, in asking the why-question, inevitably runs through a series of conditions that tends to approach completeness. The end point of each such series must be the concept of some being that is, *in itself*, a foundation and a natural stopping place for reason. We have seen how this process generates the Ideas of the soul and of the world in itself. Kant's conclusion in both cases is, of course, that these Ideas are *merely ideas*. Because we have no intuitions providing content for these concepts, knowledge of them is impossible (despite their inevitability). Experience is the only ground our intellect can cultivate. And experience is essentially open-ended; no closure, no completeness will be found there. So the Ideas are sources of illusion. We *are drawn to think* we can know something about them. But we are mistaken.

There is one more pattern of reasoning we simply cannot avoid. It leads to the concept of God. Let us see how Kant understands this. He agrees with Descartes and the tradition that the idea of God is the idea of an all-perfect being, but he has a very interesting analysis of the way reasoning necessarily leads us to that idea. Like the ideas of soul and world, the idea of God is not an arbitrary invention. Nor is it just something we *might* invent, as Hume claims. Nor is it, as some in the Enlightenment hold, a priestly or political trick foisted on people to keep them in subjection. It is, for any being that reasons, an absolutely unavoidable concept.

Every thing, a philosopher once said, is what it is and not another thing.[2] Very sensible. But what determines what a thing is? In the broadest possible perspective (which is what our reasoning seeks) a thing is only a determinate thing if, given *every possible property* together with its *contradictory opposite*, one out of each pair of such opposites belongs to the thing. That is quite a mouthful; but the idea is really quite simple. Let's take an example.

Think of an egg, an ordinary chicken egg you might have for breakfast. It has certain properties and lacks others. That is what makes it the thing it is. But it isn't fully *determinate* unless every possible question about it has an answer; if there are questions without answers, we don't know what it is, really. Questions can be put in terms of *predicates* that express all the possible properties there are. And we can ask about the egg:

- Is it living, or not living?
- Is it white, or not white?
- Does it weigh thirty pounds, or does it not?
- Is it fragile, or is it not fragile?

And the list goes on and on and on. If the egg is to be a single, determinate thing, then to each such question there must be an answer. And there must be as many questions as there are possible predicates.

For every determinate thing that there is, reason is searching for an answer to the question, What is it? And to get a clear understanding of even one thing, such as our egg, reason would have to encompass in understanding the *complete* system of *all* the properties there could possibly be. Again we have the notion of completeness, finality. And since our egg is a real egg, we are led to think that this sum total of all possibility cannot itself be merely imaginary. There must actually be, we suppose, *some being* that encompasses all these possi-

bilities. There must be a being who is the foundation for the determinate nature of all things, by being the foundation of that enormously long list of possibilities which accounts for things being the things they are.* Such a being, as Thomas Aquinas might say, we call "God."

This is how reason inevitably comes upon the Idea of God. But the Idea is empty.† The emptiness of the Idea is clear when we realize that finding the sum total of all possible properties is an infinite task we could never complete. No experience, no intuition could ever fulfill the requirements of this Idea. Moreover, it is the Idea of something that cannot just be another phenomenal being; since it is the foundation for the determinate character of all phenomenal things, it must be noumenal—a thing in itself. As we are now abundantly aware, Kant argues that things in themselves are unknowable. So the concept of God is *just* an Idea of Reason. If we keep the principles of critical philosophy firmly in mind, Kant says,

> we can easily expose the dialectical illusion which arises from our making the subjective conditions of our thinking objective conditions of objects themselves, and from making an hypothesis necessary for the satisfaction of our reason into a dogma (P, 89).

These reflections should suffice to inhibit dogmatism, while explaining at the same time how inevitable the temptation to dogmatism is. But Kant adds a critique of the major arguments that purport to show that such a being must actually exist. He divides the arguments into three types: cosmological, design, and ontological. He argues that

---

*Even this is not enough. For we can imagine other worlds than this one. And they too would need determinacy. So the being we are led to conceive must be the foundation not only for the actual world but for any other possible world as well. God, if there is a god, must account not only for what the world *is* but for what it *could be*. But this is just to emphasize that such a being could not lack any *possible* perfection.

†Remember the slogan, "Thoughts without content are empty, intuitions without concepts are blind." (See p. 379.) The Ideas are thoughts without content.

each of the first two types makes use of the principle of the ontological argument at a crucial stage.
So we will focus on that.

The Ontological Argument

We met Descartes' version of this argument in the
fifth *Meditation*; the argument is originally presented by Anselm of Canterbury in the eleventh
century.* You will remember that this argument is
unique because it presupposes nothing but our
idea of God as a most perfect being. From that idea
alone, *a priori*, as Kant would say, the existence of
God is supposed to follow; it follows just as surely
(so Descartes tells us) as a theorem about the interior angles of a triangle follows from the concept of
a triangle. Kant's critique of this argument is famous, and we will examine it with some care.

He begins with a general point.

> In all ages men have spoken of an *absolutely necessary*
> being, and in so doing have endeavoured, not so
> much to understand whether and how a thing of this
> kind allows even of being thought, but rather to
> prove its existence. There is, of course, no difficulty
> in giving a verbal definition of the concept, namely,
> that it is something the non-existence of which is im-
> possible. But this yields no insight into the condi-
> tions which make it necessary to regard the non-exis-
> tence of a thing as absolutely unthinkable. It is
> precisely these conditions that we desire to know, in
> order that we may determine whether or not, in re-
> sorting to this concept, we are thinking anything at
> all (*CPR*, 501).

Kant is again insisting on the need for critical philosophy. Previous thinkers have rushed to prove
the existence of a supremely perfect being, without
examining in a reflective way "how a thing of this
kind allows even of being thought." What we need
to do, Kant says, is to examine the status of such a
concept in our thought. We may find that through

---

this concept we are not "thinking anything at all,"
that the concept has only a "verbal definition."*

If we give the concept this kind of examination,
what do we find? We find that it is supposed to be
illuminated by several analogies. Descartes' comments about triangles and mountains without val-
leys come to mind. God is supposed to have necessary existence in just the same way that a triangle
necessarily has three angles. Kant's first criticism
shows that these are not in fact analogous.

> All the alleged examples are, without exception,
> taken from *judgments*, not from *things* and their exis-
> tence. But the unconditioned necessity of judgments
> is not the same as the absolute necessity of things. . . .
> The above proposition does not declare that three
> angles are absolutely necessary, but that, under the
> condition that there is a triangle (that is, that a trian-
> gle is given), three angles will necessarily be found
> in it. . . .
>
> If, in an identical proposition, I reject the predi-
> cate while retaining the subject, contradiction re-
> sults; and I therefore say that the former belongs nec-
> essarily to the latter. But if we reject subject and
> predicate alike, there is no contradiction; for nothing
> is then left that can be contradicted. To posit a trian-
> gle, and yet to reject its three angles, is self-contradic-
> tory; but there is no contradiction in rejecting the
> triangle together with its three angles. The same
> holds true of the concept of an absolutely necessary
> being. If its existence is rejected, we reject the thing
> itself with all its predicates; and no question of con-
> tradiction can then arise (*CPR*, 501–2).

The ontological argument is supposed to show
us that the judgment "God does not exist" is self-
contradictory because existence is one of the perfections included in the concept of God. (It is sup-

---

*For a discussion of the original argument as given by Anselm, see
pp. 248–250. Review the argument as presented by Descartes in
Meditation V.

*Kant's doubts here recall the reason that Thomas Aquinas does
not accept the ontological argument. Thomas said that the argument assumes we have an adequate grasp of the "essence" of God,
but that this is not something we can assume. (See p. 252.) The
reason Thomas gives (that all our concepts originate in the senses)
is not exactly Kant's reason; but both of them require an examination of our *title* to such a concept, and in that way both are doing
"critical" philosophy.

posed to be like saying, "Something that exists does not exist.") The aim of the argument is to show that the atheist is just not thinking coherently. But, Kant says, even if we grant that "God exists" is necessarily true, this is simply a fact about our *concepts*. If the concept of God is given, then the concept of existence is given; and we cannot consistently deny God's existence. But it is quite open to the atheist to simply reject the concept. And if he does, the argument can get no hold on him. As Kant says, "Nothing is then left that can be contradicted."*

You can probably see that defenders of the argument might have a comeback to this point. They might say it is not so clear that the atheist *can* reject the concept. An atheist, in denying God's existence, must understand what it is he is denying, in which case he does have the concept. But Kant has a second and deeper criticism of the argument, one that will reinforce the first.

The deeper criticism rests on an analysis of what we are doing when we say that something exists.

> "Being" is obviously not a real predicate: that is, it is not a concept of something which could be added to the concept of a thing. It is merely the positing of a thing, or of certain determinations, as existing in themselves (*CPR*, 504).

This is a difficult thought. But we can make it clear by reflecting on definitions. Suppose we have a certain concept *x*. If we want to know what that concept is, we are asking for a definition. And the definition will be given in terms of certain predicates, say *f*, *g*, *h*. So we will be told that an *x* is something that is *f*, *g*, and *h*. A triangle, for example, is a closed plane figure bounded by three straight lines. Could "being" or "existence" be on such a list of predicates? This is what Kant denies. To say that *a triangle is a figure* is one thing. To say that *a triangle exists* is to say something of an altogether different *kind*. If we say that a triangle exists,

we are not expressing one of the properties of the triangle; existence is not the kind of thing that should be named in a list of those properties. To say that a triangle exists is to "posit" something that has *all* the properties of a triangle. It is to say that the concept (together with the properties that define it) *applies* to something.

If Kant is right, it follows that *every* judgment of existence is *synthetic*. None of them is simply analytic of the concept expressed by the subject of the judgment—because existence is not a normal predicate and cannot be part of the subject term's definition. And that means that *in no case* is the denial of a judgment asserting existence a contradiction. But this is exactly what the ontological argument claims.*

The fundamental mistake of the argument is the assumption that existence is a predicate like others and that the concept of a perfect being would have to include it.

> If, now, we take the subject (God) with all its predicates . . . , and say "God is," or "There is a God," we attach no new predicate to the concept of God, but only posit the subject in itself with all its predicates, and indeed posit it as being an *object* that stands in relation to my *concept*. The content of both must be one and the same; nothing can have been added to the concept, which expresses merely what is possible, by my thinking its object . . . as given absolutely. Otherwise stated, the real contains no more than the merely possible. A hundred real thalers do not contain the least coin more than a hundred possible thalers (*CPR*, 505).

If I say that God does not exist, I am not denying in the predicate part of the sentence what I have implicitly asserted in the subject part. I am simply refusing to "posit" an object of the sort the subject describes. Atheism may be wrong, but it is at least not a logically incoherent view. So the ontological argument fails.

---

*So far the analysis is similar to that given by Hume. Look again at Hume's discussion on p. 357.

*Modern logic agrees with Kant here. The two propositions "Dogs bark" and "Dogs exist" may *look* very much alike. But their logic is very different. In symbolic notation, the first is $(x)(Dx \supset Bx)$. The second is $(Ex)(Dx)$.

The attempt to establish the existence of a supreme being by means of the famous ontological argument of Descartes is therefore so much labour and effort lost; we can no more extend our stock of [theoretical] insight by mere ideas, than a merchant can better his position by adding a few noughts to his cash account (*CPR*, 507).

Is it Kant's purpose to make atheism possible? Not at all. In another famous line, Kant says,

I have therefore found it necessary to deny *knowledge*, in order to make room for *faith* (*CPR*, 29).

What sort of faith he has in mind we will discover in examining his moral philosophy.

Let us sum up this section with some reflections on the *positive* function of these Ideas of Reason: soul, world, and God. We have seen that in no case can we have knowledge of the things-in-themselves these Ideas picture. Taken as sources of knowledge, the Ideas are illusory. But they do express an *ideal* that reason cannot disregard: the ideal of knowledge as a complete, unified, and systematic whole, with no loose ends and nothing left out. It is this that drives reason forward in asking its why-questions; and it is this goal that, in their various ways, the Ideas of soul, world, and God express. *If* reason could complete its search, it would have to end with such concepts. Since experience, the field in which reason can successfully labor, is essentially open-ended, the search cannot be completed. But these Ideals can serve a *regulative* purpose, representing the *goal* toward which rational creatures like ourselves are striving. We want to understand *completely*.

Reason and Morality

We are not only knowers. We are also doers. So far we have seen Kant examining in his critical way our capacities for knowing. The critical investigation into knowledge looks at reason in its *theoretical* aspect; it is concerned with the *a priori* foundations

of mathematics and physics, together with the temptations of transcendent metaphysics. As we have seen, it uncovers space and time as pure forms of intuition, the pure concepts (categories) that structure experience, and the Ideas. We are now turning to see what Kant has to say about our actions. The critical inquiry into action concerns reason in its *practical* aspect. It is concerned with the *a priori* foundations of morality.

Kant takes pains to distinguish his treatment from a common way to look at morality. We might think of morality as just one more empirical phenomenon to be understood. If we take this point of view, we examine what people *in fact* praise and blame, and what motivations (e.g., sympathy) explain these facts. To look at morality this way, Kant says, is to do "practical anthropology" (*G*, 2). This is the way Hume looks at morality.*

There is nothing wrong with studying practical life this way. But Kant is convinced that an empirical study of morality will miss the contribution of *reason* to practical life; and it will be impossible to find *the moral law*. All you will get is a collection of different, probably overlapping, practices or customs. No *universality* can be found this way; nor will the *necessity* that attaches to obligation appear.† (In fact, Kant is right about this; anthropology seems to reveal nothing but customs that vary from culture to culture. Compare the story told by Herodotus on p. 42, in the light of which he agrees with Pindar that custom—*nomos*—is "king of all." As you read Kant, you should be thinking about whether he succeeds in showing this saying to be a *mistake*.)

Kant, of course, wants to apply his Copernican revolution to practical life as well as theoretical. We need a *transcendental* inquiry into the foundations of our practical life to complement that into our theoretical life. Morality, he believes, is not just a set of practices in the phenomenal world. It has its

---

*To make sure you understand the contrast, look back at the way Hume thinks of his moral philosophy, pp. 360–363.
†For *universality* and *necessity* as marks of the *a priori* contributions of reason to experience, see p. 372. What goes for experience, goes for action, too.

foundation in *legislation by pure reason*. Morality, just as much as mathematics and natural science, is constituted in part by *a priori* elements originating in the nature of reason itself. Therefore it is necessary to work out

> a pure moral philosophy that is wholly cleared of everything which can only be empirical and can only belong to anthropology (*G*, 2).

In pursuing such a philosophy, Kant is engaged in nothing less than

> seeking out and establishing the supreme principle of morality (*G*, 5).

This is an ambitious aim. You can see that if Kant succeeds, he will have undercut the moral relativism that seems to be the result of restricting moral philosophy to empirical anthropology. He will have found a *criterion* of moral value that is *nonrelative*.

The Good Will

One way into such a "pure moral philosophy" is to ask whether there is anything at all that could be called *good* without qualification. Now there are many good things in the world.

> Intelligence, wit, judgment, and whatever talents of the mind one might want to name are doubtless in many respects good and desirable, as are such qualities of temperament as courage, resolution, perseverance. But they can also become extremely bad and harmful if the will, which is to make use of these gifts of nature and which in its special constitution is called character, is not good. The same holds with gifts of fortune; power, riches, honor, even health, and that complete well-being and contentment with one's condition which is called happiness make for pride and often hereby even arrogance, unless there is a good will to correct their influence on the mind (*G*, 7).

You can see Kant's line of argument. Money, for example, is surely something good, but it is not

good *without qualification*; it is good only if used well. Likewise, intelligence is surely good, but dangerous if put to bad use. Think of a healthy, wealthy, and smart terrorist!

> There is no possibility of thinking of anything at all in the world, or even out of it, which can be regarded as good without qualification, except a *good will* (*G*, 7).

Many earlier philosophers have suggested a connection between being a morally good person and being happy. Plato, for instance, argues that the just man *is* the happy man.* Kant, more realistic perhaps, disagrees. If happiness correlates (as Hobbes claims) with the satisfaction of desires, there is no guarantee that moral goodness will match perfectly with happiness. We can think of the image in Plato's *Republic* of the perfectly just man languishing in prison; it is just too hard, Kant seems to suggest, to imagine that he is also perfectly happy! There is a relationship, however.

> The sight of a being who is not graced by any touch of a pure and good will but who yet enjoys an uninterrupted prosperity can never delight a rational and impartial spectator. Thus a good will seems to constitute the indispensable condition of being even worthy of happiness (*G*, 7).

It may not in fact be the case that happiness correlates perfectly with a good will in this world. But it *should* be so; any "impartial spectator" will feel uneasy at the sight of some really rotten person who is really happy. Goodness may not guarantee happiness, but it seems to constitute the condition of *being worthy* of happiness, or of *deserving* it. And this opinion is reflected in common sayings, such as, "She deserves better."†

We cannot, then, solve the problem about the nature of *moral goodness* by inquiring (as Aristotle,

---

*See pp. 134–136. Plato is not the only one to pursue this tack. We find it in Aristotle (pp. 174–175), Epicurus (pp. 187–188), the Stoics (pp. 190–192), and Augustine (pp. 216–217).
†This connection between moral goodness and happiness is important for what Kant calls "rational religion." See p. 398.

Epicurus, and Augustine do) into happiness.* If the only thing good without qualification is a *good will*, we must examine that directly. So let us ask, What is a good will? And what makes a good will *good*?

We need first to clarify the notion of will. We will not go far wrong if we think of an *act of will* as a kind of internal command with a content of this kind: "Let me now do *A*!" But not every such imperative qualifies as an act of will. If I decide to do *A* on a whim, or because I want to, or for no reason at all, this will be acting from *inclination*, not from *will*. Only internal commands that come at the end of a process of rational deliberation qualify as acts of will. There is something peculiarly *rational* about will. In fact, it is not too much to say that *will is just reason in its practical employment*. Dogs and cats have inclinations, but only a rational being can have a will.† In its theoretical employment, the outcome of a process of reasoning is an indicative, descriptive statement (e.g., "Bodies fall according to the formula $v = 1/2 \, gt^2$"). When reason deliberates about practical matters, by contrast, the outcome is an imperative, a command, an act of will (e.g., "Let me now help this suffering person").

As this example makes clear, every act of will has a certain content. If we spell out the "*A*" in one of the will's commands, we get what Kant calls a *maxim*. Maxims are rules which express the *subjective intention* of the agent in doing an action. For instance, we might get maxims of the following sort: "Let me now keep the promise I made yesterday," or "Let me now break the promise I made yesterday."

We can think of Kant's moral philosophy as the search for a criterion for sorting maxims into two classes: those which are morally OK, and those which are not. If he can find such a rule (really a metarule, since it is a rule for deciding about maxims, which are themselves rules), he will have found "the supreme principle of morality."

Now we return to the question: what makes an act of will *good*? Kant first makes a negative point. It is *not the consequences* of a good will that make it

good. In determining what makes it good, we must altogether set aside what it accomplishes in the world.

> Even if, by some especially unfortunate fate or by the niggardly provision of stepmotherly nature, this will should be wholly lacking in the power to accomplish its purpose; if with the greatest effort it should yet achieve nothing, and only the good will should remain (not, to be sure, as a mere wish but as the summoning of all the means in our power), yet would it, like a jewel, still shine by its own light as something which has its full value in itself (*G*, 7–8).

If Jane acts out of a truly good will, our estimation of her moral worth is unaffected even if an uncooperative nature frustrates the intended outcome. Her will "sparkles like a jewel," even if the action it produces goes wrong.

But this just raises the question with more urgency. What is such a good will? If a good will cannot be defined by anything external to it, something about *the willing itself* must make it good. Now we have seen that every act of will has an intelligible content, expressible as the maxim of that act. Only the maxim, in fact, differentiates one act of will from another. So a good will must be one with a certain kind of maxim. But what kind?

Here we have to distinguish the *form* of a maxim from its *content*. The content of a maxim always refers to some outcome, such as keeping a promise or helping someone in need. But since we must abstract from all outcomes to evaluate its goodness, it is clear that a good will cannot be defined in terms of content. So something about the *form* of a maxim must make it morally OK or not OK. What could it be?

Kant finds a clue in the concept of *duty*. We act out of a good will when we try to do the right thing. In trying to do what is morally right, we do not have our eyes on some advantage to ourselves, but only on the rightness of the action.* We want nothing else but to do our duty. And what is duty?

---

*For another view on this issue, see the utilitarians, Chapter 23.
†Contrast this notion of will with that of Hobbes, p. 333.

*In T. S. Eliot's play, *Murder in the Cathedral*, Thomas Becket, the archbishop of Canterbury, is meditating about his possible martyrdom. He says, "The last temptation is the greatest treason:/To do the right deed for the wrong reason." A very Kantian sentiment.

Duty is the necessity of an action done out of respect for the law (*G*, 13).

Duty and law go together. Unless there is a law, there can be no duties. The law tells us what our duties are. The law says, "You *must* do *A*"—the "must" expressing the "necessity" Kant refers to. If an action is done out of a good will, then, it is one that has a peculiar motivation: "respect for law." What law? The moral law, of course. But what does that law say? The answer to this question is the heart of Kant's moral philosophy. But we are not quite ready for it yet.

Let us note that actions can be motivated into two quite distinct ways. We often act out of desires of various kinds. These are the kinds of motivations that Hobbes and Hume recognize.* Kant groups all these motivations under *inclinations*. But he recognizes one other motivator: *respect for law*. This is a purely rational motivation, quite different from and possibly opposed to even the strongest desire. For Kant, unlike Hume, reason is not just the slave of the passions. Like Plato, Kant thinks that reason can *rule*, can motivate us to override and control the desires.†

On the assumption that rational respect for law can motivate persons to do their duty, we can classify actions in four ways:

1. *As done from inclination, but contrary to duty:* I do not repay the ten dollars I borrowed because my friend has forgotten about it and I would rather keep it.
2. *As done from calculated self-interest, but according to duty:* Common proverbs, such as "Honesty is the best policy," often express this (partial) overlap of prudence and morality.
3. *As done from a direct inclination, but according to duty:* If I act to preserve my life out of fear, or am kind simply because I am overwhelmed with

pity, I am doing the right thing, but not *because it is right*.
4. *As done from duty, even if it runs contrary to inclinations:* I keep my promise to take my children on a picnic, whether I want to or not.

Only the last is a case of acting from a good will.

We have an answer, then, to the question about what makes a will good. It is not the outcome nor the particular content of the maxim implicit in it. We act from a good will when we act out of a sense of duty, doing what is right solely because it is right, from respect for the moral law. Only such acts have true moral worth.

The Moral Law

We now need to know what the moral law says. We already know that we cannot discover it by empirical investigation; the most we can get that way is anthropology—a description of the rules people *do* live by. We cannot get rules they *ought* to live by.* At best one might be able to cite examples to imitate. But, Kant says,

> worse service cannot be rendered morality than that an attempt be made to derive it from examples. For every example of morality presented to me must itself first be judged according to principles of morality in order to see whether it is fit to serve as an original example, i.e., as a model. But in no way can it authoritatively furnish the concept of morality. Even the Holy One of the gospel must first be compared with our ideal of moral perfection before he is recognized as such (*G*, 20–21).

If there is going to be a moral law, its origin must be independent of experience. It must be *a priori*; it must be an aspect of practical reason itself.

In order to understand the content of the moral law, as a rule guiding actions, we need one more distinction. Kant distinguishes two kinds of *imperatives*:

---

*For Hobbes, you will recall, desire for pleasure and aversion to pain are the sole motivators. Hume adds a nonegoistic source of action in sympathy; but this, too, is simply a passion. See pp. 332 and 363.
†See pp. 360–361 for Hume's views of passion and reason. Plato's opposed views are discussed on pp. 129–130.

---

*Note that once more Kant is trying to solve a problem that Hume poses. He is trying to answer the question, Where does the "ought" come from? Review Hume's famous challenge on pp. 362–363.

1. An imperative is *hypothetical* when it has this form: "If you want *x* in circumstances *C*, do *A*."

There are several familiar kinds of these hypothetical imperatives.* Kant distinguishes two types:

1a. *Technical* imperatives, such as those of medicine and engineering (e.g., if you want to cure a patient with these symptoms, use this drug); these Kant calls *rules of skill*.

1b. *Pragmatic* imperatives, such as advice about how to be happy; "Dear Abby" is filled with examples; Kant calls these *counsels of prudence*.

2. An imperative is *categorical* when it has this form: "Do *A* (in circumstance *C*)."

Note that there is no reference to your wishes, wants, desires, ends, or goals in a **categorical imperative**. This is what it means to call it "categorical." Given that you are in *C*, it simply says, "Do *A*." It is not "iffy."

If the moral law expresses our duty and if there is something necessary about our duty, then it seems the moral law must be *categorical*. Hypothetical imperatives are not necessary; they apply to you only if your wants are those specified in the if-clause. If you don't want to build a bridge, then the technical imperatives of engineering get no grip on you. But the moral law applies regardless of your wants.

We can sum up in this way. The moral law must

- Abstract from everything empirical
- Make no reference to consequences of actions
- Be independent of inclinations
- Be capable of inspiring respect

Now if we examine hypothetical imperatives, we find that they one and all

- Make reference to empirical facts
- Concern consequences of actions
- Express our inclinations
- Inspire, at most, approval, not respect

Therefore, the moral law must be a categorical imperative.

We are getting close. The moral law is a rule for choosing among maxims. It is supposed to be a sorting device, separating the morally acceptable maxims from those not acceptable. Since all empirical content must be left behind, it cannot refer to the *content* of maxims. So it must refer to their *form*. As an imperative, it has the character of law; and the essential feature of a law is that it has a *universal* form.*

> Hence there is only one categorical imperative, and it is this: Act only according to that maxim whereby you can at the same time will that it should become a universal law (*G*, 30).

Kant has reached his goal: "the supreme principle of morality." This is the first formulation of the famous categorical imperative. Note several features of this rule:

a. It is clearly synthetic; no contradiction is produced by denying it.
b. It is clearly *a priori*; it has no empirical content.
c. It is therefore an example of pure reason at work—this time legislating for actions.

If pure reason in its theoretical employment provides principles according to which things *do in fact happen*, we can now see that in its practical employment pure reason provides a principle according to which things *ought to happen*.

---

*Hypothetical imperatives, when they function as the conclusions of arguments, are instances of reason being "the slave of the passions." (See Hume, p. 361.) They tell you how to get what you want.

*Think of laws in science; if a proposition is claimed to be a law, but a counter-instance is found, we conclude that it is not a law after all—because it does not hold universally. Review what Kant says about universality and necessity being the criteria for the *a priori*. (See p. 372.)

Let us see how it works. You are considering, let us suppose, making a promise; but you have in mind not keeping it if it runs counter to your inclinations. The maxim of your action might be expressed this way: "Let me make this promise, intending not to keep it if I don't want to."

How does the categorical imperative get a grip on this? It tells you that this is a morally acceptable maxim only if you can *universalize* it. To universalize a maxim is to consider the case in which *everyone* acts according to it: "Let everyone make promises, intending not to keep them if they don't want to."

And now the question to ask is, Could this be a universal law? It could not; for if everyone acted according to this rule, no one would trust others to keep their promises. And if no one ever trusted others to keep a promise, the very meaning of promising would vanish. Saying "I promise" would become indistinguishable from saying "Maybe." So your original maxim is not one that can be universalized; you cannot will that everyone should act on the principle you are considering for your own action. And it must be rejected as an acceptable moral principle.

There is only one categorical imperative, but Kant thinks it can be expressed in a variety of ways. One of the most interesting makes use of the notion of an *end in itself*. All our actions have ends; we always act for the sake of some goal. If our end is one prompted by desire, the end has only *conditional value*. That is, it is worth something *only* because someone desires it. Diamonds have that sort of worth. If no one wanted them, they would be worthless; and how much they are worth depends exactly on how much people want them (taking a certain supply of them for granted). All these ends are relative, not absolute.

> But let us suppose that there were something whose existence has in itself an absolute worth, something which as an end in itself could be a ground of determinate laws. . . .
> Now I say that man, and in general every rational being, exists as an end in himself and not merely as a means to be arbitrarily used by this or that will (*G*, 35).

Rational beings—including extraterrestrial rational beings, if there are any—are different from the ends that have worth only because somebody desires them. How could they fail to be different? They are the *source* of all the relative values there are. How could they just be another case of relative values? They are ends in themselves. In terms of value, then, there are two classes of entities:

- Things, which have only a *conditional* value, which we can call *price*; their value is *relative* to the desires for them and correlates to their *use* as *means* to the satisfaction of those desires.
- Persons, who have *absolute* worth, which we can call *dignity*; their value is *not relative* to what someone desires from them; they have value as *ends* and command *respect*.

In terms of this distinction, the categorical imperative can be stated this way:

> Act in such a way that you treat humanity, whether in your own person or in the person of another, always at the same time as an end and never simply as a means (*G*, 36).

Don't treat persons like things. Don't *use* people. Don't think of others simply as means to your own ends. These are all admonitions in the spirit of Kant's categorical imperative. You can see that this form of it is merely a variant of the first (universalizing) form: by restricting the maxims of your own actions to those to which *anyone* could subscribe (the first form), you are according to *all* the dignity of personhood (the second form) by respecting them as equal sources of the moral law.

Autonomy

The moral law as categorical imperative arises from pure reason. It imposes itself imperiously upon me, saying: Do this—choose your maxims according to whether they can be universalized. But since it is a principle of reason, and I am a rational being, I am not just subject to it. I am also the *author* of it.

It expresses my nature as a rational being. And we are led naturally to

> the idea of the will of every rational being as a will that legislates universal law. . . .
>
> . . . The will is thus not merely subject to the law but is subject to the law in such a way that it must be regarded also as legislating for itself and only on this account as being subject to the law (of which it can regard itself as the author) (*G*, 38).

And this leads Kant to the momentous conclusion that with regard to the moral law each of us is **autonomous**. We each give the law to ourselves. A law to which I cannot give my rational consent according to the universalization principle cannot be a *moral* law.

There are nonmoral (and even immoral) laws; Kant calls them *heteronomous*—having their source outside ourselves. What is characteristic of such laws is that I have no intrinsic reason to obey them. If I find them binding on me, it is only because they appeal to some interest (perhaps by threatening punishment for violations). But with respect to the moral law, no such appeal to the inclinations can work. Not even promises of heaven or threats of hell are relevant. With respect to the moral law, I do not feel bound from without, for the moral law expresses my inmost nature as a rational creature.

As an autonomous legislator of the moral law, I find myself a member of a community of such legislators. This community Kant calls a *realm of ends*.

> For all rational beings stand under the law that each of them should treat himself and all others never merely as means but always at the same time as an end in himself. Hereby arises a systematic union of rational beings through common objective laws, i.e., a kingdom that may be called a kingdom of ends (certainly only an ideal), inasmuch as these laws have in view the very relation of such beings to one another as ends and means.
>
> A rational being belongs to the kingdom of ends as a member when he legislates in it universal laws while also being himself subject to these laws. He belongs to it as sovereign, when as legislator he is himself subject to the will of no other (*G*, 39–40).

Note that Kant here calls certain laws "objective." These laws contrast with "subjective" rules. A subjective rule or maxim is one that may differ from person to person. The reason is that they are *relative to inclination*. Consider the maxim, "Let me run six miles per day." Is that a good maxim? We would all agree that this depends on what you *want*; it is a good maxim for someone who wants eventually to compete in a marathon. But it is a poor maxim for someone who wants only to maintain basic fitness. Such maxims are neither objective nor universal; they are implicitly hypothetical, relative, and personal. There are many such personal maxims, and Kant has no objection to them.

But, if Kant is right, not all rules are relative and subjective like this. A law legislated by the rational will according to the categorical imperative is "objective." He means it is a law that *any rational being* will agree to. The moral law for me is the moral law for you. Any maxim approved by the universalization test will be the same for all; it is simply not acceptable unless it is fit to be a *universal* law, one that each rational being can legislate for itself. Reason is not, despite Hume, just the "slave of the passions"; reason is the source of a criterion for judging the passions. The inclinations may propose actions, together with their maxims. But reason judges which are acceptable. Reason is legislative. It is autonomous. And its laws are *absolute*.*

We can come back at last to the notion of a good will, the only thing good without qualification. We now see that a good will is governed by the categorical imperative; a good will is one that can be universalized. We can even imagine a will so much in harmony with reason that all its maxims are in natural conformity with the moral law. Such a will Kant calls a "holy" will. A holy will would never feel that it *ought* to do something it didn't want to do, because it would always want to do what was right. It would never feel duty to be a constraint.

---

*Note that in a certain way Kant again agrees with Hume, this time about the fact/value distinction. There are no values just in facts per se. Value comes from the side of the subject. But it does not follow that it is always bestowed by desire or passion; reason has a crucial role that provides a kind of objectivity in morality parallel to the objectivity in science.

Though we can imagine such a will, we must confess that it is not the will we have. We experience a continual struggle between inclination and duty. So a good will is something we may aspire to, but we can never be completely confident that we have attained it.

> We like to flatter ourselves with the false claim to a more noble motive; but in fact we can never, even by strictest examination, completely plumb the depths of the secret incentives of our actions. For when moral value is being considered, the concern is not with the actions, which are seen, but rather with their inner principles, which are not seen.
>   . . . if we look more closely at our planning and striving, we everywhere come upon the dear self, which is always turning up, and upon which the intent of our actions is based rather than upon the strict command of duty (which would often require self-denial) (G, 19–20).

As Aristotle said, "It is a hard job to be good."*

Freedom

Finally, we need to situate Kant's moral theory in the general critique of reason, to see how the moral law fits with his epistemology and metaphysics. The notion of *autonomy* is the key. An autonomous will must be one that is *free*.

> The will is a kind of causality belonging to living beings insofar as they are rational; freedom would be the property of this causality that makes it effective independent of any determination by alien causes.
>   . . . freedom is certainly not lawless, even though it is not a property of will in accordance with laws of nature. It must, rather, be a causality in accordance with immutable laws, which, to be sure, is of a special kind. . . . What else, then, can freedom of the will be but autonomy, i.e., the property that the will has of being a law to itself? The proposition that the will is in every action a law to itself expresses, however, nothing but the principle of acting according to no other maxim than that which can at the same time have itself as a universal law for its object. Now this is

precisely the formula of the categorical imperative and is the principle of morality. Thus a free will and a will subject to moral laws are one and the same (G, 49).

Freedom, Kant says, is not sheer randomness; nor is it whim or caprice; nor is it arbitrariness. Freedom is giving the law for one's action to oneself. It is not, therefore, lawless. Freedom is in fact a kind of causality—a power of producing actions according to a rule that one legislates for oneself. But this is just autonomy. And autonomy is the principle of a rational will free from the influence of the inclinations. Such a will is bound only by the requirement of lawfulness itself—i.e., by universality, by the categorical imperative. So "a free will and a will subject to moral laws are one and the same."

But this presents a problem. If all events in the world can be experienced only under the category of causality (as we saw in Kant's treatment of theoretical understanding), what *room* is there for freedom? Kant's Copernican revolution comes to the rescue. Recall the distinction between phenomena and noumena. What is impossible in the phenomenal world may be quite possible in the noumenal. We seem to have two standpoints from which to consider ourselves.

Phenomenally	Noumenally
I *appear* to myself as an *object* in the world.	I *am* the unknown *subject* to whom the world appears.
All objects are organized by the *a priori* category of causality.	The category of causality does not apply.
I appear to act under causal laws that I do not legislate for myself (heteronomy).	I may act under rational laws I legislate for myself (autonomy).
I do not appear to be free.	I am free, in that I can act on laws that I give to myself.

*See p. 177.

Since Kant insists that the world of things-in-themselves is strictly unknowable, the propositions on the right cannot be known to be true. (Knowledge is restricted to how things appear, under the pure intuitions of space and time and the categories.) But we can know that they are *possibly* true. We do know that there is a world of things-in-themselves; and we know that our categories do not apply to them, only to how they appear to us. So from a theoretical point of view, Kant's Copernican revolution creates room for autonomy, freedom, and the moral law.

As agents, Kant says, engaged in practical life, we

> cannot act in any way other than under the idea of freedom. . . . Reason must regard itself as the author of its principles independent of foreign influences. Therefore as practical reason or as the will of a rational being must reason regard itself as free (*G*, 50).

When we make a decision, we cannot help but think that it is up to us, in our freedom, to decide. And, if Kant is right, nothing in science—empirical psychology, for instance—could show us that we are wrong. For experimental science can only deal with the world as it appears, not with the world as it really is.

This does not constitute a *proof* of freedom, as Kant clearly recognizes. Freedom is a mere Idea, an Idea of Pure Reason. But we ought now to recall Kant's saying that he "found it necessary to deny *knowledge*, in order to make room for *faith*" (*CPR*, 29). Faith in freedom is one thing he has in mind—not an arbitrary faith, but one founded in that practical necessity to think of ourselves "under the idea of freedom." It is not knowledge; but it is a rational faith. And the distinction between things as they are in themselves and things as they appear to us is the metaphysical foundation that allows this freedom to be possible. We *must assume* we are free; and we *may do so*. The assumption of freedom is a *practical necessity* and a *theoretical possibility*.

Morality is the foundation of other articles of a rational faith as well. We can think of morality as giving us the command: *"Do that through which thou becomest worthy to be happy"* (*CPR*, 638). As we have seen, being worthy of happiness does not guarantee that we will be happy, at least not in the world of our experience. Yet goodness and happiness *ought* to go together. It wouldn't make good sense if we were urged by reason to qualify for a condition that would ultimately be denied to us. It seems that reason is telling us that we have *a right to hope* for happiness. The fact that we belong to the noumenal, purely intelligible, world opens up a possibility that it might be more than a mere hope.

For it to be more than a futile hope, however, it seems that a future life must be possible (since we see that goodness and happiness do not coincide in this life). It follows that we must believe in the immortality of the soul (which is, from the point of view of theoretical knowledge, a mere Idea of Reason). And we must also believe that a power exists sufficient to guarantee the eventual happiness of those who strive for moral goodness. This power, of course, is God (also, from the point of view of theory, merely an Idea).

> God and a future life are two postulates which, according to the principles of pure reason, are inseparable from the obligation which that same reason imposes upon us (*CPR*, 639).

So Kant rounds off his critical philosophy. Wisdom, Kant tells us, requires indeed a certain modesty about our rational powers—as both Socrates and Hume, in their different ways, insist. But our powers are adequate to do mathematics and empirical science, and they provide a sure and certain guide for our practical life. For the rest, faith and hope are at least not irrational. But *knowledge* is limited to the realm of possible experience. After the incisive skeptical probes of Hume, "that acute man," Kant has grounds to claim that he has indeed rehabilitated reason—but only within strict limits.

Kant's critical philosophy would have a profound influence on the course of subsequent philosophy. And, as we will see, aspects of it are still alive today.

Notes

1. References to Kant's works will be as follows:

   P: *Prolegomena to Any Future Metaphysics*, translated by Paul Carus, revised by James W. Ellington (Indianapolis: Hackett Publishing Co., 1977).

   G: *Grounding for the Metaphysics of Morals*, trans. James W. Ellington (Indianapolis: Hackett Publishing Co., 1981).

   CPR: *Immanuel Kant's Critique of Pure Reason*, trans. Norman Kemp Smith (New York: St. Martin's Press, 1956).

2. Joseph Butler, *Fifteen Sermons* (London: G. Bell and Sons Ltd., 1949), 23.

21

G. W. F. Hegel:
Taking History Seriously

Since early Greek times, it has been the ambition of those seeking wisdom to give a general account of the universe and our place in it. One after another, philosophers announce to the world that they have succeeded in solving the riddle. But each attempt, though it builds on preceding efforts and tries to correct their shortcomings, seems to raise new occasions for doubt. The persistent jabs of sophists and skeptics always find a target and keep generations of philosophers in business. Some assumptions, however, are taken for granted by most of these thinkers and by Western culture in general. We can set them out in the following way:

- There is a *truth* about the way things are.
- This truth is *eternal* and unchanging.
- This truth can, in principle, be *known* by us.
- It is the job of the *philosopher*, relying on reason and experience, to discover this truth.
- Knowing the truth about ourselves and the universe in which we live is *supremely important*, for only such truth can serve as a secure foundation on which culture can be built: science, religion, ethics, the state, and a good life for all.

As we have seen, both Hume and Kant argue for a severe limitation on these ambitions. Hume drives us toward a skeptical attitude regarding the powers of human reason. And Kant, though he rescues Newtonian science and offers us a rational morality, concedes that we can know things only as

they *appear* to us, structured by our senses and rational faculties. What we *really* are, and what reality is *in itself*, is completely and forever hidden from us.

Still, in one important respect, Kant accepts the assumptions common to most of the Western philosophical tradition: that there is a truth about the way things are and that this truth is eternal. He thinks he has found it. Kant's central truths, of course, focus on what it is to be rational. The structures of a rational mind are the same for all rational creatures (and so, of course, for all humans). They are unchanging over time—the same for ancients and moderns, primitives and enlightened philosophers. The receptive structures of Sensibility, the pattern-imposing categories of the Understanding, and the insatiable logical drive of Reason are the given features of mind, identical in every age and every place.

Nineteenth-century thinkers alter this picture and transform it in surprisingly far-reaching ways. Chief among them is Georg Wilhelm Friedrich Hegel (1770–1831), a German philosopher of encyclopedic range who is sensitive to the exciting changes surrounding him in his world. It will be worth spending a little time in setting the scene.

The French Revolution   July 14, 1789. A Paris mob storms the fortress-prison known as the Bastille, hated symbol of royal absolutism. Hegel is nineteen. Like youth all over Europe, he is enthralled.

The Revolution seems like a new start, an overthrow of the dead weight of centuries. Reason is triumphant over tradition. The people are in control.

It is true that this control turns into the Reign of Terror, that it spawns a series of wars, and that it leads to Napoleon's coup d'état and his assumption of the title of Emperor. But something deep and remarkable has happened, and Europe will never be the same again. Hegel imbibes the sense of history being made, of real change, of the possibility of progress toward a more rational society. And he never loses it.

> . . . it is not difficult to see that ours is a birth-time and a period of transition to a new era. Spirit has broken with the world it has hitherto inhabited and imagined, and is of a mind to submerge it in the past. Spirit is indeed never at rest but always engaged in moving forward. But just as the first breath drawn by a child after its long, quiet nourishment breaks the gradualness of merely quantitative growth—there is a qualitative leap, and the child is born—so likewise the Spirit in its formation matures slowly and quietly into its new shape, dissolving bit by bit the structure of its previous world, whose tottering state is only hinted at by isolated symptoms. The frivolity and boredom which unsettle the established order, the vague foreboding of something unknown, these are the heralds of approaching change. The gradual crumbling that left unaltered the face of the whole is cut short by a sunburst which, in one flash, illuminates the features of the new world (PS, 6–7).[1]

Hegel's references to the Revolution are obvious here, as is his sense of something new bursting into history. It is not, of course, absolutely new, any more than the new-born child appears from nothing. A long period of preparation marked by the people's increasing dissatisfaction has preceded it. Moreover,

> this new world is no more a complete actuality than is a new-born child; it is essential to keep this in mind. It comes on the scene for the first time in its immediacy or its Notion. Just as little as a building is finished when its foundation has been laid, so little is the achieved Notion of the whole the whole itself.

When we wish to see an oak with its massive trunk and spreading branches and foliage, we are not content to be shown an acorn instead (PS, 7).

Several crucial concepts are introduced in these two quotations, and it is important to get some preliminary understanding of them. The word translated "Spirit" is the German *Geist*. Scholars disagree about whether the best English equivalent is "Spirit," as this translator has it, or "mind." Hegel's use of *Geist* surely includes everything we mean by mind, but it has larger implications that allow Hegel to talk of the Revolution as Spirit breaking with past traditions and maturing as it moves forward in history. The term "Notion" is a translation of *Begriff* and is often rendered "concept." It is the term Kant uses for concepts, including the *a priori* concepts he calls categories. Sometimes I shall use "concept" where it seems appropriate. In this second quotation we can understand Hegel to be saying that the *concept* of a people united in "Liberty, Equality, and Fraternity" has come on the scene. But to achieve this "Notion" is not yet to achieve the *reality* of a society organized by those principles. That may take a long time, just as it takes a long time for the acorn to develop into the giant oak. Development, movement toward maturity, the sense of history going on—history with direction, purpose, aim—are central characteristics of Hegel's thought.

The Romantics Hegel lives at what is arguably the high point of German culture. Goethe is just twenty years his senior, Schiller ten. Hegel is a close friend of the poet Hölderlin. Beethoven is almost his exact contemporary. Novalis, Herder, the Schlegel brothers—all react against what they feel is the dry and cold rationality of the Enlightenment. In England it is the time of Wordsworth, Shelley, Keats, Byron, and Blake. They are called the Romantics. What do the Romantics stand for?

They champion imagination and feeling. They are suspicious of science and the picture of the world it provides, resisting "analysis" and the application of logical methods to living things. They agree with Kant that science and reason cannot reveal reality, but they look to other faculties to take us where reason falters: to intuition, to love, to passion.

The Romantics look back to classical Greece—once again! The inexhaustibility of that heritage is remarkable. There they see a somewhat idealized version of what they come to admire. It is the *unity* and *harmony* of Greek life that impresses them. As they see it, there is no conflict in these Greeks between reason and inclination, science and religion, rationality and feeling. Their morality seems to grow naturally out of their sense of being at home in the world and in their society.

This is what they hold against Kant: that he divides human beings, so that their reason is eternally at odds with their passions. For Kant, as we have seen, morally right actions cannot be motivated by inclination, passion, or feeling—not even the feeling of love. The only acts that are morally good, Kant tells us, are done out of that austere motivation of rational respect for the moral law. And this strikes the Romantics as an almost schizophrenic divisiveness. Are all of our impulses to be dismissed as of no account? Or worse—as evil? Many of them oppose the Christianity they are familiar with, setting its pessimism about sin and evil in humanity against what they perceive as the sunny, optimistic outlook of the Greeks. Kant's austere morality seems to them merely a remnant of a tradition that has outworn its usefulness. Some, including the young Hegel, explore the possibilities for a new folk religion that would express more adequately the ideals they hold dear.

Hegel cannot be classed as a Romantic; indeed, in some respects he criticizes the movement severely. As we'll see, he is himself a great champion of Reason. But this ideal of harmony within and among human beings he makes thoroughly his own. Nothing will satisfy him that leaves conflicts unresolved, that pits one aspect of a man against himself—or his neighbor.

Hegel's thought is notoriously difficult, and what you will read here is a considerable simplification. But in an introduction to philosophy, that is quite in order. The main themes and something of Hegel's contribution to the great conversa-tion should be intelligible. As you will surely see, the very idea of the history of philosophy *as* a Great Conversation owes much to Hegel. For him, this conversation *is* philosophy, and to study its history is to immerse oneself in the development of Reason itself.

Epistemology Internalized

Hume calls for the construction of a science of human nature, and Kant attempts a critique of pure reason. In each case, the motivation is to examine the "instrument" by which we gain knowledge in order to understand the nature and limits of our cognitive capacities. This seems, on the face of it, a very reasonable thing. But Hegel has an objection.

> In the case of other instruments, we can try and criticise them in other ways than by setting about the special work for which they are destined. But the examination of knowledge can only be carried out by an act of knowledge. To examine this so-called instrument is the same thing as to know it. But to seek to know before we know is as absurd as the wise resolution of Scholasticus, not to venture into the water until he had learned to swim.[2]

If we want to know whether a chisel is an adequate instrument, we can use our sense of touch as a criterion, or we can observe with our eyes how easily it parts the wood. But if we want to know whether our knowledge is an adequate instrument—whether it gets us the truth—we have only our own knowledge to depend on. For coming to know how (and what) we know is an *instance* of knowing, and cannot therefore *precede* it.

To resolve not to enter the water until one has learned to swim is absurd; you learn to swim by swimming. It is, Hegel assures us, just as absurd to think that before we can be sure that we know anything, we have to *know* what our abilities for gaining knowledge *are.*

If this criticism is correct, it completely invalidates the project of epistemology as it has been carried out since Descartes. This tradition holds that to know whether we can know anything, we have to *know* what knowing is. But to know what knowing is *presupposes* that we can know something. And so we are involved in a circle and cannot answer the question. It is obvious that Hegel is posing again the ancient problem of the criterion.* To decide whether a conscious state constitutes knowledge, we must have a criterion or standard to judge by. But by what criterion do we tell whether we have accepted the right criterion? How do we know that our "knowledge" about knowledge really is *knowledge*?

Hegel sees a second difficulty in Kant's project: it concedes too much to skepticism. Our aim in knowledge, at the outset, is to know the way things *really are*, to discover the truth about reality as it exists *in itself*. But if our reason imposes its categories on things, so that objects can exist only *for us*, then this ambition of knowing what is real and true must be given up. Kant bravely draws the consequence: all we can know is how things *appear* to us. The truth about reality is forever hidden from our sight. We can know phenomena, how things are for us. In addition, we know there are things-in-themselves; but *what* they are is forever beyond our powers to discover, since we would have to step outside ourselves and compare whatever ideas we had about them with the things themselves—without using any of the natural equipment of the rational mind! And that is not possible. But this leaves us skeptical about things-in-themselves.

Some of Kant's successors find this unsatisfactory—indeed, self-contradictory. To claim to know that there are things-in-themselves but to deny that we can know anything about them does seem self-undermining. If we don't know anything about them, how do we know there are such things? Hegel agrees with this criticism and works out an alternative view in which the distinction between consciousness and its objects is a distinction *internal* to consciousness. This is a difficult notion, but a crucial one. Let us see if we can understand it.

Amazingly, Hegel thinks he can solve both problems at once: the problem of the criterion and the problem of how we can gain knowledge of things-in-themselves. The key to his solution is the idea of *development*. As long as we think of a mind as *one* complete and finished entity and that which we intend to comprehend as a *second* complete and finished entity, there can be no solution to these problems. As long as subject and object are thought to be inherently unrelated, there can be no guarantee that they will correspond, and skepticism always looms large. Descartes does not defeat it, Hume resigns himself to it, and Kant cultivates the garden of phenomena in the midst of a vast sea of unknowables. What Hegel proposes to show is that consciousness moves through *stages* (he sometimes calls them "moments"), that it does this with a kind of *necessity*, driven by clear inadequacies at each stage, and that we can "watch" as it develops itself from the simplest and most inadequate consciousness to one that is completely adequate to its object. To "watch" in this way is to do what he calls **phenomenology**—to engage in an attempt to discern the *internal dialectic* through which consciousness moves toward ever more satisfactory relations with its objects.* Phenomenology of mind (or of Spirit) takes consciousness itself as a phenomenon; it tries to set out the *logos* of this phenomenon—its logic or internal rationale.

I have several times used the word "internal." This needs to be explained. You can see the significance of what Hegel is doing by comparing it to our "ordinary" way of thinking. For most of us, knowledge (if we think of it at all) is a certain state of mind that *represents* or *corresponds* to some object external to it. I have this idea that my bicycle is in the garage. That is one thing. I also have this bicycle. That is a second thing. These two things, idea and object, seem quite independent of one another and can vary independently.† That is why knowledge is a problem. I can believe my bicycle

---

*For earlier discussions of this problem, see Sextus Empiricus, pp. 195–197, Montaigne, p. 278, and Descartes, pp. 290–291.

*For the connection between dialectic and truth in Socrates and Plato, see pp. 62 and 117–118.
†Again we note the key elements of the representational theory. See pp. 294–295.

is in the garage when in fact it has been stolen. I believe something false about the bike; I am in error and do not have the truth. In the possibility of this discrepancy we have the origins of skepticism.*

Notice, though, that every time we are aware of an object, we take it *really to be* (in itself) what it *seems to be* (for us). As long as we are satisfied in our contemplation of this object, no dichotomy between what it really is and how it appears to us arises in our consciousness. Our concept (or Notion) of the object coincides perfectly with the object. But then how does the idea of *appearance* ever arise? How does the idea of how something *is for us* ever get distinguished from the idea of what it *is in itself*? Hegel argues that this *can* happen because consciousness is conscious not only of the object but also of itself (as related to the object); and it *does* happen whenever we become aware of some discrepancy between our "knowledge" of the object and our "experience" of the object.

> For consciousness is, on the one hand, consciousness of the object, and on the other, consciousness of itself; consciousness of what for it is the True, and consciousness of its knowledge of the truth. Since both are *for* the same consciousness, this consciousness is itself their comparison; it is for this same consciousness to know whether its knowledge of the object corresponds to the object or not (*PS*, 54).

The crucial phrase here is this: "both are *for* the same consciousness." The *object* and our *awareness of that object* are *given together*—in the same consciousness! This is why Hegel thinks a critique of knowledge can be *internal* to consciousness and why it can proceed by means of phenomenology. The comparison between concept and object is made by the same consciousness that is aware of both. The object of consciousness is not, never has been, and *could not be* some completely independent thing-in-itself. Every object, indeed, every *conceivable* object, is an object *for a subject*. The

slogan "no object without a subject" expresses the key idea in what is called **idealism**. We shall discuss this view further below.

What we discover if we just "watch" consciousness at work is that it reveals—by itself, and with a certain kind of inevitability—the discrepancies between its own awarenesses and its objects. It corrects itself to make its awareness more adequate to the object; but in changing itself, it finds that the object has not stayed put but has changed correspondingly. And what the object was previously taken to *be* is now seen only to *appear* to be. Its former status as thing-in-itself (a status it had only because the former consciousness *ascribed* that status to it) is now withdrawn, and it is now seen as having been only an object *for us*. Thus arises the distinction *within consciousness* between appearance and reality, that very distinction we naively (together with Kant and almost all previous philosophers) thought had to exist between the realm of consciousness as a whole and something entirely independent of consciousness.

As an example, think of the way human consciousness is related to "the rising of the sun" before and after Copernicus. Before Copernicus, we *saw* the sun rise and move across the sky. But then our theory changed, and with it our world. What we now see is the *apparent rising* of the sun. In our naive moments we may still be deceived, but we now know that it *really* is we ourselves who are moving.

Phenomenology is just following out the dialectic of these mutually dependent changes in object and concept.

> Consequently, we do not need to import criteria, or to make use of our own bright ideas and thoughts during the course of the inquiry; it is precisely when we leave these aside that we succeed in contemplating the matter in hand [knowledge] as it is *in and for itself* (*PS*, 54).

There is no need for us philosophers to come up with the criterion for knowledge. The problem of the criterion is in process of solving itself. Nor should we despair because it seems we cannot

---

*You should review Descartes' first *Meditation* at this point. It is the classic modern source for the way skeptical problems arise. Note that it all depends on the absolute independence of idea and object.

compare our thoughts with their objects and test definitively for their correctness. In examining its own adequacy, consciousness is continually engaged in such comparison and testing; "all that is left for us to do is simply to look on" (*PS*, 54). Hegel claims that by pursuing philosophy this way, by simply "looking on," we will see the criterion for knowledge develop naturally and necessarily *from within consciousness itself*; consciousness corrects itself.

Hegel's *Phenomenology of Spirit* can be thought of as a kind of biography of consciousness, the story of its development toward maturity. As consciousness develops, it grows ever more adequate to its object (and its object to consciousness), until at the end we discover a stage that deserves to be called **absolute knowledge**. At this point there will be no more discrepancy between reality and the knower; what there is will *be* what it is *known to be*; and what we *know* will correspond perfectly to *what there is*—because there has been a long process of mutual adjustment of each to the other. At that point Reason will be satisfied, because it will see that *what is real is what is rational, and what is rational is the real.*

> The series of configurations which consciousness goes through along this road is, in reality, the detailed *education* of consciousness itself to the standpoint of Science (*PS*, 50).

There is an ambiguity in the way I have presented Hegel to this point, but it is an ambiguity present in Hegel's thought. Is this development to be thought of as a series of stages within the life of *each human consciousness*, as it matures toward adequacy? Or is it to be regarded as a historical process, through which the *human race* travels from stages of primitive culture to the most advanced science, religion, and philosophy? The answer is that it is both. And in some sense it is a *logical* progression as well. The reason is to be found in the concept of Spirit. Individuals are manifestations of Spirit. But so are civilizations and cultures. And throughout all, Hegel holds, there is present the World Spirit, which develops in and through

individuals and cultures toward self-knowledge, rationality, and freedom. But of this, more later.

So far this is all rather abstract. We need to look at several examples. Let us begin where Hegel does in his book, *Phenomenology of Spirit*, with the simplest sort of knowledge—what he calls **sense-certainty**.*

Think of the simple presence of some object to your consciousness, e.g., the paper on which this sentence is written. Now, as Hegel says, you have to be very careful here. You may now be *thinking* of this experience. But in the *consciousness* of the piece of paper there is no thinking going on. There is just the presence of the paper to your consciousness. You are just *sensing* the presence of the paper. The fact that there is no thinking involved—no use of concepts to characterize the paper—is crucial for the *certainty* of this kind of experience. It is a very basic, extremely elementary kind of experience—an experience of the sheer presence of something to consciousness without any "work" being done on it by the consciousness. This sort of consciousness is wholly *receptive*. It is like one of Hume's *impressions*. There seem to be no Kantian "conceptual filters" at work organizing, relating, and structuring the material. The knowledge is "unmediated" by any interpretive scheme of the mind which has it. That is why this kind of experience seems to exclude the possibility of mistake. Hegel calls this kind of experience *immediate*.

We, of course, are using language and quite sophisticated concepts in doing this phenomenology of sense-certainty. But we want to characterize it "from the inside," so to speak, as it experiences it-

---

*Philosophers have often looked to something like this to serve as the *foundation for knowledge*. It may be that you are deceived that there is a dagger before you. But, apparently, you cannot be mistaken that it is *as if* there were a dagger before you. How things *seem* to you, what you *sense* (as opposed to what objects you *perceive*), seems immune from doubt and so is fit to be a foundation. Recall what Descartes claims to be certain of even if his senses deceive him about external objects. Hume's impressions also play this role (p. 344). There are later examples as well, right into the twentieth century. If Hegel is right in his critique here, a lot of modern epistemology is simply based on a mistake.

self. So we must be careful not to import our external descriptions into that consciousness itself. What, then, is it like?" All we can say by way of description is that there is a *This* presented to an *I*. And perhaps, to make the "This" more clear, we can add that it is presented *Now* and *Here*. Sense-certainty aims to pick out and experience what philosophers have called a *particular* (the *This*) in its sheer particularity, without attributing any *universal* characteristics to it.* Sense-certainty does not know this page as white, or as dotted with black marks—or, for that matter, as a page. Such characterizations import interpretive concepts into the experience, but it is wholly bare of such notions. There is just that sheer presence in your visual field. (Take a minute to see whether this description does capture an elementary aspect of your current experience.)

But now we notice that this *I* might direct its attention elsewhere, and a new *This* is presented—a can of cola, perhaps. But the cola can be characterized by *This* just as well as the paper. And there is a new *Now* and *Here* as well. The "This," "Now," and "Here," however, have not changed; they just apply to a different object. But what this shows us is that these are themselves *concepts*; they are, in fact, universals. And they are among the *most universal* of all universals, since they can apply to *every* object.

Moreover, another consciousness might become aware of this piece of paper. In that case, there is another *I* involved. It is no less an "I" than the first. And this shows that the "I" is also a universal. Like the others, it is *universally* universal. And so it is essentially empty.† It reveals nothing at all about the *nature* of the I in question.

What does all this mean? We can observe, Hegel says, that this most fundamental kind of consciousness turns into its opposite. It seemed to be the most concrete, rich, dense, real kind of knowledge there is. It seemed to be "immediate," by which Hegel means uninterpreted, unconceptualized, and unmodified by any conscious activity. It seemed to be an apprehension of the pure particularity of things. But it turns out that this "knowledge" is the most bare, most abstract, most universal, and most empty of content imaginable.

> Because of its concrete content, sense-certainty immediately appears as the *richest* kind of knowledge.... Moreover, sense-certainty appears to be the *truest* knowledge; for it has not as yet omitted anything from the object, but has the object before it in its perfect entirety. But, in the event, this very *certainty* proves itself to be the most abstract and poorest *truth* (PS, 58).

What does such a consciousness *know*? It *cannot* say. But is knowledge that cannot be expressed really knowledge at all? Imagine a world in which the only consciousnesses that exist are instances of such brute awareness; there would be no classification, no characterization, no comparison, no relating of one thing to another, no narratives, no laws, no explanations, no remembrance of things past or expectations of things to come—and virtually no language! Consciousness could not even be aware of a tree *as a tree*, for that involves the application of the concept "tree" and a classification of it with like things. Would such a world qualify as one in which *knowledge* exists? Hegel, for one, is sure that it would not.

So sense-certainty, which seemed to be the most secure form of knowledge, immune from the ravages of doubt, turns out not to be knowledge at all. And consciousness is impelled to go beyond it. Note well: It is consciousness *itself* that is forced beyond this minimal stage. Indeed, in necessarily using the universal concepts of "This" and "I," it is already beyond this stage. *We* are not imposing this from the outside. We are not supplying some criterion according to which this stage is unsatisfactory.

---

*The distinction between particulars and universals goes back at least to Plato, who notes that some things have properties in common—squareness, redness, humanity, etc. These common features, Plato thinks, are (peculiar) things themselves; he calls them "Forms." (See p. 111.) Aristotle and the medieval philosophers call the common properties of things "universals." Their status has been a perennial topic of debate. Hegel has this part of the great conversation clearly in mind here.

†There are echoes here of Kant's critique of rational psychology. Review pp. 382–384.

There is an internal dialectic at work, forcing consciousness to recognize the inadequacy of sense-certainty and to move to a new level of sophistication. We are just "looking on."

Suppose that we "personalize" consciousness for a moment (as Hegel tends to do anyway) and think of it as having intentions and goals. We can then ask, What is it that "motivates" consciousness to develop beyond this primitive stage? Hegel answers this question in a somewhat peculiar, but characteristic, way. Consciousness, in its "attempt to be" simply sense-certainty, *negates itself*. In the stage of sense-certainty, it "intends" to be nothing more than a knowledge of what is immediately present to it. But, as we have seen, it fails. The insufficiency of this attempt is *displayed* to consciousness itself in its very attempt. It *cannot* be what it tries to be, since it necessarily interprets even this minimal experience in terms of universal concepts ("This," "Here," "Now," and "I"), which, moreover, are completely inadequate to capture the experience.

But, Hegel points out, this negation of itself as certain knowledge is not a kind of blank rejection. It is not equivalent to skepticism (which can be thought of as a *general* sort of negation of knowledge). It is a quite determinate and specific negation: the negation of the sufficiency of sense certainty for knowledge. And this drives consciousness not into skepticism, but into a quite determinate new form.

What consciousness has learned is that it cannot find the certainty of true knowledge by retreating to elementary beginning points.* So it has no other alternative but to plunge ahead, make use of concepts, interpret its experience, and hope that somehow a correspondence of subject and object lies in the direction of conceptual elaboration. If knowledge is to be possible, consciousness cannot be merely receptive, for what it has discovered is that any attempt to merely "register" what is present to it *already* makes use of universal concepts, but these are concepts so poor that *what* is being

sensed cannot be expressed. Mind *must* play a more active role.*

We can learn one more thing from this first bit of the dialectic of consciousness. Sense-certainty is negated. Its pretentions to knowledge are *false*. But when consciousness goes on to another stage, it will not leave the contents of sense behind, to start afresh. When consciousness begins to interpret in terms of richer concepts, it will interpret *precisely what has been negated*: the sense experience that does not itself suffice for knowledge. So the earlier stage is not lost; what is *true* in it is preserved and incorporated in the next level.

Hegel finds this dialectical pattern repeated again and again, both in the progress of consciousness toward Absolute Knowledge and in the sequence of stages the human race goes through in history. A "moment" develops until it displays its own inadequacy. It is then negated and supplanted by a second (as the universally universal supplants the purely particular in sense-certainty). Then a stage emerges that incorporates the valuable and true in each of these stages. That stage then begins to develop, and the process repeats itself.† It is this *internal* dialectic that he thinks will supply at last the criterion for knowledge and close off the possibility of skepticism.

We cannot here follow the immensely elaborate and complex dialectic Hegel displays for us. Let us instead sketch briefly the progress of the next few stages, then discuss more fully several of the most famous and influential of them.

The inadequacy of sense-certainty leads consciousness on to the stage Hegel calls

- *Perception*, in which objects are characterized using concepts (universals) that describe their properties. Perception's structure is consciousness of *things* that *have* these properties. But what is a thing? Is it a mere collection of the

---

*Compare Descartes' project of discovering a foundation in simple certainties and Hume's recommendation to trace ideas back to impressions.

---

*Here Hegel agrees with Kant's Copernican revolution and supplies an argument to back it up. Knowledge cannot be like the wax tablet that passively receives impressions from objects. The knower cannot help but play an active role in conceptualizing the object.
†Hegelians have often called these moments the *Thesis*, the *Antithesis*, and the *Synthesis*. Hegel does not often use these terms, but this triadic structure is common in his analyses.

properties? That hardly seems right, since it misses the *unity* of a thing. Is it then something lying behind all the properties? But then it becomes an unknowable *X*, since we know things by perception only in terms of their properties. And that can't be right either. This dilemma forces consciousness on to the next stage of

• *Understanding*, in which things are understood in terms of *laws*, as in Newtonian science. These laws are thought to express the *truth of things*—their inner nature or essence. They *explain* the properties we ascribe to things in perception and give us an account of the unity of things—of why a given thing has just the properties it does have. But in producing such explanations, consciousness is *active*, not merely passive. And in recognizing this contribution by itself, consciousness reaches the stage of explicit

• *Self-consciousness*.

What Hegel says here is justly famous; let's examine it more carefully.

Self and Others

There is, within the stage of self-consciousness, a dialectic that structurally resembles the one in sense-certainty. In a passage that is the despair of commentators, Hegel seems to suggest that the most basic form of self-consciousness is *Desire*. Why should this be? Any answer, in view of the obscurity of Hegel's text here, is somewhat speculative. But perhaps this is what he has in mind.

Consciousness faces a world of objects that is *other* than itself. Yet, in the stage of Understanding, it recognizes that the inner essence or "truth" of these objects (revealed in science) is its own work. So it really isn't *other* after all. And yet, obviously, it isn't just itself. It both *is* other and it *isn't*. Consciousness wants to resolve this unsatisfactory situation and it tries to do so by *incorporating the other into itself*. And that is the essence of desire: wanting to make what is other than oneself into one's own. In this way the previous dialectic of consciousness leads inexorably to Desire as the next development.

But Desire is not merely conscious; it is explicitly *self*-conscious. Think about what it is like to desire something. You say, "*I* want a million dollars." In the very expression of your desire, there is consciousness of self, of the *I*—and also of the fact that your self is not all there is. To be conscious of your *self*, you need to have a contrast. Desire provides that contrast in abundance. It is what you do not have, but want, that defines for you what *you* are!

Still, there is something incomplete about this stage of self-consciousness. We might put it this way. Desire reveals the poignancy of being *other* than the world revealed to sense, perception, and understanding. And so it is a form of *self*-consciousness. But it does not yet reveal this self as *being self-conscious*. All we have in desire is the disclosure of a difference between two poles, between oneself and the other, together with a project to close up the gap. But the *nature* of oneself is not yet clear.

Think of the way a child develops a consciousness of herself. At first there is a stage where no distinction is made between self and other. What breaks this seamless unity of the child's world is frustration—when something *desired* is not attained. She becomes aware of the difference between herself and Mama, between herself and the bottle, between herself and the teddy bear. But this is not yet full-blown self-consciousness, explicit consciousness *of herself as a self-conscious being*. This comes much later and requires—as Hegel is among the first to recognize—another self-consciousness with which to contrast herself.

Self-consciousness achieves its satisfaction only in another self-consciousness.

Self-consciousness exists in and for itself when, and by the fact that, it so exists for another; that is, it exists only in being acknowledged (PS, 110–11).

Self-consciousness is achieved, Hegel is telling us, only by being *recognized* as such by another self-consciousness. *Recognition* of a mutual sort between persons *creates* self-conscious beings. My self-consciousness exists "in and for itself" only insofar as it "exists for another." I cannot be *for myself* a self-conscious being unless I am acknowledged as such by another self-consciousness and *recognize* this acknowledgement. Self-consciousness is a *social* fact.*

But if Hegel is right, this mutual recognition is not an easy process. It is filled with conflict of the most desperate sort. It is a dialectical achievement that involves—as does all such dialectical progress—radical negation. How does this work? We can make Hegel's tortuous and abstract discussion more intelligible if we talk of two individuals, Jones and Smith.

Jones recognizes Smith as *like himself*—as a self-consciousness constituted by Desire. But this is not a happy recognition; for it means that in a certain sense Jones has "lost" himself; he recognizes himself now as an "*other* being"—for Smith. Who is Jones? He is what Smith takes him to be. Jones becomes conscious of himself as an object of Smith's Desire. Remember that Desire is an attempt to make one's own what is felt to be alien to oneself. The ominous aspect of this attempt can be brought out if we think in terms of *control*; to make something one's own is to bring it within the sphere of one's power to control it. Jones, naturally, resists this attempt on Smith's part to control his existence. And, on the other side, Smith equally feels himself to be simply an "other being" for Jones; he too resists this status.†

But this still does not bring out the full complexity of the situation. For although Jones wants to make Smith his own, and although he recognizes that Smith has a similar project, Jones recognizes that Smith "is equally independent and self-contained, . . . something that has an independent existence" which, therefore, Jones cannot simply utilize for his own purposes if Smith does not agree. "They *recognize* themselves as *mutually recognizing* one another" (*PS*, 112). So their consciousness of each other is not the same as their consciousness of their lawn mowers.

But at first this mutual recognition is necessarily inadequate. From each side the situation is this: one is the being doing the *recognizing*, and the other is the being *being recognized*. Look at it from the side of Jones, remembering that the same can be said for Smith's point of view. Jones recognizes Smith as both *like* himself and as *other* than himself. Smith (from Jones' point of view) is the one being recognized. But Jones cannot yet recognize Smith as a *pure* self-consciousness.* He sees him as an embodied, living individual: an *object* in the world, but one who (like himself) wants to control the *other*—i.e., to control him. Jones thinks:

- Smith is like me, an independent, self-conscious being.
- Smith is aware of me.
- Smith recognizes that I am aware of him.
- He realizes that *for me*, he is just another object in the world.
- Smith is constituted, like me, by Desire.
- Hence, Smith will not be content to leave me in my independence, since that will mean I may come to control him.

---

*Contrast this with the view of Descartes, who holds that it is quite possible that *he alone* exists (the specter of solipsism—see pp. 298–299). If Hegel is right, this individualism is simply *impossible*. Humans are *made* into self-conscious individuals, persons in the full sense, by their interactions with other human beings. No one is a self-made man.

†Kant's second formulation of the categorical imperative (p. 385) commands us to treat others as ends, not as means only. What Hegel is identifying here is an unavoidable tendency in self-conscious beings to treat each other *precisely* as means. Relations between the sexes often take this dialectical form, and complaints that someone is perceived only as a "sex object," or is being "used," get a natural interpretation in this Hegelian context. Hegel agrees, of course, with the rationality and rightness of Kant's imperative; but he is pointing out how difficult it is to achieve the state in which it is actualized.

---

*Hegel has a very strong sense of "self-consciousness" in mind here. Think of it like this. You can become conscious of your height and weight, but that is a minimal self-consciousness indeed. You can go farther and become aware of your inclinations, of your character, of your personality, of your thoughts. Indeed, for *any fact* about yourself, you could become conscious of it—make it into an *object* for yourself. So being self-conscious in this strong sense is engaging in an *absolute abstraction* from *all* the facts that make you the existing individual that you are, turning every facet of yourself into an *object* for yourself. To use the title of a recent book by Thomas Nagel, this is *The View From Nowhere* (New York: Oxford University Press, 1986). With this possibility of *pure* self-consciousness, Hegel tells us, *Spirit* first makes its explicit appearance in the dialectic.

- I had better not leave Smith in his independence, lest he control me.
- I must *kill* Smith, even if this means risking my life to do so.

Smith, of course, has exactly parallel thoughts. Once again, it is the unsatisfactory nature of a stage—the immediate self-certainty of Desire—that drives self-consciousness into the next. Desire produces conflict. Each consciousness is driven to *negate* the other, to control it, to turn it into a mere means for the satisfaction of its own *Desire.** And it is this negating that reveals to each consciousness its true nature as a *pure self-consciousness.* Why? Because each is willing to risk everything worldly—even his natural *life*—in the struggle for domination.

> Thus the relation of the two self-conscious individuals is such that they prove themselves and each other through a life-and-death struggle. They must engage in this struggle, for they must raise their certainty of being *for themselves* to truth, both in the case of the other and in their own case. And it is only through staking one's life that freedom is won; only thus is it proved for self-consciousness, its essential being is not [just] being, not the *immediate* form in which it appears, not its submergence in the expanse of life, but rather that there is nothing present in it which could not be regarded as a vanishing moment, that it is only pure *being-for-itself.* The individual who has not risked his life may well be recognized as a *person,* but he has not attained to the truth of this recognition as an independent self-consciousness (*PS,* 113–14).

Hegel's thought here is an extreme one. Spirit, which comes on the scene explicitly for the first time in self-consciousness, cannot *realize itself* (become an actuality) except in mutual recognition by independent and free self-conscious individuals. But such mutual recognition is hazardous and tricky; it involves the necessity of tearing oneself— and the other—away from everything immediate and merely natural. And the only proof of that is the willingness to confront death in the struggle to demonstrate that one is *not simply an object for another.*

But what happens next is a surprise. Suppose Jones wins the struggle and kills Smith. Has he achieved what he wanted? Not at all. For in eliminating Smith, he deprives himself of precisely that source of recognition that he needs to realize himself as a self-conscious being! He has shattered the mirror in which he might have discovered who he is. In some fashion (either in the course of history or in some dim way within each developing consciousness, or perhaps in both—Hegel does not make this clear), self-conscious individuals become aware of this self-defeating character of the life-and-death struggle. And the result is a compromise.

What happens is this: the stronger makes the weaker into his slave.* Let us imagine that Jones makes himself the master. Then he has, in relation to Smith, a very real independence and freedom; and he experiences Smith as recognizing that independence. Jones, then, exists *for himself* and has apparently achieved what he needs: the recognition of himself as a free and independent self-consciousness. But has he really? Oddly enough, he has not. For consider the consciousness of the slave. It is a *dependent* consciousness—unfree and subject to the will of the master. But such a consciousness is not fit to provide the recognition that the master needs to confirm himself as free and independent. That can only be given by another free and independent individual. From Jones' own point of view, Smith (his slave) is almost indistinguishable from a mere brute. What could "recognition" by such a creature *mean?* So the master does not win what he needs by enslaving the other, any more than he could win it by killing the other.

Consider the consciousness of the slave. It is completely at its master's beck and call. The slave must work at the master's bidding. Smith's work is not done for Smith's sake, but for the sake of Jones,

---

*There are echoes here of Hobbes' description of the state of nature. See again pp. 333–334.

---

*It is worth noting that ancient societies, including Greek, Roman, and Hebrew, were all slave societies. Indeed, as we know, slavery was not abolished even in America until relatively recently. Hegel's discussion here has a historical cast that the earlier, more purely epistemological studies lack.

who rules him. It would seem that Smith, too, has failed to achieve that self-consciousness that Spirit is driving toward. But again something odd happens.

Think of Smith's work. He is oriented toward things in the world. Suppose he is a cobbler; he takes leather and nails and *changes* them until they become shoes. He does this not to satisfy his own Desire, of course, but to satisfy the Desire of his master, Jones. But in working on the things of the world, he expresses himself; he *puts himself into the products of his labor*. These products exist independently of him; but he recognizes himself in them and so achieves in his *work* a kind of self-realization that is denied the master. He *objectifies* himself and so can recognize himself in what he produces. "I," he can say, "am the one who made this; this object reveals what I can do and who I am; I have put *myself* into this object." Thus he achieves a definite kind of self-consciousness. In the independence of these objects, of the products of his labor, he recognizes his own independence.*

But that is not all. In addition to this "positive moment" in his attainment of self-consciousness, there is a pervasive fear in the slave that constitutes a "negative moment."

> For this consciousness has been fearful, not of this or that particular thing or just at odd moments, but its whole being has been seized with dread. In that experience it has been quite unmanned, has trembled in every fibre of its being, and everything solid and stable has been shaken to its foundations. But this pure universal movement, the absolute melting-away of everything stable, is the simple, essential nature of self-consciousness, absolute negativity, *pure being-for-itself*, which consequently is *implicit* in this consciousness (*PS*, 117).

The fear of the slave, a kind of universal dread, drives him back into himself, distances him from the master and even from the things on which he works. The entire material world is "negated"; the slave in his fear says "no" to it all—and discovers himself as a pure self-consciousness. In this way, too, he becomes aware of himself as something *other* than everything else that exists. Moreover, he has objectively before him an example of self-consciousness in the master, although the master fails to experience himself that way (not having an independent consciousness in which to mirror himself). He becomes what the master can never become: a being who exists as an object *for himself*. He, rather than the master, is the bearer of Spirit in its progress toward new heights of development.

And yet all is not well in the self-consciousness of the slave. It recognizes itself in the products of its labor and it has an image of itself in the self-conscious independence of the master. But, as Hegel says, these two "moments" *fall apart*. They are not brought together in one unified self-consciousness. And the dialectical story must go on.

Stoic and Skeptical Consciousness

Hegel thinks that the next stage in the development of Spirit appeared first at a definite point in our historical past. After the death of the Greek city-states came the era of empires, first Alexander's, then, after a period of uncertainty, the empire of Rome. The vastness of the empire, its impersonality and bureaucracy, and the sheer weight of established institutions caused most people to feel helpless to shape their destiny in this world. In this context, Spirit, now acutely conscious of itself, withdraws from everything that it cannot control; in effect, it withdraws *into itself*, finding there an independence and freedom that is denied it in the hostile world.

This is the key idea in Stoic thought, which distinguishes *what is in one's power* from *what is not in one's power*; it identifies as in one's power such conscious states as "opinion, aim, desire, aversion."* These Hegel calls "thinking." Why? Note that with

---

*Some forty years later, Karl Marx would take up this dialectic of master and slave. For Marx, of course, it is not consciousness that is at stake, but real material life and well-being. He accepts Hegel's point that a man objectifies himself in his labor, and goes on to emphasize that if the product of a man's labor is not his own, if it belongs to another, then that man is alienated *from himself*. From this point arises his critique of capitalism. See "Marx: Beyond Alienation and Exploitation," in Chapter 22.

---

*See p. 190.

respect to absolutely any experience—pain, pleasure, boredom, etc.—the Stoic will ask, "Now, what shall I do about that? How shall I consider that? What opinion shall I have of it?" The *immediacy* of sensory experience is completely transcended, and the self-conscious Stoic must *think* about how to respond.* This reflective self is apparently in complete control of its own happiness, since it can always "negate" or consider *as nothing* anything that threatens it. Consequently, it experiences itself as perfectly free. The Stoic claims that his way of life produces both happiness and freedom.

> This freedom of self-consciousness when it appeared as a conscious manifestation in the history of Spirit has, as we know, been called Stoicism. Its principle is that consciousness is a being that *thinks*, and that consciousness holds something to be essentially important, or true and good only in so far as it *thinks* it to be such (*PS*, 121).

As you might have guessed by now, Hegel is not content just to *describe* the Stoic form of consciousness. He proposes to show that it, too, is one-sided and inadequate, that Spirit has not yet found a satisfactory resting place. His critique of Stoicism is that its form of self-consciousness is still too *abstract*.

> The freedom of self-consciousness is *indifferent* to natural existence and has therefore *let this equally go free*: the *reflection* is a *twofold* one. Freedom in thought has only *pure thought* as its truth, a truth lacking the fullness of life. Hence freedom in thought, too, is only the Notion of freedom, not the living reality of freedom itself (*PS*, 122).

The thought of the Stoic, Hegel tells us, frees him from "natural existence"; but by the same token, it lets natural existence "go free," too. Consequently, there is a lack of *reality* in the Stoic's freedom, and his much-prized thinking lacks "the fullness of life." That is why Hegel says the Stoic has only the

"Notion" (the concept) of freedom, not its "living reality." What is still required is that this concept be embedded in the Stoic's life, so that he does not *need* to abstract himself from it in order to find his happiness. The Stoic mode of life does have a certain "truth" to it; it is possible to withdraw into "pure thought." But this truth is a partial truth, an *abstraction* from what would be the whole truth about conscious existence. This truth—perhaps *the Truth*—lies in the unity of a life where that which conceptual, rational, reflective thinking declares to be valuable is *actually realized in natural existence*. And this the Stoic conspicuously lacks.*

Again, the road toward such unity is tortuous and indirect. Things have to get worse before they can get better. Consciousness has to *experience* itself as the negation of all reality. It is not enough, as with Stoicism, to realize that one *could* set the value of everything as naught. This stage must actually be lived through.

> *Scepticism* is the realization of that of which Stoicism was only the Notion, and is the actual experience of what the freedom of thought is. This is *in itself* the negative and must exhibit itself as such (*PS*, 123).

The skeptic actually *lives* this negation of the world by thinking; he *suspends judgment* about each and every claim concerning reality. Indeed, he actively uses the resources of thought to make this possible by constructing equally plausible arguments on each side of every question.†

But once again, this stratagem on the part of Spirit proves unstable. Notoriously, the skeptic needs to find a way to *live*. He cannot make judgments about the true, the real, and the good. So how is he to manage it? The standard skeptical line at this point is to "adhere to appearances," as Sextus Empiricus puts it, to "live in accordance with the normal rules of life, undogmatically, seeing that we

---

*Epictetus says, "Men are disturbed not by things, but by the view they take of things." And what view we take is something, he says, that is in our own control. It will be helpful to review the discussion of Stoicism in Chapter 12.

*It is worth comparing this critique of Stoicism with that of St. Augustine. See p. 245. Note also that Hegel's internal critique of Stoicism (that it splits man into two halves) is akin to the Romantics' critique of Kant (p. 403).

†For an example of the techniques of the skeptics, see p. 194.

cannot remain wholly inactive."* Hegel's analysis of this tactic lays it bare as a sham. Skeptical self-consciousness at one time

> recognizes that its freedom lies in rising above all the confusion and contingency of existence, and at another time equally admits to a relapse into occupying itself with what is unessential. . . . It affirms the nullity of seeing, hearing, etc., yet it is itself seeing, hearing, etc. It affirms the nullity of ethical principles, and lets its conduct be governed by these very principles. Its deeds and its words always belie one another (*PS*, 124–25).

In short, skeptical self-consciousness is mired deep in self-deception. Priding itself on its freedom, it becomes slave to the customs of the society in which it finds itself, whatever they happen to be. This purely accidental life cannot, Hegel is convinced, be the goal of Reason and Spirit.

Hegel's Analysis of Christianity

The next transition arises naturally—necessarily, Hegel would say—out of this unsatisfactory state.† Again, as Hegel sees it, something very interesting happens.

---

*See p. 197. For a modern version of the same principle, recall Montaigne's "defense" of Raymond Sebond and its outcome, p. 278. A somewhat similar pattern is found in David Hume; see p. 365.

†It is perhaps time to pause a moment and reflect. Recall that Hegel's strategy is to discover the criterion for knowledge *from within*. The dialectic we have been tracing can be thought of as a process of sloughing off one proposed but clearly unsatisfactory criterion after another. And by now the *goal* should be getting clearer, too, though the details still need to be filled in. Nothing will do but a state in which Spirit is not *alienated* from reality, but *identifies* with it, and can see *itself* expressed in whatever it knows to be real. One further aspect of this process needs to be noted. You can see that we have moved from a purely *theoretical* sense of knowledge to one that incorporates *the entire life* of a knower. (This correlates with the increasingly historical cast to the story Hegel is telling.) Hegel, for whom the Truth is always the whole, will be satisfied with nothing less: Reason governs *all*.

In Scepticism, consciousness truly experiences itself as internally contradictory. From this experience emerges a *new form* of consciousness which brings together the two thoughts which Scepticism holds apart. Scepticism's lack of thought about itself must vanish, because it is in fact *one* consciousness which contains within itself these two modes. This new form is, therefore, one which *knows* that it is the dual consciousness of itself, as self-liberating, unchangeable, and self-identical, and as self-bewildering and self-perverting, and it is the awareness of this self-contradictory nature of itself (*PS*, 126).

Spirit recognizes its split nature. And it recognizes the split as a duality *within itself*. It no longer identifies itself only with the thinking, rational side but incorporates into itself both of the opposed aspects. This, too, is a process that takes agonizingly long. Once again, things have to get worse before they can get better. This self-divided consciousness, aware nonetheless that it is *one*, Hegel calls the *Unhappy Consciousness*.* On the one side there is the experience of free and rational thinking, of pure universality, which nothing merely contingent or natural can touch. Hegel calls this the *Unchangeable*. On the other side, consciousness experiences itself as a changeable, unessential, "self-bewildering and self-perverting" particular individual, subject to the sheerest happenstance of accident. These two sides are "alien to one another" (*PS*, 127).

Under psychological pressure to resolve this dilemma, consciousness identifies itself with the Changeable and experiences the Unchangeable as "an alien Being," as *not itself* (*PS*, 127). The Unhappy Consciousness is essentially a *religious* consciousness; as you can see, Hegel has in mind the two poles around which Augustine's thought revolves: God and the soul.† But there is an obvi-

---

*Compare Augustine's flirtation with Manicheanism and the essential move in its rejection (pp. 213–214).

†Hegel's characterization of this stage as an *Unhappy Consciousness* brings to mind St. Paul's despairing cry in Romans 7: ". . . when I want to do the right, only the wrong is within my reach. In my inmost self I delight in the law of God, but I perceive that there is in my bodily members a different law, fighting against the law that my reason approves and making me a prisoner under the law . . . of sin." A quick review of Chapter 12 will be helpful at this point.

ously radical twist in Hegel's story. The Unchangeable (experienced as God) is not *actually* a being independent of an individual's consciousness; it only seems so. Actually, it is one *pole* of Spirit's consciousness of itself in this Unhappy stage of its dialectical development. And the desperately unhappy individual, cut off from the Unchangeable (God), does not *actually* exist independently; he only seems to. But it does really seem so! It is not an illusion to be brushed aside as trivial.

Christianity appears to Hegel as a subtle and ingenious construction on the part of Spirit to reunite what has been split. What is needed is supplied: a *Mediator*. This mediator must participate in both sides of the duality—i.e., he must be both God and man. The (supposed) actuality of this mediator demonstrates that *in principle* the two sides of Spirit—eternal and temporal, infinite and finite, Unchangeable and Changeable—are one. This, Hegel holds, is what the Christian doctrine of the Incarnation really means: Jesus as truly man and truly God manifests the unity of the Spirit. The believer participates in the nature of the Unchangeable through devotion, sacrifice, and thanksgiving and hopes for the completion of this process in the life to come. The Holy Spirit is the sign that the gulf can be bridged, that sinners can become saints, and *individuals* can participate in the life divine.*

So Hegel regards Christianity as expressing a truth, or at least a part of the truth. But it does so in mythological and imaginative forms. It takes philosophy—i.e., Reason—to understand its real significance.

---

*Is Hegel a Christian theologian, explaining "the true meaning of the faith"? Or is he an atheist, proposing a secular interpretation of a religious tradition he does not accept? As is characteristic with Hegel, it is hard to answer this question unambiguously. He is convinced that every stage of consciousness has its truth (as well as its falsity) and that what is true in it will be preserved in successor stages. But there *are* successor stages, which will do more justice to the phenomena than the earlier ones do. Christianity, for Hegel, is one necessary, fruitful stage in the history of Spirit. But it is no more than that. Marx and his followers will emphasize the aspect of surpassing religion and proclaim themselves atheists. Others—"liberal" theologians—will emphasize what is true and must be preserved. Kierkegaard takes offense at the whole notion that *finite individuals* could ever "surpass" the truth in Christianity. See Chapter 22.

Reason and Reality: The Theory of Idealism

Consciousness, by its own internal development, has now reached the stage of reincorporating its *other* into itself. It recognizes that what it took to be alien—the thing sensed and perceived, the world as understood by science, the object of desire and labor, the self-consciousness of the master and the dependence of the slave, the negatively valued world of Stoic and skeptic, and finally the projection of itself into the heavens as God—is all, it now sees, nothing but its own work. Wherever consciousness looks, it sees nothing but *itself!**

> In grasping the thought that the *single* individual consciousness is *in itself* Absolute Essence, consciousness has returned into itself (*PS*, 139).

Hegel calls this stage *Reason*. It will help to understand why if we think back to Kant. For Kant, Reason is the faculty that asks and tries to answer why-questions. You will remember that the propensity to ask such questions sets us off in a search for the "condition" that explains the subject we are asking about. Since we can always ask again, we find ourselves driven toward the Idea (a technical term, for Kant, you recall) of a condition that is *unconditioned*, that neither has nor needs any further explanation. (There are in fact three such Ideas: God, the soul, and the world in itself.) But in the realm of phenomena, nothing unconditioned can be found; and noumena are closed to our inspection. So Reason is a drive that must remain

---

*It may help here to remember the *beginning* of the dialectic. Our natural resistance to this conclusion, our conviction that consciousness cannot be *all* there is, has its basis in "sense-certainty"—in the apparent *brute-fact* character of sensation. It seems absolutely *not up to us* to determine what we sense when we open our eyes. And the sense of something independent of our awareness—something *other*, something *alien*—is very powerful. Hegel does not deny this. But, he asks you to consider that as soon as you try to say *what* it is that you sense, you are in the realm of concepts, interpretation, and reason. *What it is*—even this apparently independent fact—is relative to the consciousness that comprehends it.

forever unsatisfied. This is how Kant limits knowledge to make room for faith.*

But for Hegel there is no need for faith. His elaborate dialectic *from within* has, he thinks, covered all the possibilities that any consciousness could ever be aware of. And everywhere, absolutely everywhere, consciousness discovers *itself*; in every explanation of an *other*, it finds meanings, laws, truths, values it has itself supplied. It is true that there is process involved. But it is a process that consciousness now knows must have a close; for it knows that it—it, *itself*—is the *Unconditioned*. And that is why Hegel calls the stage in which this truth is recognized *Reason*. It is Kantian Reason with this difference: it can achieve its aim!

> Now that self-consciousness is Reason, its hitherto negative relation to otherness turns round into a positive relation. Up till now it has been concerned only with its independence and freedom, concerned to save and maintain itself for itself at the expense of the *world*, or of its own actuality, both of which appeared to it as the negative of its essence. But as Reason, assured of itself, it is at peace with them, and can endure them; for it is certain that it is itself reality, or that everything actual is none other than itself; its thinking is itself directly actuality, and thus its relationship to the latter is that of idealism. . . .
>
> Reason is the certainty of consciousness that it is all reality; thus does idealism express its Notion (*PS*, 139–40).

To put it in another typically Hegelian way, the *substance* of the world is a *subject* of consciousness!

This conclusion might seem to be outrageous. How could *I*, a "*single* individual consciousness," be *all reality*? Is this some sort of mysticism? Even if we grant Hegel's controversial claim that whatever I can be aware of is something I have constituted myself, *I* am certainly not conscious of *all reality*!

Two things can be said in Hegel's defense. First, his claim is to be understood only as the outcome of the entire dialectical story that has been told up to this point. It is not something that you in your

common sense should be expected to immediately assent to. Our feeling of outrageousness may be simply a manifestation of that stage of consciousness in which most of us mostly live; that may occupy a rather lowly rung on the dialectical ladder. Common sense may have its limits, and the question we need to address is this: How sound is the dialectical path that Hegel has sketched for us?

> . . . anyone who has not trodden this path finds this assertion incomprehensible when he hears it in this pure form—although he does as a matter of fact make the assertion himself in a concrete shape [i.e., the assertion is implicit in his behavior] (*PS*, 141).

What Hegel means by this last remark is that whenever we act, we implicitly *assume* that the world is intelligible, rational, and meaningful. We bank on it. But to do that is to "make the assertion" that it is not alien to Reason—that the Reason in it is the same Reason as is in us. We are all, he seems to say, *practical* idealists, whether we admit it or not.

The second reply has to do with the *subject* of consciousness. My outrage is predicated on the assumption that I am *merely* a single, finite, limited individual. If that were so, of course, the outrage would be justified. But is that so? One thing to consider is our earlier conclusion that mind and forms of consciousness are inherently social.* A completely isolated individual consciousness is not possible. So I, as a conscious subject, represent or manifest a more general consciousness: that of my community, those who share the same language and instruments of interpretation (concepts).

Moreover, Hegel agrees with Kant that Reason is a principle of universality. What is rational cannot differ from mind to mind. If it is rational in *these* circumstances to do just exactly *that*, then it is rational for me, for you, and for anyone else. So when Hegel says that consciousness in its mode of Reason is *all reality*, he does not mean the consciousness that you happen to display today. After all, the

---

*Kant's concept of Reason is discussed on pp. 381–382.

*See p. 410.

dialectic he has led us through has shown us one after another *inadequate* form of consciousness. And your form of consciousness today is no doubt inadequate in many ways. Hegel means that consciousness, Reason *in itself* or in its *essence*, is identical with all reality. This consciousness is *implicit* in you and me, and we are part of the process in which it is *becoming explicit*. This process is history. In that (implicit) sense, even the single consciousness that *you* are is *all reality*.*

In this connection, Hegel often talks in terms of a *World Spirit*. The term has clear religious connotations, but it would be a mistake to identify it with the Christian concept of God. (Recall Hegel's critique of the "alienation" characteristic of traditional religious—unhappy—consciousness.) The World Spirit is consciousness and Reason manifesting itself in the world. Indeed, Hegel thinks history is a process in which "God" is coming to comprehend itself in and through us.

> Consciousness will determine its relationship to otherness or its object in various ways, according to the precise stage it has reached in the development of the World-Spirit into self-consciousness. How it *immediately* finds and determines itself and its object at any time, or the way in which it is *for itself*, depends on what it has already *become*, or what it already is *in itself* (PS, 141–42).

The endpoint of this process, when subject and object correspond perfectly because each recognizes the other as nothing but itself, the stage of perfect self-consciousness, is the stage Hegel calls *absolute knowledge*.

What is known in absolute knowledge? It is the Kantian *Idea*—the unconditioned explainer of all reality. But it is now known not just as an ever-receding goal serving to regulate our enquiries. It is known as it is *in itself*. For it is the World Spirit's rational consciousness of *itself* as constituting all reality—as the Unconditioned. This means that

the process of gaining knowledge is not like an infinitely long path we can never hope to traverse. It is more like a loop; it closes and comes back on itself. In absolute knowledge the problem of the criterion will be solved, because all possible grounds for skeptical doubt will have been analyzed and *surpassed* in the dialectical progression that gets us to that point. Spirit will not just know reality; it will know that it knows.

It is ultimately for the World Spirit that objects are (or rather, will be) completely intelligible and contain nothing in which the subject does not recognize itself—not for you and me (except in the sense that we are already *implicitly* Reason and this perfection of self-consciousness). It is in this sense that Hegel sponsors an *absolute* idealism. The relativity of objects to subjects is never perfect for any of us; there remains (for us) opacity and darkness and an alien character to the things in the world and even to ourselves. They continue to be experienced *as other*. But if we have followed Hegel's dialectic (and if he is *right*), we know that this is merely appearance. In themselves they are illuminated by the light of Reason and are comprehensible—without remainder! Things exist only *for* a subject. There are no dark and incomprehensible things-in-themselves. Things exist *for* the Absolute, for the self-consciousness of the World Spirit. For the World Spirit *is* all reality.

Spirit Made Objective: The Social Character of Ethics

The recognition on the part of Reason that it encompasses all reality is not yet the end of the dialectic. For this is, as we might say, "mere" recognition and has a formal or abstract character to it. Hegel would say it merely expresses the "Notion" of Reason.* It remains for Reason to *make itself* into what it recognizes that it truly is; Reason must *objectify* itself. It must come out of itself and express

---

*For an enlightening analogy, compare Aristotle's notion of potentiality. The tadpole is not yet *actually* a frog, but it already is a frog *potentially* (see pp. 157–158).

*Compare the passage about the French Revolution, p. 402.

itself in its objects, so that these objects are made to display explicitly that rationality which, so far, is theirs only implicitly. Reason must become Practical Reason and actually shape the life of the community of self-conscious beings. Reason must become ethics.

The realm of **objective spirit**, as Hegel calls it, is the realm of culture—of art, religion, custom, morality, the family, and law. Here Spirit makes itself into an actual object for itself and can comprehend itself in contemplating its products. But this process, too, is tortuous; like all the rest, it is a process involving complication, negativity, and inadequacy. Again we will simplify.

Hegel looks back to ancient Greece before the controversy between Socrates and the Sophists for an example of unity and harmony.* At this time, the judgments of individuals about what should and should not be done, what is valuable, and what the good life consists in reflect the "ethos" of the Greek city-state. Individuals simply absorb the standards of their city; these standards are theirs without question and without reflection. Citizens do not experience a conflict between their individual conscience and what is required of them by the state, since they cannot be said to have an "individual" conscience at all.† Their desires are simply molded by the customs of the community, which they take for granted. We must not think that there is anything sinister about this process. It is the most natural thing in the world, since children grow up *necessarily* internalizing the standards of the society in which they live.

There are several consequences: (a) citizens do not experience the welfare of their community as hostile to their own welfare, but naturally identify their own good with the good of the state to which they belong; so there is harmony between individual and community; (b) they experience themselves as free in their actions—so free, indeed, that they need not even remark on it, since the experience of unfreedom is not present to them as a contrast. We can call this the stage of *custom*.

But this stage, Hegel notes, is marked by an *immediate* identity between an individual and the community. And, as we should now know, immediacy is a state that needs to be overcome and will be overcome by producing some *negative* to itself. Immediacy is always simplistic, naive, and abstract, for Hegel. In this case, it lacks the character of being *for itself*, which is essential to a developed consciousness; it is not a *self-conscious* harmony and freedom. It does not represent a rational decision, just an unexamined way of life that is taken for granted.

The negative "moment" in Greek history is represented by the Sophists and Socrates. Influenced by the wider knowledge of the non-Greek world brought about through trade and warfare, the Sophists express the view that Greek customs are not "natural," not matters of *physis*, but mere matters of "convention" or *nomos*.* This represents a giant step toward becoming self-conscious, for it suggests that customs and traditions have been *invented* by consciousness and can be *changed*. Socrates, for his part, engages in his ceaseless questioning in order to discover the *reason why* something is considered just or pious or courageous.† It is self-consciousness as *Reason* that comes on the scene with Socrates. The detachment of consciousness from its immediacy in the traditional society of the Greeks is a fateful step; it detaches the individual from that sense of natural solidarity with his community, and Western civilization is never the same again. Hegel recognizes that our long history since has, in a way, been an exploration of the consequences of this step.

This negative stage of increasing individual self-consciousness reaches a culmination, according to Hegel, in modern times, when the Reformation affirms the criterion of individual conscience, En-

---

*Hegel would not want to deny that there have been many such "traditional societies" (as they are often called); but the Greeks, whom Hegel here interprets in line with the Romantic view of them, are unique because it seems to have been they who first move away from the "immediacy" of traditional modes of community to a more rational and reflective mode.

†Hegel says, "An Athenian citizen did what was required of him, as it were from instinct." (*RH*, 53). Compare Heidegger on "the One" ("The 'Who' of Dasein," in Chapter 27).

*See the discussion of the debate about *nomos* and *physis* (Chapter 6).
†Any of the earlier dialogues of Plato will give you the flavor of his questions, *Euthyphro* being a particularly good example.

lightenment thinkers debunk everything based only on tradition and privilege, and the French Revolution tries overnight to reconstruct society according to the dictates of reason.* Philosophically speaking, Hegel sees this stage reaching a climax in the ethical thinking of Immanuel Kant. He calls this stage *morality*. We need to pay some attention to Hegel's discussion of Kant, since he takes Kant to "typify" this second, self-conscious stage.

Hegel accepts much of Kant's analysis. Morality, he agrees, must be founded on Reason, not Desire. Reason, moreover, gives us universal laws telling us what our duties are. And to do one's duty is to act in a way that is both autonomous and free:[†]

> I should do my duty for duty's sake, and when I do my duty it is in a true sense my own objectivity which I am bringing to realization. In doing my duty, I am by myself and free. To have emphasized this meaning of duty has constituted the merit of Kant's moral philosophy and its loftiness of outlook (*PR*, 253).

In all these respects, Kant's thought is the culmination of that tradition of self-reflective rationality begun by Socrates. In fact, Hegel gives the Kantian emphasis on the role of reason additional support.

Think about the claim that you are free when you can do—without hindrance or constraint—what you want to do.[‡] It is a view of freedom that has been espoused by many "liberal" thinkers, from Hume and John Stuart Mill to present-day "liberal" economists. What is characteristic of the view is that desires are simply accepted as a *given*; on this view, the question a person faces in seeking happiness is just this: What shall I do to get the most satisfaction for the desires I in fact have? And I am free to the degree that no one interferes with my pursuit of that satisfaction.

It is Hegel's view that this is a very shallow kind of freedom. It is no more satisfactory than the abstract view of Stoic and skeptic. Indeed, it is equally abstract, but in a precisely opposite direction.* Just as the Stoic and skeptic abstract themselves from "living actuality" and identify themselves with pure thought, reflection, and universality, so the "liberal" theorists about freedom identify themselves solely with their nonreflective, rationally uncriticized, given desires. The former experience themselves as possessing an "infinite will," since their decisions range freely over any alternatives presented to them.[†] The will of the latter is wholly finite, being simply the set of naturally given (or culturally instilled) inclinations, yearnings, hankerings, wants, etc. Hegel calls this an "arbitrary will."

> Arbitrariness implies that the content is made mine not by the nature of my will but by chance. Thus I am dependent on this content, and this is the contradiction lying in arbitrariness. The man in the street thinks he is free if it is open to him to act as he pleases but his very arbitrariness implies that he is not free. When I will what is rational, then I am acting not as a particular individual but in accordance with the concepts of ethics in general (*PR*, 230).

To be truly free, Hegel claims, we must not be at the mercy of whatever happens to influence and form us, lest we be simply the pawns and dupes of irrational interests and forces. (Think, in this connection, of the ways advertisers or politicians try to mold and persuade us.) To be free we must be *rational*. And, since rationality is intrinsically *universal*, to be rational is to be *ethical*. This is already argued by Kant, and Hegel emphatically agrees. Reason is not, and cannot be, simply the slave of

---

*Take a quick look back at the discussions of conscience in the Reformation (p. 275), Kant on enlightenment (p. 339), and Hume on superstition (p. 341). The French Revolutionaries consciously aimed at a rational society; to this end they introduced a new religion of reason, rationalized the calendar, adopted the metric system, and cut off the king's head.

†For Kant's theory of morality, see "Reason and Morality," in Chapter 20.

‡See Hume's endorsement of this view, p. 355. It is the natural companion of the view that reason is and must be the slave of the passions.

*"The development we are studying is that whereby the abstract forms reveal themselves not as self-subsistent but as false" (*PR*, 233).

†Compare Descartes' claim in *Meditation IV* that even God's will is not more free than our own.

the passions; reason must be a determining factor in action.

Hegel thinks that the Stoic/skeptic view on the one hand and the "liberal" Humean view on the other constitute *two abstract moments* that need to interact and interpenetrate each other. Abstract reason must become concrete in action, and the arbitrary will needs to be disciplined by reason. In this way Hegel buttresses the Kantian view of reason, freedom, morality, and action.

But, in Hegel's view, Kant does not show us how to make reason actual in the world. Though Kant correctly identifies reason as the key to morality and freedom alike, his discussion remains abstract and, therefore, inadequate as a guide for life. We need to examine Hegel's critique of Kant's ethics.

Recall that Kant's criterion for the moral acceptability of a principle of action is the categorical imperative.* Suppose we are thinking of acting on a certain maxim; the categorical imperative bids us examine it by asking, Can it be universalized? The maxim will be morally acceptable as a basis for acting only if it passes this universalization test. Otherwise, it would be morally wrong to act on that principle. It is important to note that the categorical imperative is a purely *formal* rule; by itself, it does not bid us do anything in particular. What it does is to *test* proposed maxims (and hence actions) for moral acceptability.

One of Kant's clearest examples is the proposal to make a promise, intending all the while to break it if it proves inconvenient to keep. Kant argues that this maxim cannot be universalized, because if it were, promising would simply disappear. The universal practice of promising with an intention to break the promise undermines itself and so cannot be an acceptable moral practice. Acting on this maxim will work for individuals only if they can count on nearly everyone else keeping their promises; but that is to make an exception for oneself in order to satisfy some desire of one's own—*at the expense of others*—the very essence of immorality.

This seems a strong argument. What is Hegel's objection? In effect Hegel asks, And then what?

Suppose we grant the entire argument; what are we to do now? We see that the practice of false promising cannot be institutionalized in a society, but that still leaves us with two options:

a. We can make promises, intending sincerely to keep them.
b. We can dispense with the institution of promising altogether.

There seems to be no way the categorical imperative, as a purely formal rule, can decide between these two possibilities; for there seems nothing impossible or contradictory about a society that simply does not have the institution of promising. Kant's formal principle is *too abstract*, since it cannot choose between these two alternatives.*

The criticism can be put in a more politically sensitive way if we consider another example: stealing. Can a maxim that I may steal what is my neighbor's property be universalized? It again seems clear that it cannot, for were it universalized the institution of private property would disappear. Hegel grants that there is a contradiction between the institution of private property and the maxim *Thou mayest steal*. You cannot consistently have both. But again, the question is this: Shall we have the institution or not? And again we seem to be left with two consistent possibilities:

c. A society with private property and rules against stealing.
d. A society without private property.

Kant's purely formal imperative, Hegel argues, is helpless to choose between them.† And the reason is that in itself it has no *content*.

---

*The content of the categorical imperative, together with an examination of the "promising" example, is set out on pp. 394–395.

*Would a Kantian be able to reply to this argument? Might one say that if faced with the prospect of legislating for society a set of practices which either includes or excludes the practice of promising, the rational choice would be in favor of promising? If so, the same move might be possible for stealing and private property (see below). In either case, however, rationality would probably have to mean more than just absence of contradiction.

†This is obviously another one of the points Karl Marx picks up from Hegel. If a purely formal and individualistic morality like Kant's cannot be a guide in selecting *institutions*, then a guide for life must be given by *society*. And doing that is *politics*.

The absence of property contains in itself just as little contradiction as the non-existence of this or that nation, family, etc., or the death of the whole human race. But if it is already established on other grounds and presupposed that property and human life are to exist and be respected, then indeed it is a contradiction to commit theft or murder; a contradiction must be a contradiction of something, i.e., of some content presupposed from the start as a fixed principle (*PR*, 90).

The inadequacy of this stage of morality was made dramatically clear, Hegel believes, in the French Revolution. This was an attempt to *impose* on society abstract principles of a universal sort, to *force* recalcitrant reality to be rational and free. But this freedom was a purely *negative* freedom; and the result was the Terror. When negative freedom

> turns to actual practice, it takes shape in religion and politics alike as the fanaticism of destruction—the destruction of the whole subsisting social order—as the elimination of individuals who are objects of suspicion to any social order, and the annihilation of any organization which tries to rise anew from the ruins. Only in destroying something does this negative will possess the feeling of itself as existent. Of course it imagines that it is willing some positive state of affairs, such as universal equality or universal religious life, but . . . what negative freedom intends to will can never be anything in itself but an abstract idea, and giving effect to this idea can only be the fury of destruction (*PR*, 22).

The stage of *morality* is supplanted by what Hegel calls *ethics*. (These terms are often used synonymously, but they are quite distinct for Hegel.) *Ethics* is the next dialectical step in the objectification of Spirit. But let us pause a moment to review. At first there was *custom*, where an unreflective and uncritical harmony existed between the life of the individual and the life of his society. This broke down in the *Socratic*/Stoic/skeptic realization of oneself as pure reason, distinct from any natural or social realities; the apex of this stage is to be found in the *morality* of Kant.

What is required for Spirit to become what it is, however—fully rational, self-conscious, and

free—is for it to be able to recognize itself in its cultural expressions. And so the next step, *ethics*, is the recognition of rationality in institutions—in property, contracts, the family, and the state. Spirit, alienated from its products in a necessary differentiation of itself from them, must reappropriate them, see itself in them, express itself in the social dimension—but now critically, rationally, freely. The abstraction of Kantian morality is to be overcome by the objectification of reason in society.

For Hegel, ethics is virtually indistinguishable from social and political philosophy. Or rather, it is not *philosophy* at all, but the *realization* of philosophy in an actual community. As he says, "the system of right is the realm of freedom made actual, the world of mind brought forth out of itself like a second nature" (*PR*, 20). What kind of social system will this incarnation of Spirit be? How will right, duty, rationality, and freedom all manage to coalesce in the society of Spirit objectified?

We won't go into the details of Hegel's social thought; he tends too much to see his own society as approaching or having reached the ideal, and much of his discussion is thus of interest only to historians. But we need to indicate his general idea and to point out one of its consequences.

As we have already noted, an individual must be thought of as socially shaped and constructed; no one is an island. Hobbes' view of the rational origin of a state as a contract made by isolated individuals with a view to their own individual protection is, for Hegel, simply another instance of undue abstraction.* The relation between an individual and the community is more like that between a leg and the body it belongs to. If the leg were to say, "I am an independent entity, and I will go my own way," this would be manifestly absurd. It is no less absurd for individuals to consider themselves distinct from the community that nourishes, educates, shapes and forms them. Indeed, an individual per se is an *abstraction* (there's that word again) from the whole. As separate from the community, a person lacks reality. It is the community, which Hegel calls the *State*, that is the bearer of the objective

---

*For Hobbes' view of the social contract, see pp. 335–336.

reality of Spirit and as such is "higher" than the individual. The State is like an organism, and individuals are like its organs. Hegel goes as far as to say,

> A single person . . . is something subordinate, and as such he must dedicate himself to the ethical whole. Hence if the state claims life, the individual must surrender it.

> The rational end of man is life in the state, and if there is no state there, reason at once demands that one be founded. . . . It is false to maintain that the foundation of the state is something at the option of all its members. It is nearer the truth to say that it is absolutely necessary for every individual to be a citizen (PR, 241–42).

But what kind of state is it that can rightly subordinate persons like this? It must be, Hegel says, a rational state. And that means that it must be one whose laws are universal and impartial, one to which free and rational individuals can give their free and rational consent.* Citizens must be able to live freely and rationally in such a state because the state is the objective correlate of that Reason which is the essence of their very being. Here we see how Hegel thinks to surpass, and yet incorporate, the "moments" of unthinking harmony (*custom*) and rational abstraction from that harmony by individuals (*morality*). There is to be a new harmony, one now founded self-consciously on rational principles. After being merely implicit in traditional societies, and after a long estrangement from a reality that was less than fully rational, Spirit is now to find itself mirrored in the institutions and laws of the organic community. These institutions and laws will not seem restrictive to its citizens, because they express the inner nature of those citizens.

> If men are to act, they must not only intend the good but must know whether this or that particular course is good. What special course of action is good or not,

right or wrong, is determined, for the ordinary circumstances of private life, by the laws and customs of a state. It is not too difficult to know them. . . . Each individual has his position; he knows, on the whole, what a lawful and honorable course of conduct is. To assert in ordinary private relations that it is difficult to choose the right and good, and to regard it as a mark of an exalted morality to find difficulties and raise scruples on that score indicates an evil and perverse will. It indicates a will that seeks to evade obvious duties or, at least, a petty will that gives its mind too little to do (*RH*, 37).

The empty form of Kantian morality is thus to be given content by the laws and customs of the state one grows up in. It is true that "each individual is also the child of a people at a definite stage of its development" (*RH*, 37) and that none of us lives in a perfectly rational society. But Hegel seems to say that this is no excuse for trying to go off on our own individualistic tangents. Our ethical life is only realized by actualizing the norms of our society. An individual *"must bring the will demanded by his people to his own consciousness, to articulation"* (*RH*, 38).

The moral of the French Revolution (and others since then, we, in the spirit of Hegel, might add) is that Reason cannot (like Descartes in the sphere of ideas) try to sweep the board clean and begin anew. That way leads only to destruction. What is necessary is to recognize what is *already rational* in the present and to nurture and strengthen that. And there is *always* some rationality in current circumstances; Spirit is always already implicit in some stage of realization, though it is usually inadequate, one-sided, and (of course) abstract.

When Spirit becomes fully *concrete*, when its objective expression in culture matches perfectly its rational essence, then individuals—the subjective bearers of self-consciousness—will recognize themselves in the institutions of their society without hesitation. At that point they will be fully free, for the institutions shaping them will not be alien to themselves, but an expression of the rationality and universality that constitute them as persons. They will not be constrained either by their own nonrationally given desires or by the arbitrariness of irrational laws and institutions. All will be, as in

---

*It does not necessarily mean one in which each citizen has a vote; Hegel's picture of a rational state is a constitutional monarchy where decisions are made by discussion among large scale interests, such as the landed class and corporations.

the stage of *custom*, a harmony. But now it will be a rationally founded harmony, approved by the self-conscious, rational citizens of that State.

You can see that there is an uneasy ambiguity in Hegel's treatment of the ideal community. On the one hand, there is some basis for a radical critique of nearly any given society; insofar as its institutions lack rationality—and when will they not?—they are subject to criticism and potential change. On the other hand, Hegel can seem terribly conservative; for whatever there is in the way of social arrangements has *some* rationality to it, is in some way a stage on the way to the Absolute. The State at that stage, moreover, is the shaper of all the individuals who make it up; apart from it, they are mere abstractions, unrealities. Moreover, that stage is in some sense, he tells us, necessary. If it is necessary and is simply working its own way out toward a more adequate embodiment of Reason and Freedom, what sense does it make to interfere? His emphasis that the philosopher must not prescribe, but must simply "look on," seems to indicate that in the social setting, as in epistemology, Spirit takes care of itself.

This ambiguity runs throughout Hegel's thought and explains how after his death there could form two groups of Hegelians, radical and conservative, each claiming to represent the master.* It permeates, moreover, his thought about history, with which we will end our much simplified consideration of this complex system of ideas.

History and Freedom

We have seen that a central concept in Hegel's thought is that of development. Development in the realm of Spirit is complex and dialectical, because Spirit, unlike Nature, is intrinsically in relation to itself; that is why there is always negativity involved: always (a) an object standing in opposi-

tion to the subject, (b) typically experienced as *other* (alien), and (c) needing to be recovered so that the subject can recognize itself in its object. As an observer of the development of Spirit, Hegel sees this dialectical process at work everywhere: in the consciousness of the individual, in society, even in concepts themselves. Unlike nearly all previous philosophers, Hegel sees Reason itself developing its own tools, its concepts and Notions, in this dialectical and historical process. That is why it has not been possible previously to solve the problem of the criterion: each philosopher has necessarily been working in a certain stage of the development of Reason and necessarily expresses the way things look at that stage. But each of these stages has been abstract (i.e., not yet the whole, the True) and therefore inadequate. The criterion for knowledge and action, Hegel believes, is in the process of *working itself out in history*. And we "phenomenological" observers need only "look on" to see it happening.

History is meaningful; it has a direction and a purpose; it is going somewhere. And Hegel claims to know where it is going. Its goal is *Freedom*. In a schematic (and surely oversimple) way, Hegel claims we can actually see this process going on. In ancient Oriental societies (e.g., the Persian), he says, only *one* was free (the ruler); in Greek and Roman societies, *some* were free (the citizens, but not the slaves); and in his own time, it has been realized that *all* are free (though the working out of this realization may take a long time yet). But to understand this fully, we need to say a bit more about Freedom and its relation to Reason.

> The sole thought which philosophy brings to the treatment of history is the simple concept of *Reason*: that Reason is the law of the world and that, therefore, in world history, things have come about rationally (*RH*, 11).

Hegel discusses Reason in exalted terms, saying it is "both *substance and infinite power*," (*RH*, 11) and suggesting that it is what people really mean when they speak of God. Let us see if we can understand this.

---

*The most famous of the "left-wing," or radical, Hegelians is of course Karl Marx.

Reason is *substance*, Hegel says, because it is "that by which and in which all reality has its being" (*RH*, 11). This should make some sense to us by now, since we have seen that Hegel believes only the universal concepts of rational thought can determine *what something is*. Its very *being* (as that kind of thing) is a function of Reason—and *nothing* can have a nonrational existence.

Reason is *power*, he says,

for Reason is not so impotent as to bring about only the ideal, the ought, and to remain in an existence outside of reality—who knows where?—as something peculiar in the heads of a few people. . . . [Reason] is its own exclusive presupposition and absolutely final purpose, and itself works out this purpose from potentiality into actuality, from inward source to outward appearance, not only in the natural but also in the spiritual universe, in world history (*RH*, 11).

Parts of this "working out" we have traced in following the dialectical stages from implicit to explicit self-consciousness, and from a naively traditional to a self-consciously rational and organic society. Reason, then, seems to be simply another term for the Absolute, for the World Spirit.

How is Reason related to Freedom? Well, what is Freedom? Freedom, Hegel tells us, is

self-contained existence. . . . For when I am dependent, I refer myself to something else which I am not; I cannot exist independently of something external. I am free when I am within myself. This self-contained existence of Spirit is self-consciousness, consciousness of self (*RH*, 23).

You can see that if there isn't anything in reality *but* Spirit (or Reason)—its objects having existence only relative to it,* so that when Spirit becomes conscious of them it is becoming conscious of itself in them—and if to be free is to be "self-contained," then Spirit is essentially free. But being *essentially* free and being *actually* free are two different things. The former is merely the abstract essence, the latter

is the concrete reality. History is the dialectical tale by which the former becomes the latter.

. . . world history is the exhibition of spirit striving to attain knowledge of its own nature.

World history is the progress of the consciousness of freedom. . . .

We have established Spirit's consciousness of its freedom, and thereby the actualization of this Freedom as the final purpose of the world (*RH*, 23–24).

But how does this work? It sounds glorious, and perhaps it is. But how does it fit the *facts* of history, where there is so much that seems irrational and evil? Is Hegel just a "cockeyed optimist" about history? On the contrary, Hegel is acutely conscious of the negative side of the story; only, as always, he sees this negativity as an essential aspect of the dialectic leading to freedom. Reason does not conquer easily, but only with agonizing slowness and indirection. He is under no illusions about the motivations behind the acts that make history.

Passions, private aims, and the satisfaction of selfish desires are . . . tremendous springs of action. Their power lies in the fact that they respect none of the limitations which law and morality would impose on them; and that these natural impulses are closer to the core of human nature than the artificial and troublesome discipline that tends toward order, self-restraint, law, and morality.

When we contemplate this display of passions and the consequences of their violence, the unreason which is associated not only with them, but even—rather we might say *especially*—with *good* designs and righteous aims; when we see arising therefrom the evil, the vice, the ruin that has befallen the most flourishing kingdoms which the mind of man ever created, we can hardly avoid being filled with sorrow at this universal taint of corruption. And since this decay is not the work of mere nature, but of human will, our reflections may well lead us to a moral sadness, a revolt of the good will (spirit)—if indeed it has a place within us. Without rhetorical exaggeration, a simple, truthful account of the miseries that have overwhelmed the noblest of nations and polities and the finest exemplars of private virtue forms

---

*This is the key element in Hegel's absolute idealism.

a most fearful picture and excites emotions of the profoundest and most hopeless sadness, counterbalanced by no consoling result. We can endure it and strengthen ourselves against it only by thinking that this is the way it had to be—it is fate; nothing can be done (*RH*, 26–27).

Hegel compares history to a "slaughter bench," at which the happiness, wisdom, and virtue of countless individuals and peoples have been sacrificed. When this image takes hold, the question forces itself upon us:

To what principle, to what final purpose, have these monstrous sacrifices been offered? (*RH*, 27).

Hegel's answer, of course, is Freedom. But we need to say a bit more about how he thinks Freedom will come out of this protracted and bloody process.

He is under no illusions, as we have noted, about individuals acting from Reason. In fact, he goes as far as to say,

We assert then that nothing has been accomplished without an interest on the part of those who brought it about. And if "interest" be called "passion" . . . we may then affirm without qualification that *nothing great in the world* has been accomplished without passion (*RH*, 29).

But that is only half the story. The other half is equally important: Reason, or what Hegel calls the *Idea.**

Two elements therefore enter into our investigations: first the Idea, secondly, the complex of human passions; the one the warp, the other the woof of the vast tapestry of world history (*RH*, 29).

Individuals, then, act out of their passions and desires. Like the threads in a tapestry that run in one direction only, they are unaware that they are held

---

*Remember that "Idea," for Hegel, represents the unconditioned explainer of everything and that the nature of Spirit (self-conscious, universal Reason) is that it functions as the Idea.

in place by a rationality which, fixing their actions into a pattern they can scarcely discern, works out a purposeful progress toward Absolute Knowledge and Freedom.

The burden of historical development is carried particularly, Hegel thinks, by certain persons, whom he calls "world-historical individuals." Alexander, Caesar, and Napoleon are examples he cites. What is true of them is that

their own particular purposes contain the substantial will of the World Spirit.

Such individuals have no consciousness of the Idea as such. They are practical and political men. But at the same time they are thinkers with insight into what is needed and timely. They see the very truth of their age and their world, the next genus, so to speak, which is already formed in the womb of time. It is theirs to know this new universal, the necessary next stage of their world, to make it their own aim and put all their energy into it (*RH*, 40).

They do not pursue this "new universal" consciously, of course. The may simply seek to consolidate their own power. And they may do so quite ruthlessly; "so mighty a figure must trample down many an innocent flower, crush to pieces many things in its path" (*RH*, 43). But in pursuing their private aims, they unknowingly serve a larger purpose. There are unintended effects to their actions, and whether they will it or not, they serve the purposes of reason. This Hegel calls the

cunning of Reason—that it sets the passions to work for itself, while that through which it develops itself pays the penalty and suffers the loss. . . . The particular in most cases is too trifling as compared with the universal; the individuals are sacrificed and abandoned. The Idea pays the tribute of existence and transience, not out of its own funds but with the passions of the individuals (*RH*, 44).

Individuals, then, are the *means* by which the World Spirit actualizes its Reason in the world. And if we see this, we can be reconciled to the agony and the tragedy of world history. It is all worthwhile because it is necessary to realize the goal.

The insight then to which . . . philosophy should lead us is that the actual world is as it ought to be, that the truly good, the universal divine Reason is the power capable of actualizing itself. This good, this Reason, in its most concrete representation, is God. God governs the world (*RH*, 47).

What Hegel gives us in his reflections on history, is a **theodicy**, a justification of the ways of God to human beings; it is one solution to the old problem of evil. Hegel's is perhaps the most elaborate theodicy since Augustine wrote *The City of God* in the early fifth century.* But notice the price that is paid: the actual world *is as it ought to be*. Remembering Hegel's own lament over the "slaughter bench" of history, this is a remarkable conclusion. All this is worthwhile because it leads to a supremely valuable end.

And what, in particular, is that end to be? We already know. It is "the union of the subjective with the rational will; it is the moral whole, the *State*" (*RH*, 49). Once again, note that the State does not exist for the sake of satisfying the desires of its citizens.

Rather, law, morality, the State, and they alone, are the positive reality and satisfaction of freedom. The caprice of the individual is not freedom. It is this caprice which is being limited, the license of particular desires.

The subjective will, passion, is the force which actualizes and realizes. The Idea is the interior; the State is the externally existing, genuinely moral life.

It is the union of the universal and essential with the subjective will, and as such it is *Morality* (*RH*, 50).*

It is the realization of Freedom, of the absolute, final purpose, and exists for its own sake. All the value man has, all spiritual reality, he has only through the state. For his spiritual reality is the knowing presence to him of his own essence, of rationality, of its objective, immediate actuality present in and for him. Only thus is he truly a consciousness, only thus does he partake in morality, in the legal and moral life of the state. For the True is the unity of universal and particular will. And the universal in the state is in its laws, its universal and rational provisions. The state is the divine Idea as it exists on earth (*RH*, 52–53).

Here again we feel that ambiguity we noted before. When Hegel says the state is the "divine Idea as it exists on earth," does he mean *any* state? Or does he mean only the ideal, perfectly rational state? On the one hand, as we have seen, the actual world is as it ought to be. This suggests that, if things are not as good as they *might* be, still they are as good as they realistically *can* be (at this stage), and there is no sense complaining. On the other hand, there is the ideal of a rational state in which individuals will actually find themselves at home because it expresses perfectly their inner nature as rational beings. No actually existing state seems to measure up. Again we find the ambivalence between conservative and radical points of view.

But perhaps this ambivalence can be reduced if we note that Hegel is quite self-consciously *not* a "world-historical individual." He is a philosopher. And it is not the job of philosophy, he holds, to change the world; it is the philosopher's job simply to understand it. Remember that we began our consideration of Hegel's philosophy with the problem of the criterion. Hegel suggests that this problem does not need to be solved by the philosopher, because it is in process of solving itself; all the philosopher needs to do is "look on." Near the end

*See the discussion of Augustine's view of history, pp. 240–243. One crucial difference is that for Augustine the justification of history lies *beyond* it in the life to come, whereas for Hegel it lies *within* history itself in an attainable historical condition. A second difference is that Augustine looks for the *peace* of the blessed, whereas Hegel justifies everything in terms of the rational *freedom* to be enjoyed by citizens of a rational state. A third difference is in the conception of God. For Augustine, God is a being quite independent of the world he created, having his being even outside of time; for Hegel, the world *is* God coming to self-actualization in time through self-conscious knowers like ourselves.

*Hegel here uses the term "morality" to designate what he elsewhere has called "ethics," perhaps to indicate that only in the actuality of the State does Kantian morality realize its inner nature.

of his life, Hegel comes back to that same point in a memorable image.

> One more word about giving instruction as to what the world ought to be. Philosophy in any case always comes on the scene too late to give it. As the thought of the world, it appears only when actuality is already there cut and dried after its process of formation has been completed. . . . When philosophy paints its grey in grey, then has a shape of life grown old. By philosophy's grey in grey it cannot be rejuvenated but only understood. The owl of Minerva spreads its wings only with the falling of the dusk (*PR*, 12–13).

Notes

1. References to Hegel's works will be as follows:
   PS: Phenomenology of Spirit, trans. A. V. Miller (Oxford: Clarendon Press, 1977).
   PR: Hegel's Philosophy of Right, trans. T. M. Knox (Oxford: Oxford University Press, 1952).
   RH: Reason in History, trans. Robert S. Hartman (New York: The Liberal Arts Press, 1953).
2. Quoted from *The Logic of Hegel*, trans. William Wallace (Oxford, 1892), in Richard Norman, *Hegel's Phenomenology: A Philosophical Introduction* (Published for Sussex University Press by Chatto and Windus Ltd., London, 1976), 11.

22

Kierkegaard and Marx:
Two Ways to "Correct" Hegel

The influence of Hegel was enormous. Everywhere he was read and discussed, dissected and analyzed, damned and admired. The synthesis of so much learning and the forging of so many insights could hardly help but shape the next generation of philosophers.

Despite the range and depth of Hegel's thought, some readers had the sense (which perhaps you share) that this magnificent system was extravagant, that it promised more than it could deliver. In a certain way, moreover, and contrary to Hegel's explicit intentions, it seemed too *abstract*; it did not seem to deal concretely enough with the actuality of people's lives as they led them, making very specific choices in very specific circumstances. This was an ironic complaint indeed, since abstraction is Hegel's great enemy.

In this chapter we will glance at two thinkers who are deeply in Hegel's debt. They can both be considered Hegelians, but they are renegade Hegelians, each in his own way. Both have contributed in lasting ways to our thinking in many spheres of human life, from religion to politics, from art to economics, from the anxieties of individual psychology to the sociology of class struggle. Their intellectual progeny in our time go by the names of **existentialist** and Marxist. So we shall examine some of the central contributions of Søren Kierkegaard and Karl Marx to the great conversation.

Kierkegaard: On Individual Existence

The "authorship" of Søren Kierkegaard (1813–1855) is exceedingly varied and diverse. For one thing, about half of it is pseudonymous (written under other names—and quite a number of them, too). Why? Not for the usual reason, to hide the identity of the author; nearly everyone in little Copenhagen knew Kierkegaard, and they knew he had written these books. There is a deeper reason: the various "authors"—a romantic young man known simply as A; Judge William (a local magistrate), Johannes de Silentio (John the Silent), the Seducer (who writes a famous diary), Victor Eremita (the Hermit), Johannes Climacus (the Climber), to name only a few—all represent different views. Through their voices Kierkegaard means to embody some of the numerous possibilities for managing the problem of having to exist as a human being. This is a problem, he believes, that we all face. Moreover, it is a problem that cannot be solved in the abstract, by thinking about it—though it cannot be solved without thinking about it either!* A solution is worked out in one's life by

---

*Kierkegaard, who thinks of himself as the "gadfly of Copenhagen," agrees with Socrates' dictum that "the unexamined life is not worth living." (See Plato's *Apology*, 38a.)

the choices one actually makes, thereby defining and creating the self one becomes. His pseudonymous authors "present themselves" to the reader as selves in the process of such self-creation. They thereby function as models for possibilities that you or I might also actualize in our own lives; they awaken us to alternatives and stimulate us to self-examination.

Kierkegaard calls this technique "indirect communication." His motive for adopting it is his conviction that most of us live in varying forms and degrees of self-deception. We are not honest with ourselves about the categories that actually structure our lives. He attempts to provoke the shock of self-recognition by offering characters with which the reader may identify and then revealing slowly, but inexorably, what living in that way really means. He is particularly concerned with an "illusion" that he thinks many of his contemporaries in nineteenth-century Denmark suffer from: the impression that they are *Christians*. He wants to clarify what it means actually to live as a Christian. And it is his particular concern to distinguish such a life from two things: (1) from the average bourgeois life of a citizen in this state-church country, where everyone is baptized as a matter of course, and (2) from the illusion that intellectual speculation of the Hegelian type is a modern successor to faith.

In the course of this elaborate literary production, Kierkegaard offers us insights that many recent philosophers, psychologists, and theologians have recovered and used in their own work.* For our present purposes, we will sketch several of these life possibilities and then draw some conclusions about how Hegel needs to be modified, if Kierkegaard is right. We will follow Kierkegaard and call them the *esthetic*, the *ethical*, and the *religious*.

---

*We will later examine one twentieth-century thinker who owes much to Kierkegaard, Martin Heidegger. See Chapter 27.

The Esthetic

In the first part of a two-part work called *Either/Or*,* we find the somewhat chaotic papers of an unknown young man whom the editor of the volume (himself a pseudonymous character) elects simply to call "A." The fond desire of A's life is simply to *be* something. His ideal is expressed in a line by the twentieth-century poet T. S. Eliot: "You are the music while the music lasts."[1] This kind of complete absorption, which we experience occasionally in pleasurable moments, seems wonderful to him. If only the whole of life could be like that! If only he could evade reflection, self-consciousness, thought, the agony of choice, and this business of always having to *become* something! If he could just enjoy life in its *immediacy*.[†] A's dream is to live unreflectively a life of pleasure.

But A is a clever and sophisticated young man. He realizes that this is not possible. For one thing, immediacy never exists where it is sought; to take it as one's *aim* or *ideal* entails directly that one has missed the goal. As soon as you think, "What I really want is a life of pleasure," you prove that you are already beyond simply *having* such a life. You are reflecting on how nice that would be. No human, in fact, can attain the placid, self-contained immediacy of the brutes. And it is clear to A that pleasure is not his life, but the chief preoccupation of his life.

This becomes clear to A through his reflections on the figure of Don Juan. As A imagines him, he is pure, undifferentiated, unreflective desire—nothing more than embodied sensuality. Don Juan

---

*Already in the title of this early work, we see an attack on central themes in Hegel, for whom "both/and" might be an appropriate motto. As we have seen, the progress of Hegelian dialectic is a successively reiterated synthesis, gathering in the truth contained in earlier stages until we reach in the end a stage of absolute knowledge. Kierkegaard is convinced that such a stage is impossible for existing human beings. We'll see why.

†"Immediacy," of course, is a Hegelian category. Look back to pp. 406–408 for Hegel's phenomenological critique of immediacy as a foundation for knowledge.

wants women wholesale, and he gets what he wants. In Mozart's opera, *Don Giovanni*,* the Don's servant keeps a list of his conquests, which he displays in a comic aria, informing us that they number 1003 in Spain alone! The figure of Don Juan represents something analogous to a force of nature—an avalanche or hurricane—but for this very reason there is something subhuman about him. A concludes that this "pure type" can exist only in art and that music is the appropriate vehicle for its expression. Sensuality (together with its associated pleasure) is not human reality, but an aspect of human reality. It is an abstraction.†

What, then, to do? There seems to A one obvious solution: make one's life itself into a work of art. Then one could have toward it the same relation as to any fine esthetic object. The pleasures of immediacy may be vanishing, but the pleasures of esthetic appreciation are all the more available. After all, there is the famous "esthetic distance" that characterizes enjoyment in the esthetic mode. Toward this end A writes a little "how-to" manual called *Rotation of Crops*.

> People with experience maintain that proceeding from a basic principle is supposed to be very reasonable; I yield to them and proceed from the basic principle that all people are boring. Or is there anyone who would be boring enough to contradict me in this regard? . . . Boredom is the root of all evil.
>
> This can be traced back to the very beginning of the world. The gods were bored; therefore they created human beings. Adam was bored because he was alone; therefore Eve was created. Since that moment, boredom entered the world and grew in quantity in exact proportion to the growth of population. Adam was bored alone; then Adam and Eve were bored together; then Adam and Eve and Cain and Abel were bored *en famille*. After that, the population of the world increased and the nations were bored *en masse*. To amuse themselves, they hit upon the notion of building a tower so high that it would reach the sky.

This notion is just as boring as the tower was high and is a terrible demonstration of how boredom had gained the upper hand (*EO 1*, 285–86).[2]

Here we have an expression of the categories under which A organizes his life. Everything is evaluated in terms of the pair of concepts:

interesting/boring

The rotation method is a set of techniques for keeping things interesting. Let us just note a few of the recommendations.

Variety, of course, is essential, since nothing is as boring as the same old thing. But it is no use trying to achieve variety by varying one's surroundings or circumstances, though this is the "vulgar and inartistic method."

> One is weary of living in the country and moves to the city; one is weary of one's native land and goes abroad; one is europamüde [weary of Europe] and goes to America, etc; one indulges in the fanatical hope of an endless journey from star to star (*EO 1*, 291).

What one must learn to do is vary *oneself*, a task A compares to the rotation of crops by a farmer. The key idea is a developed facility for remembering and forgetting. To avoid boredom, we need to remember and forget artistically, not randomly as most of us do. Whoever develops this art will have a never-ending source of interesting experiences at hand.

> No part of life ought to have so much meaning for a person that he cannot forget it any moment he wants to; on the other hand, every single part of life ought to have so much meaning for a person that he can remember it at any moment (*EO 1*, 293).

In addition, one requires absolute freedom to break away at any time from anything, lest one be at the mercy of something or someone boring. Thus one must beware of entanglements and avoid

---

*Kierkegaard admired this opera extravagantly, attending many performances of it.

†Here A is echoing, of course, Hegel's own critique of immediacy.

commitments. The rule is no friendships (but acquaintances aplenty), no marriage (though an occasional affair adds to the interest), and no business (for what is so boring as the demands of business?).

The key notion is to stay in control. As A writes in one of a series of aphoristic paragraphs,

> Real enjoyment consists not in what one enjoys but in the idea. If I had in my service a submissive jinni who, when I asked for a glass of water, would bring me the world's most expensive wines, deliciously blended, in a goblet, I would dismiss him until he learned that the enjoyment consists not in what I enjoy but in getting my own way (*EO* 1, 31).

This project of living for the interesting is explored in a variety of ways in A's papers, but its apex is surely the lengthy manuscript known as *The Seducer's Diary*. In some prefatory remarks, A claims to have stolen the diary from the desk of an acquaintance, though the "editor" of *Either/Or*, in which it appears, doubts this. He speculates that it was written by A himself, in which case it may represent a kind of dream on the part of A, in which A explores possibilities that he knows he is capable of—and perhaps we are, too.*

The essentials of the plot are simple. Johannes, the diarist, sees a young girl, Cordelia, and is fascinated. He insinuates himself into her family. While paying little attention to her, but much to her fussy old aunt, he sets things up so that he appears interesting to Cordelia. He promotes Edward, a rather conventional and boring young man in love with Cordelia, as a suitable match; but slowly and cleverly he brings her to see Edward—in comparison with himself—as boorish and common. He manipulates an engagement with himself. But he then brings her to the point of believing that a marriage is an external impediment to true love, in such a way that *she* seems to be making the decisions. For such reasons *she* breaks the engagement. There is a passionate night together. And then he leaves her.

Everything is arranged by Johannes to intensify the interesting. As a result, the diary is a far cry from those novels of sexual athleticism whose characters are as thin as their bodies are voluptuous. The focus is on the psychological rather than the physical. And it must be so, for the Seducer is the polar opposite of Don Juan (within the sphere of the esthetic).* Whereas the latter is supposed to be wholly nonreflective, an embodiment of pure immediacy, the seducer lives so completely in reflection that he seems to touch down in reality only occasionally. All is planning, arranging, scheming, plotting, and enjoying the results, as one would enjoy a play at the theater. Johannes is at once the playwright, the actor, and the audience in the drama of his life. It is not the actual seduction that matters to him (one moment of physical conquest is much like another), but the drama leading up to that moment. That is where the art lies. That is what is really interesting. And to preserve the esthetic character of his experience, he must keep the necessary esthetic distance, even from himself.

> I scarcely know myself. My mind roars like a turbulent sea in the storms of passion. If someone else could see my soul in this state, it would seem to him that it, like a skiff, plunged prow-first down into the ocean, as if in its dreadful momentum it would have to steer down into the depths of the abyss. He does not see that high on the mast a sailor is on the lookout. Roar away, you wild forces, roar away, you powers of passion; even if your waves hurl foam toward the clouds, you still are not able to pile yourselves up over my head—I am sitting as calmly as the king of the mountain (*EO* 1, 324–25).

---

*Note how possibilities are piled up here. Kierkegaard presents Victor Eremita (the nonreal, merely possible editor of the volume), who presents A (the literary embodiment of certain possibilities, who (possibly) presents the Seducer. Everything conspires to hold the reader at a distance, as if to say: *this* is not your life; it is merely a reflection of it. By its very intensification of possibility, it accentuates—by contrast—the actual. The medium is itself part of the message.

---

*Remember that the esthetic is defined as that style of life in which everything is judged in terms of the pair of categories: interesting / boring.

Other aspects of this project to treat one's life like an esthetic object reveal themselves subtly in the diary. The project must be carried out in secret; to reveal his intentions to Cordelia would bring the whole enterprise to ruin. And so he must, necessarily, deceive Cordelia. He is, in terms Kant and Hegel would find appropriate, *using* her for ends she not only does not consent to, but of which she has not the slightest hint.

Does Johannes love Cordelia? He asks himself this question.

> Do I love Cordelia? Yes! Sincerely? Yes! Faithfully? Yes—in the esthetic sense (*EO* 1, 385).

He flatters himself that he is benefiting her. In what sense? Why, in the only sense he recognizes: he is making her life more interesting! He found her a naive young girl; he will leave her a sophisticated woman. She was innocent, uninitiated into *possibility*; he has taught her the delights and terrors of the possible. He found her nature; he will leave her spirit. So, at least, he tells himself.

Whether Cordelia agrees is another matter. A includes a letter she sent to Johannes after the break, which Johannes had returned unopened (*EO* 1, 312):

> Johannes,
> Never will I call you "my Johannes," for I certainly realize you have never been that, and I am punished harshly enough for having once been gladdened in my soul by this thought, and yet I do call you "mine": my seducer, my deceiver, my enemy, my murderer, the source of my unhappiness, the tomb of my joy, the abyss of my unhappiness. I call you "mine" and call myself "yours," and as it once flattered your ear, proudly inclined to my adoration, so shall it now sound as a curse upon you, a curse for all eternity. . . . Yours I am, yours, yours, your curse.
>
> Your Cordelia

It appears that even within the sphere of the esthetic there might be no clear answer to whether Johannes has benefited Cordelia. But, as we'll see, that is not the only kind of question that can be asked.

The Ethical

The bulk of the second part of *Either/Or* is composed of several long letters from a magistrate in one of the lower courts, a certain Judge William. They are addressed to A. The main topic is love; but the Judge has his eye on a larger issue: what it means for an existing human being to be a *self*.

To see the relevance of this issue, let us look back to another of A's aphorisms. He says,

> My life is utterly meaningless. When I consider its various epochs, my life is like the word *Schnur* in the dictionary, which first of all means a string, and second a daughter-in-law. All that is lacking is that in the third place the word *Schnur* means a camel, in the fourth a whisk broom (*EO* 1, 36).

A recognizes that there is no continuity in his life. It is as if he were a succession of different people, one interested in this, another in that. The different periods of his life have no more relation to each other than do the meanings of the word *Schnur*. In a sense, A has no self—or rather, he is splintered into a multiplicity of semi-selves, which comes to much the same thing. The Judge has a remedy.

Taking his cue from A's own preoccupations, the Judge gives us an analysis of romantic love. Its "mark" is that it is *immediate*. Its watchword is "To see her was to love her." And indeed, that is how we think about love, too; we talk about "falling in love"—something that can *happen* to one, a condition in which one may, suddenly, just find oneself. Falling in love is not something one *does* deliberately after reflection.

> Romantic love manifests itself as immediate by exclusively resting in natural necessity. It is based on beauty, partly on sensuous beauty. . . . Although this love is based essentially on the sensuous, it nevertheless is noble by virtue of the consciousness of the eternal which it assimilates, for it is this that distinguishes all love from lust: that it bears a stamp of eternity. The lovers are deeply convinced that in itself their relationship is a complete whole that will never be changed (*EO* 2, 21).

This conviction, however, since it is based merely on something natural, on *what happens to one*, is an illusion. If you can fall into love, you can fall out of it again. For this reason, it is easy to make romantic love look ridiculous; it promises what it cannot deliver: faithfulness, persistence, *eternity*. (Just listen to popular love songs.) The Judge notes that a lot of modern literature expresses cynicism about love. The culmination of this cynicism is either (1) giving in to the transience of nature, resigning the promise of lasting love, and making do with a series of affairs, or (2) the marriage of convenience, which gives up on love altogether.

The Judge deplores both alternatives. He believes A is right in valuing romantic love. But, he says to A, what you want, you can't have on your terms. The promise of eternity in romantic love can be realized, but not if you simply "go with the flow" (as we say). What is required is choice, a determination of the will.

The Judge is a defender of *conjugal* love, a defender of marriage, the mark of which is precisely the engagement of the will. The bride and groom *make promises* to each other. They promise to *love*. The Judge argues that what one hears from the Romantic poets, that marriage is the enemy of romantic love, is simply false. For what romantic love seems to offer, but cannot deliver, is exactly what the engagement of the will can provide: the continuity and permanence of love. Marriage, as an expression of the will, is not the death of romantic love; it comes to its aid and provides what it needs in order to endure. Without the will, love is simply inconstant and arbitrary nature.*

It is true, the Judge admits, that conjugal love is not a fit subject for art. Love stories usually go like this: The handsome prince falls in love with the beautiful princess, and after much opposition and struggle (ogres and dragons, wicked uncles and unwilling fathers), they are married; the last line of the story is "And they lived happily ever after." (The best recent example of this pattern is the Rob Reiner movie, *The Princess Bride*.) But, says the Judge, these stories end just where the really interesting part begins. Nevertheless, the marriage cannot be represented in art, "for the very point is time in its extension." The married person "has not fought with lions and ogres, but with the most dangerous enemy—with time."

> The faithful romantic lover waits, let us say for fifteen years; then comes the moment that rewards him. Here poetry very properly perceives that the fifteen years can easily be concentrated; now it hastens to the moment. A married man is faithful for fifteen years, and yet during these fifteen years he has had possession; therefore in this long succession he has continually acquired the faithfulness he possessed, since marital love has in itself the first love and thereby the faithfulness of the first love. But an ideal married man of this sort cannot be portrayed, for the point is time in its extension. . . .
>
> And although this cannot be portrayed artistically, then let your consolation be, as it is mine, that we are not to read about or listen to or look at what is the highest and the most beautiful in life, but are, if you please, to live it.
>
> Therefore, when I readily admit that romantic love lends itself much better to artistic portrayal than marital love, this does not at all mean that it is less esthetic than the other—on the contrary, it is more esthetic (*EO* 2, 138–39).

The Judge is defending the *esthetic* validity of marriage and, with it, the self. For marriage is seen by the Judge as an example of a style of life quite other than that which A has been leading. The ethical life requires the development of the *self*.

The crucial difference between the esthetic and the ethical is *choice*. In a certain sense, of course, the esthetic life is full of choices. But, with that clear-sighted irony that an intelligent esthete brings to his experience, A sees that none of them are *significant choices*. What this means is that any choice might as well have been the opposite—and can be tomorrow. After all, if your aim is "the interesting," you must not get stuck in commitments. None of these esthetic choices really mean any-

---

*Compare what Hegel has to say about the "artibrariness" of a will (by which he means merely natural or conditioned desires) that has not been subjected to reason. See p. 419.

thing, for the self doing the choosing. Among A's papers, this is expressed in "An ecstatic lecture."

> Marry, and you will regret it. Do not marry, and you will also regret it. . . . Whether you marry or do not marry, you will regret it either way. Laugh at the stupidities of the world, and you will regret it; weep over them, and you will also regret it. . . . Whether you laugh at the stupidities of the world or weep over them, you will regret it either way. Trust a girl, and you will regret it. Do not trust her, and you will also regret it. . . . Whether you trust a girl or do not trust her, you will regret it either way. Hang yourself, and you will regret it. Do not hang yourself, and you will also regret it. . . . Whether you hang yourself or do not hang yourself, you will regret it either way. This, gentlemen, is the quintessence of all the wisdom of life (*EO* 1, 38–39).

In a certain sense, "either/or" is A's watchword. But *how* one says this makes all the difference. And the Judge urges that A's manner of saying it means the loss of the self.

> Imagine a captain of a ship the moment a shift of direction must be made; then he may be able to say: I can do either this or that. But if he is not a mediocre captain he will also be aware that during all this the ship is ploughing ahead with its ordinary velocity, and thus there is but a single moment when it is inconsequential whether he does this or does that. So also with a person. . . there eventually comes a moment where it is no longer a matter of an Either/Or, not because he has chosen, but because he has refrained from it, which also can be expressed by saying: Because others have chosen for him—or because he has lost himself (*EO* 2, 164).

And so it is with us; if we drift, if we fail to decisively take hold of our lives, if we treat every either/or as indifferent, we will lose our selves; there will be nobody who we are.*

So the Judge pleads with A to adopt a different either/or, the mark of which is *seriousness of choice*. And when one chooses seriously, when one *engages oneself*, one chooses *ethically*.*

> Your choice is an esthetic choice, but an esthetic choice is no choice. On the whole, to choose is an intrinsic and stringent term for the ethical. Wherever in the stricter sense there is a question of an Either/Or, one can always be sure that the ethical has something to do with it. The only absolute Either/Or is the choice between good and evil, but this is also absolutely ethical (*EO* 2, 166–67).

And yet the Judge is not—at least not directly—urging A to choose the good. He just wants him to *choose*.

> What, then, is it that I separate in my Either/Or? Is it good and evil? No, I only want to bring you to the point where this choice truly has meaning for you. . . .
> Rather than designating the choice between good and evil, my Either/Or designates the choice by which one chooses good and evil or rules them out. Here the question is under what qualifications one will view all existence and personally live. That the person who chooses good and evil chooses the good is indeed true, but only later does this become manifest, for the esthetic is not evil but the indifferent. And that is why I said that the ethical constitutes the choice. Therefore, it is not so much a matter of choosing between willing good or willing evil as of choosing to will, but that in turn posits good and evil (*EO* 2, 168–69).

The Judge's either/or, then, has to do with the categories under which things are evaluated. One will lead a radically different life if everything is decided according to,

good / evil

---

*This thought is developed by Martin Heidegger, who holds that without a resolute seizing of oneself, one's life is dominated by what "they" say, or what "One" does or doesn't do. See "The 'Who' of Dasein," in Chapter 27.

*This does not mean that one necessarily chooses the right, but that one's choice, whether right or wrong, lies within the domain of the ethical; it is a choice *subject to ethical evaluation*. From the esthetic point of view, such evaluation is simply not meaningful (since the categories of evaluation are restricted to "interesting/boring").

rather than

interesting / boring

And the basic either/or, the really significant or deep one, is not either one of these alternatives, but that which poses this question:

esthetic *or* ethical?

If the Judge is right, the mark of making that choice is the *way* one chooses: with the entire seriousness and passion of the will (in which case the categories of good and evil *automatically* arise), or in that ironic, detached, amoral way in which one can say, "Choose either, you will regret both."

We can now see why marriage is for the Judge an example and symbol of the ethical. What one says at the altar is a decisive expression of the will, a choice that one makes for the future, *of oneself*. One chooses to be the sort of self who will continue to nurture and come to the aid of romantic love. It is no longer a matter of what happens to you; it is a matter of what you do with what happens to you. The ethical person gives up the futile project of simply trying to *be* something, and takes up the project of *becoming* something—of becoming a *self*.

It will be helpful before moving on to summarize some of the chief differences between these two ways of life. It is striking how different things look from the two perspectives (we have not discussed all these differences in detail).

1. *Immediacy*, which in the esthetic stage has the status of a condition to be aspired to, looks from the ethical point of view like *nature*, i.e., material for the will to act upon—to shape and form.
2. The possibility of *reflection* in the esthetic (the spectator's view of one's own life) takes on in the ethical the aspect of *practical freedom* (the ability to take the givens of one's life and make something of them).
3. The necessity for *secrecy* in the esthetic life (remember the Seducer) is supplanted by a requirement of *openness* in the ethical.
4. The prominence of the *accidental* in the esthetic (what happens to one) finds its ethical contrast in the notion of the *universal* (what duty requires of every human being).
5. The *abstraction* of the esthetic, hung as it is between the impossible immediacy of Don Juan and the incredible reflectiveness of the Seducer, is contrasted with the *concreteness* of the self-construction of the individual, where the accidental givens are taken over and given form by the universal demands of duty.
6. The attempt to *be* is given up in favor of the striving to *become*.
7. The emphasis on *the moment* is superseded by the value of *the historical* (as in an affair vs. a marriage).
8. The *fragmentariness* of an esthetic life stands in contrast to the *continuity* of the ethical.

These contrasts pave two distinct avenues for human life. The question arises: Are there any other possibilities?

The Religious

If the key characteristic of the esthetic style of life is enduring or enjoying (and perhaps arranging) what happens to one, and that of the ethical stage is taking oneself in hand and creating oneself, it seems apparent that human existence involves a tension between two poles. Kierkegaard characterizes them differently in various works: immediacy and reflection; nature and freedom; necessity and possibility; the temporal and the eternal; the finite and the infinite. On the one hand, we simply *are* something: a collection of accidental facts. On the other hand, we are an awareness of this, together with the need to do something about it; and this aspect of ourselves seems to elude all limitation, since it is not definitely this nor that. It seems to be a capacity for distancing ourselves from anything finite, temporal, and given.*

From the ethical point of view, this duality defines the task facing an individual: to become oneself. The task is to bring these two poles together so that they interpenetrate and inform each other: the immediate and finite takes a definite shape, and the reflective and infinite loses its abstract indefiniteness. One becomes a definite and unique thing: oneself.†

If one listened only to the Judge, one would think that this task of becoming oneself, though difficult, was something one could hope with confidence to accomplish. Further reflection, however, casts doubt on that optimistic assumption. A more penetrating psychology notes that the two poles providing the material out of which the self is constituted have a tendency to fall apart; indeed, one *wants* them to fall apart, one *cooperates* in identifying oneself now with this aspect, now with that. One *refuses* the anxiety-filled role of holding the two poles together. The problem is that one is *not willing to be oneself*, but wants always to be something more or something less: *either* something approaching God *or* something analogous to an unthinking brute.

As soon as this tendency is discovered, the individual is definitely beyond the ethical. What use is more determination to succeed in the task of being yourself, if you are continually undermining this determination by your unwillingness to be yourself?* All this huffing and puffing and moral seriousness begin to look like an impossible attempt to lift oneself by one's own bootstraps. Even the Judge seems to have an inkling of this, since he appends to the last letter he sends to A a "sermon" preached by an "older friend" of his, which is a meditation on the thought that "as against God, we are *always* in the wrong." Perhaps, the preacher says, we try to console ourselves by saying, "I do what I can." But, he asks, doesn't this provoke a new anxiety?

> Did you find rest in those words, "One does what one can"?
>
> So every more earnest doubt, every deeper care is not calmed by the words: One does what one can. If a person is sometimes in the right, sometimes in the wrong, to some degree in the right, to some degree in the wrong, who, then, is the one who makes that decision except the person himself, but in the decision may he not again be to some degree in the right and to some degree in the wrong?
>
> Doubt is again set in motion, care again aroused; let us try to calm it by deliberating on:
> THE *UPBUILDING* THAT LIES IN THE THOUGHT THAT IN RELATION TO GOD WE ARE ALWAYS IN THE WRONG (*EO* 2, 345–46).

With these thoughts we are in the domain of religion; it is no coincidence that they are put into the mouth of a pastor. Kierkegaard's views on religion are complex and extensive, some of them expressed by still other pseudonyms and some under his own name. He distinguishes at least two levels of religion: a basic level of what we might call religious consciousness in general (as it is shared, in different ways, by pagan figures like Socrates and Old Testament patriarchs such as Abraham) and a more intense level distinctive, he thinks, of Christianity. For our introductory purposes, we will set aside many of these complexities and focus on

---

*See the note on p. 410 where I discuss Hegel's notion of pure self-consciousness. See also Pico della Mirandola on the dignity of human beings, pp. 269–270.

†We need to be careful here. Kierkegaard does not present the ethical self as unique in the sense that it defines itself as *different from other selves*, for that would be to define it in terms external to itself. Becoming oneself involves the embodiment of those rational and universally human aspects which Kant and Hegel focus on in their treatment of morality and ethics. And these are shared by all. But the *way* in which these are embodied will depend on the particular given facts about oneself, and in that respect no one individual will be exactly like any other.

---

*Compare what Augustine has to say about the bondage of the will. See pp. 215 and 236. The "unhappy consciousness" of Hegel, at once self-liberating and self-perverting, is another expression of this stage. See p. 414.

some basic features of his treatment of *what it means to be a Christian*.

We already have the materials for the first step: the consciousness of sin—the thought that as against God we are always in the wrong. For this unwillingness to be ourselves, which one of the pseudonyms identifies as the essence of *despair*,* is, religiously understood, precisely *sin*. It is a sickness in the self; since the self is busy cooperating in making itself sick, it is not a sickness that the self can cure. I cannot *do* anything to heal myself of this continually self-inflicted wound. In the ruins of the project to *create* myself, nothing remains but to confess this. If I am to be able to be myself—without self-deception, rationalization, doublemindedness, and other forms of despair—I must give up the ethical project of trying to create myself or justify my own existence and receive it as a gift. And this I can only do by *faith*.

Kierkegaard's various discussions of religion are permeated by the paradoxical. The "author" of *Fear and Trembling*, Johannes de Silentio, confesses that he cannot *understand* Abraham, who in response to a command of God undertakes to sacrifice his only son. Ethically speaking, Abraham is a murderer; there is no excuse or justification that he can give for this action within the sphere of the universally human. To whom can he explain this behavior? He seems to be all alone, out beyond the firm ground of the ethical—just he and God. For this reason he cannot even tell his wife, Sarah, what he proposes to do; she would think him mad.†

De Silentio characterizes a figure he calls "the Knight of Faith." Such a knight makes two "movements." He makes a movement of *infinite resignation*, by which he resigns all claims to anything finite; he no longer identifies himself in terms of his possessions, worldly goods, his body, or even his own will. In making this movement of resignation, he discovers his "external consciousness" (*FT*, 48) and identifies himself with it. The religious expression of this movement of resignation is the monastery: the retreat from the world with its triple vows of poverty, chastity, and obedience. But, paradoxically—"by virtue of the absurd," as de Silentio puts it—the Knight of Faith at the very same time makes a movement by which he lives *in* the world, as much at home as any Philistine. The author imagines that he meets such a Knight of Faith.

The instant I first lay eyes on him, I set him apart at once; I jump back, clap my hands, and say half aloud, "Good Lord, is this the man, is this really the one—he looks just like a tax collector!" But this is indeed the one. I move a little closer to him, watch his slightest movement to see if it reveals a bit of heterogeneous optical telegraphy from the infinite, a glance, a facial expression, a gesture, a sadness, a smile that would betray the infinite in its heterogeneity with the finite. No! I examine his figure from top to toe to see if there may not be a crack through which the infinite would peek. No! He is solid all the way through. . . . He belongs entirely to the world; no bourgeois philistine could belong to it more. . . . He finds pleasure in everything, takes part in everything. . . . He attends to his job. . . . He goes to church. . . . In the afternoon, he takes a walk to the woods. He enjoys everything he sees, the swarms of people, the new omnibuses. . . . Toward evening, he goes home, and his gait is as steady as a postman's. On the way, he thinks that his wife surely will have a special hot meal for him when he comes home—for example, roast lamb's head with vegetables. If he meets a kindred soul, he would go on talking all the way to Østerport about this delicacy with a passion befitting a restaurant operator. It so happens that he does not have four shillings to his name, and yet he firmly believes that his wife has this delectable meal waiting for him. If she has, to see him eat would be the envy of the elite and an inspiration to the common man, for his appetite is keener than Esau's. His wife does not have it—curiously enough, he is just the same. . . . And yet, yet—yes, I could be infuriated over it if for no other reason than envy—and yet this man has made and at every moment is making the movement of infinity. He drains the deep sadness of life in infinite resignation, he knows the blessedness

---

*Kierkegaard's psychological discussion of the varieties of despair (contained in a slim volume entitled *The Sickness Unto Death*) is rich in detail and has been very influential.

†Note that there is here, as in the esthetic, an inability to be "open" about one's life. But it is different from the esthetic in being not prior to the ethical, but beyond it. Only someone who takes the ethical demands with utmost seriousness can venture beyond them with the anxiety of Abraham in obedience to God.

of infinity, he has felt the pain of renouncing everything, the most precious thing in the world, and yet the finite tastes just as good to him as one who never knew anything higher (*FT*, 38–40).

This double movement is precisely what de Silentio sees in Abraham; he has resigned Isaac entirely, yet he believes, by virtue of the absurd, in God's promise that his descendants through this son will be a great nation. De Silentio can admire moral heroes who make personal sacrifices for the sake of a greater good; these he can understand. But at Abraham he simply gapes in astonishment. Such a paradox, he says, is beyond human understanding—yet, apparently, it is possible to *live* it.

The specifically Christian form of religious life is even more paradoxical. In the recognition of sin, Christianity seems to push the individual as far away from spiritual health and wholeness as possible; but in the forgiveness of sin it offers what the individual cannot achieve. Moreover, it does this through belief in the incarnation, death, and resurrection of Jesus Christ, which embodies a paradox in itself. There is in Christianity an "objective" paradox to match the subjective paradoxicality of the life of faith: the paradox of the God-Man, a concept against which reason bangs its head fruitlessly. For who can *understand* the idea of a man who is wholly and fully a man, but at the same time, God? The idea of the eternal *become* temporal? This, Johannes Climacus (yet another pseudonym) insists, makes no rational sense at all.*

What this "absolute paradox" means is that being Christian is not a matter of *understanding* something, but of *existing* in a certain manner. Christianity resists being understood; it invites a certain form of life. It is the invitation to receive oneself in the forgiveness of sin, to forego the futile endeavor to create oneself and to rest in the forgiveness of sin. What Christianity requires is not understanding, but faith; and faith is the opposite of despair; it is nothing less than *being willing to be oneself*.

---

*You might like to look again at those last words about religion by the skeptical Hume, p. 360.

From the point of view of Christian religion, the esthetic and the ethical life both look like forms of despair. The former flip-flops between Don Juan and the Seducer, trying vainly to deny either reflective freedom or the stubbornness of given facts. The latter seems a futile attempt to get behind one's life and give it a push from outside. Neither acknowledges the reality of sin. And that is why the thought that "as against God we are always in the wrong" is an *edifying* thought. Like the alcoholic's admission that he is an alcoholic, it represents the first essential step in building up a self: the admission that one cannot build it alone. Instead of trying to *enjoy* the self or *create* the self, this admission of defeat clears the decks so that one can *receive* oneself.

The Individual

You might think that the pattern we have seen in the relations between esthetic, ethical, and religious forms of life is just the Hegelian pattern all over again. Inadequacies in earlier stages are exposed and remedied by later stages, toward which consciousness moves with a kind of inexorable logic. But this would be a serious mistake. To see why, we must examine the way Kierkegaard understands the position of the individual human being.

One reason he resorts to indirect communication is to combat the Hegelian view of the natural and necessary evolution of consciousness to ever higher levels. Each pseudonymous "author" presents to the reader a "possibility" for life; in that respect, they are all on the same level. Each invites the reader to identify with him.

- *The esthete*: You have only one life to live, so you might as well arrange to make it enjoyable. It is true that the kind of ironic detachment this requires means that life is ultimately meaningless and that there are no serious choices; but that's just how life is.
- *The ethicist*: Life *is* neither this way nor that; it all depends on what you *do* with it. And that is a

matter of choice, the sort of serious choice that constitutes a continuing self. You *are* what you *make* of yourself. And far from being meaningless, nothing could possibly matter more.

• *The Christian*: You can't successfully create yourself. We are all failures at this task. What is required is acknowledgement of this fact, together with faith in God's forgiveness through Christ. In this way we can come to accept ourselves in spite of our unacceptability; only thus can we be free simply to *be* ourselves.*

It is Kierkegaard's claim that among these three possibilities (and they may not be the only ones) existing human beings must *choose*. And they must choose without being able to attain a position in which they could know for certain which choice was the right or best one. There is no such vantage point for us as Hegel imagines absolute knowledge to be—no coincidence of subjectivity and objectivity, no identification of ourselves with Absolute Spirit, no *good reason* to choose one life rather than another, and no *knowledge* here at all. For existing human beings, the key concepts are choice, decision, and *risk*. The "movement" from one stage to another is not a natural movement, as we might imagine increasing maturity to be. Nor is it a rational or logical progression which carries itself along by a kind of inner necessity. There is no necessity here at all. A move from one kind of life to another is less like the result of rational persuasion and more like conversion. If one makes such a move it is by a *leap*.

It is true that *within* each of these frameworks, each occupant thinks it can characterize and explain the others. To the Judge, A looks like a man who has lost himself; to A, the Judge's marriage

looks overwhelmingly boring. The Christian sees them both as examples of despair—of not willing to be oneself; and no doubt the Christian could be accused, from some other framework, of irrationality and of going beyond the evidence. Where does the truth lie? In order to determine this, it seems one would have to take up a point of view outside them all and consider them all *objectively*. But it is Kierkegaard's conviction that no such point of view is available to an existing human being. You and I, he thinks, are free to choose among the possibilities. But we are not free to choose *for good reasons*—from an objective point of view. Neither are we free *not to choose*. Simply by living, we are making our choices; we cannot help it.

Hegel and the Hegelians Kierkegaard knew suppose that the process of living well can be organized in an objective and rational way. In particular, they think that philosophy can construct a *system* in which every aspect of life and reality is given its necessary and proper place. To this supposition Johannes Climacus, the philosopher among Kierkegaard's pseudonyms, responds in scathing tones.*

> I shall be as willing as the next man to fall down in worship before the System, if only I can manage to set eyes on it. Hitherto I have had no success; and though I have young legs, I am almost weary from running back and forth. . . . Once or twice I have been on the verge of bending the knee. But at the last moment, when I already had my handkerchief spread on the ground, to avoid soiling my trousers,

---

*It is worth noting that Kierkegaard's stage of *faith* is worlds away from the sort of "self-acceptance" urged upon us by so much contemporary psychology (and advertising!). The "I'm OK, you're OK" syndrome is one that is basically esthetic, in Kierkegaard's terms. What it lacks is both the seriousness of the ethical and the consciousness of sin. Dietrich Bonhoeffer, a German theologian influenced by Kierkegaard and killed by the Nazis, would have called it "cheap grace."

---

*The prospect of a possible completeness in understanding Kierkegaard identifies with Socrates, who assumes that the individual has within himself the capacity to recognize the truth. (See p. 98.) No one is more enthusiastic in admiration of Socrates than Kierkegaard. But in choosing for himself the Socratic roles of "gadfly" and "midwife," he is absolutely clear about his differences from Socrates. Whereas Socrates asks questions to provoke *recollection* of the truth (which he believes everyone implicitly knows), Kierkegaard poses possibilities to stimulate *choice* (in the conviction that no one knows). With respect to Hegel, Climacus remarks ironically (and not entirely fairly), "to go beyond Socrates when one nevertheless says essentially the same as he, only not nearly so well—that, at least, is not Socratic" (*PF*, 111).

and I made a trusting appeal to one of the initiated who stood by: "Tell me now sincerely, is it entirely finished; for if so I will kneel down before it, even at the risk of ruining a pair of trousers (for on account of the heavy traffic to and from the system, the road has become quite muddy),"—I always received the same answer: "No, it is not yet quite finished." And so there was another postponement—of the System, and of my homage.

System and finality are pretty much one and the same, so much so that if the system is not finished, there is no system. . . . A system which is not quite finished is an hypothesis; while on the other hand to speak of a half-finished system is nonsense (*CUP*, 97–98).

Climacus makes a distinction between a *logical system* and what he calls an *existential system*. And he claims that a logical system is possible, but an existential system is not. Geometry is a good example of a logical system; it is founded on axioms, postulates, and definitions, from which we can prove theorems using the rules of logic. What is characteristic of a logical system is that all the theorems are already implicit in the premises. That is the respect in which "finality" is an essential characteristic of a system—if a proposition that cannot be deduced from the axioms is introduced, it follows that a mistake has been made. Given a certain set of axioms, the set of derivable theorems is also given; no new truths can be added later, and none of the theorems can be altered. In particular, Climacus says, nothing must be incorporated into such a logical system "that has any relation to existence, that is not indifferent to existence" (*CUP*, 100). Existence, after all, makes headway, like the ship, and may always falsify any "system" that purports to describe it. So far as its relation to existence goes, a logical system merely presents a possibility, a hypothesis.*

The reason why an existential system is not possible (at least for us) is that "existence is precisely the opposite of finality" (*CUP*, 107).

Respecting the impossibility of an existential system, let us then ask quite simply . . . "Who is to write or complete such a system?" Surely a human being; unless we propose again to begin using the strange mode of speech which assumes that a human being becomes speculative philosophy in the abstract, or becomes the identity of subject and object. So then, a human being—and surely a living human being, i.e., an existing individual. . . . It is from this side . . . that objection must be made to modern philosophy; not that it has a mistaken presupposition, but that it has a comical presupposition, occasioned by its having forgotten in a sort of world-historical absent-mindedness, what it means to be a human being. Not indeed, what it means to be a human being in general; for this is the sort of thing that one might even induce a speculative philosopher to agree to; but what it means that you and I and he are human beings, each one for himself (*CUP*, 109).

The problem is that in constructing a system that supposedly captures existence, the speculative philosopher supposes that he can be finished with existence before existence is finished with him! As long as he lives, he must choose; his own existence is precisely not something finished. To suppose that at some point in his life he (or we, or the human race in its history) could attain the finality that comes with a system is simply comic.* Such a philosopher, Climacus says, "has gradually come to be so fantastic a being that scarcely the most extravagant fancy has ever invented anything so fabulous" (*CUP*, 107).

We have seen that the problem of the criterion has plagued philosophers since Sextus Empiricus, who first formulates it clearly. By what mark can

---

*About this point Climacus seems to be more correct than he could have known. Since the discovery of non-Euclidean geometries in the latter part of the nineteenth century, any system of geometry has to be regarded, as far as its application goes, as a hypothesis about the nature of space. For all these systems themselves can tell us, space may be either Euclidean or non-Euclidean.

*There is some reason to believe Kierkegaard's criticism here may be more apt against some enthusiastic "right-wing" Hegelians than against Hegel himself. You will recall that we noted several times a deep ambivalence running through Hegel's thoughts. For a strain that sounds very Kierkegaardian, see again the famous "Owl of Minerva" passage on p. 427.

we tell when we have latched onto truth and goodness? Hegel's answer to this problem is that we will know *in the end*—i.e., when we see how everything hangs together in a systematic way. What Kierkegaard is denying is that this kind of sight is possible for existing human beings. Perhaps that *would* do as a criterion. But we can't get there from here. And so we have to live without a criterion, without certainty, without good reason. We live by a *leap*.

The essential task for an existing human being, then, is not to speculate philosophically about absolute knowledge, but to become himself. As we have seen, this is a task involving risky choices, choices that must be made without the comfort of objective certainty. Speculative philosophers who try to present a *system* explaining existence imagine they can reach such a degree of objectivity that they revoke the risk in living; but this is sheer illusion. As Climacus plaintively asks, "Why can we not remember to be human beings?" (*CUP*, 104).

The tendency of modern philosophy is entirely toward objectivity. Kierkegaard sets himself absolutely against this tendency. He deplores

> . . . the objective tendency, which proposes to make everyone an observer, and in its maximum to transform him into so objective an observer that he becomes almost a ghost, scarcely to be distinguished from the tremendous spirit of the historical past (*CUP*, 118).

He endorses a saying by G. E. Lessing (a noted eighteenth-century German dramatist) to this effect: that if God held in his right hand the truth and in his left hand the striving for the truth, and asked the existing individual to choose one, the appropriate choice would be the left hand.

With respect to the individual's relation to the truth, there are two questions: (1) whether it is indeed the truth to which one is related; and (2) whether the mode of the relationship is a true one. Call the former an *objective* question and the latter a *subjective* question. The former concerns *what* is said or believed, the latter *how* it is said or believed.

For an existing individual, there is no way in which that first question can be definitively settled.

As a result, the *how* is accentuated.* For an individual, the quality of life depends on the intensity, the passion, the decisiveness with which this relation is maintained. (Remember the advice of the Judge to A about choice; remember also the way in which the consciousness of sin—of actually being already in error and separated from the truth—intensifies the situation in the Christian framework). Climacus offers a formula that expresses the appropriate knowledge relation of the individual to the truth.

> An objective uncertainty held fast in an appropriation-process of the most passionate inwardness is the truth, the highest truth available for an *existing individual* (*CUP*, 182).

Objectively speaking, the individual never has more than "uncertainty"; this uncertainty correlates subjectively with the riskiness of the choice made; and the riskier the choice the more intense the "passionate inwardness" with which it is made. For the individual, living in this subjectivity *is* living in the truth.

Kierkegaard is interested in two questions: (1) what is it to be an existing human being? and (2) what is it to be a Christian? He is convinced that unless we get an adequate answer to the first question, we will get the second one wrong. He believes most people do get it wrong. In an age in which everyone considers himself a Christian as a matter of course, Kierkegaard means to unsettle this complacency by drawing our attention back to the first question.

If the problem that faces each individual is this problem of how to manage the duality implicit in being a self, then it becomes evident that being a Christian must be a certain way of solving the problem. It cannot be just a matter of church mem-

---

*Climacus is here thinking of truth about the best life choices. But an analogy from general epistemology might be helpful. Knowledge is usually defined as *justified true belief*. Unless our belief is true—i.e., objectively correct—it cannot constitute knowledge. But the best we can do to ensure its truth is to believe *for the best reasons we have*. It is not up to us whether our belief is *true*, only whether it is *justified*.

bership, or of being baptized, or of having the right (i.e., orthodox) beliefs, or of "understanding" oneself and one's place in the "system" (in the manner of Hegelian philosophy). It is a problem that cannot be solved in any other way than by the construction of the self through the choices, momentous and trivial, that one makes when faced with life's multifarious possibilities.

In a whimsical passage, Johannes Climacus tells us the story of how he became an author. He was smoking his cigar on a Sunday afternoon in a public garden and ruminating on how he might best spend his life to be of benefit to mankind. He was thinking about all those

> "celebrated names and figures, the precious and much heralded men who are coming into prominence and are much talked about, the many benefactors of the age who know how to benefit mankind by making life easier and easier, some by railways, others by omnibusses and steamboats, others by the telegraph, others by easily apprehended compendiums and short recitals of everything worth knowing, and finally the true benefactors of the age who make spiritual existence in virtue of thought easier and easier, yet more and more significant. And what [he asks himself] are you doing?" Here my soliloquy was interrupted, for my cigar was smoked out and a new one had to be lit. So I smoked again, and then suddenly this thought flashed through my mind: "You must do something, but inasmuch as with your limited capacities it will be impossible to make anything easier than it has become, you must, with the same humanitarian enthusiasm as the others, undertake to make something harder." This notion pleased me immensely, and at the same time it flattered me to think that I, like the rest of them, would be loved and esteemed by the whole community. For when all combine in every way to make everything easier, there remains only one possible danger, namely, that the ease becomes so great that it becomes altogether too great; then there is only one want left, though it is not yet a felt want, when people will want difficulty. Out of love for mankind, and out of despair at my embarrassing situation, seeing that I had accomplished nothing and was unable to make anything easier than it had already been made, . . . I conceived it as my task to create difficulties everywhere (*CUP*, 165–66).

What sort of difficulties? Those that remind us of what a hazardous and risky business it is, this business of having to be an existing human individual.

Marx: Beyond Alienation and Exploitation

As we have noted, several themes become prominent at the close of the Enlightenment and the beginning of the nineteenth century. And in Hegel they are most systematically developed. We can summarize these themes as follows:

1. *The significance of history.* The classical quest for eternal truths, knowable at any time and in any circumstances, is replaced by the notion of the development of culture and of reason itself. Moreover, this development is thought of as *progress* toward a more encompassing truth, rationality, and freedom.

2. *The role of opposition and antagonism in this progress.* Hegel notices, indeed emphasizes the role of the *negative* in development, i.e., that struggle and loss is an essential part of any move forward.* William Blake, the English Romantic poet, puts it this way: "Without contraries is no progression."[3]

3. *The attainment of the goal by the race, not the individual.* Since the progress is a historical one and since individuals cannot jump out of their own cultural setting, the goal (self-consciousness, rationality, freedom) must be one toward which the race is moving, rather than one which an individual could attain in any completeness.

4. *The justification of the evil that accompanies this progression.* Hegel, as we have seen, acknowledges the suffering that individuals endure on the "slaughter bench" of history but argues that all is worthwhile because of the incomparable value of the end: the realization of Absolute

---

*In a way, this is a very old thought. See Heraclitus on the necessity for opposition and strife, p. 19.

Spirit in the wholly rational state. As Lenin was later to put a similar point: You can't make an omelet without breaking some eggs.

Karl Marx (1818–1883) accepts these views. Indeed, he accepts them in their Hegelian guise; as a young man, Marx was self-consciously one of the left-wing Hegelians. Like Kierkegaard, whom he did not know, he complains that Hegelian philosophy is speculative and abstract. But unlike Kierkegaard, his remedy for this abstraction is not to focus on the plight of the anxious individual, forced to make choices without rational warrant; such a focus on "subjectivity" would seem to him an abstraction of a different, but no less deplorable, kind. Marx develops his critique along other lines.

Hegel believes (1) that reality is Spirit, (2) that the human being is Spirit unknown to itself, alienated from its objects (and so from itself), and (3) that the cure for this **alienation** is the knowledge that there is nothing in the object which is not put there by the subject—by Spirit itself. The human being is God coming to consciousness of himself through history. Marx comes to believe that this is exactly right, but only in a funny kind of way. For what Hegel has done, Marx thinks, is to take reality and "etherealize" it. It is as though the real world has been transposed into another key and played back to us—all there, but with everything looking weirdly distorted. Hegel, Marx believes, has taken philosophy off its feet and turned it upside down on its head. It is Marx's determination to put philosophy back on its feet again. In an early work written with Friedrich Engels, Marx expresses this determination.

In direct contrast to German philosophy which descends from heaven to earth, here we ascend from earth to heaven. That is to say, we do not set out from what men say, imagine, conceive, nor from men as narrated, thought of, imagined, conceived, in order to arrive at men in the flesh. We set out from real, active men, and on the basis of their real life-process we demonstrate the development of the ideological reflexes and echoes of this life-process. The phantoms formed in the human brain are also, necessarily, sublimates of their material life-process, which is empirically verifiable and bound to material premises. Morality, religion, metaphysics, all the rest of ideology and their corresponding forms of consciousness, thus no longer retain the semblance of independence. They have no history, no development; but men, developing their material production and their material intercourse, alter, along with this their real existence, their thinking and the products of their thinking. Life is not determined by consciousness, but consciousness by life (GI, 118–19).[4]

Consider the last sentence. Hegel writes as if the forms of consciousness, traced in his phenomenolgy of Spirit, have a kind of independence or basic character. The various forms of life, Hegel holds, depend on the forms of consciousness, the level to which knowledge has evolved: sense-certainty, perception, understanding, desire, the unhappy consciousness, morality, and so on. But to Marx and Engels, this puts the cart before the horse. Those forms of consciousness do not have the kind of independence Hegel ascribes to them. And so they do not, in themselves, have a history. There is, however, an underlying reality that does have a history. This *material* reality has to do first and foremost with *economic* matters—with putting bread on the table. It is the reality of "men in the flesh," of "real, active men" and their "life processes." Hegel's forms of consciousness are simply "sublimates" or ideological reflections of this more basic reality.

The most essential need of such real men is the sustenance of their material life. Marx calls this the

first premise of all human existence, and therefore of all history, the premise, namely, that men must be in a position to live in order to be able to "make history." But life involves before everything else eating and drinking, a habitation, clothing and many other things. The first historical act is thus the production of the means to satisfy these needs, the production of material life itself (GI, 119–20).

This premise is followed by other no less basic points: that the production of the means of subsistence involves the need for instruments of production and thus multiplies needs; that people propagate their own kind and so create families; and, most important, that these activities involve people from the start in social relationships.

> It follows from this that a certain mode of production or industrial stage is always combined with a certain mode of co-operation, or social stage, and this mode of co-operation is itself a "productive force" (*GI*, 121).

It is Marx's intention, then, to substitute for Hegelian speculative philosophy a discipline that looks carefully at the actual, empirically ascertainable facts about human beings. Marx is one of the influential figures in the history of both sociology and economics. He holds that if you want to understand a certain form of consciousness—of religion, perhaps, or of literature—you need to understand the material (economic and social) conditions in which it is produced. It is no good simply looking at texts or practices in isolation; you need to understand the context in which they arise.*

But even more important is the emphasis Marx places on action. Understanding is not enough, even for the intellectual. What is called for is doing. Perhaps no one has put the philosopher in such a central role since Plato had proposed that philosophers should become kings and kings philosophers.† In a famous line, Marx writes,‡

> The philosophers have only *interpreted* the world, in various ways; the point, however, is to *change* it (*TF*, 109).

---

*Vigorous controversies exist among literary critics over precisely this point, the "New Critics" arguing that the text itself must speak, and more or less Marxist opponents replying that the text is not an independent entity that has a voice of its own.
†For the rationale behind this proposal of Plato's, see "The State," in Chapter 10. In a way, Marx proposes a similar role for the intellectual in the struggles of his time.
‡Look once more at the "Owl of Minerva" passage in Hegel (p. 427). This is what Marx is attacking.

In what ways is philosophy supposed to change the world? . . . To understand, we must ask what Marx sees when he undertakes to describe "real" people in their actual existence.

Alienation, Exploitation, and Private Property

In an early work (1844), unknown until the 1930s, Marx presents an analysis of the condition these "real" people had reached in the middle of the nineteenth century. We need to remind ourselves that this is the heyday of the industrial revolution—of the steam engine, the coal mine, and the knitting mill, of the twelve- or fourteen-hour work day, of child labor, and of a widening gap between those who own the means of production and the masses who give their labor in factories they have no stake in. In understanding these conditions, Marx relies heavily on the major political economists who analyze the new industrial situation, Adam Smith and David Ricardo.

Here is how Marx sees things.

> *Wages* are determined through the antagonistic struggle between capitalist and worker. Victory goes necessarily to the capitalist. The capitalist can live longer without the worker than can the worker without the capitalist (*EPM*, 65).

The capitalist, of course, owns the means of production, the factories and tools. A separation of ownership from labor is characteristic of the industrial age. In the days when cobblers made shoes, virtually every cobbler had his own shop and tools; perhaps he had an apprentice or two and maybe even a servant. But ownership and labor were typically combined in the same person. In the nineteenth century, however, there is a split between the class of people who own the very large and expensive means of industrial production and the class that provides the labor, a split that takes on the characteristics of a "struggle."

To increase their profits and meet the competition of other industrial entrepreneurs, the capitalists pay the workers no more than is necessary to keep the workers alive, working, and reproducing.

This is possible in part because there are typically more workers than jobs. So the worker takes on the characteristic of a *commodity* in the system; like all commodities, the capitalist tries to buy it as cheaply as possible. As a commodity, of course, the worker is not thought of as a human being, but "only as a working animal—as a beast reduced to the strictest bodily needs" (*EPM*, 73). The worker could be (and often is) replaced by a machine.

The worker must face not only the capitalist, but also the landlord. Formerly, the landed gentry could live solely by the productivity of the land. But the vigorous activity of the capitalist has forced competition here, too; and landowners are either driven out of this class altogether or become capitalists in their own right, seeking a profit from the land. They, therefore, seek to make rents as high as possible, and tenant farmers join the industrial workers as commodities on the market.

Private property is one fact political economy takes for granted, Marx says. But that should not be taken for granted; it needs an explanation. Marx's explanation leans heavily on his Hegelian background. For example, suppose you take a piece of wood from the floor of the forest, sit down, and painstakingly carve into it the face of Lincoln. We can say that you have "put something of yourself into it." No longer raw nature, it now is an expression of yourself. It is, in fact, your labor *objectified*. In confronting it, you are confronting yourself: you are the person who *did that*. In contemplating this object, you become aware at one and the same time of it and of yourself, for part of what you are stands there in objectified form before you. Before you put your labor into it, you would not have been harmed had someone stolen it; but now, if it is stolen, the thief steals part of *you*.*

The whole history of mankind, Marx holds, has been such a revealing of himself to himself on the part of man. Man is an active, productive, creative being. And in producing objects, he creates himself: these objects are the products of his activity and show himself to himself as in a mirror. Do you want to know what man is? Look at his art, his laws, his religion, his societies, his technologies, his industrial products; they will tell you what he is, because they are man himself in objectified form. It is in such *externalization* that man makes himself fully human—i.e., self-consciously human.

But in the industrial age this process has become perverted. For the worker labors and produces a *commodity*. What does that mean?

(1) It means that the *work* of the worker is not experienced as an affirmative production of himself; rather, it is experienced as an *alienation* from himself. The labor he performs is external to him; as Marx puts it,

> he does not affirm himself but denies himself, does not feel content but unhappy, does not develop freely his physical and mental energy but mortifies his body and ruins his mind. . . . His labor is therefore not voluntary, but coerced; it is *forced labor*. It is therefore not the satisfaction of a need; it is merely a *means* to satisfy needs external to it. Its alien character emerges clearly in the fact that as soon as no physical or other compulsion exists, labor is shunned like the plague (*EPM*, 110–11).

Rather than being an expression of himself, his work is experienced as the loss of himself. As a result he is *dehumanized*; he feels active and productive only in his *animal* functions; in his *human* functions (i.e., productive labor), he is no more than an animal—or worse, a machine.*

(2) The worker is alienated not only from his labor, but also from the *products* of his labor. They are not his. All he has are his wages, which are necessarily enough only for bare subsistence. His product stands over against him as an independent power; although he has put himself into it, he has no control over it. As a worker, he puts his life into the object, but then his life no longer belongs to him.

This is more intelligible if we note that according to the economists of the day, *value* is defined in terms of labor. The value of something (including money) represents a certain amount of labor. The

---

*Compare Hegel on master and slave, pp. 410–412.

*Those of you who have worked on an assembly line can perhaps verify from your own experience Marx's description of such work.

worker produces value, but value in the hands of another: the one with the means to purchase the labor of the worker, i.e., the capitalist. In plain words, what the worker is producing is capital, and with it the capitalist.

The worker, then, is alienated from his labor and from the products of his labor; in neither can he find himself. If we return now to the question about the origin of private property, we can see, Marx says, that it has its foundation in *alienated labor*. And since the classical political economists formulate their laws in terms of private property, we can see that they are formulating the laws of estranged labor—the laws of a condition of society in which workers are exploited, dehumanized.

> All these consequences result from the fact that the worker is related to the *product of his labor* as to an *alien* object. For on this premise it is clear that the more the worker spends himself, the more powerful becomes the alien world of objects which he creates over and against himself, the poorer he himself—his inner world—becomes, the less it belongs to him as his own. It is the same in religion. The more man puts into God, the less he retains himself. The worker puts his life into the object; but now his life no longer belongs to him but to the object. . . . The *alienation* of the worker in his product means not only that his labor becomes an object, an *external* existence, but that it exists *outside him*, independently, as something alien to him. It means that the life which he has conferred on the object confronts him as something hostile and alien. . . .
>
> It is true that labor produces for the rich wonderful things—but for the worker it produces privation. It produces palaces—but for the worker, hovels. It produces beauty—but for the worker, deformity. It replaces labor by machines, but it throws a section of the workers back to a barbarous type of labor, and it turns the other workers into machines. It produces intelligence—but for the worker stupidity, cretinism (*EPM*, 108–10).

In the condition of alienated labor—of private property—the natural human needs of people become perverted. "Man becomes ever poorer as man, his need for *money* becomes ever greater if he wants to overpower hostile being" (*EPM*, 147). The

need for money, of course, is insatiable; schemes for multiplying human needs and creating new ones are derived to increase one's money wealth. This process is fueled by *greed*. Greed and the money system, Marx says, are corollaries; devotion to money becomes a kind of secular religion.

Communism

Private property, then, has a history; it is not a natural, given fact. Private property is the result of alienated labor. And this alienation of labor itself has a history. Marx's view of this history is sketched in the well-known first part of the *Manifesto of the Communist Party*, which he wrote with Engels in 1848.

> The history of all hitherto existing society is the history of class struggles.
>
> Freeman and slave, patrician and plebian, lord and serf, guild-master and journeyman, in a word, oppressor and oppressed, stood in constant opposition to one another, carried on an uninterrupted, now hidden, now open fight, a fight that each time ended, either in a revolutionary reconstitution of society at large, or in the common ruin of the contending classes. . . .
>
> Our epoch, the epoch of the bourgeoisie, possesses, however, this distinctive feature: it has simplified the class antagonisms. Society as a whole is more and more splitting up into two great hostile camps, into two great classes directly facing each other: Bourgeoisie and Proletariat (*MCP*, 35–36).

The bourgeoisie is the class of owners, including both capitalists (in the narrower sense) and landlords. Marx characterizes it in the following way.

> The bourgeoisie, wherever it has got the upper hand, has put an end to all feudal, patriarchal, idyllic relations. It has pitilessly torn asunder the motley feudal ties that bound man to his "natural superiors," and left remaining no other nexus between man and man than naked self-interest, than callous "cash payment." It has drowned the most heavenly ecstasies of religious fervour, of chivalrous enthusiasm, of philistine sentimentalism, in the icy water of egotistical

calculation. It has resolved personal worth into exchange value, and in place of the numberless indefeasible chartered freedoms, has set up that single, unconscionable freedom—Free Trade. In one word, for exploitation, veiled by religious and political illusions, it has substituted naked, shameless, direct, brutal exploitation (*MCP*, 38).

In pursuit of its ends, the bourgeoisie constantly revolutionizes the instruments of production and thus transforms relations among people in society into competitive relations. It produces a world market and interdependence among nations. It converts all other nations, on pain of extinction, into bourgeoisie as well. It concentrates property in a few hands. And it produces its own opposition: the proletariat.

> In proportion as the bourgeoisie, *i.e.*, capital, is developed, in the same proportion is the proletariat, the modern working class, developed—a class of labourers, who live only so long as they find work, and who find work only so long as their labour increases capital (*MCP*, 42).

The proletariat is the class of nonowners, of workers who have nothing but their labor to call their own. We have already characterized the life of the worker, as Marx sees it. We can now add that the lower strata of the middle classes—small tradespeople, shopkeepers, craftsmen, peasants—tend to sink gradually into the proletariat, that as it grows in size it begins to feel its strength, and that it is the only really revolutionary class. As Marx sees it,

> The development of Modern Industry . . . cuts from under its feet the very foundation on which the bourgeoisie produces and appropriates products. What the bourgeoisie, therefore, produces, above all, is its own grave diggers. Its fall and the victory of the proletariat are equally inevitable (*MCP*, 48).

Historical development, as Marx sees it, has led us to the point where society is divided into two great classes whose interests are diametrically opposed.

The interests of the proletariat, Marx believes, are best represented by the communists, "the most advanced and resolute section of the working class parties of every country," who have "the advantage of clearly understanding the line of march, the conditions, and the ultimate general results of the proletarian movement" (*MCP*, 49). (This insight is the result of taking Hegelian dialectical philosophy off its head and setting it back on its feet.) And what communism stands for is the abolition of private property.

About this claim Marx and Engels make the following remarks.

> The distinguishing feature of Communism is not the abolition of property generally, but the abolition of bourgeois property. But modern bourgeois private property is the final and most complete expression of the system of producing and appropriating products, that is based on class antagonisms, on the exploitation of the many by the few. . . .
>
> Hard-won, self-acquired, self-earned property! Do you mean the property of the petty artisan and of the small peasant, a form of property that preceded the bourgeois form? There is no need to abolish that; the development of industry has to a great extent already destroyed it, and is still destroying it daily. . . .
>
> You are horrified at our intending to do away with private property. But in your existing society, private property is already done away with for nine-tenths of the population; its existence for the few is solely due to its non-existence in the hands of those nine-tenths. You reproach us, therefore, with intending to do away with a form of property, the necessary condition for whose existence is, the non-existence of any property for the immense majority of society.
>
> In one word, you reproach us with intending to do away with your property. Precisely so; that is just what we intend. . . .
>
> Communism deprives no man of the power to appropriate the products of society; all that it does is to deprive him of the power to subjugate the labour of others by means of such appropriation (*MCP*, 50–54).

If the history of the world has, as Marx says, been the history of class struggles, then there seems to be something final and apocalyptic about this division of society into bourgeoisie and proletariat, into the few who have all and the many who have nothing. And if this picture is taken seriously, it seems as though a final revolution, in which the workers take control of the means of production, might be the goal toward which history is moving. This is, in fact, the "theoretical advantage" that the communists claim—that they can see this line of development.

Marx agrees with Hegel about the character of the end: that for which so much suffering is all worthwhile is *freedom*.* But it is not the freedom of pure self-consciousness—knowing itself to be all there is, both subject and object—that Marx praises. Rather, it is the freedom of real, active, working men and women, who no longer find themselves alienated from their work, the products of their work, and their fellow workers.

> When, in the course of development, class distinctions have disappeared, and all production has been concentrated in the hands of a vast association of the whole nation, the public power will lose its political character. Political power, properly so called, is merely the organized power of one class for oppressing another. If the proletariat during its contest with the bourgeoisie is compelled, by the force of circumstances, to organize itself as a class, if, by means of a revolution, it makes itself the ruling class, and, as such, sweeps away by force the old conditions of production, then it will, along with these conditions, have swept away the conditions for the existence of class antagonisms and of classes generally, and will thereby have abolished its own supremacy as a class.
>
> In place of the old bourgeois society, with its classes and class antagonisms, we shall have an association, in which the free development of each is the condition for the free development of all (*MCP*, 59–60).

It is indeed not enough to understand the world; what is required is to change it. The *Manifesto* ends with a ringing call to action (*MCP*, 74):

> The Communists disdain to conceal their views and aims. They openly declare that their ends can be attained only by the forcible overthrow of all existing social conditions. Let the ruling classes tremble at a Communistic revolution. The proletarians have nothing to lose but their chains. They have a world to win.
>
> WORKING MEN OF ALL COUNTRIES, UNITE!

If things have not worked out as Marx and Engels expected, it must nonetheless be allowed that their vision of a world where the "free development of each is the condition for the free development of all," a world without exploitation and without class antagonisms, has done as much actually to change the world (in one way and another) as any system of thought has ever done.

Notes

1. T. S. Eliot, *Four Quartets: The Dry Salvages*, V, in *The Complete Poems and Plays 1909–1950* (New York: Harcourt, Brace and Co., 1958), 136.
2. References to the works of Søren Kierkegaard are as follows:
   EO: Either/Or, vols. 1 and 2, trans. Howard V. Hong and Edna H. Hong (Princeton: Princeton University Press, 1987). References in text are to volume numbers and page numbers.
   FT: Fear and Trembling, trans. Howard V. Hong and Edna H. Hong (Princeton: Princeton University Press, 1983).
   CUP: Concluding Unscientific Postscript, trans. David F. Swenson and Walter Lowrie (Princeton: Princeton University Press, 1944). *PF: Philosophical Fragments*, trans. Howard V. Hong and Edna H. Hong (Princeton: Princeton University Press, 1985).
3. William Blake, "The Marriage of Heaven and Hell," in *William Blake*, ed. J. Bronowski (New York: Penguin Books, 1958), 94.
4. References to the works of Karl Marx are as follows:
   GI: The German Ideology, in *The Marx-Engels Reader*, ed. Robert C. Tucker (New York: W. W. Norton and Co., 1972).
   TF: Theses on Feuerbach, in Tucker (ed.), *The Marx-Engels Reader*.
   EPM: The Economic and Philosophic Manuscripts of 1844, ed. Dirk J. Struik (New York: International Publishers, 1964).
   MCP: Manifesto of the Communist Party (with Friedrich Engels), trans. Samuel Moore (Moscow: Progress Publishers, 1971).

---

*See Hegel's discussion of freedom as the goal of history, pp. 423–426.

23

The Utilitarians:
Moral Rules and the Happiness of All

At about the same time that Kant is working out his views on duty and the rational justification of the moral law, a quite different orientation for ethics is being developed in England. The utilitarians, as they come to call themselves, are much more empirical than Kant or Hegel, and in their own way nearly as radical in their critique of society as Marx; however, they advocate reform rather than revolution. They draw on sources in their own English-speaking history, particularly on Hobbes and Hume, but develop these themes in a quite distinctive fashion.

Two thinkers stand out in connection with **utilitarianism**, though others contribute to the doctrine. Jeremy Bentham (1748–1832) and John Stuart Mill (1806–1873) together set out its principal tenets, though there are some basic points on which they disagree. We can begin our investigation of this still influential view of morality with a quotation from Mill's little booklet, *Utilitarianism* (1861).

> All action is for the sake of some end, and rules of action, it seems natural to suppose, must take their whole character and color from the end to which they are subservient. When we engage in a pursuit, a clear and precise conception of what we are pursuing would seem to be the first thing we need (*U*, 2).[1]

Note the *teleological* orientation here.* Suppose I want to know what I ought to do, or what would be the right thing to do. Since everything I do is intended to accomplish something, i.e., is "for the sake of some end," it seems sensible to pay attention to that end. Mill suggests that the end in fact determines whether what I do is the morally right thing. It is the consequences of my action that fix its rightness and wrongness.†

But what consequences do we look to? Every act always has many, many consequences. Which of them are morally relevant? Bentham and Mill answer this question by claiming that in everything we do, no matter what the particular end, we are aiming at a single thing: happiness. But does this help? Aristotle has already noted that people disagree widely over what happiness is.‡ If happiness means one thing to Jones and another to Smith,

---

*You may recall that this word comes from the Greek *telos*, meaning end or goal. Something is teleological if it points to an outcome. See the earlier discussion on p. 157. See also p. 172.

†Consequences are precisely what Kant says morality must *not* be concerned with. For Kant, the morally relevant facts concern only a person's intention: does the individual act out of *duty*, out of respect for the moral law. Consequences are completely irrelevant to morality. See p. 392.

‡ See pp. 172–173.

how will it help to note that all their actions are aiming at happiness?

Bentham and Mill are convinced, however, that this variability is only superficial; at its core, happiness is everywhere alike. As Bentham puts it,

> Nature has placed mankind under the governance of two sovereign masters, *pain* and *pleasure*. It is for them alone to point out what we ought to do, as well as to determine what we shall do. On the one hand the standard of right and wrong, on the other the chain of causes and effects, are fastened to their throne. They govern us in all we do, in all we say, in all we think: every effort we can make to throw off our subjection, will serve but to demonstrate and confirm it (*PML*, 1).

Our goal in whatever we do, Bentham says, is to avoid pain for ourselves and to secure pleasure. And that is what happiness is.* Note that Bentham here makes two distinct claims. The first is a thesis about motivation; this is a psychological thesis, proposing that considerations of pain and pleasure always determine our actions. This psychological or causal thesis has a name: *psychological hedonism*.†

The second thesis is an ethical or moral thesis, which holds that right and wrong are tied to pleasure and pain. That is, in judging the moral rightness of an action, we must consider the pleasure and pain that action produces. This claim is called *ethical hedonism*. As you can see, it is distinct from the former; it is a claim, not about what we in fact do, but about what we ought to do. It is in these terms that Bentham and Mill formulate the principle of utility.

> By the principle of utility is meant that principle which approves or disapproves of every action whatsoever, according to the tendency which it appears to have to augment or diminish the happiness of the party whose interest is in question: or what is the same thing in other words, to promote or oppose that happiness (*PML*, 2).

So far this doesn't have a moral ring to it. If the "party whose interest is in question" is I, then I follow this principle in doing what will make me happy, i.e., what will provide me the greatest proportion of pleasure over pain. That may be prudent, but not, it seems, especially moral. It doesn't seem to have that peculiar moral *bite*; after all, pursuing my own interests may sometimes be held to be wrong. The utilitarians, however, give the principle of utility a moral character by insisting that what is ethically relevant is not my happiness or yours, but happiness itself. In this form it is sometimes also called the greatest happiness principle and is summed up in the slogan "The greatest happiness for the greatest number." So the utilitarian standard, as Mill tells us,

> is not the agent's own greatest happiness, but the greatest amount of happiness altogether (*U*, 11).

Suppose you are facing a choice between actions and wondering what, morally speaking, you ought to do. Here is what the utilitarian advises. Estimate how much total pleasure and pain each alternative action will produce for you and everyone concerned. The action that produces the best pleasure/pain ratio overall is the one you ought to perform. Note that it is not more important that *you* should be happy as a result of your action than other people. But neither is it less important. The happiness of each is to be weighed equally.

It is of great importance to see that the utilitarians were not thinking just of private actions by individual citizens. They were one and all active in politics, in the reform of law, and in trying to produce better legislation. The principle of utility was to function not just as a moral guide, but as a tool of social criticism and reform. In the early nineteenth century many felt that the law in England was a mess—a tangled skein of contradictory precedents originating in forms of society very different from the one in which these thinkers were living. The law seemed designed chiefly to secure a livelihood for the lawyers.* All the utilitarians, Bentham

---

*This is what Hobbes calls "felicity." See p. 333.
†The term "hedonism" is discussed on p. 184.

---

*Charles Dickens details the terrible effects of interminable suits dragging through the courts in his novel *Bleak House*.

in particular, used the principle of utility to criticize this maze by asking, Does this law, this institution, this way of doing things contribute to happiness or misery? This tool was sufficiently sharp to earn them the appellation "philosophical radicals." In the name of general happiness, they demanded parliamentary reform, prison reform, the extension of the right to vote, full legal rights for women, greater democracy, ways of making government officials accountable, changes in punishments, and so on. The principle of utility is a sharp tool for reformers; it can pinpoint social evils and suggest remedies.

But how is this tool to be used? Bentham believes that one of the great advantages of the principle of utility is the detail and precision of thought it makes possible in these moral and political issues. In fact, he tries to work out something like a calculus of pleasures and pains, so that one can simply *calculate* the right thing to do by taking into account the various amounts of happiness each alternate course of action or law would produce. Though Mill and other utilitarians have doubts about how strictly this method can work, a brief glance will help us get an understanding of the movement.

One part of Bentham's project is to list the various kinds of pleasures and pains that need to be taken into account. There are a great many; among the pleasures are those of sense, wealth, skill, a good name, piety, power, memory, and so on. Among the pains are those of privation, the senses, awkwardness, a bad name, memory, expectation, and so on. Each of these is explained in sufficient degree, Bentham thinks, so that it can be recognized and taken account of by the judge, the legislator, or the private citizen in dealing with other persons.

But in considering any given pleasure, we see that it differs in several ways from another pleasure of the same kind; the same is true of pains. Pleasures and pains differ in:

- *Intensity* (some toothaches hurt worse than others)
- *Duration* (some last longer)

- *Certainty* or *uncertainty* (some are avoidable, others not)
- *Propinquity* or *remoteness* (some are expected tomorrow, others not for several years)
- *Fecundity* (some pleasures or pains bring other pleasures or pains in their wake; others do not)
- *Purity* (if a pleasure does *not* bring pains along with it, it is "pure")
- *Extent* (how many people are affected by it)

You can see how these considerations might be brought to bear on a practical problem. A more intense pleasure is preferable to one less intense. The longer pains last and the more people they affect, the worse they are judged to be. So if a law will produce quite intense pleasure for a few people but condemn a great many to pains of long duration, it is sure to be a very bad law. That law should not be passed. Actual cases are usually more complicated, but this gives the basic idea.

The utilitarians believe that legislation and moral judgment alike can approximate a science. Given the principle of utility and these rules, one should not have to *guess* which law or action is best; one can *discover* it. These thinkers assume that pleasure can be quantified; if this assumption is correct, the legislator or moral agent need only add up the sums to arrive at the right answer. Bentham allows that it may be difficult or too time consuming to engage in this deliberation before every decision. But, he says, it should be kept in view; the closer we can come to it, the more exactly correct our choices will be.

But can pleasures and pains be quantified in this exact way? Here is a point on which Mill differs from Bentham.* Though full of admiration for the older man, Mill says that Bentham is like a "one-eyed man," who sees clearly and far, but very narrowly.[2] To Bentham, pleasure is pleasure, and

---

*To understand why, it helps to know something of Mill's life. You may enjoy Mill's very readable *Autobiography*, in which he recounts his childhood and remarkable education at the hands of his father, his nervous breakdown and the cure of it, and his twenty-year Platonic love of Harriet Taylor, who became his wife only after the death of her husband. Mill's active involvement with the intellectual and political movements of the day are also detailed.

that's the end of it. In a famous line, Bentham declares that "quantity of pleasure being equal, pushpin [a children's game] is as good as poetry."[3] But Mill thinks this is obviously not true. Some pleasures are worth more than others, even if the *amount* of pleasure in each is the same (supposing that one can determine this). Pleasures, he wants to say, differ not only in quantity, but also in quality.

> It is quite compatible with the principle of utility to recognize the fact that some kinds of pleasure are more desirable and more valuable than others. It would be quite absurd that, while in estimating all other things quality is considered as well as quantity, the estimation of pleasure should be supposed to depend on quantity alone (*U*, 8).

This may well be right, but it raises two problems. First, it seems to undermine Bentham's claim that legislation and morality might be made scientific. For even if you agree that one could compare *amounts* of pleasure and pain to add up the quantities produced, it seems hard to imagine that *qualities* are likewise quantifiable. If they were, they would just be quantities again, and we would be back with Bentham. The second problem is whether there is any way to *tell* which pleasures are more desirable. To this question Mill has an answer.

> Of two pleasures, if there be one to which all or almost all who have experience of both give a decided preference, irrespective of any feeling of moral obligation to prefer it, that is the more desirable pleasure (*U*, 8).

Consult the person of experience, Mill tells us: someone who has tried both. Setting aside moral considerations, that person's preference is a sign that one exceeds the other in quality and is more desirable.*

---

*We have to set moral consideration aside in making this judgment, lest we beg the question. After all, we are trying to discover where the greatest happiness lies precisely in order to determine what our moral obligations are!

But, you might object, is there any reason to think that people will agree about which pleasure is better? Suppose we take a survey of those who have experienced each of two kinds of pleasure—a day in an amusement park, let us say, and a day spent reading poetry. Do you think we will find anything approaching unanimity? And if we don't, how are we going to take the principle of utility as a practical rule to make decisions? We are supposed to maximize happiness; but if happiness varies so much among individuals, how are we going to decide whether to build more amusement parks or more libraries?

> From this verdict of the only competent judges, I apprehend there can be no appeal. On a question which is the best worth having of two pleasures, or which of two modes of existence is the most grateful to the feelings, . . . the judgment of those who are qualified by knowledge of both, or if they differ, that of the majority among them, must be admitted as final (*U*, 11).

So, Mill tells us, democratic politics is the way to make this decision. In fact, he thinks there will be a large measure of agreement because of the similarities among people. But where there are differences, the majority must rule. In personal decisions, of course, this complication is often lacking; we may know quite well the pleasures and preferences of all those concerned, and then it is relatively simple to determine the right thing to do. We should (1) try to foresee what each action open to us would lead to, (2) compare the total happiness to all (ourselves included) produced by each, and (3) choose the one that produces the most happiness (understood as pleasure in this qualitative sense).

A key concept of utilitarian moral philosophy is its *consequentialism*: that actions are sorted into the morally acceptable and the morally unacceptable by virtue of their consequences. The early utilitarians identify as relevant the consequences bearing on happiness, understanding happiness to be pleasure and the absence of pain. Utilitarians in our century, while preserving the consequentialism, have sometimes looked to other features than pleasure to justify moral judgments.*

Suppose we ask whether the principle of utility is the right one to use in making a choice. Is it, as the utilitarians hold, the criterion for the morally right? It is not the only option available, as we already know. Aristotle would ask whether the action contributes to our excellence (virtue) as an instance of the human species. Jesus, St. Paul, and Augustine would have us ask whether what we propose to do is in accord with the will of God. Kant would urge us to submit the maxim of our action to the test of universalization. And Hegel would presumably have us look to the standards present in our current cultural situation.† Is there anything the utilitarian can say that should convince us that the principle of utility is what Kant said he was searching for: the "supreme principle of morality"?‡

Both Bentham and Mill address this question. Both insist that since the principle of utility is held to be the *first* principle of morality, it is not subject to ordinary kinds of proof. Nonetheless, each thinks he can provide arguments to convince us. Let us examine them in turn.

Bentham believes we will be converted to utilitarianism if we just consider the alternatives. There are only two, he thinks, though these two may appear in various versions and disguises. The clearest opposite to the principle of utility is what he calls the principle of asceticism. An adherent of this principle would judge many actions to be right that involve a denial of pleasure for themselves and, perhaps, for others. An ancient Stoic, who holds virtue to be the only good, may be an example.§ Others (e.g., certain religious ascetics) may

judge an actual increase of pain to be right, at least for oneself. Luther in the monastery beating himself for his sins is a vivid illustration.

Bentham has two arguments against the principle of asceticism. First, it is never applied consistently. A monk does not torture himself because he thinks it is good in itself, but because he judges it necessary to gain the incomparable pleasures of heavenly bliss. Thus, he bears witness against his will to the principle of utility. The Stoics, according to Bentham, see correctly that some pleasures are sources of pain but generalize hastily to the unwarranted claim that pleasures as such are never good. Nonetheless, they praise the virtues, which in Bentham's eyes are nothing more than producers of pleasure without the accompanying pains. Thus the Stoics, too, reject utility inconsistently.

Second, asceticism has never been applied to government. Even if one thought it would be good to minimize one's own pleasures, or perhaps to increase one's pains, no legislator has ever consciously aimed at stocking the body politic with highwaymen, housebreakers, or arsonists. And if through negligence and ignorance the misery of the populace increases, the government that allows it is justifiably criticized.

Basically, Bentham argues that the ascetic principle cannot be consistently pursued.

> The principle of utility is capable of being consistently pursued; and it is but tautology to say, that the more consistently it is pursued, the better it must ever be for humankind. The principle of asceticism never was, nor ever can be, consistently pursued by any living creature. Let but one tenth part of the inhabitants of the earth pursue it consistently, and in a day's time they will have turned it into a hell (*PML*, 13).

The other alternative to utility Bentham calls the principle of sympathy and antipathy. Most of the other claimants to the title of moral criterion reduce, he thinks, to this.

> . . . I mean that principle which approves or disapproves of certain actions, not on account of their tending to augment the happiness, nor yet on account of

---

*G. E. Moore, for instance, holds that a certain quality of *goodness* is what the moralist is to look to; while pleasure is one good thing, he says, there are numerous other goods not reducible to pleasure, such as knowledge. R. M. Hare takes as fundamental what people *prefer*; whether that is always a matter of pleasure is an open question.

†See pp. 173–174 (Aristotle); p. 206 (Jesus); pp. 237–238 (Augustine); p. 394 (Kant); and pp. 421–422 (Hegel).
‡See p. 391.
§See p. 192.

their tending to diminish the happiness of the party whose interest is in question, but merely because a man finds himself disposed to approve or disapprove of them (*PML*, 15–16).

In a way, Bentham remarks, this is not a principle, but the denial that a principle is needed. All that is required is a sentiment of approval or disapproval on the part of the moral agent. Though such judgments may often coincide with judgments of utility, they need not. People, of course, seldom are content simply to say that an action is right because they approve of it. So they cloak their decisions in fine words. They attribute their approvals and disapprovals to common sense, to a special moral sense, to understanding, to the law of nature, to the law of reason, to good order, to the voice of God, and more. But all such appeals come down in the final analysis to what the individual in question approves or disapproves. And this seems to Bentham excessively arbitrary.*

Bentham ends this defense of utility with a rhetorical flourish. Suppose you say, "This is morally right; I know it is, though I do not know whether it will bring happiness or misery; moreover, I don't care." Bentham asks you to assume it will bring misery. Then he urges you to bring that misery clearly before your mind, to feel it, become sensible of it. Can you still, in the face of that fact, persist in your conviction that to do it is the right thing? (To do the experiment right, of course, it is important that we not imagine that the misery is a means to some further happiness. It must be misery as an end. That, Bentham thinks, none of us can persist in calling right.)

Mill adds arguments of his own. Though he agrees that questions of ultimate ends do not admit of proof, he thinks convincing considerations can be brought forward. Among these considerations, unfortunately, are two arguments that nearly all subsequent philosophers have held to be remarkably poor. They are famous (perhaps even infamous) for that reason alone. We'll examine them briefly.

The only proof capable of being given that an object is visible is that people actually see it. The only proof that a sound is audible is that people hear it; and so of the other sources of our experience. In like manner, I apprehend, the sole evidence it is possible to produce that anything is desirable is that people do actually desire it (*U*, 34).

What Mill needs to show is that the general happiness is desirable, that it is what we ought to strive for. But his analogies do not work. "Visible" means "can be seen," and "audible" means "can be heard." But "desirable" is not parallel. It does not mean "can be desired," but "should be desired." So the fact that something is desired (even if that something be the greatest happiness of the greatest number) doesn't mean it *ought* to be desired.

Mill's second argument is no better. The conclusion he needs to support is that each of us, you and I, should (morally speaking) take the general happiness as our end; when we act, that is what we ought to be trying to bring about. He argues that

> happiness is a good, that each person's happiness is a good to that person, and the general happiness, therefore, a good to the aggregate of all persons (*U*, 34).

We can, perhaps, grant the premises of this argument: that happiness is a good and that for each person that person's own happiness is a good to that person. But all that follows from this premise is that each person's happiness is a good to *someone*. It does not follow that *your* happiness is a good to *me*, just because my own is. Each and every bit of the general happiness is a good to some person; but it may not be, for all the premises tell us, that the general happiness is a good to everyone—that it is what *each* of us ought to pursue. Yet that is what the principle of utility claims.*

But how important are these errors? Both Bentham and Mill, after all, admit that their first principle cannot be proved. Perhaps, then, it is a mistake to try to prove it. We may feel that their

---

*Is this convincing? Or is it altogether too superficial a treatment of alternatives to utilitarian ethics?

*Logicians have a name for this kind of mistake. They call it a fallacy of composition, since what applies to every part is erroneously applied to the whole.

consequentialist morality is pointing to something important, even if it cannot be proved correct. The lack of proof does leave open the possibility that there is more to morality than utility. But it may be hard to deny that utility plays an important role.

Let us set aside this attempt at a positive proof and look at another kind of defense of the utilitarian creed. Mill considers various sorts of objections to it and tries to show that they all rest on misunderstandings. It is worth reviewing some of those objections; we will gain a clearer view of the utility principle by seeing what it does *not* mean.

(1) Some accuse utilitarians, especially utilitarians who set pleasure as the good, of aiming too low. It is the old objection aimed already at the Epicureans. Since pleasure and pain are something we share with the animals, to make these the standard of right and wrong is to espouse a philosophy for pigs.* To this Mill replies that human beings, having higher faculties than pigs, require more to make them happy; but their happiness is still just pleasure and their unhappiness pain. In this connection Mill pens a famous line.

> It is better to be a human being dissatisfied than a pig satisfied; better to be a Socrates dissatisfied than a fool satisfied. And if the fool, or the pig, are of a different opinion, it is because they only know their own side of the question (*U*, 10).

(2) Some hold that the utilitarian standard is unrealizable. Is it possible that everyone should be happy? First, Mill replies, even if that were impossible, the principle of utility would still be valid. We can do much to minimize unhappiness, even if we cannot attain its opposite. Second, it is an exaggeration to say that happiness—even the general happiness—is impossible. The happiness that utilitarians favor is not, after all, a life of constant rapture, but

> moments of such, in an existence made up of few and transitory pains, many and various pleasures, with a decided predominance of the active over the passive,

and having as the foundation of the whole not to expect more from life than it is capable of bestowing (*U*, 13).

He believes that even now a great many people live this way. If it were not for the "wretched education and wretched social arrangements" prevailing in his society, he thinks, such a life would be attainable by almost all. And he adds,

> When people who are tolerably fortunate in their outward lot do not find in life sufficient enjoyment to make it valuable to them, the cause generally is caring for nobody but themselves (*U*, 13).

(3) Some critics object that in making happiness the end, utilitarians undercut the most noble motives and the most admirable character. Do we not, they ask, admire the individual who is willing to give up, to sacrifice personal happiness? Wouldn't this human virtue be destroyed if we all became happiness seekers?

Mill admits that we admire those who give up their personal happiness for the sake of something they prize even more. But what is this for which they renounce their happiness?

> . . . after all, this self-sacrifice must be for some end; it is not its own end; and if we are told that its end is not happiness but virtue, which is better than happiness, I ask, would the sacrifice be made if the hero or martyr did not believe that it would earn for others immunity from similar sacrifices? . . . All honor to those who can abnegate for themselves the personal enjoyment of life when by such renunciation they contribute worthily to increase the amount of happiness in the world; but he who does it or professes to do it for any other purpose is no more deserving of admiration than the ascetic mounted on his pillar (*U*, 15–16).

Utilitarians, Mill says, can admire such self-sacrifice as much as any. They only refuse to recognize that it is good in itself. It is admirable only if it tends to increase the total amount of happiness in the world. And that is exactly what the principle of utility urges.

---

*See the discussion of Epicurus on p. 188. You might also look at Aristotle's remark about pleasure on p. 173.

(4) Other critics object that it is asking too much of people to have the general happiness in view in all their actions. You can think of this as the opposite of the first objection; instead of holding that the standard is too low, some claim it is impossibly high.

To this Mill replies that it is the business of ethics to tell us what our duties are, what is right and what is wrong. But ethics does not go as far as to require that everything we do should be done from a certain *motive*.* From a utilitarian point of view, the rightness of an action is judged by what it brings about; why the agent acted in that way is irrelevant. Mill gives an example:

> He who saves a fellow creature from drowning does what is morally right, whether his motive be duty or the hope of being paid for his trouble (*U*, 18).

Does this make ethics seem altogether *too external*? Are people's motives really that irrelevant to what is right and wrong? In a footnote added in response to criticism of that sort, Mill allows that our estimate of the *agent* may vary, depending on whether he saved the drowning person out of duty or greed. In the latter case, we will think less of the man and be less likely to trust him in similar circumstances. But, Mill insists, we must allow that, for whatever motive, the right thing was done.

(5) The above objection easily turns into another. It would seem that utilitarianism

> renders men cold and unsympathizing; that it chills their moral feelings toward individuals; that it makes them regard only the dry and hard consideration of the consequences of actions, not taking into their moral estimate the qualities from which those actions emanate (*U*, 19).

Here Mill reiterates that we have to distinguish between *actions* as good or bad and *persons* as good or bad. It is possible, of course, that a good person

occasionally performs a morally bad action, just as a really bad person may do a good thing. And though some utilitarians may stress the moral estimation of action almost to the exclusion of "the other beauties of character which go toward making a human being lovable or admirable" (*U*, 20) (Mill is surely thinking of Bentham here), there is no barrier in utilitarianism itself to valuing these highly. Moreover, although goodness of character and the rightness of action may sometimes not coincide, "in the long run the best proof of a good character is good actions" (*U*, 20). So utilitarianism need have no chilling effect on us.

(6) To the objection that utilitarianism, which counts only worldly happiness as the mark of moral rightness, is a "godless" doctrine, Mill replies that it all depends on how you think of God.

> If it be a true belief that God desires, above all things, the happiness of his creatures, and that this was his purpose in their creation, utility is not only not a godless doctrine, but more profoundly religious than any other (*U*, 21).

(7) The last objection we will consider is that the principle of utility is impractical. It requires something there is usually no time to do. Very often we are called upon to act quickly in making a choice; there is no time to do the exhaustive calculations required to determine the consequences of all the alternatives available. To this Mill has a very interesting reply.

> This is exactly as if anyone were to say that it is impossible to guide our conduct by Christianity because there is not time, on every occasion on which anything has to be done, to read through the Old and New Testaments. The answer to the objection is that there has been ample time, namely the whole past duration of the human species. During all that time mankind have been learning by experience the tendencies of actions (*U*, 23).

The fact that utility functions as a first principle does not in any way rule out secondary principles. These intermediate generalizations, Mill holds, are readily available to us in the common wisdom of

---

*This is exactly what Kant thinks morality does require: that every morally right action be one that is done out of duty, from respect for the moral law. Actions done out of mere inclination are not worth anything, morally speaking. See p. 393.

our culture and in the law. We do not need to calculate each time whether *this* murder would be all right, or whether *that* lie would be justified, or whether making *this* contribution to the relief of the homeless fits with the first principle. We learn the basic moral rules as children. Such secondary rules may be subject to gradual improvement. They may be more and more perfectly adapted to produce happiness. There may be occasional exceptions to them, too; but a *moral* justification for an exception must be decided by appeal to utility.

> Nobody argues that the art of navigation is not founded on astronomy because sailors cannot wait to calculate the Nautical Almanac. Being rational creatures, they go to sea with it ready calculated; and all rational creatures go out upon the sea of life with their minds made up on the common questions of right and wrong (*U*, 24).

It is indeed not possible to calculate the utility of each of our actions on the occasion of their performance. But we don't need to. We cannot do without secondary rules in society, which can be learned and relied upon. But these can be improved only by bringing them more closely in line with the first principle: utility. For Mill, Bentham's great virtue lies in his attempt to improve these subordinate principles, particularly in social institutions and the law.

Let us round out our discussion of utilitarianism by considering a problem which Mill addresses and which seems unresolved to this day. Can the principle of utility function as the *sole* principle of an acceptable morality? The problem concerns justice. Can the demands of justice be incorporated into the utilitarian framework? Or is there something different here, something that resists the calculation of consequences?

It is easy to dream up cases where there is at least the appearance of conflict between justice and utility. Executing an innocent man may, in certain circumstances, quell a riot and prevent the death of hundreds. It is clear that to execute the innocent is *unjust*. Yet a utility calculation seems to tell us that in this circumstance executing the man is the morally right thing to do, since it would produce more pleasure and less pain overall.* So it seems there is a clash between the claims of justice and the claims of utility. In circumstances like this, justice tells us one thing, utility another. Mill tries to argue that this clash is merely apparent and that justice rightly understood can be seen to be a special case of utility. If his argument is successful, justice and utility are reconciled.

Mill allows that the subjective feeling attached to judgments about justice is different from, and stronger than, the feeling about utility. We think it is a more serious business to violate justice than simply to fail to bring about as much happiness as we can. Why? Because, Mill believes, justice is associated with *rights*. It is unjust, for instance, to violate someone's *legal* right. Or at least it is usually unjust to do so; most of us will allow that there are bad laws, which may provide persons with legal rights they *ought* not to have. In this case, perhaps it is not unjust to violate such a legal right; but a case like that is the exception.

This leads to the notion of *moral* rights—rights that laws ought to protect but sometimes may not. A person may have a moral right even in the absence of any legal protection. Injustice, then, is taking or withholding from someone something to which that person has a moral right. When injustice is done, we have a natural reaction: resentment. And we very much want the perpetrator of injustice to be punished. To be sure, we may punish other acts; but we feel that punishment is particularly appropriate when someone's moral rights have been violated.

> When we call anything a person's right, we mean that he has a valid claim on society to protect him in the possession of it (*U*, 52).

If I have a right to something, I have a "valid claim" on society to protect me by threatening to punish anyone who violates this right. That is what

---

*Discussion of such cases has made it clear that it is not so easy to be sure that the circumstances justifying an innocent man's execution from a utilitarian standpoint ever exist. For instance, one would have to be virtually certain that the fact of his innocence would never be known, lest even worse events ensue. And could you ever be certain enough of that?

it is to have a right. But this leaves Mill with further problems. What is the origin of such rights? Are such rights compatible with the principle of utility? And on what grounds can I claim that society owes me such protection?

Mill argues that no other reason can be given, and none is needed, than general utility. One part of utility is so basic, so fundamental to our happiness, that without it everything else is in jeopardy: security.

> All other earthly benefits are needed by one person, not needed by another; and many of them can, if necessary, be cheerfully foregone or replaced by something else; but security no human being can possibly do without; on it we depend for all our immunity from evil and for the whole value of all and every good, beyond the passing moment, since nothing but the gratification of the instant could be of any worth to us if we could be deprived of everything the next instant by whoever was momentarily stronger than ourselves (*U*, 53).

Security, being safe in our persons and possessions, is the "most indispensable of all necessaries," Mill says (*U*, 53).* And because it is so basic to our happiness, the feelings that attach to its protection are particularly strong. That is why it may *seem* that justice is different from utility. But far from being different from utility, let alone opposed to it, justice is its deepest and most fundamental form.

> I account the justice which is grounded on utility to be the chief part, and incomparably the most sacred and binding part, of all morality. Justice is a name for certain classes of moral rules which concern the essentials of human well-being more nearly, and are therefore of more absolute obligation, than any other rules for the guidance of life; and the notion which we have found to be of the essence of the idea of justice—that of a right residing in an individual—implies and testifies to this more binding obligation. . . . a person may possibly not need the benefits of others, but he always needs that they should not do him hurt (*U*, 58).

In this way Mill argues there is no conflict between justice and utility. If we return to our example of executing an innocent man for the sake of avoiding a riot, we can see what Mill would say. It is unjust to take his life, so it ought not to be done. To acquiesce in the violation of that man's security imperils the security of us all. And that none of us will tolerate.* The appearance of conflict can be overcome if we reflect that justice is the name we give to the deepest condition for securing our happiness.

Bentham and Mill, together with utilitarians to the present day, urge that there is only one way to decide the morally right thing to do. Think about the consequences of all the actions open to you, estimate (if you can't literally calculate) the effect each action would have on the happiness of all the persons affected (or on the goodness of their lives, or on what they would prefer), and the right thing will become apparent. What remains is simply to do it.

Notes

1. References to the works of Bentham and Mill are as follows:
   PML: Jeremy Bentham, *An Introduction to the Principles of Morals and Legislation* (Oxford: Clarendon Press, 1907).
   U: John Stuart Mill, *Utilitarianism*, ed. George Sher (Indianapolis: Hackett Publishing Co., 1979).
2. John Stuart Mill, "Bentham," in *Utilitarianism and Other Essays*, ed. Alan Ryan (New York: Penguin Books, 1987), 151.
3. Quoted in *The Encyclopedia of Philosophy*, vol. 1, ed. Paul Edwards (New York: Macmillan Co., Free Press, 1967), 283.

---

*You would be right to hear echoes of Hobbes here. See Hobbes on the deplorable "state of nature" in which no one can feel safe (p. 334).

*Critics of utilitarianism will push the point, however, that it is *possible*—however unlikely—that such an execution will actually increase the general happiness. And if one *could* be sure that the circumstances were right, then utility *would* prescribe the execution. Since this could in no case be a just act, there is in principle an unresolved conflict between justice and utility, and Mill's attempt at reconciliation fails. The principle of justice must have other, independent grounds—perhaps in something like the Kantian imperative that one is never to use a person as a means to an end. See again Kant's discussion of this on p. 395.

24

The Pragmatists:
Thought and Action

The nineteenth century is a tumultuous one, socially, politically, and intellectually. It is the century of the railroad, the newspaper, and the factory. It is the century of the British Empire, colonialism, and the conquest of the American continent. And it is the century of the principle of the conservation of energy, of non-Euclidean geometries, of non-Aristotelian logic, and of evolution. A topsy-turvy century, indeed, but one convinced on the whole that progress is being made every day.

Nothing bolsters this conviction more substantially than the progress of science; and among the accomplishments of science, none stands out more prominently than that of Darwin. A cause for controversy down to our own day, Darwin's evolutionary theory seems to capture for natural science the phenomena of *life*, in much the same way that Newton masters space, time, and gravitational forces. A basically mechanistic explanation is given for the forms of living things, for their variety, and for their tendency to alter over long spans of time. The basic outlines of Darwinian evolutionary theory are well known: genetic changes produce small variations in offspring; some of these changes are beneficial to individuals who possess them; under the pressure of population and scarcity of resources, these individuals are more likely to reproduce; and thus the advantages are passed progressively from generation to generation, leading eventually to differentiation of species in different ecological niches. The core ideas are those of *random variation* and *natural selection*.

Darwinian thought is an extension of the earlier revolution in our scientific understanding of the world, bringing the phenomena of life definitely within the scope of natural explanations. It is a momentous and influential shift, affecting intellectuals of all kinds—not least those philosophers who come to call themselves pragmatists.

Charles Sanders Peirce

Charles Peirce (1839–1914), the son of a Harvard mathematician, was trained in the techniques of science from an early age. He used to claim that he had been brought up in a laboratory. For a good part of his adult life, he worked as a scientist for the United States Coast and Geodetic Survey. He made some contributions to the theory of the pendulum and was much concerned with problems of accurate measurement. But he was early attracted to problems in logic and probability theory and made a close study of the philosophies of Kant and Hegel. His research in logic is extremely original, contributing to the expansion of logic beyond the

Aristotelian syllogism.* In addition to extending the theory of *deductive* inferences, Peirce does much to clarify *inductive* inferences; he also explores that sort of inference which starts from certain facts and leaps to a hypothesis that explains them. (He calls this last sort *abductive* inferences, a term that has not caught on.)

Peirce is also a metaphysician of some power, combining in his later thought a version of evolutionary theory with absolute idealism.† But it is not his metaphysics that has been influential, so we shall concentrate on what he calls his **pragmatism**. The word comes from a Greek root meaning "deed" or "act" and is chosen to accentuate the close ties that Peirce sees between our intellectual life (concepts, beliefs, theories) on the one hand and our practical life of actions and enjoyments on the other. Peirce also occasionally calls it *practicalism*, and sometimes *critical common-sensism*. We'll see that John Dewey thinks of **instrumentalism** as a term nearly equivalent in force, this term bringing out the tool-like character of the intellectual conceptions we use.

Others, including most prominently the psychologist and philosopher William James, adopt the term "pragmatism"; it comes to mean a number of subtly different things to different people. In 1908, an American philosopher, Arthur Lovejoy, wrote an article entitled "The Thirteen Pragmatisms." It seemed there were almost as many versions of the doctrine as there were philosophers who adopted the name. Since many of them diverged significantly from what Peirce meant by the term, he invented the term *pragmaticism* for his own views—a word, he said, ugly enough to be safe from kidnappers. He was correct; and in

fact history knows his views by the more common term "pragmatism." It is under that heading that we will examine what he has to say.

Fixing Belief

In the late 1870s, Peirce published a series of articles in *Popular Science Monthly*, in which the influence of scientific practice on this lifelong researcher is evident. He distinguishes four ways of coming to a fixed belief about some subject matter, four methods of settling opinion. These are techniques that can be used (indeed, are used) to arrive at what we think, at least, is true. They are ways of resolving doubt.

First there is the *method of tenacity*. If the aim is settlement of opinion, one might ask oneself,

> why should we not attain the desired end, by taking any answer to a question which we may fancy, and constantly reiterating it to ourselves, dwelling on all which may conduce to that belief, and learning to turn with contempt and hatred from anything which might disturb it? (FB, 248–49).[1]

Those who adopt this technique enjoy certain benefits. First, they avoid the uncomfortable state of indecision and doubt. It cannot be denied, Peirce says, "that a steady and immovable faith yields great peace of mind" (FB, 249). Moreover, there seems to be nothing that can *rationally* be said in objection; for such persons are content to set rationality aside, and reasons against their beliefs will be (from their point of view) beside the point.

Nonetheless, Peirce believes that this is not a satisfactory method of settling opinion. His reason is an interesting one and sheds light on his pragmatism. One might think that the proper objection to the method of tenacity is that it is bound to leave one with too many false beliefs. But that is not Peirce's objection. The trouble with this method is that it

> will be unable to hold its ground in practice. The social impulse is against it. The man who adopts it will find that other men think differently from him,

---

*For a brief account of Aristotle's conception of logic, which dominates Western thought for 2400 years, see pp. 145–153; the syllogism is discussed on pp. 148–150.

†For an account of absolute idealism in its Hegelian guise, see pp. 415–417. The key feature in Peirce's version is that the entire universe has the distinguishing features of mind and that it is moving toward a *rational end* out of *love*. But such a brief account hardly does it justice.

and it will be apt to occur to him, in some saner moment, that their opinions are quite as good as his own, and this will shake his confidence in his belief (FB, 250).

The right objection is that tenacity *doesn't work!** This thought, that others may well be as right as oneself, arises from the "social impulse," Peirce says, "an impulse too strong in man to be suppressed" (FB, 250). We are in fact influenced by the opinions of others. So some method must be found that will fix belief not only in the individual, but in the community.

This thought leads us to the second method, *authority*.

> Let an institution be created which shall have for its object to keep correct doctrines before the attention of the people, to reiterate them perpetually, and to teach them to the young; having at the same time power to prevent contrary doctrines from being taught, advocated, or expressed. Let all possible causes of a change of mind be removed from men's apprehensions. Let them be kept ignorant, lest they should learn of some reason to think otherwise than they do. Let their passions be enlisted, so that they may regard private and unusual opinions with hatred and horror. Then, let all men who reject the established belief be terrified into silence. Let the people turn out and tar-and-feather such men, or let inquisitions be made into the manner of thinking of suspected persons, and, when they are found guilty of forbidden beliefs, let them be subjected to some signal punishment. When complete agreement could not otherwise be reached, a general massacre of all who have not thought in a certain way has proved to be a very effective means of settling opinion in a country (FB, 250).

This method, Peirce judges, is much superior to the first; it can produce majestic results in terms of culture and art. He even allows that for the mass of humankind, there may be no better method than that of authority. But this method is also unstable:

there will always be some people who see that in other ages or countries, different doctrines have been held on the basis of different authorities. And they will ask themselves whether there is any reason to rate their beliefs higher than the beliefs of those who have been brought up differently. These reflections "give rise to doubts in their minds" (FB, 252). In the long run, authority does not *work* any better than tenacity in settling opinion.

The unsatisfactory character of the first two methods gives rise to the third, which Peirce calls both *the method of natural preferences* and the *a priori method*. Here we accept what seems "obvious," or "agreeable to reason," or "self-evident," or "clear and distinct." Our opinions are neither those we just happen to have at the beginning nor those imposed by an authority; they are those we arrive at after reflection, conversation with others, and taking thought.

The best examples of such a method, Peirce thinks, are the great metaphysical systems, from Plato through Hegel. But what is obvious from that history is that one man's self-evidence is another man's absurdity, and the method

> makes of inquiry something similar to the development of taste; but taste, unfortunately, is always more or less a matter of fashion, and accordingly metaphysicians have never come to any fixed agreement, but the pendulum has swung backward and forward between a more material and a more spiritual philosophy, from the earliest times to the latest (FB, 253).

Again we have an unstable and hence unsatisfactory method for settling our opinions.*

What we need is some method

> by which our beliefs may be caused by nothing human, but by some external permanency—by something upon which our thinking has no effect. . . . It must be something which affects, or might affect, every man. And, though these affections are necessarily as various as are individual conditions, yet the method must be such that the ultimate conclusion of

---

*Experience with certain sorts of "fanatics" may make one doubt whether Peirce is altogether correct here.

*Compare Hume's impatience with intuition as a foundation for knowledge, p. 342.

every man shall be the same. Such is the method of science. Its fundamental hypothesis, restated in more familiar language, is this: There are real things, whose characters are entirely independent of our opinions about them; those realities affect our senses according to regular laws, and, though our sensations are as different as our relations to the objects, yet, by taking advantage of the laws of perception, we can ascertain by reasoning how things really are, and any man, if he have sufficient experience and reason enough about it, will be led to the one true conclusion (FB, 253–54).

Several features of the *method of science* are distinctive. First, there is the attempt to make our beliefs responsive to something *independent* of what any of us thinks—or would like to think; in various ways, the first three methods lack precisely this feature. Second, we see that the method of science is decidedly a *public* method: there is to be no reliance on what is peculiar to you or to me; our beliefs are to be determined by what can affect you *and* me *and* anyone else who inquires. Again, this public character is lacking in the first three methods. Third, because of this essentially public character, the *social impulse* (which wrecks the first three methods) will not undermine opinion that is settled in this scientific way.

According to Peirce's conception of science, however, it rests on an assumption, or "hypothesis" that there *actually is* some reality independent of our thinking about it. Suppose we ask, Why should we grant this assumption?* For one thing, the practice of science does not itself lead us to doubt the assumption; indeed, Peirce holds, the method "has had the most wonderful triumphs in the way of settling opinion" (FB, 254). In this regard, too, it is strikingly different from the other methods: it works! But the fundamental reason to grant this assumption has to do with the very nature of belief and doubt. Peirce's thoughts on this score are original and deep. We need to look at them.

---

*After all, this seems to be the central issue in modern epistemology; it is what Descartes' methodical doubt undermines and what Hegel's idealism denies. How can Peirce be so naive?

Belief and Doubt

We have been examining methods of "fixing" belief or settling our opinions. But what is it to have a belief? And what is it like to doubt? Doubting and believing are clearly different, but how? Peirce finds three differences. (1) The sensation of believing is different from that of doubting; they just feel different. (2) We are strongly disposed to escape doubt but are content when we have a belief—at least until we are led to doubt it again by some surprise the world has in store for us. (3) The most profound difference, however, gets us to the very nature of belief and doubt. For a belief is a *habit*, and doubt is the lack of such a habit. This needs explaining.

Do you believe the world is (roughly) round? Let's assume you do. What is it to have this belief? It is not a matter of having a thought in your mind; presumably, you have believed this for a long time, although you have not been constantly thinking that thought. And it would be wrong to say that you believed it only when you had this thought actively in mind. Belief, Peirce says, "is not a momentary code of consciousness" (WPI, 279). Nor does it "make us act at once, but puts us into such a condition that we shall behave in a certain way, when the occasion arises" (FB, 247). So if you believe the world is round, you are in a "condition" that leads you to behave in the following ways: if someone asks you whether the world is flat, you say, "No, it is round"; if you win a trip "around the world," you accept it gladly; if you see a picture of the world taken from a satellite, you say, "Yes, that is what I expected it would look like." If you are on the interstate highway in Kansas, you drive confidently and do not worry about running your car off the edge. Being *disposed to behave* in these various ways—and more—is what it is to have the belief that the world is round. To have a belief is to have a habit that allows you to act confidently in the world, expecting that your actions in given circumstances will fulfill their purposes.

Doubting, on the other hand, is being in an uncertain state; it is the lack of a settled habit and so involves *not knowing* what to do in a given situation. That is why we struggle to escape doubt; it is essentially an anxious and irritating state. Peirce calls the struggle to escape doubt and attain the condition of belief *inquiry*, though he admits that sometimes it is not a very apt term. Inquiry, then, is an attempt to recover the calm satisfactoriness of knowing *what to do when*, which is characteristic of belief. And Peirce is convinced, as we have seen, that only the public, intersubjective methods of scientific inquiry will work in the long run to carry us from doubt to fixed belief.

Three things are essential to inquiry: a stimulus, an end or goal, and a method. Here is how Peirce thinks about these things:

* Stimulus: Doubt
* End: Settlement of opinion
* Method: Science

We need to explore further each of the first two factors. Let us begin with some reflections on doubt.

According to all the pragmatists, inquiry (indeed, thinking in general) always begins with a felt problem. But, they say, not everything that has been thought by philosophers to be problematic really is so.

> Some philosophers have imagined that to start an inquiry it was only necessary to utter a question whether orally or by setting it down upon paper, and have even recommended us to begin our studies with questioning everything! But the mere putting of a proposition into the interrogative form does not stimulate the mind to any struggle after belief. There must be a real and living doubt, and without this all discussion is idle (FB, 248).

Peirce obviously has Descartes in mind.* Perplexed by the contradictory things he had been taught, Descartes determines to "doubt everything" until he should come upon something "so clear and dis-

---

*Review Descartes' first *Meditation*.

tinct" that he could not possibly doubt it. Descartes is embarked on what Dewey is to call "the quest for certainty."

But Peirce simply cannot take this project of methodical doubt seriously. This is not, he thinks "a real and living doubt"; it is only a "make-believe" (WPI, 278). To propose that one begin by doubting everything, Peirce remarks, is to suppose that doubting is "as easy as lying."

> We cannot begin with complete doubt. We must begin with all the prejudices which we actually have when we enter upon the study of philosophy. These prejudices are not to be dispelled by a maxim, for they are things which it does not occur to us *can* be questioned. Hence this initial skepticism will be a mere self-deception, and not real doubt; and no one who follows the Cartesian method will ever be satisfied until he has formally recovered all those beliefs which in form he has given up. It is, therefore, as useless a preliminary as going to the North Pole would be in order to get to Constantinople by coming down regularly upon a meridian. A person may, it is true, in the course of his studies, find reason to doubt what he began by believing; but in that case he doubts because he has a positive reason for it, and not on account of the Cartesian maxim. Let us not pretend to doubt in philosophy what we do not doubt in our hearts (CII, 156–57).

> Do you call it *doubting* to write down on a piece of paper that you doubt? If so, doubt has nothing to do with any serious business. But do not make believe; if pedantry has not eaten all the reality out of you, recognize, as you must, that there is much that you do not doubt, in the least (WPI, 278).

What is the basis of Peirce's condemnation of "make-believe" doubt? It rests on his analysis of what it is to believe something. To believe, as we have seen, is to be possessed of a habit, to have a disposition to behave in certain ways in certain situations; to doubt is to be without such a habit—not to know what to do when. But if that is so, to say "I doubt everything" while going about eating bread rather than stones, opening doors rather than walking into them, and carrying on all the normal business of living is "a mere self-deception." There is *much* we do not doubt at all, and we should not "pretend" to doubt in philosophy what we do not doubt in our hearts.*

It is quite possible, of course, that our experiences will lead us to doubt things that we had not doubted before; the world often surprises us. But then these are *real doubts*, doubts that pose real problems and urge us on to inquiry because we no longer know how to act. This is very different from a philosopher who sits in his dressing gown before the fire and says, "I doubt everything."

Peirce's critique of Descartes' starting point, then, comes to this: (1) it is impossible, since we *cannot* suspend judgment about everything while continuing to live; and (2) it is futile. What we need is not an absolutely certain starting point, but a method of improving the beliefs that, to begin with, we do not imagine *can* be doubted. We must start where we are, with all the beliefs we actually have; only *real* doubts are to count in nudging us away from them. As long as our beliefs work for us, we will have no motivation to question them. You can perhaps appreciate why Peirce occasionally thinks "practicalism" would be a suitable term for his thought.

We might wonder also whether Peirce has correctly identified the end of inquiry. Can the settlement of opinion really suffice as the end or goal of our inquiries? Isn't that being satisfied with too little? Surely, we are inclined to think, what we are after in science and philosophy is the *truth*. Couldn't we settle our opinions and still be *wrong*?

Truth and Reality

Peirce points out first that we invariably think each of our beliefs to be true as long as we have no cause to doubt it.* It is only in that uneasy state of doubt that we wonder about the truth of our beliefs. Second, when doubt ceases, so does inquiry. If we are satisfied with the belief we come to, what sense does it make to wonder, abstractly, whether it might still be false?† If our belief is fixed, we wouldn't know what else to do to determine whether it is true or false.

Finally, Peirce asks us to consider what we mean by "true."

> If your terms "truth" and "falsity" are taken in such senses as to be definable in terms of doubt and belief and the course of experience (as for example they would be if you were to define the "truth" as that to a belief in which belief would tend if it were to tend indefinitely toward absolute fixity), well and good: in that case, you are only talking about doubt and belief. But if by truth and falsity you mean something not definable in terms of doubt and belief in any way, then you are talking of entities of whose existence you can know nothing, and which Ockham's razor would clean shave off (WPI, 279).

What motivates those "doubts" that we raise occasionally even when we are, for all practical purposes, satisfied with our beliefs? It is the suspicion that our beliefs may not, for all their practical usefulness, *correspond* with reality—that reality may, for all our care and investigation, still be quite different. And this might be the case, we suspect, even if we could in no way discover the discrepancy. But if that is what we mean, Peirce says, then we "are talking of entities of whose existence [we] can know nothing." **Ockham's razor**, that principle of parsimony in theorizing, would shave them clean off.‡

---

*Peirce's sarcastic comment about the detour to the North Pole refers to the fact that Descartes, shortly after "doubting everything," had once again proved—now on a certain foundation!—the existence of God and the distinctness and immortality of the soul, the existence and nature of the external world, and much more that he claimed he had "suspended judgment" about.

*Compare Hegel for a similar point: p. 405.

†Compare Descartes' reflections in *Meditation I* about dreams. Are these, as Peirce claims, just "make believe"?

‡William of Ockham, the fourteenth-century theologian and philosopher, formulates this principle: Do not multiply entities beyond necessity. It is a rule that bids us to make do with the simplest hypothesis in explaining the facts. For a brief look at some of Ockham's views, see pp. 260–262.

We do not and cannot stabilize our beliefs, Peirce argues, by noticing they are true—by seeing that they correspond with a fact. We never do see this. Peirce's argument for this is complicated, but we can get the gist of it quite simply by using an example he gives. Consider a triangle with one side horizontal at the top and its apex pointing down. And now think of it being dipped into still water.

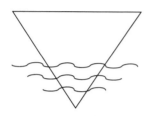

Let the water represent some fact, and let the waterline across the triangle represent some cognition of that fact. Dipping the triangle deeper into the water represents a more and more adequate understanding of the fact, and the horizontal base of the triangle may represent a highly developed cognition of that fact (as we might have in some science). The waterline will be such that, no matter how little it is dipped into the water, there will be other horizontal lines that can be drawn between it and the apex. If the distance from the apex up to the waterline is a, then other lines could be drawn at $\frac{1}{2}a$, $\frac{1}{4}a$, and so on—no matter how small a is.

The question is this: Can we get a *pure* conception of the fact, untainted by any previous theorizing about the fact? Can we see the fact *bare*, or *uncontaminated* by any previous cognitions? This is what would be necessary if it were practicable to settle our beliefs by seeing whether they correspond to reality. We would have to be able to apprehend the fact quite independently of any beliefs we already have and then compare that fact with our beliefs. But we can no more do this, Peirce argues, than we can find a waterline on the triangle below which no other line can be drawn. *All* our cognitions, beliefs, hypotheses, theories, and understandings are dependent on other items of that same kind; none of them provide a *test* of correspondence with a fact independent of the beliefs we already have whenever we have an experience of that fact.*

It would be easy to draw the wrong conclusion from this claim, however. It would be easy to suppose that this makes impossible the cognition of those "external permanencies" which it is supposed to be the genius of science to discern—of those things "upon which our thinking has no effect" (FB, 253–54). But Peirce remarks that although

> everything which is present to us is a phenomenal manifestation of ourselves, this does not prevent its being a phenomenon of something without us, just as a rainbow is at once a manifestation both of the sun and the rain (CII, 169).

What Peirce's argument does do, however, is to undercut any claim to be certain about a belief on the ground that it represents a "pure intuition," uncontaminated by prior cognitions. But this is an implication Peirce is happy to welcome, since we have seen that he has given up the project of basing our knowledge on a foundation of certain truths in any case. What counts, again, is whether we have a method to improve our beliefs, not whether we can be certain of them.†

---

*Here Peirce agrees with Hegel's attack on immediacy. To try to say what an experience is *of* without relying on the concepts and theories we *bring to* that experience is quite impossible. To think we could do that would be equivalent to thinking there could be a waterline on the triangle which is lower than any other line could possibly be. There is no *unmediated* knowledge, no "theory-free" apprehension of "the facts." Wilfrid Sellars has called the opinion to the contrary "the myth of the given." For the Hegelian view of this matter, see pp. 406–409.

†You may be reminded here of the saying of Xenophanes, the pre-Socratic. "The gods have not revealed all things from the beginning to mortals; but, by seeking, men find out, in time, what is better. No man knows the truth, nor will there be a man who has knowledge about the gods and what I say about everything. For even if he were to hit by chance upon the whole truth, he himself would not be aware of having done so, but each forms his own opinion." For a discussion of this saying, see p. 14. Peirce would add two caveats: (1) Xenophanes is right about no man knowing the truth only if knowing the truth entails having certainty about it; (2) the "seeking" must be by scientific methods if we are to find out "what is better"; that is how each is to form "his own opinion."

But now we must ask, How does Peirce think of truth? If we cannot understand fixation of belief in terms of the attainment of truth, he suggests we try to define truth in terms of belief and doubt. He offers several attempts at such a definition:

The opinion which is fated to be ultimately agreed to by all who investigate, is what we mean by the truth (HMIC, 273).

. . . that to a belief in which belief would tend if it were to tend indefinitely toward absolute fixity (WPI, 279).

. . . a state of belief unassailable by doubt (WPI, 279).

Note that each of these definitions makes truth dependent on the states of belief and doubt, not the other way around. A true belief, according to them, is a fixed belief—not fixed just for the moment, but *absolutely* fixed, not just undoubted, but *unassailable* by doubt. The truth about some subject matter is what investigators using scientific methods, if they were persistent, would eventually come to agree upon. That is what truth *means*.

Let's draw out some consequences. The truth is a kind of *ideal*, one for which we strive in our inquiries. Since it is what investigators *will* agree upon, no present agreements (no matter how broad and deep) can suffice to give us absolute confidence that what we *now* believe is true. It is always possible that further investigation will upset present beliefs. Nonetheless, it is quite possible that many of our present beliefs are true. What does this mean? It means that many of our beliefs are ones that future investigators will continue to reaffirm in the light of their inquiries; these beliefs are in fact "unassailable by doubt" because the world holds no surprises that will upset them, though again we cannot ever be certain that this is so for any given belief.

Note, moreover, that truth is something *public*. It is not the case that truth is relative to individuals or cultures. *Evidence* may be relative in such a way, and what one individual has good reason to believe may differ from what another has good reason to

believe—because the one may have access to evidence that the other lacks. But we do not have reason to claim for certain that our beliefs are true just because we believe them. It is the *community of inquirers* that defines what is true, not any individual.

We can see how this understanding of truth fits in with Peirce's practicalism by noting a further implication.

For truth is neither more nor less than that character of a proposition which consists in this, that belief in the proposition would, with sufficient experience and reflection, lead us to such conduct as would tend to satisfy the desires we should then have. To say that truth means more than this is to say that it has no meaning at all.[2]

Beliefs, being habits, invariably lead to conduct by being incorporated in and taken account of by desires that move us to act. For example, we believe there is a hamburger before us and, being hungry, pick it up and take a bite. The belief is a true one if, when acting on it at the behest of a desire, that desire can be satisfied and not frustrated. If I experience the mouth-watering flavor of a Big Mac, then the belief that it was indeed a hamburger is a true one.* If my teeth meet a rubber imitation, my belief is a false one; the falsity is testified to by the fact that my action does not satisfy my desire to eat.† True beliefs, then, are those that can be relied on in our practical activity in the world (including the world of the scientific laboratory). William James puts it this way: they are the beliefs that

---

*Of course, there are hallucinations and dreams that might make it a false belief even if it seemed as though I were eating a hamburger. But these are possibilities that future inquiry by the community will be able to detect and discount.

†This notion of satisfaction is an important one for the pragmatists. In the thought of William James, it is subject to certain ambiguities and provoked the outcry of critics: "What? Do you mean to say that any belief that *satisfies you* is to be counted a true one?" But you can see that in Peirce's hands the public nature of truth, together with the requirement of agreement by a community of scientific inquirers, makes this rebuke fairly inapplicable to him.

pay. But Peirce would be quick to add that they must pay *for* the community of inquirers and *in the long run*.

It is in terms of truth, so understood, that Peirce thinks we must also understand the concept of reality. What do we mean by "the real"? Peirce says that we may define it as

> that whose characters are independent of what anybody may think them to be (HMIC, 271).

But though that is a perfectly correct definition, it is not, he thinks, a very helpful one. It does not tell us how to recognize reality or give us any instructions about how to find it.

A more satisfactory explanation can be given in terms of truth (which, remember, is itself defined in terms of belief fixed by the methods of scientific investigation). Peirce remarks that scientists are convinced that different lines of inquiry into the same subject matter will come eventually to the same result.

> One man may investigate the velocity of light by studying the transits of Venus and the aberration of the stars; another by the oppositions of Mars and the eclipses of Jupiter's satellites; a third by the method of Fizeau; a fourth by that of Foucault; a fifth by the motions of the curves of Lissajous; a sixth, a seventh, an eighth, and a ninth, may follow the different methods of comparing the measures of statical and dynamical electricity. They may at first obtain different results, but, as each perfects his method and his processes, the results will move steadily together toward a destined centre. So with all scientific research. Different minds may set out with the most antagonistic views, but the progress of investigation carries them by a force outside of themselves to one and the same conclusion. This activity of thought by which we are carried, not where we wish, but to a foreordained goal, is like the operation of destiny. No modification of the point of view taken, no selection of other facts for study, no natural bend of mind even, can enable a man to escape the predestinate opinion. This great law is embodied in the conception of truth and reality. The opinion which is fated to be ultimately agreed to by all who investigate, is what we

mean by the truth, and the object represented in this opinion is the real. That is the way I would explain reality (HMIC, 273).

According to this view, reality is *what true opinion says it is*. And true opinion is that opinion which further scientific inquiry will never upset. But here is a problem. Doesn't this understanding of reality make it *dependent on us* in a way that the former definition (in terms of what is *independent* of what anyone may think) does not? Hasn't Peirce contradicted himself here? He considers this objection and says that

> reality is independent, not necessarily of thought in general, but only of what you or I or any finite number of men may think about it;* . . . though the object of the final opinion depends on what that opinion is, yet what that opinion is does not depend on what you or I or any man thinks. Our perversity and that of others may indefinitely postpone the settlement of opinion; it might even conceivably cause an arbitrary proposition to be universally accepted as long as the human race should last. Yet even that would not change the nature of the belief, which alone could be the result of investigation carried sufficiently far; and if, after the extinction of our race, another should arise with faculties and disposition for investigation, that true opinion must be the one which they would ultimately come to. "Truth crushed to earth shall rise again," and the opinion which would finally result from investigation does not depend on how anybody may actually think. But the reality of that which is real does depend on the real fact that investigation is destined to lead, at last, if continued long enough, to a belief in it (HMIC, 274).

Reality, then, can be independent of the inquiries of any finite number of individuals and yet be what would be revealed in inquiry, provided that inquiry is designed to be sensitive to what is independent of ourselves—i.e., provided that it is scientific. For Peirce, then, *science is the criterion of the real*; not science as it exists at any given stage, of

---

*Compare Parmenides saying that "thought and being are the same," p. 24.

course, but that ideal science toward which scientific activity is even now moving.*

> The real, then, is that which, sooner or later, information and reasoning would finally result in, and which is therefore independent of the vagaries of me and you. Thus the very origin of the conception of reality shows that this conception essentially involves the notion of a COMMUNITY, without definite limits, and capable of a definite increase of knowledge. And so those two series of cognition—the real and the unreal—consist of those which, at a time sufficiently future, the community will always continue to reaffirm; and of those which, under the same conditions, will ever after be denied. Now, a proposition whose falsity can never be discovered, and the error of which therefore is absolutely incognizable, contains, upon our principle, absolutely no error. Consequently, that which is thought in these cognitions is the real, as it really is. There is nothing, then, to prevent our knowing outward things as they really are, and it is most likely that we do thus know them in numberless cases, although we can never be absolutely certain of doing so in any special case (CII, 186–87).

Two comments: (1) Peirce is here denying the Kantian doctrine that we *cannot* know things as they really are, but only as they appear to us.† There is no essentially hidden thing-in-itself; things are as they reveal themselves to inquiry. (2) His ground

---

*Here we have a decisively different conception of the problem of the criterion; it is not a criterion *from which to start*—as though we had to solve that problem *first*, before we could do any intellectual work. Peirce would agree that if we think of the problem of the criterion in that way, it is unsolvable; it requires that we know something before we can know something, and skepticism will be the result. According to Peirce's view, however, we know enough about the nature of the criterion to know that we do not now have it in hand; yet we also know how to make definite and regular progress toward it. Peirce's view has certain similarities to Hegel's idea that "absolute knowledge" lies at the end of a process of historical development and that nothing prior to that point can be certain; it differs in recommending empirical science as the method by which to arrive at "fixed beliefs." (See the discussion of Hegel, pp. 403–406.)

†Review Kant's distinction between noumena and phenomena, pp. 379–381.

for affirming that we can know things "as they really are" is the "principle" that there is no error possible where it is impossible to discover it. Why does he believe this? To understand his reasoning here, we must turn to what Peirce has to say about *meaning.*

First let us summarize a main theme in all we have examined so far. It goes by the name of **fallibilism**: a readiness to acknowledge that one's knowledge is not yet completely satisfactory, together with an intense desire to find things out.* Peirce would wholeheartedly agree with an aphorism formulated in the early twentieth century by Otto Neurath, one of a group of thinkers known as logical positivists.

> We are like sailors who must rebuild their ship on the open sea, never able to dismantle it in dry-dock and to reconstruct it there out of the best materials.[3]

There is, perhaps, no belief of ours immune from possible revision. But, like the sailors on the open sea, we cannot replace all our beliefs at once. If we revise certain convictions, we do it only by standing on some others which, for the time being, we must regard as stable.

Meaning

Peirce says that

> pragmatism is, in itself, no doctrine of metaphysics, no attempt to determine any truth of things. It is merely a method of ascertaining the meanings of hard words and of abstract concepts (SP, 317).

We have already, as a matter of fact, seen this method at work on the concepts of belief and doubt, truth and reality. But now we must examine it directly.

Peirce restricts his doctrine of meaning to what he calls *intellectual concepts*, which he contrasts with *mere subjective feelings*. An intellectual con-

---

*Once more you should look over that fragment of Xenophanes discussed on pp. 14–15.

cept is any concept "upon the structure of which, arguments concerning objective fact may hinge" (SP, 318). Examples are concepts like "hard," "ten centimeters," "lithium," and "believes." We may get a better feel for what is distinctive about them by looking at how Peirce characterizes subjective feelings.

> Had the light which, as things are, excites in us the sensation of blue, always excited the sensation of red, and *vice versa*, however great a difference that might have made in our feelings, it could have made none in the force of any argument. In this respect, the qualities of hard and soft strikingly contrast with those of red and blue; because while red and blue name mere subjective feelings only, hard and soft express the factual behaviour of the thing under the pressure of a knife-edge. . . . My pragmatism, having nothing to do with qualities of feeling, permits me to hold that the predication of such a quality is just what it seems, and has nothing to do with anything else. Hence, could two qualities of feeling everywhere be interchanged, nothing but feelings could be affected. Those qualities have no intrinsic significations beyond themselves (SP, 318).

Peirce is here expressing a version of a thought experiment called *the inverted spectrum*. It is often given in a two-person setting. Suppose the sensation I have when I see a ripe tomato is qualitatively identical to the sensation you have when you look at the sky on a clear day, and vice versa. Could we discover this? Apparently we could not, since you cannot directly access my sensations, nor I yours—and everything else would be the same. I would have learned to call ripe tomatoes "red" (doesn't everybody?) despite the fact that the sensation they produce in me is the sensation you call blue. If someone asked me to bring them something red, I might bring a tomato. And I would call the sky "blue," even though the sensation I have when I look at it is the same as the sensation you have when looking at a ripe tomato. Such an inversion of qualities would make absolutely no difference to our behavior, our language, our reasoning, or our science. They are "mere subjective feelings only." In

a fairly clear sense, such sensations have no *meaning*. Nothing else depends on them.

Contrast such a sensation with the quality of hardness (to use Peirce's example). Whether something is hard makes a difference to all those things sensations do not affect: our behavior (we will not be able to crush it in our hand like a sponge), our language (if we call something hard, we communicate something quite definite to our hearers), our reasoning (from the premise that an item is hard, we can conclude that a knife edge will not easily divide it), and our science. "Hard" is a good example of an intellectual concept. It has *implications* that must be understood if we are to understand the concept. If you do not understand that a knife edge will not easily divide a hard object, you do not understand what "hard" means.

These implications have to do with the *behavior* of the objects that are correctly called "hard." They will behave in certain ways under certain circumstances. Indeed, even if a knife edge is never actually drawn across an object, to call it "hard" is to imply that *if* a knife edge *were* put to it, it *would not* divide easily. So the implications of an intellectual concept include what Peirce calls the "would-be's" and the "would-do's" of objects to which the concepts are applicable. These would-be's and would-do's are, of course, nothing else than *habits* or dispositions. The rock has a disposition to resist a knife edge; and by virtue of this disposition it is rightly called "hard."

We have looked at one example of an intellectual concept and have noted the ways in which it contrasts with pure subjective sensations. Only the former have meaning. But now we can ask, How can we decide what an intellectual concept means? And this is the same as to ask, How can we make our ideas clear?

> The very first lesson that we have a right to demand that logic shall teach us is, how to make our ideas clear; and a most important one it is, depreciated only by minds who stand in need of it. To know what we think, to be masters of our own meaning, will make a solid foundation for great and weighty thought. . . . It is terrible to see how a single unclear

idea, a single formula without meaning, lurking in a young man's head, will sometimes act like an obstruction of inert matter in an artery, hindering the nutrition of the brain, and condemning its victim to pine away in the fullness of his intellectual vigor and in the midst of intellectual plenty (HMIC, 260–61).

Peirce distinguishes three grades of clearness in ideas. We may first "have such an acquaintance with the idea as to have become familiar with it, and to have lost all hesitancy in recognizing it in ordinary cases" (HMIC, 258). If we can identify samples of quartz, for example, from among a variety of stones presented to us, then "quartz" is clear to us to this first degree. A second grade of clearness is provided by a verbal definition, such as one finds in a dictionary and could memorize (or write down in an exam, perhaps). But to attain the third grade of clearness we must follow this rule:

> Consider what effects, which might conceivably have practical bearings, we conceive the object of our conception to have. Then, our conception of these effects is the whole of our conception of the object (HMIC, 266).

Let us examine this rule carefully. The first thing to note is that the meaning of an intellectual concept is always something that itself has meaning. Meanings are not things; they are not brute facts; they are not sensations or actions. If you ask what "hard" means, it is not a proper answer for me to clunk you on the head with a rock. Or, if I do, then the meaning of "hard" is still not the rock; nor is it the sensation you felt when you were struck. The word "hard" is a *sign*, and its meaning must be another sign. (We will examine the nature of signs in a moment.)

Next, consider the idea of "effects, which might conceivably have practical bearings." If we ask what "hard" means, we are asking for a conception that can apply to objects that are hard; we are asking what effects these objects have that we can notice, i.e., have some impact upon us—for instance, that they will not be scratched by many other substances.

And finally, note that Peirce holds that the whole of our conception of these effects is the whole of

the conception we are trying to clarify. There is nothing in our conception of "hard" beyond our conception of these effects. Peirce offers a procedure for identifying these effects.

> Proceed according to such and such a general rule. Then, if such and such a concept is applicable to such and such an object, the operation will have such and such a general result; and conversely.
>
> . . . to predicate any such concept of a real or imaginary object is equivalent to declaring that a certain operation, corresponding to the concept, if performed upon that object, would . . . be followed by a result of a definite general description (SP, 331–32).

This is a formula for what is sometimes called *operational definition*. Note that applications of this procedure will always have two parts: there will be an operation performed and a result observed. Let us see how it might work in the case of "hard." We can define "X is hard" in these ways:

- If you apply a knife edge to x, you will not cut it.
- If you throw x forcefully at a window, the window will (probably) break.
- If you press your hand on x, x will resist the pressure of your hand.

Note that in each case the structure is the same; an operation is specified, and a result is observed. Some action is performed and in consequence we have an experience of some kind. Note also that an indefinite number of such tests can be made, and all of them together make up the meaning of the concept "hard."

By employing such operational definitions, we can attain the third grade of clearness in ideas. With such clarity we can not only apply the concept to familiar examples or give a verbal definition, but also clear away the fogginess that so often seems to surround our ideas. We sometimes hear that we know how gravity *works*—i.e., we know the laws it obeys—but we don't know what it *is*. The same is sometimes said of force—that we understand its effects, but not what it *is*. But if Peirce is right about the structure of clear ideas, this is just confusion. Once you know the laws of gravity and the equations of force, once you can predict the results of certain operations correctly so that your experience confirms your predictions, you *do know* what gravity and force are; for there is nothing more in your ideas of them than these effects, which you admit you are clear about. What else could you possibly mean?

> The idea which the word force excites in our minds has no other function than to affect our actions, and these actions can have no reference to force otherwise than through its effects. Consequently, if we know what the effects of force are, we are acquainted with every fact which is implied in saying that a force exists, and there is nothing more to know (HMIC, 270).

We have already seen this procedure at work, clarifying our ideas of belief and doubt, truth and reality. Let's review. In what does your *belief* that the earth is round consist? The answer is given in terms of operation and result: if you are offered a trip around the world, you will not say, "What? Are you crazy?" What does it mean to *doubt* whether a certain food is spoiled? If it is offered to you, you will be uncertain whether to eat it. What is it for a belief to be *true*? If the community were to inquire sufficiently long about it, there would come a point where our beliefs would stabilize. What do we mean when we claim that something is *real*? That inquiry concerning it would survive all possible tests. In each case, Peirce has been striving for that third grade of clearness, and in each case he applies that hypothetical structure of operation and result. In each case, the operations are such as any member of the community might (in principle) perform, and the results are public in the sense that anyone might observe them. There might, of course, be private associations or feelings associated with these terms—especially with "truth" and "reality"—but these are not part of the meaning of the terms. Language, after all, is a social convention we learn as children and teach others. Were its meanings not founded in something public and common, neither the learning nor the teaching of language would be explicable.

We should note one other consequence of Peirce's discussion of meaning. Consider two beliefs that seem to be different; perhaps they just have a different feel to them or are expressed in different words. Are they really different? If the practical consequences of the two are not different, "then no mere differences in the manner of consciousness of them can make them different beliefs, any more than playing a tune in different keys is playing different tunes" (HMIC, 264). William James was later to put this point in terms of this slogan:

Every difference must make a difference.

If there is no difference in practical effects, then there is no difference in meaning. Peirce draws out the radical consequence of this principle.

> It will serve to show that almost every proposition of ontological metaphysics is either meaningless gibberish—one word being defined by other words, and they by still others, without any real conception ever being reached—or else is downright absurd; so that all such rubbish being swept away, what will remain of philosophy will be a series of problems capable of investigation by the observational methods of the true sciences (WPI, 282).

This seems to be an announcement of the end of philosophy, its true work being taken over by the empirical sciences. Indeed, some twentieth-century thinkers draw just that conclusion from similar premises about meaning.* Peirce himself, however, goes on to argue for a metaphysics of absolute idealism in which mind is the fundamental fact in reality. Because he thinks this conclusion can be warranted on the basis of methods continuous with those of the sciences, he believes that his metaphysics conforms to this radical principle.

To understand the essentials of Peirce's view better, let us contrast it with that of David Hume.†

---

*Compare the logical positivists, pp. 507–511. See also Martin Heidegger for a differently motivated but similar conclusion on p. 574.

†See "The Theory of Ideas," in Chapter 19.

There are some clear similarities to be noted first. Both are interested in getting rid of what they see as fakery and quackery in metaphysics. And both are convinced that clarity about meaning will be helpful in dismissing much of it as sophistry and illusion.

But the differences are more striking than the similarities.

1. Hume's method of certifying the meaning of a term is essentially *contemplative*. The philosopher sits in his study and muses over his experiences; if he finds some sensation in his memory from which the idea in question has arisen, it is accepted—otherwise not. For Peirce, on the other hand, the method of clarifying our ideas is *active*. To find out what a term means, we have to *do* something and then experience the consequences.

2. Hume's criterion tends to be *individualistic* and *private*; the sensations I have had are not likely to be exactly the sensations you have had. Peirce's criterion is emphatically *public*; he will admit as a practical consequence nothing that could not be experienced by *anyone*.*

3. Whereas Hume's investigation of the meaning of our ideas is oriented toward the *past*, toward their origin, Peirce's is *future-looking*, toward use.

4. These differences have a consequence. Whereas for Hume the meanings of words are pretty much *fixed* in the light of our past experience, Peirce is able to think of us as much more flexible and *creative* with respect to language. What we do (together with the effects of those actions) determines the meanings of words. And what we do is under our control (though the result is not). This consequence is quite in line with Peirce's acceptance of evolution and the possibility of progress. Language, too, evolves.

In fact, therefore, men and words reciprocally educate each other; each increase of a man's information involves, and is involved by, a corresponding increase of a word's information (CII, 189).

The meanings of our words are not cut from stone once and for all; they change as relevant information about their objects changes—because for them to have meaning at all is for them to be part of a network of implications. As information changes, so do these implications. The meaning of "heat," for example, is no longer what it was in the days before modern thermodynamics.

Signs

A consideration of some elements of Peirce's doctrine of signs will bring us full circle. The entities that have meaning Peirce calls "signs." Here again Peirce is extremely original; he calls himself a "pioneer," a "backwoodsman," and "first-comer" in this area. His discussion is very complex and never thoroughly or systematically worked out. We will concentrate only on several central features.

Peirce gives the term "sign" (as he does "habit") a very wide sense. He means to include the simplest cases of communication in the animal world as well as the most sophisticated language of science. He believes there is one property which is common to all signs and which differentiates them from anything not a sign. All signs have a certain *triadic structure*: a *sign* stands for an *object* to an *interpretant*.* Being a sign, then, requires all three of these elements. We do, of course, sometimes just say that "*a* means *b*," but Peirce holds this is an incomplete formulation; if it is spelled out in full, we must say that "*a* means *b* to *c*." For *a* couldn't *mean b* except to some interpreter of *a*.

---

*In addition, remember that Peirce does not count subjective sensations as part of meaning in any case; when he refers to what anyone can experience, he is talking about something that is already interpreted, already a sign. It is not the pure *sensation* of blue that counts as the relevant experience, but the *judgment* "That is blue" elicited from us in the presence of certain objects, together with all the implications concerning its relations to other colors, to light, to what we know of the surfaces of objects, to our sensory apparatus, and so on.

*We would normally speak here of an "interpreter," thinking primarily, no doubt, of a human who understands the sign. Peirce uses this odd term "interpretant" because he wants to be able to say that there are a variety of ways in which the meaning of a sign can be apprehended, interpretation by a human mind being only one. The behavior of bees in response to a bee dance indicating the direction of nectar (they fly in a certain direction) is, in his terms, an interpretant of the dance. But it would be strange to think of the flight of bees as an "interpreter" of the dance.

It is from this triadic structure that the modern division in linguistics and philosophy of language has grown. We may consider language simply as a set of markers or tokens and investigate the permissible relations among them; such an investigation of rules relating signs to each other is called *syntax*. Second, we may pay attention to the relation between words and what they are about, i.e., what they stand for: the "word-world" relation. When we do this we are considering the *semantics* of language (or, more broadly, signs). Finally, we may think about the way signs affect their users and hearers, and this is known as *pragmatics*.

Let us think for a moment of the semantic aspect of signs. Peirce notes three different ways that a sign can be related to its object. (1) The significance of the sign may depend on an actually existing *causal relation* between it and what it signifies. For example, dark clouds are a sign of rain, and smoke a sign of fire. Thus does Robinson Crusoe infer that he is not alone on his island, for footprints in the sand *mean* another person. Signs that work in this way Peirce calls *indexes*. For example, a weather vane is an index of the direction of the wind. (2). Some signs work because they *resemble* their objects. Peirce calls these *icons*. The face in the rock at the Delaware Water Gap is an icon of an Indian. Photographs, as you should be able to see, are both indexes and icons. (3) Some signs are related to their objects in purely *conventional* or *arbitrary* ways. Peirce calls such signs *symbols*. Most of the words in human languages are like this. There is no natural relation between the color red and the word "red"—or, for that matter, "rot" or "rouge." These words stand for red things, rather than for square or heavy things, because a custom or convention of using them in that way has grown up.

But they stand for red things only *to* some interpretant. Without an interpretant, a sign is just a brute fact; nothing, in short, is a sign unless it is used as a sign. What kinds of interpretants can there be? Peirce distinguishes three important kinds. (1) There are *emotional* interpretants for signs. Some words, for instance, produce a lot of feeling when heard or uttered ("freedom," for example), others very little. But the feeling itself is not just a brute fact; it has itself the nature of a sign;

it is itself significant. The feeling of pride on observing the flag has a reference to one's nation just as surely as does the flag itself. (2) There are also *energetic* interpretants. Peirce gives the example of a drill sergeant's order, "Ground arms!" One interpretant of this command is the actual movement by the troops as they lower their muskets to the ground. But by far the most important kind of interpretant is (3) the *logical*. And we need to examine this in more detail.

The first thing to be noted about a logical interpretant is that it is itself a sign. In fact, it is a sign that has the same meaning as the sign it interprets. A dictionary definition might be a good example: "vixen" is defined as "female fox." The latter is the interpretant, and you can see it is about the same class of objects as the former. But, Peirce says, such an interpretant cannot be the *final* or *ultimate* interpretant; because it is itself a sign, it calls for further interpretants of the same kind. And those interpretants require still others, and so on. Can this potential regress be brought to a halt?*

There is an ultimate-interpretant, Peirce says. It is a *habit*. Though Peirce's discussion of these matters is somewhat obscure, we can understand his point in this way. One understands a word best when one goes beyond the first and second grades of clearness to the third.† That third grade of clearness, you recall, is given by a set of "if-then" sentences that specify a series of operations together with the results experienced in consequence of performing them. "*X* is hard" means "if you try to cut *x* with a knife, you will fail," and so on. A habit or disposition is itself precisely such a set of "if-thens." So *having the third grade of clearness* with respect to a concept is *having a habit with respect to the word* that expresses the concept. For example, if I really do understand "hard," then my behavior is such that *if* I want something I can cut with my

---

*You should be reminded here of Descartes' second rule, which prescribes analysis into simples, which are clear and distinct ideas requiring no further analysis (p. 290). And Hume, worried about the same problem, traces ideas back to their origin in sensations. Both are ways to halt the regress of meaning-giving. Peirce's way to halt this regress is distinctively different.
†See p. 472.

knife, *then* I will select a stick rather than a stone to practice my whittling.

> Consequently, the most perfect account of a concept that words can convey will consist in a description of the habit which that concept is calculated to produce. But how otherwise can a habit be described than by a description of the kind of action to which it gives rise, with the specification of the conditions and of the motive? (SP, 342).

We saw earlier that belief has the nature of a habit; we now see that coming to master the meaning of a word is itself a matter of attaining a habit. So the meaning of an intellectual concept is given by a logical interpretant, and each logical interpretant is subject to further interpretations until anchored finally in a habit of behavior. Two things follow: (1) A linguistic or conceptual sign can function *as a sign* only in the context of an entire working system of signs; nothing can be a sign in isolation; all by itself, a word has *no meaning.* This view is often called "holism." (2) Our entire intellectual life is tied to matters of behavior and experience, to action, and to the quest to establish habits (concepts and beliefs) that will serve us well. To this end, we modify the concepts and beliefs we begin with (and cannot help having), hoping to attain intellectual concepts that will prove ever more adequate to living in our community and in the world. As we have seen, Peirce recommends the methods of science as the way to attain more adequate habits—to "fix" our beliefs. And with this thought we have come full circle.

John Dewey

Intellectually speaking, John Dewey was born in the year that Darwin published *On the Origin of Species by Means of Natural Selection.* He took seriously Darwin's incorporation of human life into nature and tried to work out its consequences for epistemology, metaphysics, and ethics. He lived a long life, from 1859 to 1952, and wrote volumi-

nously on social, educational, and political matters as well as on these more traditional philosophical topics. He was born in Vermont on the eve of the Civil War and lived through the time of tremendous industrial growth in America, the expansion westward, and both world wars. He lived through the revolution in physics that we associate with Einstein and contributed to theories that made scientific methods applicable also in sociology and psychology. He said of himself that the forces that influenced him and stimulated him to think came not from books, but "from persons and from situations" (FAE, 13).[4] He is one of the classic sources of pragmatic ideas in philosophy.

The Impact of Darwin

We will scarcely be able to canvass everything Dewey contributed, even to pragmatic philosophy. But an examination of his *naturalism* in epistemology and metaphysics, together with his *theory of value*, will supplement our discussion of Peirce and give a good overview of the leading pragmatic themes. A 1909 lecture, "The Influence of Darwinism on Philosophy," sets the stage.

> That the publication of the "Origin of Species" marked an epoch in the development of the natural sciences is well known to the layman. That the combination of the very words origin and species embodied an intellectual revolt and introduced a new intellectual temper is easily overlooked by the expert. The conceptions that had reigned in the philosophy of nature and knowledge for two thousand years, the conceptions that had become the familiar furniture of the mind, rested on the assumption of the superiority of the fixed and final; they rested upon treating change and origin as signs of defect and unreality. In laying hands upon the sacred ark of absolute permanency, in treating the forms that had been regarded as types of fixity and perfection as originating and passing away, the "Origin of Species" introduced a mode of thinking that in the end was bound to transform the logic of knowledge, and hence the treatment of morals, politics, and religion (IDP, 3).

The ancient Greeks assume that to really know something, one has to grasp its essence, its form (*eidos*).* Scholastic philosophy in the Middle Ages, sharing this assumption, translates *eidos* as "species." The cardinal principle is that species (forms) are *fixed*, an assumption that would shape philosophy, science, ethics, and theology for two thousand years.

> The conception of *eidos*, species, a fixed form and final cause, was the central principle of knowledge as well as of nature. Upon it rested the logic of science. Change as change is mere flux and lapse; it insults intelligence. Genuinely to know is to grasp a permanent end that realizes itself through changes. . . . Completely to know is to relate all special forms to their one single end and good: pure contemplative intelligence. . . . The influence of Darwin upon philosophy resides in his having conquered the phenomena of life for the principle of transition, and thereby freed the new logic for application to mind and morals and life. When he said of species what Galileo had said of the earth, *e pur se muove*, he emancipated, once for all, genetic and experimental ideas as an organon of asking questions and looking for explanations (IDP, 6–8).

Obviously Dewey sees a much broader significance to the achievement of Darwin than the merely biological. He thinks there are just two fundamentally different ways to look at knowledge and our place in nature: either we must find "the appropriate objects and organs of knowledge in the mutual interactions of changing things," or we must "seek them in some transcendent and supernal region" (IDP, 6). It is Darwin's great merit, Dewey believes, that he has shown us the former path.

In the wake of Darwin's work, a great shift of attention and emphasis opens up. Intelligence becomes more concrete, more down-to-earth, more practical. And the new philosophy

forswears inquiry after absolute origins and absolute finalities in order to explore specific values and the specific conditions that generate them. . . . Interest shifts from the wholesale essence back of special changes to the question of how special changes serve and defeat concrete purposes. . . . To idealize and rationalize the universe at large is after all a confession of inability to master the courses of things that specifically concern us. As long as mankind suffered from this impotency, it naturally shifted a burden of responsibility that it could not carry over to the more competent shoulders of the transcendent cause. But if insight into specific conditions of value and into specific consequences of ideas is possible, philosophy must in time become a method of locating and interpreting the more serious of the conflicts that occur in life, and a method of projecting ways for dealing with them: a method of moral and political diagnosis and prognosis (IDP, 10–13).

Dewey sees the result of Darwin's evolutionary theory as the prospect of applying scientific, experimental methods to all the pressing, practical human problems. This can't happen overnight, he acknowledges; but he does see it happening and devotes himself to helping the process along.

> Old ideas give way slowly; for they are more than abstract logical forms and categories. They are habits, predispositions, deeply engrained attitudes of aversion and preference. Moreover, the conviction persists—though history shows it to be a hallucination—that all the questions that the human mind has asked are questions that can be answered in terms of the alternatives that the questions themselves present. But in fact intellectual progress usually occurs through sheer abandonment of questions together with both of the alternatives they assume—an abandonment that results from their decreasing vitality and a change of urgent interest. We do not solve them: we get over them. Old questions are solved by disappearing, evaporating, while new questions corresponding to the changed attitude of endeavor and preference take their place. Doubtless the greatest dissolvent in contemporary thought of old questions, the greatest precipitant of new methods, new intentions, new problems, is the one effected by the scientific revolution that found its climax in the *Origin of Species* (IDP, 14).

---

*This is most clear in the work of Plato (see "Knowledge and Opinion," in Chapter 10); for him, knowledge has to be certain and its objects eternal and unchanging: the Forms. For Aristotle, form is always embedded in concrete substances, but he is no less insistent than his teacher Plato that the object of knowledge is always the form of a thing; and, as we have noted before, the dominant form is the one toward which a substance develops: its *final cause*. The final cause of all things, for Aristotle, is that pure actuality he calls the *unmoved mover*, or God.

We have not solved all the old problems of philosophy, but that's all right. Those are problems, Dewey says, that we should just "get over." When we see how the "new methods" of the latest scientific revolution can be applied to the practical problems we already face, the old problems will simply "disappear" or "evaporate."

Dewey thus sets himself against any philosophy that would pose an impassable gulf between knowers and what is known, between subject and object, self and nonself, experience and nature, action and the good.* Human beings are to be understood as embedded without residue in the flux of natural processes—indeed, as a product of such processes. The vaunted cognitive abilities of the human species, including its capacity for sophisticated science, are to be understood as abilities developed through the evolutionary process. This view is often called *naturalism*, and John Dewey is one of the most vigorous exponents.

An epistemological corollary of this naturalistic vision in metaphysics is *giving up the quest for certainty*. All our knowledge is understood to be hypothetical and revisable in the light of future experience. What we know depends as much on our interests and capacities as it does on the objects of knowledge; if our interests shift, so will our concepts, and with them the "world" of our experience.

The same is true of our *values*, Dewey believes. Here, too, no certainty is possible, but it does not follow that all values are equally valuable, or that they are all on a par, or that whatever an individual happens to like is a value. Dewey believes that some views about value are superior to others and that we can improve our opinions about morals and values, though without ever attaining certainty. The situation here is parallel to that in the sciences. Let us explore these matters in more detail.

Naturalized Epistemology

Dewey thinks of intelligence or inquiry as a matter of problem solving. Like Peirce, he understands problem solving as the endeavor to remove doubt and establish habits we can use to advantage.

> The function of reflective thought is to transform a situation in which there is experienced obscurity, doubt, conflict, disturbance of some sort, into a situation that is clear, coherent, settled, harmonious (*HWT*, 100–101).

This is the process: We face a difficulty or perplexity; we take stock of the situation (the facts of the case); we imagine possible courses of action. This leads in turn to further reflection on the facts and thought about outcomes; this may lead to considering other possibilities for action, and that to further investigation of the situation. This interaction between the discovered facts and suggested solutions goes on until we find what moves us toward a more satisfactory state.

> Suppose you are walking where there is no regular path. As long as everything goes smoothly, you do not have to think about your walking; your already formed habit takes care of it. Suddenly you find a ditch in your way. You think you will jump it (supposition, plan); but to make sure, you survey it with your eyes (observation), and you find that it is pretty wide and that the bank on the other side is slippery (facts, data). You then wonder if the ditch may not be narrower somewhere else (idea), and you look up and down the stream (observation) to see how matters stand (test of idea by observation). You do not find any good place and so are thrown back upon forming a new plan. As you are casting about, you discover a log (fact again). You ask yourself whether you could not haul that to the ditch and get it across the ditch to use as a bridge (idea again). You judge that idea is worth trying, and so you get the log and manage to put it in place and walk across (test and confirmation by overt action). . . .

> The two limits of every unit of thinking are a perplexed, troubled, or confused situation at the beginning and a cleared up, unified, resolved situation at the close. . . .

> In between, as states of thinking, are (1) *suggestions*, in which the mind leaps forward to a possible solution; (2) an intellectualization of the difficulty or perplexity that has been *felt* (directly experienced)

---

*This theme Dewey adapts from Hegel; see p. 403.

into a *problem* to be solved, a question for which the answer must be sought; (3) the use of one suggestion after another as a leading idea, or *hypothesis*, to initiate and guide observation and other operations in collection of factual material; (4) the mental elaboration of the idea or supposition as an idea or supposition (*reasoning*, in the sense in which reasoning is a part, not the whole of inference); and (5) testing the hypothesis by overt or imaginative action (*HWT*, 105–7).

We must not misunderstand this example. Dewey means it to represent the pattern of *all* our intellectual endeavors. Several points are particularly important. First, human knowers are not passive spectators of the world they come to know. They are involved participants, part of the world. It is one of Dewey's complaints that traditional theories of knowledge make the knower an entity separate from the known, thus erecting barriers between subject and object, knower and known, that could not in any case be bridged again. His own theory, by setting human beings firmly within the natural world, claims to avoid many of the traditional problems of epistemology.* Second, there is a conscious rejection of the rule that we should "not frame hypotheses."† The mind "leaps forward" to possible solutions. Such leaps should not be condemned, but encouraged. We cannot do without framing hypotheses. And third, what is crucial is not whether a proposition represents a leap beyond present evidence, but whether it stands up to future tests by experience and action. A good hypothesis is one that *works*.

You can see that there is an intimate connection between this way of conceiving human knowledge and the futility of a quest for certainty. If the correctness of our beliefs lies open to future tests, to possible correction by future experience as mediated by actions we have not yet taken, then any claim to certainty *now* must be unjustified. Even the most firmly grounded beliefs of science and common sense may need to be modified as human experience grows more extensive and complex.*

Dewey carries on a constant dialectical debate with traditional philosophy and especially with empiricism. Like William James, he believes that pragmatism is a *via media* between the extremes of empiricism and rationalism, incorporating what is best in both. The main problem with these traditional rivals, he believes, is that each operates with an impoverished notion of what experience is. In an essay of 1917, Dewey contrasts the traditional concept of experience with one he thinks more adequate.

(i) In the orthodox view, experience is regarded primarily as a knowledge-affair. But to eyes not looking through ancient spectacles, it assuredly appears as an affair of the intercourse of a living being with its physical and social environment. (ii) According to tradition experience is (at least primarily) a psychical thing, infected throughout by "subjectivity." What experience suggests about itself is a genuinely objective world which enters into the actions and sufferings of men and undergoes modifications through their responses. (iii) So far as anything beyond a bare present is recognized by the established doctrine, the past exclusively counts. Registration of what has taken place, reference to precedent, is believed to be the essence of experience. Empiricism is conceived of as tied up to what has been, or is, "given." But experience in its vital form is experimental, an effort to change the given; it is characterized by projection, by reaching forward into the unknown; connection with

*The solipsism and skepticism that haunts Descartes and Hume, for instance, simply cannot arise on this view; they *begin* with the possibility that *my* experience might be all there is and face the problem of justifying belief in anything else. For Dewey, this is not a real possibility, since it leaves the metaphysical status and nature of the knower unclarified. He also agrees with Peirce that we must begin with the beliefs we actually have; it is not possible for us to doubt them all. Dewey rejects the principal theses of the representational theory of knowledge and perception (pp. 294—295).
†For the role of this thought in the views of Newton and David Hume, see pp. 340, 342, 349, and 353.

*You can see that Dewey, like Hegel, takes time seriously. Not only our beliefs but also our methods, concepts, and logical tools are part of history. But unlike Hegel, he does not envision a stage in which the progression comes to completion; there is no such thing as *absolute knowledge* for Dewey. In this regard, he resembles Kierkegaard more than Hegel (though he would not have liked Kierkegaard's supernatural religion nor the emphasis on non-rational choice). Compare pp. 439–443.

a future as its salient trait. (iv) The empirical tradition is committed to particularism. Connections and continuities are supposed to be foreign to experience, to be by-products of dubious validity. An experience that is an undergoing of an environment and a striving for its control in new directions is pregnant with connections. (v) In the traditional notion experience and thought are antithetical terms. Inference, so far as it is other than a revival of what has been given in the past, goes beyond experience; hence it is either invalid, or else a measure of desperation by which, using experience as a springboard, we jump out to a world of stable things and other selves. But experience, taken free of the restrictions imposed by the older concept, is full of inference. There is, apparently, no conscious experience without inference; reflection is native and constant (NRP, 23).

Important points are made here. Let us review them in order.

1. Point (i) is the denial that the knower is a disinterested spectator.
2. Point (ii) rejects any notion of experience that would locate it exclusively in a subject, leaving the question of an objective world up in the air.
3. Point (iii) captures the inherent purposiveness of experience, the fact that it is always oriented toward the future and concerned about the implications of the present on that future.*
4. Point (iv) attacks the Humean notion that experience presents all events as "loose and separate."†
5. Point (v) notes that if reason were a faculty for making inferences that is quite distinct from experience, the result would be the restriction of experience to a purely subjective realm. Then, as long as we wanted to base our knowledge on experience, we would be unable to escape the skepticism plaguing traditional empiricism. But if experience is adequately characterized, it shows itself to be a matter of interactions between an organism and its environment; it is

"full of inference" and presents itself in intimate contact with the objective world. There is no such thing as experience that is not already involved in the world.

And once we see that, many of the traditional problems of philosophy (such as the problem of the "reality" of the "external" world) simply "evaporate"; we "get over" them.

Nature and Natural Science

Experience, then, is an affair of nature, since human beings are wholly natural creatures. But what is nature? Dewey resists the imperialism, so to speak, of certain sciences that claim a unique title to reveal the essence of nature. Galileo and Descartes agree that (material) reality is what mathematical physics can tell us about, and Hobbes tries to extend that claim to human nature. The result seems to Dewey an unpalatable dichotomy: either human experience is not a part of the world of nature at all (as in Descartes' dualism), or a Hobbesian materialism reigns. But neither seems able to do justice to all we value and hold dear. We saw that "secondary qualities"—the felt, sensory, reds and blues, warms and colds, feelings of hope, love, or despair—are "kicked inside" by the early scientific revolutionaries as being merely effects *in us* of the geometrical, extended things that make up the realm of nature; many philosophers, acknowledging that physics gives us knowledge of what really is, feel compelled to join them.* This seems wholly inadequate to Dewey. If we identify science with the physical sciences (as traditionally understood), we will cut ourselves off from the uses of intelligence in the more human spheres. The problem, as he sees it, is once again a *spectator theory of knowledge*. It springs from

---

*Contrast Hume's rule about ideas: to discover whether a purported idea is a genuine one, trace it *back* to an impression. Here experience is assumed to be *given* whole and complete at any moment, and "the past exclusively counts." Compare Peirce, p. 474.
†See p. 350.

---

*The loss is poignantly expressed in the poem by John Donne. See p. 284. The pattern is an ancient one. Democritus, the contemporary of Socrates, is convinced that reality is made up of atoms and the void, but he recognizes that our access to the world is through the sensory qualities of our experience and laments that "man is cut off from the real." (See p. 31.) Dewey struggles against this conclusion.

the assumption that the true and valid object of knowledge is that which has been prior to and independent of the operations of knowing, . . . [from] the doctrine that knowledge is a grasp or beholding of reality without anything being done to modify its antecedent state—the doctrine which is the source of the separation of knowledge from practical activity (*QC*, 196).

But as we have seen, experience and knowledge are a matter of interactions (transactions) between the knower and the known; neither is left at the end exactly as it was at the beginning of the affair. What counts as intelligent intervention, Dewey holds, is a matter of *method*. And a method is legitimate if it succeeds in transforming confused situations into clear ones.

> The result of one operation will be as good and true an object of knowledge as any other, provided it is good at all: provided, that is, it satisfies the conditions which induced the inquiry. . . . One might even go as far as to say that there are as many kinds of valid knowledge as there are conclusions wherein distinctive operations have been employed to solve the problems set by antecedently experienced situations. . . .
>
> There is no kind of inquiry which has a monopoly of the honorable title of knowledge (*QC*, 197, 220).

Along these lines, Dewey attacks what some call "scientism."

> Thus, "science," meaning physical knowledge, became a kind of sanctuary. A religious atmosphere, not to say an idolatrous one, was created. "Science" was set apart; its findings were supposed to have a privileged relation to the real. In fact the painter may know colors as well as the meteorologist; the statesman, educator and dramatist may know human nature as truly as the professional psychologist; the farmer may know soils and plants as truly as the botanist and mineralogist. For the criterion of knowledge lies in the method used to secure consequences and not in metaphysical conceptions of the nature of the real. . . .
>
> That "knowledge" has many meanings follows from the operational definition of conceptions. There

are as many conceptions of knowledge as there are distinctive operations by which problematic situations are resolved (*QC*, 221).

If we add one more ingredient, we will be ready to see why Dewey thinks that intelligence can be as effective in the realms of value and morality as it is in science. That ingredient is his *instrumentalism*. Because the basic cognitive situation is the problem-situation, and because hypotheses are created to resolve such situations satisfactorily, the concepts involved in hypotheses are necessarily relative to our concerns and interests. Without interests and concerns there would be no problems! Ideas, concepts, and terms, then, are intellectual *tools* we use as long as they serve our purposes and discard when they no longer do. They are *instruments* for solving problems.

Physicists and chemists create concepts that serve the purposes of these sciences: explanation, prediction, and control. But these concepts no more reveal what the world *really* is than any other sort of concept does. They too are merely instruments serving certain purposes; there is nothing prior or more basic about them that should cast a disparaging shadow on concepts serving other purposes. Dewey believes that many philosophers have been misled in thinking that modern physics actually reveals the true nature of reality. Making that assumption seems to shunt the qualities manifest in experience (all those "secondary qualities," whose loss was mourned by John Donne) off the main line onto a siding. But, Dewey says, that is to mistake the purport of scientific knowledge.

> Only when the older theory of knowledge and metaphysics is retained, is science thought to inform us that nature in its true reality is but an interplay of masses in motion, without sound, color, or any quality of enjoyment and use. What science actually does is to show that any natural object we please may be treated in terms of relations upon which its occurrence depends, or as an event, and that by so treating it we are enabled to get behind, as it were, the immediate qualities the object of direct experience presents, and to regulate their happening, instead of having to wait for conditions beyond our control to

bring it about. Reduction of experienced objects to the form of relations, which are neutral as respects qualitative traits, is a prerequisite of ability to regulate the course of change, so that it may terminate in the occurrence of an object having desired qualities (QC, 104–5).

From the point of view of physical science, then, the world appears to be just a sequence of events in certain relations to each other. But we needn't conclude that the world *really is* just such a sequence of events, bare of every quality we prize and delight in. Scientific concepts, like all concepts, including also the concepts of "event" and "relation," are merely tools we use to satisfy certain specific interests. But the interests served by physical science are not all the interests we have, nor are they our primary interests. In fact, treating nature as physics does (in terms of events and relations between events) itself serves larger purposes: our interest in being able to "regulate the course of change, so that it may terminate in the occurrence of an object having desired qualities." The concepts of science owe their very being to the values we have; meanings and values are always relative to our purposes.

"Event" is a concept about as bare and stripped of all that is precious to us as we can find. Yet it applies to everything that happens. Even the things of common sense, such as tables and chairs, can be considered extended, slowly unfolding events. But as we experience them, they are *events with meanings*. And the meanings are multiple. Consider, Dewey suggests, a piece of paper. We call it "a piece of paper," when we are interested in it in a certain way—as something to write on, perhaps, or something to wrap the fish in. But if we consider it in terms of an event (a kind of extended happening), it is clear that it

. . . has as many other explicit meanings as it has important consequences recognized in the various connective interactions into which it enters. Since the possibilities of conjunction are endless, and since the consequences of any of them may at some time be significant, its potential meanings are endless. It signifies something to start a fire with; something like

snow; made of wood-pulp; manufactured for profit; property in the legal sense; a definite combination illustrative of certain principles of chemical science; an article the invention of which has made a tremendous difference in human history, and so on indefinitely. There is no conceivable universe of disclosure in which the thing may not figure, having in each its own characteristic meaning. And if we say that after all it is "paper" which has all these different meanings, we are at bottom but asserting that . . . paper is its ordinary meaning for human intercourse (*EN*, 7).

But suppose we insist on asking, But what is it *really*? Is it *really* wood pulp? Or a white surface for writing on? Or atoms and the void? What would Dewey say? He would tell us that we were asking a question to which there is no answer. It is all of these things—and more—since the applicability of any of these concepts merely reflects certain of our purposes and interests. No one of them can be singled out as the *essence* of the event.

We can see that for Dewey there is no sharp line demarcating science from common sense, any more than there is a gap between knower and the known. Both are ways of dealing with recalcitrant situations and making us better able to cope; they are different because they serve different purposes, but they are alike in making use of ideas and concepts as *tools* for the realization of those purposes. The same is true of philosophy. Dewey proposes

a first-rate test of the value of any philosophy which is offered us: Does it end in conclusions which, when they are referred back to ordinary life-experiences and their predicaments, render them more significant, more luminous to us, and make our dealings with them more fruitful? Or does it terminate in rendering the things of ordinary experience more opaque than they were before, and in depriving them of having in "reality" even the significance they had previously seemed to have? (*EN*, 319–20).

Value Naturalized

Let us apply this criterion to Dewey's own philosophy by looking finally at what he has to say about values.

He notes that the modern problem about values arises with the expulsion of ends and final causes from nature that takes place with the rise of modern science.

For centuries, until, say, the sixteenth and seventeenth centuries, nature was supposed to be what it was because of the presence within it of *ends*. . . . All natural changes were believed to be striving to actualize these ends as the goals toward which they moved by their own nature. Classical philosophy identified *ens* [being], *verum* [truth], and *bonum* [goodness], and the identification was taken to be an expression of the constitution of nature as the object of natural science. In such a context there was no call and no place for any *separate* problem of valuation and values, since what are now termed values were taken to be integrally incorporated in the very structure of the world. But when teleological considerations were eliminated from one natural science after another, and finally from the sciences of physiology and biology, the problem of value arose as a separate problem (*TV*, 2–3).

Our earlier discussions of Dante and the consequences of Galilean science fit this analysis. The problem of how to understand values is acute. As Dewey sees it, there are two tendencies in modern thought, both of which accept the value-neutral character of nature. On the one hand, value is thought to have its origin in something above or beyond nature: in God, perhaps, or, as Kant claims, in pure reason. At the other extreme, value is identified with the purely subjective: with pleasure, perhaps, or with whatever an individual finds enjoyable.

There is either a basic distrust of the capacity of experience to develop its own regulative standards, and an appeal to what philosophers call eternal values, in order to ensure regulation of belief and action; or there is acceptance of enjoyments actually experienced irrespective of the method or operation by which they are brought into existence. Complete bifurcation between rationalistic method and an empirical method has its final and most deeply human significance in the ways in which good and bad are thought of and acted for and upon (*QC*, 256).

Neither of these alternatives is attractive to Dewey, who wants to account for values in a wholly *naturalistic* way, but without identifying the good with the arbitrary preference of an individual. What he wants is a way of treating values parallel to the way a scientist treats hypotheses—a way that will make *progress* in valuations possible but without claiming *certainty* at any point.

The problem of restoring integration and cooperation between man's beliefs about the world in which he lives and his beliefs about the values and purposes that should direct his conduct is the deepest problem of modern life (*QC*, 255).

It is this "integration and cooperation" between facts and values that is disturbed by the rise of modern science in the sixteenth and seventeenth centuries.* Once science is no longer teleological, once it no longer gives us reason to think there are purposes embedded in things, the status of ends and goods in the world becomes problematic. Dewey thinks a pragmatic approach can best restore such integration and solve this "deepest problem." The key idea is this:

that escape from the defects of transcendental absolutism is not to be had by setting up as values enjoyments that happen anyhow, but in defining value by enjoyments which are the consequences of intelligent action. Without the intervention of thought, enjoyments are not values but problematic goods, becoming values when they re-issue in a changed form from intelligent behavior (*QC*, 259).

Let us explore this idea. Like Peirce, who holds that we must begin reflection with the beliefs we already have and cannot wipe the slate clean to start with something absolutely certain, Dewey thinks we all begin with certain values and cannot help doing so. We do so simply by virtue of the fact that there are certain things we *like* or *prize*. Some of these likings may be biologically determined, some culturally produced. But there can be no

---

*See, for instance, Hume on the gap between fact and value, pp. 362–363.

doubt that at any stage of our lives, we do have such likings, desirings, and prizings. How are these to be understood? In accord with his general theory of experience, Dewey denies that these are purely subjective states. To *like* something is to have a certain disposition to behavior; if I like chocolate ice cream, I have tendencies to choose it when buying ice cream, to eat it when it is served to me, and so on. Liking is a matter of interactions between an organism and its environment; it is a transactional matter. To like *X* is to be disposed to try to get it; or, if we already have *X*, liking it is a matter of attempts to preserve, keep, or protect it.

Now, given that we all have such likings, do they constitute values? In one sense they do, Dewey says, but in another sense not. They do represent what we antecedently or *immediately* value (to use a word of Hegel's); but it would be a big mistake to identify these values with values per se. And the reason is that there is a big difference between what we find *satisfying* and that which is *satisfactory*, between what we *desire* and what is *desirable*, between those things we *think good* and the things that *are good*. Dewey is here trying to do justice to the fairly common experience of wanting a certain thing, getting it, and discovering (once we have it) that it does not live up to its advance notices.

What makes the difference between the satisfying and the satisfactory is the intervention of intelligence.

The fact that something is desired only raises the *question* of its desirability; it does not settle it. Only a child in the degree of his immaturity thinks to settle the question of desirability by reiterated proclamation: "I want it, I want it, I want it." . . . To say that something satisfies is to report something as an isolated finality. To assert that it is satis*factory* is to define it in its connections and interactions. The fact that it pleases or is immediately congenial poses a problem to judgment. How shall the satisfaction be rated? Is it a value or is it not? Is it something to be prized and cherished, *to be* enjoyed? Not stern moralists alone but everyday experience informs us that finding satisfaction in a thing may be a warning, a summons to be on the lookout for consequences. To

declare something satis*factory* is to assert that it meets specifiable conditions. It is, in effect, a judgment that the thing "will do." It involves a prediction; it contemplates a future in which the thing will continue to serve; it *will* do. It asserts a consequence the thing will actively institute; it will *do* (QC, 260–61).

The ultimate sources of value, then, are our likings, prizings, esteemings, desirings. If we never liked anything, value would not even be on our horizon. But the things we like are always involved in a network of relations to other things. It might be that if we could just have *Y*, we would be satisfied. But *Y* never comes isolated and alone. It requires *X* as a precondition and brings along *Z* as a consequence. And *X* might require such effort and sacrifice that the luster of *Y* is considerably diminished. And *Z* might be so awful that it disqualifies *Y* as a value altogether. (The use of cocaine might be a good example.) Discovering these relations is the work of inquiry, intelligence, and scientific methods, for causal conditions and consequences are matters of fact. So science and values are not two realms forever separated from each other. Finding what is valuable involves the use of methods of intelligence similar to those used in the sciences.

It follows, then, that value judgments can be true and false, for they involve a prediction. To say that something is *good* or to urge that an action *ought* to be done is to say that it *will do*. And that means that we will continue to like it in the light of the entire context in which it is embedded. To call something satisfactory is to say that it will satisfy, given its causal conditions and consequences. And whether that is so is a matter of fact. What is desirable, then, is what is desired after intelligent inquiry and experience have had their say. So not only can value judgments be true and false, they can be supported by the methods of intelligent inquiry analogous to the methods of the sciences.

Let us consider a typical objection to this way of looking at things. Suppose we allow that intelligence and the methods of science might have bearing on *means* and on *consequences*; we might nonetheless hold that this does not show how these methods can get any grip at all on what is *good in itself*, what is *intrinsically valuable*.* Or we might say that science (sociology or anthropology) can indeed tell us what people do in fact value, but it cannot tell us what is valuable.

What is Dewey's reply? To suppose that there are such things as *ends in themselves* or things that are good no matter what is to make an illegitimate abstraction from the real context in which things are liked and enjoyed. Every end is itself a means to some further end, simply because it is located in time and has consequences. Ends, then, are never absolute; they are what Dewey calls *ends-in-view*. We may take a certain state of affairs to be an end, but that is always provisional and subject to revision in the light of further experience—of the conditions and consequences of that state of affairs. In fact, there is a continuum of ends and means, each means being a means in the light of some end, and each end a means to some further end. Furthermore, there is a reciprocity between ends and means; any actual end is what it is only as the culmination of those specific means that lead to it, and the means are means only as they lead to that particular end.

Dewey uses the story by Charles Lamb about the origin of roast pork to illustrate these points.

> The story, it will be remembered, is that roast pork was first enjoyed when a house in which pigs were confined was accidentally burned down. While searching in the ruins, the owners touched the pigs that had been roasted in the fire and scorched their

fingers. Impulsively bringing their fingers to their mouths to cool them, they experienced a new taste. Enjoying the taste, they henceforth set themselves to building houses, enclosing pigs in them, and then burning the houses down. Now, if ends-in-view are what they are entirely apart from means, and have their value independently of valuation of means, there is nothing absurd, nothing ridiculous in this procedure, for the end attained, the *de facto* termination, *was* eating and enjoying roast pork, and that was just the end desired. Only when the end attained is estimated in terms of the means employed—the building and burning-down of houses in comparison with the other available means by which the desired result in view might be attained—is there anything absurd or unreasonable about the method employed (*TV*, 40–41).

You simply cannot have ends apart from means, and every means qualifies the end you actually get.* This fact has implications, Dewey believes, for the maxim "the end justifies the means" and also for the popular objection to it. The maxim clearly involves the notion of something which is an end-in-itself, apart from the conditions and consequences of its actual existence. That end is supposed to justify the use of whatever means are necessary to its attainment—no matter how awful they may be. The maxim is plausible, however, only because we assume that only *that* end will be brought into existence, not a whole series of other consequences stemming both from the existence of that end and from the means used to achieve it. And that assumption is a mistake. A recognition that the relation of ends and means is reciprocal and ongoing clarifies the sense in which the maxim is true (nothing *could* justify a means except a certain end) and the sense in which it is false (no end in isolation from its context could ever justify *any* means to it, simply because there are no such ends). Dewey says that

---

*This objection is a version of Hume's principle that reason is and can only be the slave of the passions. (See p. 361.) According to this principle, reason can tell you how to get what you want (means), but it cannot tell you what to want (ends). We have already seen, however, that Dewey challenges just this exclusivity of reason and experience; if he is right, there is no experience that is not already interpreted in terms of certain concepts, and no reason apart from experience. In a way, this echoes Kant's famous motto about concepts and intuitions (see p. 376), but with this difference: that there are no absolutely *a priori* concepts; all concepts are instruments invented to serve certain purposes—which themselves are not absolute but develop reciprocally as a result of the application of the methods of intelligence. Again the closest historical parallel is Hegel (see "Epistemology Internalized," in Chapter 21).

---

*This is a fact that nations are apt to forget in wartime, to their own detriment. And individuals who take it as their end to be, let us say, rich sometimes discover that in the process they have created themselves as persons they are not happy to be. Means enter into, i.e., help determine, the character of the ends for which they are chosen.

nothing happens which is *final* in the sense that it is not part of an ongoing stream of events. . . . Every condition that has to be brought into existence in order to serve as means is, *in that connection*, an object of desire and an end-in-view, while the end actually reached is a means to future ends as well as a test of valuations previously made. Since the end attained is a condition of further existential occurrences, it must be appraised as a potential obstacle and potential resource. If the notion of some objects as ends-in-themselves were abandoned, human beings would for the first time in history be in a position to frame ends-in-view and form desires on the basis of empirically grounded propositions of the temporal relations of events to one another (*TV*, 43).

It is clear that Dewey has no use for the idea of something good in itself—at least not prior to intelligent reflection. If any pragmatic sense can be made of that notion at all, it will have to be along Peircean lines: that which the intelligent community ultimately comes to agree upon as desirable or good.* We have no hot line to either truth or goodness, and certainty has to be given up with respect to values as well as knowledge. But by inquiring into the conditions and consequences of ends-in-view, we bring our values more and more into line with what we ultimately *would* be satisfied with, if we knew everything there is to know about the facts. If we were to treat our values the same way we treat our scientific beliefs, then

standards, principles, rules . . . and all tenets and creeds about good and goods, would be recognized to be hypotheses. Instead of being rigidly fixed, they would be treated as intellectual instruments to be tested and confirmed—and altered—through consequences affected by acting upon them. They would lose all pretense of finality—the ulterior source of dogmatism. It is both astonishing and depressing that so much of the energy of mankind has gone into fighting for (with weapons of the flesh as well as of the spirit) the truth of creeds, religious, moral and political, as distinct from what has gone into effort to

try creeds by putting them to the test of acting upon them. The change would do away with the intolerance and fanaticism that attend the notion that beliefs and judgments are capable of inherent truth and authority; inherent in the sense of being independent of what they lead to when used as directive principles. . . . Any belief as such is tentative, hypothetical; it is not just to be acted upon, but is to be *framed* with reference to its office as a guide to action. Consequently, it should be the last thing in the world to be picked up casually and then clung to rigidly. When it is apprehended as a tool and only a tool, an instrument of direction, the same scrupulous attention will go to its formation as now goes into the making of instruments of precision in technical fields. Men, instead of being proud of accepting and asserting beliefs and "principles" on the ground of loyalty, will be as ashamed of that procedure as they would now be to confess their assent to a scientific theory out of reverence for Newton (*QC*, 277–78).

This theme, that thought and action are reciprocally dependent on each other, that no knowledge worth the name is without implications for practice, and that no action is irrelevant to the utility of our intellectual tools, may be considered the distinctive and essential theme of pragmatism.

Notes

1. References to the works of Charles Sanders Peirce are as follows:
   FB, "The Fixation of Belief," and HMIC, "How to Make Our Ideas Clear," in *Writings of Charles S. Peirce*, vol. 3 (Bloomington: Indiana University Press, 1986). WPI, "What Pragmatism Is," CII: "Cognition, Intuition, and Introspection," and SP, "Survey of Pragmatism," in *Collected Papers of Charles Sanders Peirce*, ed. Charles Hartshorne and Paul Weiss, vol. 5 (Cambridge, Mass: Harvard College, 1934).
2. Note added by Peirce in 1903 to "The Fixation of Belief," in Hartshorne and Weiss, *Collected Papers*, 232.
3. Epigraph (translated from the German) to W. V. O. Quine's *Word and Object* (New York: John Wiley and Sons, 1960).

*Review what Peirce says about truth, p. 468.

4. References to the works of John Dewey are as follows: FAE, "From Absolutism to Experimentalism," and NRP, "The Need for a Recovery of Philosophy," in *Dewey: On Experience, Nature, and Freedom*, ed. Richard Bernstein (Indianapolis: Bobbs-Merrill, 1960). IDP, "The Influence of Darwinism on Philosophy," in *John Dewey: The Middle Works (1899–1924)*, vol. 4, ed. Jo Ann Boydston (Carbondale, Ill.: Southern Illinois University Press, 1977).

QC, The Quest for Certainty: A Study of the Relation of Knowledge and Action (1929; New York: G. P. Putnam's Sons, Capricorn Books, 1960).

HWT, How We Think (Boston: D. C. Heath and Co., 1933).

EN, Experience and Nature (New York: W. W. Norton and Co., 1929).

TV, Theory of Valuation (Chicago: University of Chicago Press, 1939).

25

Ludwig Wittgenstein and the Logical Positivists: The Limits of Language

In 1889 a son was born into the wealthy and talented Wittgenstein family of Vienna. He grew up in an atmosphere of high culture; the most prominent composers, writers, architects, and artists of that great city were regular visitors to his home. His father was an engineer and industrialist, his mother was very musical, and Ludwig was talented both mechanically and musically. It was also, however, a troubled family; there were several suicides among his siblings. He himself seems to have struggled against mental illness most of his life.

Having decided to study engineering, he went first to Berlin and then to Manchester, England, where he did some experiments with kites and worked on the design of an airplane propeller. This work drew his interests toward pure mathematics and eventually to the foundations of mathematics. The early years of the century were a time of exciting developments in logic and the foundations of mathematics; Gottlob Frege and Bertrand Russell were among the most prominent contributors to a revolution that created a new logic and the beginnings of a new understanding of mathematical truth.

It was apparently Frege who advised Wittgenstein to go to Cambridge to study with Russell, which he did in the fall of 1911. Russell tells a story about Wittgenstein's first year there.

At the end of his first term at Cambridge he came to me and said: "Will you please tell me whether I am a complete idiot or not?" I replied, "My dear fellow, I don't know. Why are you asking me?" He said, "Because, if I am a complete idiot, I shall become an aeronaut; but if not, I shall become a philosopher." I told him to write me something during the vacation on some philosophical subject and I would then tell him whether he was a complete idiot or not. At the beginning of the following term he brought me the fulfillment of this suggestion. After reading only one sentence, I said to him: "No, you must not become an aeronaut."[1]

When the war broke out in 1914, Wittgenstein was working on a manuscript which was to become the *Tractatus Logico-Philosophicus*. He served in the Austrian army and spent the better part of a year in an Italian prisoner-of-war camp, where he finished writing this dense, aphoristic little work that deals with everything from logic to happiness. After the war, he gave away the fortune he had inherited from his father, designating part of it for the support of artists and poets. He considered that he had set out in the *Tractatus* the final solution of the problems addressed there and left philosophy to teach school in remote Austrian villages. He lived, at that time and afterwards, in severe simplicity and austerity.

His days as a schoolmaster did not last long, however, and for a time he worked as a gardener in a monastery. Then he took the lead in designing and building a mansion in Vienna for one of his sisters. Eventually, through conversations with friends, he came to recognize what he thought were grave mistakes in the *Tractatus* and to think he might be able to do good work in philosophy again. He was invited back to Cambridge in 1929, where he submitted the *Tractatus*—by then published and widely read—as his dissertation.

He lectured there (except for a time during the Second World War) until shortly before his death in 1951. He published nothing else in his lifetime, though several manuscripts circulated informally. A second major book, *Philosophical Investigations*, was published posthumously in 1953. Since then many other works have been published from notes and writings he left.

Subsequent developments leave no doubt that Wittgenstein is one of the century's deepest thinkers. He is also one of the most complex and fascinating human beings to have contributed to philosophy since Socrates.[2]

The New Logic

Wittgenstein's concerns early in life are fundamentally moral and spiritual; the most important question of all, he believes, is *how to live*. As we'll see, however, he also believes there is very little one can *say* about that problem. Like a number of other Viennese in the early decades of this century, he is repelled by the degree to which the hypocritical, the artificial, the ornate and merely decorative, the false and pretentious, and the striving for *effect* characterizes politics, daily life, and art at this time. He is a kindred spirit of the revolt that includes Arnold Schönberg in music and Adolf Loos in architecture. An austere lucidity and ruthless honesty are the values Wittgenstein sets against the confusion of the age. It is not, perhaps, accidental that he masters the new logic of Frege and Russell and becomes an important contributor to it. He sees in it the key by which certain fundamental problems of life and culture can be definitively solved. This new logic is a tool of very great power, incredibly magnified in our day by the speed and storage capacities of the digital computer. Without

the conceptual innovations of Frege, Russell, and Wittgenstein, the computer age in which we live would scarcely have been possible. Every college and university now teaches courses that represent the fruit of this revolution in our thinking about logic.

We cannot go into its details here. We need note only that its power derives from abstracting completely from the meaning or semantic content of assertions. It is a *formal* logic in just this sense: that the rules governing transformations from one symbolic formula to another make reference only to the syntactical structures of the formulas in question and not at all to their meaning. Aristotle's logic of the syllogism, of course, is formal in this same sense.* But it is oversimple. The new logic provides a symbolism for the internal structure of sentences that is enormously more powerful than Aristotle's and a symbolism for a much more complex set of relations among sentences. For the first time, it really seems plausible that whatever you might want to say can be represented in this formalism. Because this logic abstracts entirely from content, it can be used with equal profit in any field, from operations research to theology. It will tell us what follows from certain premises, which assertions are inconsistent with each other, and so on. Being formal in this sense, it sets out a kind of logical skeleton that can be fleshed out in any number of ways, while preserving the logical relations precisely.

The prospect opened up by the new logic is that of a language more precise and clear than the language we normally speak—a purified, *ideal language*, in which there is no ambiguity, no vagueness, no dependence on emphasis, intonation, or the many other features of our language that may mislead us and are inessential for representing the truth. Bertrand Russell expresses the appeal of such a language in this way:

> In a logically perfect language the words in a proposition would correspond one by one with the components of the corresponding fact, with the ex-

---

*See pp. 148–150. For the distinction between syntax and semantics, see p. 475.

ception of such words as 'or', 'not', 'if', 'then', which have a different function. In a logically perfect language, there will be one word and no more for every simple object, and everything that is not simple will be expressed by a combination of words, by a combination derived, of course, from the words for the simple things that enter in, one word for each simple component. A language of that sort will be completely analytic, and will show at a glance the logical structure of the facts asserted or denied. The language which is set forth in *Principia Mathematica* is intended to be a language of that sort.* It is a language which has only syntax and no vocabulary whatever. Barring the omission of a vocabulary, I maintain that it is quite a nice language. It aims at being that sort of a language that, if you add a vocabulary, would be a logically perfect language. Actual languages are not logically perfect in this sense, and they cannot possibly be, if they are to serve the purposes of daily life.[3]

Two complementary ideas make the new logic of particular interest to philosophers. The first is the conviction that natural language, such as ordinary English, does not in fact possess this sort of perfection. The language we normally speak is full of vagueness, ambiguity, and confusion. It is by no means what Russell calls "a logically perfect language." The second idea is a suspicion that these tawdry features of our natural languages tend to lead us astray in our thinking, particularly when we think about philosophical matters, which are always at some conceptual distance from everyday talk "of shoes and ships and sealing wax, of cabbages and kings."

So the dazzling idea of applying the new logic to traditional philosophical problems takes root in the imagination of many philosophers. Perhaps, if they could formulate these problems in terms of the crystalline purity of these formal logical structures, they could finally—after all these centuries—be definitively solved. The excitement is great. And indeed some very impressive analyses of

puzzling uses of language are produced. One of the most influential of these is the "theory of definite descriptions" authored by Bertrand Russell. A definite description is a phrase of the form, "the so and so." Sentences containing phrases of this form have a certain paradoxical character. Consider, for example, this sentence: "The golden mountain does not exist." We think this is a true sentence. But ask yourself: "How can it be *true* that the golden mountain does not exist unless the phrase "the golden mountain" is meaningful? And how can it be meaningful unless there is something that it means? And if there *is* something that it means— why, then, the original sentence seems to be *false*. Doesn't it? So the golden mountain must exist after all! This is a puzzle.

Russell applies the new logic to this puzzle and shows how it can be made to disappear. By getting clear about the logic of the language in which the puzzle is stated, we can see that our temptation to suppose that in some sense a golden mountain must exist is merely a confusion. This analysis has a great impact on many philosophers. It seems to show that the application of this logic to traditional problems of metaphysics and epistemology can produce clarity where before there was confusion. The logical analysis of language, then, seems to promise a definite increase in clarity of thought. Wittgenstein shares this sense that the new logic might make *all* the difference for philosophy. In the preface to the *Tractatus*, he writes:

> The book deals with the problems of philosophy, and shows, I believe, that the reason why these problems are posed is that the logic of our language is misunderstood. The whole sense of the book might be summed up in the following words: what can be said at all can be said clearly, and what we cannot talk about we must pass over in silence (*Tractatus*, p. 3).

Wittgenstein's thought here is a radical one indeed: the posing of the problems of philosophy is itself the problem. If we can just get clear about "the logic of our language," these problems will *disappear*. They will be part of "what we cannot talk about." About them we must be *silent*.

Principia Mathematica, written by Bertrand Russell and Alfred North Whitehead between 1910 and 1913, is a classic of modern logic.

And how will getting clear about the logic of our language produce such a startling result? If we get clear about the logic of our language, Wittgenstein thinks, we will see what the *limits* of language are. And we will also see that thinkers violate those limits whenever they pose and try to answer the sorts of problems we call philosophical.

> Thus the aim of the book is to set a limit to thought, or rather—not to thought, but to the expression of thoughts: for in order to be able to set a limit to thought, we should have to find both sides of the limit thinkable (i.e., we should have to be able to think what cannot be thought).
>
> It will therefore only be in language that the limit can be set, and what lies on the other side of the limit will simply be nonsense (*Tractatus*, p. 3).

This has a somewhat Kantian ring to it, and it is worth taking a moment to compare it to Kant's view of the limits of knowledge. You will recall that Kant sets himself to uncover the limits of rational knowledge and thinks to accomplish that by a critique of reason. Knowledge, Kant holds, is a product of *a priori* concepts and principles supplied by reason on the one hand and of intuitive material supplied by sensibility on the other. Its domain is phenomena, the realm of possible experience. Beyond this are things-in-themselves (noumena), thinkable, perhaps, but unknowable by us. Knowledge, Kant believes, has definite limits; and we can know what these are.*

Wittgenstein's strategy in the *Tractatus* bears a family resemblance to this Kantian project. But it is more radical on two counts. It aims to set a limit not just to knowledge, but to thought itself. And what lies on the other side of that limit is *not in any way thinkable*. Wittgenstein calls it "nonsense."

He refers, rather opaquely, to a problem standing in the way of such a strategy. In drawing boundaries, we draw a line and say, for example: Here, on this side, is Gary's land; there, on that side, is Genevieve's. But as this example shows, drawing ordinary boundaries or setting ordinary limits presupposes that both sides are thinkable, perhaps even experienceable or knowable. How, then, is it possible to set a limit to *thought*? To do so, it would seem we would have to "think what cannot be thought," survey what is on the *other* side of the boundary line, if only to know what it is we intend to exclude. Wittgenstein's ingenious notion, which we will explore in the next section, is that this limit setting must be done in language—and *from inside* language. He thinks he has found a way to draw the line that doesn't require having to *say* in language what is excluded, what lies outside the limit. One can set the limit, he thinks, by working outward from the center through what *can* be said. The center is defined by what a language *is*, by the *essence* of language. What lies out beyond the boundary *shows itself* to be linguistic nonsense.

The *Tractatus*

These are the first two sentences in Wittgenstein's youthful work, the *Tractatus Logico-Philosophicus*:

1.   The world is all that is the case.
1.1   The world is the totality of facts, not of things.*

These sayings, announced so bluntly, may seem dark. But the key to unlock these mysteries is at hand: the new logic. Wittgenstein believes that he can use this logic to reveal the *essence of language*. And the essence of language *shows us* what the world must be. But this needs explanation.

---

*A quick review of Kant's Copernican revolution and the idea of critique will bring this back to mind. See pp. 368–370.

*The *Tractatus* is arranged in short, aphoristic sentences, or small groups of sentences that express a complete thought. These sentences are numbered according to the following scheme. There are seven main aphorisms, 1, 2, 3, etc. 1.1 is supposed to be a comment on or an explanation of 1; 1.11 is to play the same role with respect to 1.1. It must be admitted that this elegant scheme is sometimes difficult to interpret.

Picturing

What is language? We are told that Wittgenstein's thinking about this question takes a decisive turn when he sees a diagram in a magazine story about an auto accident. Let us suppose it looked like this:

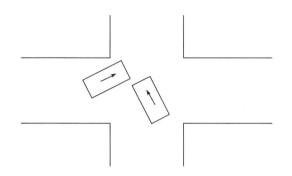

This diagram, we can say, *pictures* a *state of affairs*. It may not, of course, accurately represent what really happened. If we call the actual state of affairs *the facts*, we can say that it is a picture of a **possible state of affairs**—a picture of what might have happened and perhaps did happen. (We can imagine the lawyers on each side presenting contrasting pictures of the accident.)

2.1　　　We picture facts to ourselves.
2.12　　A picture is a model of reality.
2.131　In a picture the elements of the picture are the representatives of objects.
2.14　　What constitutes a picture is that its elements are related to one another in a determinate way.
2.141　A picture is a fact.

The diagram above is itself a fact: it is made up of actual elements (lines on the page) that are related to each other in certain ways. Moreover, each element in the diagram represents some object in the world (the edges of the streets, cars). So this fact pictures, or models, another (possible) fact: the way the objects here represented were actually (or possibly) related to each other at a certain time and place.

Every picture has a certain *structure*. By "structure" Wittgenstein means the way its elements are related to each other. Two pictures that are different in many ways might still have a similar structure. Imagine, for instance, a color photograph taken from a helicopter hovering over the corner just after the accident. The elements of this picture (blobs of color) are quite different from the elements of our drawing (black lines on a white background). But if our drawing is accurate, the two pictures have a similar structure: their elements are related to each other in similar ways.

Furthermore, the two pictures not only have a similar structure but also actually have something in common: what Wittgenstein calls **pictorial form**. It is important to note that pictorial form is not another element in addition to the lines in our drawing or the colors in the photograph, nor is it the actual structure of these two pictures. Rather, pictorial form is the *possibility* that a picture might actually have just this structure, that elements of some sort might actually be arranged in just this way. There needn't ever have been a picture, or a fact, with elements related to each other like this. But even if there never had been, there *could* have been. This possibility is actualized in our diagram; it might be actualized as well in the helicopter photo and in indefinitely many more pictures of the same state of affairs. All these pictures would have the *same* pictorial form.

But it is not just similar pictures that share the same form.

2.16　　If a fact is to be a picture, it must have something in common with what it depicts.
2.161　There must be something identical in a picture and what it depicts, to enable the one to be a picture of the other at all.
2.17　　What a picture must have in common with reality, in order to be able to depict it—correctly or incorrectly—in the way it does, is its pictorial form.

Pictures and what is pictured by them must also share the same form. So far we have been thinking of spatial pictures of objects in space. But there are other kinds of pictures, too. We can, for instance, think of an orchestra score as a picture; this is a spatial picture (the notes are laid out next to each other on a page), but what it primarily pictures is not spatial, but temporal: the succession of sounds the orchestra plays in a performance. Yet a score is also a picture, in Wittgenstein's sense, of the grooves in a recording of the work and of the magnetic tracings on a tape or compact disc. And we could think of the grooves in a recording as in turn a picture of the sound produced when it is played (see 4.0141). So while we tend to use the word "picture" rather narrowly, the concept applies very widely. Wherever there are objects in relation representing other objects, there is a Wittgensteinian picture.

Every picture, Wittgenstein claims, is a *logical* picture. And logical pictures can depict the world (2.19). As we have seen, a picture may represent reality correctly or incorrectly. That is why Wittgenstein says that logical pictures *can* depict the world: they depict ways the world might be—possible states of affairs.

If we think of a certain two-dimensional space, such as a desk top, we can see that there are a variety of possible ways the books on it can be arranged. Analogously, we can think of *logical space*. Logical space consists of all the possibilities there are for all the objects there are to be related to each other in all the possibly different ways there are. Logical space, then, comprises the form not only of all the actual states of affairs but also of all possible states of affairs. Given this notion of logical space, we can say,

2.202   A picture represents a possible situation in logical space.

Some pictures represent reality correctly, and others don't. How can we tell whether what a picture tells us is true?

2.22   What a picture represents it represents independently of its truth or falsity, by means of its pictorial form.

2.223   In order to tell whether a picture is true or false we must compare it with reality.

2.224   It is impossible to tell from the picture alone whether it is true or false.

2.225   There are no pictures that are true *a priori*.

You can't tell just by looking at our accident diagram, no matter how microscopically you inspect it, whether it represents the accident correctly. And this is the case with *all* pictures, Wittgenstein says. A *true* picture is one that represents a possible state of affairs that is also actual. And actual states of affairs are *facts*. So a true picture depicts the facts. If there were a picture true *a priori* (independent of experience), you wouldn't have to "compare it with reality" to tell whether it is true; you could discover the facts just by examining the picture. But that, Wittgenstein says, is precisely what is not possible. To tell whether a picture is true (represents the facts correctly), you have to check its fit with the facts. In no case can we tell *a priori* whether a picture is true. This is an extremely important feature of pictures.*

Thought and Language

Among the logical pictures, there is one sort that is of particular significance.

3.   A logical picture of facts is a thought.

3.001   'A state of affairs is thinkable': what this means is that we can picture it to ourselves.

3.01   The totality of true thoughts is a picture of the world.

3.02   A thought contains the possibility of the situation of which it is the thought. What is thinkable is possible too.

Our thoughts, then, are pictures, too. And, being pictures, they have all the characteristics of pic-

---

*If Wittgenstein is right, rationalist attempts to say what the world must be like based on reason alone must be mistaken. No matter how "clear and distinct" one of Descartes' ideas is, for instance, one can't deduce from this that it is true. By stressing that there are no pictures that are true *a priori*, Wittgenstein expresses one version of empiricism. Compare Hume, pp. 345–346.

tures we noted earlier: they are composed of elements in a certain arrangement, so they are facts with a certain structure; in virtue of that, they possess pictorial form; they represent possible states of affairs; and they share their pictorial and logical form with what they represent.

And now comes a crucial point.

3.1　　In a proposition a thought finds an expression that can be perceived by the senses.

3.11　　We use the perceptible sign of a proposition (spoken or written, etc.) as a projection of a possible situation.

So thought finds its expression in perceptible signs, or sentences, i.e., in *language*. Now we can understand why Wittgenstein thinks he can set a limit to thought by finding the limits of language. It is in language that thought is expressed. If there are limits to what language can express, these will be the limits of thought as well.

But what is a propositional sign, a sentence? Like all pictures, it is a fact, an arrangement of objects.

3.1431　　The essence of a propositional sign is very clearly seen if we imagine one composed of spatial objects (such as tables, chairs, and books) instead of written signs.
　　　　Then the spatial arrangement of these things will express the sense of the proposition.

Suppose you want to picture the fact that Sarah is standing to the east of Ralph. You might use a table to represent Sarah and a chair to represent Ralph. By putting the table to the east of the chair, you can picture the fact in question. This shows us, Wittgenstein says, "the essence of a propositional sign." What he means is that written or spoken sentences are like this, too; they are made up of elements standing in certain relations.

But it is not obvious that they are like this.

4.002　　Everyday language is a part of the human organism and is no less complicated than it.
　　　　It is not humanly possible to gather immediately from it what the logic of language is.
　　　　Language disguises thought.

The *essence* of language is hidden, "disguised." But it is something that can be disclosed, or shown. What is it that reveals the hidden essence of language? *Logic*. Wittgenstein agrees with Russell that the superficial grammar of what we say may not be a good indication of the logic of what we say. And he holds that Frege and Russell's logic displays for us the internal structure, the essence of language. Still, he is not tempted to discard our natural languages (German or English, for example) in favor of some artificially created "ideal" language. Nor does he have any inclination to reform our language in the direction of some postulated ideal. Since the languages we speak are *languages*, they, as much as any constructed language, must exemplify the essence of language. So logic must reside even there, in the heart of our confusing, vague, and ambiguous languages. What we need is not to junk them in favor of some ideal, but to understand them.

5.5563　　In fact, all the propositions of our everyday language, just as they stand, are in perfect logical order.

If they weren't, they wouldn't constitute a language!

But because "language disguises thought," the logical structure of our language is not apparent. To bring it to light we need *analysis*. What sort of analysis, then, can we give of a sentence? We already have the elements of an answer in hand. A sentence is a picture, and we know that a picture, like all facts, is composed of elements set in a certain structure. So there must be elements and a structure in every sentence. It only remains to determine what they are.

Let's consider again the sentence "Sarah is to the East of Ralph." We saw that this could be represented by one object in relation to another, a table and a chair, for instance. The table would in effect be a kind of name for Sarah, and the chair a name for Ralph. Wittgenstein concludes that the *only* elements needed in a language are names. Everything else—all the adjectives and prepositions, for instance—are inessential. If sentences were completely analyzed into their basic elements, all this would disappear. What would be left would be names in a structure.*

> 3.202   The simple signs employed in propositions are called names.
>
> 3.203   A name means an object. The object is its meaning. . . .
>
> 3.26   A name cannot be dissected any further by means of a definition: it is a primitive sign.

As you can see, there would be a very great difference between the "look" of a completely analyzed propositional sign and our ordinary sentences. One might have a hard time even recognizing the complete analysis of a familiar sentence, particularly because the names in question have to be *simple* signs. What we take to be names in ordinary language are invariably complex; they can be "dissected . . . by means of a definition." "Santa Claus" is short for "the jolly fat man who brings toys to good children." "George Washington" is a shorthand expression for "the first president of the United States" (and many other descriptions). These descriptions themselves need to be analyzed if we are to get to the roots of things to understand how language pictures the world.

If we get to that level of clarity, Wittgenstein thinks, we will see that sentences are composed of names in a logical structure. And names are *simple*. They cannot be further analyzed or "dissected."

The meaning of a name cannot be given in a definition using other linguistic elements; the meaning of a name is the object it stands for.*

Now we are ready to go back to the beginning and understand those first mysterious propositions of the *Tractatus*. Just as sentences represent possible states of affairs, true sentences represent facts. True sentences, moreover, are made up of names, and names stand for objects. But a sentence isn't just a list of names; it has an internal structure. And a fact isn't just a jumble of things; it has the same structure as the true sentence that pictures it. Why? Because the pictorial form of sentences mirrors the logical form of facts. The *world* is what is pictured in the totality of true sentences. The world, then, is not just a random collection of objects; it is "the totality of facts, not of things" because it shares the same logical form as the true sentences.

> 1.13   The facts in logical space are the world.

But we do not yet see how to solve the main problem Wittgenstein poses: to set a limit to thought. To do this, we have to look more closely at the logic of propositions.† As Russell shows, ordinary language often disguises the logical form of our sentences, but analysis can reveal it. A complete analysis would leave us with sentences that could not be further analyzed—simple sentences sometimes called *atomic propositions*. They would have constituents (names in a structure of possibility), but they could not be further broken down into other sentences.

---

*Here is a rough analogy. Certain notations in mathematics are merely a convenience and could be eliminated without diminishing the science. x^3, for instance, is just $x \cdot x \cdot x$. And $4y$ can be defined as $y + y + y + y$. So Wittgenstein thinks names standing in certain relations will express whatever we want to express, though we usually use more economical means.

*It is worth noting that Wittgenstein does not offer any examples of these simple names in the *Tractatus*. He argues that they must be implicit in our language and ultimately reachable by analysis; but just what they are—and what they name—is something of a mystery.

†For our purposes, I will not distinguish between sentences and propositions, though some philosophers do; a proposition is often thought of as an abstract feature several sentences can share when they mean the same thing. For example, "Mary hit Sally" and "Sally was hit by Mary" are different sentences but can be said to express the same proposition. Another example is "Snow is white" and "Schnee ist weiss."

4.221   It is obvious that the analysis of propositions must bring us to elementary propositions which consist of names in immediate combination.

But how are these simple sentences related to each other? Wittgenstein holds that

5.134   One elementary proposition cannot be deduced from another.

What this means is that the truth-value of each is independent of the truth-value of any other. An elementary proposition can remain true while the truth-values of any others (or even all the others) change. This has consequences for our view of the world as well.

2.061   States of affairs are independent of one another.
2.062   From the existence or non-existence of one state of affairs, it is impossible to infer the existence or non-existence of another.

Recall once more the beginning of the *Tractatus*:

1.2   The world divides into facts.
1.21   Each item can be the case or not the case while everything else remains the same.

This view, called **logical atomism**, is reminiscent of Hume's remark that "all events seem entirely loose and separate."* It means that relations existing between atomic facts cannot be *logical* relations. Given one true elementary proposition, it is never *necessary* that another one be true—or false.

There are, of course, logical relations between complex propositions. If we are given the truth-value of *p* and of *q*, we can infer something about the truth of the conjunction, *p and q*. To display these logical relations, Wittgenstein devises *truth tables*. A truth table for a complex proposition sets forth all the logically possible combinations of truth-values for its components and then displays

the corresponding truth-values for the whole. Here, for example, are truth tables for conjunctive, disjunctive, and negative propositions.

p	*q*	*p and q*	*p or q*	*not p*
T	T	T	T	F
T	F	F	T	F
F	T	F	T	T
F	F	F	F	T

The two columns on the left set out the possibilities; they show us that two propositions may both be true, one or the other may be true, or neither one may be true. The truth table for the conjunction shows us that the conjunction is true only when both of the components are true, and false otherwise. The truth table for the disjunction (an "or" statement) shows us that the disjunction is true unless both of the components are false. And the truth table for negation shows that negating a proposition changes its truth value.

Propositions may be of any degree of complexity. There may be a very large number of elementary propositions in its makeup, and the logic of their relations may be extremely complicated. The truth table for a proposition such as

if[if(p and q) then not (r or s)]
then (t if and only if not u)

is very large, but it is calculable. The truth-value of a complex proposition is a function of the truth-values of the component parts; this feature is called *truth functionality*. The logic of the *Tractatus* is a truth-functional logic.

Logical Truth

We noted before that no pictures are true *a priori*. To determine whether a proposition is true or false, then, we must compare it to the world. From the point of view of logic, any elementary proposition might be true, or it might be false. Such propositions are called *contingent*: their truth depends on the facts. The contingency of elementary propositions has another implication: however the world is, whatever the facts are, they *might have been different*. There is never any necessity in the facts. The negation of any true elementary proposition always pictures a possibility. Suppose it is true that it is now raining where I am; then it is false that it is not raining here and now (see the truth table above), but it is not necessarily false. It is a coherent possibility that it should not be raining here and now, even if it is. Given the configuration of the objects in the world, it is raining. But the objects of the world *could have been* otherwise configured.

We might like to ask, Just how far do these unrealized possibilities extend? How many possibilities are there? The answer is that this is what logic shows us. Our experience of the world can tell us what the actual facts are. Logic shows us what they *might be*. Logic is the science of the possible. And everything that it shows us is *necessary* (i.e., not contingent).* Consider, for example, the truth table for a proposition like this:

Either it is raining, or it is not raining.

p	not p	p or not p
T	F	T
F	T	T

The first column gives us the possibilities for the truth of *p*. The next column shows us what is the case when *p* is negated. And the third displays the results of disjoining the first two. The crucial thing to notice is that whatever the truth of *p* (and there are just these two possibilities), *p or not p* is true. In other words, there is no possibility that this proposition could be false. It is *necessarily* true; it is a

logical truth. Such a proposition Wittgenstein calls a **tautology**.*

There are three important points to notice here.

(1) The sentence represented by *p or not p* is a complex, not an elementary, proposition; *p* may or may not be elementary, but in this complex proposition, it is set in a structure defined by the logical operators, "not" and "or." Only propositions that are logically complex in this way can be necessarily true or false. (That is just another way to say that the truth of an elementary proposition is always contingent.)

(2) Logical words such as "not," "and," "or," and "if-then" are not *names*. These terms do not stand for objects; they have an entirely different function. They are part of the *structure* of sentences, not part of the content.†

> 4.0312   My fundamental idea is that the 'logical constants' are not representatives; that there can be no representatives of the *logic* of facts.

Wittgenstein illustrates this "fundamental idea" by considering double negation. There is a law of logic stating that negating the negation of a proposition is equivalent to asserting the proposition:

not not p if and only if p.

If it is not true that it is not raining, then it is raining. If the logical operator "not" were a name of something, the left side of this equivalence would picture something quite different from what the right side pictures; the law would then be false. But

---

*If something is possible, it cannot be merely contingent that it is possible, since whatever actually exists must *already* be possible; so what is possible couldn't *depend* on what the facts are.

*There are two limiting cases of propositions. Tautologies are one case; contradictions are the other. While tautologies are necessarily true, contradictions are necessarily false. Tautologies do not rule out any possibilities, contradictions rule them all out. In a sense, it is not strictly correct to call tautologies and contradictions "propositions," since propositions are pictures of reality; tautologies and contradictions do not picture states of affairs. They have a different, and very important, role to play.
†Compare Russell's description of a logically perfect language on pp. 490–491.

it doesn't. And the proof of this is that a truth table for this principle is a tautology.

(3) Suppose we interpret *p* as "It is raining"; then the tautology *p or not p* says, "Either it is raining, or it is not raining." But while "It is raining" gives us some information, the tautology tells us nothing. It says nothing; it is not a *picture*. Why is it that the proposition *p* can tell us something? It can be informative because it picks out one of several possibilities and says that that is how things are. In picking out that possibility, it excludes another. It tells us something about the world by shutting out one possibility and allowing another; *p or not p*, by contrast, excludes nothing. It does not rule out any possibilities, so it does not *say* anything.

4.461   Propositions show what they say: tautologies and contradictions show that they say nothing. A tautology has no truth conditions, since it is unconditionally true: and a contradiction is true on no condition.

4.462   Tautologies and contradictions are not pictures of reality. They do not represent any possible situations. For the former admit *all* possible situations, and the latter *none*.

Saying and Showing

We come here to a distinction that is very important to Wittgenstein: the distinction between *saying* and **showing**. Propositions do two things; they show something and they say something.

4.022   A proposition *shows* its sense.
A proposition *shows* how things stand *if* it is true, and it *says that* they do so stand.

The proposition "All crows are black" shows or presents its sense. We can see what this means if we ask what would be required to *understand* it. To understand this proposition is to grasp its sense; to grasp its sense is to understand what *would be the case* if it were *true*. When we understand the sen-

tence, we know that *if* it is true, any crow we come across will be black. Notice that understanding the sentence is not yet knowing that all crows are black. Given that we understand it, we might wonder whether it is true or doubt that it is true. It is, after all, possible that some crows aren't black; the proposition might present a possible state of affairs only, not a fact. But we grasp its sense in *knowing what would make it either true or false*. That—its sense—is what a proposition *shows*.

But a proposition like this plays another role. It not only shows its sense but also *says* things are this way, that crows actually are black. It makes an assertion and so is true or false depending on the facts of the world. According to Wittgenstein, this is the most general propositional form, i.e., what all propositions have in common:

4.5   This is how things stand.

Propositions show their sense; they say how things are.

But tautologies and contradictions *show* that they *say nothing*. If these limiting cases of propositions say nothing, however, we might wonder whether they have any importance. Couldn't we just ignore or neglect them? No. They are of the very greatest importance. They show us what is possible and what is impossible. They display for us the structure of logical space.

But they have another importance as well.

6.1   The propositions of logic are tautologies.

What Wittgenstein here calls the "propositions" of logic are sometimes called the laws of logic. Consider as an example the very basic law called the principle of noncontradiction: that no proposition can be both true and false. We can represent this as

not both p and not p.

If we write a truth table for this formula, we can see that it is a tautology—i.e., necessarily true—no matter what the truth-values of *p* are.

p	not p	p and not p	not (p and not p)
T	F	F	T
F	T	F	T

So the device of truth tables provides a justification for the laws of logic. Showing they are tautologies is equivalent to demonstrating their necessary truth. The truth table shows that there is no alternative to the laws of logic—no possibility that they might be false.* The *Tractatus* doctrine is that every principle of logical inference can be reduced to a tautology.†

Moreover,

6.113   It is the peculiar mark of logical propositions that one can recognize that they are true from the symbol alone, and this fact contains in itself the whole philosophy of logic.

What this means is that the propositions of logic can be known *a priori*. As we saw above, we can know about the actual world only by comparing a proposition with reality. It is the mark of logical propositions that this is not only unnecessary, but impossible; since they say nothing, they cannot say anything we could check out by examining the facts.

So the propositions of logic are one and all tautologies. And every valid form of inference can be expressed in a proposition of logic. This means that all possible logical relations between propositions can be known *a priori*. And in knowing them, we know the logical structure of the world—logical space, what Wittgenstein calls "the scaffolding of the world" (6.124).

---

*Of course this also shows that the laws of logic *say* nothing, i.e., are *about* nothing. The laws of logic are purely formal and empty of content. And that is exactly why they can be noncontingently true.
†In fact this claim is not correct. Truth tables constitute a decision procedure for validity only in *propositional logic*, where the analysis of structure does not go deeper than whole propositions. In *quantificational* (or *predicate*) *logic*, where the analysis reveals the internal structure of propositions, Alonzo Church later proves there is no such decision procedure.

6.1251   Hence there can *never* be surprises in logic.
6.127   All the propositions of logic are of equal status: it is not the case that some of them are essentially primitive propositions and others essentially derived propositions.
Every tautology itself shows that it is a tautology.

Setting the Limit to Thought

Finally, we are ready to understand how Wittgenstein thinks he can show us the limits of language. An operation discovered by Wittgenstein can be performed on a set of elementary propositions and can produce all the possible complex propositions (truth functions) that can be expressed by that set. Suppose we have just two elementary propositions, p and q. Using this operator, we can calculate that there are just sixteen possible truth functions combining them: *not p, not q, p or q, p and q, if p then q,* etc. Now imagine that we were in possession of *all* the elementary propositions there are; using this operation on that set, one could simply calculate all the possible truth functions there are and so generate each and every possible proposition.

Remembering the picture theory of meaning, we can see that this set of possible propositions pictures all the possible states of affairs there are, and in all their possible logical combinations. So, it represents the entirety of logical space: everything that there could possibly be in reality. Notice that there would be no proposition saying that these are all the possible facts; in fact, there couldn't be such a proposition. But there also doesn't need to be. That these are all the facts there are *shows itself* in these propositions being all there are, in there simply being no more that are possible, calculable, formulable. And we can see there are no more possible propositions, because all the possible ones are part of this set produced by this operator.

This very large set of propositions contains everything it is possible to say, plus the tautologies and contradictions (which say nothing). Beyond this set of possible propositions lies only *nonsense*. So the limit of thought is indeed set from inside.

Thought is expressed in language. The essence of language is picturing. And, given this, we can work out from the center to the periphery of language by means of logic. We do not need to take up a position outside the thinkable in order to draw a line circumscribing it. The limit *shows itself* by the lack of sense that pseudopropositions display when we try to say something unsayable. It is indeed, then, only "in language that the limit can be set, and what lies on the other side of the limit will simply be nonsense" (*Tractatus* preface, p. 3).

> 5.61 Logic pervades the world: the limits of the world are also its limits.
> So we cannot say in logic, 'The world has this in it, and this, but not that.'
> For that would appear to presuppose that we were excluding certain possibilities, and this cannot be the case, since it would require that logic should go beyond the limits of the world; for only in that way could it view those limits from the other side as well. We cannot think what we cannot think; so what we cannot think we cannot *say* either.

Value and the Self

In a letter to a potential publisher for the *Tractatus*, Wittgenstein writes,

> The book's point is an ethical one. I once meant to include in the preface a sentence which is not in fact there now but which I will write out for you here, because it will perhaps be a key to the work for you. What I meant to write, then, was this: My work consists of two parts: the one presented here plus all that I have *not* written, and it is precisely this second part that is the important one. My book draws limits to the sphere of the ethical from the inside as it were, and I am convinced that this is the ONLY *rigorous* way of drawing those limits. In short, I believe that where many others today are just *gassing*, I have managed in my book to put everything firmly in place by being silent about it.[5]

We began our consideration by suggesting that it would be a bad mistake to think of Wittgenstein as primarily a logician. Yet nearly everything we have

discussed to this point concerns logic and the logical structure of language. And this reflects the actual content of the *Tractatus*, the bulk of which is devoted to these problems. This is paradoxical. The paradox is resolved when we note that—in Wittgenstein's eyes—the really important part of the book is the part he did not write! Why didn't he write it? Was he too lazy? Did he run out of time? Of course not. He didn't write the important part because he was convinced it *couldn't be written.* What is most important—the ethical point of the book—is something that *cannot be said.*

Nonetheless, and again paradoxically, he does have some things to "say" about this sphere, which he also calls "the mystical."* Before we examine his remarks—brief and dark sayings, as many have noted—it will be helpful to set out a consequence of what we have already learned.

> 4.1 Propositions represent the existence and non-existence of states of affairs.
> 4.11 The totality of true propositions is the whole of natural science (or the whole corpus of the natural sciences).

The essence of language is picturing; and to picture is to say, "This is how things stand." The job of natural science is to tell us how things are, to give us a description of the world. And if natural science could finish its job, we would then have a *complete* picture of reality. Nothing—no object, no fact—would be left out. It would include the *totality* of true propositions.

But natural science does not contain any propositions like these: one ought to do *x*; it is wrong to *y*; the meaning of life is *z*. It follows that these are not really propositions at all; they look a lot like propositions, but, if Wittgenstein is right, they lie *beyond the limits of language.* Strictly speaking, they are unsayable. Those who utter them may be "just *gassing.*" Or they may be trying to say the most important things of all but failing, because they "run against the boundaries of language." In a "Lecture

---

*It is obviously a problem how we are to understand what he "says" about the unsayable. He makes a suggestion we will consider later.

on Ethics" Wittgenstein gave in 1929 or 1930 (not published until 1965), he says,

> This running against the walls of our cage is perfectly, absolutely hopeless. Ethics so far as it springs from the desire to say something about the ultimate meaning of life, the absolute good, the absolute valuable, can be no science. What it says does not add to our knowledge in any sense. But it is a document of a tendency in the human mind which I personally cannot help respecting deeply and I would not for my life ridicule it.[6]

Ethics "can be no science" because science consists of propositions, and

6.4   All propositions are of equal value.

6.41   The sense of the world must lie outside the world. In the world everything is as it is, and everything happens as it does happen: *in* it no value exists—and if it did exist, it would have no value.
If there is any value that does have value, it must lie outside the whole sphere of what happens and is the case.

6.42   And so it is impossible for there to be propositions of ethics.
Propositions can express nothing that is higher.

6.421   It is clear that ethics cannot be put into words.
Ethics is transcendental.

We can think of the *Tractatus* as the absolute end point of that road that begins with Copernicus and leads to the expulsion of value from the framework of the world.* The vision of the *Tractatus* is one where everything in the world is flattened out, where nothing is of any more significance than anything else, because nothing is of any significance at all. In the world is no value at all, nothing of importance. There are just the facts. And even if there were such a thing in the world as a value, that thing would itself just be another fact. It would *have* no value.

In Samuel Beckett's play *Endgame* a character named Hamm, blind and unable to move from his chair, commands his servant Clov to "Look at the earth." Clov gets his telescope, climbs a ladder, and looks out of the high window.

CLOV:
    Let's see.
    (He looks, moving the telescope.)
    Zero . . .
    (he looks)
    . . . zero . . .
    (he looks)
    . . . and zero.

HAMM:
    Nothing stirs. All is—

CLOV:
    Zer—

HAMM *(violently)*:
    Wait till you're spoken to!
    (Normal voice.)
    All is . . . all is . . . all is what?
(Violently.)
    All is what?

CLOV:
    What all is? In a word? Is that what you want to know? Just a moment.
    (He turns the telescope on the without, looks, lowers the telescope, turns toward Hamm.)
    Corpsed.[7]

Beckett's vision could not be more like Wittgenstein's. And, at the same time, it could not be more unlike. Turn the telescope to the earth (the world) and the verdict is "Zero, zero, zero." "Corpsed." In it no value exists. For Beckett, that is all there is; and that accounts for the sense of desolation and despair you find in his work. But Wittgenstein also knows another "reality."*

---

*Look back again to the discussion of how *final causes*, purposes and goals, are excluded from explanations in the new science. See pp. 283–284.

*In a phrase as opposed as possible to Beckett's conclusion that the earth is "corpsed," Wittgenstein says, "The world and life are one" (5.621). But in the light of his claim that the world consists wholly of valueless facts, this is a dark saying. It does seem, though, to be related to the idea that the self is the "limit" of the world and to the complementarity of solipsism and realism. We shall examine these ideas below.

Ethics, Wittgenstein says, "cannot be put into words." But what does it mean that ethics is something "higher," that it is "transcendental"? To understand this saying, we need to hear Wittgenstein's views of the subject, the self, the "I." He suggests that if you wrote a book called *The World as I Found It*, there is one thing that would not be mentioned in it: *you*. It would include all the facts you found, including all the facts about your body. And it would include psychological facts about yourself as well: your character, personality, dispositions, and so on. But you—the subject, the one to whom all this appears, the one who *finds* all these facts—would not be found.*

5.632   The subject does not belong to the world; rather, it is a limit of the world.

5.641   The philosophical self is not the human being, not the human body, or the human soul, with which psychology deals, but rather the metaphysical subject, the limit of the world—not a part of it.

It seems, then, that there are two "realities" in correlation: the world and the self; however, in the strict sense, the self or subject cannot be *said* to be a reality. Wittgenstein compares the situation to the relation between an eye and its visual field. The eye is not itself part of the visual field; it is not seen. In the same way, all content, all the facts, are "out there" in the world, which is the "totality of facts" (1.1).

5.64   Here it can be seen that solipsism, when its implications are followed out strictly, coincides with pure realism. The self of solipsism shrinks to a point without extension, and there remains the reality co-ordinated with it.

5.62   For what the solipsist *means* is quite correct; only it cannot be *said*, but makes itself manifest.*

What the solipsist wants to say is that only he exists, and the world only in relation to himself. But this cannot be *said*. Why? Because to say it would be to use language—propositions—to picture facts. And in picturing facts we are picturing the world, *not* the transcendental self to whom the world appears. So this self "shrinks to a point without extension." And if we ask *what there is*, the answer is the world—"all that is the case" (*Tractatus*, proposition 1). And this is just the thesis of radical **realism**, the antithesis of solipsism.

The concern of ethics is good and evil. But, as we have seen, there is no room for good and evil in the world, where everything just is whatever it is. What application, then, do these concepts have? Ethics must concern itself with the transcendental: the self, the subject. But how? Here is a clue.

6.373   The world is independent of my will.

6.374   Even if all that we wish for were to happen, still this would only be a favour granted by fate, so to speak.

I may will or intend to do something, e.g., write a check to pay a telephone bill. And usually I can do it. But it is clear that paying a bill by check depends on the cooperation of the world: the neurons have to fire just right, the nerves must transmit the neural signals reliably, the muscles must contract in

---

*Among thinkers we have studied, this should remind you most of Kant, for whom the ego is also transcendental. It is not identical with Kant's view, however. Kant believes that, though we can't come to know the nature of "this I or he or it (the thing) which thinks," we could come to know a lot about it—that it is the source of the pure intuitions, the categories, the *a priori* synthetic propositions, all of which explain the structure of the empirical world. And all this can be stated in meaningful propositions. For Wittgenstein, none of this is possible. The structure of the world is not dictated by the structure of rational minds, because the structure of reality is just logic; and logic, consisting as it does of empty tautologies, neither has nor needs a source. Kant's world needs a structure-giver because its fundamental principles are thought to be synthetic. For Wittgenstein, logic is *analytic*. It requires no source beyond itself because it has no content requiring explanation. This "scaffolding of the world" is not itself a fact in the world, nor is it a fact about the world or about rational minds. It is not a fact at all! It shows *itself*. Look again at the relevant discussions of Kant on pp. 382–384.

*Compare Descartes' struggles to overcome solipsism by proving the existence of God in *Meditation III*; see also pp. 298 and 305. Wittgenstein acknowledges there is a truth in solipsism; but such truth as there is already involves the reality of the world—of which the self is aware. So there is no need to *prove* the world's existence—or that of God, about whom in any case nothing can be said.

just the right way, the bank must not suddenly crash, and so forth. And none of that is entirely in my control. That is what Wittgenstein means when he says the world is independent of my will. If I intend to pay my telephone bill, getting it done is, in a way, a "favour granted by fate."*

Good and Evil, Happiness and Unhappiness

Wittgenstein seems to have proved that good and evil cannot lie in the world. Everything just happens as it does happen. So good and evil must pertain to the will. What I will is in my control, even if the outcome of my willing in the world is not. In a strict sense, my willing *is* my action: the rest is just the result of my action. But now we have to ask what good and evil could be, if they pertain to the will only.

> 6.422   When an ethical law of the form, 'Thou shalt . . .', is laid down, one's first thought is, "And what if I do not do it?" It is clear, however, that ethics has nothing to do with punishment and reward in the usual sense of the terms. So our question about the *consequences* of an action must be unimportant. At least those consequences should not be events. For there must be something right about the question we posed. There must indeed be some kind of ethical reward and punishment, but they must reside in the action itself. (And it is also clear that the reward must be something pleasant and the punishment something unpleasant.)

Good action (good willing) is rewarded with something pleasant, and evil action is punished with the unpleasant. But these are not rewards and punishments "in the usual sense"; they cannot be external to the action itself. They cannot, in other words, be something added by the world. How could a "favour granted by fate" have anything to do with *ethical* rewards? Such rewards and punishments must be intrinsic to the actions themselves. But what could they be?

> 6.43   If the good or bad exercise of the will does alter the world, it can alter only the limits of the world, not the facts—not what can be expressed by means of language.
> In short the effect must be that it becomes an altogether different world. It must, so to speak, wax and wane as a whole.
> The world of the happy man is a different one from that of the unhappy man.

These are difficult sayings, indeed. And I do not claim to understand fully what Wittgenstein means by them. It does seem clear that the reward for good willing is happiness and the punishment for bad is unhappiness. The good person, as Plato also thinks, is the happy person.* But this obviously does not mean that Jones, who lives righteously and well, will get whatever she wants in life. That kind of connection between willing and the world doesn't exist. (This fact is also recognized by Kant.) Goodness does not produce *that kind* of happiness.† What kind does it produce, then?

Strictly speaking, this question cannot be answered. In the *Notebooks, 1914–1918*, Wittgenstein asks:

> "What is the objective mark of the happy, harmonious life? Here it is again clear that there cannot be any such mark, that can be *described*. This mark cannot be a physical one but only a metaphysical one, a transcendental one" (*N*, 78).[8]

---

*If these reflections are going to make any sense to you at all, you will have to pause a bit and try to sink into this way of viewing things. It will not be any good to just try to learn the words, or even memorize the sentences. Wittgenstein would insist that if you are able only to parrot the words, you will have understood *nothing*. Here is an exercise that might help. Pick out some fact about your present experience. Focus on it. Try to regard it as merely a fact in the world, one fact among others. Now try to focus on some psychological state in the same way. Practice in this should make even your own psychological states have the same status as any other fact in the world; they will not be "privileged," as it were, but just facts that are *there*. And then ask yourself: for whom are they there? For ideas that are in some ways similar, see the discussion of the Stoics on p. 190.

---

*See Plato's discussion of the happiness of the just soul, pp. 133–135.
†It might help to remember here that Wittgenstein gave away the considerable fortune he inherited when his father died and lived the rest of his life simply and austerely. What the world can supply cannot *make* you happy!

And we know that nothing can be *said* about the transcendental. Still, there are clues and hints. What could it mean, for instance, that the *world* of the happy person is a different world from that of the unhappy one? That the world waxes and wanes as a whole? Here is a possibility.

Most of us, most of the time, do not occupy the position of the transcendental subject, even though that is what we essentially are—the limit of the world, not some entity within the world. We identify ourselves with a body, with certain desires, with a set of psychological facts. This is, we think, what we are. And in so identifying ourselves, our world narrows, *wanes*. We are concerned with *this* body, with satisfying *these* desires. And *our* world is just the world relevant to these concerns. It is as though the rest didn't exist. If we could, however, identify with the transcendental self, our world would wax larger. Indeed, we would see it just as it is—a limited whole and the totality of facts, none of which are of such importance that they crowd out any other. *Our* world would become *the* world. Only the world of the happy person is identical with the world as it is. The happy see the world with that disinterested enjoyment we experience when we appreciate a fine work of art. In Wittgenstein's words:

6.421 (Ethics and aesthetics are one and the same.)

and

The work of art is the object seen *sub specie aeternitatis*; and the good life is the world seen *sub specie aeternitatis*. This is the connection between art and ethics.

The usual way of looking at things sees objects as if it were from the midst of them, the view *sub specie aeternitatis* from outside (N, 84e).

and

Aesthetically, the miracle is that the world exists. That what exists does exist.

Is it the essence of the artistic way of looking at things, that it looks at the world with a happy eye? (N, 86e).

To live one's life "from the viewpoint of eternity" is to live in the present.* And here we have another clue:

Whoever lives in the present lives without fear and hope (N, 76e).

What could this mean? The thought seems to be that fear and hope essentially refer to time; one fears what *may happen*, and one hopes *for the future*. But if one lives entirely in the present, there is no past and future about which to fear and hope. If there is nothing one fears—absolutely nothing—and if there is nothing one hopes (presumably because one lacks nothing), how could one fail to be happy? In his "Lecture on Ethics," Wittgenstein tells us that when he tries to think of something with absolute value, two "experiences" come to mind.

I will describe this [first] experience in order, if possible, to make you recall the same or similar experiences, so that we may have a common ground for our investigation. I believe the best way of describing it is to say that when I have it *I wonder at the existence of the world*. And I am then inclined to use such phrases as "how extraordinary that anything should exist" or "how extraordinary that the world should exist." I will mention another experience straight away which I also know and which others of you might be acquainted with: it is, what one might call, the experience of feeling *absolutely* safe. I mean the state of mind in which one is inclined to say "I am safe, nothing can injure me what ever happens."[9][†]

Wittgenstein adds that the expression of these "experiences" in language is, strictly speaking, nonsense. One can wonder that the world contains kangaroos, perhaps; but there is no proposition that can express the "fact" that the world exists. Why not? Because this "fact" is obviously not one of the facts that make up that totality which *is* the

---

*Compare Augustine on the atemporal nature of God, p. 226.
†Such a powerful echo of Socrates! In his defense at his trial, Socrates says, "a good man cannot be harmed either in life or in death" (*Apology* 41d).

world, and beyond that totality there is nothing. And it is equally nonsense to say that one feels *absolutely* safe; one can be safe from tigers, or protected from polio. But to say, "Nothing whatever can injure me," is just a misuse of language. Yet, that is the only satisfactory expression, Wittgenstein thinks, for what is of absolute value. Here we have an example of running against the boundaries of language.

To "wonder at the existence of the world" is to experience it as a limited whole. And that Wittgenstein calls "the mystical."

6.44   It is not *how* things are in the world that is mystical, but *that* it exists.

6.45   To view the world *sub specie aeterni* is to view it as a whole—a limited whole.
Feeling the world as a limited whole—it is this that is mystical.

To live the life of the philosophical self, that metaphysical self which is not a part of the world but its limit, is to have a sense for "the mystical." This life is also the good life, the beautiful life, and the happy life. It is a life of absolute safety.

Remember, though, that all of this is not something that can properly be said. It cannot even really be asked about. It is tempting to think that we can ask, Why does the world exist? or Why is there anything at all rather than nothing? But

6.5   When the answer cannot be put into words, neither can the question be put into words.
The riddle does not exist.
If a question can be framed at all, it is also *possible* to answer it.

6.52   We feel that even when *all possible* scientific questions have been answered, the problems of life remain completely untouched. Of course there are then no questions left, and this itself is the answer.

6.521   The solution of the problem of life is seen in the vanishing of the problem.
(Is not this the reason why those who have found after a long period of doubt that the sense of life became clear to them have

then been unable to say what constituted that sense?)

6.522   There are, indeed, things that cannot be put into words. They *make themselves manifest*. They are what is mystical.

The Unsayable

If you have been following carefully, you have no doubt been wondering how Wittgenstein can manage to say all this stuff that he so explicitly "says" cannot be said. This is indeed a puzzle we must address. What he has been writing is clearly philosophy. But if, as he (philosophically) says, the totality of true propositions is science, what room is there for philosophy?

4.111   Philosophy is not one of the natural sciences.
(The word 'philosophy' must mean something whose place is above or below the natural sciences, not beside them.)
Philosophy aims at the logical clarification of thoughts.
Philosophy is not a body of doctrine but an activity.
A philosophical work consists essentially of elucidations.
Philosophy does not result in 'philosophical propositions', but rather in the clarification of propositions.
Without philosophy thoughts are, as it were, cloudy and indistinct: its task is to make them clear and to give them sharp boundaries.

The key thought here is that philosophy is an activity; its business is clarification. It follows that we should not look to philosophy for *results*, for truths, or for "a body of doctrine." To do so is to mistake the nature of philosophizing altogether. It has been one of the major failings of the philosophical tradition, Wittgenstein believes, that it has tried to produce "philosophical propositions"— that it has thought of itself as something "beside" the sciences, in the same line of work as science.

But it is *altogether different* from science. It lies, one might say, at right angles to science. Wittgenstein's view of his predecessors is severe:

4.003   Most of the propositions and questions to be found in philosophical works are not false but nonsensical.
Consequently we cannot give any answer to questions of this kind, but can only establish that they are nonsensical.
Most of the propositions and questions of philosophers arise from our failure to understand the logic of our language.
(They belong to the same class as the question whether the good is more or less identical than the beautiful.)
And it is not surprising that the deepest problems are in fact *not* problems at all.

6.53   The correct method in philosophy would really be the following: to say nothing except what can be said, i.e., propositions of natural science—i.e., something that has nothing to do with philosophy—and then, whenever someone else wanted to say something metaphysical, to demonstrate to him that he had failed to give a meaning to certain signs in his propositions. Although it would not be satisfying to the other person—he would not have the feeling that we were teaching him philosophy—*this* method would be the only strictly correct one.

Plato and Aristotle, Hume and Kant all think they are revealing or discovering truth. But, if Wittgenstein is right, all of their most important claims are nonsensical. They aren't even *candidates* for being true! Their theories—to the extent that they are not absorbable by empirical science—are pseudo-answers to pseudoquestions. They arise because these philosophers don't understand the logic of our language; Wittgenstein thinks he has, for the first time, clearly set this forth.

But there is still a worry. Wittgenstein is himself not utilizing "the correct method" in writing the *Tractatus*. How, then, are we to take his own "propositions" here?

6.54   My propositions serve as elucidations in the following way: anyone who understands me eventually recognizes them as nonsensical, when he has used them—as steps—to climb up beyond them. (He must, so to speak, throw away the ladder after he has climbed up it.)
He must transcend these propositions, and then he will see the world aright.

To "see the world aright" is surely to see it from the viewpoint of eternity, from the point of view of the philosophical self. It is not too farfetched to be reminded of that ladder the mystics talk about as leading to oneness with God. Having climbed Wittgenstein's ladder, we too can wonder at the existence of the world, feel absolutely safe, experience happiness and beauty—and do our science. But we would always have to keep in mind the last "proposition" of the *Tractatus*:

7   What we cannot speak about we must pass over in silence.

Yet, the things we must "pass over in silence" are the most important of all.

Logical Positivism

In the preface to the *Tractatus*, Wittgenstein writes,

> Perhaps this book will be understood only by someone who has himself already had the thoughts that are expressed in it—or at least similar thoughts (*Tractatus*, p. 3).

This was to prove prophetic. Russell supplied an introduction that Wittgenstein thought so misunderstood his intentions that he refused to have it printed in the German edition. And his book was studied painstakingly by a group of scientifically oriented philosophers in Vienna (a group that came to be known as the Vienna Circle) who admired its logic and philosophy of language but had no sympathy with what Wittgenstein himself thought most important. Because this latter group proved extremely influential, at least for a time, we will briefly note their major theses. The movement they began had a significant impact on scientists (both natural and social), on philosophy of science, and on the general public. These philosophers are called *logical positivists*.

Logical positivism can be identified with three claims, all of which have recognizable roots in the *Tractatus*. The first is that logic and mathematics are *analytic*. The positivists accept Wittgenstein's analysis of the basic truths of logic: that they are tautological in nature. Both mathematics and logic are empirically or factually empty, providing no knowledge of nature at all.* They are, however, extremely important: they provide a framework in which we can move from one true factual statement to another, i.e., they license inferences, just as Wittgenstein says they do.†

The second principle is a criterion for judging the meaningfulness of all nontautological assertions. It is called the **verifiability principle**. The positivists believe they can use it to sweep away not only the confusions of past philosophy, but also everything Wittgenstein holds most dear.‡ Here is Moritz Schlick's explanation of verifiability.

> When, in general, are we sure that the meaning of a question is clear to us? Evidently when and only when we are able to state exactly the conditions under which it is to be answered in the affirmative, or as the case may be, the conditions under which it is to be answered in the negative. By stating these conditions, and by this alone, is the meaning of a question defined.
>
> The meaning of a proposition consists, obviously, in this alone, that it expresses a definite state of affairs. One can, of course, say that the proposition

itself already gives this state of affairs.* This is true, but the proposition indicates the state of affairs only to the person who understands it. But when do I understand a proposition? When I understand the meanings of the words which occur in it? These can be explained by definition. But in the definitions new words appear whose meanings cannot again be described in propositions, they must be indicated directly: the meaning of a word must in the end be *shown*, it must be *given*. This is done by an act of indication, of pointing; and what is pointed at must be given, otherwise I cannot be referred to it.[10]

The definitions Schlick refers to are Wittgenstein's analyses of complex propositions into elementary or atomic propositions and ultimately into words that are not further definable. For Wittgenstein, as we have seen, elementary propositions are composed of names in a logical syntax. The names stand for objects. He never specifies exactly what objects the names name. He once said, much later, that when he wrote the *Tractatus* he thought of himself as a logician and believed that it wasn't his business to identify the objects that he on logical grounds deduced would have to be there.

But for the Positivists, the truth conditions for elementary sentences are given in *perception*. The simple objects designated by the indefinable words must be the kind of thing you can indicate, or point to. Schlick uses the Wittgensteinian word "shown" and paraphrases it by "given." The meaning of a word must be something you can *point to* or *indicate* in some way. You have to be able to *show* me what you mean. What Schlick means by "given" is "given in sense experience. This, then, is the bite of the verifiability principle. Unless you can explain what perceptual or sensed difference the truth or falsity of your assertion would make, the proposition you are asserting is *meaningless*. Clearly, logical positivism is a kind of empiricism.†

---

*Thus they correspond roughly to what Hume calls relations of ideas (see p. 345) and Kant's notion of the analytic *a priori* (see p. 371). Note how different a philosophy of mathematics this is from that of Kant, who believes arithmetic, while *a priori*, is not analytic.
†Review the discussion of the principles of logic on pp. 499–500.
‡In fact, the positivists have no clear view of just what Wittgenstein holds dear.

---

*Wittgenstein says, "A proposition *shows* its sense" (4.022).
†Like David Hume, prince of empiricists, the positivists want to base all nonanalytic knowledge on the data our senses provide. See again the discussion of "the theory of ideas" and Hume's rule, "No impression, no idea" (pp. 343–344).

The positivists have no sympathy for a "good" kind of nonsense, no tolerance for "running against the boundaries of language." All this they want to *exterminate*. They talk about the *elimination* of metaphysics. (One gets the image of lining metaphysical ideas up against the wall and gunning them down.) What is to be left as meaningful is science—science alone! Out with Plato's Forms, Aristotle's *entelechy*, Augustine's God, Descartes' Mind, Kant's noumena, Hegel's Absolute Spirit— and Wittgenstein's Mystical! Out with metaphysics altogether—that attempt to know something beyond what our senses can verify. It is to be purged from human memory.* And the instrument of this purging is the principle of meaningfulness. Since none of these notions are verifiable by sense experience, they are all meaningless.

Note that the positivists are not committed, for example, to the atheist's claim that there is no God. Such a claim they consider to be as much a metaphysical statement as the claim that there is a God. Both claims are shut out from the realm of meaning altogether; if the verifiability criterion is correct, both the believer and the atheist are uttering meaningless noises. Since their claims are without sense, one cannot sensibly ask which is true: neither one is even a possible candidate for truth.

The Positivists work at refining the verifiability principle to avoid obvious counterexamples. For instance, verifiability needn't be *direct*, as when I see something with my own eyes; it can be *indirect*, as when I rely on instrumentation, or (more important) when I test the observable consequences of a hypothesis that is not itself directly testable. And it is enough, they say, for propositions to be verifiable *in principle*. They obviously want to allow for the meaningfulness of propositions that are not now verifiable only because of technological limitations; moreover, something doesn't have to be conclusively verifiable for it to be meaningful. They draw a contrast between *strong* (conclusive) verification and *weak* verification (verification by evidence indicating that something is likely to be

true or probably true). The positivists hold that weak verifiability is enough to qualify a statement as meaningful. But unless a proposition is at least indirectly verifiable, verifiable in principle, and weakly verifiable, it is declared to have no sense.

The third plank of the positivist platform concerns the nature of philosophy. Like Wittgenstein, they hold that philosophy is not in the business of providing knowledge about the supersensible; its task is the clarification of statements. So it is an activity, as Wittgenstein says. But they are convinced that philosophy doesn't have to be classified as nonsense. If the activity of philosophy is clarification, it has certain statable results: it issues in definitions. Much of the writing of the logical positivists is devoted to clarifying what they call "the logic of science." And so they are interested in the concepts of *law* and *theory*, of *hypothesis* and *evidence*, of *confirmation* and *probability*. Much good work is produced in understanding these concepts and how they relate to each other. Under their influence the *philosophy of science* becomes a recognized and important part of philosophy; without their work in this area, it is unlikely that most academic departments would now be teaching courses in this field.*

The fate of ethical statements on positivist principles is particularly interesting. Moral judgments do not seem to be verifiable—even weakly, indirectly, and in principle. So they don't seem to meet the criterion for factual meaningfulness. That raises the question: What kind of statement is a judgment that stealing is wrong?† In an explosive

---

*For a similar sentiment, see David Hume's trenchant remarks at the end of his *Enquiry* (p. 365). It has been said with some justice that logical positivism is just Hume plus modern logic.

*Like most of the distinctive theses of logical positivism, the positivists' understanding of the logic of science is now largely surpassed. It now seems too abstract, too prescriptive, and not mindful enough to how science is actually done. The complaint is, ironically, that positivists are not empirical enough about science itself. Historical studies in the past several decades have significantly modified our understanding of that important cultural institution we call science. One of the milestones in this development is Thomas Kuhn's 1962 work, *The Structure of Scientific Revolutions*.
†Recall Wittgenstein's claim that in the world there is no value— and if there were a value in the world, it would *have* no value. The realm of facts excludes the realm of values. You should also look back to Hume's famous discussion of the distinction between *is* and *ought* (pp. 362–363).

book called *Language, Truth, and Logic*, published in 1936, the English philosopher A. J. Ayer sets out the positivist view of ethics. Ethical concepts, he says, are "mere pseudoconcepts."

Thus if I say to someone, "You acted wrongly in stealing that money," I am not stating anything more than if I had simply said, "You stole that money." In adding that this action is wrong I am not making any further statement about it. I am simply evincing my moral disapproval of it. It is as if I had said, "You stole that money," in a peculiar tone of horror, or written it with the addition of some special exclamation marks. The tone, or the exclamation marks, adds nothing to the literal meaning of the sentence. It merely serves to show that the expression of it is attended by certain feelings in the speaker.

If now I generalize my previous statement and say, "Stealing money is wrong," I produce a sentence which has no factual meaning—that is, expresses no proposition which can be either true or false. It is as if I had written "Stealing money!!"—where the shape and thickness of the exclamation marks show, by a suitable convention, that a special sort of moral disapproval is the feeling which is being expressed. It is clear that there is nothing said here which can be true or false. Another man may disagree with me about the wrongness of stealing, in the sense that he may not have the same feelings about stealing as I have, and he may quarrel with me on account of my moral sentiments. But he cannot, strictly speaking, contradict me. For in saying that a certain type of action is right or wrong, I am not making any factual statement, not even a statement about my own state of mind. I am merely expressing certain moral sentiments. And the man who is ostensibly contradicting me is merely expressing his moral sentiments. So that there is plainly no sense in asking which of us is in the right. For neither of us is asserting a genuine proposition. . . .

We can now see why it is impossible to find a criterion for determining the validity of ethical judgments. It is not because they have an "absolute" validity which is mysteriously independent of ordinary sense-experience, but because they have no objective validity whatsoever. If a sentence makes no statement at all, there is obviously no sense in asking whether what it says is true or false. And we have seen that sentences which simply express moral judgments do not say anything. They are pure expressions of feeling and as such do not come under the category of truth and falsehood. They are unverifiable for the same reason as a cry of pain or a word of command is unverifiable—because they do not express a genuine proposition.[11]

This is pretty radical stuff, at least as judged by the philosophical tradition. Its ancestry lies in the views of the Sophists, that things (at least in the moral sphere) just are as they seem to the individual human being.* If Ayer is right, there are no objective truths about the good life or about right and wrong, so reason (obviously) cannot help us find them. It follows that Socrates' search for the nature of piety, courage, and justice is misguided. And all the philosophers who build on that assumption are mistaken in what they are doing. Plato's Form of the Good, Aristotle's virtues as human excellences, Epicurus' pleasure, the Stoics' keeping of the will in harmony with nature, Augustine's ordered loves, Hobbes' social contract, Kant's categorical imperative, Mill's greatest good for the greatest number—all these are not, if Ayer is right, contributions to a theory of the right and the good for humans, but merely expressions of how these individuals feel about things.†

If we use a different measure, however, Ayer's view isn't so radical. In fact, it is the underpinning of what seems to many these days the sheerest

---

*See the motto of Protagoras on p. 41, and the relevance of rhetoric to justice as developed by Gorgias, Antiphon, and Callicles, discussed on pp. 42–46. A major portion of rhetoric might be thought of as techniques for "expressing moral sentiments" in persuasive ways.

†It is important to note that the Wittgenstein of the *Tractatus* would think this turn of events about as awful as could be imagined. While he would agree that value is not a matter of fact, he wants to locate ethics—what really matters—in the life of the transcendental or philosophical self. Positivist ethics construes value as no more than the way some empirical self happens to feel about things. What greater difference could there be? Wittgenstein says, "God does not reveal himself *in* the world" (*Tractatus* 6.432). The positivists make each of us a little god. From Wittgenstein's point of view, if Ayer is right, all we ever get in morality is "just *gassing.*" See again Wittgenstein's views on ethics, pp. 504–506.

common sense. Nearly every college freshman, in my experience, arrives with the opinion that this view of moral judgments is so obvious that it is very near absurd to question it.*(That, of course, is not a very strong argument in its favor.)

Ayer's view, sometimes called *the emotivist theory of ethics*, is stated in a brash and bold fashion. Other thinkers in the same tradition qualify and complicate it to meet obvious objections; but it is good to see it stated in its bare essentials, especially since it has been so widely adopted by the public. It is important to note that the emotivist theory of ethics depends on a stark contrast between the realm of facts and all the rest. And this contrast, at least as the positivists develop it, is based on the verifiability principle's adequacy as a theory of meaning. If that theory of meaning is flawed, we may not be able to get by with such a radically subjectivist theory of morality. We will examine the question about meaning in some detail when we turn to Wittgenstein's later philosophy.

To their credit, it should be noted that certain difficulties in the verifiability principle are noted and examined by the positivists themselves. For instance, the sharp division of meaningful propositions into the analytic statements of logic and definition on the one hand and the verifiable statements of fact on the other leads naturally to this question: What sort of statement is the verifiability principle itself? There seem to be three possibilities:

(1) The verifiability principle might be a factual statement. But—by its own terms—the principle must itself be verifiable by sense experience to be factual; it must have truth conditions in sense experience. But what sense experiences could constitute the truth conditions for this principle? The possibility of seeing red roses might constitute the meaning of "Some roses are red." And experiences in a laboratory might (in a complicated and indirect way) verify "Copper conducts electricity." But

how could experience go any way at all toward showing it to be true that the only meaningful statements are those verifiable by experience? As Wittgenstein would later remark, the standard meter bar in Paris cannot be said either to be or not to be one meter long. A criterion cannot guarantee itself. So it seems clear that it is not factual.

(2) It might be analytic, a definition of "meaningful." But it doesn't seem to capture the *ordinary* sense of meaningfulness. There are lots of unverifiable propositions we think we understand perfectly well. Consider this example: The last word in Caesar's mind, unuttered, before he died, was 'tu'. " This seems obviously sensible and it is either true or false. But the possibility of verifying it, even weakly, indirectly, and in principle, seems zero. The fact that we cannot in any way *find out* whether it is true, does not subtract from its meaningfulness in the slightest.

(3) There seems only one possibility left, given the positivist framework. If it doesn't fit either of the two main favored categories, perhaps the principle functions as a kind of recommendation that this is how we *should* use the word "meaningful," or a proposal that it would be *good* to use the word "meaningful" in this way. This understanding of the verifiability principle would associate it with the positivist view of ethical propositions. Its enunciation would express feelings of approval about this way of understanding meaning and perhaps urge others to feel the same way. But if this is what the verifiability principle amounts to, then there is no *reason* why we all should adopt it, and nonpositivists can (on positivist grounds) simply say, "Well, I feel different about it." And that is not very satisfactory.

Notes

1. Bertrand Russell, "Philosophers and Idiots," *The Listener* 52, no. 1354 (February 10, 1955): 247. Reprinted in Russell's *Portraits from Memory* (London: George Allen and Unwin, Publishers, 1956), 26–27.
2. A brief and very readable account of Wittgenstein's life can be found in Norman Malcolm's *Ludwig Witt-*

---

*This fact is one of the centerpieces of Alan Bloom's complaint about today's university education, addressed in his best-seller, *The Closing of the American Mind*.

genstein: A Memoir (Oxford: Oxford University Press, 1958).

3. Bertrand Russell, "Logical Atomism," in *Logic and Knowledge* (London: George Allen and Unwin, Publishers, 1956), 197–98.

4. Ludwig Wittgenstein, *Tractatus Logico-Philosophicus*, trans. D. F. Pears and B. F. McGuinness (London: Routledge and Kegan Paul, 1961). Quotations from the main text of the *Tractatus* will be identified by the paragraph numbers found in that work.

5. Paul Englemann, *Letters from Ludwig Wittgenstein, with a Memoir* (Oxford: Basil Blackwell, 1967), 143–44.

6. Ludwig Wittgenstein, "Lecture on Ethics," *Philosophical Review* 74 (1965): 12.

7. Samuel Beckett, *Endgame* (New York: Grove Press, 1958), 29–30.

8. Quotations from Ludwig Wittgenstein's *Notebooks, 1914–1916* (Oxford: Basil Blackwell, 1961) are cited in the text using the abbreviation *N*.

9. Wittgenstein, "Lecture on Ethics," 8.

10. Moritz Schlick, "Positivism and Realism," in *Logical Positivism*, ed. A. J. Ayer (New York: Macmillan Co., 1959), 86–87.

11. A. J. Ayer, *Language, Truth, and Logic* (New York: Dover Publications, n.d.), 107–8.

26

Ludwig Wittgenstein
and Ordinary Language:
"This Is Simply What I Do"

In the preface to the *Tractatus*, Wittgenstein writes,

> . . . the *truth* of the thoughts that are here set forth seems to me unassailable and definitive. I therefore believe myself to have found, on all essential points, the final solution of the problems.[1]

And he, with great consistency and in perfect conformity with his inexpressible ethics, leaves philosophy to teach elementary school in a remote Austrian village. As the years pass, though, he engages in conversations with other philosophers and scientists, including members of the Vienna Circle. Eventually he comes to believe that he has not after all found "the final solution" of all the problems he had addressed. The vision expressed in the *Tractatus* is powerful and elegant, but Wittgenstein gradually becomes convinced that it is not *true*. And in the first fifty pages of *Philosophical Investigations* he subjects his earlier views to devastating criticism.*

There are certainly difficulties in the *Tractatus*. For one thing, his view that logic consists solely of

tautologies is proved by Alonzo Church to be too simple.* Furthermore, there is that strange consequence of the picture theory—that all his own philosophical propositions are nonsensical, despite the fact that many of us seem to understand at least some of them rather well. But it is neither of these things that moves Wittgenstein to criticize the doctrines of the *Tractatus*. Indeed, he is already quite dissatisfied before the publication of Church's Theorem. Wittgenstein begins to feel difficulties in connection with the central thesis of the *Tractatus*—that a proposition is a picture, together with the correlated doctrine of names and simple objects. Norman Malcolm tells a story about a conversation between Wittgenstein and P. Sraffa, a lecturer in economics at Cambridge.

> One day (they were riding, I think, on a train) when Wittgenstein was insisting that a proposition and

---

*Published posthumously in 1953, two years after his death, the *Philosophical Investigations* is written in two parts, the first of which is organized in numbered sections, most of which are a paragraph or two long. Like the *Tractatus*, it is a difficult book, but it is difficult in quite a different way. Whereas you can read a sentence in the *Tractatus* half a dozen times and still be puzzled about what it means, the *Investigations*, for the most part, reads with some ease. But then you find yourself asking, What does this all amount to?

---

*Wittgenstein had held that sentences containing quantifiers were capable of analysis into elementary propositions, and so were truth functions of elementary propositions. This meant that truth tables could function as a decision procedure for determining the truth of all logically true propositions. For instance, (Ex) Fx (there exists something that has the property F) was to be analyzed as (*Fa* or *Fb* or *Fc* . . .) (i.e., object *a* is *F*, or object *b* is *F*, or object *c* is *F*, or . . .). And (x)Fx became (*Fa* and *Fb* and *Fc* . . .). This meant that in principle there could be a truth table written for any generalized sentence, and we would have a *decision procedure* for determining the truth of these sentences. But in 1930, Alonzo Church proved that no such decision procedure is possible for domains that are possibly infinite. (This is called Church's Theorem.)

that which it describes must have the same 'logical form,' the same 'logical multiplicity,' Sraffa made a gesture, familiar to Neapolitans as meaning something like disgust or contempt, of brushing the underneath of his chin with an outward sweep of the fingertips of one hand. And he asked: 'What is the logical form of *that*?' Sraffa's example produced in Wittgenstein the feeling that there was an absurdity in the insistence that a proposition and what it describes must have the same 'form.' This broke the hold on him of the conception that a proposition must literally be a 'picture' of the reality it describes.[2]

A meaningful gesture, surely! It communicates something very effectively. Or think of "Phooey!" or "Nuts!" Bits of language? Of course. But what is their logical form? And of what simple names are they composed? And what possible states of affairs do they picture? Just to ask such questions shows up a deficiency in the *Tractatus* doctrine—if it is to be taken as a description of the very *essence* of language. Even if you were to grant that the picture theory correctly analyzes an important part of language (e.g., the propositions of natural science), it would be at best only partial; it would not reach the essence of language.*

Philosophical Illusion

Wittgenstein allows that the *Tractatus* does express a possible way of seeing things. We can climb the ladder of his "nonsensical" propositions and get a certain vision of things. He had said in the *Tractatus* that we would then "see the world aright" (*Tractatus* 6.54). But he now thinks this way of seeing things is a mistake. Yet, "mistake" is not quite the right word; it is more like an illusion, he suggests, or even a superstition that held him in thrall (*PI,* 97, 110).[3] But how could he have been so de-

---

*The positivists recognize this deficiency, too; Ayer's emotivist theory of moral language (that it does nothing more than express and influence feelings) is an attempt to accommodate other uses of language than the literal and descriptive. Wittgenstein's critique, however, is far deeper and more radical.

ceived? What is the source of this illusion that the *Tractatus* presents with such clarity and power? Philosophers in general, he thinks, are peculiarly subject to this illusion. But all of us can easily be seduced into this kind of error; what trips us up is *the nature of language itself*. Here is one way that the seduction can work.

We sometimes find that others misunderstand what we mean when we talk to them. And we find that these misunderstandings can often be removed by paraphrasing what we mean, by substituting one form of expression for another. It is often helpful to use simpler terms to explain what we mean:

> this may be called an "analysis" of our forms of expression, for the process is sometimes like one of taking a thing apart (*PI*, 90).
>
> But now it may come to look as if there were something like a final analysis of our forms of language, and so a *single* completely resolved form of every expression. That is, as if our usual forms of expression were, essentially, unanalyzed; as if there were something hidden in them that had to be brought to light. When this is done the expression is completely clarified and our problem is solved.
>
> It can also be put like this: we eliminate misunderstandings by making our expressions more exact; but now it may look as if we were moving towards a particular state, a state of complete exactness; and as if this were the real goal of our investigation (*PI*, 91).

The Wittgenstein of the *Tractatus* was committed to all these notions: to the idea that there is "something hidden" in our ordinary language that can be "completely clarified" by a "final analysis" into " a *single* completely resolved form of every expression," which would gain us our "real goal"—"a state of complete exactness." The slide to these conclusions is so subtle we scarcely notice it. They seem almost *obvious*. But they are sources of the illusion.

> This finds expression in questions as to the essence of language, of propositions, of thought. . . . For they see in the essence, not something that already lies open to view and that becomes surveyable by a rearrangement, but something that lies *beneath*

the surface. Something that lies within, which we see when we look *into* the thing, and which an analysis digs out.

'The essence is hidden from us': this is the form our problem now assumes. We ask: *"What is* language?", *"What is* a proposition?" And the answer to these questions is to be given once for all; and independently of any future experience (*PI*, 92).

Language, propositions—these seem mysterious, strange. And we ask with a baffled kind of emphasis, *What is* language? *What is* thought? *What is* a name? It seems to us that these are *deep* questions, about *deeply hidden* things. (Compare this question: *What are* numbers? Or Augustine's question, *What is* time?)*

We are encouraged to suppose that there *must* be an essence of language—one essence—because it is all called by one name, "language"; further, we assume that because it is all language, every instance of it must have something in common with all the rest. This is a supposition that goes way back; Socrates, in asking about piety, is not content with answers that give him examples of pious behavior. What he wants is the essence of piety, i.e., what it is about any instance of piety that *makes* it an instance of piety.†

About this seductive idea, Wittgenstein now says,

A *picture* held us captive. And we could not get outside it, for it lay in our language and language seemed to repeat it to us inexorably (*PI*, 115).

This picture is not a *Tractatus* picture. It is a picture in an ordinary, though metaphorical, sense, as when we say, "I can't help but picture her as happy." It is a picture of language as a *calculus*, as

something possessing "the crystalline purity of logic" (*PI*, 107). This picture, Wittgenstein says, "held us captive."

It is like a pair of glasses on our nose through which we see whatever we look at. It never occurs to us to take them off (*PI*, 103).

We predicate of the thing what lies in the method of representing it (*PI*, 104).

(*Tractatus Logico-Philosophicus*, 4.5): "The general form of a proposition is: This is how things are."— That is the kind of proposition that one repeats to oneself countless times. One thinks that one is tracing the outline of the thing's nature over and over again, and one is merely tracing round the frame through which we look at it (*PI*, 114).

Captive to a picture, we cannot shake off the conviction that language *must* have an essence, that hidden in the depths of our ordinary sentences must be an exact logical structure in which simple names stand for simple objects. Logic, which sets out the structure of possibilities and is the "scaffolding of the world" (*Tractatus* 6.124), *requires* that. Propositions *really* have pictorial form, logical form, and an isomorphism with what they picture. Never mind that language doesn't actually look like that! That is the way (we think) it *must* be.

But that is just what is wrong with the *Tractatus* vision. It is not just a description of how our language (or some part of it) seems to work and how it seems to be related to the world. Rather, the *Tractatus prescribes* to language. But now we can see the way out of the illusion. We can get out of the grip of superstition about language by confining ourselves solely to *description*.

It was true to say [in the *Tractatus*] that our considerations could not be scientific ones. . . . And we may not advance any kind of theory. There must not be anything hypothetical in our considerations. We must do away with all *explanation*, and description alone must take its place. And this description gets its light, that is to say its purpose, from the philosophical problems. These are, of course, not empirical problems; they are solved, rather, by looking into the workings of our language, and that in such a way as to make us recognize those workings: *in despite of*

---

*For a discussion of Augustine's famous reflections on time, see pp. 226–229. Recall Augustine's remark about knowing what time is as long as no one asks him to explain it but being unable to say when he is asked. Wittgenstein takes this to indicate that the nature of time is something we need to be *reminded* of, just as we need to be reminded of how our language works by "arranging what we have always known" (*PI*, 109).

†See Plato's *Euthyphro* 5d–6e and p. 77.

an urge to misunderstand them. The problems are solved, not by giving new information, but by arranging what we have always known. Philosophy is a battle against the bewitchment of our intelligence by means of language (*PI*, 109).

There are clear echoes of the *Tractatus* here. Note that philosophy is still something quite different from the sciences: its problems are "not empirical." And philosophy's job is not to produce theories or explanations. Philosophy is still an activity of clarification rather than a set of results. But Wittgenstein no longer thinks that all philosophical problems can be solved at once, by analyzing "the essence of language." We must proceed in a piecemeal fashion, working patiently at one problem after another by "looking into the workings of our language," by "arranging what we have always known." It is not "new information" that we need to resolve philosophical problems. We need the ability to find our way through the many temptations to misunderstand.

> When philosophers use a word—"knowledge", "being", "object", "I", "proposition", "name"—and try to grasp the *essence* of the thing, one must always ask oneself: is the word ever actually used in this way in the language-game which is its original home?—
> What *we* do is to bring words back from their metaphysical to their everyday use (*PI*, 116).

The notion of a **language-game** is one we will have to examine closely. It is clear that philosophical *theories* of knowledge, reality, the self, and the external world are regarded with great suspicion by Wittgenstein, just as they were in the *Tractatus*. Such theories, we may imagine, he still regards as "just gassing." But the reason for suspicion is now different. The words that are being used in these theories—"know," "object," "I," "name"—all are words with common uses. Wittgenstein now suspects that as they are used in these philosophical theories, the words lose their anchors in the uses and activities that make them meaningful. They float free, without discipline, and lose their meaning; yet, it is just *because* they have no anchors in concrete life that they seem to indicate deep prob-

lems. This appearance of depth, however, is just part of the illusion. And what is needed is to "bring words back from their metaphysical to their everyday use."

Here is another point of similarity with Wittgenstein's view in the *Tractatus*. There he held that the "correct method" in philosophy was to show someone who thinks he is saying something philosophical and deep that "he had failed to give a meaning to certain signs" (*Tractatus* 6.53) and so was not saying anything at all. Here, the alternative to saying something metaphysical is not supposed to be limited to the picture propositions of natural science, as the *Tractatus* recommends. The alternative is to come back to home ground in our ordinary ways of talking.

Philosophical problems are *baffling*:

> A philosophical problem has the form: "I don't know my way about" (*PI*, 123).

But the solution is not to construct a philosophical theory about the baffling topic. What we need is to clarify the language in which the problem is posed.

> Philosophy may in no way interfere with the actual use of language; it can in the end only describe it.
> For it cannot give it any foundation either.
> It leaves everything as it is (*PI*, 124).
> Philosophy simply puts everything before us, and neither explains nor deduces anything.　—Since everything lies open to view there is nothing to explain. For what is hidden, for example, is of no interest to us.
> One might also give the name "philosophy" to what is possible *before* all new discoveries and inventions.
> The work of the philosopher consists in assembling reminders for a particular purpose.
> If one tried to advance *theses* in philosophy, it would never be possible to question them, because everyone would agree to them (*PI*, 126–28).

This is surely a radical view of philosophy, as radical in its way as that of the *Tractatus*. According to this view, the aim of the philosopher is not to solve the big problems about knowledge, reality, God, the soul, and the good. These are not real problems at all; they arise only out of misunderstanding our language. The task of the philosopher is to unmask the ways in which these problems are generated, and by putting "everything before us" and "assembling reminders" bring us back to home ground.* What is the purpose of the reminders? To show us how the language in which these "deep" questions are framed is actually used in those human activities in which they get their meaning. If we understand that, we will be freed from the temptation to suppose these are real questions. Wittgenstein offers the following rule:

> don't think, but look! (*PI*, 66).

Here are two more striking remarks on this theme.

> The philosopher's treatment of a question is like the treatment of an illness (*PI*, 255).
> What is your aim in philosophy? To shew the fly the way out of the fly-bottle (*PI*, 309).

The first remark suggests that philosophy is itself the illness for which it must be the cure. There is an old saying by Bishop Berkeley about raising a dust and then complaining that we cannot see. The posing of philosophical problems, Wittgenstein is saying, is like that. Being possessed by a philosophical problem is like being sick; only it is we ourselves who make ourselves sick—confused, trapped, perplexed by paradoxes. We foist these illusions on ourselves by misunderstanding our own language. It is so very *easy* to do that, because language itself suggests these illusions to us. Philosophy, then, is a kind of therapy for relieving mental cramps.

With the second remark we get the unforgettable image of a fly having gotten itself trapped in a narrow-necked bottle, buzzing wildly about and slamming itself frantically against the sides of the bottle, unable to find the way out that lies there open and clear if only the fly could recognize it. We get into philosophical problems so easily but then can't find our way out again.

> "But *this* isn't how it is!"   —we say, "Yet *this* is how it has to *be*!" (*PI*, 112).

Just like the fly in the bottle! It is Wittgenstein's aim to show us how to put philosophical problems behind us, to help us find the way out of the bottle, rather than to devise theories that will constitute solutions to them. This view is reasonable if we suspect that philosophy as practiced since Socrates and Plato is likely to be based on illusion, like a superstition from which we need to be awakened. And that is Wittgenstein's view.

Language-Games

Let us look in more detail at the way Wittgenstein uses the prescription "Don't think, but look!" in criticizing the characteristic theses of the *Tractatus*. We'll begin with one of the most basic notions in that work, the notion of a *name*.

Wittgenstein makes use of a device he calls "language-games." A language-game is an activity that involves spoken (or written) words. These words have a natural place in the activity; it is this place, the role they play in the activity, that makes them mean what they do mean. It is sometimes helpful, Wittgenstein suggests, to imagine a language-game more primitive than the ones we engage in.

> It disperses the fog to study the phenomena of language in primitive kinds of applications in which one can command a clear view of the aim and functioning of the words (*PI*, 5).

Here is such a primitive language-game.

> The language is meant to serve for communication between a builder A and an assistant B. A is building with building-stones: there are blocks, pillars, slabs

---

*The notion of assembling "reminders" is reminiscent of Socrates' view of the philosopher's task. As a "midwife," he can only help others recollect the truth within them. (See p. 98.) There are two differences: (a) Socrates thinks we recollect truths we were acquainted with before birth, and (b) though what we are reminded of in a Wittgensteinian way are certainties for us, it may not be possible to claim they are *true*, or that we *know* them. We will discuss this further below.

and beams. B has to pass the stones, and that in the order in which A needs them. For this purpose they use a language consisting of the words "block", "pillar," "slab," "beam." A calls them out;   —B brings the stone which he has learnt to bring at such-and-such a call.   —Conceive this as a complete primitive language (*PI*, 2).

The words in this language-game can very naturally be thought of as names. To each word there corresponds an object. Here we have an example of a language that the theory of the *Tractatus* fits. This theory

does describe a system of communication; only not everything that we call language is this system. And one has to say this in many cases where the question arises "Is this an appropriate description or not?" The answer is: "Yes, it is appropriate, but only for this narrowly circumscribed region, not for the whole of what you were claiming to describe."

It is as if someone were to say, "A game consists in moving objects about on a surface according to certain rules . . ." —and we replied: You seem to be thinking of board games, but there are others. You can make your definition correct by expressly restricting it to those games (*PI*, 3).

There are language-games in which all the words are names, in which the function of each name is to stand for an object. But not all language is like that. In the following language-game, the *Tractatus* view that names exhaust the meaningful symbols shows itself to be inadequate—if we only *look*.

I send someone shopping. I give him a slip marked "five red apples". He takes the slip to the shopkeeper, who opens the drawer marked "apples"; then he looks up the word "red" in a table and finds a colour sample opposite it; then he says the series of cardinal numbers—I assume that he knows them by heart—up to the word "five" and for each number he takes an apple of the same colour as the sample out of the drawer.   —It is in this and similar ways that one operates with words (*PI*, 1).

What is interesting in this little example is the very different way in which the shopkeeper operates

with each of the three words. "Apple" seems to be a name, like "slab." But what of "red"? And, even more significantly, what of "five"? Both of them are used in ways completely different from "apple" and completely different from each other. Can they all be *names*?* Suppose we ask:

But what is the meaning of the word "five"?   —No such thing was in question here, only how the word "five" is used (*PI*, 1).

The suggestion that "five" is a name, and that it names a number, is resisted. The point of this language-game, this little "reminder," is to cure us of the hankering to ask about the *meaning* of this word, especially since we are inclined to think its meaning must be an object analogous to apples—only a very mysterious one. We are brought back to the way in which we actually use the word. We say the numbers and take an apple for each number. And there is nothing deep or mysterious here to puzzle us. Note that this example shows us Wittgenstein doing just what he says the job of the philosopher is: to dispel puzzlement by bringing words "back from their metaphysical to their everyday use" (*PI*, 116). There is no explanation given, just description. Wittgenstein is merely "arranging what we have always known" (*PI*, 109).

Still, the idea that all words *signify* something is hard to resist. We do feel (strongly!) the temptation to ask, But what does the word "five" *mean*? And we can just feel the slide toward asking, "What *really is* a number, anyway? (Don't you feel it?) If we like, Wittgenstein says, we can agree that every word signifies something. But what is gained thereby? Once we know how the words are used, what do we add by saying, "This word signifies *that*"? Assimilating

the descriptions of the uses of words in this way cannot make the uses themselves any more like one another. For, as we see, they are absolutely unlike.

---

*Consider again Plato's theory of Forms (pp. 109–112). Is Plato someone who falls into the trap of thinking that meaningful words—"eagle," "square," "equal"—are names and that there must be something each one names?

Think of the tools in a tool-box: there is a hammer, pliers, a saw, a screw-driver, a rule, a glue-pot, glue, nails and screws. —The functions of words are as diverse as the functions of these objects. (And in both cases there are similarities.)

Of course, what confuses us is the uniform appearance of words when we hear them spoken or meet them in script and print. For their *application* is not presented to us so clearly. Especially not, when we are doing philosophy!

It is like looking into the cabin of a locomotive. We see handles all looking more or less alike. (Naturally, since they are all supposed to be handled.) But one is the handle of a crank which can be moved continuously (it regulates the opening of a valve); another is the handle of a switch, which has only two effective positions, it is either off or on; a third is the handle of a brake-lever, the harder one pulls on it, the harder it brakes; a fourth, the handle of a pump: it has an effect only so long as it is moved to and fro.

When we say: "Every word in language signifies something" we have so far said *nothing whatever*; unless we have explained exactly *what* distinction we wish to make.

Imagine someone's saying: "*All* tools serve to modify something. Thus the hammer modifies the position of the nail, the saw the shape of the board, and so on." —And what is modified by the rule, the glue-pot, the nails? —"Our knowledge of a thing's length, the temperature of the glue, and the solidity of the box." —Would anything be gained by this assimilation of expressions? (*PI*, 10–14).

What Wittgenstein is trying to drive home is that the quest for generality and for general explanations of meaning is fruitless. You can engage in this project, but what does it get you? Do you really further your understanding of tools when you say they *all* serve to modify something? Like the handles in the cabin of the locomotive, what counts is how they work; and they work in very different ways. So it is with words, also. "Five" works in an altogether different way from "red." The quest for general explanations is likely to make us forget that and to lead us into illusions about meaning and language—illusions into which the author of the *Tractatus* was led. The cure is to stick to the details, to "assemble reminders," to "bring words back from their metaphysical to their everyday use."

In the *Tractatus*, Wittgenstein had claimed to give us the *essence* of language. This claim had two implications that he now believes are baseless. The first is that language is *everywhere all-alike*; we have just been examining some reasons to give up this claim. The second is that the account of language he gave was *complete*. We might be inclined to say that these primitive language-games Wittgenstein describes are, by contrast, incomplete. But Wittgenstein now says,

ask yourself whether our language is complete; —whether it was so before the symbolism of chemistry and the notation of the infinitesimal calculus were incorporated in it; for these are, so to speak, suburbs of our language. (And how many houses or streets does it take before a town begins to be a town?) Our language can be seen as an ancient city: a maze of little streets and squares, of old and new houses, and of houses with additions from various periods; and this surrounded by a multitude of new boroughs with straight regular streets and uniform houses (*PI*, 18).

Language is something living and growing; creative language users are always adding to it. And there is no rule that new additions have to be like the old. The calculus, for instance, and the exactness of Euclidean geometry (and the new logic, for that matter) are all like "new boroughs with straight regular streets." But we must not assume that all language is like that; it is an "ancient city," with all the quirks, the twists and turns of narrow streets and different kinds of houses—like London or Vienna.

In the *Tractatus*, Wittgenstein had held that the proposition was the basic unit and that each proposition pictured a possible state of affairs. Now he asks,

But how many kinds of sentence are there? Say assertion, question, and command? —There are *countless* kinds: countless different kinds of use of what we call "symbols", "words", "sentences". And this multiplicity is not something fixed, given once for all: but new types of language, new language-games, as we may say, come into existence, and others become obsolete and get forgotten. (We can get a *rough picture* of this from the changes in mathematics.)

Here the term "language-*game*" is meant to bring into prominence the fact that the *speaking* of language is part of an activity, or of a form of life.

Review the multiplicity of language-games in the following examples, and in others:

Giving orders, and obeying them—
Describing the appearance of an object, or giving its measurements—
Constructing an object from a description (a drawing)—
Reporting an event—
Speculating about an event—
Forming and testing a hypothesis—
Presenting the results of an experiment in tables and diagrams—
Making up a story; and reading it—
Play-acting—
Singing catches [i.e., rounds]—
Guessing riddles—
Making a joke; telling it—
Solving a problem in practical arithmetic—
Translating from one language into another—
Asking, thanking, cursing, greeting, praying (*PI*, 23).

In all these ways—and more— we use language. It is absolutely unhelpful—and worse, dangerous!— to suppose that language is everywhere all-alike. It leads into pseudoproblems and illusions, the sorts of dead-ends where we are likely to say, This isn't how it is, but this is how it *must* be.

Ostensive Definitions

Let's think again about names. We are tempted to think that the process of naming is fundamental and that the rest of language can be built on that foundation. We teach the child "ball," "blue," "water." But how do we do this? And when has the child mastered the meaning of these words? We present a ball to a child and get the child to pay attention to it, while we repeat, "ball, ball." This might lead us to generalize again and claim that language gets attached to the world by means of *ostensive definitions* like this. And so we might formulate a *theory* of naming.

But if we look carefully, we see that this assumption cannot be right.

Now one can ostensively define a proper name, the name of a colour, the name of a material, a numeral, the name of a point of the compass and so on. The definition of the number two, "That is called 'two'"—pointing to two nuts—is perfectly exact. —But how can two be defined like that? The person one gives the definition to doesn't know what one wants to call "two"; he will suppose that "two" is the name given to *this* group of nuts! . . . an ostensive definition can be variously interpreted in *every* case (*PI*, 28).

Note that Wittgenstein is not denying that ostensive definitions are often useful. What he is attacking is the notion that they are a key to the essence of language, to what is basic in language use. He denies that ostensive definitions can be the simple foundation stone on which all else is built. If I try to show you what a watch is (supposing you don't know) by pointing to the device on my wrist, you may take it that "watch" means a color, a material, a device for keeping time, or a direction. My intention can be "variously interpreted." And what is true for this case is true for every case.

How do ostensive definitions work, then? Well, I could help you out by saying, "This device on my wrist is a watch." But that presumes, as you can clearly see, that you already are in possession of large portions of the language. You have to understand "device" and "on" and "wrist" if what I say is going to be helpful. So it seems clear that language cannot *begin* with ostensive definitions. And names cannot themselves be absolutely primitive: to understand a name, you have to understand what role it is supposed to play in the language-game.

So one might say: the ostensive definition explains the use—the meaning—of the word when the overall role of the word in the language is clear. . . .

One has already to know (or be able to do) something in order to be capable of asking a thing's name. But what does one have to know?

When one shews someone the king in chess and says: "This is the king", this does not tell him the use of this piece—unless he already knows the rules of the game up to this last point: the shape of the king. . . .

We may say: only someone who already knows how to do something with it can significantly ask a name (*PI*, 30–31).

An ostensive definition is of use only *within* a language-game. It is of no help in getting into the game in the first place.

But that leaves us with a problem. How do we ever get started with language, if acquiring the use of even names like "ball" and "milk" presupposes an understanding of language in general? Here Wittgenstein again advises us to *look*.

A child uses such primitive forms of language when it learns to talk. Here the teaching of language is not explanation, but training.

(I do not want to call this "ostensive definition", because the child cannot as yet *ask* what the name is. I will call it "ostensive teaching of words". . . . This ostensive teaching of words can be said to establish an association between the word and the thing (*PI*, 5–6).

Suppose that such an "association" is established between "apple" and apples by "training" little Jill in that way. Does she now *understand* the word "apple"? Well, does your dog understand "Come!" when he comes at that command? The process is similar, Wittgenstein suggests, and so are the results. The difference between Jill and Rover is that Jill can eventually go on to learn a lot more about apples by internalizing an ever more complex language in which to talk about them. Understanding comes in degrees; Jill is capable of understanding more than Rover, but they start in the same way. It is not by definitions (ostensive or not) that we enter the gate of language, but by training.

Objects

We are tempted to think, as the *Tractatus* suggests, that "a name means an object. The object is its

meaning." But if that were so, Wittgenstein "reminds" us, a word would have no meaning if nothing corresponded to it.

It is important to note that the word "meaning" is being used illicitly if it is used to signify the thing that 'corresponds' to the word. That is to confound the meaning of a name with the *bearer* of the name. When Mr. N. N. dies one says that the bearer of the name dies, not that the meaning dies. And it would be nonsensical to say that, for if the name ceased to have meaning it would make no sense to say, "Mr. N. N. is dead" (*PI*, 40).

It does, of course, make sense to say that John F. Kennedy is dead. So the name is not meaningless, even though its bearer is no longer in existence. And it follows that the meaning of a name cannot be the object it names. What, then, is the meaning of a name? It is having a place in a particular language-game, a certain role in a form of life.

For a *large* class of cases—though not for all—in which we employ the word "meaning" it can be defined thus: the meaning of a word is its use in the language (*PI*, 43).

And that is why it is important not to think, but to look and see how a word is being used.

Names in the *Tractatus* stand for objects, and these objects are said to be *simple*. In fact, Wittgenstein held at the time he wrote the *Tractatus* that there *must* be simple objects; otherwise, the definition of names could go on forever, and nothing would have any determinate sense. Definitions must come to an end! And they can only end in the absolutely simple.*

But what are the simple constituent parts of which reality is composed? —What are the simple constituent parts of a chair? —The bits of wood of which it is made? Or the molecules, or the atoms? —"Simple" means: not composite. And here the

---

*The commitment to simples has a long history. We find it already in Plato, and versions of it are found in many other thinkers— including Hume and Russell, who hold that although not every idea has to be traceable to a corresponding impression, the simple ones do. (See p. 343.)

point is: in what sense 'composite'? It makes no sense at all to speak absolutely of the 'simple parts of a chair' (*PI*, 47).

When talking of simple and composite, we must pay attention to the game we are playing with these words. To suppose that they have meaning quite independently of some concrete activity in which they are being used is to let language "go on holiday" (*PI*, 38), a sure way to generate unsolvable philosophical problems.

If I tell someone without any further explanation: "What I see before me now is composite," he will have the right to ask: "What do you mean by 'composite'? For there are all sorts of things that can mean!" . . .

But isn't a chessboard, for instance, obviously, and absolutely, composite? —You are probably thinking of the composition out of thirty-two white and thirty-two black squares. But could we not also say, for instance, that it was composed of the colours black and white and the schema of squares? (*PI*, 47).

There are circumstances in which we analyze composite things in one way and circumstances in which we analyze them in another way. This is what we find, if we *look*. Why should we insist that there must be one way in which composite things can be analyzed into elements that are absolutely simple, quite independent of context or language-game? This insistence looks like a prime case of thinking and not looking—a case of prescribing to language and the world. Once again, Wittgenstein invites us to resist the temptation.*

Family Resemblances

Here we come up against the great question that lies behind all these considerations. —For someone might object against me: "You take the easy way out! You talk about all sorts of language-games, but have nowhere said what the essence of a language-game, and hence of language, is: what is common to all

these activities, and what makes them into language or parts of language. So you let yourself off the very part of the investigation that once gave you yourself most headache, the part about the *general form of propositions* and of language."

And this is true. —Instead of producing something common to all that we call language, I am saying that these phenomena have no one thing in common which makes us use the same word for all—but that they are *related* to one another in many different ways. And it is because of this relationship, or these relationships, that we call them all "language." I will try to explain this.

Consider for example the proceedings that we call "games." I mean board-games, card-games, ballgames, Olympic games, and so on. What is common to them all? —Don't say: "There *must* be something common, or they would not be called 'games'—but *look and see* whether there is anything common to all. —For if you look at them you will not see something that is common to *all*, but similarities, relationships, and a whole series of them at that. To repeat: don't think, but look! —Look for example at board-games; here you find many correspondences with the first group, but many common features drop out, and others appear. When we pass next to ball-games, much that is common is retained, but much is lost. —Are they all 'amusing'? Compare chess with noughts and crosses [tic-tac-toe]. Or is there always winning and losing, or competition between players? Think of patience [solitaire]. In ball-games there is winning and losing; but when a child throws his ball at the wall and catches it again, this feature has disappeared. Look at the parts played by skill and luck; and at the difference between skill in chess and skill in tennis. Think now of ring-a-ring-a-roses; here is the element of amusement, but how many other characteristic features have disappeared! And we can go through the many, many other groups of games in the same way; can see how similarities crop up and disappear.

And the result of this examination is: we see a complicated network of similarities overlapping and criss-crossing: sometimes overall similarities, sometimes similarities of detail.

I can think of no better expression to characterize these similarities than "family resemblances"; for the various resemblances between members of a family: build, features, colour of eyes, gait, temperament, etc. etc. overlap and criss-cross in the same way. — And I shall say: 'games' form a family (*PI*, 65–67).

---

*Compare Dewey on the analysis of a concept like "a piece of paper," p. 482.

I have quoted this well-known passage at length because it is extremely important. The notion of **family resemblances** has been a *freeing* notion of great significance for thought. Recall that at the beginning of the Western philosophical tradition, dominating it with the kind of power that only unexamined assumptions can have, stands Socrates with his questions: What is piety? Courage? Justice? And what Socrates wants is a definition, the *essence* of the thing. What he wants to discover are those features which (1) any act of justice has, (2) any nonjust act lacks, and (3) *make* the just act just. Are Acts *A* and *B* both just? Then it seems natural to suppose that there must be something they have *in common*, something they *share*, some feature *by virtue of which* they are just. And unless we understand what that is, we will not understand justice.*

It is difficult to exaggerate the impact this assumption has had. It certainly lies beneath the *Tractatus* quest for the essence of language; it accounts for the author's certainty that there must be such a thing. But now that we are looking rather than thinking, we discover that, in very many cases, there is no such thing. There is no essence of games, nor of language. And almost surely there is no essence of justice or piety. All are matters of instances, examples, and cases loosely related to each other by crisscrossing and overlapping similarities. What we find when we look are family resemblances. What we find is exactly the kind of thing that Socrates so curtly dismisses when it is offered by Euthyphro!

It follows from this new picture that there may be no sharp boundaries for many of our concepts.

How should we explain to someone what a game is? I imagine that we should describe *games* to him,

and we might add: "This *and similar things* are called 'games'". And do we know any more about it ourselves? Is it only other people whom we cannot tell exactly what a game is? But this is not ignorance. We do not know the boundaries because none have been drawn. To repeat, we can draw a boundary—for a special purpose. Does it take that to make the concept usable? Not at all! (Except for that special purpose.) no more than it took the definition: 1 pace = 75 cm. to make the measure of length 'one pace' usable. And if you want to say "But still, before that it wasn't an exact measure", then I reply: very well, it was an inexact one. —Though you still owe me a definition of exactness (*PI*, 69).

One might say that the concept 'game' is a concept with blurred edges. —"But is a blurred concept a concept at all?" —Is an indistinct photograph a picture of a person at all? Is it even always an advantage to replace an indistinct picture by a sharp one? Isn't the indistinct one often exactly what we need?

Frege compares a concept to an area and says that an area with vague boundaries cannot be called an area at all. This presumably means that we cannot do anything with it. —But is it senseless to say: "Stand roughly there"? (*PI*, 71).

We may understand Wittgenstein's point more clearly by examining another example. What, people sometimes ask, is a religion? Is belief in a supreme being essential to religion? Then early Buddhism is not a religion. How about belief in life after death? But early Judaism seems to lack that feature. Some people suggest that Communism is essentially religious in character. But how can that be, if it lacks so many of the features of Presbyterianism? If we search for the conditions that are both necessary and sufficient to define "religion," we will probably search in vain. But suppose we proceed this way: Do you want to know what a religion is? Consider Roman Catholicism; this and similar things are called "religions." To treat the question this way is to think of "religion" as a family resemblance concept.

Someone might ask, "How 'similar' to Roman Catholicism does something have to be if it is to qualify as a religion?" We would be right to reply that there is no exact answer to that question.

Suppose someone objects, "But then you haven't drawn a sharp boundary!" We can reply

---

Euthyphro on piety is a good example. For other examples, see Plato on knowledge (pp. 106–108) and Descartes on clear and distinct ideas (p. 290). The assumption pervades nearly all of our tradition. I recall some years ago being on a committee to rethink the requirements for a bachelor of arts degree. We expended a lot of energy in trying to discern the *essence* of a bachelor of arts, just what it is that makes a certain degree a bachelor of arts degree—as though this were somehow laid up in the Platonic heaven of Forms. That this discussion was fruitless would not have surprised Wittgenstein.

that that is true. If you want, you can draw a boundary for a special purpose; but don't suppose that in doing so you are answering the original question. It is not our ignorance that makes this way of replying to the question about religion an appropriate one. We don't know more about it ourselves; no one does. The concept "religion" functions in our language in this family resemblance kind of way. And the absence of a set of necessary and sufficient conditions to mark off religions from other things does not mean that the concept is not useful and serviceable, any more than "Stand roughly there" is a useless instruction just because it isn't perfectly precise.*

When he was writing the *Tractatus*, Wittgenstein thought that every proposition had to have a determinate sense and that therefore a completely analyzed proposition would be free of all vagueness and ambiguity. (Remember the ideal presented by Russell's notion of a logically perfect language: see p. 490.) How could it be otherwise, when it was composed of simple names, each standing for a simple object? But if we look, without seeking to prescribe how it *must* be, we see that language is not everywhere exact, like a logical calculus. Like "game," many of our concepts are governed by relationships of family resemblance rather than essences.† And they are none the worse for that. So Wittgenstein assembles his reminders of how our language actually functions, bringing us back to the activities (forms of life) in which it does its varied jobs. And in so doing, he shows us the way out of various fly bottles we get ourselves into by misunderstanding the logic of our language.

---

*Notice how this sort of thing undercuts Descartes' requirement (*Meditation IV*) that we should assent only to ideas that are clear and distinct. Most of our ideas, Wittgenstein holds, are not clear and distinct. And that is not something we should try to fix. On the contrary, our concepts are "in order" as they are.

†But not all. We do have concepts that are governed by strict rules. Many scientific concepts—"triangle," for example, or "force"—are like that. We should not think of the family resemblance claim as a *theory* about the essence of meaning! It is worth noting that recent studies by cognitive psychologists about how people categorize objects have strongly supported Wittgenstein's views about the family resemblance character of many of our concepts.

The Continuity of Wittgenstein's Thought

As you can see, virtually every one of the principal theses of the *Tractatus* is undermined and rejected by the later Wittgenstein.

* There is an essence of language.
* The essence of language is picturing facts.
* There is a complete and exact analysis of every sentence.
* The basic elements of language are names.
* The meaning of a name is its bearer.
* Names are simple.
* Names name simple objects.
* The world is pictured as the totality of facts in logical space.

Other thinkers have changed their ways of thinking—Augustine after his conversion to Christianity, Kant after reading Hume—but Wittgenstein's turnabout is as deep and dramatic as any. Is there any line of continuity that one can trace through this shift? Let me suggest that three interrelated themes persist.

The first is an opposition, which seems to amount to a personal revulsion, to what Wittgenstein calls "just *gassing*." A more contemporary term for this phenomenon might be "bullshitting."[4] The second is the idea that one might "set a limit to thought" (*Tractatus*, p. 3). And the third is the notion that some things cannot be said, but only shown.

The whole point of the *Tractatus*, you will recall, was to "set a limit to thought" by delineating what can and cannot be said. Whatever can be said can be said clearly. The rest is "nonsense," which we must "pass over in silence" (*Tractatus*, p. 3). Wittgenstein felt that most talk about the meaning of life, about value and God and the soul, was "just *gassing*"—an attempt to put into words questions and answers that cannot be put into words. But it is crucial to remember that he also thought that these matters were far and away the most important. The revulsion he felt was grounded in his conviction that prattle about them demeans them, takes them out of the realm in which they properly exist. A good man, for instance, is not someone who talks about goodness, but someone who "shows" it, displays it in his life. "It is clear that ethics cannot be put into words" (*Tractatus* 6.421). But it *can* be put into a life!

That project—to set a limit to thought by identifying nonsense, gassing, and bullshit—is still the driving force of Wittgenstein's later thought. The aim has not changed, but the method by which he thinks it can be done has changed. In the *Tractatus* he tried to do it all at once—with one stroke, as it were—by constructing a theory of language and meaning that would expose nonsense for what it is. But having come to see that he had been prescribing to language, that he had been held captive by the picture of language as a logical calculus, he now gives up the attempt to create a theory. Instead, he "assembles reminders" (*PI*, 127) that bring us back from nonsense to the actual uses of language in those varied activities (forms of life) in which words get their meaning. This is something that cannot be done all at once, but requires the careful examination of case after case where language "goes on holiday" (*PI*, 38) and misleads us. And so we get the little stories, the language-games, the questions and answers, and the multitudinous examples of the *Philosophical Investigations*.

The *Tractatus* tells us there are some things that cannot be said; these things show themselves. Among them are these:

- The logical structure of language (which displays itself in every proposition)
- The nature of logical truth (manifest in tautologies)
- The relation of the philosophical subject to the world (the coincidence of solipsism and realism)
- The happiness of the good person (who has a different world from that of the unhappy person)
- "The mystical" (that the world is)*

---

*I have again just used language to talk about all these things. And, as we have seen, that is paradoxical. But we must remember that according to *Tractatus* doctrine, what I have just said is, strictly speaking, nonsense—part of that ladder that needs to be thrown away.

In the *Investigations*, are there still things that can only be shown, not said? There are, but it is not so easy to list them. Rather, the showing has become identical with the *style* of the book. Even the samples we have examined show us a very unusual style full of questions (often unanswered), conversations between the author and an interlocutor, instructions ("Compare," "Imagine"), stories, suggestions, and so on. Surely no other book in the history of philosophy contains so many questions! The aim is still, as in the *Tractatus*, to get us to "see the world aright" (*Tractatus* 6.54). But now that means to see it, and language especially, in all its incredible variety and differentiation. Still, the aim is to *see* it, or, we might almost say, to let it *show itself* to us. It is not, perhaps, by accident that in the preface, Wittgenstein compares his book to an album of sketches.*

> The philosophical remarks in this book are, as it were, a number of sketches of landscapes which were made in the course of . . . long and involved journeyings.
> . . . Thus this book is really only an album (*PI*, p. ix).

It would not be going too far to compare Wittgenstein here with an artist, trying in various ways to get us to see the "landscapes" of our language from a variety of points of view, so that we no longer get *lost* in them. There are few if any doctrines to be learned in this book. What it teaches is a way of investigating puzzles and problems—a way, Wittgenstein thinks, that will lead to clarity.

> It is not our aim to refine or complete the system of rules for the use of our words in unheard-of ways.
> For the clarity that we are aiming at is indeed *complete* clarity. But this simply means that the philosophical problems should *completely* disappear.
> The real discovery is the one that makes me capable of stopping doing philosophy when I want to.
> —The one that gives philosophy peace, so that it is no longer tormented by questions which bring *itself*

---

*Nor is it incidental that the earlier book is called a *treatise* and the later book *investigations*. The former suggests completeness and a theoretical character that is altogether lacking in the latter.

in question. —Instead, we now demonstrate a method, by examples; and the series of examples can be broken off. —Problems are solved (difficulties eliminated), not a *single* problem.

There is not a philosophical method, though there are indeed methods, like different therapies (*PI*, 133).

What would be left if the philosophical problems should completely disappear? Would we be any the worse off? And just what problems is Wittgenstein thinking about here? One can hardly escape the conclusion that Wittgenstein still thinks that most of philosophy is "just *gassing*"—that it is still transgressing the limits of thought. But now the diagnosis cannot be given once and for all by drawing a single limit; now what is required is careful attention to the multifarious language-games we actually play in our forms of life and detailed showing of how philosophical thinking tends to drift away from them into illusion.

In Wittgenstein's later work, we find a number of attempts to show us how traditional problems disappear if we look carefully at the language in which they are framed. There are discussions relevant to problems about understanding, meaning, the status of sensations, and other supposedly private mental states. We find sections dealing with the idea of seeing something, with interpretation, with rule following. These investigations are hard to summarize without doing them an injustice. A brief description of a van Gogh painting stands to the painting itself in much the same way that any summary of Wittgenstein's "conclusions" stands to his "album" of detailed investigations. Just as you really need to immerse yourself in the painting if you are going to appreciate it, so you need to follow the text of the *Investigations* really to understand it.

We can say, however, that these investigations tend to be profoundly subversive, in the sense that they undermine the foundations of many traditional views, e.g., Descartes' dualism, Hume's theory of ideas, Kant's transcendental ego. Yet none of them is presented as an *argument*. We find the characteristic examples, questions, stories, and

jokes, all designed to get us to *see* things in a different light. The whole point, we might say, is for us to give up the temptation to formulate philosophical theories about mind, reality, perception, or understanding. They are designed to get the fly out of the bottle.

There is one theme in Wittgenstein's later work, closely connected to the idea of a language-game, that we can perhaps pull out. It is a theme directly relevant to a matter that has come up repeatedly in our account of the great conversation: the question about relativism. You will recall that this issue originates in the dispute between Socrates and the Sophists (see those earlier chapters) and is expanded on by most of our philosophers. Can Wittgenstein throw any new light on that old perplexity?

Our Groundless Certainty

Think about the ubiquitous arrow, indicating to us which way to go—to the exit, on the one-way street, to Philadelphia. The arrow is a kind of rule. Let us ask a question you perhaps have never asked before: How do I know which way I am being directed to go? I do know. I am to go in the direction of the arrow's point. But how do I know this? Why, for instance, don't I go toward the tail of the arrow? Or why don't I go in different directions on different days of the week?

Here are some possible answers: (1) I *decide* in each case to go toward the arrow's head; (2) I *intuit* which way it is directing me to go; (3) I follow the *rule*: Go toward the arrow's head. But (1) is crazy; (2) seems just to put a label on what I do without giving any account of it; and (3) promises an infinite regress—for exactly the same question arises in regard to this rule! Is there a "metarule" that explains to me how *this* rule is to be obeyed?

Wittgenstein suggests a fourth possibility:

what has the expression of a rule—say a sign-post—got to do with my actions? What sort of connexion is there here? —Well, perhaps this one: I have been trained to react to this sign in a particular way, and now I do so react to it (*PI*, 198).

Training. Rather like we train a dog to heel, perhaps. But can that be right? An objection is raised by Wittgenstein's "interlocutor," the voice that so often presents our own hesitations to suggestions he makes.

> But that is only to give a causal connexion; to tell how it has come about that we now go by the signpost; not what this going-by-the-sign really consists in (*PI*, 198).

The objection is that this does not tell us what rule following *is*, but only how we come by it. To explain how we acquire a practice, it seems, is not to explain the practice itself. But Wittgenstein replies,

> On the contrary; I have further indicated that a person goes by a sign-post only in so far as there exists a regular use of sign-posts, a custom (*PI*, 198).

Without such a custom, such a "regular use," there would be no such thing as obeying the sign. If that is right, some interesting consequences follow.

> Is what we call "obeying a rule" something that it would be possible for only *one* man to do, and to do only *once* in his life: —This is of course a note on the grammar of the expression "to obey a rule".
>
> It is not possible that there should have been only one occasion on which someone obeyed a rule. It is not possible that there should have been only one occasion on which a report was made, an order given or understood; and so on. —To obey a rule, to make a report, to give an order, to play a game of chess, are *customs* (uses, institutions) (*PI*, 199).

Wittgenstein's reference to the *grammar* of obeying a rule is a comment about its "logic," in a broad sense. It is part of the concept, he means, that a rule is embedded in institutions, customs, and ways of doing things. There are no rules apart from that kind of setting. We are not to understand this as an empirical remark, as something that we conclude on the basis of observing rules. Rather, he means to say that it is not *possible* that there should

be a purely private rule.* And since obeying a rule is part of a custom, it presupposes a community in which such practices exist.

Suppose, then, that you were asked, "But why do you go in the direction of the arrow's point?" What would you say? How *do* you know that is the way to go?

> Well, how do I know? —If that means "Have I reasons?" the answer is: my reasons will soon give out. And then I shall act, without reasons (*PI*, 211).
> "How am I able to obey a rule?" —If this is not a question about causes, then it is about the justification for my following the rule in the way I do.
> If I have exhausted the justifications I have reached bedrock, and my spade is turned. Then I am inclined to say: "This is simply what I do" (*PI*, 217).

In this striking metaphor, Wittgenstein brings us back to the communal practices in which our language-games have their home. It is as if the Platonic and Kantian why-questions have made us dig deeper and deeper. But there comes a point when we can dig no more, find no more justifications for our beliefs, our knowledge claims, or our scientific methods. At that point we reach bedrock, and our "spade is turned." And what is bedrock? Is it some Cartesian clear and distinct idea I cannot possibly doubt? Is it some Humean private impression in my mind? Is it a Kantian synthetic *a priori* truth that reason legislates for itself? Or is it the Hegelian culmination of Reason's inexorable development into Absolute Spirit made explicit for itself? No. None of these things. Bedrock is "simply what I do." And what I do is part of what *we* do, we who live this form of life, engage in these activities, play these language-games, grow up in these customs.

---

*In a section of the *Investigations* we will not discuss, Wittgenstein uses this principle of the essentially public character of rules to show that there could not be a language in which I gave ostensive (private) definitions for my sensations. The supposition that such a language is possible is remarkably pervasive, both in common life and in philosophy. Accordingly, if Wittgenstein is correct there, a great deal of confusion is dismissed, and numerous philosophical theories of the mind are shown to be untenable. The sections in which this view is set out (roughly 243–351) are as famous as they are difficult.

There comes a point where explanations and justifications for behaving in a certain way come to an end. Then one just acts. We do as our linguistic community has trained us to do. In the end, it comes down to this:

> When I obey a rule, I do not choose.
> I obey the rule *blindly* (*PI*, 219).

Custom, practice, the activities that make up a form of life—these have an almost sophistic ring to them, reminding us of Protagoras who says, "Of all things, the measure is man."* Aren't we tempted to object at this point? Does Wittgenstein mean that agreeing among ourselves *makes* things true?

> "So you are saying that human agreement decides what is true and what is false?" —It is what human beings *say* that is true and false; and they agree in the *language* they use. That is not agreement in opinions but in form of life (*PI*, 241).

Think of measuring the length of a table. I do it and report my results: 30. You do it and report 76. Is one of us right and the other wrong? It turns out that my rule is graduated in inches and yours in centimeters. So what we both say can be true; the difference is that we were using different measures. If you use my measure, agree in my "language for measuring," we will (usually) agree in "opinion" too. Still, it is not our agreement on 30 that *makes* that opinion true; the length of the table does that. But there is an agreement in language-game that *makes it possible* for us to agree and disagree about opinions.

The contrast Wittgenstein draws between what we *say* and the agreement in *language* is another point of similarity and contrast between the later philosophy and the *Tractatus*. There we found the distinction between what can be said and what can only be shown. Here we find that when we get to bedrock, there is no more to say. At that point I can only *display* my form of life, the language-game I

play. Here, where the spade is turned, I just *show* you what I do: This is what I do—how I live, the way I understand, mean things, and follow rules; this is my (our) form of life. In the *Tractatus*, it was the logical hardness of tautologies that turned the spade, that could only be shown. Here it is the practice of a certain set of language-games.

But this bedrock cannot, as we have seen, be a purely private form of life, governed by private rules. And Wittgenstein now pushes this point by asking, What does it mean to "agree in language"?

> If language is to be a means of communication there must be agreement not only in definitions but also (queer as this may sound) in judgments (*PI*, 242).

Imagine that when we measure the table, our results are inconsistent, even if we use the same rule each time. At first we report 30, then 17, then 54, then 1003, and so on. Whatever it was we were doing, could we call that *measuring*? No. *That*, whatever it is, is not measuring. A measure (the yardstick) is analogous to a language. It allows us to say certain things. And just as there has to be some agreement in "results" if we are to have a measure, so also there has to be some agreement in "opinions" or "judgments" if we are to have a language. We have to hold many of the same things true and false.

But which things? Are there any judgments in particular that we need to agree about in order to communicate with one another in a language? Is there a *foundation* of agreement? And if there is, can we identify it?

In an essay called "A Defense of Common Sense," the English philosopher G. E. Moore claims to "know with certainty" a large number of propositions.[5] And he thinks we all know them, too. For instance, he claims each of us knows that

- There exists a living human body which is *my* body.
- My body was born at a certain time in the past.
- My body has existed continuously ever since.
- My body has changed in many ways.

---

*For a comparison with the Sophists' version of relativism, see "Relativism," in Chapter 6.

- My body has been since birth close to the surface of the earth.
- My body has been at various distances from other things which also exist.

And we know with certainty that

- The earth existed many years before I was born.
- There have been many other human bodies like my own.
- I have had many different experiences.
- So have other human beings.

This is not Moore's complete list, but you get the idea. It is a list of what seem to be *truisms*.

Wittgenstein says many interesting things about the claim that we *know with certainty* that these propositions are true. (He tends to think the word "know" is inappropriately used here.) But our interest is directed to his idea that these "opinions" or "judgments" might form the basis for an agreement that might define a language or a form of life.

How is that we are so *certain* of these "facts"? Have we carefully investigated each of them and come to a belief that the preponderance of evidence is in their favor? No. They do not have that kind of status. Taken together they are more like a *picture* we accept.*

> But I did not get my picture of the world by satisfying myself of its correctness; nor do I have it because I am satisfied of its correctness. No: it is the inherited background against which I distinguish between true and false (*OC*, 94).[6]

Wittgenstein compares this "inherited background" to a kind of mythology, by which he means to indicate that though the truisms making up the picture are in a way empirical, they are not acquired by empirical investigation. He also com-

pares our world picture to the banks of a river within which the water of true and false propositions can flow. The mythology can change; the banks of the river are not unalterable. And in some ways, at least, different pictures are possible for us even at a given time.

> . . . Very intelligent and well-educated people believe in the story of creation in the Bible, while others hold it as proven false, and the grounds of the latter are well known to the former (*OC*, 336).

How are we to account for this? Suppose the doubter talks to the believer. If the reasons for doubt are already well known to someone who believes the biblical story, what could the doubter say to the believer to convince him? All his reasons are already on the table—and they don't convince! Moore (and probably all of us, too) believes the earth has existed for many, many years. But

> . . . why should not a king be brought up in the belief that the world began with him? And if Moore and this king were to meet and discuss, could Moore really prove his belief to be the right one? I do not say that Moore could not convert the king to his view, but it would be a conversion of a special kind; the king would be brought to look at the world in a different way (*OC*, 92).

Different language-games (different forms of life) are possible. And arguments in favor of one of them *presuppose* the standards of argument and evidence characteristic of that very form of life. So reasons do not get a grip on a form of life with different standards and rules of reasoning.

But again we are tempted to think there must be something that would constitute a definitive justification, if not for our present view, then for some future one.* Is "conversion" really the final word? What, we might think, about *science*? Can't that serve as a foundation which isn't just a matter of "what we do"? Suppose I justify my actions by the

---

*Not a *Tractatus* picture, of course; this kind of picture is holistic rather than atomistic, imprecise rather than exact, a system of mutually supporting judgments that it doesn't occur to us *can* be doubted. These matters are explored in another posthumously published book, *On Certainty*.

*Compare Peirce's definition of truth as the opinion that investigators will eventually come to agree upon, if they continue to investigate according to scientific methods (pp. 468–469).

propositions of physics; e.g., I do not perform rain dances because science tells me dancing is ineffective in bringing rain.

> Supposing we met people who did not regard that as a telling reason. Now, how do we imagine this? Instead of the physicist, they consult an oracle. (And for that we consider them primitive.) Is it wrong for them to consult an oracle and be guided by it?   —If we call this "wrong" aren't we using our language-game as a base from which to *combat* theirs?
>
> And are we right or wrong to combat it? Of course there are all sorts of slogans which will be used to support our proceedings.
>
> Where two principles really do meet which cannot be reconciled with one another, then each man declares the other a fool and heretic.
>
> I said I would 'combat' the other man,   —but wouldn't I give him *reasons*? Certainly; but how far do they go? At the end of reasons comes *persuasion*. (Think what happens when missionaries convert natives.) (*OC*, 609–12).*

Combat does not seem to be a form of justification. And conversion is not being convinced by good reasons. Reasons, Wittgenstein reminds us, come to an end.

World pictures, then, may differ; but there is *always* a framework within which we come to believe and think certain things.

> I have a telephone conversation with New York. My friend tells me that his young trees have buds of such and such a kind. I am now convinced that his tree is. . . . Am I also convinced that the earth exists?
>
> The existence of the earth is rather part of the whole *picture* which forms the starting-point of belief for me.
>
> Does my telephone call to New York strengthen my conviction that the earth exists? (*OC*, 208–10).

Wittgenstein wants us to answer no; it does not strengthen that conviction. But that conviction is already as strong as it could possibly be! Is there anything of which I am *more* certain?* Moore's truisms, to which we all consent, are not *known* by us to be true; a claim to know is in order only where doubt is in order, and where one is ready to trot out one's evidence to resolve the doubt.

> If you tried to doubt everything you would not get as far as doubting anything. The game of doubting itself presupposes certainty (*OC*, 115).
>
> Why do I not satisfy myself that I have two feet when I want to get up from a chair? There is no why. I simply don't. That is how I act (*OC*, 148).
>
> How does someone judge which is his right and which his left hand? How do I know that my judgment will agree with someone else's? How do I know that this colour is blue? If I don't trust *myself* here, why should I trust anyone else's judgment? That is to say: somewhere I must begin with not-doubting; and that is not, so to speak, hasty but excusable: it is part of judging (*OC*, 150).
>
> I should like to say: Moore does not *know* what he asserts he knows, but it stands fast for him, as also for me; regarding it as absolutely solid is part of our *method* of doubt and enquiry (*OC*, 151).

The world picture we have is not something we have checked out; nor is it something we *could* check out. What would I do to assure myself that *this* is my right hand? Ask somebody? But if I have a doubt here, why would I credit a second person's reassurance? (This is not to deny that in certain special circumstances I might have such a doubt and be reassured; perhaps I have put on distorting spectacles.) Can I doubt—Descartes notwithstanding—that I have a body? That I have parents? That I have never been to the moon? These things "stand fast" for us. It is hard to imagine anything

---

*Compare these views with the contrast Plato draws between *knowledge* and *opinion* (pp. 106–108). Do Wittgensteinian certainties fall neatly into *either* category?

*Compare Descartes' doubt in *Meditations I* and *II*. He thinks we can be more certain that we are thinking, understanding, doubting. But is that so?

more certain than these judgments for us to use as a lever to cast doubt on them. Is it, for example, *more certain* that my senses have sometimes deceived me than that the sky I'm looking at is blue?*

> Might I not believe that once, without knowing it, perhaps in a state of unconsciousness, I was taken far away from the earth—that other people even know this, but do not mention it to me? But this would not fit into the rest of my convictions at all. Not that I could describe the system of these convictions. Yet my convictions do form a system, a structure (*OC*, 102).

> And now if I were to say "It is my unshakeable conviction that etc.", this means in the present case too that I have not consciously arrived at the conviction by following a particular line of thought, but that it is anchored in all my *questions and answers*, so anchored that I cannot touch it (*OC*, 103).

> All testing, all confirmation and disconfirmation of a hypothesis takes place already within a system. And this system is not a more or less arbitrary and doubtful point of departure for all our arguments: no, it belongs to the essence of what we call an argument. The system is not so much the point of departure, as the element in which arguments have their life (*OC*, 105).

> . . . Much seems to be fixed, and it is removed from the traffic. It is so to speak shunted onto an unused siding (*OC*, 210).

> Now it gives our way of looking at things, and our researches, their form. Perhaps it was once disputed. But perhaps, for unthinkable ages, it has belonged to the *scaffolding* of our thoughts. (Every human being has parents.) (*OC*, 211).

The use of the *Tractatus* word "scaffolding" in this connection cannot be an accident. In his earlier view, it was logic (that transparent and absolutely rigid medium) that was the scaffolding of the world. Now, in dramatic contrast, what grounds our system of beliefs includes such apparently empirical and logically accidental facts as that I have

---

*Wittgenstein's critique here should remind you of Peirce on doubt and belief. (See again, pp. 465–466.)

parents, or even that motor cars don't grow out of the earth (279). If certain people believed that, we would suppose they are so different from us as to have entirely different standards of verification and reasonableness; it is not clear we could even understand those who seriously persisted in this belief; they would seem mad. The person who claims—in the light of all our certainties about Chrysler and Honda and engineering and production lines—that cars grow out of the earth is not making a *mistake*. This person would seem *demented*.

> In order to make a mistake, a man must already judge in conformity with mankind (*OC*, 156).

The complex system of certainties that make up a world picture does not function like an ordinary foundation. The foundation of a house is that on which everything else rests, but the foundation could stand alone. Our certainties form a system of interrelated judgments.

> When we first begin to *believe* anything, what we believe is not a single proposition, it is a whole system of propositions. (Light dawns gradually over the whole.) (*OC*, 141).

> I have arrived at the rock bottom of my convictions. And one might almost say that these foundation-walls are carried by the whole house (*OC*, 248).

Here the atomism of the *Tractatus* is most thoroughly repudiated. We do not first believe a single isolated proposition, then a second, a third, and so on. "Light dawns gradually over the whole" system. And in a striking metaphor, Wittgenstein suggests that the foundation walls are themselves borne up by their connection with the rest of the house.

But, we still want to ask: what makes us so certain of this picture? What guarantees for us that these judgments are fixed, that they do stand fast? Wittgenstein's answer is that *nothing* guarantees this. There is no guarantee. We are, indeed, certain of these things; but our certainty cannot be anchored in anything objective, in anything that is more certain than they.

To be sure there is justification; but justification comes to an end (*OC*, 192).

And in what does it come to an end?

At the foundation of well-founded beliefs lies belief that is not well-founded (*OC*, 253).

The difficulty is to realize the groundlessness of our believing (*OC*, 166).

Giving grounds . . . , justifying the evidence, comes to an end;   —but the end is not certain propositions' striking us immediately as true, i.e., it is not a kind of *seeing* on our part; it is our *acting*, which lies at the bottom of the language game (*OC*, 204).*

My *life* consists in my being content to accept many things (*OC*, 344).

If the Western philosophical tradition has been a quest for certainty, we can say that Wittgenstein satisfies that quest. For he acknowledges that there are many, many things of which we are certain (many more things than most philosophers ever imagined!). But as a quest for objective certainty, for a foundation which guarantees the *truth* of the edifice of knowledge, then, in a certain sense, if Wittgenstein is right, philosophy is *over*. Epistemology is *over*. For there comes a point where the spade is turned, where one cannot dig any deeper. And bedrock comes sooner than most philosophers have wanted it to come. We find it in our form of life. Our life *consists* in "being content to accept many things." This is, Wittgenstein holds, a difficult realization; we keep wanting to ask that good old why-question. Can't we, we yearn to ask, *somehow justify our form of life*? No, says Wittgenstein. It is *groundless*. It is "simply what we do." And what *we* do may not be what *they* do. Philosophy cannot dig deeper than the practices and customs that define our form of life. We do have our certainties. But they are groundless.

Philosophy may in no way interfere with the actual use of language; it can in the end only describe it.
For it cannot give it any foundation either.
It leaves everything as it is (*PI*, 124).

Notes

1. Ludwig Wittgenstein, *Tractatus Logico-Philosophicus* (London: Routledge and Kegan Paul, 1961), 5.
2. Norman Malcolm, *Ludwig Wittgenstein: A Memoir* (Oxford: Oxford University Press, 1958), 69.
3. Quotations from Ludwig Wittgenstein's *Philosophical Investigations* (New York: Macmillan Co., 1953) are cited in the text using the abbreviation *PI*. References are to section numbers.
4. Wittgenstein is mentioned in Harry D. Frankfurt's very interesting piece, "On Bullshit," in his *The Importance of What We Care About* (Cambridge: Cambridge University Press, 1988). Frankfurt identifies the essence of bullshit as the lack of any concern for truth.
5. G. E. Moore, "A Defense of Common Sense," in *Contemporary British Philosophy*, 2d ser., ed. G. Muirhead (London: George Allen and Unwin, Publishers, 1925).
6. Quotations from Ludwig Wittgenstein's *On Certainty* (Oxford: Basil Blackwell, 1969) are cited in the text using the abbreviation *OC*. References are to paragraph numbers.

---

*Compare Kierkegaard on the unavoidability of a *leap* (p. 442).

27

Martin Heidegger:
The Meaning of Being

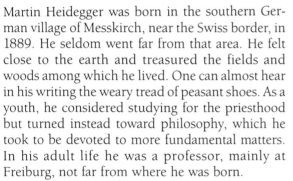

Martin Heidegger was born in the southern German village of Messkirch, near the Swiss border, in 1889. He seldom went far from that area. He felt close to the earth and treasured the fields and woods among which he lived. One can almost hear in his writing the weary tread of peasant shoes. As a youth, he considered studying for the priesthood but turned instead toward philosophy, which he took to be devoted to more fundamental matters. In his adult life he was a professor, mainly at Freiburg, not far from where he was born.

Heidegger lived through both world wars and for a time in the 1930s supported the Nazi party. This disreputable episode has been the occasion for much debate: Was it, or was it not, essentially connected to his philosophy? Opinion is divided. Although Heidegger was not in all respects an admirable person, he is nevertheless a philosopher of great power. He died in 1976.

The difficulty of his writing is legendary. Heidegger's aim is to try to say things that our tradition—the great conversation since Plato—has made it hard to say. Our language has been formed by this tradition; since Heidegger thinks the tradition has "hidden" precisely what he is most interested in, he finds it inadequate. So he devises new

terms to express what he wants to say.* Often these inventions have Greek etymological roots. Sometimes they are ordinary words put together in extraordinary ways or given extraordinary meanings.

The difficulty is compounded because translators do not always agree on the best English rendering of a German term. So the same term may be translated several ways.†

In 1927, Heidegger published a book called *Being and Time*. Actually, the work Heidegger projected was in two parts, and *Being and Time* constituted just two-thirds of the first part. The rest was never published. Why? Apparently he came to believe that the edifice for which *Being and Time* was to provide a foundation could not be built on that foundation. Consequently, there was a "turn" in his thinking, so that (as with Wittgenstein) we can speak of the early and the late philosophy. He

---

*Early in our story we see thinkers struggling to find (or invent) language adequate to what they want to say. Compare Anaximander (p. 10), Heraclitus (p. 18), and Democritus (p. 28). Though we usually assume our language is satisfactory, we see that the struggle to find the right words continues.

†I have had to make some terminological decisions; where a translation is at variance with my decision, I have put the translation I am using in brackets.

never gave up the pursuit of the issue he announced as his concern in *Being and Time*, however; in 1962, he gave a lecture entitled *Time and Being*. We will explore this "turn," but we will begin with—and give most of our attention to—the analysis of human existence as it is worked out in that partially completed 1927 book.

What Is the Question?

Tortuous though it is, Heidegger's thought has from the beginning a remarkable single-mindedness. There is one question, and only one, to which all his intellectual effort is directed. Heidegger calls it the question of the meaning of **Being**.* How to understand this question is itself a question. The concern it expresses will become richer and clearer as we explore his philosophy, but we should now address it in a preliminary way.

You have before you a piece of paper on which some words are written. The paper can be described in a variety of ways.† When we describe it, we are saying *what* it is—what kind of thing it is, what its characteristics and functions and uses are. But there is also this curious fact: *that* it is. I call it a curious fact because it tends to remain in the background, taken for granted—even, perhaps, hidden. But it is just this fact Heidegger wishes to ask about. What does it mean for the piece of paper to *be*? Kant, you will recall, urges that "being" is no ordinary predicate, and we have noted that this insight is incorporated into the quantifier of modern logic.‡ To say that the piece of paper *exists*, Kant

claims, is not further to describe it, nor to elaborate its concept, but to assert that something corresponds to the description we have given.

So far, so good. But what does this "corresponding" come to? What is it for the piece of paper to *be*? It is hard, perhaps, to get that question clearly in mind, to focus it, to pay attention to it. Heidegger is convinced that Kant doesn't satisfactorily answer this question, nor has anyone else in Western philosophy answered it. But that is precisely the question Heidegger is addressing. What does that *mean*—that the paper *is*?

Heidegger begins *Being and Time* with a quotation from Plato's dialogue *The Sophist*, in which a stranger remarks:

> For manifestly you have long been aware of what you mean when you use the expression 'being'. We, however, who used to think we understood it, have now become perplexed (*BT*, 1).[1]

That, Heidegger thinks, precisely describes *our* situation. You might think that this is odd. Even if Plato is perplexed, how can it be that all the intervening centuries of thought haven't cleared the matter up? Heidegger's answer is that the history of philosophical reflection about Being has been as much a *hiding* of the phenomenon as a revealing of it—and for deep and interesting reasons, as we will see.

We tend to have conflicting intuitions about the nature of Being. On the one hand, it seems the most obvious thing in the world: it applies to everything! We ourselves and every entity we meet *are*. How could we not know what Being is? On the other hand, if you are asked to define it, your response will probably be much like that of Augustine when asked about the nature of time.* One thing is clear, Heidegger says: Being is not itself an entity; it is not one more thing along with all the other things in the world. Imagine that you write down on a long, long list all the things that there

---

*I will follow the usual convention and capitalize the word when it is *Being* that is in question. The word "being" of course has other uses in English. Occasionally I may speak of *a being* or of *beings*; when uncapitalized, the term is the equivalent of "entity" or "item" or "thing" in a very broad sense (not just physical thing)—i.e., whatever can *be*, or have *Being*.

†You might look again at all the ways that John Dewey finds for describing such an item (p. 482).

‡See again Kant's discussion of the ontological argument (pp. 388–390).

---

*See p. 227.

are. Would you write down "apples, planets, babies, dirt, . . ., and Being"? No, you would not. Each of the entities on that list, in a strange way, has carried its Being along with it.* But what is this Being that puts humans and hammers and rocks and stars on the list but unicorns and square circles off? That is the question.

In saying that Being—the object of his inquiry—is not itself *a* being (not a thing, an entity, one of the items that exist), Heidegger means to make clear that he is not engaging in that traditional quest for *the* being who is responsible for all the rest. Heidegger is not searching for or trying to prove the existence of God—at least as God has traditionally been conceived. Heidegger is not asking about the *highest being*, but about what it is that accounts for the fact that there is *anything at all* (rather than nothing). What does it mean that entities *are*?

This sounds like an obscure question. If Heidegger is at all right, it is obscure because the tradition in which we have been raised—indeed, the very language we use—conspires to obscure it. The question seems on the one hand to be so abstract and distant from us as to be of purely academic interest, if that. Yet on the other hand, since we ourselves exist, it seems so intimate and near to us as to be almost too close to examine.† How could one make any progress in answering this question about the meaning of Being?

---

*The early Wittgenstein's contrast between (a) the totality of facts that make up the world and (b) *that* the world exists is essentially the same as Heidegger's contrast between entities (beings) and Being. (See p. 506.) Wittgenstein, of course, believes nothing can be said about this "*that* it is"; this is the "unsayable" about which we must be silent—the *mystical*. But it is just this that Heidegger commits all his intellectual energy to trying to say. A caution: what Heidegger means by "world" is *very* different from what the *Tractatus* means by it, and our relationship to it is correspondingly different.

†Again Wittgenstein comes to mind: recall the analogy of the visual field that does not include the eye that sees it (see p. 503). *Being* is so "close" to us as to be invisible to us. It is one of Heidegger's aims to get us some "distance" from it so that it can appear to us as it is.

The Clue

> Any inquiry, as an inquiry about something, has *that which is asked about*. But all inquiry about something is somehow a questioning of something. So in addition to what is asked about, an inquiry has *that which is interrogated*. . . . Furthermore, in what is asked about there lies also *that which is to be found out by the asking* (BT, 24).

The inquiry about the meaning of Being is *asking about* Being; that is the focus of our question. And what we want to find out by our asking is the meaning of Being. But what will we examine? Where will we look? If our investigation is to be a real, concrete one, it can't just hang in the air; it must tie down to something. There must be something that we *interrogate*.

> "Being is always the Being of an entity" (BT, 29).

Being, in other words, is not like the smile of the Cheshire cat, which can remain mysteriously after the cat has vanished. As we have seen, Being comes along with the entities that *are*. What Heidegger is now saying is that apart from entities, there "is" no Being. If we wanted to put this in a slangy slogan, we might say: No *be-ing* without a *be-er*. So if we want to investigate Being, we must do it in connection with some entity. But which entity do we choose? In principle, any might do, from quarks to gophers to black holes. But is there some entity that would be *best* to interrogate with respect to its Being?

At this point Heidegger notes that an inquiry like this is itself something that has Being. (Asking questions is not just *nothing*, after all.) And we would not have answered our question about the meaning of Being unless we also got clear about the Being of items like inquiries—and of the entities that inquire! This suggests that *we ourselves* might be the entity we interrogate in our inquiry, the focus of our investigation.

Heidegger recognizes, of course, that many sorts of investigation concern themselves with human beings. Many sciences have something to say about us: physics, chemistry, biology, history, psychology, anthropology. But none of these sciences takes the perspective on humans that is relevant to our question. To focus attention on the relevant aspect, he refers to the entity we will interrogate by a term that is usually left untranslated: **Dasein**. This term can be used in German to refer to almost any kind of entity, though it is usually used for human beings. Literally the term means "being there." ("Da" means "there" or sometimes "here"; "sein" is "being.") And Heidegger chooses this term to highlight the aspect of humans he is interested in: not the chemistry of the body nor the history of human society, but their Being.*

The suggestion that Dasein should be the focus of our investigation—the entity to be interrogated—is further supported by noting that we are distinctive among entities in an interesting way.

> Dasein is an entity which does not just occur among other entities. Rather it is ontically distinguished by the fact that, in its very Being, that Being is an *issue* for it. But in that case, this is a constitutive state of Dasein's Being, and this implies that Dasein, in its Being, has a relationship towards that Being—a relationship which itself is one of Being. And this means further that there is some way in which Dasein understands itself in its Being, and that to some degree it does so explicitly. It is peculiar to this entity that with and through its Being, this Being is disclosed to it. *Understanding of Being is itself a definite characteristic of Dasein's Being.* Dasein is ontically distinctive in that it *is* ontological (*BT*, 32).

This important paragraph no doubt needs some explanation. Heidegger employs a distinction between two levels at which an entity can be described; he calls them **ontic** and **ontological**. We can think of the ontic level as that of ordinary facts.

Each Dasein has a certain physical size, grows up in a certain culture, experiences moods, uses language and tools, remembers and intends, often fears death, and usually thinks its way of life is the right way: these are all ontic facts.

But there is also a deeper level at which Dasein can be described: in its *way of Being*—in the way it is "there," present to things, in the world, together with others. We can think of this level as a matter of structural features of Dasein that make possible all the ontic facts we are ordinarily aware of.* This is the ontological level.

Heidegger holds that, ontically considered, Dasein is unique among entities. And what makes it distinctive is that its own Being "is an *issue* for it." What he means is that Dasein is the being that is concerned about its own Being; it *matters* to Dasein how things are going with it, how it is doing, what the state of its Being is and will become. So Dasein already has, by virtue of its being the sort of entity that it is, a certain understanding of Being. Its own Being is always, at any given point, "disclosed to it." Because this feature of Dasein is so fundamental, Heidegger asserts that Dasein "*is* ontological." What does this mean? Ontology is the discipline concerned with Being. So to say that Dasein *is* ontological is to say that Dasein's *way of Being* involves having an *understanding* of its own Being. This openness to itself is what makes Dasein Dasein!

This feature of Dasein is so central that Heidegger points to it as the *essence* of Dasein. In each case—yours, mine—Dasein "has its Being to be" (*BT*, 33). It is as though Dasein can't just *be* (the

---

*Like the term "person" in Kant, this term doesn't specify whether human beings are the only beings with the particular *way of Being* we have. Perhaps in other galaxies . . .

*It might be helpful to recall Kant's four questions, e.g., "What makes natural science possible?" Kant is asking about the "transcendental" conditions on the side of the subject that must be assumed, given that science (or mathematics, or morality, or metaphysics) actually exists. In a similar way, Heidegger is inquiring about Dasein's basic mode of Being: what must Dasein be for the ontic facts to be what they are? As we will see, Heidegger's project differs from Kant's in two distinct ways: (1) He is not asking about a *subject*, as opposed to an object; (2) he thinks he has a way to reveal to us the very Being of Dasein. So there is no unknowable noumenal entity that has the character of a transcendental ego. Compare Kant on the soul, pp. 382–384.

way spiders are, for example); Dasein has to *decide* about its Being. How it will *be* is an *issue*; its Being this way or that is not just a given fact. Being, for Dasein, is a *problem* to be solved; but it cannot be solved in a disinterested and theoretical way; it is solved only by living—by existing.*

Heidegger searches for a term to designate the way of Being that is characteristic of Dasein. He settles on "existence." Dasein *exists*. As he uses this term, dogs and cats *are*, but they do not *exist*. Stones and stars are, but they do not exist. They have a different *kind* of Being. "Existence," then, is a technical term for Dasein's way of being. The term "exist" has etymological roots that suggest a kind of projection out from or away from the given situation. Heidegger sometimes writes it as "ek-sist" to emphasize this transcending of the given.† As we will see, Dasein ek-sists: it is always projecting itself beyond the present circumstance to future possibilities. We are aware of the present in the light of what it has been (the past) and could become (the future); we are not simply confined in it. This feature, in fact, is what makes it possible for Dasein to be concerned about its own Being. (Already we hear intimations of the importance of *time* to the question about the meaning of Being.)

Heidegger can say, then, that the essence of Dasein—what Dasein most essentially is—is its existence. And his first task is an "analytic" of Dasein. If we can get clear about Dasein's way of Being, this should be a step toward the larger question of the meaning of Being in general. Dasein is the best entity to interrogate because Dasein, in existing, already has an understanding of Being. To some degree, Being is "in the open" in Dasein, available in a way it would not be in a chemical compound. This understanding does not yet amount to the clear and comprehensive ontological understanding Heidegger is seeking; it is only an average, everyday kind of understanding, which (as we will see) may hide as much as it discloses. But Heidegger has found a clue to where to begin.*

Heidegger calls an analysis of Dasein's existence a *fundamental* ontology. The ontological analysis of Dasein (the description of Dasein's basic structures) provides "the condition for the possibility of any ontologies" (*BT*, 34). Since the essence of Dasein is its existence, this will be an *existential* analysis. And what Heidegger will be looking for is something analogous to the traditional *categories*, i.e., concepts setting out the most basic sorts of ways that things can be.† The concepts in the analysis of existence that correspond to the traditional categories Heidegger calls *existentials*. We will see what these are.

Let us summarize:

- What we are after is the meaning of Being. The name for such an inquiry is "ontology."
- The place to begin is where Being is "in the open."
- Dasein, because it is constituted by an understanding of its own Being, is such a "place."
- So, Dasein is the entity to be interrogated.
- Dasein's way of Being is existence.
- So we want an existential analysis of Dasein.
- This analysis will be formulated in terms of concepts called "existentials," which play the role for Dasein that the traditional categories

---

*Compare Kierkegaard, p. 440.
†"Ek" is a Greek particle that suggests a standing out away from some origin, as in "ecstasy"—standing outside one's normal self.

*Heidegger's reason for turning to Dasein in his attempt to discern the meaning of Being is responsive to the puzzle Plato discusses about searching for the truth: If we don't know the truth, how do we know where to look? And how will we know when we have found it? If we do know the truth, what sense does it make to search for it? See p. 97. Plato thinks learning the truth is "recollecting" what the soul had known in some preexistence. Heidegger thinks that Dasein is a profitable field for investigation, because Dasein already has a "preontological" understanding of Being. This understanding can be clarified and deepened into a genuine ontology.
†Compare Aristotle on the categories, p. 145, and Kant, p. 376. Heidegger agrees that "Being can be said in many ways." But he thinks neither of them has discovered the appropriate "categories" for Dasein, the language adequate to our existence.

play for what Heidegger will call "present-at-hand" entities—i.e., they give the most general characterizations of its way of Being.

* And this analysis will provide a fundamental ontology, from which the meaning of Being in general can be approached.

This focus on Dasein and its existence has led many to classify Heidegger as an existentialist. And perhaps there is no harm in that. But it must be clearly kept in mind that the analysis of existence is not what he is mainly interested in. Heidegger is, from first to last, intent on deciphering the meaning of Being.

Phenomenology

We now know what the aim is. But we do not yet have a very clear idea of how to pursue that goal. Even though Dasein is the kind of being that has an understanding of its own Being, we must not think that philosophy can just take that over—far from it. For one thing, there are many ways in which Dasein has been interpreted in the great conversation, and any of these are available for Dasein to use: as a soul temporarily imprisoned in a body (Plato), as a rational animal (Aristotle), as a creature of God (Augustine), as the *ego cogito* (Descartes), as a material mechanism (Hobbes), as a transcendental ego (Kant), as the absolute subject (Hegel). *None* of these interpretations, Heidegger thinks, are adequate. In one way or another, they all miss the *existence* of Dasein. And even the average, everyday, unsophisticated way in which Dasein understands itself may hide as much as it reveals about Dasein's true existential nature. Dasein always understands itself in one way or another. But philosophy cannot just take over Dasein's self-understanding. It is as likely to be a misunderstanding as to be a correct one.

You can see, however, that we have a serious problem. How are we going to approach Dasein? With what method? Heidegger suggests that the analysis should proceed in two stages. In the first stage, we should set aside all the sophisticated theories of the tradition and try just to look at Dasein's "average everydayness."* We want to grasp Dasein as it exists most obviously and naturally. Still, the results of this analysis of everyday Dasein will be merely provisional, because we suspect that Dasein understands itself to some degree *inauthentically*, self-deceptively, hiding its way of Being from itself.

For this reason, the second stage is necessary; we must ask what it would be for Dasein to grasp itself, to own up to what it really is, to exist and understand itself *authentically*. In such an adequate self-understanding of its Being, Dasein will reveal the existentials that define it, and we will have an authentic fundamental ontology. This second stage will reveal *temporality* as the meaning of the Being of Dasein; thus we'll see that *time* is of central importance for the main question. In fact, Heidegger suggests time as the "horizon" within which the meaning of Being must be understood—that Being itself is fundamentally temporal in nature.

But this is getting far ahead of our story. We are still faced with the problem of just how to go about investigating everyday existence. This must be done, Heidegger tells us, *phenomenologically*. Our understanding of the term "phenomenology" from our discussion of Hegel can serve as a clue to its meaning here.† There, the key idea is that we can "watch" consciousness as it develops through its stages toward more adequate forms. This idea of observing is central for Heidegger, too.‡ It has

---

*Compare the later Wittgenstein's motto: "Don't think, but look!" (p. 517). Heidegger goes as far as to talk of "destroying" the ontological tradition that extends from the Greeks to ourselves—so fundamentally misguided does he believe its "thinking" has been!
†See p. 404.
‡Heidegger's phenomenological method actually owes most to his teacher, Edmund Husserl, who develops phenomenological methods of inquiry. For Husserl, phenomenology is (a) a science which is (b) purely descriptive, rather than deductive or explanatory, (c) which sets aside in a systematic way all prior assumptions and presuppositions, (d) whose subject matter is consciousness—its structure, its contents, and its "intended" objects—and (e) whose outcome is a description of essences—e.g., an account of *what it is to be* an act of perception or the object of a remembering. Husserl's motto is "to the things themselves!" Heidegger takes this over, but he understands it in quite a different way.

nothing to do with bodily eyes, of course; this "watching" is more a matter of attitude, of not imposing preconceived notions on the subject in question. Phenomenology is the disclosing, or uncovering, of a phenomenon by means of discourse about it. We can think of it as the attempt to *let* entities manifest themselves as they truly are.

Phenomena are understood to be "the totality of what lies in the light of day or can be brought to light" (*BT*, 51). A phenomenon, Heidegger says, is "*that which shows itself in itself*, the manifest" (*BT*, 51). Phenomena are not "mere appearances," then. They are not just illusions. Nor are they signs for something else. They are "the things themselves" as they show themselves—and not by means of something else, but "in themselves." And that is why phenomenology is relevant to our question about Being—why phenomenology can be ontology. For what we want to do is to let Being itself appear, as it is.

Notice that Heidegger makes a subtle distinction: some matters, he says, "lie in the light of day," and others "can be brought to light." Roughly speaking, entities are what lie in the light of day—the tableware we use each day, the daily newspaper, the family dog, your brother. But (and this should be no surprise by now) their Being is not so clearly apparent to us. This is what must be brought to light, uncovered, disclosed. And this is just what phenomenology is designed to do.

Heidegger suggests three ways in which the phenomenon of Being might be hard to discern: (1) Being might be "hidden," in the sense that it is just too close to us for us to focus on it easily; (2) it might be "covered up," an idea that suggests Being was once known but has been made inaccessible by the tradition; and (3) Being might be "disguised," in the sense that Dasein, unable to face the awful truth about its existence, might draw a veil of camouflage over it (*BT*, 59–60). So the data we are after might not simply be there "in the light of day," manifesting themselves for us to see. We will have to engage in some *interpretation* to bring the phenomena to light. This interpretation Heidegger calls "hermeneutics," drawing this term from the tradition of interpreting texts, particularly Scrip-

ture. The meaning of a text is often obscure; to understand it requires an interpretation. So also is the meaning of Being obscure. And even the character of our own existence requires interpretation if we are not to be misled by the "disguises" we subject it to. To get to the meaning of Dasein, then, will require a method that is phenomenological and hermeneutical at the same time. But the aim is to let the phenomenon of Being shine forth, as it is in itself.

Being-in-the-World

We are ready now to begin the analysis of the existential structure of Dasein. Remember, what we are aiming at is an explicit understanding of Dasein's way of Being, that way which Heidegger calls "existence." The *basic state* of Dasein, he tells us, is this: that Dasein essentially, necessarily, *is-in-the-world*. The hyphens in this odd phrase are not accidental; they are supposed to tell us that we are dealing here with a *unitary* phenomenon. It is not possible, in other words, to understand Dasein apart from its world; indeed, Dasein without the world would not be "da"—i.e., *there*. To be in a world—to "have" a world—is constitutive for Dasein.

We need to unpack this very rich notion. But before we do, it might be useful to contrast it with some others. We can already see that Heidegger's phenomenological analysis of Dasein's Being is completely at variance with the view expressed most clearly by Descartes: that it is a real possibility (one that needs to be ruled out by argument) that I might be the only thing that exists.* As we have seen, this ego (or mind), which Descartes thinks could exist independently of the world, gets trapped inside itself and has a hard time finding the world again. In supposing that such an independent existence is possible for the soul, Heidegger claims,

---

*Review *Meditation I* with its skeptical arguments from sense deceptions, dreams, and the evil demon. Descartes thinks he can defeat solipsism only by *proving* the existence of God.

Descartes misses precisely the *Being* of Dasein—namely, its **Being-in-the-world**. Heidegger thinks that Descartes' notion of the *ego*, of "the *thing* which thinks," in fact attributes to Dasein a kind of Being that belongs rather to a different sort of entity, which he will call the **present-at-hand**.* This is just one dramatic example of how the Western philosophical tradition has gone wrong—one example, Heidegger thinks, of how our forgetfulness of Being has warped our perception of things. One finds this pattern, he believes, in the whole history of the conversation since Descartes—in Hume, Kant, and Hegel particularly.† But its roots can be traced back to Plato's interpretation of the true Being of entities in terms of the Forms.

Our tradition, Heidegger holds, has succumbed to a tendency toward *objectification*. As a result, we have taken the world to be made up of substances, things, objects; and the self or soul or mind has been understood as just another substance or thing. No wonder the crucial question seemed to be the epistemological one: whether the mind (understood to be a subject-kind-of-thing) can *know* the object (understood as another kind of thing). Can a subject *transcend* its subjectivity and know the truth about objects existing independently of it? We have seen how Kant's Copernican revolution "solves" this problem by making knowable objects dependent on the knowing subject, but at the price of leaving things-in-themselves unknown. All this, Heidegger believes, is a result of our having "covered over" the phenomenon of Being. And, most crucially, it has distorted our understanding of *our own* Being. It is this covering up that Heidegger means to combat. And the first shot in this battle is the notion that the basic state of Dasein (which, you will recall, is in each case *mine*) is Being-in-the-world.

---

*We will explicitly discuss this notion of the present-at-hand on pp. 544–545.

†Heidegger would think that Hume's bundle theory of the self, Kant's transcendental ego, and Hegel's infinite subject (Spirit) as the substance of the world all miss the phenomenon of the Being of Dasein. All are dominated by the heritage of Descartes, for whom the subject is a peculiar kind of *thing* (though they differ about the kind of thing it is).

What does this mean? For one thing, it means that the fundamental relation between Dasein and the world is not epistemological, but ontological. Knowing is not basic; Being is. We *are* in-the-world, and we are so in a way that is deeper and richer than any propositional knowledge could completely express. What is it to be *in* the world? We can't fully answer this question until we understand more clearly what a "world" is. But in a preliminary way, we can say this: it is not the same as the coffee being *in* the cup, or the pencil being *in* the box. In these cases, we have one "present-at-hand" thing spatially contained in another. Heidegger does not want to deny that for certain purposes the entity that is Dasein can be regarded like this: right now, for instance, I am *in* my study, which is *in* my house in exactly this sense.

But this is not the basic fact about the way I am in the world. (It is not the basic fact, for that matter, about the way I am in my study.) Dasein is *in*-the-world more in the sense in which my brother was *in* the navy, or my son is *in* love. Dasein's way of Being-in-the-world is a matter of being engaged in projects, involved with others, using tools. Dasein *dwells* in the world; it is not just *located* there. Dasein's

> Being-in-the-world has always dispersed itself or even split itself up into definite ways of Being-in. The multiplicity of these is indicated by the following examples: having to do with something, producing something, attending to something and looking after it, making use of something, giving something up and letting it go, undertaking, accomplishing, evincing, interrogating, considering, discussing, determining. . . . All these ways of Being-in have *concern* as their kind of Being—a kind of Being we have yet to characterize in detail (*BT*, 83).

Concernfully—that is the way Dasein is *in*-the-world. In all these ways and more, Dasein is concernfully engaged in the world. What this means is that there is a more basic mode of relating to the things in the world than knowing them. Knowledge we might have or lack. But Being-in is something we cannot *be* without.

From what we have been saying, it follows that Being-in is not a 'property' which Dasein sometimes has and sometimes does not have, and *without* which it could be just as well as it could with it. It is not the case that man 'is' and then has, by way of an extra, a relationship-of-Being towards the 'world'—a world with which he provides himself occasionally. Dasein is never 'proximally' an entity which is, so to speak, free from Being-in, but which sometimes has the inclination to take up a 'relationship' towards the world. Taking up relationships towards the world is possible only *because* Dasein, as Being-in-the-world, is as it is (*BT*, 84).

Being-in-the-world, in other words, is one of the *existentials* that characterizes the fundamental ontology of Dasein. It is one aspect of the essence of Dasein. The world is *given with* Dasein. But what a *world* is we are not yet clear about.

Remember that we are trying to disclose the Being of Dasein by an investigation of "average everydayness." So we now have to ask, How does this phenomenon of Being-in-the-world show itself in Dasein's average everydayness? What form does our Being-in normally take? We can get an answer, Heidegger suggests, via an interpretation of the *entities in the world* "closest" to us.

> We shall call those entities which we encounter in concern "*equipment*". In our dealings we come across equipment for writing, sewing, working, transportation, measurement. The kind of Being which equipment possesses must be exhibited (*BT*, 97).

If we try to give a phenomenological description of our everyday mode of Being, what we find is that we dwell in a world of gear, of equipment for use. We do not first understand a pen as a "mere thing," and thereafter apprehend its use as a writing instrument. That is not the right description of our way with the pen. We grasp it to *write with*, usually without a thought. It is "on hand," or, as Heidegger puts it, **ready-to-hand**. We simply turn the knob to open the door, often with our mind entirely on other matters—don't we? We deal with the things around us in an engaged, not a detached, manner. We cope with them in a variety of ways. They are

elements in our ongoing projects. The things that are phenomenologically "closest" to us are not, then, neutral "objects" which we first stare at in a disinterested way and to which we must subsequently assign some "value."

It is in this manner that we are most primordially in-the-world. Descartes worries about the problem of a transcendent reality: Is there anything "out there" beyond my mind's ideas? But if Heidegger is right, that is not a problem at all. Dasein *is* a kind of transcendence—in its very Being! Dasein is essentially *in-the-world*, engaged with the entities of the world in a concernful fashion. Kant believes that the scandal of philosophy is that philosophers have not solved this problem of transcendence. Heidegger, on the contrary, thinks the scandal is that philosophy has thought there is a problem! That there seems to be a problem about, for example, "the reality of the external world" is just a sign of how distant we are from an understanding of our own mode of Being.*

But we still need to clarify the mode of Being of these entities "closest" to us in-the-world. Let us ask, What is it to *be* a hammer? In what does its *being-a-hammer* consist? There is a certain characteristic shape for a hammer, and a hammer is usually made out of certain definite materials, though both shape and materials can vary. But it is neither shape nor composition that *makes* a hammer a hammer. What it is for something to be a hammer is for it to have a certain definite use—a function, a purpose. A hammer is (to oversimplify slightly) *to-drive-nails-with*. That is what a hammer *is*. A hammer *hammers*.

It is important to note that the Being of the hammer involves a reference to something else—to nails. What is it to be a nail? To be a nail is to be something that can be driven into boards to fasten them together. Another reference!

---

*Heidegger's analysis of Being-in-the-world is a radical rejection of what we have called the representational theory (p. 294), the central claim of which is that we are directly or immediately acquainted only with ideas in the mind. If Heidegger is right, what we are directly and immediately acquainted with are functionally understood items in the world around us.

Taken strictly, there 'is' no such thing as *an* equipment. To the Being of any equipment there always belongs a totality of equipment, in which it can be this equipment that it is. Equipment is essentially 'something in-order-to . . .' A totality of equipment is constituted by various ways of the 'in-order-to', such as serviceability, conduciveness, usability, manipulability.

In the 'in-order-to' as a structure there lies an *assignment* or *reference* of something to something (*BT*, 97).

It is not possible, in other words, that there should exist just one item of equipment. Being a hammer involves a context of other equipment and, ultimately, the world.*

Let us ask a related question. When do we *understand* something to be a hammer? In what does this understanding consist? Most basically, I understand a hammer when I know how to hammer with it—when I can use it to drive the nails into the boards. The Being of the hammer—as a hammer—reveals itself not to a disinterested observation of its appearance or to a scientific investigation of its weight and material properties. Its Being is manifest primarily and fundamentally in a skill I have, particularly when I actualize this skill in actually hammering. That is how the hammer shows itself to be what it is. Hammers are understood in virtue of a kind of "know-how," not (primarily) by way of a "theory of hammers." Its being a hammer reveals itself to my *circumspective concern*—to my care-full involvements with it in the projects I am engaged in. Heidegger calls this kind of Being "readiness-to-hand."

Tools, gear, and equipment in general have this kind of Being. And dealing with the ready-to-hand is the most fundamental mode of our Being-in-the-world. On all sides we find it, if we only have eyes to look. It is easy to miss, because it is so "close" to us, almost too familiar to notice. But our skillful coping with nearly everything we encounter during a day's dealings is a matter of encountering over and over again the ready-to-hand. Our fundamental mode of understanding is not theoretical or scientific, but practical. We *understand how* to drive a car, use a fork, put on a pair of pants, open a can. And we manifest that understanding in actually driving, hammering, using the computer, combing our hair, and so on. The Being of Dasein is in this primordial sense a Being-in-the-world.

It cannot be emphasized too much that this concernful dealing with the ready-to-hand is *basic*. If Heidegger is right about this, the question of whether there "really" are hammers and cars and cans simply cannot arise. Philosophers have thought this is a real problem only because they have missed the Being of Dasein as Being-in-the-world and Dasein's relation to the ready-to-hand.

We are making some progress, but we do not yet know what it is to be a world. A clue can be derived from the fact that the ready-to-hand never comes alone, but always in a context of references and assignments to other entities. The hammer is to pound the nails; there would be no nails if there were no boards needing joining; the boards are shaped the way they are to build a house; houses are for sheltering and for dwelling in. All these things are meaningful together—or not at all. Each has the structure of an in-order-to. But if we pay close attention to this phenomenon of interlocking in-order-to's, we can see that three other things are also manifest.

(1) Though we do not typically pay attention to the needle or the hammer directly—what we are involved in is *the work*, and the hammer is used in a way "transparently"—the work involves *making use of something* for a purpose. Consider a cobbler making shoes.

In the work there is also a reference or assignment to 'materials': the work is dependent on leather, thread, needles, and the like. Leather, moreover, is produced from hides. These are taken from animals, which someone else has raised. . . . Hammer, tongs, and needle, refer in themselves to steel, iron, metal, mineral, wood, in that they consist of these. In equipment that is used, 'Nature' is discovered along with it by that use—the 'Nature' we find in natural products (*BT*, 100).

---

*Compare the anti-atomistic remarks of the later Wittgenstein, p. 531.

As Heidegger is careful to point out, the "nature" that presents itself in this way is nature as a resource: "the wood is a forest of timber, the mountain a quarry of rock; the river is water-power, the wind is wind 'in the sails'" (*BT*, 100). This nature is part of the world of equipment "in" which Dasein essentially is. It is not quite the nature of the physicist (to which we will come shortly). Along with the ready-to-hand Being of equipment, then, there is revealed the world of nature.

(2) Along with the ready-to-hand, other entities having the same kind of being as Dasein are also manifest. I, after all, did not make the hammer I pound with, nor did I manufacture the nails, nor did I shape the boards I join with them. They did not just "happen," either. These entities reveal that I am not alone in the world but live in the world together with others who are like me.* This world, moreover, shows itself to be a *public* world. Hammers are mass produced; they are designed specifically so that *anyone* can hammer with them. The instruments in a car are intentionally designed so that the *average person* can easily read them. It would be a big mistake (we will soon see just how big) to understand Heidegger as saying that each Dasein lives in his own little world. Far from it. While we can quite properly speak of the chicken farmer's world, or the magazine publisher's world, or the cyclist's world, these are not fundamental. Each is but a modification carved out of the larger public world. These smaller worlds are not the world in which Dasein most fundamentally dwells; that world is the one and only public world. The Being of Dasein is Being-in-*the*-world. And this is a world I have in common with others.

(3) The third phenomenon that is evident together with the ready-to-hand is what Heidegger calls a "for-the-sake-of-which." Let's go back to the hammer. The hammer is what it is as equipment, ready-to-hand for hammering. As we have seen, there is a whole series of references or assignments in which the hammer is involved: it is essentially related to nails, which "refer" to boards, which "point" toward building houses. Does this set of functional relations have a terminus? Is there a point to it? Does it come to an end somewhere? Is there anything *for the sake of which* this whole set of relations exists? Yes. The totality of these involvements

> goes back ultimately to a "towards-which" in which there is *no* further involvement: this "towards-which" is not an entity with the kind of Being that belongs to what is ready-to-hand within a world; it is rather an entity whose Being is defined as Being-in-the-world, and to whose state of Being, worldhood itself belongs. . . . The primary 'toward-which' is a "for-the-sake-of-which". But the 'for-the-sake-of-which' always pertains to the Being of *Dasein*, for which in its Being, that very Being is essentially an issue (*BT*, 116–17).

Dasein, concerned for its own Being, understands the possibility that it might freeze in the winter and provides for itself a house. It is in terms of the possibilities of Dasein's Being that the entire set of functional relations attains its structure and Being. We get the image of an immensely complicated, crisscrossing network of functional assignments in which all the entities in the world are caught up and have their Being. This network is anchored in the Being of Dasein, that Being for whom its own Being is a matter of concern and whose Being has the structure of Being-in-the-world.

It is important to note that the world is not an entity; nor is it a collection of entities; nor is it a totality of facts, as the early Wittgenstein thinks.* Heidegger's thought is as far removed from the atomism of the *Tractatus* as you can imagine. It is only within the context of the world that something can *be* a hammer. The world is a prior whole, presupposed by the Being of the ready-to-hand; it is not the *sum* of lots and lots of things, each of which might equally well exist alone. There would be no hammers in a world without nails to drive; there would be no nails without boards

---

*If the problem of the reality of the "external world" seems like a pseudoproblem from Heidegger's point of view, the same is true of the problem of "other minds." It just doesn't arise!

---

*See the discussion of the first sentences of the *Tractatus*, pp. 492 and 496.

to join; there would be no boards without houses to build; and there would be none of these entities without Dasein—that for-the-sake-of-which they all exist and whose mode of Being is Being-in-the-world.

But if we are clear about what the world is *not*, we are still not clear about what it is. The world in which Dasein has its Being is one of those all-too-familiar, too-close-to-be-observed phenomena. The world is not, for instance, the earth. It would sound very odd indeed to talk about Being-in-the-earth (as though one lived underground). Nor is the world the same as the universe. (Christians talk of the "sins of the world," but "sins of the universe" makes no sense at all.) What, then, is this familiar, but strange, phenomenon of the world?

Though our immediate focus is usually on the things *in* the world, Heidegger suggests that there are certain experiences in which the phenomenon of the world itself—the *worldhood* of the world—comes to the fore. Consider working with a lever, trying to move a large and heavy box. What is manifest is the work, the project—to get *this* over *there*—and in a subsidiary (but not explicitly focused) way, the lever. Suddenly the lever breaks. It is no longer ready-to-hand. We could, in fact, call it unready-to-hand. It takes on the character of *conspicuousness*. Whereas one had hardly noticed the lever before, just using it in that transparent way, suddenly it announces itself, forces itself into awareness.

Two things happen. For one thing, "pure presence-at-hand announces itself in such [damaged] equipment" (*BT*, 103). There occurs a transition to another mode of Being. The functionality that defined the lever *as* a lever vanishes; the item is disconnected from that series of references and involvements that made it be—as a lever. It no longer *is* a lever. It just *lies there*. We no longer seize hold of it in that familiar way to use in our project. It is no longer alongside us in our work. Rather, it stands over against us. We observe it, stare at it. It has become an *object*. It now *is* merely *present-at-hand*.

Heidegger allows that in the course of our everyday lives, this moment of pure presence-at-hand-edness may not last very long; the item soon takes up a new place in our system of functional involvements, with the meaning of "to-be-fixed" or "to-be-discarded." But this glimpse into the present-at-hand is a revelation of another whole mode of Being: a realm of pure objects, suitable for contemplation and scientific investigation. It is important to note that in some sense, it is the same entity as before; however, its *mode of Being* changes. Now it is just an *object*, a *substance with properties*.* Revealed in this way, it can be a theme for investigation by the natural sciences. In fact, *nature*—in the sense dealt with by modern physics—now first makes its appearance. This is not nature as a resource, as part of the equipment character of the world; it is nature disconnected from Dasein's concern—a sheer presence.

Along with the stripping away of functional characteristics, something else takes place in the transition to presence-at-hand. Every tool has a "place," almost in an Aristotelian sense.† If you have "misplaced" your hammer, there are certain places you will look for it and certain places you won't; you won't look in the oven. There is a "region" in which it "belongs."

> In the 'physical' assertion that 'the hammer is heavy' we *overlook* not only the tool-character of the entity we encounter, but also something that belongs to any ready-to-hand equipment: its place. Its place becomes a matter of indifference. This does not mean that what is present-at-hand loses its 'location' altogether. But its place becomes a spatio-temporal position, a 'world-point', which is in no way distinguished from any other (*BT*, 413).

Heidegger is describing (1) the existential genesis of those infinite spaces whose "silence" so frightens

---

*Recall that the "substance/property" concept is one of the categories of Kant, one of the fundamental ways that objects can—*must*—be. See p. 377. Heidegger is here claiming that this mode of being is a derivative one; it belongs to the present-at-hand, which is a modification of the more basic ready-to-hand. What is fundamental is not the *object*, but the *tool*.

†See the discussion of the ancient idea that things have a "natural place" and of how "space" comes to supplant "place" as a basic concept in seventeenth-century science (p. 282).

Pascal* and (2) the *origin* of that objectifying way of understanding the world that has so dominated our tradition. The important thing to note is that the present-at-hand is not primordial, or basic. The objects of natural science have their Being in a *modification* of the more fundamental entities that are ready-to-hand. Our tradition since Plato and Aristotle, but especially since Descartes, has assumed (without proof, Heidegger insists) that the basic mode of Being for the things of the world is just this objectified presence-at-hand, in which things are available for perceiving and theorizing about, independent of their role as equipment in the world. Suppose *you* are asked, for example, "What is there—*really*?" You are likely to answer in terms of the entities described by physical science: rocks and trees and electrons and such. But that answer is, Heidegger believes, precisely backwards. The most basic mode of Being for the entities we encounter in the world is Being-ready-to-hand; objects as there for disinterested scientific inquiry ride piggyback on that.

This claim has its bite in the notion that no matter how much of the world we "objectify," we always, necessarily, do so on a background of circumspective concern, of practices that deal with the world in the ready-to-hand kind of way. Dasein cannot, if Heidegger is right, totally objectify itself. Yet, that is just the way our tradition has treated Dasein—as an *object* with *properties* of a certain sort (distinctive properties, perhaps, but an object nonetheless). That is why we tend to think that explanations of a *scientific* sort can be given for human behavior: explanations in terms of conditioning, or complexes, or drives, or peer "pressure," or any number of other analogues to explanation in physical science. And that is why the question of the meaning of Being is so obscure to us; in assimilating our own Being to that of the present-at-hand, we have lost the sense of what it is to *exist*. Since existence is our own mode of Being, that mode of Being in which and about which we are concerned, of which we do necessarily have some understanding, a misunderstanding here turns everything topsy-turvy. It is no wonder that clarifying the meaning of Being is so difficult a task.

But we still have not clarified the meaning of "the world." What is it to be a world? That is the second thing that shows up in those experiences where tools go wrong in some way. When the lever breaks, not only does the present-at-hand light up, but the whole ensemble of relations in which it was transparently embedded now comes into view. When the lever gets disconnected from this network and just lies there, the network itself becomes visible. Part of it is disturbed; what we notice is that it has been there all the time! It is this system of references, within which Dasein and the ready-to-hand have their Being, that constitutes the *worldhood of the world*. To be a world, in other words, is to be a structure within which entities *are* and have their meaning.* This entire network of in-order-to's and toward-which's and for-the-sake-of's—that is the phenomenon of the world. So the world is neither a thing, nor an entity, nor a collection of entities. It is that wherein entities have their Being, whether that Being is existence, readiness-to-hand, or presence-at-hand.

You should now have a fairly clear understanding of that basic *existential*, that most fundamental characteristic of Dasein: that Dasein is Being-in-the-world.

The "Who" of Dasein

Who is Dasein?

That may sound like a strange question, and in fact it is. Not because the term "Dasein" is a strange

---

*See p. 282.

---

*Heidegger's conception of "the world" is something like that "scaffolding of the world" that the early Wittgenstein thinks logic provides. (See p. 500.) The enormous difference, of course, is that Wittgenstein's scaffolding supports only sheer meaningless facts—what Heidegger would call the present-at-hand—whereas the worldhood of the world is rich in functionality, usefulness, meaning. But it is interesting to note a correspondence between Heidegger's claim that the phenomenon of the world is usually "too close" to us to be observed and the *Tractatus* claim that this logical structure "cannot be said," but must be "shown."

one, but because the answer seems so straightforward. If Dasein is in each case "mine," then it would seem that, in my case anyway, the answer would be *I myself*, this *person* named Norman Melchert, this *individual*, this *self* or *subject*; I am who Dasein is in this case. And each of you should be able to answer in the same way. What could be more obvious?

But Heidegger thinks this easy and familiar answer, just like our ordinary opinion about what entities constitute the world, covers up or disguises the ontological reality. To talk of self or subject is to fall prey to the temptation to suppose that I am a *thing*, a kind of "soul substance" (perhaps in the way Descartes thinks). But the *Being* of Dasein in its everydayness is not lighted up by this kind of answer; rather, it is hidden.* This question is then in order: Who is Dasein as it exists in its averageness? The answer Heidegger gives to this question is extraordinary.

> It could be that the "who" of everyday Dasein just is *not* the "I myself" (*BT*, 150).

Heidegger's phenomenological answer to the question about the "who" of Dasein in everydayness is *das Man*. This phrase is based on an ordinary German term that occurs in contexts like "Man sagt," which can be rendered as "One says," or "It is said that," or perhaps as "They say." While in the detergent aisle of the supermarket one day, I heard one woman say to another, "I think I'll try this; they say that's good." You might ask, Who is this "they"? If

you had put this question to her, she probably wouldn't have been able to tell you.*

So Heidegger finds that Dasein in its average everydayness is this "They" or "the One."† But what does that mean? We have already seen that Others are "given" along with the ready-to-hand (e.g., with this shirt, which was cut and sewn in a factory somewhere). And if our account is to be phenomenologically adequate, it must record the fact that Others are encountered as themselves Being-in-the-world. The Others, too, *exist* with that same concernful Being-in-the-world as I do.

Moreover, the existence of Others like me is not something that has to come as the conclusion of an argument, as the old problem of "other minds" suggests. I do not first start with *myself* and then conclude on the basis of similarity between observable aspects of myself and Others that they must be persons, too.‡ That would not be an accurate description of my experience of Others.

> By 'Others' we do not mean everyone else but me— those over against whom the "I" stands out. They are rather those from whom, for the most part, one does *not* distinguish oneself—those among whom one is too. . . . The world of Dasein is a *with-world*. Being-in is *Being-with* Others. Their Being-in-themselves within-the-world is *Dasein-with* (*BT*, 154–55).

Being-with is, like Being-in-the-world, an *existential*—one of the characteristics that defines Da-

---

*Hume rejects the "soul substance" of Descartes (pp. 351–354), as does Hobbes in a quite different way (p. 330). And we can interpret Kant and Hegel as denying that a person is an object; a person, they would say, is subject! (See pp. 383 and 416.) But Heidegger thinks that nonetheless—and despite Kant's explicit denial—they all are implicitly using the category of *substance* to characterize the subject; in doing so, they assimilate the Being of Dasein to that of the present-at-hand, and they one and all miss the ontological character of Dasein's Being—its *existence*. Heidegger agrees with Kierkegaard in thinking of the Self as a *task*, not something *given*. That is part of what it means that Dasein's own Being is an *issue* for it; how it is to be constituted is a matter for *decision*. See pp. 436 and 440.

*The translators of *Being and Time* render "das Man" as "the They." Hubert Dreyfus argues in an unpublished commentary that it is much better to bring it into English as "the One" (*Being-in-the-World: A Commentary on Heidegger's Being and Time, Division I*, June 1988). I will sometimes use one locution, sometimes the other.
†Dreyfus argues convincingly that Heidegger does not always distinguish clearly two facets of his own account of "the One": a positive function Dreyfus calls "conformity" or "Falling-in-with," and a negative function he calls "conformism" or "Falling-away-from." The latter, but not the former, correlates with Dasein in the mode of *inauthentic existence*. We will try to keep these aspects distinct.
‡To proceed in this way would be to assume that I *first* have an ontologically adequate grasp of myself and *thereafter* extend this understanding to others. But that is just the (very Cartesian) assumption that Heidegger says we cannot make.

sein's Being. This means that Dasein could not exist without Others, any more than it could exist without the world. It is part of Dasein's very *Being* to be with-Others-in-the-world. This is true even when Dasein is alone or neglects the Others or is indifferent to them. The anchorite in the cave is *with* Others, if only in the mode of seeking to avoid them. The anchorite carries the Others with her into the cave in her ability to speak a language, to think, to meditate in the way she does; this "carrying with" is what it means to say that Being-with is an *existential*.

The discovery of Being-with is an important step. But it does not yet get us clearly to the "who" of Dasein. There is a clue, however, in the phrase, "those from whom . . . one does *not* distinguish oneself." We could paradoxically put it this way: One is, oneself, one of the Others. In fact, Heidegger tells us, we are so much one of the "they" that we are constantly concerned lest we differ too much from them.

> In one's concern with what one has taken hold of, whether with, for, or against, the Others, there is constant care as to the way one differs from them, whether that difference is merely one that is to be evened out, whether one's own Dasein has lagged behind the Others and wants to catch up in relation to them, or whether one's Dasein already has some priority over them and sets out to keep them suppressed. The care about the distance between them is disturbing to Being-with-one-another, though this disturbance is one that is hidden from it (*BT*, 163–64).

We can think of this as the existential foundation for the familiar phenomenon of "keeping up with the Joneses." Heidegger calls it *distantiality* (still another of those invented words!); he uses this term to signify the constant concern of Dasein that it might get too far away from the norm—from what "they say" or what "one does." (Compare: "One just doesn't *do* that!") One doesn't want too large a "distance" to open up between oneself and the Others.

Heidegger suggests that this phenomenon is "hidden" from Dasein. And, indeed, I think that is

so. When I have suggested to young people that an enormous part of their lives is governed by norms they participate in but are hardly aware of, I usually get a lot of resistance. They all want to think of themselves as unique, self-made individuals! But we all hold our forks the same way, a way different from that of the English; and we all stand roughly the same distance from another person when we converse with them, a distance farther away than Latin Americans stand. If you spell "existence" as "existance," I correct you. And these examples could be multiplied indefinitely. We do as *they* do. When someone strays, they are brought back in line, usually so gently that it is scarcely noticed, but forcefully if necessary. Sociologists tell us that this establishment and enforcement of norms is one of the principal functions of gossip.

> . . . this distantiality which belongs to Being-with, is such that Dasein, as everyday Being-with-one-another, stands in *subjection* to Others. It itself *is* not; its Being has been taken away by the Others. Dasein's everyday possibilities of Being are for the Others to dispose of as they please. These Others, moreover, are not *definite* Others. On the contrary, any Other can represent them. What is decisive is just that inconspicuous domination by Others which has already been taken over unawares from Dasein as Being-with. One belongs to the Others oneself and enhances their power. . . . The "who" is not this one, not that one, not oneself, not some people, and not the sum of them all. The 'who' is the neuter, *the "they"* [the One]. . . .
>
> We take pleasure and enjoy ourselves as *they* take pleasure; we read, see, and judge about literature and art as *they* see and judge; likewise we shrink back from the 'great mass' as *they* shrink back; we find 'shocking' what *they* find shocking. The "they" [the One], which is nothing definite, and which all are, though not as the sum, prescribes the kind of Being of everydayness (*BT*, 164).

Let's take one of these "they" phenomena from everydayness and examine it: consider the "proper" distance to stand from someone you are talking with. Social scientists will tell you that there is a "norm" here based on your cultural background.

You almost certainly behave according to your cultural norm, and you are uncomfortable if it is violated. Is this something you *decided*? Certainly not. What is its ground, its reason, its justification—its *logos*? There really doesn't seem to be any. Is there a Platonic Form governing this matter? No. Is it "natural"? No, though it feels natural to us, just as other distances feel natural to people of other cultures. Where does it come from, this "naturalness"—this "rightness," even—that we are uncomfortable violating? Can there be any other answer than "that is what we do?* This is how it is done, how *One* does it. That is all the foundation it has!

Along with *distantiality*, the phenomenon of *averageness* is an existential characteristic of the One. And this involves a kind of *leveling down*, in which every kind of uniqueness, oddness, or priority is smoothed out as much as possible. We noted the *public* character of the world as manifest in ready-to-hand items. Now we see that the world is a common, public world in another sense, too. The "way things are done" is set by the One, not by each Dasein privately for itself. The world of the One is a *public* world from the start. It is into that world, moreover, that Dasein comes from the very beginning; it is the One that shapes it and makes Dasein's "who" what it is. We are all *das Man*. In a striking phrase, Heidegger puts it this way:

> Everyone is the other, and no one is himself (*BT*, 165).

The public character of the world of the One—the world of everyday Dasein (our world)—has an interesting consequence.

> . . . it deprives the particular Dasein of its answerability. The "they" . . . can be answerable for everything most easily, because it is not someone who needs to vouch for anything. It 'was' always the "they" who did it, and yet it can be said that it has been 'no one' . . . .
>
> Thus the particular Dasein in its everydayness is *disburdened* by the "they" (*BT*, 165).

---

*Compare the later Wittgenstein, pp. 527, 529, and 532.

Who is responsible for the way everyday life goes? No one. It is just the way One does it. Dasein conforms to this *way of Being*; Dasein *Falls-in-with-it*. Notice that this is not—so far—something for which Dasein is to *blame*; distantiality and averageness are *existentials*; that is, they are aspects of the very *essence* of Dasein's existence. It couldn't be otherwise for Dasein. And isn't this fortunate? To have to bear the burden of responsibility for the whole of the way one lives would be too much; the "they" is there to help out. In its average everydayness, Dasein does not feel this burden because

> the "*they*", which supplies the answer to the question of the "*who*" of everyday Dasein, is the "*nobody*" to whom every Dasein has already surrendered itself in Being-among-one-another (*BT*, 165–66).

It is important to note that Heidegger distinguishes three modes in which Dasein can relate itself to itself: **inauthenticity**, **authenticity**, and an undifferentiated mode, which is neither. We have so far been trying to describe the undifferentiated mode of Dasein's existence, though the eagerness with which Dasein accepts the "disburdening" is a hint of what inauthenticity amounts to. As a being for whom its own Being is always at issue, Dasein is always facing the *decision* between existing inauthentically or authentically; it in fact always exists predominantly in one mode or the other. We will explore these modes more fully, but we can now say that authentic existence is not a grasping of some nature or essence of oneself quite different from the "they-self"; it is, rather, a matter of coming to terms with the fact that this is what one is and that one is *no more than this*. And inauthentic existence is a way of hiding this truth from oneself. Existing as "the One" is not yet inauthentic. But "the One" constantly presents to Dasein the possibility of evading the disquieting aspects of *having to Be the being that it is* by fleeing into the security of what "they say." Thus the One is both a constitutive factor in Dasein and a temptation to inauthenticity.

For now, though, we can see that the answer to the question about the "who" of Dasein is this: in its average everydayness, Dasein exists in the mode of "the One." Dasein (you and I in our way of existing) belongs to "the They."

Modes of Disclosure

What makes Dasein seem a promising entity to analyze, given that the meaning of Being is our quarry, is the fact that Dasein's own Being is an issue for it. That means that Dasein has an understanding of its own Being, though it is not explicitly worked out. But what sort of understanding is this? In what ways is Dasein already *always* disclosed to itself? Think of a dense and dark forest, and in the midst of it imagine a clearing. The clearing opens up a space within which flowers and trees can appear; in fact, it is the clearing that is the condition for anything at all being visible. And now, with this analogy in mind, let us ask, Is there such a clearing in the *world*? Does Dasein exist in such a clearing? Not exactly, Heidegger answers. Rather, he wants to say, Dasein *is* such a clearing.*

> . . . *as* Being-in-the-world it is cleared in itself, not through any other entity, but in such a way that it *is* itself the clearing. . . . Dasein brings its "there" along with it. If it lacks its "there", it is not factically the entity which is essentially Dasein; indeed, it is not this entity at all. *Dasein is its disclosedness* (BT, 171).

A human being that was not in itself this kind of openness to beings and to Being would not yet be a Dasein; such a human would, perhaps, be a corpse. In any case, it would not be "there." Disclosedness is part of the existential constitution of

Dasein. And that is what we now have to bring more clearly to light.

Heidegger discusses this "thereness" of Dasein under three headings: **attunement**, understanding, and discourse.* These are very rich pages in *Being and Time*, and we must be content with omitting much. But it is essential to grasp something of these modes of disclosure.

Attunement

We are sometimes asked, "How are you doing?" The surprising thing is that we can always answer. And in answering, we report our *mood*. We say, "Fine," or "Awful—I think I failed the calculus exam." Heidegger holds that moods don't *just happen*; they are not just meaningless present-at-hand items we undergo, the way our heart sometimes beats faster and sometimes slower. Moods are *cognitive*. They are disclosive. But what do they disclose? They reveal how we are coping with this business of having to exist, i.e., how we are bearing the burden of having to be here. Dasein is "attuned" to its own Being.

Moreover, moods are not experienced as private states or feelings, independent of the world out there. Suppose you are in a bad mood, that (as we say) you got out of bed on the wrong side this morning. Where, phenomenologically speaking, does this mood reveal itself? In your head, while the world goes on its sunny way? Not at all. *Nothing*, you are likely to say, is going right. *Everything* seems to be against you. Your *world* is dark. And why should it not be so, if your Being is indeed Being-in-the-world? Moods are pervasive, coloring everything. Suppose you have been watching a horror movie on a video all alone, late at night.

---

*The German word here translated as "clearing" is "Lichtung." It is important that the word comes from the word for *light*—"Licht." Dasein is in itself the "light of nature" (Descartes, *Meditation III*), the condition for uncovering the truth. Compare also Augustine on the interior illumination of the soul (p. 222) and Plato on the image of the Sun (p. 120). What Augustine attributes to the Interior Teacher (Christ) and Plato to the Form of the Good, Heidegger takes to be the very essence of Dasein itself—that it is *there*.

*The term I am bringing into English as "attunement" (following Dreyfus) is *Befindlichkeit*. There is no very good equivalent; the translators of *Being and Time* translate it as "state-of-mind." But that plays right into the hands of Heidegger's opponents in the conversation who interpret the modes of disclosure as "states" belonging to a present-at-hand entity—e.g., as properties of something like Descartes' mind-substance. It is such "subjectivism" that Heidegger is combating through and through.

Thereafter, every creak in the house, every hoot of an owl, and every gust of wind in the trees takes on an ominous quality. You anxiously check the locks and make sure the windows are closed. The *world* is now a scary place! How are you now bearing the burden of having to be there? Not very well.

Dasein never exists without a mood. Even the flat, calm, easygoing character of an average day is a mood. Dasein *is*, remember, its disclosedness. In revealing its "thereness," Dasein's mood discloses how Dasein is attuned to its world. In this disclosure is revealed a further aspect of Dasein's Being: **thrownness**. We find ourselves "thrown" into our Being-in-the-world in the following sense. None of us chose to be born. Nor did we decide to be born in the twentieth century, rather than the thirteenth. Nor were we consulted about whether we would be American or Chinese or Mexican. Nor if we preferred being male or female. Nor black nor white nor any other color. Nor to be born to just *these* parents in just *that* town with just *those* relatives and neighbors, with a certain very specific kind of housing., transportation, and tools at hand. (Lucy says to Snoopy: "You've been a dog all your life, haven't you? I've often wondered what made you decide to become a dog." Snoopy, lying on his doghouse roof, replies, "I was fooled by the job description." But that is a joke, isn't it? It *belongs* in the comics!) We just *find ourselves* in existence—in a world of a particular sort, having one language rather than another and one characteristic way of looking at things rather than another. We are, as Heidegger says, "delivered over" to our "there," to our world (*BT*, 174).

We could put this idea in another way: *Who* we are is a very particular sort of *One*; there is no help for it, for we are "thrown" into one "they" rather than another. Even if we eventually reject certain features of this One, as characteristically happens when human beings mature, we do so drawing on the resources available in *this* world; we cannot make use, for instance, of the psychological and technological discoveries of the twenty-third century. We are *thrown* into the world.

This throwness is a fact. It is a fact about our Being. So it is an *ontological* fact. Heidegger uses

two words for facts. Ordinary facts (that the kiwi is a bird native to New Zealand, for instance, or that this book is written in English, or that I am five feet, ten inches tall) he calls *factual*. Facts about things present-at-hand, for instance, are factual. Ontological facts about Dasein, facts about us not as beings, but about our Being (or *way* of Being), he calls *factical*. Our being a "clearing," for instance, is factical; our Being-in-the-world is factical; our throwness is part of our **facticity**. In attempting a "fundamental ontology" of Dasein, then, Heidegger is investigating its facticity: the facts about its Being. The facticity of our being thrown is one of the things that moods reveal.

A phenomenologist could go through mood after mood and display the character of each as revealing an aspect of Dasein's Being. But Heidegger focuses on one mood in particular, which he thinks has far-reaching implications. Let us sketch his analysis of *anxiety*.

Like all moods, anxiety is cognitively significant; that is, it discloses something. Anxiety is rather like fear; but it would be a big mistake to confuse them. Fear discloses the fearful: some particular threat to a future possibility of Dasein. Anxiety, by contrast, reveals a very general feature of Dasein's Being. Anxiety is not directed to a particular entity in the world that threatens (the charging bull, the assassin relentlessly hunting one down) but to something more fundamental and far-reaching.

> . . . *that in the face of which one has anxiety is Being-in-the-world as such* (*BT*, 230).

What is Being-in-the-world? We already know; it is the most basic existential characteristic of Dasein. So what Dasein is anxious-in-the-face-of is *itself*! Heidegger is suggesting that anxiety reveals in a peculiarly conspicuous way Dasein's having-to-Be. Ordinarily, average Dasein goes along "absorbed" in the world of its concern, engaged in projects that seem unquestionably to have a point and meaning. But if we remember that the self of everyday Dasein is *the One*, we can see that these projects are those set down by the public world;

they have their meaning dictated by the "they." And normally Dasein does not notice this. In its average everydayness, Dasein is delivered over to Being-in-the-public-world-of-already-assigned-significances. Dasein has "fallen-in" with the world of what "One says," what "One does and doesn't do."*

Anxiety, Heidegger suggests, is unique among moods because it is a disclosure of that world *as such.* Unlike fear, in which some entity *within the world* is apprehended as possibly detrimental, the "object" of anxiety is no *thing.* If a person suffering from anxiety is asked what he is afraid of, he replies, "Nothing." And that, Heidegger says, is exactly right; nothing *in the world* is the object of this mood. Rather, that whole system of assignments and references that makes up the worldhood of the world, becomes present and *stands over against one.* No longer caught up in it, Dasein beholds it as something alien to itself. Dasein catches sight of itself as Being-engaged in this now alien world of the One. And it shudders.

> In anxiety what is environmentally ready-to-hand sinks away, and so, in general, do entities within-the-world. The 'world' can offer nothing more, and neither can the Dasein-with of Others. Anxiety thus takes away from Dasein the possibility of understanding itself, as it falls, in terms of the 'world' and the way things have been publicly interpreted. Anxiety throws Dasein back upon that which it is anxious about—its authentic potentiality-for-Being-in-the-world. Anxiety individualizes Dasein. . . .
>
> Anxiety makes manifest in Dasein its *Being towards* its ownmost potentiality-for-Being—that is, its *Being-free* for the freedom of choosing itself and taking hold of itself (*BT*, 232).

The meaningfulness of the world, together with that of all the projects that Dasein has heretofore cared about, slips away. The world doesn't exactly become meaningless; it is still *the world* (i.e., a set of in-order-to's). But in anxiety one is detached from it; it means nothing to the particular Dasein

that is gripped by anxiety. One can still see others going through the motions, but it seems absurd.* Anxiety distances us from our ordinary everyday *Being-in.* It makes clear that how I am to be is a matter of *choice*—that the responsibility lies squarely with *me.* As Heidegger says, anxiety "individualizes." It separates us out from the One.

Wrenched out of the familiar "falling-in" with the way of the world, Dasein experiences itself as *not-at-home-in-the-world.* Yet, it is essentially nothing but Being-in-the-world! Dasein has no other reality; it cannot repair to its own "substance" or enjoy its own "essence" apart from the world. "Just be *yourself*," we are often advised. But, if Heidegger is right, there is no one for us to be apart from the world of the One! In anxiety, then, Dasein is made aware of that fact, but in the mode of not being at home in it. There is no home but that home, yet, anxiously, we are homeless.†

On the one hand, anxiety reveals with penetrating clarity the nature of Dasein's Being. But on the other hand, it provides a powerful motivation for Dasein to hide itself from itself—to flee back into the comfortable, familiar, well-ordered, meaningful world of the One, to avoid the risky business of taking up responsibility for one's own Being. That is why Heidegger says that Dasein is anxious about its "authentic potentiality-for-Being-in-the-world." Anxiety presents Dasein with the clear choice between existing authentically or inauthentically. The temptation is to flee back into the world, to be reabsorbed in it, to shut one's eyes to the fact that a *decision* about one's way of life is called for. The

---

*It is important to remember that this feature is an *existential*; it is not something Dasein could be without .So it is not something to *blame* Dasein for or to *regret.*

---

*This is a word that I don't believe Heidegger uses in this context. But it plays a large role in the thought of French existentialist thinkers, such as Sartre and Camus. See, for instance, Sartre's novel *Nausea* and Camus' *The Myth of Sisyphus* and *The Stranger.* Heidegger does not like Sartre's version of existentialism; it essentially preserves rather than overcomes Cartesian dualism, he maintains. But the Heideggerian influence in these thinkers is strong.

†The German word here is "Unheimlichkeit," literally "not-at-homeness." The translators of *Being and Time* bring it into English as "uncanniness." It is perhaps this same sense of homelessness that Augustine has in mind when he prays, "Our hearts find no peace until they rest in you" (p. 237). Unlike Augustine, Heidegger cannot believe that there is a home for us *beyond* the world.

temptation is to think that our lives are as anteced-ently well ordered as the career of a hammer—that the meaning of life is *given* and doesn't have to be *forged*. To flee back into the pre-decided life of the One would "disburden" Dasein and quiet anxiety. But such fleeing on the part of Dasein would be "falling-away-from" itself, the *inauthentic* kind of **falling**.* Falling-away from oneself is the same as falling-prey-to the One. So Dasein "tranquilizes" itself in the familiar world of significance, fleeing *away from* its thrownness and its not-at-homeness *into* the world of the One; thus it disguises from itself its true Being (that its Being is an *issue*). For in the world of the One, all crucial decisions are al-ready made, dictated by the norms of what One does and doesn't do. The possiblities open to Da-sein are already "disposed of" beforehand. One's life is *settled*. And anxiety is covered up.

Moods, then, are cognitively significant; they al-ways tell us something about ourselves and, in par-ticular, about our Being. Among the moods, anx-iety most clearly reveals the Being of Dasein—that it is thrown-Being-in-the-world-of-the-One. And in doing so, it both distances Dasein from that Be-ing and provides a motivation for falling back into that world in an inauthentic way.

Understanding

In one way or another, Dasein is always "attuned" to its world. But every attunement carries with it an understanding of that world (and every under-standing has its mood); understanding, Heidegger says, is *equiprimordial* with attunement (meaning that they come together and that neither can be

derived from the other). We have already met "un-derstanding," of course. Dasein from the beginning has been held to be that being who—simply by virtue of Being—has an understanding of its Be-ing. To be "there," in fact, *is* to understand. But this is hard to—understand. Let us see if we can do so.

We can begin in a very familiar way by examin-ing what we mean when we say that John under-stands carburetors. We mean that he is competent with respect to carburetors, that he can adjust, tune, and probably repair them. It need not be that John could write a book about carburetors; per-haps he couldn't. But if you are having carburetor troubles, John is the man for you. He really *under-stands* carburetors! Now it is crucial to note that *possibility* or *potentiality* is involved in this kind of understanding. John can do more than just de-scribe the current present-at-hand state of your carburetor; he can see *what's wrong* with it. And this means that he has in view a potential state of the device that is different from its current state: a possibility that it might function properly. And he has the *know-how* to produce that state. John's un-derstanding is a matter of being able to bring it from a condition of not working well to one of sat-isfactory performance, a possibility not now realized.

This notion of possibility is also involved in the existential understanding that belongs to Dasein. For what does Dasein essentially understand? It-self, in its own Being. Suppose someone (God, maybe) had a list of everything factually true of you at this moment: every hair on your head, the state of every neuron in your brain, and every thought and feeling. Would this list tell us who you are? It would not. It would not even if it was extended to list every fact about you since you were born. Why not? Because you, as a case of Dasein, are not some-thing present-at-hand, a mere collection of facts; you are essentially *what you can be*. You are a certain "potentiality-for-Being," to use Heidegger's tor-tuous language. Unless I understand your *possi-bilities*, I will not understand you.

. . . Dasein is constantly 'more' than it factually is, supposing that one might want to make an inventory

---

*Remember that there are two kinds of "falling": *falling-in-with* is one of the essential characteristics of Dasein, an *existential*. Dasein's "who" is invariably and inevitably the *One*. The second kind of falling, *falling-away-from*, is Dasein's fleeing from the anxious real-ization of its own essential homelessness into the illusory security that the life of the One seems to offer. Such fleeing is the mark of *inauthentic* existence, of not appropriating the Being that is *one's own*. Heidegger does not always distinguish the two kinds of falling as clearly as one might wish, though there is plenty of support in the text for the distinction.

of it as something-at-hand and list the contents of its Being, . . . But Dasein is never more than it factically is, for to its facticity its potentiality-for-Being belongs essentially (*BT*, 185).

But now let's shift the perspective. Rather than thinking of what would be required for a third party to understand you, think about what is needed for you to understand yourself. Here is the somewhat startling answer: Nothing—beyond your Being-there. To exist *is* to understand.* Understanding (as an *existential*) is having competence over one's Being; that is not something added on "by way of an extra" (*BT*, 183). That is what it is to exist. And this understanding is an understanding of possibility. Right now, at this very moment, you *are*, a certain understanding of your possibilities (e.g., the possibility of continuing to read this chapter, of underlining this phrase, of going to the refrigerator for a cold drink, of calling a friend, of becoming an engineer or accountant, perhaps of dropping out of school and bumming around the world). You exist these potentialities in your every thought and movement. And this understanding, which you *are*, is not something that you need to conceptualize or explicitly think about. It just is a certain *competence* with respect to your Being that you cannot help manifesting.

How is it that understanding is a basic part of Dasein, not something added to it? Understanding has the structure of *projection*. We are always projecting ourselves into possibilities. Again, we must be careful not to think of this as a matter of reflecting on possibilities, of reviewing or deliberating, or of having them "in mind." It is more primordial than that. To understand a chair, for instance, is to be prepared to sit in it rather than wear it. To understand oneself as a student is to *project* oneself into potentially mastering Chinese or statistics or into the possibility of being a college graduate. Understanding oneself as a student *permeates* one's

---

*This is quite compatible, of course, with your *misunderstanding* yourself; a misunderstanding is a kind of understanding. This is why inauthentic existence is one of your possibilities.

Being. To exist in a specific situation *is* to have an understanding (or a misunderstanding) of the promise or menace of what is impending. Understanding in this fundamental sense is a matter of our *Being*. It is an aspect of what it means to *exist*. Since we are what we *can be*, possibility is even more fundamental to our Being than the actuality of the facts about us. And these possibilities are not something external to our Being. They are possibilities that we *are*.

This understanding, as a kind of competence with respect to the potentialities of our Being, is always there; just because it is always there, however, it tends to be tacit. But it can be developed more explicitly; it then takes the form of *interpretation*. Interpretation is not something different from understanding; it is understanding itself come to fruition. Consider the light switch in your room, something you understand very well in one sense; you operate with it in such a familiar way that you scarcely notice it; you probably couldn't tell me what its color is. But suppose one day it fails to function. Now its "place" in the functional ordering of the world is disturbed; you had all along been taking its role as equipment for granted— i.e., understanding it implicitly. But now it comes to the fore, and you understand it explicitly—as a device to transmit electricity. This "as" structure is already implicit in your everyday and familiar understanding. But now it is expressed; it becomes explicit in an *interpretation*. Interpretation always lays bare "the structure of *something as something*" (*BT*, 189).

The fact that interpretation (whether of a device, a text, the meaning of someone's action, etc.) is always founded on a prior understanding has an important implication for Heidegger. There is no way we can disengage ourselves from our Being-in-the-world sufficiently to guarantee a completely "objective" view of something. Every interpretation *always* inevitably takes something for granted; it is worked out on some background that is not itself available for inspection and decision. That does not mean that truth is unavailable to Dasein. But it does mean that Dasein is involved in a kind of circle it cannot get out of.* Interpreting is understanding x *as* y—e.g., the switch *as* a device for controlling the flow of electricity. But interpretation just makes explicit that prior understanding of it *as* a switch in the first place. That understanding is a matter of having a certain competence with respect to it. Such competent understanding is a matter of (largely unreflective) projection, of ways of behaving toward what *could be*. And all this exists only on the background of our Being-in-the-world in general, which involves understanding the potentialities of such equipment as light switches.

This circle is usually called **the hermeneutic circle**; all interpretation is caught up in what is understood beforehand. It is not a vicious circle, Heidegger maintains.[†] But it is one that should be recognized.

> If the basic conditions which make interpretation possible are to be fulfilled, this must . . . be done by not failing to recognize beforehand the essential conditions under which it can be performed. What is decisive is not to get out of the circle, but to come into it in the right way (*BT*, 194–95).

---

*It is interesting to compare this point with the pragmatist claim that we must give up the quest for certainty. See Peirce's triangle example on p. 467 and the summary of Dewey's view of experience, pp. 479–480. Heidegger is here combating the desire of Descartes to find an Archimedean point from which to view the world; there is, Heidegger claims, no "view from nowhere." We can also think of it as an argument against Hume's motto (taken from Newton) to frame no hypotheses (see pp. 340–342). If framing hypotheses is a matter of bringing a certain understanding *to* a situation, then we cannot help framing hypotheses—just as Kant thinks there is no getting around the *a priori* structures that make knowledge possible. There is some justice in viewing the history of modern philosophy as a conversation between the rationalists, the empiricists, and the pragmatists. In this (oversimplified) schema, Heidegger would line up with the pragmatists.

†Note that Heidegger grants one of the fundamental claims of the skeptic: The structure of our knowledge does involve a circle. He thinks this isn't damaging because Dasein, as he conceives it, does not have to *break* into the clearing (e.g., by means of some *criterion*); Dasein is already the clearing, the revealing of Being. This doesn't mean, of course, that Dasein always knows the truth for the One and individual Dasein can conspire to cover it up. For the relevance of this circle to skeptical claims, see the discussion of Sextus Empiricus, p. 196. This same problem comes up in Plato and Aristotle. See pp. 127–128, and 152.

"The right way" is to come without illusions (i.e., without imagining that one can get a kind of "bare" look at the object of interpretation) and to be as clear and explicit as possible about what one is bringing to the interpretive task. Part of Heidegger's conviction is that this background can never be made *completely* explicit.* For it is this background that Dasein *is*.

Let us summarize. Understanding, like attunement, is an *existential*. There is no Being-there that does not involve understanding. The primordial mode of understanding is a kind of know-how or competence with respect to things, particularly with respect to Dasein's own Being. This is largely implicit, but it can be spelled out in an interpretation. It is such an interpretation that Heidegger is striving to construct with respect to the meaning of Dasein's Being and ultimately for the meaning of Being in general.

Discourse

Because the world of Dasein is a world of significations (in-order-to's, toward-which's, and for-the-sake-of's, to put it in Heideggerese), Dasein exists in an *articulated* world; like a turkey, it has "joints" at which it may be carved. The hammer is distinct from the nails but is *for* pounding them into the boards, which are a third articulated item. In understanding how to use a hammer, Dasein displays a primordial understanding of this articulation. As we have seen, this primitive kind of understanding can be made explicit in interpretation. And now we must add that interpretation itself is a phenomenon *in-the-world* only in terms of *discourse*.

---

*Hubert Dreyfus is the most notable (though not the only) person to apply this point to artificial intelligence. It shows, he believes, that the work in traditional artificial intelligence was bound to fail because it was based on the assumption that all the rules by which an intelligent system operates could be made explicit and operate on items that are context-free (i.e., not in-a-world). If Heidegger is right, this is not true of us and is very likely not true for any system that has more than strictly limited capabilities. You might look at Dreyfus' book, *What Computers Can't Do* (New York: Harper and Row, 1972) and the book he wrote with his brother Stuart (a computer engineer), *Mind over Machine* (New York: Macmillan Co., The Free Press, 1985).

Discourse, Heidegger says, is equiprimordial with attunement and understanding. (Again, this means that while it cannot be reduced to either of them, it is equally basic.) Discourse, too, is an *existential*. It is an essential characteristic of Dasein. There is no Dasein that doesn't *talk*.* In talk, or discourse, the articulations of the world of Dasein are expressed in *language*. Moreover, we talk *with one another*, so discourse essentially involves Being-*with*. Discourse involves communication.

> Discoursing or talking is the way in which we articulate 'significantly' the intelligibility of Being-in-the-world. Being-with belongs to Being-in-the-world, which in every case maintains itself in some definite way of concernful Being-with-one-another. Such Being-with-one-another is discursive as assenting or refusing, as demanding or warning, as pronouncing, consulting, or interceding, as 'making assertions', and as talking in the way of 'giving a talk' (*BT*, 204).†

Again, Heidegger warns against a misunderstanding.

> Communication is never anything like a conveying of experiences, such as opinions or wishes, from the interior of one subject into the interior of another. Dasein-with is already essentially manifest in a co-state-of-mind [co-attunement] and a co-understanding. In discourse Being-with becomes 'explicitly' *shared*; that is to say, it *is* already, but it is unshared as something that has not been taken hold of and appropriated (*BT*, 205).

This remark should be understood as part of Heidegger's continuing polemic against the Cartesian picture of the isolated subject shut up within the walls of the mind and forced to find some way to "convey" a message across an empty space to another such subject. As Being-with, we already live in a common world with others—the public world of equipment and its structural articulation. In discourse we "take hold" of this common legacy and express it in language.

Falling-Away

With the analysis of the modes of disclosure, the general shape of Heidegger's fundamental ontology is coming into view. Dasein is

- Being-in-the-world
- Being-with-others
- Falling-in-with the One
- Thrown
- A Clearing, manifesting itself in attunement, understanding, and discourse

We also know that Dasein has the potentiality for existing in either an authentic or an inauthentic fashion. We need to understand these alternatives more clearly. Let us begin by discussing inauthenticity.

Dasein *is* Being-in-the-world and as such "falls-in-with" the "others" who constitute "the One." Dasein has no secret, private essence *out of which* it could fall; nor is Dasein initially "innocent," later falling into sin. As long as we are talking about the first kind of falling—falling-in-with—questions of innocence or guilt are not yet in order. This kind of falling is a constitutive, ontological characteristic of what it is to be Dasein.*

In discussing anxiety, we noted that Dasein is tempted to flee its anxious homelessness and *lose*

---

*What about newborn babies, you ask? The answer seems to be that while they are clearly human, they are not a case of Dasein. They are not (yet) *there* in that way characteristic of Dasein. As they are socialized, Dasein slowly dawns in them.

†Compare what Wittgenstein says about the ways we use language (p. 520). Heidegger, like the later Wittgenstein, is convinced that philosophy has often been led astray by supposing that *assertion* has first place in discourse.

*Despite Heidegger's protestations, some theologians suggest that we might have here the basis for an interpretation of what the Christian tradition has called "original sin." If there is no "pure" essence of Dasein to be corrupted in the first place, and if—as we will shortly see—the One which becomes the "who" of Dasein is itself inauthentic, how could Dasein *not* be "conceived and born in sin"? Rudolph Bultmann and Paul Tillich are among the theologians who have been strongly influenced by Heidegger. For Augustine on original sin, see p. 230.

itself in the tranquilizing security of the public world. But Heidegger now wants to go a step farther and claim that simply Being-in-the-world is itself *tempting*. For the world is, after all, the world of the One. And to understand why this might by its very nature tempt Dasein toward inauthenticity, we need to understand the modes of disclosure characteristic of the One. How does *One* understand? How are "they" attuned to their Being? What sort of discourse is Dasein thrown into as it takes up its Being-in-the-world?

Idle Talk

As we have seen, the Being of discourse consists in an expression in language of the articulations making up the world. Discourse is essentially revealing, disclosing. It opens up the world. But in average everydayness, discourse tends toward being just idle talk.

> We do not so much understand the entities which are talked about; we already are listening only to what is said-in-the-talk as such. What is said-in-the-talk gets understood; but what the talk is about is understood only approximately and superficially (*BT*, 212).

This is something you can test for yourself. Listen carefully to the conversations that go on among your acquaintances; see how much of their "everyday" talk is just a matter of latching on to "what-is-said" as such, without any deep commitment to the subject matter being discussed or to the truth about it. How much of it is just chatter? Or an attempt to impose opinions on others? How much is what Wittgenstein calls "just *gassing*"?*

> And because this discoursing has lost its primary relationship-of-Being towards the entity talked about, or else has never achieved such a relationship, it does not communicate in such a way as to let this entity be appropriated in a primordial manner, but communicates rather by following the route of *gossiping* and *passing the word along*. What is said-in-the-talk

as such, spreads in wider circles and takes on an authoritative character. Things are so because one says so.

> The groundlessness of idle talk is no obstacle to its becoming public; instead it encourages this. Idle talk is the possibility of understanding everything without previously making the thing one's own (*BT*, 212–13).

It is into the idle talk of the One that Dasein is thrown, when it is thrown into the world.

> This way in which things have been interpreted in idle talk has already established itself in Dasein. There are many things with which we first become acquainted in this way, and there is not a little which never gets beyond such an average understanding. This everyday way in which things have been interpreted is one into which Dasein has grown in the first instance, with never a possibility of extrication. In it, out of it, and against it, all genuine understanding, interpreting, and communicating, all re-discovering and appropriating anew, are performed (*BT*, 213).

Discourse is an existential; it is one of the essential characteristics of Dasein. Dasein is a talking entity. But when Dasein falls-in-with the others in its world, as it must, it also falls-in with this degenerate form of discourse. Note that there is no possibility of extricating ourselves from idle talk. It is the milieu in which we exist. The best we can do is to struggle against it—from within it—toward "genuine understanding." But as long as we remain inauthentically content with what-is-said, idle talk will cover over the meaning of Being, including the meaning of our own Being. That is why Heidegger can say, "Being-in-the-world is in itself tempting" (*BT*, 221).

Curiosity

Dasein, we have said, is in its very Being a "clearing" in the midst of the world. It is a clearing because *understanding* is an aspect of its essence. But in its average everydayness, understanding, too, tends to become shallow and disconnected from

*See pp. 501, 510, and 524.

Being. As long as we are absorbed in our work, hammering away on the roof, our understanding is engaged in the project. But when we take a rest, understanding idles. And then it becomes *curiosity*. Curiosity is a concern just to see—but not in order to understand what one sees.

> It seeks novelty only in order to leap from it anew to another novelty. In this kind of seeing, that which is an issue for care does not lie in grasping something and being knowingly in the truth; it lies rather in its possibilities of abandoning itself to the world. Therefore curiosity is characterized by a specific way of *not tarrying* alongside what is closest. Consequently it does not seek the leisure of tarrying observantly, but rather seeks restlessness and the excitement of continual novelty and changing encounters. In not tarrying, curiosity is concerned with the constant possibility of *distraction*. Curiosity has nothing to do with observing entities and marvelling at them. . . .* To be amazed to the point of not understanding is something in which it has no interest. Rather it concerns itself with a kind of knowing, but just in order to have known (*BT*, 216–17).

One is reminded of those folks who visit the Grand Canyon primarily, it seems, to be able to bring back slides to show their friends. Curiosity and idle talk, Heidegger says, reinforce each other; "*either* of these ways-to-be drags the other one with it" (*BT*, 217). You can see why this is so. If one never tarries anywhere, one's understanding is bound to be expressed in idle talk about what one has "seen." Together, Heidegger wryly remarks, they are supposed to guarantee a "life" which is genuinely "lively."

Ambiguity

Because of the predominance of idle talk and curiosity, ambiguity pervades Dasein's Being-in-the-world. It

---

*At this point Heidegger makes a reference to Aristotle's remark that all philosophy begins in wonder (p. 158). You should also review the "rotation method" from the first part of Kierkegaard's *Either/Or* (p. 431).

soon becomes impossible to decide what is disclosed in a genuine understanding, and what is not. . . .

> Everything looks as if it were genuinely understood, genuinely taken hold of, genuinely spoken, though at bottom it is not; or else it does not look so, and yet at bottom it is (*BT*, 217).

Genuine understanding of something is, of course, difficult. It takes time, patience, and careful attention. But in a day when the results of the most mathematically sophisticated physics are reported in the daily paper in a way that is supposed to inform the average person, who can tell what is truly understood and what is not? Since understanding is the "light of nature" in which beings and Being are "cleared," and since understanding is essential to the very Being of Dasein, a deadly ambiguity seeps into Dasein's existence.

Dasein, in its average everydayness, is *the One*. But the average everydayness of the One is characterized by idle talk, curiosity, and ambiguity. It follows that Dasein

> has mostly the character of Being-lost in the publicness of the "they". Dasein has, in the first instance, fallen away from itself as an authentic potentiality for Being its Self, and has fallen into the 'world'. "Fallenness" into the 'world' means an absorption in Being-with-one-another, in so far as the latter is guided by idle talk, curiosity, and ambiguity (*BT*, 220).

In falling-in-with the way of the world, Dasein tends to fall-away-from itself. While it is important to keep these two notions distinct, one gets the definite impression that Heidegger believes the first invariably brings the second with it. Dasein falls away from itself by failing to grasp its own Being clearly—with understanding. It understands itself the way "they" understand. It even takes its moods, its way of being attuned, from the One—what matters to Dasein is what "they say" matters. Dasein does not decisively seize itself for itself; it lets itself float, lost in the interpretations of the public "they." It is this not being at one with oneself, not being *one's own*, belonging only to the One, that is the heart of inauthenticity. And we all *are* inauthentic in this way.

This idea is driven home by a further reflection about *thrownness*. To this point we have talked about being "thrown" into the world as if it were an event that happened to us once, at birth. But Heidegger maintains that we are constantly being thrown into the world.

> Thrownness is neither a 'fact that is finished' nor a Fact that is settled. Dasein's facticity is such that *as long as* it is what it is, Dasein remains in the throw, and is sucked into the turbulence of the "they's" inauthenticity (*BT*, 223).

Dasein remains "in the throw" as long as it *is*. We are constantly being thrown into the world, and the world is always the world of the One. This has important implications for what *authentic* existence might be.

> . . . *authentic* existence is not something which floats above falling everydayness; existentially, it is only a modified way in which such everydayness is seized upon (*BT*, 224).

But we will return to that shortly.

Care

Heidegger's interpretation of the ontology of Dasein is rich and complex. We have explored quite a number of the *existentials*, or "categories" that define its way of Being. At this point, Heidegger asks whether this multiplicity of concepts is founded in a deeper unity. He thinks he can indeed point to a unifying ontological concept, in the light of which all the rest make sense.

The simplified, single phenomenon that lies at the root of Dasein's Being, Heidegger tells us, is *Care*. Care is understood as the ontological structure that makes possible Dasein's everyday *concerns* for its projects, its *solicitude* for Others, even its *willing* and *wishing*. In typical Heideggerian fashion, Care is spelled out as

- Being-ahead-of-itself by projecting toward its possibilities, while
- Being-in-the-world, and
- Being engaged with entities encountered within-the-world.

(This kind of talk should now be making some sense to you; go over these phrases carefully, making sure that it is not simply "idle talk" to you.)

It is important to note that Care is not some special "ontic" attitude that Dasein might occasionally display. Care is the *Being* of Dasein: without care, no Being-there. Care is manifest in all understanding, from the intensely practical to the most purely theoretical. It is present in attunement and in all discourse. Dasein is not fundamentally the *rational animal*, not basically the *ego cogito*, not primarily a *knower*. What is most fundamental to Dasein's Being is caring: Dasein is the being for whom things *matter*.* And that brings us right back to the very beginning, where we noted that Dasein is that being for whom its own Being is *an issue*.

Heidegger thinks to support this interpretation of the unity of Dasein's Being by quoting an old Latin fable about the creation of human beings by the gods:

> Once when 'Care' was crossing a river, she saw some clay; she thoughtfully took up a piece and began to shape it. While she was meditating on what she had made, Jupiter came by. 'Care' asked him to give it spirit, and this he gladly granted. But when she wanted her name to be bestowed upon it, he forbade this, and demanded that it be given his name instead. While 'Care' and Jupiter were disputing, Earth arose and desired that her own name be conferred on the creature, since she had furnished it with part of her body. They asked Saturn to be their arbiter, and he made the following decision, which seemed a just one: 'Since you, Jupiter, have given its spirit, you

---

*Some years ago, the rock group Queen recorded a song in which this phrase was repeated: "Nothing really matters." Is this an argument against Heidegger's claim that Care is the essence of Dasein? Not at all. It if were *true* that nothing really mattered, Queen would not bother to sing it in that poignant and nostalgic way they do. They *care* that "nothing matters," thereby proving that something *does* matter.

shall receive that spirit at its death; and since you, Earth, have given its body, you shall receive its body. But since 'Care' first shaped this creature, she shall possess it as long as it lives' (*BT*, 242).

Not long ago, my wife was recovering from a severe case of flu. Sitting on the sofa in the living room and looking about, she said, "I must be alive; I'm beginning to care that the house is a mess." Heidegger would have liked that.

We have in Care, then, a single, unitary, simple foundation for all the complexities we have so far discovered in the Being of Dasein—and for those still to come. But before we fill in the final bits of the picture, we need to pause a moment to think about *truth*.

Truth

According to the Western philosophical tradition, truth belongs to what is said, to assertions or judgments.* The tradition develops this notion into the idea that in true judgments there is a "correspondence" between the assertion and what it is about; in a similar way, St. Thomas talks about an "adequation" of the intellect to reality, and others about an "agreement." Heidegger does not want to claim these views are mistaken, exactly. But he does think they are misleadingly formulated and shallow. The problem is one we have met before in our analysis of everydayness: the items involved (assertion and object) are conceived by the tradition in terms of items present-at-hand, when this is not their mode of Being at all.

To mistake their mode of Being makes for insoluble problems; what, after all, *is* it for the assertion "Corn grows in the Midwest" to *agree* with fields of corn in Iowa? As marks on this page, that sentence doesn't seem related at all to what grows around Iowa City. So the tradition feels compelled to *supplement* that present-at-hand item with some mental state (an idea, a concept, an intention, a signifi-

*See Aristotle's incomparable definition of truth, p. 147.

cant content). But this presents three further problems: (1) Such states are also conceived as something present-at-hand; they just have a different "locus" (in the subject). But is that really their mode of Being? (2) How is the *mental state* related to the *marks on the page?* and (3) Doesn't the same question arise with regard to those mental states: What is it for *them* to "agree" with reality?

In addition, we always have this nagging problem: How could we ever *tell* if our judgments correspond to their objects?*

What is needed, Heidegger is certain, is attention to the *Being* of truth. What mode of Being does truth have? In developing an ontology of truth, Heidegger thinks we can bypass these traditional puzzles and answer the old problem posed so poignantly (or was it cynically?) by Pilate: "What is truth?" (John 18:38).

We already have the clue to untangle this mess. For we know that Dasein *is*, in its very Being, disclosure. In attunement, understanding, and discourse, Dasein *dis*-covers itself, others, the world of equipment, nature, and the present-at-hand. To "be there" *is* to *uncover* entities.

> To say that an assertion "*is true*" signifies that it uncovers the entity as it is in itself. Such an assertion asserts, points out, 'lets' the entity 'be seen' . . . in its uncoveredness. The *Being-true (truth)* of the assertion must be understood as *Being-uncovering* (*BT*, 261).

When I say that a picture is askew (supposing that it is), what I say is true. But its being true is not a matter of two present-at-hand items (my saying and the angle of the picture) having some sort of relation holding between them. It is a matter of my actually uncovering it *as it is*. That my assertion is true is demonstrated when I look at the picture; what I have "put forward in the assertion (namely the entity itself) shows itself *as that very same thing*" (*BT*, 261). What the perceiving confirms is that the

*This, you will recall, was one of the major motivations leading Kant to his Copernican revolution, in which the problem is "solved" by trying to show that objects are (partially) *constructs* by the judging mind. See pp. 368–369.

assertion is indeed an *uncovering*; it is what it purports to be.

Heidegger does not think of this notion of truth as casting away the traditional view of truth. Rather, he says, thinking of truth as *uncovering* is a way of giving that view an ontologically adequate foundation. In fact, he believes that one can detect this view of truth in the earliest pronouncements of the Greeks; only later, with Plato and Aristotle, did the notion of assertions and things "corresponding" come to prominence. This was, in Heidegger's eyes, *not* an advance.

> . . . the ultimate business of philosophy is to preserve the *force of the most elemental words* in which Dasein expresses itself, and to keep the common understanding from leveling them off to that unintelligibility which functions in turn as a source of pseudo-problems (*BT*, 262).

The "classical" view of truth as a correspondence between two independently existing items is just such a "leveling off" of the primordial phenomenon of uncovering, and it leads to the expected "pseudo-problems."

Being-true, then, is Being-uncovering. It is Dasein that uncovers entities by virtue of Being that clearing, that disclosedness, which comes along with Being-in-the-world understandingly. So Being-true is a way of Being for Dasein.

> *Dasein is 'in the truth'.* This assertion has meaning ontologically. It does not purport to say that ontically Dasein is introduced 'to all the truth' either always or just in every case, but rather that the disclosedness of its ownmost Being belongs to its existential constitution (*BT*, 263).

If this sounds too optimistic to be true, remember that Dasein is also falling-away-from itself into the world of the One, where idle talk, curiosity, and ambiguity dominate. So Dasein, while essentially "in the truth" in the sense that it is disclosive in its very Being, is also in "untruth." And in fact, since we are "thrown" into the world of the One, it is untruth that is "closer" to us than truth. In our everydayness

entities look as if. . . . That is, they have, in a certain way, been uncovered already, and yet they are still disguised.

> Truth (uncoveredness) is something that must always first be wrested from entities. Entities get snatched out of their hiddenness. The factical uncoveredness of anything is always, as it were, a kind of *robbery*. Is it accidental that when the Greeks express themselves as to the essence of truth they use a *privative* expression . . . [a-letheia]? When Dasein so expresses itself, does not a primordial understanding of its own Being thus make itself known—the understanding . . . that Being-in-untruth makes up an essential characteristic of Being-in-the-world? (*BT*, 265).

Remember that in idle talk one tends to listen only to what-is-said. This mode of One's communication in average everydayness covers over phenomena ("disguises" them) while still revealing something. A genuine insight must, after all, be communicated in assertions. But soon the assertions begin to wear out and be taken for granted and only half-understood. They suffer the leveling characteristic of the world of what "they say." As what "they say," the assertions become "what everyone knows" and take on the character first of the ready-to-hand (instruments we can use), and eventually of the present-at-hand. At that point the classical view of correspondence takes over. But if a genuine disclosure is to take place, Dasein must force its way through this everydayness and uncover the phenomenon itself—for itself. This happens in scientific revolutions and (as we will see) in art.

Heidegger finds it significant that the Greek word for truth begins with *a* ("not") and that the middle part of the word *lethe* is the same as the word for forgetfulness. (Lethe is the river in Hades whose water causes those who drink it to forget the past.) So truth is *not-forgetting*, an idea suggesting that what is uncovered is something that was previously forgotten, covered over, hidden.* And Hei-

---

*Perhaps this meaning of the word is connected with Socrates' view that coming to know the truth is a matter of "recollecting" what we once knew in a time before our birth but have since forgotten. See p. 98.

degger's view of Dasein as falling (into the world of the One and away from itself) accounts for just such a phenomenon. That is why there is something *violent* about the quest for truth; it is like, he says, robbery. For Dasein must penetrate the fog that rises up around the One—to which fog, remember, each Dasein is also contributing—to "wrest" the truth from entities. Truth is difficult to achieve.

This view of truth as an *existential*, as an essential aspect of Dasein's Being, has interesting consequences for the problem of relativism. Heidegger thinks it enables him to stake out a middle ground between the sophists, skeptics, and relativists on the one hand and the absolutists who talk of eternal truth on the other.

> *'There is' truth only in so far as Dasein is and so long as Dasein is.* Entities are uncovered only *when* Dasein *is*; and only as long as Dasein *is*, are they disclosed. Newton's laws, the principle of contradiction, any truth whatever—these are true only as long as Dasein *is*. Before there was any Dasein, there was no truth; nor will there be any after Dasein is no more. For in such a case truth as disclosedness, uncovering, and uncoveredness, *cannot* be. Before Newton's laws were discovered, they were not 'true'; it does not follow that they were false, or even that they would become false if ontically no discoveredness were any longer possible. . . .
>
> To say that before Newton his laws were neither true nor false, cannot signify that before him there were no such entities as have been uncovered and pointed out by those laws. Through Newton the laws became true; and with them, entities became accessible in themselves to Dasein. Once entities have been uncovered, they show themselves precisely as entities which beforehand already were. Such uncovering is the kind of Being which belongs to 'truth' (*BT*, 269).

Because Dasein is "in the truth," the uncovering of entities *as they really are in themselves* is a possibility. This possibility, of course, depends on Dasein-like beings: no Dasein, no truth—i.e., no uncovering of entities. All truth, as Heidegger says, "*is relative to Dasein's Being*" (*BT*, 270). In a sense, Protagoras was right in saying, "of all things, the mea-

sure is man."* But does this mean that truth is *subjective* in the sense that it depends on what a given Dasein happens to think? Not at all. For Dasein, in uncovering entities, comes "face to face with the entities themselves" (*BT*, 270). It is true, of course, that each Dasein is "thrown" into a certain language and culture; and each language and culture already has a certain understanding of entities and Being embedded in it. This is always a mixture of truth and untruth. But the possibility of genuine uncovering is given with Dasein's Being; nothing in principle stands between Dasein and the truth.

Moreover, although truth exists only in conjunction with Dasein (so that there are no eternal truths unless Dasein always existed), what is uncovered is uncovered as *already having been there*. So Heidegger is not an idealist who claims that entities are constructions on the part of a subject. The world is revealed as having antedated the emergence of Dasein. But it is revealed only *to* Dasein. Newton's laws *became* true (i.e., dis-covered) in Newton's day; but what these laws tell us, they tell us about those entities that also existed ages before Newton lived.†

Death

In spite of the extensive analysis we have been following, Heidegger is not satisfied that he has explored all the dimensions of Dasein's Being. In particular, it is not clear that we have an understanding of the *totality* of Dasein. Nor has much been said about the character of *authenticity*. So these topics remain. We will first explore the idea of totality.

Is it even possible to understand Dasein *as a whole*? We have seen that Dasein's existence is characterized by projection toward possibilities: at every stage, Dasein is what it is *not yet*; there are

---

*See p. 41.

†There are difficult passages where Heidegger says that although *entities* are not dependent upon Dasein, *Being* is. So, he thinks, Being and truth always come together. This is hard to understand; what it means must depend upon the general solution to the question of the meaning of Being.

always potentialities-for-Being that are yet unrealized. As Heidegger now puts it, this means that there is always "something *still outstanding*," something "*still to be settled*" with respect to Dasein's Being (*BT*, 279). Can that be brought into our understanding in a way that will give us an interpretation of Dasein as a totality? This obviously brings us to the topic of the *end* of Dasein: to death. It is death that makes Dasein a *whole*. But how is death to be understood?

It seems I cannot experience my own death, since to do so I would have to live through it—and then I wouldn't be dead.*

> When Dasein reaches its wholeness in death, it simultaneously loses the Being of its "there". By its transition to no-longer-Dasein, it gets lifted right out of the possibility of experiencing this transition and of understanding it as something experienced (*BT*, 281).

Death must be understood in terms of the Being of Dasein; that is, we must understand it in the light of that unitary phenomenon of Dasein's Being: Care. Dasein's death is not just its end in a physical or biological sense. Death, as a *possibility* for Dasein, is something that, in a queer sense, Dasein *lives*. Care, after all, means Dasein's Being-ahead-of-itself in an understanding of possibilities. Dasein *is* its possibilities. And among those possibilities is the possibility that Dasein will die. This is, in fact, a strange possibility, because it is one that Dasein is *bound* to realize. Unlike other possibilities, this is one about which Dasein has no choice. As Heidegger puts it, death is "not to be outstripped" (*BT*, 294).† We are *thrown* into this possibility, with never a chance of extrication.

One of the aspects of Dasein, however, is *falling*. And in falling-away-from itself into the world of the "they," Dasein exists this possibility of death in the mode of fleeing-in-the-face-of-it. Everydayness, in various ways, covers over this possibility. The One hides from Dasein the fact that *it* must die. How does it do this? By interpreting death as a mishap, an event, as something present-at-hand—but not yet!

> Death gets passed off as always something 'actual'; its character as a possibility gets concealed. . . . By such ambiguity, Dasein puts itself in the position of losing itself in the "they" as regards a distinctive potentiality-for-Being which belongs to Dasein's ownmost self. The "they" gives its approval, and aggravates the *temptation* to cover up from oneself one's ownmost Being-towards-death. This evasive concealment in the face of death dominates everydayness so stubbornly that, in Being with one another, the 'neighbors' often still keep talking the 'dying person' into the belief that he will escape death and soon return to the tranquillized everydayness of the world of his concern. Such 'solicitude' is meant to 'console' him. . . . In this manner the "they" provides a *constant tranquillization about death*. At bottom, however, this is a tranquillization not only for him who is 'dying' but just as much for those who 'console' him (*BT*, 297–98).

Everydayness transforms death from one's ownmost possibility into an event which is distant and then says it is nothing to be *afraid* of. But in so tranquilizing Dasein, it closes off the *anxiety* a genuine appropriation of this possibility generates.* Dasein's fleeing in the face of death takes the form of evasion. Our Being is a *Being-towards-death*, but everydayness *alienates Dasein from this Being*. This is one of the modes in which Dasein is in "untruth," since no matter how the One tranquilizes and evades and alienates, Dasein—each of us—will die.

So, our ontological interpretation of Dasein *can* get hold of Dasein as-a-whole; Dasein's Being is a Being-towards-death, in which Dasein's death is

---

*There are reported cases, of course, of people who "died" and came back to tell about it. They often tell of experiences they had while they were "dead." But what Heidegger would surely say about these cases is that they are not cases of death but something else. They are not death, because the persons involved did not lose their "Being-there."

†One of my own professors used to say in his raspy voice, "As soon as a man is born, he is old enough to die."

---

*See again the contrast between fear and anxiety, p. 550.

understood as a possibility that in each moment is a defining characteristic of Dasein. Dasein's Being (as a potentiality-for-Being) in a way encompasses its death. Any adequate interpretation of Dasein will necessarily have grasped Dasein's death. Being-towards-death, too, is an *existential*.

The evasion and alienation from oneself typical of absorption in the "they" is a form of inauthentic existence. Is, then, an authentic appropriation of death possible? We know what it would be like. There would be no evasion, no explaining away, no misinterpreting of the mode of Being of death. Death would be steadily apprehended as a possibility of Dasein's Being—not in brooding over it or thinking about it, but existing in every moment in the *anticipation* of death.

> Being-towards-death is the anticipation of a potentiality-for-Being of that entity whose kind of Being is anticipation itself. In the anticipatory revealing of this potentiality-for-Being, Dasein discloses itself to itself as regards its uttermost possibility (*BT*, 307).

This authentic anticipation of death wrenches Dasein away from the One. It *individualizes* Dasein, brings each Dasein before a possibility that belongs to it alone: it says, "I must die." It forces the realization that one is *finite* and so lights up all the possibilities that lie between the present and death. They, too, are uniquely *mine*. Anticipation grasps both the certainty of death and the uncertainty about when it will come. We are certain to die, but we know not when. Anticipation is a mode of understanding; in anticipation of death, Dasein authentically understands itself as a finite, limited whole. This understanding of itself on the part of Dasein is accompanied by an attunement. (Remember that every understanding has its mood, every mood an understanding.) The mood that accompanies anticipation is *anxiety*. Again, anxiety is displayed as the mood in which Dasein comes face to face with itself—and *doesn't* flee.

> We may now summarize our characterization of authentic Being-towards-death as we have projected it existentially: *anticipation reveals to Dasein its lostness*

in the they-self, and brings it face to face with the possibility of being itself, primarily unsupported by concernful solicitude, but of being itself, rather in an impassioned freedom towards death—a freedom which has been released from the illusions of the "they" and which is factical, certain of itself, and anxious (*BT*, 311).

Because anticipation releases us from bondage to the interpretations of the One and puts us "in the truth," we are "freed" to *Be ourselves as a whole*—but only as Being-towards-death. Any evasion casts us back into the "they" and inauthenticity.

Conscience, Guilt, and Resoluteness

Authentic existence is now our theme. But there is a problem. Dasein is caught up in the life of the One, living wholly by what "they say." Remember that there is no private essence to Dasein, no "interior" self with contents of its own. In everydayness, Dasein acquiesces in the way "they" understand its possibilities; it goes-along with the mood and understanding and discourse of the One; it has not "taken hold" of itself. How then does Dasein know there is anything *but* the life of the "they-self"? How does it become *aware* that it is not being *itself* but is fleeing itself by falling-into-the-world inauthentically? What resources does Dasein have to enable it to come to itself in authentic existence?

> . . . because Dasein is *lost* in the "they," it must first *find* itself. In order to find *itself* at all, it must be 'shown' to itself in its possible authenticity. In terms of its possibility, Dasein is already a potentiality-for-Being-its-Self, but it needs to have this potentiality attested (*BT*, 313).

What is it that can "show" Dasein to *itself* as a possibly authentic Self? What "attests" to this possibility? The voice of *conscience*, Heidegger says (*BT*, 313). But we have to be careful here, as elsewhere, not to interpret this "voice" in the way it is ordinarily understood. By now we should be sufficiently on guard against this problem: conscience, like understanding, attunement, and discourse, has an everyday form that hides as much as it discloses. And, in any case, what we are looking for is the *existential ground* on the basis of which ordinary experiences of conscience are *possible*.

So conscience in this existential or ontological sense is not to be identified with that nagging little voice that occasionally tells us we have done something wrong or that warns us not to do what we might like to do. The deep sense of conscience must have the same sort of Being as Dasein; it is not occasional, but constant. It is, moreover, a mode of disclosure, in which something is presented to be understood. And what we need is an interpretation of this phenomenon that makes it clear where this "voiceless voice" comes from, to whom it is addressed, and what it "says."

In the mode of average everydayness, Heidegger says, Dasein is constantly listening. But it "listens away" from itself and hears only the voice of the "they." As a result, it "fails to hear" itself. As we have seen, Dasein *is* the One; each of us is one of "the others" (from whom, for the most part, we do not distinguish ourselves); and this indefinite One is what generally determines how life goes in the world.

Conscience is a "call" to this One (who we are). So conscience is a call to oneself in the mode of the One and is a mode of discourse. But it is a wordless discourse; it does not chastise you for lying, for example. Yet, like all discourse, it has a content. But it doesn't convey information; it is more like a *summons*.

> *What* does the conscience call to him to whom it appeals? Taken strictly, nothing. The call asserts nothing, gives no information about world-events, has nothing to tell. Least of all does it try to set going a 'soliloquy' in the Self to which it has appealed. 'Nothing' gets called to this Self, but it has been *summoned* to itself—that is, to its ownmost potentiality-for-Being. (*BT*, 318).

As we have seen, Dasein *is* just such a potentiality-for-Being. That is what *existing* is—having certain possibilities in the mode of already-understandingly-being-them. And existence is the essence of

Dasein. But this Being of Dasein is hidden to Dasein itself as long as it is governed by the "they." What conscience does is to disclose Dasein to itself as such a potentiality for being. Conscience requires that Dasein *choose* among possibilities. So conscience "calls Dasein forth to its possibilities" (*BT*, 319). In effect, it says, "You cannot hide behind the 'they' any longer; *you* are responsible for your existence!" (In putting words in the mouth of conscience, I am of course falsifying somewhat Heidegger's insistence that the call is "wordless," but not in a damaging way, I hope.)

We now know to whom the call of conscience is addressed: to Dasein in its everydayness. And we know what the call "says": *you must become yourself!* The call, then, summons inauthentic Dasein to take hold of itself, to take itself over, and in so doing to be itself authentically. But who is doing the calling?

> *In conscience Dasein calls itself* (*BT*, 320).

Well, we might have known! Still, that is not exactly clear. How can Dasein call itself in this way? If it is Dasein to whom the call comes, how can it be Dasein that is doing the calling? Indeed, as Heidegger acknowledges, the call typically seems to come from *beyond* oneself. It seems to be

> something which *we ourselves* have neither planned for nor prepared for nor voluntarily performed, nor have we ever done so. 'It' calls, against our expectations and even against our will. On the other hand, the call undoubtedly does not come from someone else who is with me in the world. The call comes *from* me and yet *from beyond me* (*BT*, 320).

This seems phenomenologically accurate; it is the basis, Heidegger suggests, for interpretations of the call as the voice of God or for attempts to give a sociological or biological interpretation of conscience. None of these will do, however, since these causal accounts all try to locate conscience in *something*—i.e., in something present-at-hand. And the call has to have the kind of Being of Dasein.

The puzzle can be solved if we recall the not-at-homeness that is revealed in the mood of anxiety. Anxiety, you will remember, individualizes Dasein, pulls it out of the "they," and makes clear that it is its own *having to be*. In anxiety, Dasein feels alienated from the world of the One, yet recognizes that it has no other home. It comes to understand itself as *thrown into existence*. With this contrast between Dasein as *at home in the world on the terms set out by the "they"* and Dasein as *cast out of that familiar home* we can solve the problem. The "it" that calls is "uncanny" Dasein in its mode of not-being-at-home-in-the-world; and "it" calls to Dasein in the mode of the "they," summoning it *to itself*.

And now we can also see why authentic existence is not a wholly different kind of existence than inauthentic but just a modified way in which such everydayness is seized upon. To exist authentically is to take responsibility for the self that one is. And that is inevitably, inextricably, and for as long as one lives, the self that has been (and is being) shaped by the particular "they" into which one has been "thrown." There is no "true self" other than this.

Conscience, then, is a call: a summons. It summons Dasein, lost in the "they," to take up responsibility for itself. It is true that you are not responsible for yourself "from the bottom up," so to speak; you are not responsible for how and where you were "thrown" into existence. But in authentic existence you shoulder the burden. The authentic self does not excuse itself, blaming parents, society, or circumstance for its shortcomings. Authentic Dasein *makes itself responsible*; it says, "Yes, this is who I am, who I have been; and this is who I will become."

Conscience summons Dasein to Be itself, to turn away from the rationalizations and self-deceptions of the "they." It summons lost Dasein back to its thrownness and forth into existence—into an understanding that projects itself into the peculiar possibilities of its own future. The summons issues from Dasein itself. And Dasein hears the verdict: Guilty. Why "guilty"? Because Dasein, in fleeing itself into the world of the "they," has not been what

it is now called to; Dasein has not been *itself*. Yet we are not summoned to a kind of wallowing around in self-recrimination; we are to realize our essence—i.e., for the first time truly to *exist*.

The existential interpretation of conscience, then, is what "attests" to inauthentic Dasein that there is another possibility and calls it to exist authentically by taking over this having-to-be-itself into which it has been thrown. Dasein takes it over in a certain *understanding* of its own authentic possibilities, in the *mood* of anxiety (since the tranquilizing of the "they" is set aside), and with a reticence that answers to the wordless *discourse* of conscience. There is nothing to be said; there is everything to be done.

> This distinctive and authentic disclosedness, which is attested in Dasein itself by its conscience—*this reticent self-projection upon one's ownmost Being-guilty, in which one is ready for anxiety*—we call "resoluteness." . . .
>
> In resoluteness we have now arrived at that truth of Dasein which is most primordial because it is *authentic* (BT, 343).

Resoluteness is the term for authentic Being-in-the-world. To be resolute is to *be oneself*. In resoluteness, Dasein exists in that disclosedness which puts it "in the truth." But since what Dasein grasps in the understanding of resoluteness is its own Being-guilty, it understands that in truth it has been, and perhaps will soon again be, "in untruth."*

We can put the results of the last two sections together in the following way. In *anticipation*, authentic Dasein grasps and does not hide its Being-toward-death. In answering the call of conscience, Dasein sets aside the temptations of the One and *resolutely* takes up the burden of Being-itself as thrown, existing, falling, guilty Being-in-the-world. But in resolutely Being-itself, a finite whole, Dasein must anticipate its death. And anticipation, for its part, is not a kind of free-floating imagination, but a way of Being that has come to itself and

---

*See p. 560.

has become transparent to itself. So anticipation and resoluteness, if understood deeply enough, imply each other.

In **anticipatory resoluteness**, Dasein comes at last authentically to itself.

We don't often hear Heidegger speak of "joy." But in the section where he discusses anticipatory resoluteness, he writes:

> Along with the sober anxiety which brings us face to face with our individualized potentiality-for-Being, there goes an unshakable joy in this possibility (*BT*, 358).

Temporality as the Meaning of Care

Imagine that you know a secret and are *very* sure that Peter doesn't know it. But on Thursday afternoon he makes an extremely puzzling remark. At first you can't figure out what his remark *means*; nor (which is not the same) what it *means* that Peter made the remark. But as you think about it, you realize that he must know the secret, too. Only on that background does his remark make any sense. What Peter said is *intelligible* only on that assumption. It is that background—Peter knowing the secret—that made it *possible* for him to say what he did.

This example brings us to Heidegger's sense of *meaning*. This is, of course, an everyday example, and Heidegger's interest is directed to the meaning of Being. That is the fox we have been hunting through all these hills and dales and twisty paths. It is for the sake of uncovering the meaning of Being that Heidegger engages in the analysis of Dasein. But so far we have asked, What is the meaning of *Dasein's* Being? In particular, we have been asking, What is the meaning of everydayness? In asking this, we have been constructing an *ontology*. This ontology (the *existentials*) serves as a background against which the phenomena of average everydayness become *intelligible*. We can now say that it is

the articulated structure of Care that makes everyday Dasein *possible*. And we can summarize this structure:

- Existence (Being-ahead-of-itself-in projecting possibilities)
- Facticity (thrownness into-the-world and to-ward-death)
- Falling (in-with-the-Others and away-from-itself)

Taken together as a totality, these features define Care as the essence of Dasein's Being. But have we reached rock bottom with the concept of Care? Or can we ask once again, What is the *meaning of Care*? At this point, we need to pay explicit attention to meaning. Heidegger's discussions of meaning are difficult. Here is an example:

> What are we seeking ontologically with the meaning of care? What does "*meaning*" signify? . . . meaning is that wherein the understandability of something maintains itself—even that of something which does not come into view explicitly and thematically. "Meaning" signifies the "upon-which" of a primary projection in terms of which something can be conceived in its possibility as that which it is. Projecting discloses possibilities—that is to say, it discloses the sort of thing that makes possible (*BT*, 370–71).

That is hard to understand. But if you think back to our example, you should be able to grasp it. What does it *mean* that Peter makes this remark? To uncover the meaning of the remark, we "project" his remark on a background (or larger context) that makes it understandable—i.e., that Peter knows the secret. This background is (in Heideggerese) the "upon-which" of the projection of Peter's remark; it is that "upon which" we project the remark. In this larger context, Peter's remark makes perfect sense; it is meaningful. So meaning is "that wherein the understandability" of the remark "maintains itself."

Moreover, it seems that only if Peter knows the secret is it *possible* for him to say what he does. So "projecting discloses possibilities"—the "sort of thing that makes possible." It is Peter's knowing the secret that makes possible his saying what he does.

Here is another analogy. Some think that human life is meaningful only if it is projected on a larger background, perhaps of immortality or divine purposes. In that context life has, perhaps, the meaning of a *test*. Without such a background, they say, life is meaningless—pointless. The meaningfulness of life is possible only if it is embedded in a larger context. Whether this is so is an interesting question we will not directly address (though Heidegger's views are relevant to an answer). But the sense of meaning is the same as the one in Heidegger's question about the meaning of Care—and, ultimately, of the meaning of Being.

So if we are now asking about the meaning of Care, we are asking about a deeper background, or larger context, in the light of which the phenomenon of Care becomes intelligible. We are asking about that upon which Care can be projected to make it understandable and to show it as possible. Is there a still more fundamental (more primordial) structure to Dasein's Being that makes possible existence, facticity, and falling? That is the question.

We are still not ready for the general question about the meaning of Being. But what can be said about the meaning of Care? Heidegger takes as his clue the Being of Dasein when it is most "true," or most itself: authentic existence. (This is legitimate, since the other modes of Dasein's Being have been displayed as a falling-away from this truth; even though inauthentic everydayness is the mode of Being that is "closest" to us, it is nonetheless *ontologically* derivative.) We have seen authentic existence spelled out in terms of anticipatory resoluteness. Anticipatory resoluteness, for its part, is

Being towards one's ownmost, distinctive, potentiality-for-Being (*BT*, 372).

What makes this "Being towards" possible? Time—and in particular, the future.

For anticipatory resoluteness to be *possible*, it must be that Dasein is in itself, in its very Being, *futural*—temporal. This doesn't mean that Dasein is "located" in time, any more than Dasein's Being-*in*-the-world means that Dasein is "located" in an objective space.* Dasein is "futural" in that it *comes towards itself* in that projecting of possibilities that defines existence. Dasein is always ahead-of-itself-in-time.

We have seen that anticipatory resoluteness also fastens onto itself as Being-guilty. Dasein takes over its facticity—makes its thrownness its own—by taking responsibility for itself.

> But taking over thrownness signifies *being* Dasein authentically *as it already was*. . . . Only in so far as Dasein *is* as an "I-*am*-as-having-been", can Dasein come towards itself futurally in such a way that it comes *back*. Anticipation of one's uttermost and ownmost possibility is coming back understandingly to one's ownmost "been." Only so far as it is futural can Dasein *be* authentically as having been. The character of "having been" arises, in a certain way, from the future (*BT*, 373).

You "are" your possibilities. But what these possibilities are depends on what you have been. You can only project yourself authentically into the future by "coming back" to yourself as having been something.

What does it mean, though, that this "having been" itself arises from the future? That seems strange. I think we can understand Heidegger's thought here in this way. What you have been (and now are, as a result) is not just a set of dead facts. These facts take life and meaning from your projects. You are now, let us say, a college student; as each moment slips away, this is something you have been. But *have you been* preparing for a job? Or *have you been* learning to understand yourself? Or laying a foundation for a scholarly life? Or inching up the ladder of monetary reward? Four people who answer these questions differently might have taken exactly the same courses and read exactly the

---

*Review the discussion of Being-in on p. 540.

same books to this point. But the *meaning* of what they have done is radically different; it is projected against a different background (and notice that each background essentially makes reference to the future!). Because the meaning of what they have done is different, what they "have been" is also different. The difference is defined by the different futures they project. That is how the character of "having been" arises from the future.* We can now see that since it is futural, Dasein also essentially has a past. But once again we must be careful. This is an *existential* past, not one that is composed of moments that have added up and then dropped away into nothingness. It is a past that one constantly *is*.

Finally, anticipatory resoluteness plants one firmly in the current situation. It does not live in daydreams or fantasy; it is not lost in nostalgia. Authentic Dasein resolutely takes action in the light of an attuned understanding of its potentialities and its having been. It encounters what *has presence* by *making present* the entities that define its situation and dealing with them. An unblinkered, clear, disclosive *sight* of what is present is essential to Dasein's authentic appropriation of itself.

> Only as the *Present* in the sense of making present, can resoluteness be what it is: namely, letting itself be encountered undisguisedly by that which it seizes upon in taking action (*BT*, 374).

Those who live in illusion do not act decisively and effectively, because they do not "make present" the entities about them; they veil them over and hide them, disguise and misunderstand them. Authentic "making present" is the existential meaning of the Present as a mode of temporality. This present is not a neutral "now," through a series of which a life must pass. It is not just the knife-edge dividing future from past. It is the rich activity of authentic dealing with things by *making-present* the things that are, in the light of our potentialities and what we have been.*

And now we can say that

> *Temporality reveals itself as the meaning of authentic care* (*BT*, 374).

So that "upon which" Care becomes intelligible is the structure of temporality. Temporality involves projecting into the future, coming back to one's past, and making present. It is important to note that this structure is not itself an entity; it is not a thing or a being. Most importantly, it is not like an empty container in which temporal items can be placed.† Temporality is the most fundamental structure of Dasein's Being-there. Dasein is essentially temporal and essentially *finite*, since authentic Dasein anticipates its end in death. Time, in the sense of existential temporality, is the framework within which something like Care is possible. Time is, to put it in Heidegger's terms, the *horizon* of Dasein's Being. Just as whatever is visible to you now is within the horizon, the framework of temporality defines the horizon for Dasein. All the features of Dasein's Being we have examined are possible only against this background.

Heidegger's analysis of Dasein is now virtually complete. Nothing has yet been said about birth, as the beginning of Dasein. Not much needs to be said, except that between birth and death Dasein "stretches itself along" (*BT*, 423). One gets the image of a rubber band fastened down at birth and stretching out towards the future. Dasein is at any moment not just what it is *then*, but also what it has

---

*For reasons like this, Sartre claims that we are *radically free* and that any kind of causal determination of our actions is ruled out. If what we have been depends on what it means, and if what it means depends on what we project ourselves to be in the future, then there is no neutral causal description "at-hand" to serve as a basis for deterministic laws. If Heidegger is right, there is no call for the reconciliation projects of Hume and Kant, since the kind of causal determinism with which freedom needs to be reconciled cannot even gain a foothold. But is he right? (See pp. 354–356 for Hume and pp. 384–386 for Kant.)

*Compare Augustine's famous discussion of time, pp. 226–229.
†Clock time, or ordinary everyday time, which looks rather like this, is the result of a kind of "leveling off" of this rich existential temporality. It gets a kind of objectivity in much the same way that present-at-hand items do: by abstracting away the meaningfulness of Dasein's Being-in-time.

been and will be. This "connectedness" of Dasein in its stretching along Heidegger calls *historicality*. And he thinks the proper understanding of that phenomenon—enlightened by the entire analysis of the Being of Dasein—is essential to the proper writing of "history." These are interesting matters, but we will stop here and turn to the big question for which all this has been preliminary: the question about the meaning of Being.

The Priority of Being

I write about the thought of the later Heidegger with some caution. If you thought things were difficult to this point, try to read some of the later essays, which contain sentences one can read over and over with hardly a glimmer of an idea of what they might mean.* Part of the difficulty, too, is that Heidegger's thought undergoes some development from the early 1930s until the time near his death in 1976, but he almost never acknowledges that it does. Moreover, he looks back to *Being and Time* and reinterprets some of the things he said there—but without admitting that this is what he is doing. He says over and over that the understanding of the *question* is the most important thing and stresses the tentativeness of his formulations. And he uses the same terms in somewhat different ways in different periods, again without telling us that this is what he is doing.

But throughout he insists that he is trying to say always the same thing: to give expression in language to the *meaning of Being*. And he maintains that what he is trying to say is very *simple*. It is its simplicity, in fact, that is the cause of so much obscurity. He even suggests occasionally that the proper way to express what he wants to say is

through *silence*.* Yet he writes a great deal, struggling again and again to put it in words. Certain lines of thought do stand out with some clarity, however, and I will try to give you some idea of how the problem about the meaning of Being fares in his hands after the period of *Being and Time*.

I will simplify all this drastically and focus on one central theme. We are reminded of this theme in an image that Heidegger borrows from Descartes, the image of philosophy as a tree.† The roots of the tree, Descartes says, are metaphysics, the trunk is physics, and all the other sciences are the branches.

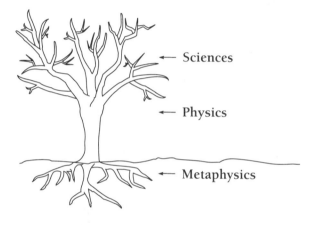

Heidegger accepts this image. But what he wants to ask about (and has been asking about since the first page of *Being and Time*) is the *ground* in which the roots are sunk. Metaphysics is concerned with *beings, entities, substances, things*. It wants to know what kinds of entities there are and whether the fact that they are what they are has an explanation (perhaps in God, the "highest being"). Metaphysics is more general than the special sciences and goes deeper. Each science deals with a certain *kind* of being and orders it, describes it, and gives an account of how and why it changes. Biology deals with living things, for example, history with historical things; metaphysics, by contrast, deals with things or substances in general. But everywhere, in

---

*Consider the last sentence in a lecture called "The Turning": "May world in its worlding be the nearest of all nearing that nears, as it brings the truth of Being near to man's essence, and so gives man to belong to the disclosing bringing-to-pass that is a bringing into its own." This work can be found in *The Question Concerning Technology: Heidegger's Critique of the Modern Age*, translated by William Lovitt (New York: Harper and Row, 1977).

---

*Compare Wittgenstein on the unsayable, pp. 506–507.
†See p. 293.

science and in metaphysics alike, beings (entities) are the focus of attention.

Beings always appear, says Heidegger, in the light of *Being*. Amoeba *are*, and biology can tell us a lot about them; but biology does not tell us what it means for amoeba to *be*. A mountain *is*, and geology can explain how it came to have the shape it has; but geology does not explain what it is for a mountain to *be*. It may be that Platonic Forms *are*, that Aristotelian substances *are*, that Augustine's God *is*, that Cartesian minds *are*, that Hobbesian matter *is*, that the Hegelian subject-Spirit *is*, and so on, throughout the history of the great conversation. What makes all these entities available for investigation and understanding (if they are) is that they *are*. But if Heidegger is right, in no case has a metaphysician directly approached the question of *what that means*. What does it *mean* for something—anything—to *Be*? This, he thinks, is the question he alone first asks.

Note again that *this* question is not answered by an appeal to God or a first cause understood as the highest being. If such a first cause *is*, the very same question applies to it. What does it mean for God to *Be*? As we have seen, the published parts of *Being and Time* are devoted to what Heidegger calls "fundamental ontology," an analysis of that peculiar entity whose very mode of Being involves an understanding of what that means—even if that understanding is inadequate and distorted. A quick review of the results will be useful.

* *Temporality* makes possible
* *Care*, which is the essence of
* *Dasein*, which is a
* *Clearing*, in the light of which there come to presence
* *Beings* (Dasein itself, the ready-to-hand, and the present-at-hand, each of which has a mode of
* *Being* (Care, Functionality, Objectness)

Temporality (primordial time) is the meaning of Dasein's Being—i.e., the deepest structure in Dasein through which everything else is seen to make sense. By projecting itself into future possibilities while being firmly anchored in the past of its thrownness, Dasein makes present the situation in which it acts and stretches itself along, caringly, in time. The published parts of *Being and Time* end with the suggestion that this primordial temporality might be the horizon for understanding Being itself. So time might be not only the meaning of Dasein's Being, but also of Being in general. And the title of the book makes one think that this is how the unpublished part would have gone.

Now what's wrong with this?* Why does Heidegger not follow out this lead and publish the rest of what he had planned to write? What causes this "turn" in his thinking? I think the answer must be that the pattern in this thinking makes Being too dependent on Dasein. And there are two things wrong with this.

(1) It is too subjective. Throughout *Being and Time*, Heidegger struggles against subjectivism in philosophy, against the idea that Being is somehow dependent on the subject. The whole analysis of Dasein as a clearing and as Being-in-the-world is designed to show that the terror of being trapped inside our own minds is a "put-up job," the solipsistic consequence of a mistaken starting point. Dasein is *in its very essence* beyond itself, transcendent, *in* the world among entities. But now at the end it suddenly looks as though subjectivism has not been escaped at all. If the meaning of Being is time and if time is a structure of Dasein's Being, then it seems obvious that Being itself is dependent on Dasein's understanding of it.

(2) It is too *metaphysical*. Dasein is after all *a* being, one entity among others. And if Being itself is dependent upon Dasein, then it seems the metaphysical pattern of trying to find a ground for Being *in some entity* is repeating itself in Heidegger's thought. And this is intolerable! His objection to traditional metaphysics is that it neglects Being by concentrating on beings, searching *among beings* for a ground or first principle that accounts for them. In a way, this outcome of *Being and Time* is even worse. Traditional metaphysics, in Heidegger's view, is *oblivious* of the question about Being. He, by contrast, devoting all his intellectual energies to clarify the meaning of Being, has fallen directly into the metaphysical trap.

---

*See p.533–534.

So a new direction is called for. It is not that the work done in *Being and Time* has to be repudiated, but that it all gets transposed into a new key, so to speak. Without exactly taking anything back, everything is transformed. Let me try to say how. Dasein is no longer thought of as fundamental in the project to discern the meaning of Being, so the correlative notion of a "fundamental ontology" disappears. The term "Dasein" itself tends to give way to the term "man," or "human being." And the human being now is thought of not as "a clearing," but as one element in a clearing that is now called *the truth of Being*. The other elements of the truth of Being are variously identified but always involve time and Being itself. The idea in *Being and Time* that truth is a kind of "robbery," that it has to be "wrested" resolutely out of its hiddenness, is replaced by the notion that truth is a gift we need only receive. The Open, the Clearing, the Unhiddenness of Being is not something we have to create, just to recognize (not that this is easy). And the initiative is not with us; it is on the side of Being, which "sends" to us various ways of unveiling itself. These various "sendings" of Being constitute historical epochs, which are defined by the understanding of Being they have. And what "they say," the opinion of the faceless "one," is replaced by the very particular and specific understanding of Being in an epoch—e.g., in our day. Authentic existence, too, is transformed; the focus is not on the anxious individual who has to appropriate the self in anticipatory resoluteness, but on Being, which graciously "calls" or offers itself. And the thought is that if this call could be accepted, the very essence of the human being might alter. The key throughout is that the priority and the initiative shift from the human being to Being.

But we need to fill in at least some of the details that constitute this "turn." A good place to start is Heidegger's understanding of the present age. It is an age dominated, he says, by science and technology. This is a kind of truism, but Heidegger understands this in a peculiar way, one we need to grasp.

We often think of technology as a matter of instruments we can use for one purpose or another. Sometimes we hear that technology in itself is "neutral" and can be used for either good or evil, just as a poison may be used to kill disease-infested rats or one's wealthy aunt Matilda. That is not a mistaken way to think about technology, but, Heidegger claims, it is shallow. It may be "correct," but is it "true"? Does it disclose the *essence* of technology? Today we are battling many ills brought on by technology: air and water pollution, the population explosion, the extinction of species, the depletion of the ozone layer, waste disposal, the threat of nuclear war. But we tend to think that we can master them: what we need is more and better technology! So we equip our cars with catalytic converters and spend much money on antiballistic missile systems. We think we can *master* technology by devising technological "fixes" for technological problems.

But what, Heidegger asks, if the essence of technology is not this business of devising means to desired ends? What if technology is fundamentally something quite different? What if technology is basically a way of revealing, of bringing forth, of unconcealing? What if technology were a "place" —a clearing—where *truth* happens?

And so in fact it is. What is distinctive about *modern* technology is that it does not just use means that nature supplies, as the windmill makes use of the wind. What it does is *store up* energy in a way the older technology could not. It is

a challenging, which puts to nature the unreasonable demand that it supply energy which can be extracted and stored as such.

. . . a tract of land is challenged in the hauling out of coal and ore. The earth now reveals itself as a coal mining district, the soil as a mineral deposit. . . . Agriculture is now the mechanized food industry. Air is now set upon to yield nitrogen, the earth to yield ore, ore to yield uranium, for example; uranium is set upon to yield atomic energy, which can be released either for destruction or for peaceful use (*QCT*, 296).[2]

Technology reveals *everything* as what Heidegger calls the **standing-reserve**. What is characteristic of this mode of openness is that everything presents itself as something to be "set upon" and "ordered" and "stored" for *use*. He gives a particular example.

The hydroelectric plant is set into the current of the Rhine. It sets the Rhine to supplying its hydraulic pressure, which then sets the turbines turning. This turning sets those machines in motion whose thrust sets going the electric current for which the long-distance power station and its network of cables are set up to dispatch electricity. In the context of the interlocking processes pertaining to the orderly disposition of electrical energy, even the Rhine itself appears to be something at our command. . . . What the river is now, namely a water-power supplier, derives from the essence of the power station. In order that we may even remotely consider the monstrousness that reigns here, let us ponder for a moment the contrast that is spoken by the two titles: "The Rhine," as dammed up into the *power* works, and "The Rhine," as uttered by the *art* work, in Hölderlin's hymn by that name. But, it will be replied, the Rhine is still a river in the landscape, is it not? Perhaps. But how? In no other way than as an object on call for inspection by a tour group ordered there by the vacation industry (*QCT*, 297).

What is "monstrous" about this is not that the Rhine supplies power, but that whatever we behold presents itself as "standing reserve," something to be mastered and ordered, to be unlocked and exposed, to be set upon and challenged to provide "the maximum yield at the minimum expense" (*QCT*, 297). What the Rhine *is*, within this mode of revealing, is *defined* by the possibility of damming it up for power. Imagine a lovely valley being "challenged," "set upon," to supply lots for subdivisions for suburban housing. This valley is "standing-reserve" for development. If we were to use the terminology from *Being and Time*, we could say that this is just the way "One" sees it or that this is how "they" experience the world.*

But Heidegger does not now put it that way. To put it that way makes it seem too much as though this way of experiencing the world is in our control, as though we could simply change it if we wished to. He does not believe this is so.

Who accomplishes the challenging setting upon through which what we call the real is revealed as standing-reserve? Obviously, man. To what extent is man capable of such a revealing? Man can, indeed, conceive, fashion, and carry through this or that in one way or another. But man does not have control over unconcealment itself, in which at any given time the real shows itself or withdraws.

Wherever man opens his eyes and ears, unlocks his heart, and gives himself over to meditating and striving, shaping and working, entreating and thanking, he finds himself everywhere already brought into the unconcealed. The unconcealment of the unconcealed has already come to pass whenever it calls man forth into the modes of revealing allotted to him (*QCT*, 299–300).

I cannot decide to "unconceal" the real; nor can you; nor can we together. Nor can we simply decide to reveal it in a new and different way. That is not something in our power. As soon as we meditate or strive, shape or work, ask or thank, as soon as we do anything at all we are *already* within the clearing of unconcealment. (This corresponds to Dasein's being "in the truth" in *Being and Time*.) A certain "mode of revealing" has been "allotted" to us. We have not *decided* to see things in this technologically relevant way; that is the way they *present* themselves to us. The origins of a revealing are no more in our control than the thrownness of Dasein.

Heidegger calls this challenging of nature that orders it as the storehouse of standing-reserve **enframing**. Enframing is a mode of disclosure, of revealing the real. It reveals the real as orderable for use. Enframing, while itself nothing technological in the ordinary sense, is the *essence* or *meaning* of technology. It is what makes ordinary technology possible. If you recall our discussion of "meaning," you can see that to call enframing the meaning of technology is to say that enframing is "that wherein the understandability of [technology] maintains itself" (*BT*, 370). We live in a technological world in precisely this sense: that everything in it is revealed as standing-reserve. This is *our* meaning for Being.

It has not always been so, of course. Other epochs have experienced the world differently. And this fact suggests that the "revealing" characteristic of our time, enframing, hides as much as it discloses. We are "in untruth" as well as in the truth. What accounts for the different ways in which Be-

---

*Review the discussion of Dasein as "the One," pp. 545–549.

ing presents (and hides) itself in different ages? Heidegger's answer is that there is *no explanation* for this. Whatever explanations we have already presuppose a certain revealing of reality; they are internal to a mode of grasping Being. In our case, explanations have the scientific/technological character they do because they are internal to enframing. They *express* our fundamental relation to reality, so they cannot *explain* it.*

Enframing is our *destiny*. We are ourselves "challenged forth" to order things in the mode of standing-reserve. This *comes* to us; we do not invent it. It is *given* to us. It is "too late" to ask whether we should or should not approach reality this way. The Greeks did not *decide* to experience reality as *physis*, a kind of production (Aristotle's actualization of potentialities), a *bringing forth* of things into appearance—as opposed to *challenging forth*. It was not up to the Medievals to understand reality as the creation of almighty God; this way of experiencing things seemed so natural that it was hard to imagine it could be otherwise. Nor was it the conscious decision of those early Moderns who applied calculation to nature to experience the world as a world of *objects*. These ways of unconcealing are "sent" to us; we participate in them without ever having them totally in our power. And no *reason* can be given for the shifts from one mode of revealing to another.

Heidegger uses the word "monstrous" in his description of the Rhine as a power source. We need to say a bit more about this. Any "destining" of a mode of revealing brings along with it a *danger*. Within a given revealing, much that is correct may be asserted; however, the danger is that "in the midst of all that is correct, the true will withdraw" (*QCT*, 308). With respect to enframing, this danger is intensified; in fact, Heidegger thinks enframing is so dangerous that it is worthy of being called "the supreme danger" (*QCT*, 308). What is this danger?

This danger attests itself to us in two ways. As soon as what is unconcealed no longer concerns man even as object, but exclusively as standing-reserve, and man in the midst of objectlessness is nothing but the orderer of the standing-reserve, then he comes to the very brink of a precipitous fall, that is, he comes to the point where he himself will have to be taken as standing-reserve. Meanwhile, man, precisely as the one so threatened, exalts himself to the posture of lord of the earth. In this way the illusion comes to prevail that everything man encounters exists only insofar as it is his construct. This illusion gives rise in turn to one final delusion: it seems as though man everywhere and always encounters only himself. Heisenberg has with complete correctness pointed out that the real must present itself to contemporary man in this way. *In truth, however, precisely nowhere does man today any longer encounter himself, i.e., his essence. . . .*

Thus, the challenging-enframing not only conceals a former way of revealing, bringing-forth, but it conceals revealing itself and with it that wherein unconcealment, i.e., truth, comes to pass (*QCT*, 308–9).

We are back again to the forgetfulness of Being with which *Being and Time* begins, but now it is in a different guise. The danger in enframing is twofold, Heidegger tells us.

(1) We ourselves may be taken simply as standing-reserve, to be ordered forth for use.* But as we relate to ourselves in this technological/scientific way, we miss what is peculiar to us: our essence, our Being-open (what Heidegger earlier calls Dasein). Heidegger goes as far as to say that *nowhere* do we today encounter ourselves in this essence. Enframing is a drastic and extreme mode of *hiding* our Being from ourselves.

(2) Since everything looks like material-for-use ordered by our science and technology, it seems we *nowhere* can get beyond ourselves: again, subjectivism triumphs! And this, Heidegger consistently holds, is a "delusion." Enframing exalts man to the

---

*Compare the later Wittgenstein's remarks about justification coming to an end and about the "spade turning" on "what I do." See pp. 527 and 532. Heidegger sees a kind of "history of Being" in the successive modes of its being revealed. This reminds us of Hegel— except that there is no dialectical necessity posited for the shifts.

*Compare Kant's distinction between persons and things, and his second formulation of the categorical imperative: that rational beings must never be used as means only, but always treated as an end. (See p. 395.) Enframing human beings means taking them to be available as standing-reserve for use, not respecting them as persons.

position of "lord of the earth" and so *misses* the phenomenon of enframing as itself a mode of revealing—as a way the truth of Being is made manifest. We are plunged so deep in enframing that it is difficult for us to realize that this is what we are doing. Again we "forget" our Being and the fact that other modes of revealing are possible.

> Enframing blocks the shining-forth and holding sway of truth. The destining that sends into ordering is consequently the extreme danger. What is dangerous is not technology. Technology is not demonic; but its essence is mysterious. The essence of technology, as a destining of revealing, is the danger. . . .
>
> The rule of enframing threatens man with the possibility that it could be denied to him to enter into a more original revealing and hence to experience the call of a more primal truth (*QCT*, 309).

Heidegger is not purely negative about science and technology, however. For one thing, it *is* a way in which entities become "unhidden." He is willing to allow that results in the sciences may be "correct." For another, the technological/scientific way of understanding reality is, he thinks, the legitimate heir of the entire Western philosophical tradition. Philosophy has always been, in Heidegger's view, fundamentally metaphysics. As the individual sciences mature and separate from their mother, as they set up business on their own (or, to use Descartes' image, as the branches of the tree flourish), they take over the task of telling us what entities there are in reality. *This* job can now be done *better* by the scientist in the laboratory than by the metaphysician in an armchair. As Heidegger tells us more than once, philosophy as metaphysics is *finished*. And we are left with enframing, which is the way we have been granted to understand what there is.

So technology and its companion, modern science, have a positive role to play. They constitute the "extreme danger," however, in what we might call their "imperialism": in the claim that there is no other way to reveal reality than this. Remember, this is *our* way of experiencing the world, one we cannot simply step out of, any more than the authentic individual of *Being and Time* has a private

reality into which she can repair to "be herself," leaving behind the world of the "One."

But now Heidegger quotes the poet Hölderlin.

> But where danger is, grows
> The saving power also (*QCT*, 310).

As the *extreme* danger, enframing seems to close off all modes of revealing but itself. But if we can just concentrate our attention on enframing's *being a revealing* we may catch sight of *its coming to presence*. This attempt to let Being *Be* and to express it in language Heidegger calls *thinking*. This may not seem very illuminating, since we imagine that thinking is something we all do every day. But he (typically) understands thinking in a very particular and peculiar way. Thinking is *recalling Being out of its hiddenness*. It is through this kind of thinking that we may come to understand ourselves as part of that "constellation" in which modes of revealing are "sent" or "granted" to humans, in which beings are lighted up in their becoming *present*. Philosophy and metaphysics, then, must be *replaced* by thinking. And thinking must *supplement* enframing.

And yet this way of putting it is still too subjective. It makes it seem as though this "turning" toward the presence of things is something that is up to us. It makes it seem as though we can just *decide* to think. But even this turning is a granting we cannot manage by ourselves; it is one we can at most be ready for.*

We can ask, though, where we might look for such a revealing of the Being of things and ourselves. Heidegger has two answers to this question: in the thinking of the thinker and in poetry and art. We cannot discuss his understanding of art in detail here. But it is significant, he thinks, that the Greek word for art is *techne*. In the "technology" of the artist, however, what is produced is not something for use, to be stored and transformed and

---

*You might like to compare the contrast between the early and the late Heidegger (between anticipatory resoluteness and receptive openness) with the contrast between Pelagius and Augustine. See pp. 236–237. There are also obvious echoes of Plato's Myth of the Cave, in which what is required is a *turning* away from shadows toward the light of the sun (pp. 121–123).

used up. What is produced is a *work*. A work *stands there*. In and through the work, a *world* opens up; and a world is (roughly) the way things present themselves. So art, too, is a mode of unveiling, revealing, unconcealing. But it is not a challenging, a forcing, an imposing and mastering of things. Rather, it *lets things appear* as they are. And in being a *work*—i.e., something that has been *worked* into being—it reveals its *presencing* of the world in a way that enframing finds hard to do.

Art is a

"letting happen of the advent of the truth of beings, . . . the setting-into-work of truth (*OWA*, 184).[3]

Art "opens up a world" (*OWA*, 169); it *lets the truth happen*. It is truth setting *itself* into the work to reveal a world. Art, moreover, is not concerned (or should not be concerned) with the beautiful, which is just a by-product. In the form of a Greek temple, or in Hölderlin's poetry, art unveils the *Being* of things. Art is a matter of *truth*.

But again, we must be careful. For great art is no more a matter for individual decision than any mode of revealing is. Notice that art is understood as the setting-*itself*-into-work of truth. Art is not entirely in the control of the artist, any more than we are in control of enframing. Talk of the "muses" may be an expression of this idea. The work is *given* to the artist, or through the artist to us. Art, too, is a gift, a granting of unveiledness that the human cannot be the master of.

We have spoken again and again of a "sending" or a "destining" of a "gift" that must be received and cannot be forced, invented, or created. Every mode of revealing, Heidegger holds, has this character. Let us now, at the end of our consideration, ask, Who does the sending? From whom is this gift received? In asking this question, we approach the clearest answer Heidegger has given as to the *meaning of Being*. Here is his most explicit statement.

From the dawn of Western-European thinking until today, Being means the same as presencing. . . . Being is determined as presence by time.[4]

Again, Heidegger reminds us that we must not think of Being as a *thing* (or entity). Nor is time a *thing*. Nor is it strictly correct to say that Being *is*.* What there *is* are things: this book is, the sun is, your brother is. Being is what these entities *have*. But to say that they have it suggests again that it is a *thing*, like the purse or credit card that you have, or a property they might have or lack, like being brown or heavy. But neither of these can be right. See how hard it is to say what Heidegger wants to express!

Being is not what is present. Being, he tells us, is the *presencing* of things. The notion of "presencing" seems clearly to involve time. Presencing is "making-present" or (better) "letting-be-present." But it would be a mistake, too, to think that Being—presencing—is itself temporal. What is temporal (in time) are entities: this book, the sun, your brother. These things begin, are present for a while, and end. Entities (beings) have a past, a present, and a future.

Nor is time something temporal. Time does not "have" a past, a present, and a future—though my car does. Nor is it strictly correct to say of time that it *is*. Entities *are*. But entities are—*in time*.

Entities *are* precisely in their *presencing*. And presencing is being-present. And being-present is one mode of temporality, or time. So it is *Being and Time*, or *Time and Being*, after all—but without the priority given to Dasein! And yet presencing must involve that which is open to and receives it; Being involves humans. You can see how Heidegger is struggling to clarify and understand in an authentic way the relations of Being, beings, humans (or Dasein), and time. As he sees it, each one involves the others.[†]

We have seen that entities are present in one mode of revealing or another; currently, the mode is scientific/technological, what Heidegger calls enframing. This is how things *present themselves* now to us. This is something not in our control; it

---

*It is interesting to compare here what Plato says about the Form of the Good as "beyond being." See p. 120.

†Compare again Augustine on time, pp. 227–229.

is "sent" to us. And we asked, Who does the sending? And now we can see two possible answers: either Being or time.

But neither is adequate, Heidegger thinks. To think of either Being or time as the "giver" of the gift of Being, of presencing, is to turn them back into entities. And that is precisely the wrong way to think. Better, he thinks, is the German phrase *es gibt*. Literally, this means "it gives," but a more idiomatic translation is "there is." So we can say that "it gives Being" or "there is time." There is no "sender" of the gift of Being, if by "sender" we mean "thing that sends." To suppose there is would be to ground Being in *a* being—precisely the error that metaphysics has made all these centuries. We must just acknowledge that "there is time" and "there is Being."

But that acknowledgement is hidden from us under the domination of enframing. Intent on control and mastery of entities, even thinking of human beings as part of the standing-reserve, we pass right over the mystery and wonder of their *presence*. Were we to "turn" from our preoccupation with "challenging" and "setting-upon," this would be an event—perhaps the event of events! It would be the "gathering together" of Being as presencing, of time as the horizon within which presencing occurs, and of man. This would be the true clearing, in which Being and time are *appropriated* by man, and by which man could come into his true essence as the entity that is *open to Being*. Heidegger calls this the *event of appropriation*.

If this were to occur, human beings would no longer think of themselves as lords of the earth, but as guardians or shepherds of Being. They would take it as their responsibility to preserve and protect Being, recognizing that *presencing* is a gift they cannot master or control. We are not, Heidegger says, the masters of Being but its "neighbors."

In the age of enframing, where everything is understood as standing-reserve, there is no "room" for God. (Or perhaps even God is thought of as "standing-reserve," a kind of public utility that can be used to gain the satisfaction of one's desires; one often gets this impression from the television

evangelists.* Heidegger does not talk much about God. He thinks of the present time as

> the time of the gods that have fled *and* of the god that is coming.[5]

And he is clear that he does not regard Being as God or a god. But in the event of appropriation, where a man opens up to the mystery of presencing, there is also uncovered the "space" in which God (or "the god," as he sometimes says, echoing Socrates), might become meaningful again. He speaks of this as the sphere of "the holy" and suggests that this is what the poet is particularly apt to reveal.

> Only from the truth of Being can the essence of the holy be thought. Only from the essence of the holy can the essence of divinity be thought. Only in the light of the essence of divinity can it be thought and said what the word "God" is to signify. Or must we not first be able to understand and hear these words carefully if we as men, i.e., as existing beings, are to have the privilege of experiencing a relation of God to man? How, then, is the man of the present epoch even to be able to ask seriously and firmly whether God approaches or withdraws when man omits the primary step of thinking deeply in the one dimension where this question can be asked: that is, the dimension of the holy, which, even as dimension, remains closed unless the openness of Being is cleared and in its clearing is close to man.[†] Perhaps the distinction of this age consists in the fact that the dimension of grace has been closed. Perhaps this is its unique dis-grace.[6]

We await the event of appropriation, a gracious new gift of "sending," a mode of revealing in which Being is not forgotten or hidden, in which we ap-

---

*Compare Augustine on the contrast between use and enjoyment, pp. 237–238.
†One way to understand Heidegger is to see him addressing a question very similar to the one Kierkegaard thinks is *preliminary* to the question of what it is to be a Christian. See p. 442. You might also compare the "dimension of the holy" to what Wittgenstein calls *the mystical* (p. 506).

propriate what is "given," namely, Being as presence. In this *truth of Being*, this disclosedness, man will come to himself not by force or resolute willing, but in simply *letting Being be*. If this should take place, we will be transformed as we experience

the marvel of all marvels: that what-is *is*.[7]

Notes

1. Quotations from Martin Heidegger's *Being and Time*, trans. John Macquarrie and Edward Robinson (Oxford: Basil Blackwell, 1967), are cited in the text using the abbreviation *BT*.
2. Quotations from Martin Heidegger, *The Question Concerning Technology*, trans. William Lovitt, in *Basic Writings*, ed. David Farrell Krell (New York: Harper and Row, 1977), are cited in the text using the abbreviation *QCT*.
3. Quotations from Martin Heidegger, *The Origin of the Work of Art*, trans. Albert Hofstadler, in *Basic Writings*, are cited in the text using the abbreviation *OWA*.
4. Martin Heidegger, *On Time and Being*, trans. Joan Stambough (New York: Harper and Row, 1972), 2.
5. Martin Heidegger, *Hölderlin and the Essence of Poetry*, trans. Douglas Scott, in *Existence and Being*, ed. Werner Brock (Chicago: Henry Regnery Company, 1949), 289.
6. Martin Heidegger, *Letter on Humanism*, trans. Edgar Lohner, in *Philosophy in the Twentieth Century*, v. 2, ed. William Barrett and Henry D. Aiken (New York: Random House, 1962), 294.
7. Martin Heidegger, *Postscript to What is Metaphysics?* in *Existence and Being*, 355.

Afterword

We have come to the end of our survey of Western philosophy. But have we come to the end of philosophy? Although Wittgenstein and Heidegger suggest that philosophy as we have known it is over, the great conversation still seems to be flourishing. As always, it is stimulated both by changes in the world outside itself and by internal developments. Here I want simply to set down a few notes from a philosophy watcher, indicating some interesting things currently happening, hoping to convince you that philosophy is not just its history—that it is *not* all in the past. The situation is somewhat chaotic, as always; only from a later historical perspective could someone say with any assurance what it all means. Remember Hegel's owl. So here are a few impressions.

(1) The development of the computer has provided a dramatic new stimulus for thinking about the mind. Here we have a model of something that is clearly a machine but may hold the promise of being genuinely intelligent. This prospect obviously has implications for the quarrel between Descartes and Hobbes about the nature of mind. Philosophers are engaged in fruitful conversations with psychologists, computer scientists, linguists, and neuroscientists in what may become a new discipline: cognitive science. It may be too soon to promise a unified science of the mind, but the work in this area is the most exciting since the heady days of Hume and Kant.

(2) There has been intense activity in practical or applied ethics. The stimulus of new technolo-gies in medicine and the worries about nuclear war, poverty and starvation, the environment, and shady business practices, together with those seemingly intractable problems of abortion and capital punishment, have led to much interesting work. There has even been a clamor for help by professionals in various fields; philosophers not only write books and articles, but also serve on hospital ethics committees, lead seminars on business ethics, and even serve as aides in Congress.

(3) Historical and sociological studies of the history of science have raised this question: To what extent—if at all—can we regard the deliverances of the sciences as "objective"? Perhaps (this is the most radical suggestion) they are ideological through and through, governed in their choice of problems and favored solutions by social values they are loath to acknowledge. Perhaps physics is just another kind of literature that tells us more about its creators than about the world! Naturally, this view is not without its critics. And voices in this part of the conversation are sometimes less than calm and measured.

(4) Feminist critics have raised worries about the degree to which moral theories have been shaped by male values. Do the Kantian and utilitarian emphases on rules and universality, for instance, reflect the fact that these theories were devised by men living in a world of male dominance? What does this "ethics of impartiality" have to say about the more intimate spheres of personal and

family relationships? Should these, too, be governed by a moral law that applies universally? Or would this be the death of them and of something precious to us that makes our lives worthwhile? Have the values of caring and nourishing been unduly neglected by our tradition?

(5) The fact that we now live in a "global village," where very different cultural, religious, and philosophical assumptions confront each other daily, is leading to a broader context in which to ask philosophical questions. This book is a history of *Western* philosophy; one might think that it is oblivious to those broader contexts. But, as Heidegger urges, unless we understand our own tradition in some depth, we will be shallow and unpromising partners in the broader conversation between East and West. We can look to an intensification of the conversation on this front.

(6) The old antagonism between the relativists and the objectivists seems no nearer resolution. Currently, the sophists seem to be in the ascendancy, and devotees of Socrates on the defensive. But many are struggling to see whether there may be a way to acknowledge a truth in relativism without giving up the Socratic quest altogether.

We can hardly say that Kant's four questions have been settled to everyone's satisfaction. We are still asking and must continue to ask

1. What can we know?
2. What ought we to do?
3. For what can we hope?
4. What is man?

And if we are now somewhat uncomfortable in asking the fourth question using the term "man" in just this way, we acknowledge one result of how the conversation has gone recently.

Philosophy isn't everything. Daniel Dennett has said that if the unexamined life is not worth living, the overexamined life is nothing to write home about, either (*Elbow Room: The Varieties of Free Will Worth Wanting* [Oxford: Clarendon Press, 1984], 87). But philosophy has the peculiar characteristic of being inescapable for us all. And so we should try to do it with something approaching Aristotelian "excellence" to the extent possible for each of us, remembering what my own German professor once said: "Whether you will philosophize or won't philosophize, you *must* philosophize."

Glossary

a posteriori   A term applied primarily to statements, but also to ideas or concepts; knowledge of the *a posteriori* is derived from (comes *after*) experience (e.g., "Trees have leaves").

a priori   A term applied primarily to statements, but also to ideas or concepts, that can be known *prior to* and independently of appeal to experience (e.g., "Two and three are five," or "All bodies are extended").

absolute knowledge   A term in Hegel's philosophy designating the state of consciousness when everything "other" has been brought into itself and Spirit knows itself to be all of reality.

alienation   Hegelian term appropriated by Marx to describe the loss of oneself and control over what properly belongs to oneself in capitalist social structures. One's work and the products of one's labor, for instance, are made "alien" to oneself and belong to another. Existentialism stresses the general feeling of alienation among modern human beings.

analytic   A term applied to statements the denial of which is a contradiction (e.g., "All bachelors are unmarried").

anticipatory resoluteness   Heideggerian term for authentically facing the fact that one is destined for death.

appearance   The way things present themselves to us, often contrasted with the way they really are (e.g., the oar in water appears bent but is really straight). Kant holds that all we can ever come to know is how **things-in-themselves** *appear* to our senses and understanding; appearance is the realm of **phenomena** versus **noumena**.

argument   A set of statements, some of which (the premises) function as reasons to accept another (the conclusion).

atomism   From a Greek word meaning "uncuttable"; the ancient Greek view of Democritus and others that all of reality is composed of tiny indivisible bits and the void (or empty space). See also **logical atomism**.

attunement   In Heidegger's thought, the term for a mode of disclosure that manifests itself in a mood; e.g., the mood of anxiety discloses Dasein's not-being-at-home in the world of its ordinary concern. See **Dasein**.

authenticity   Being oneself, taking responsibility for oneself in accepting the burden of having to "be here"— i.e., thrown into this particular existence with just these possibilities (Heidegger).

autonomy   Self-rule or giving the law to oneself, as opposed to heteronomy or being under the control of another. A key principle in Kant's **ethics**.

Being   The fundamental concept of **metaphysics**. Doctrines of **categories** such as those of Aristotle and Kant attempt to set forth the most general ways that things can *be*. The meaning of Being is the object of Heidegger's quest.

Being-in-the-world   The most general characteristic of **Dasein**, according to Heidegger; more fundamental than knowing, it is being engaged in the use of gear or equipment in a world functionally organized.

categorical imperative   The key principle in Kant's moral theory, bidding us always to act in such a way that the maxim (principle) of our action could be universally applied.

categories   Very general concepts describing the basic modes of being. Aristotle distinguishes ten, including "substance," "quantity," and "quality." Kant lists twelve, the most important of which are "substance" and "causality."

causation   What accounts for the occurrence or character of something. Aristotle distinguishes four kinds of cause: material, formal, efficient, and final. According to most recent theories, influenced by Hume, causation is a relationship between events where the first is regularly or lawfully related to the second.

compatibilism   The view that human liberty (or freedom of the will) can coexist with determinism—the universal **causation** of all events. Classic sources are Hobbes and Hume.

convention   The Sophists contrast what is true by nature (*physis*) with what is true by convention or agreement (*nomos*) among humans. The latter, but not the former, can also be changed by human decision.

correspondence   A view of truth; a statement is said to be true provided that it "corresponds" with what it is about—i.e., it *says* that reality is such and such, and reality *is in fact* such and such.

criterion   A mark or standard by which something is known. The "problem of the criterion" is posed by skeptics who ask by what criterion we can tell that we know something and, if an answer is given, by what criterion we know that this is the correct criterion.

Dasein   Heidegger's term for the way of being characteristic of humans. Literally meaning "Being there," it designates that way to be in which one's own **Being** is a matter of concern.

determinism   The view that there is a causal condition for every event, without exception, sufficient to produce that event just as it is. The philosophical relevance of determinism lies particularly in relation to human action.

dialectic   A term of many meanings. For Socrates, it is a progression of questions and answers, driving toward less inadequate opinions. For Plato, it is the sort of reasoning that moves from **Forms** to more basic Forms, and at last to the Form of the Good. For Hegel, it is the progress of both thought and reality by the reconciliation of opposites and the generation of new opposites. Marxists apply the Hegelian doctrine to the world of material production.

dogmatism   A term applied by philosophers to the holding of views for no adequate reason.

empiricism   The view that all knowledge of facts must be derived from sense experience; a rejection of the view that any knowledge of nature is innate or constructable by reasoning alone. Exemplified by Hume and the **logical positivists**.

enframing   Heidegger's term for the technological understanding of **Being** as "**standing-reserve**," where everything is "set upon" to produce the maximum yield at minimum expense. Enframing is the essence or *meaning* of technology.

entelechy   A goal or end residing within a thing, guiding its development from potentiality to the actuality of its **essence** (Aristotle).

epistemology   Theory of knowledge, addressing the questions of what knowledge is, whether we have any, what its objects may be, and how we can reliably get more.

essence   That set of properties which makes each thing uniquely the kind of thing that it is.

esthetics   The theory of art and the beautiful and/or the sublime. The word originally comes from the Greek term for sense experience. Kierkegaard calls the style of life that pursues sensual pleasure "esthetic."

ethics   The study of good and evil, right and wrong, moral rules, virtues, and the good life; their status, meaning, and justification.

existentialism   The philosophy that focuses on what it means to exist in the way human beings do—usually stressing choice, risk, and freedom. Kierkegaard is a main figure, as is Heidegger.

facticity   The way of Being of **Dasein** (Heidegger). One aspect of our facticity, for instance, is our **Being-in-the-world**; another is our **thrownness**—simply finding ourselves in existence in some particular way.

fallibilism   The view expressed by Peirce, and earlier by Xenophanes, that though we may know the truth in certain cases, perhaps in many cases, we can never be certain that we do.

falling   Heideggerian term for the phenomenon of being defined by others. **Dasein** inevitably *falls-in-with* what "they" say and tends strongly to *fall-away-from* itself.

family resemblance   Wittgenstein's term for the way many of our concepts get their meaning. There is no set of necessary and sufficient conditions for an item to be a *game*, for instance, only overlapping and crisscrossing resemblances among instances of things we call games.

Forms   Those ideal realities Plato takes to be both the objects of knowledge and the source of the derived reality of the sensible world: the Square Itself, for instance, and the Forms of Justice and the Good.

great chain of being   The view that reality is stretched between God (or the One) and nothingness, with each kind of thing possessing its own degree of being and goodness. Found in Plotinus and Augustine; widespread for many centuries.

hedonism   The view that pleasure is the sole objective of motivation (psychological hedonism) or that it is the only thing good in itself (ethical hedonism)

hermeneutic circle   The idea that any interpretation takes something for granted; e.g., understanding part of a text presupposes an understanding of the whole, and vice versa. Every understanding lights up its objects only against a background that cannot at the same time be brought into the light. It follows that complete objectivity is impossible.

hubris   A Greek word meaning arrogance or excessive self-confidence, particularly of mortals in relation to the gods.

idealism   The view that objects exist only relative to a subject that perceives or knows them. There are many forms; in Hegel's *absolute idealism*, for instance, mind or Spirit (the Absolute) is the only ultimate reality, everything else having only a relative reality.

inauthenticity   Heidegger's word for Dasein's fleeing from itself into the average everyday world of what "they" say and do; not being oneself.

induction   A method of reasoning that infers from a series of single cases to a new case or to a law or general principle concerning all such cases.

innate ideas   Ideas that any mature individual can acquire independently of experience. Defended in different ways by Plato and Descartes, attacked by the empiricists.

instrumentalism   Dewey's term for his own philosophy, according to which all our intellectual constructions (concepts, laws, theories) have the status of tools for solving problems.

language-games   Comparing words to pieces in a game such as chess. What defines a rook are the rules according to which it moves; what characterizes a word are the jobs it does in those activities and forms of life in which it has its "home." Language is a game we play with words (the later Wittgenstein).

light of nature   Descartes' term for reason, in the light of which things can appear so clear and distinct that they cannot possibly be doubted.

logical atomism   A view expressed by the early Wittgenstein, in which language is thought of as a logical calculus built up from simple unanalyzable elements called names. Names stand for simple objects, which are the substance of the world.

logical positivism   A twentieth-century version of **empiricism** that stresses the **tautological** nature of logic and mathematics, together with the criterion of **verifiability** for factual statements: if they are not verifiable by sense experience, the statements are not meaningful.

logical truth   Truths that are true by virtue of logic alone. Wittgenstein explains logical truths as **tautologies**.

logos   Greek term meaning word, utterance, rationale, argument, structure. In Heraclitus, the ordering principle of the world; in St. John, that according to which all things were made and which became incarnate in Jesus.

materialism   The view that the fundamental reality is matter, as understood by the sciences—primarily physics. Mind or spirit has no independent reality.

metaphysics   The discipline that studies **being** as such, its kinds and character, often set out in a doctrine of **categories**. Also called by some "first philosophy."

naturalism   A view that locates human beings wholly within nature and takes the results of the natural and human sciences to be our best idea of what there is; since Darwin, naturalists in philosophy insist that the human world is a product of the nonpurposive process of evolution.

noumena   Kant's term for things as they are in themselves, quite independently of how they may appear to us; he believes they are unknowable. Contrasted with **phenomena** or **appearance**.

nous   Greek term usually translated as "mind." In Aristotle, *nous* is the active and purely formal principle that engages in thinking and contemplation; he argues that *nous* is more than just the form of a living body; it is a reality in its own right and is eternal.

objective spirit   That realm in which Spirit expresses itself externally, giving rationality to institutions, law, and culture (Hegel).

Ockham's razor   A principle stated by William of Ockham demanding parsimony in the postulation of entities for the purpose of explanation; often formulated as "Do not multiply entities beyond necessity."

One, the   1. In Plotinus and Neoplatonic thought, the source from which the rest of reality emanates. 2. A translation of Heidegger's term "das Man," designating **Dasein** as not differentiated from "the others," the crowd, the anonymous many who dictate how life goes and what it means.

ontic   Heidegger's term for the realm of ordinary and scientific facts; contrasted with **ontological**.

ontological   1. Having to do with **being**, with what there is in the most general sense. 2. In Heidegger, having to do with that deep structure of **Dasein's Being** which makes possible the **ontic** facts about average everydayness; disclosed in *fundamental ontology*.

ontological argument   An argument for God's existence that proceeds solely from an idea of what God is, from his **essence**. Different versions found in Anselm and Descartes; criticized by Aquinas and Kant.

phenomena   What appears, just as it appears. In Kant, contrasted with **noumena**. The object of study by **phenomenology**.

phenomenology   The attempt to describe what appears to consciousness; a science of consciousness: its structures, contents, and objects. In Hegel and later in Husserl and Heidegger.

pictorial form   What a picture and the pictured have in common that allows the first to picture the second (early Wittgenstein).

possible experience   In Kant, a term designating the extent to which sensibility and understanding can reach, structured as they are by the *a priori* intuitions of space and time, together with the *a priori* concepts or **categories**.

possible state of affairs   In early Wittgenstein, the way in which objects could relate to each other to constitute a fact.

pragmatism   A view developed by Peirce, James, and Dewey in which all of our intellectual life is understood in relation to our practical interests. What a concept means, for instance, depends wholly on the practical effects of the object of our concept.

present-at-hand   A Heideggerian term for things understood as bereft of their usual functional relation to our interests and concerns; what "objective" science takes as its object. A modification of our usual relation to things as **ready-to-hand**.

primary qualities   In Galileo and other early Moderns, qualities which a thing actually has—e.g., size, shape, location—and which account for or explain certain effects in us (*secondary qualities*), such as sweetness, redness, warmth.

rational psychology   Kant's term for that discipline which attempts to gain knowledge of the self or soul in nonempirical ways, relying on rational argument alone; Kant thinks it an illusion that rational psychology produces knowledge.

rationalism   The philosophical stance that is distrustful of the senses, relying only on reason and rational argument to deliver the truth (Parmenides and Descartes).

ready-to-hand   Heidegger's term for the mode of **Being** of the things that are most familiar to **Dasein**; gear or equipment in its functional relation to Dasein's concerns.

realism   A term of many meanings; central is the contention that reality is both logically and causally independent of even the best human beliefs and theories.

relativism   A term of many meanings; central is the view that there are no objective standards of good or bad to be discovered and that no objective knowledge of reality is possible; all standards and knowledge claims are valid only relative to times, individuals, or cultures.

representational theory   The view that our access to reality is limited to our perceptions and ideas, which function as representations of things beyond themselves; a problem associated with this theory is how we can ever know that there are things beyond these representations.

rhetoric   The art of persuasive speaking developed and taught by the **Sophists** in ancient Greece, whose aim was to show how a persuasive *logos* could be constructed on each side of a controversial issue.

secondary qualities   Those qualities, such as taste and color, produced in us by the *primary qualities* of objects—size, shape, etc.

semantics   Study of word-world relationships; how words relate to what they are about.

sense-certainty   What is left if we subtract from sensory experience all interpretation in terms of concepts, e.g., the sheer blueness we experience when we look at a clear sky; the immediate; where Hegel thinks philosophy must start, though it is forced to go on from there.

showing   Contrasted in Wittgenstein's early philosophy with *saying*; logic, for instance, shows itself in every bit of language; a proposition *shows* (displays) its sense, and it *says* that this is how things stand.

skepticism The view that for every claim to know, reason can be given to doubt it; the skeptic suspends judgment about reality (Sextus Empiricus, Montaigne). Descartes uses skeptical arguments to try to find something that cannot be doubted.

social contract The theory that government finds its justification in an agreement or contract either among individuals or between individuals and a sovereign power (Hobbes and others).

solipsism The view, which must be stated in the first person, that only I exist; the worry about solipsism motivates Descartes to try to prove the existence of God.

Sophist From a Greek word meaning "wise one." The Sophists were teachers in ancient Greece who taught many things to ambitious young men but specialized in **rhetoric**.

standing-reserve Heidegger's term for the way **Being** is apprehended in a technological society—as entities ready for rational ordering, stockpiling, and use.

Stoicism The view that happiness and freedom is at hand for the asking if we but distinguish clearly what properly belongs to ourselves and what is beyond our power, limiting our desires to the former and thus keeping our wills in harmony with nature.

substance What is fundamental and can exist independently; that which has or underlies its qualities. There is disagreement about what is substantial, Plato taking it to be the **Forms**, Aristotle the individual things of our experience. Some philosophers (e.g., Spinoza) argue that there is but *one* substance, God.

syllogism An **argument** of two premises and a conclusion composed of categorical subject-predicate statements; the argument contains just three terms, each of which appears in just two of the statements (Aristotle).

synthetic A term applied to statements the denial of which is not contradictory; according to Kant, in a synthetic statement the predicate is not "contained" in the subject but adds something to it (e.g., "Mount Cook is the highest mountain in New Zealand").

tautology A statement the truth table for which contains only *T*'s. Wittgenstein uses the concept to explain the nature of logical truth and the laws of logic.

teleology Purposiveness or goal-directedness; a teleological explanation of some fact is an explanation in terms of what it is for or what end it serves.

theodicy The justification of the ways of God to man, especially in relation to the problem of evil: What would justify an all-powerful, wise, and good God in creating a world containing so many evils?

things-in-themselves In Kantian philosophy, things as they are quite independent of our apprehension of them, of the way they appear to us; **noumena**. Things-in-themselves are unknowable.

Third Man Term for a problem with Plato's **Forms**: we seem to be forced into an infinite regress of Forms to account for the similarity of two men.

thrownness Heideggerian term for **Dasein's** simply finding itself in existence under certain conditions, without ever having a choice about that.

transcendental Term for the conditions on the side of the subject that make knowing or doing possible. Kant's critical philosophy is a transcendental investigation; it asks about the *a priori* conditions for experience and action in general.

utilitarianism Moral philosophy that takes consequences as the criteria for the moral evaluation of action; of two alternative actions open to one, it is right to choose that one that will produce the best consequences for all concerned—e.g., the most pleasure or happiness.

validity A term for logical goodness in deductive arguments; an **argument** is valid whenever, if the premises are true, it is not possible for the conclusion to be false. An argument can be valid, however, even if the premises are false.

verifiability principle The rule adopted by the **logical positivists** to determine meaningfulness in factual statements; if no sense experience can count in favor of the truth of a statement (can verify it at least to some degree), it is declared meaningless, since meaning is said to consist in such verifiability.

Credits

Index